36th Congress, 1st Session. | HOUSE OF REPRESENTATIVES. | Ex. Doc. No. 55.

RESULTS

OF

METEOROLOGICAL OBSERVATIONS,

MADE UNDER THE DIRECTION OF THE

UNITED STATES PATENT OFFICE AND THE SMITHSONIAN INSTITUTION,

FROM THE

YEAR 1854 TO 1859, INCLUSIVE,

BEING A REPORT OF THE

COMMISSIONER OF PATENTS

MADE AT

THE FIRST SESSION OF THE THIRTY-SIXTH CONGRESS.

VOL. II.--PART I.

WASHINGTON.
GOVERNMENT PRINTING OFFICE.
1864.

CONTENTS.

INTRODUCTION.

The Results of Meteorological Observations made under the direction of the United States Patent Office and the Smithsonian Institution up to the year 1859 were presented to Congress in January, 1860, and ordered to be printed. The *first volume* was published in 1861, and contained the reductions of observations for six years, viz: 1854, 1855, 1856, 1857, 1858 and 1859, and included the following results:

1. The average height of the barometer.
2. The maximum and minimum of the same instrument, and the day when they occurred in each month.
3. The average temperature for the hours of 7 a. m., 2 p. m., and 9 p. m.; and the mean for the month.
4. The highest and lowest degree of temperature, and when they occurred.
5. The warmest and coldest days as a whole.
6. The average maximum and minimum force of vapor.
7. The relative humidity.
8. The number of times the wind blew from each quarter.
9. The amount of rain and snow.
10. The average amount of cloudiness.
11. Summaries for each year.

The *second volume* has remained uncompleted until the present time, on account of the great amount of printing required by the several departments of government in the prosecution of the war; and as the same cause may still further delay the completion of the work, it has been thought advisable to issue the portions already in type, as the first part of the second volume.

The following pages comprise two parts of the reductions, viz: The observations of periodical phenomena; and the materials for the critical investigation of three remarkable storms of 1859.

PERIODICAL PHENOMENA.

The periodical phenomena were classified and prepared for publication, at the expense of the Smithsonian Institution, by Dr. Franklin B. Hough, of New York. The following are his introductory remarks:

"The general results here given form a series of observations on plants and animals, made principally by the meteorological observers of the Smithsonian Institution from 1851 to 1859. From the list of objects specified as worthy of record—the dates of putting forth and fall of leaves, blossoming, ripening of fruit, times of appearance and disappearance of animals, &c.—two hundred and twenty-nine distinct subjects of observation were selected as presenting sufficient extent and diversity for this inquiry.

"The primary object of the observations furnishing the data for these tables was stated in the earlier circulars of the Institution, to be the construction of a series of tables showing the geographical distribution of the animal and vegetable kingdoms in North America. This object has since been pursued, in part, by special researches under the auspices of the Smithsonian Institution, as regards the distribution of the forests and trees of North America, and the geographical range of various animals. That the following pages may afford data auxiliary to such an object is evident; but it may be suggested, that a careful comparison of extended catalogues of plants and animals, prepared by competent persons in localities properly selected, will be necessary for a full investigation of this important subject.

"These results will be found to have a more direct application to meteorological science, by indicating the progress of the seasons in different localities, and their relative variability in different years. For this purpose plants and animals afford indications as significant as meteorological instruments as to temperature and other climatic conditions, because strictly dependent upon them, and in the absence of all other records they would furnish a reliable chronicle of the passing year. A comparison of the dates will, in many cases, show the prevalence of certain conditions over large areas, and observations upon one plant are often confirmed by many others. From the tender or hardy varieties introduced by cultivation, it will generally be found that indigenous plants are more reliable indicators of comparative earliness or lateness of season than those dependent upon tillage; and for observations made from year to year in any given locality, trees and shrubs are more suitable for this purpose than herbaceous plants.

"Another obvious result derived from these observations is the determination of the mean time of flowering or maturity of plants as a botanical characteristic, and as leading to a knowledge of the habits and range of birds and other animals. It is well known that a difference in the time of blossoming often forms a specific character in plants, as in the familiar example of two species of *Sambucus*, (elder.) The *S. pubens* is an early blooming shrub, and the *S. canadensis* does not blossom until the former is ripening its fruit.

"The accompanying tables embrace observations upon the foliation of eighty-seven species; the blossoming of ninety-two species; the ripening of fruit of ten species; and the defoliation of eighteen species of plants; and upon the first appearance of sixteen species of birds, one of reptiles, three of fishes, and two of insects. The remaining records were considered too few and disconnected for useful comparison, and seldom amounted to a dozen entries to any subject for the whole period.

"To these have been added several tables of the opening and closing of lakes, rivers, canals and harbors, collected from various sources, and tending to illustrate the same leading features of climate as the records of organic phenomena. Of similar use would have been dates of the progress of husbandry, as of seed time, harvest, and other labors of the farm, which are in a certain degree dependent upon the seasons. The few data of this class, which were reported in the absence of any special request, were deemed too scattered and imperfect for classification. An inquiry for copies of records of these facts, which have long been kept by intelligent agriculturists in many sections of the country as matters of personal reference and use, might be productive of valuable results.

"It cannot be doubted that systematic observations by careful observers upon the growth of similar seeds under exactly similar conditions of soil, exposure, time, and depth of sowing, &c., with the view of determining the dates of germination, blossoming, ripening and decay of plants, as governed by climatic influences alone, in widely different localities, would be productive of great benefit to science. The adaptation of different localities to special agricultural products would thus be determined with much certainty, and results of practical utility to the agriculturist would be obtained. The florist, gardener and farmer would be largely interested in these results, and it is believed a sufficient number of these could be found for conducting a series of careful and systematic observations of this kind.

"In the blank circulars issued for obtaining the following data, two columns were usually provided for entering the dates of flowering of plants. One of these was designed to include the dates of first appearance of blossoms, and the other those of general flowering of the species. The former was more generally filled, and has therefore been selected for our classification; and in cases where no entry was made in the first column, that of the second has been adopted, by applying, in most cases, a correction of from two to six days. Entries presenting apparent errors have generally been omitted, and in doubtful cases such disposition was made of the record as the circumstances required.

"It is to be regretted that these observations do not present that continuity and uniformity which would enable us to arrive accurately at the mean dates of the events recorded. The period is itself too short to enable us to obtain this important information, which can only be procured by a long course of careful observation."

The following tables are inserted at the beginning of the periodical phenomena for facilitating reference:

1. List of stations and names of observers.
2. Alphabetical list of plants, animals, &c., of which observations are given.

STORMS.

The materials for the critical study of three storms of 1859, one of which occurred in the month of March, and the other two in September, were collected from the records in the Institution, and prepared for publication by Professor J. H. Coffin, of Lafayette College, Easton, Pennsylvania.

One of the important objects aimed at in establishing the meteorological observations of the Smithsonian Institution was the collection of data for the critical examination of the development and progress of the extended commotions of the atmosphere which occur during the autumn, winter and spring, over the middle or temperate portions of North America.

It is well known that two hypotheses as to the direction and progress of the wind in these storms have been advocated with an exhibition of feeling unusual in a problem of a purely scientific character, and which, with sufficient available data, is readily susceptible of a definite solution. According to one hypothesis, the motion of the air in these storms is gyratory; according to the other, it is in right lines toward a central point, or toward an irregular elongated middle space. It is hoped that the data here given will be considered of importance in settling, at least approximately, these questions as to the general phenomena of American storms.

The plan adopted for studying this subject is to construct a series of maps representing at definite intervals the face of the sky, direction of the wind, pressure and temperature of the air, &c., over the whole country during the interval from the beginning of the commotion until its end.

Prefixed to the reductions of storms are the following tables:

1. List of Stations and counties arranged by States, with Index to pages.
2. Alphabetical list of Stations, giving their latitudes and longitudes.

JOSEPH HENRY,
Secretary Smithsonian Institution.

WASHINGTON, *March*, 1864.

OBSERVATIONS

UPON

PERIODICAL PHENOMENA

IN

PLANTS AND ANIMALS,

FROM 1851 TO 1859,

WITH

TABLES OF THE DATES OF OPENING AND CLOSING OF LAKES, RIVERS, HARBORS, ETC.

ARRANGED BY FRANKLIN B. HOUGH, M. D.

LIST OF STATIONS AND NAMES OF OBSERVERS.

	STATIONS.	OBSERVERS.
Maine	Brunswick, (Bowdoin College,) Cumberland county	A. S. Packard, jr.
	Carmel, Penobscot county	John J. Bell.
	Castine, Hancock county	Joseph L. Stevens, M. D.
	Cornishville, York county	Silas West. G. W. Guptill.
	Gardiner, Kennebeck county	W. Gardiner.
	Monson, Piscataquis county	Benjamin F. Wilbur.
	Naples, Cumberland county	Samuel F. Perley.
	Perry, Washington county	W. D. Dana.
	Steuben, Washington county	J. D. Parker.
New Hampshire	Concord, Merrimack county	Dr. William Prescott.
	Francestown, Hillsborough county	H. E. Sawyer.
	Londonderry, Rockingham county	Robert C. Mack.
	Manchester, Hillsborough county	Samuel M. Bell.
	North Barnstead, Belknap county	R. F. Hanscam.
	Salmon Falls, Rollinsford, Stafford county	George B. Sawyer.
	Shelburne, Coos county	Fletcher Odell.
	Somersworth, (Great Falls,) Stratford county	H E Sawyer.
	Stratford, Coos county	B. Gould Brown.
	West Enfield, Grafton county	Nathaniel Purmont.
Vermont	Bennington, Bennington county	Joseph Barker.
	Brandon, Rutland county	David Buckland.
	Brattleborough, Windham county	John Lewis Russell.
	Burlington, Chittenden county	Prof. Zadock Thompson.
	Castleton, Rutland county	D. Underwood.
	Craftsbury, Orleans county	James A. Paddock.
	Lunenburg, Essex county	Hiram A. Cutting.
	Newark, Caledonia county	D. F. Johnson.
	Shelburn, Chittenden county	George Bliss.
	Stockbridge, Windsor county	W. C. Belcher.
	West Rupert, Bennington county	Joseph Parker.
Massachusetts	Boston, (and vicinity,) Suffolk county	John L. Russell.
	Bridgewater, Plymouth county	L. A. Darling.
	Cambridge, (Harvard College Observatory,) Middlesex county	W. C. Bond.
	Canton, Norfolk county	D. H. Ellis.
	Florida, Berkshire county	L F. Whitcomb.
	Lawrence, Essex county	John Fallon.
	Mendon, Worcester county	John George Metcalf.
	New Ashford, Berkshire county	Phinehas Harmon.
	North Attleborough, Bristol county	Henry Rice.
	Richmond, Berkshire county	William Bacon.
	Uxbridge, Worcester county	James W. Robbins, M. D.
	Waltham, Middlesex county	Thomas Hill.
	Westfield, Hampden county	Rev. Emmerson Davis.
	Williamstown, Berkshire county	Samuel E. Elmore. Irving Magee.
	Worcester, Worcester county	F. H. Rice, M. D. John S. Sargent.
Rhode Island	Acquidneset	E. G. Arnold.
	Point Judith, (4 miles north of lighthouse,) Washington county	Joseph P. Hazard.
Connecticut	Columbia, Tolland county	William H. Yeomans.
	East Windsor Hill, Hardford county	P. A. Chadbourne.
	Fairfield, Fairfield county	J. M. Shaffer.
	Georgetown, Fairfield county	Aaron B. Hull.
	Middletown, Middlesex county	Prof. John Johnston.
	Norwich, New London county	N. Scholfield.
	Preston, New London county	William W. Meech.
	Saybrook, Middlesex county	James Rankin.
New York	Angelica, Alleghany county	Dr. E. M. Alba.
	Baldwinsville, Onondaga county	John Bowman.
	Cazenovia, Madison county	Aaron White.
	Ceres, Alleghany county	Dr. R. P. Stevens.
	Chatham, Columbia county	Cornelius Chase.
	Clinton, Oneida county	Dr. H. N. Paine.
	Constableville, Lewis county	L L. Fairchilds.
	Eden, Erie county	Anna Landon. Stephen Landon.
	Elmira, Chemung county	Ira F. Hart.
	Fishkill Landing, Dutchess county	William K. Denning.

LIST OF STATIONS AND NAMES OF OBSERVERS.

STATIONS.		OBSERVERS.
New York	Flatbush, King's county	John L. Zabriskie. Peter J. Neefus.
	Geneva, Ontario county	Rev. W. D. Wilson.
	Lake (P. O.), Greenwich, Washington county	Peter Reid.
	Lowville, Lewis county	J. Carroll House.
	Mexico, Oswego county	John R. French.
	New Lebanon, Columbia county	Joseph Bates, M. D.
	New York, (Institution for Deaf and Dumb,) New York county	Oran W. Morris.
	Nichols, Tioga county	Robert Howell.
	North Salem, Westchester county	John F. Jenkins. Mrs. M. Jenkins Lobdell.
	Ogdensburg, St. Lawrence county	William E. Guest.
	Oswego, Oswego county	William S. Malcolm.
	Ovid, Seneca county	J. W. Chickering.
	Penn Yan, Yates county	Dr. Henry P. Sartwell.
	Philipstown, (Beverly,) Putnam county	Thomas B. Arden.
	Plainville, Onondaga county	J. H. Norton.
	Plattsburg, Clinton county	W. C. Belcher.
	Rochester, Monroe county	Prof. Chester Dewey. William C. Pratt.
	Sag Harbor, Suffolk county	Ephraim M. Bryam.
	Sennett, Cayuga county	Henry B. Fellows.
	Somerville, St. Lawrence county	Franklin B. Hough, M. D.
	Spencertown, Columbia county	A. W. Morehouse.
	Waterloo, Seneca county	A. E. Bishop.
	Wellsville, Alleghany county	H. M. Sheerar.
	West Concord, Erie county	Lewis Woodward.
	West Day, Saratoga county	Jude M. Young.
	West Point, Orange county	John Bratt.
	White Plains, Westchester county	John F. Jenkins.
	Williamsville, Erie county	William Van Pelt.
New Jersey	Burlington, (Burlington College,) Burlington county	Adolph Frost.
	Freehold, Monmouth county	O. R. Willis.
	Moorestown, Burlington county	S. C. Thornton, jr.
	Newark, Essex county	William A. Whitehead.
	Readington, Hunterdon county	John Fleming.
	Sergeantsville, Hunterdon county	John T. Sergeant.
Pennsylvania	Bedford, Bedford county	Samuel Brown.
	Bellefonte, Centre county	J. I. Burrell.
	Ceres, (adjacent to New York State line)	R. P Stevens.
	Chambersburg, Franklin county	R. Weiser.
	Darby, (Sharon Female Seminary,) Delaware county	John Jackson.
	Easton, (Lafayette College,) Northampton county	Prof. James H. Coffin.
	Fleming, Centre county	James M. McPinn. Samuel Brugger.
	Freeport, Armstrong county	Andrew Roulston.
	Gettysburg, Adams county	Prof. M. Jacobs.
	Hollidaysburg, Blair county	J. R. Lowrie.
	Huntingdon, Luzerne county	Jesse Gorsuch.
	Indiana, Indiana county	David Peelor.
	Lancaster, Lancaster county	Thomas C. Porter.
	Lima, Delaware county	Minshall Painter.
	Meadville, Crawford county	T. F. Thickstun. Prof. L. D. Williams.
	Mercersburg, Franklin county	Thomas C. Porter.
	Middletown, Delaware county	Minshall Painter.
	Morrisville, Bucks county	E. Hance.
	Murrysville, Westmoreland county	Robert L. Stewart.
	Nazareth, Northampton county	E. T. Kluge. H. A. Brickenstein.
	North Whitehall, Lehigh county	Edward Kohler.
	Orwigsburg, Schuylkill county	J. S. Keller.
	Philadelphia, (vicinity of,) Philadelphia county	A. Zumbrock, M. D.
	Radnor, Delaware county	John Evans.
	Reading, Adams county	John Schoener.
	Shamokin, (Lancaster colliery,) Northumberland county	P. Friel.
	Somerset, Somerset county	George Mowry.
	Sugar Grove, Warren county	Lorin Blodget.
	Upper Darby, Delaware county	Dr. George Smith.
	Valley Forge, Montgomery county	C. P. Jones.

LIST OF STATIONS AND NAMES OF OBSERVERS.

	STATIONS.	OBSERVERS.
Pennsylvania	West Chester, Chester county	Dr. William Darlington.
Maryland	Easton, Talbot county	Samuel T. Rodgers.
	Frederick, Frederick county	Henry E. Hanshew.
	Hagerstown, Washington county	John H. Heyser.
	Ridge, St. Mary's county	T. G. Stagg.
	Sykesville, (Schellman Hall,) Carroll county	Miss Harriott M. Baer.
Virginia	Berryville, Clarke county	Miss Ellen Kownslar.
	Buffalo, Putnam county	Samuel A. Couch.
	Clarke county	William T. Allen.
	Crack Whip, Hardy county	D. H. Ellis.
	Crichton's Store, Brunswick county	R. F. Astrop.
	Diamond Grove, Brunswick county	R. F. Astrop.
	Doddridge county	W. C. Quincy.
	Genito, Powhatan county	R. F. Astrop.
	Kanawha Saline, Kanawha county	W. C. Reynolds.
	Madison C. H., Madison county	A. G. Grinnan.
	Meadow Dale, Highland county	J. Slaven.
	Mossy Creek, Augusta county	Jed. Hotchkiss.
	Mount Solon, Augusta county	James T. Clarke.
	Peach Grove, Fairfax county	W. C. Quincy.
	Poplar Grove, Kanawha county	James E. Kendall.
	Portsmouth, Norfolk county	Prof. N. B. Webster.
	Rose Hill, Essex county	Geo. Wythe Upshaw.
	Salem, Roanoke county	J. Carson Wells.
	Smithfield, Isle of Wight county	Dr. John R. Purdie.
	The Plains, Fauquier county	John Pickett.
	Trout Run Valley, Hardy county	D. H. Ellis.
	Wardensville, Hardy county	D. H. Ellis.
	Winchester, Frederick county	Thomas Allen.
	Wirt C. H., Wirt county	Josiah W. Hoff.
North Carolina	Chapel Hill, Orange county	Prof. James Phelps. R. P. Battle. R. H. Battle.
	Gaston, Northampton county	Dr. Geo. F. Moore.
	Green Plains, Northampton county	Dr. Geo. F. Moore.
South Carolina	Aiken, Barnwell district	H. W. Ravenel.
	Black Oak, Charleston district	H. W. Ravenel.
	Camden, Kershaw district	J. A. Young, M. D.
	Charleston, Charleston district	Jos Johnson, M. D.
	Edisto Island, Colleton district	E. N. Fuller, M. D.
	Fulton, Clarendon district	J. Dyson.
	Georgetown, Georgetown district	Rev. Alex. Glennie.
	St. John's, Berkly	F. Peyse Poucher, M. D. H. W. Ravenel.
	Waccaman, All Saints	Rev Alex. Glennie.
Georgia	Savannah, Chatham county	John F. Posey. Rev. C. W. Rogers.
	Sparta, Hancock county	Dr. E. M. Pendleton.
	Varnell's Station, Whitfield county	Alexander Gerhardt.
	Zebulon, Pike county	Mrs. J. T. Arnold.
Florida	Alligator, Columbia county	Edward R. Ives.
	Cedar Keys, Levy county	Augustus Steele.
	Key West, Monroe county	Wm. C. Dennis.
	Knox Hill, Walton county	J. Newton.
	Seville, (near Tallahasse,) Leon county	Lardner Gibbon.
Alabama	Carlowville, Dallas county	H. L. Alison, M. D.
	Childersburg, Talladega county	Benjamin F. Holley.
	Eutaw, Greene county	Alex. Winchell.
	Greensborough, Greene county	Robert B. Waller.
	Greene Springs, Greene county	Henry Tutwiller.
	Weewokaville, Talladega county	Benjamin F. Holley.
Mississippi	Columbus, Lowndes county	James S. Lull.
	Jasper, Clark county	E. S. Robinson. Rankin Smith.
	Oktibbehah county	S. B. Hollinshead.
	Oxford, (University of Mississippi,) Lafayette county	L. Harper.
	Port Gibson, Claiborne county	A. H. Peck, M. D.
Louisiana	Big Pond, Avoyelles parish	Benjamin W. Kimball.
	Trinity, Chatahoula parish	A. R. Kilpatrick, M. D.
Texas	Austin, Travis county	Dr S. K. Jennings.

LIST OF STATIONS AND NAMES OF OBSERVERS.

	STATIONS.	OBSERVERS.
Texas	Cross Roads, Williamson county	F. S. Wade.
	Goliad, Goliad county	John C. Brightman.
	Helena, Karnes county	E. Walker, M. D. John C. Brightman.
	New Wied, Comal county	L. C. Ervendberg.
	Union Hill, Washington county	Wm. H. Gantt.
Arkansas	Perryville, Johnson county	H. F. Hardy.
Tennessee	Glenwood, (near Clarksville,) Montgomery county	Wm. M. Stewart.
	Knoxville, Knox county	Oran W. Morris.
	Lebanon, (Cumberland University,) Wilson county	Prof. A. P. Stewart.
	Nashville, (Tyre Springs,) Davidson county	T. C. Downie.
	Walnut Grove, Greene county	James B. Bean.
Kentucky	Fairview, (near Bloomfield,) Nelson county	John R. Jones.
	Maysville, Mason county	E. L. Berthoud.
Missouri	Hannibal, Marion county	O. H. P. Lear.
	Rockport, Atchison county	Charles Quarles Chandler, M. D.
	St. Louis, St. Louis county	Dr. A. Wislizenus. George Engelmann, M. D.
	Trenton, (Grand River College,) Grundy county	John M. Ordway.
	Westport, Jackson county	Not stated.
Ohio	Ashtabula, Ashtabula county	Dr. J. C. Hubbard.
	Belle Centre, (Geneva Hall,) Logan county	Robert Shields.
	Bowling Green, Wood county	Wm. R. Peck, M. D.
	Cheviot, Hamilton county	Ebenezer Hannaford.
	Cincinnati, (College Hill,) Hamilton county	Prof. A. Wood
	Cleveland, Cuyahoga county	Gustavus A. Hyde. J. Kirkpatrick.
	Edinburgh, Portage county	Smith Sanford.
	Elkrun, Columbiana county	Smith B. McMillan.
	Germantown, Montgomery county	J. L. Binkerd. L. Groneway.
	Hamilton, Butler county	Ebenezer Hannaford.
	Hiram, Portage county	S. M. Luther.
	Hockingport, Athens county	James Fraser.
	Jefferson, Ashtabula county	James D. Herrick.
	Keene, Coshocton county	Miss P. D. Childs. Dr. E. C. Bidwell.
	Madison, Lake county	Rev. L. S. Atkins.
	Marietta, Washington county	Wm. Holden.
	Mount Healthy, Hamilton county	Carlos Shepard.
	Poland, Mahoning county	Not stated.
	Ripley, Brown county	J. Ammen.
	Rockport, Cuyahoga county	Edward Colburn.
	Savannah, Ashland county	John Ingram.
	Troy, Miami county	Charles L. McClung.
	Welchfield, Geauga county	B. F. Abell.
	West Bedford, Coshocton county	H. D. McCarty.
	Windham, Portage county	Samuel W. Treat.
Indiana	Indianapolis, Marion county	James Furguson.
	Laconia, Harrison county	Edw. S. Crosier. Adam Crosier.
	New Albany, Floyd county	C. Barnes.
	New Harmony, Posey county	John Chappellsmith.
	Richmond, Wayne county	Dr. John T. Plummer.
Illinois	Athens, Menard county	Joel Hall. Elihu Hall.
	Augusta, Hancock county	S. B. Mead, M. D.
	Batavia, Kane county	Thompson Mead.
	Brighton, Macoupin county	Wm. V. Eldredge.
	Carthage, Hancock county	Samuel Jacob Wallace.
	Chicago, Cook county	C. D. [illegible].
	Edgington, Rock Island county	Dr. E. H. Bowman.
	Galesburgh, Knox county	M. K. Taylor, M. D.
	Manchester, Scott county	John Grant.
	Marengo, McHenry county	O. P. Rogers & Son.
	Ottawa, La Salle county	J. O. Harris, M. D. C. H. Brush.
	Pekin, Tazewell county	J. W. Riblet.
	Peoria, (Orchard Farm,) Peoria county	Jacob H. Riblet.
	Riley, McHenry county	E. Babcock.

LIST OF STATIONS AND NAMES OF OBSERVERS.

STATIONS.		OBSERVERS.
Illinois	Warsaw, Hancock county	Benjamin Whittaker.
	Waynesville, De Witt county	J. E. Cantril.
	West Northfield, (The Grove,) Cook county	Robert W. Kennicott.
	West Salem, Edwards county	Henry A. Titze.
	Winnebago, Winnebago county	James W. Tolman.
Michigan	Ann Arbor, Washtenaw county	Lum. Woodruff. Mary H. Clark.
	Brest, Monroe county	Thomas Whelpley.
	Cooper, Kalamazoo county	Mrs. Octavia C. Walker.
	Flint, Genesee county	Dr. Clark and M. Miles.
	Grand Rapids, Kent county	Alfred O. Currier.
	Holland, Ottawa county	L. H. Streng.
	Romeo, Macomb county	Seth L. Andrews, M. D.
	St. James, (Beaver Island,) Emmet county	James J. Strang.
	Washington, Macomb county	Dennis Cooley.
	Wyandotte, Wayne county	E. P. Christian.
Wisconsin	Appleton, Ontagamie county	Prof. R. Z Mason.
	Baraboo, Sauk county	Dr. B. F. Mills.
	Greenfield, Mikwaukee county	Edward Hasse.
	Madison, Dane county	J. H B Matts.
	Milwaukee, Milwaukee county	I. A. Lapham.
	Norway, Racine county	John E. Himoe.
	Platteville, Grant county	J. L. Pickard, M. D.
Minnesota	Beaver Bay, Lake county	Thomas Clark.
	Burlington, Lake county	A. A. Hibbard.
	Cass Lake Mission	Benjamin F. Odell.
	Fort Ripley, Wanahtah county	Dr. J. F. Head.
	Kaposie, (7 miles east of Fort Snelling)	Not stated.
	Lac qui Parle	Alfred L. Riggs.
	Princeton, Benton county	O. E. Garrison.
	Red Wing, Goodhue county	Rev. Jabez Brooks.
Iowa	Bellevue, Jackson county	John C. Fory.
	Border Plains, Webster county	Wm. K. Goss.
	Dubuque, Dubuque county	Asa Horr, M. D.
	Eagle, Bremer county	Dexter Beal.
	Fairbank, Buchanan county	Dexter Beal.
	Fairfield, Jefferson county	J. M. Shaffer, M. D.
	Fort Madison, Lee county	Daniel McCready.
	Franklin, Buchanan county	Dexter Beal.
	Keokuk, Lee county	J. L. Zabriskie.
	Muscatine, Muscatine county	F. S. Parvin.
	Pleasant Plains, Jefferson county	Townsend McConnell.
	Plum Spring, Delaware county	B F. Odell.
Kansas	Leavenworth city, Leavenworth county	E L. Berthoud.
California	Sacramento, Sacramento county	Thomas M. Logan, M. D.
Oregon	Salem Prairie, Marion county	Thomas T. Eyre.
Washington Terr.	Shoalmette Bay	J. G. Cooper.
Nova Scotia	Horton	A. P. S. Stuart.
	Windsor, (King's College	Rev. J. M. Hensley.
	Wolfville, (Acadia College)	Prof. C. F. Hartt.
Canada East	Stanbridge, (near Saxe's Mills P. O., Vermont)	J. C. Baker.
Rupert's Land	Red River Settlement	Donald Gunn.
Saxony	Leipsig	Dr. Hofmeister.

DATES OF FOLIATION

OR

LEAFING OF PLANTS.

2*

ACER DASYCARPUM.—*White or Silver Maple.*

Name of Station.	1851.	1852.	1853.	1854.	1855.	1856.	1857.	1858.	1859.
Brunswick ... Maine								June 7	
Gardiner ... do							May 24		
Perry ... do									May 25
Steuben ... do				May 15	June 1			June 4	
Shelburne ... New Hamp								May 14	
Somersworth ... do				May 3					
Brandon ... Vermont								May 15	
Castleton ... do				May 7					
Florida ... Massachusetts								May 15	
Mendon ... do				May 12					
Columbia ... Connecticut							May 1		
Fishkill Landing ... New York							May 4	April 30	
New York city ... do								April 15	April 26
Rochester ... do							May 20	April 29	
West Point ... do			April 27						
Freehold ... New Jersey									May 6
Moorestown ... do					April 28				
Darby ... Pennsylvania			May 2						
Easton ... do				April 23					
Gettysburg ... do		May 5							
Lancaster ... do				April 10					
North Whitehall ... do							May 10		
Radner ... do		March 29	Feb. 13	March 1			April 9	Feb. 26	Mar. 23
Shamokin ... do							May 30		
Somerset ... do								May 20	
Upper Darby ... do				April 26					
Sykesville ... Maryland							May 25		
Buffalo ... Virginia					April 18				
Crichton's Store ... do								April 12	
Kanawha Salines ... do								March 25	
Chapel Hill ... N. Carolina								March 30	
Greensborough ... Alabama						March 31		March 22	
Jasper ... Mississippi					March 24				
Cleveland ... Ohio				April 21	April 25				
Hocking Port ... do							May 10		
Laconia ... Indiana								April 4	
Augusta ... Illinois				May 1			May 15		
Brighton ... do							May 4	March 30	
Peoria ... do								April 24	
Riley ... do							May 18		
Warsaw ... do							April 30	April 1	
Waynesville ... do								May 2	
West Northville ... do				April 25					
Ann Arbor ... Michigan			May 20						
Flint ... do					April 26				
Wyandotte ... do								May 1	May 10
Princeton ... Minnesota							May 5		
Stanbridge ... Canada							May 10	April 17	

ACER RUBRUM.—*Red or Soft Maple.*

Name of Station.	1851.	1852.	1853.	1854.	1855.	1856.	1857.	1858.	1859.
Brunswick ... Maine						June 2	June 2	June 5	
Cornish ... do						May 10	May 8		
Gardiner ... do							May 23		
Naples ... do							May 9		
Perry ... do									May 25
Steuben ... do	May 26					June 7			May 23
Londonderry ... New Hamp		May 8	May 8						
Manchester ... do		May 1							
North Barnstead ... do							May 23		
Salmon Falls ... do				May 7					
Somersworth ... do				May 3					
Stratford ... do						May 19			
Brandon ... Vermont			May 10	May 10		May 14	May 22	May 14	
Castleton ... do				May 6					
Craftsbury ... do						May 16	May 23		

ACER RUBRUM.—*Red or Soft Maple*—Continued.

Name of Station.	1851.	1852.	1853.	1854.	1855.	1856.	1857.	1858.	1859.
Newark ... Vermont							May 18		
Shelburn ... do						April 28			
Stockbridge ... do			May 8						
West Rupert ... do						April 25			
Bridgewater ... Massachusetts							May 12		
Florida ... do							May 8	May 10	
Lawrence ... do							May 27		
North Attleborough ... do		May 8							
Richmond ... do		May 10							
Uxbridge ... do				May 14					
Worcester ... do						May 12			
Columbia ... Connecticut							May 26	May 27	
East Windsor Hill ... do			May 6						
Fairfield ... do								May 15	
Georgetown ... do						May 1			
Middletown ... do		May 5							
Preston ... do						May 15			
Baldwinsville ... New York								May 22	
Chatham ... do		May 8							
Eden ... do						May 17	May 28		
Elmira ... do						April 29			
Fishkill Landing ... do							May 2	April 30	April 21
Flatbush ... do			April 15		April 24	May 18			
Lake ... do							May 23	May 15	May 12
Lowville ... do								May 26	
Mexico ... do						May 5			
New Lebanon ... do			May 5						
New York city ... do								April 12	
Nichols ... do								May 10	May 4
Ogdensburg ... do			May 15			May 12			
Oswego ... do						April 27			
Ovid ... do	May 11					May 12			
Plattsburg ... do		May 13							
Rochester ... do			April 28	April 25	May 1	April 28	May 11	May 4	
Spencertown ... do					May 12	May 19			
Waterloo ... do		May 1							
Wellsville ... do							April 4		
West Point ... do		May 5	April 28						
Williamsville ... do				April 22					
Burlington ... New Jersey		April 28							
Freehold ... do									May 5
Sergeantsville ... do							May 7		
Ceres ... Pennsylvania		May 8							
Easton ... do		May 3		April 25					
Fleming ... do							May 2		
Freeport ... do				April 2					
Gettysburg ... do		May 8	April 30	April 26		April 29			
Hollidaysburg ... do		May 6	April 28						
Huntingdon ... do						April 25	May 12		
Indiana ... do		May 9							
Meadville ... do		May 8				May 5			
Mercersburg ... do		May 6							
Murrysville ... do							May 24		
Nazareth ... do						May 3	May 10		
Orwigsburg ... do		May 7							
Shamokin ... do							May 27		
Somerset ... do								May 20	
Upper Darby ... do			April 24	April 29					
Easton ... Maryland				April 10					
Sykesville ... do			April 21	March 20			May 4		
Buffalo ... Virginia					April 25	April 19			
Crichton's Store ... do			April 15			April 15		April 15	
Mossy Creek ... do		April 25							
Poplar Grove ... do							April 16	April 20	April 3
Portsmouth ... do		April 10				April 19			
Rose Hill ... do						April 20	April 23		Mar. 24
Chapel Hill ... N. Carolina			April 2						
Savannah ... Georgia						March 31			
Sparta ... do							March 31		
Alligator ... Florida							Feb. 20		

ACER RUBRUM.—*Red or Soft Maple*—Continued.

Name of Station.	1851.	1852.	1853.	1854.	1855.	1856.	1857.	1858.	1859.
Greene Springs ... Alabama						April 12			
Greensborough ... do						April 4	March 21	March 22	
Weewokaville ... do		March 15	April 5						
Columbus ... Mississippi								March 14	
Jasper ... do					March 26	March 26			
Big Pond ... Louisiana						Feb 20			
Trinity ... do							March 5	March 20	
Union Hill ... Texas							March 1		
Hannibal ... Missouri				April 6					
Fairview ... Kentucky									May 10
Maysville ... do			April 22						
Ashtabula ... Ohio				May 3					
Belle Centre ... do		May 1						April 27	
Cheviot ... do						April 21			
Cleveland ... do				April 22	April 24				
Germantown ... do						April 25			
Hiram ... do						May 3	May 4	May 8	
Hocking Port ... do							May 15		
Keene ... do		March 28							
Marietta ... do								April 29	
Poland ... do					May 5				
Savannah ... do							May 10		
Laconia ... Indiana								April 2	
New Albany ... do						April 21			
Athens ... Illinois		April 26				April 7			
Batavia ... do								May 1	
Brighton ... do								April 6	
Edgington ... do							May 10		
Warsaw ... do						April 15	May 4	April 10	
West Salem ... do						April 20	May 21	April 21	
Ann Arbor ... Michigan			May 20						
Cooper ... do						April 14			
Flint ... do					April 26				
Saint James ... do			May `10			May 19			
Wyandotte ... do								April 25	May 1
Madison ... Wisconsin						May 13			
Norway ... do						May 15			
Cass Lake Mission ... Minnesota							May 15		
Lac qui Parle ... do			May 9	April 28					
Princeton ... do							May 1		
Border Plains ... Iowa								April 28	May 2
Eagle ... do							May 14		
Fairfield ... do									May 3
Fort Madison ... do		April 30				April 19			
Muscatine ... do			April 25	May 7	May 10	April 23			
Pleasant Plain ... do				April 15		May 20			
Leavenworth ... Kansas								April 23	
Windsor ... Nova Scotia							May 30		
Horton ... do					May 25				
Stanbridge ... Canada						May 6	May 10	April 17	

ACER SACCHARINUM.—*Sugar Maple.*

Name of Station.	1851.	1852.	1853.	1854.	1855.	1856.	1857.	1858.	1859.
Brunswick ... Maine							June 2	June 4	
Cornish ... do							May 9		
Gardiner ... do							May 16		
Naples ... do							May 12		
Perry ... do									May 25
Londonderry ... New Hamp		May 1	May 12						
Manchester ... do		May 10		May 11					
North Barnstead ... do							May 20		
Salmon Falls ... do				May 7					
Shelburne ... do								May 17	
Somersworth ... do				May 12					
West Enfield ... do							May 12		
Brandon ... Vermont			May 5	May 10			May 22		

ACER SACCHARINUM.—*Sugar Maple*—Continued.

Name of Station.	1851.	1852.	1853.	1854.	1855.	1856.	1857.	1858.	1859.
Burlington Vermont			May 10						
Castleton do.				May 7					
Newark do.							May 23		
Stockbridge do.			May 7						
Florida Massachusetts							May 20	May 10	
Mendon do.				May 15					
North Attleborough do.		May 8		May 12	May 13				
Richmond do.		May 10							
Williamstown do.							May 19		
Columbia Connecticut							May 25	May 20	
East Windsor Hill do.			May 8						
Fairfield do.								May 18	
Middletown do.		May 6	May 3						
Baldwinsville New York		May 8							
Chatham do.		May 12							
Fishkill Landing do.							May 4	April 30	April 20
Flatbush do.		May 1							
Lake do.							May 12	May 15	May 8
New Lebanon do.			May 4						
New York city do.					May 6			May 2	
Nichols do.								May 18	May 4
Ogdensburg do.			May 15			May 12			
Ovid do.				May 17					
Plattsburg do.		May 11							
Rochester do.				May 10	May 7		May 24	May 24	
Spencertown do.					May 12				
Waterloo do.		May 7							
Wellsville do.							April 10		
West Day do.									May 6
West Point do.			May 5						
Williamsville do.				April 30					
Burlington New Jersey		May 6							
Freehold do.									May 12
Ceres Pennsylvania		May 8							
Darby do.			May 2						
Easton do.				May 5					
Fleming do.							May 15		
Gettysburg do.			April 22						
Hollidaysburg do.		May 6	April 23						
Indiana do.		May 13							
Meadville do.		May 10							
Murrysville do.							May 11		
Nazareth do.							May 16		
Shamokin do.							May 30		
Somerset do.								May 20	
Upper Darby do.		May 1	April 26	April 24					
Easton Maryland		April 21							
Buffalo Virginia					April 20				
Crichton's Store do.			April 15					April 10	
Kanawha Salines do.								March 30	
Mossy Creek do.		April 25					May 20		
Poplar Grove do.								April 26	April 13
Greensborough Alabama						April 4		March 25	
Weewokaville do.		March 15	April 5						
Hannibal Missouri				April 10					
Glenwood Tennessee			April 1						
Fairview Kentucky									April 26
Maysville do.			April 25						
Ashtabula Ohio				May 5					
Belle Centre do.		May 6		May 1				May 1	
Cleveland do.				May 1	April 20				
Germantown do.		April 29	April 12	April 19					
Hiram do.								May 16	
Hocking Port do.							May 1		
Mount Healthy do.				April 10					
Poland do.					April 29				
Ripley do.							April 25		
Savannah do.							May 15		
Troy do.									April 15
Indianapolis Indiana									April 18

ACER SACCHARINUM.—*Sugar Maple*—Continued.

Name of Station.		1851.	1852.	1853.	1854.	1855.	1856.	1857.	1858.	1859.
Laconia	Indiana								April 8	April 11
Augusta	Illinois		May 5		May 1	April 28		May 20		
Batavia	do								May 1	
Brighton	do							April 30	April 12	
Marengo	do							May 22	April 20	
Pekin	do								May 20	
Peoria	do								April 26	
Warsaw	do							April 20	April 12	
Waynesville	do								May 6	
West Northville	do				May 0					
Winnebago	do							May 23		May 8
Ann Arbor	Michigan			May 20						
Flint	do					April 28				
Romeo	do						May 12			
Saint James	do			May 16						
Wyandotte	do								May 5	
Greenfield	Wisconsin									April 15
Princeton	Minnesota							May 1		
Border Plains	Iowa								May 11	May 5
Dubuque	do				May 7					
Fort Madison	do		May 3	April 21						
Keokuk	do						April 24			
Muscatine	do		May 10	May 1	May 7					
Pleasant Plain	do				April 15					
Stanbridge	Canada							May 10	May 10	
Leipsig	Saxony								April 16	

ACHILLEA MILLEFOLIUM.—*Millefoil, Yarrow.*

Name of Station.		1851.	1852.	1853.	1854.	1855.	1856.	1857.	1858.	1859.
Brunswick	Maine								May 25	
Steuben	do	May 15			May 25			May 4		
North Barnstead	New Hamp.							May 10		
Shelburne	do								May 9	
Florida	Massachusetts							May 16	May 19	
North Attleborough	do				April 25					
Waltham	do				April 10					
Columbia	Connecticut							April 25	April 28	
New York city	New York								May 8	
Ovid	do				May 13					
Spencertown	do					May 1				
West Point	do		May 10							
Ceres	Pennsylvania		May 28							
Darby	do		March 13							
Gettysburg	do			March 17						
Hollidaysburg	do		March 30	March 19						
Shamokin	do							April 25		
Buffalo	Virginia					April 9				
Mossy Creek	do							April 24		
Poplar Grove	do								April 4	
New Wied	Texas			Feb. 5						
Maysville	Kentucky			May 20						
Ashtabula	Ohio				July 10					
Bowling Green	do								April 5	
Keene	do		April 24							
Mount Healthy	do				May 1					
Poland	do					March 28				
Savannah	do							June 3		
Laconia	Indiana								April 10	
Edgington	Illinois							May 2		
Peoria	do								April 22	
Wyandotte	Michigan								May 28	
Pleasant Plain	Iowa				April 1	April 9	April 2			
Leavenworth	Kansas								April 8	
Horton	Nova Scotia					May 17				
Stanbridge	Canada							April 20	April 20	
Leipsig	Saxony								April 20	

ÆSCULUS FLAVA.—*Yellow Buckeye.*

Name of Station.	1851.	1852.	1853.	1854.	1855.	1856.	1857.	1858.	1859.
Rochester, New York			May 17		May 3		May 20	May 6	
West Point, do.			May 6						
Freehold, New Jersey									April 30
Easton, Pennsylvania				April 20					
Upper Darby, do.			April 15	April 25					
Chapel Hill, N. Carolina			March 23						
All Saints, S. Carolina					March 22				
Greensborough, Alabama						March 20	March 10		
Weewokaville, do.		April 1	March 5						
New Wied, Texas			March 15	March 10					
Maysville, Kentucky			April 22						
Belle Centre, Ohio		April 15							
Germantown, do.				April 8					
Indianapolis, Indiana									April 12
Fort Madison, Iowa		May 3							
Leipsig, Saxony								April 22	

ÆSCULUS GLABRA.—*Ohio Buckeye.*

Name of Station.	1851.	1852.	1853.	1854.	1855.	1856.	1857.	1858.	1859.
Rochester, New York			May 21		May 3		May 20	May 6	
Waterloo, do.		April 25							
West Point, do.			May 6						
Freehold, New Jersey									April 25
Nazareth, Pennsylvania							May 15		
Buffalo, Virginia					April 13				
Poplar Grove, do.								April 12	March 31
Greensborough, Alabama						March 20	March 10		
Jasper, Mississippi					March 16	March 20			
Oktibbehah county, do.							Feb. 19		
Hannibal, Missouri				April 8					
Ashtabula, Ohio				April 13					
Belle Centre, do.		April 15		April 10				April 5	
Cleveland, do.					April 22				
Germantown, do.		April 15	April 17	April 6					
Keene, do.		April 20							
Mount Healthy, do.				April 1					
Poland, do.					April 26				
Ripley, do.							April 20		
Savannah, do.							May 7		
Laconia, Indiana								March 1	
Augusta, Illinois		April 20	April 22	April 23	April 21				
Pekin, do.								May 14	
Warsaw, do.							May 3	April 14	
Waynesville, do.								April 12	
West Northville, do.				April 28					
Flint, Michigan					April 23				
Fairfield, Iowa									May 8
Fort Madison, do.		April 30		May 20					
Keokuk, do.						April 26			
Muscatine, do.		April 27	April 25	April 18	May 5				
Leavenworth, Kansas								May 2	

ÆSCULUS HIPPOCASTANUM.—*Horse Chestnut.*

Name of Station.	1851.	1852.	1853.	1854.	1855.	1856.	1857.	1858.	1859.
Brunswick, Maine							May 20	June [illegible]	
Gardiner, do.							May 22		
Naples, do.							May 16		
Perry, do.									May 20
Steuben, do.							May 25	May 16	
Francestown, New Hamp.			April 28						
Manchester, do.		May 7		May 11					
Salmon Falls, do.				May 11					
Somersworth, do.				May 2					
Castleton, Vermont				May 9					

ÆSCULUS HIPPOCASTANUM.—*Horse Chestnut*—Continued.

Name of Station.	1851.	1852.	1853.	1854.	1855.	1856.	1857.	1858.	1859.
Boston ... Massachusetts		May 24							
Lawrence ... do							May 6		
Mendon ... do				May 3					
North Attleborough ... do		May 6		May 1	May 2				
Uxbridge ... do				May 13					
Richmond ... do		May 15							
Waltham ... do				May 9					
Williamstown ... do							May 27		
Worcester ... do							May 9		
Columbia ... Connecticut							May 17	May 10	
Middletown ... do		May 5	April 30	May 7					
Chatham ... New York		May 9							
Fishkill Landing ... do							May 6		
Flatbush ... do		May 1	April 14	April 24	April 23				
New York city ... do				April 30	April 26			May 18	
Nichols ... do								May 28	April 21
Plattsburg ... do		May 13							
Ovid ... do				May 10					
Rochester ... do			April 27		April 26		May 18	May 6	
Spencertown ... do					May 1				
Waterloo ... do		April 28							
West Point ... do			April 26						
Freehold ... New Jersey									April 20
Moorestown ... do					April 21				
Newark ... do	April 13	May 4							
Ceres ... Pennsylvania		May 14							
Easton ... do		April 25		April 13					
Gettysburg ... do		May 11		May 3					
Hollidaysburg ... do			April 15						
Lancaster ... do				April 13					
Meadville ... do		April 6							
Philadelphia ... do								April 14	
Darby ... do			April 22						
Easton ... Maryland				March 29					
Green Plains ... N. Carolina							April 12		
Alligator ... Florida								Jan. 9	
Savannah ... Ohio							May 20		
Indianapolis ... Indiana									April 25
Batavia ... Illinois								April 27	
Marengo ... do							May 20	May 12	
West Northville ... do				April 25					
Muscatine ... Iowa		April 27	April 30	April 24	May 5				
Horton ... Nova Scotia					May 24				
Leipsig ... Saxony								April 10	

AILANTHUS GLANDULOSA.—*Tree of Heaven.*

Name of Station.	1851.	1852.	1853.	1854.	1855.	1856.	1857.	1858.	1859.
Burlington ... Vermont			May 10						
Mendon ... Massachusetts				May 20					
North Attleborough ... do				May 27	May 20				
Point Judith ... Rhode Island				May 25					
Columbia ... Connecticut							May 29	June 5	
Middletown ... do		May 15	May 8	May 10					
Fishkill Landing ... New York							May 15		
Flatbush ... do		May 18	May 8	May 10	May 15				
New York city ... do				May 16	May 16			May 19	
Plattsburg ... do		May 25							
Rochester ... do			May 21		May 24		May 30	May 27	
Spencertown ... do					May 24				
Waterloo ... do		May 15							
West Point ... do		May 17	May 9						
Burlington ... New Jersey		April 24							
Easton ... Pennsylvania		May 13		May 12					
Gettysburg ... do		May 9	April 30	May 3					
Hollidaysburg ... do		May 4							
Lancaster ... do				May 6					
Meadville ... do		May 22							

AILANTHUS GLANDULOSA.—*Tree of Heaven*—Continued.

Name of Station.		1851.	1852.	1853.	1854.	1855.	1856.	1857.	1858.	1859.
Mercersburg	Pennsylvania		May 6							
Murrysville	do							June 1		
Shamokin	do							May 30		
Darby	do			May 3						
Upper Darby	do			May 2						
Easton	Maryland				May 2					
Buffalo	Virginia				April 25					
Clark county	do							May 17	May 14	
Madison C. H.	do		April 24							
Mossy Creek	do		May 1					May 12		
Portsmouth	do		April 15							
Rose Hill	do						April 23			April 3
Chapel Hill	N. Carolina			April 20					April 8	
Camden	S. Carolina		March 28							
Alligator	Florida								March 5	
Greensborough	Alabama						April 6	March 25	April 10	
Hannibal	Missouri				April 26					
Glenwood	Tennessee			April 10						
Knoxville	do		April 29							
Maysville	Kentucky			May 5						
Ashtabula	Ohio				May 16					
Belle Centre	do		May 20						May 20	
Cleveland	do				May 10					
Germantown	do		May 8	May 1	May 5					
Keene	do		May 10							
Mount Healthy	do				May 1					
Poland	do					May 22				
Ripley	do							May 14		
Savannah	do							May 1		
Brighton	Illinois							May 3	March 17	
West Northville	do				May 17					
West Salem	do							May 26		
Romeo	Michigan						May 24			
Fort Madison	Iowa		May 15							
Muscatine	do		May 7	May 16	May 20	May 7				

AMELANCHIER CANADENSIS.—*Shad Bush—Serviceberry.*

Name of Station.		1851.	1852.	1853.	1854.	1855.	1856.	1857.	1858.	1859.
Brunswick	Maine								June 9	
Cornish	do							May 10		
Gardiner	do							May 30		
Perry	do						May 5			
Manchester	New Hamp.		May 15		May 12					
West Enfield	do							May 12		
Brandon	Vermont			May 6	May 9					
Newark	do							May 12		
Stockbridge	do			May 10						
Florida	Massachusetts							May 20	May 20	
Lawrence	do							May 26		
North Attleborough	do				May 1	May 10				
Richmond	do		May 15							
Columbia	Connecticut							May 20	May 8	
East Windsor Hill	do			April 26						
Middletown	do		May 6							
Chatham	New York		May 12							
Lake	do							May 11	May 19	May 3
New York city	do								May 6	
Plattsburg	do		May 8							
Ovid	do				May 16					
Rochester	do			May 5	May 10	May 2		May 22	May 7	
Burlington	New Jersey		April 20							
Ceres	Pennsylvania		April 30							
Fleming	do							May 15		
Freeport	do				April 10					
Gettysburg	do		May 5	April 28	April 22					
Hollidaysburg	do			April 15						

AMELANCHIER CANADENSIS.—*Shad Bush—Serviceberry.*—Continued.

Name of Station.		1851.	1852.	1853.	1854.	1855.	1856.	1857.	1858.	1859.
Meadville	Pennsylvania		May 3							
Somerset	do								April 29	
Upper Darby	do			April 26	April 22					
Sykesville	Maryland			April 11	March 11					
Buffalo	Virginia					April 17				
Mossy Creek	do		April 25							
Poplar Grove	do								April 12	April 10
Chapel Hill	N. Carolina			April 18						
Weewokaville	Alabama		April 2	March 20						
Ashtabula	Ohio				April 17					
Belle Centre	do								April 20	
Hocking Port	do							May 3		
Poland	do					May 14				
Savannah	do							May 11		
Laconia	Indiana								April 9	
Augusta	Illinois					April 25				
Warsaw	do							April 18	April 4	
Saint James	do			May 5						
Lac qui Parle	Minnesota			May 10	May 1					
Princeton	do							May 10		
Border Plains	do								April 27	May 7
Leavenworth	Kansas								April 14	

AMPELOPSIS QUINQUEFOLIA.—*Virginia Creeper—American Ivy.*

Name of Station.		1851.	1852.	1853.	1854.	1855.	1856.	1857.	1858.	1859.
Manchester	New Hamp		May 17							
East Windsor Hill	Connecticut			May 2						
Flatbush	New York		May 1	April 16						
West Point	do		May 10	April 28						
Burlington	New Jersey		May 8							
Gettysburg	Pennsylvania		May 3	April 28	May 1					
Upper Darby	do			April 24						
Crichton's Store	Virginia			April 10						
Genito	do		April 25							
Mossy Creek	do		May 5							
Maysville	Kentucky			April 26						
Belle Centre	Ohio		May 6							
Muscatine	Iowa		May 12	May 2						

AMYGDALUS NANA.—*Flowering Almond.*

Name of Station.		1851.	1852.	1853.	1854.	1855.	1856.	1857.	1858.	1859.
Brunswick	Maine							June 3	June 7	
Gardiner	do							June 1		
Steuben	do				May 16					
Manchester	New Hamp		May 17							
Burlington	Vermont					May 10				
Stockbridge	do			May 8						
Mendon	Massachusetts				May 2					
North Attleborough	do		May 10			May 5				
Worcester	do						May 13	May 20		
Columbia	Connecticut							May 13	May 9	
Fairfield	do								May 16	
Angelica	New York						May 10			
Chatham	do		May 1							
Flatbush	do		May 1	April 25	April 25	May 5				
New York city	do				April 28					
Nichols	do									May 10
Ogdensburg	do			May 5						
Ovid	do				May 18					
Plattsburg	do		May 12							
Rochester	do						May 14	May 24	May 22	
Spencertown	do					May 8	May 6			
Burlington	New Jersey		May 20							

AMYGDALUS NANA.—*Flowering Almond*—Continued.

Name of Station.	1851.	1852.	1853.	1854.	1855.	1856.	1857.	1858.	1859.
Ceres .... Pennsylvania..		May 14							
Easton .... do				April 20					
Gettysburg .... do		May 3	April 25	April 20					
Hollidaysburg .... do			May 3						
Meadville .... do		May 6							
Morrisville .... do						May 25			
Murrysville .... do						May 18			
Nazareth .... do						May 7			
Easton .... Maryland...				May 17					
Sykesville .... do			April 4				May 15		
Buffalo .... Virginia....					April 15				
Clark County .... do							April 25	April 7	
Crichton's Store .... do			March 30				April 10	April 12	March 20
Kanawha Salines .... do								March 28	
Mossy Creek .... do		April 25					May 10		
Poplar Grove .... do								April 6	March 30
Rose Hill .... do						April 13			March 23
Chapel Hill .... N. Carolina..			March 23						
Camden .... S. Carolina..		March 8							
Sparta .... Georgia....						March 5			
Alligator .... Florida....								March 1	
Greensborough .... Alabama...						April 5	March 24	Feb. 28	
Weewokaville .... do		April 10	March 30						
Jasper .... Mississippi..					March 8	March 20			
Union Hill .... Texas....							Feb. 8		
Glenwood .... Tennessee..			March 27						
Maysville .... Kentucky..			April 24						
Ashtabula .... Ohio....				April 25					
Belle Centre .... do		May 3						May 5	
Bowling Green .... do								April 11	
Cleveland .... do				April 20	April 22				
Germantown .... do						April 21			
Keene .... do		May 10							
Mount Healthy .... do				May 1					
Ripley .... do							April 10		
Savannah .... do							May 10		
Indianapolis .... Indiana...									April 18
Laconia .... do								April 10	
Athens .... Illinois....						April 16			
Augusta .... do		April 30	April 15	April 20	April 19		May 7		
Batavia .... do								April 2	
Brighton .... do							March 12		
Warsaw .... do						April 25	April 13	April 8	
Waynesville .... do								April 2	
West Northville .... do				April 23					
Ann Arbor .... Michigan...			May 4						
Wyandotte .... do								April 30	
Madison .... Wisconsin...						April 28			
Border Plains .... Iowa....									May 5
Eagle .... do							May 20		
Fairfield .... do									May 2
Muscatine .... do		May 10	May 2	April 26	May 1				
Horton .... Nova Scotia..					May 27				
Stanbridge .... Canada....							May 13	May 10	
Leipsig .... Saxony....								April 16	

ANEMONE NEMOROSA.—*Wind Flower—Wood Anemone.*

Name of Station.	1851.	1852.	1853.	1854.	1855.	1856.	1857.	1858.	1859.
Brunswick .... Maine....							May 6	May 13	
Londonderry .... New Hamp..		May 4							
Manchester .... do		May 7							
Mendon .... Masssachusetts..				May 1					
Worcester .... do							May 12		
Fairfield .... Connecticut..								May 1	
Chatham .... New York...		May 10							
Ovid .... do				May 9					
West Point .... do		April 10							

ANEMONE NEMOROSA.—*Wind Flower—Wood Anemone*—Continued.

Name of Station.		1851.	1852.	1853.	1854.	1855.	1856.	1857.	1858.	1859.
Ceres	Pennsylvania		April 27							
Hollidaysburg	do			April 18						
Sykesville	Maryland			April 3	April 1					
Buffalo	Virginia					April 12				
Mossy Creek	do		March 25					April 20		
Ashtabula	Ohio				April 15					
Cleveland	do				April 15	April 11				
Keene	do		April 10							
Poland	do					April 1				
Fort Ripley	Minnesota		May 9							
Princeton	do							April 30		
Fairfield	Iowa									April 9
Keokuk	do						April 22			
Leavenworth	Kansas								Feb. 5	
Leipsig	Saxony								March 30	

AQUALEGIA CANADENSIS.—*Wild Columbine.*

Name of Station.		1851.	1852.	1853.	1854.	1855.	1856.	1857.	1858.	1859.
Cornish	Maine							May 28		
Lawrence	Massachusetts							May 12		
North Attleborough	do		April 29		April 28	May 3				
Columbia	Connecticut							Feb. 25	April 22	
Fairfield	do								May 13	
Chatham	New York		May 8							
New York city	do					April 26				
Ovid	do				May 6					
West Point	do		April 20							
Burlington	New Jersey		May 5							
Ceres	Pensylvania		May 15							
Freeport	do				April 2					
Hollidaysburg	do		April 3	April 7						
Buffalo	Virginia					March 15				
Clark County	do							May 1	April 15	
Mossy Creek	do		March 30					March 30		
Belle Centre	Ohio		May 1							
Ripley	do							April 6		
Laconia	Indiana								March 1	
Wyandotte	Michigan								March 20	
Lac qui Parle	Minnesota			April 19	April 14					
Princeton	do							May 6		
Fairfield	Iowa									April 27
Muscatine	do		April 19	April 23	April 10	May 1				
Pleasant Plains	do				May 1					
Leavenworth	Kansas								March 26	
Stanbridge	Canada							May 10	April 10	

ASCLEPIAS CORNUTI.—*Milkweed.*

Name of Station.		1851.	1852.	1853.	1854.	1855.	1856.	1857.	1858.	1859.
Naples	Maine							May 27		
West Enfield	New Hamp.							May 3		
Florida	Massachusetts.							May 15		
North Attleborough	do		May 21		May 20	May 25				
Waltham	do				May 18					
Columbia	Connecticut							May 14	May 22	
Flatbush	New York				May 20					
Ovid	do				May 19					
Waterloo	do		April 20							
West Point	do		June 4							
Burlington	New Jersey		May 12							
Darby	Pennsylvania.			May 13						
Easton	Maryland		Feb. 25							
Clark county	Virginia							May 28		
Crichton's Store	do			April 25				May 10		
Genito	do		April 30							
Mossy Creek	do		May 1							

ASCLEPIAS CORNUTI.—*Milkweed.*—Continued.

Name of Station.		1851.	1852.	1853.	1854.	1855.	1856.	1857.	1858.	1859.
Chapel Hill	N. Carolina			May 7						
Weewokaville	Alabama		April 4	April 2						
Union Hill	Texas							May 10		
Ashtabula	Ohio				May 16					
Cleveland	do			May 3						
Germantown	do				May 5					
Hocking Port	do							May 15		
Mount Healthy	do				May 15					
Savannah	do							May 18		
Augusta	Illinois							May 25		
Brighton	do							May 3		
Warsaw	do							May 15		
Lac qui Parle	Minnesota			June 1	May 24					
Fort Madison	Iowa				May 6					
Stanbridge	Canada							June 1	June 10	

ASIMINA TRILOBA.—*Papaw.*

Name of Station.		1851.	1852.	1853.	1854.	1855.	1856.	1857.	1858.	1859.
Radnor	Pennsylvania			May 9						
Buffalo	Virginia					April 25				
Clark county	do							May 23	May 18	
Crichton's Store	do							April 12	April 10	
Poplar Grove	do								April 23	April 18
All Saints	S. Carolina					April 9				
Alligator	Florida								March 1	
Greensborough	Alabama							March 26	March 28	
Ashtabula	Ohio				May 14					
Belle Centre	do				May 5				May 15	
Germantown	do				April 28					
Hocking Port	do							May 29		
Hount Healthy	do				April 20					
Poland	do					May 16				
Savannah	do							May 24		
Laconia	Indiana								April 17	
Brighton	Illinois							April 29		
Warsaw	do							April 20	April 16	
Waynesville	do								May 15	
Muscatine	Iowa				May 7					
Leavenworth	Kansas								April 30	

BIGNONIA RADICANS—*Trumpet Creeper.*

Name of Station.		1851.	1852.	1853.	1854.	1855.	1856.	1857.	1858.	1859.
Gardiner	Maine							May 25		
Steuben	do					May 29			May 5	
Mendon	Massachusetts				May 13					
Point Judith	Rhode Island				May 30					
New York city	New York					May 20				May 14
Ovid	do				May 26					
Burlington	New Jersey		May 16							
Gettysburg	Pennsylvania			May 3						
Meadville	do		May 26							
Darby	do			May 6						
Crichton's Store	Virginia			April 24					April 12	
Genito	do		April 28							
Poplar Grove	do								April 24	April 26
Alligator	Florida								Jan. 5	
Cleveland	Ohio				May 12	May 5				
Mount Healthy	do				May 1					
Poland	do					May 19				
Laconia	Indiana								May 1	
Augusta	Illinois		May 15	May 15	May 14	May 3		June 2		
Warsaw	do							May 10	April 26	
West Northville	do				May 15					
Flint	Michigan					May 3				
Muscatine	Iowa		May 15							
Leipsig	Saxony								April 26	

CARPINUS AMERICANA.—*Hornbeam—Ironwood.*

Name of Station.		1851.	1852.	1853.	1854.	1855.	1856.	1857.	1858.	1859.
Waterloo	New York		May 6							
West Point	do			April 30						
Ceres	Pennsylvania		May 10							
Easton	do			May 4						
Gettysburg	do		May 9							
Hollidaysburg	do			April 28						
Indiana	do		May 13							
Meadville	do		May 8							
Mercersburg	do		May 4							
Radnor	do			April 28	May 4					
Upper Darby	do		May 8	April 29						
Madison Court-house	Virginia		April 19							
Weewokaville	Alabama		April 3	March 29						
Trenton	Missouri			April 25						
Glenwood	Tennessee			April 10						
Belle Centre	Ohio		April 29							
Warsaw	Illinois							May 2		

CARYA ALBA.—*Shellbark Hickory.*

Name of Station.		1851.	1852.	1853.	1854.	1855.	1856.	1857.	1858.	1859.
Gardiner	Maine							May 30		
Salmon Falls	New Hamp				May 17					
Brandon	Vermont								May 16	
Castleton	do			May 12						
Mendon	Massachusetts				May 19					
North Attleborough	do				May 18					
Uxbridge	do				May 21					
Columbia	Connecticut							May 27	May 26	
Fairfield	do								May 23	
Chatham	New York		May 15							
Fishkill Landing	do								May 10	
Flatbush	do				May 3	May 8				
Lake	do							May 24	May 24	May 13
New York city	do								May 12	
Nichols	do								May 30	May 14
Ovid	do				May 20					
Spencertown	do					May 20				
Moorestown	New Jersey					April 26				
Easton	Pennsylvania				May 7					
Fleming	do							May 20		
Freeport	do				May 10					
Indiana	do		May 10							
Murrysville	do							May 21		
North Whitehall	do							May 23		
Orwigsburg	do		May 7							
Shamokin	do							May 29		
Somerset	do								May 20	
Upper Darby	do				May 6					
Easton	Maryland				May 4					
Buffalo	Virginia					April 26				
Clark county	do							May 15	May 8	
Crichton's Store	do							May 2	April 7	Mar. 16
Poplar Grove	do								May 12	April 28
Rose Hill	do						April 17			April 7
Chapel Hill	N. Carolina								April 3	
Greensborough	Alabama						April 4		Mar. 24	
Jasper	Mississippi					April 7				
Hannibal	Missouri				April 23					
Ashtabula	Ohio				May 13					
Belle Centre	do				May 1				April 22	
Bowling Green	do								May 14	
Cleveland	do				May 7	May 3				
Hiram	do							May 24	May 10	
Mount Healthy	do				April 25					
Poland	do					May 13				
Savannah	do							May 24		

CARYA ALBA.—*Shellbark Hickory.*—Continued.

Name of Station.		1851.	1852.	1853.	1854.	1855.	1856.	1857.	1858.	1859.
Laconia	Indiana								April 18	
Augusta	Illinois				May 3	April 28		May 20		
Batavia	do								May 15	
Brighton	do							May 17	April 29	
Edgington	do							May 15		
Marengo	do								April 20	
Pekin	do								May 20	
Peoria	do								May 15	
Warsaw	do							May 13	April 30	
West Northville	do				May 12					
West Salem	do							May 16		
Ann Arbor	Michigan			May 20						
Wyandotte	do								May 11	
Princeton	Minnesota							May 15		
Border Plains	Iowa								May 20	May 12
Eagle	do							May 28		
Fairfield	do									May 10
Fort Madison	do				April 22					
Keokuk	do						April 28			
Muscatine	do				May 10	May 15				
Pleasant Plain	do					May 7	May 25	June 1		
Leavenworth	Kansas								April 30	
Stanbridge	Canada								May 24	

CASTANEA VESCA.—*Chestnut.*

Name of Station.		1851.	1852.	1853.	1854.	1855.	1856.	1857.	1858.	1859.
Gardiner	Maine							May 29		
Florida	Massachusetts							May 20		
Mendon	do				May 21					
North Attleborough	do		May 10		May 13	May 3				
Uxbridge	do				May 15					
Richmond	do		May 20							
Waltham	do				May 13					
Columbia	Connecticut							May 24	May 23	
Middletown	do			May 4						
Fishkill Landing	New York							May 12	May 1	April 4
Flatbush	do		May 8	May 3	May 6	May 9				
Lake	do									May 18
New Lebanon	do			May 14						
New York city	do								May 13	
Nichols	do									May 12
Spencertown	do					May 20				
West Point	do		May 5	April 27						
Burlington	New Jersey		May 8							
Ceres	Pennsylvania		May 13							
Darby	do		May 10	April 30						
Easton	do		May 6		May 5					
Fleming	do							May 25		
Freeport	do				May 10					
Gettysburg	do				April 29					
Indiana	do		May 8							
Meadville	do		May 10							
Nazareth	do							May 10		
North Whitehall	do							May 21		
Orwigsburg	do		May 7							
Shamokin	do							May 25		
Somerset	do								May [illegible]0	
Upper Darby	do		May 9	April 30	May 10					
Valley Forge	do		May 5							
Easton	Maryland				April 29					
Sykesville	do		May 1	April 20	May 5			May 20		
Madison C. H.	Virginia		April 30							
Poplar Grove	do								April 26	April 28
Rose Hill	do						April 14			April 13
Greensborough	Alabama						April 12	April 2	April 12	
Weewokaville	do		April 4	Mar. 30						

CASTANEA VESCA.—*Chestnut*—Continued.

Name of Station.		1851.	1852.	1853.	1854.	1855.	1856.	1857.	1858.	1859.
Ashtabula	Ohio				May 15					
Bowling Green	do								May 10	
Cleveland	do				May 14	May 6				
Hiram	do							May 24	May 14	
Hocking Port	do							May 18		
Poland	do					May 14				
Savannah	do							June 2		
Laconia	Indiana								April 18	
West Northville	Illinois				April 29					
Muscatine	Iowa		May 2	May 1	May 10	May 18				
Leipsig	Saxony								April 30	

CELASTRUS SCANDENS.—*Bitter-sweet.—Wax-work.*

Name of Station.		1851.	1852.	1853.	1854.	1855.	1856.	1857.	1858.	1859.
Manchester	New Hamp.		May 22							
Middletown	Connecticut		May 6							
Burlington	New Jersey		May 7							
Gettysburg	Pennsylvania				April 30					
Hollidaysburg	do			May 1						
Mossy Creek	Virginia		May 1							
Augusta	Illinois		May 1							
St. James	Michigan			May 3						
Lac qui Parle	Minnesota			May 21						

CERASUS CERASUS.—*Garden Cherry.*

Name of Station.		1851.	1852.	1853.	1854.	1855.	1856.	1857.	1858.	1859.
Carmel	Maine						May 21			
Perry	do						June 1			
Concord	New Hampshire						May 18			
Salmon Falls	do				May 12					
Stratford	do						May 12			
Craftsbury	Vermont						May 13	May 28		
Newark	do						May 31			
Shelburn	do						May 17			
West Rupert	do						May 12	May 18		
Bridgewater	Massachusetts							May 20		
East Weymouth	do						May 8			
Westfield	do						May 12			
Worcester	do						April 29			
Columbia	Connecticut								May 15	
Georgetown	do						April 30			
Norwich	do						May 1			
Weston	do						May 16			
Angelica	New York						May 19			
Clinton	do							May 4		
Eden	do						May 14	June 2		
Flatbush	do							May 4		
Lake	do						May 17			
Lowville	do						May 20	April 24	May 1	
New York city	do							May 7		
Rochester	do						May 10	May 23		
Spencertown	do						May 10			
Wellsville	do								April 10	
West Concord	do						May 23			
Sergeantsville	New Jersey							May 9		
Bellefonte	Pennsylvania								May 12	
Gettysburg	do		May 3							
Huntingdon	do						April 29	May 2		
Indiana	do		April 29							
Lima	do						April 26			
Morrisville	do						May 10			
Nazareth	do						April 29			
North Whitehall	do							May 7		

CERASUS CERASUS.—*Garden Cherry*—Continued.

Name of Station.	1851.	1852.	1853.	1854.	1855.	1856.	1857.	1858.	1859.
Shamokin .... Pennsylvania.							May 2		
Ridge .... Maryland...						April 24			
Sykesville .... do......						May 14			
Buffalo .... Virginia....						April 30			
Crack Whip .... do......							April 30		
Crichton's Store .... do......						April 15			
Poplar Grove .... do......									March 28
Winchester .... do......						April 28			
Wirt C H .... do......						May 10			
Aiken .... South Carolina.						April 9			
Zebulon .... Georgia....						April 21			
Alligator .... Florida...							Feb. 1		
Greene Springs .... Alabama...						April 1			
Oxford .... Mississippi..						April 7			
Helena .... Texas....							Feb. 25		
Rockport .... Missouri...						April 14			
Westport .... do......						April 15			
Cheviot .... Ohio.....						April 18			
Edinburg .... do......							May 24		
Germantown .... do......						April 18			
Hamilton .... do......							May 3		
Hiram .... do......						May 4			
Jefferson .... do......						May 10			
Welchfield .... do......							June 6		
New Albany .... Indiana...						April 28			
New Harmony .... do......						April 8			
Manchester .... Illinois....						April 19			
Ottawa .... do......								April 11	
Pekin .... do......								May 14	
Warsaw .... do......						April 19	May 8	April 1	
West Salem .... do......						April 23		April 18	
Cooper .... Michigan...						April 29			
St. James .... do......						May 20			
Madison .... Wisconsin...						May 3	May 13		
Norway .... do......						May 1			
Fort Madison .... Iowa.....						April 21			
Muscatine .... do......				April 22		May 5			
Pleasant Plain .... do......						May 20			
Stanbridge .... Canada...						May 18			

CERASUS SEROTINA.—*Wild Black Cherry.*

Name of Station.	1851.	1852.	1853.	1854.	1855.	1856.	1857.	1858.	1859.
Brunswick .... Maine.....								June 9	
Gardiner .... do......							May 28		
Naples .... do......							May 8		
Perry .... do......									May 8
Steuben .... do......				May 28					
Salmon Falls .... New Hampshire.				May 3					
West Enfield .... do......							May 14		
Brandon .... Vermont...			May 3				May 10	May 5	
Castleton .... do......			May 7						
Newark .... do......							May 20		
Florida .... Massachusetts.							May 10	May 5	
Mendon .... do......				May 10					
North Attleborough .... do......				May 4	May 3				
Williamstown .... do......							May 25		
Worcester .... do......							May 13		
Point Judith .... Rhode Island.				May 26					
Columbia .... Connecticut.							May 3	May 10	
Fairfield .... do......								May 21	
Fishkill Landing .... New York...							May 10		April 24
Flatbush .... do......				April 10	April 21				
Lake .... do......								May 8	May 5
New York city .... do......				May 5	May 2			May 8	
Spencertown .... do......					May 1				
Moorestown .... New Jersey.					April 19				
Easton .... Pennsylvania.				April 13					

CERASUS SEROTINA.—*Wild Black Cherry*—Continued.

Name of Station.	1851.	1852.	1853.	1854.	1855.	1856.	1857.	1858.	1859.
Fleming ..... Pennsylvania							May 15		
Murrysville ..... do							May 11		
North Whitehall ..... do							May 7		
Somerset ..... do								May 5	
Sykesville ..... Maryland				May 10			May 14		
Clarke county ..... Virginia					April 15				
Crichton's Store ..... do							April 10	April 10	March 10
Mossy Creek ..... do							May 15		
Poplar Grove ..... do								April 3	March 29
Rose Hill ..... do						April 12			April 10
Alligator ..... Florida								Jan. 21	
Greensborough ..... Alabama						March 22	March 13	Feb. 28	
Jasper ..... Mississippi					March 22				
Hannibal ..... Missouri				April 10					
Ashtabula ..... Ohio				April 30					
Belle Centre ..... do								April 15	
Poland ..... do					April 28				
Ripley ..... do							April 22		
Savannah ..... do							May 27		
Augusta ..... Illinois					April 20				
Batavia ..... do								April 28	
Brighton ..... do							May 7	May 6	
Marengo ..... do							May 18	April 13	
Warsaw ..... do							May 4	April 14	
Waynesville ..... do								April 15	
West Northville ..... do				April 20					
West Salem ..... do							May 10		
Flint ..... Michigan					April 23				
Wyandotte ..... do								April 30	
Princeton ..... Minnesota							May 10		
Eagle ..... Iowa							May 20		
Fairfield ..... do									May 10
Muscatine ..... do				April 24					
Pleasant Plain ..... do				April 23	April 16		May 28		
Leavenworth ..... Kansas								March 29	
Stanbridge ..... Canada							May 12	May 8	

CERASUS VIRGINIANA.—*Choke Cherry.*

Name of Station.	1851.	1852.	1853.	1854.	1855.	1856.	1857.	1858.	1859.
Brunswick ..... Maine								June 9	
Cornish ..... do							April 26		
Gardiner ..... do							June 3		
Somersworth ..... New Hamp.				May 10					
West Enfield ..... do							May 12		
Brandon ..... Vermont			April 30				May 9		
Castleton ..... do			May 10						
Florida ..... Massachusetts							May 18		
Waltham ..... do				May 8					
Columbia ..... Connecticut							May 16		
Lake ..... New York							May 9	May 7	May 4
New York city ..... do				May 15	April 30			June 4	
Spencertown ..... do					May 1				
Fleming ..... Pennsylvania							May 20		
Indiana ..... do		May 8							
Murrysville ..... do							May 14		
Alligator ..... Florida								Jan. 20	
Poland ..... Ohio					May 1				
Laconia ..... Indiana								March 31	
Riley ..... Illinois							May 7		
Waynesville ..... do								May 4	
West Northville ..... do				April 23					
Lac qui Parle ..... Minnesota				April 25					
Princeton ..... do							May 10		
Border Plains ..... Iowa									May 1
Eagle ..... do							May 20		
Muscatine ..... do				April 23					

CERASUS VIRGINIANA.—*Choke Cherry*—Continued.

Name of Station.	1851.	1852.	1853.	1854.	1855.	1856.	1857.	1858.	1859.
Pleasant Plain ....Iowa....				April 20	April 10		May 28		
Stanbridge ....Canada....							May 15	June 1	
Leipsig................Saxony....								April 10	

CERCIS CANADENSIS.—*Redbud.*—*Judas Tree.*

Name of Station.	1851.	1852.	1853.	1854.	1855.	1856.	1857.	1858.	1859.
Columbia ....Connecticut..							May 17		
Rochester..............New York...			May 28		May 20		June 6	May 28	
Burlington ....New Jersey..		May 20							
Freehold ....do.....									April 25
Gettysburg ....Pennsylvania..		May 11		May 8					
Nazareth ....do.....							May 26		
Upper Darby.................do.....		May 12	May 3	May 1					
Hagerstown ....Maryland...			April 22						
Buffalo ....Virginia....					April 15				
Crichton's Store ....do.....			April 18					April 15	
Genito ....do.....		April 10							
Mossy Creek ....do.....		May 10					May 28		
Poplar Grove ....do.....								April 30	April 16
Chapel Hill............N. Carolina..			April 20					April 10	
All Saints.............S. Carolina..					March 22				
Alligator ....Florida....								April 2	
Greensborough ....Alabama...							March 25	April 1	
Weewokaville...............do.....		March 15	April 26						
Jasper ....Mississippi..					March 12	March 21			
Trenton................Missouri...				April 22					
Fairview ....Kentucky..									April 20
Maysville..................do.....			May 8						
Belle Centre ....Ohio.....		May 13		May 1				May 5	
Hocking Port ....do.....							May 25		
Mount Healthy ....do.....				April 30					
Poland ....do.....					May 19				
Laconia.................Indiana....								April 15	May 9
Augusta.................Illinois....			May 15		April 28		May 28		
Brighton ....do.....							May 21	April 1	
Edgington ....do.....							May 10		
Peoria.....................do.....								May 15	
Warsaw ....do.....							May 14	April 29	
Waynesville ....do.....								April 20	
West Northville............do.....				May 2					
West Salem ....do.....							May 28		
Ann Arbor ....Michigan...			May 23						
Muscatine ....Iowa....			April 30						
Leavenworth ....Kansas....								April 10	

CHELIDONIUM MAJUS.—*Celandine.*

Name of Station.	1851.	1852.	1853.	1854.	1855.	1856.	1857.	1858.	1859.
Manchester ....New Hamp...		May 7							
Burlington............New Jersey...		April 20							
Hollidaysburg ...... Pennsylvania..			April 7						
Mossy Creek .... Virginia....		March 15							

CHIONANTHUS VIRGINICA.—*Fringe Tree.*

Name of Station.	1851.	1852.	1853.	1854.	1855.	1856.	1857.	1858.	1859.
Flatbush ....New York...		May 8	April 21	April 27					
Burlington ....New Jersey...	April 18								
Moorestown.................do.....					May 15				
Gettysburg...........Pennsylvania..		May 6							
Hollidaysburg ....do.....			May 3						
Darby ....do.....		May 10	May 7						
Radnor ....do.....		June 5		May 27	June 8	June 8	June 14	June 13	

CHIONANTHUS VIRGINICA.—*Fringe Tree*—Continued.

Name of Station.	1851.	1852.	1853.	1854.	1855.	1856.	1857.	1858.	1859.
Buffalo ... Virginia					April 30				
Chapel Hill ... N. Carolina			April 20					April 15	
All Saints ... S. Carolina					April 18				
Camden ... do		April 10							
Alligator ... Florida								Jan. 30	
Greensborough ... Alabama							March 29	April 6	
Ashtabula ... Ohio				April 24					
Cleveland ... do				May 17	May 15				
Poland ... do					May 12				
Muscatine ... Iowa		May 12	May 2	May 12					

CIMICIFUGA RACEMOSA.—*Blacksnake Root.*—*Rattlesnake Root.*

Name of Station.	1851.	1852.	1853.	1854.	1855.	1856.	1857.	1858.	1859.
Columbia ... Connecticut							April 26	April 22	
Moorestown ... New Jersey					April 13				
Easton ... Pennsylvania				April 8					
Gettysburg ... do				April 28					
Hollidaysburg ... do		May 24	May 9						
North Whitehall ... do							May 7		
Shamokin ... do							May 27		
Sykesville ... Maryland			April 3						
Buffalo ... Virginia					April 27				
Clarke county ... do								April 28	
Crichton's Store ... do			May 3						
Mossy Creek ... do		April 25							
Camden ... S. Carolina		March 13							
Aligator ... Florida								Jan. 5	
Weewokaville ... Alabama		April 15	April 5						
Ashtabula ... Ohio				May 6					
Poland ... do					May 12				
Brighton ... Illinois							May 25	April 29	
Princeton ... Minnesota							May 20		
Stanbridge ... Canada							May 1	May 1	

CLETHRA ALNIFOLIA.—*White Alder.*—*Sweet Pepperbush.*

Name of Station.	1851.	1852.	1853.	1854.	1855.	1856.	1857.	1858.	1859.
Gardiner ... Maine							May 29		
Florida ... Massachusetts							May 5		
Waltham ... do				May 15					
Columbia ... Connecticut								May 1	
New York city ... New York									May 8
Spencertown ... do					May 1				
Freehold ... New Jersey									May 1
Crichton's Store ... Virginia									March 22
Alligator ... Florida								Jan. 3	
Fairfield ... Iowa									May 10

CORNUS FLORIDA.—*Flowering Dogwood.*

Name of Station.	1851.	1852.	1853.	1854.	1855.	1856.	1857.	1858.	1859.
Cornish ... Maine						May 20			
Francestown ... New Hamp.			April 23						
Stratford ... do						May 11			
West Enfield ... do							May 20		
West Rupert ... Vermont						May 10	May 20		
Bridgewater ... Massachusetts							May 12		
Florida ... do							May 10	May 10	
Mendon ... do				May 12					
Waltham ... do				May 19					
Columbia ... Connecticut							May 18	May 17	
Georgetown ... do						May 5			
Fishkill Landing ... New York								May 16	

CORNUS FLORIDA—*Flowering Dogwood*—Continued.

Name of Station.		1851.	1852.	1853.	1854.	1855.	1856	1857.	1858.	1859.
Flatbush	New York		May 1	April 25	May 7					
Lake	do						May 22			
New York city	do							May 15	May 18	
Ovid	do				May 25					
Rochester	do			May 12					May 15	
Spencertown	do					May 1				
Waterloo	do		May 6							
Wellsville	do								May 4	
West Point	do		May 12	May 9						
Burlington	New Jersey		April 28							
Freehold	do									May 1
Sergeantsville	do							May 11		
Fleming	Pennsylvania							May 26		
Freeport	do				May 15					
Gettysburg	do			April 30	April 30					
Hollidaysburg	do			May 1						
Huntingdon	do						May 8	May 23		
Indiana	do		May 12							
Meadville	do		May 12							
Murrysville	do							May 26		
Nazareth	do						May 14	May 21		
Shamokin	do							June 1		
Darby	do		May 8	April 27						
Upper Darby	do			April 26						
Valley Forge	do		May 7							
Easton	Maryland				April 20					
Ridge	do						April 15			
Sykesville	do		May 3	May 8	April 1		May 5	May 24		
Berryville	Virginia						April 16			
Buffalo	do					April 24				
Crichton's Store	do			April 14				April 15	April 20	March 22
Genito	do		March 16							
Mossy Creek	do		May 1					May 30		
Poplar Grove	do								April 18	April 16
Rose Hill	do						April 18	April 27		April 7
Wirt Court-House	do						May 10			
Chapel Hill	N. Carolina			April 18					April 5	
Alligator	Florida								Jan. 9	
Greensborough	Alabama						April 18	March 17	March 22	
Greene Springs	do						April 5			
Weewokaville	do		April 4	April 15						
Jasper	Mississippi					March 24				
New Wied	Texas			March 8						
Union Hill	do							March 2		
Maysville	Kentucky			April 23						
Ashtabula	Ohio				May 11					
Belle Centre	do		May 8		May 5					
Cleveland	do				April 30	May 1				
Edinburg	do							May 29		
Mount Healthy	do				April 25					
Poland	do					May 2				
Savannah	do							May 20		
Laconia	Indiana								April 18	
West Salem	Illinois							May 29		
Ann Arbor	Michigan			May 18						
Wyandotte	do								May 8	
Appleton	Wisconsin						May 23			
Lac qui Parle	Minnesota				April 28					
Princeton	do							May 5		
Muscatine	Iowa			May 2	May 1	May 12				
Stanbridge	Canada								May 0	

CRATÆGUS COCCINEA.—*Scarlet Fruited Thorn.*

Name of Station.		1851.	1852.	1853.	1854.	1855.	1856	1857.	1858.	1859.
Brunswick	Maine								June 9	
Cornish	do							May 27		
Naples	do							May 22		
Steuben	do	May 25	May 11	May 16	May 19				May 6	

CRATÆGUS COCCINEA—*Scarlet Fruited Thorn*—Continued.

Name of Station.	1851.	1852.	1853.	1854.	1855.	1856.	1857.	1858.	1859.
Salmon Falls, New Hamp.				May 2					
Somersworth, do.				May 11					
Castleton, Vermont.			May 9						
Stockbridge, do.			May 10						
Florida, Massachusetts.								May 8	
North Attleborough, do.		May 8		May 8	April 25				
Columbia, Connecticut.							May 23	May 15	
Middletown, do.			May 4						
Plattsburg, New York.		May 12							
Ovid, do.				May 12					
Rochester, do.								May 15	
Waterloo, do.		May 10							
Ceres, Pennsylvania.		May 4							
Gettysburg, do.			May 2						
Indiana, do.		May 11							
Meadville, do.		May 8							
Philadelphia, do.								April 15	
Shamokin, do.							June 1		
Buffalo, Virginia.					April 30				
Clarke county, do.							May 7	May 29	
Crichton's Store, do.			April 17				April 15	April 25	April 1
Poplar Grove, do.								April 11	March 30
Rose Hill, do.						April 13			March 15
Camden, S. Carolina.		April 3							
Greensborough, Alabama.						March 27			
Weewokaville, do.			March 20						
Jasper, Mississippi.					March 26				
Belle Centre, Ohio.		May 4		May 5				April 24	
Mount Healthy, do.				April 10					
Indianapolis, Indiana.									April 18
Laconia, do.								April 14	
Augusta, Illinois.		April 19		April 20	April 21				
Warsaw, do.							May 9	April 19	
West Northville, do.				April 20					
Ann Arbor, Michigan.			May 21						
Flint, do.					May 24				
Princeton, Minnesota.							May 15		
Fairfield, Iowa.									May 2
Pleasant Plain, do.							June 1		
Leavenworth, Kansas.								May 20	

CRATÆGUS CRUS-GALLI.—*Cockspur Thorn.*

Name of Station.	1851.	1852.	1853.	1854.	1855.	1856.	1857.	1858.	1859.
Castleton, Vermont.			May 10						
Florida, Massachusetts.							May 25	May 10	
Columbia, Connecticut.							May 18		
Middletown, do.		May 2	May 4						
Ovid, New York.				May 11					
Rochester, do.								May 18	
Waterloo, do.		May 1							
Freehold, New Jersey.									May 1
Gettysburg, Pennsylvania.		May 8							
Hollidaysburg, do.			April 10						
Indiana, do.		May 6							
Meadville, do.		May 10							
Middletown, do.							May 19		
Radnor, do.		May 24				June 4	June 14		
Buffalo, Virginia.					April 26				
Rose Hill, do.						April 13			March 15
Chapel Hill, N. Carolina.								March 29	
Alligator, Florida.								Jan. 3	
Greensborough, Alabama.						March 27		March 20	
Weewokaville, do.		April 10							
New Wied, Texas.		March 15	April 2	March 5					
Maysville, Kentucky.			May 6						
Belle Centre, Ohio.		May 6							

CRATÆGUS CRUS-GALLI.—*Cockspur Thorn*—Continued.

Name of Station.	1851.	1852	1853.	1854.	1855.	1856.	1857.	1858.	1859.
Cleveland ...... Ohio				April 22	April 21				
Poland ...... do					May 4				
Lac qui Parle ...... Minnesota				May 4					
Princeton ...... do							May 10		
Pleasant Plain ...... Iowa					April 16		June 5		

CRATÆGUS OXYCANTHA.—*English Hawthorn.*

Name of Station.	1851.	1852	1853.	1854.	1855.	1856.	1857.	1858.	1859.
Castleton ...... Vermont			May 12						
Fairfield ...... Connecticut								May 16	
Middletown ...... do		May 4	April 28						
New York city ...... New York					May 25				
Ovid ...... do				May 11					
Rochester ...... do								May 25	
Waterloo ...... do		May 3							
West Point ...... do			April 27						
Burlington ...... New Jersey		April 10							
Gettysburg ...... Pennsylvania			May 2						
Hollidaysburg ...... do			April 16						
Middletown ...... do							May 17		
Clarke county ...... Virginia							May 8	April 20	
Genito ...... do		April 12							
Rose Hill ...... do						April 13	March 20	April 11	March 15
Chapel Hill ...... N. Carolina								April 7	
Alligator ...... Florida								March 15	
Ashtabula ...... Ohio				May 1					
Cleveland ...... do				April 21	April 20				
Savannah ...... do							May 28		
Augusta ...... Illinois		April 13		April 20	April 21		May 10		
Leipsig ...... Saxony								April 20	

ERYTHRONIUM AMERICANUM.—*Dogtooth Violet—Adder-tongue.*

Name of Station.	1851.	1852	1853.	1854.	1855.	1856.	1857.	1858.	1859.
Brunswick ...... Maine							May 12		
Manchester ...... New Hampshire		April 20							
Brandon ...... Vermont			April 20	April 20					
Castleton ...... do			April 25						
Newark ...... do							May 1		
Florida ...... Massachusetts							May 1		
East Windsor Hill ...... Connecticut			May 10						
Chatham ...... New York		April 24							
New York city ...... do								April 12	
Nichols ...... do								May 5	
Ovid ...... do				April 30					
Rochester ...... do			April 16						
Spencertown ...... do					April 26				
Waterloo ...... do		April 13							
Williamsville ...... do				April 14					
Ceres ...... Pennsylvania		May 4							
Darby ...... do		April 10	April 3						
Fleming ...... do							April 25		
Gettysburg ...... do			April 10	April 10					
Hollidaysburg ...... do		April 22	April 3						
Mossy Creek ...... do		May 5							
Murrysville ...... do							April 12		
Nazareth ...... do							April 24		
Chapel Hill ...... N. Carolina			March 20						
Weewokaville ...... Alabama			March 20						
Ashtabula ...... Ohio				May 20					
Belle Centre ...... do		March 27		April 10				March 28	
Hiram ...... do								April 15	
Keene ...... do		April 1							

ERYTHRONIUM AMERICANUM.—*Dogtooth Violet.—Adder-tongue*—Continued.

Name of Station.		1851.	1852.	1853.	1854.	1855.	1856.	1857.	1858.	1859.
Poland	Ohio					April 1				
Athens	Illinois			April 8						
St. James	Michigan			April 9						
Pleasant Plain	Iowa				April 15					
Plum Spring	do					April 17				
Leavenworth	Kansas								March 24	
Stanbridge	Canada							May 1	April 8	

FRAGARIA VESCA.—*Field Strawberry.*

Name of Station.		1851.	1852.	1853.	1854.	1855.	1856.	1857.	1858.	1859.
Carmel	Maine						May 5			
Cornish	do						May 1			
Stratford	New Hamp						May 1			
Craftsbury	Vermont						April 27	May 5		
West Rupert	do						April 27			
Bridgewater	Mass							May 12		
Florida	do							May 4		
North Attleborough	do		May 1							
Westfield	do						May 10			
Worcester	do						April 25			
Acquidneset	Rhode Island						April 25			
Georgetown	Connecticut						April 15			
Middletown	do			April 15						
Norwich	do						April 21			
Preston	do						April 26			
Angelica	New York						May 2			
Clinton	do							June 1		
Eden	do						April 20	May 16		
Elmira	do						April 14			
Flatbush	do							May 9		
Geneva	do						May 5			
Lowville	do						May 7	April 29	May 9	
New York city	do							May 8		
Ogdensburg	do			May 1			May 3			
Spencertown	do						April 26			
Waterloo	do		April 2							
Wellsville	do								April 15	
West Point	do		April 1	March 31						
Burlington	New Jersey		March 15							
Sergeantsville	do							April 2		
Ceres	Pennsylvania		May 5							
Gettysburg	do			April 7	April 10					
Hollidaysburg	do			April 1						
Lima	do						April 17			
Meadville	do						April 28			
Morrisville	do						May 2			
Nazareth	do						April 26			
Shamokin	do							April 29		
Darby	do			March 25						
Frederick	Maryland							April 19		
Ilidge	do						April 2			
Buffalo	Virginia						April 24			
Crack Whip	do							April 27		
Crichton's Store	do			March 20			April 17			
Genito	do		March 9							
Mossy Creek	do		April 15					April 20		
Poplar Grove	do									March 15
Portsmouth	do		Feb. 27							
Chapel Hill	N. Carolina			April 1						
Sparta	Georgia						Feb. 29	March 1		
Zebulon	do							Feb. 28		
Weewokaville	Alabama		Feb. 26							
Oxford	Mississippi						March 10			
Trinity	Louisiana								March 2	
Helena	Texas							Feb. 25		

FRAGARIA VESCA.—*Field Strawberry*—Continued.

Name of Station.	1851.	1852.	1853.	1854.	1855.	1856.	1857.	1858.	1859.
Trenton, Missouri			March 27	April 6					
Belle Centre, do		March 24							
Germantown, do						April 6			
Hiram, do							March 21		
Jefferson, do						April 26			
Welchfield, do							March 31		
Marengo, Illinois						April 12			
Ottawa, do								March 20	
Warsaw, do						April 23	May 3	April 7	
West Salem, do						April 4	April 10	April 1	
Cooper, Michigan						April 13			
Saint James, do						May 1			
Appleton, Wisconsin						April 14			
Madison, do						April 17			
Norway, do						April 3			
Platteville, do						April 20			
Beaver Bay, Minnesota								May 10	
Fort Ripley, do		April 23							
Red Wing, do						April 11			
Fort Madison, Iowa						April 10			
Muscatine, do		April 20	April 10			April 20			
Pleasant Plain, do						April 15			
Stanbridge, Canada						April 30			
Red River Settlement, Rupert's Land						May 5			

FRAXINUS AMERICANA.—*White Ash.*

Name of Station.	1851.	1852.	1853.	1854.	1855.	1856.	1857.	1858.	1859.
Cornish, Maine							May 27		
Gardiner, do							June 3		
Naples, do							May 23		
Manchester, New Hamp.				May 15					
West Enfield, do							May 28		
Brandon, Vermont			May 16				May 26	May 30	
Castleton, do			May 10						
Newark, do							June 1		
Florida, Massachusetts							May 25	May 20	
Lawrence, do							May 27		
Mendon, do				May 19					
North Attleborough, do				May 15	May 10				
Uxbridge, do				May 16					
Williamstown, do							May 28		
Point Judith, Rhode Island				May 26					
Columbia, Connecticut							May 27	May 30	
Fairfield, do								May 21	
Fishkill Landing, New York							May 10	May 10	
Lake, do									March 19
New York city, do					April 29			May 14	
Nichols, do									May 12
Ovid, do				May 20					
Spencertown, do					May 24				
Fleming, Pennsylvania							May 20		
Middletown, do							May 26		
Philadelphia, do								April 14	
Upper Darby, do			May 12						
Buffalo, Virginia					April 20				
Crichton's Store, do									April 25
Mossy Creek, do							May 25		
Poplar Grove, do									April 26
Chapel Hill, North Carolina								April 9	
Childersburg, Alabama								April 1	
Greensborough, do						April 4	Mar. 26	April 3	
Trinity, Louisiana								May 1	
Hannibal, Missouri				April 22					
Ashtabula, Ohio				May 12					
Belle Centre, do				May 10					
Cleveland, do					May 2				

FRAXINUS AMERICANA.—*White Ash*—Continued.

Name of Station.	1851.	1852.	1853.	1854.	1855.	1856.	1857.	1858.	1859.
Germantown, Ohio				April 28					
Hiram, do								May 10	
Hocking Port, do							May 20		
Mount Healthy, do				April 28					
Poland, do					May 14				
Savannah, do							May 20		
Laconia, Indiana								March 27	
Augusta, Illinois				April 30	April 28		3		
Batavia, do								April 18	
Marengo, do							April 15		
Pekin, do								May 14	
Riley, do							May 28		
Warsaw, do							May 9	April 13	
Wyandotte, Michigan								May 11	
Lac qui Parle, Minnesota				May 12					
Princeton, do							May 15		
Border Plains, Iowa								May 20	
Eagle, do							May 26		
Fairfield, do									May 9
Muscatine, do				May 10	May 7				
Pleasant Plain, do				April 25					May 10
Leavenworth, Kansas								April 29	
Stanbridge, Canada							May 26	May 25	

GLEDITSCHIA TRIACANTHUS.—*Honey Locust.*

Name of Station.	1851.	1852.	1853.	1854.	1855.	1856.	1857.	1858.	1859.
Flatbush, New York			May 10						
Rochester, do			May 25						
Waterloo, do		May 12							
West Point, do			May 10						
Burlington, New Jersey		May 15							
Gettysburg, Pennsylvania				May 1					
Hollidaysburg, do			May 1						
Meadville, do		May 22							
Upper Darby, do			May 7						
Sykesville, Maryland		May 15							
Crichton's Store, Virginia			April 13						
Genito, do		April 8							
Camden, S. Carolina		Mar. 28							
Weewokaville, Alabama		Mar. 28	April 20						
Maysville, Kentucky			April 28						
Belle Centre, Ohio		May 7							
Keene, do		May 10							
Indianapolis, Indiana									May 2
Augusta, Illinois		May 10	May 15						

HALESIA TETRAPTERA.—*Snowdrop Tree.*

Name of Station.	1851.	1852.	1853.	1854.	1855.	1856.	1857.	1858.	1859.
Steuben, Maine	May 16	May 11	May 17	May 18	May 20		May 20	May 24	
Castleton, Vermont			May 3						
North Attleborough, Massachusetts				May 1	May 6				
Columbia, Connecticut							May 3		
Nichols, New York								May 15	
Waterloo, do		April 19							
Williamsville, do				April 20					
Burlington, New Jersey		April 20							
Darby, Pennsylvania			April 7						
Easton, do				April 11					
Fleming, do							May 1		
Freeport, do				May 22					
Gettysburg, do		May 10							
Indiana, do		April 22							

HALESIA TETRAPTERA.—*Snowdrop Tree*—Continued.

Name of Station.	1851.	1852.	1853.	1854.	1855.	1856.	1857.	1858.	1859.
Nazaerth .... Pennsylvania.							May 10		
Upper Darby .... do......		May 16	April 26	May 3					
Poplar Grove .... Virginia ...								April 22	
Ashtabula .... Ohio.....				April 23					
Belle Centre .... do......		May 1							
Mount Healthy .... do......				April 10					
Savannah .... do......							May 15		
Brighton .... Illinois....							May 24	April 1	
Saint James .... Michigan...			May 15						
Fairfield .... Iowa.....									May 1

HAMAMELIS VIRGINICA.—*Witch Hazel.*

Name of Station.	1851.	1852.	1853.	1854.	1855.	1856.	1857.	1858.	1859.
Londonderry .... New Hamp..			May 2						
Salmon Falls .... do......				May 12					
Brandon .... Vermont....			May 13						
Stockbridge .... do......			May 11						
Burlington .... New Jersey .		April 20							
Ceres .... Pennsylvania.		May 12							
Hollidaysburg .... do......			April 28						
Indiana .... do......		May 11							
Meadville .... do......		May 1							
Valley Forge .... do......		May 5							
Genito .... Virginia....		April 2							
Portsmouth .... do......		Mar. 13							
Camden .... S. Carolina..		Mar. 29							
Weewokaville .... Alabama...		Mar. 25	April 5						
Maysville .... Kentucky ..			April 5						
Muscatine .... Iowa.....		April 27							

HEPATICA TRILOBA.—*Round-lobed Liverwort.*

Name of Station.	1851.	1852.	1853.	1854.	1855.	1856.	1857.	1858.	1859.
Burlington .... Vermont....			April 20		May 4				
Columbia .... Connecticut..							May 25		
East Windsor Hill .... do......			May 7						
Ovid .... New York ..				May 5					
Rochester .... do......			April 20	Mar. 28	April 13		May 25	May 4	
Spencertown .... do......					May 1				
Ceres .... Pennsylvania.		April 30							
Fleming .... do......							May 1		
Gettysburg .... do......		April 12	Mar. 28	April 14					
Mossy Creek .... Virginia ...		Mar. 20					April 30		
Poplar Grove .... do......								Perenn'l.	Perenn'l.
Maysville .... Kentucky..			Mar. 25						
Belle Centre .... Ohio.....		April 15		April 10				April 20	
Keene .... do......		April 6							
Athens .... Illinois....			April 9						
Waynesville .... do......								April 6	
Horton .... Nova Scotia .					May 22				
Leipsig .... Saxony....								May 2	

HEDYOTIS CÆRULEA.—*Bluets.—Innocence.*

NAME OF STATION.	1851.	1852.	1853.	1854.	1855.	1856.	1857.	1858.	1859.
Brunswick ... Maine							May 4		
Mendon ... Massachusetts				April 21					
Columbia ... Connecticut							May 1	April 20	
Gettysburg ... Pennsylvania			April 20						
Darby ... do		April 20							
Buffalo ... Virginia					April 15				
Mossy Creek ... do		May 1					May 20		
Chapel Hill ... N. Carolina			Feb. 25						
Keene ... Ohio		April 20							
Savannah ... do							May 18		
Brighton ... Illinois								April 12	
Fairfield ... Iowa									April 25

HYPERICUM PERFORATUM.—*St. John's Wort.*

NAME OF STATION.	1851.	1852.	1853.	1854.	1855.	1856.	1857.	1858.	1859.
Cornish ... Maine							May 10		
Columbia ... Connecticut							May 16	June 1	
Flatbush ... New York		May 20							
New York city ... do								May 19	
Plattsburg ... do		May 10							
Sykesville ... Maryland							May 27		
Crichton's Store ... Virginia			May 3					April 30	April 12
Genito ... do		April 1							
Mossy Creek ... do							May 20		
Poplar Grove ... do								April 8	
Cleveland ... Ohio					April 18				
Stanbridge ... Canada							May 10	May 15	

IRIS VERSICOLOR.—*Large Blue Flag.*

NAME OF STATION.	1851.	1852.	1853.	1854.	1855.	1856.	1857.	1858.	1859.
Brunswick ... Maine							May 9		
Cornish ... do							June 12		
Steuben ... do		May 5	May 11	May 14			May 1	May 1	
Manchester ... N. Hampshire		May 20							
Castleton ... Vermont			May 4						
Mendon ... Massachusetts				May 5					
North Attleborough ... do		May 5		April 28	May 6				
Columbia ... Connecticut							April 28	April 22	
New York city ... New York					April 23				
Gettysburg ... Pennsylvania			March 1						
Hollidaysburg ... do		May 7	April 3						
Darby ... do		March 14	March 26						
Sykesville ... Maryland			March 1	March 2			Feb. 20		
Crichton's Store ... Virginia								April 1	March 13
Genito ... do		March 30							
Mossy Creek ... do		April 20							
Poplar Grove ... do								March 19	March 8
Chapel Hill ... N. Carolina			April 12						
Ashtabula ... Ohio				April 10					
Belle Centre ... do		April 24							
Ripley ... do							March 25		
Savannah ... do							May 5		
Laconia ... Indiana								March 25	
Brighton ... Illinois							May 9	April 21	
Marengo ... do								April 4	
Riley ... do							May 16		
Lac qui Parle ... Minnesota				May 5					
Pleasant Plain ... do				April 25					
Fairfield ... Iowa									April 25
Leavenworth ... Kansas								April 7	
Horton ... Nova Scotia					May 14				
Stanbridge ... Canada							May 1	May 4	

JUGLANS NIGRA.—*Black Walnut.*

Name of Station.	1851.	1852.	1853.	1854.	1855.	1856.	1857.	1858.	1859.
Londonderry ... N. Hampshire			May 4						
Flatbush ... New York		May 9	May 2						
New Lebanon ... do			May 12						
Burlington ... New Jersey		May 25							
Ceres ... Pennsylvania		May 18							
Easton ... do		May 12							
Freeport ... do				May 15					
Gettysburg ... do			May 2	May 4					
Hollidaysburg ... do			May 4						
Indiana ... do		May 13							
Meadville ... do		May 12							
North Whitehall ... do							May 14		
Orwigsburg ... do		May 8							
Darby ... do			April 27						
Upper Darby ... do			April 27						
Valley Forge ... do		May 7							
Hagerstown ... Maryland			April 30						
Sykesville ... do		May 6	May 10						
Crichton's Store ... Virginia			April 14						
Genito ... do		April 15							
Madison C. H. ... do		April 26							
Poplar Grove ... do									April 28
Mossy Creek ... do		May 1							
Camden ... S. Carolina		April 18							
Eutaw ... Alabama		March 30							
Weewokaville ... do		April 6	April 20						
New Wied ... Texas			March 12						
Glenwood ... Tennessee			April 14						
Knoxville ... do		May 6							
Maysville ... Kentucky			May 6						
Belle Centre ... Ohio		May 12							
Germantown ... do		May 1	April 25						
Indianapolis ... Indiana									May 3
Augusta ... Illinois		May 10	May 18						
Warsaw ... do							May 20		
Fort Madison ... Iowa		May 2	April 29						
Muscatine ... do		May 12	May 9						

KALMIA LATIFOLIA.—*Mountain Laurel.*

Name of Station.	1851.	1852.	1853.	1854.	1855.	1856.	1857.	1858.	1859.
Castleton ... Vermont			May 10						
Worcester ... Massachusetts							May 1		
Columbia ... Connecticut							May 17		
Fishkill Landing ... New York							May 15	May 17	
Burlington ... New Jersey		May 10							
Moorestown ... do					May 15				
Easton ... Pennsylvania				May 17					
Hollidaysburg ... do			May 1						
Shamokin ... do							May 28		
Mossy Creek ... Virginia		May 15					May 30		
Poplar Grove ... do								Perennial	Perennial
Poland ... Ohio					May 12				

LAURUS BENZOIN.—*Spice Bush.*

Name of Station.	1851.	1852.	1853.	1854.	1855.	1856.	1857.	1858.	1859.
Gardiner ... Maine							May 23		
Newark ... Vermont							May 5		
Columbia ... Connecticut							May 15	May 22	
New York city ... New York								May 15	
Ovid ... do				May 18					
Rochester ... do								May 10	
Spencertown ... do					May 15				
Burlington ... New Jersey		May 1							

LAURUS BENZOIN.—*Spice Bush*—Continued.

Name of Station.		1851.	1852.	1853.	1854.	1855.	1856.	1857.	1858.	1859.
Gettysburg	Pennsylvania		May 6	April 20	April 26					
Hollidaysburg	do			April 10						
Mercersburg	do		May 6							
Nazareth	do							May 21		
Shamokin	do							May 30		
Upper Darby	do				April 9					
Sykesville	Maryland			April 26						
Buffalo	Virginia					April 18				
Crichton's Store	do			April 15				April 4	April 10	
Genito	do		April 5							
Mossy Creek	do		May 1					May 20		
Poplar Grove	do								April 12	April 6
Chapel Hill	North Carolina			April 20					April 8	
Weewokaville	Alabama		March 25	April 5						
New Wied	Texas		Feb. 15	March 1						
Belle Centre	Ohio		May 5							
Cleveland	do				April 30	May 6				
Mount Healthy	do				May 10					
Savannah	do							May 8		
Laconia	Indiana								April 10	
West Northville	Illinois				April 26					
Wyandotte	Michigan								May 13	
Muscatine	Iowa		May 12							
Pleasant Plain	do				May 1					

LEUCANTHEMUM VULGARE.—*Ox-eye Daisy.*

Name of Station.		1851.	1852.	1853.	1854.	1855.	1856.	1857.	1858.	1859.
Brunswick	Maine							April 15	June 1	
Cornish	do							May 3		
Steuben	do							May 6		
West Enfield	New Hampshire							May 7		
Castleton	Vermont			June 5						
Newark	do							June 1		
Florida	Massachusetts							May 5		
Columbia	Connecticut							May 14	May 10	
New York city	New York								May 20	
Ovid	do				May 13					
Spencertown	do					April 30				
Sykesville	Maryland							April 28		
Buffalo	Virginia					May 4				
Poplar Grove	do									April 8
Hiram	Ohio							May 24		
Savannah	do							May 20		
Laconia	Indiana								April 18	
Princeton	Minnesota							May 25		
Stanbridge	Canada							May 20	May 1	

LIRIODENDRON TULIPIFERA.—*Tulip Tree.—American Poplar.*

Name of Station.		1851.	1852.	1853.	1854.	1855.	1856.	1857.	1858.	1859.
Cornish	Maine							May 15		
Perry	do									May 20
Steuben	do	May 25	May 10	May 19	May 16				June 5	
Londonderry	New Hampshire		May 5	May 2						
Stratford	do								May 26	
Castleton	Vermont			May 7						
Newark	do							May 23		
Florida	Massachusetts							May 15		
North Attleborough	do				May 1	May 13				
Richmond	do		May 20							
Williamstown	do							May 28		
Columbia	Connecticut							May 14	May 15	
Fishkill Landing	New York							May 6		April 24
Flatbush	do		May 7	April 19	April 27	April 29				

LIRIODENDRON TULIPIFERA.—*Tulip Tree.—American Poplar*—Continued.

Name of Station.	1851.	1852.	1853.	1854.	1855.	1856.	1857.	1858.	1859.
New York city, New York				May 18				May 12	
Ovid, do				May 20					
Rochester, do					May 8		May 20	May 24	
Waterloo, do		May 4							
West Point, do			May 1						
Burlington, New Jersey		April 28							
Freehold, do									May 1
Moorestown, do					May 1				
Ceres, Pennsylvania		May 16							
Darby, do		April 2	April 16						
Fleming, do							May 18		
Gettysburg, do		May 7		April 26					
Indiana, do		May 6							
Meadville, do		May 7							
Mercersburg, do		April 29							
Middletown, do							May 1		
Murrysville, do							May 20		
Nazareth, do							May 8		
North Whitehall, do							May 22		
Philadelphia, do								April 13	
Upper Darby, do		May 2	April 19	April 24					
Easton, Maryland				May 9					
Sykesville, do		April 30	April 22	May 1			May 23		
Buffalo, Virginia					April 18				
Clarke county, do								April 22	
Crichton's Store, do			April 3				April 4	April 7	March 16
Genito, do		March 17							
Kenawha Salines, do								April 2	
Madison C. H., do		April 9							
Mossy Creek, do		April 25					May 5		
Poplar Grove, do								April 12	April 3
Rose Hill, do						April 12	April 5	April 5	April 10
Chapel Hill, North Carolina			March 28					March 29	
All Saints, South Carolina					March 22				
Eutaw, Alabama		Feb. 27							
Greensborough, do						March 23	March 20	Feb. 28	
Weewokaville, do		March 27	April 15						
Columbus, Mississippi								March 15	
Jasper, do					March 26				
Glenwood, Tennessee			March 29						
Knoxville, do		April 25							
Maysville, Kentucky			May 6						
Ashtabula, Ohio				May 10					
Belle Centre, do		May 12							
Cincinnati, do			April 20						
Cleveland, do				April 23	April 15				
Hiram, do							May 23		
Keene, do		May 6							
Savannah, do							May 26		
Laconia, Indiana								March 31	
Batavia, Illinois								April 20	
Brighton, do							May 19	April 11	
Marengo, do							May 15	April 5	
Warsaw, do							May 1		
West Northville, do				April 25					
Wyandotte, Michigan								April 27	
Princeton, Minnesota							May 10		
Eagle, Iowa							May 9		
Muscatine, do		May 10	May 4	April 28	May 18				
Pleasant Plain, do				April 28		May 10			
Stanbridge, Canada								May 20	
Leipsig, do								April 25	

LONICERA PERICLYMENUM.—*Foreign spurs.*

Name of Station.	1851.	1852.	1853.	1854.	1855.	1856.	1857.	1858.	1859.
Steuben.......... Maine			June 1						
Plattsburg.......... New York...		May 17							
Burlington.......... New Jersey ..		May 1							
Darby .... Pennsylvania..			March 17						
Easton .... do......		April 24							
Hollidaysburg .... do......			April 14						
Mossy Creek .... Virginia ..		May 1							

LONICERA SEMPERVIRENS.—*Trumpet Honeysuckle.*

Name of Station.	1851.	1852.	1853.	1854.	1855.	1856.	1857.	1858.	1859.
Steuben.......... Maine	May 15	May 11	May 19						
Plattsburg.......... New York...		May 10							
West Point .... do......		April 23							
Darby .... Pennsylvania..			March 20						
Easton .... do......		April 24							
Gettysburg .... do......			March 27	April 20					
Hollidaysburg.......... do......			May 2						
Sykesville.......... Maryland...		March 11							
Chapel Hill .... N. Carolina..			March 1						
Belle Centre.......... Ohio		May 8							
Keene.......... do......		April 12							
Muscatine.......... Iowa		May 7	April 20						

LONICERA TARTARICA.—*Foreign spurs.*

Name of Station.	1851.	1852.	1853.	1854.	1855.	1856.	1857.	1858.	1859.
Brunswick .... Maine							May 14	May 25	
Castine .... do......		May 25							
Boston .... Massachusetts.		June 1							
Ovid .... New York...				May 25					
Rochester .... do......			April 28		May 6		May 1	May 23	
Darby .... Pennsylvania..			March 30						
Lima .... do......			March 13						
Middletown.......... do......							May 1		
Mossy Creek.......... Virginia ...							May 10		
Cleveland.......... Ohio.....				May 14	April 14				
Poland .... do......					April 10				
West Northville .... Illinois....				April 10					
Leipsig.......... Saxony....								April 5	

MAGNOLIA GLAUCA.—*Sweet-bay.—Laurel Magnolia.*

Name of Station.	1851.	1852.	1853.	1854.	1855.	1856.	1857.	1858.	1859.
North Attleborough.. Massachusetts.				May 16	May 13				
Freehold.......... New Jersey ..									April 28
Hollidaysburg.......... Pennsylvania.			May 8						
Middletown.......... do......							May 20		
Radnor.......... do......			May 24	May 20	May 24		June 7		
Upper Darby.......... do......		May 12	May 8	May 10					
Easton.......... Maryland...				May 4					
Crichton's Store.......... Virginia ...								April 23	April 15
Mossy Creek.......... do......		April 30							
All Saints.......... S. Carolina..					April 17				
Greensborough .... Alabama...						Evergr'n			
Cleveland .... Ohio....				May 6	May 6				
West Northville .... Illinois ...				April 30					

MITCHELLA REPENS.—*Partridge Berry.*

Name of Station.	1851.	1852.	1853.	1854.	1855.	1856.	1857.	1858.	1859.
Naples ... Maine							June 17		
Florida ... Massachusetts							May 10		
Worcester ... do							April 28		
Columbia ... Connecticut							May 1		
Poland ... Ohio					May 1				

MORUS RUBRA.—*Red Mulberry.*

Name of Station.	1851.	1852.	1853.	1854.	1855.	1856.	1857.	1858.	1859.
Londonderry ... New Hamp			May 16						
Stockbridge ... Vermont			May 11						
Columbia ... Connecticut								May 17	
Fairfield ... do								May 21	
Waterloo ... New York		May 7							
West Point ... do			May 12						
Burlington ... New Jersey		May 15							
Moorestown ... do					May 10				
Darby ... Pennsylvania			May 5						
Gettysburg ... do				May 5					
Indiana ... do		May 14							
Meadville ... do		May 18							
Murrysville ... do							June 1		
North Whitehall ... do							May 24		
Upper Darby ... do		May 13	April 29	May 12					
Hagerstown ... Maryland			April 23						
Sykesville ... do		April 30	May 2						
Buffalo ... Virginia					April 24				
Clarke county ... do							May 20		
Crichton's Store ... do			April 15				May 1	April 10	Mar. 22
Genito ... do		April 15							
Kanawha Salines ... do								May 1	
Poplar Grove ... do								May 1	April 25
Rose Hill ... do						April 17			April 15
Chapel Hill ... N. Carolina			April 25					April 6	
Camden ... S. Carolina		Mar. 10							
Alligator ... Florida								Jan. 12	
Greensborough ... Alabama						April 10	Mar. 30		
Weewokaville ... do		Mar. 28	April 15						
Trinity ... Louisiana							Mar. 26	April 7	
New Wied ... Texas		Mar. 20	Mar. 25						
Union Hill ... do							Mar. 10		
Maysville ... Kentucky			May 6						
Belle Centre ... Ohio		May 15		May 10					
Germantown ... do		May 6	May 2						
Hocking Port ... do							May 20		
Mount Healthy ... do				April 30					
Poland ... do				May 14					
Savannah ... do							May 12		
Laconia ... Indiana								April 17	
Brighton ... Illinois							May 20	April 9	
Peoria ... do								May 8	
Warsaw ... do							May 3	April 25	
West Salem ... do							May 27		
Fairfield ... Iowa									May 6
Muscatine ... do		May 15	May 8	May 1	May 7				
Leavenworth ... Kansas								May 12	

PERSICA VULGARIS.—*Peach.*

Name of Station.	1851.	1852.	1853.	1854.	1855.	1856.	1857.	1858.	1859.
Steuben ... Maine					June 1	June 8	June 1		
Londonderry ... New Hamp		May 8	May 7						
Manchester ... do		May 20		May 12					
Salmon Falls ... do				May 7					
Somersworth ... do				May 13					
West Rupert ... Vermont						May 7			

PERSICA VULGARIS.—*Peach*—Continued.

Name of Station.	1851.	1852.	1853.	1854.	1855.	1856.	1857.	1858.	1859.
Bridgewater ....Massachusetts.							May 31		
East Weymouth..........do......						May 9			
Mendon..................do......				May 16					
North Attleborough ....do......		May 7		May 2	May 13				
Worcester ....do......						May 2	May 9		
Columbia.............Connecticut .							May 26	May 22	
Fairfield....................do......								May 26	
Georgetown ....do......						April 29			
Norwich ....do......						April 25	April 26		
Preston ....do......						May 17			
Angelica.............New York ..						May 15			
Chatham ....do......		May 12							
Eden..........................do......							June 5		
Fishkill Landing..........do......									April 17
Flatbush ....do......		May 6	April 19	April 23	April 27		May 20		
Geneva ....do......						May 25			
New Lebanon..............do......			May 3						
New York city.............do......				May 12	May 9			April 29	
Ovid ....do......				May 18		May 26			
Rochester ....do......					May 8		May 22		
Waterloo ....do......		May 2							
Wellsville ....do......							April 6	April 6	
West Point ....do......			May 1						
Burlington.........New Jersey.		April 29							
Sergeantsville..............do.....							April 26		
Bellefonte ....Pennsylvania.								April 24	
Darby ....do......		May 14	April 20						
Easton ....do......		May 1		April 16					
Fleming......................do......							May 20		
Freeport ....do......				April 12					
Gettysburg ....do......		May 5	April 27	April 26		April 30			
Huntingdon ....do......							May 3		
Indiana ....do......		May 9							
Lima...........................do......						May 1			
Meadville ....do......		May 6				April 25			
Morrisville ....do......						May 15			
Murrysville.................do......							May 12		
Nazareth ....do......						May 7			
Orwigsburg ....do......		May 3							
Shamokin ....do......							May 25		
Upper Darby................do......		May 3		April 13					
Ridge.................Maryland...						May 6			
Sykesville ....do......		April 21	April 21	April 25		May 14	May 10		
Buffalo ....Virginia ...					April 15				
Clarke county...............do......						May 5			
Crack Whip..................do......							April 30		
Crichton's Store............do......			April 15			April 16	May 1	April 20	Mar. 24
Doddridge county..........do......						April 18			
Genito ....do......		Mar. 20							
Kanawha Salines...........do......								April 12	
Madison C. H...............do......		Mar. 30							
Mossy Creek ....do......		April 22					May 1		
Mount Solon................do......						April 30			
Poplar Grove ....do......							April 21	April 8	April 4
Portsmouth..................do......						April 13			
Rose Hill.....................do......						April 22	April 14		April 20
Winchester ....do......						April 3			
Aiken................S. Carolina ..						April 11			
All Saints ....do......					Mar. 22	April 13			
Camden ....do......		Mar. 19							
Sparta..................Georgia....						Mar. 8	Mar. 25		
Zebulon ....do......						April 1			
Alligator ....Florida....							Feb. 1	Jan. 8	
Greensborough.........Alabama ...						April 4	Mar. 18	Mar. 3	
Greene Springs.............do......						April 10			
Weewokaville ....do......		Mar. 1							
Columbus ....Mississippi..								Mar. 15	
Jasper..........................do......					Mar. 1	Mar. 22			
Oxford ....do......						April 2			

PERSICA VULGARIS.—*Peach*—Continued.

Name of Station.	1851.	1852.	1853.	1854.	1855.	1856.	1857.	1858.	1859.
Big Pond .... Louisiana						Mar. 21	Mar. 4		
Trinity .... do								Mar. 4	
Helena .... Texas							Feb. 7		
New Wied .... do			Mar. 10						
Union Hill .... do							Feb. 28		
Hannibal .... Missouri				April 20					
Westport .... do						April 31			
Maysville .... Kentucky			April 8						
Belle Centre .... Ohio		April 26		April 24				April 26	
Bowling Green .... do								April 15	
Cheviot .... do						April 25			
Cleveland .... do				April 23	April 26				
Edinburg .... do							May 25		
Germantown .... do		April 20	April 8	April 5		April 16			
Hiram .... do						April 30	May 8	April 20	
Hocking Port .... do							May 1		
Jefferson .... do						May 11			
Keene .... do		May 8							
Marietta .... do								April 16	
Mount Healthy .... do				April 15					
Poland .... do				April 21					
Ripley .... do							April 22		
Savannah .... do							May 22		
Welchfield .... do							June 7		
Indianapolis .... Indiana									April 4
Laconia .... do								April 4	
New Albany .... do						April 26	April 30		
Athens .... Illinois		April 25	April 10			April 25			
Augusta .... do		May 1		April 30	April 30		May 14		
Batavia .... do								April 29	
Brighton .... do							May 14	April 10	
Marengo .... do							May 12	April 15	
Ottawa .... do								April 12	
Pekin .... do								May 20	
Peoria .... do								April 4	
Warsaw .... do						April 21	May 14		
Waynesville .... do								April 15	
West Northville .... do				April 22					
West Salem .... do						April 24	May 8	April 10	
Winnebago .... do							May 20	May 6	
Cooper .... Michigan						April 29			
Flint .... do					May 2				
Romeo .... do						May 12			
St. James .... do						May 20			
Wyandotte .... do								May 13	
Appleton .... Wisconsin						May 5			
Border Plains .... Iowa								April 15	May 7
Eagle .... do							May 16		
Fairfield .... do									May 9
Fort Madison .... do			April 14	April 15		April 25			
Keokuk .... do						April 26			
Muscatine .... do		May 7	April 24	April 20	April 24	May 8			
Pleasant Plains .... do				April 25					
Leavenworth .... Kansas								April 3	
Sacramento .... California						Mar. 10			
Salem .... Oregon						April 29			
Leipsig .... Saxony								April 15	

PLATANUS OCCIDENTALIS.—*Buttonwood.*—*Sycamore.*

Name of Station.	1851.	1852.	1853.	1854.	1855.	1856.	1857.	1858.	1859.
Stockbridge .... Vermont			May 18						
North Attleborough. Massachusetts		May 10							
Flatbush .... New York		May 12	May 10						
New Lebanon .... do			May 16						
Rochester .... do			May 21						
West Point .... do		May 14	May 6						
Burlington .... New Jersey		May 10							

PLATANUS OCCIDENTALIS.—*Buttonwood.—Sycamore*—Continued.

Name of Station.	1851.	1852.	1853.	1854.	1855.	1856.	1857.	1858.	1859.
Ceres ....Pennsylvania..		May 14							
Darby ....do.....			May 5						
Gettysburg ....do.....			May 2	May 2					
Hollidaysburg........do.....		May 16							
Mercersburg ....do.....		May 7							
Upper Darby........do.....		May 15	May 7						
Valley Forge........do.....		May 8							
Sykesville ....Maryland...		April 30							
Crichton's Store........Virginia....			April 10						
Genito ....do.....		April 6							
Mossy Creek ....do.....		May 5							
Chapel Hill........N. Carolina..			April 10						
Camden ....S. Carolina..		March 29							
Weewokaville ....Alabama...		April 15	April 2						
New Wied ....Texas....		March 15							
Glenwood........Tennessee..			April 8						
Maysville........Kentucky..			April 28						
Belle Centre ....Ohio.....		May 10							
Germantown........do.....		May 2	May 1						
Indianapolis ....Indiana.....									May 1
Augusta ....Illinois....		May 10							
Fort Madison ....Iowa.....		May 2							

POPULUS TREMULOIDES.—*American Aspen.*

Name of Station.	1851.	1852.	1853.	1854.	1855.	1856.	1857.	1858.	1859.
Steuben ....Maine....	May 18		May 13						
Manchester ....New Hamp..		May 15							
Salmon Falls........do.....				May 11					
Brandon ....Vermont...			May 10						
Stockbridge........do.....			May 8						
North Attleborough.Massachusetts..		May 8							
Flatbush ....New York...		May 1							
Plattsburg ....do.....		May 14							
Rochester........do.....								May 26	
Waterloo ....do.....		May 6							
Burlington ....New Jersey..		May 10							
Indiana........Pennsylvania..		May 6							
Meadville........do.....		May 8							
Upper Darby........do.....		May 1							
Portsmouth........Virginia....		April 8							
Camden ....S. Carolina...		March 29							
Belle Centre ....Ohio.....		May 3							
Indianapolis........Indiana....									April 27
Augusta........Illinois....		April 28	April 22						
Fort Ripley ....Minnesota...		May 10							
Muscatine ....Iowa.....		May 12	May 2						
Pleasant Plain........do.....						May 15			

PRUNUS DOMESTICA.—*lum.*

Name of Station.	1851.	1852.	1853.	1854.	1855.	1856.	1857.	1858.	1859.
Carmel ....Maine....						May 21			
Cornish........do.....							May 28		
Perry ....do.....						May 3			
Concord ....New Hamp..						May 20			
Stratford ....do.....						June 6			
Brandon ....Vermont...						May 14			
Craftsbury ....do.....						May 20	May 27		
Newark ....do.....						May 23			
Shelburn ....do.....						May 18			
West Rupert ....do.....						May 12			
Bridgewater ....Massachusetts..							May 20		
East Weymouth........do.....						May 10			
Florida ....do.....							May 20		

PRUNUS DOMESTICA.—*Plum*—Continued.

Name of Station.	1851.	1852.	1853.	1854.	1855.	1856	1857.	1858.	1859.
New Ashford .... Massachusetts						May 14			
Westfield .... do						May 17			
Worcester .... do						May 5			
Columbia .... Connecticut							May 15		
Georgetown .... do						May 5			
Hartford .... do	May 9								
Norwich .... do						May 2			
Angelica .... New York						May 21			
Clinton .... do							June 2		
Eden .... do						May 14	May 30		
Lowville .... do						May 23	April 19	May 15	
New York city .... do							May 13		
Ovid .... do						May 17			
Rochester .... do							May 23		
Wellsville .... do								April 12	
Sergeantsville .... New Jersey							May 13		
Bellefonte .... Pennsylvania								May 15	
Gettysburg .... do						April 30			
Huntingdon .... do						May 1			
Lima .... do						May 1			
Morrisville .... do						May 10			
Nazareth .... do						May 5			
Buffalo .... Virginia						April 30			
Crack Whip .... do							April 30		
Crichton's Store .... do						April 15			
Poplar Grove .... do							April 23	April 8	
Winchester .... do						April 26			
Wirt Court-House .... do						May 12			
Aiken .... S. Carolina						April 4			
Savannah .... Georgia						April 1			
Sparta .... do						March 15	March 30		
Zebulon .... do						April 1			
Alligator .... Florida							Feb. 1		
Greene Springs .... Alabama						April 10			
Oxford .... Mississippi						March 24			
Helena .... Texas							Feb. 25		
Edinburg .... Ohio							May 26		
Germantown .... do						April 28			
Hiram .... do						May 2			
Jefferson .... do						May 14			
Welchfield .... do							June 8		
New Albany .... Indiana						April 28			
Warsaw .... Illinois						April 20	May 9	April 4	
West Salem .... do						April 16	May 20	April 30	
St. James .... Michigan						May 30			
Wyandotte .... do								May 8	
Appleton .... Wisconsin						May 7			
Madison .... do						May 1	May 23		
Norway .... do						May 21			
Fort Madison .... Iowa						April 22			
Muscatine .... do				April 21					
Pleasant Plain .... do						May 10			
Stanbridge .... Canada						May 15			

PYRUS COMMUNIS.—*Pear*.

Name of Station.	1851.	1852.	1853.	1854.	1855.	1856	1857.	1858.	1859.
Brunswick .... Maine								June 7	
Carmel .... do						May 23			
Gardiner .... do							May 25		
Naples .... do							May 15		
Perry .... do						May 29			May 20
Steuben .... do					June 2	June 8	May 31	June 6	
Concord .... New Hamp						May 16			
Londonderry .... do		May 6							
Somersworth .... do				May 12					
West Enfield .... do							May 16		

PYRUS COMMUNIS.—*Pear*—Continued.

Name of Station.		1851.	1852.	1853.	1854.	1855.	1856.	1857.	1858.	1859.
Brandon	Vermont			May 10	May 10		May 15			
Castleton	do			May 4						
Craftsbury	do						May 20	May 28		
Shelburn	do						May 17			
Stockbridge	do			May 12						
West Rupert	do						May 15			
Boston	Massachusetts		May 27							
Bridgewater	do							May 19		
East Weymouth	do						May 13			
Florida	do							May 25	May 15	
Lawrence	do							May 26		
Mendon	do				May 8					
New Ashford	do						May 23			
North Attleborough	do		May 5		May 9	May 13				
Richmond	do		May 25							
Waltham	do				May 10					
Westfield	do						May 18			
Worcester	do						May 1	May 9		
Columbia	Connecticut							May 12	May 13	
East Windsor Hill	do			April 30						
Fairfield	do								May 13	
Georgetown	do						May 1			
Middletown	do		May 7	April 29						
Norwich	do						May 1	April 24		
Preston	do						May 16			
Angelica	New York						May 23			
Chatham	do		May 12							
Clinton	do							May 29		
Eden	do						May 12			
Fishkill Landing	do							May 6	May 1	April 17
Flatbush	do		May 1	April 18	April 26	April 28		May 8		
Geneva	do						May 6			
Lake	do							May 23	May 11	May 6
Lowville	do						May 21		May 10	
New Lebanon	do			May 3						
New York city	do				May 5	April 30		May 12	May 5	
Ovid	do				May 10		May 12	May 27		
Rochester	do			May 4		May 6	May 10	May 23		
Spencertown	do					April 30	May 6			
Waterloo	do		May 1							
Wellsville	do							April 5	April 5	
West Concord	do						May 22			
West Point	do		May 1	April 27						
Williamsville	do				May 2					
Burlington	New Jersey		April 29							
Moorestown	do					April 20				
Newark	do	April 6								
Sergeantsville	do							May 11		
Bellefonte	Pennsylvania								May 12	
Ceres	do		May 15							
Darby	do		April 2	April 12						
Easton	do				April 16					
Fleming	do							May 10		
Gettysburg	do		April 28	April 20	April 20		April 23			
Hollidaysburg	do			April 15						
Huntingdon	do						April 28	May 2		
Indiana	do		April 26							
Lima	do						April 27			
Meadville	do		May 8				April 27			
Morrisville	do						May 14			
Murrysville	do							May 10		
Nazareth	do						May 3			
North Whitehall	do							May 5		
Shamokin	do							May 26		
Upper Darby	do		May 2	April 24	April 23					
Valley Forge	do		May 1							
Easton	Maryland				April 19					
Sykesville	do		May 1	April 23	April 23			May 10		
Buffalo	Virginia					April 16	April 27			
Clarke county	do							April 29		

PYRUS COMMUNIS.—*Pear*—Continued.

Name of Station.	1851.	1852.	1853.	1854.	1855.	1856.	1857.	1858.	1859.
Crack Whip ... Virginia							April 30		
Crichton's Store ... do			March 25			April 14	April 14	April 7	March 25
Genito ... do		April 6							
Madison C. H. ... do		March 30							
Mossy Creek ... do		April 20							
Mount Solon ... do						April 29			
Rose Hill ... do						April 15			
Winchester ... do						April 23			
Wirt C. H ... do						May 10			
Chapel Hill ... N. Carolina			March 16					March 27	
Aiken ... S. Carolina						April 10			
All Saints ... do					April 7	April 13			
Camden ... do		March 19							
Savannah ... Georgia						April 1			
Sparta ... do						March 8			
Greene Springs ... Alabama						April 1			
Greensborough ... do						April 4	March 16	March 3	
Weewokaville ... do		March 20	March 20						
Jasper ... Mississippi					March 20	March 22			
Helena ... Texas							Feb. 28		
New Wied ... do			April 6	April 1					
Hannibal ... Missouri				April 5					
Westport ... do						April 21			
Glenwood ... Tennessee			March 24						
Maysville ... Kentucky			April 10						
Ashtabula ... Ohio				April 25					
Belle Centre ... do		May 9		April 23				April 24	
Bowling Green ... do								April 29	
Cleveland ... do				April 21	April 24				
Edinburg ... do							May 12		
Germantown ... do		April 13	April 6	April 7		April 20			
Hiram ... do								April 24	
Jefferson ... do						May 16			
Keene ... do		May 7							
Marietta ... do								April 15	
Mount Healthy ... do				April 12					
Poland ... do					April 20				
Ripley ... do							April 7		
Savannah ... do							May 17		
Welchfield ... do							June 4		
Indianapolis ... Indiana									April 13
Laconia ... do								April 12	
New Albany ... do						April 28			
Athens ... Illinois						April 26			
Augusta ... do		May 5	May 7		April 22		May 10		
Batavia ... do								April 20	
Brighton ... do							May 11	April 20	
Marengo ... do						May 15	May 20	April 21	
Ottawa ... do								April 12	
Peoria ... do								April 17	
Warsaw ... do						April 30		April 4	
West Northville ... do				April 23					
West Salem ... do						April 29	May 14	April 16	
Winnebago ... do							May 23	April 27	
Ann Arbor ... Michigan			May 4						
Flint ... do					April 23				
Romeo ... do						May 10			
St. James ... do						May 26			
Wyandotte ... do								April 29	
Madison ... Wisconsin						May 10			
Dorder Plains ... Iowa									May 1
Fairfield ... do									May 4
Fort Madison ... do				April 17		April 24			
Muscatine ... do		May 3	May 1	April 20	April 24	May 13			
Pleasant Plain ... do				April 25			May 22		
Sacramento ... California						March 15			
Salem ... Oregon						April 21			
Horton ... Nova Scotia					May 24				
Stanbridge ... Canada							May 20	May 16	
Leipsig ... Saxony								April 28	

PYRUS MALUS.—*Apple.*

Name of Station.		1851.	1852.	1853.	1854.	1855.	1856.	1857.	1858.	1859.
Brunswick	Maine								June 8	
Carmel	do						May 23			
Cornish	do						May 25	May 26		
Gardiner	do							May 25		
Naples	do							May 12		
Perry	do						May 20			May 20
Steuben	do	May 25	May 5	May 23	May 19	May 15		May 28	May 17	
Concord	N. Hampshire						May 22			
Francestown	do			May 11						
Londonderry	do		May 7	April 29						
Manchester	do		May 17		May 11					
North Barnstead	do							May 21		
Salmon Falls	do				May 11					
Shelburne	do								May 10	
Somersworth	do				May 10					
Stratford	do								May 28	
West Enfield	do							May 14		
Brandon	Vermont			May 6	May 12			May 22	May 12	
Burlington	do					May 8				
Castleton	do			May 8						
Craftsbury	do						May 16	May 25		
Newark	do						May 20	May 26		
Shelburn	do						May 18			
Stockbridge	do			May 8						
West Rupert	do						May 14	May 18		
Cambridge	Massachusetts						May 7			
Florida	do							May 8	May 9	
Lawrence	do							May 27		
Mendon	do				May 6					
New Ashford	do						May 21			
North Attleborough	do		May 5		May 2	May 2				
Richmond	do		May 20							
Waltham	do				May 10					
Worcester	do						May 4	May 9		
Columbia	Connecticut							May 9	May 10	
East Windsor Hill	do			April 27						
Fairfield	do								May 15	
Georgetown	do						April 28			
Middletown	do		May 6	April 27						
Norwich	do						May 1	April 24		
Preston	do						May 13			
Angelica	New York						May 20			
Baldwinsville	do		May 8						May 18	
Chatham	do		May 12							
Clinton	do							June 2		
Eden	do						May 13	May 24		
Fishkill Landing	do							May 6	May 2	April 17
Flatbush	do		May 3	April 18	April 24	April 27	May 8			
Geneva	do						May 13			
Lake	do						May 19	May 15	May 10	May 6
Lowville	do						May 17	April 25	May 17	
Mexico	do						May 1			
New Lebanon	do			May 2						
New York city	do				May 5	May 8		May 11	May 5	
Nichols	do								May 10	April 25
Ogdensburg	do						May 13			
Ovid	do				May 11		May 15	May 23		
Plattsburg	do		May 12							
Rochester	do					April 28	May 4	May 20	May 5	
Spencertown	do					May 1	May 20			
Waterloo	do		May 4							
Wellsville	do							April 15	April 20	
West Concord	do						May 20			
West Point	do		May 1	April 26						
Burlington	New Jersey		April 29							
Freehold	do									April 28
Moorestown	do					April 15				
Sergeantsville	do							April 27		
Bellefonte	Pennsylvania								May 15	
Ceres	do		May 14							

PYRUS MALUS.—*Apple*—Continued.

Name of Station.	1851.	1852.	1853.	1854.	1855.	1856.	1857.	1858.	1859.
Darby ... Pennsylvania		April 30	April 19						
Easton ... do		April 30		April 16					
Fleming ... do							May 10		
Freeport ... do				April 24					
Gettysburg ... do		May 3	April 20	April 26		April 25			
Hollidaysburg ... do		April 27	April 14						
Huntingdon ... do						April 27	May 1		
Indiana ... do		April 27							
Lancaster ... do				April 10					
Lima ... do						May 1			
Meadville ... do		May 4				April 26			
Mercersburg ... do		April 22							
Morrisville ... do						May 14			
Murrysville ... do							April 30		
Nazareth ... do						April 30	May 4		
North Whitehall ... do							May 7	May 7	
Orwigsburg ... do		May 2							
Shamokin ... do							May 25		
Upper Darby ... do		May 1	April 25	April 23					
Valley Forge ... do		April 26							
Easton ... Maryland				April 20					
Ridge ... do						April 12			
Spencerville ... do							April 25		
Sykesville ... do			April 22	April 14		May 12	May 3		
Buffalo ... Virginia					April 15	April 29			
Clarke county ... do							April 24	April 10	
Crack Whip ... do							April 30		
Crichton's Store ... do			March 30			April 14	April 11	April 17	March 22
Doddridge county ... do						April 16			
Genito ... do		March 10							
Madison C. H. ... do		March 26							
Mossy Creek ... do		April 20				April 30	April 20		
Mount Solon ... do						April 20			
Poplar Grove ... do							April 14	April 8	March 28
Portsmouth ... do						April 16			
Rose Hill ... do						April 11	April 5	April 12	
Wardensville ... do						April 17			
Winchester ... do						April 25			
Wirt C. H ... do						May 10			
Chapel Hill ... N. Carolina			March 28					March 25	
Camden ... S. Carolina		March 10							
Savannah ... Georgia						April 1			
Sparta ... do						March 8	March 20		
Alligator ... Florida								Jan. 20	
Carlowville ... Alabama							March 29		
Childersburg ... do								April 4	
Greene Springs ... do						April 26			
Greensborough ... do						March 23	March 17	March 4	
Weewokaville ... do		March 18	April 8						
Columbus ... Mississippi								March 15	
Jasper ... do					March 22				
Trinity ... Louisiana								April 1	
Helena ... Texas							Feb. 28		
New Wied ... do		April 1	March 29	April 5					
Hannibal ... Missouri				April 5					
Trenton ... do				April 15					
Westport ... do						April 25			
Glenwood ... Tennessee			March 26						
Maysville ... Kentucky			April 23						
Ashtabula ... Ohio				April 27					
Belle Centre ... do		April 23		April 22				April 12	
Bowling Green ... do								April 10	
Cheviot ... do						April 22			
Cleveland ... do				April 23	April 21				
Edinburg ... do							May 17		
Germantown ... do		April 16	April 10	April 8		April 23			
Hamilton ... do							May 6		
Hiram ... do						April 26	May 10	April 21	
Hocking Port ... do							May 4		
Jefferson ... do						May 10			

PYRUS MALUS.—*Apple*—Continued.

Name of Station.		1851.	1852.	1853.	1854.	1855.	1856.	1857.	1858.	1859.
Keene	Ohio		May 7							
Marietta	do								April 4	
Mount Healthy	do				April 10					
Poland	do					April 20				
Ripley	do							April 5		
Savannah	do							May 22		
Troy	do									April 30
Welchfield	do							June 5		
Indianapolis	Indiana									April 8
Laconia	do							March 30		
New Albany	do						April 29			
New Harmony	do						April 12			
Athens	Illinois						April 16			
Augusta	do		April 19			April 20	April 17	May 5		
Batavia	do								April 21	
Brighton	do							May 3	April 16	
Manchester	do						April 19			
Marengo	do						May 8	May 18	April 20	
Ottawa	do						April 21		April 12	
Pekin	do								May 10	
Peoria	do								April 21	
Riley	do							May 21		
Warsaw	do						April 18	May 11	April 8	
Waynesville	do								April 10	
West Northville	do				April 21					
West Salem	do						April 24	May 10	April 10	
Winnebago	do							May 15	April 27	
Ann Arbor	Michigan		May 18							
Cooper	do						April 24			
Flint	do					April 23				
Romeo	do						April 30			
St. James	do			May 28			April 22			
Madison	Wisconsin						May 10	May 15		
Lac qui Parle	Minnesota			May 4						
Border Plains	Iowa								April 12	April 29
Eagle	do							May 9		
Fairfield	do									May 1
Fort Madison	do		May 8	April 9	April 16		April 23			
Keokuk	do						April 21			
Muscatine	do		April 27	April 20	April 20	April 20	May 1			
Pleasant Plain	do				April 15		May 10	May 22		
Sacramento	California						March 15			
Horton	Nova Scotia					May 24				
Stanbridge	Canada						May 15	May 20	May 14	
Leipsig	Saxony								April 30	

QUERCUS ALBA.—*White Oak.*

Name of Station.		1851.	1852.	1853.	1854.	1855.	1856.	1857.	1858.	1859.
Brunswick	Maine								June 9	
Gardiner	do							May 30		
Naples	do							May 29		
Londonderry	New Hamp.		May 11	May 14						
Salmon Falls	do				May 12					
West Enfield	do							May 24		
Brandon	Vermont			May 14	May 12			May 23	May 24	
Castleton	do			May 17						
Florida	Massachusetts								May 9	
Mendon	do				May 22					
North Attleborough	do		May 8		May 13	May 14				
Uxbridge	do				May 21					
Waltham	do				May 13					
Worcester	do							May 27		
Point Judith	Rhode Island				May 25					
Columbia	Connecticut							May 17	May 18	
Middletown	do			May 8	May 11					
Chatham	New York		May 8							
Fishkill Landing	do								April 27	April 24

QUERCUS ALBA.—*White Oak*—Continued.

Name of Station.		1851.	1852.	1853.	1854.	1855.	1856.	1857.	1858.	1859.
Flatbush	New York		May 12	May 3	May 7					
Lake	do							May 24		May 18
New York city	do								May 20	
Nichols	do								May 31	May 15
Ovid	do				May 15					
Rochester	do							May 10	May 20	
Sag Harbor	do		May 17							
Spencertown	do					May 24				
Waterloo	do		May 12							
West Point	do			May 5						
Burlington	New Jersey		May 15							
Ceres	Pennsylvania		May 30							
Fleming	do							May 20		
Freeport	do		May 15	May 6	May 5					
Gettysburg	do		May 11	April 29	May 1					
Hollidaysburg	do		May 10	May 4						
Indiana	do		May 15							
Meadville	do		May 20							
Mercersburg	do		May 6							
Murrysville	do							May 26		
North Whitehall	do							May 23		
Orwigsburg	do		May 10							
Shamokin	do							June 1		
Darby	do		May 4	April 28						
Somerset	do								May 20	
Upper Darby	do		May 10	April 26	April 29					
Valley Forge	do		May 7							
Hagerstown	Maryland			April 23						
Sykesville	do			April 26	May 20					
Buffalo	Virginia					April 26				
Clarke county	do								May 5	
Crichton's Store	do			April 2				April 30	April 9	March 25
Genito	do		April 1							
Madison C. H.	do		April 27							
Mossy Creek	do		May 1					May 10		
The Plains	do									May 1
Poplar Grove	do								April 25	May 4
Chapel Hill	N. Carolina			April 12					April 9	
Camden	S. Carolina		March 28							
Alligator	Florida								Jan. 1	
Seville	do									Feb. 25
Greensborough	Alabama						April 1	March 17	April 3	
Weewokaville	do		March 15							
Jasper	Mississippi					March 26	March 26			
Cross Roads	Texas									March 15
New Wied	do			March 20						
Hannibal	Missouri				April 22					
Glenwood	Tennessee			April 11						
Fairview	Kentucky									May 5
Maysville	do			May 16						
Ashtabula	Ohio				May 12					
Belle Centre	do		May 10		May 12				May 20	
Bowling Green	do								April 11	
Cleveland	do				May 12	May 6				
Germantown	do				April 26					
Hiram	do							May 26	May 16	
Hocking Port	do							May 25		
Keene	do		May 7							
Mount Healthy	do				April 30					
Poland	do					May 14				
Rockport	do									May 10
Savannah	do							June 1		
Laconia	Indiana								April 10	May 4
Athens	Illinois		May 1							
Augusta	do		May 12	May 9	May 3	April 28		May 25		
Batavia	do								April 28	
Brighton	do							May 16	May 10	
Marengo	do							May 23	May 24	
Pekin	do								May 25	
Peoria	do								May 4	

QUERCUS ALBA.—*White Oak*—Continued.

Name of Station.		1851.	1852.	1853.	1854.	1855.	1856.	1857.	1858.	1859.
Riley	Illinois							May 30		
Warsaw	do							May 17	April 26	
Waynesville	do								May 6	
West Salem	do							May 28		
Winnebago	do							May 13	May 12	May 13
Ann Arbor	Michigan			May 20						
Flint	do					May 2				
Wyandotte	do									May 3
Lac qui Parle	Minnesota				May 18					
Princeton	do							May 6		
Border Plains	Iowa								May 5	May 9
Eagle	do							May 20		
Fairfield	do									May 10
Fort Madison	do		May 8	April 28	May 2					
Keokuk	do						April 28			
Muscatine	do			May 8	May 7	May 10				
Pleasant Plain	do				May 1					
Leavenworth	Kansas								April 4	
Stanbridge	Canada							May 20	May 20	

RHODODENDRON MAXIMUM.—*Great Laurel.*

Name of Station.		1851.	1852.	1853.	1854.	1855.	1856.	1857.	1858.	1859.
Columbia	Connecticut							May 24		
Fairfield	do								May 30	
Poplar Grove	Virginia								Perennial	
Poland	Ohio					May 26				
Leavenworth	Kansas								April 6	
Stanbridge	Canada									May 24

RHODODENDRON NUDIFLORA AZALEA.—*Common Red Honeysuckle.*

Name of Station.		1851.	1852.	1853.	1854.	1855.	1856.	1857.	1858.	1859.
Gardiner	Maine							May 29		
Steuben	do				May 18	June 1		April 11		
Castleton	Vermont				April 24					
Lawrence	Massachusetts							April 24		
Richmond	do		June 1							
Columbia	Connecticut							May 10	April 20	
Fairfield	do								June 2	
Flatbush	New York			April 12		April 18				
New York city	do								May 14	
Ovid	do				June 1					
Rochester	do			May 10		May 14		June 1	May 24	
Wellsville	do							June 12		
Moorestown	New Jersey					April 10				
Newark	do		April 15							
Ceres	Pennsylvania		May 18							
Darby	do		May 14							
Gettysburg	do		May 11		April 30					
Nazareth	do							March 28		
Shamokin	do							May 26		
Easton	Maryland				March 29					
Sykesville	do			April 19						
Clarke county	Virginia								March 16	
Crichton's Store	do			April 12					April 20	April 8
Genito	do		April 20							
Mossy Creek	do		May 1					May 20		
Poplar Grove	do								April 18	April 13
Rose Hill	do						April 12			March 6
Chapel Hill	N. Carolina			April 20						
All Saints	S. Carolina					April 2				
Camden	do		March 21							
Alligator	Florida								Jan. 5	
Greensborough	Alabama								April 6	
Weewokaville	do		March 28	April 2						

RHODODENDRON NUIDFLORA AZALEA.—*Common Red Honeysuckle*—Continued.

Name of Station.	1851.	1852.	1853.	1854.	1855.	1856.	1857.	1858.	1859.
Jasper Mississippi					March 26				
Ashtabula Ohio				April 14					
Mount Healthy do				April 25					
Poland do					May 4				
Ripley do							March 25		
Savannah do							May 20		
Indianapolis Indiana									April 10
Laconia do								March 1	
Brighton Illinois								April 6	
Warsaw do							April 25	April 1	
Waynesville do								March 30	
Wyandotte Michigan								March 28	
Lac qui Parle Minnesota			April 23	April 23					
Princeton do							May 20		
Border Plains Iowa								April 7	May 1
Fairfield do									May 3
Muscatine do		April 30	April 24	April 10	May 1				
Pleasant Plain do				April 20	April 17				
Plum Spring do					April 20				
Stanbridge Canada							May 10	April 16	

RHUS GLABRA.—*Smooth Sumach.*

Name of Station.	1851.	1852.	1853.	1854.	1855.	1856.	1857.	1858.	1859.
Stockbridge Vermont			May 18						
Burlington New Jersey		May 15							
Easton Pennsylvania			May 3						
Hollidaysburg do			May 4						
Sykesville Maryland		March 11	May 8						
Crichton's Store Virginia			April 18						
Genito do		April 10							
Mossy Creek do		May 1							
Camden S. Carolina		April 18							
Weewokaville Alabama		April 15	April 20						
Maysville Kentucky			May 6						
Indianapolis Indiana									May 1
Augusta Illinois		May 5	May 7						

RIBES GROSSULARIA.—*Gooseberry.*

Name of Station.	1851.	1852.	1853.	1854.	1855.	1856.	1857.	1858.	1859.
Brunswick Maine						May 12			
Carmel do						May 5			
Cornish do						May 5	May 16		
Perry do						May 5			
Steuben do	May 3	May 8	May 10						May 3
Concord New Hamp.						May 9			
Londonderry do			April 25						
Manchester do		May 10							
Brandon Vermont			May 4						
Burlington do					April 25				
Craftsbury do						May 5	May 9		
Newark do						May 9	May 10		
Shelburn do						May 1			
Stockbridge do			May 2						
West Rupert do							May 8		
East Weymouth Massachusetts						May 5			
Florida do							May 8		
Mendon do				May 3					
North Attleborough do		April 27		April 25					
Worcester do						April 30			
Columbia Connecticut								May 4	
East Windsor Hill do			April 23						
Georgetown do						April 20			
Middletown do		May 1	April 14						
Norwich do							April 12		

RIBES GROSSULARIA.—*Gooseberry*—Continued.

Name of Station.		1851.	1852.	1853.	1854.	1855.	1856.	1857.	1858.	1859.
Preston	Connecticut						April 27			
Angelica	New York						May 5			
Chatham	do		May 12							
Eden	do						May 8	May 17		
Elmira	do						April 23			
Flatbush	do		April 20	April 2				April 19		
Geneva	do						May 3			
Lake	do						May 16			
Lowville	do						May 2	April 20	April 28	
Mexico	do						April 26			
New Lebanon	do			April 27						
Ogdensburg	do			May 1						
Oswego	do						April 27			
Ovid	do						May 12	May 23		
Plattsburg	do		May 9							
Rochester	do						May 1	May 8		
West Point	do		April 15	March 24						
Burlington	New Jersey		April 15							
Sergeantsville	do							April 6		
Bellefonte	Pennsylvania								May 1	
Bucks county	do						April 15			
Ceres	do		May 10							
Darby	do		April 20	March 29						
Easton	do		April 25	April 11						
Gettysburg	do		April 11	April 7	April 3					
Hollidaysburg	do		April 3	April 1						
Huntingdon	do						April 25			
Indiana	do		April 12							
Lima	do						April 26			
Meadville	do		April 20				April 13			
Nazareth	do						May 1			
North Whitehall	do								April 24	
Shamokin	do							April 29		
Upper Darby	do		April 10	April 22						
Ridge	Maryland						April 15			
Sykesville	do		March 10				April 11			
Berryville	Virginia						April 14			
Buffalo	do						April 24			
Crack Whip	do							April 28		
Crichton's Store	do						April 14			
Genito	do		March 8							
Madison C. H	do		March 15							
Mossy Creek	do		March 20					April 5		
Mount Solon	do						April 9			
The Plains	do									March 15
Winchester	do						April 15			
Camden	S. Carolina		March 10							
Sparta	Georgia						March 8			
Weewokaville	Alabama		April 8							
Rockport	Missouri						April 3			
Westport	do						April 16			
Fairview	Kentucky									April 5
Maysville	do			April 2						
Belle Centre	Ohio		April 15							
Cleveland	do						April 20			
Edinburgh	do							May 9		
Germantown	do			April 3			April 16	May 4		
Hiram	do						April 18			
Jefferson	do						April 25			
Keene	do		April 10							
Troy	do									March 30
Welchfield	do							May 26		
Laconia	Indiana									March 15
Athens	Illinois			March 18			April 9			
Augusta	do		April 5	April 3			April 8			
Manchester	do						April 4		March 17	March 15
Ottawa	do						April 27		March 26	
Warsaw	do						April 10	April 29	April 15	
West Salem	do						April 8	March 27	April 1	
Winnebago	do									April 25

RIBES GROSSULARIA.—*Gooseberry*—Continued.

Name of Station.		1851.	1852.	1853.	1854.	1855.	1856.	1857.	1858.	1859.
Cooper	Michigan						April 13			
Grand Rapids	do						April 24			
Saint James	do						May 12			
Appleton	Wisconsin						May 1			
Greenfield	do									April 25
Madison	do						April 16	May 11		
Norway	do						April 23			
Platteville	do						April 26			
Beaver Bay	Minnesota								May 15	
Cass Lake Mission	do							May 13		
Fort Ripley	do		May 4							
Lac qui Parle	do			April 20						
Red Wing	do						April 24			
Fairfield	Iowa									April 25
Fort Madison	do			March 25	March 24			April 12		
Muscatine	do		April 21	April 26						
Pleasant Plain	do						April 12			
Salem	Oregon						March 22			
Windsor	Nova Scotia						May 3	May 4		
Red River	Rupert's Land						May 7			

RIBES RUBRUM.—*Red Currant.*

Name of Station.		1851.	1852.	1853.	1854.	1855.	1856.	1857.	1858.	1859.
Brunswick	Maine						May 22	May 22	May 23	
Carmel	do						May 5			
Cornish	do						May 12	May 17		
Naples	do							May 7		
Perry	do						May 9			May 3
Steubene	do	May 18	May 8	May 5	May 12	May 12		May 6	May 1	May 16
Concord	New Hamp						May 8			
Londonderry	do		May 5	April 27						
Manchester	do		May 8		April 28					
North Barnstead	do							May 9		
Salmon Falls	do				May 11					
Shelburn	do								May 7	
Somersworth	do				May 2					
Stratford	do						May 8			
West Enfield	do							May 6		
Brandon	Vermont			May 4	May 11			May 9	May 7	
Burlington	do					May 8				
Castleton	do			May 5						
Craftsbury	do						May 10	May 10		
Newark	do						May 11	May 21		
Shelburn	do						May 1			
Stockbridge	do			May 2						
West Rupert	do							May 12		
East Weymouth	Massachusetts						May 5			
Florida	do							May 8	April 27	
North Attleborough	do		April 25		April 25	April 24				
Richmond	do		May 12							
Worcester	do						April 30	April 28		
Columbia	Connecticut							May 9	May 7	
East Windsor Hill	do			April 25						
Fairfield	do								May 12	
Georgetown	do						April 25			
Middletown	do		May 4	April 14						
Norwich	do							April 12		
Preston	do						April 27			
Angelica	New York						May 8			
Chatham	do		May 8							
Eden	do						May 10	May 22		
Elmira	do						April 27			
Fishkill Landing	do						May 2			April 12
Flatbush	do		April 20	April 4	April 6	April 17		April 21		
Geneva	do						May 10			
Lake	do						May 17	May 7	May 6	May 3

RIBES RUBRUM.—*Red Currant*—Continued.

Name of Station.		1851.	1852.	1853.	1854.	1855.	1856.	1857.	1858.	1859.
Lowville	New York						May 5	May 8	May 13	
Mexico	do						April 29			
New Mexico	do			May 1						
New York city	do				April 28	April 24			April 20	
Nichols	do								May 1	
North Salem	do						April 27			
Ogdensburg	do			May 1						
Oswego	do						April 27			
Plattsburg	do		May 9							
Ovid	do				May 6		May 11	May 23		
Rochester	do			April 22		April 28	April 25	May 6	April 20	
Spencertown	do					April 26				
Wellsville	do							April 5	April 15	
West Concord	do						May 15			
West Point	do		April 23	April 2						
Williamsville	do				April 27					
Burlington	New Jersey		April 15							
Freehold	do									Mar. 20
Moorestown	do					April 21				
Newark	do	April 4								
Bellefonte	Pennsylvania								May 1	
Bucks county	do						April 25			
Ceres	do		May 10							
Darby	do		April 15	April 3						
Easton	do		April 28		April 22					
Fleming	do							May 1		
Freeport	do				April 12					
Gettysburg	do		April 30	April 9	April 16		April 27			
Huntingdon	do						April 25			
Indiana	do		April 22							
Lima	do						April 21			
Meadville	do		May 1				April 18			
Murrysville	do							May 1		
Nazareth	do						May 1	April 27		
North Whitehall	do							April 29		
Orwigsburg	do		April 26							
Shamokin	do							April 29		
Somerset	do								April 18	
Upper Darby	do		April 22	April 25						
Valley Forge	do		April 20							
Easton	Maryland				Mar. 1					
Ridge	do						April 15			
Sykesville	do		Mar. 10	Mar. 23	April 20		April 13	April 10		
Berryville	Virginia						April 14			
Buffalo	do					April 10	April 25			
Clark county	do							April 24	April 16	
Crack Whip	do							April 28		
Crichton's Store	do			Mar. 18			April 14	April 1	April 1	
Genito	do		Mar. 8							
Mossy Creek	do		April 20					April 20		
Mount Solon	do						April 12			
Plains	do									April 1
Poplar Grove	do							April 25	April 10	Mar. 30
Rose Hill	do						April 12			April 30
Winchester	do						April 22			
Sparta	Georgia						Mar. 8			
Columbus	Mississippi								Mar. 15	
Jasper	do					Mar. 20				
Helena	Texas							Feb. 5		
Westport	Missouri						April 9			
Glenwood	Tennessee			April 2						
Fairview	Kentucky									April 10
Maysville	do			April 9						
Ashtabula	Ohio				April 26					
Belle Centre	do		April 21		April 20				April 12	
Bowling Green	do								April 10	
Cheviot	do					April 19				
Cleveland	do				April 20	April 18	April 21			
Edinburg	do							May 11		
Germantown	do			April 1	Mar. 31		April 15			

RIBES RUBRUM.—*Red Currant*—Continued.

Name of Station.		1851.	1852.	1853.	1854.	1855.	1856.	1857.	1858.	1859.
Hamilton	Ohio							April 27		
Hiram	do						April 21	May 4	April 6	
Hocking Port	do							May 8		
Jefferson	do						April 30			
Keene	do		April 25							
Marietta	do								April 14	
Poland	do					April 10				
Ripley	do							April 5		
Rockport	do									Mar. 15
Savannah	do							May 5		
Troy	do									April 13
Welchfield	do							May 30		
Indianapolis	Indiana									April 10
Laconia	do								April 12	April 13
Athens	Illinois						April 9			
Augusta	do		April 10	April 4		April 12	April 9	May 2		
Batavia	do								April 2	
Brighton	do							May 5	April 15	
Edgington	do							May 2		
Manchester	do						April 6			Mar. 15
Marengo	do							May 10	April 6	
Ottawa	do						April 16		April 1	
Pekin	do								May 2	
Peoria	do								April 10	
Riley	do							May 5		
Warsaw	do						April 16	April 30	April 5	
Waynesville	do								April 8	
West Northville	do				April 10					
West Salem	do						April 14	April 20	April 23	
Winnebago	do							May 16	April 27	May 1
Ann Arbor	Michigan			May 21						
Cooper	do						April 17			
Flint	do					April 15				
Grand Rapids	do						April 27			
Romeo	do						April 23			
St. James	do			May 6			May 12			
Wyandotte	do									April 20
Greenfield	Wisconsin									May 15
Madison	do						April 17	May 11		
Norway	do						April 23			
Platteville	do						April 30			
Beaver Bay	Minnesota						May 15			
Lac qui Parle	do				May 1					
Princeton	do							June 10		
Red Wing	do						April 22			
Border Plains	Iowa								April 12	April 27
Eagle	do							May 9		
Fairfield	do									April 28
Fort Madison	do				April 22		April 24			
Muscatine	do		April 27	April 24	April 20	May 5	April 26			
Pleasant Plain	do				April 26		April 5			
Salem	Oregon						Mar. 29			
Horton	Nova Scotia					May 17				
Windsor	do							May 4		
Stanbridge	Canada						May 2	May 3	May 24	
Leipsig	Saxony								April 10	

ROBINIA PSEUD ACACIA.—*Common Locust.*

Name of Station.		1851.	1852.	1853.	1854.	1855.	1856.	1857.	1858.	1859.
Brunswick	Maine								June 17	
Gardiner	do							June 2		
Naples	do							May 25		
Steuben	do	June 4		May 30				June 3	June 9	
Londonderry	New Hampshire		May 11	May 14						
Castleton	Vermont			May 14						
Stockbridge	do			May 18						

ROBINIA PSEUD-ACACIA.—*Common Locust*—Continued

NAME OF STATION.		1851.	1852.	1853.	1854.	1855.	1856.	1857.	1858.	1859.
Mendon	Massachusetts				May 22					
North Attleborough	do		May 15		May 11	May 15				
Richmond	do		June 1							
Waltham	do				May 13					
Worcester	do							May 13		
Point Judith	Rhode Island				May 26					
Columbia	Connecticut							May 26	May 21	
Fairfield	do								May 25	
Chatham	New York		May 23							
Fishkill Landing	do							May 20		May 1
Flatbush	do		May 15	May 2	May 7	May 10				
Lake	do							May 31	June 3	May 20
New York city	do				May 19	May 21			May 20	
Ogdensburg	do			May 20						
Plattsburg	do		May 20							
Ovid	do				May 17					
Rochester	do			May 20		May 24		May 3	May 18	
Spencertown	do					May 15				
Waterloo	do		May 8							
West Point	do		May 18	May 6						
Burlington	New Jersey		May 15							
Freehold	do									May 10
Moorestown	do					May 11				
Ceres	Pennsylvania		June 1							
Darby	do		May 8	May 2						
Easton	do				April 29					
Gettysburg	do		May 11	May 3	May 4					
Hollidaysburg	do		May 20	May 6						
Indiana	do		May 11							
Lancaster	do				May 4					
Meadville	do		May 16							
Mercersburg	do		May 6							
Murrysville	do							May 24		
Nazareth	do							May 24		
Somerset	do								May 16	
Upper Darby	do				May 7					
Hagerstown	Maryland			April 25						
Sykesville	do		May 1	April 27	April 27			May 1		
Buffalo	Virginia					April 20				
Clark county	do							May 10	May 10	
Crichton's Store	do			April 17					April 15	April 10
Genito	do		April 13							
Kanawha Salines	do								April 12	
Madison C. H.	do		April 30							
Mossy Creek	do		May 1					May 12		
Poplar Grove	do								April 15	April 18
Rose Hill	do						April 10		April 10	Mar. 30
Chapel Hill	North Carolina			April 2						
Camden	South Carolina		May 29							
Alligator	Florida								April 16	
Greensborough	Alabama						Mar. 30	Mar. 20	Mar. 4	
Weewokaville	do		April 15	April 18						
Trinity	Louisiana								April 1	
Hannibal	Missouri				April 22					
Trenton	do				April 23					
Glenwood	Tennessee			April 10						
Knoxville	do		April 15							
Maysville	Kentucky			April 27						
Ashtabula	Ohio				May 13					
Belle Centre	do		May 10		May 1				May 10	
Bowling Green	do								April 18	
Cleveland	do				May 10	May 3				
Germantown	do		May 5	May 1	May 2					
Hiram	do							May 24	May 16	
Hocking Port	do							May 20		
Mount Healthy	do				May 1					
Poland	do					May 14				
Ripley	do							May 8		
Savannah	do							June 5		
Indianapolis	Indiana									May 2

ROBINIA PSEUD-ACACIA.—*Common Locust*—Continued.

Name of Station.	1851.	1852.	1853.	1854.	1855.	1856.	1857.	1858.	1859.
Laconia ....Indiana....								April 12	
Augusta..........Illinois ...		May 12	May 13	May 5	May 7		May 18		
Brighton ....do......							April 25	April 8	
Marengo ....do......							May 20	April 21	
Pekin ....do......								May 14	
Warsaw ....do......								May 12	
Waynesville ....do......								May 15	
West Northville ....do......				May 3					
West Salem..........do......							May 29		
Winnebago ....do......								May 15	
Ann Arbor ....Michigan...			May 21						
Flint..........do......					May 1				
Romeo ....do......						May 20			
Fairfield ....Iowa.....									May 9
Fort Madison..........do......				May 2					
Muscatine ....do......		May 11		May 10	May 7				
Pleasant Plain ....do......				May 1			June 5		
Horton ....Nova Scotia..					May 31				
Stanbridge..........Canada....							May 18	May 15	
Leipsig ....Saxony....								May 10	

ROBINIA VISCOSA.—*Clammy Locust.*

Name of Station.	1851.	1852.	1853.	1854.	1855.	1856.	1857.	1858.	1859.
Brunswick ....Maine....								June 17	
Gardiner ....do......							May 30		
Waltham..........Massachusetts.				May 13					
Columbia ....Connecticut..							May 27	May 21	
Fairfield..........do......								May 20	
Nichols ....New York..									May 12
Rochester ....do......								May 15	
Spencertown ....do......					May 15				
Gettysburg ....Pennsylvania.			May 3	May 2					
Hollidaysburg..........do......			May 4						
Buffalo..........Virginia....					April 29				
Clark county ....do......								May 10	
Weewokaville..........Alabama...		April 15							
Trinity..........Louisiana ..								April 1	
Poland ....Ohio......				May 2					
Waynesville ....Illinois ...								May 18	
West Northville..........do......				May 3					
Winnebago ....do......							May 24		
Ann Arbor ....Michigan...			May 1						
Fairfield ....Iowa.....									May 6
Fort Madison ....do......			April 29						

ROSA CENTIFOLIA.—*Hundred-leaved Rose.—Cabbage Rose.*

Name of Station.	1851.	1852.	1853.	1854.	1855.	1856.	1857.	1858.	1859.
East Windsor Hill....Connecticut..			April 22						
Chatham..........New York..		May 8							
Plattsburg..........do......		May 8							
Waterloo..........do......		May 1							
Burlington ....New Jersey..		May 7							
Darby..........Pennsylvania.		March 28	April 3						
Gettysburg ....do......			March 31	April 17					
Hollidaysburg..........do......		May 11							
Meadville ....do......		May 6							
Sykesville..........Maryland...		April 27	April 5						
Madison C. H...........Virginia...		March 20							
Mossy Creek ....do......		May 1							
New Wied..........Texas......			March 5						
Glenwood ....Tennessee...			March 26						
Belle Centre..........Ohio.....		May 1							
Germantown..........do......		April 18	April 1						
Augusta..........Illinois ...		April 20	April 22						
Muscatine..........Iowa......		May 14	May 4						

ROSA RUBIGINOSA.—*Sweet Brier.*

NAME OF STATION.	1851.	1852.	1853.	1854.	1855.	1856.	1857.	1858.	1859.
Steuben .... Maine....			May 14						
Londonderry .... New Hamp..		May 7	April 29						
Middletown .... Connecticut..			April 28						
Chatham .... New York..		May 4							
New Lebanon .... do......			May 3						
Plattsburg .... do......		May 11							
Waterloo .... do......		May 1							
West Point .... do......		April 25							
Burlington .... New Jersey..		April 20							
Ceres .... Pennsylvania..		May 5							
Darby .... do......		May 1	April 18						
Gettysburg .... do......			May 10	May 10					
Indiana .... do......		April 26							
Meadville .... do......		May 5							
Sykesville .... Maryland..		April 27							
Madison C. H. .... Virginia...		March 28							
Mossy Creek .... do......		April 1							
Chapel Hill .... N. Carolina..			April 1						
Camden .... S. Carolina..		March 4							
Belle Centre .... Ohio.....		April 26							
Indianapolis .... Indiana....									April 10
Augusta .... Illinois....		April 22	April 22						
Muscatine .... Iowa.....			May 4						

RUBUS ODORATUS.—*Purple Flowered Raspberry.*

NAME OF STATION.	1851.	1852.	1853.	1854.	1855.	1856.	1857.	1858.	1859.
Londonderry .... New Hamp..			April 25						
Stockbridge .... Vermont...			May 6						
Flatbush .... New York..		May 1							
Plattsburg .... do......		May 10							
Burlington .... New Jersey..		April 20							
Easton .... Pennsylvania..		May 1							
Gettysburg .... do......				April 26					
Hollidaysburg .... do......			April 23						
Crichton's Store .... Virginia....			March 25						
Genito .... do......		March 16							
Madison C. H. .... do......		April 10							
Mossy Creek .... do......		May 1							
Chapel Hill .... N. Carolina..			April 10						
Weewokaville .... Alabama..			April 20						
Muscatine .... Iowa.....		April 28	April 26						

RUBUS STRIGOSUS.—*Red Raspberry.*

NAME OF STATION.	1851.	1852.	1853.	1854.	1855.	1856.	1857.	1858.	1859.
Brunswick .... Maine....						May 28			
Carmel .... do......						May 7			
Cornish .... do......						May 20	May 15		
Perry .... do......						May 13			
Concord .... New Hamp..						May 28			
Salmon Falls .... do......				May 7					
Sherburne .... do......				May 11					
Stratford .... do......						May 10			
Craftsbury .... Vermont...						May 5	May 12		
Newark .... do......						May 14			
Shelburn .... do......						May 12			
West Rupert .... do......						May 14	May 21		
Bridgewater .... Massachusetts..							May 12		
East Weymouth .... do......						May 12			
Florida .... do......							May 16		
Worcester .... do......						May 1			
Acquidneset .... Rhode Island..						April 23			
Columbia .... Connecticut..								May 27	
Angelica .... New York..						May 4			
Clinton .... do......							May 28		

RUBUS STRIGOSUS.—*Red Raspberry*—Continued.

Name of Station.		1851.	1852.	1853.	1854.	1855.	1856.	1857.	1858.	1859.
Eden	New York						May 18	May 22		
Lowville	do						May 7	April 30	May 16	
New York city	do							May 1		
Oswego	do						April 27			
Ovid	do							May 24		
Spencertown	do						May 15			
Sergeantsville	New Jersey							April 24		
Bellefonte	Pennsylvania								April 15	
Gettysburg	do						April 25			
Morrisville	do						May 5			
Nazareth	do						May 4			
Ridge	Maryland						April 4			
Buffalo	Virginia						April 28			
Crichton's Store	do						April 12			
Cheviot	Ohio						April 16			
Cleveland	do						April 21			
Edinburg	do							May 12		
Germantown	do						April 11			
Hamilton	do						May 7			
Athens	Illinois						April 15			
Warsaw	do							April 30	April 16	
West Salem	do						April 15	May 9	April 10	
Cooper	Michigan						April 21			
St. James	do						May 5			
Beaver Bay	Minnesota								May 10	
Red Wing	do						April 23			
Fort Madison	Iowa						April 21			
Muscatine	do						April 25			
Stanbridge	Canada						May 8			

RUBUS VILLOSUS—*Blackberry.*

Name of Station.		1851.	1852.	1853.	1854.	1855.	1856.	1857.	1858.	1859.
Brunswick	Maine							May 28	June 13	
Gardiner	do							May 16		
Naples	do							May 16		
Perry	do									May 10
North Barnstead	N. Hamp							May 11		
Salmon Falls	do				May 11					
Somersworth	do				May 10					
West Enfield	do							May 14		
Castleton	Vermont			May 3						
Stockbridge	do			May 5						
Florida	Massachusetts							May 18	April 27	
Mendon	do				May 13					
North Attleborough	do		May 7		April 27	May 6				
Waltham	do				June 2					
Columbia	Connecticut							May 13	May 14	
Fairfield	do								May 12	
Georgetown	do						April 25			
Preston	do						May 4			
Chatham	New York		May 14							
Fishkill Landing	do							May 2	April 27	
Flatbush	do			April 9						
Lake	do							May 14	May 16	
New Lebanon	do			May 4						
New York city	do				April 26				April 30	
Plattsburg	do		May 12							
Ovid	do				May 15					
Spencertown	do					May 5				
Wellsville	do							May 10		
West Point	do		May 6							
Burlington	New Jersey		April 20							
Moorestown	do					April 15				
Ceres	Pennsylvania		May 9							
Easton	do		May 7		April 20					
Fleming	do							May 15		
Gettysburg	do			April 2	April 20					
Hollidaysburg	do			April 10						
Meadville	do		May 1							

RUBUS VILLOSUS—*Blackberry*—Continued.

Name of Station.		1851.	1852.	1853.	1854.	1855.	1856.	1857.	1858.	1859.
North Whitchall	Pennsylvania							May 11		
Philadelphia	do								April 15	
Shamokin	do							May 28		
Darby	do			April 18						
Somerset	do								May 14	
Upper Darby	do			April 24						
Easton	Maryland				April 30					
Sykesville	do		April 4	April 16	April 20			May 10		
Buffalo	Virginia					April 28				
Clark county	do								April 20	
Crichton's Store	do			March 25					April 7	March 10
Genito	do		March 16							
Madison C. H.	do		April 8							
Mossy Creek	do		April 20					May 5		
Poplar Grove	do							April 10	March 28	
Chapel Hill	N. Carolina			March 26					April 1	
Camden	S. Carolina		March 10							
Childersburg	Alabama								March 25	
Greensborough	do						March 23	March 10	March 1	
Weewokaville	do		Feb. 27	April 20						
Jasper	Mississippi						March 26			
Trinity	Louisiana							March 1	March 4	
Hannibal	Missouri				April 18					
Glenwood	Tennessee			March 26						
Maysville	Kentucky			April 20						
Ashtabula	Ohio				April 30					
Belle Centre	do		April 27		May 10					
Bowling Green	do								April 4	
Cleveland	do					April 23				
Germantown	do			April 3	March 28					
Mount Healthy	do				April 10					
Poland	do					April 23				
Laconia	Indiana								March 30	
Augusta	Illinois		April 25							
Batavia	do								April 22	
Brighton	do							April 19	April 13	
Edgington	do							May 10		
Marengo	do							May 20		
Pekin	do								May 20	
Peoria	do								April 24	
Warsaw	do							May 15	April 15	
Waynesville	do								April 8	
West Northville	do				April 23					
West Salem	do							May 26		
Wyandotte	Michigan								April 30	
Fairfield	Iowa									May 4
Pleasant Plain	do				April 25					
Leavenworth	Kansas								April 9	
Stanbridge	Canada							May 20	April 28	

SAMBUCUS CANADENSIS—*Common Black Elder.*

Name of Station.		1851.	1852.	1853.	1854.	1855.	1856.	1857.	1858.	1859.
Naples	Maine							May 4		
Perry	do									May 10
Londonderry	New Hamp			April 22						
Salmon Falls	do				May 7					
Shelburne	do								May 16	
West Enfield	do							May 8		
Castleton	Vermont			May 8						
Newark	do							May 10		
Stockbridge	do			May 13						
Florida	Massachusetts							April 28		
Mendon	do				May 16					
North Attleborough	do		May 8		May 4	May 2				
Columbia	Connecticut							May 15	May 9	
Middletown	do			April 30						
Chatham	New York		May 8							
Flatbush	do		May 18	April 8		April 14				
Lake	do							May 15	May 14	May 11
New Lebanon	do			May 2						

SAMBUCUS CANADENSIS—*Common Black Elder*—Continued.

Name of Station.	1851.	1852.	1853.	1854.	1855.	1856.	1857.	1858.	1859.
New York city .... New York								May 18	
Plattsburg .... do		May 13							
Ovid .... do				May 12					
Rochester .... do			May 10				May 25	May 12	
Spencertown .... do					May 1				
Waterloo .... do		April 21							
West Point .... do			April 27						
Burlington .... New Jersey		May 1							
Moorestown .... do					April 19				
Newark .... do		April 29							
Ceres .... Pennsylvania		May 6							
Easton .... do		May 2		April 13					
Fleming .... do							April 25		
Gettysburg .... do			April 27	April 30					
Hollidaysburg .... do			April 3						
Indiana .... do		April 26							
Meadville .... do		May 5							
Murrysville .... do							April 20		
North Whitehall .... do							May 5		
Orwigsburg .... do		May 7							
Philadelphia .... do								April 15	
Shamokin .... do							June 1		
Darby .... do		March 22	April 8						
Somerset .... do								May 12	
Upper Darby .... do		May 8	April 25						
Valley Forge .... do		April 20							
Sykesville .... Maryland		April 9	April 3	April 7			May 20		
Buffalo .... Virginia					April 13				
Clark county .... do							April 24	April 18	
Crichton's Store .... do			March 13				April 15	April 2	March 5
Genito .... do		March 16							
Madison C. H. .... do		March 27							
Mossy Creek .... do		April 15					April 17		
Poplar Grove .... do								April 10	March 24
Chapel Hill .... N. Carolina			March 11						
All Saints .... S. Carolina					March 24				
Camden .... do		April 10							
Alligator .... Florida								April 5	
Greensborough .... Alabama							March 10	March 20	
Weewokaville .... do		Feb. 28	March 5						
Columbus .... Mississippi								Jan. 10	
Trinity .... Louisiana							March 1	Feb. 25	
New Wied .... Texas		March 20	March 20	March 15					
Trenton .... Missouri				April 8					
Glenwood .... Tennessee			March 26						
Maysville .... Kentucky			April 17						
Ashtabula .... Ohio				May 3					
Belle Centre .... do		April 21		April 1					
Bowling Green .... do								April 10	
Cleveland .... do				April 14	April 13				
Germantown .... do		April 26	March 30	March 28					
Hiram .... do								April 2	
Hocking Port .... do							April 8		
Keene .... do		April 20							
Mount Healthy .... do				April 1					
Poland .... do					April 10				
Ripley .... do							May 1		
Savannah .... do							May 18		
Laconia .... Indiana								March 27	
Athens .... Illinois		April 10							
Pekin .... do								May 20	
Peoria .... do								April 17	
Lac qui Parle .... Minnesota			May 1	April 25					
Border Plains .... Iowa								April 2	May 5
Fairfield .... do									May 4
Fort Madison .... do				April 15					
Pleasant Plain .... do				April 25			May 20		
Leavenworth .... Kansas								April 5	
Horton .... Nova Scotia					May 25				
Stanbridge .... Canada							May 20	April 20	

SAMBUCUS PUBENS.—*Red-berried Elder.*

Name of Station.		1851.	1852.	1853.	1854.	1855.	1856.	1857.	1858.	1859.
Naples	Maine							May 4		
North Barnstead	New Hamp							May 6		
Castleton	Vermont			May 5						
New York city	New York								May 20	
Nichols	do									April 14
Plattsburg	do		May 10							
Ovid	do				May 7					
Rochester	do			May 12		May 4			May 10	
Spencertown	do					May 1				
Fleming	Pennsylvania							April 25		
Meadville	do		April 30							
Murrysville	do							April 10		
Shamokin	do							June 1		
Upper Darby	do			April 25						
Ashtabula	Ohio				May 8					
Hiram	do							May 3	April 6	
Augusta	Illinois		April 23	April 30		April 20				
Brighton	do							May 17	April 19	
Flint	Michigan					April 26				
St. James	do			April 25						
Wyandotte	do								April 25	
Stanbridge	Canada								May 1	

SANGUINARIA CANADENSIS.—*Bloodroot.*

Name of Station.		1851.	1852.	1853.	1854.	1855.	1856.	1857.	1858.	1859.
Brandon	Vermont			April 22	April 26	April 26		April 30	April 24	
Burlington	do			April 24						
Castleton	do			May 8						
Worcester	Massachusetts							May 15		
Columbia	Connecticut							April 25	April 26	
Ovid	New York				May 5					
Spencertown	do					May 1				
Waterloo	do		April 10							
West Point	do		May 20							
Burlington	New Jersey		May 1							
Ceres	Pennsylvania		May 1							
Easton	do				April 21					
Hollidaysburg	do			April 28						
Upper Darby	do		April 15	April 4						
Valley Forge	do		April 15							
Buffalo	Virginia					April 10				
Clark county	do							April 15	March 24	
Crichton's Store	do			April 14				May 1		April 8
Genito	do		April 13							
Mossy Creek	do		March 20							
Chapel Hill	N. Carolina			March 20					March 30	
Alligator	Florida								Jan. 12	
Weewokaville	Alabama			March 20						
Trenton	Missouri			April 8	April 6					
Maysville	Kentucky			April 10						
Ashtabula	Ohio				April 26					
Belle Centre	do		March 27		April 1				April 1	
Keene	do		April 24							
Mount Healthy	do				May 12					
Poland	do					April 1				
Savannah	do							May 12		
Laconia	Indiana								March 10	
Athens	Illinois			April 9						
Augusta	do		April 15	April 13		April 15		May 14		
Edgington	do							May 3		
Waynesville	do								April 8	
West Northville	do				April 13					
Wyandotte	Michigan								April 25	
Lac qui Parle	Minnesota			May 1	April 21					
Border Plains	Iowa								April 18	April 28

SANGUINARIA CANADENSIS.—*Bloodroot*—Continued.

Name of Station.		1851.	1852.	1853.	1854.	1855.	1856.	1857.	1858.	1859.
Pleasant Plain	Iowa				May 10	April 30				
Stanbridge	Canada							May 15	April 18	
Leipsig	Saxony								May 1	

SASSAFRAS OFFICINALE.—*Sassafras.*

Name of Station.		1851.	1852.	1853.	1854.	1855.	1856.	1857.	1858.	1859.
Londonderry	New Hamp.		May 9							
Flatbush	New York		May 8	May 8						
West Point	do			April 28						
Burlington	New Jersey		May 1							
Darby	Pennsylvania		May 10							
Gettysburg	do			April 27	May 5					
Meadville	do		May 19							
Murrysville	do							May 20		
Orwigsburg	do		May 9							
Radnor	do		May 16	April 28	April 28			May 13		
Valley Forge	do		May 13							
Genito	Virginia		March 14							
Madison C. H	do		April 17							
Mossy Creek	do		May 1							
Chapel Hill	N. Carolina			April 17						
All Saints	S. Carolina					April 7				
Camden	do		April 15							
Weewokaville	Alabama		April 6	March 5						
Belle Centre	Ohio		May 12							

SAXIFRAGA VIRGINIENSIS.—*Virginia Saxifrage.*

Name of Station.		1851.	1852.	1853.	1854.	1855.	1856.	1857.	1858.	1859.
Brunswick	Maine							April 21		
New York city	New York					April 14			April 15	
Plattsburg	do		April 30							
Ovid	do				April 25					
Rochester	do					April 28		May 12		
Burlington	New Jersey		May 1							
Gettysburg	Pennsylvania		April 27	March 18	April 15					
Hollidaysburg	do			April 2						
Shamokin	do							June 1		
Upper Darby	do		April 15							
Clark county	Virginia								April 15	
Mossy Creek	do		April 20							
Poland	Ohio					April 15				
Brighton	Illinois								April 16	
West Salem	do							May 21		

SMILACINA BIFOLIA.—*Two-leaved Solomon's Seal.*

Name of Station.		1851.	1852.	1853.	1854.	1855.	1856.	1857.	1858.	1859.
Brunswick	Maine							May 20	May 20	
Castleton	Vermont			May 10						
Columbia	Connecticut							May 8	May 19	
Ovid	New York				May 12					
Burlington	New Jersey		May 15							
Ceres	Pennsylvania		May 28							
Gettysburg	do			April 23	April 29					
Hollidaysburg	do			May 1						
Darby	do		May 5							
Clark county	Virginia								April 23	
Crichton's Store	do			April 13				April 19		April 5
Genito	do		April 13							
Weewokaville	Alabama		April 5	April 1						
Mount Healthy	Ohio				April 21					
Savannah	do							May 20		
Marengo	Illinois								April 12	
Princeton	Minnesota							May 10		
Pleasant Plain	Iowa							May 10		
Horton	Nova Scotia					May 17				

STAPHYLEA TRIFOLIA.—*American Bladder Nut.*

Name of Station.	1851.	1852.	1853.	1854.	1855.	1856.	1857.	1858.	1859.
Burlington ....New Jersey..		May 15							
Hollidaysburg........Pennsylvania.		April 28	April 19						
Upper Darby...............do		May 10	April 23						
New Wied ....Texas			April 2						
Belle Centre ....Ohio.....		March 1							
Augusta................Illinois ...		April 28							

SYRINGA VULGARIS.—*Lilac.*

Name of Station.	1851.	1852.	1853.	1854.	1855.	1856.	1857.	1858.	1859.
Brunswick ....Maine							May 25	May 31	
Gardiner ....do......							May 15		
Naples ....do......							May 6		
Steuben ....do......	May 17	May 6	May 10	May 15	May 25		May 12	May 4	
Francestown..........New Hamp..			April 23						
Londonderry ....do......		May 1	April 17						
Manchester ....do......		May 6		May 1					
Salmon Falls...............do......				May 2					
Shelburne ....do......								May 7	
Somersworth ....do......				April 24					
Stratford ....do......								May 24	
West Enfield...............do......							May 10		
Brandon ....Vermont...			April 28	May 8			May 9	May 2	
Burlington ....do......					May 6				
Newark ....do......							May 12		
Stockbridge ....do......			May 5						
Lawrence ....Massachusetts.							April 24		
Mendon ....do......				May 2					
North Attleborough.......do......		April 29		April 25	April 25				
Waltham ....do......				April 23					
Williamstown ....do......							May 23		
Worcester ....do......							April 30		
Columbia ....Connecticut .							May 9	April 26	
East Windsor Hill..........do......			April 18						
Fairfield ....do......								May 7	
Middletown..................do......		April 21	April 10	May 1					
Baldwinsville ....New York ..								May 12	
Chatham ....do......		May 3							
Fishkill Landing ....do......							May 1	April 13	April 12
Flatbush ....do......		April 20	April 9	April 8	April 15				
Lake ....do......								May 4	May 1
Mexico ....do......						April 27			
New Lebanon ....do......			May 1						
New York city..............do......				May 2	April 26			May 16	
Plattsburg ....do......		May 12							
Ovid ....do......				April 30					
Rochester ....do......			April 18		April 24	April 23	May 8	April 6	
Spencertown ....do......					April 24				
Waterloo ....do......		April 1							
West Point ....do......		April 21	April 25						
Williamsville ....do......				April 17					
Burlington ....New Jersey..		April 1							
Moorestown ....do......					April 16				
Newark ....do......	May 3	May 16							
Ceres ....Pennsylvania.		May 3							
Easton ....do......		April 25		April 28					
Fleming ....do......							April 25		
Gettysburg ....do......		April 11	April 1	April 2					
Hollidaysburg ....do......		April 10	April 6						
Indiana ....do......		April 20							
Meadville ....do......		April 22							
Middletown ....do......							May 9		
Murrysville ....do......							April 3		
Nazareth ....do......							April 23		
Philadelphia ....do......								April 8	
Darby ....do......			April 7						
Somerset ....do......								April 17	
Upper Darby ....do......		April 18	April 10						
Valley Forge..................do......		April 20							

SYRINGA VULGARIS.—*Lilac*—Continued.

Name of Station.	1851.	1852.	1853.	1854.	1855.	1856.	1857.	1858.	1859.
Easton .... Maryland				April 6					
Sykesville .... do		March 14	March 30	March 1			April 26		
Buffalo .... Virginia					April 10				
Clark county .... do							April 1	April 3	
Crichton's Store .... do			March 13				April 1	April 1	March 13
Genito .... do		March 15							
Kanawha Salines .... do								March 30	
Madison C. H. .... do		March 24							
Mossy Creek .... do		March 30					April 1		
Poplar Grove .... do								April 5	March 18
Portsmouth .... do		Feb. 27				April 4			
Rose Hill .... do						April 9	Feb. 26	March 19	March 8
Chapel Hill .... N. Carolina			March 23					March 28	
Camden .... S. Carolina		March 9							
Greensborough .... Alabama						March 20	March 19	March 1	
Columbus .... Mississippi								March 13	
Hannibal .... Missouri				March 25					
Glenwood .... Tennessee			March 22						
Knoxville .... do		March 28							
Ashtabula .... Ohio				April 20					
Belle Centre .... do		April 22		April 12				March 27	
Bowling Green .... do								April 4	
Cleveland .... do				April 12	April 17				
Germantown .... do			March 30	March 28					
Hiram .... do							May 6	April 7	
Keene .... do		May 1							
Marietta .... do									April 1
Mount Healthy .... do				April 25					
Poland .... do					April 3				
Ripley .... do							March 19		
Savannah .... do							May 3		
Indianapolis .... Indiana									April 8
Laconia .... do								March 1	
Augusta .... Illinois		March 14	April 4		April 12				
Batavia .... do								April 10	
Brighton .... do							May 4	April 14	
Edgington .... do							May 4		
Marengo .... do							May 10	April 1	
Pekin .... do								May 14	
Peoria .... do								March 24	
Riley .... do							May 8		
Waynesville .... do								March 23	
West Northville .... do				April 18					
West Salem .... do							April 20		
Ann Arbor .... Michigan			April 10						
Flint .... do					April 14				
Romeo .... do						April 23			
Wyandotte .... do								March 30	
Fairfield .... Iowa									April 26
Muscatine .... do		April 20	April 20	April 12	May 7				
Pleasant Plain .... do				April 20		April 9	May 15		
Horton .... Nova Scotia					May 15				
Stanbridge .... Canada							May 2	April 24	
Leipsig .... Saxony								April 12	

TARAXACUM DENS-LEONIS.—*Dandelion.*

Name of Station.	1851.	1852.	1853.	1854.	1855.	1856.	1857.	1858.	1859.
Brunswick .... Maine							April 17		
Perry .... do									May 10
Steuben .... do							May 7		
Londonderry .... N. Hampshire		May 15							
Manchester .... do				May 1					
North Barnstead .... do							May 18		
Shelburne .... do								May 7	
Stratford .... do								May 12	
West Enfield .... do							May 3		
Florida .... Massachusetts							May 5	May 15	

TARAXACUM DENS-LEONIS.—*Dandelion*—Continued.

Name of Station.	1851.	1852.	1853.	1854.	1855.	1856.	1857.	1858.	1859.
Mendon .... Massachusetts.				April 28					
North Attleborough ...... do		April 30		April 20	April 23				
Williamstown .... do							May 27		
Worcester .... do							April 4		
Columbia .... Connecticut.							April 26	April 15	
Chatham .... New York		May 5							
Flatbush .... do		March 10							
Lake .... do							April 28		April 28
New York city .... do								May 2	
Ovid .... do				May 5					
Rochester .... do			April 16				May 12		
Spencertown .... do					April 25				
Waterloo .... do		April 4							
West Point .... do		April 10							
Burlington .... New Jersey		May 10							
Ceres .... Pennsylvania.		May 5							
Darby .... do		March 26	March 26						
Easton .... do				April 8					
Fleming .... do							April 20		
Gettysburg .... do		April 8	March 21						
Hollidaysburg .... do		April 3	April 2						
Shamokin .... do							April 10		
Somerset .... do								April 15	
Valley Forge .... do		April 10							
Easton .... Maryland				April 17					
Sykesville .... do			April 10	April 20			April 27		
Buffalo .... Virginia					April 10				
Clark county .... do								April 12	
Mossy Creek .... do		April 7					April 20		
Poplar Grove .... do								April 1	March 22
Rose Hill .... do						April 6			
Chapel Hill .... N. Carolina			April 1						
Camden .... S. Carolina		March 4							
Maysville .... Kentucky			March 15						
Ashtabula .... Ohio				April 12					
Belle Centre .... do		March 24						March 20	
Cleveland .... do					April 15				
Germantown .... do			March 30	March 28					
Keene .... do		April 1							
Mount Healthy .... do				April 10					
Ripley .... do							Feb. 20		
Savannah .... do							May 15		
Laconia .... Indiana								March 28	
Batavia .... Illinois								April 10	
Brighton .... do							May 10	April 20	
Marengo .... do								April 1	
Pekin .... do								May 23	
Riley .... do							May 8		
St. James .... Michigan			April 16						
Keokuk .... Iowa						April 26			
Muscatine .... do			April 22	April 20	May 9				
Stanbridge .... Canada							April 25	April 8	
Leipsig .... Saxony								April 1	

TILIA AMERICANA.—*Linden.—Basswood.*

Name of Station.	1851.	1852.	1853.	1854.	1855.	1856.	1857.	1858.	1859.
Brunswick .... Maine							May 31	June 9	
Gardiner .... do							June 5		
Naples .... do							May 20		
Londonderry .... New Hampshire.		May 9	May 10						
North Barnstead .... do							May 10		
Salmon Falls .... do				May 7					
Brandon .... Vermont				May 13				May 24	
Stockbridge .... do			May 11						
Mendon .... Massachusetts				May 7					
North Attleborough .... do				May 11	May 13				
Columbia .... Connecticut							May 11	May 22	

TILIA AMERICANA.—*Linden.—Basswood*—Continued.

Name of Station.		1851.	1852.	1853.	1854.	1855.	1856.	1857.	1858.	1859.
Fishkill Landing	New York							May 10		
Flatbush	do		May 7	April 29	April 27	April 27				
Lake	do							May 25	May 24	May 7
New York city	do				May 15	May 10			May 15	
Nichols	do								May 24	May 8
Ogdensburg	do			May 20						
Ovid	do				May 18					
Plattsburg	do		May 9							
Rochester	do								May 10	
Spencertown	do					May 20				
West Point	do		May 6	May 6						
Burlington	New Jersey		May 15							
Moorestown	do					April 25				
Ceres	Pennsylvania		May 6							
Darby	do			May 1						
Easton	do				May 12					
Fleming	do							May 20		
Gettysburg	do		May 5	April 26	April 26					
Hollidaysville	do			April 20						
Meadville	do		May 8							
Mercersburg	do		April 29							
Middletown	do							May 20		
Murrysville	do							May 23		
Upper Darby	do			May 7	May 10					
Mossy Creek	Virginia		May 1							
Poplar Grove	do								April 25	April 18
Greensborough	Alabama							March 30	April 1	
New Wied	Texas		April 1	April 1						
Maysville	Kentucky			April 28						
Ashtabula	Ohio				May 6					
Belle Centre	do		May 7						May 1	
Cleveland	do				April 30					
Hocking Port	do							May 31		
Mount Healthy	do				April 28					
Poland	do					May 14				
Indianapolis	Indiana									May 3
Laconia	do								April 13	
Augusta	Illinois		May 10	May 15		May 12		May 20		
Batavia	do								April 20	
Pekin	do								May 23	
Warsaw	do							May 10	April 18	
West Northville	do				May 7					
Wyandotte	Michigan								May 5	
Fort Ripley	Minnesota		May 24							
Lac qui Parle	do				May 8					
Princeton	do							May 5		
Border Plains	Iowa								May 9	May 4
Dubuque	do				May 6					
Eagle	do							May 27		
Fairfield	do									May 10
Keokuk	do						May 1			
Pleasant Plain	do				May 10					
Leavenworth	Kansas								April 27	
Stanbridge	Canada							May 20	May 26	

ULMUS AMERICANA.—*American Elm.*

Name of Station.		1851.	1852.	1853.	1854.	1855.	1856.	1857.	1858.	1859.
Brunswick	Maine							June 4	June 5	
Gardiner	do							May 15		
Naples	do							May 17		
Perry	do						May 25			June 1
Steuben	do	May 27								
Londonderry	New Hamp.		May 6	May 4						
Manchester	do		May 20		May 11					
North Barnestead	do							May 19		
Salmon Falls	do				May 11					
Somersworth	do				May 13					

ULMUS AMERICANA.—*American Elm*—Continued.

NAME OF STATION.		1851.	1852.	1853.	1854.	1855.	1856.	1857.	1858.	1859.
Stratford	New Hamp.								May 14	
West Enfield	do							May 10		
Brandon	Vermont				May 12				May 20	
Stockbridge	do			May 9						
Lawrence	Massachusetts							May 27		
Mendon	do				April 20					
North Attleborough	do		May 10		May 15	May 12				
Uxbridge	do				May 16					
Waltham	do				May 10					
Williamstown	do							May 26		
Worcester	do							April 28		
Columbia	Connecticut							May 15		
Fairfield	do								May 12	
Middletown	do		May 5	April 30	May 8					
Fishkill Landing	New York							May 20	April 25	May 1
Flatbush	do		May 8	April 23	May 7					
New York city	do				May 12	April 10			May 15	
Nichols	do								May 22	
Ogdensburg	do			May 20						
Plattsburg	do		May 10							
Ovid	do				May 16					
Rochester	do							May 20	May 1	
Spencertown	do					May 15				
Waterloo	do		May 7							
West Point	do		May 8	May 5						
Burlington	New Jersey		May 6							
Newark	do	April 24								
Ceres	Pennsylvania		May 14							
Easton	do				April 28					
Fleming	do							May 22		
Gettysburg	do		May 8	April 20	April 26					
Meadville	do		May 12							
Mercersburg	do		May 7							
Philadelphia	do								April 14	
Upper Darby	do				May 3					
Easton	Maryland				May 1					
Hagerstown	do			April 22						
Buffalo	Virginia					April 16				
Clark county	do								May 1	
Crichton's Store	do			April 17				April 10		
Genito	do		April 13							
Mossy Creek	do		May 1							
Poplar Grove	do								April 11	April 10
Rose Hill	do						April 20			
Chapel Hill	N. Carolina			April 1					April 3	
Camden	S. Carolina		March 29							
Greensborough	Alabama						April 4	March 22	March 24	
Weewokaville	do		March 1							
Columbus	Mississippi								March 14	
Trinity	Louisiana								March 4	
Union Hill	Texas							March 1		
Hannibal	Missouri				April 1					
Maysville	Kentucky			March 18						
Ashtabula	Ohio				May 10					
Belle Centre	do		May 4						May 1	
Cleveland	do					April 27				
Germantown	do				May 1					
Hiram	do								April 25	
Keene	do		May 6							
Mount Healthy	do				April 30					
Poland	do					May 14				
Ripley	do							April 20		
Savannah	do							May 21		
Indianapolis	Indiana									April 30
Laconia	do								April 10	
Augusta	Illinois		May 3	May 7	May 4			May 15		
Batavia	do								April 22	
Brighton	do							May 13	April 19	
Edgington	do							May 1		

ULMUS AMERICANA.—*American Elm*—Continued.

Name of Station.	1851.	1852.	1853.	1854.	1855.	1856.	1857.	1858.	1859.
Marengo .... Illinois							May 20	May 25	
Pekin .... do								May 23	
Peoria .... do								April 17	
Warsaw .... do							May 14	April 18	
West Salem .... do							May 18		
Winnebago .... do							May 23	May 8	
Flint .... Michigan					April 26				
Romeo .... do						April 26			
Wyandotte .... do								May 10	
Fort Ripley .... Minnesota		May 18							
Lac qui Parle .... do			May 16	April 20					
Princeton .... do							May 5		
Eagle .... Iowa							May 21		
Fairfield .... do									May 2
Keokuk .... do						April 24			
Muscatine .... do		April 30	May 1	May 4					
Pleasant Plain .... do				May 10	May 9	May 20			
Leavenworth .... Kansas								April 25	
Horton .... Nova Scotia					May 25				
Stanbridge .... Canada							May 20	May 24	

VIBURNUM LENTAGO.—*Sweet Viburnum.*

Name of Station.	1851.	1852.	1853.	1854.	1855.	1856.	1857.	1858.	1859.
Brunswick .... Maine								June 2	
New York city .... New York				May 7					May 16
Middletown .... Pennsylvania							May 9		
Philadelphia .... do								April 14	
Poland .... Ohio					April 10				
West Northville .... Illinois				April 20					
Flint .... Michigan					April 23				
Wyandotte .... do								April 28	
Princeton .... Minnesota							May 1		
Pleasant Plain .... Iowa				May 1					
Stanbridge .... Canada								May 10	

VIBURNUM OPULIFOLIUM.—*Ninebark.*

Name of Station.	1851.	1852.	1853.	1854.	1855.	1856.	1857.	1858.	1859.
Burlington .... New Jersey		April 25							
Hollidaysburg .... Pennsylvania			April 19						
Indiana .... do		May 9							
Crichton's Store .... Virginia			April 15						
Weewokaville .... Alabama			April 15						
Augusta .... Illinois					April 21				

VIBURNUM OPULUS.—*Snowball.*

Name of Station.	1851.	1852.	1853.	1854.	1855.	1856.	1857.	1858.	1859.
Londonderry .... New Hamp.			April 26						
Manchester .... do		May 15							
Chatham .... New York		May 1							
Ogdensburg .... do			May 6						
Plattsburg .... do		May 10							
Rochester .... do			April 26						
Waterloo .... do		April 11							
Burlington .... New Jersey		May 1							
Newark .... do		May 1							
Ceres .... Pennsylvania		May 11							
Gettysburg .... do			April 18	April 30					
Hollidaysburg .... do			April 8						
Indiana .... do		April 28							
Meadville .... do		May 8							

VIBURNUM OPULUS.—*Snowball*—Continued.

NAME OF STATION.	1851.	1852.	1853.	1854.	1855.	1856.	1857.	1858.	1859.
Crichton's Store........Virginia			March 28						
Genito........do		April 3							
Mossy Creek........do		April 30							
Chapel Hill........N. Carolina			April 10						
Camden........S. Carolina		March 11							
Weewokaville........Alabama		April 8							
Glenwood........Tennessee			April 9						
Belle Centre........Ohio		May 1							
Augusta........Illinois		April 20							
Muscatine........Iowa		April 29	April 30						

VITIS AESTIVALIS.—*Summer Grape.*

NAME OF STATION.	1851.	1852.	1853.	1854.	1855.	1856.	1857.	1858.	1859.
Manchester........New Hamp.		May 25							
Brandon........Vermont			May 18						
Stockbridge........do			May 18						
North Attleborough..Massachusetts		May 13							
Flatbush........New York			May 8						
New Lebanon........do			May 16						
New York city........do							May 14		
Rochester........do					May 25		May 25		
West Point........do			May 15						
Burlington........New Jersey		May 15							
Ceres........Pennsylvania		June 2							
Gettysburg........do			April 30	April 30					
Hollidaysburg........do			May 2						
Meadville........do		May 20							
Darby........do			April 29						
Sykesville........Maryland		May 2	April 30						
Crichton's Store........Virginia			April 17						
Genito........do		April 16							
Madison C. H........do		April 30							
Mossy Creek........do		May 5							
Chapel Hill........N. Carolina			May 1						
Camden........S. Carolina		March 18							
Weewokaville........Alabama		April 15	April 15						
Belle Centre........Ohio		May 12							
Keene........do		May 10							
Augusta........Illinois		May 4	May 16						

DATES

OF

BLOSSOMING OF PLANTS.

ACER RUBRUM.—*Red or Soft Maple.*

Name of Station.		1851.	1852.	1853.	1854.	1855.	1856.	1857.	1858.	1859.
Brunswick	Maine							May 9	May 8	
Castine	do		May 5							
Carmel	do						April 24			
Cornish	do						May 2	May 3		
Gardiner	do							April 30		
Naples	do							April 28		May 2
Perry	do						May 1			
Steuben	do		May 6	May 5				May 13	May 14	May 10
Francestown	N. Hampshire			April 30						
Londonderry	do		May 1	April 19						
Manchester	do	May 10	April 26		April 27					
North Barnstead	do						May 1	May 3		
Salmon Falls	do				May 1					
Somersworth	do				May 11					
Stratford	do						May 6			
Brandon	Vermont			April 27	May 2			May 1	April 18	
Brattleborough	do	April 7								
Burlington	do			April 23		May 1				
Castleton	do				May 1					
Craftsbury	do						May 26	May 18		
Stockbridge	do			May 17						
West Rupert	do						April 29	April 29		
Boston	Massachusetts		May 1							
Bridgewater	do							May 1		
Florida	do							May 9	May 10	
Mendon	do				April 20					
North Attleborough	do		April 26		April 20	April 21				
Richmond	do		May 8							
Waltham	do				April 21					
Worcester	do						May 1	April 20		
Acquidneset	Rhode Island						April 22			
Columbia	Connecticut							May 7	April 20	
East Windsor Hill	do			April 10						
Georgetown	do						April 19			
Middletown	do		April 19	April 4	April 12					
Baldwinsville	New York	April 6	May 2				April 26			
Ceres	do	May 27								
Chatham	do	April 8	May 1							
Eden	do						April 20	May 6		
Flatbush	do							April 26		
Geneva	do						May 8			
Lake	do						April 29	April 30	April 23	April 29
Lowville	do						May 16		May 16	
Mexico	do						April 28			
New Lebanon	do	April 20	May 8	April 26						
New York city	do				March 26	April 13			April 1	
Nichols	do			April 26					April 13	March 23
North Salem	do	April 1	April 20			April 15				
Ogdensburg	do	April 24	May 6	April 20			April 22			
Ovid	do				April 20					
Penn Yan	do							May 20		
Plattsburg	do	May 1	May 24							
Rochester	do	April 2	April 19	March 28	March 24	April 12	April 18	April 20	April 1	
Sag Harbor	do	April 10	April 16							
Somerville	do	April 30								
Spencertown	do					April 20	April 30			
Wellsville	do							April 10	April 10	
West Point	do		April 20	April 7						
White Plains	do					April 20				
Freehold	New Jersey							Feb. 25		March 12
Readington	do								April 15	May 4
Bucks county	Pennsylvania						April 17			
Ceres	do		May 14							
Chambersburg	do	March 25	April 25							
Chester	do	March 29								
Darby	do		April 10							
Easton	do				April 13					
Fleming Centre	do	April 2						April 5		
Freeport	do		April 25	March 23	April 11					
Gettysburg	do		April 2	March 30	April 1		April 12			

ACER RUBRUM.—*Red or Soft Maple*—Continued.

Name of Station.	1851.	1852.	1853.	1854.	1855.	1856.	1857.	1858.	1859.
Hollidaysburg........Pennsylvania		April 10	April 7						
Huntington ....do							April 15		
Indiana ....do		April 16							
Lancaster ....do							April 20		
Lima ....do		March 29	March 24	March 18	April 15	April 16	March 28		
Meadville ....do	April 1	April 17				April 21			
Mercersburg ....do		April 2							
Morrisville ....do						March 25			
Mungersville ....do							April 20		
Nazareth ....do	April 25					April 20	April 12		
Orwigsburg ....do		April 20							
Philadelphia ....do								March 25	
Radnor ....do		March 26	March 26	March 17	April 13	April 14	March 25	March 28	
Reading ....do	March 22								
Sugar Grove ....do	April 14								
Upper Darby ....do		April 1	March 27	March 25					
Easton ....Maryland				Feb. 28					
Hagerstown ....do		March 25	March 25						
Sykesville ....do	March 28	March 20	April 1			April 3	April 3		
Buffalo ....Virginia					March 26	March 25			
Crichton's Store ....do			March 12					March 16	
Diamond Grove ....do	March 10								
Doddridge county ....do						April 10			
Genito ....do		Feb. 5							
Madison Court-house ....do	April 4	March 19							
Mossy Creek ....do		March 10					April 1		
Mount Solon ....do						April 1			
Plains ....do									March 10
Poplar Grove ....do							April 3	March 23	March 15
Rose Hill ....do						April 6	Feb. 25	March 19	March 10
Smithfield ....do		Feb. 25							
Chapel Hill ....N. Carolina			March 3					April 1	
Gaston ....do						March 1			
Green Plains ....do							Feb. 22		
Aiken ....S. Carolina			March 18			March 10			
All Saints Parish ....do					March 23				
Black Oak ....do		Jan. 29							
Camden ....do		March 7				March 23			
Fulton ....do					Feb. 8	Feb. 26			
Georgetown ....do						March 28			
Savannah ....Georgia						Jan. 3			
Sparta ....do						March 3	Feb. 28	Feb. 25	
Varnell's Station ....do									Feb. 5
Zebulon ....do							Feb. 19		
Alligator ....Florida								Jan. 3	
Knox Hill ....do		Feb. 7							
Carlowville ....Alabama							Feb. 23		
Childersburg ....do							Feb. 20		
Eutaw ....do		Feb. 21							
Greensborough ....do						March 10	Feb. 9	Feb. 4	
Weewokaville ....do			March 20						
Columbus ....Mississippi						March 3	Feb. 20	Feb. 21	
Jasper county ....do						March 26			
Oxford ....do						March 14			
Big Pond ....Louisiana						Feb. 1			
Trinity ....do							Feb. 1	Feb. 1	
New Wied ....Texas		Feb. 15							
Union Hill ....do							Feb. 27		
Knoxville ....Tennessee		Feb. 24							
Lebanon ....do	March 25								
Walnut Grove ....do						April 8			
Fairview ....Kentucky									May 5
Maysville ....do			March 25						
Ashtabula ....Ohio				April 26					
Belle Centre ....do		March 15						March 28	
Cincinnati ....do			April 1						
Cleveland ....do				April 20	April 18				
Hiram ....do						April 29	May 4	April 9	
Jefferson ....do						April 24			
Keene ....do		March 28							

ACER RUBRUM.—*Red or Soft Maple*—Continued.

NAME OF STATION.	1851.	1852.	1853.	1854.	1855.	1856.	1857.	1858.	1859.
Madison ... Ohio							May 4		
Marietta ... do								March 21	March 9
Mount Healthy ... do					April 18				
Poland ... do					May 3				
Welchfield ... do							May 20		
Laconia ... Indiana								March 25	March 6
New Albany ... do						April 6	April 1		
Richmond ... do	Feb. 15								
Athens ... Illinois		March 16	March 27						
Chicago ... do							April 25		
Warsaw ... do						April 24	April 28	April 1	
West Salem ... do						April 8	Feb. 15		
Flint ... Michigan					April 5				
St. James ... do						May 11			
Wyandotte ... do								March 24	April 14
Madison ... Wisconsin						April 21			
Milwaukee ... do	April 1								
Kaposia ... Minnesota	April 1								
Lac qui Parle ... do			May 2	April 19					
Princeton ... do							April 25		
Border Plains ... Iowa								March 19	April 21
Dubuque ... do	March 28								
Eagle ... do							May 4		
Fairbanks ... do						April 28			
Pleasant Plain ... do				March 25		April 15	April 13		
Leavenworth City ... Kansas								April 18	
Horton ... Nova Scotia					May 8		April 30		
Windsor ... do							May 9		
Stanbridge ... Canada							May 20		

ACER SACCHARINUM.—*Sugar Maple.*

NAME OF STATION.	1851.	1852.	1853.	1854.	1855.	1856.	1857.	1858.	1859.
Castine ... Maine		May 8							
Cornish ... do							May 15		
Naples ... do							May 23		
Manchester ... New Hamp		May 11							
Salmon Falls ... do				May 1					
Brandon ... Vermont			May 7				May 20		
Burlington ... do			May 8						
Castleton ... do				May 12					
Stockbridge ... do			April 29						
Florida ... Massachusetts							May 27	May 15	
North Attleborough ... do		May 10							
Richmond ... do		May 14							
Waltham ... do				May 8					
Columbia ... Connecticut							May 11	May 14	
East Windsor Hill ... do			May 4						
Middletown ... do			May 3						
Lake ... New York							May 15		
New Lebanon ... do		May 12							
Nichols ... do			May 4					May 3	May 2
North Salem ... do	May 11	May 2			May 10				
Ovid ... do				May 12					
Plattsburg ... do	April 27	May 6							
Rochester ... do			April 28	April 25	April 18		May 18	May 20	
Somerville ... do	May 13								
Spencertown ... do					May 7				
Wellsville ... do							April 5		
West Point ... do			April 28						
White Plains ... do					May 10				
Williamsville ... do				May 13					
Ceres ... Pennsylvania		May 14							
Darby ... do			April 15						
Fleming Centre ... do	April 9								
Freeport ... do			March 24						
Gettysburg ... do			April 7						
Hollidaysburg ... do		April 15	April 29						

ACER SACCHARINUM.—*Sugar Maple*—Continued.

Name of Station.	1851.	1852.	1853.	1854.	1855.	1856	1857.	1858.	1859.
Lima........Pennsylvania..		May 7	April 29	April 24		May 5	May 6		
Meadville........do......	May 2	May 12							
Morrisville........do......						April 10			
Mungersville........do......							May 10		
Nazareth........do......	May 1						May 12		
Radnor........do......		May 8			May 2		May 11		
Reading........do......	March 29								
Sugar Grove........do......	April 28								
Upper Darby........do......	April 25	May 1	April 22	April 24					
Easton........Maryland..				March 10					
Buffalo........Virginia....					April 12				
Crichton's Store........do......			March 9					March 17	Feb. 12
Genito........do......	April 16	March 5							
Mossy Creek........do......		April 1					March 25		
Poplar Grove........do......								April 30	March 28
Green Plains........N. Carolina..							Feb. 20		
Knox Hill........Florida....		March 8							
Greensborough........Alabama...						March 24			
Weewokaville........do......		April 5	March 24						
Knoxville........Tennessee..		March 20							
Lebanon........do......	March 26								
Maysville........Kentucky..			March 29						
Trenton........Missouri..			April 25	April 15					
Ashtabula........Ohio.....				May 8					
Belle Centre........do......		April 27		April 23					
Cincinnati........do......			April 10						
Germantown........do......			May 1	April 23					
Madison........do......							May 18		
Marietta........do......									March 25
Mount Healthy........do......				April 10	April 22				
Poland........do......					April 28				
Troy........do......									April 29
Laconia........Indiana....								April 7	April 23
Indianapolis........do......									April 20
Athens........Illinois....			April 20						
Augusta........do......			April 20		April 20				
Pekin........do......								May 8	
Warsaw........do......							May 6	April 20	
Ann Arbor........Michigan..			April 30						
Flint........do......					April 25				
Wyandotte........do......								May 1	
Baraboo........Wisconsin...	April 24								
Burlington........Minnesota...								May 5	
Princeton........do......							May 1		
Border Plains........Iowa.....								May 4	May 5
Horton........Nova Scotia..					May 19				
Stanbridge........Canada....							May 20		
Leipsig........Saxony....								April 19	

ACHILLEA MILLEFOLIUM.—*Millefoil.—Yarrow.*

Name of Station.	1851.	1852.	1853.	1854.	1855.	1856.	1857.	1858.	1859.
Brunswick........Maine....								July 3	
Cornish........do......							July 13		
Naples........do......							June 21		
Francestown........New Hamp..			June 15						
Manchester........do......		June 24							
North Barnstead........do......							June 20		
Salmon Falls........do......				June 7					
Shelburne........do								June 25	
Brattleborough........Vermont....	June 29								
Stockbridge........do......			June 2						
Florida........Massachusetts..							July 25	July 25	
Uxbridge........do......			June 5						
Point Judith........Rhode Island..				June 12					
Columbia........Connecticut..							July 9	July 1	
East Windsor Hill........do......		June 25							
Middletown........do......		June 26							

ACHILLEA MILLEFOLIUM.—*Millefoil.*—*Yarrow*—Continued.

Name of Station.		1851.	1852.	1853.	1854.	1855.	1856.	1857.	1858.	1859.
Ceres	New York	June 24								
Chatham	do	June 20								
New Lebanon	do	July 5								
Nichols	do									June 4
North Salem	do	June 10								
Plattsburg	do		July 3							
Rochester	do		July 1						July 6	
Somerville	do	June 14								
Spencertown	do					July 20				
West Point	do			June 14						
Chester	Pennsylvania	June 10								
Darby	do		June 18	June 12						
Easton	do				June 22					
Gettysburg	do		June 4	June 3	June 1					
Hollidaysburg	do		June 2	June 16						
Lima	do		June 12							
Meadville	do	June 10	June 17							
Mungersville	do							June 16		
Reading	do	June 14								
Sugar Grove	do	June 20								
Upper Darby	do	June 24	June 21	June 26	June 20					
Hagerstown	Maryland		June 14	June 15						
Buffalo	Virginia					June 4				
Madison C. H	do	June 25								
Mossy Creek	do		Aug. 1							
Poplar Grove	do								July 20	
Portsmouth	do		May 20							
Eutaw	Alabama		May 13							
New Wied	Texas	May 20	April 10	April 20						
Nashville	Tennessee				June 4					
Maysville	Kentucky			May 25						
Trenton	Missouri		May 27		May 25					
Cincinnati	Ohio			May 29						
Keene	do		June 20							
Mount Healthy	do				June 1					
Savannah	do							June 20		
Athens	Illinois		May 31	May 26	May 30					
Augusta	do	June 10	May 26		May 25			June 10		
Peoria	do								May 10	
West Northfield	do				July 1					
Flint	Michigan					June 25				
Wyandotte	do								June 28	
Milwaukee	Wisconsin	July 10								
Kaposia	Minnesota	June 16								
Pleasant Plain	Iowa				May 25		June 30			
Stanbridge	Canada							June 1	June 18	
Leipsig	Saxony								June 6	

ÆSCULUS GLABRA—*Ohio Buckeye.*

Name of Station.		1851.	1852.	1853.	1854.	1855.	1856.	1857.	1858.	1859.
New York city	New York				May 20					
Rochester	do			May 24	May 20	May 25		June 3	May 26	
Waterloo	do		May 22							
Lima	Pennsylvania			May 5						
Buffalo	Virginia					May 2				
Poplar Grove	do								May 12	May 2
Chapel Hill	N. Carolina								April 10	
All Saints	S. Carolina					April 5				
Greensborough	Alabama						April 1	March 20	March 24	
Jasper	Mississippi					March 6	March 26			
Belle Centre	Ohio		May 5		April 28				May 10	
Cincinnati	do			May 1						
Germantown	do		May 5		April 28					
Hocking Port	do							May 14		
Mount Healthy	do				April 25					

ÆSCULUS GLABRA.—*Ohio Buckeye*—Continued.

Name of Station.		1851.	1852.	1853.	1854.	1855.	1856.	1857.	1858.	1859.
Poland	Ohio					May 27				
Ripley	do							May 15		
Savannah	do							May 20		
Laconia	Indiana								April 20	
Athens	Illinois		May 6	May 4	April 25	April 24				
Augusta	do		May 5	May 1	May 6	April 25		May 20		
Flint	Michigan					May 5				
Fort Madison	Iowa				May 7					

ÆSCULUS HIPPOCASTANUM.—*Horse Chestnut.*

Name of Station.		1851.	1852.	1853.	1854.	1855.	1856.	1857.	1858.	1859.
Brunswick	Maine							June 7	June 8	
Castine	do		June 5							
Gardiner	do							June 8		
Naples	do							June 5		
Manchester	New Hamp.	May —	May 18		May 21					
Salmon Falls	do				May 24					
Somersworth	do				May 22					
Brattleborough	Vermont	May 30								
Castleton	do				June 15					
Boston	Massachusetts		May 24							
Mendon	do				May 22					
North Attleborough	do		May 19		May 20	May 20				
Richmond	do		June 1							
Uxbridge	do				May 28					
Worcester	do							May 26		
Columbia	Connecticut							May 26	May 26	
Middletown	do		May 2	May 14	May 20					
Chatham	New York		May 28							
Fishkill Landing	do									May 15
Flatbush	do		May 20	May 10	May 12	May 13				
New Lebanon	do			May 13						
New York city	do				May 13	May 15			May 20	
Nichols	do								June 1	June 1
Ovid	do				May 20					
Plattsburg	do	May 21	May 26							
Rochester	do		May 17	May 20	May 22	May 23	May 23	June 1	May 26	
Sag Harbor	do		May 29							
Spencertown	do					May 24				
West Point	do			May 12						
Moorestown	New Jersey					May 12				
Burlington	do		May 10							
Newark	do	May 12	May 20							
Easton	Pennsylvania				May 12					
Gettysburg	do		May 12		May 14					
Hollidaysburg	do			May 6						
Mercersburg	do		May 14							
Lancaster	do				May 9					
Lima	do							May 14		
Radnor	do		May 22	May 20	May 16	May 20	May 22	May 25	May 24	
Darby	do			May 5						
Easton	Maryland				April 24					
Hagerstown	do			April 27						
Alligator	Florida								Feb. 23	
St. Louis	Missouri						May 1			
Mount Healthy	Ohio					April 26				
Ann Arbor	Michigan			June 2						
Wyandotte	do								June 2	
Milwaukee	Wisconsin	May 20								
Muscatine	Iowa	April 27								
Horton	Nova Scotia					June 10				
Leipsig	Saxony								April 30	

AILANTHUS GLANDULOSA.—*Tree of Heaven.*

Name of Station.	1851.	1852.	1853.	1854.	1855.	1856.	1857.	1858.	1859.
North Attleborough..Massachusetts.				July 1	July 7				
Middletown ....Connecticut..			June 19	June 26					
Flatbush................New York ..		June 26	June 17						
New York city.............do......				May 19					
Ovid ....do......				July 1					
Rochester....................do......					July 7		July 10	July 8	
Spencertown.................do......					July 1				
West Point ....do......		May 18	June 25						
Darby ....Pennsylvania.			June 14						
Easton ....do......		June 22		June 19					
Fleming.......................do......	April 22								
Gettysburg ....do......			June 13	June 7					
Lancaster ....do......				June 12					
Lima ....do......			June 10						
Mercersburg ....do......		June 14							
Upper Darby..................do......		June 21	June 15	June 20					
Easton ....Maryland ..				May 25					
Hagerstown...................do......			June 17						
Buffalo ....Virginia ...					June 17				
Madison C. H ....do......		June 6							
Rose Hill......................do......							June 16		
Chapel Hill.............N. Carolina..			May 26						
Greensborough ....Alabama...						May 10			
Jasper ....Mississippi..						April 6			
Glenwood ....Tennessee ..			May 24						
Maysville...............Kentucky ..			May 21						
Ashtabula ....Ohio				June 27					
Belle Centre ....do......				June 25					
Cincinnati ....do......			June 10						
Mount Healthy ....do......				July 1					
Augusta..................Illinois ...				June 19					
West Salem...................do......							June 25		

AMELANCHIER CANADENSIS.—*Shadbush.—Serviceberry.*

Name of Station.	1851.	1852.	1853.	1854.	1855.	1856.	1857.	1858.	1859.
Brunswick ....Maine....									May 27
Castine ....do......		May 19							
Cornish........................do......							May 7		
Gardiner ....do......							May 23		
Perry ....do......						May 20			May 24
Francestown............New Hamp..			May 11						
Manchester ....do......	May 7	May 10		May 12					
Salmon Falls.................do......				May 14					
Somersworth ....do......				May 14					
West Enfield..................do......							May 25		
Brandon ....Vermont...			May 10	May 12					
Brattleborough...............do......	April 29								
Burlington.....................do......			May 8						
Newark ....do......							May 27		
Stockbridge ....do......			May 9						
Florida ....Massachusetts..							May 25	May 25	
Haverhill ....do......	May 12								
Mendon ....do......				May 3					
North Attleborough ....do......		May 10		May 6	May 6				
Richmond ....do......		May 10							
Uxbridge ....do......				May 6					
Waltham ....do......				May 10					
Worcester ....do......							May 22		
Columbia ....Connecticut..							May 23	May 6	
Middletown....................do......		May 7	May 5	May 8					
Ceres.....................New York..	April 19								
Chatham ....do......	April 28	May 7							
Fishkill Landing.............do......							May 9	May 3	
Lake ....do......							May 19	May 8	May 7
New Lebanon ....do......			May 3						
New York city ....do......								May 6	
Nichols..........................do......			May 6					May 5	May 3

AMELANCHIER CANADENSIS.—*Shadbush.—Serviceberry*—Continued.

Name of Station.	1851.	1852.	1853.	1854.	1855.	1856.	1857.	1858.	1859.
North Salem ....New York..	April 21	April 28							
Ovid ....do......				May 10					
Penn Yan..........do......							May 26		
Plattsburg ....do......	May 12	May 10							
Rochester..........do......	April 28	May 10	May 3	May 6	May 4		May 16	April 20	
Somerville..........do......	May 13								
Spencertown..........do......					May 1				
White Plains..........do......					May 4				
Burlington ....New Jersey..		May 2							
Freehold ....do......									March 20
Ceres ....Pennsylvania..		May 1							
Chester ....do......	April 17								
Darby ....do......			April 16						
Fleming Centre ....do......	May 12						May 15		
Freeport..........do......		May 1	April 26	April 23					
Gettysburg..........do......		April 25	April 17	April 16					
Hollidaysburg ....do......		May 2	April 22						
Indiana..........do......		May 5							
Lima ....do......		May 4	April 22			April 28			
Meadville..........do......	April 20	May 7							
Mercersburg ....do......		April 22							
Mungersville..........do......							May 9		
Radnor ....do......		May 6	April 28						
Reading ....do......	April 12								
Somerset ....do......								May 2	
Sugar Grove ....do......	April 27								
Upper Darby..........do......	April 9	May 3	April 23	April 22					
Valley Forge..........do......		April 28							
Sykesville ....Maryland...	April 11	April 24	April 24	April 30					
Buffalo ....Virginia ...					April 16				
Kanawha Salines ....do......								March 31	
Madison C. H..........do......		April 7							
Mossy Creek ....do......		April 7							
Poplar Grove..........do......								April 4	March 24
Chapel Hill..........N. Carolina..			March 20						
Childersburg ....Alabama...								March 25	
Eutaw..........do......	March 12	March 15							
Weewokaville..........do......		April 14	March 15						
Knoxville..........Tennessee...		March 24							
Trenton ....Missouri ...			April 13	April 8					
Ashtabula ....Ohio....				April 28					
Belle Centre ....do......		April 26						April 20	
Cincinnati ....do......			April 10						
Hocking Port..........do......							May 3		
Keene ....do......	April 4	April 20							
Marietta..........do......									April 1
Poland ....do......					April 20				
Windham ....do......						April 28			
Laconia ....Indiana....								March 20	
Richmond ....do......	March 20								
Athens..........Illinois....		April 18	April 18		April 21				
Augusta ....do......			April 15		April 20				
Warsaw ....do......							May 3	April 12	
Ann Arbor..........Michigan....			May 2						
Flint ....do......					April 25				
Romeo ....do......						May 4			
St. James..........do......			April 12						
Washington ....do......		April 16							
Baraboo ....Wisconsin...	May 4								
Kaposia..........Minnesota ..	May 15								
Lac qui Parle ....do......			May 16	May 1					
Princeton..........do......							May 20		
Border Plains..........Iowa.....								April 28	May 4
Fort Madison ....do......		April 24	April 20						
Pleasant Plain ....do......				April 20					
Leavenworth City.......Kansas....								April 9	
Horton ....Nova Scotia..					May 26				

AMPELOPSIS QUINQUEFOLIA.—*Virginia Creeper.—American Ivy.*

Name of Station.	1851.	1852.	1853.	1854.	1855.	1856.	1857.	1858.	1859.
Londonderry.......... New Hamp..		Aug. 21							
Manchester .... do.....	July 26	July 11							
East Windsor Hill.....Connecticut..		July 10							
Middletown.............. do.....		July 8	July 7						
New Lebanon.......... New York..			July 10						
North Salem.............. do.....	July 24								
Rochester .... do.....			June 15						
Somerville .... do.....	July 4								
West Point .... do.....			May 21						
Gettysburg.......... Pennsylvania..			May 22						
Genito.................. Virginia...		June 16							
Belle Centre .... Ohio.....		July 24							
Athens .... Illinois....		July 18							
Dubuque .... Iowa.....	May 10								

AMYGDALUS NANA.—*Flowering Almond.*

Name of Station.	1851.	1852.	1853.	1854.	1855.	1856.	1857.	1858.	1859.
Brunswick.............. Maine.....							June 4	June 5	
Castine.................... do.....		June 20							
Gardiner .... do.....							May 26		
Manchester.......... N. Hampshire.		May 20		May 20					
Brattleborough.......... Vermont...	May 16								
Stockbridge................ do.....			May 24						
Mendon.............. Massachusetts.				May 14					
North Attleborough....... do.....		May 18		May 13	May 15				
Uxbridge.................. do.....				May 18					
Waltham................... do.....				May 15					
Worcester .... do.....						May 22	May 25		
Point Judith......... Rhode Island .				May 28					
Columbia .... Connecticut..							May 22	May 18	
East Windsor Hill......... do.....		May 20	May 9						
Fairfield................... do.....							May 23		
Middletown .... do.....		May 15	May 5	May 13					
Angelica............ New York..						May 22			
Ceres...................... do.....	May 12								
Chatham .... do.....	May 16								
Fishkill Landing .... do.....							May 14		
Flatbush .... do.....		May 10	May 3	May 5	May 12				
New Lebanon.............. do.....	May 10								
New York city............ do.....				April 28	April 28			April 16	
Nichols.................... do.....									May 7
North Salem.............. do.....	May 1	May 16							
Ogdensburg............... do.....	June 1		May 16						
Ovid...................... do.....				May 13					
Penn Yan .... do.....							May 28		
Plattsburg .... do.....	May 21	May 24							
Rochester................. do.....			May 10		May 16		May 25	May 18	
Sag Harbor .... do.....	May 1	May 6							
Spencertown .... do.....					May 17	May 19			
West Point .... do.....		May 16							
Burlington .... New Jerey..		May 7							
Moorestown............... do.....					April 21				
Ceres............... Pennsylvania.		May 23							
Chester.................... do.....	May 1								
Easton .... do.....				May 7					
Fleming Centre .... do.....							May 20		
Freeport................... do.....			May 7						
Gettysburg .... do.....		May 5	April 28	April 25					
Hollidaysburg............. do.....			May 3						
Indiana .... do.....		May 1							
Lima...................... do.....		May 10			May 12	May 10	May 10		
Meadville .... do.....	May 2	May 17							
Morrisville................ do.....						April 15			
Mungersville.............. do.....							May 10		
Sugar Grove .... do.....	May 20								
Upper Darby.............. do.....		May 8	April 29	April 25					
Valley Forge .... do.....		May 5							

AMYGDALUS NANA.—*Flowering Almond*—Continued.

Name of Station.	1851.	1852.	1853.	1854.	1855.	1856.	1857.	1858.	1859.
Easton Maryland				April 12					
Hagerstown do		May 6	April 24						
Spencerville do							April 26		
Sykesville do	April 29	May 2	April 4				May 11		
Buffalo Virginia					April 20				
Clark county do							May 22	April 12	
Crichton's Store do			Mar. 30				April 10	April 7	Mar. 26
Diamond Grove do	Mar. 29								
Genito do		Mar. 11							
Kanhawa Salines do								April 3	
Madison C. H. do	April 10								
Mossy Creek do		April 20					May 1		
Peach Grove do						April 8			
Poplar Grove do								April 10	April 4
Portsmouth do		Mar. 10				April 15			
Rose Hill do						April 15		April 3	Mar. 23
Chapel Hill North Carolina			Mar. 20						
Green Plains do							April 5		
Camden South Carolina		Mar. 8							
Fulton do					Mar. 20				
Alligator Florida								Mar. 10	
Knox Hill do		Feb. 7							
Childersburg Alabama							Mar. 1		
Greensborough do						Mar. 27	Mar. 1	Mar. 17	
Weewokaville do		April 3	Mar. 10						
Columbus Mississippi							Feb. 23	Mar. 14	
Jasper county do					Mar. 17	Mar. 24			
Union Hill Texas							Mar. 1		
Glenwood Tennessee			April 1						
Knoxville do		Mar. 12							
Lebanon do	Mar. 28								
Maysville Kentucky			April 24						
Hannibal Missouri				April 21					
St. Louis do						April 25			
Ashtabula Ohio				April 28					
Belle Centre do		May 3		April 25				April 25	
Bowling Green do								May 5	
Cincinnati do			April 20						
Cleveland do				May 4	May 6				
Hiram do							May 28	May 11	
Keene do	April 10	May 4							
Mount Healthy do				April 10					
Poland do					April 10				
Ripley do							April 26		
Savannah do							May 7		
Indianapolis Indiana									April 18
Laconia do								Mar. 31	
Augusta Illinois	April 20	April 30	April 25		April 22		May 11		
Brighton do							May 21		
Marengo do							May 15	May 25	
Warsaw do							May 1	April 18	
Waynesville do								April 25	
West Northfield do				May 3					
Ann Arbor Michigan			May 16						
Brest do	May 11								
Flint do					May 2				
Romeo do						May 22			
Wyandotte do								May 23	
Milwaukee Wisconsin	May 13								
Border Plains Iowa									May 13
Fairfield do									May 9
Muscatine do		May 10	May 3	April 23	May 1				
Pleasant Plain do				April 23					
Horton Nova Scotia					June 6				
Stanbridge Canada							May 20		
Leipsig Saxony								April 26	

ANEMONE NEMOROSA.—*Wind Flower.—Wood Anemone.*

Name of Station.		1851.	1852.	1853.	1854.	1855.	1856.	1857.	1858.	1859.
Brunswick	Maine							May 19	May 25	
Castine	do		May 2							
Gardiner	do							May 4		
Londonderry	New Hamp		May 7	April 29						
Manchester	do		May 9		May 11					
Salmon Falls	do				May 10					
Somersworth	do				May 13					
Brattleborough	Vermont	May 3								
Stockbridge	do			May 16						
Mendon	Massachusetts				May 10					
North Attleborough	do		April 20		May 2	April 30				
Uxbridge	do				May 8					
Waltham	do				May 4					
Worcester	do							May 12		
East Windsor Hill	Connecticut			May 2						
Fairfield	do							May 1		
Ceres	New York	April 20								
Chatham	do	April 25	May 11							
New Lebanon	do	May 15		May 6						
New York city	do								May 3	
North Salem	do	April 5	May 4			April 25				
Plattsburg	do	May 1	May 9							
White Plains	do					April 25				
West Point	do		May 3	April 25						
Freehold	New Jersey									March 30
Ceres	Pennsylvania		April 30							
Chambersburg	do	April 6	April 25							
Chester	do	March 17								
Upper Darby	do	March 31	May 7	April 26	April 26					
Easton	do				April 5					
Fleming Cĕntre	do	May 5						May 1		
Gettysburg	do				April 16					
Hollidaysburg	do		May 2	April 28						
Lima	do		April 27							
Meadville	do	April 12	May 3							
Mungersville	do							May 5		
Nazareth	do							May 4		
Radnor	do							May 3	April 10	
Reading	do	April 12								
Darby	do		April 23							
Sugar Grove	do	April 28								
Hagerstown	Maryland			April 24						
Sykesville	do		April 17	April 9	April 20					
Buffalo	Virginia					April 15				
Madison C. H.	do	April 5	April 26							
Mossy Creek	do		April 5					April 24		
Jasper county	Mississippi					March 31				
New Wied	Texas	March 5								
Glenwood	Tennessee			April 2						
Knoxville	do		March 12							
Trenton	Missouri		April 16	April 11	April 6					
Ashtabula	Ohio				May 11					
Hiram	do						April 28	April 16		
Keene	do		April 15							
Marietta	do								April 5	April 3
Augusta	Illinois					April 20				
West Northfield	do				April 25					
Ann Arbor	Michigan			April 26						
Flint	do					April 21				
Romeo	do						April 26			
Baraboo	Wisconsin	May 4								
Milwaukee	do	April 10								
Fort Ripley	Minnesota		May 1							
Kaposia	do	April 15								
Princeton	do							May 1		
Fairfield	Iowa									April 10
Pleasant Plain	do				May 18					
Leavenworth City	Kansas								April 3	

AQUALEGIA CANADENSIS.—*Wild Columbine.*

Name of Station.		1851.	1852.	1853.	1854.	1855.	1856.	1857.	1858.	1859.
Brunswick	Maine							June 3	June 5	
Castine	do		May 25							
Cornish	do							May 31		
Gardiner	do							May 19		
Manchester	New Hamp.	May 25	May 27		May 30					
Salmon Falls	do				May 29					
Brattleborough	Vermont	May 1								
Burlington	do			May 16						
Hingham	Massachusetts		May 5							
North Attleborough	do		May 9		May 12	May 15				
Uxbridge	do				May 16					
Waltham	do				May 2					
Columbia	Connecticut							May 18	May 13	
East Windsor Hill	do		June 1							
Middletown	do				May 10					
Chatham	New York	May 16	May 18							
New Lebanon	do	May 14		May 26						
New York city	do				May 5				May 12	
North Salem	do	April 21	May 5							
Ovid	do				May 16					
Penn Yan	do							May 21		
Plattsburg	do	May 4	May 14							
Rochester	do		May 15	May 20		May 20		May 20	June 1	
Somerville	do	May 20								
Waterloo	do		May 15							
West Point	do		May 10	May 16						
White Plains	do					April 28				
Burlington	New Jersey		May 20							
Moorestown	do					May 5				
Ceres	Pennsylvania		June 10							
Fleming Centre	do	April 20								
Freeport	do		May 15	May 7						
Hollidaysburg	do		May 12	May 7						
Mercersburg	do		May 10							
Lancaster	do				April 27					
Lima	do		May 13							
Meadville	do	April 18	May 25							
Morrisville	do						May 10			
Mungersville	do							May 10		
Radnor	do			May 1	May 11			May 23		
Reading	do	April 18								
Darby	do		April 15	April 18						
Sugar Grove	do	June 1								
Upper Darby	do	May 13	April 24	April 29	April 23					
Hagerstown	Maryland		May 3	April 27						
Buffalo	Virginia					May 14				
Clark county	do							May 5	April 22	
Madison C. H.	do		May 10							
Mossy Creek	do		April 25					April 30		
Camden	S. Carolina		March 13							
Glenwood	Tennessee			April 3						
Lebanon	do	April 15								
Trenton	Missouri			May 20						
Belle Centre	Ohio		June 10							
Bowling Green	do								May 25	
Cincinnati	do			May 1						
Marietta	do								May 8	May 3
Laconia	Indiana								April 8	
Richmond	do	April 30								
Athens	Illinois		May 7	May 8	May 2					
Augusta	do	April 27	May 10		May 10					
Pekin	do								June 22	
Peoria	do								May 20	
West Northfield	do				May 24					
Ann Arbor	Michigan			June 1						
Brest	do	May 14								
Flint	do					May 22				
Wyandotte	do								May 25	
Milwaukee	Wisconsin	May 1								

AQUALEGIA CANADENSIS.—*Wild Columbine*—Continued.

Name of Station.		1851.	1852.	1853.	1854.	1855.	1856.	1857.	1858.	1859.
Fort Ripley	Minnesota		June 1							
Kaposia	do	May 20								
Lac qui Parle	do			May 20	June 3					
Princeton	do							May 25		
Dubuque	Iowa	May 12								
Fairfield	do									May 20
Muscatine	do			May 20	May 7					
Plum Spring	do					May 1				
Leavenworth City	Kansas								April 2	
Stanbridge	Canada							June 1	June 8	

ASCLEPIAS CORNUTI.—*Milk Weed.*

Name of Station.		1851.	1852.	1853.	1854.	1855.	1856.	1857.	1858.	1859.
Cornish	Maine							July 14		
Naples	do							July 26		
Londonderry	New Hamp.		July 6	July 9						
Manchester	do	July 8								
Stockbridge	Vermont			June 26						
Boston	Massachusetts		July 5							
Florida	do							July 15		
North Attleborough	do		June 30		June 26	June 27				
Uxbridge	do				June 24					
Point Judith	Rhode Island				July 23					
Columbia	Connecticut							July 9	July 1	
Baldwinsville	New York	July 20								
Chatham	do	July 9								
Nichols	do								July 10	July 7
North Salem	do	June 19	June 12							
Ovid	do				June 15					
Penn Yan	do							June 8		
Plattsburg	do		July 9							
Rochester	do							July 5	July 1	
West Point	do			June 28						
Mercersburg	Pennsylvania		June 22							
Mungersville	do							July 8		
Reading	do	June 28								
Sugar Grove	do	July 10								
Hagerstown	Maryland		June 27							
Clark county	Virginia							June 27	June 21	
Crichton's Store	do			May 20						June 1
Madison C. H.	do	July 6								
Rose Hill	do						July 1			July 1
Chapel Hill	N. Carolina			May 20						
Weewokaville	Alabama		April 25							
Union Hill	Texas							May 2		
Glenwood	Tennessee			May 30						
Maysville	Kentucky			July 10						
Trenton	Missouri		June 15	June 23						
Ashtabula	Ohio				July 10					
Belle Centre	do		June 19							
Cleveland	do				July 2	July 5				
Germantown	do				June 20					
Madison	do							July 20		
Marietta	do								June 28	
Mount Healthy	do				July 10	July 1				
Athens	Illinois		June 29	June 15	June 12					
Augusta	do				June 20	June 25				
Brest	Michigan	June 28								
Wyandotte	do								July 1	
Milwaukee	Wisconsin	July 3								
Lac qui Parle	Minnesota				June 24					
Princeton	do							June 10		
Fort Madison	Iowa				June 19					
Keokuk	do						June 30			

ASIMINA TRILOBA.—*Papaw.*

Name of Station.		1851.	1852.	1853.	1854.	1855.	1856.	1857.	1858.	1859.
New York city	New York				May 15					
Buffalo	Virginia					April 28				
Clark county	do							May 20	May 6	
Crichton's Store	do							May 15		March 16
Kanawha Salines	do								April 9	
Poplar Grove	do								April 18	April 4
All Saints	S. Carolina					April 4				
Alligator	Florida								April 1	
Childersburg	Alabama								April 3	
Greensborough	do						April 1	March 20	March 17	
Ashtabula	Ohio				May 16					
Belle Centre	do								May 18	
Hocking Port	do							May 14		
Marietta	do								April 24	April 7
Mount Healthy	do				May 22					
Poland	do					May 15				
Laconia	Indiana								April 8	
Brighton	Illinois							May 25		

BIGNONIA RADICANS.—*Trumpet Creeper.*

Name of Station.		1851.	1852.	1853.	1854.	1855.	1856.	1857.	1858.	1859.
Gardiner	Maine							Aug. 26		
Dover	New Hamp.		May 25							
North Attleborough	Massachusetts				June 8					
Point Judith	Rhode Island				July 29					
Columbia	Connecticut							July 9		
Middletown	do		July 12		July 5					
North Salem	New York	Aug. 1								
Ovid	do				July 5					
Spencertown	do					July 4				
Burlington	New Jersey		Aug. 10							
Darby	Pennsylvania			Aug. 10						
Gettysburg	do			July 10						
Lima	do				June 30					
Meadville	do	July 20	July 10							
Upper Darby	do		July 26							
Sykesville	Maryland	June 25								
Buffalo	Virginia					July 6				
Crichton's Store	do			June 15					June 28	
Diamond Grove	do	June 10								
Madison C. H	do	June 1	June 1							
Mossy Creek	do		July 1							
Poplar Grove	do								July 20	July 4
Rose Hill	do						June 13			June 10
St. John's	S. Carolina	June 4								
Alligator	Florida								March 16	
Eutaw	Alabama		June 6							
Jasper county	Mississippi						April 20			
Maysville	Kentucky			June 20						
Cleveland	Ohio				July 9	July 12				
Marietta	do								July 15	
Mount Healthy	do				June 20	June 25				
Laconia	Indiana								May 15	
Athens	Illinois		June 28	June 23	June 30					
Augusta	do	July 11	July 5	July 4	June 25	July 10		July 10		
Marengo	do								July 3	
[illegible]	do							June 15		
Wyandotte	Michigan								July 20	
Milwaukee	Wisconsin	June 3								
Leipsig	Saxony								July 8	

CALTHA PALUSTRIS.—*Marsh Marigold.—Cowslip.*

Name of Station.		1851.	1852.	1853.	1854.	1855.	1856.	1857.	1858.	1859.
Manchester	New Hamp.	May 2	May 8							
Brattleborough	Vermont.	May 1								
Burlington	do			May 12						
North Attleborough	Massachusetts.		April 2							
Middletown	Connecticut.		May 5							
Ceres	New York.	April 16								
Chatham	do	April 20								
New Lebanon	do	May 1	May 5	May 2						
North Salem	do	April 21	April 26							
Penn Yan	do							May 2		
Plattsburg	do	May 3	May 9							
Rochester	do		May 3	April 25						
Somerville	do	April 30								
West Point	do		May 18	May 4						
Ceres	Pennsylvania.		May 7							
Fleming Centre	do	April 26								
Gettysburg	do		May 1		April 24					
Hollidaysburg	do		April 23	April 20						
Mercersburg	do		April 19							
Meadville	do	April 16								
Darby	do		April 20							
Sugar Grove	do	April 28								
Upper Darby	do		April 28	April 25						
Hagerstown	Maryland		April 16	April 16						
Mossy Creek	Virginia		April 15							
Belle Centre	Ohio		April 16							
Cincinnati	do			April 21						
Keene	do	April 5	April 18							
Richmond	Indiana	April 1								
Brest	Michigan	April 23								
Washington	do		May 2							
Baraboo	Wisconsin	May 7								
Kaposia	Minnesota	May 1								
Lac qui Parle	do				April 20					
Dubuque	Iowa	April 17								
Fairbanks	do						April 24			

CARYA ALBA.—*Shell-bark Hickory.*

Name of Station.		1851.	1852.	1853.	1854.	1855.	1856.	1857.	1858.	1859.
Gardiner	Maine							June 29		
Castleton	Vermont				June 5					
Uxbridge	Massachusetts				June 1					
Columbia	Connecticut							May 24	June 2	
Flatbush	New York				June 3					
Nichols	do								June 5	
Ovid	do				June 1					
Rochester	do				May 30					
Spencertown	do					June 1				
Easton	Pennsylvania				May 17					
Freeport	do				May 15					
Buffalo	Virginia					April 30				
Clark county	do								May 6	
Crichton's Store	do							May 2	April 17	April 12
Poplar Grove	do									May 12
Chapel Hill	N Carolina			April 7						
Fulton	S. Carolina					April 18				
Cross Roads	Texas									March 10
Hannibal	Missouri				May 5					
Fairview	Kentucky									May 10
Ashtabula	Ohio				May 26					
Belle Centre	do				April 28				May 16	
Hiram	do							June 4		
Marietta	do								May 8	
Poland	do					June 3				
Rockport	do									June 10
Laconia	Indiana								April 24	April 24
Athens	Illinois				May 10					

CARYA ALBA.—*Shell-bark Hickory*—Continued.

Name of Station.		1851.	1852.	1853.	1854.	1855.	1856.	1857.	1858.	1859.
Augusta	Illinois					April 28				
Pekin	do								May 23	
Peoria	do								April 20	
Warsaw	do							May 18	April 30	
West Northfield	do				May 28					
West Salem	do							May 14		
Wyandotte	Michigan								June 8	May 15
Princeton	Minnesota							May 20		
Border Plains	Iowa								May 28	May 27
Fairfield	do									May 22
Keokuk	do						May 12			
Pleasant Plain	do				April 28	May 1				
Leavenworth City	Kansas								May 13	
Stanbridge	Canada								June 15	

CASTANEA VESCA—*Chestnut.*

Name of Station.		1851.	1852.	1853.	1854.	1855.	1856.	1857.	1858.	1859.
Gardiner	Maine							June 29		
Londonderry	New Hamp.		July 15							
Manchester	do	July 19	July 8							
Florida	Massachusetts							Aug. 5		
North Attleborough	do		June 23		June 25	July 5				
Richmond	do		July 10							
Point Judith	Rhode Island				July 5					
Columbia	Connecticut							July 10	July 2	
Middletown	do		July 5							
Fishkill Landing	New York							Aug. 15	Aug. 25	
Flatbush	do		June 20							
Lake	do									June 30
Nichols	do			July 6					July 8	July 12
Penn Yan	do							June 26		
Rochester	do			July 6	July 4	July 10	July 14	July 10	July 6	
Spencertown	do					July 8				
West Day	do									July 1
West Point	do		July 1	June 28						
Ceres	Pennsylvania		June 24							
Fleming Centre	do							July 4		
Freeport	do		July 2		July 6					
Hollidaysburg	do		July 20	June 20						
Mercersburg	do		June 29							
Lima	do		June 30		June 30	July 4		July 5		
Mungersville	do							July 10		
North Whitehall	do							July 12		
Radnor	do			June 20		July 4	July 2			
Darby	do			June 18						
Somerset	do								July 15	
Upper Darby	do			June 20	June 27					
Sykesville	Maryland		June 17	June 18	June 25			July 21		
Crack Whip	Virginia							July 2		
Kanawha Salines	do								June 20	
Madison C. H	do		June 12							
Poplar Grove	do								July 4	June 25
Eutaw	Alabama		May 28							
Greensborough	do						June 1		May 25	
Trenton	Missouri		June 24							
Ashtabula	Ohio				June 13					
Cleveland	do				July 2	July 5				
Elk Run	do									July 6
Hiram	do							July 19	July 12	
Keene	do		July 9							
Madison	do							July 10		
Rockport	do									June 10

CERASSUS CERASSUS.—*Garden Cherry.*

Name of Station.	1851.	1852.	1853.	1854.	1855.	1856.	1857.	1858.	1859.
Brunswick ... Maine								June 2	
Carmel ... do						May 30			
Cornish ... do						May 21	May 26		
Naples ... do							May 23		
Perry ... do						June 7			
Steuben ... do						June 12			
Concord ... New Hamp.						May 13			
Manchester ... do				May 30					
North Barnstead ... do						May 26			
Salmon Falls ... do				May 19					
West Enfield ... do							May 26		
Castleton ... Vermont				May 20					
Craftsbury ... do						May 30	May 31		
Stanbridge ... do						May 20			
Shelburn ... do						May 20			
West Rupert ... do						May 18	May 24		
Bridgewater ... Massachusetts							May 15		
Cambridge ... do						May 12			
Florida ... do								June 9	
Lawrence ... do							May 11		
North Attleborough ... do		May 8							
Uxbridge ... do				May 19					
Waltham ... do				May 19					
Westfield ... do						May 7			
Worcester ... do						May 8			
Point Judith ... Rhode Island				May 25					
Clinton ... Connecticut							May 26		
Georgetown ... do						May 12			
Norwich ... do						May 15			
Preston ... do						May 17			
Eden ... New York						May 17	May 25		
Flatbush ... do							May 9		
Geneva ... do						May 12			
Lake, (Washington county) ... do						May 23			
Lowville ... do						May 28	May 18	May 20	
New York city ... do							May 7		
North Salem ... do						May 15			
Ovid ... do				May 20		May 12	May 23		
Rochester ... do						April 30		May 1	
Spencertown ... do					May 20	May 19			
Wellsville ... do								May 20	
West Concord ... do						May 24			
West Day ... do									May 17
Readington ... New Jersey							May 10	May 1	April 28
Sergeantsville ... do							May 12		
Bellefonte ... Pennsylvania								May 6	
Fleming Centre ... do	May 28								
Gettysburg ... do						April 30			
Huntingdon ... do						May 6	May 7		
Indiana ... do		May 2							
Lancaster ... do								May 2	
Lima ... do		April 30	April 22		April 30	April 29			
Nazareth ... do						May 5			
North Whitehall ... do							May 9		
Morrisville ... do						May 7			
Radnor ... do		May 12							
Frederick ... Maryland							April 29		
Ridge ... do						April 24			
Spencerville ... do							April 22		
Sykesville ... do						April 29			
Buffalo ... Virginia						April 29			
Crack Whip ... do							May 5		
Crichton's Store ... do						April 14			
Mossy Creek ... do							April 30		
Mount Solon ... do						April 30			
Plains ... do									March 26
Poplar Grove ... do									April 9
Wardensville ... do						April 29			
Winchester ... do						April 23			
Wirt C. H. ... do						May 1			

CERASSUS CERASSUS.—*Garden Cherry*—Continued.

Name of Station.		1851.	1852.	1853.	1854.	1855.	1856.	1857.	1858.	1859.
Aiken	S. Carolina						March 30			
Camden	do						March 26			
Sparta	Georgia							March 25		
Varnell's Station	do									March 20
Seville	Florida									March 8
Carlowville	Alabama							March 16	March 15	
Columbus	Mississippi						April 9			
Oxford	do						April 10			
Cross Roads	Texas									March 21
Walnut Grove	Tennessee						May 4			
Fairview	Kentucky									March 20
Rockport	Missouri						April 21			
Cheviot	Ohio						April 25			
Edinburg	do							May 22		
Germantown	do						April 28			
Hamilton	do							May 15		
Hiram	do						May 11	May 24		
Jefferson	do						May 12			
Rockport	do									May 1
Welchfield	do							May 27		
Windham	do						May 7			
Laconia	Indiana									March 30
New Albany	do						April 20	April 24		
New Harmony	do						April 20			
Athens	Illinois						April 27			
Augusta	do						April 29			
Carthage	do						May 2			
Manchester	do						April 22	May 11	April 15	April 16
Marengo	do						May 17			
Ottawa	do								April 28	
Riley	do						May 14			
Warsaw	do						April 27	May 17	April 4	
West Salem	do						April 25	May 5		
Winnebago	do									May 10
Cooper	Michigan						May 12			
Grand Rapids	do						May 6			
Washington	do		May 11							
Wyandotte	do									May 2
Madison	Wisconsin						May 19	May 28		
Norway	do						May 15			
Platteville	do						May 10			
Beaver Bay	Minnesota								May 19	
Fairbanks	Iowa						May 4			
Fort Madison	do						April 29			
Muscatine	do			May 1	April 24		May 9			
Pleasant Plain	do						May 25			
Salem Prairie	Oregon						April 23			
Windsor	Nova Scotia							May 25		

CERASSUS SEROTINA.—*Wild Black Cherry.*

Name of Station.		1851.	1852.	1853.	1854.	1855.	1856.	1857.	1858.	1859.
Gardiner	Maine							May 23		
Naples	do							June 20		
Perry	do									May 24
Stratford	New Hampshire						May 28			
West Enfield	do							May 26		
Castleton	Vermont				May 20					
Boston	Massachusetts		May 27							
Florida	do							June 10	June 1	
North Attleborough	do		June 4		May 31	June 6				
Uxbridge	do				May 26					
Waltham	do				June 1					
Worcester	do							May 31		
Point Judith	Rhode Island				June 11					
Columbia	Connecticut							June 14	June 1	
Fishkill Landing	New York								April 27	
Lake	do							June 2	June 7	

CERASSUS SEROTINA.—*Wild Black Cherry*—Continued.

Name of Station.		1851	1852.	1853.	1854.	1855.	1856.	1857.	1858.	1859.
New York city	New York				May 5	May 13			April 28	
Nichols	do			May 9						
Spencertown	do					May 15				
Easton	Pennsylvania				April 29					
Mungersville	do							May 10		
Philadelphia	do								April 20	
Radnor	do		June 3	May 21	May 13	May 18	May 29			
Somerset	do								June 3	
Schellman Hills	Maryland							May 10		
Buffalo	Virginia					May 28				
Clark county	do							June 1	May 20	
Crichton's Store	do							April 25	April 21	April 8
Mossy Creek	do							May 25		
Poplar Grove	do								May 14	May 8
Rose Hill	do						April 16			April 15
Alligator	Florida								Jan. 30	
Childersburg	Alabama								April 1	
Greensborough	do						April 6	March 18	March 16	
Jasper	Mississippi					April 3				
New Wied	Texas				April 2					
Ashtabula	Ohio				May 9					
Belle Centre	do								May 20	
Bowling Green	do								April 25	
Madison	do							June 13		
Marietta	do								May 8	
Poland	do					May 27				
Brighton	Illinois							May 16		
Marengo	do							June 10	May 30	
Riley	do							June 15		
Waynesville	do								May 18	
West Northfield	do				May 24					
Flint	Michigan					May 10				
Romeo	do						June 2			
Wyandotte	do								June 8	
Princeton	Minnesota							May 10		
Eagle	Iowa							May 20		
Fairfield	do									May 23
Keokuk	do						May 21			
Pleasant Plain	do				May 20	April 29	June 7			
Stanbridge	Canada							May 20	June 12	

CERCIS CANADENSIS.—*Red-bud.—Judas Tree.*

Name of Station.		1851	1852.	1853.	1854.	1855.	1856.	1857.	1858.	1859.
Hagerstown	Maryland		May 6	April 26						
Sykesville	do		May 10							
Buffalo	Virginia					April 19				
Clark county	do								May 1	
Crichton's Store	do			April 1				April 4	April 5	March 15
Genito	do		March 15							
Kanawha Salines	do								April 9	
Madison C. H.	do	April 10	April 6							
Mossy Creek	do		April 10					April 30		
Plains	do									April 27
Poplar Grove	do								April 12	April 12
Rose Hill	do						April 16		April 1	April 10
Chapel Hill	N. Carolina	April 1		March 30					March 30	
Aiken	S. Carolina			March 19						
All Saints	do					March 15				
Black Oak	do		March 2							
Camden	do		March 11							
Fulton	do					March 16				
St. John's	do	March ..								
Varnell's Station	Georgia									March 20
Alligator	Florida								Feb. 15	
Childersburg	Alabama								March 20	
Greensborough	do						March 27	Feb. 27	March 13	
Weewokaville	do		March 10	March 20						

CERCIS CANADENSIS.—*Red-bud.—Judas Tree*—Continued.

Name of Station.	1851.	1852.	1853.	1854.	1855.	1856.	1857.	1858.	1859.
Columbus, Mississippi							Feb. 20	March 21	
Oktibbeha county, do							Feb. 24		
New Wied, Texas			March 7						
Glenwood, Tennessee			April 5						
Lebanon, do	March 20								
Fairview, Kentucky									March 25
Maysville, do			April 18						
Hannibal, Missouri				April 12					
Trenton, do		April 28	April 22	April 20					
Belle Centre, Ohio		April 27		April 20				May 1	
Cincinnati, do			April 23						
Germantown, do		April 28	April 26						
Keene, do	April 20	May 1							
Marietta, do								April 13	April 12
Mount Healthy, do				April 20					
Poland, do					May 12				
Indianapolis, Indiana									April 17
Laconia, do								March 31	April 13
Richmond, do	May 2								
Athens, Illinois		April 25	April 20	April 20	April 21				
Augusta, do	April 12	May 1	April 22	April 24	April 21		May 15		
Brighton, do							May 12		
Pekin, do								May 24	
Warsaw, do							May 7		
Waynesville, do								April 20	
West Northfield, do				May 9					
West Salem, do							May 8		
Ann Arbor, Michigan			May 23						
Fort Madison, Iowa		April 30	April 29						
Muscatine, do			April 30	April 22					
Leavenworth, Kansas								April 1	

CHIONANTHUS VIRGINICA.—*Fringe Tree.*

Name of Station.	1851.	1852.	1853.	1854.	1855.	1856.	1857.	1858.	1859.
Flatbush, New York		June 18	June 10	June 17					
Rochester, do				June 12					
Gettysburg, Pennsylvania			June 15						
Lima, do		June 4	May 28	May 30					
Middletown, do					June 7				
Radnor, do		June 5							
Upper Darby, do			June 4	May 28					
Easton, Maryland				May 1					
Buffalo, Virginia					May 18				
Madison C. H., do		May 18							
Rose Hill, do						May 20			May 19
Chapel Hill, N. Carolina								April 20	
All Saints, S. Carolina					April 18				
Camden, do		April 11							
Alligator, Florida								Jan. 31	
Eutaw, Alabama		March 30							
Greensborough, do						April 15	April 2	March 29	
Poland, Ohio					May 27				

CLETHRA ALNIFOLIA.—*White Alder.—Sweet Pepper-bush.*

Name of Station.	1851.	1852.	1853.	1854.	1855.	1856.	1857.	1858.	1859.
Gardiner, Maine							Aug. 28		
Florida, Massachusetts							Aug. 1		
Point Judith, Phode Island				Aug. 3					
Easton, Pennsylvania				June 16					
Radner, do					Aug. 7	Aug. 7	Aug. 16		
Fairfield, Iowa									May 23

CONVOLVULUS PURPUREUS.—*Purple Morning Glory.*

Name of Station.		1851.	1852.	1853.	1854.	1855.	1856.	1857.	1858.	1859.
Castine	Maine		July 5							
Darby	Pennsylvania			July 1						
Sugar Grove	do	June 10								
Sykesville	Maryland	July 25	July 8	June 18						
New Wied	Texas	May 10								
Belle Centre	Ohio		July 1							
Keene	do		July 3							
Athens	Illinois			June 18						
Augusta	do		July 25							
Brest	Michigan	July 15								
Milwaukee	Wisconsin	July 5								
Lac qui Parle	Minnesota			June 5	July 1					
Dubuque	Iowa	July 20								

CORNUS FLORIDA.—*Flowering Dogwood.*

Name of Station.		1851.	1852.	1853.	1854.	1855.	1856.	1857.	1858.	1859.
Cornish	Maine						June 15			
Stratford	New Hamp.						May 18			
West Enfield	do							June 20		
Newark	Vermont						June 17			
West Rupert	do						June 13	June 14		
Bridgewater	Massachusetts							May 15		
Florida	do							June 25	July 20	
Mendon	do				May 17					
North Attleborough	do		May 30		May 22					
Uxbridge	do				May 18					
Columbia	Connecticut							May 26	May 26	
Georgetown	do						May 26			
Middletown	do			May 19	May 24					
Chatham	New York	May 28								
Eden	do							May 22		
Flatbush	do		May 26	May 17				May 29		
Lake, (Washington county)	do								June 7	
New Lebanon	do	May 18		May 25						
New York city	do				May 16	May 22		May 29		
North Salem	do	May 10				May 10				
Ovid	do				May 20		May 16			
Penn Yan	do							May 16		
Rochester	do		May 20	May 30	May 22	June 1	May 18		May 25	
Sag Harbor	do		June 3							
Spencertown	do					June 1	June 15			
West Point	do		June 1	May 16						
Moorestown	New Jersey					May 15				
Burlington	do		May 16							
Freehold	do									May 10
Readington	do							May 20	May 20	May 12
Sergeantsville	do							May 25		
Chester	Pennsylvania	May 20								
Easton	do				May 1					
Fleming Centre	do	May 15								
Freeport	do		May 17	May 18	May 17					
Gettysburg	do			May 10	May 5					
Hollidaysburg	do		May 20	May 18						
Huntingdon	do						May 12	May 26		
Indiana	do		May 17							
Lima	do			May 4		May 15	May 15	May 26		
Meadville	do	May 23	May 20							
Morrisville	do						May 10			
Mungersville	do							May 20		
Nazareth	do						June 1			
Radnor	do		May 15	May 9	May 13	May 24	May 22	May 31	May 17	
Reading	do	May 12								
Darby	do		May 10	May 9						
Somerset	do								June 3	
Sugar Grove	do	May 26								
Upper Darby	do	May 12	May 17	May 14	May 11					

CORNUS FLORIDA.—*Flowering Dogwood*—Continued.

Name of Station.	1851.	1852.	1853.	1854.	1855.	1856.	1857.	1858.	1859.
Easton ... Maryland				April 26					
Hagerstown ... do		May 14							
Ridge ... do						April 15			
Sykesville ... do	May 5	May 15	May 5	May 16		May 21	May 10		
Buffalo ... Virginia					May 1				
Clark county ... do								May 2	
Crack Whip ... do							May 17		
Crichton's Store ... do			April 5			April 15	May 1	April 17	April 8
Doddridge county ... do						April 30			
Genito ... do		April 6							
Kanawha Salines ... do								April 23	
Madison C. H. ... do	April 30	April 29							
Mossy Creek ... do		May 1					May 15		
The Plains ... do									April 25
Poplar Grove ... do							May 15	April 22	April 14
Rose Hill ... do						April 28	May 1		April 18
Wardensville ... do						May 6			
Wirt C. H. ... do						May 1			
Chapel Hill ... N. Carolina	April 19		April 14					April 12	
Aiken ... S. Carolina			April 1			April 18			
All Saints Parish ... do					April 7	April 18			
Black Oak ... do		March 21							
Camden ... do		March 22				April 11			
Fulton ... do					April 9				
St. John's ... do	March 15								
Savannah ... Georgia						March 20			
Sparta ... do							March 27		
Varnell's Station ... do									March 26
Alligator ... Florida								Jan. 31?	
Carlowville ... do							March 18	March 5	
Seville ... do									Feb. 28
Childersburg ... Alabama							March 27	March 24	
Eutaw ... do	March 21	March 6							
Greensborough ... do						April 4	March 24	March 25	
Weewokaville ... do		April 20	April 1						
Columbus ... Mississippi						April 9	March 28		
Jasper county ... do						March 22			
Oxford ... do						April 8			
Big Pond ... Louisiana						March 1			
Glenwood ... Tennessee			April 18						
Knoxville ... do		April 7							
Lebanon ... do	April 25								
Fairview ... Kentucky									April 10
Maysville ... do			April 23						
Ashtabula ... Ohio				May 13					
Belle Centre ... do		May 17		May 8					
Cincinnati ... do			May 1						
Cleveland ... do				May 21	May 19				
Edinburg ... do							May 30		
Elk Run ... do									May 5
Germantown ... do		May 5	May 1	April 25		May 6			
Hocking Port ... do							May 10		
Keene ... do	May 10	May 14							
Madison ... do							June 1		
Mount Healthy ... do				May 3	May 15				
Poland ... do					May 16				
Rockport ... do									May 7
Savannah ... do							May 28		
Laconia ... Indiana							April 13		April 22
West Salem ... Illinois						May 2	May 22	April 24	
Ann Arbor ... Michigan			May 25						
Brest ... do	May 18								
Wyandotte ... do								June 4	May 22
Milwaukee ... Wisconsin	May 24								
Lac qui Parle ... Minnesota				May 24					
Princeton ... do							May 25		
Muscatine ... Iowa			May 27						
Pleasant Plain ... do						June 5			
Stanbridge ... Canada								June 10	

CRATÆGUS COCCINEA.—*Scarlet Fruited Thorn.*

NAME OF STATION.	1851.	1852.	1853.	1854.	1855.	1856.	1857.	1858.	1859.
Brunswick .... Maine								June 10	
Cornish .... do							June 6		
Gardiner .... do							May 31		
Naples .... do							June 8		
Steuben .... do	June 10		June 6		June 10				
Salmon Falls .... New Hamp				May 24					
Castleton .... Vermont				May 25					
Stockbridge .... do			May 25						
Florida .... Massachusetts								May 12	
North Attleborough .... do		May 27		May 10					
Point Judith .... Rhode Island				June 1					
Columbia .... Connecticut							June 5	June 7	
Middletown .... do		May 27							
Chatham .... New York	June 5								
New Lebanon .... do		June 6	May 21						
Nichols .... do								June 5	
North Salem .... do	May 16	May 13							
Penn Yan .... do							June 6		
Plattsburg .... do		May 25							
Rochester .... do		June 1	May 30	May 20	June 1		May 29	May 24	
Ceres .... Pennsylvania		May 20							
Fleming Centre .... do	May 23								
Mercersburg .... do		May 21							
Meadville .... do	May 14	May 17							
Philadelphia .... do								April 20	
Radnor .... do		May 24	May 3	May 16			May 16	May 14	
Somerset .... do								June 1	
Hagerstown .... Maryland		May 15	May 15						
Buffalo .... Virginia					May 12				
Clark county .... do							May 9	April 29	
Crichton's Store .... do			May 12				May 15		
Poplar Grove .... do								April 29	April 25
Greensborough .... Alabama						April 1			
Weewokaville .... do			March 15						
Knoxville .... Tennessee		March 15							
Trenton .... Missouri		May 1							
Belle Centre .... Ohio		May 10		May 10					
Cincinnati .... do			April 30						
Madison .... do							June 10		
Mount Healthy .... do				April 25	May 10				
Laconia .... Indiana								April 25	
Athens .... Illinois			April 29	April 20					
Augusta .... do	April 10	May 10	May 3	April 30	May 8		May 20		
Peoria .... do								May 8	
Warsaw .... do							May 23		
West Northfield .... do				May 11					
Ann Arbor .... Michigan			May 20						
Flint .... do					May 28				
Milwaukee .... Wisconsin	May 17								
Princeton .... Minnesota							May 20		
Fairfield .... Iowa									May 7
Fort Madison .... do		May 3	April 13						
Horton .... Nova Scotia					June 8				

CRATÆGUS OXYCANTHA.—*English Hawthorn.*

Gardiner .... Maine							June 16		
Steuben .... do							June 19		
Manchester .... New Hamp		May 31		May 20					
Fishkill Landing .... New York							May 30		
New York city .... do				May 15					
Ovid .... do				May 28					
Penn Yan .... do							June 8		
Rochester .... do			May 30					June 1	
West Point .... do			June 10						
Burlington .... New Jersey		May 26							
Lima .... Pennsylvania							June 2		

CRATÆGUS OXYCANTHA.—*English Hawthorn*—Continued.

Name of Station.	1851.	1852.	1853.	1854.	1855.	1856.	1857.	1858.	1859.
Radnor .... Pennsylvania		May 24	May 21	May 16			June 3	May 25	
Upper Darby .... do		May 17							
Buffalo .... Virginia					May 2				
Clark county .... do							June 1	May 25	
Genito .... do		April 12							
Rose Hill .... do						April 22	May 5		April 15
Alligator .... Florida								March 20	
Jasper county .... Mississippi						April 4			
Lebanon .... Tennessee	May 9								
Cleveland .... Ohio				May 14	May 16				
Augusta .... Illinois			May 5	May 8	May 13		May 30		
West Northfield .... do				May 27					
Horton .... Nova Scotia					June 8				
Leipsig .... Saxony								May 10	

DIGITALIS PURPUREA.—*Foxglove.*

Name of Station.	1851.	1852.	1853.	1854.	1855.	1856.	1857.	1858.	1859.
Castine .... Maine		July 25							
Brattleborough .... Vermont	June 30								
North Attleborough .. Massachusetts		July 14							
Ceres .... New York	July 1								
Penn Yan .... do							June 14		
West Point .... do			June 10						
Burlington .... New Jersey		July 15							
Chester .... Pennsylvania	July 1								
Delaware county .... do	June 6								
Meadville .... do	June 8	June 12							
Sykesville .... Maryland	May 24	May 25	May 20						
Mossy Creek .... Virginia		June 1							
New Wied .... Texas	April 10		April 18						

EPIGÆA REPENS.—*Trailing Arbutus.*

Name of Station.	1851.	1852.	1853.	1854.	1855.	1856.	1857.	1858.	1859.
Brunswick .... Maine							May 1	May 11	
Cornish .... do							May 3		
Gardiner .... do							May 13		
Naples .... do							May 1		
Francestown .... New Hamp			April 10						
Manchester .... do	April 13	April 23		April 28					
Salmon Falls .... do				April 21					
Somersworth .... do				April 22					
Brattleborough .... Vermont	April 2								
Burlington .... do			April 14		April 24				
Stockbridge .... do			April 20						
Boston .... Massachusetts		April 12							
Lawrence .... do							May 1		
Mendon .... do				May 20					
Uxbridge .... do				May 11					
Worcester .... do							April 2		
Columbia .... Connecticut							April 28	April 3	
East Windsor Hill .... do			May 31						
Middletown .... do		April 11	April 10	April 10					
Chatham .... New York	April 4	April 27							
Lake, (Washington county) . do							April 22		
New Lebanon .... do	April 14	May 2	April 19						
Plattsburg .... do	April 12	April 24							
Rochester .... do	April 11	April 27	April 9	April 24	April 15			April 15	
Somerville .... do	May 12								
West Point .... do		April 18	April 20						
Burlington .... New Jersey		May 5							
Moorestown .... do					April 20				
Ceres .... Pennsylvania		April 30							
Chambersburg .... do	April 5	April 25							

EPIGÆA REPENS.—*Trailing Arbutus*—Continued.

Name of Station.	1851.	1852.	1853.	1854.	1855.	1856.	1857.	1858.	1859.
Chester, Pennsylvania	March 26								
Fleming Centre, do	April 4								
Gettysburg, do		April 20	April 11	April 25					
Hollidaysburg, do		April 20							
Mercersburg, do		April 26							
Lancaster, do				April 10					
Meadville, do	April 1	April 18							
Lima, do					June 12				
Mungersville, do							May 4		
Philadelphia, do								April 8	
Reading, do	April 7								
Sugar Grove, do	March 30								
Upper Darby, do	April 9	April 22	April 19	April 13					
Hagerstown, Maryland		April 1	April 1						
Sykesville, do		April 25							
Mossy Creek, Virginia		March 20							
Chapel Hill, N. Carolina								March 20	
Aiken, South Carolina			March 1						
Camden, do		March 8							
Poland, Ohio					April 13				
Horton, Nova Scotia					April 18				

EPILOBIUM SPICATUM.—*Willow Herb.*

Name of Station.	1851.	1852.	1853.	1854.	1855.	1856.	1857.	1858.	1859.
Brunswick, Maine							July 31	Aug. 8	
Manchester, New Hamp	July 1	July 10							
Chatham, New York		July 8							
Penn Yan, do							July 1		
Plattsburg, do		July 2							
Rochester, do			July 4				July 10		
Reading, do	June 25								
Leipsig, Saxony								July 1	

ERYTHRONIUM AMERICANUM.—*Dog-tooth Violet.—Adder Tongue.*

Name of Station.	1851.	1852.	1853.	1854.	1855.	1856.	1857.	1858.	1859.
Brunswick, Maine							May 15	May 27	
Cornish, do							May 30		
Gardiner, do							April 30		
Naples, do							May 13		
Manchester, New Hamp		May 1		May 5					
Brandon, Vermont			May 11						
Brattleborough, do	April 22								
Burlington, do			May 12						
Castleton, do				April 30					
Newark, do							May 10		
Stockbridge, do			April 30						
Florida, Massachusetts							May 15		
West Cambridge, do				May 4					
Worcester, do							May 9		
Middletown, Connecticut		April 23	April 21						
Ceres, New York	April 20								
Chatham, do	April 20	May 8							
Lake, (Washington county), do							April 30		
New Lebanon, do	May 4		April 20						
New York city, do								May 4	
Nichols, do								May 12	
North Salem, do	April 11	April 25			May 1				
Ovid, do				May 7					
Penn Yan, do							May 24		
Plattsburg, do	April 29	May 4							
Rochester, do		April 30	April 20	April 24				April 25	
Somerville, do	April 21								
Spencertown, do					May 10				
West Point, do		April 26							
White Plains, do					May 2				

ERYTHRONIUM AMERICANUM.—*Dog-tooth Violet.—Adder Tongue*—Continued.

Name of Station.		1851.	1852.	1853.	1854.	1855.	1856.	1857.	1858.	1859.
Burlington	New Jersey		March 20							
Ceres	Pennsylvania		May 6							
Chester	do	April 8								
Fleming Centre	do	May 12						April 28		
Gettysburg	do		April 28		April 18					
Hollidaysburg	do		May 2	May 1						
Mercersburg	do		April 15							
Lima	do		April 27	April 28	April 21			May 1		
Meadville	do	April 10	April 24							
Myersville	do							April 28		
Philadelphia	do								April 18	
Radnor	do					April 21	April 25			
Reading	do	April 7								
Darby	do		April 15	April 6						
Sugar Grove	do	April 23								
Upper Darby	do	April 12	April 24	April 22	April 22					
Chapel Hill	N. Carolina			March 21					April 3	
Weewokaville	Alabama			March 23						
Jasper county	Mississippi					April 6	April 1			
Ashtabula	Ohio				May 3					
Belle Centre	do		April 17		April 22				April 20	
Bowling Green	do								April 20	
Hiram	do							May 1		
Keene	do	April 16	April 18							
Richmond	Indiana	April 6								
Athens	Illinois				April 13					
Marengo	do								May 1	
Brest	Michigan	April 15								
Flint	do					April 21				
Romeo	do						May 5			
Wyandotte	do								April 26	
Pleasant Plain	Iowa				April 23					
Stanbridge	Canada							May 4		

FRAGARIA VESCA.—*Field Strawberry.*

Name of Station.		1851.	1852.	1853.	1854.	1855.	1856.	1857.	1858.	1859.
Castine	Maine		June 10							
Carmel	do						May 15			
Cornish	do						May 20	May 16		
Perry	do						May 25			May 15
Steuben	do		May 22	May 12						May 5
Francestown	New Hamp.			May 15						
Londonderry	do		May 10	May 12						
Manchester	do	May 12	May 14							
North Barnstead	do						May 26			
Salmon Falls	do				May 14					
Somersworth	do				May 19					
Stratford	do						May 22			
Brandon	Vermont			May 14			May 15			
Brattleborough	do	May 1								
Craftsbury	do						May 18	May 25		
Newark	do						May 20			
Stanbridge	do						May 10			
Shelburn	do						May 18			
Stockbridge	do			May 2						
West Rupert	do						May 8			
Bridgewater	Massachusetts							May 16		
Cambridge	do						May 6			
Florida	do						May 4			
North Attleborough	do		May 5							
Westfield	do						May 19			
Worcester	do						May 25			
East Windsor Hill	do			May 12						
Georgetown	do						May 8			
Middletown	do		May 5	April 27						
Norwich	do						May 18			
Preston	do						May 20			

FRAGARIA VESCA.—*Field Strawberry*—Continued.

NAME OF STATION.	1851.	1852.	1853.	1854.	1855.	1856.	1857.	1858.	1859.
Angelica New York						May 20			
Chatham do		May 4							
Clinton do							June 6		
Eden do						May 18	May 24		
Flatbush do		May 4							
Geneva do						May 16			
Lake, (Washington county) do						May 19			
Lowville do						June 14	June 7	June 19	
Mexico do						May 17			
New Lebanon do			May 2						
New York city do							May 20		
North Salem do		May 7							
Ogdensburg do						May 15			
Ovid do							May 26		
Penn Yan do							May 20		
Plattsburg do		May 12	May 6						
Spencertown do						May 20			
Somerville do	May 10								
Waterloo do		May 12							
West Day do									May 8
West Point do		May 18	May 9						
White Plains do					May 1				
Burlington New Jersey		April 26							
Readington do							May 20	May 10	
Sergeantsville do							May 21		
Bellefonte Pennsylvania								May 10	
Ceres do		May 20							
Easton do				May 7					
Fleming Centre do	April 16								
Gettysburg do		May 6	May 8	April 26					
Hollidaysburg do		May 13	May 4						
Mercersburg do		May 6							
Indiana do		May 13							
Lima do			May 2	April 25		May 16			
Meadville do		May 8				May 20			
Morrisville do						May 9			
Nazareth do						May 14			
North Whitehall do							May 6		
Radnor do		April 28							
Reading do	April 18								
Darby do			April 20						
Upper Darby do		May 6	April 25						
Valley Forge do		May 4							
Hagerstown Maryland			April 12						
Ridge do						April 27			
Sykesville do			April 21						
Buffalo Virginia						April 29			
Crichton's Store do						April 21			
Genito do		March 30							
Madison C. H. do		April 10							
Mossy Creek do		April 25					April 30		
The Plains do									April 13
Poplar Grove do							April 30		April 12
Portsmouth do		March 15							
Wardensville do						May 4			
Winchester do						April 30			
Chapel Hill N. Carolina			April 4						
Aiken S. Carolina						April 7			
Camden do		March 13				March 23			
Savannah Georgia						March 3			
Sparta do						March 16	March 20		
Varnell's Station do									March 20
Zebulon do						April 10			
Seville Florida									Feb. 1
Carlowville Alabama							March 17	March 1	
Eutaw do	March 21	March 10							
Greensborough do						April 3			
Weewokaville do		March 25	March 15						
Fairview Kentucky									April 25
Columbus Mississippi						March 20			

FRAGARIA VESCA.—*Field Strawberry*—Continued.

Name of Station.	1851.	1852.	1853.	1854.	1855.	1856.	1857.	1858.	1859.
Glenwood .... Tennessee ..	....	....	April 14	....	....	....	....	....	....
Knoxville .... do	....	April 12	....	....	....	....	....	....	....
Walnut Grove........ do......	....	....	....	....	....	April 10	....	....	....
Trenton .... Missouri ...	....	April 22	April 24	April 20	....	....	....	....	....
Belle Centre .... Ohio.....	....	May 8	....	....	....	....	....	....	....
Cincinnati .... do......	....	....	May 1	....	....	....	....	....	....
Germantown........ do......	....	....	....	....	....	April 24	....	....	....
Hiram........ do......	....	....	....	....	....	May 19	May 25	....	....
Jefferson .... do......	....	....	....	....	....	May 12	....	....	....
Troy .... do......	....	....	....	....	....	....	....	....	April 12
Windham .... do......	....	....	....	....	....	May 8	....	....	....
Indianapolis .... Indiana....	....	....	....	....	....	....	....	....	May 21
Laconia .... do......	....	....	....	....	....	....	....	....	April 5
New Harmony........ do......	....	....	....	....	....	April 25	....	....	....
Athens........ Illinois....	....	April 13	April 17	....	....	....	....	....	....
Augusta .... do......	....	....	April 18	....	....	May 30	....	....	....
Carthage .... do......	....	....	....	....	....	April 25	....	....	....
Manchester .... do......	....	....	....	....	....	May 10	....	....	....
Marengo .... do......	....	....	....	....	....	April 21	....	....	....
Ottawa .... do......	....	....	....	....	....	May 6	....	April 27	....
Warsaw .... do......	....	....	....	....	....	....	May 13	April 18	....
West Salem........ do......	....	....	....	....	....	April 27	May 9	April 24	....
Winnebago .... do......	....	....	....	....	....	....	....	....	May 16
Ann Arbor .... Michigan...	....	May 1	....	....	....	....	....	....	....
Cooper .... do......	....	....	....	....	....	May 14	....	....	....
Grand Rapids........ do......	....	....	....	....	....	May 8	....	....	....
St. James........ do......	....	....	....	....	....	May 23	....	....	....
Wyandotte .... do......	....	....	....	....	....	....	....	April 7	May 7
Appleton .... Wisconsin...	....	....	....	....	....	May 16	....	....	....
Norway .... do......	....	....	....	....	....	April 27	....	....	....
Platteville .... do......	....	....	....	....	....	May 25	....	....	....
Madison .... do......	....	....	....	....	....	May 7	May 20	....	....
Beaver Bay........ Minnesota ..	....	....	....	....	....	....	....	May 11	....
Cass Lake Mission........ do......	....	....	....	....	....	....	May 24	....	....
Fort Ripley........ do......	....	May 17	....	....	....	....	....	....	....
Lac qui Parle .... do......	....	....	May 16	April 25	....	....	....	....	....
Fairbanks .... Iowa.....	....	....	....	....	....	May 11	....	....	....
Fort Madison .... do......	....	April 30	May 13	....	....	....	....	....	....
Muscatine .... do......	....	May 7	May 5	....	....	May 13	....	....	....
Pleasant Plain .... do......	....	....	....	....	....	May 11	....	....	....
Salem Prairie........ Oregon....	....	....	....	....	....	March 20	....	....	....
Horton........ Nova Scotia..	....	....	....	....	....	....	May 10	....	....
Windsor........ do......	....	....	....	....	....	....	May 1	....	....
Red River Settlement, Rupert's Land.	....	....	....	....	....	May 10	....	....	....

FRAXINUS AMERICANA.—*White Ash.*

Name of Station.	1851.	1852.	1853.	1854.	1855.	1856.	1857.	1858.	1859.
Naples .... Maine....	....	....	....	....	....	....	May 24	....	....
Florida .... Massachusetts.	....	....	....	....	....	....	Aug. 1	July 30	....
Uxbridge .... do......	....	....	....	May 25	....	....	....	....	....
Columbia .... Connecticut..	....	....	....	....	....	....	May 12	May 1	....
New York city .... New York ..	....	....	....	....	....	....	....	May 14	....
Spencertown .... do......	....	....	....	....	May 12	....	....	....	....
Fleming Centre........ Pennsylvania.	May 12	....	....	....	....	....	....	....	....
Lima .... do......	....	May 15	....	....	May 10	....	....	....	....
Radnor .... do......	....	....	....	....	May 8	....	May 13	....	....
Buffalo........ Virginia...	....	....	....	....	April 20	....	....	....	....
Crichton's Store........ do......	....	....	....	....	....	....	May 20	....	May 1
Poplar Grove........ do......	....	....	....	....	....	....	....	....	May 16
Childersburg .... Alabama...	....	....	....	....	....	....	....	April 4	....
Greensborough .... do......	....	....	....	....	....	March 26	....	....	....
Belle Centre .... Ohio.....	....	....	....	May 10	....	....	....	....	....
Germantown........ do......	....	....	May 5	....	....	....	....	....	....
Troy .... do......	....	....	....	....	....	....	....	....	April 12
Laconia........ Indiana....	....	....	....	....	....	....	....	March 9	....
Athens .... Illinois....	....	....	....	April 30	....	....	....	....	....
Augusta .... do......	....	....	....	....	April 28	....	May 20	....	....

FRAXINUS AMERICANA.—*White Ash*—Continued.

Name of Station.		1851.	1852.	1853.	1854.	1855.	1856.	1857.	1858.	1859.
Pekin	Illinois								May 14	
Warsaw	do							May 9	April 16	
Flint	Michigan					April 20				
Lac qui Parle	Minnesota				May 1					
Princeton	do							May 25		
Border Plains	Iowa								May 8	
Leavenworth City	Kansas								May 12	
Stanbridge	Canada							June 1	June 16	

GAYLUSSACIA RESINOSA.—*Whortleberry.*

Name of Station.		1851.	1852.	1853.	1854.	1855.	1856.	1857.	1858.	1859.
North Attleborough	Massachusetts		May 30		May 20	May 27				
Uxbridge	do				May 20					
Waltham	do				June 1					
Point Judith	Rhode Island				June 1					
Columbia	Connecticut							May 26	June 10	
New York city	New York								May 23	
Nichols	do								May 10	
Rochester	do					June 3				
Fleming Centre	Pennsylvania	May 27								
Lancaster	do							May 28		
Lima	do			May 21						
Sykesville	Maryland				May 6			May 5		
Buffalo	Virginia					May 12				
Crichton's Store	do								May 11	April 22
Poplar Grove	do								May 12	April 29
Rose Hill	do						April 28	May 10		April 28
Alligator	Florida								Feb. 9	
Flint	Michigan					May 25				
Princeton	Minnesota							May 25		
Stanbridge	Canada								June 15	

GERANIUM MACULATUM.—*Cranesbill.*

Name of Station.		1851.	1852.	1853.	1854.	1855.	1856.	1857.	1858.	1859.
Gardiner	Maine							June 4		
Manchester	New Hamp.	June 11								
Salmon Falls	do				May 28					
Uxbridge	Massachusetts				May 29					
Waltham	do				May 29					
Point Judith	Rhode Island				May 27					
East Windsor	Connecticut		June 4							
Ceres	New York	May 14								
Chatham	do	May 16	May 20							
New Lebanon	do	May 18	June 1	May 18						
New York city	do				May 16	May 24			May 16	
Nichols	do								May 20	May 11
North Salem	do	May 12	May 17							
Ovid	do				May 18					
Penn Yan	do							May 18		
Rochester	do		May 13	May 14	May 22	May 18		June 1	May 25	
Freehold	New Jersey									April 15
Chester	Pennsylvania	May 15								
Fleming Centre	do	May 12						May 25		
Gettysburg	do		May 4	May 20	April 25					
Hollidaysburg	do		May 20	May 4						
Mercersburg	do		May 20							
Lancaster	do				May 9					
Lima	do		May 13	May 7			May 15	May 22		
Meadville	do		May 16							
Morrisville	do						May 15			
Mungersville	do							May 14		
Radnor	do			May 17		May 20	May 26	May 23	May 12	
Reading	do	May 17								

GERANIUM MACULATUM.—*Cranesbill*—Continued.

Name of Station.		1851.	1852.	1853.	1854.	1855.	1856.	1857.	1858.	1859.
Darby	Pennsylvania		May 10	April 26						
Sugar Grove	do	May 18								
Upper Darby	do	May 9	May 12	May 10	May 10					
Hagerstown	Maryland		May 6	May 6						
Sykesville	do	May 20	May 20							
Madison C. H.	Virginia	June 13	May 15							
Mossy Creek	do		April 28					May 5		
Chapel Hill	N. Carolina			April 20						
St. John's	S. Carolina	April 29								
New Wied	Texas				March 18					
Knoxville	Tennessee		April 20							
Belle Centre	Ohio		May 4		May 10					
Bowling Green	do								May 15	
Cincinnati	do			May 1						
Germantown	do		May 15							
Hiram	do							May 20	May 10	
Keene	do	May 16								
Madison	do							May 18		
Marietta	do								May 8	
Richmond	Indiana	May 5								
Athens	Illinois		April 27	April 30	April 27	April 28				
Augusta	do	May 10	May 10	May 6	April 24	May 10		May 30		
West Northfield	do				May 14					
Ann Arbor	Michigan			May 21						
Brest	do	May 16								
Wyandotte	do								May 30	
Baraboo	Wisconsin	May 12								
Kaposia	Minnesota	May 21								
Dubuque	Iowa	May 12								
Eagle	do							May 30		

HALESIA TETRAPTERA.—*Snowdrop Tree.*

Name of Station.		1851.	1852.	1853.	1854.	1855.	1856.	1857.	1858.	1859.
Steuben	Maine	July 3		July 14						
North Attleborough	Massachusetts		June 14		June 8	June 16				
Point Judith	Rhode Island				May 25					
Middletown	Connecticut		May 19	May 10	May 15					
Fishkill Landing	New York							May 30		
Nichols	do								June 20	June 25
Burlington	New Jersey		June 12							
Freeport	do		June 6		May 22					
Gettysburg	Pennsylvania		May 10							
Lima	do		May 10	May 4	April 25	May 15		May 16		
Radnor	do		May 12	May 7						
Darby	do			May 25						
Upper Darby	do	May 4	May 16	May 6	May 8					
Sykesville	Maryland	May 26								
Poplar Grove	Virginia								May 8	
All Saints	S. Carolina					March 15				
Belle Centre	Ohio		May 26							
Mount Healthy	do				April 30					
Brighton	Illinois							June 2	May 6	
Milwaukee	Wisconsin	June 13								
Fort Madison	Iowa				May 10					

HAMAMELIS VIRGINIANA.—*Witch Hazel.*

Name of Station.		1851.	1852.	1853.	1854.	1855.	1856.	1857.	1858.	1859.
Manchester	New Hamp.	Oct. 10	Sept. 20							
Brandon	Vermont			Oct. 19						
Stockbridge	do			Oct. 5						
Hollidaysburg	Pennsylvania		Sept. 24							
Meadville	do		Oct. 12							
Maysville	Kentucky			Nov. 29						

HEPATICA TRILOBA.—*Round-lobed Liverwort.*

Name of Station.		1851.	1852.	1853.	1854.	1855.	1856.	1857.	1858.	1859.
Castine	Maine		May 1							
Gardiner	do							April 9		
Francestown	New Hamp.			April 22						
Brattleborough	Vermont	April 22								
Burlington	do			April 25		May 1				
Stockbridge	do			April 24						
Boston	Massachusetts.		April 5							
Worcester	do							May 19		
Middletown	Connecticut		April 23							
Ceres	New York	April 1								
Chatham	do	April 4	April 26							
Lake	do							April 24		
New Lebanon	do	May 8		April 22						
North Salem	do	April 1	April 20			May 1				
Ovid	do				April 21					
Penn Yan	do							April 27		
Plattsburg	do	April 19	May 1							
Rochester	do	April 11	April 27	April 20	April 5	April 13		May 12	April 15	
Somerville	do	April 6								
Spencertown	do					April 20				
West Point	do		April 20	April 20						
White Plains	do					April 28				
Freehold	New Jersey									March 25
Ceres	Pennsylvania.		May 6							
Chester	do	March 27								
Easton	do		March 13		April 8?					
Fleming Centre	do	April 2						April 15		
Gettysburg	do		April 14	April 10	April 17					
Hollidaysburg	do		April 18	April 2						
Mercersburg	do		April 2							
Indiana	do				March 15					
Lima	do		April 23	April 8	April 11	April 20		April 12		
Meadville	do	April 1	April 15							
Mungersville	do							April 21		
Nazareth	do							April 18		
Philadelphia	do								April 12	
Radnor	do								April 14	
Reading	do	April 3								
Darby	do		April 10	March 28						
Sugar Grove	do	March 30								
Upper Darby	do	April 3	April 22	April 11	April 7					
Hagerstown	Maryland		April 16	April 16						
Sykesville	do	March 31	April 1							
Madison C. H.	Virginia	April 5	April 6							
Mossy Creek	do		March 15					April 20		
Poplar Grove	do								April 12	March 31
Knoxville	Tennessee		March 24							
Maysville	Kentucky			March 30						
Trenton	Missouri			April 13	April 6					
Belle Centre	Ohio		April 1		April 1				April 1	
Germantown	do		April 20							
Keene	do	April 3	April 14							
Poland	do					April 12				
Richmond	Indiana	March 27								
Athens	Illinois		March 13	March 21	March 16	April 13				
Waynesville	do								April 8	
West Northfield	do				April 10					
Ann Arbor	Michigan			April 15						
Brest	do	April 23								
Flint	do					April 18				
Romeo	do						April 25			
Washington	do		April 16							
Baraboo	Wisconsin	April 18								
Kaposia	Minnesota	April 28								
Pleasant Plain	Iowa				April 10					
Plum Spring	do					April 16				
Horton	Nova Scotia					May 15				
Leipsig	Saxony								March 20	

HOUSTONIA CÆRULEA.—*Bluets.—Innocence.*

Name of Station.		1851.	1852.	1853.	1854.	1855.	1856.	1857.	1858.	1859.
Brunswick	Maine							May 14	May 10	
Naples	do							May 30		
Francestown	New Hamp.			April 23						
Manchester	do		May 11		May 7					
Salmon Falls	do				May 2					
Somersworth	do				May 13					
Brattleborough	Vermont	April 7								
Stockbridge	do			May 1						
Mendon	Massachusetts				May 5					
North Attleborough	do		May 10		May 11					
Uxbridge	do				May 10					
Worcester	do							May 5		
Columbia	Connecticut							May 6	April 29	
East Windsor Hill	do		May 10	April 20						
Middletown	do		April 10	April 8	April 20					
Fishkill Landing	New York								April 12	
New Lebanon	do	May 18								
New York city	do				May 3					
North Salem	do	May 16								
Penn Yan	do							May 30		
Plattsburg	do	May 6	May 8							
Somerville	do	April 20								
Fleming Centre	Pennsylvania	May 12								
Gettysburg	do		May 1	April 20	April 18					
Hollidaysburg	do		May 2	April 28						
Mungersville	do							April 8		
Nazareth	do							May 10		
Philadelphia	do							April 12		
Reading	do	April 3								
Darby	do		April 21	April 10						
Sugar Grove	do	May 16								
Upper Darby	do	March 27	April 27	April 22	May 1					
Buffalo	Virginia					April 20				
Madison C. H	do	April 1	March 20							
Mossy Creek	do		May 1					May 20		
Chapel Hill	N. Carolina			Feb. 30				March 19		
All Saints	S. Carolina					April 5				
Black Oak	do		March 28							
Eutaw	Alabama		March 14							
Greensborough	do					April 1	March 20			
Jasper county	Mississippi						April 1			
Knoxville	Tennessee		May 1							
Nashville	do				April 15					
Cincinnati	Ohio			May 1						
Hiram	do							May 11	May 7	
Keene	do		May 20							
Marietta	do								March 29	March 15
Poland	do					April 12				
Brighton	Illinois								May 6	
Winnebago	do							May 15	April 19	
Wyandotte	Michigan								May 1	
Milwaukee	Wisconsin	May 5								
Fairfield	Iowa									May 1

HYPERICUM PERFORATUM.—*St. John's Wort.*

Name of Station.		1851.	1852.	1853.	1854.	1855.	1856.	1857.	1858.	1859.
Cornish	Maine							July 10		
Naples	do							July 26		
Londonderry	New Hamp.		July 10	June 20						
Manchester	do	July 11	July 8							
Salmon Falls	do				June					
Stockbridge	Vermont			June 25						
Uxbridge	Massachusetts				June 21					
Point Judith	Rhode Island				July 3					
Columbia	Connecticut							June 27	July 1	
East Windsor Hill	do		July 1							
Middletown	do			June 30						

HYPERICUM PERFORATUM.—*St. John's Wort*—Continued.

Name of Station.		1851.	1852.	1853.	1854.	1855.	1856.	1857.	1858.	1859.
New Lebanon	New York	June 4								
Nichols	do								June 28	July 6
North Salem	do	June 26	June 18							
Penn Yan	do							June 20		
Plattsburg	do	July 1								
Rochester	do			July 10				July 6	July 16	
Somerville	do	July 2								
Chester	Pennsylvania	June 5								
Gettysburg	do			July 1						
Hollidaysburg	do		Aug. 14							
Mercersburg	do		June 22							
Lima	do					July 24				
Mungersville	do							June 30		
Sugar Grove	do	July 6								
Upper Darby	do	June 30	June 15	June 25	June 20					
Hagerstown	Maryland		June 18	June 18						
Sykesville	do		July 8					June 30		
Clarke county	Virginia							June 22		
Madison C. H.	do	June 15								
Mossy Creek	do		Aug. 1							
Poplar Grove	do								July 10	
Cleveland	Ohio				July 2	July 3				
Athens	Illinois		July 12	July 15						
Wyandotte	Michigan								June 8	
Stanbridge	Canada							June 10	June 16	
Leipsig	Saxony								June 20	

IRIS TRICOLOR.—*Fleur de Lis.*

Name of Station.		1851.	1852.	1853.	1854.	1855.	1856.	1857.	1858.	1859.
Brunswick	Maine								June 22	
Salmon Falls	New Hamp.				June 3					

IRIS VERSICOLOR.—*Large Blue Flag.*

Name of Station.		1851.	1852.	1853.	1854.	1855.	1856.	1857.	1858.	1859.
Castine	Maine		June 29							
Cornish	do							June 11		
Gardiner	do							June 26		
Naples	do							June 14		
Londonderry	New Hamp.		June 16	June 8						
Manchester	do	June 26	June 12							
North Barnstead	do							June 6		
Salmon Falls	do				June 1					
Brattleborough	Vermont	May 30								
Stockbridge	do			June 4						
North Attleborough	Massachusetts		June 3		June 1	July 15				
Uxbridge	do				June 16					
Waltham	do				June 2					
Point Judith	Rhode Island				June 4					
Columbia	Connecticut							June 4	June 10	
East Windsor Hill	do		June 1							
Fairfield	do							May 20		
Middletown	do		June 6		June 4					
Ceres	New York	June 5								
Chatham	do	May 27	May 29							
Flatbush	do		May 25	May 24						
New Lebanon	do	May 26		June 3						
Nichols	do								June 16	
North Salem	do	June 3	June 5							
Ovid	do				June 10					
Plattsburg	do	June 8								
Rochester	do			June 5	May 1	June 3			June 10	
Sag Harbor	do		May 25							
Somerville	do	June 10								
West Point	do			June 9						

IRIS VERSICOLOR.—*Large Blue Flag*—Continued.

Name of Station.	1851.	1852.	1853.	1854.	1855.	1856.	1857.	1858.	1859.
Burlington .... New Jersey..		April 15							
Moorestown .... do.....					May 10				
Chester .... Pennsylvania..	May 16								
Fleming Centre .... do.....	May 28								
Freeport .... do.....			April 29						
Gettysburg .... do.....		April 28	May 6	May 8					
Hollidaysburg .... do.....		June 10							
Indiana .... do.....		May 4							
Lima .... do.....		May 24					June 2		
Meadville .... do.....	May 26	May 28							
Morrisville .... do.....						May 5			
Radnor .... do.....			June 17						
Darby .... do.....			May 11						
Sugar Grove .... do.....	June 23								
Upper Darby .... do.....	May 27	May 30	May 29						
Easton .... Maryland...				April 28					
Hagerstown .... do.....			May 8						
Sykesville .... do.....	May 6		May 6	May 20					
Clarke county .... Virginia....							April 15		
Crichton's Store .... do.....			March 30						
Genito .... do.....		May 15							
Madison C. H. .... do.....	April 20								
Mossy Creek .... do.....		May 10							
Poplar Grove .... do.....								May 22	May 12
Portsmouth .... do.....	April 15								
Rose Hill .... do.....						March 28			
Chapel Hill .... N. Carolina..			April 16						
All Saints .... S. Carolina..					April 22				
Camden .... do.....		March 28							
St. John's .... do.....	April 1								
Childersburg .... Alabama..								April 1	
Eutaw .... do.....		March 20							
Weewokaville .... do.....		March 28	April 1						
Jasper county .... Mississippi..					March 31	April 9			
New Wied .... Texas				March 20					
Glenwood .... Tennessee ..			April 12						
Knoxville .... do.....		April 15							
Lebanon .... do.....	April 11								
Hannibal .... Missouri...				May 4					
Ashtabula .... Ohio.....				June 10					
Belle Centre .... do.....		May 20							
Cincinnati .... do.....			May 3						
Savannah .... do.....							May 20		
Laconia .... Indiana...								May 1	
Athens .... Illinois ..		May 20	June 9	May 15					
Batavia .... do.....								April 22	
Brighton .... do.....							May 15	May 7	
West Northfield .... do.....				May 25					
Ann Arbor .... Michigan ..		June 4							
Flint .... do.....					May 27				
Wyandotte .... do.....								June 20	
Baraboo .... Wisconsin..	June 1								
Milwaukee .... do.....	May 28								
Kaposia .... Minnesota..	May 15								
Princeton .... do.....							June 15		
Dubuque .... Iowa	June 12								
Eagle .... do.....							June 14		
Fairfield .... do.....									May 2
Keokuk .... do.....						April 21			
Pleasant Plain .... do.....				May 25	April 28				
Horton .... Nova Scotia..					May 11				
Stanbridge .... Canada....							June 1		

JUGLANS NIGRA.—*Black Walnut.*

Name of Station.		1851.	1852.	1853.	1854.	1855.	1856.	1857.	1858.	1859.
Flatbush	New York			May 23						
Darby	Pennsylvania		May 25							
Fleming	do	May 24								
Freeport	do		May 27		May 17					
Lima	do		June 15	May 17						
Mercersburg	do		May 21							
North Whitehall	do							June 5		
Upper Darby	do			May 14						
Hagerstown	Maryland			May 25						
Sykesville	do			May 14						
Mossy Creek	Virginia		April 20							
Poplar Grove	do									May 12
Fulton	S. Carolina					April 21				
Eutaw	Alabama		May 3							
Weewokaville	do		April 6							
Cross Roads	Texas									March 15
New Wied	do			April 5						
Fairview	Kentucky									April 15
Maysville	do			May 16						
Belle Centre	Ohio		May 18							
Germantown	do		May 7							
Rockport	do									June 8
Laconia	Indiana									May 1
Athens	Illinois		May 20			May 15				
Augusta	do		May 10	May 20						

KALMIA LATIFOLIA.—*Mountain Laurel.*

Name of Station.		1851.	1852.	1853.	1854.	1855.	1856.	1857.	1858.	1859.
Gardiner	Maine							June 30		
Manchester	New Hamp	July 1	June 20		June 15					
Salmon Falls	do				June 12					
Brattleborough	Vermont	June 20								
Uxbridge	do				June 14					
Worcester	do							June 24		
Point Judith	Rhode Island				June 17					
Columbia	Connecticut							June 27	July 1	
East Windsor	do		June 16							
Middletown	do		June 18	June 6	June 8					
Chatham	New York		June 20							
New Lebanon	do	July 5								
Nichols	do									June 22
North Salem	do	June 13								
Spencertown	do					July 4				
West Point	do			June 2						
Freehold	New Jersey									June 1
Chester	Pennsylvania	May 15								
Easton	do				May 27					
Fleming	do							June 20		
Gettysburg	do				May 26					
Hollidaysburg	do		June 22	June 13						
Mercersburg	do		May 29							
Lancaster	do							June 10		
Lima	do			May 31	May 30	June 12	June 10	June 15		
Meadville	do	June 29								
Radnor	do				June 9		June 16	June 17	June 19	
Reading	do	June 1								
Somerset	do								June 25	
Sugar Grove	do	June 26								
Upper Darby	do		June 12	June 4	June 4					
Hagerstown	Maryland			June 1						
Sykesville	do	June 9								
Madison C. H.	Virginia	May 20	May 21							
Mossy Creek	do		May 20							
Poplar Grove	do								July 1	June 5
Chapel Hill	N. Carolina	April 23								
Aiken	S. Carolina			April 20						
Fulton	do					April 28				
Nashville	Tennessee				May 7					
Keene	Ohio	May 28								
Poland	do					June 3				

LAURUS BENZOIN.—*Spice Bush.*

Name of Station.	1851.	1852.	1853.	1854.	1855.	1856.	1857.	1858.	1859.
Gardiner........Maine							June 4		
Brattleborough........Vermont	May 20								
Newark........do							May 12		
Richmond........Massachusetts		May 1							
Waltham........do				May 5					
Columbia........Connecticut							May 18	April 28	
Chatham........New York	May 1								
New York city........do								May 10	
North Salem........do	April 9								
Ovid........do				May 2					
Rochester........do				May 2				April 25	
Spencertown........do					May 5				
Chester........Pennsylvania	April 3								
Easton........do				April 22					
Gettysburg........do		April 28	April 18	April 18					
Hollidaysburg........do		April 28	April 27						
Mercersburg........do		April 17							
Lancaster........do				April 5					
Lima........do		April 27	April 1	April 4	April 20		April 11		
Meadville........do	April 18								
Morrisville........do						April 10			
Mungersville........do							May 10		
Philadelphia........do								April 4	
Radnor........do			April 17		May 8			April 14	
Reading........do	April 7								
Darby........do		April 15	March 28						
Sugar Grove........do	April 11								
Upper Darby........do	April 5	April 17	April 10	April 9					
Hagerstown........Maryland			April 12	April 13					
Sykesville........do	April 9	April 23	April 6						
Buffalo........Virginia					April 16				
Crichton's Store........do			March 15					April 1	March 10
Genito........do		March 9							
Madison C. H.........do		March 20							
Mossy Creek........do		March 18							
Poplar Grove........do								April 2	March 20
Chapel Hill........N. Carolina			March 12					April 18	
St. John's........S. Carolina	March 10								
Weewokaville........Alabama		March 31	March 20						
New Wied........Texas	March 5	Feb. 1	Feb. 12	Feb. 2					
Belle Centre........Ohio		April 13		April 1				April 20	
Bowling Green........do								April 15	
Cincinnati........do			April 10						
Cleveland........do				April 20	April 23				
Hiram........do								April 15	
Hocking Port........do							May 15		
Keene........do	April 6								
Laconia........Indiana								March 31	
Athens........Illinois		April 1	April 10	March 21	April 20				
West Northfield........do				April 21					
Ann Arbor........Michigan			April 25						
Brest........do	April 23								
Wyandotte........do								April 27	

LEUCANTHEMUM VULGARE.—*Ox-eye Daisy.*

Name of Station.	1851.	1852.	1853.	1854.	1855.	1856.	1857.	1858.	1859.
Brunswick........Maine								June 30	
Castine........do							June 7		
Gardiner........do							June 5		
Naples........do							June 16		
Perry........do									June 25
Manchester........New Hamp.	June 12								
Salmon Falls........do				May 28					
West Enfield........do							June 25		
Castleton........Vermont				June 5					
Newark........do							May 15		

LEUCANTHEMUM VULGARE.—*Ox-eye Daisy*—Continued.

Name of Station.	1851.	1852.	1853.	1854.	1855.	1856.	1857.	1858.	1859.
Boston .... Massachusetts.		June 5							
Florida .... do							July 1	July 1	
North Attleborough .... do		June 1		June 5	June 6				
Uxbridge .... do				May 30					
Waltham .... do				June 1					
Worcester .... do							May 8		
Point Judith .... Rhode Island.				June 7					
Columbia .... Connecticut							June 4	June 10	
Middletown .... do				June 2					
Nichols .... New York								June 14	June 5
Ovid .... do				June 20					
Rochester .... do				June 10	June 8		June 23		
Spencertown .... do					June 10				
Lima .... Pennsylvania.		June 4							
Mungersville .... do							June 18		
Nazareth .... do							June 1		
Upper Darby .... do				May 21					
Sykesville .... Maryland							May 25		
Buffalo .... Virginia					May 31				
Clark county .... do							June 5	June 1	
Poplar Grove .... do								June 24	June 1
Cleveland .... Ohio					June 5				
Hiram .... do							July 26	June 23	
Marietta .... do								June 6	
Savannah .... do							June 2		
Laconia .... Indiana								May 1	
Wyandotte .... Michigan								June 20	
Princeton .... Minnesota							July 15		
Horton .... Nova Scotia					June 23				
Stanbridge .... Canada							June 4	June 20	
Leipsig .... Saxony								May 20	

LILIUM PHILADELPHICUM.—*Wild Lily.*

Name of Station.	1851.	1852.	1853.	1854.	1855.	1856.	1857.	1858.	1859.
Manchester .... New Hamp.	July 18	July 19							
Brattleborough .... Vermont	June 24								
Stockbridge .... do			June 26						
North Attleborough .. Massachusetts.		July 8							
East Windsor .... Connecticut.		July 5							
Chatham .... New York	July 1								
New Lebanon .... do			June 17						
North Salem .... do	June 26								
Penn Yan .... do							June 22		
Somerville .... do	June 24								
West Point .... do		June 9	June 20						
Burlington .... New Jersey		July 15							
Chester .... Pennsylvania.	June 10								
Hollidaysburg .... do		June 15	June 10						
Meadville .... do	July 4	July 4							
Reading .... do	June 29								
Sugar Grove .... do	July 5								
Upper Darby .... do		July 25							
Trenton .... Missouri		June 18	June 20	June 7					
Athens .... Illinois		June 29	June 18						
Augusta .... do	June 22								
Ann Arbor .... Michigan		July 10							
Milwaukee .... Wisconsin	July 1								
Lac qui Parle .... Minnesota			June 27	June 26					

LINNÆA BOREALIS.—*Twin Flower.*

Name of Station.		1851.	1852.	1853.	1854.	1855.	1856.	1857.	1858.	1859.
Brunswick	Maine								July 3	
Gardiner	do							Aug. 7		
Naples	do							June 18		
Manchester	New Hamp	June 11								
Brattleborough	Vermont	June 1								
Castleton	do				May 10					
Radnor	Pennsylvania							June 2		
Wyandotte	Michigan								May 30	
Horton	Nova Scotia					June 11				

LIRIODENDRON TULIPIFERA.—*Tulip Tree.—American Poplar.*

Name of Station.		1851.	1852.	1853.	1854.	1855.	1856.	1857.	1858.	1859.
Steuben	Maine			May 15						
Londonderry	New Hamp			April 13						
Stratford	do								May 4	
Castleton	Vermont				May 20					
North Attleborough	Massachusetts				June 15	June 23				
Worcester	do							May 9		
Columbia	Connecticut							June 16	July 1	
East Windsor	do		June 15							
Middletown	do			June 5	June 16					
Ceres	New York	June 22								
Chatham	do	June 13	June 12							
Flatbush	do		June 20	June 1	June 9					
Penn Yan	do							May 30		
Rochester	do		June 16		June 16	June 25		July 4	June 18	
West Point	do			June 6						
Burlington	New Jersey		June 5							
Chester	Pennsylvania	May 15								
Fleming Centre	do							June 20		
Freeport	do				June 6					
Gettysburg	do		June 4							
Lancaster	do				May 22					
Lima	do			May 25	May 22	June 4		June 10		
Meadville	do	June 6	June 12							
Radnor	do		June 5	May 21	June 6			June 10	June 4	
Darby	do		May 31	May 20						
Sugar Grove	do	May 25								
Upper Darby	do	May 24	June 1	May 23	May 26					
Sykesville	Maryland	May 23	May 26	May 26	May 25			June 15		
Buffalo	Virginia					May 8				
Clark county	do								May 28	
Crichton's Store	do			May 1				May 14	May 1	April 27
Diamond Grove	do	May 10								
Genito	do		April 30							
Kanawha Salines	do								May 20	
Madison C. H	do		May 15							
Mossy Creek	do		May 20					June 20		
Poplar Grove	do								June 12	May 19
Portsmouth	do		May 9							
Rose Hill	do						May 16	May 26		May 14
Chapel Hill	N. Carolina			May 1					April 25	
All Saints	S. Carolina					April 26				
Black Oak	do		April 8							
Camden	do		March 11							
Fulton	do					April 24				
St. John's	do	April 8								
Greensborough	Alabama						April 20	April 6	April 30	
Weewokaville	do		April 1	April 20						
Glenwood	Tennessee			April 29						
Knoxville	do		May 10							
Lebanon	do	May 9								
Nashville	do				April 25					
Ashtabula	Ohio				June 3					
Cleveland	do				June 8					
Germantown	do				May 25					

LIRIODENDRON TULIPIFERA.—*Tulip Tree.—American Poplar*—Continued.

NAME OF STATION.	1851.	1852.	1853	1854.	1855.	1856.	1857.	1858.	1859.
Hiram .... Ohio							June 20		
Keene .... do	May 26								
Madison .... do							June 25		
Mount Healthy .... do					June 10				
Poland .... do					June 4				
Wyandotte .... Michigan								June 10	
Princeton .... Minnesota							May 30		
Stanbridge .... Canada								June 12	
Leipsig .... Saxony								June 20	

LOBELIA CARDINALIS.—*Cardinal Flower.*

NAME OF STATION.	1851.	1852.	1853	1854.	1855.	1856.	1857.	1858.	1859.
Gardiner .... Maine							Aug. 26		
Naples .... do							July 28		
Point Judith .... Rhode Island				Aug. 12					
Ceres .... New York	Aug. 1								
Chatham .... do	July 28								
Fishkill Landing .... do								Aug. 2	
North Salem .... do	Aug. 1								
Penn Yan .... do							July 14		
Chester .... Pennsylvania	July 20								
Lima .... do		Aug. 20							
Meadville .... do	July 15	July 18							
Sugar Grove .... do	Aug. 3								
Upper Darby .... do		Aug. 2							
Madison C. H .... Virginia	July 12								
Mossy Creek .... do		Aug. 1							
Rose Hill .... do						Aug. 10			
All Saints .... S. Carolina					Aug. 1				
New Wied .... Texas		Aug. 25	Aug. 12						
Belle Centre .... Ohio		July 20							
Poland .... do					June 2				
Athens .... Illinois		Sept. 1							
Augusta .... do	Aug. 20								
West Northfield .... do				July 22					
Flint .... Michigan					Aug. 10				
Romeo .... do						July 25			
Wyandotte .... do								July 15	

LONICERA SEMPERVIRENS.—*Trumpet Honeysuckle.*

NAME OF STATION.	1851.	1852.	1853	1854.	1855.	1856.	1857.	1858.	1859.
Steuben .... Maine	July 15								
Chatham .... New York	June 2								
New Lebanon .... do			June 13						
Penn Yan .... do							May 30		
Plattsburg .... do		June 23							
West Point .... do			May 26						
Ceres .... Pennsylvania		June 14							
Gettysburg .... do			May 9	May 8					
Lima .... do			May 5						
Meadville .... do	May 23	June 4							
Radnor .... do		June 1	May 22	May 26			May 24	June 9	
Darby .... do			May 12						
Sugar Grove .... do	June 14								
Sykesville .... Maryland	May 12	May 20							
Mossy Creek .... Virginia		May 15							
Aiken .... S. Carolina			April 2						
St. John's .... do	April 1								
Lebanon .... Tennessee	April 30								
Belle Centre .... Ohio		June 10							
Keene .... do	June 20								
Marietta .... do								May 8	
Muscatine .... Iowa			June 8						

LONICERA TARTARICA.—*Foreign Spurs.*

Name of Station.	1851.	1852.	1853.	1854.	1855.	1856.	1857.	1858.	1859.
Brunswick ... Maine								June 16	
Castine ... do		June 20							
Uxbridge ... Massachusetts				May 27					
Ovid ... New York				June 5					
Penn Yan ... do							June 8		
Rochester ... do			May 20	May 15	May 22		May 27	May 26	
Chester ... Pennsylvania	April 30								
Lima ... do		May 11	May 1	May 4	May 12	May 21	May 16		
Upper Darby ... do				May 7					
Hagerstown ... Maryland			May 1						
Mossy Creek ... Virginia							May 25		
Cleveland ... Ohio				May 14	May 11				
West Northfield ... Illinois				May 8					
Leipsig ... Saxony								May 2	

LUPINUS PERENNIS.—*Lupine.*

Name of Station.	1851.	1852.	1853.	1854.	1855.	1856.	1857.	1858.	1859.
Londonderry ... New Hamp			June 1						
Manchester ... do		May 29							
Burlington ... do			May 28						
Boston ... Massachusetts	May 3	June 6							
North Attleborough ... do		July 2							
Uxbridge ... do				May 27					
East Windsor ... Connecticut		June 7							
Chatham ... New York	June 7								
Rochester ... do		May 20	May 20	June 4	May 18		June 8	May 25	
Burlington ... New Jersey		June 5							
Mercersburg ... Pennsylvania		May 26							
Upper Darby ... do		May 16	May 16						
Madison C. H ... Virginia	May 1								
Mossy Creek ... do		May 5					May 20		
All Saints ... S. Carolina					April 5				
Black Oak ... do		March 30							
St. John's ... do	April 6								
Alligator ... Florida								April 20	
New Wied ... Texas	March 25		April 1						
Union Hill ... do							March 5		
Poland ... Ohio					May 14				
Ann Arbor ... Michigan			May 6						
Flint ... do					May 20				
Romeo ... do						June 10			
Wyandotte ... do								June 6	
Horton ... Nova Scotia					June 11				

MAGNOLIA GLAUCA.—*Sweet Bay.—Laurel Magnolia.*

Name of Station.	1851.	1852.	1853.	1854.	1855.	1856.	1857.	1858.	1859.
North Attleborough . Massachusetts					June 5				
Easton ... Maryland				May 17					
Crichton's Store ... Virginia									May 20
Madison C. H ... do		June 8							
Mossy Creek ... do		May 20							
Portsmouth ... do		April 30				May 10			
All Saints ... S. Carolina					April 17				
Camden ... do		May 1							
Fulton ... do					May 1				
St. John's ... do	April 20								
Alligator ... do								March 15	
Eutaw ... Alabama		May 24							
Greensborough ... do						May 20	May 9	May 1	
Columbus ... Mississippi							May 8	April 20	
Lebanon ... Tennessee	May 18								
West Northfield ... Illinois				June 19					

MITCHELLA REPENS.—*Partridge Berry.*

NAME OF STATION.	1851.	1852.	1853.	1854.	1855.	1856.	1857.	1858.	1859.
Castine ..... Maine							July 12		
Naples ..... do							July 8		
Manchester ..... New Hamp.	June 26								
Salmon Falls ..... do				June 24					
Florida ..... Massachusetts							May 25		
Ovid ..... do				June 16					
Lima ..... New York		June 17							
Reading ..... do	June 16								
All Saints ..... S Carolina					May 3				
Alligator ..... Florida								April 3	
Poland ..... Ohio					May 14				

MITELLA DIPHYLLA.—*Currant Leaf.*

NAME OF STATION.	1851.	1852.	1853.	1854.	1855.	1856.	1857.	1858.	1859.
Stockbridge ..... Vermont			May 16						
Chatham ..... New York		May 25							
New Lebanon ..... do		May 7	May 10						
North Salem ..... do	April 25	May 5							
Penn Yan ..... do							May 2		
Plattsburg ..... do		May 10							
Rochester ..... do			May 15						
Somerville ..... do	April 30								
Fleming Centre ..... Pennsylvania	May 17						July 4		
Hollidaysburg ..... do			April 28						
Mercersburg ..... do		May 6							
Lima ..... do		May 24	May 15						
Meadville ..... do		May 15							
Reading ..... do	April 22								
Upper Darby ..... do		May 15							
Mossy Creek ..... Virginia		May 10							

MORUS RUBRA.—*Red Mulberry.*

NAME OF STATION.	1851.	1852.	1853.	1854.	1855.	1856.	1857.	1858.	1859.
Columbia ..... Connecticut							Aug. 9		
Burlington ..... New Jersey		July 25							
Darby ..... Pennsylvania			May 9						
Fleming ..... do	May 16								
Freeport ..... do		May 21	May 10	June 4					
Meadville ..... do		May 30							
Upper Darby ..... do		May 20	May 16	May 15					
Hagerstown ..... Maryland			May 10						
Sykesville ..... do		May 14							
Buffalo ..... Virginia					May 2				
Clark county ..... do							May 25	May 20	
Crichton's Store ..... do			April 20				May 10		April 5
Genito ..... do		May 1							
Kanawha Salines ..... do								April 20	
Poplar Grove ..... do								May 20	May 10
Rose Hill ..... do						June 25			
Chapel Hill ..... N. Carolina			April 28						
Camden ..... S. Carolina		April 12							
Fulton ..... do					April 20				
Alligator ..... Florida								March 3	
Childersburg ..... Alabama								March 30	
Greensborough ..... do						April 4	March 22	March 30	
Weewokaville ..... do		March 28	April 2						
New Wied ..... Texas			March 30	March 5					
Maysville ..... Kentucky			May 20						
Belle Centre ..... Ohio		May 17		May 24					
Cincinnati ..... do			May 2						
Germantown ..... do		May 14	May 14						
Mount Healthy ..... do				May 1					
Poland ..... do					May 26				

MORUS RUBRA.—*Red Mulberry*—Continued.

Name of Station.	1851.	1852.	1853.	1854.	1855.	1856.	1857.	1858.	1859.
Indianapolis .... Indiana									May 8
Laconia .... do								May 1	
Athens .... Illinois		May 15							
Brighton .... do							June 1		
Fairfield .... Iowa									May 20

NUPHAR ADVENA.—*Yellow Pond Lily.*

Name of Station.	1851.	1852.	1853.	1854.	1855.	1856.	1857.	1858.	1859.
Castine .... Maine		July 20							
Londonderry .... New Hamp.		June 8							
Manchester .... do	June 14	June 1							
Salmon Falls .... do				May 28					
North Attleborough .. Massachusetts.		June 6							
East Windsor .... Connecticut		June 7							
New Lebanon .... New York	June 12								
North Salem .... do	June 12								
Penn Yan .... do							June 15		
Plattsburg .... do	June 24								
Rochester .... do			June 8						
Somerville .... do	June 16								
Chester .... Pennsylvania.	May 15								
Gettysburg .... do		May 10							
Hollidaysburg .... do		June 1							
Meadville .... do	May 10								
Darby .... do		May 20							
Sugar Grove .... do	June 26								
Upper Darby .... do		May 18	May 16						
Mossy Creek .... do		May 15							
All Saints .... S. Carolina					April 20				
St. John's .... do	April 20								
Belle Centre .... Ohio		May 1							
Brest .... Michigan	July 28								
Milwaukee .... Wisconsin	May 31								
Fort Ripley .... Minnesota		June 27							

NYMPHÆA ODORATA.—*White Pond Lily.*

Name of Station.	1851.	1852.	1853.	1854.	1855.	1856.	1857.	1858.	1859.
Castine .... Maine		July 20							
Gardiner .... do							July 31		
Naples .... do							July 12		
Perry .... do									July 8
Londonderry .... New Hamp.		July 10	June 17						
Manchester .... do	July 26	July 10							
Salmon Falls .... do				June 25					
Stockbridge .... Vermont			June 25						
Boston .... Massachusetts.		July 5							
Florida .... do							July 8		
North Attleborough .... do		June 22		June 16	June 22				
Uxbridge .... do				June 11					
Worcester .... do							July 10		
Columbia .... Connecticut							July 18	June 20	
Lake .... New York									June 22
New Lebanon .... do	June 20								
North Salem .... do	Aug. 21								
Penn Yan .... do							June 15		
Plattsburg .... do	July 3								
Rochester .... do			June 15		June 25		July 10		
Somerville .... do	June 24								
Ceres .... Pennsylvania		June 26							
All Saints .... S. Carolina					April 15				
Black Oak .... do		April 25							
St. John's .... do	April 25								
Columbus .... Mississippi							May 1		
Belle Centre .... Ohio		June 20							

NYMPHÆA ODORATA.—*White Pond Lily*—Continued.

Name of Station.		1851.	1852.	1853.	1854.	1855.	1856.	1857.	1858.	1859.
West Northfield	Illinois				June 2					
Wyandotte	Michigan								June 4	
Milwaukee	Wisconsin	June 21								
Fort Ripley	Minnesota		June 27							

OXALIS VIOLACEA.—*Violet Wood Sorrel.*

Name of Station.		1851.	1852.	1853.	1854.	1855.	1856.	1857.	1858.	1859.
Darby	Pennsylvania		May 25							
Hollidaysburg	do		June 2							
Meadville	do		June 1							
Mercersburg	do		May 21							
Murrysville	do							May 23		
Upper Darby	do		May 12	May 6						
Madison C. H	Virginia		May 15							
Mossy Creek	do		May 15							
Chapel Hill	N. Carolina			April 17						
Camden	S. Carolina		May 1							
Eutaw	Alabama		March 1							
Weewokaville	do		Feb. 24	March 20						
New Wied	Texas			April 5						
Glenwood	Tennessee			April 20						
Knoxville	do		April 20							
Trenton	Missouri			April 30						
Germantown	Ohio		May 11							
Athens	Illinois		April 25			April 17				
Augusta	do		May 1							

PERSICA VULGARIS.—*Peach.*

Name of Station.		1851.	1852.	1853.	1854.	1855.	1856.	1857.	1858.	1859.
Cornish	Maine						June 1			
Naples	do							May 24		
Francestown	New Hamp.			May 7						
Londonderry	do		May 17	May 1						
Manchester	do		May 10		May 12					
Salmon Falls	do				May 20					
Brattleborough	Vermont	May 6								
Burlington	do			May 16						
West Rupert	do						May 12			
Boston	Massachusetts		May 12							
Bridgewater	do							May 10		
Cambridge	do						May 22			
Florida	do								May 25	
Mendon	do				May 8					
North Attleborough	do		May 10		May 9	May 7				
Uxbridge	do				May 9					
Worcester	do						May 13	May 14		
Point Judith	do				May 10					
Columbia	Connecticut							May 17	May 8	
East Windsor	do			April 25						
Fairfield	do							May 24		
Georgetown	do						May 15			
Middletown	do		April 30	May 8	May 7					
Norwich	do							May 10		
Preston	do						May 24			
Baldwinsville	New York	May 11	May 14				May 19	May 28		
Ceres	do	May 14								
Chatham	do	May 5	May 16							
Eden	do							May 24		
Fishkill Landing	do							May 10	April 24	April 24
Flatbush	do		May 7	April 21	May 3	May 6		May 9		
Lake	do						May 18			
New Lebanon	do	May 10		May 8						
New York city	do				May 3	May 7			April 25	
Nichols	do								May 7	

PERSICA VULGARIS.—*Peach*—Continued.

NAME OF STATION.	1851.	1852.	1853.	1854.	1855.	1856.	1857.	1858.	1859.
North Salem, New York	April 10	May 2			May 2	May 10			
Ovid, do				May 6		May 16	May 25		
Penn Yan, do							May 27		
Rochester, do	May 1	May 8	May 5	May 10			May 20	May 6	
Sag Harbor, do	April 29	May 10							
Waterloo, do		May 13							
Wellsville, do								April 15	
West Point, do		May 8	April 27						
Williamsville, do				May 10					
White Plains, do					May 1				
Burlington, New Jersey		May 1							
Newark, do	April 15	May 3							
Readington, do							May 12	May 4	
Sergeantsville, do							May 9		
Bellefonte, Pennsylvania								May 15	
Ceres, do		May 30							
Chester, do	April 4								
Easton, do		May 4		May 1					
Freeport, do		May 5		April 24					
Gettysburg, do		April 30	April 10	April 16		April 28			
Hollidaysburg, do		May 4	April 20						
Mercersburg, do		April 27							
Huntingdon, do						May 12	May 5		
Indiana, do		May 3							
Lancaster, do				April 10			May 1		
Lima, do		April 30	April 8	April 8	April 25	April 28	May 2		
Meadville, do	April 15	May 7				May 6			
Nazareth, do						May 12	May 10		
North Whitehall, do							May 9	April 22	
Orwigsburg, do		May 3							
Philadelphia, do								April 10	
Radnor, do				April 22			May 8		
Reading, do	April 9								
Darby, do		April 29	April 10						
Somerset, do								April 28	
Sugar Grove, do	April 27								
Upper Darby, do	April 5	May 6	April 15	April 13					
Hagerstown, Maryland		April 25	April 10						
Ridge, do						April 18			
Spencerville, do							April 21		
Sykesville, do	April 1	April 20	April 9	April 5			April 25		
Buffalo, Virginia					April 18	April 26			
Clark county, do							April 26	April 3	
Crichton's Store, do			March 13			April 13	April 15	March 28	March 9
Doddridge county, do						April 29			
Genito, do		March 10							
Kanawha Salines, do								March 23	
Madison C. H., do		March 17							
Mossy Creek, do		April 1					April 30		
Mount Solon, do						April 26			
Plains, do									March 23
Poplar Grove, do							April 3	April 3	March 23
Portsmouth, do		March 18				April 9			
Rose Hill, do						April 14	March 25	March 26	March 12
Smithfield, do		March 9							
Wardensville, do						April 26			
Winchester, do						April 25			
Chapel Hill, N. Carolina	Feb. 27		Feb. 28					March 15	
Gaston, do						March 19			
Green Plains, do							March 15		
Aiken, S. Carolina						March 16			
All Saints, do					Feb. 25				
Black Oak, do		Feb. 25							
Camden, do		Feb. 26				March 20			
Fulton, do					March 12	March 24			
Georgetown, do						March 16			
Savannah, Georgia						Feb. 10			
Sparta, do						March 28	March 17		
Varnell's Station, do									Feb. 28

PERSICA VULGARIS.—*Peach*—Continued.

NAME OF STATION.	1851.	1852.	1853.	1854.	1855.	1856.	1857.	1858.	1859.
Zebulon .... Georgia							Feb. 26		
Alligator .... Florida							Feb. 12	Feb. 10	
Knox Hill .... do		Feb. 6							
Seville .... do									Feb. 3
Carlowville .... Alabama							Feb. 27	March 13	
Childersburg .... do							Feb. 27	March 12	
Eutaw .... do		Feb. 20							
Greensborough .... do						March 25	Feb. 19	Feb. 18	
Weewokaville .... do		Feb. 27	Feb. 25						
Columbus .... Mississippi						March 27	Feb. 24	March 15	
Jasper county .... do					March 6	March 16			
Oktibbeha county .... do							Feb. 28		
Oxford .... do						March 25			
Big Pond .... Louisiana						Feb. 15			
Trinity .... do						Feb. 10	Feb. 5	Feb. 10	
Cross Roads .... Texas									March 5
New Wied .... do	Feb. 28	Feb. 15	March 1	Feb. 8					
Union Hill .... do							Feb. 15		
Glenwood .... Tennessee			March 19						
Knoxville .... do		March 13							
Lebanon .... do	March 16								
Nashville .... do				April 1					
Walnut Grove .... do						May 2			
Fair View .... Kentucky									March 18
Maysville .... do			April 10						
Hannibal .... Missouri				April 8					
St. Louis .... do						April 21			
Trenton .... do			April 23	April 16					
Ashtabula .... Ohio				April 23					
Belle Centre .... do		May 5		April 12				April 15	
Bowling Green .... do								May 20	
Cheviot .... do						April 27			
Cincinnati .... do			April 10						
Cleveland .... do				April 23	April 27				
Edinburg .... do							May 16		
Germantown .... do			April 17	April 7		April 30			
Hamilton .... do							May 2		
Hiram .... do							May 13	April 24	
Keene .... do	April 30	May 2							
Madison .... do							May 21		
Marietta .... do								April 5	March 23
Mount Healthy .... do				April 10	April 20				
Poland .... do					April 21				
Ripley .... do							April 25		
Rockport .... do									April 13
Savannah .... do							May 9		
Welchfield .... do							April 24		
Indianapolis .... Indiana									April 1
Laconia .... do								March 27	March 24
New Albany .... do						April 22	April 17		
Richmond .... do	March 23								
Athens .... Illinois		April 29	April 16	April 13	April 19				
Augusta .... do	May 5	May 1	April 20	May 14	April 20		May 14		
Batavia .... do								May 8	
Brighton .... do							May 1	April 1	
Manchester .... do							May 11	April 19	April 11
Pekin .... do								May 10	
Warsaw .... do						May 1	May 16		
West Northfield .... do				May 4					
West Salem .... do							April 27	April 1	
Ann Arbor .... Michigan		May 22							
Brest .... do	April 23								
Cooper .... do						May 14			
Grand Rapids .... do						May 7			
Washington .... do		May 12							
Wyandotte .... do								May 9	May 3
Greenfield .... Wisconsin									May 12
Milwaukee .... do	April 26								
Dubuque .... Iowa	May 10								

PERSICA VULGARIS.—*Peach*—Continued.

Name of Station.	1851.	1852.	1853.	1854.	1855.	1856.	1857.	1858.	1859.
Fairbanks .... Iowa						May 9			
Fairfield .... do									May 2
Fort Madison .... do	April 26		April 20	April 19					
Muscatine .... do		May 10	April 30	April 22	May 1				
Pleasant Plain .... do				April 20	May 7				
Sacramento .... California						March 1			
Salem Prairie .... Oregon						March 26			
Leipsig .... Saxony								March 3	

PODOPHYLLUM PELTATUM.—*Mandrake.*

Name of Station.	1851.	1852.	1853.	1854.	1855.	1856.	1857.	1858.	1859.
Ovid .... New York				May 14					
Penn Yan .... do							May 20		
Rochester .... do			May 30	May 25				April 26	
Darby .... Pennsylvania		May 14	May 9						
Easton .... do				May 15					
Fleming .... do	May 24						May 28		
Freeport .... do		May 21							
Gettysburg .... do		May 10		May 11					
Hollidaysburg .... do		May 20	May 7						
Lancaster .... do				May 10					
Lima .... do		May 13	May 7				May 15		
Meadville .... do		May 25							
Middletown .... do							May 25		
Murrysville .... do							May 23		
Upper Darby .... do		May 14	May 10	May 10					
Hagerstown .... Maryland		May 5	May 5						
Buffalo .... Virginia					May 2				
Clark county .... do							May 15		
Crichton's Store .... do									April 10
Genito .... do		April 16							
Kanawha Salines .... do								April 18	
Mossy Creek .... do		May 4							
Poplar Grove .... do								May 2	May 4
Chapel Hill .... N. Carolina			April 13						
All Saints .... S. Carolina					March 21				
Alligator .... Florida								Feb. 20	
Childersburg .... Alabama								March 25	
Eutaw .... do		March 12							
Greensborough .... do						April 5	March 24	March 24	
Weewokaville .... do		March 3	April 1						
Glenwood .... Tennessee			April 21						
Knoxville .... do		April 28							
Maysville .... Kentucky			April 18						
Ashtabula .... Ohio				May 27					
Belle Centre .... do		April 27		May 12				May 8	
Bowling Green .... do								May 18	
Mount Healthy .... do				May 12					
Poland .... do					May 15				
Laconia .... Indiana								April 24	
Athens .... Illinois		May 7		May 5	May 6				
Augusta .... do		May 10	May 5	May 10			May 25		
Brighton .... do							May 9	May 3	
Edgington .... do							May 5		
Marengo .... do								May 15	
Pekin .... do								May 20	
West Salem .... do							May 18		
Ann Arbor .... Michigan			May 22						
Flint .... do					May 18				
Wyandotte .... do								May 27	
Fairfield .... Iowa									May 23

POGONIA OPHIOGLOSSOIDES.—*Adder's Tongue.*

Name of Station.	1851.	1852.	1853.	1854.	1855.	1856.	1857.	1858.	1859.
Brunswick ... Maine								July 5	
West Enfield ... New Hamp.							May 10		
Brattleborough ... Vermont	July 6								
Burlington ... do			May 16						
Castleton ... do				May 1					
Florida ... Massachusetts							May 15	May 10	
Richmond ... do		May 10							
Ceres ... New York	July 1								
Chatham ... do	May 1								
Nichols ... do								May 10	
Penn Yan ... do							June 14		
Sugar Grove ... Pennsylvania	June 26								
Upper Darby ... do	June 25								
All Saints ... S. Carolina					May 20				
Pekin ... Illinois								May 5	
Stanbridge ... Canada							May 1		

PONTEDERIA CORDATA.—*Pickerel Weed.*

Name of Station.	1851.	1852.	1853.	1854.	1855.	1856.	1857.	1858.	1859.
Brunswick ... Maine							Aug. 12		
North Attleborough .. Massachusetts				July 5	July 10				
North Salem ... New York	July 15								
Chester ... Pennsylvania	July 1								
Lancaster ... do				July 1					
All Saints ... S. Carolina					May 25				
Black Oak ... do		May 5							
St. John's ... do	April 28								
Trenton ... Missouri		June 29							
Milwaukee ... Wisconsin	July 8								
Princeton ... Minnesota							June 25		

PRUNUS DOMESTICA.—*Plum.*

Name of Station.	1851.	1852.	1853.	1854.	1855.	1856.	1857.	1858.	1859.
Carmel ... Maine						May 30			
Cornish ... do							May 26		
Perry ... do						June 6			
Concord ... New Hamp.						May 18			
Salmon Falls ... do				May 14					
Stratford ... do						May 24			
Brandon ... Vermont						May 18			
Craftsbury ... do						May 26	June 3		
Newark ... do						May 28			
Stanbridge ... do						May 20			
Shelburne ... do						May 21			
Bridgewater ... Massachusetts							May 17		
New Ashford ... do		May 9				May 20			
Westfield ... do						May 12			
Worcester ... do						May 14			
Georgetown ... Connecticut						May 13			
Hartford ... do	May 9								
Clinton ... New York							May 26		
Eden ... do						May 18	May 26		
Flatbush ... do							May 10		
Lake, Washington county .. do						May 20			
Lowville ... do						May 31	May 3	May 22	
Mexico ... do						May 15			
New Lebanon ... do		May 10							
New York city ... do							May 13		
Ogdensburg ... do		May 18							
Ovid ... do						May 14	May 23		
Spencertown ... do						May 19			
Readington ... New Jersey							May 14	May 8	May 5
Sergeantsville ... do							May 10		
Bellefonte ... Pennsylvania								May 12	
Huntington ... do						May 9			
Lancaster ... do							April 29		

PRUNUS DOMESTICA.—*Plum*—Continued.

Name of Station.	1851.	1852.	1853.	1854.	1855.	1856.	1857.	1858.	1859.
Lima ... Pennsylvania		May 5	April 17	April 14	May 1				
Meadville ... do						May 20			
Morrisville ... do						May 7			
Nazareth ... do						May 6			
North Whitehall ... do								April 29	
Radnor ... do			April 23		May 1	May 4	May 8	April 24	
Reading ... do	April 9								
Frederick ... Maryland							April 28		
Spencerville ... do							April 26		
Buffalo ... Virginia						April 29			
Crack Whip ... do							May 5		
Crichton's Store ... do						April 14			
Doddridge county ... do						April 25			
Mount Solon ... do						April 26			
Poplar Grove ... do							May 6	April 6	
Wardensville ... do						April 28			
Winchester ... do						April 23			
Wirt C. H ... do						May 1			
Gaston ... N. Carolina						March 10			
Aiken ... S. Carolina						March 30			
Camden ... do						March 27			
Fulton ... do					Feb. 25	March 18			
Savannah ... Georgia						Jan. 31			
Sparta ... do						March 24	March 22		
Varnell's Station ... do									March 20
Zebulon ... do							Feb. 25		
Alligator ... Florida							Feb. 6		
Cedar Keys ... do						March 1			
Seville ... do									Feb. 22
Carlowville ... Alabama							Feb. 21	March 3	
Greensborough ... do						March 20			
Columbus ... Mississippi						March 20			
Oxford ... do						March 31			
Big Pond ... Louisiana						Feb. 14			
Trinity ... do								Feb. 16	
Cross Roads ... Texas									March 5
Goliad ... do								Jan. 31	
Fairview ... Kentucky									March 10
St Louis ... Missouri						April 20			
Edinburg ... Ohio							May 22		
Hiram ... do						May 13	May 22		
Jefferson ... do						May 17			
Troy ... do									May 1
Welchfield ... do							May 25		
Laconia ... Indiana									March 29
New Albany ... do						April 23	April 24		
New Harmony ... do						April 10			
Athens ... Illinois						April 27			
Marengo ... do						May 16			
Ottawa ... do								April 29	
Riley ... do						May 15			
Warsaw ... do						April 28	May 18	April 10	
West Salem ... do						April 24	May 9	April 10	
Winnebago ... do									May 7
Cooper ... Michigan						May 12			
Grand Rapids ... do						May 10			
St. James ... do						May 24			
Wyandotte ... do								May 6	May 5
Appleton ... Wisconsin						May 18			
Greenfield ... do									May 9
Norway ... do						May 2			
Platteville ... do						May 17			
Madison ... do						May 7	May 13		
Fairbanks ... Iowa						May 15			
Fort Madison ... do						April 29			
Muscatine ... do			May 3	April 24		May 12			
Pleasant Plain ... do						May 6			
Salem Prairie ... Oregon						April 14			
Horton ... Nova Scotia							May 28		
Windsor ... do							May 28		

PYRUS COMMUNIS.—*Pear.*

Name of Station.	1851.	1852.	1853.	1854.	1855.	1856.	1857.	1858.	1859.
Castine ... Maine		June 1							
Cornish ... do.							June 5		
Gardiner ... do.							May 28		
Naples ... do.							May 30		
Perry ... do.									June 10
Steuben ... do.		May 25				June 15			
Concord ... New Hamp.						May 19			
Londonderry ... do.		May 22	May 15						
Manchester ... do.		May 15							
West Enfield ... do.							June 4		
Brandon ... Vermont							May 26	May 26	
Burlington ... do.			May 19						
Brattleborough ... do.	May 14								
Castleton ... do.				May 20					
Shelburne ... do.						May 21			
West Rupert ... do.						May 24			
Bridgewater ... Massachusetts.							May 17		
Cambridge ... do.						May 22			
Florida ... do.							June 1	June 1	
Mendon ... do.				May 14					
New Ashford ... do.		May 9				May 26			
North Attleborough ... do.				May 13	May 16				
Uxbridge ... do.				May 12					
Waltham ... do.				May 10					
Richmond ... do.		May 25							
Westfield ... do.						May 13			
Worcester ... do.						May 19	May 20		
Columbia ... Connecticut.							May 14	May 18	
Fairfield ... do.							May 23		
Georgetown ... do.						May 17			
Middletown ... do.		May 15	May 11	May 13					
Norwich ... do.							May 24		
Preston ... do.						May 19			
Ceres ... New York.	May 10								
Chatham ... do.	May 12								
Clinton ... do.							June 3		
Eden ... do.						May 18	May 27		
Fishkill Landing ... do.							May 10	May 7	April 26
Flatbush ... do.		May 5	April 19	May 4	May 12		May 12		
Geneva ... do.						May 19			
Lake ... do.						May 19	May 28	May 30	May 20
Lowville ... do.						May 29			
Mexico ... do.						May 16			
New Lebanon ... do.	May 8		May 12						
New York city ... do.				May 3	May 4		May 12	May 8	
North Salem ... do.	May 10	May 15							
Ovid ... do.				May 10		May 15	May 30		
Penn Yan ... do.							June 1		
Rochester ... do.		June 4	May 7	May 11	May 10	May 15	May 23	May 7	
Sag Harbor ... do.	May 10	May 22							
Spencertown ... do.					May 15	May 19			
Waterloo ... do.		May 14							
Wellsville ... do.							April 10		
West Concord ... do.						May 24			
West Point ... do.			May 1						
Burlington ... New Jersey.		May 10							
Moorestown ... do.					April 20				
Newark ... do.	April 25	May 7							
Readington ... do.							May 16	May 5	May 2
Sergeantsville ... do.							May 13		
Bellefonte ... Pennsylvania.								May 28	
Chester ... do.	April 19								
Easton ... do.				May 1					
Gettysburg ... do.		May 1	May 2	April 20		April 28			
Hollidaysburg ... do.		May 7	April 29						
Huntington ... do.						May 7			
Indiana ... do.		May 4							
Lancaster ... do.				April 23			May 4		
Lima ... do.		May 7	April 28		May 1	May 1	May 4		
Meadville ... do.	April 26	May 12							

PYRUS COMMUNIS.—*Pear*—Continued.

Name of Station.	1851.	1852.	1853.	1854.	1855.	1856.	1857.	1858.	1859.
Morrisville Pennsylvania						May 11			
Mungersville do							May 10		
North Whitehall do							May 10	May 7	
Philadelphia do								April 14	
Radnor do		May 8		April 28	May 2	May 10	May 10	April 30	
Reading do	April 19								
Darby do		May 3							
Somerset do								May 1	
Sugar Grove do	May 10								
Upper Darby do	April 23	May 7	April 27	April 25					
Valley Forge do		May 3							
Easton Maryland				April 20					
Frederick do							April 30		
Hagerstown do		April 30	April 22						
Sykesville do	April 10	April 20	April 22	April 19		May 1	May 4		
Buffalo Virginia					April 20	April 29			
Clark county do							April 24	April 10	
Crichton's Store do			April 12			April 18	April 4	April 10	March 30
Kanawha Salines do								April 6	
Madison C. H. do		April 3							
Mossy Creek do		April 10							
Plains do									April 15
Rose Hill do						April 20	March 19	April 10	March 31
Smithfield do		March 15							
Wirt C. H. do						May 5			
Chapel Hill N. Carolina			March 28					April 1	
Aiken S. Carolina						April 3			
All Saints do					March 27				
Black Oak do		March 25							
Camden do		March 10							
Fulton do					March 25	April 3			
St. John's do	March 15								
Savannah Georgia						March 31			
Sparta do						March 15	March 22		
Varnell's Station do									March 20
Zebulon do						April 9			
Carlowville Alabama							March 12	March 13	
Childersburg do								April 4	
Eutaw do		March 3							
Greensborough do						March 28	March 1	March 14	
Weewokaville do		March 13	April 5						
Columbus Mississippi						April 4	March 18	March 20	
Jasper county do						March 26			
Glenwood Tennessee			April 3						
Lebanon do	April 1								
Fairview Kentucky									March 1
Maysville do			April 9						
Hannibal Missouri				April 19					
Ashtabula Ohio				April 29					
Belle Centre do		May 1		April 23				April 24	
Bowling Green do								May 1	
Cheviot do						April 28			
Cleveland do				April 26	May 1				
Edinburg do							May 18		
Germantown do		April 20	April 20	April 19		April 27			
Hiram do						May 12	May 14		
Jefferson do						May 18			
Keene do	April 4	May 7							
Madison do							June 5		
Marietta do								April 9	April 9
Mount Healthy do				April 12	April 22				
Poland do					April 28				
Ripley do							April 22		
Rockport do									May 1
Savannah do							May 9		
Troy do									May 11
Welchfield do							May 26		
Indianapolis Indiana									April 15
Laconia do								April 3	April 4
Richmond do	April 12								

PYRUS COMMUNIS.—*Pear*—Continued.

NAME OF STATION.	1851.	1852.	1853.	1854.	1855.	1856.	1857.	1858.	1859.
Athens ..... Illinois		April 28	April 19	April 21	April 21				
Augusta ..... do	April 20	May 1	April 26	May 14	April 22		May 14		
Brighton ..... do							May 13		
Marengo ..... do							May 25	May 8	
Ottawa ..... do								April 28	
Pekin ..... do								May 10	
Peoria ..... do								April 17	
Riley ..... do							May 29		
Warsaw ..... do							May 17	April 18	
West Northfield ..... do				April 26					
Winnebago ..... do									May 8
Ann Arbor ..... Michigan			May 5						
Brest ..... do	May 17								
Flint ..... do					May 1				
Romeo ..... do						May 12			
Wyandotte ..... do								May 12	May 5
Appleton ..... Wisconsin						May 18			
Milwaukee ..... do	May 10								
Madison ..... do						May 21			
Dubuque ..... Iowa	May 11								
Fairbanks ..... do						May 9			
Fairfield ..... do									May 2
Fort Madison ..... do				April 21					
Muscatine ..... do			May 3	April 22	May 1	May 15			
Pleasant Plain ..... do							May 22		
Horton ..... Nova Scotia					June 4		May 31		
Windsor ..... do							May 28		
Stanbridge ..... Canada							June 1		
Leipsig ..... Saxony								April 30	

PYRUS MALUS.—*Apple*.

NAME OF STATION.	1851.	1852.	1853.	1854.	1855.	1856.	1857.	1858.	1859.
Brunswick ..... Maine									June 7
Castine ..... do		June 3							
Cornish ..... do						June 1	June 6		
Gardiner ..... do							May 29		
Naples ..... do							June 6		
Perry ..... do									June 10
Steuben ..... do	June 6	May 25	May 29	June 3	May 29	June 14	June 6	June 5	May 31
Concord ..... New Hamp.						May 25			
Londonderry ..... do		May 22	May 15						
Manchester ..... do	May 20	May 20		May 18					
North Barnstead ..... do						June 1	June 1		
Salmon Falls ..... do				May 18					
Shelburne ..... do								May 31	
Somersworth ..... do				May 18					
Stratford ..... do								June 5	
West Enfield ..... do							June 2		
Brandon ..... Vermont			May 22	May 22		May 24	May 29	May 29	
Brattleborough ..... do	May 16								
Burlington ..... do			May 25						
Castleton ..... do				May 10					
Craftsbury ..... do						June 5	June 8		
Lunenburg ..... do									June 1
Newark ..... do						June 16	June 10		
Stanbridge ..... do						May 25			
Shelburne ..... do						May 24			
Stockbridge ..... do			May 17						
West Rupert ..... do						May 27	May 31		
Cambridge ..... Massachusetts						May 25			
Florida ..... do						June 10	June 8		
Mendon ..... do				May 15					
New Ashford ..... do		May 16				May 25			
North Attleborough ..... do				May 14	May 20				
Uxbridge ..... do				May 14					
Waltham ..... do				May 16					
Richmond ..... do		May 27							

PYRUS MALUS.—*Apple*—Continued.

Name of Station.	1851.	1852.	1853.	1854.	1855.	1856.	1857.	1858.	1859.
Westfield .... Massachusetts.						May 16			
Worcester .... do						May 17	May 22		
Point Judith .... Rhode Island.				May 25					
Columbia .... Connecticut							May 23	May 16	
Fairfield .... do							May 22		
Georgetown .... do						May 19			
Middletown .... do		May 15	May 10	May 13					
Norwich .... do							May 20		
Preston .... do						May 22			
Angelica .... New York						May 22			
Baldwinsville .... do	May 18					May 25	June 1		
Ceres .... do	May 14								
Chatham .... do	May 14	May 23							
Clinton .... do							May 30		
Eden .... do						May 26	June 1		
Fishkill Landing .... do							May 20	May 10	May 7
Flatbush .... do		May 12	April 19	May 6	May 12		May 18		
Geneva .... do						May 22			
Lake .... do						May 26	May 29	May 28	May 21
Lowville .... do						June 2	May 15		
Mexico .... do						May 23			
New Lebanon .... do	May 16	May 10	May 14						
New York city .... do				May 3	May 12		May 14		
Nichols .... do			May 18					May 13	May 8
North Salem .... do	May 15	May 13				May 20			
Ogdensburg .... do	May 20					May 18			
Ovid .... do				May 15		May 20	May 27		
Penn Yan .... do							June 1		
Plattsburg .... do	May 15	May 22							
Rochester .... do	May 15		May 14	May 13	May 6	May 14	May 23	May 7	
Sag Harbor .... do	May 13	May 10							
Somerville .... do	May 21								
Spencertown .... do					May 17	May 26			
Waterloo .... do		May 20							
Wellsville .... do							April 21		
West Day .... do									May 16
West Point .... do			May 10						
White Plains .... do					May 12				
Burlington .... New Jersey		May 12							
Moorestown .... do					April 20				
Newark .... do		May 5							
Readington .... do							May 21	May 12	May 8
Sergeantsville .... do							May 23		
Bellefonte .... Pennsylvania.								May 28	
Ceres .... do		May 20							
Easton .... do		May 8		May 5					
Fleming Centre .... do							May 20		
Freeport .... do		May 7	May 2	April 23					
Gettysburg .... do		May 7	April 29	April 27		April 23			
Hollidaysburg .... do		May 11	May 1						
Mercersburg .... do		May 6							
Huntington .... do						May 13	May 18		
Indiana .... do		May 5							
Lancaster .... do				April 25			May 6		
Lima .... do		May 7		April 24	May 5		May 9		
Meadville .... do	May 6	May 15				May 17			
Morrisville .... do						May 12			
Mungersville .... do							May 10		
Nazareth .... do						May 10	May 5		
North Whitehall .... do							May 25	May 7	
Orwigsburg .... do		May 10							
Radnor .... do		May 0	May 1	May 6	May 13	May 10	May 15	May 1	
Reading .... do	April 21								
Darby .... do		May 4	May 29						
Somerset .... do								May 3	
Sugar Grove .... do	May 15								
Upper Darby .... do	May 2	May 8	May 3	April 28					
Valley Forge .... do		May 5							
Easton .... Maryland				April 18					
Hagerstown .... do		May 2	April 27						

PYRUS MALUS.—*Apple*—Continued.

Name of Station.	1851.	1852.	1853.	1854.	1855.	1856.	1857.	1858.	1859.
Ridge, Maryland						April 21			
Sykesville, do	April 20	May 2	April 27	April 26			May 9		
Buffalo, Virginia					April 22	April 30			
Clark county, do							April 27	April 20	
Crack Whip, do							May 1		
Crichton's Store, do			April 8				April 1	April 10	April 8
Doddridge county, do						April 30			
Kanawha Salines, do								April 11	
Madison C. H., do	April 15	March 28							
Mossy Creek, do		April 20					May 10		
Mount Solon, do						April 29			
The Plains, do									April 6
Poplar Grove, do							May 7	April 20	April 12
Portsmouth, do		March 29				April 19			
Rose Hill, do						April 12	April 12		April 6
Wardensville, do						April 30			
Winchester, do						April 31			
Wirt C. H, do						May 3			
Chapel Hill, N. Carolina			March 29					March 31	
Camden, S. Carolina		March 17							
Fulton, do					March 30	April 5			
St. John's, do	March 25								
Savannah, Georgia						March 31			
Sparta, do						March 15	March 31		
Varnell's Station, do									March 20
Zebulon, do						April 6			
Alligator, Florida								April 18	
Knox Hill, do		March 10							
Carlowville, Alabama							March 21	March 20	
Childersburg, do							April 1	April 1	
Eutaw, do		March 6							
Greensborough, do						April 3	March 3	March 22	
Weewokaville, do		March 12	April 5						
Columbus, Mississippi						April 9	March 22	March 29	
Jasper county, do						March 26			
Trinity, Louisiana							March 26		
Cross Roads, Texas									March 28
Glenwood, Tennessee			April 5						
Knoxville, do		March 21							
Lebanon, do	April 8								
Nashville, do				April 8					
Walnut Grove, do						May 7			
Fairview, Kentucky									April 25
Maysville, do			April 20						
Hannibal, Missouri				April 21					
St. Louis, do						April 22			
Trenton, do			April 29	April 22					
Ashtabula, Ohio				May 6					
Belle Centre, do		May 5		April 24				May 1	
Bowling Green, do								May 1	
Cheviot, do						April 27			
Cincinnati, do			April 23						
Cleveland, do				May 8	May 2				
Edinburg, do							May 27		
Elk Run, do									May 6
Germantown, do		April 26	April 25	April 15		April 29			
Hamilton, do							May 14		
Hiram, do						May 17	May 24	May 16	
Jefferson, do						May 17			
Keene, do		May 6							
Madison, do							June 5		
Marietta, do								April 9	March 28
Mount Healthy, do				April 15	April 25				
Poland, do					May 1				
Ripley, do							April 27		
Rockport, do									May 2
Savannah, do							May 10		
Welchfield, do								May 31	
Windham, do						May 12			
Laconia, Indiana								April 4	April 8

PYRUS MALUS.—*Apple*—Continued.

Name of Station.	1851.	1852.	1853.	1854.	1855.	1856.	1857.	1858.	1859.
New Albany ....Indiana ...						April 26			
New Harmony ....do......						April 23			
Athens ....Illinois....		April 25	April 21	April 22	April 24	April 29			
Augusta ....do......	April 26	May 1	April 27		April 23	April 29	May 8		
Batavia...................do......								May 4	
Brighton ....do......							May 2	April 7	
Carthage ....do......						May 3			
Manchester ....do......						April 22	May 14	April 19	April 19
Marengo...................do......						May 18	May 22	May 15	
Ottawa ....do......						April 29		April 30	
Peoria....................do......								April 24	
Riley.....................do......						May 20			
Warsaw ....do......						April 31	May 20	April 20	
Waynesville ....do......								April 25	
West Northfield ....do......				May 4					
West Salem ....do......							May 8	April 18	
Winnebago ....do......							May 28	May 10	May 13
Ann Arbor ....Michigan...		May 22							
Brest.....................do......	May 18								
Flint ....do......					May 1				
Romeo ....do......						May 19			
Washington ....do......		May 25							
Wyandotte ....do......									May 3
Appleton.............Wisconsin ..						May 25			
Milwaukee.................do......	May 14								
Platteville ....do......						May 20			
Madison ....do......						May 21	May 30		
Eagle ....Iowa.....							May 27		
Fairbanks ....do......						May 24			
Fairfield.................do......									May 2
Fort Madison ....do......	April 24	May 5	April 28	April 20					
Keokuk ....do......						May 8			
Muscatine ....do......		May 10	May 4	April 24	April 29	May 12			
Pleasant Plain ....do......				April 20	April 26	May 20	May 22		
Salem Prairie...........Oregon....						April 26			
Horton ....Nova Scotia..					June 4		May 31		
Windsor ....do......							May 28		
Stanbridge ....Canada....							May 26	May 26	
Leipsig ....Saxony....								May 1	

QUERCUS ALBA.—*White Oak.*

Name of Station.	1851.	1852.	1853.	1854.	1855.	1856.	1857.	1858.	1859.
Naples ....Maine....							June 5		
Londonderry...........New Hamp...		May 30	June 3						
Manchester ....do......	June 8	June 1		May 30					
Boston ....Massachusetts.		May 23							
Florida...................do......								May 25	
North Attleborough ....do......		May 21		May 19	May 18				
Uxbridge ....do......				May 25					
Columbia ....Connecticut..							May 26	May 28	
Middletown................do......			May 23	May 20					
Ceres...................New York..	May 25								
Chatham ....do......		May 27							
New Lebanon ....do......			May 21						
Ovid ....do......				May 20					
Rochester ....do......							June 1	May 25	
Sag Harbor ....do......	May 10								
West Point ....do......			May 10						
Fleming Centre .....Pennsylvania..	May [illegible]								
Freeport..................do......				May 15					
Gettysburg ....do......			May 3						
Mercersburg ....do......		May 10							
Lima ....do......		May 15	May 15						
Meadville ....do......	May 25	May 22							
Darby ....do......			May 1						
Sugar Grove ....do......	May 23								
Upper Darby...............do......		May 14		May 12					

QUERCUS ALBA.—*White Oak*—Continued.

Name of Station.		1851.	1852.	1853.	1854.	1855.	1856.	1857.	1858.	1859.
Hagerstown	Maryland		May 15	May 15						
Sykesville	do	May 19								
Buffalo	Virginia					May 1				
Clark county	do							May 10	May 5	
Crichton's Store	do							May 5	April 15	
Diamond Grove	do	April 10								
Madison C. H.	do	April 14	April 30							
Poplar Grove	do									May 1
Mossy Creek	do							May 20		
Chapel Hill	N. Carolina			April 4						
Green Plains	do							April 13		
Camden	S. Carolina		March 17							
Fulton	do					April 6				
Alligator	Florida								March 3	
Knox Hill	do		March 11							
Sevilla	do									March 9
Eutaw	Alabama		March 11				March 28	March 24		
Jasper county	Mississippi						April 6			
New Wied	Texas			April 1						
Knoxville	Tennessee		April 4							
Lebanon	do	April 10								
Fairview	Kentucky									May 10
Maysville	do			April 18						
Belle Centre	Ohio		May 15		May 20					
Cincinnati	do			May 3						
Cleveland	do				May 15					
Poland	do					May 21				
Laconia	Indiana								April 25	
Athens	Illinois		May 6	May 6	April 25	April 28				
Augusta	do	May 12	May 20	May 6	May 10	April 26		May 24		
Warsaw	do							May 26		
Waynesville	do								May 10	
West Salem	do							May 31		
Flint	Michigan					May 20				
Milwaukee	Wisconsin	May 26								
Fort Ripley	Minnesota		May 20							
Princeton	do							May 10		
Border Plains	Iowa								May 20	May 14
Dubuque	do	May 19								
Eagle	do							May 27		
Fort Madison	do		May 1							
Muscatine	do				May 10					
Pleasant Plain	do				May 1	May 5				
Leavenworth	Kansas								April 24	
Stanbridge	Canada							June 1	June 15	

RHODODENDRON MAXIMUM.—*Great Laurel.*

Name of Station.		1851.	1852.	1853.	1854.	1855.	1856.	1857.	1858.	1859.
Gardiner	Maine							June 18		
Troy	New Hamp.	July 8								
Boston	Massachusetts		June 29							
Point Judith	Rhode Island				July 8					
Columbia	Connecticut							June 4		
Fairfield	do							June 9		
Fleming Centre	Pennsylvania							July 1		
Lima	do					July 11		July 10		
Radnor	do				June 27	June 30	June 20	June 27	July 1	
Reading	do	June 26								
Poplar Grove	Virginia								June 29	
Chapel Hill	N. Carolina								April 20	
Poland	Ohio					May 26				

RHODODENDRON NUDIFLORA AZALEA.—*Common Red Honeysuckle.*

Name of Station.	1851.	1852.	1853.	1854.	1855.	1856.	1857.	1858.	1859.
Castine, Maine		June 20							
Gardiner, do							June 24		
Manchester, New Hamp.	May 31	June 1		May 30					
Brattleborough, Vermont	June 3								
Castleton, do				May 5					
Lawrence, Massachusetts							May 27		
Richmond, do		June 10							
Uxbridge, do				May 23					
Worcester, do							May 19		
Point Judith, Rhode Island				May 25					
Columbia, Connecticut							May 18	June 1	
East Windsor Hill, do		June 1							
Middletown, do		May 20		May 15					
Ceres, New York	May 25								
Chatham, do	May 20								
New Lebanon, do	May 15		May 25						
New York city, do								May 14	
Flushing, do				May 6					
Nichols, do								June 12	
North Salem, do	May 5	May 18							
Ovid, do				May 25					
Penn Yan, do							June 8		
Rochester, do		May 15	May 20	May 24	May 16		June 8	May 28	
West Point, do		May 16	May 29						
Moorestown, New Jersey					May 12				
Easton, Pennsylvania		May 23		May 8					
Fleming Centre, do	May 12						May 31		
Freeport, do		May 28	May 23	May 21					
Gettysburg, do		May 10		May 3					
Hollidaysburg, do		May 17	May 20						
Mercersburg, do		May 14							
Lancaster, do							May 25		
Indiana, do		May 17							
Lima, do		May 13	May 5			May 16	May 26		
Meadville, do	May 18	May 20							
Radnor, do		May 16	May 12	May 19		May 22	May 25	May 15	
Darby, do		May 14	May 1						
Sugar Grove, do	May 15								
Upper Darby, do		May 11	May 5	May 10					
Easton, Maryland				April 20					
Hagerstown, do		May 13	May 13						
Sykesville, do	May 12	May 14	April 30						
Crichton's Store, Virginia			April 15				April 15	April 8	April 6
Diamond Grove, do	April 5								
Genito, do		April 18							
Kanawha Salines, do								April 23	
Madison C. H, do	April 20	May 2							
Mossy Creek, do		May 5					May 25		
Poplar Grove, do								May 8	April 18
Chapel Hill, N. Carolina	April 12		April 17						
Aiken, S. Carolina			April 2						
All Saints, do					April 2				
Black Oak, do		March 20							
Camden, do		April 1							
Fulton, do					April 14				
St. John's, do	March 20								
Alligator, do								Jan. 14	
Childersburg, Alabama								March 25	
Eutaw, do		March 23							
Greensborough, do						April 25	April 28		
Weewokaville, do			March 25						
Jasper county, Mississippi					April 0	April 17			
Knoxville, Tennessee		April 10							
Lebanon, do	April 19								
Mount Healthy, Ohio				May 20	April 20				
Poland, do					May 26				
Indianapolis, Indiana									May 15
Laconia, do								April 8	
Brighton, Illinois								May 16	
Milwaukee, Wisconsin	May 1								

RHODODENDRON NUDIFLORA AZALEA.—*Common Red Honeysuckle*—Continued.

Name of Station.		1851.	1852.	1853.	1854.	1855.	1856.	1857.	1858.	1859.
Lac qui Parle	Minnesota			June 3	May 19					
Princeton	do							May 25		
Border Plains	Iowa								May 26	May 27
Eagle	do							June 14		
Fairfield	do									June 5
Fort Madison	do				April 1					
Muscatine	do			June 8	May 18					
Pleasant Plain	do				May 15	April 24				
Stanbridge	Canada							May 20	June 5	

RIBES GROSSULARIA.—*Gooseberry.*

Name of Station.		1851.	1852.	1853.	1854.	1855.	1856.	1857.	1858.	1859.
Castine	Maine		May 12							
Carmel	do						May 15			
Cornish	do						May 16	May 20		
Perry	do						May 25			
Steuben	do	May 24		May 20						May 30
Concord	New Hamp.						May 15			
Francestown	do			May 10						
Manchester	do		May 19							
Brandon	Vermont			May 16						
Burlington	do			May 11		May 13				
Craftsbury	do						May 30	May 31		
Newark	do							May 29		
Stanbridge	do						May 10			
Shelburn	do						May 14			
Stockbridge	do			May 10						
Bridgewater	Massachusetts							May 9		
Cambridge	do						May 12			
North Attleborough	do		May 11							
Richmond	do		May 10							
Worcester	do						May 7			
East Windsor	Connecticut			May 1						
Georgetown	do						May 4			
Middletown	do			May 4	May 12					
Norwich	do						May 14			
Preston	do						May 18			
Angelica	New York						May 11			
Ceres	do	May 1								
Chatham	do		May 20							
Eden	do						May 18			
Flatbush	do		May 7	April 20				May 7		
Geneva	do						May 9			
Lake	do						May 22			
Lowville	do						May 11	May 2	May 3	
New Lebanon	do	May 4		May 5						
North Salem	do		May 6							
Ovid	do						May 15	May 25		
Penn Yan	do							May 21		
Plattsburg	do		May 10							
Rochester	do						May 1			
Sponoortown	do						May 12			
Waterloo	do		May 10							
Wellsville	do								April 12	
West Point	do		May 5	April 24						
Burlington	New Jersey		April 15							
Sergeantsville	do							May 15		
Bellefonte	Pennsylvania								May 8	
Ceres	do		May 16							
Freeport	do		May 6	April 20						
Gettysburg	do		May 2	April 22	April 23					
Mercersburg	do		April 23							
Indiana	do		May 1							
Lancaster	do							April 29		
Lima	do		May 4				April 27			
Meadville	do	April 18	May 4				May 8			
Radnor	do			April 23						

RIBES GROSSULARIA.—*Gooseberry*—Continued.

Name of Station.	1851.	1852.	1853.	1854.	1855.	1856.	1857.	1858.	1859.
Darby ... Pennsylvania		April 27	April 19						
Sugar Grove ... do	April 23								
Upper Darby ... do		May 2	April 25						
Hagerstown ... Maryland		April 19	April 13						
Ridge ... do						April 15			
Schellman Hills ... do						May 2			
Sykesville ... do	April 7	April 20							
Buffalo ... Virginia						April 26			
Diamond Grove ... do	April 6								
Genito ... do		March 25							
Madison C. H ... do		April 7							
Mossy Creek ... do		April 20					April 20		
Mount Solon ... do						April 26			
The Plains ... do									April 1
Wardensville ... do						May 3			
Wirt C. H ... do						May 1			
Oxford ... Mississippi						April 4			
Lebanon ... Tennessee	April 23								
Fairview ... Kentucky									April 15
Belle Centre ... Ohio		May 1							
Edinburg ... do							May 21		
Germantown ... do		April 24	April 24	April 20					
Hiram ... do						May 1	May 13		
Jefferson ... do						May 18			
Keene ... do		April 25							
Troy ... do									April 15
Welchfield ... do							May 18		
Laconia ... Indiana									April 10
Richmond ... do	April 6								
Athens ... Illinois		April 26				April 26			
Augusta ... do		April 25	April 18			April 25			
Carthage ... do						April 27			
Manchester ... do						April 7	April 27	March 23	
Ottawa ... do								April 26	
Warsaw ... do						April 26	May 6	April 20	
West Salem ... do							May 1	April 8	
Winnebago ... do									April 29
Brest ... Michigan	May 5								
Cooper ... do						May 11			
Grand Rapids ... do						May 10			
St. James ... do						May 28			
Baraboo ... Wisconsin	May 4								
Greenfield ... do									May 1
Norway ... do						May 3			
Platteville ... do						May 1			
Madison ... do						April 27	May 26		
Beaver Bay ... Minnesota								May 19	
Lac qui Parle ... do			June 9	April 28					
Dubuque ... Iowa	April 15								
Fairfield ... do									May 3
Fort Madison ... do	April 23	April 25	April 9	April 23		April 29			
Muscatine ... do		May 17	May 2			May 14			
Pleasant Plain ... do						May 7			
Salem Prairie ... Oregon						March 30			
Horton ... Nova Scotia							May 19		
Windsor ... do							May 14		
Red River Settlement, Rupert's Land						May 15			

RIBES RUBRUM.—*Red Currant.*

Name of Station.	1851.	1852.	1853.	1854.	1855.	1856.	1857.	1858.	1859.
Brunswick ... Maine							May 25		May 25
Castine ... do		May 12							
Carmel ... do						May 15			
Cornish ... do						May 18	May 21		
Gardiner ... do							May 21		
Naples ... do							May 21		
Perry ... do						May 25			May 15
Steuben ... do	May 30			June 2	May 20			June 3	

RIBES RUBRUM.—*Red Currant*—Continued.

Name of Station.	1851.	1852.	1853.	1854.	1855.	1856.	1857.	1858.	1859.
Concord .... New Hamp.						May 12			
Francestown .... do.			May 10						
Londonderry .... do.		May 17	May 8						
Manchester .... do.	May 20	May 11		May 16					
North Barnstead .... do.						May 22			
Salmon Falls .... do.				May 19					
Shelburne .... do.								May 23	
Somersworth .... do.				May 13					
Stratford .... do.						May 19			
West Enfield .... do.							May 28		
Brandon .... Vermont.			May 15			May 12			
Burlington .... do.			May 12		May 12				
Castleton .... do.				May 14					
Craftsbury .... do.						May 23	May 25		
Newark .... do.						May 31	June 1		
Stanbridge .... do.						May 12			
Shelburn .... do.						May 14			
Stockbridge .... do.			May 11						
West Rupert .... do.							May 21		
Bridgewater .... Massachusetts.							May 15		
Cambridge .... do.						May 12			
Florida .... do.							May 25	May 17	
North Attleborough .... do.		May 10		May 9	May 17				
Uxbridge .... do.				May 9					
Waltham .... do.				May 10					
Richmond .... do.		May 10							
Westfield .... do.						May 5			
Worcester .... do.						May 6	May 15		
Columbia .... Connecticut.							May 12	May 9	
East Windsor .... do.		May 2							
Fairfield .... do.							May 20		
Georgetown .... do.						May 2			
Middletown .... do.			May 4						
Norwich .... do.						May 14	May 16		
Angelica .... New York.						May 14			
Baldwinsville .... do.		May 10							
Ceres .... do.	May 3								
Chatham .... do.		May 14							
Clinton .... do.							May 33		
Eden .... do.							May 18	May 25	
Fishkill Landing .... do.							May 12		May 10
Flatbush .... do.		May 7	April 20	April 24	April 30		May 4		
Geneva .... do.						May 13			
Lake .... do.						May 15	May 14	May 10	May 6
Lowville .... do.						May 17	May 23	June 2	
Lowville .... do.						May 12			
New Lebanon .... do.	May 1		May 6						
New York city .... do.				May 1	May 3			April 20	
Nichols .... do.								May 8	May 4
North Salem .... do.	May 8	May 6			May 5	May 17			
Ogdensburg .... do.			April 20			May 8			
Ovid .... do.				May 9		May 6	May 27		
Penn Yan .... do.							May 21		
Plattsburg .... do.		May 10							
Rochester .... do.	May 6	May 10	April 25	May 6	May 1	May 6	May 18	May 21	
Sag Harbor .... do.	April 25	May 10							
Somerville .... do.	April 30								
Spencertown .... do.					May 12	May 10			
Wellsville .... do.							April 10	April 20	
West Concord .... do.						May 17			
West Day .... do.									May 15
West Point .... do.		May 6	April 24						
Williamsville .... do.				May 14					
White Plains .... do.					May 10				
Burlington .... New Jersey.		April 15							
Newark .... do.		May 6							
Bucks county .... Pennsylvania.						April 29			
Ceres .... do.		May 20							
Chester .... do.	April 10								
Easton .... do.		May 4		May 4					

RIBES RUBRUM.—*Red Currant*—Continued.

Name of Station.	1851.	1852.	1853.	1854.	1855.	1856.	1857.	1858.	1859.
Freeport .... Pennsylvania.		May 6	April 20	May 2					
Gettysburg .... do		May 1	April 22	April 23		April 30			
Indiana .... do		May 1							
Lancaster .... do							May 4		
Lima .... do		May 10	April 22			April 29	May 10		
Meadville .... do	April 25	May 7				May 7			
Morrisville .... do						May 6			
Mungersville .... do							May 10		
Nazareth .... do							May 6		
North Whitehall .... do							April 25	May 4	
Orwigsburg .... do		May 9							
Darby .... do		April 26	April 14						
Sugar Grove .... do	May 13								
Upper Darby .... do	April 12	April 29	April 25	April 27					
Valley Forge .... do		May 5							
Easton .... Maryland				April 19					
Hagerstown .... do		April 28	April 21						
Ridge .... do						April 15			
Sykesville .... do	April 7	April 20		April 23		May 2	April 28		
Buffalo .... Virginia					April 29	April 27			
Clark county .... do							May 3	May 6	
Crichton's Store .... do			April 2				April 11	April 10	March 20
Diamond Grove .... do	April 6								
Genito .... do		March 25							
Mossy Creek .... do		April 15					April 30		
Mount Solon .... do						April 22			
The Plains .... do									April 12
Poplar Grove .... do							May 1	April 23	April 14
Rose Hill .... do						April 20	March 28		April 20
Wardensville .... do						May 2			
Winchester .... do						May 3			
Wirt C. H. .... do						May 1			
Camden .... S. Carolina		March 17				April 11			
Sparta .... Georgia						March 15			
Knox Hill .... Florida		Feb. 23							
Childersburg .... Alabama								March 30	
Columbus .... Mississippi						April 4	March 21	March 21	
New Wied .... Texas	April 1								
Fairview .... Kentucky									April 25
Maysville .... do			April 9						
Hannibal .... Missouri				April 20					
Trenton .... do		April 28							
Ashtabula .... Ohio				May 8					
Belle Centre .... do		May 4		April 22				April 18	
Cheviot .... do						May 5			
Cleveland .... do				April 25	April 29	April 28			
Edinburg .... do							May 19		
Elk Run .... do									May 8
Germantown .... do			April 21	April 20		April 28			
Hiram .... do						May 1	May 21	May 4	
Jefferson .... do						May 1			
Keene .... do	April 2	April 25							
Marietta .... do								April 13	
Poland .... do					April 26				
Ripley .... do							April 29		
Rockport .... do									March 25
Savannah .... do							May 10		
Troy .... do									April 25
Welchfield .... do							May 23		
Laconia .... Indiana								April 15	April 25
New Harmony .... do						April 18			
Richmond .... do	April 7								
Athens .... Illinois		April 28				April 25			
Augusta .... do	April 25	April 24	April 20		April 23	April 26	May 8		
Batavia .... do								April 30	
Brighton .... do							June 1		
Carthage .... do						April 26			
Manchester .... do						April 10	April 27		
Marengo .... do						April 30	May 22	May 1	
Ottawa .... do						April 26		April 25	

RIBES RUBRUM.—*Red Currant*—Continued.

Name of Station.		1851.	1852.	1853.	1854.	1855.	1856.	1857.	1858.	1859.
Peoria	Illinois								April 17	
Warsaw	do						April 26	May 4	April 20	
Waynesville	do								April 22	
West Northfield	do				April 26					
West Salem	do						April 23	May 1	April 18	
Winnebago	do							May 27		May 5
Ann Arbor	Michigan		May 18	May 18						
Brest	do	April 26								
Flint	do					May 1				
Grand Rapids	do						May 1			
Romeo	do						May 8			
St. James	do						May 29			
Wyandotte	do									May 1
Appleton	Wisconsin						May 11			
Baraboo	do	April 4								
Greenfield	do									May 15
Milwaukee	do	May 5								
Norway	do						May 3			
Platteville	do						May 5			
Madison	do						April 27	May 26		
Border Plains	Iowa								April 25	May 9
Dubuque	do	April 15								
Fairfield	do									May 2
Fort Madison	do	May 5	May 1		May 2		April 29			
Muscatine	do			May 2			May 11			
Pleasant Plain	do						May 4			
Salem Prairie	Oregon						March 18			
Horton	Nova Scotia					May 24		May 25		
Windsor	do							May 10		
Stanbridge	Canada							May 12	May 15	
Leipsig	Saxony								April 20	

ROBINIA PSEUD-ACACIA.—*Common Locust.*

Name of Station.		1851.	1852.	1853.	1854.	1855.	1856.	1857.	1858.	1859.
Brunswick	Maine								June 28	
Gardiner	do							June 27		
Naples	do							June 22		
Steuben	do								July 6	
Londonderry	New Hamp		June 17	June 10						
Manchester	do				June 4					
Salmon Falls	do				June 7					
Somersworth	do				June 8					
Brattleborough	Vermont	June 15								
Castleton	do				May 15					
North Attleborough	Massachusetts		June 10		June 4	June 10				
Uxbridge	do				June 6					
Waltham	do				June 5					
Richmond	do		June 10							
Worcester	do							June 24		
Point Judith	Rhode Island				June 15					
Columbia	Connecticut							June 10	June 19	
East Windsor	do		June 10							
Fairfield	do							June 9		
Middletown	do		June 5		June 4					
Baldwinsville	New York	June 14								
Ceres	do	June 20								
Chatham	do	June 15	June 6							
Flatbush	do		June 8	May 31	June 1					
Lake	do							June 15	June 17	June 4
New Lebanon	do	June 28	June 12	June 10						
New York city	do				May 29				June 6	
Nichols	do									May 28
North Salem	do	June 8	June 5							
Ovid	do				June 7					
Penn Yan	do							May 28		
Plattsburg	do	June 3	June 14							

ROBINIA PSEUD-ACACIA.—*Common Locust*—Continued.

Name of Station.	1851.	1852.	1853.	1854.	1855.	1856.	1857.	1858.	1859.
Rochester ....New York...		June 13	June 8	June 6	June 8	June 10	June 21	June 15	
Spencertown ....do......					June 10				
West Point ....do......		June 3	May 26						
White Plains..............do......					June 2				
Burlington ....New Jersey..		May 30							
Freehold ....do......									June 1
Chester.............Pennsylvania.	May 27								
Easton ....do......				May 26					
Gettysburg ....do......		May 25	May 25	May 28					
Hollidaysburg............do......		May 28	May 25						
Mercersburg ....do......		May 24							
Lancaster ....do......				May 21					
Lima ....do......		June 2	May 30	May 30	May 29	June 1	May 14		
Meadville.................do......	May 30	June 6							
Radnor ....do......		June 2	May 27	May 27		June 2	June 8		
Darby ....do......		May 26	May 20						
Somerset...................do......								June 10	
Sugar Grove ....do......	June 10								
Upper Darby ....do......	May 27	June 2	May 26	May 26					
Hagerstown ....Maryland...		May 23	May 19						
Sykesville ....do......	May 19	May 24	May 18	May 22			June 1		
Buffalo ....Virginia....					May 10				
Clark county..............do......							May 28	June 6	
Crack Whip................do......							June 9		April 20
Crichton's Store...........do......			May 11					April 27	
Diamond Grove ....do......	April 28								
Kanawha Salines..........do......								May 6	
Madison C. H ....do......	May 7	May 3							
Mossy Creek ....do......		May 15							
Poplar Grove ....do......								May 12	
Portsmouth ....do......		April 2							
Rose Hill ....do......									May 9
Wardensville ....do......						May 15			
Chapel Hill............N. Carolina..	April 22								
Aiken ....S. Carolina..			April 10						
Fulton ....do......					April 27				
St. John's ....do......	April 20								
Eutaw ....Alabama....		April 7							
Greensborough ....do......						April 18	April 1		
Trinity...................Louisiana...							March 24		
Glenwood...............Tennessee...			April 24						
Knoxville....................do......		May 1							
Lebanon ....do......	April 29								
Nashville ....do......				May 5					
Maysville...............Kentucky...			May 4						
Trenton ....Missouri....			May 23	May 15					
Belle Centre ....Ohio.....		May 28		May 20					
Cincinnati ....do......			May 18						
Cleveland ....do......				June 3	May 28				
Germantown ....do......			May 19	May 20					
Hiram.........................do......							June 16		
Keene ....do......	May 19								
Marietta ....do......								May 13	May 12
Mount Healthy..............do......				May 15	May 15				
Poland ....do......					May 27				
Savannah ....do......							June 10		
Indianapolis..............Indiana....									May 10
Laconia ....do......								May 1	
Athens ....Illinois....		May 15	May 26	May 15					
Augusta ....do......		May 22	May 20	May 10	May 7		June 5		
Pekin ....do......								June 11	
Riley ....do......							June 18		
West Northfield............do......				June 3					
West Salem..................do......							May 31		
Ann Arbor ....Michigan...		June 10							
Flint ....do......					May 25				
Romeo ....do......						June 8			
Milwaukee.............Wisconsin...	June 10								
Fairfield ....Iowa.....									May 22

ROBINIA PSEUD-ACACIA.—*Common Locust*—Continued.

Name of Station.		1851.	1852.	1853.	1854.	1855.	1856.	1857.	1858.	1859.
Fort Madison	Iowa	May 20								
Keokuk	do						May 9			
Pleasant Plain	do							June 8		
Stanbridge	Canada							June 1		
Leipsig	Saxony								June 5	

ROBINIA VISCOSA.—*Clammy Locust.*

Name of Station.		1851.	1852.	1853.	1854.	1855.	1856.	1857.	1858.	1859.
Brunswick	Maine								June 29	
Gardiner	do							July 10		
Naples	do							July 7		
Francestown	New Hamp.			June 17						
Uxbridge	Massachusetts.				June 6					
Point Judith	Rhode Island.				June 22					
Columbia	Connecticut							June 26	June 17	
East Windsor	do		June 16							
Middletown	do		June 14		June 10					
Chatham	New York		June 24							
Nichols	do								June 20	
North Salem	do	June 17								
Penn Yan	do							June 12		
Plattsburg	do		June 20							
Rochester	do		June 17	June 13	June 10	June 14	June 16	July 3	June 20	
Spencertown	do					June 20				
Gettysburg	Pennsylvania.		June 8	May 25						
Lima	do		June 17	June 10						
Radnor	do			June 2	June 2	June 10		June 13	June 9	
Upper Darby	do		June 8	June 1	May 29					
Buffalo	Virginia					May 20				
Mossy Creek	do		May 20							
Portsmouth	do						April 16			
Chapel Hill	N. Carolina								April 25	
Poland	Ohio					May 27				
Augusta	Illinois				May 20	May 15				
Riley	do							June 22		
West Northfield	do				June 19					
Winnebago	do							June 20		
Ann Arbor	Michigan			May 13						
Flint	do					June 25				

ROSA CENTIFOLIA.—*Hundred-leaved Rose.—Cabbage Rose.*

Name of Station.		1851.	1852.	1853.	1854.	1855.	1856.	1857.	1858.	1859.
Castine	Maine		July 10							
Brattleborough	Vermont	June 25								
North Attleborough	Massachusetts		June 19							
Chatham	New York		June 26							
Plattsburg	do		June 26							
Burlington	New Jersey		June 10							
Newark	do	June 9								
Freeport	Pennsylvania.		June 10							
Gettysburg	do		June 1	May 25	May 25					
Hollidaysburg	do		May 28							
Meadville	do	June 8	June 15							
Sugar Grove	do	June 30								
Hagerstown	Maryland			May 28						
Sykesville	do	May 31	May 29	May 27						
Madison C. H.	Virginia		May 21							
Mossy Creek	do		May 1							
Portsmouth	do		May 15							
Glenwood	Tennessee			May 9						
Belle Centre	Ohio		May 30							
Germantown	do		June 5							
Augusta	Illinois	May 29	June 5	June 3						
Milkaukee	Wisconsin	June 20								
Muscatine	Iowa			June 5						

ROSA RUBIGINOSA.—*Sweet Brier.*

Name of Station.	1851	1852.	1853.	1854.	1855.	1856.	1857.	1858.	1859.
Steuben ....Maine....			July 16						
Francestown..........New Hamp..			June 14						
Londonderry.................do......		June 27	June 18						
Salmon Falls................do......				June 17					
Stockbridge...............Vermont...			June 19						
North Attleborough..Massachusetts		June 16							
Middletown..........Connecticut..			June 8						
Chatham..............New York ..		June 19							
Penn Yan ....do......							June 9		
Plattsburg ....do......		June 24							
Gettysburg.... ......Pennsylvania.		June 5							
Meadville.... ....do......		June 20							
Radnor ....do......			May 27				June 21		
Darby ....do......			June 8						
Upper Darby................do......		June 28	June 1						
Madison C. H..........Virginia....		May 25							
Mossy Creek ....do......		May 20							
Belle Centre ....Ohio.....		June 28							
Cincinnati ....do......			May 15						
Augusta...................Illinois....	July 20	July 3							

RUBUS STRIGOSUS.—*Red Raspberry.*

Name of Station.	1851	1852.	1853.	1854.	1855.	1856.	1857.	1858.	1859.
Perry.................Maine....						June 21			
Manchester ....New Hamp..	June 4								
Stratford....................do......						June 15			
Craftsbury ....Vermont...						June 22	June 30		
Newark ....do......						June 22			
Shelburn ....do......						May 25			
West Rupert................do						June 9	June 12		
Bridgewater ....Massachusetts.							May 17		
North Attleborough ....do......		June 13							
Columbia...... ......Connecticut..							June 9		
Georgetown...... ....do......						June 5			
Norwich.......................do......						May 30			
Preston......... ....do......						June 13			
Angelica.... ....New York..						June 10			
Clinton.......................do......							June 11		
Eden ....do......							June 15		
Flatbush ....do......							June 8		
Lowville ....do......						July 10	July 9	July 10	
Spencertown ....do......					June 21				
Sergeantsville ....do......							May 30		
Fleming Centre ......Pennsylvania.	May 26								
Lima ....do......			May 19			June 5			
Meadville ....do......						June 12			
Nazareth.... ....do......						June 1			
Ridge.................Maryland...						May 27			
Germantown.... ....Ohio						May 15			
Jefferson ....do......						June 5			
Welchfield...................do......							June 18		
Carthage ....Illinois....						May 23			
Cooper...... ....Michigan ..						May 16			
Wyandotte ....do......								May 13	
Madison.... ....Wisconsin ..						May 25			
Burlington...... ......Minnesota ..								July 10	
Lac qui Parle ....do......			June 10						
Wolfsville...........Nova Scotia..							June 17		

RUBUS VILLOSUS—*Blackberry.*

Name of Station.		1851.	1852.	1853.	1854.	1855.	1856.	1857.	1858.	1859.
Brunswick	Maine								June 26	
Cornish	do							June 25		
Naples	do							June 17		
Londonderry	New Hamp.		June 9	June 1						
Manchester	do	June 4			June 8					
Salmon Falls	do				June 7					
Shelburne	do								June 20	
West Enfield	do							June 24		
Stockbridge	Vermont			June 3						
North Attleborough	Massachusetts		June 5							
Waltham	do				May 31					
Worcester	do							June 25		
Point Judith	Rhode Island				June 11					
Columbia	Connecticut							June 10	June 12	
East Windsor	do		June 5							
Fairfield	do							June 1		
Chatham	New York		June 19							
Flatbush	do		June 6	June 1						
Lake	do							June 15	June 15	
New York city	do					May 20			June 1	
Nichols	do								June 10	May 25
Penn Yan	do							May 29		
Plattsburg	do		June 8							
Rochester	do			June 20	May 31					
Spencertown	do					June 7				
Fleming Centre	Pennsylvania	May 26						June 20		
Gettysburg	do		May 24	May 20	May 14					
Lancaster	do				May 20					
Lima	do		May 27	May 18		May 29		June 6		
Meadville	do		June 6							
Mungersville	do							June 15		
Nazareth	do							June 25		
North Whitehall	do							June 10		
Radnor	do			May 26			June 2	June 4	June 4	
Darby	do		May 25	May 17						
Upper Darby	do		May 30	May 12	May 19					
Easton	Maryland				May 10					
Hagerstown	do			May 16						
Sykesville	do		May 20	May 17	May 19			May 28		
Buffalo	Virginia					May 15				
Clark county	do							May 29		
Crichton's Store	do			April 25				May 20	May 10	May 10
Genito	do		May 1							
Kanawha Salines	do								May 4	
Madison C. H.	do		May 8							
Mossy Creek	do		May 15							
The Plains	do									May 15
Poplar Grove	do								May 13	May 8
Winchester	do						June 7			
Wirt C. H	do						May 10			
Chapel Hill	N. Carolina			April 18					April 28	
Aiken	S. Carolina			April 18			April 8			
Camden	do		May 3							
Fulton	do					April 18				
Alligator	Florida								Jan. 1	
Childersburg	Alabama								April 10	
Eutaw	do		April 16							
Greensborough	do						April 16	May 1	April 2	
Columbus	Mississippi						April 15			
Jasper county	do					March 24	April 9			
Trinity	Louisiana							March 29	April 1	
Glenwood	Tennessee			April 28						
Knoxville	do		May 3							
Nashville	do				May 3					
Maysville	Kentucky			May 18						
Hannibal	Missouri				May 5					
Trenton	do		May 17							
Ashtabula	Ohio				May 28					
Belle Centre	do		May 24		May 16					
Cheviot	do						May 25			

RUBUS VILLOSUS—*Blackberry*—Continued.

Name of Station.		1851.	1852.	1853.	1854.	1855.	1856.	1857.	1858.	1859.
Cincinnati	Ohio			May 15						
Germantown	do			May 17						
Jefferson	do						June 6			
Marietta	do								May 15	
Mount Healthy	do				May 15	May 20				
Poland	do					May 27				
Athens	Illinois		May 19	May 17	May 12					
Augusta	do		May 12	May 20	May 10	May 20		June 10		
Brighton	do							May 20	May 12	
Marengo	do							June 18		
Pekin	do								June 15	
Peoria	do								June 1	
Warsaw	do							May 10	May 1	
West Northfield	do				May 24					
West Salem	do						May 28	June 4		
Wyandotte	Michigan								June 6	
Fairfield	Iowa									May 23
Pleasant Plain	do				May 1					
Leavenworth City	Kansas								May 20	
Stanbridge	Canada							June 20		

SAMBUCUS CANADENSIS—*Common Black Elder.*

Name of Station.		1851.	1852.	1853.	1854.	1855.	1856.	1857.	1858.	1859.
Brunswick	Maine								July 21	
Cornish	do							July 18		
Gardiner	do							June 7?		
Naples	do							July 8		
Manchester	New Hamp.	July 6			June 25					
Salmon Falls	do				June 21					
Shelburne	do								July 18	
West Enfield	do							June 29		
Brattleborough	Vermont	June 15								
Newark	do							June 8		
Stockbridge	do			June 24						
North Attleborough	Massachusetts		June 27		June 21	June 25				
Uxbridge	do				June 24					
Point Judith	Rhode Island				July 4					
Columbia	Connecticut							July 9	July 1	
East Windsor	do		June 20							
Middletown	do		June 26	July 1	June 24					
Chatham	New York		June 24							
Flatbush	do		June 25	June 20	June 20					
Lake	do							July 13	June 30	July 6
New Lebanon	do	June 20		June 14						
Nichols	do								June 26	June 22
North Salem	do	June 20	June 20							
Penn Yan	do							June 16		
Plattsburg	do		July 1							
Rochester	do			July 1			July 1	May 27	June 25	
Somerville	do	July 2								
Spencertown	do					July 10				
West Point	do		June 5	June 14						
Chester	Pennsylvania	June 15								
Easton	do		June 19		June 17					
Fleming Centre	do							June 20		
Freeport	do		June 10							
Gettysburg	do			June 7	June 1					
Hollidaysburg	do		June 20	July 2						
Lancaster	do				June 10					
Lima	do		June 17	June 14	June 29	June 24		July 1		
Meadville	do	June 12	June 25							
Mungersville	do							July 4		
North Whitehall	do							July 1		
Radnor	do			June 17	June 16		June 24	June 27	June 21	
Reading	do	June 12								
Darby	do			June 17	June 12					

SAMBUCUS CANADENSIS.—*Common Black Elder*—Continued.

Name of Station.		1851.	1852.	1853.	1854.	1855.	1856.	1857.	1858.	1859.
Sugar Grove	Pennsylvania	June 3								
Upper Darby	do		June 20	June 12	June 20					
Hagerstown	Maryland		June 2	June 8						
Sykesville	do	June 6	June 10	June 11	June 14			June 20		
Buffalo	Virginia					June 17				
Clark county	do							June 20	June 16	
Crack Whip	do							July 7		
Crichton's Store	do			June 30					July 1	June 1
Diamond Grove	do	May 20								
Madison C. H	do		June 9							
Mossy Creek	do		May 30							
Poplar Grove	do								June 1	June 1
Portsmouth	do		May 28							
Chapel Hill	N. Carolina			June 1						
Aiken	S. Carolina			May 24						
All Saints	do					May 15				
Black Oak	do		May 8							
St. John's	do	May 2								
Alligator	Florida								March 20	
Knox Hill	do		Feb. 20							
Eutaw	Alabama		June 1							
Greensborough	do								May 18	
Trinity	Louisiana							June 18	May 29	
New Wied	Texas		May 10							
Glenwood	Tennessee			June 10						
Lebanon	do	June 9								
Maysville	Kentucky			June 25						
Trenton	Missouri		June 12							
Belle Centre	Ohio		May 30		June 1					
Cleveland	do				June 17	June 20				
Germantown	do			June 20	June 16					
Hiram	do								May 20	
Hocking Port	do							June 9		
Keene	do		June 22							
Madison	do							June 3		
Marietta	do								June 8	
Mount Healthy	do				June 10	June 5				
Poland	do					May 27				
Indianapolis	Indiana									June 5
Athens	Illinois		June 12	June 18	June 15					
Augusta	do	June 18	June 14							
West Northfield	do				July 4					
Ann Arbor	Michigan		June 26	June 2						
Flint	do					May 18				
Romeo	do						July 2			
Wyandotte	do								June 29	
Milwaukee	Wisconsin	June 20								
Kaposia	Minnesota	June 6								
Lac qui Parle	do			May 16	May 25					
Dubuque	Iowa	May 25								
Fairfield	do									May 2
Horton	Nova Scotia					June 4				
Stanbridge	Canada							June 20	June 10	

SAMBUCUS PUBENS.—*Red-berried Elder.*

Name of Station.		1851.	1852.	1853.	1854.	1855.	1856.	1857.	1858.	1859.
Cornish	Maine							June 1		
Gardiner	do							May 25		
Naples	do							May 25		
Manchester	New Hamp.	May 10								
Castleton	do				May 10					
Mendon	Massachusetts				April 26					
Ceres	New York	May 20								
New Lebanon	do			May 20						
Nichols	do									April 18
Rochester	do	May 17	May 15	May 25	May 13	May 20		July 8	May 17	

SAMBUCUS PUBENS.—*Red-berried Elder*—Continued.

NAME OF STATION.	1851.	1852.	1853.	1854.	1855.	1856.	1857.	1858.	1859.
Spencertown........New York...					April 30				
Fleming Centre .....Pennsylvania..	April 26						May 18		
Meadville.................do......		May 30							
Mungersville ....do......							May 8		
Radnor ....do......		May 15	May 4					May 9	
Romeo ....Michigan...						May 23			
Wyandotte ....do......								May 13	
Stanbridge ....do......								May 26	

SANGUINARIA CANADENSIS.—*Bloodroot.*

NAME OF STATION.	1851.	1852.	1853.	1854.	1855.	1856.	1857.	1858.	1859.
Gardiner...............Maine....							May 2		
Brandon ....Vermont...			April 27	April 30			April 30	April 24	
Brattleborough ....do......	April 15								
Burlington ....do......			April 26		May 1				
Castleton ....do......				May 10					
Waltham ....Massachusetts.				May 5					
Richmond ....do......		May 4							
Worcester ....do......							May 13		
Columbia ....Connecticut..							May 5	May 1	
Flatbush ....New York ..					April 23				
New Lebanon..............do......	April 26								
North Salem..............do......	April 3	April 15							
Ovid ....do......				April 23					
Penn Yan ....do......							April 19		
Plattsburg ....do......	April 24	May 10							
Rochester.................do......				April 20					
Somerville................do......	April 12								
Spencertown ....do......					May 5				
Ceres...............Pennsylvania.		May 2							
Chambersburg ....do......	April 6	April 24							
Chester ....do......	March 15								
Easton ....do......		April 20		April 20					
Fleming Centre ....do......	May 2						May 1		
Gettysburg ....do......				April 25					
Hollidaysburg.............do......		May 1	April 29						
Lancaster ....do......				March 15					
Lima......................do......		April 18	April 8	April 4	April 20		April 11		
Meadville.................do......	April 1	April 1							
Nazareth ....do......							April 23		
Philadelphia ....do......								April 4	
Radnor ....do......		April 25	April 1	April 8	April 13		April 26	April 10	
Reading ....do......	April 3								
Darby ....do......		April 10	March 29						
Sugar Grove ....do......	April 14								
Upper Darby...............do......	April 3	April 17	April 3	April 4					
Valley Forge..............do......		April 24							
Hagerstown ....Maryland...			March 30						
Sykesville ....do......	March 20	April 3	April 3						
Buffalo ....Virginia ...					April 14				
Clark county..............do......							April 15	April 1	
Madison C. H..............do......	April 10								
Mossy Creek...............do......		March 15							
Chapel Hill..........N. Carolina..			March 20					March 30	
Black Oak ....S. Carolina..		March 1							
Eutaw.................Alabama...		Feb. 15							
Knoxville ....Tennessee ..		March 24							
Maysville ....Kentucky ..			April 19						
Trenton. ....Missouri ...		April 12	April 8	April 6					
Belle Centre ....Ohio.....		April 8		April 1				April 3	
Cincinnati ....do......			March 25						
Germantown................do......		April 20	April 15	April 16					
Keene.....................do......	April 3	April 10							
Marietta..................do......								April 5	March 30
Mount Healthy ....do......				May 20					
Laconia ....Indiana....								March 15	
Richmomd..................do......	March 27								

SANGUINARIA CANADENSIS.—*Bloodroot*—Continued.

NAME OF STATION.	1851.	1852.	1853.	1854.	1855.	1856.	1857.	1858.	1859.
Athens, Illinois		April 6	April 9						
Augusta, do	April 12	April 20	April 13	April 12	April 20				
Batavia, do								April 25	
West Northfield, do				April 17					
Brest, Michigan	April 15								
Flint, do					April 21				
Wyandotte, do								May 2	
Baraboo, Wisconsin	April 18								
Kaposia, Minnesota	April 28								
Lac qui Parle, do			May 8	April 21					
Border Plains, Iowa								April 18	April 18
Plum Spring, do					April 16				
Stanbridge, Canada								April 24	
Leipsig, Saxony								April 8	

SAPONARIA OFFICINALIS.—*Soapwort.*

NAME OF STATION.	1851.	1852.	1853.	1854.	1855.	1856.	1857.	1858.	1859.
East Windsor Hill, Connecticut		July 3							
North Salem, New York	July 1								
Sag Harbor, do	July 20	July 20							
West Point, do			June 20						
Burlington, New Jersey		July 15							
Chester, Pennsylvania	July 15								
Freeport, do		July 29	July 26						
Gettysburg, do		June 30							
Meadville, do		July 10							
Upper Darby, do		July 18	July 1						
Sykesville, Maryland	June 28	July 8	July 1						
Lebanon, Tennessee	June 15								
Belle Centre, Ohio		July 10							
Athens, Illinois		July 4	July 29						
Augusta, do	July 18	July 17	June 28						
Brest, Michigan	July 10								

SASSAFRAS OFFICINALE.—*Sassafras.*

NAME OF STATION.	1851.	1852.	1853.	1854.	1855.	1856.	1857.	1858.	1859.
Flatbush, New York			April 15						
Burlington, New Jersey		May 9							
Darby, Pennsylvania		May 9							
Fleming, do	April 20								
Gettysburg, do			May 2	April 30					
Hollidaysburg, do		May 22							
Indiana, do		May 7							
Meadville, do		May 19							
Murrysville, do							May 20		
Radnor, do		May 16							
Upper Darby, do		May 4	April 26						
Hagerstown, Maryland			April 14						
Genito, Virginia		March 29							
Madison C. H, do		April 5							
Mossy Creek, do		April 20							
Chapel Hill, N. Carolina			March 20						
Fulton, S. Carolina					March 23				
Eutaw, Alabama		March 3							
Weewokaville, do		March 7	March 25						
Glenwood, Tennessee			April 8						
Belle Centre, Ohio		May 1							
Athens, Illinois		April 29							
Ann Arbor, Michigan		May 18							

SAXIFRAGA VIRGINIENSIS.—*Virginia Saxifrage.*

Name of Station.		1851.	1852.	1853.	1854.	1855.	1856.	1857.	1858.	1859.
Brunswick	Maine							May 9	May 9	
Cornish	do							May 12		
Brattleborough	Vermont	April 15								
Castleton	do				May 10					
Stockbridge	do			April 27						
Boston	Massachusetts		April 21							
Mendon	do				May 3					
Uxbridge	do				May 23					
Waltham	do				April 28					
Worcester	do							April 30		
Middletown	Connecticut		April 22							
New York city	New York								April 15	
North Salem	do	April 11	May 1							
Ovid	do				May 2					
Penn Yan	do							May 3		
Plattsburg	do	April 29	May 8							
Rochester	do		April 30	April 25	April 20	May 3		May 16		
Somerville	do	April 22								
Burlington	New Jersey		March 30							
Chester	Pennsylvania	March 30								
Fleming Centre	do	April 12						May 1		
Gettysburg	do		April 26	May 2	April 18					
Hollidaysburg	do		April 23	April 10						
Mercersburg	do		April 17							
Lancaster	do				April 5					
Lima	do				April 11					
Meadville	do	April 12	April 28							
Mungersville	do							April 14		
Nazareth	do							May 7		
Philadelphia	do								April 8	
Darby	do		April 1	March 25						
Upper Darby	do	March 17	April 17	April 14	April 9					
Hagerstown	Maryland			April 14						
Sykesville	do		April 29							
Clark county	Virginia							May 9	April 13	
Madison C. H	do	April 10								
Mossy Creek	do		April 25							
Chapel Hill	N. Carolina								April 2	
Knoxville	Tennessee		May 1							
Cincinnati	Ohio			April 15						March 24
Marietta	do								March 28	
West Salem	Illinois							May 8		
Dubuque	Iowa	April 1								

SILENE PENNSYLVANICA.—*Wood Pink.*

Name of Station.		1851.	1852.	1853.	1854.	1855.	1856.	1857.	1858.	1859.
Fleming	Pennsylvania	May 10								
Freeport	do		May 17							
Gettysburg	do			May 3	May 10					
Mercersburg	do		May 7							
Mossy Creek	Virginia		May 4							
Belle Centre	Ohio		June 5							

SMILACINA BIFOLIA.—*Two-leaved Solomon's Seal.*

Name of Station.		1851.	1852.	1853.	1854.	1855.	1856.	1857.	1858.	1859.
Brunswick	Maine								June 20	
Gardiner	do							May 30		
Naples	do							June 3		
Manchester	New Hamp.		May 10							
Brandon	Vermont			May 10						
Castleton	do				May 15					
Stockbridge	do			May 26						
Uxbridge	do				May 23					
Waltham	do				May 17					

SMILACINA BIFOLIA.—*Two-leaved Solomon's Seal*—Continued.

Name of Station.	1851.	1852.	1853.	1854.	1855.	1856.	1857.	1858.	1859.
East Windsor........Connecticut..		June 1							
Middletown ......do......		May 15							
Ceres........New York ..	May 14								
Chatham ......do......	June 8								
North Salem......do......	May 15								
Ovid ......do......				May 20					
Plattsburg ......do......	May 14	May 25							
Rochester ......do......			May 4				June 1		
Somerville ......do......	May 16								
Ceres ....Pennsylvania.		June 5							
Fleming Centre ......do......	May 31								
Gettysburg ......do......			May 7	May 15					
Mercersburg ......do......		May 20							
Meadville ......do......	May 25								
Lima ......do......							May 16		
Darby ......do......		May 25							
Sugar Grove ......do......	May 11								
Upper Darby......do......	May 16	May 28							
Crichton's Store......Virginia....			April 26				May 12		
Genito ......do......		April 25							
Weewokaville........Alabama...		April 20	April 6						
Athens ....Illinois....			May 10						
Ann Arbor ....Michigan...		June 8							
Wyandotte ......do......								May 16	
Princeton ....Minnesota ..							May 30		
Horton ....Nova Scotia..					May 24				

SYRINGA VULGARIS.—*Lilac.*

Name of Station.	1851.	1852.	1853.	1854.	1855.	1856.	1857.	1858.	1859.
Brunswick........Maine....							June 6	June 3	
Castine ......do......		June 10							
Gardiner......do......							June 3		
Naples......do......							June 7		
Perry......do......									June 10
Steuben ......do......	June 9	June 6	June 6	June 1	June 13		June 10	June 4	
Londonderry........New Hamp..		May 21	May 27						
Manchester ......do......		May 25		May 20					
Salmon Falls......do......				May 22					
Shelburne......do......								June 6	
Somersworth......do......				May 21					
Stratford ......do......								June 8	
West Enfield......do......							June 16		
Brandon ....Vermont...			May 25				May 29	June 1	
Burlington ......do......			June 3						
Newark......do......							June 15		
Stockbridge......do......			May 17						
Boston ....Massachusetts..		May 23							
Lawrence ......do......							May 27		
Mendon......do......				May 17					
North Attleborough ......do......		May 20		May 20	May 25				
Uxbridge ......do......				May 10					
Waltham ......do......				May 19					
Worcester ......do......							May 26		
Point Judith ....Rhode Island..				June 1					
Columbia ....Connecticut..							June 1	May 27	
East Windsor Hill......do......		May 28							
Fairfield......do......							May 23		
Middletown......do......		May 18	May 13	May 15					
Baldwinsville ....New York ..	May 19	May 25							
Ceres......do......	May 23								
Chatham ......do......	May 21	May 23							
Fishkill Landing ......do......								May 15	May 6
Flatbush ......do......		May 18	May 14	May 12	May 17				
Lake ......do......								June 2	May 21
New Lebanon......do......	May 18	May 24	May 20						
New York city......do......				May 12	April 26				May 16
Nichols ......do......								May 23	May 14

SYRINGA VULGARIS.—*Lilac*—Continued.

Name of Station.		1851.	1852.	1853.	1854.	1855.	1856.	1857.	1858.	1859.
North Salem	New York	May 15	May 15							
Ogdensburg	do			April 24			May 18			
Ovid	do				May 16					
Penn Yan	do							June 8		
Plattsburg	do	May 25	May 24							
Rochester	do	May 22	May 15	May 17	May 16	May 18	May 25	May 29	May 20	
Sag Harbor	do	May 22	June 1							
Somerville	do	May 22								
Spencertown	do					May 20				
Waterloo	do		May 14							
West Point	do		May 18	May 11						
White Plains	do					May 12				
Burlington	New Jersey		May 1							
Moorestown	do					May 1				
Ceres	Pennsylvania		May 18							
Chester	do	April 15								
Easton	do				May 12					
Fleming Centre	do							May 25		
Gettysburg	do		May 4	May 2	April 28					
Hollidaysburg	do		May 18	May 10						
Mercersburg	do		May 7							
Indiana	do		May 12							
Lancaster	do				May 2			May 15		
Lima	do		May 10	May 2	May 5	May 12		May 19		
Meadville	do	May 12	May 26							
Morrisville	do						May 1			
Darby	do			May 4						
Somerset	do								May 20	
Sugar Grove	do	May 13								
Upper Darby	do	May 5	May 12	May 6	May 7					
Valley Forge	do		May 8							
Easton	Maryland				April 23					
Hagerstown	do		May 6	April 28						
Sykesville	do	April 27	May 1	April 19	April 26			May 10		
Buffalo	Virginia					April 26				
Clark county	do							May 8	April 24	
Crichton's Store	do			March 25				May 10	April 10	March 24
Genito	do		March 14							
Kanawha Salines	do								April 12	
Madison C. H.	do		April 15							
Mossy Creek	do		April 25					May 20		
Poplar Grove	do								April 14	Killed
Portsmouth	do						April 22			
Rose Hill	do						April 20		April 15	March 30
Chapel Hill	North Carolina			April 1					April 9	
Camden	South Carolina		March 14							
Eutaw	Alabama		March 20							
Greensborough	do							March 16	March 30	
Columbus	Mississippi							March 27	March 30	
Jasper county	do						April 6			
Glenwood	Tennessee			April 13						
Knoxville	do		April 5							
Lebanon	do	April 1								
Hannibal	Missouri				April 23					
Trenton	do		May 3							
Ashtabula	Ohio				May 10					
Belle Centre	do		May 10		April 20				May 12	
Cincinnati	do			April 25						
Cleveland	do				May 9	May 5				
Hiram	do							May 30	May 24	
Keene	do	April 20	May 10							
Madison	do							June 1		
Marietta	do									April 22
Mount Healthy	do				April 30	April 30				
Poland	do					May 11				
Ripley	do							May 10		
Windham	do						May 15			
Indianapolis	Indiana									April 8
Laconia	do								April 10	
Richmond	do	May 1								

SYRINGA VULGARIS.—*Lilac*—Continued.

Name of Station.		1851.	1852.	1853.	1854.	1855.	1856.	1857.	1858.	1859.
Athens	Illinois			April 28	April 30					
Augusta	do		May 1	April 30	April 23	April 25		May 21		
Brighton	do							May 14	April 18	
Marengo	do							June 1	May 25	
Pekin	do								May 25	
Riley	do							June 5		
Waynesville	do								May 3	
West Northfield	do				May 10					
West Salem	do							May 1		
Ann Arbor	Michigan			May 14						
Flint	do					May 5				
Wyandotte	do								May 24	
Milwaukee	Wisconsin	May 15								
Fairfield	Iowa									May 8
Muscatine	do			May 13	May 7					
Pleasant Plain	do				April 25		May 15			
Horton	Nova Scotia				June 6					
Stanbridge	Canada							May 30	May 20	
Leipsig	Saxony								May 10	

TARAXACUM DENS-LEONIS.—*Dandelion.*

Name of Station.		1851.	1852.	1853.	1854.	1855.	1856.	1857.	1858.	1859.
Brunswick	Maine								May 28	
Castine	do		May 13							
Cornish	do							May 22		
Gardiner	do							May 2		
Naples	do							May 21		
Perry	do									May 12
Steuben	do			May 12		May 25				
Francestown	New Hamp.			April 28						
Londonderry	do		May 27	April 24						
Manchester	do		May 11		May 13					
Salmon Falls	do				May 9					
Shelburne	do								May 19	
Somersworth	do				May 14					
Stratford	do								May 12	
West Enfield	do							May 23		
Brandon	Vermont			May 18	May 14				May 8	
Brattleborough	do	April 23								
Burlington	do			May 1						
Castleton	do				May 8					
Newark	do							May 28		
Stockbridge	do			May 6						
Florida	Massachusetts							May 25	May 20	
Lawrence	do							May 11		
Mendon	do				May 10					
North Attleborough	do		May 5		April 27	May 2				
Uxbridge	do				May 9					
Waltham	do				May 1					
Richmond	do		May 10							
Worcester	do							April 16		
Columbia	Connecticut							May 6	April 22	
East Windsor	do		May 10							
Middletown	do		April 27	March 26	April 25					
Baldwinsville	New York		May 15							
Chatham	do		May 10							
Fishkill Landing	do							May 15		
Flatbush	do		May 4	April 12	April 25	April 28				
Lake	do							May 9	May 2	May 6
Mexico	do						May 15			
New Lebanon	do			April 19						
New York city	do				May 5	May 3			May 12	
Nichols	do								May 5	April 27
North Salem	do		April 18							
Ogdensburg	do			May 6						
Ovid	do				May 10					
Penn Yan	do							April 23		

TARAXACUM DENS-LEONIS.—*Dandelion*—Continued.

Name of Station.		1851.	1852.	1853.	1854.	1855.	1856.	1857.	1858.	1859.
Plattsburg	New York		May 9							
Rochester	do			April 16	April 15	May 1		May 15		
Spencertown	do					May 15				
Somerville	do	May 6								
Waterloo	do		May 12							
West Point	do		May 6	April 27						
Williamsville	do				May 10					
White Plains	do					April 16				
Burlington	New Jersey		April 26							
Freehold	do									March 30
Moorestown	do					April 19				
Ceres	Pennsylvania		May 15							
Easton	do		May 5		May 1					
Fleming Centre	do	March 26						May 8		
Freeport	do		May 13	May 8	April 25					
Gettysburg	do		May 1	April 20	April 24					
Hollidaysburg	do		May 3	April 26						
Mercersburg	do		April 27							
Indiana	do		May 6							
Lima	do			May 2	April 2	April 24		April 22		
Meadville	do		April 6							
Mungersville	do							April 24		
Philadelphia	do								April 13	
Radnor	do				April 22	May 1	May 10	April 18	April 29	
Darby	do		April 27	March 30						
Somerset	do								May 13	
Upper Darby	do		May 1	April 19	April 18					
Valley Forge	do		May 4							
Easton	Maryland				April 19					
Hagerstown	do			April 15						
Sykesville	do		May 4	April 23	April 21			May 10		
Buffalo	Virginia					April 20				
Clark county	do								April 12	
Kanawha Salines	do								April 10	
Madison C. H.	do		April 10							
Mossy Creek	do		April 10					May 1		
Poplar Grove	do								April 20	April 12
Portsmouth	do		March 10				April 2			
Rose Hill	do						April 26	May 3	April 7	April 5
Chapel Hill	N. Carolina			April 3					April 7	
Camden	S. Carolina		May 5							
Glenwood	Tennessee			April 16						
Knoxville	do		March 20							
Maysville	Kentucky			April 23						
Trenton	Missouri		May 1		April 22					
Ashtabula	Ohio				April 30					
Belle Centre	do		April 29		April 24				April 23	
Bowling Green	do								April 20	
Cincinnati	do			April 20						
Cleveland	do				April 23	May 2				
Germantown	do		April 20	April 20	April 16					
Hiram	do							April 28	April 20	
Keene	do		April 13							
Madison	do							May 5		
Marietta	do								April 5	April 2
Mount Healthy	do				April 20	April 28				
Poland	do					April 22				
Ripley	do							April 12		
Savannah	do							May 20		
Windham	do						May 2			
Indianapolis	Indiana									April 25
Laconia	do								April [illegible]0	
Richmond	do	April 9								
Athens	Illinois		April 16	April 25	April 25	April 24				
Augusta	do		April 28	April 28	April 20	April 25		May 14		
Batavia	do								April 26	
Brighton	do							May 14	April 24	
Pekin	do								May 23	
Peoria	do								May 2	
Waynesville	do								May 5	

TARAXACUM DENS-LEONIS—*Dandelion*—Continued.

Name of Station.	1851.	1852.	1853.	1854.	1855.	1856.	1857.	1858.	1859.
West Northfield .... Illinois				April 26					
Winnebago .... do								May 10	
Flint .... Michigan				April 27					
Romeo .... do						May 3			
Wyandotte .... do								April 25	
Keokuk .... Iowa						May 3			
Muscatine .... do			May 10	April 30					
Horton .... Nova Scotia					May 6				
Stanbridge .... Canada							May 2	May 8	
Leipsig .... Saxony								April 1	

TILIA AMERICANA.—*Linden.*—*Basswood.*

Name of Station.	1851.	1852.	1853.	1854.	1855.	1856.	1857.	1858.	1859.
Brunswick .... Maine								July 12	
Gardiner .... do							June 28		
Naples .... do							July 25		
Manchester .... New Hamp		July 1							
Stockbridge .... Vermont			July 12						
North Attleborough .. Massachusetts		June 28		June 28	June 26				
Middletown .... Connecticut		July 10							
Chatham .... New York	June 25								
Lake .... do							July 23	July 15	
Nichols .... do								July 9	
Plattsburg .... do		July 15							
Rochester .... do		July 17	June 10	July 25	June 30	July 14	July 12	July 3	
Spencertown .... do					June 17				
West Point .... do		June 20	June 17						
Burlington .... New Jersey		June 20							
Gettysburg .... Pennsylvania		June 24	June 11	June 2					
Mercersburg .... do		June 29							
Lancaster .... do				June 24					
Lima .... do		June 14		June 30		June 10	July 1		
Meadville .... do		July 15							
Radnor .... do			July 1	June 30	July 4	July 3	July 11	July 3	
Sugar Grove .... do	June 23								
Sykesville .... Maryland	June 20								
Poplar Grove .... Virginia								July 2	June 29
New Wied .... Texas	May 10	May 18	May 2	June 1					
Maysville .... Kentucky			July 12						
Ashtabula .... Ohio				June 12					
Belle Centre .... do		June 13		June 8					
Germantown .... do				June 24					
Poland .... do					June 8				
Athens .... Illinois		June 29	June 28	June 25					
Augusta .... do			May 23		May 28		July 5		
West Northfield .... do				July 11					
Wyandotte .... Michigan								June 20	
Fort Ripley .... Minnesota		May 20							
Lac qui Parle .... do			July 18	July 10					
Princeton .... do							May 30		
Border Plains .... Iowa									June 12
Pleasant Plain .... do				July 1					
Stanbridge .... Canada							June 20		

ULMUS AMERICANA.—*American Elm.*

Name of Station.	1851.	1852.	1853.	1854.	1855.	1856.	1857.	1858.	1859.
Brunswick .... Maine							May 9	May 12	
Cornish .... do							May 4		
Gardiner .... do							May 23		
Naples .... do							May 3		
Perry .... do						May 5			
Francestown .... New Hamp			April 28						
Londonderry .... do		May 2	April 15						
Manchester .... do		April 29		April 28					

ULMUS AMERICANA.--*American Elm*—Continued.

Name of Station.	1851.	1852.	1853.	1854.	1855.	1856.	1857.	1858.	1859.
Salmon Falls, New Hamp.				May 20					
Shelburne, do.								May 9	
Stratford, do.								May 14	
Brandon, Vermont			May 2					April 20	
Brattleborough, do.	April 3								
Burlington, do.			April 22		May 4				
Castleton, do.				May 8					
Boston, Massachusetts		April 22							
Mendon, do.				April 21					
North Attleborough, do.		April 26		April 14	April 28				
Waltham, do.				April 22					
Worcester, do.							May 4		
Columbia, Connecticut								May 7	
East Windsor, do.			April 4						
Middletown, do.		April 15	April 4	April 20					
Chatham, New York	April 1	May 1							
Flatbush, do.		April 28	April 2						
New Lebanon, do.	April 28		April 20						
New York city, do.				May 7	April 19				
Nichols, do.								April 15	March 30
North Salem, do.	March 26	April 13							
Ovid, do.				April 10					
Penn Yan, do.							May 1		
Plattsburg, do.	April 21	May 4							
Rochester, do.	April 1		April 20	April 20	April 13	April 25	May 8	April 1	
Sag Harbor, do.	April 12								
Somerville, do.	April 19								
Spencertown, do.					April 20				
West Point, do.		April 20	April 10						
White Plains, do.					April 12				
Freehold, New Jersey									March 15
Ceres, Pennsylvania		May 20							
Easton, do.				April 20					
Fleming Centre, do.	March 20								
Gettysburg, do.		April 2		April 1					
Hollidaysburg, do.		April 3	April 1						
Mercersburg, do.		April 2							
Lancaster, do.				March 11					
Meadville, do.	April 3								
Mungersville, do.							April 1		
Radnor, do.		March 26	April 6				April 10	April 10	
Reading, do.	March 23								
Sugar Grove, do.	April 9								
Upper Darby, do.			March 31						
Hagerstown, Maryland		March 16	March 29						
Sykesville, do.	April 23								
Buffalo, Virginia					April 6				
Clark county, do.								April 10	
Crichton's Store, do.			Feb. 7					April 7	March 10
Genito, do.		March 15							
Kanawha Salines, do.								March 21	
Mossy Creek, do.		March 10					March 25		
Poplar Grove, do.								March 21	March 15
Rose Hill, do.							Feb. 25	April 1	March 14
Smithfield, do.		Feb. 22							
Chapel Hill, N. Carolina			Feb. 6					March 25	
Black Oak, S Carolina		Jan. 6							
Camden, do.		April 11							
Fulton, do.					Feb. 8				
Greensborough, Alabama						March 20	Feb. 28		
Weewokaville, do.			March 8	March 12					
Trinity, Louisiana							Feb. 1	Feb. 25	
Knoxville, Tennessee		March 1							
Maysville, Kentucky			March 23						
St. Louis, Missouri						April 6			
Trenton, do.				March 15					
Belle Centre, Ohio		March 14		April 1				March 15	
Cincinnati, do.			April 5						
Cleveland, do.					April 20				
Hiram, do.							April 30		

ULMUS AMERICANA.—*American Elm*—Continued.

Name of Station.		1851.	1852.	1853.	1854.	1855.	1856.	1857.	1858.	1859.
Marietta	Ohio								March 28	March 14
Laconia	Indiana								March 20	
Richmond	do	April 10								
Athens	Illinois		March 14	March 26	March 15	April 10				
Augusta	do					April 10				
Batavia	do								May 15	
Warsaw	do							May 30		
Waynesville	do							March 19		
Ann Arbor	Michigan			April 8						
Flint	do					April 12				
Wyandotte	do								April 7	
Milwaukee	Wisconsin	April 1								
Fort Ripley	Minnesota		May 2							
Lac qui Parle	do			April 29	April 17					
Princeton	do							May 30		
Dubuque	Iowa	April 1								
Pleasant Plain	do					April 16		April 13		
Leavenworth City	Kansas								March 16	
Horton	Nova Scotia					April 26				
Stanbridge	Canada							June 1	June 20	

VIBURNUM LENTAGO.—*Sweet Viburnum.*

Name of Station.		1851.	1852.	1853.	1854.	1855.	1856.	1857.	1858.	1859.
Brunswick	Maine								June 28	
Gardiner	do							May 18		
Naples	do							June 22		
Manchester	New Hamp	June 1								
Uxbridge	Massachusetts				May 30					
Worcester	do							May 23		
East Windsor	Connecticut		June 5							
New York city	New York								May 16	
Fleming Centre	Pennsylvania	May 26								
Radnor	do		May 26	May 20		May 24		May 31	May 30	
Hagerstown	Maryland		May 9							
Poland	Ohio					May 20				
Augusta	Illinois					April 30				
West Northfield	do				May 19					
Flint	Michigan					May 18				
Wyandotte	do								June 15	
Princeton	Minnesota							May 15		
Pleasant Plain	Iowa				May 10					
Stanbridge	Canada								June 20	

VIBURNUM OPULUS.—*Snowball.*

Name of Station.		1851.	1852.	1853.	1854.	1855.	1856.	1857.	1858.	1859.
Castine	Maine		July 4							
Londonderry	New Hamp			June 3						
Manchester	do	June 18	June 3							
Brattleborough	Vermont	June 4								
Burlington	do			June 3						
North Attleborough	do		May 28							
Ceres	New York	May 27								
Chatham	do	June 1								
Flatbush	do		May 25							
New Lebanon	do			May 28						
North Salem	do	May 26								
Ogdensburg	do	June 1								
Penn Yan	do							June 8		
Plattsburg	do		June 7							
Rochester	do		June 3	May 31						
Somerville	do	May 30								
Waterloo	do		May 20							
West Point	do		May 25	May 28						
Burlington	New Jersey		May 15							

VIBURNUM OPULUS.—*Snowball*—Continued.

Name of Station.	1851.	1852.	1853.	1854.	1855.	1856.	1857.	1858.	1859.
Ceres ....Pennsylvania..		May 6							
Chester ....do......	May 25								
Fleming Centre ....do......	May 26								
Freeport.....................do......		May 26	May 23						
Gettysburg ....do......			May 10						
Hollidaysburg..............do......			May 15						
Mercersburg ....do......		May 15							
Lima ....do......		May 31							
Meadville....................do......	May 20	June 2							
Darby ....do......		May 20							
Upper Darby................do......	May 20	May 24	May 20						
Hagerstown ....Maryland....		May 11	May 6						
Sykesville ....do......	May 19	May 20							
Crichton's Store.......Virginia....			April 24						
Diamond Grove ....do......	April 10								
Genito ....do......		April 26							
Madison C. H ....do......	April 30	April 30							
Mossy Creek ....do......		May 10							
Portsmouth ....do......		April 10							
Black Oak..............S. Carolina..		April 10							
Camden ....do......		March 17							
St. John's ....do......	April 26								
Eutaw ....Alabama....		March 31							
Weewokaville ....do......		April 16							
New Wied..................Texas.....	March 25								
Glenwood ....Tennessee...			April 24						
Knoxville ....do......		April 15							
St. Louis..................Missouri....						May 8			
Belle Centre ....Ohio.....		May 17							
Cincinnati ....do......			May 5						
Germantown ....do......		May 6							
Keene ....do......	May 6								
Indianapolis..............Indiana....									May 1
Augusta.....................Illinois....	May 14	May 10	May 14	May 6					
Brest ....Michigan...	May 23								
Wyandotte.....................do......								May 27	
Milwaukee ....Wisconsin...	May 23								
Dubuque ....Iowa.....	May 20								
Fort Madison ....do......	May 18								
Muscatine......................do......		May 17	May 20						

VIOLA CUCULLATA.—*Hooded Violet.*

Name of Station.	1851.	1852.	1853.	1854.	1855.	1856.	1857.	1858.	1859.
Steuben ....Maine....	May 11								
Manchester ....New Hamp...	May 8								
Salmon Falls.................do......				May 10					
Somersworth ....do......				May 13					
Brattleborough..............do......	April 26								
North Attleborough..Massachusetts.		May 3							
East Windsor..........Connecticut..			April 22						
Middletown...................do......		April 21							
Ceres.....................New York...	April 25								
Chatham ....do......	May 1	May 13							
New Lebanon................do......	May 1		May 1						
North Salem ....do......	April 11								
Penn Yan ....do......							May 20		
Plattsburg ....do......	May 4	May 10							
Rochester ....do......			May 12						
Somersville ....do......	May 10								
Waterloo ....do......		April 25							
Burlington.............New Jersey...		April 20							
Chester ....Pennsylvania..	May 7								
Freeport.........................do......		May 13	May 10						
Gettysburg ....do......		May 4							
Hollidaysburg ....do......		April 25	April 28						
Mercersburg ....do......		April 28							
Lima ....do......		April 30	April 14	April 21	April 25				

VIOLA CUCULLATA.—*Hooded Violet*—Continued.

Name of Station.	1851.	1852.	1853.	1854.	1855.	1856.	1857.	1858.	1859.
Meadville .... Pennsylvania..	April 15								
Radnor .... do......							April 18		
Reading .... do......	April 12								
Darby .... do......		April 17	April 30						
Sugar Grove .... do......	May 21								
Upper Darby .... do......		April 29	April 12						
Hagerstown .... Maryland...		April 26	April 24						
Sykesville .... do......	April 8	April 29							
Mossy Creek .... Virginia....		April 20							
Eutaw .... Alabama....		March 9							
Knoxville .... Tennessee....		March 26							
Lebanon .... do......	April 1								
Maysville .... Kentucky...			April 18						
Trenton .... Missouri....		April 15	April 12	April 8					
Belle Centre .... Ohio.....		April 20							
Cincinnati .... do......			April 11						
Germantown .... do......		May 6							
Keene .... do......	April 6								
Richmond .... Indiana....	April 4								
Athens .... Illinois....		April 12	April 11						
Augusta .... do......	April 10	April 13	April 16						
Kaposia .... Minnesota...	May 12								
Lac qui Parle .... do......			May 5						
Dubuque .... Iowa.....	May 10								
Pleasant Plain .... do......					April 22				

VITIS ÆSTIVALIS.—*Summer Grape.*

Name of Station.	1851.	1852.	1853.	1854.	1855.	1856.	1857.	1858.	1859.
Manchester .... New Hamp..	June 29	June 17							
Salmon Falls .... do......				June 21					
North Attleborough.. Massachusetts.		June 18							
Flatbush .... New York...			June 10						
Rochester .... do......				June 6					
West Point .... do......			June 14						
Burlington .... New Jersey...		June 10							
Darby .... Pennsylvania..			June 2						
Fleming .... do......	May 27								
Gettysburg .... do......		June 16	May 20	June 2					
Radnor .... do......			June 10						
Upper Darby .... do......		April 16							
Genito .... Virginia....		April 25							
Madison C. H .... do......		May 26							
Mossy Creek .... do......		May 20							
Chapel Hill .... N. Carolina..			May 24						
Camden .... S. Carolina..		April 18							
Weewokaville .... Alabama...		April 15	May 15						
Knoxville .... Tennessee...		May 20							
Belle Centre .... Ohio.....		June 20							
Athens .... Illinois....		May 23			May 17				
Augusta .... do......			May 26						

DATES

OF

RIPENING OF FRUITS.

CERASUS CERASUS.—*Garden Cherry.*

NAME OF STATION.	1851.	1852.	1853.	1854.	1855.	1856.	1857.	1858.	1859.
Cornish ... Maine						July 20	July 30		
Monson ... do						July 25			
Perry ... do						July 30			
Craftsbury ... Vermont						July 25	July 28		
Newark ... do						July 30			
Stanbridge ... do						July 15			
West Rupert ... do						Aug. 24	Aug. 4		
Westfield ... Massachusetts						June 30			
Columbia ... Connecticut							July 10	June 29	
Georgetown ... do						June 25			
Norwich ... do						June 30	June 28		
Preston ... do						July 8			
Clinton ... New York							July 19		
Eden ... do						July 15	July 21		
Flatbush ... do							July 8		
Geneva ... do						July 15			
Lake ... do						July 16			
Lowville ... do						July 25	Aug. 10	July 15	
Mexico ... do						July 16			
Ovid ... do						June 30			
Plainville ... do						July 18			
Rochester ... do						July 10			
Spencertown ... do						July 15			
Huntington ... Pennsylvania						June 6			
Lima ... do		June 12	July 1	June 10	June 30				
Nazareth ... do						July 10			
Ridge ... Maryland						June 26			
Sykesville ... do						June 29			
Berryville ... Virginia						June 11			
Crack Whip ... do							July 5		
Crichton's Store ... do						June 15			
Poplar Grove ... do						June 22			June 8
Winchester ... do						June 12			
Sparta ... Georgia						April 30			
Zebulon ... do						June 20			
Fairview ... Kentucky									May 25
St. Louis ... Missouri						June 2			
Edinburg ... Ohio							July 11		
Elk Run ... do									June 25
Germantown ... do						June 20			
Hamilton ... do						June 15			
Hiram ... do						July 13	July 27		
Jefferson ... do						July 8			
Rockport ... do									Aug. 1
Troy ... do									June 1
Welchfield ... do							July 24		
Augusta ... Illinois						June 18			
Manchester ... do						June 28		June 20	
Riley ... do						July 4			
Warsaw ... do						June 17			
West Salem ... do						June 13	June 30		
Winnebago ... do									July 1
Cooper ... Michigan						June 29			
Norway ... Wisconsin						June 25			
Platteville ... do						June 30			
Madison ... do						July 29			
Wyandotte ... do									June 25
Beaver Bay ... Minnesota								Aug. 20	
Muscatine ... Iowa						June 26			
Pleasant Plain ... do						Aug. 1			
Wolfsville ... Nova Scotia							July 11		

FRAGARIA VESCA.—*Field Strawberry.*

NAME OF STATION.	1851.	1852.	1853.	1854.	1855.	1856.	1857.	1858.	1859.
Cornish ... Maine						June 21	June 25		
Monson ... do						July 1			
Perry ... do						July 4			June 25

FRAGARIA VESCA.—*Field Strawberry*—Continued.

Name of Station.	1851.	1852.	1853.	1854.	1855.	1856.	1857.	1858.	1859.
Steuben .... Maine....		June 20	June 20			July 8			
Londonderry .... New Hamp..		June 15	June 14						
Manchester .... do......		June 25							
Salmon Falls .... do......				June 17					
Stratford .... do......						June 26			
Brandon .... Vermont...						June 20			
Craftsbury .... do......						June 28	July 1		
Newark .... do......						June 30			
Stanbridge .... do......						June 29			
Shelburne .... do......						June 17			
Stockbridge .... do......			June 8						
West Rupert .... do......						June 2[illegible]	June 25		
North Attleborough.. Massachusetts.		June 12							
Westfield .... do......						June 22			
Columbia .... Connecticut..								June 26	
East Windsor Hill .... do......			June 7						
Georgetown .... do......						June 12			
Middletown .... do......		June 9	June 7						
Norwich .... do......						June 23	June 28		
Preston .... do......						June 18			
Angelica .... New York ..						June 4			
Clinton .... do......							June 29		
Eden .... do......						June 10			
Flatbush .... do......							June 10		
Lake .... do......						June 24			
Lowville .... do......						July 4	July 3	July 6	
Mexico .... do......						June 24			
North Salem .... do......		June 8							
Ogdensburg .... do......						June 22			
Ovid .... do......						June 28			
Plattsburg .... do......		June 20							
Rochester .... do......						June 14			
Spencertown .... do......						June 25			
West Day .... do......									June 10
West Point .... do......		June 10	June 18						
Burlington .... New Jersey..		June 2							
Bellefonte .... Pennsylvania.								June 11	
Easton .... do......				June 12					
Gettysburg .... do......		June 4	June 10	June 3					
Hollidaysburg .... do......		June 25							
Huntington .... do......						June 9	June 16		
Lima .... do......						June 7			
Meadville .... do......		June 12							
Morrisville .... do......						June 10			
Nazareth .... do......						June 25			
Darby .... do......			May 24						
Ridge .... Maryland...						June 5			
Hagerstown .... do......			May 22						
Sykesville .... do......		May 25	May 20						
Berryville .... Virginia....						May 30			
Crack Whip .... do......							June 7		
Crichton's Store .... do......			April 21			May 24			
Madison C. H .... do......		May 28							
Mossy Creek .... do......		May 25							
Peach Grove .... do......						June 4			
Plains .... do......									June 5
Poplar Grove .... do......						June 2	June 8		
Portsmouth .... do......		May 9							
Wardensville .... do......						May 31			
Winchester .... do......						June 4			
Chapel Hill .... N. Carolina..			May 18						
Camden .... S. Carolina..		April 17							
Savannah .... Georgia ...						April 3			
Sparta .... do......						April 1			
Varnell's Station .... do......									April 29
Zebulon .... do......						May 1			
Seville .... Florida...									April 4
Greensborough .... Alabama ...						May 2			
Weewokaville .... do......		April 15	May 12						
Columbus .... Mississippi ..						May 1			

FRAGARIA VESCA.—*Field Strawberry*—Continued.

Name of Station.	1851.	1852.	1853.	1854.	1855.	1856.	1857.	1858.	1859.
Glenwood .... Tennessee ..			May 9						
Walnut Grove .... do						June 6			
Fair View .... Kentucky ..									May 25
Trenton .... Missouri ...			May 26	May 20					
Belle Centre .... Ohio		June 19							
Cheviot .... do						May 30			
Elk Run .... do									May 25
Germantown .... do						May 28			
Hiram .... do						June 12	June 27		
Jefferson .... do						June 19			
Troy .... do									May 21
Welchfield .... do							July 7		
Richmond .... do	April 22								
Indianapolis .... Indiana ...									May 20
Athens .... Illinois						May 30			
Carthage .... do						May 31			
Galesburg .... do									June 15
Manchester .... do						May 31			
Marengo .... do						June 18			
Ottawa .... do								June 5	
Warsaw .... do						June 2			
West Salem .... do						June 1	June 7		
Winnebago .... do									June 15
Cooper .... Michigan ...						June 19			
Romeo .... do						June 15			
Wyandotte .... do								June 10	June 4
Appleton .... Wisconsin ..						June 9			
Greenfield .... do									June 25
Norway .... do						June 10			
Platteville .... do						June 20			
Madison .... do						June 30			
Beaver Bay .... Minnesota ..								June 20	
Fort Ripley .... do		June 18							
Lac qui Parle .... do			June 15	June 11					
Franklin .... Iowa						June 6			
Muscatine .... do			June 10			June 8			
Pleasant Plain .... do						June 9			
Salem Prairie .... Oregon ...						April 31			
Wolfville .... Nova Scotia.							June 27		

GAYLUSSACIA RESINOSA.—*Whortleberry.*

Name of Station.	1851.	1852.	1853.	1854.	1855.	1856.	1857.	1858.	1859.
Naples .... Maine							Aug. 12		
North Attleborough .. Massachusetts.				July 13	July 14				
Worcester .... do							Aug. 5		
Columbia .... Connecticut ..							Aug. 10	Aug. 1	
Nichols .... New York ..								Aug. 20	
Spencertown .... do					May 15				
Sykesville .... Maryland ..				July 12			July 20		
Crack Whip .... Virginia ...							July 20		
Crichton's Store .... do							July 20		
Poplar Grove .... do								July 4	June 24
Rose Hill .... do						June 28			June 25
Ashtabula .... Ohio				July 3					
Burlington .... Minnesota ..								July 10	
Princeton .... do							Aug. 1		

PERSICA VULGARIS—*Peach.*

Name of Station.	1851.	1852.	1853.	1854.	1855.	1856.	1857.	1858.	1859.
Londonderry .... New Hamp ..		Sept. 12	Sept. 15						
Manchester .... do		Sept. 25							
West Rupert .... Vermont ...						Sept. 20			
North Attleborough .. Massachusetts.				Aug. 25	Aug. 1				
Columbia .... Connecticut ..							Sept. 23	Aug. 24	

PERSICA VULGARIS.—*Peach*—Continued.

Name of Station.	1851.	1852.	1853.	1854.	1855.	1856.	1857.	1858.	1859.
Georgetown … Connecticut						Aug. 31			
Norwich … do							Aug. 28		
Eden … New York						Sept. 14	Sept. 25		
Fishkill Landing … do								Aug. 4	Aug. 10
Flatbush … do		Aug. 1			Aug. 15		Sept. 19		
Nichols … do								Sept. 12	
Plainville … do						Aug. 28			
Bellefonte … Pennsylvania								Sept. 20	
Hollidaysburg … do		Sept. 10							
Ridge … Maryland						Aug. 14			
Sykesville … do		Aug. 18	Aug. 20				Sept. 20		
Buffalo … Virginia					Aug. 10				
Crichton's Store … do									Aug. 10
Mossy Creek … do							Aug. 25		
Poplar Grove … do								Aug. 22	Aug. 28
Rose Hill … do						Aug. 20			Aug. 20
Winchester … do						Aug. 15			
Chapel Hill … N. Carolina			Aug. 1						
Seville … Florida									July 15
Eutaw … Alabama		July 20							
Greensborough … do						July 5	July 1	June 27	
Columbus … Mississippi						June 30			
Big Pond … Louisiana						July 23			
Cross Roads … Texas									June 15
Walnut Grove … Tennessee						Aug. 28			
Fairview … Kentucky									Aug. 1
Maysville … do			July 25						
Ashtabula … Ohio				Sept. 8					
Cleveland … do				Aug. 30	Aug. 30				
Germantown … do			Aug. 5						
Hiram … do							Sept. 21	Sept. 10	
Hocking Port … do							Aug. 30		
Madison … do							Sept. 30		
Mount Healthy … do				Aug. 4	Aug. 1				
Rockport … do									Aug. 1
Troy … do									Aug. 20
Laconia … Indiana									Aug. 15
Richmond … do	July 25								
Augusta … Illinois			Aug. 20						
Brighton … do							Sept. 12	Sept. 6	
Manchester … do							Sept. 15		
Warsaw … do						Sept. 22			
Ann Arbor … Michigan		Oct. 6							
Cooper … do						Aug. 6			
Wyandotte … do									Sept. 10
Keokuk … Iowa						Aug. 15			
Fairfield … do									Sept. 19
Leipsig … Saxony								Sept. 20	

PRUNUS DOMESTICA.—*Plum.*

Name of Station.	1851.	1852.	1853.	1854.	1855.	1856.	1857.	1858.	1859.
Monson … Maine						Sept. 21			
Perry … do						July 30			
Newark … Vermont						Aug. 30			
Stanbridge … do						Aug. 30			
Bridgewater … Massachusetts						Aug. 30			
Westfield … do						Aug. 28			
Columbia … Connecticut							Sept 8?		
Georgetown … do						Aug. 28			
Eden … New York						Aug. 26	Aug. 31		
Flatbush … do							Sept. 24		
Lowville … do						Sept. 3	Sept. 12	Sept. 1	
Plainville … do						Sept. 11			
Bellefonte … Pennsylvania								Sept. 1	
Crichton's Store … Virginia						July 1			
Poplar Grove … do						July 20		Aug. 10	
Salem … do							Aug. 28		

PRUNUS DOMESTICA.—*Plum*—Continued.

Name of Station.		1851.	1852.	1853.	1854.	1855.	1856.	1857.	1858.	1859.
Savannah	Georgia						May 3			
Zebulon	do						May 29			
Greensborough	Alabama						June 6			
Big Pond	Louisiana						May 16			
Cross Roads	Texas									June 5
Fairview	Kentucky									Aug. 1
Galesburg	Illinois									Sept. 1
Riley	do						Sept. 10			
Wyandotte	Michigan									April 13
Madison	Wisconsin						Aug. 28			
Pleasant Plain	Iowa						June 19			
Wolfville	Nova Scotia						Sept. 15			

PYRUS COMMUNIS.—*Pear.*

Name of Station.		1851.	1852.	1853.	1854.	1855.	1856.	1857.	1858.	1859.
Gardiner	Maine							Sept. 29		
Londonderry	New Hamp.		Sept. 1	Sept. 3						
West Enfield	do							Sept. 12		
West Rupert	Vermont						Aug. 26	Oct. 4		
Bridgewater	Massachusetts						Aug. 31			
New Ashford	do						Oct. 5			
North Attleborough	do		Aug. 16		Aug. 20	Aug. 10				
Westfield	do						Aug. 24			
Worcester	do							Aug. 5		
Columbia	Connecticut							Sept. 7	Sept. 4	
Georgetown	do						Aug. 29			
Norwich	do						Aug. 15	Sept. 1		
Eden	New York							Sept. 4		
Fishkill Landing	do								Aug. 20	Aug. 15
Flatbush	do		July 20			Aug. 7		Aug. 7		
Lake	do						Sept. 27	Oct. 12	Sept. 18	Sept. 29
Lowville	do						Oct. 1		Sept. 28	
Plainville	do						Sept. 4			
Spencertown	do						Aug. 15	Sept. 15		
West Concord	do						Sept. 15			
Bellefonte	Pennsylvania								Aug. 31	
Lima	do							Aug. 1		
Nazareth	do						Aug. 1			
Darby	do			July 20						
Sykesville	Maryland		Sept. 15	Aug. 4	Sept. 4			Sept. 5		
Buffalo	Virginia					Aug. 21				
Crichton's Store	do						July 31		July 31	Aug. 15
Poplar Grove	do						Aug. 30			
Savannah	Georgia						Sept. 3			
Greensborough	Alabama						June 15	July 10	June 24	
Greene Springs	do						June 25			
Columbus	Mississippi						June 31			
Fairview	Kentucky									Aug. 10
Maysville	do			July 22						
Ashtabula	Ohio				Aug. 1					
Cheviot	do						Aug. 10			
Cleveland	do				July 30					
Edinburg	do							Aug. 22		
Germantown	do		Aug. 8	Aug. 1						
Hiram	do							Aug. 30	Aug. 25	
Mount Healthy	do				Aug. 1	Aug. 1				
Rockport	do									Sept. 1
Troy	do									July 10
Pekin	Illinois								Aug. 8	
Wyandotte	Michigan								June 30	April 25
Madison	Wisconsin						Sept. 24			
Fairfield	Iowa									Aug. 26
Keokuk	do						Sept. 5			
Horton	Nova Scotia					Sept. 16				
Wolfville	do						Sept. 16			
Leipsig	Saxony							Aug. 20		

PYRUS MALUS.—*Apple.*

Name of Station.		1851.	1852.	1853.	1854.	1855.	1856.	1857.	1858.	1859.
Cornish	Maine							Oct. 15		
Gardiner	do							Sept. 1		
Naples	do							Oct. 10		
Steuben	do		Oct 1			Sept. 20		Oct. 10		
Londonderry	New Hampshire		Sept. 28	Sept. 20						
Manchester	do		Sept. 20							
West Enfield	do							Sept. 20		
Lunenburg	Vermont									July 31
Newark	do						Oct. 4			
Stanbridge	do						Oct. 1			
West Rupert	do							Oct. 9		
Bridgewater	Mass						Aug. 10			
North Attleborough	do		July 1		Aug. 25	July 20				
Westfield	do						Aug. 18			
Worcester	do							Aug. 8		
Columbia	Connecticut							Sept. 26	Sept. 30	
Georgetown	do						Aug. 15			
Norwich	do						Aug 20			
Eden	New York							Aug. 15		
Fishkill Landing	do								Aug. 20	Sept. 10
Flatbush	do		Aug. 10							
Lake	do						Sept. 30	Oct. 6	Sept. 25	Oct. 1
Lowville	do						Oct. 9			
Nichols	do									Aug. 3
Ogdensburg	do						Aug. 17			
Plainville	do						Aug. 17			
Plattsburg	do		July 20							
Spencertown	do					Oct. 1	Oct. 15			
Bellefonte	Pennsylvania								Sept. 20	
Huntingdon	do						July 14			
Lima	do							Aug. 1		
Darby	do			July 18						
Ridge	Maryland						Sept. 22			
Sykesville	do		Oct. 1	Sept. 25	Oct. 4		Oct. 1	Oct. 4		
Buffalo	Virginia					Aug. 1				
Crichton's Store	do								Aug. 1	Aug. 15
Poplar Grove	do								July 20	July 10
Chapel Hill	N. Carolina			Aug. 1						
Savannah	Georgia						Sept. 3			
Greensborough	Alabama						Aug. 1	July 15		
Greene Springs	do						June 20			
Columbus	Mississippi						June 16			
Cross Roads	Texas									June 15
Fairview	Kentucky									July 18
Maysville	do			July 20						
Ashtabula	Ohio				Aug. 15					
Cleveland	do				July 26					
Edinburg	do							Sept. 12		
Elk Run	do									Aug. 1
Germantown	do		July 20	Aug. 6						
Hamilton	do						July 7			
Hiram	do							Sept. 4	Aug. 30	
Hocking Port	do							Aug. 20		
Mount Healthy	do				Aug. 1	Aug. 1				
Rockport	do									Aug. 20
Troy	do									Aug. 1
West Bedford	do							Oct. 3		
Brighton	Illinois							Sept. 1		
Manchester	do						July 12			
West Salem	do							Sept. 4		
Cooper	Michigan						Aug. 20			
Wyandotte	do									July 18
Madison	Wisconsin						Sept. 24			
Fairfield	Iowa									Sept. 18
Keokuk	do						Oct. 1			
Salem Prairie	Oregon						Oct. 9			
Horton	Nova Scotia							April 28		
Wolfville	do						Sept. 28			
Stanbridge	Canada							Oct. 20		
Leipsig	Saxony								Sept. 10	

RIBES GROSSULARIA.—*Gooseberry.*

Name of Station.		1851.	1852.	1853.	1854.	1855.	1856.	1857.	1858.	1859.
Cornish	Maine						July 30			
Monson	do						Aug. 1			
Perry	do						Aug. 16			
Londonderry	New Hampshire			July 18						
Craftsbury	Vermont						Aug. 15			
Newark	do						July 31			
Stanbridge	do						Aug. 15			
Stockbridge	do			Aug. 5						
West Rupert	do							Aug. 17		
Georgetown	Connecticut						July 12			
Eden	New York						July 22			
Flatbush	do		July 10					July 13		
Geneva	do						July 21			
Lake	do						July 31			
Lowville	do						Aug. 19		Sept. 11	
Mexico	do						July 20			
Plainville	do						Aug. 3			
Plattsburg	do		July 30							
Spencertown	do						July 4			
Waterloo	do		July 25							
West Point	do		July 6							
Burlington	New Jersey		July 20							
Bellefonte	Pennsylvania								July 31	
Gettysburg	do		June 30	July 4						
Lima	do			July 1			July 9			
Meadville	do						July 18			
Morrisville	do						June 20			
Nazareth	do						July 6			
Darby	do			Aug. 7						
Ridge	Maryland						June 20			
Sykesville	do		June 22	June 16						
Berryville	Virginia						June 30			
Poplar Grove	do						June 17			
Fairview	Kentucky									June 10
Belle Centre	Ohio		July 24							
Edinburg	do							Aug. 10		
Elk Run	do									July 10
Germantown	do			July 15						
Jefferson	do						July 17			
Troy	do									June 29
Indianapolis	Indiana									June 21
Warsaw	Illinois						June 29			
Norway	Wisconsin						July 31			
Madison	do						July 20			
Beaver Bay	Minnesota								Aug. 20	
Lac qui Parle	do			July 6						
Fairfield	Iowa									June 21
Pleasant Plain	do						July 14			
Salem Prairie	do						July 15			
Wolfville	Nova Scotia							July 24		

RIBES RUBRUM.—*Red Currant.*

Name of Station.		1851.	1852.	1853.	1854.	1855.	1856.	1857.	1858.	1859.
Cornish	Maine						July 20	July 15		
Monson	do						July 25			
Naples	do							Aug. 5		
Perry	do						July 25			July 25
Steuben	do					Sept. 10	July 26			
Londonderry	New Hamp		July 6	July 6						
Stratford	do						July 20			
West Enfield	do							July 25		
Brandon	Vermont						July 12			
Craftsbury	do						July 18	July 25		
Newark	do						July 26			
Stanbridge	do						Aug. 20			
Stockbridge	do			July 5						
West Rupert	do							Aug. 26		

RIBES RUBRUM.—*Red Currant*—Continued.

Name of Station.		1851.	1852.	1853.	1854.	1855.	1856.	1857.	1858.	1859.
Florida	Massachusetts.						Aug. 10	Aug. 10	Aug. 10	
North Attleborough	do.		July 4		July 5	July 13				
Point Judith	Rhode Island.				July 15					
Columbia	Connecticut.							July 18	July 16	
East Windsor	do.		July 5							
Georgetown	do.						July 2			
Norwich	do.							July 14		
Preston	do.						July 11			
Chatham	New York.		July 18							
Clinton	do.							July 23		
Eden	do.						July 20	July 16		
Fishkill Landing	do.									July 1
Flatbush	do.		July 11					July 8		
Geneva	do.						July 24			
Lake	do.						July 14	July 14	July 11	July 7
Lowville	do.						July 24	Aug. 11	July 20	
Mexico	do.						July 11			
Nichols	do.								July 4	July 6
Ovid	do.				July 8		July 7			
Plainville	do.						July 21			
Plattsburg	do.		July 4							
Rochester	do.						July 6			
Spencertown	do.					July 15	Aug. 15			
West Point	do.		June 25	June 10						
Burlington	New Jersey.		July 20							
Gettysburg	Pennsylvania.			July 4	July 4					
Lima	do.			July 1			June 29	June 22		
Meadville	do.						July 24			
Morrisville	do.						July 15			
Nazareth	do.						July 7	July 17		
Darby	do.			June 28						
Easton	Maryland.				June 12					
Ridge	do.						June 26			
Sykesville	do.		June 18	June 16	June 25		June 26	July 1		
Berryville	Virginia.						June 26			
Buffalo	do.					June 26				
Clark county	do.							June 25		
Crack Whip	do.							July 13		
Crichton's Store	do.									July 10
Mossy Creek	do.		June 1							
Peach Grove	do.						June 2			
Poplar Grove	do.						June 19	June 21	June 13	June 8
Rose Hill	do.						June 5			
Winchester	do.						July 5			
Fairview	Kentucky.									June 1
Ashtabula	Ohio.				June 28					
Belle Centre	do.		June 22		July 1				July 1	
Cleveland	do.				July 12	July 18				
Edinburg	do.							July 20		
Elk Run	do.									July 4
Germantown	do.				June 29		June 16			
Hiram	do.						July 11	July 26	July 12	
Hocking Port	do.							July 8		
Savannah	do.							June 1		
Troy	do.									June 15
Indianapolis	Indiana.									June 15
Augusta	Illinois.		June 25				June 15	July 1		
Galesburg	do.									June 15
Manchester	do.						June 10			
Marengo	do.							July 20	July 10	
Ottawa	do.								June 27	
Warsaw	do.						June 6			
West Salem	do.						June 12	June 28		
Winnebago	do.									July 4
Ann Arbor	Michigan.		July 4							
Cooper	do.						June 25			
Flint	do.					July 1				
Romeo	do.						July 8			
Wyandotte	do.									June 20

RIBES RUBRUM.—*Red Currant*—Continued.

Name of Station.		1851.	1852.	1853.	1854.	1855.	1856.	1857.	1858.	1859.
Norway	Wisconsin						July 1			
Platteville	do						June 28			
Madison	do						July 5			
Border Plains	Iowa								July 10	July 9
Fairfield	do									June 18
Keokuk	do						June 28			
Muscatine	do						June 27			
Pleasant Plain	do						June 24			
Salem Prairie	Oregon						July 8			
Wolfville	Nova Scotia							July 17		
Stanbridge	Canada							June 1		
Leipsig	Saxony								July 15	

RUBUS STRIGOSUS.—*Red Raspberry.*

Name of Station.		1851.	1852.	1853.	1854.	1855.	1856.	1857.	1858.	1859.
Cornish	Maine						July 19	July 17		
Monson	do						July 26			
Perry	do						July 25			
Steuben	do						July 30			
Stratford	New Hamp.						July 15			
Brandon	Vermont						July 11			
Craftsbury	do							July 30		
Newark	do						July 25			
Stanbridge	do						July 29			
Columbia	Connecticut							July 10		
Georgetown	do						July 5			
Norwich	do							July 22		
Preston	do						July 14			
Clinton	New York							July 15		
Eden	do							July 19		
Flatbush	do							July 12		
Geneva	do						July 29			
Lake	do						July 6			
Lowville	do						July 26	July 30	July 29	
Mexico	do						July 11			
Ovid	do						July 17			
Plainville	do						July 20			
Spencertown	do					Aug 11				
West Concord	do						Sept. 1			
Lima	Pennsylvania						July 4			
Meadville	do						July 28			
Nazareth	do						July 15			
Ridge	Maryland						June 29			
Sykesville	do						June 26			
Edinburg	Ohio							July 27		
Germantown	do						June 28			
Hiram	do						July 7	July 20		
Jefferson	do						July 9			
Cooper	Michigan						July 11			
Wyandotte	do								June 6	
Madison	Wisconsin						July 22			
Lac qui Parle	Minnesota			July 19						
Franklin	Iowa						July 1			
Muscatine	do						June 30			
Wolfville	Nova Scotia							July 25		

RUBUS VILLOSUS.—*Blackberry.*

Name of Station.		1851.	1852.	1853.	1854.	1855.	1856.	1857.	1858.	1859.
Gardiner	Maine							Sept. 1		
Naples	do							Sept. 2		
Londonderry	New Hamp.		July 30	July 14						
Shelburne	do								Sept. 1	
West Enfield	do							Aug. 18		
Lunenburg	Vermont									Sept. 1
Stockbridge	do			Aug. 1						

RUBUS VILLOSUS.—*Blackberry*—Continued.

Name of Station.	1851.	1852.	1853.	1854.	1855.	1856.	1857.	1858.	1859.
North Attleborough .. Massachusetts		July 10			July 20				
Columbia .. Connecticut							Aug. 15	Aug. 10	
Eden .. New York						July 21			
Lake .. do									Aug. 11
Mexico .. do						July 31			
Nichols .. do								Aug 2	July 30
North Salem .. do		July 10							
Plattsburg .. do		July 27							
Rochester .. do						July 4			
Spencertown .. do					July 15				
West Point .. do			Aug. 5						
Fleming Centre .. Pennsylvania							Aug. 15		
Lima .. do				July 17			Aug. 1		
Meadville .. do		July 25							
Radnor .. do			June 18						
Easton .. Maryland				June 25					
Sykesville .. do		July 11	July 17	July 11			Aug. 1		
Berryville .. Virginia						June 30			
Buffalo .. do					July 13				
Crack Whip .. do							July 18		
Crichton's Store .. do						June 25		July 25	July 10
Poplar Grove .. do						June 29		July 1	
Winchester .. do						July 2			
Chapel Hill .. N. Carolina			July 1						
Fulton .. S. Carolina					June 15				
Greensborough .. Alabama						June 6	June 10	May 28	
Columbus .. Mississippi						May 22			
Trinity .. Louisiana							June 5		
Knoxville .. Tennessee		June 18							
Maysville .. Kentucky			July 3						
Hannibal .. Missouri				July 25					
Belle Centre .. Ohio		July 24							
Cleveland .. do				Aug. 16					
Hiram .. do							Aug. 24	Aug. 4	
Jefferson .. do						July 19			
Mount Healthy .. do				Aug. 1	Aug. 1				
Augusta .. Illinois		July 22	July 10				July 10		
Brighton .. do							Aug. 7		
Pekin .. do								Aug. 16	
West Salem .. do							Aug. 1		
Wyandotte .. Michigan								Aug. 1	
Beaver Bay .. Wisconsin								Aug. 20	
Fairfield .. Iowa									Aug. 4
Stanbridge .. Canada							July 30		

DATES OF DEFOLIATION

OR

FALL OF LEAF IN PLANTS.

22*

ACER DASYCARPUM.—*White or Silver Maple.*

Name of Station.		1851.	1852.	1853.	1854.	1855.	1856.	1857.	1858.	1859.
Brunswick	Maine							Nov. 6	Nov. 5	
Gardiner	do							Oct. 20		
Brandon	Vermont								Oct. 21	
Castleton	do				Nov. 1					
Florida	Massachusetts								Oct. 15	
Worcester	do							Nov. 1		
Point Judith	Rhode Island				Nov. 15					
Columbia	Connecticut								Oct. 20	
Fishkill Landing	New York							Nov. 2		Oct. 10
Rochester	do							Oct. 20		
West Point	do			Oct. 25						
Sykesville	Maryland							Oct. 30		
Buffalo	Virginia					Oct. 25				
Crichton's Store	do									Oct. 25
Greensborough	Alabama						Nov. 30			
Cleveland	Ohio				Nov. 13	Nov. 5				
Hiram	do							Oct. 14		
Hocking Port	do							Oct. 25		
Brighton	Illinois								Oct. 4	
Riley	do							Oct. 12		
Princeton	Minnesota							Oct. 10		
Stanbridge	Canada							Nov. 10	Oct. 10	

ACER RUBRUM.—*Red or Soft Maple.*

Name of Station.		1851.	1852.	1853.	1854.	1855.	1856.	1857.	1858.	1859.
Cornish	Maine							Oct. 25		
Brunswick	do							Oct. 21	Oct. 24	
Monson	do						Oct. 15			
Gardiner	do							Oct. 17		
Naples	do							Oct. 12		
Steuben	do		Oct. 5							
Londonderry	New Hamp.			Oct. 12						
Manchester	do		Oct. 15		Oct. 15					
West Enfield	do						Oct. 10			
Brandon	Vermont			Oct. 21	Oct. 16			Oct. 15	Oct. 15	
Castleton	do				Oct. 1					
Craftsbury	do						Oct. 10			
West Rupert	do						Oct. 30			
Bridgewater	Massachusetts						Nov. 2			
Florida	do							Oct. 20	Oct. 15	
North Attleborough	do				Oct. 5					
Richmond	do		Oct. 25							
Worcester	do							Oct. 31		
Point Judith	Rhode Island				Nov. 2					
Columbia	Connecticut							Oct. 7	Oct. 15	
Georgetown	do						Oct. 19			
Middletown	do		Oct. 4							
Eden	New York						Oct. 16			
Fishkill Landing	do							Nov. 2		Oct. 10
Lake	do						Oct. 18	Oct. 8		
Lowville	do						Oct. 20			
Mexico	do						Oct. 27			
Nichols	do								Oct. 20	
North Salem	do		Oct. 18							
Ogdensburg	do			Oct. 15						
Rochester	do							Oct. 10		
Spencertown	do					Nov. 1				
West Point	do		Nov. 3	Oct. 25						
Fleming	Pennsylvania							Oct. 12		
Hollidaysburg	do		Oct. 2							
Meadville	do		Oct. 10				Oct. 8			
Murrysville	do							Oct. 25		
Shamokin	do							Oct. 1		
Darby	do			Nov. 5						
Easton	Maryland				Oct. 12					
Sykesville	do		Oct. 1	Oct. 15	Oct. 29			Oct. 27		

ACER RUBRUM.—*Red or Soft Maple*—Continued.

Name of Station.	1851.	1852.	1853.	1854.	1855.	1856.	1857.	1858.	1859.
Buffalo … Virginia					Oct. 25				
Crichton's Store … do			Nov. 1			Oct. 6			
Mossy Creek … do		Oct. 20							
Poplar Grove … do						Sept. 30		Sept. 26	Oct. 1
Rose Hill … do						Oct. 31	Oct. 20		Oct. 30
Savannah … Georgia						Sept. 5			
Sparta … do							Nov. 5		
Alligator … Florida							Oct. 1		
Greensborough … Alabama						Nov. 25			
Weewokaville … do		Nov. 5							
Big Pond … Louisiana						Oct. 27			
Concordia … do							Nov. 19		
Walnut Grove … Tennessee						Oct. 21			
Maysville … Kentucky			Nov. 2						
Belle Centre … Ohio		Oct. 26						Oct. 10	
Cleveland … do				Oct. 27	Oct. 25				
Hiram … do						Oct. 7	Oct. 14	Oct. 15	
Hocking Port … do							Oct. 28		
Jefferson … do						Oct. 23			
Madison … do							Nov. 1		
Savannah … do							Oct. 10		
West Bedford … do						Oct. 3			
Athens … Illinois						Oct. 15			
Brighton … do							Oct. 9	Oct. 4	
Edgington … do							Oct. 19		
West Salem … do						Oct. 19	Nov. 1		
Holland … Michigan						Sept. 21			
Madison … Wisconsin						Oct. 24			
Lac qui Parle … Minnesota			Oct. 15						
Princeton … do							Oct. 10		
Border Plains … Iowa						Sept. 17	Oct. 15		
Leavenworth City … Kansas								Oct. 18	
Wolfsville … Nova Scotia						Oct. 15			
Stanbridge … Canada						Nov. 29	Nov. 10	Oct. 10	

ACER SACCHARINUM.—*Sugar Maple.*

Name of Station.	1851.	1852.	1853.	1854.	1855.	1856.	1857.	1858.	1859.
Cornish … Maine							Oct. 28		
Brunswick … do							Oct. 22	Oct. 26	
Naples … do							May 12		
Londonderry … New Hampshire			Oct. 17						
Manchester … do		Oct. 16		Oct. 15					
West Enfield … do							Oct. 15		
Brandon … Vermont			Oct. 22	Oct. 28			Oct. 22		
Castleton … do				Nov. 1					
Newark … do							Oct. 15		
Florida … Massachusetts								Oct. 15	
Richmond … do		Oct. 30							
Williamstown … do							Oct. 12		
Point Judith … Rhode Island				Nov. 3					
Columbia … Connecticut							Oct. 15		
Fishkill Landing … New York							Nov. 2		Oct. 10
Lake … do							Oct. 24	Oct. 25	
Mexico … do						Oct. 23			
Nichols … do								Oct. 15	
North Salem … do		Sept. 29							
Rochester … do							Nov. 1		
Spencertown … do					Nov. 1	Oct. 16			
West Point … do		Nov. 15	Oct. 25						
Fleming … Pennsylvania							Oct. 16		
Meadville … do		Oct. 15							
Murrysville … do							Oct. 30		
Darby … do			Oct. 24						
Easton … Maryland				Oct. 12					
Buffalo … Virginia					Oct. 25				
Crichton's Store … do			Oct. 25						Oct. 20
Mossy Creek … do		Oct. 20							

ACER SACCHARINUM.—*Sugar Maple*—Continued.

Name of Station.	1851.	1852.	1853.	1854.	1855.	1856	1857.	1858.	1859.
Poplar Grove, Virginia								Oct. 3	Oct. 10
Greensborough, Alabama						Nov. 25			
Weewokaville, do		Nov. 15							
Glenwood, Tennessee			Oct. 14						
Maysville, Kentucky			Nov. 2						
Belle Centre, Ohio		Nov. 1		Oct. 20				Oct. 20	
Cheviot, do						Oct. 20			
Cleveland, do				Oct. 30	Oct. 26				
Germantown, do		Oct. 20	Oct. 26	Oct. 29					
Hocking Port, do							Nov. 8		
Madison, do							Nov. 10		
Ripley, do							Nov. 1		
Savannah, do							Oct. 5		
Brighton, Illinois							Oct. 14	Oct. 3	
Marengo, do								Oct. 20	
Pekin, do								Oct. 24	
St. James, Michigan			Nov. 9						
Princeton, Minnesota							Oct. 10		
Border Plains, Iowa								Oct. 18	Oct. 18
Stanbridge, Canada							Nov. 10	Oct. 18	
Leipsig, Saxony								Nov. 1	

ÆSCULUS HIPPOCASTANUM.—*Horse Chestnut.*

Name of Station.	1851.	1852.	1853.	1854.	1855.	1856	1857.	1858.	1859.
Brunswick, Maine							Oct. 17	Oct. 25	
Castleton, Vermont				Nov. 10					
North Attleborough, do				Oct. 1					
Williamstown, Massachusetts							Oct. 16		
Worcester, do							Nov. 1		
Point Judith, Rhode Island				Oct. 27					
Columbia, Connecticut							Oct. 5	Oct. 25	
Middletown, do				Sept. 30					
Fishkill Landing, New York							Nov. 12		Oct. 1
Flatbush, do			Oct. 14						
Mexico, do						Oct. 27			
Nichols, do								Oct. 20	
Rochester, do							Oct. 20		
Spencertown, do					Nov. 1				
West Point, do			Oct. 25						
Meadville, Pennsylvania		Nov. 1							
Darby, do			Oct. 23						
Leipsig, Saxony								Oct. 28	

CARYA ALBA.—*Shell-bark Hickory.*

Name of Station.	1851.	1852.	1853.	1854.	1855.	1856	1857.	1858.	1859.
Brandon, Vermont							Oct. 22	Oct. 19	
Castleton, do				Oct. 15					
Columbia, Connecticut							Oct. 14	Oct. 25	
Lake, New York							Oct. 10	Oct. 10	
Nichols, do								Oct. 20	
Spencertown, do					Nov. 1				
Easton, Pennsylvania				Nov. 4					
Fleming, do							Oct. 20		
Murrysville, do							Nov. 5		
Buffalo, Virginia					Oct. 12				
Clark county, do							Nov. 1	Nov. 5	
Crichton's Store, do							Nov. 1		Oct. 20
Poplar Grove, do								Oct. 1	Oct. 12
Greensborough, Alabama						Oct. 31			
Belle Centre, Ohio				Oct. 12				Oct. 20	
Cleveland, do				Nov. 3	Oct. 29				
Hiram, do							Oct. 15		
Hocking Port, do							Oct. 20		
Savannah, do							Oct. 25		

CARYA ALBA.—*Shell-bark Hickory*—Continued.

Name of Station.	1851.	1852.	1853.	1854.	1855.	1856.	1857.	1858.	1859.
Brighton .... Illinois							Oct. 21	Oct. 30	
Edginton .... do							Nov. 1		
Pekin .... do								Oct. 25	
West Salem .... do							Nov. 7		
Border Plains .... Iowa								Oct. 12	Oct. 11
Fairfield .... do									Oct. 8
Fort Madison .... do				Nov. 1					
Leavenworth City .... Kansas								Oct. 20	

CASTENA VESCA.—*Chestnut.*

Name of Station.	1851.	1852.	1853.	1854.	1855.	1856.	1857.	1858.	1859.
Manchester .... New Hampshire		Oct. 10		Oct. 15					
Florida .... Massachusetts							Oct. 20		
Worcester .... do							Nov. 1		
Columbia .... Connecticut							Oct. 29	Oct. 14	
Fishkill Landing .... New York							Nov. 2		Oct. 7
Flatbush .... do			Nov. 5						
Lake .... do							Oct. 25		
Nichols .... do								Oct. 20	
Spencertown .... do					Nov. 1				
West Point .... do		Nov. 25	Oct. 25						
Fleming .... Pennsylvania							Oct. 25		
Meadville .... do		Oct. 25							
Darby .... do			Oct. 25						
Easton .... Maryland				Nov. 20					
Sykesville .... do		Oct. 1	Nov. 10	Oct. 29			Nov. 4		
Poplar Grove .... Virginia								Oct. 10	Oct. 12
Greensborough .... Alabama						Nov. 17			
Cleveland .... Ohio				Nov. 5					
Hiram .... do							Oct. 18	Oct. 20	
Madison .... do							Nov. 1		
Savannah .... do							Oct. 15		
Leipsig .... Saxony								Nov. 1	

CERASUS CERASUS.—*Garden Cherry.*

Name of Station.	1851.	1852.	1853.	1854.	1855.	1856.	1857.	1858.	1859.
Brunswick .... Maine							Oct. 22		
Monson .... do						Oct. 15			
Newark .... Vermont						Oct. 31			
West Rupert .... do						Oct. 29			
Bridgewater .... Massachusetts						Nov. 4			
Columbia .... Connecticut							Oct. 13		
Georgetown .... do						Oct. 31			
Norwich .... do						Oct. 11			
Angelica .... New York						Sept. 9			
Eden .... do						Oct. 20			
Flatbush .... do							Nov. 1		
Lowville .... do						Oct. 22	Oct. 21		
Bellefonte .... Pennsylvania								Oct. 25	
Crichton's Store .... Virginia						Oct. 3			
Poplar Grove .... do						Sept. 30			Oct. 16
Winchester .... do						Oct. 15			
Sparta .... Georgia							Nov. 10		
Zebulon .... do						Sept. 15			
Alligator .... Florida							Oct. 15		
Germantown .... Ohio						Oct. 7			
Hiram .... do							Oct. 19		
Jefferson .... do						Oct. 23			
West Bedford .... do						Oct. 10			
Marengo .... Illinois						Oct. 1			
West Salem .... do						Oct. 20			
Holland .... Michigan						Sept. 28			
Madison .... Wisconsin						Sept. 29			
Norway .... do						Oct. 5			
Pleasant Plain .... Iowa						Oct. 30			
Salem .... Oregon						Nov. 1			
Stanbridge .... Canada						Nov. 24			

CERCIS CANADENSIS.—*Red-bud.—Judas Tree.*

Name of Station.	1851.	1852.	1853.	1854.	1855.	1856.	1857.	1858.	1859.
Brunswick, Maine							Oct. 16		
Columbia, Connecticut							Oct. 12	Oct. 19	
Crichton's Store, Virginia			Nov. 1				Oct. 25		Oct. 25
Poplar Grove, do								Oct. 1	Oct. 16
Maysville, Kentucky			Nov. 3						
Belle Centre, Ohio		Oct. 24							
Brighton, Illinois								Sept. 27	
Pekin, do								Oct. 25	
Leavenworth City, Kansas								Oct. 22	

FRAXINUS AMERICANA.—*White Ash.*

Name of Station.	1851.	1852.	1853.	1854.	1855.	1856.	1857.	1858.	1859.
Cornish, Maine							Oct. 10		
Gardiner, do							Sept. 20		
Naples, do							Oct. 10		
Manchester, New Hamp				Oct. 1					
West Enfield, do							Oct. 15		
Brandon, Vermont			Oct. 16				Oct. 16	Oct. 18	
Florida, Massachusetts								Oct. 10	
Columbia, Connecticut							Oct. 8	Oct. 15	
Fishkill Landing, New York							Oct. 15		Nov. 1
Lake, do							Oct. 17		
Spencertown, do					Oct. 15				
Fleming, Pennsylvania							Oct. 10		
Buffalo, Virginia					Oct. 28				
Crichton's Store, do							Oct. 15		
Poplar Grove, do									Oct. 12
Concordia, Louisiana							Nov. 5		
Belle Centre, Ohio				Oct. 20					
Cleveland, do				Oct. 20					
Hiram, do							Oct. 12		
Hocking Port, do							Oct. 8		
Savannah, do							Oct. 10		
Riley, Illinois							Oct. 16		
Princeton, Minnesota							Oct. 1		
Border Plains, Iowa								Oct. 7	Oct. 8

LIRIODENDRON TULIPIFERA.—*Tulip Tree.—American Poplar.*

Name of Station.	1851.	1852.	1853.	1854.	1855.	1856.	1857.	1858.	1859.
Steuben, Maine		Oct. 18							
Worcester, Massachusetts							Nov. 20		
Columbia, Connecticut								Oct. 28	
Flatbush, New York			Nov. 8						
Fleming, Pennsylvania							Oct. 20		
Hollidaysburg, do		Oct. 27							
Meadville, do		Nov. 1							
Murrysville, do							Nov. 6		
Darby, do			Oct. 23						
Sykesville, Maryland		Oct. 15	Nov. 1	Nov. 24			Oct. 27		
Buffalo, Virginia					Nov. 8				
Crichton's Store, do			Oct. 25				Oct. 15		Oct. 20
Poplar Grove, do									Oct. 8
Rose Hill, do						Nov. 5			Nov. 1
Greensborough, Alabama						Nov. 20			
Glenwood, Tennessee			Oct. 15						
Belle Centre, Ohio		Oct. 24							
Cleveland, do				Oct. 29	Oct. 28				
Hiram, do							Oct. 15		
Madison, do							Nov. 5		
Savannah, do							Oct. 30		
Brighton, Illinois							Oct. 21	Sept. 6	
Marengo, do								Oct. 23	
Princeton, Minnesota							Sept. 20		
Stanbridge, Canada							Oct. 10		
Leipsig, Saxony								Oct. 31	

PERSICA VULGARIS.—*Peach.*

Name of Station.	1851.	1852.	1853.	1854.	1855.	1856.	1857.	1858.	1859.
Londonderry..........New Hamp..			Oct. 21						
Manchester..................do......		Oct. 17							
West Rupert...........Vermont...						Oct. 27			
Bridgewater...........Massachusetts.						Nov. 6			
North Attleborough.........do......				Oct. 1					
Point Judith..........Rhode Island.				Nov. 15					
Columbia.............Connecticut.							Oct. 13	Oct. 20	
Georgetown..................do......						Oct. 31			
Norwich......................do......						Oct. 18			
Eden....................New York..						Oct. 20			
Flatbush.....................do......			Nov. 4				Oct. 15		
Mexico........................do......						Oct. 13			
Nichols........................do......								Oct. 12	
Fleming...............Pennsylvania.							Oct. 30		
Meadville....................do......						Oct. 15			
Darby..........................do......			Oct. 20						
Ridge....................Maryland..						Sept. 8			
Sykesville....................do......		Oct. 14	Oct. 28	Nov. 25			Nov. 1		
Buffalo....................Virginia..					Nov. 8				
Clark county................do......								Nov. 10	
Crichton's Store............do......			Oct. 10				Oct. 15		Nov. 1
Mossy Creek.................do......							Oct. 10		
Poplar Grove................do......						Oct. 24		Oct. 8	Oct. 1
Rose Hill.....................do......						Nov. 1			
Winchester...................do......						Oct. 22			
Savannah................Georgia...						Oct. 1			
Sparta..........................do......							Nov. 10		
Zebulon........................do......						Sept. 30			
Alligator.................Florida....							Oct. 15		
Greensborough..........Alabama...						Nov. 15			
Columbus..............Mississippi..							Nov. 10		
Port Gibson..................do......						Oct. 15			
Big Pond...............Louisiana..						Nov. 3			
Concordia....................do......							Dec. 30		
Walnut Grove...........Tennessee..						Oct. 8			
Belle Centre................Ohio....				Nov. 1				Nov. 12	
Germantown..................do......		Nov. 10				Oct. 7			
Hiram..........................do......						Oct. 4		Oct. 25	
Hocking Port.................do......						Nov. 6	Nov. 20		
Jefferson......................do......						Oct. 23			
Madison.......................do......							Oct. 15		
Savannah......................do......							Oct. 30		
West Bedford.................do......						Oct. 8			
Athens....................Illinois....						Nov. 11			
Brighton.......................do......							Oct. 21	Oct. 12	
Marengo.......................do......								Oct. 30	
Pekin...........................do......								Oct. 20	
West Salem....................do......						Nov. 10	Nov. 7		
Border Plains..............Iowa.....								Nov. 9	
Fairfield.......................do......									Nov. 3
Fort Madison.................do......			Sept. 12	Oct. 30					
Keokuk.........................do......						Sept. 6			
Pleasant Plain...............do......						Nov. 1			
Sacramento............California..						Nov. 3			
Salem....................Oregon...						Nov. 11			
Leipsig...................Saxony...								Nov. 1	

PYRUS COMMUNIS.—*Pear.*

Name of Station.	1851.	1852.	1853.	1854.	1855.	1856.	1857.	1858.	1859.
Brunswick..................Maine....							Nov. 5		
Cornish........................do......							Oct. 25		
Mouson........................do......						Oct. 15			
Naples.........................do......							Oct. 19		
Steuben........................do......		Oct. 10							
West Enfield..........New Hamp..							Oct. 25		
Brandon.................Vermont...				Oct. 30			Nov. 6		
Bridgewater...................do......						Sept. 29			

PYRUS COMMUNIS.—*Pear*—Continued.

Name of Station.	1851.	1852.	1853.	1854.	1855.	1856.	1857.	1858.	1859.
Craftsbury … Vermont						Oct. 23			
Florida … Massachusetts							Oct. 20	Oct. 15	
New Ashford … do						Oct. 28			
North Attleborough … do				Oct. 5					
Worcester … do							Nov. 6		
Columbia … Connecticut							Oct. 10	Oct. 27	
Norwich … do						Oct. 14			
Eden … New York						Oct. 16			
Fishkill Landing … do									Oct. 4
Flatbush … do			Oct. 20				Oct. 15		
Lake … do						Oct. 29	Nov. 6		
Lowville … do						Oct. 4		Oct. 5	
Spencertown … do					Oct. 15	Sept. 30			
Fleming … Pennsylvania							Nov. 10		
Meadville … do						Oct. 10			
Darby … do			Oct. 21						
Easton … Maryland				Dec. 1					
Sykesville … do		Sept. 20	Oct. 29	Oct. 25		Oct. 15	Oct. 29		
Buffalo … Virginia					Nov. 8				
Crichton's Store … do						Oct. 20	Oct. 15	Sept. 25	
Winchester … do						Oct. 25			
Sparta … Georgia							Nov. 15		
Greensborough … Alabama						Nov. 16			
Port Gibson … Mississippi						Oct. 15			
Glenwood … Tennessee			Oct. 22						
Belle Centre … Ohio				Nov. 1					
Cleveland … do				Nov. 8	Oct. 29				
Germantown … do		Oct. 29	Oct. 25			Oct. 2			
Hiram … do								Oct. 1	
Jefferson … do						Oct. 23			
Savannah … do							Oct. 10		
Athens … Illinois						Oct. 11			
Brighton … do							Oct. 30	Oct. 26	
Marengo … do								Oct. 16	
West Salem … do						Oct. 31			
Winnebago … do							Nov. 1		
Holland … Michigan						Oct. 15			
Appleton … Wisconsin						Nov. 1			
Madison … do						Oct. 15			
Fairfield … Iowa									Oct. 10
Fort Madison … do				Oct. 20					
Keokuk … do						Oct. 12			
Sacramento … California						Nov. 5			
Salem … Oregon						Nov. 1			
Stanbridge … Canada							Oct. 25	Oct. 20	
Leipsig … Saxony								Nov. 1	

PYRUS MALUS.—*Apple*.

Name of Station.	1851.	1852.	1853.	1854.	1855.	1856.	1857.	1858.	1859.
Cornish … Maine							Oct. 25		
Brunswick … do							Nov. 18		
Naples … do							Oct. 10		
Londonderry … New Hamp.			Oct. 26						
Manchester … do		Oct. 20							
West Enfield … do							Oct. 25		
Brandon … Vermont				Oct. 30		Oct. 30	Nov. 6	Oct. 27	
Craftsbury … do						Nov. 5			
Newark … do						Oct. 20	Oct. 20		
West Rupert … do						Oct. 29			
Bridgewater … Massachusetts						Nov. 1			
Canton … do							Oct. 1		
Florida … do							Oct. 25		
New Ashford … do						Oct. 27			
North Attleborough … do				Oct. 3					
Point Judith … Rhode Island				Nov. 5					
Columbia … Connecticut							Oct. 15	Oct. 27	
Georgetown … do						Oct. 31			

PYRUS MALUS.—*Apple*—Continued.

Name of Station.	1851.	1852.	1853.	1854.	1855.	1856.	1857.	1858.	1859.
Norwich, Connecticut						Oct. 14			
Angelica, New York						Oct. 18			
Eden, do						Oct. 16			
Fishkill Landing, do									Oct. 14
Flatbush, do			Nov. 10				Oct. 25		
Lake, do						Oct. 31	Nov. 11	Oct. 30	
Lowville, do						Oct. 27		Oct. 20	
Mexico, do						Oct. 25			
Nichols, do								Oct. 25	
Spencertown, do					Oct. 15				
Bellefonte, Pennsylvania								Oct. 31	
Fleming, do							Nov. 10		
Hollidaysburg, do		Oct. 7							
Meadville, do						Oct. 13			
Murrysville, do							Nov. 10		
Darby, do			Oct. 20						
Sykesville, Maryland		Oct. 2	Oct. 29	Oct. 28		Oct. 29	Nov. 1		
Buffalo, Virginia					Nov. 8				
Crichton's Store, do			Nov. 1			Oct. 31	Oct. 20		
Poplar Grove, do								Oct. 8	Oct. 12
Rose Hill, do						Nov. 2			Nov. 2
Winchester, do						Oct. 28			
Sparta, Georgia							Nov. 5		
Greensborough, Alabama						Nov. 15			
Concordia, Louisiana							Dec. 30		
Maysville, Kentucky			Oct. 30						
Belle Centre, Ohio				Nov. 12				Oct. 24	
Cleveland, do				Nov. 26	Nov. 5				
Germantown, do		Nov. 14	Nov. 4			Oct. 12			
Hiram, do						Oct. 12	Oct. 19		
Hocking Port, do						Nov. 14	Nov. 18		
Jefferson, do						Oct. 23			
Madison, do							Nov. 1		
West Bedford, do						Oct. 11			
Athens, Illinois						Oct. 9			
Brighton, do							Nov. 7	Oct. 29	
Marengo, do						Nov. 1		Oct. 23	
Pekin, do								Oct. 20	
Riley, do							Oct. 24		
Winnebago, do							Nov. 1		
Holland, Michigan						Oct. 10			
Wyandotte, do								Sept. 10	
Appleton, Wisconsin						Nov. 1			
Madison, do						Oct. 15			
Border Plains, Iowa								Oct. 20	
Fairfield, do									Nov. 4
Fort Madison, do			Sept. 20						
Keokuk, do						Oct. 20			
Pleasant Plain, do						Nov. 15			
Sacramento, California						Nov. 5			
Salem, Oregon						Nov. 16			
Wolfsville, Nova Scotia						Oct. 25			
Stanbridge, Canada						Nov. 22	Oct. 25		
Leipsig, Saxony								Nov. 1	

QUERCUS ALBA.—*White Oak.*

Name of Station.	1851.	1852.	1853.	1854.	1855.	1856.	1857.	1858.	1859.
Brunswick, Maine							Nov. 5	Nov. 2	
Naples, do							Oct. 24		
West Enfield, New Hamp.							Oct. 15		
Brandon, Vermont			Oct. 25	Oct. 16				Oct. 18	
North Attleborough, Massachusetts				Oct. 1					
Columbia, Connecticut							Oct. 18	Oct. 28	
Lake, New York							Oct. 30	Oct. 22	
Spencertown, do					Nov. 1				
Fleming, Pennsylvania							Nov. 1		
Murrysville, do							Nov. 6		

QUERCUS ALBA.—*White Oak*—Continued.

Name of Station.	1851.	1852.	1853.	1854.	1855.	1856.	1857.	1858.	1859.
Sykesville, Maryland			Nov. 3	Oct. 28					
Buffalo, Virginia					Nov. 8				
Crichton's Store, do.									Nov. 10
Poplar Grove, do.								Oct. 8	Oct. 20
Greensborough, Alabama						Nov. 25			
Maysville, Kentucky			Nov. 1						
Ashtabula, Ohio				Oct. 20					
Belle Centre, do.		Nov. 6		Oct. 27					
Cleveland, do.				Nov. 14	Nov. 3				
Hiram, do.							Oct. 16		
Hocking Port, do.							Nov. 10		
Athens, Illinois		Oct. 25			Oct. 31				
Brighton, do.							Nov. 9	Oct. 16	
Marengo, do.								Oct. 23	
Pekin, do.								Oct. 20	
Riley, do.							Oct. 24		
West Salem, do.							Nov. 8		
Princeton, Minnesota							Oct. 10		
Border Plains, Iowa								Oct. 25	
Fort Madison, do.				Oct. 25					
Leavenworth City, Kansas								Oct. 20	
Stanbridge, Canada							Oct. 25		

ROBINIA PSEUD-ACACIA.—*Common Locust.*

Name of Station.	1851.	1852.	1853.	1854.	1855.	1856.	1857.	1858.	1859.
Brunswick, Maine							Oct. 20	Oct. 28	
Naples, do.							Oct. 26		
Londonderry, New Hamp.			Oct. 28						
North Attleborough, Massachusetts				Sept. 19					
Point Judith, Rhode Island				Oct. 31					
Columbia, Connecticut							Oct. 12	Oct. 20	
Fishkill Landing, New York									Oct. 1
Flatbush, do.			Nov. 6						
Lake, do.							Oct. 27		
Nichols, do.								Oct. 15	
Spencertown, do.					Nov. 1				
Easton, Pennsylvania				Nov. 1					
Fleming, do.							Nov. 5		
Hollidaysburg, do.		Oct. 27							
Murrysville, do.							Nov. 1		
Darby, do.			Oct. 24						
Sykesville, Maryland		Oct. 1	Oct. 27	Oct. 25			Nov. 4		
Buffalo, Virginia					Nov. 7				
Clark county, do.								Oct. 25	
Crichton's Store, do.								Oct. 20	Nov. 1
Poplar Grove, do.								Oct. 8	Oct. 21
Rose Hill, do.						Oct. 25			Oct. 20
Greensborough, Alabama						Nov. 10			
Concordia, Louisiana							Oct. 30		
Glenwood, Tennessee			Oct. 22						
Maysville, Kentucky			Nov. 4						
Belle Centre, Ohio		Oct. 27		Oct. 27					
Cleveland, do.				Oct. 30	Nov. 5				
Germantown, do.		Nov. 10							
Hiram, do.							Oct. 15	Oct. 20	
Hocking Port, do.							Nov. 1		
Savannah, do.							Oct. 20		
Brighton, Illinois								Oct. 1	
Fairfield, Iowa									Oct 30
Fort Madison, do.				Oct. 1					
Stanbridge, Canada							Oct. 1		
Leipsig, Saxony								Nov. 5	

SYRINGA VULGARIS.—*Lilac.*

Name of Station.	1851.	1852.	1853.	1854.	1855.	1856.	1857.	1858.	1859.
Cornish .... Maine....							Nov. 15		
Londonderry .... New Hamp..			Nov. 6						
Manchester .... do......		Oct. 20							
West Enfield .... do......							Nov. 3		
Brandon .... Vermont...			Nov. 7	Nov. 10				Nov. 12	
North Attleborough.. Massachusetts.				Oct. 1					
Columbia .... Connecticut..							Oct. 31		
Middletown .... do......				Oct. 15					
Easton .... Maryland...				Oct. 12					
Sykesville .... do......		Nov. 1	Nov. 1	Oct. 28			Nov. 1		
Buffalo .... Virginia...					Nov. 11				
Crichton's Store .... do......							Sept. 20		Sept. 20
Genito .... do......		Sept. 15							
Poplar Grove .... do......								Oct. 29	Oct. 28
Greensborough .... Alabama...						Nov. 20			
Belle Centre .... Ohio.....		Oct. 20		Nov. 12					
Cleveland .... do......				Nov. 20	Nov. 10				
Madison .... do......							Oct. 21		
Savannah .... do......							Oct. 20		
Brighton .... Illinois....								Sept. 29	
Stanbridge .... Canada....							Nov. 15		
Leipsig .... Saxony....								Nov. 1	

TILIA AMERICANA.—*Linden.—Basswood.*

Name of Station.	1851.	1852.	1853.	1854.	1855.	1856.	1857.	1858.	1859.
Cornish .... Maine....							Oct. 20		
Brunswick .... do......							Oct. 4	Oct. 4	
Naples .... do......							Nov. 2		
Londonderry .... New Hamp..			Oct. 17						
Manchester .... do......				Oct. 15					
Brandon .... Vermont...				Oct. 14					
North Attleborough.. Massachusetts.				Sept. 20					
Point Judith .... Rhode Island.				Oct. 26					
Flatbush .... New York ..			Nov. 5						
Lake .... do......							Oct. 30		
Spencertown .... do......					Oct. 1				
West Point .... do......		Nov. 20							
Easton .... Pennsylvania..				Oct. 31					
Fleming .... do......							Oct. 20		
Crichton's Store .... Virginia...							Sept. 25		
Poplar Grove .... do......								Oct. 1	Oct. 8
Greensborough .... Alabama ..						Oct. 15			
Maysville .... Kentucky ..			Oct. 29						
Ashtabula .... Ohio.....				Oct. 18					
Belle Centre .... do......		Oct. 26		Oct. 15					
Cleveland .... do......				Nov. 7					
Hocking Port .... do......							Oct. 10		
Brighton .... Illinois....								Oct. 12	
Edgington .... do......							Oct. 20		
Pekin .... do......								Oct. 20	
Princeton .... Minnesota ..							Oct. 25		
Border Plains .... Iowa								Oct. 10	Oct. 18
Leavenworth City .... Kansas....								Sept. 24	
Stanbridge .... Canada....							Oct. 15	Oct. 20	

ULMUS AMERICANA. *American Elm.*

Name of Station.	1851.	1852.	1853.	1854.	1855.	1856.	1857.	1858.	1859.
Cornish .... Maine....							Oct. 15		
Brunswick .... do......							Oct. 14	Oct. 19	
Naples .... do......							Oct. 14		
Londonderry .... New Hamp..			Oct. 15						
Manchester .... do......		Oct. 10							
West Enfield .... do......							Oct. 15		
Brandon .... Vermont...			Oct. 21	Oct. 20				Oct. 21	

ULMUS AMERICANA.—*American Elm*—Continued.

NAME OF STATION.	1851.	1852.	1853.	1854.	1855.	1856.	1857.	1858.	1859.
North Attleborough..Massachusetts.				Sept. 25					
Flatbush..............New York ..			Nov. 5						
Spencertown ....do......					Nov. 1				
West Point ....do......			Oct. 25						
Easton ....Pennsylvania.				Oct. 27					
Fleming . ...do......							Oct. 21		
Buffalo ....Virginia...					Nov. 5				
Crichton's Store..........do......									Oct. 25
Genito ....do......		Sept. 25							
Poplar Grove ....do......								Oct. 1	Oct. 1
Greensborough ....Alabama...						Nov. 20			
Maysville ....Kentucky ..			Nov. 8						
Belle Centre ....Ohio.....		Nov. 1		Oct. 12					
Cleveland ....do......				Nov. 6	Oct. 28				
Madison . ...do......							Nov. 5		
Savannah ....do......							Oct. 25		
Princeton ....Minnesota ..							Oct. 10		
Leavenworth City ...... Kansas....								Sept. 24	
Stanbridge ....Canada....							Nov. 20	Oct. 20	

DATES

OF

FIRST APPEARANCE OF BIRDS.

CHÆTURA PELASGIA.—*Chimney Birds.*

Name of Station.	1851.	1852.	1853.	1854.	1855.	1856.	1857.	1858.	1859.
Brunswick ... Maine								May 25	
Cornish ... do							May 10		
Perry ... do									May 20
Steuben ... do				May 30	June 1				
Concord ... New Hamp.					May 11				
Londonderry ... do		May 22							
Manchester ... do		May 6							
Brattleborough ... Vermont	May 12								
Burlington ... do					May 6				
Newark ... do							May 20		
Boston ... Massachusetts		May 26							
Florida ... do								May 25	
Mendon ... do				April 28					
North Attleborough ... do				May 1	May 3				
Uxbridge ... do				May 7					
Worcester ... do							May 4		
Columbia ... Connecticut							May 6	April 22	
East Windsor ... do			April 22						
Saybrook ... do					May 13				
Fishkill Landing ... New York							May 17	May 10	May 7
Flatbush ... do					April 20				
Lake ... do							May 18	May 4	May 4
New York city ... do				May 18	April 27			May 12	
Nichols ... do			May 2					May 12	May 3
North Salem ... do		March 11			April 15				
Ogdensburg ... do						April 6			
Waterloo ... do		May 5							
Wellsville ... do							April 15		
West Point ... do		May 1							
Burlington ... New Jersey		May 10							
Moorestown ... do					May 1				
Freeport ... Pennsylvania			April 27	April 24					
Gettysburg ... do				May 1					
Indiana ... do		May 3							
Lancaster ... do							May 25		
Lima ... do		April 18	April 22	April 7		April 26	April 29		
Meadville ... do		May 7							
Nazareth ... do							April 27		
Radnor ... do						May 1	May 3	April 29	
Somerset ... do								May 14	
Upper Darby ... do		April 26	April 29	May 1					
Easton ... Maryland				May 1					
Frederick ... do							April 25		
Hagerstown ... do		April 28	April 26						
Sykesville ... do		May 1	April 29	April 24			May 10		
Buffalo ... Virginia					April 19				
Clark county ... do							May 9	April 22	
Poplar Grove ... do								May 3	May 1
Rose Hill ... do						April 28			April 25
Chapel Hill ... N. Carolina								April 2	
Green Plains ... do							May 3		
Varnell's Station ... Georgia									April 9
Alligator ... Florida								Feb. 14	
Eutaw ... Alabama									March 28
Greensborough ... do						April 4	April 4		
Union Hill ... Texas							April 20		
Glenwood ... Tennessee			April 8						
Fairview ... Kentucky									April 20
Ashtabula ... Ohio				May 1					
Belle Centre ... do				April 23					
Bowling Green ... do								May 8	
Germantown ... do			April 18	April 21					
Hiram ... do							May 9	April 25	
Mount Healthy ... do				April 15					
Poland ... do					April 26				
Ripley ... do							May 9		
Savannah ... do							May 2		
Troy ... do									May 4
Indianapolis ... Indiana									May 2
Laconia ... do								April 9	April 11

CHÆTURA PELASGIA.—*Chimney Birds*—Continued.

Name of Station.	1851.	1852.	1853.	1854.	1855.	1856.	1857.	1858.	1859.
Richmond ...... Indiana	April 6								
Athens ...... Illinois		May 1	May 6		April 22				
Augusta ...... do		April 23							
Brighton ...... do							May 1	March 9	
Washington ...... Michigan		May 11							
Princeton ...... Minnesota							May 10		
Fort Madison ...... Iowa		May 1							
Keokuk ...... do						April 24			
Muscatine ...... do			April 20						
Leavenworth City ...... Kansas								April 20	
Horton ...... Nova Scotia					May 13				
Stanbridge ...... Canada							June 1	May 15	

AGELAIUS PHŒNICEUS.—*Red-winged Blackbird.*

Name of Station.	1851.	1852.	1853.	1854.	1855.	1856.	1857.	1858.	1859.
Londonderry ...... New Hamp		March 12	March 18						
Manchester ...... do		May 7		April 22					
Mendon ...... Massachusetts				March 10					
North Attleborough ...... do		March 9		March 14	March 17				
Waltham ...... do				May 16					
Columbia ...... Connecticut							March 29	April 22	
East Windsor ...... do			March 24						
Fairfield ...... do							March 20		
Saybrook ...... do					March 16				
Ceres ...... New York	March 26								
Fishkill Landing ...... do							May 25	April 1	
Lake ...... do							March 25	March 18	March 13
New Lebanon ...... do			March 27						
Nichols ...... do			March 18					April 2	March 14
North Salem ...... do	Feb. 28				May 1				
Ogdensburg ...... do	March 23								
Plattsburg ...... do		April 23							
Spencertown ...... do					April 20				
Waterloo ...... do		March 28							
West Point ...... do		April 30							
Burlington ...... New Jersey		March 10							
Moorestown ...... do					May 5				
Ceres ...... Pennsylvania		March 9							
Fleming Centre ...... do							March 20		
Freeport ...... do		March 5	April 13	April 2					
Gettysburg ...... do			March 13						
Lancaster ...... do				March 13			March 28		
Lima ...... do		March 6					May 3		
Meadville ...... do		March 20							
Mungersville ...... do							Feb. 27		
Nazareth ...... do							March 30		
Orwigsburg ...... do		March 12							
Radnor ...... do		March 14	March 13			March 29			
Darby ...... do			March 10						
Sugar Grove ...... do	March 25								
Upper Darby ...... do			March 1						
Easton ...... Maryland				March 7					
Hagerstown ...... do		March 6	March 1						
Sykesville ...... do	April 20	March 8		April 26					
Buffalo ...... Virginia					March 9				
Clark county ...... do								March 15	
Genito ...... do		Feb. —							
Kanawha Salines ...... do								March 15	
Madison C. H ...... do	March 20	Feb. 24							
Mossy Creek ...... do		March 3							
Plains ...... do									March 15
Poplar Grove ...... do								Wintered	March 3
Rose Hill ...... do						Wintered		Wintered	Wintered
Smithfield ...... do		Wintered							
Varnell's Station ...... Georgia									Feb. 14
Alligator ...... Florida								Wintered	

AGELAIUS PHŒNICEUS.—*Red-winged Blackbird*—Continued.

Name of Station.	1851.	1852.	1853.	1854.	1855.	1856.	1857.	1858.	1859.
Seville, Florida									April 15
Jasper county, Mississippi					March 17				
Union Hill, Texas							April 10		
Glenwood, Tennessee			March 28						
Ashtabula, Ohio				May 5					
Cleveland, do				May 30					
Hiram, do								March 29	
Poland, do					March 6				
Savannah, do							April 5		
Indianapolis, Indiana									May 4
Athens, Illinois		March 5	March 15		Feb. 10				
Augusta, do		April 30	March 18	May 5	April 10				
Batavia, do								March 23	
Brighton, do							March 6	March 7	
Edgington, do							April 20		
Galesburg, do									March 9
Marengo, do							April 15	April 20	
Pekin, do								April 19	
Riley, do							March 26		
Winnebago, do								March 15	May 13
Ann Arbor, Michigan			April 14						
Flint, do					April 3				
Washington, do		March 12							
Wyandotte, do								May 17	
Milwaukee, Wisconsin	Feb. 24								
Burlington, Minnesota								April 4	
Lac qui Parle, do				April 12					
Princeton, do							May 10		
Border Plains, Iowa									March 18
Dubuque, do	April 11								
Eagle, do							March 23		
Fairfield, do									April 22
Fort Madison, do		March 16	March 20						
Muscatine, do			April 1						
Pleasant Plain, do				March 10			May 2		
Leavenworth City, Kansas								April 18	
Stanbridge, Canada							May 25	May 25	

BERNICLA CANADENSIS.—*Wild Goose.*—(Passes North.)

Name of Station.	1851.	1852.	1853.	1854.	1855.	1856.	1857.	1858.	1859.
Brunswick, Maine							March 27	March 28	
Castine, do		March 26							
Naples, do							March 27		
Perry, do						April 9			April 6
Steuben, do	March 19	March 19	April 6	March 17	April 7	April 8	March 19	March 3	March 20
Londonderry, New Hamp.		March 20	March 17						
Manchester, do		March 20							
Somersworth, do				April 15					
Stratford, do						April 2		March 29	
Brandon, Vermont						March 24			
Castleton, do				March 12					
Lunenburg, do									April 3
Newark, do							March 25		
Boston, Massachusetts		April 1							
Cambridge, do						March 25			
Mendon, do				March 9					
New Ashford, do						March 11			
North Attleborough, do		March 14		March 17	April 8				
Richmond, do		March 10							
Worcester, do						April 10	Feb. 15		
Williamstown, do						March 29			
Acquidneset, Rhode Island						March 22			
Columbia, Connecticut							March 31		
East Windsor, do			March 15						
Fairfield, do							March 14		
Georgetown, do						March 22			
Middletown, do		March 12							

BERNICLA CANADENSIS.—*Wild Goose.*—(Passes North)—Continued.

Name of Station.		1851.	1852.	1853.	1854.	1855.	1856.	1857.	1858.	1859.
Norwich	Connecticut						April 6			
Preston	do						April 7			
Saybrook	do					April 10				
Eden	New York						April 3			
Fishkill Landing	do									March 9
Flatbush	do							April 2		
Lake	do						March 24	March 18		March 10
Lowville	do						April 3			
New Lebanon	do			March 26						
New York city	do					April 14				
North Salem	do		March 14							
Ogdensburg	do						April 6			
Ovid	do				April 10					
Philipstown	do						April 3			
Rochester	do				March 10					
Sag Harbor	do		March 15							
Spencertown	do					April 20				
West Point	do		March 20							
White Plains	do					April 8				
Burlington	New Jersey		March 13							
Moorestown	do					April 1				
Bellefonte	Pennsylvania								April 31	
Ceres	do		March 15							
Freeport	do				March 5					
Gettysburg	do			March 23						
Hollidaysburg	do			March 9						
Huntington	do						April 2			
Indiana	do		March 10							
Meadville	do		March 9							
Lima	do							March 23		
North Whitehall	do								March 25	
Orwigsburg	do		March 8							
Philadelphia	do								March 28	
Darby	do		April 14							
Somerset	do								March 13	
Upper Darby	do				April 17					
Sykesville	Maryland			March 30				March 28		
Buffalo	Virginia					March 15	March 18			
Crichton's Store	do			March 12					March 25	Feb. 28
Genito	do		March 3							
Meadow Vale	do									Feb. 11
Mossy Creek	do		March 1							
Plains	do									March 3
Poplar Grove	do							Feb. 20	March 13	Feb. 21
Trout Run Valley	do						March 21			
Chapel Hill	N. Carolina									April 6
Gaston	do						March 30			
Greene Plains	do							March 19		
Varnell's Station	Georgia									Feb. 5
Alligator	Florida								Wintered	
Cedar Keys	do						March 15			
Seville	do									Feb. 15
Childersburg	Alabama								Feb. 20	
Eutaw	do		Jan. 24							
Big Pond	Louisiana						March 1			
Trinity	do								Feb. 18	
Rockport	Missouri						April 1			
Ashtabula	Ohio				May 10					
Hiram	do						March 19	Feb. 24	March 17	
Jefferson	do						March 24			
Madison	do							March 20		
Rockport	do									March 1
Savannah	do							Feb. 23		
Troy	do									Feb. 1
Welchfield	do							March 18		
Windham	do						March 22			
Laconia	Indiana								March 26	Feb. 19
Athens	do		Feb. 22	Wint'd?.	Feb. 11	Wint'd?.				
Augusta	Illinois			Feb. 23	Feb. 12		April 10	Feb. 14		

BERNICLA CANADENSIS.—*Wild Goose.*—(Passes North)—Continued.

Name of Station.		1851.	1852.	1853.	1854.	1855.	1856.	1857.	1858.	1859.
Batavia	Illinois								March 12	
Brighton	do							March 17	March 10	
Chicago	do							April 7		
Edgington	do							March 18		
Galesburg	do									Feb. 18
Manchester	do						March 8	Jan. 30	March 2	Feb. 18
Marengo	do						March 25	Feb. 17	May 20	
Ottawa	do								March 13	
Pekin	do								Feb. 6	
Riley	do						March 21	Feb. 17		
Warsaw	do						April 1			
Waynesville	do								March 9	
West Northfield	do				March 1					
West Salem	do						March 1	Feb. 4		
Winnebago	do							Feb. 27	March 16	March 2
Ann Arbor	Michigan			April 7						
Cooper	do						April 1			
Flint	do					May 20				
Grand Rapids	do						April 20			
St. James	do			April 2						
Wyandotte	do									March 7
Appleton	Wisconsin						April 8			
Greenfield	do									March 13
Milwaukee	do	March 28								
Norway	do						March 19			
Platteville	do						April 6			
Madison	do						March 31			
Burlington	Minnesota								April 7	
Fort Ripley	do		April 10							
Lac qui parle	do			March 23	March 12					
Princeton	do							March 18		
Red Wing	do						April 5			
Bellevue	Iowa							March 26		
Border Plains	do							March 21	March 14	March 5
Eagle	do							March 20		
Fairbanks	do						March 18			
Fairfield	do									March 2
Fort Madison	do		Feb. 7	Feb. 21	Feb. 19					
Franklin	do							March 20		
Keokuk	do						March 12			
Muscatine	do		March 10	March 10	March 1	March 2	March 18			
Pleasant Plain	do				March 1	March 9	March 17	Feb. 14		
Leavenworth City	Kansas								Jan. 14	
Horton	Nova Scotia					April 4		March 28		
Stanbridge	Canada							April 1	April 1	
Red River	Rupert Land						April 2			

ANTROSTOMUS VOCIFERUS.—*Whip-poor-will.*

Name of Station.		1851.	1852.	1853.	1854.	1855.	1856.	1857.	1858.	1859.
Cornish	Maine						April 24	May 19		
Naples	do							May 30		
Perry	do						May 15			June 20
Steuben	do					June 8				
Concord	New Hamp.						May 30			
Londonderry	do		May 26							
North Barnstead	do						May 18	May 6		
Stratford	do								May 25	
Brandon	Vermont				May 20		May 13	May 5		
Brattleborough	do	June 3								
Castleton	do				May 15					
Boston	Massachusetts		June 1							
Bridgewater	do							May 6		
Mendon	do				May 12					
North Attleborough	do		May 6		May 13	May 16				
Waltham	do				May 22					
Westfield	do						May 15			
Worcester	do							June 3		

ANTROSTOMUS VOCIFERUS.—*Whip-poor-will*—Continued.

Name of Station.		1851.	1852.	1853.	1854.	1855.	1856.	1857.	1858.	1859.
South Windsor	Connecticut						April 25			
Columbia	do								May 27	
Fairfield	do							April 29		
Georgetown	do						April 28			
Preston	do						May 6			
Chatham	New York	May 11								
Eden	do						May 13			
Fishkill Landing	do								April 30	April 29
Flatbush	do							May 8		
Lake	do						April 28	May 7	May 9	May 11
Nichols	do								April 19	May 11
North Salem	do					May 2				
Ovid	do				May 18					
Spencertown	do					April 20	April 16			
West Day	do									May 25
West Point	do		June 1	May 16						
Moorestown	New Jersey					May 10				
Sergeantsville	do							May 10		
Bellefonte	Pennsylvania								April 31	
Fleming Centre	do							May 9		
Huntington	do						April 12	May 7		
Lancaster	do							May 5		
Lima	do		May 3	April 17	April 27		April 16	June 6		
Meadville	do						May 13			
Morrisville	do						May 4			
Mungersville	do							April 30		
North Whitehall	do							May 8	April 24	
Orwigsburgh	do		April 28							
Radnor	do							April 30	May 20	
Upper Darby	do		May 1							
Ridge	Maryland						April 22			
Spencerville	do							April 28		
Sykesville	do				April 26		April 13	May 5		
Buffalo	Virginia					April 18	April 9			
Crack Whip	do							April 30		
Crichton's Store	do			April 14			April 9	April 4	March 28	March 28
Mossy Creek	do							May 5		
Mount Solon	do						April 17			
The Plains	do									April 26
Poplar Grove	do							April 30	April 10	April 12
Portsmouth	do						April 11			
Rose Hill	do						April 16	April 1	April 22	April 19
Chapel Hill	N. Carolina								April 9	
Green Plains	do							April 1		
Savannah	Georgia						March 15			
Sparta	do						March 16	March 31		
Varnell's Station	do									March 27
Alligator	Florida							Feb. 29		
Cedar Keys	do						March 26			
Seville	do									April 2
Childersburg	Alabama							March 27	April 15	
Greene Springs	do						April 10			
Weewokaville	do		April 8	April 6						
Columbus	Mississippi						April 16			
Trinity	Louisiana							Feb. 15		
Austin	Texas						April 1			
Union Hill	do							April 14		
Glenwood	Tennessee			April 13						
Hannibal	Missouri				April 12					
Rockport	do						April 2			
Ashtabula	Ohio				May 4					
Belle Centre	do				April 22					
Bowling Green	do								April 22	
Edinburg	do							May 14		
Germantown	do						May 12			
Hiram	do						April 26	May 9	April 30	
Jefferson	do						May 27			
Madison	do							May 7		
Marietta	do									May 26
Mount Healthy	do				May 10					

ANTROSTOMUS VOCIFERUS.—*Whip-poor-will*—Continued.

Name of Station.	1851.	1852.	1853.	1854.	1855.	1856.	1857.	1858.	1859.
Rockport ... Ohio									May 7
Welchfield ... do							May 8		
Laconia ... Indiana								May 3	April 11
Athens ... Illinois				April 12	April 15	April 12			
Augusta ... do				May 4		April 12	May 13		
Brighton ... do							April 20	April 25	
Carthage ... do						May 29			
Edgington ... do							May 1		
Manchester ... do						April 16	May 9	April 20	April 12
Marengo ... do						April 22	May 2	April 28	
Ottawa ... do								April 25	
Pekin ... do								May 5	
Peoria ... do								March 29	
Riley ... do							May 8		
Warsaw ... do						April 9	April 3		
Waynesville ... do								April 20	
West Northfield ... do				April 25					
West Salem ... do						April 8	April 25		
Winnebago ... do								April 30	
Ann Arbor ... Michigan		April 18							
Brest ... do	April 3								
Cooper ... do						April 14			
Flint ... do					April 29				
Romeo ... do						April 25			
St. James ... do						May 18			
Wyandotte ... do								April 20	
Appleton ... Wisconsin						May 17			
Greenfield ... do									May 3
Norway ... do						May 26			
Platteville ... do						May 1			
Madison ... do						April 20	May 19		
Princeton ... Minnesota							May 2		
Red Wing ... do						April 21			
Border Plains ... Iowa								April 28	May 2
Eagle ... do							May 4		
Fairbanks ... do						May 11			
Fairfield ... do									April 20
Fort Madison ... do	May 12	April 26							
Muscatine ... do				April 17	April 17	April 17			
Pleasant Plain ... do				April 10	June 1	May 23	May 1		
Stanbridge ... Canada							May 20	May 20	

CHORDEILES POPETUE.—*Night Hawk.*

Name of Station.	1851.	1852.	1853.	1854.	1855.	1856.	1857.	1858.	1859.
Brunswick ... Maine								May 25	
Steuben ... do									May 9
Radnor ... Pennsylvania								May 12	
Hagerstown ... Maryland		May 4							
Crack Whip ... Virginia							May 29		
Glenwood ... Tennessee			April 28						
Laconia ... Indiana									May 2
Winnebago ... Illinois									April 17

DOLICHONYX ORYZIVORUS.—*Reed-Bird, Rice-Bird, or Bob-o-Link.*

Name of Station.	1851.	1852.	1853.	1854.	1855.	1856.	1857.	1858.	1859.
Brunswick ... Maine							May 22		
Cornish ... do							May 9		
Gardiner ... do							May 23		
Naples ... do							May 22		
Steuben ... do			May 25		June 8			May 25	
Londonderry ... New Hamp.		May 7							
North Barnstead ... do							May 13		
Shelburne ... do								May 11	
West Enfield ... do							May 13		

DOLICHONYX ORYZIVORUS.—*Reed-Bird*, *Rice-Bird*, or *Bob-o-Link*—Continued.

Name of Station.		1851.	1852.	1853.	1854.	1855.	1856.	1857.	1858.	1859.
Brandon	Vermont				May 10					
Castleton	do				May 7					
Lunenburg	do									June 5
Newark	do							May 26		
Florida	Massachusetts							May 10	May 20	
Mendon	do				May 13					
Waltham	do				May 17					
Worcester	do							June 3		
Columbia	Connecticut							May 10	May 7	
Middletown	do				May 8					
Chatham	New York	May 12								
Lake	do							May 10	May 20	May 16
New York city	do								June 2	
Nichols	do								May 12	May 20
North Salem	do		May 1			May 8				
Ovid	do				May 15					
Spencertown	do					May 12				
Wellsville	do							May 16		
Easton	Maryland				May 15					
Clark county	Virginia							May 18		
Varnell's Station	Georgia									May 9
Seville	Florida									April 26
Columbus	Mississippi								Jan. 10	
Union Hill	Texas							Nov. 18		
Glenwood	Tennessee			May 6						
Hannibal	Missouri				April 1					
Ashtabula	Ohio				May 20					
Hiram	do								March 29	
Madison	do							May 2		
Poland	do					May 12				
Welchfield*	do							May 20		
Batavia	Illinois								April 21	
Marengo	do							May 8	May 10	
Riley	do							May 5		
West Northfield	do				May 6					
Winnebago	do							May 8	May 8	May 6
Border Plains	Iowa								March 14	
Eagle	do							May 4		
Leavenworth City	Kansas								May 17	
Horton	Nova Scotia					May 24				
Stanbridge	Canada							May 21	April 20	

PRROGNE PURPUREA.—*Martin.*

Name of Station.		1851.	1852.	1853.	1854.	1855.	1856.	1857.	1858.	1859.
Brunswick	Maine							May 1	April 25	
Castine	do		April 29							
Cornish	do							May 10		
Naples	do							May 8		
Perry	do									May 5
Steuben	do	May 2	May 6	May 21	May 19	May 25				
Francestown	New Hamp.			April 22						
Londonderry	do		May 13	April 10						
Manchester	do		April 17		April 17					
Brattleborough	Vermont	May 3								
Castleton	do				May 1					
Lunenburg	do									June 15
Boston	Massachusetts		May 17							
Florida	do							May 5	May 10	
Mendon	do				May 20					
North Attleborough	do		April 17		April 13	April 19				
Waltham	do				March 16					
Columbia	Connecticut							April 16	April 10	
East Windsor	do			April 28						
Fairfield	do							May 7		
Middletown	do		May 1							
Saybrook	do					April 23				

* This bird was never observed at this place before the above date.

PROGNE PURPUREA.—*Martin*—Continued.

Name of Station.	1851.	1852.	1853.	1854.	1855.	1856.	1857.	1858.	1859.
Flatbush, New York		May 2							
Lowville, do.								April 20	
New York city, do.					May 19				
Nichols, do.								May 1	
North Salem, do.	April 28				May 26				
Ogdensburg, do.	April 24	April 17			April 23	April 16			
Ovid, do.				April 21					
Plattsburg, do.		April 21							
Rochester, do.						April 25			
Sag Harbor, do.	April 10	April 16							
Spencertown, do.					April 18				
Waterloo, do.		April 17							
Wellsville, do.							May 1		
West Point, do.			May 3						
Burlington, New Jersey		May 10							
Freeport, Pennsylvania		March 30	April 8	April 11					
Gettysburg, do.		April 11	March 27	April 9					
Hollidaysburg, do.			April 20						
Mercersburg, do.		April 10							
Indiana, do.		May 7							
Lancaster, do.				April 12			May 20		
Meadville, do.	May 20								
Mungersville, do.							April 26		
Orwigsburg, do.		April 11							
Philadelphia, do.								April 14	
Darby, do.		March 14	April 8						
Somerset, do.								March 10	
Easton, Maryland				April 20					
Frederick, do.							April 3		
Hagerstown, do.		March 31	April 2						
Ridge, do.						April 29			
Sykesville, do.	May 13		May 3						
Buffalo, Virginia					April 6				
Diamond Grove, do.	April 24								
Genito, do.		April 15							
Madison C. H., do.		April 15							
Mossy Creek, do.		March 30					May 1		
The Plains, do.									April 2
Poplar Grove, do.								April 11	April 18
Portsmouth, do.						April 7			
Rose Hill, do.						April 27			April 25
Smithfield, do.		April 3							
Chapel Hill, N. Carolina	April 2		March 9					April 4	
Green Plains, do.							March 22		
Camden, S. Carolina		March 19							
Varnell's Station, Georgia									March 29
Alligator, Florida								Feb. 9	
Cedar Keys, do.						March 25			
Childersburg, Alabama								April 7	
Eutaw, do.		March 29							
Greensborough, do.						March 24		March 27	
Weewokaville, do.		April 12	March 21						
Trinity, Louisiana							March 16	March 10	
Cross Roads, Texas									April 24
Union Hill, do.							March 1		
Glenwood, Tennessee			March 21						
Lebanon, do.	April 15								
Fairview, Kentucky									April 20
Cincinnati, Ohio		March 24							
Germantown, do.		April 18	April 6						
Hiram, do.							May 9		
Hocking Port, do.							April 30		
Marietta, do.									April 2
Mount Healthy, do.				May 12					
Poland, do.					April 5				
Savannah, do.							May 12		
Troy, do.									March 1
Indianapolis, Indiana									May 2
Laconia, do.								March 26	March 22
Richmond, do.	April 2								

PROGNE PURPUREA.—*Martin*—Continued.

Name of Station.	1851.	1852.	1853.	1854.	1855.	1856.	1857.	1858.	1859.
Athens .... Illinois		April 8	April 1	April 25	April 17				
Augusta .... do		April 25	March 28				April 25		
Brighton .... do							April 2	March 20	
Edgington .... do							April 25		
Manchester .... do						March 29	March 30	March 25	April 9
Manchester .... do							May 8	May 21	
Riley .... do							May 5		
Waynesville .... do								March 18	
West Northfield .... do				April 15					
Winnebago .... do							May 2	May 7	April 19
Brest .... Wisconsin	April 18								
Flint .... Michigan					April 13				
Washington .... do		April 16							
Border Plains .... Minnesota								April 17	
Dubuque .... Iowa	April 1								
Fairfield .... do									April 25
Fort Madison .... do		April 13	April 9	April 9		April 5			
Keokuk .... do						March 23			
Muscatine .... do		April 1	April 1	April 1	April 5				
Leavenworth City .... Kansas									April 1
Stanbridge .... Canada									June 1

HIRUNDO HORREORUM.—*Barn Swallow.*

Name of Station.	1851.	1852.	1853.	1854.	1855.	1856.	1857.	1858.	1859.
Brunswick .... Maine							May 7	May 14	
Castine .... do		May 1							
Carmel .... do						April 23			
Cornish .... do							April 29		
Naples .... do							April 30		
Perry .... do						May 3			May 8
Steuben .... do		May 14	May 4	May 10	May 15	April 29	May 9		
Francestown .... New Hamp.			May 10						
Londonderry .... do		May 2	April 22						
Manchester .... do		May 5		April 25					
North Barnstead .... do						May 1	May 5		
Shelburn .... do								May 6	
Stratford .... do						May 7			
West Enfield .... do							May 6		
Brandon .... Vermont			April 28			April 26	May 9		
Burlington .... do			April 29		April 30				
Brattleborough .... do	April 29								
Castleton .... do				April 25					
Craftsbury .... do						April 26	May 3		
Newark .... do						May 7	May 1		
Stanbridge .... do						May 15			
Shelburne .... do						April 25			
Stockbridge .... do			April 8						
West Rupert .... do						April 26	April 30		
Florida .... Massachusetts								May 10	
Mendon .... do				April 27					
New Ashford .... do						April 2			
North Attleborough .... do		March 28		April 5	May 6				
Richmond .... do		May 20							
Westfield .... do						May 14			
Worcester .... do						May 21			
Acquidneset .... Rhode Island						April 4			
South Windsor .... Connecticut						April 26			
Columbia .... do							May 3	May 8	
East Windsor .... do			April 21						
Georgetown .... do						April 26			
Middletown .... do			April 23						
Norwich .... do							April 26		
Preston .... do						May 13			
Saybrook .... do					April 25				
Angelica .... New York						May 11			
Baldwinsville .... do		April 28				April 25	May 5		
Ceres .... do	May 9								

HIRUNDO HORREORUM.—*Barn Swallow*—Continued.

Name of Station.		1851.	1852.	1853.	1854.	1855.	1856.	1857.	1858.	1859.
Chatham	New York	May 7	May 1							
Constableville	do		May 1							
Eden	do						April 26			
Fishkill Landing	do							May 15	May 15	
Flatbush	do			April 28		April 17		April 28		
Lake	do						April 27	April 29	May 2	April 21
New Lebanon	do		May 10	April 27						
New York city	do								May 12	
Nichols	do								May 11	May 8
North Salem	do		April 29			May 1				
Ogdensburg	do	April 7	April 9			April 14				
Plattsburg	do		April 18							
Rochester	do						April 25	April 28		
Senneth	do							April 29		
Spencertown	do					April 25	April 29			
Waterloo	do		April 17							
Wellsville	do							May 1	May 1	
West Day	do									May 2
West Point	do		April 27							
Williamsville	do				April 10					
Burlington	New Jersey		May 10							
Freehold	do									May 10
Moorestown	do					April 28				
Readington	do							April 25	April 28	May 8
Sergeantsville	do							April 27		
Bellefonte	Pennsylvania								May 15	
Ceres	do		April 28							
Freeport	do		April 13	April 10	April 11					
Gettysburg	do				April 28		April 24			
Huntington	do						April 29	April 28		
Lancaster	do							May 25		
Meadville	do		May 3							
Morrisville	do						May 6			
Mungersville	do							April 27		
Nazareth	do						May 1	May 6		
North Whitehall	do							April 30		
Orwigsburg	do		April 25							
Radnor	do						May 3			
Darby	do		March 14	April 12						
Somerset	do								April 30	
Upper Darby	do		April 23		April 9					
Easton	Maryland				April 20					
Frederick	do							April 25		
Hagerstown	do		April 15	April 9						
Sykesville	do	April 20	April 26	April 25	March 15		April 1			
Buffalo	Virginia					April 14	April 3			
Clarke county	do							April 22	April 19	
Doddridge county	do						April 19			
Mossy Creek	do		April 10					April 20		
Mount Solon	do						April 25			
Poplar Grove	do							April 25	April 27	April 22
Rose Hill	do						May 1			April 28
Wardensville	do						May 9			
Chapel Hill	N. Carolina			April 21						
Green Plains	do							March 30		
Georgetown	S. Carolina						March 16			
Savannah	Georgia						March 1			
Sparta	do						March 15	April 1		
Varnell's Station	do									April 26
Alligator	Florida							Feb. 14	Feb. 9	
Cedar Keys	do						March 15			
Seville	do									March 25
Carlowville	Alabama							March 27	March 25	
Greensborough	do						April 2			
Greene Springs	do						April 10			
Oxford	Mississippi						March 8			
Austin	Texas						April 1			
Union Hill	do							March 10		
Lebanon	Tennessee	April 15								
Fairview	Kentucky									April 25

HIRUNDO HORREORUM.—*Barn Swallow*—Continued.

Name of Station.	1851.	1852.	1853.	1854.	1855.	1856.	1857.	1858.	1859
Ashtabula, Ohio				May 6					
Belle Centre, do		March 30		April 22					
Bowling Green, do								April 29	
Cleveland, do					April 14				
Edinburg, do							April 30		
Germantown, do		April 16		April 21		April 22			
Hamilton, do							April 23	April 27	
Hiram, do							April 27	May 1	
Hocking Port, do							May 5		
Jefferson, do						May 2			
Madison, do							May 8		
Marietta, do									April 14
Mount Healthy, do				April 25					
Poland, do					April 21				
Savannah, do							May 7		
Welchfield, do							March 21		
Windham, do						April 28			
Laconia, Indiana								March 27	April 1
New Albany, do						April 1			
Augusta, Illinois		May 5	March 30	April 1			May 14		
Brighton, do							April 12	March 30	
Chicago, do							April 5		
Manchester, do							April 30	April 26	
Warsaw, do						May 8			
West Northfield, do				April 24					
West Salem, do						April 8	April 1		
Winnebago, do							April 30	May 7	May 3
Ann Arbor, Michigan			April 3						
Cooper, do						April 15			
Flint, do					May 4				
Grand Rapids, do						May 8			
St. James, do			May 1						
Washington, do		April 28							
Greenfield, Wisconsin									May 5
Platteville, do						May 16			
Madison, do						April 7	May 18		
Burlington, Minnesota								April 16	
Fort Ripley, do		May 6							
Eagle, Iowa							May 1		
Fairbanks, do						May 27			
Fort Madison, do		May 3	March 20	April 9					
Muscatine, do		April 12	April 2	April 19					
Leavenworth City, Kansas								April 26	
Sacramento, California						April 1			
Horton, Nova Scotia					April 28		May 1		
Windsor, do							May 1		
Stanbridge, Canada							May 19	May 30	
Red River Settlement, Rupert's Land						May 17			

MIMUS FELIVOX.—*Cat Bird.*

Name of Station.	1851.	1852.	1853.	1854.	1855.	1856.	1857.	1858.	1859
Shelburne, New Hampshire								May 28	
Mendon, Massachusetts				May 5					
North Attleborough, do				May 1	May 1				
Uxbridge, do				May 10					
Worcester, do							May 12		
Columbia, Connecticut							May 15	May 1	
Fairfield, do							April 17		
Middletown, do				May 5					
Fishkill Landing, New York							May 6	May 16	
Flatbush, do					May 12				
Lake, do							May 21	May 11	May 10
New York city, do				May 20				June 3	
Nichols, do								May 8	May 6
Spencertown, do					April 30				
Wellsville, do							May 10		
Freehold, New Jersey									April 30

MIMUS FELIVOX.—*Cat Bird*—Continued.

Name of Station.	1851	1852.	1853.	1854.	1855.	1856.	1857.	1858.	1859.
Moorestown ... New Jersey					April 31				
Freeport ... Pennsylvania				May 2					
Nazareth ... do							April 28		
North Whitehall ... do								March 24	
Radnor ... do		May 1	May 1	May 6	April 31	April 29	May 5	April 30	
Somerset ... do								May 12	
Upper Darby ... do			May 1						
Easton ... Maryland				April 28					
Sykesville ... do				April 26			April 15		
Buffalo ... Virginia					April 17				
Clark county ... do							May 7	May 1	
Crichton's Store ... do							May 6	April 26	April 28
Kanawha Salines ... do								April 20	
Poplar Grove ... do								April 19	April 22
Rose Hill ... do						April 12			April 19
Chapel Hill ... N. Carolina								April 10	
Jasper ... Mississippi					March 22				
Glenwood ... Tennessee			April 21						
Ashtabula ... Ohio				May 5					
Belle Centre ... do								March 16	
Germantown ... do				April 24					
Hiram ... do							May 12	May 4	
Marietta ... do									May 2
Mount Healthy ... do				May 1					
Poland ... do					May 1				
Ripley ... do							April 24		
Laconia ... Indiana								April 10	
Athens ... Illinois				April 25	May 2				
Batavia ... do								April 20	
Brighton ... do							March 30		
Marengo ... do							May 10	May 10	
Riley ... do							April 29		
Waynesville ... do								May 1	
West Northfield ... do				April 24					
Flint ... Michigan					May 9				
Wyandotte ... do								April 12	
Burlington ... Minnesota								June 15	
Princeton ... do							April 29		
Eagle ... Iowa							May 9		
Fairfield ... do									April 1
Keokuk ... do						May 26			
Muscatine ... do					April 20				
Pleasant Plain ... do				May 10			April 30		
Leavenworth City ... Kansas								April 20	
Stanbridge ... Canada							June 1	June 10	

PANDION CAROLINUS.—*Fish Hawk.*

Name of Station.	1851	1852.	1853.	1854.	1855.	1856.	1857.	1858.	1859.
Brunswick ... Maine							April 1	April 6	
Steuben ... do	May 11		May 26						May 6
Manchester ... do		April 23		April 18					
Castleton ... Vermont				April 24					
Mendon ... Massachusetts				April 2					
North Attleborough ... do					March 27				
Worcester ... do							June 1		
Acquidneset ... Rhode Island						April 4			
East Windsor ... Connecticut			March 30						
Ceres ... New York	Feb. 20								
Lake ... do							April 27	April 14	April 15
Nichols ... do								April 20	May 15
Ogdensburg ... do	April 28								
Spencertown ... do					April 20				
Waterloo ... do		March 26							
Wellsville ... do							April 12		
Ceres ... Pennsylvania		Jan. 4							
Gettysburg ... do				May 2					
Easton ... Maryland				Feb. 27					

PANDION CAROLINUS.—*Fish Hawk*—Continued.

Name of Station.	1851.	1852.	1853	1854.	1855.	1856.	1857.	1858.	1859.
Hagerstown ... Maryland		April 10	April 8						
Sykesville ... do	April 6								
Buffalo ... Virginia					April 18				
Clark county ... do							April 20		
Crichton's Store ... do								April 1	
The Plains ... do									March 17
Poplar Grove ... do								April 22	March 28
Rose Hill ... do						March 15			March 14
Smithfield ... do		March 21							
Charleston ... S. Carolina							Wintered		
Alligator ... Florida								Wintered	
Hocking Port ... Ohio							May 1		
Athens ... Illinois		April 8							
Augusta ... do			March 23						
Brighton ... do							April 17		
Princeton ... Minnesota							May 6		
Stanbridge ... Canada								May 1	

QUISCALUS FERRUGINEUS.—*Rusty Black Bird.*

Name of Station.	1851.	1852.	1853	1854.	1855.	1856.	1857.	1858.	1859.
Brunswick ... Maine							April 30		
Cornish ... do							March 28		
Manchester ... New Hampshire		March 15							
Brandon ... Vermont			March 27	March 12					
Castleton ... do				March 9					
Newark ... do							May 5		
Mendon ... Massachusetts				April 25					
North Attleborough ... do		March 15							
Waltham ... do				April 21					
Worcester ... do							April 23		
Acquidneset ... Rhode Island						March 16			
Columbia ... Connecticut							March 26	April 26	
East Windsor ... do			March 25						
Fairfield ... do								May 16	
Fishkill Landing ... New York							May 20		April 17
New Lebanon ... do			April 1						
New York city ... do								May 16	
Nichols ... do								April 2	April 26
Ogdensburg ... do		April 12			April 14				
Spencertown ... do					April 10				
Waterloo ... do		April 1							
Moorestown ... New Jersey					April 1				
Sergeantsville ... do							Feb. 18		
Ceres ... Pennsylvania		April 18							
Easton ... do		April 4	March 10						
Freeport ... do				April 27					
Gettysburg ... do		March 9	March 23						
Indiana ... do		April 16							
Lancaster ... do							March 28		
Lima ... do						March 23			
Morrisville ... do						March 18			
Orwigsburg ... do		April 16							
Darby ... do		March 25	March 28						
Valley Forge ... do		April 20							
Sykesville ... Maryland			April 4						
Clark county ... Virginia								March 20	
Crichton's Store ... do									Feb. 4
Poplar Grove ... do									Feb. 21
Rose Hill ... do									Wintered
Fairfield ... Iowa									March 20

QUISCALUS VERSICOLOR.—*Crow Blackbird.*

Name of Station.	1851.	1852.	1853.	1854.	1855.	1856.	1857.	1858.	1859.
Perry, Maine									March 20
Castleton, Vermont			Feb. 20						
Lawrence, Massachusetts							April 8		
Mendon, do.				May 16					
North Attleborough, do.				April 8	May 1				
Waltham, do.				March 15					
Worcester, do.							March 25		
Columbia, Connecticut							March 21	March 14	
Middletown, do.		March 15	March 12						
Saybrook, do.					March 11				
Lake, New York							March 26		March 16
New York city, do.								March 20	
Nichols, do.			March 21					March 17	
North Salem, do.					April 12				
Rochester, do.						April 1			
Spencertown, do.					April 11				
Moorestown, New Jersey					March 15				
Easton, Pennsylvania		March 11							
Fleming Centre, do.							March 20		
Freeport, do.				April 8					
Lima, do.				March 1	March 18	March 9			
Mungersville, do.							March 23		
Nazareth, do.							April 1		
Philadelphia, do.								April 19	
Radnor, do.		March 3	March 2	March 3	March 16	March 16	March 13		
Easton, Maryland				March 20					
Sykesville, do.				May 4			March 7		
Buffalo, Virginia					March 14				
Clark county, do.								March 1	
Crichton's Store, do.							April 24		April 24
Rose Hill, do.									Wintered
Marietta, Ohio									March 4
Fairfield, Iowa									April 20
Border Plains, do.									March 16

SIALIA SIALIS.—*Blue Bird.*

Name of Station.	1851.	1852.	1853.	1854.	1855.	1856.	1857.	1858.	1859.
Brunswick, Maine							March 23		
Cornish, do.							March 18		
Naples, do.							March 24		
Londonderry, New Hamp.		March 11	March 14						
Manchester, do.		March 13		March 12					
North Barnstead, do.							Feb. 24		
West Enfield, do.							April 20		
Brandon, Vermont			March 21	March 12			March 17		
Burlington, do.					April —				
Brattleborough, do.	March 5								
Castleton, do.				March 8					
Newark, do.							April 20		
Boston, Massachusetts		March 11							
Cambridge, do.						March 24			
Florida, do.							March 25	March 18	
Lawrence, do.							Feb. 24		
Mendon, do.				March 6					
North Attleborough, do.		March 9		March 8	March 12				
Richmond, do.		March 9							
Waltham, do.				March 1					
Worcester, do.							Feb. 23		
Williamstown, do.						March 18			
Columbia, Connecticut						Feb. 22	March 14		
East Windsor, do.			March 4						
Fairfield, do.							Feb. 25		
Hartford, do.	March 4								
Middletown, do.		March 11	March 4	March —					
Saybrook, do.					March 11				
Baldwinsville, New York	March 14	March 14				April 4	March 15		
Ceres, do.	March 5								

SIALIA SIALIS.—*Blue Bird*—Continued.

Name of Station.	1851.	1852.	1853.	1854.	1855.	1856.	1857.	1858.	1859.
Chatham ... New York	March 15	March 8							
Constableville ... do		March 15							
Fishkill Landing ... do							March 10	March 15	Feb. 23
Flatbush ... do					March 8				
Lake ... do						March 24	Feb. 25	March 16	Feb. 27
New Lebanon ... do			March 10						
New York city ... do				May 15	April 17			March 21	
Nichols ... do			March 8					March 15	Feb. 23
North Salem ... do	Feb. 22				March 1	March 17			
Ogdensburg ... do	April 15				April 14				
Ovid ... do				March 8					
Penn Yan ... do							April 2		
Plattsburg ... do		April 30							
Rochester ... do	March 14	March 11		March 9			April 3	March 18	
Sag Harbor ... do	March 12	March 13							
Spencertown ... do					March 18				
Waterloo ... do		March 13							
Wellsville ... do							April 1		
West Day ... do									March 5
West Point ... do		Feb. 27	March 3						
Burlington ... New Jersey		March 20							
Freehold ... do									Feb. 20
Moorestown ... do					March 1				
Newark ... do		March 9							
Sergeantsville ... do							Feb. 12		
Ceres ... Pennsylvania		April 16							
Easton ... do		March 6							
Fleming Centre ... do			Feb. 11				April 1		
Freeport ... do		March 4	March 9	March 20					
Gettysburg ... do		Feb. 24	Feb. 20	Feb. 20					
Lancaster ... do				March 8			Feb. 26		
Lima ... do		March 9	Feb. 28	Feb. 9		Feb. 24			
Meadville ... do	March 10	March 6							
Morrisville ... do						March 18			
Mungersville ... do							Feb. 17		
Nazareth ... do							March 1		
Orwigsburg ... do		March 3							
Philadelphia ... do								March 28	
Radnor ... do		March 3		March 6	March 4			Feb. —	
Darby ... do		Feb. 24	Feb. 4						
Somerset ... do								March 15	
Sugar Grove ... do	Feb. 26								
Upper Darby ... do	April 12		March 1	Feb. 21					
Easton ... Maryland				March 11					
Sykesville ... do							March 7		
Buffalo ... Virginia					March 11				
Clark county ... do								Feb. 27	
Critchton's Store ... do									Wintered
Diamond Grove ... do	April 4								
Genito ... do		Feb. —							
Madison C. H. ... do	Wintered								
Mossy Creek ... do		Feb. 15							
Poplar Grove ... do								Wintered	Wintered
Rose Hill ... do						Wintered		Wintered	Wintered
Smithfield ... do		Wintered							
Chapel Hill ... N. Carolina			Jan. —					Wintered	
Green Plains ... do							Wintered		
Camden ... S. Carolina		March 14							
Varnell's Station ... Georgia									Feb. 14
Alligator ... Florida								Wintered	
Seville ... do									Jan. 20
Eutaw ... Alabama		Wintered							
Greensborough ... do						Wintered		Jan 27	
Weewokaville ... do		Wintered	March 29						
Jasper county ... Mississippi					March 15				
Trinity ... Louisiana							Jan. 30	Feb. 10	
Lebanon ... Tennessee	April 8								
Hannibal ... Missouri				March 1					
Fairview ... Kentucky									April 1
Ashtabula ... Ohio				March 1					

SIALIA SIALIS.—*Blue Bird*—Continued.

Name of Station.		1851.	1852.	1853.	1854.	1855.	1856.	1857.	1858.	1859.
Belle Centre	Ohio		March 6		March 4				March 14	
Bowling Green	do								March 14	
Cincinnati	do			Feb. 25						
Cleveland	do				March 5	March 11				
Germantown	do		April 12	Feb. 27	March 8					
Hiram	do							Feb. 6	March 12	
Mount Healthy	do				Wintered					
Poland	do					Feb. 1				
Ripley	do							March 10		
Rockport	do									Feb. 23
Savannah	do							Feb. 22		
Troy	do									Feb. 18
Windham	do						March 24			
Indianapolis	Indiana									March 15
Laconia	do								March 27	Wintered
Athens	Illinois		Jan. 29	Jan. 30	Feb. 25	Wintered				
Augusta	do		March 5	March 1	Feb. 27			Feb. 15		
Batavia	do								March 4	
Brighton	do							March 19	March 27	
Galesburg	do									March 4
Marengo	do								May 12	
Waynesville	do								March 10	
West Northfield	do				March 6					
West Salem	do							Feb. 1		
Winnebago	do							April 12	March 17	Feb. 23
Ann Arbor	Michigan			March 17						
Flint	do					March 20				
Romeo	do						April 1			
Wyandotte	do								March 12	March 9
Greenfield	Wisconsin									March 6
Milwaukee	do	Feb. 24								
Burlington	Minnesota								April 15	
Princeton	do							April 29		
Border Plains	Iowa									March 19
Eagle	do							March 21		
Fairfield	do									Feb. 22
Fort Madison	do		April 12	March 22	March 1		April 3			
Keokuk	do						March 19			
Muscatine	do		April 1	March 15	March 5	April 1				
Pleasant Plain	do				March 25	May 7		Feb. 22		
Leavenworth City	Kansas								March 19	
Stanbridge	Canada							April 30	May 30	

TROCHILLUS COLUBRIS.—*Humming Bird.*

Name of Station.		1851.	1852.	1853.	1854.	1855.	1856.	1857.	1858.	1859.
Londonderry	New Hamp.		May 18	May 15						
Brandon	Vermont				May 21					
North Attleborough	Massachusetts		May 9							
Lima	Pennsylvania		May 7							
Radnor	do					May 14	May 4			
Hagerstown	Maryland		May 18							
Greenfield	Wisconsin									May 14

TROGLODYTES AEDON.—*House Wren.*

Name of Station.		1851.	1852.	1853.	1854.	1855.	1856.	1857.	1858.	1859.
Brunswick	Maine							May 20		
Cornish	do							April 26		
Brandon	Vermont				May 10			May 6		
Castleton	do				May 15					
Newark	do							May 8		
Florida	Massachusetts								April 25	
Columbia	Connecticut							May 1	May 1	
Fishkill Landing	New York							May 15	May 10	
Flatbush	do					May 10				

TROGLODYTES AEDON.—*House Wren*—Continued.

Name of Station.		1851.	1852.	1853.	1854.	1855.	1856.	1857.	1858.	1859.
Lake	New York									March 10
New York city	do				May 6	May 13			May 16	
Nichols	do								April 16	
Spencertown	do					April 18				
Wellsville	do							May 15		
Moorestown	New Jersey					April 25				
Lancaster	Pennsylvania							April 21		
Lima	do		May 7	May 2						
Orwigsburg	do		April 11							
Radnor	do				May 11			May 9		
Sykesville	do				April 24			April 29		
Clark county	Virginia							May 5	April 24	
Crichton's Store	do								Feb. 20	Feb. 5
Poplar Grove	do								Wintered	Wintered
Chapel Hill	N. Carolina								April 1	
Green Plains	do							Wintered		
Trinity	Louisiana							Feb. 4		
Ashtabula	Ohio				April 30					
Cleveland	do					April 9				
Hiram	do							May 8	April 4	
Madison	do							May 8		
Savannah	do							May 10		
Laconia	Indiana								April 10	
Athens	Illinois				April 5					
Augusta	do							May 11		
Batavia	do								April 22	
Brighton	do								April 1	
West Northfield	do				April 25					
Wyandotte	Michigan								April 10	
Lac qui Parle	Minnesota				June 1					
Border Plains	Iowa									May 4
Eagle	do							April 24		
Keokuk	do						May 5			
Muscatine	do				April 29	May 1				
Pleasant Plain	do				May 10	May 1		May 9		
Stanbridge	Canada							May 20		

TURDUS MIGRATORIUS.—*Robin.*

Name of Station.		1851.	1852.	1853.	1854.	1855.	1856.	1857.	1858.	1859.
Brunswick	Maine							March 24		
Cornish	do							March 25		
Gardiner	do							March 23		
Naples	do							March 28		
Perry	do						April 7			March 15
Steuben	do	March 28	March 20	March 30	April 6	April 9	April 7	April 5	March 22	April 15
Francestown	New Hamp.			March 30						
Londonderry	do		March 12	March 20						
Manchester	do		March 15		March 23					
North Barnstead	do							May 27		
Shelburn	do								March 30	
Somersworth	do				March 16					
Stratford	do								March 26	
Brandon	Vermont			March 21	March 12					
Burlington	do			March 22		March 31				
Castleton	do				March 9					
Lunenburg	do									April 1
Newark	do							April 1		
Stockbridge	do			March 23						
Florida	do							March 24	March 18	
Lawrence	Massachusetts							Feb. 24		
Mendon	do				March 7					
North Attleborough	do		March 9		March 14	March 8				
Richmond	do		March 13							
Waltham	do				March 15					
Westfield	do						April 1			
Williamstown	do						April 1	March 19		
Worcester	do							Feb. 1		
Acquidneset	Rhode Island						March 20			
Columbia	Connecticut							Feb. 24	March 14	

TURDUS MIGRATORIUS.—*Robin*—Continued.

NAME OF STATION.	1851.	1852.	1853.	1854.	1855.	1856.	1857.	1858.	1859.
East Windsor........Connecticut..			March 15						
Fairfield ....do......							March 26		
Middletown..................do......		March 11	March 17	March 11					
Saybrook ....do......					March 25				
Baldwinsville ....New York..	March 15	March 13				April 4	March 15		
Ceres........................do......	March 4								
Chatham ....do......	March 15	March 9							
Constableville...............do......		March 15							
Fishkill Landing ....do......							March 30	March 25	March 17
Flatbush ....do......		March 13			March 9				
Lake ....do......						April 2	Feb. 16	March 17	
New Lebanon.................do......		March 12	March 19						
New York city ....do......					April 29			March 20	
Nichols ....do......			March 22					April 18	March 8
North Salem.................do......	March 5				March 22	March 18			
Ogdensburg ....do......	March 23				March 20	April 3			
Ovid ....do......				March 7					
Penn Yan ....do......							March 27		
Plattsburg ....do......	March 27	March 20							
Rochester....................do......	March 15	March 12		March 9		April 1	March 21	March 15	
Sag Harbor ....do......	Feb. 25	March 13							
Spencertown ....do......					March 30				
Waterloo ....do......		May 11							
Wellsville ....do......							April 1		
West Day....................do......									March 12
West Point ....do......		March 14	March 18						
Williamsville ....do......				April 16					
White Plains ....do......					March 11				
Moorestown ....New Jersey..					March 25				
Burlington ....do......		Wintered							
Freehold ....do......									March 13
Sergeantsville ....do......								Feb. 28	
Ceres ....Pennsylvania.		March 11							
Easton ....do......		March 11	March 6						
Freeport ....do......		March 1	March 10	March 29					
Gettysburg ....do......		March 4	Feb. 2	March 18					
Hollidaysburg ....do......			March 13						
Indiana.......................do......		March 1							
Lancaster ....do......							March 12		
Lima ....do......		March 9	March 9	Feb. 25					
Meadville ....do......	Feb. 26	March 2							
Morrisville ....do......						March 18			
Mungersville.................do......							Feb. 28		
Nazareth ....do......							March 3		
Orwigsburg ....do......		March 1							
Radnor ....do......		March 13						March 19	
Darby ....do......		March 9	Feb. 28						
Sugar Grove ....do......	Feb. 28								
Upper Darby.................do......	April 1	April 7	Wint'd?.	Wint'd?.					
Easton ....Maryland ..				March 1					
Hagerstown ....do......			March 2						
Sykesville ....do......	March 10	Feb. 27	March 14	March 1					
Buffalo ....Virginia ...					March 6				
Clark county.................do......							March 1		
Crichton's Store ....do......			Feb. 26			March 2		Wintered	Feb. 8
Diamond Grove ....do......	Wintered								
Genito ....do......		Wintered							
Madison C. H.................do......	Wintered	Feb. 20							
Mossy Creek ....do......		Feb. 21							
The Plains....................do......									Jan. —
Poplar Grove ....do......								Wintered	Wintered
Rose Hill.....................do......						Wintered		Wintered	Wintered
Smithfield ....do......		Wintered							
Trout Run Valley............do......						March 20			
Chapel Hill ....N. Carolina..			Feb. —						
Green Plains.................do......							Wintered		
Camden ....S. Carolina..		Feb. 1							
Varnell's Station.......Georgia ...									Feb. 26
Eutaw ....Alabama...		Wintered							
Greensborough ....do......						Wintered		Jan. 27	
Weewokaville.................do......		Wintered	March 20						

TURDUS MIGRATORIUS.—*Robin*—Continued.

Name of Station.		1851.	1852.	1853.	1854.	1855.	1856.	1857.	1858.	1859.
Seville	Florida									Feb. 20
Jasper county	Mississippi					March 23				
Oktibbeha county	do							Wintered		
Trinity	Louisiana							Feb. 27	Jan. 20	
Glenwood	Tennessee			March 2						
Lebanon	do	Feb. 5								
Ashtabula	Ohio				March 1					
Belle Centre	do		March 6		March 9				March 16	
Bowling Green	do								March 14	
Cleveland	do				March 9	March 14				
Germantown	do		April 16	March 10	March 9					
Hiram	do							Feb. 10	March 1	
Marietta	do									March 7
Poland	do					Feb. 1				
Rockport	do									March 4
Savannah	do							April 25		
Troy	do									Feb. 15
Windham	do						March 24			
Indianapolis	Indiana									March 22
Laconia	do								Wintered	Wintered
Richmond	do	March 1								
Athens	Illinois		March 7		March 1	March 6				
Augusta	do			March 11	March 14	March 6		March 16		
Batavia	do								March 22	
Brighton	do							April 11	March 17	
Edgington	do							April 20		
Galesburg	do									March 5
Marengo	do							March 24	March 18	
Riley	do							March 23		
Waynesville	do								March 16	
West Northfield	do				March 8					
West Salem	do							March 1		
Winnebago	do							March 20	May 15	Feb. 23
Ann Arbor	Michigan		March 8	March 17						
Brest	do	Feb. 28								
Flint	do					March 20				
Grand Rapids	do						March 21			
Romeo	do						March 28			
St. James	do			March 25						
Washington	do		March 10							
Wyandotte	do								March 12	
Milwaukee	Wisconsin	Feb. 24								
Burlington	Minnesota								April 4	
Fort Ripley	do		April 18							
Lac qui Parle	do				May 11					
Princeton	do							April 6		
Border Plains	Iowa								April 2	April 1
Dubuque	do	April 1								
Eagle	do							March 20		
Fairbanks	do						April 4			
Fairfield	do									March 10
Fort Madison	do			April 17	March 9		April 6			
Keokuk	do						April 22			
Muscatine	do		April 1	March 17	March 1					
Pleasant Plain	do				April 10			March 21		
Horton	Nova Scotia					April 1				
Stanbridge	Canada							April 1	March 23	

TYRANNULA FUSCA.—*Pewee.*

Name of Station.		1851.	1852.	1853.	1854.	1855.	1856.	1857.	1858.	1859.
Cornish	Maine							April 9		
Naples	do							Feb. 17		
Steuben	do		March 17							
Francestown	New Hamp			March 21						
Londonderry	do		March 27	March 22						
Manchester	do		May 17							
West Enfield	do							April 10		
Brandon	Vermont			April 1	April 6					
Burlington	do			April 26						
Castleton	do				March 14					

TYRANNULA FUSCA.—*Pewee*—Continued.

Name of Station.	1851.	1852.	1853.	1854.	1855.	1856.	1857.	1858.	1859.
Mendon .... Massachusetts.				March 10					
North Attleborough .... do		March 25		April 9					
Waltham .... do				March 15					
Columbia .... Connecticut							May 15	May 6	
East Windsor .... do			April 25						
Baldwinsville .... New York		March 14							
Chatham .... do	March 25	April 20							
Flatbush .... do					May 24				
Lake .... do						April 4	March 30	March 18	March 20
Nichols .... do			March 25						
Ogdensburg .... do	March 24	April 14			April 14				
Ovid .... do				April 6					
Rochester .... do				March 9					
Spencertown .... do					April 20				
Waterloo .... do		March 13							
Wellsville .... do							April 1		
Williamsville .... do				April 19					
Moorestown .... New Jersey					April 7				
Burlington .... do		April 1							
Freehold .... do									March 15
Easton .... Pennsylvania.		March 13							
Fleming Centre .... do							April 1		
Freeport .... do		March 8	March 21	March 29					
Gettysburg .... do		March 11	March 20	March 21					
Indiana .... do		March 9							
Lancaster .... do				March 8			March 29		
Lima .... do		March 11					May 1		
Mungersville .... do							March 24		
North Whitehall .... do							March 29	March 25	
Orwigsburg .... do		March 12							
Radnor .... do		March 9	March 14	March 3	March 31	March 23	March 29	March 19	
Darby .... do		March 9	March 17						
Hagerstown .... Maryland			March 9						
Sykesville .... do		March 7	March 21	March 5					
Buffalo .... Virginia					March 1				
Clark county .... do								March 23	
Crichton's Store .... do								March 21	
Genito .... do		Wintered							
Kanawha Salines .... do								March 14	
Mossy Creek .... do		March 1							
Poplar Grove .... do								March 14	Feb. 5
Rose Hill .... do						March 4	Feb. 23	March 17	March 10
Trout Run Valley .... do						March 31			
Chapel Hill .... N. Carolina								May 1	
Glenwood .... Tennessee			Feb. 20						
Belle Centre .... Ohio		March 26							
Cincinnati .... do		March 26	March 1						
Cleveland .... do					March 4				
Germantown .... do			March 18						
Hiram .... do								March 16	
Madison .... do							May 28		
Poland .... do					April 4				
Savannah .... do							May 10		
Laconia .... Indiana								March 1	
Athens .... Illinois		March 12	March 17	March 14	March 31				
Marengo .... do							May 15	March 24	
Waynesville .... do								April 20	
West Salem .... do							March 15		
Ann Arbor .... Michigan		March 8	April 1						
Flint .... do					April 2				
Romeo .... do						April 1			
Fort Ripley .... Minnesota		April 10							
Princeton .... do							March 18		
Border Plains .... Iowa								March 20	
Eagle .... do							March 25		
Muscatine .... do		April 7	March 25						
Pleasant Plain .... do							March 29		
Leavenworth City .... Kansas								April 2	
Horton .... Nova Scotia					May 20				
Stanbridge .... Canada							April 15	April 16	

TYRANNUS INTREPIDUS.—*King Bird.*

Name of Station.	1851.	1852.	1853.	1854.	1855.	1856.	1857.	1858.	1859.
Brunswick.........Maine							May 14		
Cornish.........do							May 8		
West Enfield.........New Hamp.							May 14		
Newark.........Vermont							May 10		
Mendon.........Massachusetts.				May 16					
Worcester.........do							May 28		
Columbia.........Connecticut								May 15	
Saybrook.........do					May 14				
Fishkill Landing.........New York								May 17	May 30
Lake.........do							June 1	May 9	May 15
Nichols.........do								May 14	May 15
Spencertown.........do					April 20				
Freeport.........Pennsylvania.			May 18						
Mungersville.........do							May 17		
Nazareth.........do							May 5		
Hagerstown.........Maryland		May 3							
Crichton's Store.........Virginia							April 27	April 21	April 15
Kanawha Salines.........do								April 26	
Poplar Grove.........do								May 3	
Rose Hill.........do						May 1			April 28
Glenwood.........Tennessee			April 22						
Hiram.........Ohio								May 1	
Madison.........do							May 16		
Poland.........do					April 13				
Laconia.........Indiana								April 21	
Batavia.........Illinois								April 7	
Marengo.........do								May 11	
Riley.........do							May 6		
West Northfield.........do				April 27					
Winnebago.........do							May 22	May 15	
Flint.........Michigan					May 20				
Wyandotte.........do								May 5	
Princeton.........Minnesota							May 10		
Border Plains.........Iowa									May 3
Eagle.........do							May 10		
Fairfield.........do									May 3
Pleasant Plain.........do				April 15					
Leavenworth City.........Kansas								Feb. 12	
Stanbridge.........Canada							June 1		

DATES

OF

FIRST APPEARANCE OF OTHER ANIMALS.

RANA, (*various species.*)—*Frogs.*—(First heard.)

Name of Station.	1851.	1852.	1853.	1854.	1855.	1856.	1857.	1858.	1859.
Brunswick, Maine							May 1		
Castine, do		April 30							
Cornish, do							April 9		
Gardiner, do							April 9		
Perry, do									May 3
Steuben, do	April 8	April 23	April 11	April 25	April 19		April 12	April 14	April 14
Francestown, New Hamp.			April 13						
Manchester, do		April 23		April 20					
North Barnstead, do							April 8		
Shelburne, do								April 15	
Somersworth, do				April 20					
Stratford, do								April 23	
West Enfield, do							April 15		
Burlington, Vermont					May 1				
Castleton, do				April 21					
Newark, do							April 28		
Stockbridge, do			April 22						
Boston, Massachusetts		March 27							
Florida, do								April 10	
Lawrence, do							May 29		
Mendon, do				April 21					
North Attleborough, do		March 28		April 6	March 31				
Richmond, do		April 27							
Waltham, do				April 26					
Westfield, do						April 16			
Williamstown, do							April 12		
Worcester, do							March 31		
Acquidneset, Rhode Island						April 5			
Columbia, Connecticut							Feb. 23	March 29	
East Windsor, do			March 21						
Middletown, do		April 11	April 2	April 12					
Saybrook, do					April 5				
Baldwinsville, New York	March 27	April 16				April 16	April 5		
Chatham, do	March 29	April 12							
Fishkill Landing, do							March 30	March 31	March 10
Lake, do							March 7	April 11	April 5
New Lebanon, do			April 9						
New York city, do				April 6	April 25			April 1	
Nichols, do			April 6						March 26
North Salem, do	March 22								
Ogdensburg, do	April 7				April 29	April 22			
Ovid, do				April 8					
Rochester, do			April 1	April 7	April 15	April 22			
Sag Harbor, do	March 1	March 15							
Somerville, do	April 1								
Spencertown, do					April 19				
Waterloo, do		April 11							
West Day, do									April 3
West Point, do		March 29	March 25						
Williamsville, do				April 5					
White Plains, do					Feb. 26				
Burlington, New Jersey		Feb. 10							
Freehold, do									March 14
Moorestown, do					March 2				
Newark, do	April 4								
Sergeantsville, do							March 3		
Ceres, Pennsylvania		March 29							
Easton, do		April 17		April 8					
Fleming Centre, do							April 6		
Freeport, do		March 13	March 30	March 20					
Gettysburg, do		March 1		March 21					
Indiana, do		March 14							
Lancaster, do							April 1		
Lima, do		April 12	March 13		March 18	April 7	March 23		
Meadville, do	March 15								
Morrisville, do						March 26			
Orwigsburg, do		March 6							
Philadelphia, do								March 28	
Radnor, do		March 16	March 19	March 10	March 23	April 3			

RANA, (*various species.*)—*Frogs.*—(First heard)—Continued.

Name of Station.		1851.	1852.	1853.	1854.	1855.	1856.	1857.	1858.	1859.
Darby	Pennsylvania		March 11							
Somerset	do								March 26	
Sugar Grove	do	April 1								
Upper Darby	do		March 13	March 20	March 11					
Valley Forge	do		May 1							
Frederick	Maryland							April 1		
Hagerstown	do		March 9	March 7						
Sykesville	do	March 31	March 12	March 5				March 21		
Buffalo	Virginia					March 8				
Crichton's Store	do			Feb. 4			Feb. 2	Feb. 6	Jan. 11	
Genito	do		Feb. 10							
Mossy Creek	do		March 10							
Plains	do									January.
Poplar Grove	do							Feb. 3	March 13	Feb. 19
Portsmouth	do		March 7				April 7			
Rose Hill	do						March 18		March 15	March 17
Chapel Hill	N. Carolina	Feb. 8		Jan. 23						
Varnell's Station	Georgia									April 3
Eutaw	Alabama		Feb. 3							
Greensborough	do						March 17	Feb. 13		
Columbus	Mississippi							Feb. 2	Jan. 14	
Jasper county	do					March 4				
Trinity	Louisiana							Jan. 29	January.	
Goliad	Texas								Jan. 10	
Glenwood	Tennessee			Feb. 26						
Lebanon	do	April 23								
Nashville	do				Feb. 13					
Fairview	Kentucky									March 25
Hannibal	Missouri				March 8					
St. Louis	do						April 2			
Trenton	do				April 5					
Ashtabula	Ohio				Feb. 20					
Belle Centre	do		March 8		March 14				March 19	
Cincinnati	do			March 29						
Cleveland	do					March 1				
Germantown	do			April 13	March 15					
Hiram	do							Feb. 12	March 20	
Hocking Port	do							April 30		
Marietta	do									March 7
Mount Healthy	do				April 10					
Poland	do					March 6				
Rockport	do									March 8
Savannah	do							March 23		
Troy	do									Jan. 21
Windham	do						April 6			
Indianapolis	Indiana									March 25
Laconia	do									March 22
Richmond	do	March 11								
Athens	Illinois		March 8	Feb. 26	March 2	March 29				
Augusta	do		March 7	March 11	March 10	April 13		March 20		
Batavia	do								March 23	
Brighton	do							April 7	March 7	
Galesburg	do									March 10
Marengo	do							March 27	March 15	
Pekin	do								March 23	
Peoria	do								March 17	
Waynesville	do								March 14	
West Salem	do							Feb. 10		
Winnebago	do								March 17	March 25
Ann Arbor	Michigan		March 25	April 1						
Brest	do	March 1								
Washington	do		March 15							
Wyandotte	do								March 15	
Greenfield	Wisconsin									March 2
Burlington	Minnesota								April 15	
Fort Ripley	do		April 25							
Kaposia	do	April 1								
Lac qui Parle	do			April 18						
Princeton	do							April 29		

RANA, (*various species.*)—*Frogs.*—(First heard)—Continued.

Name of Station.	1851.	1852.	1853.	1854.	1855.	1856.	1857.	1858.	1859.
Border Plains............Iowa.....	....	....	....	....	....	....	....	March 11	March 16
Eagle ....do......	....	....	....	....	....	....	March 30	....	....
Fairfield.................do......	....	....	....	....	....	....	....	....	March 11
Fort Madison ....do......	....	....	March 20	....	....	....	....	....	....
Muscatine ....do......	....	....	April 15	April 10	April 10	....	....	....	....
Pleasant Plain ....do......	....	....	....	Feb. 25	....	....	March 28	....	....
Horton...............Nova Scotia .	....	....	....	....	April 17	....	....	April 20	....
Stanbridge ....Canada....	....	....	....	....	....	....	April 12	April 2	....

ACIPENSER.—*Sturgeon.*—(First caught.)

Name of Station.	1851.	1852.	1853.	1854.	1855.	1856.	1857.	1858.	1859.
Brunswick ... Maine								May 20	
Gardiner ... do							June 27		
Saybrook ... Connecticut					April 10				
New York city ... New York									May 20
Ogdensburg ... do	April 18					April 20			
Burlington ... New Jersey		May 15							
Moorestown ... do					May 5				
Freeport ... Pennsylvania		May 13							
Morrisville ... do						May 5			
Crichton's Store ... Virginia			March —					April 18	March 15
Rose Hill ... do						April 1			March 30
Smithfield ... do		April 2							
Green Plains ... N. Carolina							April 29		
Camden ... S. Carolina		April 15							
Red River ... Rupert Land						April 19			

ALOSA.—*Shad.*—(First caught.)

Name of Station.	1851.	1852.	1853.	1854.	1855.	1856.	1857.	1858.	1859.
Brunswick ... Maine							May 8	May 17	
Castine ... do		April 27							
Steuben ... do							April 15		
Lawrence ... Massachusetts							May 1		
Hartford ... Connecticut						April 25			
East Windsor ... do			April 6						
Middletown ... do		May 1	March 30						
Norwich ... do						April 15	April 23		
Saybrook ... do					April 7	April 7			
Fishkill Landing ... New York									March 24
New York city ... do					April 7				
Philipstown ... do						April 21			
Burlington ... New Jersey		April 10							
Moorestown ... do					April 10				
Sergeantsville ... do							April 9		
Bucks county ... Pennsylvania						April 2			
Chester ... do	March 10								
Upper Darby ... do			March 12						
Easton ... Maryland				March 4					
Ridge ... do						April 1			
Crichton's Store ... Virginia						March 7		March 20	March 10
Genito ... do		March 10							
Rose Hill ... do						March 15	March 10	Jan. 20	Feb. 25
Smithfield ... do		March 4							
Gaston ... N. Carolina						March 1			
Green Plains ... do							April 29		
Aiken ... S. Carolina						Jan. 9			
Camden ... do		Feb. 24				March 1			
Savannah ... Georgia						Dec. 31			
Sparta ... do						March 1			
Wolfville ... Nova Scotia							June 2		

CLUPEA.—*Herring.*—(First caught.)

Name of Station.	1851.	1852.	1853.	1854.	1855.	1856.	1857.	1858.	1859.
Brunswick ... Maine								May 10	
Castine ... do		April 29							
Perry ... do						April 23			April 20
Lawrence ... Massachusetts							April 20		
North Attleborough ... do				April 11					
Rocky Hill ... Connecticut			April 1						
Saybrook ... do					April 5	April 7			
Bucks county ... Pennsylvania						April 26			
Morrisville ... do						May 14			
Easton ... Maryland				March 10					
Ridge ... do						April 1			
Crichton's Store ... Virginia			March 16					March 20	March 10
Genito ... do		March 1							
Rose Hill ... do						March 24	March 16	Feb. 20	March 20
Gaston ... N. Carolina						March 1			
Green Plains ... do							April 29		
Horton ... Nova Scotia							April 22		

Bees.—(First swarm.)

Name of Station.	1851.	1852.	1853.	1854.	1855.	1856.	1857.	1858.	1859.
Steuben, Maine									June 17
Londonderry, New Hamp.		June 13	June 5						
West Day, New York									June 12
Crichton's Store, Virginia			May 12						
Genito, do.		May 5							
The Plains, do.									May 20
Trinity, Louisiana							March 26	March 22	
Cross Roads, Texas									March 25
Fairview, Kentucky									June 6
Troy, Ohio									June 1

Fire Flies.—(First seen.)

Name of Station.	1851.	1852.	1853.	1854.	1855.	1856.	1857.	1858.	1859.
Brunswick, Maine								June 10	
Cornish, do.						June 3	June 8		
Gardiner, do.							June 17		
Naples, do.							June 20		
Perry, do.						June 21			June 10
Steuben, do.		June 30		June 19			June 19		
Francestown, New Hamp.			June 18						
Londonderry, do.		June 8	June 2						
North Barnstead, do.						June 8	June 7		
Stratford, do.						June 18		June 5	
West Enfield, do.							June 16		
Brandon, Vermont						June 3			
Brattleborough, do.	June 3								
Craftsbury, do.						June 13	July 11		
Newark, do.						June 15	June 25		
Stanbridge, do.						May 23			
Shelburn, do.						June 10			
Stockbridge, do.		June 14							
West Rupert, do.						June 19	June 18		
North Attleborough, Massachusetts		June 15		June 7	June 23				
Richmond, do.		June 30							
Worcester, do.							July 1		
Columbia, Connecticut							June 9	June 3	
Georgetown, do.						June 5			
Middletown, do.			June 4	May 22					
Norwich, do.							June 12		
Preston, do.						June 8			
Angelica, New York						June 9			
Chatham, do.		June 4							
Clinton, do.							June 24		
Fishkill Landing, do.							June 13	June 18	
Flatbush, do.		June 15					June 20		
Geneva, do.						June 22			
Lake, do.						June 6	June 6	June 5	
New Lebanon, do.			June 6						
Nichols, do.								June 5	
North Salem, do.	May 26	June 5			June 8				
Ogdensburg, do.	June 15								
Ovid, do.				June 10					
Rochester, do.						July 14	July 20		
Somerville, do.	June 1								
Spencertown, do.					June 15				
West Point, do.		June 8	May 29						
Burlington, New Jersey		June 30							
Newark, do.	June 11	June 21							
Readington, do.								June 4	
Bellefonte, Pennsylvania								June 1	
Ceres, do.		June 2							
Easton, do.		June 11		June 2					
Fleming Centre, do.							June 12		
Freeport, do.		June 18	June 16	June 17					
Gettysburg, do.		June 11		June 3					
Mercersburg, do.		June 14							
Huntington, do.						June 1	June 9		

Fire Flies.—(First seen)—Continued.

Name of Station.	1851.	1852.	1853.	1854.	1855.	1856.	1857.	1858.	1859.
Lancaster, Pennsylvania				May 29			June 1		
Lima, do.		June 2	May 27		June 7	May 26	June 6		
Meadville, do.	June 1					June 17			
Morrisville, do.						June 2			
Mungersville, do.							June 27		
Nazareth, do.						June 9			
North Whitehall, do.							June 13	June 5	
Darby, do.		June 2	May 27						
Sugar Grove, do.	June 6								
Upper Darby, do.	May 26	June 1	May 27	May 29					
Hagerstown, Maryland		May 27	May 23						
Ridge, do.						May 24			
Sykesville, do.	May 17	May 24	May 21	May 23			June 6		
Buffalo, Virginia					May 8				
Crack Whip, do.							May 26		
Crichton's Store, do.			May 1			May 20	May 14	May 7	
Diamond Grove, do.	April 27								
Genito, do.		May 10							
Mossy Creek, do.		May 25							
Peach Grove, do.						May 13			
The Plains, do.									May 27
Poplar Grove, do.							May 13	April 29	April 27
Portsmouth, do.		May 8				May 20			
Rose Hill, do.						May 20	June 1		May 25
Wardensville, do.						May 23			
Wirt C. H., do.						June 3			
Chapel Hill, N. Carolina	April 27		April 9					May 1	
Green Plains, do.							June 1		
Aiken, S. Carolina						May 8			
All Saints, do.						April 9			
Camden, do.		May 2				April 28			
St. John's, do.	March 25								
Savannah, Georgia						May 30			
Sparta, do.						March 10	May 3		
Varnell's Station, do.									April 8
Alligator, Florida							Feb. 12		
Seville, do.									March 22
Carlowville, Alabama							March 23		
Childersburg, do.								April 3	
Eutaw, do.		March 22							
Greensborough, do.						May 9		April 20	
Greene Springs, do.						April 9			
Weewokaville, do.		March 22	March 31						
Jasper county, Mississippi					April 10	April 5			
Trinity, Louisiana							March 24	March 25	
Goliad, Texas								Jan. 29	
Union Hill, do.							April 2		
Glenwood, Tennessee			April 18						
Lebanon, do.	April 27								
Fairview, Kentucky									April 12
Trenton, Missouri			May 25	May 23					
Belle Centre, Ohio		June 1		May 26				June 1	
Cincinnati, do.		June 8							
Cleveland, do.					July 12				
Germantown, do.		June 15	June 4	June 5		June 3			
Hamilton, do.						June 5			
Hiram, do.								June 2	
Hocking Port, do.							June 10		
Jefferson, do.						May 31			
Keene, do.	May 17								
Madison, do.							July 7		
Poland, do.					May 14				
Troy, do.									May 16
Indianapolis, Indiana									June 6
Laconia, do.									May 2
New Albany, do.						June 14			
Richmond, do.	June 15								
Athens, Illinois		May 29	June 1	May 29	May 6	May 22			
Augusta, do.	May 12	May 22	May 22	May 24	May 25	May 23	June 14		
Brighton, do.							June 17	May 5	

Fire Flies.—(First seen)—Continued.

Name of Station.		1851.	1852.	1853.	1854.	1855.	1856.	1857.	1858.	1859.
Carthage	Illinois						May 21			
Manchester	do						May 28	June 9	June 15	April 24
Marengo	do						May 21	July 1	June 18	
Ottawa	do								June 16	
Pekin	do								June 26	
Peoria	do								June 18	
Riley	do							June 25		
Warsaw	do						May 23			
Waynesville	do								July 3	
West Salem	do						April 26	June 4	April 30	
Winnebago	do							June 12	June 7	May 31
Ann Arbor	Michigan		June 2							
Brest	do	May 16								
Washington	do		June 18							
Appleton	Wisconsin						June 15			
Greenfield	do									June 1
Milwaukee	do	June 20								
Norway	do						June 2			
Platteville	do						June 15			
Madison	do						June 3			
Burlington	Minnesota								June 5	
Cass Lake Mission	do							May 14		
Princeton	do							June 1		
Border Plains	Iowa									June 7
Eagle	do							June 11		
Fairbanks	do						May 20			
Fairfield	do									May 23
Fort Madison	do		May 27	June 18	May 20					
Franklin	do						June 3			
Keokuk	do						June 24			
Muscatine	do			April 17						
Pleasant Plain	do				May 19	July 1		June 23		
Horton	Nova Scotia					June 23				
Wolfville	do							June 10		
Stanbridge	Canada							June 8	June 20	

MISCELLANEOUS RECORDS.

Observations upon the first blossoming of plants not included in the foregoing tables; made at Radnor, Delaware county, Pennsylvania.

[By John Evans.]

NAMES OF PLANTS.	1852.	1853.	1854.	1855.	1856.	1857.	1858.
Acer Negundo	May 6	April 9	--------	April 22	May 9	April 10	--------
spicatum	May 26	May 21	May 20	May 24	May 26	June 2	June 4
striatum	--------	--------	May 13	--------	May 16	May 24	--------
Alnus glutinosa	March 17	March 19	March 15	April 17	--------	--------	--------
serrulata	--------	March 14	--------	--------	April 10	March 21	March 23
Amelanchier florida	May 16	--------	--------	May 6	--------	--------	--------
sanguinea	May 22	--------	April 28	--------	--------	--------	--------
Andromeda calyculata	April 26	April 23	--------	--------	--------	--------	--------
arborea	--------	July 19	July 10	July 18	July 12	July 24	--------
Azalea calendulacea	--------	May 14	May 19	--------	May 23	--------	--------
viscosa	--------	July 4	June 27	June 30	July 1	July 8	--------
Berberis Aquifolium	May 6	April 18	April 22	--------	--------	--------	--------
Canadensis	May 27	--------	--------	--------	--------	May 25	--------
empetrifolium	--------	May 5	--------	--------	--------	--------	--------
repens	--------	--------	April 22	--------	--------	--------	--------
vulgaris	May 17	May 17	--------	May 16	--------	May 25	May 14
Betula alba	--------	March 19	April 26	May 2	May 4	--------	April 23
populifolia	--------	May 4	--------	--------	--------	--------	--------
Buxus sempervirens	--------	April 9	April 10	--------	--------	--------	April 16
Ceanothus Americana	--------	June 20	June 21	--------	--------	July 5	June 28
Cephalanthus occidentalis	--------	July 4	July 5	July 4	--------	July 24	July 12
Cerasus sylvestris	--------	April 23	April 28	--------	May 6	May 10	April 30
Clematis montana	--------	May 19	--------	--------	--------	--------	--------
serotina	--------	May 17	--------	--------	--------	--------	--------
viorna	--------	June 17	--------	--------	--------	--------	--------
Virginiana	--------	Aug. 8	--------	--------	--------	Aug. 21	--------
Coriacea myrtifolia	--------	June 13	--------	--------	--------	--------	--------
Cornus alba	--------	May 19	--------	--------	--------	--------	--------
alternifolia	May 27	May 21	--------	May 24	--------	June 3	May 30
circinata	June 3	May 29	May 27	--------	June 3	June 10	--------
mast	April 20	April 1	April 4	April 15	--------	May 1	April 4
stolonifera	--------	May 29	May 26	June 4	June 14	--------	--------
Corylus Americana	--------	April 1	--------	--------	--------	--------	--------
Avellana	--------	March 14	March 9	--------	April 6	Feb. 23	March 20
Cratægus cordata	--------	May 21	--------	--------	--------	--------	--------
flava	--------	--------	May 16	--------	--------	--------	--------
Pyracantha	June 3	June 1	May 31	--------	June 8	June 12	June 7
pyrifolia	--------	May 20	May 19	--------	--------	--------	--------
Crocus	March 14	March 8	March 6	March 31	April 3	March 21	March 19
Cydonia Japonica	May 6	--------	April 22	April 31	May 6	May 9	--------
Cytisus Laburnum	--------	May 21	--------	--------	--------	--------	--------
Daphne Mezereum	March 24	March 26	March 15	April 13	April 10	March 21	March 28
Dicentra Cucullaria	April 19	April 9	April 10	April 20	--------	April 26	--------
Dirca palustris	April 21	April 11	April 10	April 20	April 14	May 3	April 16
Draba verna	--------	April 6	--------	--------	--------	--------	--------
Eranthis hyemalis	Feb. 22	Jan. 30	Feb. 2	Feb. 26	March 4	Feb. 19	Jan. 27
Euonymus atropurpureus	--------	June 20	June 23	--------	--------	--------	--------
Forsythia viridissima	--------	April 9	April 10	April 18	--------	--------	--------
Galanthus nivalis	March 2	Feb. 6	Feb. 26	March 5	Feb. 26	Feb. 19	March 8
Gordonia pubescens	--------	--------	Aug. 13	Aug. 18	Aug. 23	Aug. 30	Aug. 29
Hedera Helix	--------	Aug. 20	--------	--------	--------	--------	--------
Helleborus nigra	March 24	Feb. 6	March 4	--------	April 1	March 21	March 23
rubescens	--------	--------	Jan. 14	--------	--------	--------	--------
viridis	March 16	--------	--------	--------	--------	--------	--------
Hesperis Germanica	May 24	--------	--------	--------	--------	--------	--------
Hydrangea quercifolia	--------	June 20	June 16	--------	--------	July 7	--------
Hydrophyllum Canadense	May 22	--------	May 20	--------	--------	--------	--------
Ilex Canadense	--------	--------	April 30	--------	--------	--------	--------
opaca	--------	June 2	May 31	June 4	--------	June 14	--------
Itea Virginica	--------	June 13	June 11	--------	June 18	June 28	--------
Juglans cinerea	--------	May 9	May 14	--------	--------	--------	--------
Kœlruteria paniculata	--------	July 1	--------	--------	--------	--------	--------
Lamium amplexicaule	--------	April 4	--------	--------	--------	--------	--------
Leiophyllum buxifolium	--------	May 19	May 16	May 24	--------	--------	--------
Leontice thalictroides	--------	--------	May 11	--------	--------	--------	--------
Lonicera pubescens	--------	--------	June 6	--------	--------	--------	--------

OBSERVATIONS UPON THE FIRST BLOSSOMING OF PLANTS—Continued.

Names of Plants.	1852.	1853.	1854.	1855.	1856.	1857.	1858.
Maclura aurantia		June 11				July 3	
Magnolia auriculata	May 17	May 4		May 16	May 14	May 23	
acuminata			May 13	May 16	May 16	May 18	
conspicua	April 25	April 9		April 18	April 24	April 30	
macrophylla	June 3	May 29	May 26	June 4	June 7	June 14	June 1[illegible]
purpurea	May 8		April 27		May 7		May 1[illegible]
Soulangeana	May 2	April 17	April 27	April 25		May 6	April 1[illegible]
Mahonia repens		April 23		May 2			
Melia Azederach		June 10					
Mespilus Smithii			May 19		May 26	May 26	
Narcissus	April 6	March 27	March 17	April 13	April 10	March 31	
Ornus Europæa		May 17					
Palinurus aculeatus		June 18					
Paulownia imperialis		May 19					
Philadelphus coronarius	June 2	May 24	May 25	June 1			
Pæonia Moutan		May 7	May 13		May 20		
officinalis	May 27					June 2	
Potentilla fruticosa		May 21	May 26				
Prinos glabra		June 17			June 26	June 28	
verticillata		June 17	June 16			June 28	
Prunus Americana	May 6	April 28	April 27	May 13	May 10	May 11	May [illegible]
borealis	May 10	May 3	May 3	May 6	May 16	May 13	
candicans	May 12	May 4		May 13	May 17		
Chicasa	May 15	April 28	April 30	May 6			
Mahaleb	May 10						May [illegible]
maritima		May 3	May 3	May 14	May 16		
myrobalanus	April 29	April 13	April 10	April 25	April 25	April 30	
spinosa	May 6		April 22	May 1	May 5		
Susquehanna	May 15	April 28	May 4	May 6	May 15		
Virginiana	May 16	May 14	May 3				
Pulmonaria Virginica			April 26				
Pyrus Aria		May 21					
arbutifolia	May 16	May 9					
Cydonia	May 22	May 9	May 13	May 18	May 20		
pinnatifida	May 22						
salicifolia		April 28					
Rhamnus Caroliniana		June 20	June 27				
Frangula	May 27	May 21	May 26				
Ribes alpinum			April 26				
aureum			April 22				
Gordianum		May 1					
niveum		May 1					
petræum		May 1					
rotundifolium		April 23	April 30				
saxatile		May 1	April 30				
Rosa blanda	May 30	May 21	May 26			June 8	
ferox			May 19				
Rubus fruticosus		June 17					
occidentalis	May 27						
Salix annularis		April 1					
caprea	March 29	April 9					
Croweana		April 9	April 5				
cordata			April 12				
cratægifolia	May 22						
Corbiana		April 9					
Forsteriana		April 9					
lucida			May 13			April 18	
pomeranica			April 5				
rostrata	March 29	April 9	April 5	April 15	April 14	March 31	April 24
Russelliana	May 1	April 18					
Villarsiana	March 30	April 1	April 5	April 17	April 14	March 31	April 4
Shepherdia argentea			March 15	April 13	April 10		
Spartium junceum		May 21					
Spiræa lanceolata	May 24						
opulifolia		June 4	May 26	June 4			
prunifolia		April 23	April 30				
salicifolia		June 4					
tomentosa		July 19					
Stokesia cyanea		July 23					
Syringa Persica	May 22	May 9					

OBSERVATIONS UPON THE FIRST BLOSSOMING OF PLANTS—Continued.

NAMES OF PLANTS.	1852.	1853.	1854.	1855.	1856.	1857.	1858.
Tiarella cordifolia	--------	May 1	May 11	--------	--------	--------	--------
Tussilago Farfara	April 20	April 11	--------	--------	--------	--------	--------
Viburnum acerifolium	--------	June 2	May 27	--------	--------	--------	--------
Lantana	May 15	May 9	May 11	--------	--------	--------	--------
Oxycoccus	May 30	May 21	--------	May 24	--------	--------	May 15
prunifolium	May 22	May 12	May 13	May 18	May 22	--------	May 20
Vinca minor	May 22	April 11	--------	--------	--------	May 6	--------
Viola odorata	--------	--------	April 10	--------	--------	--------	--------
Vitis vulpina	--------	June 10	--------	--------	--------	--------	--------
Wistaria Chinensis	--------	May 4	--------	May 14	May 20	May 29	--------
frutescens	--------	June 2	May 26	June 1	--------	June 14	--------
Yucca stricta	--------	July 1	--------	--------	--------	--------	--------

Observations upon the first blossoming of indigenous and cultivated plants, made at Somerville, St. Lawrence county, New York.

[By Franklin B. Hough, M. D.]

	1848.	1849.	1850.
Abies balsamifera			June 6
Abutilon Avicennæ	May 12		
Acer rubrum	May 4	April 21	April 28
saccharinum	May 4	May 18	May 6
spicatum	May 25	June 14	June 13
striatum	May 25	June 14	
Achillea Millefolium		June 13	June 13
Aconitum uncinatum			June 20
Acorus Calamus		June 6	
Actæa alba	May 20	May 28	June 1
rubra	May 20	May 26	May 27
Adlumia cirrhosa			July 5
Agrostis vulgaris			June 1
Agrimonia Eupatoria	July 15	July 28	
Alisma Plantago	June 26	July 9	June 28
Allium Cepa			June 25
tricoccum			June 25
Alnus serrulata		April 6	April 10
Althæa rosea	July 2	July 12	July 6
Ambrosia trifida	July 7	July 13	July 17
Ampelopsis quinquefolia	June 3	July 5	
Andromeda calyculata	May 6	May 3	May 25
racemosa			June 14
Anemone nemorosa			May 21
Pennsylvanica	May 25	June 6	June 8
Antennaria plantagiinifolia	May 9	May 28	May 7
margaritacea	July 13	July 17	Aug. 1
Anthoxanthum odoratum	May 20	June 9	May 26
Apios tuberosa	July 16		
Apocynum androsæmifolium		July 9	July 5
cannabinum	July 12	July 5	July 1
Aquilegia Canadensis	May 28	June 2	May 27
vulgaris			June 8
Arabis Canadensis			May 28
lævigata			June 5
lyrata		June 6	May 27
Aralia hispida	June 27	June 29	July 5
nudicaulis	May 25	May 27	May 22
racemosa		July 10	
Arenaria stricta	June 14	June 18	
Arisaema triphyllum	May 7		May 19
Artemisia Absynthium	July 21		
Abrotanum	July 21		
Asarum Canadense	May 7	May 20	May 26
Asclepias Cornuti	June 25	July 4	June 28
incarnata	June 24	July 9	July 5
quadrifolia		July 20	
Asparagus officinale	May 31	June 22	June 18
Aster prenanthoides	July 13		
Avena sativa	July 7	July 9	
Barbarea vulgaris	June 8	June 14	May 27
Berberis vulgaris			June 13
Betula excelsa		April 15	April 25
papyracea		April 1	
populifolia		April 1	April 28
Bidens frondosa	Aug. 16	Aug. 17	
Blephilia hirsuta	July 24		
Blitum capitatum	July 4	June 26	June 8
Boehmeria cylindrica	July 14	Aug. 10	
Borago officinalis	July 21		
Brasenia peltata	Aug. 10	July 5	June 18
Brassica olivacea			June 17
Rapa			June 17
Bromus secalinus	June 25		July 1
Calendula officinalis	June 26		
Calla palustris			June 13
Caltha palustris	May 7	May 10	May 2
Campanula Americana	July 6	July 27	June 20
rotundifolia	June 27	July 9	July 5
Cannabis sativa	July 13	Aug. 9	
Capsella Bursa-pastoris			May 1
Cardamine hirsuta	May 15	June 6	
rhomboidea		June 6	May 27
Carex anceps	May 4	May 1	April 26
Pennsylvanica	May 5	May 6	April 28
Carpinus Americana		April 9	
Carthamus tinctorius	July 24	July 27	
Carum Carui			June 6
Carya amara	May 31		May 25
Ceanothus Americanus	June 17	June 29	June 13
Celastrus scandens		June 8	
Centaurea Cyanus			June 17
Cephalanthus occidentalis	Aug. 11	Aug. 11	July 26
Cerassus vulgaris			May 27
Pennsylvanica	May 9	May 21	May 25
serotina	May 19	June 6	May 24
Virginiana	May 23	June 6	June 6
Cerastium viscosum		May 6	May 7
Chelone glabra		Aug. 10	
Chenopodium album	June 25	July 9	July 17
Chimaphila umbellata	July 7		July 6
Chiogenes hispidula			June 18
Chrysosplenium Americanum		April 7	May 2
Cichorium Intybis	July 13		
Cicuta maculata	June 26	July 1	July 2
Circea lutetiana	June 29	July 6	June 28
Cirsium arvense	June 26	June 29	June 28
lanceolatum	July 30	July 5	July 17
Claytonia Virginica		April 21	April 25
Clematis Virginiana	Aug. 7	July 30	
Clintonia borealis			June 9
Cochlearia Armoracia	June 3	June 7	July 13
Comptonia asplenifolia	May 11		
Comandra umbellata			June 5
Conium maculatum	June 26	July 11	June 20
Convolvulus panduratus	June 26	July 9	July 14
Coptis trifolia	May 7		May 21
Coriandrum sativum	June 26		
Cornus Canadensis		June 11	June 12
circinata	June 24	June 15	
paniculata		June 13	
sericea	June 7	June 6	
Corydalis aurea			May 27
glauca	May 14		June 1
Corylus Americana		May 9	April 22
Crataegus coccinea	May 29	June 6	June 5
punctata	May 22	June 6	June 5
Cryptotaenia Canadensis		June 2	June 7
Cuscuta Gronovii	July 13		
Cynoglossum officinale	May 29	June 2	June 5
Cypripedium acaule	June 3	June 12	June 18
parviflorum			June 13
pubescens			June 13
spectabile	July 7		June 18
Dactylis glomerata			June 21
Datura Stramonium	June 30	Aug. 12	
Daucus Carota			July 6
Delphinium Ajacis			July 16
Consolida			July 16
Dentaria diphylla	May 11	May 13	April 28
laciniata			May 12
Desmodium acuminatum			July 5

OBSERVATIONS UPON THE FIRST BLOSSOMING OF PLANTS—Continued.

	1848.	1849.	1850.
Desmodium Dillenii	July 19	Aug. 12	
Dianthus barbatus	June 19	June 27	July 1
caryophyllus	June 13	June 22	June 18
Dicentra cucullaria		April 21	April 25
Diervilla trifida	June 14	June 16	June 24
Dipsacus sylvestris		Aug. 12	
Dirca palustris	May 14	May 6	April 28
Draba verna		June 14	
Drosera rotundifolia			July 5
Echinospermum Lappula	June 27	July 6	
Elodea Virginica	Aug. 10		
Epigaea repens		April 19	
Epilobium angustifolium	June 22	June 29	July 5
palustre	June 22	June 20	June 20
Erigeron strogosum	June 6	June 6	June 13
Eriophorum alpinum	July 21	July 28	June 19
polystachyum	June 2	June 14	June 18
Erysimum cheiranthoides	July 31	July 9	
Erythronium Americanum	May 4	May 1	April 26
Eupatorium ageratoides	July 31	Aug. 12	
perfoliatum			July 26
purpureum	July 14	July 7	July 5
Fagus ferruginea	May 6	May 31	May 26
Fragaria Canadensis	May 6	May 18	
vesca			May 7
Fraxinus Americana	May 25	May 20	May 21
Fritillaria imperialis			June 20
Galeopsis Tetrahit	July 25	July 17	
Galium Aparine	May 25	June 2	
asprellum		June 8	
trifidum			May 12
triflorum	May 31	June 2	
Gaylussacia resinosa			June 1
Gentiana Andrewsii		Sept. 8	
quinqueflora		Sept. 8	
Geranium Carolinianum			June 22
Robertianum	May 24	June 8	May 29
Geum rivale			June 13
strictum	June 27		June 28
Virginianum	June 22	June 29	June 28
Gnaphalium polycephalum	July 13	Aug. 22	
uliginosum	July 13	July 9	Aug. 2
Goodyera pubescens	July 13		
Gratiola aurea			July 15
Hedyotis caerulea	May 25	May 12	May 12
Helianthus annuus	July 20	July 31	Aug. 2
tuberosus	Sept. 15	Sept. 22	
Helenium autumnale		July 30	
Heliopsis laevis	Aug. 7		
Hemerocallis flava			June 20
fulva			June 24
Hepatica triloba		April 11	April 25
Heracleum lanatum	June 26	June 14	
Hibiscus Trionum		July 9	
Hieracium Gronovii	July 19	Aug. 7	
Holcus lanatus			July 5
Hordeum hexastachyon	June 26	July 4	
Humulus Lupulus	July 15	July 21	Aug. 3
Hydrophyllum Virginianum	May 25		June 7
Hydrocotyle Americana		June 2	
Hypericum Canadense	July 15	July 21	
corymbosum	July 16		
perforatum	June 25	July 3	
punctatum			July 1
pyramidatum	July 19	Aug. 3	
Impatiens pallida	July 16	July 31	
fulva	Aug. 7	July 31	
Inula Helenium	July 12	July 15	July 17
Iris versicolor	May 30	June 1	June 9
Juglans cinerea	May 15	May 28	May 21

	1848.	1849.	1850.
Juncus acuminatus		June 13	June 13
effusus		June 16	June 13
filiformis		June 14	
Juniperus communis			June 5
Kalmia angustifolia			July 5
Lappa major	Aug. 2	Aug. 5	Aug. 1
Lemna minor	June 10	June 16	
Leonurus Cardiaca	June 19	June 27	June 26
Leontice thalictroides	May 4	May 1	May 2
Leucanthemum vulgare	June 17	June 15	June 20
Ligusticum Levisticum	June 25	July 25	June 27
Linaria vulgare	June 29	July 9	June 18
Lilium Canadense			July 5
Linnaea borealis	June 4		June 9
Lithospermum arvense		June 13	
officinale		June 13	
Lobelia cardinalis	July 23	Aug. 13	Aug. 2
inflata	July 12	July 27	Aug. 3
Lonicera hirsuta	June 14	July 3	June 24
parviflora	May 30	June 14	
ciliata	May 1	May 3	May 2
Luzula pilosa		May 9	
Lychnis Githago	June 26	June 29	June 28
Lycopus sinuatus	Aug. 1	Aug. 12	July 15
Lycium Carolinianum			June 20
Lysimachia ciliata	June 22	July 9	July 5
stricta	July 6		July 5
thyrsiflora	July 6		July 5
Malva moschata	June 25	June 27	June 20
rotundifolia	May 29	June 15	June 10
Maruta Cotula	June 25	June 28	June 20
Medeola Virginica		June 8	
Medicago lupulina			June 14
sativa			July 17
Melampyrum Americanum		July 12	
Melilotus leucantha	July 4	July 20	July 19
Mentha Canadensis	July 8	July 27	July 17
viridis		Aug. 23	
piperita		Aug. 15	
Menyanthes trifoliata		June 5	June 13
Mitchella repens	June 17		July 5
Mitella diphylla	May 5	May 11	May 7
Mimulus ringens	June 24	July 6	June 28
Moehringia lateriflora	June 5	June 18	June 5
Monarda didyma	July 5	July 9	July 17
Monotropa lanuginosa	July 13		
uniflora	July 6		
Myosotis arvensis	May 25		
Narcissus Pseudo-narcissus			May 7
Tazetta			May 11
Nardosmia palmata	July 13		
Nepeta Cataria	June 25	June 30	July 1
Glechoma	May 22	May 26	May 10
Nymphaea odorata		July 9	July 5
Nuphar advena	June 7	June 15	June 13
lutea	June 22	June 15	June 7
Œnothera biennis			June 28
Osmorhiza longystilis		June 22	
Ostrya Virginica	May 4		
Oxalis Acetosella	June 25		June 18
stricta	June 3	June 8	June 13
Panax quinquefolium	June 6		
trifolium	May 10	May 11	May 12
Panicum capillare	Aug. 16	Aug. 14	Aug. 2
Crus galli			July 19
Parnassia Caroliniana		Sept. 8	
Papaver somniferum			June 22
Pastinaca sativa	June 15	June 26	June 17
Pedicularis Canadensis	May 25	June 6	May 26
Pennisetum glaucum	July 7	July 13	

OBSERVATIONS UPON THE FIRST BLOSSOMING OF PLANTS—Continued.

	1848.	1849.	1850.
Pentstemon pubescens	June 14		
Penthorum sedoides	July 21	July 21	Aug. 1
Phaseolus perennis			July 11
Phleum pratense	June 11	June 22	June 28
Phlox divaricata	May 7	May 28	May 15
subulata			May 25
Phytolacca decandra		Aug. 12	
Pisum sativum	June 18	June 17	June 19
Plantago major	June 25	July 9	
Platanthera bracteata			June 13
psycodes	July 24	Aug. 12	
Poa annua			May 28
Podophyllum peltatum	June 2		
Pæonia officinalis			June 10
Pogonia ophiglossoides			July 5
Polygonatum multiflorum	June 3	June 8	June 13
Polygonum aviculare	June 29	June 15	Aug. 3
dumetorum	July 13	June 27	June 28
Fagopyrum	July 5	June 27	June 24
Persicaria	June 30	July 30	
sagittatum	Aug. 10		
Polymnia Canadensis	July 14	July 20	July 17
Pontederia cordata	Aug. 1	July 20	Aug. 2
Populus balsamifera		April 21	April 30
grandidentata		April 9	April 28
tremuloides		April 21	April 10
Portulaca olivacea	July 6	July 20	
Potentilla argentea	July 14	July 1	June 21
Canadensis	June 15	June 13	June 13
norvegica	July 14	June 13	July 1
Prunella vulgaris	June 3	June 26	June 27
Prunus domestica	May 6	May 18	May 15
Pycnanthemum incanun	June 27	June 26	June 23
Pyrola elliptica	July 7		July 5
rotundifolia	July 7		
secunda	July 7	June 29	
Pyrus Americana			June 18
arbutifolia	May 6	May 13	May 7
Malus	May 15	May 28	May 27
Ranunculus abortivus	May 4	May 21	May 7
acris	May 18	May 13	May 2
fascicularis	June 28	July 5	June 5
Pennsylvanica			July 9
recurvatus	May 23	May 12	May 28
Raphanus sativus			June 24
Rheum Rhaponticum	May 23	May 31	June 8
Rhus typhina	June 26	July 5	July 6
Ribes Cynosbati			May 10
Grossularia	May 7	May 21	
floridum	May 23	May 21	May 22
lacustre	May 15	May 22	
rubrum	May 5	May 10	May 14
Robinia Pseudacacia			June 20
Rosa Carolina			July 5
cinnamomea	June 3	June 16	June 15
Gallica	June 25	June 18	June 22
Rubus occidentalis		June 10	
odoratus			July 5
strigosus	May 16	May 24	June 7
triflorus	May 7	May 24	May 27
villosus	June 1	June 10	June 7
Rudbeckia laciniata	July 25	Aug. 11	
Rumex Acetosella	May 9	May 22	May 17
crispus	June 17	June 16	June 13
obtusifolius			June 13
Sagittaria sagittifolia	July 7	July 8	June 27
Salix myricoides		April 9	
tristis		April 9	
vitellina		May 3	May 6
Salvia officinalis			June 21

	1848.	1849.	1850.
Sambucus Canadensis	June 23	June 26	July 1
Sanguinaria Canadensis		April 20	April 28
Sanicula Marilandica	July 21	June 8	June 13
Saponaria officinalis		Aug. 12	
Satureja hortensis	July 21	July 21	
Saxifraga Virginiana	May 15	May 6	May 10
Scirpus atrovirens	June 27	June 15	
debilis		June 14	
lacustris		June 14	June 8
Scrophularia Marilandica			June 13
Scutellaria galericulata	July 24	Aug. 22	July 6
lateriflora	July 23	Aug. 12	
Secale cereale	June 2	May 29	June 7
Senecio aureus		June 6	
Sinapis arvensis	June 19	June 22	June 14
nigra	May 29	June 7	June 17
Sisymbrium officinale	June 26	June 28	June 1
Sium latifolium	July 16	Aug. 1	
Smilacina bifolia			June 4
racemosa	May 30	May 28	June 11
trifolia			June 4
stellata		May 28	June 13
Solanum Dulcamara			June 22
nigrum			June 20
Lycopersicum			July 15
tuberosum	June 26	July 8	July 9
Solidago Canadensis	July 14	July 21	
Sonchus arvensis	July 5	July 20	July 18
oleraceous	June 30	July 23	
Sparganium ramosum	June 9	June 27	July 6
Spiræa salicifolia	July 12	Aug. 6	July 25
tomentosa	July 21	Aug. 3	July 26
Ulmaria	July 29	July 20	
Stachys aspera	July 13	July 26	July 17
Staphylea trifolia	June 2		June 5
Stellaria borealis	May 27	June 2	
longifolia	May 26	June 14	June 15
media		April 6	April 3
Streptopus roseus			May 27
Symphytum officinale		June 22	June 20
Symphoricarpus racemosus	June 14	June 27	
Syringa Persica			June 1
vulgaris	May 19	May 28	May 29
Tanacetum vulgare	Aug. 1	July 27	July 27
Taraxacum Dens-leonis	May 4	May 9	May 7
Taxus Canadensis	May 25		May 12
Thalictrum dioicum	May 15	May 9	May 2
Thlaspi arvense	May 4	May 17	
Tiarella cordifolia	May 9	May 18	May 13
Tilia Americana	July 12	July 20	July 1
Tradescantia Virginica			June 22
Trientalis Americana	May 25	June 10	June 3
Trifolium pratense	May 29	June 12	June 9
repens	May 30	June 5	May 31
Trillium erectum	May 7	May 6	April 28
erythrocarpum	May 10	May 13	May 2
grandiflorum	May 7	May 1	May 2
Triosteum perfoliatum	May 22	June 2	
Triticum repens	June 26	June 26	June 20
Tropæolum majus			June 20
Tulipa			May 25
Typha angustifolia	July 7	July 26	July 6
Ulmus Americana		April 27	April 22
fulva		April 28	April 28
Urtica dioica	June 25	July 4	July 1
Canadensis	July 18		
Uvularia grandiflora	May 7	May 9	May 12
perfoliata			May 10
sessilifolia	May 7	May 9	May 2
Veratrum viride			June 17

OBSERVATIONS UPON THE FIRST BLOSSOMING OF PLANTS—Continued.

	1848.	1849.	1850.
Verbascum Thapsus	June 25	June 29	June 13
Lychnitis	....	....	Aug. 2
Verbena hastata	June 25	June 28	July 5
urticifolia	July 2	July 20	July 21
Veronica Anagallis	May 30	June 14	June 11
serpyllifolia	May 19	May 21	May 18
scutellata	....	....	June 14
peregrina	May 6	May 26	May 27
Viburnum acerifolium	June 7	June 15	June 13
lantanoides	May 8	June 6	May 21
Lentago	May 30	June 6	....
Opulus	May 29	June 15	June 7
pubescens	May 9	....	....
Vinca minor	May 19	May 16	....
Viola blanda	....	April 29	May 6
Canadensis	May 5	May 19	May 6
cucullata	May 4	May 11	May 10
Muhlenbergii	....	June 6	....
pubescens	May 7	May 26	May 10
rostrata	May 3	May 6	May 2
rotundifolia	May 4	May 6	May 10
Waldesteinia fragarioides	May 4	....	May 10
Xanthoxylum Americanum	June 1	....	May 27
Zea Mays	July 5	July 13	July 19
Zizia aurea	....	June 6	June 17

Dates of Periodical Phenomena observed at Hartford, Connecticut, prior to the period embraced in the foregoing tables.

[By C. Hoadley.]

	1837.	1838.	1839.	1840.	1841.	1842.	1843.
Frogs peep	....	April 7	March 28	March 29	March 26 and 27	....	April 15
Bluebirds appear	....	....	....	....	....	....	April 4
Robbins appear	....	....	....	....	....	....	April 4
Daffas blossom	....	....	....	....	....	March 26	April 21
Apricots blossom	May 5	April 28	April 9	....	....	April 5	April 30
Bloodroot blossom	....	....	April 7	April 15	....	April 10	April 25
Cherries blossom	May 4	....	April 19	April 26	....	April 16	May 4
Peaches blossom	....	May 3	April 25	....	....	April 11	May 5
Plums blossom	May 7	May 12	April 24	April 26	....	April 21	....
Early apples blossom	May 14	....	April 29	April 26	....	April 26	May 12
Crab apples blossom	....	....	April 27	....	May 18	....	May 13
Roxbury russetts blossom	....	....	April 28	....	May 16	April 30	May 15
Greenings blossom	....	....	....	....	May 17	April 30	....
Pears blossom	....	....	....	....	....	April 23	May 12
Gooseberries	....	....	....	....	....	....	....
Myrtle	....	....	....	....	....	....	....

Dates of Periodical Phenomena at Hartford—Continued.

	1844.	1845.	1846.	1847.	1848.	1849.	1850.
Frogs peep	April 4, 8 frogs lively.	March 31	March 26	April 21	March 26	March 30	....
Bluebirds appear	March 7	....	March 15	March 20	....	....	....
Robbins appear	March 14	....	....	March 23	March 12	....	....
Daffas blossom	April 13	April 6	April 11	April 22	April 8	April 8	April 3
Apricots blossom	April 14	April 7	....	April 29	April 7	....	....
Bloodroot blossoms	April 14	April 11	April 9	April 23	....	....	....
Cherries blossom	April 17	April 20 & May 1	April 21	May 5	April 25	April 30	May 3
Peach blossoms	April 20	April 21	April 22	May 8	April 29	....	April 30
Plums blossom	April 17	April 24	April 20	April 29	April 28	May 7	....
Early apples blossom	April 28	April 29	April 28	May 9	....	....	....
Crab apples blossom	....	May 1	May 2	May 14	....	May 15	....
Roxbury russetts blossom	....	May 2	May 1	May 15	....	....	....
Greenings blossom	....	May 2	May 2	May 14	May 1	....	May 13
Pears blossom	April 25	....	April 28	....	April 28	....	May 10
Goosberries	....	....	....	....	April 12	....	....
Myrtle	....	....	....	....	Jan. 1 & 6	....	....

Dates of Blossoming of Plants at West Chester, Chester county, Pennsylvania, according to the observations of forty years.

[By Dr. William Darlington.]

Acer rubrum, last of March.
saccharinum, last of April.
Achillea Millefolium, first of June to September.
Actæa alba, beginning of May.
Asclepias Cornuti, last of June.
Æsculus Hippocastanum, middle of May.
Ailantus glandulosa, June.
Amelanchier Canadensis, middle of April.
Ampelopsis quinquefolia, middle of July.
Alisma Plantago, middle of July.
Anagallis arvensis, last of June.
Anemone nemorosa, middle of April.
Aplectrum hyemale, last of May.
Apocynum androsaemifolium, last of June.
Aquilegia Canadensis, beginning of May.
Arethusa bulbosa, May.
Arum triphyllum, middle of May.
Catalpa bignonioides, last of June.
Caltha palustris, middle of April.
Carpinus Americana, middle of April.
Celastrus scandens, beginning of June.
Convolvulus purpureus, July and after.
Cercis Canadensis, last of April.
Chelidonium majus, beginning of May.
Chionanthus Virginica, beginning of June.
Cimicifuga racemosa, last of June.
Claytonia Virginica, middle of April.
Cornus florida, middle of May.
Cratægus coccinea, middle of May.
Crus galli, beginning of June.
Oxyacantha, middle of May.
Cynoglossum officinale, last of May.
Dentaria laciniata, middle of April.
Dicentra Cucullaria, last of April.
Digitalis purpurea, last of June.
Draba verna, beginning of April.
Epigæa repens, middle of April.
Erythronium Americanum, middle of April.
Geranium maculatum, beginning of May.
Gentiana Andrewsii, middle of September.
Gillenia trifoliata, beginning of June.
Hepatica triloba, last of March.
Houstonia cærulea, middle of April.
Hypericum perforatum, beginning of June.
Hydrangea arborescens, July.
Iris versicolor, last of May.
Juglans regia, middle of May.
nigra, middle of May.
Kalmia latifolia, last of May.
Lamium amplexicaule, middle of April.
Laurus Benzoin, beginning of April.
Lappa major, middle of July.
Ligustrum vulgare, beginning of June.
Lobelia cardinalis, last of July.
Linaria vulgaris, last of May.
Lupinus perennis, beginning of June.
Lilium Philadelphicum, last of June.
Liriodendron Tulipifera, last of May.
Morus rubra, middle of May.
Nuphar advena, middle of May.
Orontium aquaticum, last of April.
Oxalis violacea, last of May.
Platanus occidentalis, last of April.
Persica vulgaris, beginning of April.
Podophyllum peltatum, beginning of May.
Pontederia cordata, last of July.
Populus tremuloides, middle of April.
Pogonia ophiglossoides, last of June.
Pulmonaria Virginica, last of April.
Pyrus communis, beginning of May.
Malus, beginning of May.
Quercus alba, middle of May.
Rhododendron nudiflorum, beginning of May.
Rhus typhina, last of June.
glabra, last of June.
Ribes rubrum, middle of April.
Grossularia, middle of April.
Robinia Pseud-acacia, last of May.
Rosa Carolina, beginning of June.
Rubus odoratus, last of June.
Sagittaria sagittifolia, beginning of August.
Sambucus Canadensis, beginning of June.
Sanguinaria Canadensis, last of March.
Saponaria officinalis, beginning of July.
Saxifraga Virginiensis, middle of April.
Sassafras officinale, last of April.
Smilacina bifolia, last of May.
Staphylea trifolia, middle of May.
Syringa vulgaris, middle of May.
Symplocarpus foetidus, beginning of March.
Tilia Americana, last of June.
Tradescantia Virginica, middle of May.
Ulmus Americana, beginning of April.
Verbena hastata, middle of July.
Viola cucullata, last of April.
Vitis aestivalis, beginning of June.

NOTE.—The extreme variation in the time of blossoming of the *same plants in different years* is from ten days to two weeks.

Dates of opening and closing of the Hudson River at Albany.

[From the reports of the Regents of the University and other sources.]

Seasons.	River free from ice.	River closed by ice.	Seasons.	River free from ice.	River closed by ice.
1646	....	November 25	1824	March 3	Jan. 5, (1825)
1675-6	February 26	....	1825	March 6	December 13
1786	March 23	....	1826	February 26	December 24
1789	....	Feb. 3, (1790)	1827	March 20	December 25
1790	March 27	December 8	1828	February 8	December 23
1791	March 17	December 8	1829	April 1	Jan. 11, (1830)
1792	....	December 12	1830	March 15	December 23
1793	March 6	December 26	1831	March 15	December 5
1794	March 17	Jan 12, (1795)	1832	March 25	December 21
1795	....	Jan. 23 (1706)	1833	March 21	December 13
1796	....	November 28	1834	February 21	December 15
1797	....	November 26	1835	March 25	November 30
1798	....	November 23	1836	April 4	December 7
1799	....	Jan. 6, (1800)	1837	March 28	December 13
1800	....	Jan. 3, (1801)	1838	March 19	November 25
1801	February 28	Feb. 3, (1802)	1839	March 21	December 18
1802	....	December 16	1840	February 21	December 5
1803	....	Jan. 12, (1804)	1841	March 24	December 19
1804	April 6	December 13	1842	February 4	November 29
1805	....	Jan. 9, (1806)	1843	April 13	December 9
1806	February 20	December 11	1844	March 14	December 11
1807	April 8	Jan. 4, (1808)	1845	February 24	December 4
1808	March 10	December 9	1846	March 15	December 15
1809	....	Jan. 19, (1810)	1847	April 6	December 24
1810	....	December 14	1848	March 22	December 27
1811	....	December 20	1849	March 19	December 25
1812	....	December 21	1850	March 9	December 17
1813	March 12	December 22	1851	February 25	December 13
1814	....	December 10	1852	March 28	December 22
1815	....	December 2	1853	March 21	December 21
1816	....	December 16	1854	March 17	December 8
1817	....	December 7	1855	March 20	December 20
1818	March 25	December 14	1856	April 10	December 16
1819	April 3	December 13	1857	February 27	December 27
1820	March 25	November 13	1858	March 20	December 18
1821	March 15	December 13	1859	March 13	December 10
1822	March 15	December 24	1860	March 6	....
1823	March 24	December 16			

NOTES.

1639.—Heavy flood at Albany.

1647.—Disastrous flood in the spring.

1740-'41. }
1765-'66. } River closed as far down as Paulus Hook, now Jersey City.
1779-'80. }

1817-'18.—Winter long and intensely cold. The ice moved March 3, but soon became fixed. River remained closed 108 days.

1820.—River closed November 13; opened on the 20th, and finally closed on the 1st of December. River closed this winter to New York bay.

1824 —River clear of ice January 11, and remained thus several days.

1827-'28.—River opened and closed repeatedly at Albany during this winter. It closed the second time December 21.

1830-'31.—Opened by heavy rains, but closed again January 10.

1832-'33.—River opened January 3, and closed again January 11.

1834-'35.—River open at Albany March 17. A steamer came up as far as Van Wie's Point (5 miles below Albany) on the 18th.

1847-'48.—River closed December 24, and opened on the 31st.

1856.—Closed at Fort Washington, December 19, for 12 days.

1857—February 9.—The ice broke up in the Hudson, at Albany, early in the morning and formed a dam a few miles below, overflowing the lower part of the city to an extent never before known. The water arose about twenty feet above mean summer level and there remained several days. Steamers arrived from New York on the last day of February, but navigation was subsequently interrupted several days by ice.

1858-'59.—River frozen at Fishkill Landing January 1, so that people crossed on foot. Broke up February 21. Stopped 7 weeks, 3 days. Only 1 week good crossing with teams.

Dates of beginning and end of Navigation on the Erie Canal in New York.

[From the official reports of canal commissioners.]

Years.	Canal opened.	Canal closed.	Years.	Canal opened.	Canal closed.
1824	April 20	Dec. 4	1841	April 24	Nov. 30
1825	April 12	Dec. 5	1842	April 20	Nov. 28
1826	April 20	Dec. 18	1843	May 1	Nov. 30
1827	April 22	Dec. 18	1844	April 18	Nov. 26
1828	March 27	Dec. 20	1845	April 15	Nov. 29
1829	May 2	Dec. 17	1846	April 16	Nov. 25
1830	April 20	Dec. 17	1847	May 1	Nov. 30
1831	April 16	Dec. 1	1848	May 1	Dec. 9
1832	April 25	Dec. 21	1849	May 1	Dec. 5
1833	April 19	Dec. 12	1850	April 22	Dec. 11
1834	April 17	Dec. 12	1851	April 15	Dec. 5
1835	April 15	Nov. 30	1852	April 20	Dec. 16
1836	April 25	Nov. 26	1853	April 20	Dec. 20
1837	April 20	Dec. 9	1854	May 1	Dec. 3
1838	April 12	Nov. 25	1855	May 1	Dec. 10
1839	April 20	Dec. 16	1856	May 5	Dec.
1840	April 20	Dec. 3	1857	May 6	Dec. 1

NOTE.—The dates of opening, above given, were usually fixed upon several days in advance, and were determined to some extent by the terms of special contracts for repairs rather than the state of forwardness of the season. The dates of closing are mostly those of the first severe and protracted frost at the beginning of winter.

Dates of first Arrivals at Quebec.

[Received from Prof. Kingston, of Toronto.]

Date of arrival.	Description of vessel.	Where from.	Date of arrival.	Description of vessel.	Where from.
1760, May 9	H. M. S		1812, May 2	Ship	London
1765, May 16	Snow	Glasgow and Belfast	1813, May 5	H. M. S	Portsmouth
1766, May 29	Sloop	Boston	1814, May 8	Schooner	Halifax
1767, May 6	Sloop	Boston	1815, May 10	Ship	Alicant
1771, May 12	Brig	London	1816, May 12	Ship	Liverpool
1772, May 13	Brigantine	London	1817, May 13	Ship	Hull
1773, May 20	Ship	London	1818, May 7	Brig	Aberdeen
1777, May 5	T. ship	Newfoundland	1819, May 1	Brig	Aberdeen
1778, May 20	Snow	Cadiz	1820, May 9	Brig	Alicant
1781, May 7		London	1821, May 8	Brig	Grenada
1786, May 14	Ship	Downs	1822, April 29	Brig	St. Vincent
1787, May 11	H. M. S	Halifax	1823, May 9	Brig	Belfast
1789, May 14	Ship	Liverpool	1824, May 1	Barque	London
1795, June 2	Brig	Trinity Bay	1825, April 24	Ship	Plymouth
1796, May 20	Brig	Greenock	1826, April 25	Ship	London
1797, May 15	Schooner	St. Domingo	1827, April 30	Ship	Aberdeen
1798, May 11	Schooner	Jamaica	1828, May 8	Ship	Gibraltar
1799, May 8	Brig	St. Vincent	1829, May 2	Brig	Bristol
1800, May 17		Halifax	1830, April 26	Ship	Liverpool
1801, April 25	Ship	Liverpool	1831, April 16	Brig	Poole
1802, May 12	Brig	Newcastle	1832, May 4	Ship	Greenock
1803, May 4	Brig	Jamaica	1833, May 10	Brig	Greenock
1801, April 25	Ship	Liverpool	1834, May 6	Barque	London
1805, May 5	Ship	London	1835, May 2	Brig	Bordeaux
1806, May 9	Brig	Ayr	1836, May 11	Ship	Greenock
1807, April 28	Brig	Liverpool	1837, April 29	Barque	London
1808, April 19	Brig	Hull	1838, May 3		Poole
1809, May 4	Ship	Portsmouth	1839, May 8	Ship	Poole
1810, May 3	Ship	Newcastle	1840, April 25	Ship	Poole
1811, April 26	Ship	London	1841, April 29	Ship	Poole

Dates of first Arrivals ai Quebec—Continued.

Date of arrival.	Description of vessel.	Where from.	Date of arrival.	Description of vessel.	Where from.
1842, May 2	Barque	Gibraltar	1850, April 28	Ship	Liverpool
1843, April 18	Barque	London	1851, April 20	Ship	Liverpool
1844, May 3	Barque	London	1852, April 15	Ship	Liverpool
1845, May 1	Barque	London	1853, April 24	Ship	Greenock
1846, April 24	Ship	Glasgow	1854, April 29	Brigantine	Liverpool
1847, May 8	Ship	Forbes	1855, April 6	Ship	Glasgow
1848, May 1	Ship	Greenock	1856, April 29	Ship	Liverpool
1849, April 28	Ship	Glasgow	1857, April 20	Ship	Glasgow

Dates of first Entry and last Clearance of vessels at Ogdensburg upon the St. Lawrence.

[From the records of the custom-house, by Wm. E. Guest.]

Years.	Entered.	Cleared.	Years.	Entered.	Cleared.
1832		Dec 20	1845	April 1	Dec. 15
1833	April 12	Dec 21	1846	April 6	Dec. 25
1834	April 2	Dec. 17	1847	April 20	Dec. 8
1835	April 4	Nov. 28	1848	April 4	Dec. 25
1836	April 20	Dec. 7	1849	April 14	Dec. 21
1837	April 20	Dec. 20	1850	March 30	Dec. 12
1838	April 12	Dec. 7	1851	April 8	Dec. 16
1839	April 11	Dec. 26	1852	April 5	Dec. 25
1840	April 1	Dec. 9	1853	April 4	Dec. 21
1841	April 16	Dec. 8	1854	April 13	Dec. 13
1842	March 24	Dec. 1	1855	April 17	Dec. 21
1843	May 3	Dec. 20	1856	April 18	Dec. 11
1844	April 6	Dec. 16	1857	April 17	

NOTES.

1838.—January 26, river closed. April 5, river opened, and first boat left for Lewiston. Closed December 26.
1844.—April 8, loaded sleighs crossed the St. Lawrence. On the 14th a single sleigh crossed
1850.—January 13, teams crossed on the ice. River frozen on December 24, and crossing on the ice January 1, 1851.
1851.—December 21, river frozen. Footmen crossed on the 22d, and teams on the 23d.

Dates of opening of Lake Erie at Buffalo.

[From the official reports of canal commissioners and other sources.]

Year.	Date of opening.	Year.	Date of opening.	Year.	Date of opening.
1827	April 21	1838	March 31	1849	March 25
1828	April 1	1839	April 11	1850	March 25
1829	May 10	1840	April 27	1851	April 2
1830	April 6	1841	April 14	1852	April 20
1831	May 8	1842	March 7	1853	April 14
1832	April 27	1843	May 6	1854	April 29
1833	April 23	1844	March 14	1855	April 21
1834	April 6	1845	April 3	1856	May 2
1835	May 8	1846	April 11	1857	April 27
1836	April 27	1847	April 23	1859	March 2
1837	May 16	1848	April 9		

Dates of beginning of Navigation at Cleveland, Ohio.

[From report of Cleveland Herald and other sources.]

Year.	Date of beginning.	Year.	Date of beginning.	Year.	Date of beginning.
1830	April 3	1834	Feb. 1	1837	March 20
1831	March 29	1835	March 26	1838	March 25
1832	March 28	1836	April 14	1839	March 21
1833	April 2				

Dates of opening of Navigation at Detroit, Michigan.

[From the Detroit Advertiser.]

Year.	Date.	Arrivals and departures.
1839	March 12	Steamer Erie left for Toledo.
1840	March 8	Steamer Star arrived from Cleveland.
1841	April 18	Steamer General Wayne arrived from Buffalo.
1842	March 8	Steamer General Scott left for Buffalo.
1843	April 23	Steamer Fairport left for Cleveland.
1844	March 11	Steamer Red Jacket left for Port Gratiot.
1845	Jan. 4	Steamer United States arrived from Buffalo.
1846	March 14	Steamer J. Owen arrived from Cleveland.
1847	March 30	Steamer United States arrived from Cleveland.
1848	March 22	Propeller Manhattan left for Buffalo.
1849	March 21	Steamer J. Owen left for Cleveland.
1850	March 25	Steamer Southerner arrived from Buffalo.
1851	March 19	Steamer Hollister arrived from Toledo.
1852	March 22	Steamer Arrow left for Toledo.
1853	March 14	Steamer Bay City arrived from Sandusky.
1854	March 21	Steamer May Queen arrived from Cleveland.
1855	April 1	Steamer Arrow left for Toledo.
1856	April 15	Steamer May Queen and Arrow cleared.
1857	March 24	Steamer Ocean left for Cleveland.
1858	March 17	Steamer Dart left for Toledo.
1859	March 8	Steamer Forester left for Port Huron.

Dates of opening and closing of Milwaukee river and first arrival of steamers at Milwaukee.

[By I. A. Lapham]

Year.	Milwaukee river.		Days closed.	First steamers from lower lake.	
	Opened.	Closed.		Date.	Name.
1836	....	Nov. 20	....	....	
1837	April 13	Nov. 25	144	May 28	James Madison.
1838	March 25	Nov. 15	121	April 26	Pennsylvania.
1839	March 27	Nov. 21	132	April 30	Columbus.
1840	March 6	Nov. 17	106	April 11	Chesapeake.
1841	March 24	Nov. 25	127	April 25	Great Western.
1842	March 9	Nov. 17	104	March 26	Chesapeake.
1843	April 14	Dec. 1	148	May 8	Bunker Hill.
1844	March 10	Nov. 25	100	April 10	Missouri.
1845	March 3	Nov. 27	98	April 5	Hercules.
1846	March 9	Dec. 8	102	April 10	Bunker Hill.
1847	April 2	Nov. 28	115	April 29	Louisiana.
1848	Feb. 16	Nov. 30	80	April 13	Manhattan.
1849	March 13	Dec. 6	103	April 12	Petrel.
1850	March 12	Dec. 6	98	April 4	Republic.
1851	March 13	Dec. 13	99	April 4	Republic.
1852	March 24	Dec. 12	102	May 9	Wisconsin.
1853	March 20	Dec. 20	98	April 18	Forest City.
1854	March 10	Dec. 4	80	April 25	Globe.
1855	April 4	Dec. 18	96	May 2	Republic.

Dates of the closing and opening of the inner part of Gardiner's bay, Long Island, New York.

[By Ephraim N. Bryam, of Sag Harbor.]

Years.	Date of closing.	Date of opening.	Years.	Date of closing.	Date of opening.
1841	Jan. 5	Feb. 19	1850	Not frozen.	----------
1844	Jan. 9	Feb. 23	1851-2	Dec. 25	Feb. 10
1845	Feb. 2	Feb. 16	1853	Not frozen.	----------
1846	Jan. 18	March 10	1854	Jan. 29	Feb. 7
1847	Not frozen.	----------	1855	Feb. 6	Feb. 20
1849	Jan. 10	March 1	1856	Jan. 6	March 12

Dates of Disappearance of the Ice from Otsego lake, at Cooperstown, New York.

[From the Freeman's Journal.]

Years.	Date.	Years.	Date.
1841	April 25	1851	March 30
1842	March 30	1852	April 26
1843	April 26	1853	April 9
1844	April 13	1854	April 20
1845	April 1	1855	April 24
1846	April 7	1856	April 26
1847	April 25	1857	April 6
1848	April 10	1858	April 5
1849	April 7	1859	March 30
1850	April 24		

Dates of opening of Navigation at Plattsburg, upon Lake Champlain.

[From the reports of Regents of the New York University.]

Years.	Date.	Years.	Date.
1837	April 29	1847	May 2
1838	April 18	1848	April 1
1841	April 27	1849	April 8

Dates of opening and closing of Lake Linckloen, at Cazenovia, Madison county, New York.

[From the reports of the Regents of the New York University.]

Years.	Date of opening.	Date of closing.	Years.	Date o opening.	Date of closing.
1836	April 21	---------	1843	April 25	---------
1837	---------	Dec. 15	1844	April 10	---------
1838	April 12	Nov. 30	1845	March 31	Dec. 7
1841	April 25	---------	1846	April 7	Dec. 17

Frosts, &c., at Edisto island, South Carolina.

[E. M. Fuller, observer.]

Years.	Latest frost in spring.	Earliest frost in autumn.	Cotton caterpillar first observed, and remarks.	Years.	Latest frost in spring.	Earliest frost in autumn.	Cotton caterpillar first observed, and remarks.
1840	....	Oct. 26	August 25.	1847	March 28	Nov. 16	
1841	....	Oct. 23		1848	March 16	Nov. 2	
1842	....	Nov. 11		1849	April 19	Nov. 10	August 22.
1843	....	Oct. 18	August 18.	1850	April 1	Nov. 18	
1844	April 1	Oct. 30		1851	....	Oct. 27	
1845	March 21	April 10		1852	March 20	Nov. 8	August 20.
1846	....	Oct. 29	July 20. By September 10 the entire crop was devastated The island made less than half an average crop.	1853	....	Oct. 25	September 6; very few.
				1854	April 19	Nov. 14	
				1855	....	Oct. 8	

Number of days on which it rained in the cotton season.

Months.	1847.	1851.	1852.	1853.	Months.	1847.	1851.	1852.	1853.
April	5	9	12	4	August	19	16	5	12
May	15	3	7	6	September	11	7	14	9
June	19	12	7	8	October	2	6	7	12
July	21	16	13	17					

Spring of 1828.—This season was remarkably early in South Carolina, and followed a winter equally memorable for its extreme mildness. From November, 1827, till January 16, 1828, it was not sufficiently cool to save meat while curing into bacon, and on only four or five days a light frost occurred. In the middle of January plum trees were starting to bloom, and on the 2d of February were in full bloom. Cotton planted in warm, rich soil, and protected localities, was not killed at the roots, and put forth in the spring as *ratoon* cotton.

J. DYSON, *Fulton, South Carolina.*

OBSERVATIONS

RELATIVE TO

THREE STORMS

IN THE YEAR 1859.

REDUCED AND ARRANGED BY PROFESSOR J. H. COFFIN.

LIST OF STATIONS, ARRANGED BY STATES,

AND

INDEX FOR THE OBSERVATIONS OF THREE STORMS

IN THE YEAR 1859.

BRITISH AMERICA.

UNITED STATES.

UNITED STATES—Continued.

* Parishes.

UNITED STATES—Continued.

UNITED STATES—Continued.

MEXICO.

SOUTH AMERICA.

* Districts.

ALPHABETICAL LIST OF STATIONS

FOR THE

OBSERVATIONS OF THREE STORMS DURING 1859.

NAME OF STATION.	North latitude.	West longitude from Greenwich.
	° ′	° ′
Adams Centre, N. Y	43 48	75 52
Aiken, S. C	33 32	81 34
All Saints, S. C	33 40	79 17
Amherst, Mass	42 22	72 34
Annapolis, Md	38 58	76 29
Appleton, Wis., (Lawrence University)	44 10	88 35
Arkadelphia, Ark	34 08	92 58
Athens, Ga	33 58	83 30
Atlanta, Ga	33 43	84 18
Atsena Otie, Fla	29 07	83 02
Augusta, Ga	33 28	81 54
Augusta, Ill	40 12	89 45
Augusta, Mo	38 36	90 30
Aurora, Ill	41 40	88 16
Aurora, Ind	39 04	84 47
Austin, Texas	30 20	97 46
Austin, Texas	30 15	97 47
Avon, Ohio	41 27	82 04
Baldwinsville, N. Y	43 04	76 41
Baltimore, Md	39 18	76 37
Bardstown, Ky	37 52	85 18
Batavia, Ill	41 48	88 23
Battle Creek, Mich	42 20	85 10
Bay City, Wis	46 33	91 00
Bayfield, Wis	46 18?	90 50?
Beaver Bay, Minn	47 12	91 19
Belair, Fla	30 24	84 20
Belfast, Me	44 22	69 06
Bellefontaine, Ohio	40 21	83 40
Bellefonte, Pa	40 50	77 49
Bellevue, Iowa	42 15	90 25
Bellevue, Neb	41 08	95 50
Bellport, N. Y	40 44	72 54
Beloit, Wis	42 30	89 04
Bentonville, Ark	36 23	94 00
Berwick, Pa	41 05	76 15
Bethany, Mo	40 16	94 02
Bethel, Ohio	....	....
Beverly, N. Y	41 22	74 00
Black River Plantation, La	31 30	91 46
Bladensburg, Md	38 57	76 58
Bloomington, Ill	40 27	89 08
Bolivar, Mo	37 37	93 20
Boonville, Mo	38 55	92 40
Border Plains, Iowa	42 36	94 05
Boston, Texas	33 25	94 24
Bowling Green, Ohio	41 27	83 45
Brandon, Vt	43 45	73 00
Bridgewater, Mass	42 00	71 00
Brownsville, Ark	34 50	92 00
Brownsville, Neb	40 24	95 33
Buffalo, N. Y	42 50	79 33

NAME OF STATION.	North latitude.	West longitude from Greenwich.
	° ′	° ′
Burkeville, Texas	31 00	93 34
Burlingame, Kansas	38 35	96 45
Burlington, Iowa	40 48	91 12
Burlington, Minn	47 01	91 30
Burlington, Vt., (University of Vermont)	44 29	73 11
Cahaba, Ala	32 19	87 15
Cambridge, Mass., (Harvard University)	42 24	71 07
Cannelton, Ind	37 58	86 40
Cannonsburg, Pa	40 17	80 10
Carbon Cliff, Ill	41 31	90 29
Carlisle, Pa., (Dickinson College)	40 12	77 11
Carlowville, Ala	32 10	87 15
Carrolton, Mo	39 21	93 27
Carthage, Ill	40 23	91 17
Cassville, Mo	36 41	93 56
Catharina Sophia, Surinam, S. A	5 48	56 47
Cazenovia, N. Y	42 55	75 46
Celestville, Kan.—(See Spring Hill.)		
Chambersburg, Pa	39 58	77 45
Chapel Hill, N. C., (University of North Carolina)	35 54	79 17
Charleston, S. C	32 46	80 00
Charlotte, N. Y	43 14	77 51
Cleaverville, Ill	....	....
Chatfield, Minn	43 50	92 25
Chestertown, Md	39 14	76 02
Cincinnati, Ohio, (Woodward High School)	39 06	84 27
Cinnaminson, N. J	40 01	75 03
Claremont, N. H	43 29	72 22
Clarksville, Ga	34 41	....
Cleveland, Ohio	41 30	81 40
Clinton, N. Y	43 00	75 20
Clyde, N. Y	43 10	77 10
College Hill, Ohio, (Farmers' College)	39 19?	84 25?
Collingwood, Ohio	41 49	83 34
Columbia, Ct	41 42	72 16
Columbia, S. C	33 57	81 07
Columbus, Miss	33 30	88 29
Cornish, Me	43 40	70 44
Corunna, Mich	42 57	84 06
Covington, Ga	33 34	84 00
Craftsbury, Vt	44 40	72 29
Crichton's Store, Va	36 40	77 46
Cross Creek, Va	40 19?	80 31?
Dallasburg, Ohio	39 17	84 07
Danville, Ky	37 40	84 30
Dansville, N. Y	42 34	77 46
Davenport, Iowa	41 30	90 37
Detroit, Mich	42 24	83 00
Dexter, Me	44 55	69 32
Dixon, Ill	41 50	89 36

NAME OF STATION.	North latitude.	West longitude from Greenwich.
	° ′	° ′
Dubuque, Iowa	42 30	90 52
East Henrietta, N. Y.—(See Henrietta.)	....	....
Eden, N. Y.	42 38	79 07
Edgington, Ill.	41 25	90 46
Elgin, Ill.	42 00	88 15
Elkhorn, Neb.	41 22	96 12
Elk Run Township, Ohio.—(See East Fairfield.)		
Emerson, Mo.	39 56	91 40
Evansville, Ind.	38 08	87 29
Fairfield, Iowa	41 01	91 57
Falmouth, Va.	38 15	77 34
Farmington, Mo.	37 48	90 24
Fayette Village, Iowa	42 50	91 50
Fishkill, N. Y.	41 34	74 18
Flatbush, N. Y.	40 37	74 01
Fleming, Pa.	40 55	77 53
Florida, Mass.	42 42	73 10
Fordham, N. Y.	40 54	74 03
Forest City, Minn.	45 45	96 00
Forestville, Iowa	42 40	91 50
Fort Edward, N. Y.	43 13	73 42
Fort Madison, Iowa	40 37	91 28
Fort Niagara, N. Y.	43 18	79 08
Fort Riley, Kansas	39 02	97 00
Fort Simpson, British America	61 51	121 25
Frederick, Md.	39 24	77 18
Fredericksburg, Va.	38 20	77 28
Freedom, Ohio	41 13	81 08
Freehold, N. J.	40 15	74 21
Gainesville, Fla.	29 35	82 26
Galena, Ill.	42 25	90 33
Gardiner, Me.	44 11	69 46
Gaston, N. C.	36 32	77 45
Germantown, Pa.	40 03	75 10
Gettysburg, Pa.	39 49	77 15
Gilmer, Texas	32 46	94 48
Glenwood, Tenn.	36 28	87 13
Gonzales, Texas	29 28	97 39
Grand Haven, Mich.	43 01	86 11
Grand Rapids, Mich.	43 00	86 00
Great Salt Lake City, Utah	40 45	112 10
Great Valley, N. Y.	42 12	78 45
Green Bay, Wis.	44 30	88 00
Greencastle, Ind.	39 39	86 46
Greene Springs, Ala.	32 50	89 46
Greenfield, Mo.	37 24	93 48
Green Plains, N. C.—(See Gaston.)		
Greensborough, Ala.	32 40	87 40
Greenville, Mo.	37 07	90 30
Greenville, Texas	33 10	97 22
Hamilton, Canada	43 15	79 57
Hardinsburg, Ky., (Mt. Alba College)	37 45	86 24
Harrisburg, Pa.	40 16	76 50
Harrisonville, Mo.	38 36	94 17
Hartland, Me.	44 51	69 30
Hartwood, Va.—(See Falmouth.)		
Havana, N. Y.	42 20	76 54
Hazlewood, Minn.	45 00	95 30
Henrietta, N. Y.	43 06	77 51
Hermann, Mo.	38 40	91 27
Hillsborough, Ohio	39 00	....
Hiram, Ohio	41 20	81 15
Hocking Port, Ohio	39 18	81 41
Hornersville, Mo.	36 03	90 00
Houseville, N. Y.	43 40	75 32
Hudson, Ohio, (Western Reserve College)	41 15	81 24

NAME OF STATION.	North latitude.	West longitude from Greenwich.
	° ′	° ′
Iberia, Ohio	40 46	82 51
Ilion, N. Y.	43 01	75 14
Jackson, Jackson county, Ohio	39 07	82 30
Jacksonport, Ark.	35 36	91 15
Jacksonville, Fla.	30 30	82 00
Janesville, Wis.	42 42	89 91
Kanawha, Va.	38 53	81 25
Kanosha, Neb.	40 51	95 53
Kaufman, Texas	32 37	96 20
Kelley's Island, Ohio	41 36	82 43
Kenosha, Wis.	42 35	87 50
Kirksville, Mo.	40 11	92 33
La Grange, Tenn.		
Lake City, Fla.—(See Alligator.)		
Lake George, Mich.	46 15?	85 00?
Lake Mills, Wis.	43 00	89 00
Lambertville, N. J.	40 23	74 56
Lancaster, Mo.	40 30	92 30
Lansing, Mich., (State Agricultural College)	42 44	84 15
Larissa, Texas	31 45	95 50
Lawrence, Kansas	38 58	95 12
Lawrence, Mass.	42 42	71 11
Leavenworth City, Kansas	39 20	94 33
Lecompton, Kansas	39 02	95 10
Leitersburg, Md., (near)	39 35	77 30
Leonardtown, Md.	38 17	76 43
Lewinsville, Va.	38 56	77 04
Lewisburg, Pa., (University)	40 58	76 58
Lewisburg, Va.	38 00	80 00
Lexington, Ky.	38 06	84 18
Lexington, Mo.	39 10	93 50
Limington, Me.	43 40	70 40
Linden, Pa.	41 10	77 11
Lisbon, Me.	44 00	70 04
Livingston, Ala.	32 35	88 19
Logansport, Ind.	40 45	86 25
Louisville, Ky.	38 03	85 30
Lunenburg, Vt.	44 28	71 41
Luray, Mo., (near)	40 28	91 55
Lyons City, Iowa	41 50	90 10
Lyons, N. Y.	43 04	77 04
Madison, Ohio	41 49	81 10
Madison, Wis.	43 05	90 13
Madrid, N. Y.	44 43	75 33
Manchester, Ill.	39 33	90 34
Manhattan, Kansas	39 13	96 45
Manitowoc, Wis.	44 07	87 37
Marengo, Ill.	42 14	88 38
Marquette, Mich.	46 32	87 41
Marysville, Cal.	39 12	121 42
Memphis, Tenn.	35 06	90 08
Mendon, Mass.	42 06	71 34
Micanopy, Fla.	29 35	82 31
Michigan City, Ind.	41 41	86 53
Middletown, Ct., (Wesleyan University)	41 33	72 39
Milwaukee, Wis.	43 03	87 57
Minatitlan, Mexico	17 59	94 07
Mishawaka, Ind.	41 39	86 02
Moneka, Kansas	38 19	94 49
Monroe, Mich.	41 58	83 24
Monroe Piers, Mich.	41 53	83 19
Montgomery, Ala.	32 25	86 22
Montreal, Canada	45 30	73 36
Montross, Va.	38 07	76 46
Mont View, Va.	38 00	78 30
Montville, Ohio	41 07	81 47
Moorestown, N. J.	39 58	75 02

NAME OF STATION.	North latitude.	West longitude from Greenwich.
	° ′	° ′
Morrisania, N. Y., (Fairmount Institute)	40 53	74 01
Morrisville, Pa	40 12	74 53
Moulton, Ala	34 32	87 25
Mount Joy, Pa	40 08	77 32
Mount Washington, N. H	44 15	71 16
Murfreesborough, N. C	36 30	77 06
Murrysville, Pa	40 28	79 35
Muscatine, Iowa	41 26	91 05
Mustapha, Va	39 20	81 41
Nantucket, Mass	41 16	70 06
Naperville, Ill	41 46	88 10
Natchez, Miss	31 34	91 24
Nazareth, Pa	40 43	75 21
Nebraska City, Neb	40 40	95 43
Neosho Falls, Kansas	38 03	95 31
New Albany, Ind	38 17	85 45
Newark, N. J	40 45	74 10
Newark, Ohio	40 06	82 28
New Bedford, Mass	41 39	70 56
New Braunfels, Texas	29 42	98 15
New Brunswick, N. J	40 30	75 31
New Buffalo, Mich	41 45	86 46
New Castle, Me	44 07	69 36
New Danemora, Wis	44 17	90 38
New Harmony, Ind	38 08	87 50
New Haven, Ct	41 18	72 57
New Lisbon, Ohio	40 45	80 46
New Orleans, La	29 57	90 00
New York city, N. Y	40 42	74 01
Nichols, N. Y	42 00	76 32
Norristown, Pa	40 08	75 19
North Belgrade, Me	44 30	69 53
North Bend, Ohio	39 08	84 35
North Whitehall, Pa	40 40	75 26
Northwood, Ohio	40 28	83 45
Norway, Me	44 12	70 39
Norwich, Ct	41 32	72 03
Ogdensburg, N. Y	44 43	75 26
Omaha, Neb	41 15	96 10
Ontonagon, Mich	46 52	89 30
Oswego, N. Y	43 25	76 35
Otsego, Mich	42 27	85 40
Otsego, Wis	43 27	89 13
Ottawa, Ill	41 20	88 47
Ottawa Point, Mich	44 16	83 25
Paducah, Ky	37 06	88 36
Paris, Ky	38 16	84 07
Paris, Mo	39 30	92 00
Paulding, Miss	32 03	89 10
Pekin, Ill	40 36	89 45
Penn Yan, N. Y	42 42	77 11
Peoria, Ill	40 36	89 30
Perry, Me	45 00	67 06
Perryville, Ark	35 00	92 46
Philadelphia, Pa., (Central High School)	39 57	75 11
Pioneer Grove, Neb.—(See Omaha.)		
Pittsburg, Pa	40 30	80 00
Platteville, Wis	42 45	90 00
Pleasant Plain, Iowa	41 07	91 54
Pocopson, Pa	39 54	75 37
Point Pleasant, Va	38 50	82 31
Pomfret, Ct	41 52	72 00
Poplar Grove, Va	38 20	81 21
Port Huron, Mich	42 53	82 24
Portland, Me	43 37	70 19
Portsmouth, Ohio	38 50	82 49
Portsmouth, Va	36 50	76 19
Poydras College, La	......	......
Princeton, Minn	45 50	93 45
Providence, R. I., (Brown University)	41 49	71 25

NAME OF STATION.	North latitude.	West longitude from Greenwich.
	° ′	° ′
Raleigh, N. C	35 47	78 48
Red River Settlement, Hudson's Bay Terr'y	50 06	97 00
Richmond, Ind	39 47	84 47
Richmond, Mass	42 23	73 20
Riley, Ill	42 08	88 33
Rochester, N. Y	43 08	77 51
Rocky Run, Wis	43 26	89 19
Rossville, Iowa	43 10	91 21
Rougemont, Va	38 05	78 21
Rupert, Vt	43 15	73 11
Ruthven, Va	37 21	77 33
Sackett's Harbor, N. Y	43 55	75 57
Sacramento, Cal	38 34	121 40
St. Augustine, Fla	29 48	81 35
St. John's, Newfoundland	47 35	52 38
St. John's, S. C	33 00	80 00
St. Johnsbury, Vt	44 25	72 00
St. Louis, Mo	38 37	90 16
St. Martin, Canada	45 32	73 36
Salt Ponds, Fla., 2½ miles NE. from Key West	24 33	81 48
Sandwich, Ill	41 31	88 30
San Francisco, Cal	38 00	122 00
San Patricio, Texas	27 55	97 50
Saratoga, N. Y	43 06	74 00
Savannah, Ga	32 05	81 07
Savannah, Ohio	41 12	82 31
Saybrook, Ct., (Lynde Point light-house)	41 18	72 20
Schenectady, N. Y., (Union College)	42 49	73 55
Selma, Ala	32 25	86 51
Seville, Fla	30 29	84 07
Shamokin, Pa	40 45	76 31
Sharonville, Ohio	33 12	84 35
Shelburne, N. H	44 23	71 06
Shelbyville, Ind	39 30	85 43
Sisterdale, Texas	29 54	98 35
Smithfield, Va	37 02	76 37
Somerset, Pa	40 02	79 02
South Bend, Ind	41 37	86 08
Sparta, Ga	33 17	83 09
Spencertown, N. Y	43 19	73 41
Springdale, Ky	38 07	85 24
Springfield, Mass	42 06	72 35
Spring Hill, Ark	33 33	93 35
Spring Hill, Kansas	38 37	94 56
Stanbridge, Canada East	45 00	73 00
Steuben, Me	44 44	67 50
Stockton, Mo	37 36	93 48
Stratford, N. H	44 40	71 34
Stratham, N. H	43 00	70 54
Stribling Springs, Va	38 17	79 12
Superior, Wis	46 38½	92 03½
Sykesville, Md	39 20	70 57
Tarentum, Pa	40 37	79 19
Tarrant, Texas	33 16	95 34
The Plains, Va	38 50	77 51
Thomaston, Ga	32 56	84 30
Thomson, Ga	33 26	82 28
Thunder Bay Island, Mich	45 02	83 09
Tickfaw Station, La	30 30	90 32
Tiskilwa, Ill	41 15	89 30
Toledo, Ohio	41 45	83 36
Topsham, Me	44 00	70 00
Toronto, Canada	43 39	79 21
Troy, Ohio	40 03	84 06
Tuscumbia, Mo	38 13	92 23
Union Hill, Texas	30 30	96 31
Upper Alton, Ill	38 55	90 10
Urbana, Ohio, (Urbana University)	40 06	83 43
Vassalborough, Me	40 27	69 42

NAME OF STATION.	North latitude.	West longitude from Greenwich.	NAME OF STATION.	North latitude.	West longitude from Greenwich.
	° ′	° ′		° ′	° ′
Waldron, Ark	34 53	94 00	West Urbana, Ill	40 09	88 17
Wallingford, Ct	41 27	72 50	Westville, Miss	31 52	90 00
Wampsville, N. Y	43 04	75 50	Wet au Glaize, Mo	38 06	92 17
Warren, Me	44 05	59 15	Wheaton, Ill., (Illinois Institute)	41 49	88 06
Warrenton, Mo	38 45	91 11	Wheelock, Texas	30 55	96 27
Warrington, Fla., (navy yard)	30 20	87 16	Whitemarsh Island, Ga	32 04	81 05
Washington, Ark	33 43	93 37	Williamstown, Mass	42 43	73 13
Washington, D. C.	38 56	76 58	Willow Creek, Ill	41 45	89 05
Washington, Texas	30 26	96 15	Wilson, N. Y	43 20	78 56
Waterford, N. Y	42 48	73 41	Winchester, Tenn	35 12	86 00
Waukesha, Wis	42 50	88 11	Winchester, Va	39 15	78 10
Wausau, Wis	45 00	89 40	Windham, Ohio	41 10	81 05
Waynesville, Ill	40 16	89 07	Windsor, Nova Scotia, (King's College)	44 59	64 07
Waynesville, Mo	37 50	92 07	Winnebago, Ill	42 17	89 11
Webberville, Texas	30 14	97 34	Wolfville, Nova Scotia, (Acadia College)	45 06	64 25
Welshfield, Ohio	41 23	81 12	Woodstock, Ill	42 20	88 30
West Day, N. Y	43 20	74 16	Worcester, Mass	42 16	71 48
Westerville, Ohio	40 04	83 10	Worthington, Pa	40 52	79 39
Westfield, Mass	42 06	72 48			
West Haverford, Pa	40 00	75 21	Ypsilanti, Mich	42 15	83 47
West Salem, Ill	38 30	88 00			
Westtown, Pa	39 57	75 34	Zebulon, Ga	33 07	84 26

INDEX

TO

OBSERVATIONS ON PERIODICAL PHENOMENA.

STORMS OF 1859.

STORM No. 1, MARCH, 1859.

ST. JOHN'S, NEWFOUNDLAND.

Month and day.	Hour.	Barom'r corrected to 32° F.	Thermometer.	Force of vapor.	Cloudiness.	Motion of clouds.	Winds.	Relative humidity.	REMARKS.
March 14	2 p. m.	29.62	40		Cu. 4	NNW. 3	NNW. 2		14th. Morning soft and calm.
	9 p. m.	29.93	26		Cu. st. 10	NW. 0	NW. 3		15th. Fine all day; cool.
March 15	7 a. m.	29.86	20		Cu. st. 3	SW. 2	SW. 1		16th. Morning, blowing strong; rain, with high wind, at night; amount, 0.22 inch.
	2 p. m.	29.87	48		9	S. 2	S. 8		
	9 p. m.	29.38	40				S 3		
March 16	7 a. m.	29.84	30				W. 2		17th and 18th. Fine weather; stars very brilliant.
	2 p. m.	29.68	38				SW. 3		
	9 p. m.	29.61	40				S. 4		19th. Soft and mild; slight rain in the evening.
March 17	7 a. m.	29.26	38				NW. 2		
	2 p. m.	29.26	42				NW. 2		20th. Strong wind all day; heavy rain in the evening; amount, 0.25 inch.
	9 p. m.	29.26	35				NW. 2		
March 18	7 a. m.	29.45	34		Cu. 4	NNW. 6	NW. 3		
	2 p. m.	29.55	40		Cu. 3	NNW. 9	NW. 3		
	9 p. m.	29.56	32				NW. 3		
March 19	7 a. m.	29.76	34		Cu. st. 7	0	0		
	2 p. m.	29.41	46			NW	W. 2		
	9 p. m.	29.49	36		Cu. st. 10	NW	S. 3		
March 20	7 a. m.	29.30	38		St. 9	S. 0	S. 2		

STANBRIDGE, CANADA.

Month and day.	Hour.	Barom'r corrected to 32° F.	Thermometer.	Force of vapor.	Cloudiness.	Motion of clouds.	Winds.	Relative humidity.	REMARKS.
March 14	7 a. m.		27		0		SE. 1		15th Rain at 1 a. m.
	2 p. m.		47		10		SE. 2		18th. Rain in the a. m.
	9 p. m.		41		10		SE. 4		20th. Snow.
March 15	7 a. m.		40		10		S. 3		
	2 p. m.		45		10		SE. 1		
	9 p. m.		38		10		SW. 1		
March 16	7 a. m.		33		10		W. 3		
	2 p. m.		34		10		W. 3		
	9 p. m.		32		0		0		
March 17	7 a. m.		31		0		0		
	2 p. m.		46		10		SE. 2		
	9 p. m.		41		10		S. 0		
March 18	7 a. m.		44		10		SE. 1		
	2 p. m.		46		10		SE. 2		
	9 p. m.		47		10		SE. 3		
March 19	7 a. m.		49		10		S. 4		
	2 p. m.		46		10		S. 4		
	9 p. m.		25		10		NW. 4		

HAMILTON, CANADA.

Month and day.	Hour.	Barom'r corrected to 32° F.	Thermometer.	Force of vapor.	Cloudiness.	Motion of clouds.	Winds.	Relative humidity.	REMARKS.
March 14	9 a. m.	29.65	38						14th. Cloudy; rainy p. m.
	9 p. m.	29 07	52						15th. Cloudy; some hail and snow in the evening.
March 15	9 a. m.	29.16	42						
	9 p. m.	29.47	35						16th. Fair and clear.
March 16	9 a. m.	29.80	36						17th. Mostly cloudy.
	9 p. m.	29.82	38						18th. Misty; stormy at night and rained heavily, ending in snow.
March 17	9 a. m.	29.73	38						
	9 p. m.	29.50	42						19th. Cloudy and windy.
March 18	9 a. m.	29.00	40						
	9 p. m.	28.44	40						
March 19	9 a. m.	28.66	34						
	9 p. m.	29.30	32						

STORM No. 1, MARCH, 1859.

MONTREAL, CANADA.

Month and day.	Hour.	Barom'r corrected to 32° F.	Thermometer.	Force of vapor.	Cloudiness.	Motion of clouds.	Winds.	Relative humidity.	REMARKS.
March 14	2 p. m.	30.062	44	.265	Cu. st. 10	WNW. 1	WNW. 1	92	14th. Cloudy night.
	9 p. m.	29.959	41	.235	Cu. st. 10	WNW. 1	WNW. 1	91	15th. Rain from 8 to 12 p. m.;
March 15	7 a. m.	29.679	38	.186	Cu. st. 10	SW. 1	SW. 1	81	amount, 0.46 inch.
	2 p. m.	29.558	47	.298	Cu. st. 10	SW. 1	S. 1	92	16th. Aurora.
	9 p. m.	29.586	36	.191	Nim. 10	S. 1	S. 1	90	17th. Cloudy during night.
March 16	7 a. m.	29.684	34.3	.155	Cu. 8	WNW. 2	WNW. 2	79	18th. Slight rain at intervals dur-
	2 p. m.	29.744	40	.182	Cu. 6	WNW. 2	WNW. 2	73	ing the day.
	9 p. m.	29.912	38	.186	Cu. 6	WNW. 2	WNW. 2	81	19th. Rain, hail, and snow; amount,
March 17	7 a. m.	30.022	33	.150	0	0	W. 1	80	in water, 0.96 inch.
	2 p. m.	29.893	46	.169	Cir. 3	W. 1	W. 1	54	
	9 p. m.	29.658	44	.150	Cu. st. 10	W. 1	W. 1	80	
March 18	7 a. m.	29.621	43	.254	Nim. 10	S. 1	S. 1	92	
	2 p. m.	29.446	50.5	.348	Nim. 10	S. 1	SE. 1	93	
	9 p. m.	29.172	50	.267	Nim. 10	S. 1	SE. 1	100	
March 19	7 a. m.	29.282	39.8	.248	Nim. 10	SW. 1	SW. 2	100	
	2 p. m	29.663	40	.248	Nim. 3	WNW. 10	SW. 3	100	
	9 p. m.	29.906	33	.188	Nim. 10	SW. 1	WNW. 6	100	
March 20	7 a. m.	29.932	28	.135	Cu. 8	WNW. 4	WNW. 4	88	

RED RIVER SETTLEMENT, BRITISH AMERICA.

Month and day.	Hour.	Barom'r corrected to 32° F.	Thermometer.	Force of vapor.	Cloudiness.	Motion of clouds.	Winds.	Relative humidity.	REMARKS.
March 14	2 p. m.	------	32	----------	Cir. 3	----------	W. 1	----	
	9 p. m.	------	------	----------	----------	----------	----------	----	
March 15	7 a. m.	------	20	----------	0	----------	0	----	
	2 p. m.	------	24	----------	Cir. 3	E. 1	0	----	
	9 p. m.	------	------	----------	----------	----------	----------	----	
March 16	7 a. m.	------	------	----------	----------	----------	----------	----	
	2 p. m.	------	24	----------	----------	----------	----------	----	
	9 p. m.	------	------	----------	----------	----------	----------	----	
March 17	7 a. m.	------	21	----------	----------	----------	----------	----	
	2 p. m.	------	23	----------	----------	----------	----------	----	
	9 p. m.	------	12	----------	----------	----------	----------	----	
March 18	7 a. m.	------	− 2	----------	Cu. st. 10	S. 2	N. 2	----	
	2 p. m.	------	33	----------	Cir. 4	E. 2	NW. 1	----	
	9 p. m.	------	24	----------	0	0	NW. 1	----	
March 19	7 a. m.	------	31	----------	0	----------	S. ----------	----	
	2 p. m.	------	42	----------	Cir. 4	NE. 1	S. 1	----	
	9 p. m.	------	29	----------	0	0	0	----	
March 20	7 a. m.	------	32	----------	0	----------	SE ----------	----	

WOLFVILLE, NOVA SCOTIA.

Month and day.	Hour.	Barom'r corrected to 32° F.	Thermometer.	Force of vapor.	Cloudiness.	Motion of clouds.	Winds.	Relative humidity.	REMARKS.
March 14	2 p. m.	30.166	38	----------	Cir. st. 3	NNE. 2	NE. 2	----	Rain from $6\frac{1}{2}$ p. m. the 15th, to
	9 p. m.	30.159	31	----------	----------	----------	----------	----	a. m. on the 16th; amount,
March 15	7 a. m.	30.141	32	----------	St. 10	NW. 3	NW. 2	----	0.25 inch.
	2 p. m.	30.070	39	----------	St. 10	----------	----------	----	Rain from $7\frac{1}{4}$ p. m. the 18th, to
	9 p. m.	29.757	42	----------	Nim. 10	SW. 4	SW. 4	----	$4\frac{1}{2}$ p. m. on the 19th; amount,
March 16	7 a. m.	29.435	45	----------	St. 10	SW. 4	SW. 5	----	0.62 inch.
	2 p. m	29.503	47	----------	St. 10	NW. 4	NW. 4	----	
	9 p. m.	29.596	36	----------	----------	----------	NW. 4	----	
March 17	7 a. m.	29.840	35	----------	St. 5	NW. 4	NW. 4	----	
	2 p. m.	29.872	45	----------	----------	----------	NW. 5	----	
	9 p. m.	29.988	41	----------	Cir. st. 10	----------	NW. 2	----	
March 18	7 a. m.	29.971	31	----------	Cir. cu. 5	----------	----------	----	
	2 p. m.	29.952	48	----------	Cir. st. 10	----------	----------	----	
	9 p. m.	------	------	----------	----------	----------	----------	----	
March 19	7 a. m.	29.384	49	----------	Nim. 10	----------	SW. 3	----	
	2 p. m.	29.221	47	----------	Nim. 10	----------	SW. 4	----	
	9 p. m.	29.280	38	----------	----------	----------	SW. 2	----	
March 20	7 a. m.	29.301	39	----------	St. 10	W. 4	W. 3	----	

STORM No. 1, MARCH, 1859.

ST. MARTIN, CANADA.

Month and day.	Hour.	Barom'r corrected to 32° F.	Thermometer.	Force of vapor.	Cloudiness.	Motion of clouds.	Winds.	Relative humidity.	REMARKS.
March 14	2 p. m.	29.994	44.5	.231	Cir. st. 6	----------	NE. by E	80	15th. Rain; amount, 0.23 inch.
	10 p. m.	29.879	39.7	.210	Cir. st. 10	----------	NE. by E	86	18th. Rain; amount, 0.217 inch.
March 15	6 a. m.	29.458	38.2	.201	Rain	----------	SE	87	19th. Rain; amount, 0.346 inch.
	2 p. m.	29.439	45.0	.248	Cir. st. 10	----------	SE. by E	88	
	10 p. m.	29.476	37.0	.199	Cir. st. 9	----------	SW.	80	
March 16	6 a. m.	29.600	32.0	.149	Cir. st. 9	----------	WSW	84	
	2 p. m.	29.819	36.1	.170	Cir. st. 4	----------	W. by S.	80	
	10 p. m.	29.990	34.1	.162	Clear	----------	SW.	84	
March 17	6 a. m.	29.999	29.4	.136	Clear	----------	SSW	85	
	2 p. m.	29.967	48.3	.285	Cir. st 8	----------	SE by S.	84	
	10 p. m.	29.911	37.4	.193	Cir. st. 10	----------	SE. by S.	86	
March 18	6 a. m.	29.650	36.3	.184	Cir. st. 10	----------	E.	88	
	2 p. m.	29.294	44.7	.258	Rain	----------	NE. by S.	88	
	10 p. m.	29.194	37.7	.198	Cir. st. 10	----------	NE.	86	
March 19	6 a. m.	28.62	42.6	.137	Cir. st. 10	----------	SW.	87	
	2 p. m.	28.635	46.1	.286	Rain	----------	S. by E.	92	
	10 p. m.	29.078	22.5	.084	Cir. st. 10	----------	W. by S.	71	
March 20	6 a. m.	29.317	19.8	.087	Rain	----------	W. by N	84	

TORONTO, CANADA.

Month and day.	Hour.	Barom'r corrected to 32° F.	Thermometer.	Force of vapor.	Cloudiness.	Motion of clouds.	Winds.	Relative humidity.	REMARKS.
March 14	6 a. m.	29.732	35.3	.185	----------	----------	E. byN. 18.0	90	14th. Rain; amount, 0.385 inch.
	2 p. m.	29.434	38.6	.197	----------	----------	ENE. 14.8	84	15th. Snow; amount inappreciable.
	10 p. m.	29.042	50.7	.285	----------	----------	SSE. 15.0	76	17th. Lunar halo, 3 to 4 a. m., solar halo, 9 to 10 a. m.; both well defined. Amount of rain, 0.285 inch.
March 15	6 a. m.	29.146	38.9	.205	----------	----------	SSW 12.0	89	18th. Fog at 2 p. m.; sheet lightning in SW., 7.30 to 8 p. m. Amount of rain, 1.615 inch.
	2 p. m.	29.189	40.2	.168	----------	----------	SW. 13.4	67	19th. Violent storm of wind, continuing all day with great fury. Mean velocity from midnight of the 18th to midnight of the 19th, 34.37 miles per hour.
	10 p. m.	29.434	32.8	.118	----------	----------	W. by N. 20.9	64	
March 16	6 a. m.	29.696	33.0	.168	----------	----------	WNW. 13.0	89	
	2 p. m.	29.828	41.1	.156	----------	----------	S. by W. 11.0	60	
	10 p. m.	29.828	35.0	.175	----------	----------	S. by W. 5.2	85	
March 17	6 a. m.	29.774	32.4	.161	----------	----------	S. by W. 2.8	87	
	2 p. m.	29.605	46.5	.183	----------	----------	E. by S. 8.6	57	
	10 p. m.	29.440	44.9	.164	----------	----------	ENE. 5.4	54	
March 18	6 a. m.	29.137	42.4	.254	----------	----------	ENE. 19.6	94	
	2 p. m.	28.839	47.6	.325	----------	----------	ESE. 0.5	98	
	10 p. m.	28.512	50.7	.357	----------	----------	N. by E. 10.5	96	
March 19	6 a. m.	28.318	32.4	.151	----------	----------	WNW. 47.0	81	
	2 p. m.	28.892	32.1	.121	----------	----------	WNW. 30.8	65	
	10 p. m.	29.267	31.0	.111	----------	----------	WNW. 32.0	63	

WINDSOR, NOVA SCOTIA.

Month and day.	Hour.	Barom'r corrected to 32° F.	Thermometer.	Force of vapor.	Cloudiness.	Motion of clouds.	Winds.	Relative humidity.	REMARKS.
March 14	2 p. m.	30.275	37.5	----------	Cir. 3	----------	W. 2	....	16th. Rain during the night.
	9 p. m.	30.401	27.5	.216	0	----------	----------	91	18th. Showers in the p. m.
March 15	7 a. m.	30.317	28.5	.251	Nim. 10	----------	SW. 1	96	19th. Heavy fall of rain from 2 a. m. to 11 p. m.
	2 p. m.	30.073	------	.218	Nim. 10		SW. 2	76	20th. Slight snow squall.
	9 p. m.	29.812	39	.162	Nim. 10	----------	S. 5	68	
March 16	7 a. m.	29.286	41.5	.121	Nim. 10	----------	S. 6	58	
	2 p. m.	29.503	44	.138	Cir. & nim. 8	----------	W. 3	50	
	9 p. m.	29.671	39	.178	Nim. 9	----------	NW. 4	73	
March 17	7 a. m.	29.896	35.5	.142	Cu. 4	----------	NW. 4	88	
	2 p. m.	29.928	42.5	.198	St. & cir. 1	----------	NW. 3	65	
	9 p. m.	29.997	39.5	.174	St. 2	----------	SW. 1	80	
March 18	7 a. m.	30.106	29	.288	St. 3	----------	SW 1	96	
	2 p. m.	30.095	45.5	.335	Nim. 10	----------	SW. 2	93	
	9 p. m.	29.898	36.5	.195	Nim. 10	----------	SW. 3	90	
March 19	7 a. m.	29.475	45	.184	Nim. 10	----------	SW. 4	85	
	2 p. m.	29.304	50	.155	Nim. 8	----------	S. 4	68	
	9 p. m.	29.292	36.5	.171	Nim. 3	----------	SW. 3	100	
March 20	7 a. m.	29.204	36.5	.144	Nim. 10	----------	SW. 2	100	

STORM No. 1, MARCH, 1859.

CORNISH, MAINE.*

Month and day.	Hour.	Barom'r corrected to 32° F.	Thermometer.	Force of vapor.	Cloudiness.	Motion of clouds.	Winds.	Relative humidity.
March 14	7 a. m.	......	34	....	0	....	W. 2	....
	2 p. m.	......	44	....	Cir. st. 5	....	S. 2	....
	9 p. m.	......	36	....	Nim. 10	....	SE. 3	....
March 15	7 a. m.	......	36	....	Nim. 10	....	SE. 3	....
	2 p. m.	......	40	....	Nim. 10	....	S. 2	....
	9 p. m.	......	38	....	Nim. 10	....	NW. 2	....
March 16	7 a. m.	......	35	....	Nim. 5	....	NW. 2	....
	2 p. m.	......	38	....	Cu. 5	....	NW. 3	....
	9 p. m.	......	33	....	0	....	NW. 2	....
March 17	7 a. m.	......	34	....	0	....	NW. 1	....
	2 p. m.	......	42	....	Cir. st. 5	....	W. 1	....
	9 p. m.	......	40	....	Nim. 10	....	SW. 2	....
March 18	7 a. m.	......	40	....	Nim. 10	....	S. 2	....
	2 p. m.	......	38	....	St. 10	....	SE. 2	....
	9 p. m.	......	38	....	St. 10	....	W. 1	....
March 19	7 a. m.	......	42	....	Nim. 5	....	S. 4	....
	2 p. m.	......	41	....	Cu. 5	....	S. 3	....
	9 p. m.	......	34	....	Cu. 5	....	NW. 3	....

REMARKS.

14th. Lunar halo from 8 to 10 p. m.

15th. Rain from 4 a. m. to 9 p. m.; amount, 2.20 inches.

17th. Solar halo from 11 a. m. to 3 p. m.

Rain from 9 a. m. the 18th to 4 a. m. on the 19th; amount, 1.60 inch.

CORNISH, MAINE.†

Month and day.	Hour.	Barom'r corrected to 32° F.	Thermometer.	Force of vapor.	Cloudiness.	Motion of clouds.	Winds.	Relative humidity.
March 14	7 a. m.	......	30	....	Nim. 10	....	S. 4	....
	2 p. m.	......	46	....	Nim. 10	....	SE. 4	....
	9 p. m.	......	34	....	Nim. 10	....	W. 1	....
March 15	7 a. m.	......	34	....	Cir. cu. 3	....	W. 3	....
	2 p. m.	......	41	....	Cir. 4	....	W. 3	....
	9 p. m.	......	35	....	0	....	SW. 1	....
March 16	7 a. m.	......	34	....	Cir. 1	....	W..........	....
	2 p. m.	......	36	....	Cir. st. 4	....	SW. 2	....
	9 p. m.	......	34	....	9	....	SW..........	....
March 17	7 a. m.	......	31	....	Nim. 10	....	S. 3	....
	2 p. m.	......	43	....	Nim 10	....	E. 2	....
	9 p. m.	......	39	....	Nim. 10	....	E. 1	....
March 18	7 a. m.	......	39	....	Cir. st. 5	....	S. 5	....
	2 p. m.	......	36	....	Nim. 9	....	SW. 4	....
	9 p. m.	......	36	....	Cir. st. 9	....	SW. 5	....
March 19	7 a. m.	......	43	....	Cir. st. 8	....	W. 4	....
	2 p. m.	......	40	....	Nim. 9	....	W. 3	....
	9 p. m.	......	32	....	Cir. st. 5	....	NW. 4	....

REMARKS.

14th. Solar halo at night; winds easterly; hazy; lunar halo in the evening.

15th. Foggy all day; wind variable; rain and hail during the day, and a portion of the previous night.

16th. Fair, wind and clouds NW; luminous arch, with dark clouds beneath, during the evening streamers, at 9 p. m.

17th. Hazy; solar halo most of the day; wind and clouds SW.; thick at night.

18th. Commenced raining at 8 a. m., wind nearly S.; veered to the east at 8½ a. m.; foggy; rain continued all day.

19th. Rain till 5 a. m.; began to clear, wind SW., from 5 to 6; squall at 4 p. m.

20th. Squally most of the day. Amount of rain on the 15th, 2 + ? inches; on the 18th and 19th, 1.81 inch.

DEXTER, MAINE.

Month and day.	Hour.	Barom'r corrected to 32° F.	Thermometer.	Force of vapor.	Cloudiness.	Motion of clouds.	Winds.	Relative humidity.
March 14	7 a. m.	......	......	....	0	....	E. 2	....
	2 p. m.	......	......	....	0	....	S. 1	....
	9 p. m.	......	......	....	Nim. 10	....	S. 2	....
March 15	7 a. m.	......	......	....	Nim. 10	....	S. 4	....
	2 p. m.	......	......	....	Nim. 10	....	S. 4	....
	9 p. m.	......	......	....	Nim. 10	....	S. 2	....
March 16	7 a. m.	......	......	....	Cir. st. 8	....	NW. 2	....
	2 p. m.	......	......	....	Cir st. 9	....	NW. 4	....
	9 p. m.	......	......	....	0	....	NW. 2	....
March 17	7 a. m.	......	......	....	0	....	NW. 2	....
	2 p. m.	......	......	....	Cir. st. 8	....	NW. 3	....
	9 p. m.	......	......	....	Cir. cu. 8	....	NW. 1	....
March 18	7 a. m.	......	......	....	Nim. 10	....	S. 1	....
	2 p. m.	......	......	....	Nim. 10	....	S. 1	....
	9 p. m.	......	......	....	Nim. 10	....	SE 3	....
March 19	7 a. m.	......	......	....	Nim. 10	....	SE. 3	....
	2 p. m.	......	......	....	Cir. st. 6	....	SW. 4	....
	9 p. m.	......	......	....	Cir. st. 7	....	NW. 3	....

REMARKS.

Rain from 7.45 a. m. the 15th to 1 a. m. on the 16th; amount, 2.00 inches.

Rain from 7.35 a. m. the 18th to 8.30 a. m. on the 19th; amount, 0.75 inch.

* G. W. Guptill, observer.

† Silas West, observer.

STORM No. 1, MARCH, 1859.

GARDINER, MAINE.

Month and day.	Hour.	Barom'r corrected to 32° F.	Thermometer.	Force of vapor.	Cloudiness.	Motion of clouds.	Winds.	Relative humidity.	REMARKS.
March 14	7 a. m.	30. 29	30	----------	Clear 0	----------	Calm ------	----	15th. Rain from 7 a. m. till midnight; amount, 2.658 inches.
	2 p. m.	30. 26	46	----------	Cir. st. 3	----------	S. 1	----	16th. Aurora.
	9 p. m.	30. 26	35	----------	Overcast 10	----------	S. 1	----	18th. Rain from noon till midnight; amount, 2.244 inches.
March 15	7 a. m.	29. 92	37	----------	Rain 10	----------	SE. 4	----	
	2 p. m.	29. 64	42	----------	Rain 10	----------	SE. 3	----	
	9 p. m.	29. 39	40	----------	Rain 10	----------	SE. 2	----	
March 16	7 a. m.	29. 53	38	----------	Cir. cu. 5	NW. 3	NW. 2	----	
	2 p. m.	29. 78	40	----------	Cir. cu. 8	NW. 3	WNW. 3	----	
	9 p. m.	29. 98	33	----------	Clear 0	----------	W. 2	----	
March 17	7 a. m.	30. 15	31	----------	Clear 0	----------	WSW. 1	----	
	2 p. m.	30. 11	48	----------	Cir. cu. 5	----------	SW. 2	----	
	9 p. m.	30. 10	36	----------	Cir. cu. 10	W. 1	S. 1	----	
March 18	7 a. m.	29. 97	38	----------	Overcast 10	----------	S. 1	----	
	2 p. m.	29. 79	41	----------	Rain 10	----------	SE. 3	----	
	9 p. m.	29. 45	40½	----------	Rain 10	----------	SSW. 1	----	
March 19	7 a. m.	29. 05	42	----------	Cir. 5	SSW. 4	SSW. 4	----	
	2 p. m.	29. 01	45	----------	Cir. cu. 10	SW. 3	SSW. 3	----	
	9 p. m.	29. 07	37	----------	Clear 0	----------	SSW. 2	----	

PERRY, MAINE.

Month and day.	Hour.	Barom'r corrected to 32° F.	Thermometer.	Force of vapor.	Cloudiness.	Motion of clouds.	Winds.	Relative humidity.	REMARKS.
March 14	7 a. m.	30. 21	36	----------	0	----------	NW. 1	----	15th. Commenced raining at 10 a. m., and ended in the night; amount, 2. 46 inches.
	2 p. m.	30. 30	44	----------	0	----------	NE. 1	----	16th. Aurora. Rain from 7 p. m. the 18th to 9 a. m. on the 19th; amount, 2. 66 inches.
	9 p. m.	30. 34	33	----------	St. 2	----------	SE. 3	----	
March 15	7 a. m.	30. 18	33	----------	St. 10	----------	SE. 1	----	
	2 p. m.	29. 91	39	----------	Thick 10	----------	SE. 5	----	
	9 p. m.	29. 54	43	----------	Thick----	----------	S. 8	----	
March 16	7 a. m.	29. 31	38	----------	Cir. cu. 10	W. 5	NW. 5	----	
	2 p. m.	29. 50	44	----------	Cir. cu. 8	NW. 5	NW. 7	----	
	9 p. m.	29. 79	36	----------	0	----------	NW. 6	----	
March 17	7 a. m.	29. 32	32	----------	0	----------	NW. 3	----	
	2 p. m.	29. 98	47	----------	0	----------	SW. 4	----	
	9 p. m.	30. 05	38	----------	1	----------	W. 1	----	
March 18	7 a. m.	30. 05	34. 5	----------	St 8	SW. 1	SW. 1	---	
	2 p. m.	29. 99	41	----------	10	SE. 1	SE. 2	----	
	9 p. m.	29. 66	37	----------	Thick 10	----------	SE. 3	----	
March 19	7 a. m.	29. 18	47	----------	St. 10	SW. 5	SW. 7	----	
	2 p. m.	29. 14	45	----------	Cir. cu. 4	SW. 5	SW. 7	----	
	9 p. m.	29. 07	39	----------	Cir. cu. 10	SW-------	SW. 6	----	

PORTLAND, MAINE.

Month and day.	Hour.	Barom'r corrected to 32° F.	Thermometer.	Force of vapor.	Cloudiness.	Motion of clouds.	Winds.	Relative humidity.	REMARKS.
March 14	7 a. m.	30. 27	31	. 136	0	----------	N. 1	78	Commenced raining in the night of the 14th, and ended in the night of the 15th; amount, 2. 01 inches.
	2 p. m.	30. 25	42	. 155	4	NW. 1	NE. 2	58	Rain from 11 a. m. the 18th to 6 a. m. on the 19th; amount, 1. 687 inch.
	9 p. m.	30. 24	36	. 191	Fog 10	----------	SE. 1	90	
March 15	7 a. m.	29. 83	37	. 199	Rain 10	----------	SE. 3	90	
	2 p. m.	29. 60	41	. 235	Rain 10	----------	SE. 2	91	
	9 p. m.	29. 28	41	. 257	Rain 10	----------	SE. 1	100	
March 16	7 a. m.	29. 58	37	. 168	Cu. 6	NW. 2	W. 3	76	
	2 p. m.	------	------	------------	Cu. 4	NW. 1	W. 3	----	
	9 p. m.	29. 97	34	. 155	0	----------	W. 1	79	
March 17	7 a. m.	30. 13	31	. 146	0	----------	W. 1	84	
	2 p. m.	30. 13	44	. 130	Haze 8	----------	N. 2	45	
	9 p. m.	30. 08	48	. 165	Cu. 10	----------	S. 1	72	
March 18	7 a. m.	29. 95	37. 5	. 193	Cu. 10	SSW. 2	SSW. 1	86	
	2 p. m.	29. 71	39	. 228	Rain 10	----------	SE. 3	95	
	9 p. m.	29. 49	41	. 257	Rain 10	----------	ESE. 2	100	
March 19	7 a. m.	29. 03	42. 5	. 249	Cu. 2	S. 4	S. 3	91	
	2 p. m.	29. 01	44	. 265	Cu. 9	W. 3	SW. 2	92	
	9 p. m.	29. 10	36. 5	. 132	Cu. 10	----------	W. 2	61	

STORM No. 1, MARCH, 1859.

STEUBEN, MAINE.

Month and day.	Hour.	Barom'r corrected to 32° F.	Thermometer.	Force of vapor.	Cloudiness.	Motion of clouds.	Winds.	Relative humidity.	REMARKS.
March 14	7 a. m.	30.21	35	.142	0	0	NW. 1	70	14th. Lunar halo.
	2 p. m.	30.23	44	.218	St. 0	0	SW. 2	76	15th. Begun to rain at 9½ a. m., and ended in the night; amount, 1.70 inch.
	9 p. m.	30.30	30	.148	Nim. 6	0	SW. 1	89	Rain from 2½ p. m. on the 18th to 7 a. m. on the 19th; amount, 2.10 inches.
March 15	7 a. m.	30.07	35	.183	Nim. 10	SW. 1	SE. 3	90	A severe gale of wind during the 19th.
	2 p. m.	29.74	39	.216	Rain 10	Thick----	SE. 5	91	
	9 p. m.	29.49	44	.289	Thick & r. 10	----------	SE. 6	100	
March 16	7 a. m.	29.42	36	.191	Nim. 9	W. 2	W. 3	90	
	2 p. m.	29.61	40	.160	Nim. 9	W. 2	W. 3	64	
	9 p. m.	29.85	32	.143	0	0	NW. 2	79	
March 17	7 a. m.	30.03	33	.131	Hazy & st. 2	0	NW. 1	70	
	2 p. m.	30.07	45	.204	2	0	SW. 2	68	
	9 p. m.	30.06	36	.129	Nim. 9	W. 3	0	61	
March 18	7 a. m.	30.02	36	.191	Nim. 10	0	SE ----------	90	
	2 p. m.	29.86	42	.177	Cir. st. 10	SW. 3	SW. 3	66	
	9 p. m.	29.56	39	.238	Thick & r. 10	----------	S. 4	100	
March 19	7 a. m.	29.17	44	.265	Fog & rain 10	----------	SW. 3	92	
	2 p. m.	29.16	43	.209	Cir. 1	SW. 6	SW. 6	75	
	9 p. m.	29.08	38	.186	Nim. 10	SW. 4	SW. 3	81	

SHELBURNE, NEW HAMPSHIRE.

Month and day.	Hour.	Barom'r corrected to 32° F.	Thermometer.	Force of vapor.	Cloudiness.	Motion of clouds.	Winds.	Relative humidity.	REMARKS.
March 14	7 a. m.	30.00	33	----------	0	0	W. 2	----	15th. 7½ a. m., ½ inch damp snow; 7½ to 8½ a. m., hail and sleet; large flakes of snow till 9 a. m.; from 9 a. m. to 2 p. m., rain; heavy rain at 9 p. m.; wind W. 2.
	2 p. m.	30.00	54	----------	----------	----------	W. 2	----	16th. High wind from 10 to 11 a. m.
	9 p. m.	------	38	----------	10	0	E. 3	----	
March 15	7 a. m.	29.78	33	----------	10	0	E. 3	----	
	2 p. m.	29.47	41	----------	10	0	E. 2	----	
	9 p. m.	29.24	39	----------	10	0	W. 2	----	
March 16	7 a. m.	29.37	35	----------	Cu. 8	W 4	W. 3	----	
	2 p. m.	29.44	40	----------	Cu. 10	W. 4	W. 5	----	
	9 p. m.	29.67	32	----------	0	0	W. 5	----	
March 17	7 a. m.	29.91	37	----------	St. 1	0	W. 2	----	
	2 p. m.	29.90	61	----------	Light 10	0	W. 1	----	
	9 p. m.	29.88	35	----------	Nim. 10	NW. 2	0	----	
March 18	7 a. m.	29.80	35	----------	Nim. 10	S. 2	0	----	
	2 p. m.	29.61	39	----------	10	0	0	----	
	9 p. m.	------	------	----------	----------	----------	----------	----	
March 19	7 a. m.	29.91	45	----------	Nim. 9	S. 3	W. 3	----	
	2 p. m.	------	------	----------	----------	----------	----------	----	
	9 p. m.	------	------	----------	----------	----------	----------	----	

STRATFORD, NEW HAMPSHIRE.

Month and day.	Hour.	Barom'r corrected to 32° F.	Thermometer.	Force of vapor.	Cloudiness.	Motion of clouds.	Winds.	Relative humidity.	REMARKS.
March 14	7 a. m.	------	22	----------	0	----------	0	----	15th. Rain from 5 to 10 p. m.; amount, 1.62 inch.
	2 p. m.	------	44	----------	0	----------	SW. 2	----	18th. Rain from 7 a. m to 9 p. m.; amount, 0.82 inch.
	9 p. m.	------	38	----------	Nim. 10	----------	E. 3	----	
March 15	7 a. m.	------	35	----------	Nim. 10	----------	E. 4	----	
	2 p. m.	------	40	----------	Nim. 10	----------	NE. 4	----	
	9 p. m.	------	34	----------	Nim. 10	----------	W. 3	----	
March 16	7 a. m.	------	32	----------	Nim. 10	W. 3	W. 3	----	
	2 p. m.	------	32	----------	Nim. 9	NW. 4	NW. 4	----	
	9 p. m.	------	24	----------	0	----------	S. 1	----	
March 17	7 a. m.	------	24	----------	0	----------	0	----	
	2 p. m.	------	35	----------	Cir. st. 5	----------	S. 2	----	
	9 p. m.	------	34	----------	Cir. st. 9	SW. 2	NE. 1	----	
March 18	7 a. m.	------	36	----------	Nim. 10	----------	N. 2	----	
	2 p. m.	------	42	----------	Nim. 10	----------	E. 4	----	
	9 p. m.	------	41	----------	Nim. 10	----------	NE. 3	----	
March 19	7 a. m.	------	46	----------	Nim. 9	S. 4	S. 4	----	
	2 p. m.	------	40	----------	Nim. 10	----------	SW. 3	----	
	9 p. m.	------	30	----------	Nim. 10	----------	SW. 4	----	

STORM No. 1, MARCH, 1859.

BRANDON, VERMONT.

Month and day.	Hour.	Barom'r corrected to 32° F.	Thermometer.	Force of vapor.	Cloudiness.		Motion of clouds.		Winds.		Relative humidity.	REMARKS.
March 14	7 a. m.	------	28	----------		0	----------		S. ----------		------	Rain from 10 p. m. on the 14th to 8 p. m. on the 15th; amount, 0.735 inch.
	2 p. m.	------	50	----------	Cu.	10	----------		S.	1	------	
	9 p. m.	------	42	----------	Cu.	10	SW.	1	SSE.	4	------	
March 15	7 a. m.	------	40	----------	Cu.	10	SW.	2	SSE.	4	------	Rain from 7 a. m. on the 18th to 3 p. m. on the 19th; amount, 0.56 inch.
	2 p. m.	------	47	----------	Cu.	10	SW.	2	S.	2	------	
	9 p. m.	------	38	----------	Cu.	10	SW.	2	N.	1	------	
March 16	7 a. m.	------	34	----------	Cu.	7	NW.	2	NW.	3	------	
	2 p. m.	------	40	----------		1	----------		NW.	1	------	
	9 p. m.	------	33.5	----------		0	----------		NW ----------		------	
March 17	7 a. m.	------	30	----------		0	----------		SE ----------		------	
	2 p. m.	------	56.5	----------		10	NW.	1	S.	1	------	
	9 p. m.	------	42	----------	Cir. cu.	10	NW.	1	S.	1	------	
March 18	7 a. m.	------	44	----------	Nim.	10	----------		S.	1	------	
	2 p. m.	------	47	----------	Cu.	10	SSW.	3	SSE.	4	------	
	9 p. m.	------	50	----------	Cu.	9	SSW.	3	SSE.	3	------	
March 19	7 a. m.	------	45	----------	Cu.	9	SW.	1	SW.	3	------	
	2 p. m.	------	38.5	----------	Cu.	10	SW.	2	S.	3	------	
	9 p. m.	------	30.5	----------	Cu.	10	SW.	1	W.	3	------	

BURLINGTON, VERMONT.

Month and day.	Hour.	Barom'r corrected to 32° F.	Thermometer.	Force of vapor.	Cloudiness.	Motion of clouds.	Winds.		Relative humidity.	REMARKS.
March 14	7 a. m.	29.92	30	.174	0	----------	NE.	1	100	
	2 p. m.	29.80	46	.202	6	----------	N.	1	62	
	9 p. m.	29.65	40	.177	8	----------	N.	2	66	
March 15	7 a. m.	29.37	38	.225	10	----------	SW.	1	91	
	2 p. m.	29.16	47	.160	9	----------	SW.	1	78	
	9 p. m.	29.20	40	.147	9	----------	NW.	1	57	
March 16	7 a. m.	29.41	33	.142	9	----------	W.	2	70	
	2 p. m.	29.55	36	.116	8	----------	W.	2	53	
	9 p. m.	29.77	34	.129	0	----------	W.	1	61	
March 17	7 a. m.	29.88	31.5	.126	0	----------	SW.	1	65	
	2 p. m.	29.76	45.5	.225	8	----------	SW.	1	70	
	9 p. m.	29.66	43	.138	8	----------	SW.	1	46	
March 18	7 a. m.	29.27	45	.225	10	----------	S.	1	70	
	2 p. m.	29.16	49.5	.321	10	----------	SE.	2	86	
	9 p. m.	28.89	46	.291	10	----------	SE.	1	89	
March 19	7 a. m.	28.46	46.5	.272	10	----------	SW.	4	78	
	2 p. m.	28.55	39	.049	10	----------	SW.	4	20	
	9 p. m.	28.87	28	.105	10	----------	NW.	4	66	

CRAFTSBURY, VERMONT.

Month and day.	Hour.	Barom'r corrected to 32° F.	Thermometer.	Force of vapor.	Cloudiness.		Motion of clouds.		Winds.		Relative humidity.	REMARKS.
March 14	7 a. m.	------	26	----------		0	----------		SE.	1	------	Rain on the 14th; amount, 0.54 inch.
	2 p. m.	------	44	----------	Cir. st.	3	W.	2	S.	2	------	Snow on the 15th; amount in water, 0.10 inch.
	9 p. m.	------	38	----------	Nim.	10	----------		S.	2	------	19th. Rain; commencing at 9½ a. m.; amount, 0.58 inch.
March 15	7 a. m.	------	35	----------	Nim.	10	SW.	3	SE.	2	------	
	2 p. m.	------	40	----------	Nim.	10	S.	2	S.	2	------	
	9 p. m.	------	36	----------	Nim.	10	----------		S.	1	------	
March 16	7 a. m.	------	29	----------	Nim.	10	----------		NW.	3	------	
	2 p. m.	------	31	----------	Nim.	10	NW.	4	NW.	4	------	
	9 p. m.	------	30	----------		0	----------		SW.	1	------	
March 17	7 a. m.	------	29	----------	Cir. st.	1	----------			0	------	
	2 p. m.	------	48	----------	Cir. st.	5	SW.	2	S.	2	------	
	9 p. m.	------	37	----------	Nim.	10	----------		S.	2	------	
March 18	7 a. m.	------	37	----------	Nim.	10	----------		S.	1	------	
	2 p. m.	------	44	----------	Nim.	10	----------		S.	4	------	
	9 p. m.	------	42	----------	Nim.	10	----------		S.	2	------	
March 19	7 a. m.	------	46	----------	Nim.	8	SW.	4	S.	4	------	
	2 p. m.	------	39	----------	Nim.	9	SW.	4	S.	4	------	
	9 p. m.	------	26	----------	Nim.	10	----------		NW.	4	------	

STORM No. 1, MARCH, 1859.

RUPERT, VERMONT.

Month and day.	Hour.	Barom'r corrected to 32° F.	Thermometer.	Force of vapor.	Cloudiness.	Motion of clouds.	Winds.	Relative humidity.	REMARKS.
March 14	7 a. m.	......	28	....	Cir. 3	W. 1	....	......	
	2 p. m.	......	50	....	Cu. st. 8	SW. 2	....	......	
	9 p. m.	......	50	....	0	0	....	......	
March 15	7 a. m.	......	48	....	0	0	....	......	
	2 p. m.	......	56	....	Cu st. 3	SW. 2	....	......	
	9 p. m.	......	44	....	Nim. 10	S. 2	....	......	
March 16	7 a. m.	......	34	....	Nim. 10	S. 2	....	......	
	2 p. m.	......	58	....	Nim 10	S. 2	....	......	
	9 p. m.	......	42	....	Cu. st. 1	W. 2	....	......	
March 17	7 a. m.	......	30	....	Cir. 6	W. 2	....	......	
	2 p. m.	......	50	....	Cu. 7	W. 1	....	......	
	9 p. m.	......	50	....	0	0	....	......	
March 18	7 a. m.	......	48	....	0	0	....	......	
	2 p. m.	......	58	....	Cu. st. 9	W. 1	....	......	
	9 p. m.	......	56	....	Cu. st. 7	W. 2	....	......	
March 19	7 a. m.	......	50	....	Nim. 10	S. 3	....	......	
	2 p. m.	......	48	....	Nim. 10	S. 2	....	......	
	9 p. m.	......	36	....	Nim. 10	S. 2	....	......	

ST. JOHNSBURY, VERMONT.

Month and day.	Hour.	Barom'r corrected to 32° F.	Thermometer.	Force of vapor.	Cloudiness.	Motion of clouds.	Winds.	Relative humidity.	REMARKS.
March 14	7 a. m.	29.74	20	....	0	0	N. 1	......	15th. Rain from 1 a. m. to 10 p. m.; amount, 1.25 inch.
	2 p. m.	29.60	46	....	Hazy	....	S. 1	......	16th. Snow squall in a. m.
	9 p. m.	29.53	38	....	Nim. 10	0	S. 2	......	18th. Rain from 9 a. m. to 5 p. m.; amount, 0.65 inch.
March 15	7 a. m.	29.19	36	....	Nim. 10	0	N. 1	......	19th. Snow and rain squalls.
	2 p. m.	28.94	40	....	Nim. 10	0	S. 1	......	20th. Snow squalls.
	9 p. m.	28.91	36	....	Nim. 10	0	NW. 1	......	
March 16	7 a. m.	29.10	34	....	Nim. 10	0	N. 2	......	
	2 p. m.	29.25	37	....	Nim. 8	E. 3	W. 4	......	
	9 p. m.	29.60	31	....	0	0	W. 2	......	
March 17	7 a. m.	29.60	26	....	0	0	S. 1	......	
	2 p. m.	29.50	44	....	Thick	Haze	SE. 2	......	
	9 p. m.	29.44	33	....	Nim. 10	0	S. 2	......	
March 18	7 a. m.	29.30	35	....	Nim. 10	0	0	......	
	2 p. m.	28.89	45	....	Nim. 10	0	SE. 4	......	
	9 p. m.	28.73	36	....	Nim. 10	Foggy	N. 1	......	
March 19	7 a. m.	28.26	45	....	Nim. 8	N. 5	S. 5	......	
	2 p. m.	28.34	38	....	Nim. 10	0	SE. 5	......	
	9 p. m.	28.54	32	....	Nim. 10	0	N. 4	......	

NORWICH, CONNECTICUT.

Month and day.	Hour.	Barom'r corrected to 32° F.	Thermometer.	Force of vapor.	Cloudiness.	Motion of clouds.	Winds.	Relative humidity.	REMARKS.
March 14	7 a. m.	29.950	64	....	....	....	....	......	
	2 p. m.	......	......	....	....	....	....	......	
	9 p. m.	29.796	63	....	....	....	....	......	
March 15	7 a. m.	29.431	67	....	....	....	....	......	
	2 p. m.	......	......	....	....	....	....	......	
	9 p. m.	29.203	64	....	....	....	....	......	
March 16	7 a. m.	29.432	62	....	....	....	....	......	
	2 p. m.	......	......	....	....	....	....	......	
	9 p. m.	29.743	65	....	....	....	....	......	
March 17	7 a. m.	29.863	61	....	....	....	....	......	
	2 p. m.	......	......	....	....	....	....	......	
	9 p. m	29.733	64	....	....	....	....	......	
March 18	7 a. m.	29.580	69	....	....	....	....	......	
	2 p. m.	......	......	....	....	....	....	......	
	9 p. m.	29.038	65	....	....	....	....	......	
March 19	7 a. m.	......	......	....	....	....	....	......	
	2 p. m.	......	......	....	....	....	....	......	
	9 p. m.	......	......	....	....	....	....	......	

STORM No. 1, MARCH, 1859.

AMHERST, MASSACHUSETTS.

Month and day.	Hour.	Barom'r corrected to 32° F.	Thermometer.	Force of vapor.	Cloudiness.	Motion of clouds.	Winds.	Relative humidity.	REMARKS.
March 14	7 a. m.	30. 087	29	. 149	0	....	NW. 1	94	Rain from 10½ p m. the 14th to 7 p. m. on the 15th; amount, 1. 665 inch.
	2 p. m.	30. 03	48	. 199	St. 7	....	W. 2	60	
	9 p m.	29. 938	39	. 174	St. 10	....	SW. 3	70	
March 15	7 a. m.	29. 485	46	. 318	Nim. 10	....	SE. 3	100	Rain from 7½ a. m. the 18th to the night of the 19th; amount, 0. 962 inch.
	2 p. m.	29. 284	49	. 347	Nim. 10	SE. 6	SE. 4	100	
	9 p. m.	29. 310	40. 4	. 192	St. 7	SW. 3	NW. 4	74	
March 16	7 a. m.	29. 616	36	. 122	St. 8	NW. 3	NW. 4	57	
	2 p m.	29. 725	38. 8	. 144	St. 3	NW. 5	NW. 4	61	
	9 p. m.	29. 918	33	. 144	0	....	NW. 1	74	
March 17	7 a. m.	30. 008	32	. 133	St. 1	....	NW. 2	77	
	2 p. m.	29. 925	54. 7	. 209	St. 5	SW. 3	SE. 2	49	
	9 p. m.	29. 883	43	. 189	St. 9	....	SE. 2	68	
March 18	7 a. m.	29. 711	40. 7	. 203	St. 10	SE. 5	SE. 1	80	
	2 p. m	29. 330	49	. 359	Nim. 10	SE.	SE. 3	100	
	9 p. m.	29. 102	53. 5	. 406	Nim. 10	....	SE. 5	100	
March 19	7 a. m.	28. 817	44	. 245	Nim. 7	SW. 6	SW. 5	82	
	2 p. m.	28. 884	45. 8	. 191	St. 8	W. 4	W. 5	61	
	9 p. m.	29. 084	36	. 131	St. 9	....	W. 5	60	

BRIDGEWATER, MASSACHUSETTS.

Month and day.	Hour.	Barom'r corrected to 32° F.	Thermometer.	Force of vapor.	Cloudiness.	Motion of clouds.	Winds.	Relative humidity.	REMARKS.
March 14	7 a. m.	30. 15	38	. 161	0	0	NE. 1	64. 5	Commenced raining in the night of the 15th and ended at 8½ p. m. on the 16th; amount, 2. 016 inches. Commenced again in the night of the 17th and ended during the night of the 18th; amount, 1. 144 inch.
	2 p. m.	30. 12	50	. 145	0	0	E. 3	36. 5	
	9 p. m.	......	......	....	....	....	....	......	
March 15	7 a. m.	29. 67	49	. 313	Nim. 10	S. 5	S. 5	81	
	2 p. m.	29. 42	53	. 363	Nim. 1	0	S. 5	80	
	9 p. m.	......	......	....	....	....	....	......	
March 16	7 a. m.	29. 65	38	. 101	Cu. 7	NW. 2	NW. 5	39	
	2 p. m.	29. 78	45	. 128	Cu. st. 6	W. 2	W. 4	42	
	9 p. m.	......	......	....	....	....	....	......	
March 17	7 a. m.	30. 02	64	. 520	Cir. st. 4	W. 1	W. 2	87. 5	
	2 p. m.	30. 00	57	. 129	Cir. st. 4	W. 1	W. 2	28	
	9 p. m.	......	......	....	....	....	....	......	
March 18	7 a. m.	29. 84	57	. 364	Nim. 10	S. 5	S. 4	78	
	2 p. m.	29. 88	50	. 348	Nim. 10	S. 5	S. 4	96. 5	
	9 p. m.	......	......	....	....	....	....	......	
March 19	7 a. m.	29. 05	47	. 315	Cu. st. 5	NW. 5	NW. 4	96	
	2 p. m.	29. 02	47	. 191	Cu. st. 10	NW. 5	SW. 4	59. 5	
	9 p. m.	......	......	....	....	....	....	......	

CAMBRIDGE, MASSACHUSETTS.

Month and day.	Hour.	Barom'r corrected to 32° F.	Thermometer.	Force of vapor.	Cloudiness.	Motion of clouds.	Winds.	Relative humidity.	REMARKS.
March 14	7 a. m.	30. 35	35	....	Clear 0	....	N. 1	......	15th. Severe rain storm; amount, 2. 204 inches.
	2 p. m.	30. 23	45	....	Cir. 7	....	E. 1	78. 2	
	9 p. m.	30. 21	30	....	Cir. 7	....	SE. 1	87. 5	18th. Violent southerly wind, with heavy rain; amount, 1.159 inch.
March 15	7 a. m.	29. 75	47	....	Rain 10	....	S. 3	101	
	2 p. m.	29. 50	54	....	Rain 10	....	S. 3	103. 5	
	9 p. m.	29. 34	45	....	Rain 10	....	SW. 3	103	
March 16	7 a. m.	29. 75	38	....	Cir. cu. 4	....	SW. 3	86	
	2 p. m.	29. 82	43	....	Cu. 1	....	SW. 3	77	
	9 p. m.	30. 05	38	....	Clear 0	....	SW. 1	80	
March 17	7 a. m.	30. 17	34	....	Clear 0	....	SW. 1	82. 8	
	2 p. m.	30. 13	57	....	Cir. 7	....	W. 1	62. 5	
	9 p. m.	30. 13	47	....	Cir. cu. 7	....	SW. 1	75	
March 18	7 a. m.	29. 94	45	....	Cu. st. 8	....	S. 1	87. 4	
	2 p. m.	29. 63	52	....	Rain 10	....	S. 3	99	
	9 p. m.	29. 34	56	....	Nim. 10	....	S. 4	102	
March 19	7 a. m.	29. 05	47	....	Cu. 1	....	W. SW. 3	99. 9	
	2 p. m.	29. 04	49	....	Cu. 7	....	W. 3	74	
	9 p. m	29. 27	38	....	Cu. 10	....	W. 3	79. 8	

STORM No. 1, MARCH, 1859.

FLORIDA, MASSACHUSETTS.

Month and day.	Hour.	Barom'r corrected to 32° F.	Thermometer.	Force of vapor.	Cloudiness.	Motion of clouds.	Winds.	Relative humidity.	REMARKS.
March 14	7 a. m.	......	......	....	Cir. 2	SE. 1	SE. 2	......	15th. A thunder shower passed over from NW. to SE., at 5 p. m , one flash of lightning, two claps of thunder; duration, five minutes.
	2 p. m.	......	......	....	Cir. st. 10	SE. 3	SE. 3	......	
	9 p. m.	......	......	....	Nim. 10	SE. 3	SE. 4	......	
March 15	7 a. m.	......	......	....	Nim. 10	SE. 3	SE. 3	......	
	2 p. m.	......	......	....	Nim. 10	SE. 3	SE. 3	......	
	9 p. m.	......	......	....	Cu. 10	NW. 5	SW. 3	......	
March 16	7 a. m.	......	......	....	Cu. 10	NW. 6	NW. 9	......	
	2 p. m	......	......	....	Cu. 7	NW. 6	NW. 7	......	
	9 p. m.	......	......	....	Cu. 3	NW. 5	NW. 6	......	
March 17	7 a. m.	......	......	....	Cir. st. 2	W. 3	W. 2	......	
	2 p. m.	......	......	....	Cir. st. 7	E. 1	E. 1	......	
	9 p. m.	......	......	....	Nim. 10	E. 1	E. 2	......	
March 18	7 a. m.	......	......	....	Nim. 10	SE. 2	SW. 2	......	
	2 p. m.	......	......	....	Nim. 10	SE. 3	SE. 4	......	
	9 p. m.	......	......	....	Nim. 10	SE. 9	SE. 4	......	
March 19	7 a. m	......	......	....	Nim. 10	SW. 4	SW. 4	......	
	2 p. m.	......	......	....	Nim. 10	SW. 4	SW. 4	......	
	9 p. m.	......	......	....	Nim. 10	NW. 6	NW. 6	......	

LAWRENCE, MASSACHUSETTS

Month and day.	Hour.	Barom'r corrected to 32° F.	Thermometer.	Force of vapor.	Cloudiness.	Motion of clouds.	Winds.	Relative humidity.	REMARKS.
March 14	7 a. m.	30. 16	31	. 118	St. 1	....	NW. 0	68	15th. Rain; amount, 1. 65 inch. Rain from 6. 30 p. m. the 18th to 4. 30 a. m. on the 19th; amount, 0. 99 inch.
	2 p. m.	30. 14	45	. 160	0	....	E. 1	53	
	9 p. m.	30. 11	37	. 199	Fog 10	....	SE. 1	90	
March 15	7 a. m.	29. 72	41	. 257	Rain 10	....	SE. 3	100	
	2 p. m.	29. 19	51	. 374	Rain 10	....	SE. 1	100	
	9 p. m.	29. 31	45	. 300	Nim. 8	....	NW. 2	100	
March 16	7 a. m.	29. 64	38	. 144	St. 6	....	NW. 4	63	
	2 p. m.	29. 73	44	. 151	Cu. 7	....	NW. 4	52	
	9 p. m.	30. 01	34	. 138	0	....	NW. 2	71	
March 17	7 a. m.	30. 08	32	. 106	St. cu. 7	....	SW. 1	58	
	2 p. m.	30. 07	49½	. 124	....	....	NW. 1	35	
	9 p. m.	30. 03	42	. 177	Overcast 10	....	SW. 1	66	
March 18	7 a. m.	29. 87	41	. 212	Overcast 10	....	SE. 1	82	
	2 p. m.	29. 73	44	. 265	Rain 10	....	SE. 1	92	
	9 p. m.	29. 31	54	. 390	Rain 10	....	SW. 3	93	
March 19	7 a. m.	29. 95	48	. 260	Cu. st. 6	....	SW. 4	78	
	2 p. m.	29. 01	58	. 309	St. 3	....	SW. 4	64	
	9 p. m.	29. 14	40	. 181	Cu. st. 5	....	SW. 5	73	

MENDON, MASSACHUSETTS.

Month and day.	Hour.	Barom'r corrected to 32° F.	Thermometer.	Force of vapor.	Cloudiness.	Motion of clouds.	Winds.	Relative humidity.	REMARKS.
March 14	7 a. m.	......	34	....	Cir. 1	NW. 1	NW. 1	......	Rain on the 16th and 19th.
	2 p. m.	......	48	....	N. 1	NW. 1	NW. 1	......	
	9 p. m.	......	46	....	N. 1	NW. 1	NE. 1	......	
March 15	7 a. m.	......	50	....	N. 10	S. 1	S. 1	......	
	2 p. m.	......	55	....	N. 10	S. 2	S. 1	......	
	9 p. m.	......	45	....	N. 10	S. 1	S. 1	......	
March 16	7 a. m.	......	38	....	Cir. 10	NW. 3	NW. 3	......	
	2 p. m.	......	42	....	Cir. 10	NW. 2	NW. 2	......	
	9 p. m.	......	34	....	Cir. 1	NW. 1	NW. 1	......	
March 17	7 a. m	......	34	....	Cir. 1	W. 1	W. 1	......	
	2 p. m.	......	56	....	Cir. 1	NW. 1	NW. 1	......	
	9 p. m.	......	48	....	N. 10	S. 1	S. 1	......	
March 18	7 a. m.	......	42	....	N. 10	NE. 1	NE. 1	......	
	2 p. m.	......	61	....	N. 10	S. 3	S. 3	......	
	9 p. m.	......	58	....	N. 10	S. 3	S. 3	......	
March 19	7 a. m.	......	45	....	Cir. 10	SW. 3	SW. 2	......	
	2 p. m.	......	44	....	Cir. 10	NW. 4	NW. 4	......	
	9 p. m.	......	38	....	Cir. 10	NW. 2	NW. 1	......	

STORM No. 1, MARCH, 1859.

NANTUCKET, MASSACHUSETTS.

Month and day.	Hour.	Barom'r corrected to 32° F.	Thermometer.	Force of vapor.	Cloudiness.	Motion of clouds.	Winds.	Relative humidity.	REMARKS.
March 14	7 a. m.	30. 31	40	. 203	....	....	E. by N. 1	82	15th. Rain; amount, 0. 78 inch.
	2 p m.	30. 32	50	. 186	....	....	E. 2	51	18th. Rain; amount, 0.783 inch.
	9 p. m.	30. 25	40	. 203	....	....	ESE. 2	82	
March 15	7 a. m.	29. 96	46. 5	. 256	....	....	SSE. 5	81	
	2 p. m.	29. 77	50	. 309	....	....	SSE. 6	85	
	9 p. m.	29. 49	48	. 310	....	....	SSW. 4	92	
March 16	7 a. m.	29. 84	42	. 222	....	....	WSW. 4	83	
	2 p. m.	30. 02	47. 5	. 150	....	....	WNW. 5	45	
	9 p. m.	30. 16	40. 5	. 164	....	....	W. 3	64	
March 17	7 a. m.	30. 28	40. 5	. 154	....	....	W. 1	61	
	2 p. m.	30. 23	50	. 186	....	....	SW. 2	51	
	9 p. m.	30. 21	43	. 209	....	....	SSW. 2	75	
March 18	7 a. m.	30. 08	44	. 206	....	....	S. 2	71	
	2 p. m.	29. 81	48	. 272	....	....	SE. 5	81	
	9 p. m.	29. 60	50	. 335	....	....	S. 6	93	
March 19	7 a. m.	29. 33	45. 5	. 221	....	....	SSW. 5	72	
	2 p. m.	29. 33	47. 5	. 184	....	....	SW. 6	55	
	9 p. m.	29. 38	42	. 177	....	....	SW. 7	66	

NEW BEDFORD, MASSACHUSETTS.

Month and day.	Hour.	Barom'r corrected to 32° F.	Thermometer.	Force of vapor.	Cloudiness.	Motion of clouds.	Winds.	Relative humidity.	REMARKS.
March 14	7 a. m.	30. 26	39	. 173	0	....	N. 1	73	15th. Rain from early morning till evening; amount, 1. 80 inch.
	2 p m.	30. 24	46	. 192	Haze 5	....	SE. 1	62	18th. Commenced raining at 9 a. m., and ended in the night; Amount, 1. 01 inch.
	9 p. m.	30. 14	39	. 195	Haze 10	....	SE. 1	82	
March 15	7 a. m.	29. 76	46. 5	. 305	Rain 10	....	SE. 2	96	
	2 p m.	29. 58	50	. 361	Rain 10	....	Southerly 2	100	
	9 p. m.	29. 43	47	. 323	10	....	W. 4	100	
March 16	7 a. m.	29. 77	39. 5	. 124	6	....	WNW. 4	51	
	2 p. m.	29. 86	45	. 138	3	....	NW. 4	46	
	9 p. m.	30. 08	37	. 157	0	....	W. 1	71	
March 17	7 a. m.	30. 18	39	. 131	1	....	W. NW. 1	55	
	2 p. m.	30. 12	52	. 190	3	....	W. SW. ½	57	
	9 p. m.	30. 10	42. 5	. 222	Lt. clouds 10	....	SW. 1	83	
March 18	7 a. m.	29. 93	44	. 265	10	SSW. 1	S. by E. 1	92	
	2 p. m.	29. 59	58	. 483	Rain 10	....	SSE. 3	100	
	9 p. m.	29. 41	50	. 361	Fog 10	....	S. 4	100	
March 19	7 a. m.	29. 14	44	. 248	Haze 3	....	SW. 5	88	
	2 p. m.	29. 15	46	. 192	Cir. st. 9	WSW. 2	SW. 5	62	
	9 p. m.	29. 27	40	. 160	6	W. 1	W. by S. 4	64	

RICHMOND, MASSACHUSETTS.

Month and day.	Hour.	Barom'r corrected to 32° F.	Thermometer.	Force of vapor.	Cloudiness.	Motion of clouds.	Winds.	Relative humidity.	REMARKS.
March 14	7 a. m.	......	27	....	0	....	NE. 2	......	Heavy rain from 9 p. m. on the 14th to 5 p. m. on the 15th; amount, 3. 25 inches.
	2 p. m.	......	48	....	Nim. 10	SE. 3	SE. 4	......	18th. Rain from 5 a. m. to 3 p. m.; amount, 1. 75 inch.
	9 p. m.	......	40	....	Nim. 10	SW. 3	SW. 2	......	19th. Snow from 3 to 6 p. m.; amount in water, 0. 06 inch.
March 15	7 a. m.	......	18	....	Nim. 10	SW. 4	SW. 4	......	
	2 p. m.	......	50	....	Nim. 10	SE. 2	SW. 3	......	
	9 p. m.	......	37	....	Nim. 10	NW. 3	NW. 4	......	
March 16	7 a. m.	......	30	....	Cu. 10	NW. 3	NW. 4	......	
	2 p. m.	......	42	....	0	....	NW. 3	......	
	9 p. m.	......	30	....	0	....	NW. 2	......	
March 17	7 a. m.	......	32	....	St. 5	SW. 1	SW. 1	......	
	2 p. m.	......	46	....	Cu. 5	SE. 2	SW. 3	......	
	9 p. m.	......	40	....	Nim. 10	SE. 3	SE. 2	......	
March 18	7 a. m.	......	37	....	Nim. 10	SE. 4	SE. 4	......	
	2 p. m.	......	48	....	Nim. 10	SE. 3	SE. 4	......	
	9 p. m.	......	43	....	Nim. 10	SW. 4	SW. 8	......	
March 19	7 a. m.	......	38	....	Nim. 10	SW. 4	SW. 7	......	
	2 p. m.	......	35	....	Nim. 10	SW. 3	SW. 4	......	
	9 p. m.	......	32	....	Nim. 10	NW. 4	NW. 4	......	

STORM No. 1, MARCH, 1859.

WESTFIELD, MASSACHUSETTS.

Month and day.	Hour.	Barom'r corrected to 32° F.	Thermometer.	Force of vapor.	Cloudiness.		Motion of clouds.	Winds.		Relative humidity.	REMARKS.
March 14	7 a. m.	30. 09	29	. 113	Cir.	5	....	NW.		100	15th. Rain from 1 a. m. to 6 p. m.; amount, 1. 45 inch.
	2 p. m.	30. 12	47	. 160	Cir.	10	....	NE.		100	18th. Rain from 6 a. m. to 6 p. m.; amount, 1. 10 inch.
	9 p. m.	30. 07	41	. 164	Cir.	10	....	E.		62	
March 15	7 a. m.	29. 62	38	. 232	Nim.	10	....	SW.		51	
	2 p. m.	29. 41	49	. 349	Nim.	10	....	SW.		42	
	9 p. m.	29. 48	41	. 164	Cu.	5	....	NW.	3	51	
March 16	7 a. m.	29. 73	36	. 108	Cu.	5	....	W.	4	55	
	2 p. m.	29. 90	42	. 115	Cu.	5	....	NW.	3	41	
	9 p. m.	30. 03	38	. 118		0	....	W.	3	92	
March 17	7 a. m.	30. 12	31	. 104	Cir.	5	....	W.		100	
	2 p. m.	30. 05	52	. 157	Cir.	5	....	SE.		100	
	9 p. m.	30. 00	45	. 283	Cir.	5	....	SE.		100	
March 18	7 a. m.	29. 83	38	. 232	Nim.	10	....	SE		65	
	2 p. m.	29. 49	44	. 295	Nim.	10	....	W.		56	
	9 p. m.	29. 25	52	. 398	Nim.	10	....	S.		66	
March 19	7 a. m.	29. 02	45	. 198	Cu.	5	....	SW.	3	81	
	2 p. m.	29. 09	42	. 154	Cu.	5	....	SW.	3	42	
	9 p. m.	29. 27	47	. 148	Cu.	5	....	SW.	3	72	

WORCESTER, MASSACHUSETTS.

Month and day.	Hour.	Barom'r corrected to 32° F.	Thermometer.	Force of vapor.	Cloudiness.		Motion of clouds.	Winds.		Relative humidity.	REMARKS.
March 14	7 a. m.	29. 754	33	. 125	Cir. st.	1	....	NW.	1	69	15th. Heavy rain from 3 a. m. to 4 p. m., and from 5 to 8½ p. m.; amount, 1. 96 inch.
	2 p. m.	29. 699	52	. 170	Cir. st.	9	....	SE.	1	42	18th. Commenced raining at 7¾ a. m., long intermission in the forenoon, and ended early on the 19th; amount, 1.20 inch.
	9 p. m.	29. 668	41	. 175	St.	10	....	SE.	1	69	
March 15	7 a. m.	29. 22	46½	. 305	Nim.	10	....	SE.	1	96	
	2 p. m.	28. 98	54½	. 411	Nim.	10	....	SE.	1	97	
	9 p. m.	28. 936	45	. 258	St.	9	NW	NW.	1	88	
March 16	7 a. m.	29. 236	38	. 165	Cir. st.	7	NW	NW.	2	72	
	2 p. m.	29. 361	43	. 186	Cir. cu.	6	NW	NW.	3	67	
	9 p. m.	29. 567	37	. 157		0	0	NW.	1	71	
March 17	7 a. m.	29. 675	35	. 149	Cir.	2	....	NW.	1	74	
	2 p. m.	29. 59	58	. 255	Cir. st.	9	....	NW.	1	53	
	9 p. m.	29. 564	48	. 242	Cir. cu.	10	....	NW.	1	74	
March 18	7 a. m.	29. 421	43½	. 209	St.	10	....	SW.	1	75	
	2 p. m.	29. 065	50½	. 361	Nim.	10	....	SE.	1	100	
	9 p. m.	28. 828	56	. 443	Nim.	10	....	SE.	1	97	
March 19	7 a. m.	28. 555	46½	. 256	Cir. cu.	6	SW.......	SW.	3	81	
	2 p. m.	28. 554	46½	. 232	Cir. st.	8	SW.......	SW.	3	73	
	9 p. m.	28. 733	40	. 167	Cir. st.	9	SW.......	SW.	2	68	

WILLIAMSTOWN, MASSACHUSETTS.

Month and day.	Hour.	Barom'r corrected to 32° F.	Thermometer.	Force of vapor.	Cloudiness.		Motion of clouds.	Winds.		Relative humidity.	REMARKS.
March 14	7 a. m.	29. 46	45	....	St.	10	....	E.	2	......	Rain on the 14th, commencing at 9¼ p. m.; amount, 0. 30 inch.
	2 p. m.	29. 47	45	....	Nim.	10	....	E.	4	......	Rain on the 15th; amount, 1.25 inch.
	9 p. m.	29. 09	44	....	Nim.	10	....	E.	3	......	Began to rain at 11¼ p. m. on the 17th, and ended on the 18th; amount 0. 79 inch.
March 15	7 a. m.	28. 97	47	....	Nim.	10	....	E.	2	......	
	2 p. m.	28. 79	46	....	Nim.	10	....	E.	2	......	
	9 p. m	28. 93	35	....	Nim.	10	....	W.	2	......	
March 16	7 a. m.	29. 12	33	....	Nim.	10	....	W.	2	......	
	2 p. m.	29. 30	38	....	Cu.	4	....	W.	3	......	
	9 p. m.	29. 38	35	....		0	....	W.	1	......	
March 17	7 a. m.	29. 53	33	....		0	....	W.	1	......	
	2 p. m.	29. 47	45	....	St.	4	....	W.	1	......	
	9 p. m.	29. 27	41	....	Nim.	10	....	E.	1	......	
March 18	7 a. m.	29. 12	42	....	Nim.	10	....	E.	2	......	
	2 p. m.	28. 76	47	....	Nim.	10	....	E.	2	......	
	9 p. m.	28. 37	42	....	Nim.	10	....	SE.	2	......	
March 19	7 a. m.	28. 33	43	....	Cu.	10	....	S.	4	......	
	2 p. m.	28. 52	46	....	Cu.	10	....	SW.	2	......	
	9 p. m.	28. 68	32	....	Nim.	10	....	SW.	4	......	

STORM No. 1, MARCH, 1859.

PROVIDENCE, RHODE ISLAND.

Month and day.	Hour.	Barom'r corrected to 32° F.	Thermometer.	Force of vapor.	Cloudiness.	Motion of clouds.	Winds.	Relative humidity.	REMARKS.
March 14	Sunrise.	30.19	34	....	0	....	NE. 1	......	14th. Pleasant a. m.; rain to-
	1 p. m.	30.20	50	....	7	....	Sly. 2	......	wards night.
	10 p. m.	30.10	41	....	10	....	Sly. 1	......	15th. Steady rain all day; am't,
March 15	Sunrise.	29.72	48	....	Rain......	....	SW. 5	......	2.50 inches; barometer began
	1 p. m.	29.50	51	....	Rain......	....	Sly. 2	......	to rise at 8 p. m.; evening
	10 p. m.	29.46	45	....	10	....	Wly. 3	......	cloudy, with rain.
March 16	Sunrise.	29.68	40	....	9	....	NW. 3	......	16th. Fine; evening splendid.
	1 p. m.	29.83	45	....	2	....	NW. 3	......	17th. Pleasant; indications of
	10 p. m.	30.08	37	....	0	....	NW. 1	......	storm in the evening.
March 17	Sunrise.	30.13	34	....	0	....	NW. 1	......	18th. Began to rain at 8 a. m;
	1 p. m.	30.10	59	....	8	....	Sly. 1	......	wind brisk SE.; rain continued
	10 p. m.	30.06	45	....	10	....	Sly. 1	......	through the day and evening,
March 18	Sunrise.	29.86	44	....	10	....	Sly. 2	......	with wind heavy; amount,
	1 p. m.	29.56	52	....	Rain......	....	SE. 4	......	1.40 inch.
	10 p. m.	29.26	52	....	Rain......	....	SE. 4	......	19th. Extremely blustering all
March 19	Sunrise.	29.07	46	....	1	....	SW. 4	......	day.
	1 p. m.	29.09	48	....	5	....	SW. 5	......	
	10 p. m.	29.24	45	....	8	....	SW. 3	......	

COLUMBIA, CONNECTICUT.

Month and day.	Hour.	Barom'r corrected to 32° F.	Thermometer.	Force of vapor.	Cloudiness.	Motion of clouds.	Winds.	Relative humidity.	REMARKS.
March 14	7 a. m.	......	38	....	0	0	....	......	14th. Commenced raining at 11
	2 p. m.	......	50	....	Nim. 10	NW. 2	SE. 2	......	p. m., and continued till 3
	9 p. m.	......	40	....	Nim. 10	SW. 1	SE. 2	......	p. m. on the 15th; wind SE.
March 15	7 a. m.	......	48	....	Nim. 10	NW. 2	SE. 3	......	and S.
	2 p. m.	......	51	....	Nim. 10	NW. 1	SE. 3	......	18th. Rain from 7 to 9 p. m;
	9 p. m.	......	40	....	Nim. 10	SE. 2	NW. 3	......	wind strong SW.
March 16	7 a. m.	......	40	....	Nim. 10	SE. 3	NW. 3	......	
	2 p. m.	......	44	....	0	0	NW. 4	......	
	9 p. m.	......	34	....	0	0	....	......	
March 17	7 a. m.	......	43	....	Cu. 5	SE. 2	NW. 1	......	
	2 p. m.	......	56	....	St. 5	SE. 1	NW. 1	......	
	9 p. m.	......	43	....	Nim. 10	0	SW. 1	......	
March 18	7 a. m.	......	42	....	Nim. 10	NW. 3	SE. 3	......	
	2 p. m.	......	52	....	Nim. 10	NW. 2	SE. 3	......	
	9 p. m.	......	55	....	Nim. 10	NE. 3	SW. 5	......	
March 19	7 a. m.	......	43	....	Cu. 8	SE. 3	NW. 4	......	
	2 p. m.	......	42	....	Cu. 8	SE. 4	NW. 4	......	
	9 p. m.	......	38	....	Cu. 10	SE. 3	NW. 4	......	

MIDDLETOWN, CONNECTICUT.

Month and day.	Hour.	Barom'r corrected to 32° F.	Thermometer.	Force of vapor.	Cloudiness.	Motion of clouds.	Winds.	Relative humidity.	REMARKS.
March 14	7 a. m.	30.134	30.5	.146	0	....	N.	86	Rain from 11 p. m. the 14th to
	2 p. m.	29.092	53.4	.162	Cir. 5	....	SE. 2	40	7 p. m. on the 15th; amount,
	9 p. m.	20.063	10.6	.105	Cir. st. 10	....	SE. 2	65	2.31 inches.
March 15	7 a. m.	29.569	53	.361	Nim. 10	....	S.SW. 5	90	18th. Rain from 7 a. m. to 7
	2 p. m.	29.366	53.5	.372	Nim. 10	....	S.SW. 4	91	p. m.; amount, 1.20 inch.
	9 p. m.	29.406	43	.175	Cir. st. 10	W. 2	NW. 3	62	
March 16	7 a. m.	29.725	37.4	.115	Cir. st. 5	NW. 3	NW. 3	52	
	2 p. m.	29.808	48	.141	0	....	NW. 4	42	
	9 p. m.	30.016	38.4	.139	0	....	W. 1	60	
March 17	7 a. m.	30.084	32	.136	0	....	S.	75	
	2 p. m.	30.007	59	.170	Cir. 2	W. 2	SW. 3	34	
	9 p. m.	29.972	44.5	.234	Cir. st. 9	W.........	S. 2	80	
March 18	7 a. m.	29.758	44.2	.283	Cir. st. 10	SW. 3	SE. 1	98	
	2 p. m.	29.360	53.5	.368	Nim. 10	....	S.SE. 5	90	
	9 p. m.	29.171	55.6	.425	10	....	SW. 5	96	
March 19	7 a. m.	28.91	43.5	.220	Cir. 2	SW. 4	SW. 5	78	
	2 p. m.	29.042	43	.160	Cir. cu. 10	W. 4	SW. 5	57	
	9 p. m.	29.189	39.1	.125	Cir. 8	W. 3	NW. 4	52	

STORM No. 1, MARCH, 1859.

NEW HAVEN, CONNECTICUT.

Month and day.	Hour.	Barom'r corrected to 32° F.	Thermometer.	Force of vapor.	Cloudiness.	Motion of clouds.	Winds.	Relative humidity.	REMARKS.
March 14	7 a. m.	30.307	36	.115	------	------	------	54	
	2 p. m.	30.272	49	.175	------	------	------	50	
	9 p. m.	30.402	41	.212	------	------	------	82	
March 15	7 a. m.	29.722	39	.238	------	------	------	100	
	2 p. m	29.474	50	.361	------	------	------	100	
	9 p. m.	29.612	45	.204	------	------	------	68	
March 16	7 a. m.	29.939	39	.090	------	------	------	38	
	2 p. m.	30.033	46	.125	------	------	------	40	
	9 p. m.	30.209	40	.082	------	------	------	26	
March 17	7 a. m.	30.293	39	.090	------	------	------	38	
	2 p. m.	30.188	52	.208	------	------	------	53	
	9 p. m.	30.171	45	.204	------	------	------	68	
March 18	7 a. m.	------	------	------	------	------	------	------	
	2 p. m.	29.496	52	.388	------	------	------	100	
	9 p. m.	------	------	------	------	------	------	------	
March 19	7 a. m.	29.166	48	.014	------	------	------	4	
	2 p. m.	29.252	44	.231	------	------	------	55	
	9 p. m.	29.419	42	.113	------	------	------	42	

POMFRET, CONNECTICUT.

Month and day.	Hour.	Barom'r corrected to 32° F.	Thermometer.	Force of vapor.	Cloudiness.	Motion of clouds.	Winds.	Relative humidity.	REMARKS.
March 14	7 a. m.	29.680	34	.155	0	------	N. 2	79	15th. Began to rain at 3 a. m., and ended in the night; am't, 3.00 inches.
	2 p. m.	------	------	------	------	------	------	------	
	9 p. m.	------	------	------	------	------	------	------	
March 15	7 a. m.	29.171	48.5	.348	Nim. 10	S. 3	S. 3	100	18th. Began to rain at 7 a. m., and ended in the night; am't, 1.590 inch.
	2 p. m.	28.939	51.5	.388	Nim. 10	SE. 3	SE. 3	100	
	9 p. m.	28.901	42	.254	Cir. cu. 8	SW. 3	NW. 2	92	
March 16	7 a. m.	29.234	35	.142	Cu. 7	NW. 3	NW. 3	70	
	2 p. m.	29.329	39.5	.182	Cu. 4	NW. 4	NW. 4	73	
	9 p. m	29.532	35	.142	0	------	NW. 1	70	
March 17	7 a. m.	29.615	33.5	.138	Cir. 3	W. 1	W. 1	71	
	2 p. m.	29.551	55	.269	Cir. st. 4	W. 1	SW. 1	62	
	9 p. m.	29.523	42.3	.231	Cir. st. 10	S. 2	S. 2	83	
March 18	7 a. m.	29.333	41	.257	Cu. st. 10	SE. 2	SE. 2	100	
	2 p. m.	28.998	50	.361	Nim. 10	SE. 3	SE. 3	100	
	9 p. m.	28.849	53	.403	Nim. 10	S. 4	S. 4	100	
March 19	7 a. m.	28.520	42.5	.254	Cu. 10	SW. 4	SW. 4	92	
	2 p. m.	28.561	42.5	.209	Cu. 5	SW. 4	SW. 4	75	
	9 p. m.	28.688	38	.196	Cu. st. 10	SW. 4	SW. 4	74	

SAYBROOK, CONNECTICUT.

Month and day.	Hour.	Barom'r corrected to 32° F.	Thermometer.	Force of vapor.	Cloudiness.	Motion of clouds.	Winds.	Relative humidity.	REMARKS.
March 14	7 a. m.	------	37	------	St. 1	------	N. 1	------	15th. Rain from 1 a.? m. to 7 p. m.; amount, 2.77 inches.
	2 p. m.	------	46	------	Nim. 10	------	E. 3	------	
	9 p. m.	------	39	------	------	------	E. 4	------	18th. Rain from 4 a. m. to 11 p. m.; amount, 0.79 inch.
March 15	7 a. m.	------	46	------	Fog. 10	------	SSE. 7	------	
	2 p. m.	------	48	------	Fog. 10	------	SE. 4	------	
	9 p. m.	------	44	------	Cir. cu. 8	W. 4	NW. 4	------	
March 16	7 a. m.	------	39	------	Cir. cu. 7	W. 3	W. 5	------	
	2 p. m.	------	48	------	Cir. 2	NW. 5	NW. 6	------	
	9 p. m.	------	40	------	0	0	NW. 1	------	
March 17	7 a. m.	------	31	------	Cir. st. 1	W. 1	0	------	
	2 p. m.	------	51	------	Cir. st. 3	SW. 1	0	------	
	9 p. m.	------	42	------	Nim. 10	------	0	------	
March 18	7 a. m.	------	42	------	Nim. 10	W. 1	E. 3	------	
	2 p. m.	------	50	------	Fog. 10	S. 8	S. 8	------	
	9 p. m.	------	50	------	Fog. 10	------	S. 7	------	
March 19	7 a. m.	------	42	------	Cir. 3	SW. 7	SW. 7	------	
	2 p. m.	------	45	------	Cir. cu. 10	SW. 6	SW. 7	------	
	9 p. m.	------	40	------	Cu. 10	------	SW. 6	------	

STORM No. 1, MARCH, 1859.

WALLINGFORD, CONNECTICUT.

Month and day.	Hour.	Barom'r corrected to 32° F.	Thermometer.	Force of vapor.	Cloudiness.	Motion of clouds.	Winds.	Relative humidity.	REMARKS.
March 14	7 a. m.	30. 19	33	. 168	0	0	N. 0	89	14th. Began to rain at 9 p. m.; wind SE., 2; nim clouds, 10.
	2 p. m.	30. 11	51	. 161	Cu. 6	----------	SE. 2	42	
	9 p. m.	30. 04	41. 5	. 177	Nim. 10	----------	SE. 2	66	15th. At 2.30 a. m. bar. 29.75; wind SE., 6; clouds, 10; rain; 3 a m. bar. 29.82, uncorrected for temperature. 3 15 a. m. bar. 29.73; wind SE., 6. 3.30 a. m. bar. 29.71; wind, in gusts, SE., 6. 8 a. m. bar. 29.62; south wind, in gusts, 4; still raining; nim. clouds, scuds SW. 8.40 a. m., amount of rain, 1.17 inch. 10.30 a. m. bar. 29.52; wind SE., 4, scuds SW., 6; raining. 11 a m. bar. 29,51; wind SSW., 3; clouds, 10; nim. SW.; temperature 54°, wet bulb, 53½. 12 m. bar. 29.47; wind S., 3; clouds, 10; scuds SW., 7; raining. 1 p. m. bar. 29,45; wind S., 2; clouds, 10. 4 p. m. bar. 29.35; wind SSE., 3; clouds, 10. 5 p. m. bar. 29.31; wind S., 2. 5.12 p. m. bar. 29.35; profuse shower of rain, wind SW., 2. 6 p. m. bar. 29.34; wind NW., 1; clouds, 9; a brilliant bow in the east; amount of water during the storm, 2.42 inches.
March 15	7 a. m.	29. 58	53	. 389	Nim. scu. 10	SW. 10	SSE. 4	96	
	2 p. m.	29. 42	51	. 374	Nim. scu. 10	SW. 7	S. 2	100	
	9 p. m.	29. 49	42. 5	. 231	7	W. 4	NNW. 3	83	
March 16	7 a. m.	29. 81	38	. 123	Cu. st. 3	W. 3	WNW. 4	54	
	2 p. m.	29. 91	46. 5	. 139	Cu. 1	W. 3	NW. 4	44	
	9 p. m.	30. 09	37	. 149	0	0	SW. 0	71	
March 17	7 a. m.	30. 17	29	. 148	Cir. 1	W. 1	SSE. 0	89	
	2 p. m.	30. 17	59. 5	. 190	Cir. 2	W. 2	S. 2	38	
	9 p. m.	30. 03	44	. 218	Cir. 7	----------	S. 2	76	
March 18	7 a. m.	29. 83	45. 5	. 286	Nim. scu. 10	SW. 4	SW. 1	92	
	2 p. m.	29. 41	52. 5	. 388	Nim. scu. 10	SSW. 8	SSE. 5	100	
	9 p. m.	29. 24	54. 5	. 418	Scuds 10	SW. 9	S. 4	100	
March 19	7 a. m.	29. 04	43. 5	. 209	Cu st. 2	SW. 4	SW. 3	75	
	2 p. m.	29. 12	44	. 151	Nim. scu. 10	SW. 5	SW. 5	52	
	9 p. m.	29. 27	40	. 118	9	----------	W. 6	48	

18th. The sky last evening was covered with thick cir. clouds; wind S., 2. At 6 a. m this morning it began to rain, wind light south, clouds in scuds. 8 a. m. bar 29.78; wind and rain increasing. 11.15 a. m. bar. 29.57; wind, 5. 11.45 a. m. bar. 29.54. 12 m. bar. 29 53; violent wind and rain from SE and SSE. 1 p. m. bar. 29.46; storm moderating a little; heavy showers, with strong wind since 8 a m. 1.30 p. m. bar. 29.42; wind and rain from SSE. 2 p m. wind and rain strong from SSE. 4 p. m. bar. 29.38; wind, 3; scuds SW. 4.30 p. m. bar. 29 36; wind SSW., 3; scuds W. and SW. 5 p. m. bar. 29.33; wind S, 3; clouds, 10; scuds W. and SW. swift; amount of water to this hour, 1.28 inch. 7 p. m. bar. 29.29; wind S., 3; rain. 10 p. m. bar. 29.21; wind S., 4; clouds, 10; nim. scuds; no rain.

19th. 8 a m. bar. 29.07; wind strong SW.; cu. st. clouds SW., 5. 9 a. m. bar. 29.09; wind strong SW.

BALDWINSVILLE, NEW YORK.

Month and day.	Hour.	Barom'r corrected to 32° F.	Thermometer.	Force of vapor.	Cloudiness.	Motion of clouds.	Winds.	Relative humidity.	REMARKS.
March 14	7 a. m.	------	30	----------	Cir. st. 2	W. 0	E. 2	------	13th. Rain in the night.
	2 p. m.	------	51	----------	Cir. st. 8	W. 1	SE. 4	------	17th. Light rain at intervals during the day.
	9 p. m.	------	47	----------	Cir. st. 10	W. 1	S. 4	------	19th. Snow squalls during the day and night; depth of snow, 2 inches.
March 15	7 a. m.	------	46	----------	Cu. 2	W. 3	W. 2	------	
	2 p. m.	------	43	----------	Cu. 10	W. 3	W. 3	------	
	9 p. m.	------	37	----------	Cu. 10	W. 1	W. 3	------	
March 16	7 a. m.	------	32	----------	Cu. 10	NW. 3	NW. 3	------	
	2 p. m.	------	38	----------	Cu. 2	NW. 3	NW. 4	------	
	9 p. m.	------	32	----------	0	----------	NW. 1	------	
March 17	7 a. m.	------	30	----------	Cir. 2	W. 0	E. 0	------	
	2 p. m.	------	54	----------	Cir. st. 6	W. 0	E. 1	------	
	9 p. m.	------	50	----------	Cir. st. 8	W. 0	E. 1	------	
March 18	7 a. m.	------	47	----------	Nim. 10	S. 4	SE. 1	------	
	2 p. m.	------	53	----------	Nim. 10	S. 4	S. 2	------	
	9 p. m.	------	50	----------	Nim. 10	E. --------	E. 1	------	
March 19	7 a. m.	------	38	----------	Nim. 10	W. 5	SW. 5	------	
	2 p. m.	------	30	----------	Nim. 10	W. 5	W. 5	------	
	9 p. m.	------	28	----------	Nim. 10	NW. 4	NW. 5	------	

BELLPORT, NEW YORK.

Month and day.	Hour.	Barom'r corrected to 32° F.	Thermometer.	Force of vapor.	Cloudiness.	Motion of clouds.	Winds.	Relative humidity.	REMARKS.
March 14	7 a. m.	29. 54	40	----------	0	----------	E. 3	------	Rain from 11½ a. m. the 14th to 6 p. m. on the 15th; amount, 3.10 inches.
	2 p. m.	29. 51	48	----------	10	----------	SE. 5	------	19th. Rain from 6 a. m. to 4 p. m; amount, 0.54 inch.
	9 p. m.	29. 29	46	----------	10	----------	SE. 6	------	
March 15	7 a. m.	29. 12	49	----------	10	----------	SE. 5	------	
	2 p. m.	28. 93	50	----------	10	----------	SE. 5	------	
	9 p. m.	29. 04	47	----------	5	----------	WNW. 5	------	

STORM No. 1, MARCH, 1859.

BELLPORT, NEW YORK—Continued.

Month and day.	Hour.	Barom'r corrected to 32° F.	Thermometer.	Force of vapor.	Cloudiness.		Motion of clouds.		Winds.		Relative humidity.	REMARKS.
March 16	7 a. m.	29. 31	41	----------		8	----------		NW.	6	------	
	2 p. m.	29. 36	50	----------		5	----------		NW.	6	------	
	9 p. m.	29. 49	39	----------		0	----------		NW.	3	------	
March 17	7 a. m.	29. 55	37	----------		0	----------		NW.	0	------	
	2 p. m.	29. 49	50	----------		0	----------		SW.	2	------	
	9 p. m.	29. 41	45	----------		0	----------		S.	3	------	
March 18	7 a. m.	29. 22	45	----------		10	----------		NE.	5	------	
	2 p. m.	28. 90	51	----------		10	----------		SW.	9	------	
	9 p. m.	28. 78	51	----------		10	----------		S.	8	------	
March 19	7 a. m.	28. 68	45	----------		2	----------		WSW.	9	------	
	2 p. m.	28. 73	46	----------		9	----------		WSW.	8	------	
	9 p. m.	28. 89	40	----------		8	----------		W.	7	------	

BEVERLY, NEW YORK.

Month and day.	Hour.	Barom'r corrected to 32° F.	Thermometer.	Force of vapor.	Cloudiness.		Motion of clouds.		Winds.		Relative humidity.
March 14	7 a. m.	------	35	----------		2	----------		NE.	1	------
	2 p. m.	------	53	----------	St.	10	SE.	2	SE.	3	------
	9 p. m.	------	43	----------	Cu.	10	S.	2	SE.	1	------
March 15	7 a. m.	------	53	----------	Cu.	10	SE.	5	SE.	5	------
	2 p. m.	------	50	----------	Cu.	10	E.	1	NE.	2	------
	9 p. m.	------	46	----------	Cu.	8	SW.	1	SW.	2	------
March 16	7 a. m.	------	36	----------	Cu.	9	NW.	2	NW.	2	------
	2 p. m.	------	44	----------	Cu.	3	NW.	3	NW.	4	------
	9 p. m.	------	------	----------	----------		----------		----------		------
March 17	7 a. m.	------	31	----------	St.	6	NW.	1	NE.	1	------
	2 p. m.	------	59	----------	Cu.	4	S.	2	SW.	3	------
	9 p. m.	------	48	----------	Cu.	10	SE.	4	SE.	4	------
March 18	7 a. m.	------	46	----------	Cu.	10	E.	4	NE.	2	------
	2 p. m.	------	52	----------	Cu.	10	SE.	6	SE.	5	------
	9 p. m.	------	52	----------		10	SE.	------	SE.	7	------
March 19	7 a. m.	------	41	----------	Cu.	9	SW.	5	SW.	5	------
	2 p. m.	------	43	----------	Cu.	10	SW.	3	SW.	4	------
	9 p. m.	------	39	----------	Cu.	9	SW.	3	SW.	4	------

Remarks: Rain from 7 p. m. the 14th, with a violent gale during the night, to 5 p. m. on the 15th; amount, 1. 34 inch.
17th. Commenced raining in the night, accompanied by a gale of wind which continued all night; storm ended in the night of the 18th. Amount, 1. 52 inch.

BUFFALO, NEW YORK.

Month and day.	Hour.	Barom'r corrected to 32° F.	Thermometer.	Force of vapor.	Cloudiness.		Motion of clouds.		Winds.		Relative humidity.
March 14	8 a. m.	29. 331	43	. 164	Cir. st.	8		3	NE.	2	59
	2 p. m.	29. 078	55	. 243	Cir. st.	10		4	SE.	4	56
	9 p. m.	28. 844	56	. 308	St.	10		5	S.	4	69
March 15	8 a. m.	28. 936	39	. 195	St.	10		4	SW.	3	82
	2 p. m.	28. 953	38	. 165	St.	10		5	SW.	4	72
	9 p. m.	29. 151	36	. 129	St.	8		5	SW.	4	61
March 16	8 a. m.	29. 503	35	. 127	St.	5		4	W.	3	62
	2 p m.	29. 549	37	. 157		0	----------		SW.	3	71
	9 p. m.	29. 559	36	. 149		0	----------		W.	1	71
March 17	8 a. m.	29. 437	40	. 160	Cir. st.	8		1	SE.	1	64
	2 p. m.	29. 303	57	. 142	Cir. st.	4		1	SW.	1	30
	9 p. m.	------	54	. 206	St.	10	----------		SE.	2	49
March 18	8 a. m.	28. 717	52	. 361	Nim.	10	----------		S.	3	93
	2 p. m.	28. 537	54	. 362	Cir. st.	8		3	S.	2	87
	9 p. m.	28. 25	50	. 361	Nim.	10	----------		SE.	3	100
March 19	8 a. m.	28. 366	32	. 181	Nim.	10	----------		------------		100
	2 p. m.	28. 655	32	. 181	St.	10	----------		------------		100
	9 p. m.	28. 996	32	. 125	----------		----------		------------		69

Remarks: 14th. Slight rain from SE. at 2 p. m.; strong S. wind all the afternoon and evening; showers during the night; amount, 0. 228 inch.
15th. Snow squalls from 3. 30 to 7 p. m.; a high SW. wind during the p. m. and evening.
16th. Aurora at 8. 30, consisting of bright streamers of a yellow and greenish tinge, moving rapidly from NNW. to NE.; the streamers seemed to burst from faint patches of light 20° above the horizon, and extending nearly to the zenith; a crimson cloud formed at 9 p. m. 75° above the horizon, through which stars were visible; the cloud and streamers disappeared at 9. 30 p. m.
17th. Rain began at 11. 30 p. m., and continued during the night; amount, 0. 467 inch.
18th. Thunder shower from SSE., continued 15 minutes; 9 p. m. wind fresh; 10 p. m. wind high, and increased to a strong gale from SW.; bar. fell 04 per hour from 2 to 10 p. m., and with less rapidity till 6 a. m. on the 19th; amount, 4. 75 inches.
19th. At 2 a. m. wind blew with great violence, accompanied by rain, which changed to a thick driving snow; gale continued, with squalls of snow; 11 a. m. wind hauled to W, and continued in strong puffs during the day; 8 inches of snow fell during the storm; amount in water, 1. 239 inch.

STORM No. 1, MARCH, 1859.

EAST HENRIETTA, NEW YORK.

Month and day.	Hour.	Barom'r corrected to 32° F.	Thermometer.	Force of vapor.	Cloudiness.	Motion of clouds.	Winds.	Relative humidity.	REMARKS.
March 14	7 a. m.	29.48	37	......	Cir. 3	SW. 1	W. 1	......	19th. Snowy.
	2 p. m.	......	......	......	Cir. 8	W. 5	......	......	
	9 p. m.	28.83	52	......	......	......	SW. 8	......	
March 15	7 a. m.	28.74	72	......	Cu. 9	NE. 2	SW. 1	......	
	2 p. m.	28.78	40	......	Cir. 2	W. 1	NW. 3	......	
	9 p. m.	28.87	34	......	......	......	W. 1	......	
March 16	7 a. m.	29.37	31	......	Cir. 3	S. 1	N. 2	......	
	2 p. m.	29.50	45	......	Cir. cu. 3	S. 1	W. 2	......	
	9 p. m.	......	......	......	......	......	......	......	
March 17	7 a. m.	29.51	46	......	Cu. 9	S. 6	S. 1	......	
	2 p. m.	29.30	66	......	......	......	S. 1	......	
	9 p. m.	29.13	......	......	......	......	......	......	
March 18	7 a. m.	28.67	52	......	Cu. 7	W. 3	S. 4	......	
	2 p. m.	......	......	......	......	......	......	......	
	9 p. m.	28.29	54	......	......	......	......	......	
March 19	7 a. m.	27.90	32	......	......	......	W. 5	......	
	2 p. m.	......	......	......	......	......	......	......	
	9 p. m.	28.68	28	......	......	......	W. 1	......	

EDEN, NEW YORK.

Month and day.	Hour.	Barom'r corrected to 32° F.	Thermometer.	Force of vapor.	Cloudiness.	Motion of clouds.	Winds.	Relative humidity.	REMARKS.
March 14	7 a. m.	......	46	......	Cu. 10	N. 1	SW. 2	......	Snow storm from 3½ p. m. the 15th to 8 a. m. on the 17th. 18th. Snow at 6 p. m., thunder in the evening.
	2 p. m.	......	50	......	Cir. 8	N. 3	SW. 4	......	
	9 p. m.	......	45	......	Cu. 7	N. 2	SW. 4	......	
March 15	7 a. m.	......	42	......	Cu. 8	NE. 1	SW. 2	......	
	2 p. m.	......	36	......	Cu. 8	E. 2	SW. 3	......	
	9 p. m.	......	33	......	Nim. 9	E. 2	W. 3	......	
March 16	7 a. m.	......	36	......	Cu. 7	E. 2	SE. 2	......	
	2 p. m.	......	40	......	Cu. 1	......	S. 1	......	
	9 p. m.	......	32	......	......	......	SE. 1	......	
March 17	7 a. m.	......	40	......	Cir. cu. 6	E. 1	SE. 1	......	
	2 p. m.	......	64	......	Cu. 4	E. 1	......	......	
	9 p. m.	......	56	......	Cu. 8	......	SE. 1	......	
March 18	7 a. m.	......	46	......	Nim. 8	NE. 2	W. 2	......	
	2 p. m.	......	62	......	Cu. 6	E. 1	SE. 1	......	
	9 p. m.	......	54	......	Nim. 6	NE. 2	SW. 2	......	
March 19	7 a. m.	......	30	......	Nim. 10	......	W. 3	......	
	2 p. m.	......	28	......	Nim. 10	......	W. 3	......	
	9 p. m.	......	30	......	Nim. 10	......	W. 3	......	

FISHKILL LANDING, NEW YORK.

Month and day.	Hour.	Barom'r corrected to 32° F.	Thermometer.	Force of vapor.	Cloudiness.	Motion of clouds.	Winds.	Relative humidity.	REMARKS.
March 14	7 a. m.	30.42	33	......	St. 2	......	NE. 1	......	15th. Rain from 1 a. m. to 4 p. m.; amount, 0.21 inch. 18th Rain from 4 a. m. to 4 p. m.; amount, 0.34 inch.
	2 p. m.	30.42	56	......	St. 7	......	SE. 4	......	
	9 p. m	30.37	45	......	Nim. 8	......	SE. 4	......	
March 15	7 a. m.	29.85	35	......	10	......	S. 4	......	
	2 p. m.	29.60	53	......	10	......	S. 3	......	
	9 p. m.	29.75	45	......	Cu. 6	......	SW. 4	......	
March 16	7 a. m.	30.10	37	......	Cu. 6	......	NW. 4	......	
	2 p. m.	30.20	42	......	Cu. 6	......	NW. 5	......	
	9 p. m.	30.40	32	......	0	......	W. 3	......	
March 17	7 a. m.	30.45	33	......	St. 4	......	E. 1	......	
	2 p. m.	30.40	57	......	St. 3	......	SE. 3	......	
	9 p. m.	30.30	50	......	Nim. 10	......	SE. 5	......	
March 18	7 a. m.	30.05	48	......	10	......	SE. 3	......	
	2 p. m.	29.70	55	......	10	......	SE. 8	......	
	9 p. m.	29.60	52	......	Nim. 7	......	SE. 7	......	
March 19	7 a. m.	29.50	42	......	Cu. st. 6	......	SW. 6	......	
	2 p. m.	29.42	46	......	Cu. st. 6	......	SW. 6	......	
	9 p. m.	29.66	30	......	Cu. st. 6	......	SW. 4	......	

STORM No. 1, MARCH, 1859.

FLATBUSH, NEW YORK.

Month and day.	Hour.	Barom'r corrected to 32° F.	Thermometer.	Force of vapor.	Cloudiness.	Motion of clouds.	Winds.	Relative humidity.	REMARKS.
March 14	7 a. m.	30. 19	39	----------	St. 1	----------	NE. 1	------	14th. Cloudy all day; rain in the evening.
	2 p m	30. 16	51	----------	Nim. 10	----------	SE. 2	------	
	9 p. m.	30. 04	41	----------	Nim. 10	S. 3	E. 3	------	15th. Violent storm; wind and rain from 3 to 5 a. m.; rain continued till 9 p. m.; ceased with W. wind; amount, 1. 50 inch.
March 15	7 a. m.	29. 61	51	----------	Nim. 10	S. 10	S. 3	------	
	2 p. m.	29. 40	51	----------	Nim. 10	S. 2	S. 1	------	
	9 p m.	29. 59	48	----------	Cir. cu. 9	W. 2	W. 2	------	
March 16	7 a. m.	29. 96	40	----------	Cir cu st. 10	NW. 3	NW. 1	------	
	2 p. m.	30. 05	48	----------	Cir. 1	W. 2	W. 3	------	16th. Pleasant.
	9 p m.	30. 16	44	----------	0	----------	NW. 1	------	17th. White frost; pleasant a. m.; hazy p. m.; began to rain in the night.
March 17	7 a m.	30. 23	36	----------	Cir st cir. 3	W. 2	W. 1	------	
	2 p. m.	30. 13	54	----------	Cir. 8	NW. 2	S. 2	------	
	9 p m.	30. 10	46	----------	Cir. 9	SW. 1	S. 1	------	18th. Violent rain a. m.; little, if any, after 2 p. m.; amount, 0. 67 inch.
March 18	7 a. m.	29. 76	47	----------	Nim. 10	W. 1	SE. 3	------	
	2 p. m.	29. 37	52	----------	Nim. 10	----------	S. 3	------	
	9 p. m.	29. 18	50	----------	Nim. 10	SW. 5	S. 3	------	19th. Windy.
March 19	7 a. m.	29. 17	42	----------	Cir. cu. 10	W. 3	SW. 3	------	
	2 p. m.	29. 27	42	----------	Nim. 10	W. 4	W. 3	------	
	9 p. m.	29. 43	40	----------	Nim. 10	NW. 3	NW. 3	------	

FORDHAM, NEW YORK.

Month and day.	Hour.	Barom'r corrected to 32° F.	Thermometer.	Force of vapor.	Cloudiness.	Motion of clouds.	Winds.	Relative humidity.	REMARKS.
March 14	7 a. m.	------	------	----------	----------	----------	----------	------	
	2 p. m.	30. 01	47	. 238	----------	----------	----------	77	
	9 p. m.	29. 88	41	. 257	----------	----------	----------	100	
March 15	7 a. m.	29. 54	53	. 403	----------	----------	----------	100	
	2 p. m.	------	------	----------	----------	----------	----------	------	
	9 p. m.	29. 45	49	. 205	----------	----------	----------	60	
March 16	7 a. m.	------	------	----------	----------	----------	----------	------	
	2 p. m.	29 81	46. 5	. 156	----------	----------	----------	48	
	9 p. m.	29. 98	45	. 144	----------	----------	----------	49	
March 17	7 a. m.	30. 01	40	. 173	----------	----------	----------	73	
	2 p. m.	29. 96	56	. 230	----------	----------	----------	52	
	9 p. m.	29. 91	46. 5	. 257	----------	----------	----------	77	
March 18	7 a. m.	29. 63	50. 5	. 368	----------	----------	----------	100	
	2 p. m.	29. 41	52. 5	. 388	----------	----------	----------	100	
	9 p. m.	29. 37	51	. 374	----------	----------	----------	100	
March 19	7 a. m.	29. 39	43. 5	. 142	----------	----------	----------	51	
	2 p. m.	29. 34	41. 5	----------	----------	----------	----------	------	
	9 p. m.	29. 43	41	. 160	----------	----------	----------	64	

FORT EDWARD, NEW YORK.

Month and day.	Hour.	Barom'r corrected to 32° F.	Thermometer.	Force of vapor.	Cloudiness.	Motion of clouds.	Winds.	Relative humidity.	REMARKS.
March 14	7 a. m.	30. 22	36	. 191	Cir. st. 5	----------	NE. 1	90	Rain from 8½ p. m. the 15th to 9 a. m. on the 16th; amount, 0. 78 inch.
	2 p. m.	30. 04	45	. 160	Nim. 10	----------	N. 2	53	
	9 p. m.	30. 04	43	. 186	0	----------	SW. 4	66	
March 15	7 a. m.	30. 06	41	. 257	Nim. 10	----------	SW. 1	100	18th. Rain at intervals during the day, commencing at 3½ a. m., and ending in the night; amount, 0. 75 inch.
	2 p. m.	30. 20	44	. 278	Nim. 10	NE -------	SW. 2	100	
	9 p. m.	29. 39	40	. 248	Nim. 10	E. 1	W. 4	100	
March 16	7 a. m.	29. 66	36	. 129	Cu. 5	SE -------	W. 4	61	
	2 p. m.	29. 81	43	. 164	Cir. cu. 5	NE -------	SW. 1	58	19th. A severe squall of frozen rain, snow, and sleet at 11. 45 a. m.; wind SW. 7 to 8; very chilly.
	9 p. m.	30. 05	37	. 116	0	----------	W. 1	52	
March 17	7 a. m.	30. 06	29	. 142	0	----------	S. 1	88	
	2 p. m.	30. 04	57	. 179	Cir. cu. 5	E 2	SE. 1	55	
	9 p. m.	29. 84	37	. 178	Cu. st. 5	SW -------	SW. 1	80	
March 18	7 a. m.	29. 65	40	. 248	Nim. 10	W. 2	E. 2	100	
	2 p. m.	29. 31	46	. 311	Nim. 10	----------	SE. 1	100	
	9 p. m.	29. 02	45	. 299	Nim. 10	NW. 1	SE. 1	100	
March 19	7 a. m.	28. 75	44	. 195	Cu. st. 10	SW. 2	SW. 3	67	
	2 p. m.	28. 92	44	. 195	Nim. 10	----------	W. 5	67	
	9 p. m.	29. 11	37	. 116	Nim. 10	----------	SW. 4	52	

STORM No. 1, MARCH, 1859.

CAZENOVIA, NEW YORK.

Month and day.	Hour.	Barom'r corrected to 32° F.	Thermometer.	Force of vapor.	Cloudiness.	Motion of clouds.	Winds.	Relative humidity.	REMARKS.
March 14	7 a. m.	28. 78	35	....	Cir. 5	S. 2	SE. 2	......	14th. Commenced to rain at 6 p. m., ended in the night; amount, 0. 23 inch.
	2 p. m.	28. 63	49	....	St. 10	SE. 2	SE. 3	......	
	9 p. m.	28. 39	44	....	Nim. 10	SE. 3	SE. 4	......	
March 15	7 a. m.	28. 23	47	....	Cu. st. 5	SW. 2	SW. 2	......	Commenced raining during the night of the 17th, and ended at noon on the 18th.
	2 p. m.	28. 19	42	....	St. 9	NW. 3	NW. 3	......	
	9 p. m.	28. 29	33	....	St. 9	W. 3	W. 3	......	
March 16	7 a. m.	28. 56	28	....	St. 10	W. 4	W. 4	......	Storm commenced at 7 a. m. on the 19th, and ended at 8 a. m. on the 20th; amount on the 19th, 0. 23 inch; amount on the 20th, 0. 46 inch.
	2 p. m.	28. 69	36	....	St. 3	NW. 3	NW. 3	......	
	9 p. m.	28. 81	33	....	0	....	NW. 1	......	
March 17	7 a. m.	28. 78	31	....	Cir. 3	W. 1	SW. 1	......	
	2 p. m.	28. 63	54	....	Cir. st. 2	W. 2	S. 3	......	
	9 p. m.	28. 57	49	....	St. 9	S. 2	S. 3	......	
March 18	7 a. m.	28. 23	46	....	Nim. 10	SE. 4	SE. 4	......	
	2 p. m.	27. 96	53	....	Nim. 10	SE. 4	SE. 3	......	
	8 p. m.	27. 74	54	....	Cu. st. 5	S. 3	S. 3	......	
	9 p. m.	27. 74	54	....	Cu. st. 5	S. 3	S. 3	......	
	12 p. m.	27. 60	51	....	St. nim. 9	SW. 3	SW. 4	......	
March 19	5 a. m.	27. 54	39	....	St. nim. 10	SSW. 5	SSW. 4	......	
	7 a. m.	27. 52	36	....	Nim. 10	SSW. 5	SSW. 4	......	
	8 a. m.	27. 52	35	....	Nim. 10	SW. 5	SSW. 4	......	
	9 a. m.	27. 56	33	....	Nim. 10	SW. 5	WSW. 5	......	
	11 a. m.	27. 62	52	....	Nim. 10	W. 4	WSW. 5	......	
	2 p. m.	27. 76	29	....	Nim. 10	W. 5	W. 5	......	
	9 p. m.	28. 03	25	....	Nim. 10	W. 5	W. 5	......	

WAMPSVILLE, NEW YORK.

Month and day.	Hour.	Barom'r corrected to 32° F.	Thermometer.	Force of vapor.	Cloudiness.	Motion of clouds.	Winds.	Relative humidity.	REMARKS.
March 14	7 a. m.	......	28	....	....	SE. 1	SE. 1	......	15th. Rain from 9 p. m. till 5 a. m. on the 16th; amount, 0. 40 inch.
	2 p. m.	......	49	....	Cu. st. 6	E. 1	E. 1	......	
	9 p. m.	......	46	....	Cu. 10	E. 3	E. 4	......	
March 15	7 a. m.	......	46	....	Cir. 4	SW. 1	SW. 2	......	18th. Rain in the night; am't, 0. 40 inch.
	2 p. m.	......	43	....	Cu. 10	W. 2	W. 3	......	
	9 p. m.	......	34	....	Cu. 9	W. 2	W. 3	......	
March 16	7 a. m.	......	30	....	Cu. 10	W. 2	W. 3	......	
	2 p. m.	......	36	....	Cir. cu. 4	W. 2	W. 3	......	
	9 p. m.	......	30	....	0	0	W. 1	......	
March 17	7 a. m.	......	34	....	0	0	E. 2	......	
	2 p. m.	......	60	....	Cir. cu. 4	E. 1	E. 2	......	
	9 p. m.	......	49	....	Cu. st. 8	E. 2	E. 2	......	
March 18	7 a. m.	......	45	....	Cu. 6	E. 2	E. 2	......	
	2 p. m.	......	50	....	Cu. 10	E. 2	E. 2	......	
	9 p. m.	......	50	....	Cu. 10	SE. 3	SE. 3	......	
March 19	7 a. m.	......	38	....	Cu. 10	S. 3	S. 4	......	
	2 p. m.	......	32	....	Cu. 10	W. 4	W. 5	......	
	9 p. m.	......	26	....	Cu. 10	W. 3	W. 4		

HOUSEVILLE, NEW YORK.

Month and day.	Hour.	Barom'r corrected to 32° F.	Thermometer.	Force of vapor.	Cloudiness.	Motion of clouds.	Winds.	Relative humidity.	REMARKS.
March 14	7 a. m.	......	34	....	Cir. 7	W. 3	S. 3	......	14th. Hoar frost at 3 a. m.; solar halo at 10 a. m.; commenced to rain at 5 p. m., ending the next morning; amount on the 14th, 0. 46 inch.
	2 p. m.	......	47	....	Cir. st. 10	S. 3	S. 5	......	
	9 p. m.	......	40	....	Nim. 10	?	S. 6	......	
March 15	7 a. m.	......	42	....	Cir. cu. 7	SW. 3	S. 3	......	
	2 p. m.	......	44	....	Cir. st. 9	SW. 3	SW. 4	......	
	9 p. m.	......	33	....	Nim. 10	?	W. 5	......	15th. Commenced raining at 5 p. m., ended in the night; am't on the 15th, 0. 05 inch; am't on the 16th, 0. 10 inch.
March 16	7 a. m.	......	29	....	Cir. st. 7	W. 2	W. 4	......	
	2 p. m.	......	38	....	Cir. st. 5	W. 3	W. 4	......	
	9 p. m.	......	31	....	0	....	S. 1	......	
March 17	7 a. m.	......	33	....	Cir. st. 7	W. 3	S. 3	......	17th. Solar halo in the morning from 7 a. m. until noon.
	2 p. m.	......	57	....	Cir. st. 10	W. 3	S. 4	......	

STORM No. 1, MARCH, 1859.

HOUSEVILLE, NEW YORK—Continued.

Month and day.	Hour.	Barom'r corrected to 32° F.	Thermometer.	Force of vapor.	Cloudiness.		Motion of clouds.		Winds.		Relative humidity.	REMARKS.
March 17	9 p. m.	------	45	----------	Cir. st.	10	?		S.	5	------	Commenced to rain in the night
March 18	7 a. m.	------	47	----------	Nim.	10	?		S.	3	------	of the 17th–18th, ended the
	2 p. m.	------	51	----------	Nim.	10	?		S.	4	------	following night; amount on
	9 p. m.	------	52	----------	Nim.	7	?		S.	4	------	the 17th, 0. 30 inch; amount
March 19	7 a. m.	------	38	----------	Cu. st.	10	?		S.	5	------	on the 18th, 0. 50 inch.
	2 p. m.	------	29	----------	Nim.	10	?		SW.	6	------	19th. Stormed from 7½ a. m. until night; amount, 0. 40 inch;
	9 p. m.	------	23	----------	Nim.	10	?		W.	6	------	depth of snow, 4 inches.

MORRISANIA, NEW YORK.

Month and day.	Hour.	Barom'r corrected to 32° F.	Thermometer.	Force of vapor.	Cloudiness.		Motion of clouds.		Winds.		Relative humidity.	REMARKS.
March 14	7 a. m.	------	38	----------		0	----------		NE.	2	------	Storm commenced at 8 p. m. the
	2 p. m.	------	53	----------	Cu.	3	----------		NE.	2	------	14th, and ended at 2 p. m. on
	9 p. m.	------	43	----------	Nim.	10	----------		NE.	3	------	the 15th.
March 15	7 a. m.	------	52	----------	Nim.	10	----------		SE.	5	------	18th. Rain from 5 a. m. to 12 m.,
	2 p. m.	------	54	----------	Nim.	10	----------		W.	1	------	and 2 to 4 p. m.
	9 p. m.	------	49	----------	Cu. st.	10	----------		W.	4	------	
March 16	7 a. m.	------	40	----------	Nim.	8	----------		W.	5	------	
	2 p. m.	------	47	----------	Cu.	3	----------		W.	4	------	
	9 p. m.	------	43	----------		0	----------		W.	1	------	
March 17	7 a. m.	------	37	----------	St.	5	----------		NW.	1	------	
	2 p. m.	------	60	----------	Cu.	7	----------		NW.	2	------	
	9 p. m.	------	49	----------		0	----------		N.	2	------	
March 18	7 a. m.	------	49	----------	Nim.	10	----------		E.	3	------	
	2 p. m.	------	54	----------	Nim.	10	----------		SE.	4	------	
	9 p. m.	------	51	----------	Nim.	10	----------		SE.	5	------	
March 19	7 a. m.	------	43	----------	Cu.	7	----------		SW.	4	------	
	2 p. m.	------	42	----------	Cu.	10	----------		SW.	7	------	
	9 p. m.	------	40	----------	St.	10	----------		SW.	5	------	

NEW YORK CITY, NEW YORK.

Month and day.	Hour.	Barom'r corrected to 32° F.	Thermometer.	Force of vapor.	Cloudiness.		Motion of clouds.		Winds.		Relative humidity.	REMARKS.
March 14	7 a. m.	30. 213	43	. 151	St.	1	W.	1	NE.	1	54	Rain from 7. 15 p. m. the 14th to
	2 p. m.	30. 242	54. 6	. 188	Cir.	9	SW.	1	E.	2	44	3. 25 p. m. on the 15th; amount,
	9 p. m.	30. 000	49. 7	. 255	Nim.	10	SW.	1	NE.	3	71	1. 64 inch. Thunder and lightning at 12. 15 p. m. the 14th.
March 15	7 a. m.	29. 678	53. 8	. 370	Nim.	10	SW.	1	SE.	5	89	
	2 p. m.	29. 517	57	. 367	Nim.	10	SW.	1	SW.	3	79	18th. Rain till 5 p. m., com-
	9 p. m.	29. 634	51. 1	. 197	Cir. cu.	10	SW.	1	W.	3	52	menced in the night; amount,
March 16	7 a. m.	29. 945	41. 9	. 122	Cir. cu.	10	W.	2	NW.	3	46	0. 88 inch.
	2 p. m.	30. 062	51	. 189	Cu.	5	NW.	4	NW.	3	51	
	9 p. m.	30. 237	47	. 126		0	----------		NW.	2	40	
March 17	7 a. m.	30. 266	40	. 171		0	----------		SE.	1	68	
	2 p. m.	30. 219	58	. 213	Cir.	2	SW.	1	SE.	2	44	
	9 p. m.	30. 099	51. 8	. 181	Cir., nim.	10	SW.	1	SE.	2	47	
March 18	7 a. m.	29. 810	50	. 301	Nim.	10	SW.	1	SE.	3	83	
	2 p. m.	29. 546	55	. 419	Nim.	10	SW.	1	SE.	4	97	
	9 p. m.	29. 361	53	. 348	Cir.	5	S.	2	SE.	5	86	
March 19	7 a. m.	29. 190	45	. 204	Cir. cu.	7	SW.	2	SW.	6	68	
	2 p. m.	29. 337	44	. 138	Cir. cu.	9	SW.	2	SW.	6	48	
	9 p. m.	29. 654	44	. 119	Cir. cu.	9	SW.	2	SW.	6	41	

NICHOLS, NEW YORK.

Month and day.	Hour.	Barom'r corrected to 32° F.	Thermometer.	Force of vapor.	Cloudiness.		Motion of clouds.		Winds.		Relative humidity.	REMARKS.
March 14	7 a. m.	------	30	----------	Fog	0		0	W.	1	------	14th. Slight rain from the NW.
	2 p. m.	------	55	----------	Nim.	10		0	N.	4	------	in the evening.
	9 p. m.	------	48	----------	Nim.	10	S.	2	NW.	3	------	15th. Heavy rain from 1 to 3 a.
March 15	7 a. m.	------	48	----------	Cir.	7	SE.	3	NW.	4	------	m.; violent wind from SE.;
	2 p. m.	------	51	----------	Cir. st.	10	SE.	4	NW.	2	------	mist in the evening.
	9 p. m.	------	38	----------	Cir. st.	9	SE.	3	NW.	4	------	18th. Heavy rain from 4 to 11 a.

STORM No. 1, MARCH, 1859.

NICHOLS, NEW YORK—Continued.

Month and day.	Hour.	Barom'r corrected to 32° F.	Thermometer.	Force of vapor.	Cloudiness.	Motion of clouds.	Winds.	Relative humidity.	REMARKS.
March 16	7 a. m.	......	34	....	Cu st. 10	SE. 2	NW. 3	......	m ; commenced again at dark
	2 p. m.	......	48	....	Cu. 2	SE. 3	NW. 2	......	and continued two or three
	9 p. m.	......	30	....	Clear 0	0	NW. 1	......	hours from SE.
March 17	7 a. m.	......	28	....	Cir., cu. st. 5	0	SE. 2	......	19th. Snow squalls, with high
	2 p. m.	......	64	....	Cir. 7	0	SE. 3	......	wind from SE. during the fore-
	9 p. m.	......	51	....	Nim. 10	0	SE. 4	......	noon.
March 18	7 a. m.	......	50	....	Nim. 10	NW. 5	SE. 5	......	
	2 p. m.	......	60	....	Cu. st. 10	N. 5	SE. 3	......	
	9 p. m.	......	59	....	Cu. st. 10	N. 4	SW. 3	......	
March 19	7 a. m.	......	37	....	Nim. 10	SE. 1	NW. 4	......	
	2 p. m.	......	39	....	Cu. st. 10	SE. 5	W. 4	......	
	9 p. m.	......	31	....	Cir. st. 8	SE. 3	W. 5	......	

OGDENSBURG, NEW YORK.

REMARKS.—14th. Clear; wind, NE. 2; SW. gale and thunder storm in the night. 15th. Springlike; wind, SW. 3. 16th. Fine; SW. wind, 2; beautiful auroral display after 9 p. m.; some of the tints gentle red. 17th. Wind N. 18th. Fine rain, springlike; heavy rain in the night; wind NE. 19th. Cloudy and mild; sprinkle of rain; snow at 5 p. m.; wind N. and NW.; gale most of the night.

OSWEGO, NEW YORK.

Month and day.	Hour.	Barom'r corrected to 32° F.	Thermometer.	Force of vapor.	Cloudiness.	Motion of clouds.	Winds.	Relative humidity.	REMARKS.
March 14	7 a. m.	29.493	34	....	10	....	SE. 2	......	15th. Rain; amount, 0.40 inch.
	2 p. m.	29.354	50	....	10	....	SE. 4	......	18th. Rain at night; amount,
	9 p. m.	29.041	47	....	10	....	SE. 6	......	0.45 inch.
March 15	7 a. m.	28.943	44	....	5	....	W. 3	......	19th. Amount of rain 1.50 inch.
	2 p. m.	28.948	41	....	10	....	W. 4	......	
	9 p. m.	29.043	37	....	10	....	W. 5	......	
March 16	7 a. m.	29.311	33	....	10	....	NW. 5	......	
	2 p. m.	29.474	39	....	0	....	NW. 5	......	
	9 p. m.	29.547	33	....	0	....	SW. 2	......	
March 17	7 a. m.	29.493	31	....	10	....	SE. 2	......	
	2 p. m.	29.312	57	....	0	....	SE. 2	......	
	9 p. m.	29.262	47	....	10	....	SE. 3	......	
March 18	7 a. m.	28.903	47	....	10	....	SE. 5	......	
	2 p. m.	28.689	54	....	10	....	S. 4	......	
	9 p. m.	28.384	53	....	10	....	SW. 6	......	
March 19	7 a. m.	28.212	37	....	10	....	W. 7	......	
	2 p. m.	28.426	30	....	10	....	W. 7	......	
	9 p. m.	28.800	28	....	10	....	NW. 7	......	

ROCHESTER, NEW YORK.

Month and day.	Hour.	Barom'r corrected to 32° F.	Thermometer.	Force of vapor.	Cloudiness.	Motion of clouds.	Winds.	Relative humidity.	REMARKS.
March 14	7 a. m.	29.59	35	....	Cir. cu. 10	W. 2	W. 2	......	14th. Frost; rain from 4 to 5 p.
	2 p. m.	29.34	59	....	Cir. cu. 10	W. 2	W. 1	......	m.; windy; high wind at 7½
	9 p. m.	29.08	52	....	Cir. 5	W. 1	....	......	p. m.
March 15	7 a. m.	29.03	40	....	Cir. st. 10	W. 3	W. 5	......	15th. Rain from 2 to 3 a. m.,
	2 p. m.	29.09	42	....	0	0	W. 4	......	wind SE., and 1 to 1½ p. m.
	9 p. m.	29.23	35	....	Cir. st. 10	W. 2	....	......	wind W.; windy night.
March 16	7 a. m.	29.54	52	....	Cir. cu. 10	W. 2	W. 2	......	16th. Frost; fine day.
	2 p. m.	29.62	42	....	Cir. cu. 10	NW. 1	W. 2	......	17th. Rain from 3 to 6½ a. m.;
	9 p. m.	29.66	30	....	0	0	....	......	fine showers at 6½ p. m. and
March 17	7 a. m.	29.62	34	....	Cu. 8	W. 1	W. 1	......	10½ p. m.; wind rose to a gale
	2 p. m.	29.44	62	....	Cir. cu. 10	W. 2	E. 1	......	at 11 p. m.
	9 p. m.	29.30	53	....	Cir. 10	NW. 1	....	......	19th. Heavy gale from mid-
March 18	7 a. m.	28.98	49	....	Cir. st. 10	NW. 1	NW. 1	......	night; rain at 6 a. m.; snow
	2 p. m.	28.72	66	....	0	0	W. 2	......	and rain at 6½, and snow at 7
	9 p. m.	28.40	56	....	0	0	....	......	a. m.; snow squalls during the
March 19	7 a. m.	28.12	33	....	1	0	W. 1	......	day. *Barometer lowest ever known.*
	2 p. m.	28.56	32	....	Cir. cu. 10	NW. 1	W. 1	......	
	9 p. m.	28.88	30	....	0	0	....	......	

STORM No. 1, MARCH, 1859.

SARATOGA, NEW YORK.

Month and day.	Hour.	Barom'r corrected to 32° F.	Thermometer.	Force of vapor.	Cloudiness.	Motion of clouds.	Winds.	Relative humidity.	REMARKS.
March 14	7 a. m.	29. 82	32	. 337	St. 0	W. 0	W. 1	70	Rain from 5 a. m. the 18th to 5 a. m. on the 19th; amount, 2 inches.
	2 p. m.	29. 62	45	. 456	St. 0	NE. 0	NE. 1	88	
	9 p. m.	29. 42	40	----------	St. 5	NE. 0	SW. 1	------	
March 15	7 a. m.	29. 12	35	. 394	St. 10	SW. 0	SW. 1	82	
	2 p. m.	29. 01	45	. 618	St. 10	NE. 0	NE. 1	100	
	9 p. m.	29. 04	40	----------	St. 5	NE. 10	NE. 2	------	
March 16	7 a. m.	29. 38	35	. 433	St. 0	NW. 0	NW. 3	100	
	2 p. m.	29. 50	43	----------	Cu. st. 0	NW. 10	SW. 2	------	
	9 p. m.	29. 62	40	. 189	St. 0	SW. 0	SW. 2	33	
March 17	7 a. m.	29. 78	35	----------	Cir. 0	SW. 0	SW. 1	------	
	2 p. m.	29. 62	52	. 456	Cir. 0	SW. 0	SW. 1	88	
	9 p. m.	29. 60	32	. 389	St. 0	NE. 0	NE. 1	63	
March 18	7 a. m.	29. 27	40	. 367	St. 10	NE. 0	NE. 1	71	
	2 p. m.	29. 11	45	. 399	Cir. 10	SW. 0	SW. 3	72	
	9 p. m.	28. 92	40	. 242	St. 10	SW. 0	SW. 3	48	
March 19	7 a. m.	28. 52	45	----------	Cu. 5	SW. 10	SW. 3	------	
	2 p. m.	28. 66	36	. 451	Cu. 5	SW. 10	SW. 3	73	
	9 p. m.	28. 91	34	----------	St. 5	SW. 0	SW. 1	------	

SCHENECTADY, NEW YORK.

Month and day.	Hour.	Barom'r corrected to 32° F.	Thermometer.	Force of vapor.	Cloudiness.	Motion of clouds.	Winds.	Relative humidity.	REMARKS.
March 14	7 a. m.	30. 086	32	----------	Cir. 10	----------	W. 1	------	14th. Began to rain at 9 p. m. and ended in the night. 15th. Sprinkle all day. 16th. Light fall of snow at 7 a. m. 16th. Auroral arch at 9.40 p. m., 1½° broad, 9° high in centre, and extending 120° on the horizon.
	2 p. m.	29. 987	51	----------	Cu. st. 10	----------	E. to S. 2	------	
	9 p. m.	29. 797	43	----------	10	----------	E. to S. 2½	------	
March 15	7 a. m.	29. 433	49	----------	Nim. 10	NE. 4	N. 4	------	
	2 p. m.	29. 273	46	----------	10	----------	N. 1	------	
	9 p. m.	29. 394	39	----------	7	E. 5	3	------	
March 16	7 a. m.	29. 647	36	----------	10	E. 5	W. 6	------	
	2 p. m.	29. 836	41	----------	3	E. 4	SW. to NW. 4	------	
	9 p. m.	------	------	----------	----------	----------	----------	------	
March 17	7 a. m.	30. 033	32	----------	Cir. 10	----------	S. 1	------	
	2 p. m.	29. 891	53	----------	Cir. cu. 7	----------	SE. 1	------	
	9 p. m.	29. 831	50	----------	10	----------	S. 1	------	
March 18	7 a. m.	------	------	----------	10	----------	----------	------	
	2 p. m.	29. 212	51	----------	10	NW. 8	SE. 1	------	
	9 p. m.	28. 948	56	----------	10	----------	SE. 2	------	
March 19	7 a. m.	28. 743	47	----------	Cu. 1	NE. 3	S. 3	------	
	2 p. m.	28. 891	41	----------	10	ENE ------	S. to W. 4	------	
	9 p. m.	29. 109	35	----------	10	E. 4	SW. to W. 4	------	

SPENCERTOWN, NEW YORK.

Month and day.	Hour.	Barom'r corrected to 32° F.	Thermometer.	Force of vapor.	Cloudiness.	Motion of clouds.	Winds.	Relative humidity.	REMARKS.
March 14	7 a. m.	29. 623	35	----------	0	----------	NW. 2	------	Rain from 10 p. m. the 14th to 4½ p. m. on the 15th; amount, 0.68 inch. 16th. Brilliant aurora at 9½ p. m. 18th. Rain in the night; amount, 0.40 inch. 19th. Snow from 3 to 5 p. m.; amount in water, 0.038 inch.
	2 p. m.	29. 551	47. 6	----------	Cu. st. 10	----------	SW. 4	------	
	9 p. m.	29. 352	40. 5	----------	Cu. 10	----------	SW. 12	------	
March 15	7 a. m.	28. 952	55. 3	----------	Cu. 10	----------	SW. 10	------	
	2 p. m.	28. 825	52. 8	----------	Nim. 10	----------	W. 1	------	
	9 p. m.	28. 936	36. 5	----------	Cu. 10	----------	N. 4	------	
March 16	7 a. m.	29. 242	34	----------	Cu. 10	----------	NW. 6	------	
	2 p. m.	29. 244	36	----------	Cu. 9	----------	NW. 4	------	
	9 p. m.	29. 527	30. 1	----------	0	----------	NW. 1	------	
March 17	7 a. m.	29. 603	32. 1	----------	St. 2	----------	N. 1	------	
	2 p. m.	29. 446	57. 4	----------	Cu. cir. 3	----------	SW. 2	------	
	9 p. m.	29. 306	49. 5	----------	Cu. cir. 9	----------	SW. 2	------	
March 18	7 a. m.	29. 108	44. 9	----------	Nim. 10	----------	S. 6	------	
	2 p. m.	28. 856	50. 6	----------	Nim. 10	----------	SW. 12	------	
	9 p. m.	28. 557	57. 5	----------	Cu. cir. 9	----------	S. 25	------	
March 19	7 a. m.	28. 267	39. 2	----------	Cu. 9	----------	S. 25	------	
	2 p. m.	28. 450	39. 2	----------	Cu. 8	----------	W. 16	------	
	9 p. m.	28. 655	33. 5	----------	----------	----------	N. 18	------	

STORM No. 1, MARCH, 1859.

WATERFORD, NEW YORK.

Month and day.	Hour.	Barom'r corrected to 32° F.	Thermometer.	Force of vapor.	Cloudiness.	Motion of clouds.	Winds.	Relative humidity.	REMARKS.
March 14	7 a. m.	30.25	31		0		E		14th. Rain in the night.
	2 p. m.	30.19	54		0		SW		18th. Rain in the night; amount, 1.24 inch.
	9 p. m.	30.03	45		0				
March 15	7 a. m.	29.61	49		10		S.		
	2 p. m.	29.49	47		10		NW		
	9 p. m.	29.58	45		6				
March 16	7 a. m.	29.84	35		10		W.		
	2 p. m.	30.00	42		5		W.		
	9 p. m.	30.19	34		0				
March 17	7 a. m.	30.23	38		0		NE		
	2 p. m.	30.13	56		0		S.		
	9 p. m.	29.99	51		0				
March 18	7 a. m.	29.83	45		10		S.		
	2 p. m.	29.46	53		10		SE.		
	9 p. m.	29.19	60		0				
March 19	7 a. m.	28.94	48		7		S.		
	2 p. m.	29.11	48		10		S. 5		
	9 p. m.	29.34	34		10				

WEST DAY, NEW YORK.

Month and day.	Hour.	Barom'r corrected to 32° F.	Thermometer.	Force of vapor.	Cloudiness.	Motion of clouds.	Winds.	Relative humidity.	REMARKS.
March 14	7 a. m.		30		0		W. 1		14th. Rain at 8 p. m.
	2 p. m.		45		Nim. 9	S. 1	SE. 3		16th. Northern lights, very beautiful, red predominating.
	9 p. m.		34		Nim. 10	S. 3	S.		17th. Solar halo at 10 a. m.
March 15	7 a. m.		29		Cu. 7	W. 2	W. 2		18th. Heavy rain most of the day.
	2 p. m.		40		Cu. 4	W. 3	W. 2		19th. Snow squalls during the day, commencing with sleet and ending in snow; wind furious.
	9 p. m.		30		Nim. 8	W. 3	W.		
March 16	7 a. m.		27		Nim. 10	W. 3	W. 5		
	2 p. m.		40		Cu. 4	W. 3	W. 3		
	9 p. m.		46		0		W.		
March 17	7 a. m.		28		Cir. 2		SW. 1		
	2 p. m.		46		Cir. cu. 9		S. 2		
	9 p. m.		50		Nim. 10	S. 1	S.		
March 18	7 a. m.		44		Nim. 10	S. 4	S. 4		
	2 p. m.		46		Nim. 10	SE	SE. 3		
	9 p. m.		26		Nim. 10		SE		
March 19	7 a. m.		38		Nim. 2	SW. 4	SW. 4		
	2 p. m.		30		Nim. 10	W. 5	W. 5		
	9 p. m.		24		Nim. 10	W. 5	W.		

WILSON, NEW YORK.

Month and day.	Hour.	Barom'r corrected to 32° F.	Thermometer.	Force of vapor.	Cloudiness.	Motion of clouds.	Winds.	Relative humidity.	REMARKS.
March 14	7 a. m.		39		St. 10		E. 2		14th. Rain from 1.5 p. m. to 3.30 p. m., and at midnight.
	2 p. m.		50		Nim. 10		SW. 1		16th. Faint aurora between 9 and 10 p. m.
	9 p. m.		57		Cir. cu. 10	SW. 2	S. 4		19th. Rain in the night.
March 15	7 a. m.		42		Nim. 10	SW. 3	SW. 2		
	2 p. m.								
	9 p. m.								
March 16	7 a. m.		34		Nim. 9	NW. 4	W. 4		
	2 p. m.		38				WSW. 3		
	9 p. m.		33		Cir. 1		WSW. 1		
March 17	7 a. m.		35		St. 10		S. 1		
	2 p. m.		46		Nim. 9	W. 2	E. 3		
	9 p. m.								
March 18	7 a. m.		47		Nim. 10	SW. 3	SE. 2		
	2 p. m.		58		Nim. 10	SW. 3	SW. 3		
	9 p. m.		42		Nim. 10		NE. 2		
March 19	7 a. m.		32		Nim. 10		W. 8		
	2 p. m.		32		Nim. 10	W	W. 7		
	9 p. m.		32		Cu. 9	NW. 3	NW. 6		

STORM No. 1, MARCH, 1859.

PENN YAN, NEW YORK.

Month and day.	Hour.	Barom'r corrected to 32° F.	Thermometer.	Force of vapor.	Cloudiness.	Motion of clouds.	Winds.	Relative humidity.	REMARKS.
March 14	Sunrise.	29. 63	26	----------	10	----------	S.----------	------	14th. Rain and snow; amount, 0. 04 inch.
	2 p. m.	29. 40	55	----------	4	----------	S.----------	------	17th. Amount of rain, 0.74 inch.
	Sunset.	29. 27	49	----------	0	----------	SE.----------	------	18th. Snow; amount in water, 0. 05 inch.
March 15	Sunrise.	28. 94	44	----------	0	----------	S.----------	------	
	2 p. m.	29. 05	42	----------	0	----------	NW.----------	------	
	Sunset	29. 19	36	----------	0	----------	NW.----------	------	
March 16	Sunrise.	29. 45	31	----------	0	----------	W.----------	------	
	2 p. m.	29. 51	46	----------	8	----------	W.----------	------	
	Sunset.	29. 60	34	----------	6	----------	W.----------	------	
March 17	Sunrise.	29. 62	27	----------	8	----------	SW.----------	------	
	2 p. m.	29. 47	65	----------	9	----------	S.----------	------	
	Sunset.	29. 43	54	----------	0	----------	S.----------	------	
March 18	Sunrise.	29. 07	48	----------	0	----------	S.----------	------	
	2 p. m.	28. 80	69	----------	0	----------	S.----------	------	
	Sunset.	28. 63	57	----------	0	----------	S.----------	------	
March 19	Sunrise.	28. 40	38	----------	0	----------	SW.----------	------	
	2 p. m.	28. 65	52	----------	0	----------	W.----------	------	
	Sunset.	28. 85	31	----------	0	----------	W.----------	------	

CLINTON, NEW YORK.

Month and day.	Hour.	Barom'r corrected to 32° F.	Thermometer.	Force of vapor.	Cloudiness.	Motion of clouds.	Winds.	Relative humidity.	REMARKS.
March 14	7 a. m.	------	27	. 129	0	----------	NW. 1	88	Rain from 6 p. m. the 14th to 7 a. m. on the 15th; amount, 0. 18 inch.
	2 p. m.	------	49	. 152	Nim. 10	----------	E. 2	44	16th. Snow till 9 a. m.
	9 p. m.	------	48	. 212	Nim. 10	S. 4	SW. 4	63	18th. Rain most of the day; amount, 0. 35 inch.
March 15	7 a. m.	------	46	. 286	Nim. 10	SW. 3	SW. 2	92	19th. Snow.
	2 p. m.	------	45	. 182	Nim. 10	NW. 3	NW. 4	61	20th. Snow till noon.
	9 p. m.	------	38	. 186	Nim. 10	NW. 3	NW. 3	81	
March 16	7 a. m.	------	32	. 162	Nim. 10	NW. 4	NW. 4	89	
	2 p. m.	------	39	. 131	Nim. 5	NW. 4	NW. 5	55	
	9 p. m.	------	30	. 148	0		NW. 3	89	
March 17	7 a. m.	------	32	. 125	0	----------	N. 1	69	
	2 p. m.	------	60	. 203	Nim. 8	S. 3	SE. 2	39	
	9 p. m.	------	43	. 209	Nim. 10	----------	SE. 2	75	
March 18	7 a. m.	------	44	. 265	Nim. 10	SE. 3	NE. 2	92	
	2 p. m.	------	52	. 334	Nim. 10	SE. 3	E. 2	86	
	9 p. m.	------	52	. 334	Nim. 8	{ Up SW. 3 L. SE. 4 }	E. 3	86	
March 19	7 a. m.	------	42	. 134	Nim. 10	SW. 4	SW. 6	50	
	2 p. m.	------	35	. 162	Nim. 10	W. 4	W. 6	80	
	9 p. m.	------	28	. 117	Nim. 10	W. 4	W. 6	76	

LAMBERTVILLE, NEW JERSEY.

Month and day.	Hour.	Barom'r corrected to 32° F.	Thermometer.	Force of vapor.	Cloudiness.	Motion of clouds.	Winds.	Relative humidity.	REMARKS.
March 14	7 a. m.	30. 18	36. 5	----------	10	----------	ENE. 1	------	Rain from 6¼ p. m. the 14th to 11 a. m. on the 15th; amount, 1. 075 inch.
	2 p. m.	30. 15	59	----------	9	----------	ESE. 2	------	18th. Began to rain before day, and ended in the night; am't, 0. 530 inch.
	9 p. m.	30. 02	47. 2	----------	10	----------	SE. 2	------	
March 15	7 a. m.	29. 70	57. 5	----------	----------	----------	S. 2	------	
	2 p. m.	29. 57	60	----------	0	----------	NW. 1	------	
	9 p. m.	29. 66	45. 2	----------	0	----------	NW. 3	------	
March 16	7 a. m.	29. 96	39. 2	----------	0	----------	NW. 1	------	
	2 p. m.	30. 08	51	----------	0	----------	NW. 1	------	
	9 p. m.	30. 22	38. 1	----------	1	----------	W. 1	------	
March 17	7 a. m.	30. 23	32. 5	----------	0	----------	W. 1	------	
	2 p. m.	30. 21	62. 1	----------	9	----------	SW. 1	------	
	9 p. m.	30. 12	47. 5	----------	10	----------	SSE. 1	------	
March 18	7 a. m.	29. 74	52	----------	9	----------	SE. 3	------	
	2 p. m.	29. 51	63. 2	----------	6	----------	S. 2	------	
	9 p. m.	29. 30	56. 2	----------	0	----------	SSW. 2	------	
March 19	7 a. m.	29. 24	41. 5	----------	0	----------	WSW. 2	------	
	2 p. m.	29. 39	41. 8	----------	0	----------	W. 3	------	
	9 p. m.	29. 58	39. 2	----------	1	----------	NW. 3	------	

STORM No. 1, MARCH, 1859.

FREEHOLD, NEW JERSEY.

Month and day.	Hour.	Barom'r corrected to 32° F.	Thermometer.	Force of vapor.	Cloudiness.	Motion of clouds.	Winds.	Relative humidity.	REMARKS.
March 14	7 a. m.	......	44	......	......	......	......	......	
	2 p. m.	......	56	......	......	......	......	......	
	9 p. m.	......	48	......	......	......	......	......	
March 15	7 a. m.	......	56	......	......	......	......	......	
	2 p. m.	......	57	......	......	......	......	......	
	9 p. m.	......	52	......	......	......	......	......	
March 16	7 a. m.	......	40	......	......	......	......	......	
	2 p. m.	......	52	......	......	......	......	......	
	9 p. m.	......	44	......	......	......	......	......	
March 17	7 a. m.	......	40	......	......	......	......	......	
	2 p. m.	......	56	......	......	......	......	......	
	9 p. m.	......	48	......	......	......	......	......	
March 18	7 a. m.	......	52	......	......	......	......	......	
	2 p. m.	......	62	......	......	......	......	......	
	9 p. m.	......	57	......	......	......	......	......	
March 19	7 a. m.	......	......	......	......	......	......	......	
	2 p. m.	......	......	......	......	......	......	......	
	9 p. m.	......	......	......	......	......	......	......	

MOORESTOWN, NEW JERSEY.

Month and day.	Hour.	Barom'r corrected to 32° F.	Thermometer.	Force of vapor.	Cloudiness.	Motion of clouds.	Winds.	Relative humidity.	REMARKS.
March 14	7 a. m.	29.98	40	......	Cir. 5	E.	E. 3	......	Rain from 5 p. m. the 14th to
	2 p. m.	29.98	50	......	10	......	E. 3	......	12¼ p. m. on the 15th.
	9 p. m.	29.88	50	......	10	......	E. 4	......	18th. Rain from 2 a. m. to 1
March 15	7 a. m.	29.48	45	......	10	......	SW. 2	......	p. m.
	2 p. m.	29.46	56	......	7	......	WSW. 2	......	
	9 p. m.	29.76	48	......	5	......	4	......	
March 16	7 a. m.	29.98	40	......	5	......	NNW. 3	......	
	2 p. m.	30.07	52	......	Cir. 1	SE. 1	W. 2	......	
	9 p. m.	30.06	40	......	0	......	2	......	
March 17	7 a. m.	29.98	40	......	Cir. 1	......	W. 1	......	
	2 p. m.	29.96	60	......	9	......	S. 1	......	
	9 p. m.	29.98	48	......	7	......	W. 3	......	
March 18	7 a. m.	29.49	50	......	10	......	SSE. 5	......	
	2 p. m.	29.36	63	......	Cu. 8	NW. 10	SSE. 4	......	
	9 p. m.	29.17	55	......	5	......	SE. 5	......	
March 19	7 a. m.	29.05	43	......	7	NW. 5	SSE. 4	......	
	2 p. m.	29.36	41	......	Nim. 10	5	WNW. 5	......	
	9 p. m.	29.48	40	......	Nim. 10	......	NW. 5	......	

NEWARK, NEW JERSEY.

Month and day.	Hour.	Barom'r corrected to 32° F.	Thermometer.	Force of vapor.	Cloudiness.	Motion of clouds.	Winds.	Relative humidity.	REMARKS.
March 14	7 a. m.	30.20	......	......	......	......	NE. 2	......	Rain from 7½ p. m. the 14th to
	6 p. m.	30.12	......	......	......	......	SE. 2	......	12 m. on the 15th; amount,
March 15	7 a. m.	29.69	......	......	......	......	S. 2	......	1.36 inch.
	6 p. m.	29.47	......	......	......	......	NW. 2	......	18th. Rain from early morn to
March 16	7 a. m.	30.00	......	......	......	......	NW. 3	......	11 a. m.; amount, 0.73 inch.
	6 p. m.	30.08	......	......	......	......	NW. 2	......	
March 17	7 a. m.	30.21	......	......	......	......	SW. 2	......	
	6 p. m.	30.09	......	......	......	......	SW. 3	......	
March 18	7 a. m.	29.75	......	......	......	......	SE. to S. 4	......	
	6 p. m.	29.46	......	......	......	......	S. to SW. 4	......	
March 19	7 a. m.	29.19	......	......	......	......	WSW. 6	......	
	6 p. m.	29.41	......	......	......	......	SW. 5	......	

STORM No. 1, MARCH, 1859.

BELLEFONTE, PENNSYLVANIA.

Month and day.	Hour.	Barom'r corrected to 32° F.	Thermometer.	Force of vapor.	Cloudiness.	Motion of clouds.	Winds.	Relative humidity.	REMARKS.
March 14	7 a. m.	------	37	------	Cir. st. 3	SW. 2	N. 12	------	Rain from 12½ p. m. the 14th to 3 a. m. on the 15th.
	2 p. m.	------	52	------	Cir. st. 8	W. 4	S. 4	------	
	9 p. m.	------	52	------	Cir. st. 10	W. 4	S. 12	------	Rain from 8 p. m. the 17th to 10 p. m. on the 18th.
March 15	7 a. m.	------	46	------	Nim. 8	NW. 3	SW. 4	------	
	2 p. m.	------	50	------	0	0	W. 25	------	
	9 p. m.	------	42	------	0	0	W. 12	------	
March 16	7 a. m.	------	40	------	Cir. st. 6	0	W. 12	------	
	2 p. m.	------	52	------	Cir. 8	NW. 2	W. 12	------	
	9 p. m.	------	36	------	Nim. 10	0	W. 4	------	
March 17	7 a. m.	------	32	------	Nim. 10	S. 1	SW. 2	------	
	2 p. m.	------	62	------	Nim. 9	S. 5	S. 4	------	
	9 p. m.	------	50	------	Nim. 10	S. 6	0	------	
March 18	7 a. m.	------	50	------	Nim. 10	NW. 4	S. 2	------	
	2 p. m.	------	58	------	Nim. 9	NW. 8	S. 2	------	
	9 p. m.	------	45	------	Nim. 10	NW. 4	NW. 35	------	
March 19	7 a. m.	------	36	------	Cir. 2	NW. 4	NW. 60	------	
	2 p. m.	------	40	------	0	0	W. 60	------	
	9 p. m.	------	40	------	0	0	W. 35	------	

BERWICK, PENNSYLVANIA.

Month and day.	Hour.	Barom'r corrected to 32° F.	Thermometer.	Force of vapor.	Cloudiness.	Motion of clouds.	Winds.	Relative humidity.	REMARKS.
March 14	7 a. m.	29. 50	38	. 178	Cir. st. 2	----------	E. 2	81	Rain from 7 p. m. the 14th to 4 a. m. on the 15th.
	2 p. m.	29. 50	55	. 206	Cir. st. 7	----------	E. 3	49	
	9 p. m.	29. 17	47	. 273	Nim. 10	----------	E. 5	85	Rain from 3 a. m. the 18th to 9 a. m. on the 19th.
March 15	7 a. m.	28. 92	53	. 348	Nim. 7	----------	N. 1	86	
	2 p. m.	28. 83	57	. 230	Cir. st. 6	----------	W. 4	51	
	9 p. m.	29. 00	44	. 173	Cu. st. 6	----------	W. 4	60	
March 16	7 a. m.	29. 17	42	. 177	Cu. st. 2	----------	E. 3	66	
	2 p. m.	29. 33	52	. 232	0	----------	E. 4	60	
	9 p. m.	29. 50	56	. 083	0	----------	E. 2	19	
March 17	7 a. m.	29. 50	43	. 209	0	----------	SW. 1	75	
	2 p. m.	29. 50	63	. 340	Cu. st. 2	----------	SW. 3	61	
	9 p. m.	29. 33	54	. 362	Nim. 5	----------	S. 5	87	
March 18	7 a. m.	28. 83	55	. 349	Nim. 10	----------	E. 7	81	
	2 p. m.	28. 67	63	. 491	Nim. 10	----------	SE. 5	88	
	9 p. m.	28. 42	54	. 362	Nim. 10	----------	NW. 5	87	
March 19	7 a. m.	28. 42	41	. 190	Nim. 10	----------	W. 6	74	
	2 p. m.	28. 58	40	. 160	Nim. 10	----------	W. 7	64	
	9 p. m.	28. 75	37	. 136	Nim. 9	----------	W. 5	62	

CANNONSBURG, PENNSYLVANIA.

Month and day.	Hour.	Barom'r corrected to 32° F.	Thermometer.	Force of vapor.	Cloudiness.	Motion of clouds.	Winds.	Relative humidity.	REMARKS.
March 14	7 a. m.	28. 74	48	------	Overcast 10	----------	E. 1	------	14th. Rain from 8½ a. m. to 12 m.; amount, 0. 175 inch.
	2 p. m.	28. 52	56	------	Overcast 10	----------	SE. 5	------	
	9 p. m.	28. 39	55	------	Mottled 9	----------	SE. 5	------	17th. Rain at 5 p. m.; amount, 0. 345 inch.
March 15	7 a. m.	28. 44	44	------	0	----------	NW. 3	------	
	2 p. m.	28. 54	40	------	Overcast 10	----------	NW. 5	------	18th. Thunder, rain, and hail, with strong wind from SW., 3 to 3½ p. m.; amount, 0. 45 inch.
	9 p. m.	28. 75	37	------	Overcast 10	----------	NW. 5	------	
March 16	7 a. m.	29. 01	34	------	0	----------	W. 2	------	
	2 p. m.	29. 01	53	------	0	----------	W. 2	------	
	9 p. m.	29. 02	47	------	Cir. 1	----------	NE. 1	------	
March 17	7 a. m.	28. 90	40	------	Overcast 10	----------	E. 1	------	
	2 p. m.	28. 78	56	------	Overcast 10	----------	SW. 1	------	
	9 p. m.	28. 66	55	------	Overcast 10	----------	SE. 2	------	
March 18	7 a. m.	28. 27	53	------	Overcast 10	----------	S. 2	------	
	2 p. m.	------	------	------	St. & cir. cu. 9	----------	SW. 3	------	
	9 p. m.	28. 01	42	------	Overcast 9	----------	SW. 7	------	
March 19	7 a. m.	28. 19	30	------	Overcast 10	----------	W. 7	------	
	2 p. m.	28. 39	30	------	Overcast 10	----------	W. 6	------	
	9 p. m.	28. 61	29	------	Overcast 10	----------	W. 6	------	

STORM No. 1, MARCH, 1859.

CARLISLE, PENNSYLVANIA.

Month and day.	Hour.	Barom'r corrected to 32° F.	Thermometer.	Force of vapor.	Cloudiness.	Motion of clouds.	Winds.	Relative humidity.	REMARKS.
March 14	7 a. m.	29. 32	42. 5	. 193	St. 10	0	0	71	14th. Began to rain at 2 p. m. and ended in the night; amount, 0. 772 inch.
	2 p. m.	29. 25	56	. 282	Nim. 10	SE. 1	SE. 1	63	
	9 p. m.	29. 00	47	. 298	Rain 10	----------	0	92	
March 15	7 a. m.	28. 80	54	. 282	Cir. st. 8	W. 1	W. 1	67	Rain from 9½ p. m. the 17th till in the night of the 18th; amount, 1. 56 inch.
	2 p. m.	28. 76	55	. 168	Cu. st. 5	W. 2	W. 3	39	
	9 p. m.	28. 97	43. 5	. 202	Cu. 10	NW. 4	NW. 4	71	
March 16	7 a. m.	29. 24	38	. 103	Cir. st 2	NW. 2	NW. 3	45	
	2 p. m.	29. 30	53	. 146	0	----------	NW. 2	36	
	9 p. m.	29. 36	42	. 134	0	----------	0	50	
March 17	7 a. m.	29. 37	36	. 170	Hazy, cir st. 10	0	SE. 1	80	
	2 p. m.	29. 23	60	. 177	Hazy -------	----------	SE. 1	34	
	9 p. m.	29. 18	58	. 255	Hazy -------	----------	0	53	
March 18	7 a. m.	28. 63	52	. 334	Nim. 10	SE. 2	SE. 1	86	
	2 p. m.	28. 54	67	. 522	Cir. cu. 9	SE. 2	SE. 1	79	
	9 p. m.	28. 30	52	. 334	Cu. st. 9	SE. 2	SE. 2	86	
March 19	7 a. m.	28. 38	40	. 118	Cir. cu. 10	SW. 3	SW. 4	48	
	2 p. m.	28. 51	40	. 139	Cir. cu. 10	SW. 3	SW. 4	56	
	9 p. m.	28. 67	37	. 116	Cir. cu. 10	W. 2	W. 3	53	

FLEMING, PENNSYLVANIA.

Month and day.	Hour.	Barom'r corrected to 32° F.	Thermometer.	Force of vapor.	Cloudiness.	Motion of clouds.	Winds.	Relative humidity.	REMARKS.
March 14	7 a. m.	------	34	------	Cir. st. 10	0	SW. 1	------	14th. Rain from 12 m. to 10 p. m.; amount, 0. 50 inch.
	2 p. m.	------	54	------	Nim. 10	S. 3	SW. 2	------	
	9 p. m.	------	50	------	Nim. 10	0	SE. 1	------	Constant rain from 9 p. m. the 17th to 10 p. m. on the 18th; amount, 1. 40 inch.
March 15	7 a. m.	------	40	------	0	----------	NW. 1	------	
	2 p. m.	------	46	------	Nim. 10	W. 2	NW. 3	------	
	9 p. m.	------	42	------	Nim. 10	W. 3	NW. 5	------	
March 16	7 a. m.	------	35	------	Cu. 4	NW. 2	NW. 2	------	
	2 p. m.	------	53	------	0	----------	NW. 2	------	
	9 p. m.	------	35	------	0	----------	NW. 1	------	
March 17	7 a. m.	------	28	------	Cir. 5	W. 1	E. 2	------	
	2 p. m.	------	64	------	Cir. st. 8	NW. 1	E. 2	------	
	9 p. m.	------	55	------	Nim. 10	W. 2	NW. 2	------	
March 18	7 a. m.	------	49	------	Nim. 10	NW. 3	------------	----	
	2 p. m.	------	62	------	------------	----------	------------	------	
	9 p. m.	------	47	------	------------	----------	------------	------	
March 19	7 a. m.	------	36	------	------------	----------	------------	------	
	2 p. m.	------	36	------	------------	----------	------------	------	
	9 p. m.	------	32	------	------------	----------	------------	------	

GETTYSBURG, PENNSYLVANIA.

Month and day.	Hour.	Barom'r corrected to 32° F.	Thermometer.	Force of vapor.	Cloudiness.	Motion of clouds.	Winds.	Relative humidity.	REMARKS.
March 14	7 a. m.	29. 65	38	------	Cir. st. 10	W. 1	NE. 1	------	14th. Rain from 1 to 11 p. m.; amount, 0. 885, inch.
	2 p. m.	29. 55	53	------	Cir. st. 10	SSW. 2	SE. 1	------	
	9 p. m.	29. 29	50	------	10	E -------	NE. 1	------	16th. Aurora at 10 p. m.; red streamers N. and NW.; soon rendered invisible by the brightness of the moon; there were two narrow bands of cirrus clouds, one 45° the other 95°, stretching from E. to W. above the horizon, at the same time a lunar halo was visible.
March 15	7 a. m.	29. 12	54	------	Cu. st. 8	SSW. 3	W. 1	------	
	2 p. m.	29. 07	52	------	Cu. 3	W. 3	NW. 3	------	
	9 p. m.	29. 31	43	------	Cu. 10	WNW. 3	WNW. 3	------	
March 16	7 a. m.	29. 56	36	------	Cu. 0	NW. 1	NW. 1	------	
	2 p. m.	29. 62	54	------	0	----------	NW. 3	------	
	9 p. m.	29. 70	38	------	0	----------	NE. 1	------	
March 17	7 a. m.	29. 69	33	------	Cir. st. 2	W. 2	SW. 1	------	
	2 p. m.	29. 56	63	------	Cir. st. 5	W. 1	SW. 2	------	
	9 p. m.	29. 48	50	------	Cir. st. 10	W. 1	SSE. 1	------	Rain from 8 p. m. the 17th to 9 p. m. on the 18th; amount, 0.975 inch.
March 18	7 a. m.	28. 95	52	------	Cu. st. 10	SSE. 2	SSE. 2	------	
	2 p. m.	28. 74	66	------	Cu. st. 10	SSW. 2	SW. 2	------	
	9 p. m.	28. 63	50	------	Cu. 10	SSW. 3	SSW. 3	------	Rain from 6 to 8 p. m. the 18th; amount, 0.114 inch.
March 19	7 a. m.	28. 76	38	------	Cu. st. 10	W. 3	SW. 3	------	
	2 p. m.	28. 97	38	------	Cu. st. 10	W. 3	WSW. 4	------	
	9 p. m.	29. 12	35	------	Cu. st. 10	W. 3	NW. 4	------	

STORM No. 1, MARCH, 1859.

HARRISBURG, PENNSYLVANIA.*

Month and day.	Hour.	Barom'r corrected to 32° F.	Thermometer.	Force of vapor.	Cloudiness.	Motion of clouds.	Winds.	Relative humidity.	REMARKS.
March 14	7 a. m.	29. 94	44	......	Nim. 9	E. 1	E. 1	......	Rain from 2¼ p. m. the 14th to 5¼ a. m. on the 15th; amount, 0. 848 inch. 18th. Rain, ending at 1½ p. m.; amount, 1. 133 inch.
	2 p. m.	29. 86	57	......	10	....	E. 2	......	
	9 p. m.	29. 61	51	......	10	....	SE. 1	......	
March 15	7 a. m.	29. 39	59	......	Cir. st. 8	0	0	......	
	2 p. m.	29. 33	57	......	Cir. st. 8	NW. 3	NW. 3	......	
	9 p. m.	.9. 57	47	......	Cu. st. 6	NW. 5	NW. 5	......	
March 16	7 a. m.	29. 82	42	......	Cu. 3	NW. 3	NW. 2	......	
	2 p. m.	29. 89	55	......	0	....	NW. 2	......	
	9 p. m.	29. 96	48	......	0	....	NW. 1	......	
March 17	7 a. m.	29. 97	39	......	Cir. st. 6	E. 1	E. 1	......	
	2 p. m.	29. 85	61	......	Cir. st. 5	S. 2	S. 2	......	
	9 p. m.	29. 80	55	......	10	....	SE. 1	......	
March 18	7 a. m.	29. 37	55	......	10	....	SE. 1	......	
	2 p. m.	29. 10	63	......	10	....	S. 2	......	
	9 p m.	28. 87	56	......	10	....	S. 1	......	
March 19	7 a. m.	29. 00	43	......	10	....	NW. 3	......	
	2 p. m.	29. 16	42	......	10	....	NW. 4	......	
	9 p. m.	29. 38	40	......	Cu. st. 9	NW. 5	NW. 5	......	

HARRISBURG, PENNSYLVANIA.†

Month and day.	Hour.	Barom'r corrected to 32° F.	Thermometer.	Force of vapor.	Cloudiness.	Motion of clouds.	Winds.	Relative humidity.	REMARKS.
March 14	7 a. m.	29. 91	41	. 180	Nim. 10	....	E.---- ------	69. 5	Rain from 2½ p. m. the 14th to 3 a. m. on the 15th; amount, 0. 92 inch. 17th. Rain at 10 p. m., continued till 11½ a. m. on the 18th, began again at 7 p. m. and ended at 2½ a. m. on the 19th; amount, 1. 53 inch; very high wind during the night of the 18th.
	2 p. m.	29. 99	57	. 216	Nim. 10	....	NE. 1	46	
	9 p. m.	29. 90	48	. 310	Rain 10	....	NE. 1	92	
March 15	7 a. m.	29. 79	58	. 394	Cu. 10	E.---- ----	W.----------	82	
	2 p. m.	29. 64	57	. 118	Cir. cu. 8	E.---- ----	W. 2	25	
	9 p. m.	29. 64	45. 5	. 245	Nim. 10	E.---- ----	W. 3	80	
March 16	7 a. m.	29. 81	40. 5	. 111	Cir. st. 9	E.---- ----	W. 2	44	
	2 p. m.	29. 85	52	. 113	0	....	W. 2	29	
	9 p. m.	29. 92	44	. 173	Cir. 1	....	W.----------	60	
March 17	7 a. m.	29. 96	36. 5	. 143	Cir. 7	....	N.----------	66	
	2 p. m.	29. 89	62	. 202	Cir. 4	....	SE. 1	36	
	9 p. m.	30. 01	53	. 244	Nim. 10	....	SE. 1	60	
March 18	7 a. m.	29. 66	54	. 390	Rain 10	....	E. 1	93	
	2 p. m.	29. 33	64	. 497	Nim. 10	N. 3	SE. 2	83	
	9 p. m.	29. 24	54	. 335	Nim. 10	....	SW. 1	80	
March 19	7 a. m.	29. 20	42	. 134	Cir. st. 10	E.---- ----	SW. 3	50	
	2 p. m.	29. 19	40	. 139	Nim. 10	NE ---- --	NW. 3	56	
	9 p. m.	29. 34	39	. 090	10	....	NW. 3 to 5	38	

LEWISBURG, PENNSYLVANIA.

Month and day.	Hour.	Barom'r corrected to 32° F.	Thermometer.	Force of vapor.	Cloudiness.	Motion of clouds.	Winds.	Relative humidity.	REMARKS.
March 14	7 a. m.	29. 713	31. 5	. 162	Cr. st., cr. cu. 5	W. 5	0	91	Began to rain at 3 p. m. the 14th and ended in the night of the 15th; amount, 0. 98 inch. 18th. About 8 p. m. the wind blew a hurricane; commenced raining in the night, and ended in the night of the 19th; amount, 1. 69 inch.
	2 p. m.	29. 716	55	. 193	Cr. cu., cr. st. 7	W. 3	W. 3	44	
	9 p. m.	29. 724	47. 7	. 304	0	....	0	91	
March 15	7 a. m.	29. 723	48. 3	. 269	Cr. cu., nim. 10	....	W. 1	79	
	2 p. m.	29. 626	51. 8	. 136	Cu st., nim. 10	S. 6	SE. 3	35	
	9 p. m.	29. 367	41. 5	. 132	Nim. 10	....	SE. 3	50	
March 16	7 a. m.	29. 179	37. 8	. 106	Cu. st., cr. cu., cir. st. 7	S. 3	S. 1	47	
	2 p. m.	29. 128	51. 8	. 107	Cu. st., nim. 10	SW. 4	W. 6	28	
	9 p. m.	29 345	37. 3	. 155	10	....	NW. 4	70	
March 17	7 a. m.	29. 629	30. 1	. 168	Cu. st., nim. 9	....	N. 4	100	
	2 p. m.	29. 681	60. 5	. 165	0	....	NW. 3	31	
	9 p. m.	29. 743	52. 9	. 230	0	....	0	57	
March 18	7 a. m.	29. 789	51. 1	. 355	Cr. st., cr. cu. 8	Hazy -----	0	94	
	2 p. m.	29. 601	57. 7	. 444	Nim., cir. 9	....	S. 4	93	
	9 p. m.	29. 536	49. 5	. 306	10	....	S. 3	86	
March 19	7 a. m.	29. 135	40	. 152	Nim. 10	....	0	61	
	2 p. m.	28. 862	39	. 137	Nim. 10	....	0	58	
	9 p. m.	28. 652	36. 3	. 110	Nim. 10	....	....	52	

* Heisley, observer.

† Hickok, observer.

STORM No. 1, MARCH, 1859.

CHAMBERSBURG, PENNSYLVANIA.

Month and day.	Hour.	Barom'r corrected to 32° F.	Thermometer.	Force of vapor.	Cloudiness.	Motion of clouds.	Winds.	Relative humidity.	REMARKS.
March 14	7 a. m.	29. 452	44	. 322	St. 10	W. 1	Calm	69. 2	
	2 p. m.	29. 398	54	. 489	Nim. 10	E. 1	N. 1	74	
	9 p. m.	29. 027	50	. 524	Nim. 10	S. 4	E. 3	66. 8	
March 15	7 a. m.	29. 098	52	. 476	Cir. cu. 6	S. 2	E. 1	69. 5	
	2 p. m.	29. 072	58	. 449	Cu. st. 7	W. 2	E. 2	61. 3	
	9 p. m.	29. 241	45	. 482	Cu. st. 10	W. 2	Calm	65. 8	
March 16	7 a. m.	29. 446	49	. 403	Cir. 2	W. 2	E. 3	67. 5	
	2 p. m.	29. 546	54	. 411	Clear	....	E. 2	60. 1	
	9 p. m.	29. 558	40	. 393	Clear	....	Calm	59. 5	
March 17	7 a. m.	29. 546	38	. 411	Cir. st. 9	W. 1	Calm	60. 1	
	2 p. m.	29. 396	64	. 443	Cir. st. 9	W. 1	N. 1	64. 7	
	9 p. m.	29. 291	51	. 462	Nim. 10	E. 1	W. 1	65	
March 18	7 a. m.	28. 895	50	. 529	Nim. 9	S. 2	N. 1	74. 7	
	2 p. m.	28. 612	68	. 532	Nim. 10	S. 2	N. 1	63. 4	
	9 p. m.	28. 514	50	. 516	Nim. 10	SW. 2	W. 3	70. 4	
March 19	7 a. m.	28. 635	38	. 451	Cu. st. 10	W. 1	W. 2	73. 1	
	2 p. m.	28. 848	38	. 457	Nim. 10	W. 2	W. 3	69	
	9 p. m.	29. 053	36	. 420	Nim. 10	W. 3	E. 1	68	

LINDEN, PENNSYLVANIA.

Month and day.	Hour.	Barom'r corrected to 32° F.	Thermometer.	Force of vapor.	Cloudiness.	Motion of clouds.	Winds.	Relative humidity.	REMARKS.
March 14	7 a. m.	......	......	......	....	....	....	......	Began to rain at 2½ p. m. the 14th and ended before 7 a. m. on the 15th—high wind in the night; amount, 0. 265 inch.
	1 p. m.	29. 515	50	. 239	Rain 10	....	E. 3	65	17th. Frost.
	9 p. m.	29. 312	47	. 285	Rain 10	....	E. 4	85	18th. Rain from early morn to 11 a. m., 4 to 8 p. m., and in the night; amount, 1. 83 inch; at 4 p. m., wind S.; 7 p. m, wind W. Barometer, 28. 60.
March 15	7 a. m.	29. 180	44. 5	. 251	3	....	W. ½	84	19th. Flakes of snow at intervals during the day.
	1 p. m.	29. 104	50	. 156	10	....	W. 5	42	
	9 p. m.	29. 324	40	. 154	10	....	W. 5	61	
March 16	7 a. m.	29. 611	36	. 116	10	....	W. 4	53	
	1 p. m.	29. 656	48	. 139	0	....	W. 3	39	
	9 p. m.	29. 744	35. 5	. 184	0	....	W. ¼	85	
March 17	7 a. m.	29. 763	29	. 148	Hazy 6	....	0	89	
	1 p. m.	29. 618	59	. 177	Hazy 9	....	SE. 3	34	
	9 p. m.	29. 505	53	. 237	10	....	SE. 3	58	
March 18	7 a. m.	29. 110	51	. 361	Rain 10	....	NE. 3	93	
	1 p. m.	28. 911	56	. 407	Fog 10	....	NE. 2	87	
	9 p. m.	28. 639	48	. 297	10	....	W. 4	85	
March 19	7 a. m.	28. 652	37. 5	. 180	• 10	....	W. 6	77	
	1 p. m.	......	......	......	....	....	....	......	
	9 p. m.	......	......	......	....	....	....	......	

MORRISVILLE, PENNSYLVANIA.

Month and day.	Hour.	Barom'r corrected to 32° F.	Thermometer.	Force of vapor.	Cloudiness.	Motion of clouds.	Winds.	Relative humidity.	REMARKS.
March 14	7 a. m.	30. 32	38	......	Cir. 1	SW. 1	E. 2	......	Rain from 6 p. m. the 14th to 2 p. m. the 15th—gale of wind in the night; amount, 1. 20 inch.
	2 p. m.	30. 28	60	......	Cir. 5	SW. 1	SE. 2	......	16th. Solar halo.
	9 p. m.	30. 08	49	......	Nim. 10	SE. 3	SE. 2	......	18th. Rain, with high wind, from 3 a. m. to 10 p. m.; amount, 0. 50 inch.
March 15	7 a. m.	29. 80	58	......	Nim. 10	S. 4	S. 4	......	
	2 p. m.	29. 57	58	......	Nim. 9	SW. 3	E. 1	......	
	9 p. m.	29. 87	46	......	Cu. 5	SW. 4	NW. 4	......	
March 16	7 a. m.	30. 13	40	......	Cir. st. 5	NW. 4	NW. 4	......	
	2 p. m.	30. 20	52	......	Cu. 2	NW. 3	NW. 3	......	
	9 p. m.	30. 33	40	......	0	....	W. 1	......	
March 17	7 a. m.	30. 35	34	......	Cir. 1	W. 1	W. 1	......	
	2 p. m.	30. 28	62	......	Cir. 3	W. 1	S. 2	......	
	9 p. m.	30. 20	46	......	Cir. 5	SW. 2	SE. 2	......	
March 18	7 a. m.	29. 88	53	......	Nim. 10	SE. 3	SE. 3	......	
	2 p. m.	29. 58	63	......	Nim. 10	SE. 4	SE. 4	......	
	9 p. m.	29. 38	59	......	Nim. 10	SW. 6	S. 6	......	
March 19	7 a. m.	29. 37	41	......	Cir. 5	SW. 4	SW. 4	......	
	2 p. m.	29. 47	42	......	Cu. 5	W. 4	W. 4	......	
	9 p. m.	29. 67	39	......	Cu. 5	W. 4	W. 4	......	

STORM No. 1, MARCH, 1859.

MOUNT JOY, PENNSYLVANIA.

Month and day.	Hour.	Barom'r corrected to 32° F.	Thermometer.	Force of vapor.	Cloudiness.	Motion of clouds.	Winds.	Relative humidity.	REMARKS.
March 14	7 a. m.	29. 82	42	------	Nim. 9	Thin------	------------	------	Rain from 4½ p. m. the 14th to 7 a. m. on the 15th; amount, 0.32 inch.
	2 p. m.	29. 73	62	------	9	SE. 2	SE. 1	------	18th. Rain from 1 a. m. to 7 p. m.; amount, 0.70 inch.
	9 p. m.	29. 50	54	------	Nim. 10	----------	SE. 3	------	
March 15	7 a. m.	29. 29	62	------	Nim. 9	----------	------------	------	
	2 p. m.	29. 24	64	------	2	----------	NW. 2	------	
	9 p. m.	29. 46	49	------	5	----------	NW. 3	------	
March 16	7 a. m.	29. 82	42	------	3	----------	NW. 1	------	
	2 p. m.	29. 82	55	------		----------	1	------	
	9 p. m	29. 89	42	------	------------	----------	------------	------	
March 17	7 a. m.	29. 88	40	------	3	Thin------	SE. 1	------	
	2 p. m.	29. 78	60	------	10	Very thin..	SE. 2	------	
	9 p. m.	29. 73	54	------	Nim. 10	Thin------	------------	------	
March 18	7 a. m.	29. 24	57	------	Nim. 10	----------	3	------	
	2 p. m.	28. 75	73	------	7	----------	S. 2	------	
	9 p. m.	28. 82	61	------	8	----------	S. 2	------	
March 19	7 a. m.	28. 90	45	------	10	SW. 3	SW. 5	------	
	2 p. m.	29. 08	44	------	10	SW. 3	SW. 5	------	
	9 p. m.	29. 26	40	------	9	NW. 3	NW. 5	------	

MURRYSVILLE, PENNSYLVANIA.

Month and day.	Hour.	Barom'r corrected to 32° F.	Thermometer.	Force of vapor.	Cloudiness.	Motion of clouds.	Winds.	Relative humidity.	REMARKS.
March 14	7 a. m.	28. 71	38	. 165	Nim. 10	----------	SE. 2	72	14th. Rain from 9.30 a. m. to 2 p. m, and in the night; amount, 0.28 inch.
	2 p. m.	28. 57	56	. 336	10	SW. 1	SE. 3	75	15th. Rain; amount, 0.5 inch.
	9 p. m.	28. 36	57	. 322	Cu. nim. 8	SW. 2	S. 1	69	17th. Shower at 9 p. m.; amount, 0.05 inch.
March 15	7 a. m.	28. 39	47	. 133	0	----------	S. 2	41	18th. Rain from 3 to 7 p. m; amount, 0.56 inch. Rain and snow in the night; amount in water, 0.12 inch; barometer, 27.90 at 3¼ p. m.; wind W. at 3½ p. m.; strong from SW. at 4 p. m.; continued all night.
	2 p. m.	------	------	------	Cu. 9	SW. 2	SW. 2	------	19th. Slight snow during the day.
	9 p. m.	28. 70	37	. 199	0	----------	SW. 3	90	
March 16	7 a. m.	28. 92	37	. 116	0	----------	W. 1	53	
	2 p. m.	28. 90	49	. 107	0	----------	SW. 3	31	
	9 p. m.	28. 94	35	. 108	Nim. 10	SW. 2	0	53	
March 17	7 a. m.	28. 84	35	. 127	Nim. 10	----------	SE. 1	62	
	2 p. m.	28. 72	63	. 189	Nim. 10	----------	NE. 2	33	
	9 p. m.	28. 60	52	. 282	Nim. 10	SW. 4	E. 2	73	
March 18	7 a. m.	28. 24	55	. 376	Nim. 10	SE. 3	SE. 2	87	
	2 p. m.	27. 95	67	. 333	Nim. 8	SW. 5	SE 3	50	
	9 p. m	27. 93	45	. 204	Nim. 10	SW. 5	SW. 5	68	
March 19	7 a. m.	28. 20	33	. 113	Nim. 10	SW. 5	SW. 6	60	
	2 p. m.	28. 34	33	. 113	Nim. 10	SW. 5	SW. 5	60	
	9 p. m.	28. 57	31	. 100	Nim. 10	----------	SW. 4	57	

NORRISTOWN, PENNSYLVANIA.

Month and day.	Hour.	Barom'r corrected to 32° F.	Thermometer.	Force of vapor.	Cloudiness.	Motion of clouds.	Winds.	Relative humidity.	REMARKS.
March 14	7 a. m.	30. 161	43	. 186	St. 2	W. 1	E. 1	67	Rain from 7½ p. m. the 14th to 10 a. m on the 15th; amount, 0.81 inch.
	2 p. m.	30. 028	58	. 229	Nim. 10	E. 1	E. 1	47	Rain from 11½ p. m. the 17th to 11½ p. m. on the 18th; amount, 0.60 inch.
	9 p. m.	29. 793	49	. 322	Nim. 10	E. 2	E. 3	92	
March 15	7 a. m.	29. 523	59	. 462	Cir. cu. 10	SW. 3	SW. 2	91	
	2 p. m.	29. 413	59	. 269	Cu. st. 8	W. 2	W. 2	54	
	9 p. m.	29. 593	46	. 146	Cu. st. 5	SW. 2	W. 3	47	
March 16	7 a. m.	29. 951	46	. 169	Cu. 8	W. 2	W. 3	54	
	2 p. m.	30. 021	51	. 245	St. 2	W. 1	W. 3	65	
	9 p. m.	30. 160	42	. 177	0	0	E. 1	66	
March 17	7 a. m.	30. 183	42	. 155	St. 2	W. 1	W. 1	58	
	2 p. m.	30. 031	58	. 203	St. 3	W. 1	W. 2	42	
	9 p. m.	30. 013	48	. 189	St. 3	W. 1	W. 1	56	
March 18	7 a. m.	29. 583	53. 8	. 369	Nim. 10	E. 4	E. 3	90	
	2 p. m.	29. 293	65	. 549	Cu. st. 10	S. 3	S. 2	89	
	9 p. m.	29. 097	57	. 329	Nim. 10	S. 4	SSW. 5	72	
March 19	7 a. m.	29. 170	43. 8	. 114	Nim. 9	W. 3	SW. 4	40	
	2 p. m.	29. 303	41	. 126	Cu. st. 10	W. 5	W. 4	49	
	9 p. m.	29. 475	39	. 152	Nim. 10	W. 2	W. 3	63	

STORM No. 1, MARCH, 1859.

NORTH WHITEHALL, PENNSYLVANIA.

Month and day.	Hour.	Barom'r corrected to 32° F.	Thermometer.	Force of vapor.	Cloudiness.	Motion of clouds.	Winds.	Relative humidity.	REMARKS.
March 14	Sunrise	......	37	......	Overc't,nm. 10	....	0	......	14th. Began to rain at 6 p. m., continued in the night.
	Noon	......	55	......	Nim. 10	....	E. 2	......	15th. Thunder shower at 8 a. m.; high wind in the night.
	Sunset	......	54	......	Nim. 10	....	E. 2	......	17th. Considerable rain during the night.
March 15	Sunrise	......	54	......	Cu. st. 10	S.	S. 1	......	18th. Rain in the a. m.; high wind in the night.
	Noon	......	58	......	Cu. st. 8	S.	0	......	19th. Strong wind.
	Sunset	......	49	......	Cu. st. 8	NW.	NW. 3	......	
March 16	Sunrise	......	37	......	Cu. st. 8	NW.	NW. 2	......	
	Noon	......	54	......	Cu. 4	NW.	NW. 1	......	
	Sunset	......	42	......	Clear 0	....	0	......	
March 17	Sunrise	......	32	......	Cir. 5	NW.	0	......	
	Noon	......	60	......	Cir. cu. 4	W.	W. 2	......	
	Sunset	......	56	......	Nim. 10	....	0	......	
March 18	Sunrise	......	52	......	Rain 10	E.	E. 2	......	
	Noon	......	60	......	Rain 10	....	S. 2	......	
	Sunset	......	60	......	Cu. st. 10	S.	S. 2	......	
March 19	Sunrise	......	38	......	Cu. st 10	SW.	SW. 4	......	
	Noon	......	38	......	Cu. st. 10	SW.	SW. 4	......	
	Sunset	......	38	......	Cu. st. 10	W.	W. 4	......	

PHILADELPHIA, PENNSYLVANIA.

Month and day.	Hour.	Barom'r corrected to 32° F.	Thermometer.	Force of vapor.	Cloudiness.	Motion of clouds.	Winds.	Relative humidity.	REMARKS.
March 14	7 a. m.	30.085	43	.186	Hazy 6	....	NNE. 2	67	Rain from 5 a. m. on the 14th to 1 p. m. on the 15th; amount, 1.30 inch.
	2 p. m.	30.000	63	.188	? 8	....	ESE. 2	33	Began to rain in the night of the 17th, and ended at 1 p. m. on the 18th; amount, 0.368 inch. Commenced again at 8½ p. m., and ended in the night; amount, 0.094 inch.
	9 p. m.	29.867	52	.348	Nim. 10	....	SE. 2	90	
March 15	7 a. m.	29.588	59	.469	Nim. 10	....	SSW. 2	94	
	2 p. m.	29.462	60	.367	Cu. 10	W. 1	SW. 1	71	
	9 p. m.	29.618	48	.165	Cu. 10	W. 2	W. 2	49	
March 16	7 a. m.	29.933	42	.155	Cu., cu. st. 10	WNW. 2	W. 2	58	
	2 p. m.	29.938	56	.179	Cir., cir. cu. 2	NW. 2	WNW. 3	40	
	9 p. m.	30.078	48	.212	0	....	W. 1	63	
March 17	7 a. m.	30.109	41	.201	Haze 2	....	W. 1	78	
	2 p. m.	30.008	62	.201	Cu. 8	SW. 2	SW. 2	36	
	9 p. m.	29.986	50	.209	Cu. 10	SW. 1	SSW. 1	58	
March 18	7 a. m.	29.599	54	.390	Nim. 10	....	SE. 3	93	
	2 p. m.	29.425	65	.549	Nim. 10	....	SE. 2	89	
	9 p. m.	29.268	57	.407	Nim. 10	....	SSE. 2	87	
March 19	7 a. m.	29.228	44	.129	Cu. 10	....	SW. 3	45	
	2 p. m.	29.323	43	.142	Cu. 10	SW. 3	SW. 3	51	
	9 p. m.	29.454	40	.138	Cu. 10	....	SSW. 3	56	

PITTSBURG, MARINE HOSPITAL, PENNSYLVANIA.

Month and day.	Hour.	Barom'r corrected to 32° F.	Thermometer.	Force of vapor.	Cloudiness.	Motion of clouds.	Winds.	Relative humidity.	REMARKS.
March 14	7 a. m.	28.86	42	......	Fog	0	ESE. 1	......	14th. Rain from 9 a. m. to 1.35 p. m; amount, 0.117 inch.
	2 p. m.	28.72	56	......	9	N. 2	ESE. 3	......	17th. Began to rain at 5.30 p. m.; amount, 0.342 inch.
	9 p. m.	28.53	56	......	10	NW. 2	SE. 2	......	18th. Began to rain at 3.20 p. m.; amount, 0.236 inch.
March 15	7 a. m.	28.55	48	......	1	0	S. 2	......	19th. Began to rain at 4.45 p. m.; amount, 0.010 inch.
	2 p. m.	28.65	45	......	9	E. 3	SW. 3	......	
	9 p. m.	28.85	41	......	9	0	W. 2	......	
March 16	7 a. m.	29.08	37	......	0	0	NW. 1	......	
	2 p. m.	29.14	49	......	0	0	SW. 1	......	
	9 p. m.	29.16	42	......	0	0	NW. 1	......	
March 17	7 a. m.	29.07	38	......	10	NW. 2	SE. 1	......	
	2 p. m.	28.92	56	......	10	0	SSW. 1	......	
	9 p. m.	28.83	54	......	10	NW. 2	SE. 2	......	
March 18	7 a. m.	28.43	54	......	9	NE. 3	SE. 2	......	
	2 p. m.	28.30	65	......	9	NE. 2	SE. 3	......	
	9 p. m.	28.15	50	......	10	NE. 2	SW. 3	......	
March 19	7 a. m.	28.28	36	......	10	NE. 5	SW. 3	......	
	2 p. m.	28.48	36	......	10	NE. 5	W. 3	......	
	9 p. m.	28.68	35	......	9	E. 3	W. 3	......	

STORM No. 1, MARCH, 1859.

POCOPSON, PENNSYLVANIA.

Month and day.	Hour.	Barom'r corrected to 32° F.	Thermometer.	Force of vapor.	Cloudiness.	Motion of clouds.	Winds.	Relative humidity.	REMARKS.
March 14	7 a. m.	------	46	------	Cir. st. 10	----------	SW. 1	------	Moderate rain from 4½ p. m. the 14th to 10½ a. m. on the 15th; amount, 0.75 inch. 18th. Began to rain at 1½ a. m., and continued till near morning; amount, 0.70 inch.
	2 p. m.	------	64	------	Cu. 10	S. 3	SE. 4	------	
	9 p. m.	------	49	------	10	----------	SE. 4	------	
March 15	7 a. m.	------	59	------	10	----------	SW. 3	------	
	2 p. m.	------	60	------	Cu. 7	SW. 4	SW. 4	------	
	9 p. m.	------	47	------	Cir. 5	W. 5	W. 5	------	
March 16	7 a. m.	------	42	------	Cu. 8	W. 2	W. 2	------	
	2 p. m.	------	52	------	Cu. 1	W. 2	W. 5	------	
	9 p. m.	------	41	------	0	----------	SW. 1	------	
March 17	7 a. m.	------	35	------	Cir. st. 8	----------	W. 1	------	
	2 p. m.	------	59	------	Cir. st. 10	----------	SW. 5	------	
	9 p. m.	------	50	------	Cu. 9	SW. 2	S. 5	------	
March 18	7 a. m.	------	54	------	10	SE. 3	SE. 4	------	
	2 p. m.	------	63	------	Cu. 10	SW. 4	SW. 5	------	
	9 p. m.	------	56	------	10	S. 4	S. 7	------	
March 19	7 a. m.	------	42	------	Cu. 7	SW. 4	SW. 7	------	
	2 p. m.	------	41	------	Cu. 10	W. 5	W. 6	------	
	9 p. m.	------	40	------	Cu. 9	W. 4	W. 6	------	

SHAMOKIN, PENNSYLVANIA.

Month and day.	Hour.	Barom'r corrected to 32° F.	Thermometer.	Force of vapor.	Cloudiness.	Motion of clouds.	Winds.	Relative humidity.	REMARKS.
March 14	7 a. m.	------	34	------	Cir. 5	E. 1	E. 1	------	14th. Rain from 4½ p. m. till in the night; amount, 0.733 inch. 15th. Light sprinkle of rain at 6 p. m. 17th. Rain in the night. 18th. Ceased to rain at 2 p. m.; light sprinkle at 6 p. m; am't, 0.576 inch. 19th. Rain the previous night; sprinkling snow all day; cold rain and windy.
	2 p. m.	------	52	------	Cir. 8	E. 1	E. 2	------	
	9 p. m.	------	48	------	Nim. 10	E. 1	SE. 5	------	
March 15	7 a. m.	------	52	------	Cir. 5	E. 1	S. 1	------	
	2 p. m.	------	58	------	Cir. cu. 5	E. 1	W. 1	------	
	9 p. m.	------	42	------	Cir. 5	E. 1	W. 4	------	
March 16	7 a. m.	------	36	------	Cir. cu. 7	E. 2	W. 3	------	
	2 p. m.	------	49	------	Cir. 1	E. 1	W. 2	------	
	9 p. m.	------	48	------	0	----------	W. 1	------	
March 17	7 a. m.	------	26	------	Cir. 6	E. 1	W. 2	------	
	2 p. m.	------	59	------	Cir. cu. 5	E. 1	W. 2	------	
	9 p. m.	------	54	------	Cir. cu. 10	E. 1	SW. 3	------	
March 18	7 a. m.	------	51	------	Nim. 10	E. 2	E. 2	------	
	2 p. m.	------	58	------	Nim. 10	E. 2	E. 1	------	
	9 p. m.	------	64	------	Cir. st. 10	E. 2	E. 6	------	
March 19	7 a. m.	------	38	------	Cu. st. 10	E. 3	W. 3	------	
	2 p. m.	------	37	------	Cu. st. 10	E. 2	SW. 6	------	
	9 p. m.	------	37	------	Cu. st. 10	E. 2	W. 6	------	

SOMERSET, PENNSYLVANIA.

Month and day.	Hour.	Barom'r corrected to 32° F.	Thermometer.	Force of vapor.	Cloudiness.	Motion of clouds.	Winds.	Relative humidity.	REMARKS.
March 14	7 a. m.	27.684	49	.247	Cir. st. 10	S. 2; SW. 3	SE. 2	71	14th. Rain from 9 a. m. to 6 p. m.; amount, 0.257 inch. Rain and snow from 7 p. m. the 17th, to 7 a. m. on the 18th; amount, 1.032 inch.
	2 p. m.	27.541	48	.310	Nim. 10	SE. 7; SW. 3	SSE. 6	92.5	
	9 p. m.	27.349	51	.348	Cu. 9	SSE. 7	SW. 4	92.9	
March 15	7 a. m.	27.293	41	.168	0	----------	WSW. 2	65.3	
	2 p. m.	27.298	44	.202	Cu. st. 10	W. 6	W. 5	71.3	
	9 p. m.	27.509	34	.166	Cu. st. 10	W. 6	W. 6	84.1	
March 16	7 a. m.	27.731	30	.167	Cu. 1	NW. 5	WNW. 5	100	
	2 p. m.	27.784	45	.160	0	----------	W. 2	53.3	
	9 p. m.	27.793	38	.144	0	----------	0	62.8	
March 17	7 a. m.	27.772	37	.178	Nim. 10	----------	SE. 1	80.7	
	2 p. m.	27.653	66	.316	Cir. st. 10	W. 2	SW. 1	49.5	
	9 p. m.	27.508	45	.299	Nim. 10	----------	SW. 2	100	
March 18	7 a. m.	27.194	51	.374	Cu. st. 10	E. 5	S. 1	100	
	2 p. m.	26.802	54	.362	Cu. st. 10	SW. 5	S. 2	86.7	
	9 p. m.	26.905	43	.231	Cu. st. 10	SW. 5	SW. 5	83.3	
March 19	7 a. m.	26.971	28	.153	Nim. 10	----------	W. 6	100	
	2 p. m.	27.151	28	.153	Nim. 10	----------	W. 6	100	
	9 p. m.	27.364	26	.141	Nim. 10	W. 7	W. 6	100	

STORM No. 1, MARCH, 1859.

TARENTUM, PENNSYLVANIA.

Month and day.	Hour.	Barom'r corrected to 32° F.	Thermometer.	Force of vapor.	Cloudiness.	Motion of clouds.	Winds.	Relative humidity.	REMARKS.
March 14	7 a. m.	......	40	......	Cu. st. 10	SW. 8	0	......	14th. Rain from 8.50 a. m. to 12.30 p. m. Began to rain at 6 p. m. the 17th, and ended at 7 a. m. on the 18th; commenced again, accompanied by thunder, at 2 50 p. m., and ended in the night. 19th. Began to snow at 7 a. m., and ended in the night.
	2 p. m.	......	58	......	Cu. st. 10	SW. 7	SE. 3	......	
	9 p. m.	......	57	......	Cu. st. 10	SW. 1	S. 1	......	
March 15	7 a. m.	......	36	......	Cir. st. 2	NW. 3	SW. 2	......	
	2 p. m.	......	45	......	Cu. st. 10	SW. 7	SW. 3	......	
	9 p. m.	......	38	......	Cu. st. 10	W. 3	NW. 3	......	
March 16	7 a. m.	......	35	......	0	....	SW. 1	......	
	2 p. m.	......	51	......	0	....	SW. 2	......	
	9 p. m.	......	35	......	0	....	NW. 1	......	
March 17	7 a. m.	......	36	......	Cu. st. 10	SW. 3	0	......	
	2 p. m.	......	65	......	Cu. st. 10	W. 4	SW. 2	......	
	9 p. m.	......	53	......	Nim. 10	SW. 5	0	......	
March 18	7 a. m.	......	55	......	Nim. 10	SW. 8	0	......	
	2 p. m.	......	68	......	Cir. st. 10	SE. 6	SE. 3	......	
	9 p. m.	......	48	......	Nim. 10	SW. 8	SW. 3	......	
March 19	7 a. m.	......	35	......	Nim. 10	W. 10	SW. 3	......	
	2 p. m.	......	35	......	Nim. 10	SW. 8	SW. 3	......	
	9 p. m.	......	34	......	Cu. st. 10	W. 3	SW. 3	......	

WEST HAVERFORD, PENNSYLVANIA.

Month and day.	Hour.	Barom'r corrected to 32° F.	Thermometer.	Force of vapor.	Cloudiness.	Motion of clouds.	Winds.	Relative humidity.	REMARKS.
March 14	7 a. m.	......	41	......	Cir. 2	W. 2	E. 3	......	14th. Rain from 5¼ p. m. to 10½ a. m. on the following day; amount, 1. 80 inch.
	2 p. m.	......	65	......	Cu. 6	SE. 1	SE. 3	......	
March 15	7 a. m.	......	60	......	Cu. 10	S. 5	S. 3	......	
	2 p. m.	......	62	......	Cu. 10	NW. 3	W. 0	......	
March 16	7 a. m.	......	47	......	Cu. 7	NW. 5	NW. 4	......	
	2 p. m.	......	52	......	Cu. 2	NW. 4	NW. 4	......	
March 17	7 a. m.	......	41	......	Cir. st. 3	W. 2	S. 1	......	
	2 p. m.	......	63	......	Cir. cu. 8	NW. 4	SW. 3	......	
March 18	7 a. m.	......	54	......	10	....	SE. 4	......	
	2 p. m.	......	64	......	10	....	NW. 5	......	
March 19	7 a. m.	......	42	......	Cu. 9	NW. 6	NW. 6	......	
	2 p. m.	......	54	......	Cu. 4	NW. 5	NW. 5	......	

WESTTOWN, PENNSYLVANIA.

Month and day.	Hour.	Barom'r corrected to 32° F.	Thermometer.	Force of vapor.	Cloudiness.	Motion of clouds.	Winds.	Relative humidity.	REMARKS.
March 14	7 a. m.	29. 65	39	. 210	St. 5	....	E. 1	86	Rain from 5 p. m. the 14th to 8 a. m. on the 15th; amount, 1. 15 inch. 17th. Commenced raining in the night, and ended at 5 p. m. on the 18th; amount, 0. 805 inch.
	2 p. m.	29. 56	60	. 456	St. 8	....	SE. 1	88	
	9 p. m.	29. 29	52	. 392	Nim. 10	....	SW. 3	100	
March 15	7 a. m.	29. 06	59	. 500	Nim. 10	SW. 3	S. 2	100	
	2 p. m.	28. 94	59	. 242	Cu. 9	W. 2	W. 3	48	
	9 p. m.	29. 21	44	. 180	Cu. 5	NW. 3	NW. 3	63	
March 16	7 a. m.	29. 49	40	. 150	Cu. nim. 9	NW. 3	NW. 2	61	
	2 p. m.	29. 56	51	. 173	Cu. 1	....	NW. 3	46	
	9 p. m.	29. 67	39	. 190	0	....	W. 1	80	
March 17	7 a. m.	29. 63	33	. 178	Cir. st. 5	SW. 1	SE. 1	94	
	2 p. m.	29. 55	58	. 234	St. 10	NW. 2	SE. 2	48	
	9 p. m.	29. 51	47	. 225	Cu. st. 9	W. 3	S. by E. 3	70	
March 18	7 a. m.	29. 06	53	. 406	Nim. 10	W. 3	S. by E. 5	100	
	2 p. m.	28. 82	64	. 565	Nim. 10	SW. 4	SW. 3	94	
	9 p. m.	28. 66	54	. 418	Nim. 10	SW. 3	SW. 4	100	
March 19	7 a. m.	28. 70	40	. 160	Cu. st. 10	NW. 3	SW. 4	64	
	2 p. m.	28. 87	39	. 135	St. 10	W. 3	W. by N. 5	55	
	9 p. m.	29. 05	38	. 130	St. 10	W. 3	W. by N. 5	58	

STORM No. 1, MARCH, 1859.

ANNAPOLIS, MARYLAND.

Month and day.	Hour.	Barom'r corrected to 32° F.	Thermometer.	Force of vapor.	Cloudiness.	Motion of clouds.	Winds.	Relative humidity.	REMARKS.
March 14	7 a. m.	30.01	42.5	.237	10	....	0	87	14th. Sprinkle of rain at 2.55 to 3.20 p. m., and at intervals from 3.40 to 8 p. m.; amount, 0.12 inch.
	2 p. m.	29.91	59	.352	10	....	S. 1	70	
	9 p. m.	29.67	58	.452	10	....	S. 3	94	
March 15	7 a. m.	29.46	55	.433	10	....	S. 1	100	
	2 p. m.	29.38	63.5	.292	Cu.st. & cir cu. 6	SW. 2	N. 2	50	Rain at intervals from 9 p. m. to 10.10 a. m. on the following morning; amount, 1.24 inch.
	9 p. m.	29.68	49	.152	Cir. & cu. 2	WSW. 2	WNW. 4	44	
March 16	7 a. m.	29.93	40	.160	0	....	SW. 1	64	15th. Hail for half a minute at 1 55 p. m.; sprinkle of rain at intervals at 2½ p. m.; amount, 0.01 inch.
	2 p. m.	29.98	55	.168	0	....	W. 3	39	
	9 p. m.	30.05	47.5	.242	0	....	SW. 1	74	
March 17	7 a. m.	30.09	44	.265	Cir., Cir.st, and cu. 5	WSW. 1	S. 1	92	17th. Rain at 8.50 p. m., and at intervals till 10 a. m. the 18th; amount, 0.50 inch.
	2 p. m.	29.98	57	.295	Cir., cir.st., and cu. 8	SW. 1	S. 3	63	
	9 p. m.	29.86	53	.321	10	....	S. 2	80	18th. Rain at intervals from 6.35 to 10 p. m.; amount, 0.07 inch.
March 18	7 a. m.	29.44	57	.466	10	....	S. 4	100	
	2 p. m.	29.21	60	.487	10	....	S. 2	94	
	9 p. m.	29.05	57	.378	10	....	SSW. 4	81	
March 19	7 a. m.	29.23	41	.147	Cir. & cu. 1	WSW. 2	SW. 3	57	
	2 p. m.	29.37	46.5	.163	10	....	W. 3	51	
	9 p. m.	29.56	40	.139	Cir. & cu. 3	WNW. 2	WSW. 4	56	

BLADENSBURG, MARYLAND.

Month and day.	Hour.	Barom'r corrected to 32° F.	Thermometer.	Force of vapor.	Cloudiness.	Motion of clouds.	Winds.	Relative humidity.	REMARKS.
March 14	7 a. m.	......	39	......	10	....	....	......	18th. Rain.
	2 p. m.	......	62	......	10	....	SE.	......	
	9 p. m.	......	59	......	10	....	SE.	......	
March 15	7 a. m.	......	......	......	....	....	....	......	
	2 p. m.	......	......	......	....	....	....	......	
	9 p. m.	......	......	......	....	....	....	......	
March 16	7 a. m.	......	39	......	0	....	W.	......	
	2 p. m.	......	56	......	0	....	NW	......	
	9 p. m.	......	39	......	....	....	....	......	
March 17	7 a. m.	......	36	......	5	....	....	......	
	2 p. m.	......	65	......	10	....	SW.	......	
	9 p. m.	......	30	......	10	....	SE.	......	
March 18	7 a. m.	......	59	......	10	....	SE	......	
	2 p. m.	......	69	......	8	....	S.	......	
	9 p. m.	......	53	......	10	....	SW.	......	
March 19	7 a. m.	......	44	......	7	....	SW.	......	
	2 p. m.	......	......	......	....	....	....	......	
	9 p. m.	......	......	......	....	....	....	......	

CHESTERTOWN, MARYLAND.

Month and day.	Hour.	Barom'r corrected to 32° F.	Thermometer.	Force of vapor.	Cloudiness.	Motion of clouds.	Winds.	Relative humidity.	REMARKS.
March 14	7 a. m.	30.21	42	.197	Nim. 9	....	NE. 2	63	Rain from 6 p. m. the 14th to 10 a. m. on the 15th; amount, 1.78 inch.
	2 p. m.	30.11	61	.256	Nim. 10	....	SE. 2	44	
	9 p. m.	29.89	58	.441	Nim. 10	....	SE. 4	85	
March 15	7 a. m.	29.66	59	.482	Nim. 10	SW. 3	SW. 3	88	Thunder on the 15th.
	2 p. m.	29.56	61	.212	Cir. st. nim. 7	NW. 1	NW. 3	36½	18th. Rain at intervals during the day; amount, 0.48 inch.
	9 p. m.	29.83	46	.131	St. nim. 6	NW.	NW. 5	39½	
March 16	7 a. m.	30.22	41	.104	St. 1	....	NW. 2	36	
	2 p. m.	30.17	53	.115	0	....	NW. 3	27	
	9 p. m.	30.24	46	.134	0	....	NW. 2	38	
March 17	7 a. m.	30.26	45	.249	St. haze 4	....	NW. 2	77	
	2 p. m.	30.16	61	.209	Cir. st. 5	SE. 1	SE. 3	36	
	9 p. m.	30.07	50	.201	St. nim. 7	SE. 1	SE. 2	51	
March 18	7 a. m.	29.62	57	.439	Nim. 10	SE. 4	SE. 5	88	
	2 p. m.	29.41	66	.509	Nim. cu. st. 9	SW. 1	SW. 3	75	
	9 p. m.	29.24	54	.315	Nim. 10	....	SE. 5	71	
March 19	7 a. m.	29.40	41	.104	Cu. st. nim. 3	NW. 2	NW. 4	36½	
	2 p. m.	29.54	42	.108	Nim. cu. st. 9	NW. 1	WNW. 4	37	
	9 p. m.	29.71	38	.080	Nim. 9	....	W. 4	32	

STORM No. 1, MARCH, 1859.

FREDERICK CITY, MARYLAND.

Month and day.	Hour.	Barom'r corrected to 32° F.	Thermometer.	Force of vapor.	Cloudiness.		Motion of clouds.		Winds.		Relative humidity.	REMARKS.
March 14	7 a. m.	29.915	42.5	.249	St.	10	SW.	2		0	91	14th. Began to rain at 0.45 p. m.,
	2 p. m.	29.752	56.8	.381	Cir. st.	10	S.	3	NE.	1	82	and ended in the night; amount,
	9 p. m.	29.508	58.5	.460	Nim.	10	----------		NE.	3	94	0.518 inch.
March 15	7 a. m.	29.352	56.7	.396	Cir. cu.	9	SW.	4	W.	2	86	Rain from 8.30 p. m. the 17th to
	2 p. m.	29.405	59	.224	Cu	2	W.	2	NW.	4	45	10 a. m. on the 18th; amount,
	9 p. m.	29.613	47	.190	Cu. st.	9	W.	2	NW.	4	58	0.865 inch.
March 16	7 a. m.	29.883	42	.167		0		0	W.	2	62	Commenced again at 4.30, and
	2 p. m.	29.910	55	.180		0		0	W.	3	41	ended at 10 p. m.; amount, 0.203
	9 p. m.	29.975	44.5	.211		0		0	NW.	1	72	inch.
March 17	7 a. m.	29.985	40	.203	Cir.	8	W.	2	SW.	2	82	
	2 p. m.	29.809	60	.229	Cir. st.	10	----------		S.	3	44	
	9 p. m.	29.721	53	.308	Nim.	10	----------		S.	2	76	
March 18	7 a. m.	29.287	56.5	.428	Nim.	10	S.	4	S.	2	94	
	2 p. m.	28.995	65	.483	Cir. cu.	8	S.	2	SW.	3	78	
	9 p. m.	28.896	53.5	.320	Nim.	10	W.	1	SW.	2	78	
March 19	7 a. m.	29.109	41.5	.212	Cir. st.	8	W.	3	SW.	5	82	
	2 p. m	29.282	39.5	.167	Cir. st.	9	W.	3	W.	5	68	
	9 p. m.	29.466	38	.155	Cu. st.	10	W.	4	W.	5	68	

LEITERSBURG, MARYLAND.

Month and day.	Hour.	Barom'r corrected to 32° F.	Thermometer.	Force of vapor.	Cloudiness.		Motion of clouds.		Winds.		Relative humidity.	REMARKS.
March 14	7 a. m.	------	38	------	St.	9	W.	2	SW.	1	------	14th. Began to rain at 12 m., and
	2 p. m.	------	56	------	Nim.	10	SW.	3	SW.	1	------	ended in the night; amount,
	9 p. m.	------	59	------	Nim.	10	S.	4	S.	4	------	0.42 inch.
March 15	7 a. m.	------	54	------	Cir. st.	7	SW.	3	W.	3	------	17th. Strong S. wind in the after-
	2 p. m.	------	60	------	Cu. st.	4	NW.	3	NW.	4	------	noon and evening; commenced
	9 p. m.	------	44	------	Cu. st.	9	NW.	4	NW.	4	------	raining at 9 p. m.
March 16	7 a. m.	------	38	------	Cir.	1	NW.	3	W.	2	------	18th. Continued showers; at 6 p m.
	2 p. m.	------	52	------		0		0	NW.	3	------	strong SW. wind, and driving
	9 p. m.	------	38	------		0		0		0	------	rain; amount, 0.61 inch.
March 17	7 a. m.	------	36	------	Cir. st.	5	W.	2	W.	1	------	19th. Snow squalls, with high
	2 p. m.	------	65	------	Cir. st.	5	SW.	2	S.	3	------	wind.
	9 p. m.	------	54	------	Nim.	10	?		S.	3	------	
March 18	7 a. m.	------	58	------	Nim.	10	SW. S.	3 5	S.	4	------	
	2 p. m.	------	69	------	Cir. cu.	10	SW. S.	2 4	S.	3	------	
	9 p. m.	------	49	------	Nim.	10	W.	3	SW.	2	------	
March 19	7 a. m.	------	38	------	Cu. st.	9	NW.	6	W.	6	------	
	2 p. m.	------	36	------	Cu. st.	10	NW.	5	NW.	5	------	
	9 p. m.	------	34	------	Cu. st.	10	NW.	4	NW.	5	------	

LEONARDTOWN, MARYLAND.

Month and day.	Hour.	Barom'r corrected to 32° F.	Thermometer.	Force of vapor.	Cloudiness.		Motion of clouds.		Winds.		Relative humidity.	REMARKS.
March 14	7 a. m.	29.75	51	------	Haze	10		0	SE.	0	------	Rain from 3.30 p. m. the 14th to
	2 p. m.	29.73	63	------		10		0	SE.	5	------	10 a. m. on the 15th.
	9 p. m.	29.56	59	------		10		0	SE.	3	------	15th. Thunder storm at 5 a. m.;
March 15	7 a. m.	29.37	59	------		10		0	SW.	2	------	very heavy thunder clouds pass-
	2 p. m.	29.27	62	------	Cu. st.	5	SE.	1	W.	3	------	ing from E. to W.
	9 p. m.	29.49	50	------		0		0	NW.	4	------	17th. Rain.
March 16	7 a. m.	29.77	45	------		0		0	NW.	2	------	18th. Rain at 3 a. m.
	2 p. m.	29.80	55	------		0		0	W.	7	------	
	9 p. m.	29.80	42	------	Cir. st.	2	SE.	1	SE.	0	------	
March 17	7 a. m.	29.83	45	------	Cir. st.	7	SE.	1	S.	1	------	
	2 p. m.	29.75	52	------	St.	10	NE.	1	SE.	4	------	
	9 p. m.	29.67	------	------		10		0	SE.	4	------	
March 18	7 a. m.	29.34	58	------		10		0	SE.	5	------	
	2 p. m.	29.18	69	------	Cir. cu.	9		0	SE.	4	------	
	9 p. m.	29.00	52	------		10		0	SW.	3	------	
March 19	7 a. m.	29.04	44	------	Cir. st.	4	E.	0	W.	8	------	
	2 p. m.	29.23	47	------	Cu. st.	9	SE.	3	W.	9	------	
	9 p. m.	29.38	42	------	Cu. st.	8	SE.	3	W.	7	------	

STORM No. 1, MARCH, 1859.

SYKESVILLE, MARYLAND.

Month and day.	Hour.	Barom'r corrected to 32° N.	Thermometer.	Force of vapor.	Cloudiness.		Motion of clouds.		Winds.		Relative humidity.
March 14	7 a. m.	------	45	------	Cu. st.	6	NE.	2	E.	2	------
	2 p. m.	------	58	------	Cu.	8	W.	3	W.	2	------
	9 p. m.	------	58	------	St.	10	SE.	1	SE.	3	------
March 15	7 a. m	------	60	------	Cu.	9	SW.	3	SW.	2	------
	2 p. m.	------	60	------	Cir. cu.	4	W.	3	W.	4	------
	9 p. m.	------	45	------	Cu.	5	W.	3	W.	4	------
March 16	7 a. m.	------	40	------		0	----------		W.	2	------
	2 p. m.	------	55	------		0	----------		SW.	3	------
	9 p. m.	------	40	------	St.	2	SW.	1	W.	2	------
March 17	7 a. m.	------	38	------	Cu. st.	4	W.	2	SW.	2	------
	2 p. m.	------	62	------	Cir.	5	W.	2	SW.	3	------
	9 p. m.	------	50	------	Cu.	8	SW.	3	E	2	------
March 18	7 a. m.	------	56	------	Nim.	10	E.	2	W.	2	------
	2 p. m.	------	70	------	Cir. cu.	4	SW.	3	SW.	3	------
	9 p. m.	------	55	------	Cu.	7	SW.	3	SW.	4	------
March 19	7 a. m.	------	43	------	Cu.	5	SW.	3	SW.	5	------
	2 p. m.	------	45	------	Cu.	8	W.	4	W.	5	------
	9 p. m.	------	35	------	Cu.	6	W.	3	W.	4	------

REMARKS. Rain from 2 p. m. the 14th to 7 a. m. on the 15th; amount, 1 00 inch.
17th. Rain during the night to 10 a. m. next morning; amount, 1.50 inch. Began to rain again at 6 p. m. and ceased during the night; strong wind from 6 to 8 p. m.; amount, 2.00 inches.

BALTIMORE, MARYLAND.

Month and day.	Hour.	Barom'r corrected to 32° N.	Thermometer.	Force of vapor.	Cloudiness.		Motion of clouds.	Winds.		Relative humidity.
March 14	7 a. m.	30. 13	46	. 192		10	----------	E.	2	62
	2 p. m.	29. 99	60	. 338	St. nim.	10	----------	E.	3	65
	9 p. m.	------	59	. 439	Raining	10	----------	S.	4	88
March 15	7 a. m.	29. 55	61	. 473	Nim. 10,	fog	----------	NW.	2	88
	2 p. m.	29. 48	62	. 150	Nim.	9	----------	NW.	5	27
	9 p. m.	------	50	. 117	Nim.	9	----------	NW.	5	32
March 16	7 a. m.	30. 07	43	. 121		6	----------	W.	3	43
	2 p. m.	30. 10	55	. 120		0	----------	W.	4	28
	9 p. m.	------	46. 5	. 185		2	----------	S.	2	58
March 17	7 a. m.	30. 21	42	. 177	Cir.	5	----------	NE.	1	66
	2 p. m.	30. 05	63	. 189	Cir. cu. st.	9	----------	S.	3	33
	9 p. m.	------	54	. 231	Nim. st.	10	----------	SE.	3	55
March 18	7 a. m.	29. 48	59	. 439	Rain'g, nim.	10	----------	S.	5	88
	2 p. m.	29. 21	66	. 502	Nim. cir.	9	----------	SE.	2	78
	9 p. m.	------	59. 5	. 388	Nim. 10, rain'g		----------	S.	4	76
March 19	7 a. m.	29. 31	44	. 108	Nim. cir.	9	----------	SW.	4	37
	2 p. m.	29. 43	44	. 108	Nim.	10	----------	W.	6	37
	9 p. m.	------	40	. 097	----------		----------	----------		39

REMARKS. 18th. Amount of rain, 0.60 inch.

WASHINGTON, D. C.

Month and day.	Hour.	Barom'r corrected to 32° N.	Thermometer.	Force of vapor.	Cloudiness.		Motion of clouds.	Winds.		Relative humidity.
March 14	7 a. m.	30. 155	43	. 231	Cir.	10	----------	SE ----------		83
	2 p. m.	30. 009	62	. 370	Nim.	10	----------	SE.	3	66
	9 p. m.	29. 804	63	. 510	Nim.	10	----------	S.	4	88
March 15	7 a. m.	29. 620	60	. 487	Nim.	10	----------	SW.	3	94
	2 p. m.	29. 547	62	. 176	Cu. st.	6	----------	NW.	4	32
	9 p. m.	29. 897	48	. 165	Cu.	8	----------	NW.	5	49
March 16	7 a. m.	30. 117	44	. 108		0	----------	W.	4	37
	2 p. m	30. 157	55	. 097		0	----------	NW.	4	22
	9 p. m.	30. 215	47	. 225		0	----------	SE.	1	70
March 17	7 a. m.	30. 241	42	. 199	Cir.	4	----------		0	74
	2 p. m.	30. 093	61	. 269	Cu.	10	----------	S.	3	50
	9 p. m.	30. 007	54	. 308	Nim.	10	----------	SE.	3	74
March 18	7 a. m.	29. 572	60	. 456	Nim.	10	----------	S.	4	88
	2 p. m.	29. 333	67	. 522	Cir. cu.	9	----------	S.	4	79
	9 p. m.	29. 185	58	. 365	Nim.	10	----------	S.	5	76
March 19	7 a. m.	29. 404	47	. 179	Cu.	10	----------	SW.	5	55
	2 p. m.	29. 551	45	. 117	Cu. st.	10	----------	W.	5	39
	9 p. m.	29. 752	38	. 123	Cu.	6	----------	W.	5	54

REMARKS. 14th. Began to rain at 3 p. m. and ended in the night; amount, 0.28 inch.
Rain at intervals from 8 p. m. the 17th to 6 a. m. on the 18th; amount, 0.54 inch.
18th. Thunder and lightning at 4 a. m. Rain from 5½ to 8 p. m.; amount, 0.15 inch.

STORM No. 1, MARCH, 1859.

CRICHTON'S STORE, VIRGINIA.

Month and day.	Hour.	Barom'r corrected to 32° F.	Thermometer.	Force of vapor.	Cloudiness.	Motion of clouds.	Winds.	Relative humidity.	REMARKS.
arch 14	8 a. m.	......	51	......	St. 10	W. 2	SE. 1	......	Began to rain at 10 a. m. the 14th. After 8 p. m. dashing showers of large drops at irregular intervals during the night. Thunder at 6 a. m. on the 15th; ceased raining at 9 a. m.; amount, 1.75 inch.
	12 m.	......	67	......	Hid 10	....	SE. 1	......	
	5 p. m.	......	67	......	10	....	S. 1	......	
arch 15	8 a. m.	......	62	......	Cir. st. 10	SW. 2	S..........	......	
	12 m.	......	66	......	None 1	....	SW. 4	......	
	5 p. m.	......	63	......	1	....	W. 4	......	
arch 16	8 a. m.	......	49	......	1	....	SW. 2	......	16th. A much larger halo around the moon than usual. No stars in the circle.
	12 m.	......	58	......	1	....	SW. 2	......	
	5 p. m.	......	60	......	9	....	SW. 1	......	
arch 17	8 a. m.	......	50	......	10	....	E. 1	......	18th. 3 p. m. two strata of (cu.) clouds from S., the lower one moving with less rapidity than the upper; wind, S. 6; at 5.45 p. m. a fully developed iris and a faint imitation 10° above it; wind S., 4 to 6, all night.
	12 m.	......	60	......	10	....	S. 2	......	
	5 p. m.	......	64	......	10	....	S..........	......	
arch 18	8 a. m.	......	68	......	Cir. st. 10	SW. 2	S. 3	......	
	12 m.	......	65	......	Cir. st. 9	S. 2	S. 3	......	
	5 p. m.	......	60	......	Hid 10	....	S. 4	......	
arch 19	8 a. m.	......	43	......	5	....	SW. 4	......	
	12 m.	......	47	......	St. 3	....	W. 6	......	
	5 p. m.	......	45	......	7	....	W. 5	......	

CROSS CREEK, VIRGINIA.

Month and day.	Hour.	Barom'r corrected to 32° F.	Thermometer.	Force of vapor.	Cloudiness.	Motion of clouds.	Winds.	Relative humidity.	REMARKS.
arch 14	7 a. m.	......	37	......	....	SE	1	......	Rain from 9 a. m. the 14th to 4 p. m. on the 15th; amount, 0.35 inch.
	2 p. m.	......	62	......	....	SE	2	......	
	9 p. m.	......	59	......	....	S.........	1	......	
arch 15	7 a. m.	......	35	......	....	S.........	1	......	Snow and rain from 4 p. m. the 17th to 5 p. m. on the 19th; amount in water, 1.11 inch.
	2 p. m.	......	63	......	....	W........	2	......	
	9 p. m.	......	42	......	....	W........	3	......	
arch 16	7 a. m.	......	27	......	....	0	0	......	
	2 p. m	......	......	......	....	0	1	......	
	9 p. m.	......	31	......	....	0	0	......	
arch 17	7 a. m.	......	35	......	....	S.........	1	......	
	2 p. m.	......	63	......	....	S.........	0	......	
	9 p. m.	......	50	......	....	S.........	1	......	
arch 18	7 a. m	......	55	......	....	SW.......	1	......	
	2 p. m.	......	70	......	....	SW.......	2	......	
	9 p. m.	......	44	......	....	SW.......	2	......	
arch 19	7 a. m.	......	31	......	....	W........	3	......	
	2 p. m.	......	32	......	....	W........	3	......	
	9 p. m.	......	31	......	....	W........	3	......	

THE PLAINS, VIRGINIA.

Month and day.	Hour.	Barom'r corrected to 32° F.	Thermometer.	Force of vapor.	Cloudiness.	Motion of clouds.	Winds.	Relative humidity.	REMARKS.
arch 14	7 a. m.	......	......	......	10		....	......	Rain from 9 a. m. the 14th to 3 a. m. on the 15th.
	2 p. m.	......	......	......	....	....	....	......	
	9 p. m.	......	......	......	....	....	....	......	16th. An unusual bow or arch, spanning the heavens from E. to W., at 7 p. m.; a few shooting stars at 5 a. m.
arch 15	7 a. m.	......	58	......	5	NW. to SE. 2	NW. 2	......	
	2 p. m.	......	62	......	5	3	NW. 3	......	
	9 p. m.	......	48	......	5	3	NW. 3	......	
arch 16	7 a. m.	......	42	......	0	2	NW. 2	......	17th. Rain at 7 p. m.
	2 p m.	......	58	......	0	4	NW. 4	......	
	9 p. m.	......	47	......	0	3	NW. 3	......	
arch 17	7 a. m.	......	47	......	5	2	SW. 2	......	
	2 p. m.	......	60	......	10	5	SE. 5	......	
	9 p. m.	......	52	......	10	5	SE. 5	......	
arch 18	7 a. m.	......	59	......	10	3	SW. 4	......	
	2 p m.	......	67	......	10	4	SW. 3	......	
	9 p. m.	......	54	......	10	6	SE. 6	......	
arch 19	7 a. m.	......	40	......	5	2	NW. 2	......	
	2 p. m.	......	43	......	5	4	NW. 4	......	
	9 p. m.	......	36	......	5	5	NW. 5	......	

STORM No. 1, MARCH, 1859.

HARTWOOD, VIRGINIA.

Month and day.	Hour.	Barom'r corrected to 32° F.	Thermometer.	Force of vapor.	Cloudiness.	Motion of clouds.	Winds.	Relative humidity.	REMARKS.
March 14	7 a. m.	......	48	......	......	......	......	......	Rain from 2 p. m. the 14th to 3 a. m. on the 15th; amount, 0. 40 inch.
	2 p. m.	......	66	......	......	......	......	......	Rain from 9 p. m. the 17th to 6 p. m. on the 18th; amount, 0. 70 inch.
	9 p. m.	......	64	......	......	......	......	......	Thin ice formed on the 19th.
March 15	7 a. m.	......	60	......	......	......	......	......	
	2 p. m.	......	64	......	......	......	......	......	
	9 p. m.	......	46	......	......	......	......	......	
March 16	7 a. m.	......	40	......	......	......	......	......	
	2 p. m.	......	58	......	......	......	......	......	
	9 p. m.	......	49	......	......	......	......	......	
March 17	7 a. m.	......	44	......	......	......	......	......	
	2 p. m.	......	62	......	......	......	......	......	
	9 p. m.	......	54	......	......	......	......	......	
March 18	7 a. m.	......	60	......	......	......	......	......	
	2 p. m.	......	68	......	......	......	......	......	
	9 p. m.	......	51	......	......	......	......	......	
March 19	7 a. m	......	38	......	......	......	......	......	
	2 p. m.	......	42	......	......	......	......	......	
	9 p. m.	......	39	......	......	......	......	......	

LEWINSVILLE, VIRGINIA.

Month and day.	Hour.	Barom'r corrected to 32° F.	Thermometer.	Force of vapor.	Cloudiness.	Motion of clouds.	Winds.	Relative humidity.	REMARKS.
March 14	7 a. m.	......	59½	......	Nim. 8	Dim clouds.	ESE. 1	......	14th. Rain, ending at 10 p. m.; amount, 0. 17 inch.
	2 p. m.	......	65	......	Nim. 10	Rain at 11.	SE. 3	......	17th. Rain; amount, 0. 48 inch.
	9 p. m.	......	62	......	Nim. 10	Rain......	S., oscillat'g, 5	......	18th. Rain; amount, 0. 37 inch.
March 15	7 a. m.	......	58	......	Nim. cu. 10	....	NW. 1	......	
	2 p. m.	......	60	......	Nim. cu. 8	....	NW., oscill'g, 5	......	
	9 p. m.	......	46	......	Cu. 4	Wind fierce	SW., oscill'g, 4	......	
March 16	7 a. m.	......	43	......	0	....	WNW. 1	......	
	2 p. m.	......	57	......	0	0	W., oscill'g, 4	......	
	9 p. m.	......	51	......	0	....	SE., S. 0	......	
March 17	7 a. m.	......	48	......	Cir. st. 6	Mirky	SE., S. 1	......	
	2 p. m.	......	63	......	Cu. 8	Dim	ESE. 3	......	
	9 p. m.	......	48	......	Nim. 10	Rain......	SE. 1	......	
March 18	7 a. m.	......	60½	......	Nim. 10	Rain......	S. 4, W., osc'g, 4	......	
	2 p. m.	......	69	......	Cir. cu. 8	Showery ..	SE., S., osc'g, 3 W., osc'g, 5	......	
	9 p. m.	......	54½	......	Cu. nim. 10	Sprinkling.	SE. 5, NW., os., 5	......	
March 19	7 a. m.	......	43	......	Cu. st. 8	....	WNW. 2	......	
	2 p. m.	......	41	......	Cir. 10	Mack'l cl'ds	WNW., osc'g, 6	......	
	9 p. m.	......	36	......	Cir. st. 5	Blustering .	W. 2	......	

LEWISBURG, VIRGINIA.

Month and day.	Hour.	Barom'r corrected to 32° F.	Thermometer.	Force of vapor.	Cloudiness.	Motion of clouds.	Winds.	Relative humidity.	REMARKS.
March 14	7 a. m.	......	50	......	10	....	E..........	......	14th. Constant rain all day; am't, 0. 64 inch.
	2 p. m.	......	54	......	10	....	E..........	......	15th. Clear and cool, with a brisk wind all day.
	9 p. m.	......	50	......	9	....	S..........	......	17th. Pleasant a. m.; rain in the evening; amount, 0. 90 inch.
March 15	7 a. m.	......	46	......	0	....	SW..........	......	18th. Constant rain; amount, 0. 48 inch.
	2 p. m.	......	54	......	2	....	SW..........	......	19th. Cold blustery morning; slight snow.
	9 p. m.	......	41	......	2	....	N..........	......	
March 16	7 a. m.	......	35	......	0	....	NW..........	......	
	2 p. m	......	59	......	0	....	NW..........	......	
	9 p. m.	......	41	......	4	....	N..........	......	
March 17	7 a. m.	......	42	......	8	....	NW..........	......	
	2 p. m.	......	60	......	10	....	NW..........	......	
	9 p. m	......	49	......	9	....	NW..........	......	
March 18	7 a. m	......	56	......	10	....	S..........	......	
	2 p. m.	......	62	......	10	....	SW..........	......	
	9 p. m.	......	35	......	9	....	SW..........	......	
March 19	7 a. m.	......	31	......	10	....	NW..........	......	
	2 p. m.	......	31	......	10	....	SW..........	......	
	9 p. m.	......	31	......	9	....	SW..........	......	

STORM No. 1, MARCH, 1859.

KANAWHA, VIRGINIA.

Month and day.	Hour.	Barom'r corrected to 32° F.	Thermometer.	Force of vapor.	Cloudiness.	Motion of clouds.	Winds.	Relative humidity.	REMARKS.
March 14	7 a. m.	......	59	......	Rain 10	....	S. 2	......	14th. Rain from — a. m. to 12 m.; amount, 0. 203 inch.
	2 p. m.	......	61	......	Rain 10	....	S. 4	......	17th. Rain from 10 a. m. to — p. m.; amount, 0. 50 inch.
	9 p. m.	......	63	......	Cir. st. 5	....	....	......	18th. Rain from 12 m. to — p. m.; amount, 0. 28 inch.
March 15	7 a. m.	......	49	......	Cu. 4	SW......	S..........	......	19th. Snow; amount in water, 0. 10 inch.
	2 p. m.	......	53	......	Nim. 5	SW......	S. 4	......	
	9 p. m.	......	......	......	0	....	....	......	
March 16	7 a. m.	......	33	......	....	....	....	......	
	2 p. m.	......	......	......	....	....	....	......	
	9 p. m.	......	......	......	....	....	....	......	
March 17	7 a. m.	......	46	......	Nim. 8	....	S. 3	......	
	2 p. m.	......	58	......	Rain 10	....	S. 2	......	
	9 p. m.	......	55	......	Rain 10	....	S. 2	......	
March 18	7 a. m.	......	56	......	Nim. 10	....	0	......	
	2 p. m.	......	65	......	Rain 10	....	W. 5	......	
	9 p. m.	......	38	......	Snow 10	....	E. 5	......	
March 19	7 a. m.	......	34	......	Rain 10	W........	S. 3	......	
	2 p. m.	......	36	......	Snow 10	....	SW. 4	......	
	9 p. m.	......	38	......	Nim. 9	W........	W. 2	......	

MONTROSS, VIRGINIA.

Month and day.	Hour.	Barom'r corrected to 32° F.	Thermometer.	Force of vapor.	Cloudiness.	Motion of clouds.	Winds.	Relative humidity.	REMARKS.
March 14	7 a. m.	......	43	......	Nim. 10	0	0	......	Rain from 3 p. m. the 14th to 8½ a. m. on the 15th; amount, 2. 40 inches.
	2 p. m.	......	64	......	Cir. 10	N. 3	SE. 6	......	18th. Rain from 5¾ to 10 p. m.; amount, 0. 12 inch.
	9 p. m.	......	60	......	Nim. 10	0	SE. 8	......	
March 15	7 a. m.	......	59	......	0	0	0	......	
	2 p. m.	......	66	......	St. 3	E. 2	W. 15	......	
	9 p. m.	......	48	......	0	0	W. 4	......	
March 16	7 a. m.	......	38	......	Cir. 9	NE. 1	0	......	
	2 p. m.	......	54	......	0	0	SW. 6	......	
	9 p. m.	......	44	......	0	0	0	......	
March 17	7 a. m.	......	46	......	Nim. 10	0	SW. 2	......	
	2 p. m.	......	60	......	Cu. 10	0	SE. 2	......	
	9 p. m.	......	53	......	Cir. 10	N. 3	SE. 8	......	
March 18	7 a. m.	......	58	......	St. 3	NE. 1	SE. 18	......	
	2 p. m.	......	68	......	Cir. st. 8	N. 1	S. 12	......	
	9 p. m.	......	45	......	Nim. 10	0	SW. 12	......	
March 19	7 a. m.	......	42	......	0	0	SW. 50	......	
	2 p. m.	......	46	......	St. 9	NE. 1	W. 25	......	
	9 p. m.	......	38	......	St. 5	NE. 1	W. 15	......	

MONT VIEW, VIRGINIA.

Month and day.	Hour.	Barom'r corrected to 32° F.	Thermometer.	Force of vapor.	Cloudiness.	Motion of clouds.	Winds.	Relative humidity.	REMARKS.
March 14	7 a. m.	......	46	......	Cir. st. 10	....	SE. 2	......	14th. Rain from 10 a. m. to 7 p. m.; heavy shower at 10 p. m.; amount, 1. 50 inch.
	2 p. m.	......	50	......	Nim. 10	N. 2	SE. 4	......	17th. Appearance of rain.
	9 p. m.	......	54	......	Nim. 10	N. 1	SW. 2	......	18th. Showery.
March 15	7 a. m.	......	57	......	Cu. st. 5	E. 1	W. 2	......	
	2 p. m.	......	58	......	Cu. 6	E. 1	W. 5	......	
	9 p. m.	......	48	......	0	....	W. 6	......	
March 16	7 a. m.	......	46	......	0	....	W. 2	......	
	2 p. m.	......	64	......	0	....	SW. 4	......	
	9 p. m.	......	58	......	0	....	SE. 2	......	
March 17	7 a. m.	......	44	......	Cir. st. 8	....	NE. 2	......	
	2 p. m.	......	60	......	Cir. st. 10	N. 1	SE. 2	......	
	9 p. m.	......	56	......	Nim. 10	N. 1	S. 2	......	
March 18	7 a. m.	......	60	......	Nim. 10	N. 2	S. 6	......	
	2 p. m.	......	72	......	Nim. 10	N. 2	S. 5	......	
	9 p. m.	......	50	......	Cu. 4	E. 2	W. 6	......	
March 19	7 a. m.	......	38	......	Cir. st. 8	SE. 3	SW. 2	......	
	2 p. m.	......	42	......	Cu. cir. 8	SE. 3	NW. 6	......	
	9 p. m.	......	38	......	Cu. st. 4	E. 1	W. 6	......	

STORM No. 1, MARCH, 1859.

POINT PLEASANT, VIRGINIA.

Month and day.	Hour.	Barom'r corrected to 32° F.	Thermometer.	Force of vapor.	Cloudiness.		Motion of clouds.		Winds.		Relative humidity.	REMARKS.
March 14	7 a. m.	29.80	40	------		0		0	E.	2	------	16th. Rain from 11 a. m. to 12 m.;
	2 p. m.	29.80	56	------		0		0	E.	2	------	amount, 0.1875 inch.
	9 p. m.	29.80	44	------		0		0	E.	1	------	17th Rain from 11.40 a. m. to
March 15	7 a. m.	29.60	40	------	St.	5	W.	5	S.	2	------	12 m.; amount, 0.175 inch.
	2 p. m.	29.60	55	------	Nim.	5	W.	5	S.	3	------	19th. Snow.
	9 p. m.	29.50	42	------	Nim.	5	W.	5	W.	2	------	
March 16	7 a. m.	29.40	45	------	Nim.	10	W.	5	S.	2	------	
	2 p. m.	29.30	55	------	Nim.	10	W.	10	S.	3	------	
	9 p. m.	29.30	40	------	Nim.	10	W.	10	E.	2	------	
March 17	7 a. m.	29.20	46	------	Nim.	10	W.	10	E.	2	------	
	2 p. m.	29.30	50	------	Nim.	10	W.	5	E.	3	------	
	9 p. m.	29.40	40	------	Nim.	10	W.	5	E.	2	------	
March 18	7 a. m.	29.00	44	------	St.	5	E.	5	E.	2	------	
	2 p. m.	29.00	50	------	St.	5	W.	5	E.	3	------	
	9 p. m.	29.00	38	------		0		0	E.	2	------	
March 19	7 a. m.	29.00	37	------	St.	5	E.	5	E.	2	------	
	2 p. m.	29.00	41	------	St.	5	W.	5	E.	3	------	
	9 p. m.	29.00	40	------	Nim.	10	E.	5	E.	2	------	

POPLAR GROVE, VIRGINIA.

Month and day.	Hour.	Barom'r corrected to 32° F.	Thermometer.	Force of vapor.	Cloudiness.		Motion of clouds.		Winds.		Relative humidity.	REMARKS.
March 14	7 a. m.	------	52	------	St.	10	S.	4		0	------	14th. Drizzling rain from 6 a. m.
	2 p. m.	------	58	------	St.	10	SW.	4	SE.	2	------	to 2 p. m.; amount, 0.75 inch.
	9 p. m.	------	52	------	Cir. cu.	5	SW.	7	SW.	2	------	17th. Rain at 1 p. m.; amount,
March 15	7 a. m.	------	44	------		0		0	W.	1	------	0.25 inch.
	2 p. m.	------	55	------	Cu. st.	9	NW.	6	NW.	6	------	18th. Storm from 11 a. m. to 4
	9 p. m.	------	39	------	Cir.	2	W.	4	NW.	3	------	p. m; amount, 0.50 inch.
March 16	7 a. m.	------	29	------		0		0		0	------	
	2 p. m.	------	66	------		0		0	NW.	1	------	
	9 p. m.	------	42	------	Cir.	2	W.	2	W.	1	------	
March 17	7 a. m.	------	45	------	St.	10		0		0	------	
	2 p. m.	------	55	------	Cir.	10	S.	5	NE.	2	------	
	9 p. m.	------	52	------	St.	10	S.	4	W.	2	------	
March 18	7 a. m.	------	52	------	Cir. st.	10	SW.	3		0	------	
	2 p. m.	------	52	------	Cu. st.	10	S.	5	W.	3	------	
	9 p. m.	------	39	------	Cu. st.	9	SW.	4	NW.	4	------	
March 19	7 a. m.	------	34	------	Cu. st.	10	W.	6	NW.	5	------	
	2 p. m.	------	36	------	Cu. st.	10	W.	4	NW.	4	------	
	9 p. m.	------	34	------	St.	10		0	NW.	2	------	

PORTSMOUTH, VIRGINIA.

Month and day.	Hour.	Barom'r corrected to 32° F.	Thermometer.	Force of vapor.	Cloudiness.	Motion of clouds.	Winds.		Relative humidity.	REMARKS.
March 14	7 a. m.	30.14	56	------	1	----------	SW.	1	------	Rain from 11 p. m. the 14th to 15th;
	2 p. m.	29.90	61	------	7	----------	SE.	3	------	showers; amount, 0.57 inch.
	9 p. m.	29.83	57	------	10	----------	SE.	5	------	16th. Lunar halo.
March 15	7 a. m.	29.62	56	------	10	----------	SE.	3	------	17th. Rain at night; amount, 0.76
	2 p. m.	29.63	62	------	3	----------	SW.	4	------	inch.
	9 p. m.	29.80	56	------	1	----------	NW.	2	------	18th. Showers; amount, 0.10 inch.
March 16	7 a. m.	30.20	48	------	0	----------	N.	2	------	
	2 p. m.	30.21	60	------	0	----------	NW.	2	------	
	9 p. m.	30.28	48	------	3	----------	NW.	2	------	
March 17	7 a. m.	30.29	50	------	6	----------	S.	1	------	
	2 p. m.	30.10	59	------	6	----------	SE.	2	------	
	9 p. m.	30.02	57	------	7	----------	SE.	2	------	
March 18	7 a. m.	29.65	60	------	7	----------	SW.	2	------	
	2 p. m.	29.49	68	------	4	----------	SW.	4	------	
	9 p. m.	29.38	52	------	6	----------	SW.	6	------	
March 19	7 a. m.	29.60	42	------	1	----------	SW.	4	------	
	2 p. m.	29.64	50	------	2	----------	SW.	4	------	
	9 p. m.	29.89	40	------	7	----------	W.	4	------	

STORM No. 1, MARCH, 1359.

ROUGEMENT, VIRGINIA.

Month and day.	Hour.	Barom'r corrected to 32° F.	Thermometer.	Force of vapor.	Cloudiness.	Motion of clouds.	Winds.	Relative humidity.	REMARKS.
March 14	7 a. m.	......	50	......	Cir. st. 10	0	NE. 2	......	14th. Began to rain at 9¾ a. m., and ended in the night; amount, 0. 80 inch.
	2 p m.	......	55	......	Nim. 10	SE. 6	NE. 2	......	
	9 p. m.	......	58	......	Rain 10	....	NE. 2	......	
March 15	7 a. m.	......	58	......	Cir. st. 8	S. 3	S. 2	......	Rain from 6¼ p. m. the 17th to 9 a. m. on the 18th; amount, 0.51 inch.
	2 p m.	......	64	......	Cu 8	W. 2	W. 5	......	
	9 p. m.	......	48	......	Cir. 1	W. 3	W. 2	......	
March 16	7 a. m.	......	40	......	0	0	W. 1	......	19th. Showery; amount, 0.40 inch.
	2 p. m.	......	61	......	Cir. st. 1	0	W. 3	......	
	9 p m.	......	52	......	Cu. st. 7	W. 1	W. 1	......	
March 17	7 a. m.	......	47	......	Cir. st. 9	0	SW. 2	......	
	2 p. m.	......	63	......	Cir. st. 10	0	S. 2	......	
	9 p. m.	......	55	......	Nim. 10	S. 3	S. 2	......	
March 18	7 a. m.	......	62	......	Nim. 10	S. 6	S. 2	......	
	2 p. m.	......	69	......	Cu. 9	S. 6	S. 6	......	
	9 p. m.	......	51	......	Cu. 3	W. 2	W. 4	......	
March 19	7 a. m.	......	39	......	Cu. 8	W. 5	W. 6	......	
	2 p. m.	......	41	......	Cu. 9	W. 4	W. 5	......	
	9 p. m.	......	34	......	Cu. 3	W. 4	W. 5	......	

RUTHVEN, VIRGINIA.

Month and day.	Hour.	Barom'r corrected to 32° F.	Thermometer.	Force of vapor.	Cloudiness.	Motion of clouds.	Winds.	Relative humidity.	REMARKS.
March 14	7 a. m.	29. 79	50	......	10	....	....	......	Rain from 2 p. m. the 14th to 8 a. m. on the 15th; amount, 1.20 inch.
	2 p. m.	......	......	......	0	....	....	......	
	9 p m.	29. 54	64	......	0	....	....	......	
March 15	7 a. m.	29. 34	59	......	0	....	....	......	18th. Showery; amount, 0. 49 inch.
	2 p. m.	29. 30	64	......	0	....	....	......	
	9 p. m.	29. 62	48	......	1	....	....	......	
March 16	7 a. m.	29. 82	41	......	5	....	....	......	
	2 p. m.	29. 81	59	......	....	....	....	......	
	9 p. m.	29. 83	41	......	9	....	....	......	
March 17	7 a. m.	29. 85	45	......	10	....	....	......	
	2 p. m.	......	......	......	7	....	....	......	
	9 p. m.	29. 65	57	......	3	....	....	......	
March 18	7 a. m.	29. 26	63	......	1	....	....	......	
	2 p m.	28. 98	69	......	....	....	....	......	
	9 p. m.	28. 99	51	......	3	....	....	......	
March 19	7 a. m.	29. 19	43	......	....	....	....	......	
	2 p. m.	......	......	......	....	....	....	......	
	9 p. m.	29. 53	39	......	0	....	....	......	

SMITHFIELD, VIRGINIA.

Month and day.	Hour.	Barom'r corrected to 32° F.	Thermometer.	Force of vapor.	Cloudiness.	Motion of clouds.	Winds.	Relative humidity.	REMARKS.
March 14	7 a. m.	......	46. 7	......	Cir. nim. 10	S. 1	NE. 1	......	14th. Began to rain at 1.45 p. m., and ended in the night; amount, 0. 216 inch.
	2 p. m.	......	72	......	Cu. nim. 10	S. 2	S. 2	......	
	9 p. m.	......	65	......	Cu. nim. 10	S. 1	S. 2	......	
March 15	7 a. m.	......	64. 8	......	Cu. nim. 10	S. 2	S. 2	......	15th. Rain from 8 to 10 a. m.; heavy, distant thunder from 9 to 9. 20 a. m.; amount, 0.475 inch.
	2 p. m.	......	67. 8	......	Cir. cu. 3	W. 1	W. 3	......	
	9 p. m.	......	51	......	0	....	NW. 1	......	
March 16	7 a. m.	......	39	......	0	....	NW. 1	......	17th. Rain from the preceding night to 6. 30 a. m.; amount, 0. 45 inch.
	2 p. m.	......	60	......	Cir. st. 1	....	NW. 1	......	
	9 p. m.	......	44	......	Nim. st. 3	S. 1	SE. 1	......	
March 17	7 a. m.	......	45. 4	......	Cir. st. 9	W. 1	S. 1	......	18th. Rain from 8 a. m. to 7. 30 p. m.; amount, 0. 69 inch.
	2 p. m.	......	66	......	Cu. nim. 10	SW. 1	S. 1	......	
	9 p. m.	......	54	......	Cir. nim. 9	S. 1	SE. 1	......	
March 18	7 a. m.	......	65	......	Cu. nim. 10	SW. 1	S. 2	......	
	2 p. m.	......	69	......	Cu. nim. 9	S. 2	S. 2	......	
	9 p. m.	......	54	......	Cir. cu. 9	SW. 2	SW. 4	......	
March 19	7 a. m.	......	41. 2	......	0	....	SW. 3	......	
	2 p. m.	......	50	......	Cir. cu. 8	W. 2	SW. 3	......	
	9 p. m.	......	40	......	Cu. st. 7	NW. 1	W. 2	......	

STORM No. 1, MARCH, 1859.

STRIBLING SPRINGS, VIRGINIA.

Month and day.	Hour.	Barom'r corrected to 32° F.	Thermometer.	Force of vapor.	Cloudiness.	Motion of clouds.	Winds.	Relative humidity.	REMARKS.
March 14	7 a. m.	------	38	------	Cu. 3	SW. 3	NW. 2	------	14th. Rain from 10 a. m. to 10 p. m.; very heavy in the evening. 15th. Fine day; wind high; chilly in p. m. 16th. Large halo, very distinct at 6½ p. m. 17th. Hazy part of the day; steady rain at night, commencing at 6 p. m. 18th. Blustering, stormy day. 19th. Snow squalls during the day; wind high.
	2 p. m.	------	45	------	Cu. 1	SW. 4	NW. 2	------	
	9 p. m.	------	47	------	Cu. 1	SW. 4	SW. 3	------	
March 15	7 a. m.	------	42	------	0	0	NW. 2	------	
	2 p. m.	------	56	------	Cu. cir. 10	SW. 3	SW. 4	------	
	9 p. m.	------	37	------	Cu. st. 10	SW. 1	SW. 2	------	
March 16	7 a. m.	------	32	------	Cu. 10	SW. 1	SW. 2	------	
	2 p. m.	------	57	------	Cu. 10	SW. 1	SW. 3	------	
	9 p. m.	------	33	------	Nim. 10	0	SW. 1	------	
March 17	7 a. m.	------	35	------	Nim. cu. 10	SE. 2	NW. 2	------	
	2 p. m.	------	67	------	Nim. 10	SW. 4	SW. 3	------	
	9 p. m.	------	44	------	Nim. 6	SW. 4	SW. 1	------	
March 18	7 a. m.	------	52	------	Nim. 10	NW. 4	NE. 2	------	
	2 p. m.	------	62	------	Nim. 6	NW. 4	SW. 4	------	
	9 p. m.	------	37	------	Nim. 3	SW. 4	SW. 5	------	
March 19	7 a. m.	------	27	------	0	0	NW. 5	------	
	2 p. m.	------	36	------	Cir. st. 4	SW. 1	NW. 5	------	
	9 p. m.	------	31	------	0	0	SW. 5	------	

WESTWOOD, VIRGINIA.

Month and day.	Hour.	Barom'r corrected to 32° F.	Thermometer.	Force of vapor.	Cloudiness.	Motion of clouds.	Winds.	Relative humidity.	REMARKS.
March 14	7 a. m.	------	47	------	------------	----------	------------	------	14th. Cloudy. 15th. Rain till 9 a. m.; cleared off windy. 16th. Fine day. 17th. Cloudy; rain in the night. 18th. Cloudy; light rain in the morning; wind and rain at 5.20 p. m. 19th. Clear and windy.
	2 p. m.	------	65	------	------------	----------	E ----------	------	
	9 p. m.	------	64	------	------------	----------	SE ----------	------	
March 15	7 a. m.	------	62	------	------------	----------	------------	------	
	2 p. m.	------	64	------	------------	----------	W. 35	------	
	9 p. m.	------	51	------	------------	----------	------------	------	
March 16	7 a. m.	------	39	------	------------	----------	------------	------	
	2 p. m.	------	58	------	------------	----------	------------	------	
	9 p. m.	------	50	------	------------	----------	------------	------	
March 17	7 a. m.	------	45	------	------------	----------	------------	------	
	2 p. m.	------	------	------	------------	----------	------------	------	
	9 p. m.	------	57	------	------------	----------	SE. 12	------	
March 18	7 a. m.	------	61	------	------------	----------	35	------	
	2 p. m.	------	71	------	------------	----------	S. 35	------	
	9 p. m.	------	55	------	------------	----------	W. 12	------	
March 19	7 a. m.	------	41	------	------------	----------	------------	------	
	2 p. m.	------	47	------	------------	----------	SW. 35	------	
	9 p. m.	------	40	------	------------	----------	SW. 35	------	

WINCHESTER, VIRGINIA.

Month and day.	Hour.	Barom'r corrected to 32° F.	Thermometer.	Force of vapor.	Cloudiness.	Motion of clouds.	Winds.	Relative humidity.	REMARKS.
March 14	7 a. m.	------	44	------	8	----------	0	------	14th. Rain; amount, 0.52 inch. 17th and 18th. Rain; amount, 0.80 inch.
	2 p. m.	------	54	------	10	----------	0	------	
	9 p. m.	------	55	------	10	----------	0	------	
March 15	7 a. m.	------	54	------	2	----------	S. 1	------	
	2 p. m.	------	64	------	3	----------	SW. 2	------	
	9 p. m.	------	46	------	4	----------	W. 4	------	
March 16	7 a. m.	------	40	------	0	----------	W. 4	------	
	2 p. m.	------	56	------	0	----------	W. 3	------	
	9 p. m.	------	40	------	0	----------	0	------	
March 17	7 a. m.	------	42	------	4	----------	0	------	
	2 p. m.	------	64	------	6	----------	0	------	
	9 p. m.	------	55	------	10	----------	0	------	
March 18	7 a. m.	------	55	------	10	----------	0	------	
	2 p. m.	------	72	------	8	----------	W. 2	------	
	9 p. m.	------	55	------	10	----------	------------	------	
March 19	7 a. m.	------	40	------	8	----------	W. 4	------	
	2 p. m.	------	40	------	10	----------	W. 4	------	
	9 p. m.	------	36	------	4	----------	W. 4	------	

STORM No. 1, MARCH, 1859.

MUSTAPHA, VIRGINIA.

REMARKS.—March 14th. Heavy thunder shower last night, accompanied by vivid lightning; the rain came down in torrents. 15th. Heavy rain for about two hours. 17th. Rain half of the day and night. 18th. Ceased to rain at 2 a. m., when a heavy thunder cloud came up, discharging wind and rain at a furious rate; wind very high, resembling a tempest at sunset, and continued all night. 19th. Ground covered with snow till 10 a. m.

CHAPEL HILL, NORTH CAROLINA.

Month and day.	Hour.	Barom'r corrected to 32° F.	Thermometer.	Force of vapor.	Cloudiness.	Motion of clouds.	Winds.	Relative humidity.	REMARKS.
March 14	7 a. m.	29. 645	51	------	10	S. 2	S. 2	------	Rain from 7 p. m. the 14th to 5 a. m. on the 15th; amount, 2. 647 inches. 18th. Rain during the past night; heavy shower at 3 p. m.; wind SW. 4 or 5; amount, 0. 924 inch.
	2 p. m.	29. 520	71	------	10	S. 2	S. 1	------	
	9 p. m.	29 450	62	------	10	Invisible --	SW. 2	------	
March 15	7 a. m.	29. 228	60	------	9	SW. 2	W. 2	------	
	2 p. m.	29. 297	63	------	0	----------	W. 4	------	
	9 p. m.	29. 527	52	------	0	----------	W. 3	------	
March 16	7 a. m.	29. 682	38	------	0	----------	W. 2	------	
	2 p. m.	29. 783	61	------	7	W. 1	W. 2	------	
	9 p. m.	29. 797	49	------	5	W. 1	SE. 1	------	
March 17	7 a. m.	29. 803	46	------	10	Invisible --	E. 1	------	
	2 p. m.	29. 684	69	------	10	S. 1	S. 1	------	
	9 p. m.	29. 486	60	------	10	S. 2	S. 3	------	
March 18	7 a. m.	29. 158	64	------	10	SW. 3	S. 3	------	
	2 p. m.	28. 923	70	------	7	S. 2	S. 3	------	
	9 p. m.	29. 130	45	------	8	SW. 2	SW. 3	------	
March 19	7 a. m.	29. 266	38	------	0	----------	W. 3	------	
	2 p. m.	29. 353	46	------	6	W. 2	W. 3	------	
	9 p. m.	29. 515	39	------	0	----------	N. 2	------	

GASTON, NORTH CAROLINA.

Month and day.	Hour.	Barom'r corrected to 32° F.	Thermometer.	Force of vapor.	Cloudiness.	Motion of clouds.	Winds.	Relative humidity.	REMARKS.
March 14	7 a. m.	------	52	------	------	------	------	------	14th. Rain; thunder in SW.; am't, 1. 76 inch. 15th. Rain; amount, 0. 16 inch. 17th. Rain; amount, 0. 60 inch. 18th. Rain; lightning in SW.; amount, 0. 27 inch.
	2 p. m.	------	72	------	------	------	------	------	
	9 p. m.	------	64	------	------	------	------	------	
March 15	7 a. m.	------	64	------	------	------	------	------	
	2 p. m.	------	68	------	------	------	------	------	
	9 p. m.	------	56	------	------	------	------	------	
March 16	7 a. m.	------	52	------	------	------	------	------	
	2 p. m.	------	61	------	------	------	------	------	
	9 p. m.	------	42	------	------	------	------	------	
March 17	7 a. m.	------	44	------	------	------	------	------	
	2 p. m.	------	47	------	------	------	------	------	
	9 p. m.	------	59	------	------	------	------	------	
March 18	7 a. m.	------	61	------	------	------	------	------	
	2 p. m.	------	65	------	------	------	------	------	
	9 p. m.	------	52	------	------	------	------	------	
March 19	7 a. m.	------	45	------	------	------	------	------	
	2 p. m.	------	52	------	------	------	------	------	
	9 p. m.	------	40	------	------	------	------	------	

STORM No. 1, MARCH, 1859.

MURFREESBOROUGH, NORTH CAROLINA.

Month and day.	Hour.	Barom'r corrected to 32° F.	Thermometer.	Force of vapor.	Cloudiness.	Motion of clouds.	Winds.	Relative humidity.	REMARKS.
March 14	7 a. m.	29.44	50	.382	Cir. 2	W. 2	E. 1	96	Rain from 2 p. m. the 14th to 9½ a. m. on the 15th; amount, 0.90 inch.
	2 p. m.	29.24	70	.658	Nim. 10	SE. 2	SE. 2	90	
	9 p. m.	29.30	67	.626	Nim. 8	SW. 6	SW. 4	95	
March 15	7 a. m.	29.05	66	.626	Nim. 10	SW. 3	SW. 2	95	16th. Slight frost; lunar halo, very distinct at 10 p. m.
	2 p. m.	28.99	69	.551	Cu. 2	W. 3	W. 5	75	
	9 p. m.	29.22	57	.378	0	0	W. 1	81	Heavy rain, commencing in the night of the 17th and ending at 7 p. m. on the 18th; amount, 0.90 inch.
March 16	7 a. m.	29.51	42	.244	0	0	0	91	
	2 p. m.	29.46	60	.442	Cu. 1	W. 1	W. 2	83	
	9 p. m.	29.49	49	.335	Cir. 3	W. 3	0	93	
March 17	7 a. m.	29.60	45	.309	Cir. cu. 8	W. 2	0	96	
	2 p. m.	29.39	65	.536	St. 8	W. 1	SE. 2	84	
	9 p. m.	29.26	60	.505	Cir. cu. 10	SW. 1	SE. 2	94	
March 18	7 a. m.	29.00	46	.626	Nim. 10	SW. 3	SE. 3	95	
	2 p. m.	28.79	69	.658	St. 8	W. 1	SW. 4	90	
	9 p. m.	28.88	55	.391	Cu. 8	W. 4	SW. 5	87	
March 19	7 a. m.	29.08	43	.273	0	0	SW. 3	85	
	2 p. m.	29.14	50	.296	Cu. 3	W. 3	SW. 4	79	
	9 p. m.	29.31	42	.222	St. 1	W. 2	W. 4	83	

AIKEN, SOUTH CAROLINA.

Month and day.	Hour.	Barom'r corrected to 32° F.	Thermometer.	Force of vapor.	Cloudiness.	Motion of clouds.	Winds.	Relative humidity.	REMARKS.
March 14	7 a. m.	------	------	------	------------	----------	------------	------	Rain on the 17th; amount, 2.032 inches.
	2 p. m.	------	------	------	------------	----------	------------	------	
	9 p. m.	------	------	------	------------	----------	------------	------	
March 15	7 a. m.	------	50	------	0	----------	------------	------	
	2 p. m.	------	------	------	------------	----------	------------	------	
	9 p. m.	------	52	------	0	----------	------------	------	
March 16	7 a. m.	------	54	------	0	----------	------------	------	
	2 p. m.	------	64	------	5	----------	------------	------	
	9 p. m.	------	54	------	0	----------	------------	------	
March 17	7 a. m.	------	60	------	10	----------	------------	------	
	2 p. m.	------	61	------	10	----------	------------	------	
	9 p. m.	------	62	------	10	----------	------------	------	
March 18	7 a. m.	------	62	------	9	----------	------------	------	
	2 p. m.	------	------	------	------------	----------	------------	------	
	9 p. m.	------	41	------	0	----------	------------	------	
March 19	7 a. m.	------	42	------	1	----------	------------	------	
	2 p. m.	------	------	------	------------	----------	------------	------	
	9 p. m.	------	45	------	0	----------	------------	------	

ALL SAINTS, SOUTH CAROLINA.

Month and day.	Hour.	Barom'r corrected to 32° F.	Thermometer.	Force of vapor.	Cloudiness.	Motion of clouds.	Winds.	Relative humidity.
March 14	7 a. m.	30.04	62	.523	Cir. st. 3	W. 2	S. 2	94
	2 p. m.	29.98	70	.658	Cir.st., nim. 10	W. 1	S. 4	90
	9 p. m.	29.94	67	.626	Cir cu., nim. 10	SW. 4	S. 4	95
March 15	7 a. m.	29.76	68	.612	Cir.st.,cir.cu. 8	SW. 3	SW. 3	90
	2 p. m.	29.83	67	.246	0	---------	W. 5	37
	9 p. m.	29.97	66	.470	0	---------	W. 1	73
March 16	7 a. m.	30.16	46	.192	Cir. 1	W. 1	N. 2	62
	2 p. m.	30.19	60	.255	Cir., cir. st. 5	W. 2	SE. 3	49
	9 p. m.	30.20	54	.335	Cir. st., haze 5	W. 1	S. 1	80
March 17	7 a. m.	30.20	54	.390	Cr.st.,cr.cu. 10	S. 3	N. 2	93
	2 p. m.	30.02	68	.509	Cr.st.,cr.cu. 10	SW. 2	SE. 3	75
	9 p. m.	29.92	66	.570	Cir.st., nim. 10	SW. 2	S. 4	89
March 18	7 a. m.	29.71	67	.626	Nim. 10	SW. 3	SW. 5	95
	2 p. m.	29.55	66	.570	Cir.cu.,nim. 10	SW. 4	SW. 5	89
	9 p. m.	29.70	51	.149	Cir. cu. 1	W. 3	W. 5	40
March 19	7 a. m.	29.88	43	.142	Cir. cu. 1	W. 2	W. 4	51
	2 p. m.	29.85	54	.157	Cir. cu. 1	W. 3	W. 5	38
	9 p. m.	29.97	58	.212	0	----------	W. 2	63

REMARKS.

14th. Fine morning; rain from 9.30 to 10.30 a. m.; variable a. m. and p. m.; rain 5.30 to 8.30 p. m., and 11 to 12 p. m.; amount, 0.78 inch.

15th. Fine morning; about 8 a. m. became cloudy and threatening in the W.; 8.30 a. m. wind W., strong; clouds cleared away; high wind during the day.

16th. Fine day; at night a large halo around the moon.

17th. Variable, cloudy, afternoon and night; rain from 11 p. m. through the night; high wind.

18th. Rain, with high wind till 10.30 a. m., wind at times a strong gale; about 3 p. m. clouds cleared away; at 5 p. m. a very heavy cloud rose from W., giving a sprinkling of rain; barometer reached its minimum, 29.60, at 5 p. m.; night clear, with high wind from W.; amount, 0.60 inch.

19th. Fine; high wind, in gusts, at times till 4 or 5 p. m.

STORM No. 1, MARCH, 1859.

CHARLESTON, SOUTH CAROLINA.

Month and day.	Hour.	Barom'r corrected to 32° F.	Thermometer.	Force of vapor.	Cloudiness.	Motion of clouds.	Winds.	Relative humidity.	REMARKS.
March 14	7 a. m.	30. 14	64	......	....	....	SW........	......	14th. Rain; amount, 0.06 inch.
	2 p. m.	29. 88	76	......	....	....	Cloudy......	......	17th. Rain, with thunder; amount, 0.20 inch.
	9 p. m.	30. 02	69	......	....	....	....	......	
March 15	7 a. m.	30. 03	66	......	....	....	SW........	......	
	2 p. m.	29. 99	67	......	....	....	Cloudy......	......	
	9 p. m	30. 12	61	......	....	....	....	......	
March 16	7 a. m.	30. 39	52	......	....	....	NW........	......	
	2 p. m.	30. 31	61	......	....	....	Clear........	......	
	9 p m.	30. 29	59	......	....	....	NE........	......	
March 17	7 a. m.	30. 38	59	......	....	....	SE........	......	
	2 p. m.	30. 13	70	......	....	....	Clear........	......	
	9 p m.	30. 00	68	......	....	....	Cloudy......	......	
March 18	7 a. m.	29. 87	66	......	....	....	SW........	......	
	2 p m.	29. 79	67	......	....	....	Cloudy......	......	
	9 p. m	29. 91	52	......	....	....	Gusty......	......	
March 19	7 a. m.	29. 96	45	......	....	....	W........	......	
	2 p m.	30. 01	56	......	....	....	Clear........	......	
	9 p. m.	30. 14	54	......	....	....	NW........	......	

COLUMBIA, SOUTH CAROLINA.*

Month and day.	Hour.	Barom'r corrected to 32° F.	Thermometer.	Force of vapor.	Cloudiness.		Motion of clouds.		Winds.		Relative humidity.	REMARKS.
March 14	7 a. m.	29. 83	60	. 390	Cu.	10	SE.	3	SE.	2	74	14th. Rain from 5½ to 7 p. m. and in the night; amount, 0.69 inch.
	2 p m.	29. 75	74	. 210	Cu.	10	W.	2	SE.	3	25	16th and 19th. Frost.
	9 p. m.	29. 72	64	. 579	Cu.	10	W.	2		0	97	
March 15	7 a. m.	29. 67	59	. 222	St.	2	W.	2	SW.	3	45	
	2 p m.	29. 71	63	. 106		0	....		W.	3	18	
	9 p. m.	29. 84	55	. 132		0	....		NW.	1	30	
March 16	7 a. m.	29. 97	38	. 204	St.	2	W.	1		0	90	
	2 p. m.	30. 01	64	. 169	Cir. st.	7	W.	1	SE.	1	28	
	9 p. m.	30. 02	55	. 224		10	....		SE.	2	52	
March 17	7 a. m.	30. 01	52	. 276	Cu.	10	W.	1	SE.	2	72	
	2 p. m.	29. 78	68	. 476	Cu.	10	S.	3	SE.	3	69	
	9 p. m.	29. 66	66	. 580		10	....		SE.	4	89	
March 18	7 a. m.	29. 50	67	. 591	Cu.	10	SW.	3	S.	2	89	
	2 p m.	29. 30	62	. 256		7	SW.	3	S.	3	46	
	9 p. m.	29. 62	44	. 189	Cu.	1	W.	3	W.	4	64	
March 19	7 a. m.	29. 69	39	. 131		0	....		W.	3	55	
	2 p. m.	29. 73	54	. 116		0	....		W.	3	28	
	9 p. m.	29. 81	48	. 143		0	....		W.	2	43	

COLUMBIA, (ARSENAL ACADEMY,) SOUTH CAROLINA.

Month and day.	Hour.	Barom'r corrected to 32° F.	Thermometer.	Force of vapor.	Cloudiness.		Motion of clouds.		Winds.		Relative humidity.	REMARKS.
March 14	7 a. m.	29. 86	62	. 491	Nim.	9		0	SW.	0	88	14th Began to rain at 5.30 p. m. and ended in the night; amount, 0.60 inch.
	2 p. m.	29. 88	75	. 785	Nim.	10		0	SW.	8	90	Rain from 4.15 p. m. the 17th to 2 p. m. on the 18th; amount, 0.70 inch.
	9 p. m.	28. 75	66	. 536	Nim.	10		0		0	84	
March 15	7 a. m.	28. 78	57	. 407		0		0	W.	0	87	
	2 p. m.	28. 74	65	. 583		0		0	W.	12	94	
	9 p. m.	28. 87	55	. 376		0		0		0	87	
March 16	7 a. m.	28. 93	49	. 272		0		0	N.	0	78	
	2 p. m.	28. 99	68	. 543	Cir. st.	3		0	E.	2	79	
	9 p. m.	29. 02	59	. 410		0		0		0	82	
March 17	7 a. m.	29. 02	53	. 375	Nim.	10		0	SW.	0	93	
	2 p. m.	28. 80	66	. 570	Nim.	10		0	SE.	0	89	
	9 p. m.	28. 70	68	. 577	Nim.	10		0		0	85	
March 18	7 a m.	28. 56	65	. 583	Nim.	10		0	S.	0	94	
	2 p. m.	28. 43	61	. 505	Cir. st.	2	NE.	4	SW.	18	94	
	9 p. m.	28. 59	44	. 265		0		0		0	92	
March 19	7 a. m.	28. 76	39	. 216		0		0	W.	8	91	
	2 p. m.	28. 78	53	. 375		0		0	W.	9	93	
	9 p. m.	28. 84	48	. 310		0		0		0	92	

* Dr. E. H. Barton, observer.

STORM No. 1, MARCH, 1859.

ST. JOHN'S, SOUTH CAROLINA.

Month and day.	Hour.	Barom'r corrected to 32° F.	Thermometer.	Force of vapor.	Cloudiness.	Motion of clouds.	Winds.	Relative humidity.	REMARKS.
March 14	7 a. m.	30. 12	60	. 505	Nim. 10	E. 1	SE. 1	94	14th. Rain from 4. 5 to 5. 15 p. m., and sprinkle at 9. 15 p. m ; amount, 0. 32 inch.
	2 p m.	30. 10	74	. 604	Nim. 10	NE. 2	SE. 4	73	
	9 p. m.	30. 02	69	. 671	Nim. 10	N. 4	S. 5	95	
March 15	7 a. m.	29. 92	66	. 502	Nim. 10	E. 3	NW. 4	78	17th. Began to rain at 10.30 p. m., and ended in the night; amount, 0. 29 inch.
	2 p. m.	29. 88	68	. 295	St. 1	----------	NW. 5	63	
	9 p. m.	29. 99	47	. 247	Cir. st. 1	----------	E. 2	71	
March 16	7 a. m.	30. 20	42	. 222	Cir. st. 2	----------	NE. 2	83	18th. Raining from 6. 30 a. m. till evening ; amount, 0. 18 inch.
	2 p. m.	30. 32	67	. 230	Nim 7	E. 1	SE. 2	38	
	9 p. m.	30. 30	52	. 335	Cir. st. 5	E. 1	NW. 2	80	
March 17	7 a. m.	30. 26	53	. 362	Nim. 10	E. 1	E. 2	87	
	2 p. m.	30. 12	73	. 489	Nim. 10	NE. 2	SE. 4	62	
	9 p. m.	29. 96	70	. 658	Nim. 10	NE. 5	SW. 6	90	
March 18	7 a. m.	29. 84	67	. 626	Nim. 10	NE. 4	SW. 4	95	
	2 p. m.	29.58	68	. 509	Nim. 1	NE. 3	SW. 5	75	
	9 p. m.	29. 86	46	. 156	Cir. 1	----------	NW. 6	48	
March 19	7 a. m.	29. 93	------	. 265	0	----------	NW. 5	92	
	2 p. m.	29. 96	55	. 181	Cir. 1	E. 1	NW. 5	43	
	9 p. m.	------	46	. 156	0	----------	SW. 2	48	

ATHENS, GEORGIA.

Month and day.	Hour.	Barom'r corrected to 32° F.	Thermometer.	Force of vapor.	Cloudiness.	Motion of clouds.	Winds.	Relative humidity.	REMARKS.
March 13	9 p. m	29. 38	60	9. 83	Cu. st. 10	W. 1	· 0	76	14th. Drizzling rain began at 11½ a. m., and ended in the night; amount, 0. 906 inch.
March 14	7 a. m.	29. 23	62. 5	13. 67	Cu. st. 9	W. 1	SE. 2	95	
	2 p. m.	29. 18	59. 7	13. 04	Nim. 10	----------	SE. 2	100	
	9 p. m.	29. 14	60	12. 93	Nim. 9	----------	S. 1	90	16th. Commenced raining in the night, and continued till 8 p. m. on the 17th; amount, 1.557 inch.
March 15	7 a. m.	29. 20	50	4. 35	Nim. 10	----------	NW. 3	50	
	2 p. m.	29. 24	59. 9	2. 94	Nim. 10	----------	S. 1	22. 5	
	9 p. m	29. 35	50	3. 02	0	----------	SW. 3	33	18th. Rain, ending at 10 a. m. ; high wind from the W. all day ; a sudden shower at 4½ p. m., beginning with a brisk fall of hail ; amount, 0. 948 inch.
March 16	7 a. m.	29. 46	39. 5	4. 48	0	----------	NW. 4	72	
	2 p. m.	29. 44	61. 7	3. 47	Cir. st. 2	0	SE. 1	25	
	9 p. m.	29. 45	54. 5	4. 86	Cir. 3	W. 1	NE. 1	45	
March 17	7 a. m.	29. 39	48. 3	6. 79	Cir. st. 8	0	SE. 1	78	
	2 p. m.	29. 17	51. 8	9. 79	Cir. cu. 9	W. 3	SE. 1	100	19th. Frost.
	9 p. m.	28. 98	62. 6	14. 36	Nim. 10	S. 2	E. 2	99	
March 18	7 a. m.	28. 87	56. 8	11. 49	Nim. 10	----------	SE. 1	98	
	2 p. m.	29. 10	46. 4	4. 22	Nim. 10	S. 4	S. 4	53	
	9 p. m.	29. 13	40. 2	3. 75	Nim. 10	SW. 1	SW. 1	59	
March 19	7 a. m.	29. 21	40. 1	3. 43	Nim. 9	W. 1	W. 6	54	
	2 p. m.	29. 24	53	3. 05	Cu. st. 1	0	W. 2	29. 5	

ATLANTA, GEORGIA.

Month and day.	Hour.	Barom'r corrected to 32° F.	Thermometer.	Force of vapor.	Cloudiness.	Motion of clouds.	Winds.	Relative humidity.	REMARKS.
March 13	9 p. m.	30. 07	58	------	10	----------	E	------	14th. Rain ; amount, 0.50 inch.
March 14	7 a. m.	29. 95	60	------	10	----------	SE	------	17th. Rain ; amount, 1. 50 inch.
	2 p. m.	29. 93	58	------	10	----------	SE	------	18th. Rain ; amount, 0. 25 inch.
	9 p. m.	29. 90	60	------	5	----------	W	------	
March 15	7 a. m.	29. 90	44	------	0	----------	NW	------	
	2 p. m.	30. 00	58	------	0	----------	NW	------	
	9 p. m.	30. 00	50	------	0	----------	NW	------	
March 16	7 a. m.	30. 05	40	------	0	----------	NW	------	
	2 p m.	30. 18	58	------	5	----------	SE	------	
	9 p. m.	30. 10	54	------	5	----------	E	------	
March 17	7 a. m.	30. 00	48	------	10	----------	E	------	
	2 p. m.	29. 82	54	------	10	----------	SE	------	
	9 p. m.	29. 70	60	------	10	----------	S	------	
March 18	7 a. m.	29. 55	56	------	10	----------	S	------	
	2 p. m.	29. 58	42	------	5	----------	W	------	
	9 p. m.	29. 70	40	------	5	----------	NW	------	
March 19	7 a. m.	29. 82	34	------	0	----------	NW	------	
	2 p. m.	29. 95	50	------	0	----------	NW	------	

STORM No. 1, MARCH, 1859.

AUGUSTA, GEORGIA.

Month and day.	Hour.	Barom'r corrected to 32° F.	Thermometer.	Force of vapor.	Cloudiness.		Motion of clouds.		Winds.		Relative humidity.	REMARKS.
March 13	9 p. m.	30.04	64.5	.519	Cu. st.	10	SW.	2	SW.	0	75	14th. Rain; amount, 0.45 inch.
March 14	7 a. m.	30.00	65	.522	Cu. st.	10	SE.	3	SE.	0	79	16th. Light frost.
	2 p. m.	20.00	76.5	.623	Cu. st.	8	S.	2	SW.	2	75	17th. Heavy fall of rain in the p. m., wind and clouds from SE.; frequent thunderings at a distance in the SE., going eastward; amount, 2.05 inch.
	9 p. m.	29.87	66	.597	Cir. cu.	10	S. by W.	1	SW.	0	80	
March 15	7 a. m.	30.02	57	.255		0		0	SW.	2	53	
	2 p. m.	29.97	68	.251		0		0	SW.	4	39	
	9 p. m.	30.06	58	.296	Cu. st.	1	SW.	1	W.	3	57	
March 16	7 a. m.	30.14	44	.264		0		0	W.	0	72	
	2 p. m.	30.13	71	.351	Cu. st.	7	SW.	1	NE.	2	57	
	9 p. m.	30.18	59	.373	Cu. st.	10	SW.	1	NE.	0	62	
March 17	7 a. m.	30.20	57	.354	Cu. st.	9	SW.	1	NE.	0	66	
	2 p. m.	30.16	66	.512	Cu.	10	SE.	2	SE.	2	72	
	9 p. m.	30.05	67	.572	Cu. st.	10	SE.	3	SE.	1	76	
March 18	7 a. m.	29.94	64.5	.430	Cu. st.	10	SE.	3	SE.	1	43	
	2 p. m.	29.86	63	.359		0		0	SW.	4	58	
	9 p. m.	29.94	46	.308		0		0	SW.	4	79	
March 19	7 a. m.	29.98	43.5	.160		0		0	SW.	0	53	
	2 p. m.	30.01	59	.179		0		0	W.	0	38½	

SAVANNAH, GEORGIA.

Month and day.	Hour.	Barom'r corrected to 32° F.	Thermometer.	Force of vapor.	Cloudiness.		Motion of clouds.		Winds.		Relative humidity.	REMARKS.
March 13	9 p. m.	30.17	63.3	.593	H.	9	W.	----	E.	----	95	14th. Rain from 1 to 4 p. m.; amount, 0.043 inch.
March 14	7 a. m.	30.06	64.3	.705	Hin.	9	----------		SE.	----	92	17th. Rain in the night; amount, 0.093 inch.
	2 p. m.	30.02	71	.654	Mk.	10	----------		SE.	----	94	18th. Shower at 7 a. m.; amount, 0.017 inch.
	9 p. m.	30.00	67.8	.430	Dark	10	----------		SE.	----	71	
March 15	7 a. m.	30.00	63.6	.145	Hi.	9	----------		WNW.	3	22	
	2 p. m.	29.99	67.1	.219		0	----------		WNW.	3	45	
	9 p. m.	30.12	58	.254		0	----------		WNW.	1	76	
March 16	7 a. m.	30.22	48.3	.295		0	----------		NW.	2	52	
	2 p. m.	30.28	62.6	.391	Cgh.	4	----------		E.	3	80	
	9 p. m.	30.23	58.2	.463	H.	5	W.	----	ENE.	1	89	
March 17	7 a. m.	30.18	59	.538	Hi.	10	----------		E.	1	74	
	2 p. m.	30.05	69.6	.667	M.	10	----------		SE.	3	91	
	9 p. m.	29.91	69.5	.621	M.	10	----------		SSE.	4	94	
March 18	7 a. m.	29.93	66.6	.264	Mk.	10	----------		S.	2	34	
	2 p. m.	29.61	70.7	.152	Hgd.	5	----------		S.	4	43	
	9 p. m.	29.97	49.5	.122		0	----------		WSW.	2	43	
March 19	7 a. m.	30.07	43.3	.107		0	----------		W.	3	23	
	2 p. m.	30.02	57.9	.184		0	----------		W.	4	48	

SPARTA, GEORGIA.

Month and day.	Hour.	Barom'r corrected to 32° F.	Thermometer.	Force of vapor.	Cloudiness.		Motion of clouds.		Winds.		Relative humidity.	REMARKS.
March 13	9 p. m.	------	60	------	Cir. cu.	10	W.	2	E.	1	------	14th. Rain from 2½ to 3½ p. m.; amount, 0.71 inch.
March 14	7 a. m.	------	65	------	Cir.	1	W.	2	S.	4	------	17th. Rain during the day and night; amount, 1.53 inch.
	2 p. m.	------	73	------		0	----------		SW.	3	------	18th. Rain from 10 to 10½ a. m.; amount, 0.20 inch.
	9 p. m.	------	64	------	Cir.	0	NW.	1	SW.	1	------	
March 15	7 a. m.	------	52	------	{ Cir. cu. / Cir. st. }	2	NW.	1	W.	3	------	
	2 p. m.	------	63	------	Nim.	10	----------		W.	4	------	
	9 p. m.	------	55	------	Cir. cu.	10	W.	2	NW.	1	------	
March 16	7 a. m.	------	41	------	Nim.	10	S.	1	NE.	1	------	
	2 p. m.	------	66	------	Nim.	10	SE.	5	E.	1	------	
	9 p. m.	------	58	------	Nim.	10	SW.	2	SE.	3	------	
March 17	7 a. m.	------	55	------	Nim.	10	SW.	4	SE.	2	------	
	2 p. m.	------	60	------	Cu. & nim.	10	W.	2	SE.	2	------	
	9 p. m.	------	64	------		0	----------		SE.	4	------	
March 18	7 a. m.	------	61	------		0	----------		S.	2	------	
	2 p. m.	------	51	------		0	----------		W.	5	------	
	9 p. m.	------	42	------		0	----------		W.	1	------	
March 19	7 a. m.	------	40	------	Cir. st.	3	NW.	1	W.	2	------	
	2 p. m.	------	55	------		7	NW.	2	W.	4	------	

STORM No. 1, MARCH, 1859.

THOMASTON, GEORGIA.

Month and day.	Hour.	Barom'r corrected to 32° F.	Thermometer.	Force of vapor.	Cloudiness.	Motion of clouds.	Winds.	Relative humidity.
March 13	9 p. m.	29. 16			10		NE	
March 14	7 a. m.	29. 06			10		SE	
	2 p. m.	29. 06			10		S	
	9 p. m.	29. 07			10		S	
March 15	7 a. m.	29. 05			1		SW	
	2 p. m.	29. 07			4		SW	
	9 p. m.	29. 09			6		W	
March 16	7 a. m.	29. 21			7		NE	
	2 p. m.	29. 16			4		E	
	9 p. m.	29. 17			8		SE	
March 17	7 a. m.	29. 08			10		S	
	2 p. m.	28. 84			10		SW	
	9 p. m.	28. 71			9		W	
March 18	7 a. m.	28. 69			10		W	
	2 p. m.	28. 79			9		W	
	9 p. m.	28. 96			0		W	
March 19	7 a. m.	29. 02			0		W	
	2 p. m.	29. 04			0		W	

REMARKS.—14th. Rain; amount, 0. 75 inch. 18th. Rain; amount, 0. 75 inch. 19th. Rain, with a sprinkling of snow; amount, 0. 75 inch.

THOMSON, GEORGIA.

Month and day.	Hour.	Barom'r corrected to 32° F.	Thermometer.	Force of vapor.	Cloudiness.	Motion of clouds.	Winds.	Relative humidity.
March 13	9 p. m.	29. 61	60½		Nim. 10		N. 6, E. 1	
March 14	7 a. m.	29. 50	61		Nim. 10	N. 3	S. 44, E. 1	
	2 p. m.	29. 44	75		Nim. 10		S. 6, E. 4	
	9 p. m.	29. 37	62		Cir., nim. 9		S. 71, W. 1	
March 15	7 a. m.	29. 42	50		Cir., cir. st. 1		S. 76, W. 3	
	2 p. m.	29. 49	63		Cu. 1		S. 82, W. 5	
	9 p. m.	29. 58	53		Cir., cir. st. 2		W. 3	
March 16	7 a. m.	29. 67	38		Cir., cir. st. 5		N. 85, W. 0	
	2 p. m.	29. 79	68				N. 57, E. 2	
	9 p. m.	29. 70	56		Nim. 10		S. 61, E. 1	
March 17	7 a. m.	29. 70	52½		Nim. 10		S. 62, E. 0	
	2 p. m.	29. 49	59		Nim. 10		S. 65, E. 1	
	9 p. m.	29. 29	65		Nim. 10		S. 30, E. 5	
March 18	7 a. m.	29. 20	59		Nim. 10	NE. 2	S. 5, E. 2	
	2 p. m.	29. 18	56		Cu., nim. 8		S. 50, W. 7	
	9 p. m.	29. 36	42		Cu., cir. cu. 4		S. 60, W. 6	
March 19	7 a. m.	29. 44	37		0		S. 59, W. 3	
	2 p. m.	29. 52	54		0		S. 68, W. 5	

REMARKS.—14th. At 3. 20 p. m. the heavens were covered with large masses of nim. clouds, passing NE., with a velocity of 2; several peals of thunder NW., accompanied by lightning; 3. 35 p. m. a distant flash of lightning NW.; began to rain moderate sized drops; wind set in from NW., and rapidly brought up and diffused the mass of nim. lying upon the NW. horizon; before the diffusion was completed observed the masses of nim. going NE.; the rain increased, until it poured down in great gusts, according to the wind which reached a velocity of 7; soon passed to S. of E.; vivid flashes of lightning, followed by thunder; 7 to 9 p. m. occasional flashes of lightning S. of E.; no thunder; amount, 0. 544 inch. 16th. Rain, commencing at 8. 56 a. m.; amount, 0. 55 inch. 17th. 5. 45 a. m. heavens covered with broken nim. 10, passing NE.; velocity, 1; beneath detached flakes crossed nim., pursuing same direction; velocity, 3.

WHITEMARSH ISLAND, GEORGIA.

Month and day.	Hour.	Barom'r corrected to 32° F.	Thermometer.	Force of vapor.	Cloudiness.	Motion of clouds.	Winds.	Relative humidity.
March 13	9 p. m.		64		Nim. 10	W. 3	S. 2	
March 14	7 a. m.		69		Cir. cu. 10	W. 2	SSE. 3	
	2 p. m.		71		Nim. 10		SE. 3	
	9 p. m.		68		Nim. 10		S. 3	
March 15	7 a. m.		66		Cir. cu. 9	W. 3	NW. 5	
	2 p. m.		68		Cir. st. 2		NW. 4	
	9 p. m.		57		Cir. st. 1		NW. 1	
March 16	7 a. m.		51		Cir. 2	W. 2	N. 2	
	2 p. m.		62		Cir. 3	W. 2	NE. 4	
	9 p. m.		60		Nim. 9	W. 2	NE. 4	
March 17	7 a. m.		60		Cir. cu. 10	SW. 2	NE. 3	
	2 p. m.		70		Nim. 10		ESE. 4	
	9 p. m.		68		Nim. 10	S. 4	SE. 4	
March 18	7 a. m.		66		Nim. 10	SSW. 4	S. 3	
	2 p. m.		70		Cir. cu. 4	SW. 3	SW. 5	
	9 p. m.		50		Cir. st. 1		NW. 3	
March 19	7 a. m.		44		Cir. st. 1		W. 3	
	2 p. m.		57		0		WNW. 5	

REMARKS.—14th. Fog towards night. 15th. Cleared off about 7 a. m.; only a sprinkle of rain; amount, 0. 15 inch. 16th. After 7 a. m. wind fresh, NE. all day; cloudy p. m. 17th. Cloudy and warm; rain in the night. 18th. Rain in the morning; clouds began to break about 12 m.; wind violent during the afternoon; amount, 0. 08 inch. 19th. Wind fresh all day.

STORM No. 1, MARCH, 1859.

ZEBULON, GEORGIA.

Month and day.	Hour.	Barom'r corrected to 32° F.	Thermometer.	Force of vapor.	Cloudiness.	Motion of clouds.	Winds.	Relative humidity.	REMARKS.
March 13	9 p. m.	......	61	......	Cir. st., nim. 9	SE. 8	E. 3	......	14th. Moderate rain from 10 a. m. to 2. 05 p. m.
March 14	7 a. m.	......	60	......	Cir. st., nim. 10	S. 5	E. 4	......	16th. Light frost; small lunar halo.
	2 p. m.	......	61	......	Cir. st. 10	SW. 5	E. 2	......	Rain from 6 a. m. the 17th to 8. 10 a. m. on the 18th.
	9 p. m.	......	60	......	Cu. st., nim., cir. st. 8	SW. 10	E. 4	......	18th. Corona round the moon at 7. 10 p. m.
March 15	7 a. m.	......	53. 5	......	Nim., cu. st. 0	....	W. 4	......	
	2 p. m.	......	62	......	Nim., cu. 0	7	W. 2	......	
	9 p. m.	......	53. 5	......	Cu., nim. 7	W. 1	W. 3	......	
March 16	7 a. m.	......	45	......	Cir. cu. 2	W. 1	E. 3	......	
	2 p. m.	......	60	......	Cir. cu. 2	S. 2	E. 3	......	
	9 p. m.	......	58. 5	......	Cu., cu. st. 8	SW. 10	E. 3	......	
March 17	7 a. m.	......	55. 5	......	Cir. st., nim. 10	S. 5	E. 3	......	
	2 p. m.	......	63	......	Nim. 10	SW. 10	E. 3	......	
	9 p. m.	......	64	......	Nim. 10	S. 10	E. 3	......	
March 18	7 a. m.	......	61	......	Cu. st., nim. 10	SW. 10	W. 4	......	
	2 p. m.	......	47. 5	......	Cu. 5	SW. 10	SW. 3	......	
	9 p. m.	......	44	......	Cu. 5	SW. 8	SW. 3	......	
March 19	7 a. m.	......	42	......	0	....	NW. 3	......	
	2 p. m.	......	56. 5	......	0	....	NW. 3	......	

GAINESVILLE, FLORIDA.

Month and day.	Hour.	Barom'r corrected to 32° F.	Thermometer.	Force of vapor.	Cloudiness.	Motion of clouds.	Winds.	Relative humidity.	REMARKS.
March 13	9 p. m.	......	73	......	10	....	SE. 1	......	18th. Rain, commencing at 1 a. m.; amount, 1. 40 inch.
March 14	6 a. m.	......	69	......	5	....	SE. 1	......	
	2 p. m.	......	77	......	8	....	SE. 1	......	
	9 p. m.	......	72	......	10	....	SW. 1	......	
March 15	6 a. m.	......	69	......	10	....	SW. 1	......	
	2 p. m.	......	74	......	5	....	SW. 2	......	
	9 p. m.	......	63	......	0	....	NW. 1	......	
March 16	6 a. m.	......	53	......	0	....	NE. 2	......	
	2 p. m.	......	70	......	5	....	E. 2	......	
	9 p. m.	......	66	......	0	....	SE. 2	......	
March 17	6 a. m.	......	65	......	10	....	S. 2	......	
	2 p. m.	......	77	......	8	....	SE. 2	......	
	9 p. m.	......	75	......	5	....	SW. 2	......	
March 18	6 a. m.	......	65	......	10	....	SW. 1	......	
	2 p. m.	......	69	......	8	....	SW. 4	......	
	9 p. m.	......	55	......	0	....	NW. 1	......	
March 19	6 a. m.	......	41	......	0	....	NW. 1	......	
	2 p. m.	......	62	......	0	....	NW. 2	......	

ATSENA, FLORIDA.

Month and day.	Hour.	Barom'r corrected to 32° F.	Thermometer.	Force of vapor.	Cloudiness.	Motion of clouds.	Winds.	Relative humidity.	REMARKS.
March 13	9 p. m.	29. 87	72	......	7	SSE. 2	SSE. 1	......	Began to rain in the night of the 17th, and ended at 7 a. m. the following morning; thunder storm at 4 a. m.; amount, 1. 00 inch.
March 14	6 a. m.	29. 81	70	......	Cir. 4	SE. 2	SE. 3	......	
	2 p. m.	29. 81	73	......	Cu. 10	SW. 2	SW. 3	......	
	9 p. m.	29. 82	72	......	Cu. 10	W. 2	W. 2	......	
March 15	6 a. m.	29. 81	68	......	Cu. 10	NW. 3	NW. 3	......	
	2 p. m.	29. 81	68	......	Cir. 2	NW. 2	NW. 4	......	
	9 p. m.	29. 86	65	......	0	0	N. 3	......	
March 16	6 a. m.	29. 87	56	......	Cir. 2	0	NE. 4	......	
	2 p. m.	29. 88	75	......	Cir. 5	ENE. 1	ENE. 2	......	
	9 p. m.	29. 90	70	......	5	W. 1	W. 3	......	
March 17	6 a. m.	29. 85	69	......	Cu. 10	E. 3	E. 3	......	
	2 p. m.	29. 77	75	......	Nim. 10	S. 4	S. 4	......	
	9 p. m.	29. 73	72	......	Cu. 10	S. 4	S. 4	......	
March 18	6 a. m.	29. 67	64	......	Cu. 10	SSW. 4	SSW. 4	......	
	2 p. m.	29. 68	64	......	Cu. 9	W. 4	W. 5	......	
	9 p. m.	29. 77	58	......	2	WNW. 5	WNW. 5	......	
March 19	6 a. m.	29. 76	53	......	0	0	NW. 3	......	
	2 p. m.	29. 77	61	......	0	0	W. 3	......	

STORM No. 1, MARCH, 1859.

BELAIR, FLORIDA.

Month and day.	Hour.	Barom'r corrected to 32° F.	Thermometer.	Force of vapor.	Cloudiness.	Motion of clouds.	Winds.	Relative humidity.	REMARKS.
March 13	9 p. m.	------	72	-----	Cir. 7	W--------	SE. 1	------	14th. Rain from 2½ a. m. to 12 p. m. 15th. From 1 to 2 a. m. the wind suddenly drew to the NW.; violent for a few moments, bringing with it a heavy shower of rain; temperature became 10 or 12° colder. 17th. Rain from 7 a. m. to 7 p. m., and all night. 18th. Rain at 2 p. m.
March 14	7 a. m.	------	70	-----	Nim. 7	W--------	E. 3	------	
	2 p. m.	------	74	-----	Nim. 10	SW-------	E. 2	------	
	9 p. m.	------	71	-----	Nim. 8	SW-------	SE. 3	------	
March 15	7 a. m.	------	59	-----	Cir. 4	W--------	NW. 3	------	
	2 p. m.	------	70	-----	Clear 0	W--------	N. 2	------	
	9 p. m.	------	60	-----	Clear 0	----------	NE. 1	------	
March 16	7 a. m.	------	52	-----	Cir. st. 8	W--------	E. 2	------	
	2 p. m.	------	70	-----	St 5	W--------	E. 2	------	
	9 p. m.	------	66	-----	Cir. 3	W--------	E. 1	------	
March 17	7 a. m.	------	66	-----	Nim. 10	SW-------	SE. 2	------	
	2 p. m.	------	74	-----	Nim. 10	SW-------	S. 4	------	
	9 p. m.	------	69	-----	Cu. st. 7	W--------	NW. 2	------	
March 18	7 a. m.	----	66	-----	Nim. st. 10	W--------	N. 3	------	
	2 p. m.	------	64	-----	Cir. 3	SW-------	NW. 1	------	
	9 p. m.	------	54	-----	Clear 0	----------	NW. 1	------	
March 19	7 a. m.	------	41	-----	Clear 0	----------	Calm -------	------	
	2 p. m.	------	66	-----	Clear 0	W--------	N. 2	------	

LAKE CITY, FLORIDA.

Month and day.	Hour.	Barom'r corrected to 32° F.	Thermometer.	Force of vapor.	Cloudiness.	Motion of clouds.	Winds.	Relative humidity.	REMARKS.
March 13	9 p. m.	------	68	------	Nim. 10	0	0	------	17th. Commenced raining at 5½ p. m.; diffused lightning in E. 7 to 8 p. m.; lightning with thunder till 10 p. m.; ceased to rain at 7 a. m. on the following morning; amount, 0. 60 inch. 19th. Light frost; lunar halo at night.
March 14	7 a. m.	------	66	------	Cir. cu. 8	0	0	------	
	2 p. m.	------	83	------	Nim. 8	NE. 2	SW. 1	------	
	9 p. m.	------	68	------	0	0	0	------	
March 15	7 a. m.	------	66	------	Cu. 6	E. 2	W. 3	------	
	2 p. m.	------	71	------	0	0	NE. 3	------	
	9 p. m.	------	52	------	0	0	0	------	
March 16	7 a. m.	------	50	------	Cir. 4	NE. 1	NE. 2	------	
	2 p. m.	------	72	------	Cir. cu. 7	0	E. 4	------	
	9 p. m.	------	60	------	Cir. cu. 8	0	E. 2	------	
March 17	7 a. m.	------	63	------	Cir. cu. 7	NE. 1	SW. 2	------	
	2 p. m.	------	87	------	Cu. 5	0	SW. 1	------	
	9 p. m.	------	72	------	Cir. cu. 7	NE. 2	SW. 5	------	
March 18	7 a. m.	------	65	------	Nim. 10	NE. 5	S. 5	------	
	2 p. m.	------	64	------	Cir. cu. 7	NE. 4	SW. 5	------	
	9 p. m.	------	47	------	0	0	NW. 1	------	
March 19	7 a. m.	------	39	------	0	0	NW. 2	------	
	2 p. m.	------	65	------	0	0	NW. 4	------	

JACKSONVILLE, FLORIDA.

Month and day.	Hour.	Barom'r corrected to 32° F.	Thermometer.	Force of vapor.	Cloudiness.	Motion of clouds.	Winds.	Relative humidity.	REMARKS.
March 13	9 p. m.	30. 088	70	. 695	Overcast ----	----------	SW. 1	95	18th. Rain at 2 p. m.; amount, 1. 00 inch.
March 14	7 a. m.	30. 106	70	. 695	Cu. st. 9	SW. 2	S. 2	95	
	2 p. m.	------	------	------	------------	----------	------------	------	
	9 p. m.	------	------	------	------------	----------	------------	------	
March 15	7 a. m.	------	------	------	------------	----------	------------	------	
	2 p. m.	------	------	------	------------	----------	------------	------	
	9 p. m.	------	------	------	------------	----------	------------	------	
March 16	7 a. m.	30. 226	53	. 348	Cir. st. 8	NW. 1	N. 1	86	
	2 p. m.	30. 259	72	. 524	Cu. st. 7	SW. 2	N. 2	66	
	9 p. m.	30. 252	62	. 491	Cir. cu. 3	SW. 1	N. 1	88	
March 17	7 a. m.	30. 185	66	. 570	Cir. st. 9	S. 1	NE. 1	89	
	2 p. m.	30. 028	76	. 731	Cu. st. 8	SW. 3	NE. 2	81	
	9 p. m.	30. 021	72	. 745	8	SE. 1	SE. 1	95	
March 18	7 a. m.	29. 914	66	. 604	Overcast ----	----------	S. 5	94	
	2 p. m.	29. 845	70	. 449	Calm -------	S. 2	S. 6	61	
	9 p. m.	30. 093	54	. 256	0	0	N. 1	61	
March 19	7 a. m.	30. 212	50	. 283	Cir. 3	WSW. 1	NW. 1	78	
	2 p. m.	30. 118	64	. 373	Cir. 3	SW. 2	NW. 1	62	

STORM No. 1, MARCH, 1859.

MICANOPY, FLORIDA.

Month and day.	Hour.	Barom'r corrected to 32° F.	Thermometer.	Force of vapor.	Cloudiness.	Motion of clouds.	Winds.	Relative humidity.	REMARKS.
March 13	9 p. m.	......	73	.617	Cu., cir st. 10	....	SE. 3	77	15th. Kind of clouds at 7 a. m.; cu., cir. cu., and cu st. 16th. Frost. 17th. Clouds at 7 a. m.; cu., cu. st, cir. st; rain from 4 to 4¼ p. m; amount, 0.18 inch. 18th. Rain from 3 to 10 a. m.; amount, 1.10 inch; clouds at 9 p. m. cir., cir. st., and cu.
March 14	7 a. m.	......	69	.635	Cu. & cu. st. 5	....	SE. 2	90	
	2 p. m.	......	......	......	Cu. 10	....	SW. 2	......	
	9 p. m.	......	70	.658	Cu. 10	....	0	90	
March 15	7 a. m.	......	69	.635	9	W. 1	W. 3	90	
	2 p. m.	......	......	......	Cu., cu. st. 1	....	W. 3	......	
	9 p. m.	......	58	.483	Cu. st. 1	....	0	100	
March 16	7 a. m.	......	49	.348	Cir. st., st. 1	....	W. 1	100	
	2 p. m.	......	76	.505	Cir., cir. cu. 2	W. 1	NE. 2	56	
	9 p. m.	......	64	.563	0	....	E. 2	94	
March 17	7 a. m.	......	65	......	9	W. 1	SE. 2	......	
	2 p. m.	......	85	.733	10	....	S. 3	61	
	9 p. m	......	......	......	Cu., cu. st. 10	....	W. 2	......	
March 18	7 a. m.	......	......	......	Nim. 10	....	W. 4	......	
	2 p. m.	......	......	......	9	....	W. 5	......	
	9 p. m.	......	53	.321	Cu. st., st. 1	....	W. 2	80	
March 19	7 a. m.	......	40	.225	0	....	SW. 2	91	
	2 p. m.	......	64	.257	0	....	W. 3	43	

ST. AUGUSTINE, FLORIDA.

Month and day.	Hour.	Barom'r corrected to 32° F.	Thermometer.	Force of vapor.	Cloudiness.	Motion of clouds.	Winds.	Relative humidity.	REMARKS.
March 13	9 p. m.	30.08	69	......	Cu. 5	NE. 2	NE. 2	......	Rain from 10 p. m. the 17th to 9 a. m. on the 18th; amount, 0.30 inch.
March 14	7 a. m.	29.95	72	......	Cu. 10	SE. 2	SE. 1	......	
	2 p. m.	29.95	74	......	Cu. 10	SE. 2	SE. 3	......	
	9 p. m.	29.98	73	......	Cu. 8	SW. 1	SW. 2	......	
March 15	7 a. m.	29.98	74	......	Cu. 7	NW. 2	NW. 3	......	
	2 p. m.	29.98	80	......	Cu. 4	NW. 2	NW. 2	......	
	9 p. m.	29.88	64	......	0	0	NW. 2	......	
March 16	7 a. m.	30.04	65	......	St. 1	NE. 1	NE. 3	......	
	2 p. m.	30.08	68	......	Cu. 4	NE. 2	NE. 3	......	
	9 p. m.	30.09	68	......	Cu. 7	NE. 2	NE. 2	......	
March 17	7 a. m.	30.07	71	......	Cu. 6	SE. 2	SE. 3	......	
	2 p. m.	29.97	74	......	Cu. 8	SE. 2	SE. 3	......	
	9 p. m.	29.88	74	......	Cu. 10	SE. 2	SE. 2	......	
March 18	7 a. m.	29.81	68	......	Cu. 10	SW. 2	SW. 2	......	
	2 p. m.	29.73	72	......	Cu. 8	SW. 3	SW. 5	......	
	9 p. m.	29.91	55	......	St. 2	NW. 1	NW. 2	......	
March 19	7 a. m.	30.02	53	......	Cir. 2	NW. 1	NW. 4	......	
	2 p. m.	30.00	64	......	0	0	NW. 4	......	

SALT PONDS, FLORIDA.

Month and day.	Hour.	Barom'r corrected to 32° F.	Thermometer.	Force of vapor.	Cloudiness.	Motion of clouds.	Winds.	Relative humidity.	REMARKS.
March 14	7 a. m.	29.69	76	......	2	....	SE. 3	......	14th. Wind veered to N. at 7 p. m.; lightning in the N. at 8 p. m. 15th. Rainbow in the morning; wind came round to N. at 8 a. m. 16th. Circle round the sun. 17th. Sprinkle of rain at 8 a. m. 18th. Heavy squall from SW. at 2½ p. m.; light rain from 3 to 5 p. m.; amount, 0.02 inch.
	2 p. m.	29.71	84	......	2	....	S. 3	......	
March 15	7 a. m.	29.72	78	......	3	....	Calm 0	......	
	2 p. m.	29.77	81	......	8	....	N. 1	......	
March 16	7 a. m.	29.73	76	......	3	....	N. 3	......	
	2 p. m.	29.79	83	......	4	....	SE. 3	......	
March 17	7 a. m.	29.75	78	......	3	....	SE. 4	......	
	2 p. m.	29.78	82	......	1	....	SE. 5	......	
March 18	7 a. m.	29.67	78	......	3	....	SE. 4	......	
	2 p. m.	29.74	81	......	8	....	SW. 4	......	
March 19	7 a. m.	29.78	67	......	10	....	NW. 4	......	
	2 p. m.	29.87	68	......	3	....	N. 4	......	

STORM No. 1, MARCH, 1859.

SEVILLE, FLORIDA.

Month and day.	Hour.	Barom'r corrected to 32° F.	Thermometer.	Force of vapor.	Cloudiness.	Motion of clouds.	Winds.	Relative humidity.	REMARKS.
March 14	7 a. m.	......	68	......	Cu. st. 5	SE. 4	SE. 5	......	Light showers from 4 p. m. the 14th till midnight on the 15th. 17th. Rain, accompanied by thunder and lightning, commenced at 4 p. m. and continued at intervals till 4 a. m. on the following morning; lightning vivid, thunder not very loud, rain in large drops at first, followed by small ones in heavy showers. 19th. Frost.
	2 p. m.	......	......	......	......	......	......	......	
March 15	7 a. m.	......	54	......	Cir. st. 3	......	NW. 4	......	
	2 p. m.	......	......	......	......	......	......	......	
March 16	7 a. m.	......	52	......	Cu. st. 8	......	NE. 4	......	
	2 p. m.	......	70	......	Cir. 2	......	SW. 3	......	
March 17	7 a. m.	......	64	......	Cu. st. 9	......	Calm	......	
	2 p. m.	......	......	......	......	......	......	......	
March 18	7 a. m.	......	65	......	Cu. st. 8	SW.	SW. 6	......	
	2 p. m.	......	......	......	......	......	......	......	
March 19	7 a. m.	......	45	......	0	......	Calm	......	

CARLOWVILLE, ALABAMA.

Month and day.	Hour.	Barom'r corrected to 32° F.	Thermometer.	Force of vapor.	Cloudiness.	Motion of clouds.	Winds.	Relative humidity.	REMARKS.
March 13	9 p. m.	......	69	......	0	......	W. 3	......	Rain from 8 p. m the 18th to 3 p. m. on the 19th; amount, 2.01 inch.
March 14	7 a. m.	......	67	......	0	0	E. 0	......	
	2 p. m.	......	76	......	0	0	E. 0	......	
	9 p. m.	......	69	......	0	0	W. 0	......	
March 15	7 a. m.	......	64	......	0	0	W. 1	......	
	2 p. m.	......	73	......	0	0	W. 1	......	
	9 p. m.	......	68	......	0	0	S. 0	......	
March 16	7 a. m.	......	64	......	0	0	SW. 1	......	
	2 p. m.	......	70	......	Cu. 4	0	S. 0	......	
	9 p. m.	......	63	......	0	......	S. 1	......	
March 17	7 a. m.	......	61	......	Nim. 10	......	NW. 2	......	
	2 p. m.	......	69	......	Nim. 10	E. 1	N. 2	......	
	9 p. m.	......	64	......	Nim. 10	......	E. 2	......	
March 18	7 a. m.	......	60	......	Nim. 10	......	W. 1	......	
	2 p. m	......	69	......	Nim. 10	0	W. 0	......	
	9 p. m.	......	62	......	Cu. 4	N. 1	W. 3	......	
March 19	7 a. m.	......	60	......	0	......	W. 1	......	
	2 p. m.	......	68	......	0	......	SW. 0	......	

GREENE SPRINGS, ALABAMA.

Month and day.	Hour.	Barom'r corrected to 32° F.	Thermometer.	Force of vapor.	Cloudiness.	Motion of clouds.	Winds.	Relative humidity.	REMARKS.
March 13	9 p. m.	......	66	......	St. 10	......	SE. 3	......	15th. Beautiful lunar halo, radius about 15°. Rain from 10 p. m. the 16th to early morning on the 17th; amount, 1.71 inch. 19th. Lunar halo; radius about 20°.
March 14	7 a. m.	......	61	......	St. 10	......	0	......	
	2 p. m.	......	64	......	Cu. st. 8	W. 3	W. 2	......	
	9 p. m.	......	55	......	St. 6	SW. 1	SW. 3	......	
March 15	7 a. m.	......	44	......	0	......	0	......	
	2 p. m.	......	60	......	0	......	W. 3	......	
	9 p. m.	......	47	......	0	......	0	......	
March 16	7 a. m.	......	54	......	St. 10	......	0	......	
	2 p. m.	......	58	......	Cu. st. 10	S. 1	SW. 1	......	
	9 p. m.	......	53	......	St. 10	......	S. 2	......	
March 17	7 a. m.	......	54	......	St. 10	SW. 3	SE. 3	......	
	2 p. m.	......	59½	......	St. 10	......	SE. 1	......	
	9 p. m.	......	......	......	......	......	......	......	
March 18	7 a. m.	......	45	......	Cu. st. 10	SW. 4	W. 5	......	
	2 p. m.	......	53	......	Cu. 5	NW. 4	W. 6	......	
	9 p. m.	......	39	......	0	......	0	......	
March 19	7 a. m.	......	38	......	0	......	0	......	
	2 p. m.	......	60	......	0	......	W. 2	......	

MONTGOMERY, ALABAMA.

Month and day.	Hour.	Barom'r corrected to 32° F.	Thermometer.	Force of vapor.	Cloudiness.	Motion of clouds.	Winds.	Relative humidity.	REMARKS.
March 13	9 p. m.	......	64.5	......	8	W. 1	......	......	17th. Rain from early morn to 4½ p. m.; amount, 1.50 inch. And from 5½ p. m. to 4 a. m. on the 18th; amount, 0.84 inch.
March 14	7 a. m.	......	65	......	Nim. 10	SW. 1	......	......	
	2 p. m.	......	65	......	Nim. 9	W. 1	......	......	
	9 p. m.	......	59	......	10	W. 1	......	......	
March 15	7 a. m.	......	48	......	Nim. 10	SW. 2	......	......	
	2 p. m.	......	69.5	......	9	SW. 3	......	......	
	9 p. m.	......	53	......	9	W. 2	......	......	

STORM No. 1, MARCH, 1859.

MONTGOMERY, ALABAMA—Continued.

Month and day.	Hour.	Barom'r corrected to 32° F.	Thermometer.	Force of vapor.	Cloudiness.	Motion of clouds.	Winds.	Relative humidity.	REMARKS.
March 16	7 a. m.	------	48	------	Cir. 2	W 2	------	------	
	2 p. m.	------	------	------	Cir. 3	W. 2	------	------	
	9 p. m.	------	57	------	Cir. 3	W. 1	------	------	
March 17	7 a. m.	------	56	------	Cir. 4	------	------	------	
	2 p. m.	------	66	------	8	------	------	------	
	9 p. m.	------	66	------	10	S. 1	------	------	
March 18	7 a. m.	------	51	------	Nim. 10	SW. 3	W. and NW. 5	------	
	2 p. m.	------	52	------	Nim. 10	SW. 5	NW. 4	------	
	9 p. m.	------	42	------	------	------	------	------	
March 19	7 a. m.	------	40	------	6	W. 5	------	------	
	2 p. m.	------	62	------	4	NW. 4	------	------	

MOULTON, ALABAMA.

Month and day.	Hour.	Barom'r corrected to 32° F.	Thermometer.	Force of vapor.	Cloudiness.	Motion of clouds.	Winds.	Relative humidity.	REMARKS.
March 13	9 p. m.	29.21	59.5	.269	0	------	SE. 2	88	Rain from 5 p. m. the 13th to 10 a. m. on the 14th; amount, 2 972 inches.
March 14	7 a. m.	29.12	60	.269	Rain 10	S. 2	S. 2	90	
	10 a. m.	29.16	------	------	------	------	------	------	
	2 p. m.	29.15	60	.374	Cir.cu.,cr.st. 5	SW. 1	SW. 3	61	17th. Rain at 4 p. m.; amount, 0.910 inch.
	4 p. m.	29.18	------	------	------	------	------	------	
	9 p. m.	29.32	56	.456	Cir. st., st. 2	------	W. 2	63	18th. Rain commenced at 6 a. m.; lasted half an hour; amount, 0.100 inch.
March 15	7 a. m.	29.42	53	.474	0	------	W. 2	52	
	10 a. m.	29.48	------	------	------	------	------	------	
	2 p. m.	29.46	53	.320	0	------	NW. 2	42	
	4 p. m.	29.45	------	------	------	------	------	------	
	9 p. m.	29.50	52	.282	Cir st, st. 5	------	0	60	
March 16	7 a. m.	29.53	47	.212	Cir. st., st. 9	0	0	77	
	10 a. m.	29.54	------	------	------	------	------	------	
	2 p. m.	29.50	54	.170	10	------	SE. 1	52	
	4 p. m.	29.42	------	------	------	------	------	------	
	9 p. m.	29.42	53	.232	10	SW. 1	SE. 1	52	
March 17	7 a. m.	29.28	53	.221	Rain 10	0	E. 2	73	
	10 a. m.	29.22	------	------	------	------	------	------	
	2 p. m.	29.01	55	.218	Rain 10	0	0	69	
	9 p. m.	28.92	56	.212	0	------	SE. 2	84	
March 18	7 a. m.	28.98	53	.295	Rain 9	SW. 1	SW. 3	67	
	10 a. m.	29.06	------	------	------	------	------	------	
	2 p. m.	29.15	47	.322	Cu. st., cu. 9	W. 1	NW. 5	52	
	4 p. m.	29.19	------	------	------	------	------	------	
	9 p. m.	29.32	46	.385	Cir.cu.,cu st.5	W. 3	NW. 2	54	
March 19	7 a. m.	29.42	45	.269	0	0	NW. 2	57	
	10 a. m.	29.47	------	------	------	------	------	------	
	2 p. m.	29.43	49	.172	Cir. 1	0	NW. 2	35	

SELMA, ALABAMA.

Month and day.	Hour.	Barom'r corrected to 32° F.	Thermometer.	Force of vapor.	Cloudiness.	Motion of clouds.	Winds.	Relative humidity.	REMARKS.
March 13	9 p. m.	29.55	68	.433	Nim. 10	SW. 2	SE. 2	73	14th. Diffuse lightning and heavy thunder, NW. and SW., 4 a. m. to $9\frac{1}{4}$ a. m., passing over to NE. and SE; rain 5 40 to 10 10 a.m.; amount, 1.48 inch.
March 14	7 a. m.	29.54	66	.423	Nim. 10	SW. 3	SE. 3	88	
	2 p. m.	29.53	65	.628	Cu. st. 10	W. 2	NW. 2	73	
	9 p. m	29.64	62	.631	Cu. st. 10	W. 2	NW. 2	81	
March 15	7 a. m.	29.75	48	.639	Cir. 1	NW. 1	NW. 2	100	
	2 p. m.	29.76	61	.551	Cir. 3	NW. 1	NW. 3	75	15th. Large and beautiful circle around the moon, 8 to $9\frac{1}{2}$ p. m.
	9 p. m.	29.78	56	.476	Cu. st. 7	NW. 1	NW. 2	69	
March 16	7 a. m	29.78	46	.282	Cu. st. 10	SE. 1	E. 3	73	16th. Light sprinkle of rain, 7 to $9\frac{1}{4}$ p. m.
	2 p. m.	29.75	58	.503	Cu. nim. 10	SE. 1	E 3	66	
	9 p. m	29.72	56	.396	Nim. 10	SE. 1	E. 2	76	17th. Dash of rain before day, light showers from $7\frac{1}{2}$ to $10\frac{1}{2}$ a. m., then heavy thunder and hard rain; thunder, SW. to NE., $10\frac{1}{2}$ a. m. to $1\frac{3}{4}$ p. m.; rain continued from $7\frac{1}{2}$ a. m. to $3\frac{3}{4}$ p. m, and 7.55 to $10\frac{1}{2}$ p. m.; amount, 2.585 inches.
March 17	7 a. m.	29.54	55	.285	Nim. 10	SW. 2	SE. 2	82	
	2 p. m.	29.31	64	.376	Nim. 10	SW. 2	SW. 2	59	
	9 p. m.	29.31	61	.423	Nim. 10	SW. 2	SW. 2	88	
March 18	7 a. m.	29.40	48	.420	Nim 9	W. 2	NW. 4	94	
	2 p. m.	29.54	51	.596	Cu. st. 8	NW. 1	NW. 5	100	
	9 p. m.	29.70	48	.537	0	------	NW. 3	100	
March 19	7 a. m.	29.78	41	.335	0	------	NW. 2	100	
	2 p. m.	29.77	57	.335	0	------	NW. 3	80	

STORM No. 1, MARCH, 1859.

GREENSBOROUGH, ALABAMA.

Month and day.	Hour.	Barom'r corrected to 32° F.	Thermometer.	Force of vapor.	Cloudiness.	Motion of clouds.	Winds.	Relative humidity.	REMARKS.
March 13	9 p. m.	......	67	.573	St. 10	....	SE. 3	87	
March 14	7 a. m.	......	60	.518	Nim. 10	W. 4	S. 2	100	
	2 p. m.	......	64	.285	Cir. 7	WSW. 4	WSW. 2	48	
	9 p. m.	......	56	.155	St. 10	....	W. 2	34	
March 15	7 a. m.	......	44.5	.166	0	0	NW. 1	56	
	2 p. m.	......	60	.152	St. 1	W.......	NW. 3	29	
	9 p. m.	......	49	.234	Nim., cir. st. 4	....	NW. 2	67	
March 16	7 a. m.	......	47.5	.195	St. 10	....	NE. 1	59	
	2 p. m.	......	56.5	.249	St. 10	....	SE. 2	54	
	9 p. m.	......	53.5	.288	St. 10	....	SE. 1	70	
March 17	7 a m.	......	53	.389	St. 10	SW. 5	E. 2	96	
	2 p. m	......	58.5	.491	St. 10	....	W. 2	100	
	9 p. m.	......	58.5	.491	St 10	....	SE. 2	100	
March 18	7 a. m.	......	46	.210	St. 9	W. 4	W. 4	78½	
	2 p. m.	......	49.5	.047	W. 5	W. 3	WNW. 5	13	
	9 p. m.	......	41	.169	0	0	W. 1	65	
March 19	7 a m.	......	39	.141	0	0	W. 1	60	
	2 p. m.	......	59	.140	Nim. st. 1	W. 3	W. 2½	28	

NATCHEZ, MISSISSIPPI.

Month and day.	Hour.	Barom'r corrected to 32° F.	Thermometer.	Force of vapor.	Cloudiness.	Motion of clouds.	Winds.	Relative humidity.	REMARKS.
March 13	9 p. m.	29.30	71	......	10	....	SE. 12	......	A severe thunder storm from 12 m.
March 14	7 a. m.	29.45	56	......	Cu. 5	SW. 1	NW. 4	......	the 13th to 3 a. m. on the 14th;
	2 p. m.	29.50	62	......	Cu. 5	W. 1	NW. 4	......	amount, 1.59 inch.
	9 p. m.	29.60	54	......	Cir. 5	....	NW. 2	......	14th. Large halo around the moon.
March 15	7 a. m.	29.70	42	......	0	0	NW. 2	......	15th. Cir. hazy, cir. cu., cir, st. at
	2 p. m.	29.90	66	......	Cir. 5	SW. 1	NW. 2	......	9 p. m
	9 p. m.	29.70	56	......	Cir. 8	....	NW. 2	......	16th. Overcast and drizzly all day.
March 16	7 a m.	29.65	60	......	10	....	E. 2	......	17th. Overcast; at 2 p. m. thunder
	2 p. m.	29.60	65	......	10	....	SE. 4	......	and heavy showers of rain; ceased
	9 p. m.	29.50	57	......	10	....	SE. 2	......	at 3.30 p.m.; amount, 0.80 inch;
March 17	7 a. m.	29.27	58	......	10	....	SE. 2	......	in the evening large cu. clouds;
	2 p m.	29.20	72	......	10	....	S. 2	......	at 9 p. m. snowy cu.
	9 p. m.	29.30	58	......	Cu. 5	W. 2	NW. 25	......	18th. Frost at daylight; a few cu-
March 18	7 a. m.	29.30	42	......	0	0	NW. 12	......	muli clouds; brilliant and cloud-
	2 p. m.	29.55	56	......	0	0	NW. 12	......	less sunset.
	9 p. m.	29.65	50	......	0	0	NW. 2	......	19th. White frost, clear; a few
March 19	7 a. m.	29.65	34	......	0	0	NW. 2	......	wavy cirri in the evening; dense
	2 p. m.	29.70	70	......	0	0	SW. 2	......	haze at 9 p. m.

COLUMBUS, MISSISSIPPI.

Month and day.	Hour.	Barom'r corrected to 32° F.	Thermometer.	Force of vapor.	Cloudiness.	Motion of clouds.	Winds.	Relative humidity.	REMARKS.
March 13	9 p. m.	29.65	63.5	.566	Nim. 10	....	S. 2	96	13th. Began to rain at 5 a. m.;
March 14	7 a. m.	29.66	61.6	.527	Nim 10	NW. 4	W. 2	96	frequent thunder during the day
	2 p. m.	29.70	62.6	.257	Cir. st. 2	W. 2	W. 3	45	and night; violent rain, with
	9 p. m	29.85	51.4	.233	St. 1	....	W. 1	64	high wind; continued till 6 a. m.
March 15	7 a. m.	29.96	46.2	.179	0	....	W. 2	57	on the 14th; amount, 4.16
	2 p m.	29.98	57.7	.178	St. 1	....	NW. 2	37	inches.
	9 p. m.	29.98	48.3	.294	Cir. st. 3	NW. 2	NE. 1	87.4	17th. Rain from 5 a. m. to 8.1 p.
March 16	7 a. m.	30.01	45.1	.246	Cu. st. 9	....	NE. 1	81	m; amount, 1.555 inch.
	2 p. m.	29.93	58.7	.259	Cu. st. 10	....	SE. 2	53	
	9 p. m.	29.89	52.3	.284	Cir. cu. 7	S.........	SE. 1	72	
March 17	7 a. m.	29.73	60	.351	Nim. 10	....	E. 1	96	
	2 p. m.	29.50	56.8	.448	Nim. 10	S. 3	SE. 2	96	
	9 p. m.	29.45	56.8	.451	Cir. cu 6	....	SE. 1	97	
March 18	7 a. m.	29.61	41.9	.199	St. 7	W. 4	W. 4	74	
	2 p. m.	29.75	47.3	.119	Cu. st. 7	W. 4	W. 4	36	
	9 p m.	29.86	42.9	.167	0	....	W. 2	61.2	
March 19	7 a m.	29.97	40.3	.153	0	....	W. 2	61	
	2 p. m.	29.95	57.8	.203	Cir. 1	W. 2	W. 2	42	

STORM No. 1, MARCH, 1859.

BLACK RIVER, LOUISIANA.

Month and day.	Hour.	Barom'r corrected to 32° F.	Thermometer.	Force of vapor.	Cloudiness.	Motion of clouds.	Winds.	Relative humidity.	REMARKS.
March 13	9 p. m.	......	74	......	Nim. 10	SW. 6	S. 5	......	13th. Rain from 12 m. to 12 p. m.; amount, 1. 12 inch.
March 14	7 a. m.	......	57	......	Cu. 4	SW. 5	NW. 4	......	
	2 p. m.	......	63	......	Cir. 4	SW. 3	NW. 3	......	14th. Lunar halo at night, large and distinct.
	9 p. m.	......	55	......	Cir. 4	SW. 1	S. 1	......	
March 15	7 a. m.	......	45	......	Cir. 1	SW. 1	NE. 1	......	Rain from 11 a. m. the 16th to 3 p. m. on the 17th; amount, 0 61 inch.
	2 p. m.	......	68	......	Cir. 7	SW. 3	NE. 2	......	
	9 p. m.	......	67	......	Cir. 5	0	S. 0	......	
March 16	7 a. m.	......	53	......	Cu. st. 10	SW. 1	S. 1	......	
	2 p. m.	......	60	......	Nim. 10	S. 3	S. 3	......	
	9 p. m.	......	57	......	Nim. 10	0	S. 1	......	
March 17	7 a. m.	......	60	......	Nim. 10	0	SE. 0	......	
	2 p. m.	......	70	......	Nim. 10	SW. 5	NW. 6	......	
	9 p. m.	......	60	......	Cu. 4	W. 5	W. 7	......	
March 18	7 a. m.	......	46	......	0	0	NW. 4	......	
	2 p. m.	......	58	......	Cu. 3	NW. 5	NW. 6	......	
	9 p. m.	......	50	......	0	0	S. 1	......	
March 19	7 a. m.	......	41	......	0	0	SE. 0	......	
	2 p. m.	......	69	......	Cir. 8	W. 1	SW. 3	......	

NEW ORLEANS, LOUISIANA.

Month and day.	Hour.	Barom'r corrected to 32° F.	Thermometer.	Force of vapor.	Cloudiness.	Motion of clouds.	Winds.	Relative humidity.	REMARKS.
March 13	3 p. m.	......	78	......	....	....	SE	......	13th, 14th, and 15th. Clear.
March 14	9 a. m.	......	69	......	....	....	NW........	......	16th. Rain.
	12 m.	......	68	......	....	....	NW	......	17th. Rain.
	3 p m.	......	68	......	....	....	NE..........	......	18th and 19th. Clear.
March 15	9 a. m.	......	61	......	....	....	NW........	......	
	12 m.	......	65	......	....	....	NW	......	
	3 p. m.	......	68	......	....	....	NW........	......	
March 16	9 a. m.	......	59	......	....	....	NE..........	......	
	12 m.	......	60	......	....	....	NE.	......	
	3 p. m.	......	61	......	....	....	NE	......	
March 17	9 a. m.	......	67	......	....	....	SE	......	
	12 m.	......	68	......	....	....	SE	......	
	3 p. m.	......	70	......	....	....	SE..........	......	
March 18	9 a. m.	......	57	......	....	....	NW........	......	
	12 m.	......	58	......	....	....	NW	......	
	3 p. m.	......	59	......	....	....	NW........	......	
March 19	9 a. m.	......	58	......	....	....	NW	......	
	12 m.	......	62	......	....	....	NW........	......	

AUSTIN, TEXAS.*

Month and day.	Hour.	Barom'r corrected to 32° F.	Thermometer.	Force of vapor.	Cloudiness.	Motion of clouds.	Winds.	Relative humidity.	REMARKS.
March 13	7 a. m.	29. 23	65	. 576	Nim. 10	0	SW. 0	100	13th. Falling fog.
	2 p. m.	29. 21	81	. 369	Cu. 2	0	SW. 1	35	17th. Rain from 6 to 6¾ a. m.; amount, 0. 10 inch.
	9 p m.	29. 48	63	. 009	Cir. st. 3	0	W. 5	1	
March 14	7 a. m.	29. 02	44	. 087	Cir. 1	0	NE. 3	30	
	2 p. m.	29. 60	65	. 025	Cir. 3	0	N. 3	3	
	9 p. m.	29. 71	49	. 107	Cir. 1	0	S. 1	31	
March 15	7 a. m.	29. 74	40	. 160	Cir. 6	0	SW. 1	64	
	2 p m.	29. 67	70	. 123	Cir. st. 8	0	SW. 1	17	
	9 p. m.	29. 61	53	. 123	Cir. 3	0	SW. 2	30	
March 16	7 a. m.	29. 47	45	. 204	Cir. st. 8	0	SW. 0	68	
	2 p. m.	29. 37	63	. 416	Cu. st. 10	0	SW. 0	72	
	9 p. m.	29. 32	59	. 469	Nim. 10	0	S. 2	94	
March 17	7 a. m.	29. 29	61	. 339	Nim. 4	0	SW. 3	63	
	2 p. m.	29. 52	66	. 098	0	0	SW. 5	15	
	9 p. m.	29. 62	53	. 078	0	0	NW. 2	19	
March 18	7 a. m.	29. 78	40	. 139	0	0	SW. 1	56	
	2 p. m.	29. 71	66	. 048	0	0	NE. 2	7	
	9 p. m.	29. 66	51	. 149	0	0	NW. 1	40	

* Swante Palm, observer.

STORM No. 1, MARCH, 1859.

AUSTIN, TEXAS.*

Month and day.	Hour.	Barom'r corrected to 32° F.	Thermometer.	Force of vapor.	Cloudiness.	Motion of clouds.	Winds.	Relative humidity.	REMARKS.
March 13	7 a. m.	------	64	.562	Nim. 10	0	SE. 1	94	13th. Rain; diffused lightning E. and SE. at 7 p. m.; amount, 0.04 inch.
	2 p. m.	------	84	.356	Cir. cu. 3	NE. 1	S. 2	30	
	9 p. m.	------	66	.044	Cir. 2	N. 2	NW. 6	17	
March 14	7 a. m.	------	47	.112	Cir. st. 2	NE. 1	NW. 4	34	17th. Rain; amount, 0.14 inch.; thunder and lightning at 6 a. m.
	2 p. m.	------	70	.094	Cir. 4	SE. 1	NW. 3	13	
	9 p. m.	------	50	.162	Cir. 1	0	0	45	
March 15	7 a. m.	------	40	.181	Cir. st. 6	NE. 1	S. 1	73	
	2 p. m.	-----	71	.083	Cir. 7	N. 2	S. 2	11	
	9 p. m.	------	51	.149	Cir. 4	NE. 1	S. 3	40	
March 16	7 a. m.	------	44	.240	Cir. 1, nim. 9	N --------	0	84	
	2 p. m.	------	64	.396	Nim. 10	N. 3	S. 3	65	
	9 p. m.	------	59	.462	Nim. 10	0	SE. 3	91	
March 17	7 a. m.	------	59	.377	Nim. cu. 6	NE. 2	W. 3	74½	
	2 p. m.	------	68	.130	Cir. 1	NE. 1	NW. 4	19	
	9 p. m	------	53	.122	0	----------	NW. 3	30	
March 18	7 a. m.	------	41	.184	0	----------	W. 2	70	
	2 p. m.	------	71	.060	0	----------	NW. 3	8	
	9 p. m.	------	51	.149	0	----------	N. 1	40	

LARISSA, TEXAS.

Month and day.	Hour.	Barom'r corrected to 32° F.	Thermometer.	Force of vapor.	Cloudiness.	Motion of clouds.	Winds.	Relative humidity.	REMARKS.
March 13	7 a. m.	------	62	.491	Nim. 10	----------	SE. 2	88	13th. Rain from 10 a. m. to 3 p. m; thunder at 10 a. m., 2 and 6 p. m.
	2 p. m.	------	73	.693	Nim. 10	----------	SW. 2	85	
	9 p. m.	------	62	.460	Nim. 3	----------	NW. 3	83	15th. Large lunar halo.
March 14	7 a. m.	------	41	.169	0	0	NW. 3	65	17th. Rain at 7½ a. m.
	2 p. m.	------	60	.229	Cir. 1	----------	NW. 3	44	
	9 p. m.	------	50½	.226	0	0	0	57	
March 15	7 a. m.	------	45	.204	Cir. 1	----------	0	68	
	2 p. m.	------	69	.367	Cir. 3	----------	NE. 1	52	
	9 p. m.	------	57	.295	0 8	0	SE. 1	63	
March 16	7 a. m.	------	49	.272	Cir. cu. 3	----------	SE. 1	78	
	2 p. m.	------	67	.425	Nim. 5	----------	SE. 2	64	
	9 p. m.	------	58	.423	Nim. 10	----------	SE. 3	88	
March 17	7 a. m.	------	57	.466	Nim. 10	SW-------	SW. 1	100	
	2 p. m.	------	61½	.347	Cir. st. 1	W. 4	W. 4	64	
	9 p. m.	------	43	.278	0	0	SE. 5	100	
March 18	7 a. m.	------	40	.248	0	0	E. 1	100	
	2 p. m.	------	60½	.222	0	0	NW. 4	42	
	9 p. m.	------	52	.208	0	0	SW. 1	53	

KAUFMAN, TEXAS.

Month and day.	Hour.	Barom'r corrected to 32° F.	Thermometer.	Force of vapor.	Cloudiness.	Motion of clouds.	Winds.	Relative humidity.	REMARKS.
March 13	7 a. m.	------	------	------	10	----------	S. 2	------	14th. Heavy frost.
	2 p. m.	------	------	------	5	----------	S. 2	------	15th. Very pleasant.
	9 p. m.	------	------	------	0	----------	N. 4	------	
March 14	7 a. m.	------	------	------	0	----------	N. 3	------	
	2 p. m.	------	------	------	0	----------	N. 3	------	
	9 p. m.	------	------	------	0	----------	N. 2	------	
March 15	7 a. m.	------	------	------	0	----------	N. 2	------	
	2 p. m.	------	------	------	0	----------	NE. 2	------	
	9 p. m.	------	------	------	0	----------	S. 1	------	
March 16	7 a. m.	------	------	------	0	----------	S. 2	------	
	2 p. m.	------	------	------	0	----------	S. 2	------	
	9 p. m.	------	------	------	0	----------	S. 2	------	
March 17	7 a. m.	------	------	------	0	----------	------------	------	
	2 p. m.	------	------	------	0	----------	------------	------	
	9 p. m.	------	------	------	0	----------	------------	------	
March 18	7 a. m.	------	------	------	0	----------	------------	------	
	2 p. m.	------	------	------	0	----------	------------	------	
	9 p. m.	------	------	------	0	----------	------------	------	

* Van Nostrand, observer.

STORM No. 1, MARCH, 1859.

SISTERDALE, TEXAS.

Month and day.	Hour.	Barom'r corrected to 32° F.	Thermometer.	Force of vapor.	Cloudiness.	Motion of clouds.	Winds.	Relative humidity.	REMARKS.
March 13	7 a. m.	28.44	65	......	Nim. 7	0	S. 2	......	13th. Dry fog; 7 p. m. heat light-
	2 p. m.	28.34	82	......	Cu. st. 1	0	NE. 3	......	ning.
	9 p. m.	28.67	58	......	0	0	NW. 5	......	15th. Lunar halo.
March 14	7 a. m.	28.79	40	......	0	0	NW. 2	......	17th. Rain and hail from 4½ to 5
	2 p. m.	28.75	68	......	St. 1	0	NW. 3	......	a. m.; amount, 0.35 inch.
	9 p. m.	28.89	41	......	Cir. 1	0	NW. 2	......	
March 15	7 a. m.	28.90	36	......	Cir. 8	0	NW. 1	......	
	2 p. m.	28.79	69	......	Cir. 9	0	SE. 3	......	
	9 p. m.	28.75	51	......	Cir. 7	0	SW. 2	......	
March 16	7 a. m.	28.63	50	......	Cir. 10	0	SW. 1	......	
	2 p. m.	28.48	68	......	Cu. st. 10	0	S. 3	......	
	9 p. m.	28.48	61	......	Nim. 10	0	SE. 2	......	
March 17	7 a. m.	28.48	53	......	Cir. st. 7	0	NW. 1	......	
	2 p. m.	28.67	64	......	0	0	NW. 5	......	
	9 p. m.	28.81	51	......	0	0	N. 2	......	
March 18	7 a. m.	28.95	32	......	0	0	NW. 1	......	
	2 p. m.	28.85	70	......	0	0	NW. 2	......	
	9 p. m.	28.83	43	......	0	0	NW. 2	......	

WEBBERVILLE, TEXAS.

Month and day.	Hour.	Barom'r corrected to 32° F.	Thermometer.	Force of vapor.	Cloudiness.	Motion of clouds.	Winds.	Relative humidity.	REMARKS.
March 13	7 a. m.	29.44	68	......	Drizzling 10	....	S. 1	......	15th. Frost.
	2 p. m.	29.57	80	......	5	....	S. 1	......	17th. Thunder storm; slight shower
	9 p. m.	29.50	68	......	0	....	NW. 3	......	from SW.
March 14	7 a. m.	29.64	43	......	0	....	NW. 2	......	
	2 p. m.	29.70	68	......	0	....	NW. 1	......	
	9 p. m.	29.78	58	......	0	....	NW. 1	......	
March 15	7 a. m.	29.83	42	......	0	....	S. 1	......	
	2 p. m.	29.72	62	......	0	....	S. 1	......	
	9 p. m.	29.75	66	......	0	....	S. 1	......	
March 16	7 a. m.	29.73	55	......	5	....	S. 2	......	
	2 p. m.	29.64	67.5	......	10	....	S. 2	......	
	9 p. m.	29.57	65	......	10	....	S. 3	......	
March 17	7 a. m.	29.61	65	......	10	....	SW. 1	......	
	2 p. m.	29.58	68	......	5	....	N. 2	......	
	9 p. m.	29.70	52	......	0	....	N. 2	......	
March 18	7 a. m.	29.75	49	......	0	....	0	......	
	2 p. m.	29.76	61	......	0	....	0	......	
	9 p. m.	29.79	56	......	0	....	0	......	

UNION HILL, TEXAS.

Month and day.	Hour.	Barom'r corrected to 32° F.	Thermometer.	Force of vapor.	Cloudiness.	Motion of clouds.	Winds.	Relative humidity.	REMARKS.
March 13	7 a. m.	......	54	......	Fog	....	S. 2	......	13th. Severe norther at 8 p. m.;
	2 p. m.	......	82	......	Cu. st. 8	S. 1	S. 2	......	wind, 7; continued two hours,
	9 p. m.	......	68	......	Cu. 4	N. 1	SE. 5	......	and fell to about 5.
March 14	7 a. m.	......	42	......	St. 3	N. 1	N. 3	......	14th. Frost.
	2 p. m.	......	60	......	0	0	N. 2	......	15th. Very large lunar halo.
	9 p. m.	......	50	......	0	0	E. 1	......	16th. Norther at 8 a. m.; sprinkle
March 15	7 a. m.	......	51	......	Cir. 3	W. 1	N. 1	......	of rain.
	2 p. m.	......	60	......	Cu. st. 9	S. 2	NE. 1	......	
	9 p. m.	......	51	......	St. 8	S. 1	NW. 2	......	
March 16	7 a. m.	......	48	......	St. 10	S. 1	SE 2	......	
	2 p. m.	......	62	......	Nim. 10	S. 1	E. 3	......	
	9 p. m.	......	51	......	Nim. 10	S. 2	S. 2	......	
March 17	7 a. m.	......	62	......	Nim. 9	S. 1	S. 3	......	
	2 p. m.	......	65	......	0	0	NW. 6	......	
	9 p. m.	......	50	......	0	0	S. 4	......	
March 18	7 a. m.	......	40	......	0	0	NW. 2	......	
	2 p. m.	......	68	......	0	0	NW. 2	......	
	9 p. m.	......	52	......	0	0	S. 1	......	

STORM No. 1, MARCH, 1859.

NEW BRAUNFELS, TEXAS.

Month and day.	Hour.	Barom'r corrected to 32° F.	Thermometer.	Force of vapor.	Cloudiness.	Motion of clouds.	Winds.	Relative humidity.	REMARKS.
March 13	7 a. m.	27. 68	68	------	0	----------	S.----------	------	13th. Fog at 6 a. m.; lightning in the E. and SE. from 7 to 10 p. m.
	2 p. m	27. 60	81. 5	------	0	----------	W----------	------	15th. Lunar halo at 9 p. m.
	9 p m.	27. 70	54. 5	------	0	----------	N. 5	------	
March 14	7 a. m.	27. 73	41	------	0	----------	N----------	------	
	2 p. m.	27. 85	72. 5	------	0	----------	NE----------	------	
	9 p. m.	27. 85	52	------	0	----------	S.----------	------	
March 15	7 a. m.	27. 90	39.	------	St. 5	----------	W----------	------	
	2 p. m.	27. 88	72. 5	------	St. 5	----------	S.----------	------	
	9 p m.	27. 82	50	------	0	----------	SE----------	------	
March 16	7 a. m	27. 80	45. 5	------	0	----------	SE----------	------	
	2 p. m.	27. 63	68	------	0	----------	SE. 2	------	
	9 p. m.	27. 72	57	------	0	----------	SE. 2	------	
March 17	7 a. m.	27. 68	63	------	Cu. 5	----------	N----------	------	
	2 p. m.	27. 75	71	------	0	----------	NW----------	------	
	9 p. m.	27. 80	52	------	0	----------	NW----------	------	
March 18	7 a. m.	27. 90	38	------	0	----------	NW----------	------	
	2 p. m.	27. 85	74. 5	------	0	----------	W----------	------	
	9 p. m.	27. 90	55. 5	------	0	----------	SW----------	------	

WASHINGTON, TEXAS.

Month and day.	Hour.	Barom'r corrected to 32° F.	Thermometer.	Force of vapor.	Cloudiness.	Motion of clouds.	Winds.	Relative humidity.	REMARKS.
March 13	7 a. m.	29. 44	50	------	Nim. 10	0	S. 2	------	13th. Rain; amount, 0. 38 inch.
	2 p. m.	29. 34	72	------	Cu., nim. 5	0	S. 2	------	16th. Drizzling rain; amount, 0. 02 inch.
	9 p. m.	29. 52	44	------	Nim. 10	0	NW. 3	------	
March 14	7 a. m.	29. 77	68	------	0	0	N. 2	------	
	2 p. m.	29. 74	68	------	Cir. 4	0	N. 2	------	
	9 p. m.	29. 83	60	------	Cir. 1	0	0	------	
March 15	7 a. m.	29. 88	46	------	Cir. 1	0	0	------	
	2 p. m.	29. 80	86	------	Cir. 4	0	S. 1	------	
	9 p. m.	29. 76	64	------	Cir. 3	0	S. 1	------	
March 16	7 a. m.	29. 69	38	------	Nim. 10	0	S. 1	------	
	2 p. m.	29. 56	65	------	Nim. 10	0	S. 2	------	
	9 p. m.	29. 55	44	------	Nim. 10	0	S. 2	------	
March 17	7 a. m.	29. 44	51	------	Nim. 10	0	S. 2	------	
	2 p. m.	29. 50	74	------	0	0	NW. 3	------	
	9 p. m.	29. 72	52	------	0	0	NW. 3	------	
March 18	7 a. m.	29. 94	64	------	0	0	NW. 2	------	
	2 p. m.	29. 84	62	------	0	0	NW. 2	------	
	9 p m.	29. 82	60	------	0	0	0	------	

WASHINGTON, ARKANSAS

Month and day.	Hour.	Barom'r corrected to 32° F.	Thermometer.	Force of vapor.	Cloudiness.	Motion of clouds.	Winds.	Relative humidity.	REMARKS.
March 13	Sunrise..	------	62	------	10	----------	NW ----------	------	13th. Heavy rain most of the day, accompanied by thunder and lightning; amount, 2. 60 inches.
	2 p. m.	------	64	------	10	----------	----------	------	14th and 15th. Cool and pleasant; gentle breeze from N.
	9 p. m.	------	------	------	----------	----------	----------	------	15th. Cloudy; rain and thunder at night; amount, 0. 30 inch.
March 14	Sunrise..	------	40	------	0	----------	----------	------	16th. Fair and cool.
	2 p. m.	------	57	------	----------	----------	----------	------	17th. Frost; warm at 2 p. m.; clouds at night.
	9 p. m.	------	------	------	----------	----------	----------	------	18th. Warm rain, accompanied by thunder; amount, 0. 60 inch.
March 15	Sunrise..	------	38	------	0	----------	----------	------	
	2 p. m.	------	63	------	----------	----------	----------	------	
	9 p. m.	------	------	------	----------	----------	----------	------	
March 16	Sunrise..	------	40	------	10	----------	NW ----------	------	
	2 p. m.	------	58	------	10	----------	----------	------	
	9 p. m.	------	------	------	10	----------	----------	------	
March 17	Sunrise..	------	56	------	10	----------	NW ----------	------	
	2 p. m.	------	70	------	10	----------	----------	------	
	9 p. m.	------	------	------	10	----------	----------	------	
March 18	Sunrise..	------	38	------	0	----------	N ----------	------	
	2 p. m.	------	38	------	0	----------	----------	------	
	9 p. m.	------	------	------	----------	----------	----------	------	

STORM No. 1, MARCH, 1859.

GLENWOOD COTTAGE, TENNESSEE.

Month and day.	Hour.	Barom'r corrected to 32° F.	Thermometer.	Force of vapor.	Cloudiness.		Motion of clouds.		Winds.		Relative humidity.
March 13	9 p. m.	29. 40	63	. 408	St.	10	SSE.	2	SSE.	2	72
March 14	7 a. m.	29. 25	60	. 487	Nim.	10	SW.	2	SW.	2	94
	2 p. m.	29. 24	59. 7	. 146		0		0	SW.	6	28
	9 p. m.	29. 43	49. 5	. 182		0		0	SW.	5	61
March 15	7 a. m.	29. 54	42	. 078		0		0	WNW.	1	80
	2 p. m.	29. 64	52	. 068		0		0	NW.	3	17
	9 p. m.	29. 70	43	. 204		0		0	SE.	1	74
March 16	7 a. m.	29. 76	35	. 183	Cir.	1	W.	1	SSE.	1	90
	2 p. m.	29. 62	62	. 176	St.	10	W.	1	SE.	1	32
	9 p. m.	29. 58	54	. 206	St.	10	W.	1	SSE.	1	49
March 17	7 a. m.	29. 51	51	. 283	St.	10	S.	3	S.	1	75
	2 p. m.	29. 26	57	. 361	Nim.	10	SE.	3	SE.	1	96
	9 p. m.	29. 07	53	. 388	St.	10	?			0	100
March 18	7 a. m.	29 05	39	. 206	Nim.	10	WNW.	4	WNW.	4	86
	2 p. m.	29. 27	34	. 175	Nim.	10	NW.	3	NW.	3	89
	9 p. m.	29. 46	36	. 115	St.	10	W.	2	W.	3	54
March 19	7 a. m.	29. 58	34	. 120		0		0	NW.	2	61
	2 p. m.	29. 60	49	. 107	Cir.	1	W.	1	W.	3	31

REMARKS.

14th. A gentle rain from 11¾ a. m. to 12¼ p. m., and during the night from 9¼ p. m.

15th. Rain ceased at 9 a. m., and cleared off, with high wind; blowing a gale at 2 p. m.; amount, 1. 35 inch.

16th. White frost.

17th. A few drops of rain at 7¼ a. m., increased to a gentle, steady rain, which continued till about dark; occasional sprinkle in the evening; patches of fog at 9 p. m.; showers during the night.

18th. Drizzling rain at intervals during the morning; wind, WNW.; at 10¼ a. m. rain changed to snow, which continued falling till 2 p. m., sometimes in copious showers; ceased snowing at 4 p. m.; amount, in water, 0. 672 inch. 19th. Ice ¼-inch thick.

MEMPHIS, TENNESSEE.

Month and day.	Hour.	Barom'r corrected to 32° F.	Thermometer.	Force of vapor.	Cloudiness.	Motion of clouds.	Winds.	Relative humidity.
March 13	9 p. m.	29. 60	61	. 537	------	------	------	100
March 14	7 a. m.	29. 67	51	. 196	------	------	------	52
	2 p. m.	29. 79	54	. 157	------	------	------	38
	9 p. m.	29. 81	53	. 123	------	------	------	30
March 15	7 a. m.	29. 97	46	. 192	------	------	------	62
	2 p. m.	30. 00	59	. 091	------	------	------	18
	9 p. m.	29. 98	45	. 275	------	------	------	92
March 16	7 a. m.	29. 96	44	. 218	------	------	------	76
	2 p. m	29. 91	63	. 216	------	------	------	37
	9 p. m.	29. 82	56	. 230	------	------	------	51
March 17	7 a. m.	29. 71	50	. 361	------	------	------	100
	2 p. m.	29. 48	53	. 403	------	------	------	100
	9 p. m.	29. 41	54	. 418	------	------	------	100
March 18	7 a. m.	29. 60	37	. 221	------	------	------	100
	2 p. m.	29. 73	44	. 130	------	------	------	45
	9 p m.	29. 84	44	. 151	------	------	------	52
March 19	7 a. m.	29. 94	43	. 164	------	------	------	59
	2 p. m.	29. 93	57	. 191	------	------	------	41

13th. Rain from 7 to 12 p. m.; amount, 1. 09 inch.

17th. Rain, commencing at 7 a. m.; amount, 1. 02 inch.

LA GRANGE, TENNESSEE.

Month and day.	Hour.	Barom'r corrected to 32° F.	Thermometer.	Force of vapor.	Cloudiness.		Motion of clouds.		Winds.		Relative humidity.
March 13	9 p. m.	29. 01	62	. 491		?10	?		SW.	2	88
March 14	7 a. m.	29. 07	52	. 183	Nim.	9	NE.	2	SW.	3	47
	2 p. m.	29. 13	54	. 157		0		0	SW.	4	38
	9 p. m.	29. 24	49	. 175		0		0	SW.	2	50
March 15	7 a. m.	29. 36	42	. 155		0		0	SW.	2	58
	2 p. m.	29. 43	50	. 210		0		0	NW.	2	58
	9 p. m.	29. 43	52	. 232	Cir. st.	1		0		0	60
March 16	7 a. m.	29. 41	46	. 169	Cir. st.	3	NE.	1	SE.	2	54
	2 p. m.	29. 37	60	. 229	Nim.	5	N.	1	S.	1	44
	9 p. m.	29. 29	55	. 295	Nim.	10	N.	2	S.	2	68
March 17	7 a. m.	29. 18	51	. 348	Nim.	10	NW.	3	SE.	2	93
	2 p. m.	29. 00	52	. 388	Nim.	10	NW.	3	SE.	2	100
	9 p. m.	28. 92	55	. 405	Nim.	10	?		SW.	1	94
March 18	7 a. m.	28. 96	36	. 170	Nim.	10	NE.	2	SW.	3	80
	2 p. m.	29. 15	46	. 311	Cu.	4	E.	2	W.	4	100
	9 p. m.	29. 26	40	. 139		0		0	W.	2	56
March 19	7 a. m.	29. 30	40	. 139		0		0	W.	2	56
	2 p. m.	29. 34	55	. 168	Cir. st.	2	NE.	2	SW.	2	39

Heavy rain from 5 p. m. the 13th to 4 a. m. on the 14th.

17th. Storm at 4 a. m.

18th. Slight snow from 7 to 9 a. m.

STORM No. 1, MARCH, 1859.

BARDSTOWN, KENTUCKY.

Month and day.	Hour.	Barom'r corrected to 32° F.	Thermometer.	Force of vapor.	Cloudiness.	Motion of clouds.	Winds.	Relative humidity.	REMARKS.
March 13	9 p. m.	29.48	60	.283	Nim. 10	SW. 1	S. 1	54	13th. Ring around the moon at 8½ p. m.
March 14	7 a. m.	29.15	58	.423	St. 9	SW. 2	S. 1	88	18th. Rain at 6 a. m.; thunder storm at 7½ a. m; high wind at 8 a. m.; snow storm at 2 p m; storm ended in the night; am't in water, 0.97 inch.
	2 p. m.	29.05	60	.338	Cu. 7	SW. 3	W. 1	65	
	9 p. m.	29.22	50	.117	0	----------	W. 3	32	
March 15	7 a. m.	29.28	44	.151	Cu. st. 4	SW. 2	SW. 2	52	
	2 p. m.	29.44	49	.130	Cir. cu. 2	SW. 3	SW. 2	37	
	9 p. m.	29.57	42	.113	0	----------	SW. 1	42	
March 16	7 a. m.	29.65	35	.162	0	----------	S. 1	80	
	2 p. m.	29.56	58	.153	Cir. st. 1	SW. 1	SW. 1	32	
	9 p. m	29.52	52	.183	0	----------	SW. 1	47	
March 17	7 a. m.	29.45	51	.270	Nim. 10	SE. 2	SE. 2	72	
	2 p. m.	29.29	51	.321	Nim. 10	SE. 2	SE. 1	86	
	9 p. m.	29.05	50	.354	Nim. 10	SE. 2	SE. 1	96	
March 18	7 a. m.	28.85	54	.390	Nim. 10	SW. 3	SW. 2	93	
	2 p. m.	28.92	48	.285	Nim. 10	W. 3	W. 3	85	
	9 p. m.	29.21	33	.175	Nim. 10	W. 2	W. 3	94	
March 19	7 a. m.	29.34	32	.143	St. 10	W. 2	W. 3	79	
	2 p. m.	29.44	42	.222	Cu. 3	W. 3	W. 2	83	

DANVILLE, KENTUCKY.

Month and day.	Hour.	Barom'r corrected to 32° F.	Thermometer.	Force of vapor.	Cloudiness.	Motion of clouds.	Winds.	Relative humidity.	REMARKS.
March 13	9 p. m.	29.01	60	------	St. 3	----------	S. 1	------	13th. Rain in the night; amount, 0.763 inch.
March 14	7 a. m.	28.77	58	------	Cu. st. 8	SW. 3	SE. 3	------	15th. Rain; amount, 0.12 inch.
	2 p. m.	28.67	63	------	Cu. st. 9	SW. 3	SW. 3	------	17th. Began to rain at 5 p. m., and ended in the night; amount, 0.564 inch.
	9 p. m.	28.80	52	------	St. 1	SW. 3	SW. 5	------	18th. Showery; amount, 0.614 inch.
March 15	7 a. m.	28.84	46	------	St. 9	SW. 3	W. 4	------	
	2 p. m.	28.97	51	------	Cu. st. 2	W. 3	W. 4	------	
	9 p. m.	29.14	43	------	0	----------	W. 1	------	
March 16	7 a. m.	29.21	32	------	0	----------	W. 1	------	
	2 p. m.	29.19	63	------	St. 2	----------	E. 1	------	
	9 p. m.	29.10	55	------	St. 7	----------	SE. 1	------	
March 17	7 a. m.	29.10	50	------	St. 10	----------	S. 2	------	
	2 p. m.	28.91	55	------	St. 10	SW. 3	SE. 1	------	
	9 p. m.	28.62	55	------	St. 10	SW. 1	SE. 1	------	
March 18	7 a. m.	28.46	58	------	Cu. st. 4	S. 5	S. 2	------	
	2 p. m.	28.43	47	------	Cu. st. 8	SW. 4	W. 5	------	
	9 p. m.	28.73	40	------	St. 10	----------	W. 6	------	
March 19	7 a. m.	28.91	32	------	St. 10	NW. 4	W. 3	------	
	2 p. m.	28.99	42	------	Cu. st. 5	NW. 5	W. 4	------	

LOUISVILLE, KENTUCKY.

Month and day.	Hour.	Barom'r corrected to 32° F.	Thermometer.	Force of vapor.	Cloudiness.	Motion of clouds.	Winds.	Relative humidity.	REMARKS.
March 13	9 p. m.	29.40	55	------	Imp. 5	----------	SE. 1	------	13th. Lunar halo at 9 p. m.
March 14	7 a. m.	29.17	56	------	9	SW. 1	S. 2	------	14th. Rain from 2½ to 5 a. m.; amount, 0.388 inch.
	3 p. m.	29.04	67	.246	1	S. 3	S. 4	37	16th. Light frost; distant halo at 3 p. m.; lunar halo at 7½ p. m.
	9 p. m.	29.22	51	------	0	----------	S. 4	------	17th. Began to rain at 8.30 a. m., continued during the night; changed to snow and rain at 1½ p. m. the following day, and ended at 9 p. m.; amount, 0.74 inch.
March 15	7 a. m.	29.34	43	------	5	W. 4	SW. 4	------	
	3 p. m.	29.51	53	.146	4	SW. 3	SW. 4	36	
	9 p. m.	29.56	42	------	0	----------	SW. 1	------	
March 16	7 a. m.	29.74	33	------	0	----------	S. 2	------	
	3 p. m.	29.60	63	.243	Imp. 1	----------	SE. 2	42	
	9 p. m.	29.58	52	------	Haze 3	----------	SE. 1	------	
March 17	7 a. m.	29.51	54	------	10	SW. 2	S. 2	------	
	3 p. m.	29.27	53	.308	10	SE. 2	SE. 2	74	
	9 p. m.	29.06	51	------	Imp. 10	----------	S. 2	------	
March 18	7 a. m.	28.83	53	------	10	S. 4	S. 2	------	
	3 p. m.	28.95	37	.165	Imp. 10	----------	W. 4	72	
	9 p. m.	29.23	33	------	Imp. 10	----------	W. 4	------	
March 19	7 a. m.	29.39	32	------	10	W. 4	W. 4	------	
	3 p. m.	29.51	43	.130	5	W. 3	W. 3	45	

STORM No. 1, MARCH, 1859.

SPRINGDALE, KENTUCKY.

Month and day.	Hour.	Barom'r corrected to 32° F.	Thermometer.	Force of vapor.	Cloudiness.	Motion of clouds.	Winds.	Relative humidity.	REMARKS.
March 13	6 p. m.	29.46	59	.423	4	----------	0	88	Began to rain in the night of the 13th, and ended at 1 p. m. on the 14th; amount, 0.63 inch.
March 14	5 a. m.	29.09	54	.375	8	----------	E. 3	93	
	2 p. m.	28.94	62	.360	0	----------	S. 3	68	
	6 p. m.	29.03	55	.390	1	----------	SW. 5	93	Began to rain at 10 a. m. the 17th; changed to snow on the 18th, and ended in the night; amount in water, 0.82 inch.
March 15	5 a. m.	29.20	43	.267	9	----------	WSW. 5	100	
	2 p. m.	29.39	51	.143	3	----------	WSW. 3	43	
	6 p. m.	29.48	46	.124	0	----------	WSW. 3	42	
March 16	5 a. m.	29.64	28½	.135	0	----------	WSW. 1	88	
	2 p. m.	29.52	62	.203	1	----------	SE. 2	39	
	6 p. m.	29.47	54	.321	9	----------	ENE. 1	80	
March 17	5 a. m.	29.43	53½	.232	10	----------	S. 3	60	
	2 p. m.	29.21	50½	.315	10	----------	E. 2	89	
	6 p. m.	29.05	49½	.322	10	----------	E. 1	92	
March 18	5 a. m.	28.77	52	.361	10	----------	S. 1	96	
	2 p. m.	28.78	36½	.170	10	----------	W. 5	80	
	6 p. m.	28.83	32½	.162	10	----------	WSW. 5	89	
March 19	5 a. m.	29.22	31	.136	10	----------	WSW. 2	78	
	2 p. m.	29.37	40	.219	6	----------	W. 5	95	

PARIS, KENTUCKY.

Month and day.	Hour.	Barom'r corrected to 32° F.	Thermometer.	Force of vapor.	Cloudiness.	Motion of clouds.	Winds.	Relative humidity.	REMARKS.
March 13	9 p. m.	29.16	57	------	-----------	----------	SW. 1	------	13th. Lunar halo; hazy at 9 p. m.; storm commenced the night preceding, and ended at 7 a. m. on the 14th; amount, 0.63 inch.
March 14	7 a. m.	28.88	53	------	Nim. 10	NW ------	SE. 4	------	
	2 p. m.	28.75	63	------	Cu. nim. 10	NE. 3	SW. 3	------	
	9 p. m.	28.79	52	------	Cir. 2	NE. 4	SW. 6	------	
March 15	7 a. m.	28.89	43	------	Cu. 10	NE. 3	SW. 3	------	14th. Shower at 3 p. m.; amount, 0.13 inch.
	2 p. m.	29.13	49	------	Cu. 3	E --------	NW. 5	------	
	9 p. m.	29.26	41	------	0	----------	SW. 1	------	15th. Morning cloudy, night clear.
March 16	7 a. m.	29.32	31½	------	0	----------	NW. 1	------	16th. Morning clear; p. m. cloudy; night hazy; lunar halo.
	2 p. m.	29.35	64	------	Cu. & cir. st. 1	----------	E. 1	------	
	9 p. m.	29.23	53	------	Hazy 0	----------	SW. 1	------	Rain from 9 p. m. to 7 a. m. on the 17th; amount, 0.038 inch.
March 17	7 a. m.	29.18	50	------	Nim. 10	----------	SW. 2	------	
	2 p. m.	28.99	52	------	Nim. 10	----------	SE. 1	------	Rain from 11 a. m. the 17th to 7 a. m. on the 18th; amount, 0.87 inch.
	9 p. m.	28.76	53	------	Nim. 10	----------	SE. 1	------	
March 18	7 a. m.	29.54	55	------	Nim. 10	NE -------	SW. 1	------	
	2 p. m.	28.46	50	------	Cu. 8	E --------	W. 6	------	19th. Rain and snow till 7 a. m.; amount, 0.33 inch.
	9 p. m.	28.73	31	------	Nim. 1	NE -------	NW. 6	------	
March 19	7 a. m.	29.25	30	------	Cu. 10	SE -------	NW. 2	------	
	2 p. m.	29.07	37	------	Cu. 8	SE -------	NW. 4	------	

AVON, OHIO.

Month and day.	Hour.	Barom'r corrected to 32° F.	Thermometer.	Force of vapor.	Cloudiness.	Motion of clouds.	Winds.	Relative humidity.	REMARKS.
March 13	9 p. m.	29.20	40	.092	-----------	----------	W. 4	30	15th. Rain all day; amount, 0.80 inch.
March 14	7 a. m.	28.85	56	.282	Cu. 10	SE. 1	SW. 2	63	
	2 p. m.	28.57	60	.391	Cir. cu. 10	SW. 2	SW. 4	74	Rain on the 17th, commencing at 7 a. m., and on the 18th, beginning at 2 p. m.; amount, 1.84 inch.
	9 p. m.	------	------	------	-----------	----------	SW. 6	------	
March 15	7 a. m.	------	------	------	Cir. cu. 10	W. 1	W. 3	------	
	2 p. m.	28.93	57.7	.190	Cu. cir. 10	W. 1	W. 2	85	
	9 p. m.	29.03	36.5	.153	-----------	----------	W. 2	71	
March 16	7 a. m.	29.28	32.5	.171	0	----------	SW. 1	92	
	2 p. m.	29.23	68	.543	0	----------	NE. 1	79	
	9 p. m.	29.21	43	.132	-----------	----------	NE. 1	48	
March 17	7 a. m.	28.16	52.5	.251	Cu. st. 10	SW. 1	-----------	63	
	2 p. m.	28.86	------	------	Cu. st. 10	----------	SE. 2	------	
	9 p. m.	28.69	57.5	.315	Nim. 10	----------	SE. 1	83	
March 18	7 a. m.	28.33	60	.456	Cu. st. 10	SW -------	SW. 1	88	
	2 p. m.	28.26	50	.350	Nim. 10	SW. 1	NE. 1	96	
	9 p. m.	28.26	39.7	.173	Nim. 10	W. 1	W. 2	89	
March 19	7 a. m.	29.47	32	.162	Nim. 10	SW. 3	W. 4	89	
	2 p. m.	28.85	33.5	.144	Cu. st., nim. 10	W. 1	W. 2	75	

STORM No. 1, MARCH, 1859.

BELLEFONTAINE, OHIO.

Month and day.	Hour.	Barom'r corrected to 32° F.	Thermometer.	Force of vapor.	Cloudiness.		Motion of clouds.		Winds.		Relative humidity.	REMARKS.
March 13	9 p. m.	-----	50. 6	-----	------------		----------		SE.	3	-----	14th. Rain from 6¼ a. m. to 2 p. m.;
March 14	7 a. m.	----	47	-----	Nim.	10	SW.	5	SE.	4	-----	amount, 0. 47 inch.
	2 p. m.	-----	59	-----	Nim.	9	NE.	2	SW.	3	-----	16th. Halo round the moon at 9
	9 p. m.	-----	51	-----	Nim.	9	NW.	4	W.	4	-----	p. m.
March 15	7 a. m.	-----	36	-----	Nim.	10	NE.	4	SW.	5	-----	Began to rain at 11 a. m. on the
	2 p. m.	-----	34	-----	Cir.	7	NW.	5	W.	4	-----	17th; continued till 6½ p. m. on
	9 p. m.	-----	33	-----	------------		----------		NW.	2	-----	the 18th, when it gave place to
March 16	7 a. m.	-----	40	-----	------------		----------		E.	2	-----	a heavy snow; amount, 1. 15 inch.
	2 p. m.	-----	52	-----	Cir.	2	SE.	1	SW.	2	-----	
	9 p. m.	-----	45	-----	Cir. st.	4	SE	1	NE.	3	-----	
March 17	7 a. m.	-----	48	-----	Nim.	10	NE.	1	NW.	3	-----	
	2 p. m.	-----	50	-----	Nim.	10	SE.	1	SE.	2	-----	
	9 p. m.	-----	49. 5	-----	Nim.	10	SE.	2	SE.	3	-----	
March 18	7 a. m.	-----	49	-----	Cir. cu.	10	NE.	2	SE	2	-----	
	2 p. m.	-----	48	-----	Nim.	10	NE.	2	SE.	1	-----	
	9 p. m.	-----	30	-----	Nim.	10	SE.	1	NW.	4	-----	
March 19	7 a. m.	-----	25	-----	Nim.	10	E.	3	NW.	3	-----	
	2 p. m.	-----	29	-----	Cir. cu.	10	NE.	3	W.	3	-----	

CLEVELAND, OHIO.

Month and day.	Hour.	Barom'r corrected to 32° F.	Thermometer.	Force of vapor.	Cloudiness.		Motion of clouds.		Winds.		Relative humidity.	REMARKS.
March 13	9 p. m.	29. 13	37	-----		0	----------			0	-----	14. Slight rain from 8½ a. m. to 11½
March 14	7 a. m.	28. 87	47	-----		10	----------		SE.	2	-----	a. m.; showers from 7½ to 8½
	2 p. m.	28. 60	59	-----	Cu. st.	10	S.	5	S.	4	-----	p. m.; amount, 0. 21 inch.
	9 p. m.	28. 53	57	-----	Cir. cu.	7	SW.	4	SW.	4	-----	16th. Large lunar halo in the
March 15	7 a. m.	28. 68	41	-----	Cu. st.	10	SW.	4	SW.	3	-----	evening.
	2 p. m.	28. 79	38	-----	Cu. st.	10	----------		W.	4	-----	17th. Rain in the evening and
	9 p. m.	29. 00	36½	-----	Cu. st.	10	----------		W.	4	-----	night; amount, 0. 34 inch.
March 16	7 a. m.	29. 20	34½	-----		0	----------		NW.	3	-----	Began to rain at 3½ p. m. the 18th,
	2 p. m.	29. 21	40	-----		1	----------		N.	2	-----	changed to snow in the night,
	9 p. m.	29. 17	40½	-----		0	----------		SE -------		-----	and continued till — a. m. on the
March 17	7 a. m.	29. 06	43	-----		10	----------		SE.	3	-----	19th; amount in water, 1.77
	2 p. m.	28. 93	62	-----		10	----------		S.	3	-----	inch.
	9 p. m.	28. 74	48	-----		10	----------		S.	2	-----	
March 18	7 a. m.	28. 45	53	-----		10	----------		S.	2	-----	
	2 p. m.	28. 30	59	-----	Cu. st.	10	S.	3	N.	1	-----	
	9 p. m.	28. 29	37	-----		10	----------		W.	2	-----	
March 19	7 a. m.	28. 45	32½	-----		10	W.	5	W.	5	-----	
	2 p. m.	28. 71	36	-----	Cu. st.	10	W.	5	W.	5	-----	

BOWLING GREEN, OHIO.

Month and day.	Hour.	Barom'r corrected to 32° F.	Thermometer.	Force of vapor.	Cloudiness.		Motion of clouds.		Winds.		Relative humidity.	REMARKS.
March 13	9 p. m.	29. 305	44	-----	Cir. cu.	5	SW.	2	NE.	2	-----	14th. Several smart showers;
March 14	7 a. m.	29. 017	45	-----	Nim.	10	SW.	1		0	-----	amount, 0. 74 inch.
	2 p. m.	28. 784	58. 6	-----	Nim.	10	S.	2	S.	3	-----	Began to rain at 8½ p. m. the 17th,
	9 p. m.	28. 719	45. 7	-----	Cu. st.	9	SW.	2		0	-----	and continued till 2 a. m. on the
March 15	7 a. m.	28. 836	30	-----	Cu. st.	10	SW.	3	W.	3	-----	18th; amount, 0. 235 inch.
	2 p. m.	29. 012	40	-----	Cu.	10	SW.	3	W.	3	-----	18th. Showers during the day;
	9 p. m.	29. 237	34	-----		0		0		0	-----	began to snow at 6½ p. m.; next
March 16	7 a. m.	29. 452	36. 5	-----		0		0		0	-----	morning snow 2 inches in depth,
	2 p. m.	29. 411	55	-----		0		0		0	-----	notwithstanding the warm and
	9 p. m.	29. 331	48	-----		0		0		0	-----	wet state of the ground; amount
March 17	7 a. m.	29. 229	47. 5	-----	Cir. st.	10		0	SW.	1	-----	in water, 0. 75 inch.
	2 p. m.	29. 094	58	-----	Cir. st.	10	SW.	2	SE.	3	-----	
	9 p. m.	28. 882	58. 4	-----	Nim.	10	----------		NE.	1	-----	
March 18	7 a. m.	28. 565	------	-----	Cu. st.	10	SW.	3	SW.	1	-----	
	2 p. m.	28. 382	------	-----	Cu. st.	10	NW.	3		0	-----	
	9 p. m.	28. 504	34. 5	-----	Nim.	10	----------		NE.	1	-----	
March 19	7 a. m.	28. 737	34	-----	Cu. st.	10	NW.	3	NW.	3	-----	
	2 p. m.	28. 994	36. 4	-----	Nim.	6	W.	3	W.	2	-----	

STORM No. 1, MARCH, 1859.

CINCINNATI, OHIO.*

Month and day.	Hour.	Barom'r corrected to 32° F.	Thermometer.	Force of vapor.	Cloudiness.		Motion of clouds.		Winds.		Relative humidity.	REMARKS.
March 13	9 p. m.	29. 58	54	------		0		0		0	------	13th. Rain ; amount. 0.262 inch.
March 14	7 a. m.	29. 40	52	------	Nim.	10	N ------			0	------	14th. Rain from 1.20 to 2.20 p. m.; amount, 0. 15 inch.
	2 p. m.	29. 15	62	------	Nim.	10	E ------		W.	2	------	
	9 p. m.	29. 30	50	------	Cir.	7	NE. ------		S.	50	------	Began to rain at 2. 30 p. m. the 17th; continued, accompanied by snow on the 18th, and ended at 3 a. m. on the 19th ; amount in water, 1.155 inch.
March 15	7 a. m.	29. 40	42	------	Nim.	10	E ------		W.	15	------	
	2 p. m.	29. 57	43	------	Nim.	8	E ------		W.	5	------	
	9 p. m.	29. 79	40	------		0		0		0	------	
March 16	7 a. m.	29. 90	34	------		0		0	NE.	2	------	
	2 p. m.	29. 81	60	------		0		0	S.	2	------	
	9 p. m.	29. 76	50	------		0		0		0	------	
March 17	7 a. m.	29. 65	50	------	Nim.	10	N ------		S.	2	------	
	2 p. m.	29. 54	54	------	Nim.	10	N ------		S.	2	------	
	9 p. m.	29. 14	50	------	Nim.	10	N ------		S.	2	------	
March 18	7 a. m.	28. 89	50	------	Nim.	10	NE. ------		S.	2	------	
	2 p. m.	28. 79	56	------	Nim.	10	NE. ------		S.	4	------	
	9 p. m.	29. 21	32	------	Nim.	10	NE. ------		W.	25	------	
March 19	7 a. m.	29. 39	32	------	Nim.	10	E ------		W.	12	------	
	2 p. m.	29. 54	37	------	ir.	5	E ------		NW.	30	------	

CINCINNATI, OHIO.†

Month and day.	Hour.	Barom'r corrected to 32° F.	Thermometer.	Force of vapor.	Cloudiness.		Motion of clouds.	Winds.		Relative humidity.	REMARKS.
March 13	9 p. m.	29. 48	57	. 378	Nim.	10	------	S. ------		81	15th. Rain from $3\frac{1}{2}$ to $5\frac{3}{4}$ a. m , and $2\frac{1}{4}$ to $2\frac{1}{2}$ p. m. ; amount, 0. 54 inch.
March 14	7 a. m.	29. 25	56	. 391	Nim.	10	------	S. ------		87	
	2 p. m.	29. 09	63	. 510	Nim.	10	------	S. ------		88	
	9 p. m.	29. 19	52	. 159	Cu.	5	------	W.	4	41	Storm commenced at $2\frac{1}{2}$ p. m. the 17th, and ended at $7\frac{3}{4}$ a. m. on the 19th; amount, 0. 99 inch.
March 15	7 a. m.	29. 35	44	. 173	Nim.	10	------	W.	4	60	
	2 p. m.	29. 49	46	. 192	Nim.	10	------	W.	4	62	
	9 p. m.	29. 62	42	. 155		0	------	W.	3	58	
March 16	7 a. m.	29. 74	36	. 149		0	------	S. ------		71	
	2 p. m.	29. 67	73	. 509		0	------	S. ------		50	
	9 p. m.	29. 61	52	. 232		0	------	S. ------		62	
March 17	7 a. m.	29. 57	51	. 245		0	------	S. ------		65	
	2 p. m.	29. 44	58	. 309	Nim.	10	------	S. ------		64	
	9 p. m.	29. 03	54	. 362	Nim.	10	------	S. ------		87	
March 18	7 a. m.	28. 88	54	. 362	Cu.	5	------	SW. ------		87	
	2 p. m.	28. 71	58	. 309	Cu.	5	------	SW.	3	64	
	9 p. m.	29. 03	33	. 142	Nim.	10	------	W.	4	92	
March 19	7 a. m.	29. 24	33	. 150	Nim.	10	------	W.	3	80	
	2 p. m.	29. 46	44	. 218	Cu.	5	------	W.	3	76	

COLLINGWOOD, OHIO.

Month and day.	Hour.	Barom'r corrected to 32° F.	Thermometer.	Force of vapor.	Cloudiness.	Motion of clouds.	Winds.	Relative humidity.	REMARKS.
March 13	9 p. m.	------	44	------	------	------	------	------	
March 14	7 a. m.	------	44	------	------	------	------	------	
	2 p. m.	------	56	------	------	------	------	------	
	9 p. m.	------	45	------	------	------	------	------	
March 15	7 a. m.	------	38	------	------	------	------	------	
	2 p. m.	------	38	------	------	------	------	------	
	9 p. m.	------	34	------	------	------	------	------	
March 16	7 a. m.	------	36	------	------	------	------	------	
	2 p. m.	------	56	------	------	------	------	------	
	9 p. m.	------	46	------	------	------	------	------	
March 17	7 a. m.	------	48	------	------	------	------	------	
	2 p. m.	------	60	------	------	------	------	------	
	9 p. m.	------	50	------	------	------	------	------	
March 18	7 a. m.	------	48	------	------	------	------	------	
	2 p. m.	------	46	------	------	------	------	------	
	9 p. m.	------	36	------	------	------	------	------	
March 19	7 a. m.	------	34	------	------	------	------	------	
	2 p. m.	------	34	------	------	------	------	------	

* Phillips, observer. † Harper, observer.

STORM No. 1, MARCH, 1859.

COLLEGE HILL, OHIO.

Month and day.	Hour.	Barom'r corrected to 32° F.	Thermometer.	Force of vapor.		Cloudiness.	Motion of clouds.		Winds.		Relative humidity.	REMARKS.
March 13	9 p. m.	28. 65	54	------		0		0	SE.	2	------	14th. Rain in the night; amount, 0. 36 inch.
March 14	7 a. m.	28. 40	50	------		10	SE.	2	SE.	2	------	
	2 p. m.	28. 23	62	------		10	SE.	2	SE.	2	------	17th. Commenced raining at 1 p. m., and ended in the night; amount, 0. 72 inch.
	9 p. m.	28. 24	52	------		10	SE.	2	SW.	4	------	
March 15	7 a. m.	28. 42	40	------		10	SW.	4	SW.	4	------	
	2 p. m.	28. 60	46	------		8	SW.	4	SW.	3	------	18th. Rain and snow; amount, 0. 72 inch.
	9 p. m.	28. 64	44	------		0		0	SW.	3	------	
March 16	7 a. m.	28. 85	34	------		0		0	SW.	3	------	16th. Halo around the moon.
	2 p. m.	28. 80	60	------		0		0	SW.	3	------	
	9 p. m.	28. 80	40	------		0		0	SW.	2	------	
March 17	7 a. m.	28. 70	46	------		10	SW.	2	SW.	1	------	
	2 p. m.	28. 61	60	------		10	SW.	2	SW.	2	------	
	9 p. m.	28. 60	44	------		10	SW.	2	SW.	2	------	
March 18	7 a. m.	28. 16	52	------		10	SW.	1	SW.	1	------	
	2 p. m.	28. 05	46	------		10	SW.	3	SW.	3	------	
	9 p. m.	28. 12	32	------		10	SW.	3	SW.	3	------	
March 19	7 a. m.	28. 39	28	------		10	SW.	4	SW.	4	------	
	2 p. m.	28. 55	`38	------		5	SW.	4	SW.	4	------	

HILLSBOROUGH, OHIO.

Month and day.	Hour.	Barom'r corrected to 32° F.	Thermometer.	Force of vapor.		Cloudiness.	Motion of clouds.		Winds.		Relative humidity.	REMARKS.
March 13	9 p. m.	28. 84	55	. 131		0	----------		SE.	2	29	14th. Rain a.m. and p m.; amount, 0. 415 inch.
March 14	7 a. m.	28. 56	48½	. 322	Nim.	10	----------		SE.	4	92	
	2 p. m.	28. 38	59½	. 396	St.	10	----------		SW.	5	76	17th. Rain a.m. and p.m.; amount, 0. 991 inch.
	9 p. m.	28. 46	52	. 136	Cir.	1	----------		W.	6	35	
March 15	7 a. m.	28. 58	40	. 132	St.	10	----------		W.	6	52	18th. Storm of sleet, rain, wind, and thunder at 11 a. m.; snow storm at night; amount, 0. 235 inch.
	2 p. m.	28. 72	39	. 152	St.	9	----------		W.	6	63	
	9 p. m.	28. 90	38	. 103		0	----------		NW.	4	45	
March 16	7 a. m.	29. 05	36	. 122		0	----------		SE.	1	58	
	2 p. m.	29. 03	50	. 126		0	----------		SE.	3	34	
	9 p. m.	28. 94	47½	. 120	St.	8	----------		SE.	2	36	
March 17	7 a. m.	28. 89	50	. 144	St.	10	----------		SW.	2	39	
	2 p. m.	28. 74	50	. 328	Nim.	10	----------		SE.	3	89	
	9 p. m.	28. 44	50	. 301	Nim.	10	----------		SE.	2	100	
March 18	7 a. m.	28. 25	51½	. 388	Nim.	10	----------		SW.	2	100	
	2 p. m.	28. 05	48½	. 297	St.	10	----------		SW.	2	85	
	9 p. m.	28. 22	31	. 174	Nim.	10	----------		NW.	6	100	
March 19	7 a. m.	28. 52	28	. 123	St.	9	----------		SW.	6	77	
	2 p. m.	28. 68	32	. 106	St.	9	----------		SW.	5	58	

HIRAM, OHIO.

Month and day.	Hour.	Barom'r corrected to 32° F.	Thermometer.	Force of vapor.		Cloudiness.	Motion of clouds.		Winds.		Relative humidity.	REMARKS.
March 13	9 p. m.	------	45	------		0		0	SE.	2	------	14th. Rain from 8 to 9 p. m.; amount, 0. 27 inch.
March 14	7 a. m.	------	45	------	Cir. st.	10	SE.	2	SE.	2	------	
	2 p. m.	------	56	------	Cir. st.	9	----------		S.	3	------	17th. Rain at 4 p. m.
	9 p. m.	------	41	------	Cu.	9	----------		S.	3	------	18th. Thunder storm at 2 a. m ; amount, 0. 62 inch.
March 15	7 a. m.	------	41	------	Cir. st.	9	----------		SW.	3	------	
	2 p. m.	------	39	------	Cir. st.	10	NW.	3	SW.	4	------	19th Snow storm; amount, in water, 0. 80 inch.
	9 p. m.	------	32	------	Cu. st.	10	----------		SW.	3	------	
March 16	7 a. m.	------	31	------	Cu.	1	W.	2	SW.	2	------	
	2 p. m.	------	48	------		0		0	SW.	2	------	
	9 p. m.	------	88	------		0		0	SW.	1	------	
March 17	7 a. m.	------	51	------	Cir. st.	9	----------		S.	1	------	
	2 p. m.	------	59	------	Cir. st.	9	----------		S.	2	------	
	9 p. m.	------	48	------	Nim.	10	----------		SW.	2	------	
March 18	7 a. m.	------	54	------	Nim.	10	SW.	3	SW.	2	------	
	2 p. m.	------	58	------	Nim.	10	S.	2	S.	1	------	
	9 p. m.	------	40	------	Nim.	10	W.	3	W.	3	------	
March 19	7 a. m.	------	31	------	Nim.	10	NW.	4	NW.	4	------	
	2 p. m.	------	31	------	Nim.	10	NW.	3	NW.	6	------	

STORM No. 1, MARCH, 1859.

HUDSON, OHIO.

Month and day.	Hour.	Barom'r corrected to 32° F.	Thermometer.	Force of vapor.	Cloudiness.	Motion of clouds.	Winds.	Relative humidity.	REMARKS.
March 13	9 p. m.	28. 92	49	......	0	....	E. 1	......	14th. Rain began at 9 a. m., and ended in the night; amount, 0. 22 inch. Commenced raining at 5 p. m. the 17th, and ended on the 18th, in the night; amount, 1. 00 inch. 19th. Rain.
March 14	7 a. m.	28. 70	49	......	Amorphous 10	....	E. 3	......	
	2 p. m.	28. 38	57	......	Nim. 10	....	SE. 3	......	
	9 p. m.	28. 29	56	......	Nim. 10	....	SW. 3	......	
March 15	7 a. m.	28. 42	44	......	St., cu. 10	....	W. 4	......	
	2 p. m.	28. 61	40	......	Cir. st. 10	....	W. 4	......	
	9 p. m.	28. 78	35	......	Cu. 10	....	W. 4	......	
March 16	7 a. m.	28. 99	31	......	0	....	W. 0	......	
	2 p. m.	29. 00	48	......	0	....	SW. 0	......	
	9 p. m.	29. 00	45	......	0	....	SW. 1	......	
March 17	7 a. m.	28. 87	42	......	St., cu. 10	....	SE. 1	......	
	2 p. m.	28. 75	60	......	Amorphous 10	....	SW. 1	......	
	9 p. m.	28. 54	49	......	Nim. 10	....	SE. 2	......	
March 18	7 a. m.	28. 20	54	......	Nim. 10	....	SW. 1	......	
	2 p. m.	27. 99	60	......	Nim. 10	....	SE. 1	......	
	9 p. m.	27. 96	47	......	Nim. 10	....	W. 2	......	
March 19	7 a. m.	28. 14	33	......	Amorphous 10	....	W. 4	......	
	2 p. m.	28. 38	34	......	Cu. 10	....	W. 4	......	

JACKSON, (MONROE COUNTY,) OHIO.

Month and day.	Hour.	Barom'r corrected to 32° F.	Thermometer.	Force of vapor.	Cloudiness.	Motion of clouds.	Winds.	Relative humidity.	REMARKS.
March 13	9 p. m.	......	......	......	....	....	....	......	14th. Rain from 7 a. m. to 1 p. m.; amount, 0. 50 inch. Rain from 4 p. m. the 17th to — p. m. on the 18th; a violent storm of wind, rain, and hail at 2 and 3 p. m. on the 18th; amount, 0. 70 inch. 19th. Snow storm from — a. m. to 2 p. m.; amount, in water, 0. 30 inch.
March 14	7 a. m.	......	48	......	....	....	....	......	
	2 p. m.	......	......	......	....	....	....	......	
	9 p. m.	......	......	......	....	....	....	......	
March 15	7 a. m.	......	40	......	....	....	....	......	
	2 p. m.	......	41	......	....	....	....	......	
	9 p. m.	......	40	......	....	....	....	......	
March 16	7 a. m.	......	32	......	5	....	....	......	
	2 p. m.	......	52	......	....	....	....	......	
	9 p. m.	......	41	......	....	....	0	......	
March 17	7 a. m.	......	40	......	10	....	S. 1	......	
	2 p. m.	......	63	......	10	....	NE. 1	......	
	9 p. m.	......	52	......	10	....	W. 1	......	
March 18	7 a. m.	......	55	......	Cu. 10	E. 2	0	......	
	2 p. m.	......	......	......	....	....	....	......	
	9 p. m.	......	......	......	....	....	....	......	
March 19	7 a. m.	......	31	......	....	....	....	......	
	2 p. m.	......	55	......	....	....	....	......	

MADISON, OHIO.*

Month and day.	Hour.	Barom'r corrected to 32° F.	Thermometer.	Force of vapor.	Cloudiness.	Motion of clouds.	Winds.	Relative humidity.	REMARKS.
March 13	9 p. m.	......	......	......	....	....	....	......	16th. Magnificent display of aurora borealis. 17th. Rain at 6 p. m. 18th. Showery. 19th. Snow and frozen rain at night.
March 14	7 a. m.	......	......	......	....	....	....	......	
	2 p. m.	......	......	......	....	....	....	......	
	9 p. m.	......	......	......	....	....	....	......	
March 15	7 a. m.	......	......	......	....	....	....	......	
	2 p. m.	......	......	......	....	....	....	......	
	9 p. m.	......	......	......	....	....	....	......	
March 16	7 a. m.	......	36	......	Cu. st. 1	0	NW. 2	......	
	2 p. m.	......	46	......	0	....	W. 2	......	
	9 p. m.	......	34	......	Cir. 1	0	0	......	
March 17	7 a. m.	......	44	......	St. 10	0	S. 2	......	
	2 p. m.	......	67	......	St. 10	0	S. 2	......	
	9 p. m.	......	52	......	Nim. 10	....	S. 3	......	
March 18	7 a. m.	......	55	......	St. 10	SW. 2	S. 2	......	
	2 p. m.	......	64	......	Cir. st. 10	....	S. 1	......	
	9 p. m.	......	40	......	Nim. 10	....	W. 2	......	
March 19	7 a. m.	......	33	......	St. 10	0	W. 7	......	
	2 p. m.	......	34	......	St. 10	W. 2	W. 7	......	

* Atkins, observer.

STORM No. 1, MARCH, 1859.

MONTVILLE, OHIO.

Month and day.	Hour.	Barom'r corrected to 32° F.	Thermometer.	Force of vapor.	Cloudiness.		Motion of clouds.		Winds.		Relative humidity.
March 13	9 p. m.	28. 794	50	. 186		0	----------		S.----------		51
March 14	7 a. m.	28. 526	52	. 207		10	----------		SE ---------		53
	2 p. m.	28. 280	56	. 336		9	----------		SE ---------		80
	9 p. m.	28. 175	55	. 376		9	----------		SW---------		86
March 15	7 a. m.	28. 310	39. 5	. 145		10	----------		SW---------		59
	2 p. m.	28. 415	38	. 144		9	----------		W----------		62
	9 p. m.	28. 635	35	. 142		8	----------		SW---------		69
March 16	7 a. m.	28. 860	30	. 167		0	----------		S.----------		100
	2 p. m.	28. 881	49	. 223		0	----------		S.----------		63
	9 p. m.	28. 852	43	. 142	Cir.	4	----------		S.----------		51
March 17	7 a. m.	28. 765	43	. 164	Cir. cu.	10	----------		S.	1	58
	2 p. m.	28. 601	57	. 268	Cir. cu.	10	----------		S.	1	57
	9 p. m.	28. 406	47	. 297	Cu. st.	10	----------		SE.	1	92
March 18	7 a. m.	28. 085	53	. 375	Cu. st.	10	SW.	1	S.	1	93
	2 p. m.	27. 850	58	. 393	Cu. st.	7	SW.	1	SE.	1	81
	9 p. m.	27. 854	40	. 225	Cu. st.	10	SW.	1	SW.	2	91
March 19	7 a. m.	28. 115	30	. 187	St.	10	----------		NW.	4	94
	2 p. m.	28. 301	34	. 155	Cu. st.	9	SW.	1	W.	3	79

REMARKS.

14th. Showers from 9 to 11 a. m.
17th. Rain began at 5 p. m. and ended in the night.
18th Thunder shower at 2 p. m., wind SE.; snow in the night, wind W.; amount in water, 0.605 inch.
19th. Somewhat blustering, wind variable, SW. to NW.; occasional snow squalls.

NEW LISBON, OHIO.

Month and day.	Hour.	Barom'r corrected to 32° F.	Thermometer.	Force of vapor.	Cloudiness.		Motion of clouds.		Winds.		Relative humidity.
March 13	9 p. m.	28. 75	52	------	------------		----------		S.	0	------
March 14	7 a. m.	28. 55	50	------	Nim.	10	SE.	0	SE.	0	------
	2 p. m.	28. 32	72	------	Nim.	6	SE.	3	SE.	1	------
	9 p. m.	28. 20	64	------	Nim.	5	W.	1	SE.	0	------
March 15	7 a. m.	28. 25	62	------	Nim.	5	SW.	0	S.	0	------
	2 p. m.	28. 34	48	------	Nim.	6	SW.	3	SW.	2	------
	9 p. m.	28. 60	45	------	Nim.	5	NW.	3	NW.	3	------
March 16	7 a. m.	28. 81	35	------		0		0	SW.	0	------
	2 p. m.	28. 83	57	------		0		0	SW.	0	------
	9 p. m.	28. 80	41	------		0		0	SW.	0	------
March 17	7 a. m.	28. 75	45	------	Nim.	6	SE.	2	SE.	0	------
	2 p. m.	28. 60	70	------	Nim.	8	SE.	0	SE.	0	------
	9 p. m.	28. 45	44	------	Nim.	10	SE.	0	SE.	0	------
March 18	7 a. m.	28. 10	63	------	Nim.	10	S.	1	S.	0	------
	2 p. m.	27. 70	70	------	Nim.	10	SSE.	4	SE.	0	------
	9 p. m.	27. 81	52	------	Nim.	5	W.	3	W.	3	------
March 19	7 a. m.	28. 00	40	------	Nim.	10	SW.	3	SW.	3	------
	2 p. m.	28. 22	43	------	Nim.	8	SW.	3	W.	2	------

13th. Frost.
14th and 15th Fair.
16th. Changeable; storm from 6.30 p. m. the 17th to 4 p. m. on the 18th; amount in water, 0.85 inch.
19th. Snow and rain in the night; amount in water, 0.20 inch.

NORTHWOOD, OHIO.

Month and day.	Hour.	Barom'r corrected to 32° F.	Thermometer.	Force of vapor.	Cloudiness.		Motion of clouds.		Winds.		Relative humidity.
March 13	9 p. m.	28. 81	------	------	St.	1	----------		NW.	1	------
March 14	7 a. m.	28. 53	------	------	Nim.	10	N.	2	NW.	3	------
	2 p. m.	28. 23	------	------	Nim.	10	N.	2	NW.	3	------
	9 p. m.	28. 34	------	------	Nim.	10	----------		E.	4	------
March 15	7 a. m.	28. 49	------	------	Nim.	10	E.	2	NE.	3	------
	2 p. m.	28. 69	------	------	Nim.	10	SW.	2	SW.	2	------
	9 p. m.	28. 82	------	------		0	----------		SW.	1	------
March 16	7 a. m.	28. 98	------	------		0	----------		NE.	1	------
	2 p. m.	28. 81	------	------	------------		----------		NE.	1	------
	9 p. m.	28. 89	------	------	------------		----------		NE.	1	------
March 17	7 a. m.	28. 80	------	------	Nim.	10	N.	1	NW.	1	------
	2 p. m.	28. 49	------	------	Nim.	10	N.	1	W.	1	------
	9 p. m.	------	------	------	Nim.	10	N.	1	NW.	1	------
March 18	7 a. m.	28. 20	------	------	Nim.	10	----------		NE.	1	------
	2 p. m.	27. 97	------	------	Nim.	10	----------		NW.	2	------
	9 p. m.	27. 96	------	------	Nim.	10	SE.	2	SW.	3	------
March 19	7 a. m.	28. 43	------	------	Nim.	10	----------		SE.	2	------
	2 p. m.	28. 59	------	------	Nim.	10	SE.	2	SE.	3	------

14th. Storm commenced in the preceding night and ended at 4 p. m.; amount, 0.32 inch.
Snow storm from 12 m. the 17th to the 18th at night; amount in water, 1.63 inch.

STORM No. 1, MARCH, 1859.

PORTSMOUTH, OHIO.

Month and day.	Hour.	Barom'r corrected to 32° F.	Thermometer.	Force of vapor.	Cloudiness.		Motion of clouds.	Winds.		Relative humidity.	REMARKS.
March 13	9 p. m.	29.38	50	------		0	----------	SW.	---------	------	13th. Lunar halo 40° in diameter; rain in the night.
March 14	7 a. m.	29.21	52	------	Nim	10	----------	SE.	3	------	
	2 p. m.	29.13	70	------	Nim.	10	----------	SW.	2	------	14th. Rain from 1 to 9 a. m.; amount, 0.32 inch.
	9 p. m.	29.12	55	------		0	----------	SW.	5	------	
March 15	7 a. m.	29.21	46	------	Nim.	10	----------	SW.	3	------	16th. Lunar halo 45° in diameter.
	2 p. m.	29.27	48	------	Nim.	10	----------	SW.	2	------	Storm began at 12 m. the 17th; thunder and lightning at 11 a. m. the 18th, ended at 8 a. m. on the 19th; amount, 1.23 inch.
	9 p. m.	29.46	38	------		0	----------	SW.	1	------	
March 16	7 a. m.	29.56	30	------		0	----------	E.	1	------	
	2 p. m.	29.51	59	------		0	----------	NE.	1	------	
	9 p. m.	29.44	46	------		0	----------	SE.	1	------	
March 17	7 a. m.	29.43	45	------	Nim.	10	----------	NE.	1	------	
	2 p. m.	29.28	51	------	Nim.	10	----------	NE.	2	------	
	9 p. m.	29.04	54	------	Nim.	10	----------	SE.	3	------	
March 18	7 a. m.	28.90	60	------	Nim.	8	----------	SW.	1	------	
	2 p. m.	28.82	49	------	Nim.	9	----------	SW.	3	------	
	9 p. m.	28.93	34	------	Nim.	10	----------	SW.	5	------	
March 19	7 a. m.	29.21	32	------	Nim.	10	----------	NW.	4	------	
	2 p. m.	29.20	40	------	Nim.	9	----------	NW.	4	------	

TROY, OHIO.

Month and day.	Hour.	Barom'r corrected to 32° F.	Thermometer.	Force of vapor.	Cloudiness.		Motion of clouds.		Winds.		Relative humidity.	REMARKS.
March 13	9 p. m.	29.46	56	------		0		0	Calm	-------	------	13th. Lunar halo.
March 14	7 a. m.	29.74	50	------	Nim.	10	W. to E.	4	Calm	-------	------	14th. Rain from 11 p. m. to 2 p. m.; amount, 0.60 inch.
	2 p. m.	29.52	60	------	Nim.	10	W. to E.	5	W.	2	------	
	9 p. m	29.53	54	------	Nim.	10	W. to E.	4	W.	4	------	17th. Amount of rain, 0.50 inch.
March 15	7 a. m.	29.67	39	------	Nim.	10	W. to E.	4	W.	12	------	18th. Storm from 10 a. m. to 7 p. m.; amount, 1.70 inch.
	2 p m.	29.77	39	------	Cir.	10	W. to E.	4	W.	12	------	
	9 p. m.	29.89	40	------	Cir.	6	W. to E.	4	W.	4	------	
March 16	7 a. m.	30.10	27	------		0		0	Calm	-------	------	
	2 p. m.	30.14	54	------		0		0	W.	2	------	
	9 p. m.	30.14	52	------		0		0	W.	2	------	
March 17	7 a. m.	29.96	44	------	Nim.	10	W. to E.	2	Calm	-------	------	
	2 p. m.	29.93	56	------	Nim.	10	W. to E.	2	W.	2	------	
	9 p. m.	29.74	50	------	Nim.	10	S. to N.	4	S.	2	------	
March 18	7 a. m.	29.34	50	------	Nim.	10	W. to E.	4	Calm	-------	------	
	2 p. m.	29.13	53	------	Nim.	10	W. to E.	3	W.	2	------	
	9 p. m.	29.17	36	------	Nim.	10	W. to E	4	W.	12	------	
March 19	7 a. m.	29.60	28	------	Cir.	10	W. to E.	4	W.	8	------	
	2 p. m.	29.78	36	------	Cir.	10	W. to E.	3	W.	12	------	

SAVANNAH, OHIO.

Month and day.	Hour.	Barom'r corrected to 32° F.	Thermometer.	Force of vapor.	Cloudiness.		Motion of clouds.		Winds.		Relative humidity.	REMARKS.
March 13	9 p. m.	29.044	45	.241		0	----------		SW.	1	84	14th. Rain from 7½ a. m. to 7½ p. m.; thunder in the evening; amount, 0.21 inch.
March 14	7 a. m.	28.768	51	.272	St.	10	SW.	3	SE.	3	78	
	2 p. m.	28.448	63	.429	St.	10	S.	5	S.	5	77	
	9 p. m.	28.424	55	.321	Cir. st.	8	SW.	5	SW.	4	80	15th. Cold and blowing.
March 15	7 a. m.	28.604	39	.186	St.	10	SW.	4	SW.	4	81	16th. Lunar halo, indications of rain.
	2 p. m.	28.696	38	.178	St.	10	W.	4	SW.	4	81	
	9 p. m.	28.936	33	.168		0	----------		W.	3	89	17th. Cloudy all day; rain from 6 to 11 p. m.; amount, 0.425 inch.
March 16	7 a. m.	29.140	32	.143		0	----------		SE.	2	79	
	2 p. m.	29.118	54	.269		0	----------		SW.	3	67	18th. Heavy thunder and very heavy rain in the afternoon.
	9 p. m.	29.068	41	.225	Cir.	10	SW.	1	SW.	1	91	
March 17	7 a. m.	28.976	49	.215	St.	10	S.	3	SE.	2	69	19th. Cold and snowy all day till 4 p. m., began again at 9 p. m.; amount in water, 1.285 inch.
	2 p. m.	28.850	60	.357	St.	10	S.	3	S.	3	78	
	9 p. m.	28.634	51	.374	Nim.	10	S.	3	S.	3	100	
March 18	7 a. m.	28.308	55	.349	St.	10	SW.	3	SW.	3	81	
	2 p. m.	28.066	55	.362	Nim.	10	SW.	3	SW.	3	87	
	9 p. m.	28.132	36	.212	Nim.	10	NW.	3	NW.	3	100	
March 19	7 a. m.	28.378	30	.148	St.	10	NW.	5	NW.	5	89	
	2 p. m.	28.664	35	.155	Nim.	8	W.	4	W.	4	79	

STORM No. 1, MARCH, 1859.

URBANA, OHIO.

Month and day.	Hour.	Barom'r corrected to 32° F.	Thermometer.	Force of vapor.	Cloudiness.	Motion of clouds.	Winds.	Relative humidity.
March 13	9 p. m.	28.93	50	------	0	0	ESE. 2	------
March 14	7 a. m.	28.63	49	------	0	0	SSE. 6	------
	2 p. m.	28.40	61	------	0	0	S. 7	------
	9 p. m.	28.41	51	------	0	0	------------	------
March 15	7 a. m.	28.57	38	------	Nim. 10	S. 5	WSW. 7	------
	2 p. m.	28.70	37	------	St. 10	S. 7	WSW. 6	------
	9 p. m.	28.92	32	------	St. 3	SW. 5	W. 2	------
March 16	7 a. m.	29.07	33	------	0	0	0	------
	2 p. m.	29.07	58	------	0	0	SSE. 3	------
	9 p. m.	29.09	46	------	Cir. 3	W. 1	SE. 2	------
March 17	7 a. m.	29.02	49	------	St. 10	SW. 1	SE. 2	------
	2 p. m.	28.81	52	------	Rain 10	S. 2	S. 2	------
	9 p. m.	28.51	50	------	Rain 10	SE. 7	SE. 3	------
March 18	7 a. m.	28.32	50	------	St. 10	SW. 8	SW. 2	------
	2 p. m.	28.12	51	------	Rain 10	W. 5	WNW. 1	------
	9 p. m.	28.22	34	------	Snow 10	W. -------	WNW. 5	------
March 19	7 a. m.	28.52	28	------	10	W. 8	W. 5	------
	2 p. m.	28.70	34	------	10	W. 5	W. 6	------

REMARKS.

14th. Storm began at 4 a. m. and ended at 4½ p. m.; amount, 0.36 inch.
15th. Snowy, 10 a m. to 2 p. m.
16th. Halo round the moon.
Storm commenced at 11½ a. m. the 17th, and ended at 6 a. m. on the 19th.
18th. Thunder, 11 a. m. to 12 m; 5¾ p. m. rain changed to snow; continued all night.
19th. Spitting snow all day; am't in water, 1.04 inch.

WELCHFIELD, OHIO.

Month and day.	Hour.	Barom'r corrected to 32° F.	Thermometer.	Force of vapor.	Cloudiness.	Motion of clouds.	Winds.	Relative humidity.
March 13	9 p. m.	------	46	------	0	----------	SE. 1	------
March 14	7 a. m.	------	48	------	Nim. 10	0	SE. 2	------
	2 p. m.	------	56	------	Nim. 10	0	SE. 4	------
	9 p. m.	------	53	------	Nim. 10	0	SE. 4	------
March 15	7 a. m.	------	40	------	Nim. 10	0	SW. 3	------
	2 p. m.	------	37	------	Nim. 10	0	SW. 3	------
	9 p. m.	------	33	------	Nim. 10	0	SW. 4	------
March 16	7 a. m.	------	32	------	0	----------	W. 1	------
	2 p. m.	------	55	------	0	----------	SW. 1	------
	9 p. m.	------	38	------	0	----------	SW. 1	------
March 17	7 a. m.	------	41	------	Nim. 10	0	SE. 1	------
	2 p. m.	------	63	------	Cir. 5	0	SW. 2	------
	9 p. m.	------	48	------	Nim. 10	0	SE. 2	------
March 18	7 a. m.	------	53	------	Nim. 10	0	SW. 1	------
	2 p. m.	------	63	------	Nim. 10	0	SE. 1	------
	9 p. m.	------	40	------	Nim. 10	0	W. 3	------
March 19	7 a. m.	------	31	------	Nim. 10	0	W. 5	------
	2 p. m.	------	33	------	Nim. 10	0	W. 5	------

REMARKS.

14th. Began to rain at 9 a. m.; occasional claps of thunder in the evening, followed by high wind; velocity, 4 and 5; storm ended at 1 a. m. on the 15th; amount, 0.427 inch.
Rain from 6 p. m. the 16th to 1 a. m. on the 20th.; amount, 2.30 inch.

WESTERVILLE, OHIO.

Month and day.	Hour.	Barom'r corrected to 32° F.	Thermometer.	Force of vapor.	Cloudiness.	Motion of clouds.	Winds.	Relative humidity.
March 13	9 p. m.	28.91	52½	.226	0	----------	S. 1	57
March 14	7 a. m.	28.68	50½	.354	St. 10	SW. 2	SW. 2	96
	2 p. m.	28.41	60	.396	St. 10	SW. 4	S. 3	76
	9 p. m.	28.45	52	.159	0	----------	SW. 6	41
March 15	7 a. m.	28.56	42	.155	St. 10	SW. 5	SW. 5	58
	2 p. m.	28.70	38	.144	Cu. st. 9	W. 2	SW. 5	63
	9 p. m.	28.93	35	.142	0	----------	W. 1	70
March 16	7 a. m.	29.09	31	.155	0	----------	SE. 1	89
	2 p. m.	29.05	55	.193	0	----------	SW. 1	44
	9 p. m.	28.99	42½	.215	Cu. 8	W. 1	SW. 1	79
March 17	7 a. m.	28.92	45	.228	St. 10	SW. 1	SW. 1	76
	2 p. m.	28.77	52	.334	St. 10	W. 1	SW. 1	86
	9 p. m.	28.51	52	.361	St. 10	SE. 1	SE. 1	93
March 18	7 a. m.	28.27	53½	.396	St. 10	SW. 1	SW. 1	96
	2 p. m.	28.10	50	.309	St. 10	W. 1	SW. 2	85
	9 p. m.	28.15	35	.183	St. 10	W. 4	W. 4	90
March 19	7 a. m.	28.46	31	.155	St. 10	W. 5	W. 5	89
	2 p. m.	28.66	32½	.119	St. 10	W. 3	W. 3	64

REMARKS.

14th. Showery and squally from 5 a. m. to 6 p. m.; strong wind in the evening; amount, 0.36 inch.
15th. Snow squalls, with high wind.
16th. Frost; temperature at 6 a. m., 27°; pleasant during the day; in the evening a singular class of clouds, very light cirrus floating in riffles from W. to E.; halo round the moon about 25° in diameter.
17th. Began to rain at 12 m. and ceased during the night; amount, 0.712 inch.
18th. Thunder shower at 12 m.; rained furiously at 12½ p. m., accompanied by lightning and wind, 4 and 5; changed to snow in the night, and continued till 7 a. m. on the 19th; amount in water, 0.531 inch.

STORM No. 1, MARCH, 1859.

WINDHAM, OHIO.

Month and day.	Hour.	Barom'r corrected to 32° F.	Thermometer.	Force of vapor.	Cloudiness.	Motion of clouds.	Winds.	Relative humidity.	REMARKS.
March 13	9 p. m.	......	50	......	......	......	......	......	14th. Rain, with high wind at 9 p. m.
March 14	7 a. m.	......	40	......	......	......	......	......	
	2 p. m.	......	57	......	......	......	......	......	15th. Cloudy.
	9 p. m.	......	53	......	......	......	......	......	16th. Snowy.
March 15	7 a. m.	......	40	......	......	......	......	......	17th. Cloudy.
	2 p. m.	......	51	......	......	......	......	......	18th. Frequent showers.
	9 p. m.	......	34	......	......	......	......	......	19th. One inch of snow on ground in the morning; blustering.
March 16	7 a. m.	......	30	......	......	......	......	......	
	2 p. m.	......	55	......	......	......	......	......	
	9 p. m.	......	40	......	......	......	......	......	
March 17	7 a. m.	......	35	......	......	......	......	......	
	2 p. m.	......	57	......	......	......	......	......	
	9 p. m.	......	53	......	......	......	......	......	
March 18	7 a. m.	......	52	......	......	......	......	......	
	2 p. m.	......	57	......	......	......	......	......	
	9 p. m.	......	43	......	......	......	......	......	
March 19	7 a. m.	......	30	......	......	......	......	......	
	2 p. m.	......	33	......	......	......	......	......	

MADISON, OHIO.*

Month and day.	Hour.	Barom'r corrected to 32° F.	Thermometer.	Force of vapor.	Cloudiness.	Motion of clouds.	Winds.	Relative humidity.	REMARKS.
March 13	9 p. m.	......	34	......	0	0	SE. 1	......	14th. Began to rain at 9½ a. m. and ended in the night; am't, 0.25 inch.
March 14	7 a. m.	......	46	......	Cir. cu. 10	SW. 2	SE. 2	......	
	2 p. m.	......	56	......	Nim. 10	S. 5	SE. 4	......	
	9 p. m.	......	50	......	Nim. 10	SW. 4	SW. 5	......	16th. Began to rain at 6 p. m. and ended in the night; am't, 0.25 inch.
March 15	7 a. m.	......	40	......	Cir. cu. 10	SW. 3	SW. 4	......	
	2 p. m.	......	46	......	Nim. 10	SW. 3	SW. 3	......	
	9 p. m.	......	35	......	Nim. 10	SW. 4	W. 4	......	Commenced raining at 10 a. m. the 17th and ended at 5 p. m. on the 18th; amount, 2.200 inc's.
March 16	7 a. m.	......	34	......	0	0	W. 3	......	
	2 p. m.	......	42	......	0	0	W. 2	......	
	9 p. m.	......	33	......	......	S.	SW. 2	......	
March 17	7 a. m.	......	36	......	0	......	SE. 1	......	
	2 p. m.	......	64	......	0	......	SE. 2	......	
	9 p. m.	......	52	......	Nim. 10	......	S. 1	......	
March 18	7 a. m.	......	32	......	Nim. 10	S. 3	S. 2	......	
	2 p. m.	......	62	......	Nim. 10	S. 4	S. 3	......	
	9 p. m.	......	39	......	Nim. 10	SW. 3	W. 3	......	
March 19	7 a. m.	......	32	......	Nim. 10	SW. 4	W. 5	......	
	2 p. m.	......	33	......	Nim. 10	W. 4	W. 5	......	

BATTLE CREEK, MICHIGAN.

Month and day.	Hour.	Barom'r corrected to 32° F.	Thermometer.	Force of vapor.	Cloudiness.	Motion of clouds.	Winds.	Relative humidity.	REMARKS.
March 13	9 p. m.	29.09	46	......	Cir. st. 6	SW. 2	SE. 3	......	14th. Rain from 5 a. m. to 1 p. m.; amount, 0.40 inch, (an approximation.)
March 14	7 a. m.	28.72	43	......	Nim. 10	SW. 2	SE. 2	......	
	2 p. m.	28.54	48	......	Cir. st. 8	SW. 3	SW. 4	......	
	9 p. m.	28.55	38	......	St. 10	W. 3	SW. 4	......	Storm commenced at 10½ p. m. the 17th and ended at 8 a. m. on the 18th; amount, 0.20 inch.
March 15	7 a. m.	28.70	34	......	Cir. st. 10	W. 2	W. 4	......	
	2 p. m.	28.87	36	......	St. 9	W. 2	W. 3	......	
	9 p. m.	29.08	33	......	0	......	W. 2	......	19th. Snow squalls.
March 16	7 a. m.	29.24	33	......	0	......	0	......	
	2 p. m.	29.19	42	......	0	......	S. 2	......	
	9 p. m.	29.14	33	......	Cir. 1	SW. 1	SE. 2	......	
March 17	7 a. m.	29.05	36	......	Cir. 1	SW. 2	S. 1	......	
	2 p. m.	28.89	66	......	Cir. 2	SW. 2	S. 2	......	
	9 p. m.	28.72	49	......	Nim. 10	SW. 2	S. 2	......	
March 18	7 a. m.	28.41	43	......	Nim. 10	W. 2	N. 2	......	
	2 p. m.	28.46	36	......	Cir. st. 10	NW. 2	NW. 4	......	
	9 p. m.	28.51	33	......	Cir. st. 10	NW. 3	NW. 5	......	
March 19	7 a. m.	28.65	31	......	St. 10	NW. 3	W. 5	......	
	2 p. m.	28.87	35	......	St. 4	NW. 2	NW. 4	......	

* Mrs. King, observer.

STORM No. 1, MARCH, 1859.

DETROIT, MICHIGAN.

Month and day.	Hour.	Barom'r corrected to 32° F.	Thermometer.	Force of vapor.	Cloudiness.	Motion of clouds.	Winds.	Relative humidity.	REMARKS.
March 13	9 p. m.	29.07	39	.136	St. 1	SW. 1	SW. 1	62	Rain from 9 a. m the 14th to 6 p.
March 14	7 a. m.	29.05	43	.147	Cu. st. 8	NW. 1	NE. 2	57	m. on the 15th; amount, 0.50
	2 p. m.	28.94	53	.183	Nim. 10	S. 2	SE. 3	47	inch.
	9 p. m.	28.83	38	.123	Nim. 10	SE. 3	SE. 2	54	Rain from 8 a. m. the 18th to 3.10
March 15	7 a. m.	28.67	44	.100	Nim. 10	SE. 3	SW. 2	36	p. m. on the 19th; amount, 0.68
	2 p. m.	28.74	45	.053	Nim. 10	SE. 3	SW. 3	17	inch.
	9 p. m.	29.00	31	.108	Cu. st. 8	SW. 2	SW. 1	59	
March 16	7 a. m.	29.10	34	.168	Cir. 2	SW. 1	SW. 1	89	
	2 p. m.	29.05	46	.074	Cu. st. 3	SW. 1	SW. 2	24	
	9 p. m.	29.02	41	.092	Cu. st. 4	SW. 1	SW. 1	34	
March 17	7 a. m.	28.97	44	.151	Cu. st. 7	SE. 1	S. 1	52	
	2 p. m.	28.88	63	.125	Cu. st. 5	NW. 2	SW. 2	22	
	9 p. m.	28.77	44	.121	St. 3	W. 1	SW. 2	43	
March 18	7 a. m.	28.05	48	.297	Nim. 8	W. 3	SW. 3	85	
	2 p. m.	27.95	52	.219	Nim. 10	W. 3	W. 3	54	
	9 p. m.	27.97	38	.165	Nim. 10	W. 3	W. 2	72	
March 19	7 a. m.	28.70	34	.139	Nim. 10	W. 3	SW. 3	71	
	2 p. m.	28.79	35	.142	Nim. 8	W. 3	SW. 3	70	

GRAND RAPIDS, MICHIGAN.

Month and day.	Hour.	Barom'r corrected to 32° F.	Thermometer.	Force of vapor.	Cloudiness.	Motion of clouds.	Winds.	Relative humidity.	REMARKS.
March 13	9 p. m.	------	46	------	Cir. 1	SW. 1	NE. 1	------	Rain at intervals from 3 a. m. the
March 14	7 a. m.	------	41	------	Nim. 10	S. 2	E. 1	------	14th to 10 a. m. on the 15th;
	2 p. m.	------	43	------	Nim. 10	SW. 2	SW. 3	------	amount, 0.56 inch.
	9 p. m.	------	38	------	Nim. 10	SW. 2	SW. 3	------	16th. Lunar halo.
March 15	7 a. m.	------	32	------	Nim. 10	NW. 2	NW. 3	------	17th. Fine day; solar halo. Began
	2 p. m.	------	34	------	Cu. st. 10	NW. 2	NW. 3	------	to rain at 11.30 p. m.
	9 p. m.	------	30	------	0	----------	NE. 0	------	18th. Rain at intervals during the
March 16	7 a. m.	------	24	------	0	----------	SE. 0	------	day. Snow in the night
	2 p. m.	------	55	------	Cir. 1	W. 1	SE. 1	------	19th. Cold and windy. Snow in the
	9 p. m.	------	46	------	Cir. 1	W. 1	E. 0	------	forenoon; storm ended at 0.30
March 17	7 a. m.	------	48	------	Cir. cu. 2	W. 1	SE. 0	------	p. m.; amount in water, 0.41
	2 p. m.	------	64	------	Cir. cu. 3	W. 1	S. 1	------	inch.
	9 p. m.	------	48	------	Cir. 2	W. 1	S. 0	------	
March 18	7 a. m.	------	37	------	Nim. 10	N. 3	N. 1	------	
	2 p. m.	------	36	------	Nim. 10	NE. 3	N. 2	------	
	9 p. m.	------	33	------	Nim. 10	NW. 3	NW. 3	------	
March 19	7 a. m.	------	32	------	Cu. st. 10	NW. 3	NW. 3	------	
	2 p. m.	------	35	------	Cu. st. 10	NW. 3	NW. 3	------	

MARQUETTE, MICHIGAN.

Month and day.	Hour.	Barom'r corrected to 32° F.	Thermometer.	Force of vapor.	Cloudiness.	Motion of clouds.	Winds.	Relative humidity.	REMARKS.
March 13	9 p. m.	29.54	28	------	Nim. 10	----------	SE. 1	------	14th. Severe snow storm; depth of
March 14	7 a. m.	29.17	29	------	Nim. 10	----------	E. 4	------	snow, 10.25 inches.
	2 p. m.	28.72	32	------	Nim. 10	----------	SE. 2	------	16th. Depth of snow in woods, 3
	9 p. m.	28.56	32	------	Nim. 10	----------	SE. 1	------	10 feet.
March 15	7 a. m.	28.78	21	------	Nim. 10	----------	W. 2	------	18th. Snow; depth, 1.00 inch.
	2 p. m.	28.97	30	------	Cir. 3	----------	WNW. 4	------	
	9 p. m.	29.28	27	------	0	----------	WNW. 2	------	
March 16	7 a. m.	29.39	13	------	0	----------	W. 1	------	
	2 p. m.	29.12	39	------	St. 2	NW. 3	SE. 5	------	
	9 p. m.	29.16	33	------	Nim. 10	----------	ESE. 1	------	
March 17	7 a. m.	29.16	35	------	Cir. st. 6	----------	WNW. 1	------	
	2 p. m.	29.16	38	------	Nim. 10	----------	WNW. 1	------	
	9 p. m.	29.14	33	------	Cir. 9	NE. 4	E. 1	------	
March 18	7 a. m.	29.04	32	------	Nim. 10	----------	N. 4	------	
	2 p. m.	28.94	30	------	Nim. 10	----------	NW. 5	------	
	9 p. m.	29.00	32	------	Nim. 10	----------	NW. 5	------	
March 19	7 a. m.	29.18	24	------	Nim. 0	----------	NW. 3	------	
	2 p. m.	29.17	29	------	Nim. 0	----------	NW. 2	------	

STORM No. 1, MARCH, 1859.

LANSING, MICHIGAN.

Month and day.	Hour.	Barom'r corrected to 32° F.	Thermometer.	Force of vapor.	Cloudiness.		Motion of clouds.		Winds.		Relative humidity.	REMARKS.
March 13	8 p. m.	------	44	------	------		------		------		------	14th. Rain from 6 a. m. to 4 p. m.
March 14	7 a. m.	------	43	------	------		------		------		------	15th. Snow from 8 a. m. to 3 p. m.
	2 p. m.	------	51	------	------		------		------		------	18th. Rain from 5 to 10 a. m.
	8 p. m.	------	41	------	------		------		------		------	19th. Snow from 6 to 8 a m.
March 15	7 a. m.	------	34	------	------		------		------		------	
	2 p. m.	------	36	------	------		------		------		------	
	8 p m.	------	32	------	------		------		------		------	
March 16	7 a. m.	------	32	------	------		------		------		------	
	2 p. m.	------	48	------	------		------		------		------	
	8 p. m.	------	47	------	------		------		------		------	
March 17	7 a. m.	------	43	------	------		------		------		------	
	2 p. m.	------	61	------	------		------		------		------	
	8 p. m.	------	52	------	------		------		------		------	
March 18	7 a. m.	------	46	------	------		------		------		------	
	2 p. m.	------	39	------	------		------		------		------	
	8 p. m.	------	35	------	------		------		------		------	
March 19	7 a. m.	------	32	------	------		------		------		------	
	2 p. m.	------	34	------	------		------		------		------	

MONROE, MICHIGAN.

Month and day.	Hour.	Barom'r corrected to 32° F.	Thermometer.	Force of vapor.	Cloudiness.		Motion of clouds.		Winds.		Relative humidity.	REMARKS.
March 13	9 p. m.	------	------	------		0		0	SE.	1	------	14th. Drizzling rain and sleet from 7 a. m. to 4 p. m. Storm commenced at 9 p m the 17th and ended at 5 a. m. on the 18th.
March 14	7 a. m.	------	------	------	Nim.	10	NE.	3	NE.	4	------	
	2 p. m.	------	------	------	Nim.	10	NE.	3	NE.	5	------	
	9 p. m.	------	------	------	Cu. st.	4	NE.	2	NE.	2	------	
March 15	7 a. m.	------	------	------	Cir.	4	NW.	2	NW.	4	------	
	2 p m.	------	------	------	Cir. cu.	5	NW.	3	NW.	4	------	
	9 p. m.	------	------	------	Cir. cu.	3	NW.	4	NW.	4	------	
March 16	7 a. m.	------	------	------	Cir.	3	SW.	2	SW.	3	------	
	2 p. m.	------	------	------	Cir. cu.	4	SW.	2	SW.	3	------	
	9 p. m.	------	------	------		0		0	SW.	1	------	
March 17	7 a. m.	------	------	------	Cir.	6	SE.	1	SE.	1	------	
	2 p. m.	------	------	------	Cu. st.	7	SW.	2	SW.	2	------	
	9 p. m.	------	------	------	Nim.	10	SW.	2	SW.	2	------	
March 18	7 a. m.	------	------	------	Nim.	10	SW.	2	SW.	2	------	
	2 p. m.	------	------	------	------		------		------		------	
	9 p. m.	------	------	------	------		------		------		------	
March 19	7 a. m.	------	------	------	------		------		------		------	
	2 p. m.	------	------	------	------		------		------		------	

NEW BUFFALO, MICHIGAN.

Month and day.	Hour.	Barom'r corrected to 32° F.	Thermometer.	Force of vapor.	Cloudiness.		Motion of clouds.		Winds.		Relative humidity.	REMARKS.
March 13	9 p. m.	29. 24	52	------	Cir. cu.	10	SW.	1	------		------	14th. Rain from 10 a m. to 3 p. m ; amount, 0. 26 inch now storm from 10 p m the 17th to 9 p m. on the 18th ; amount in water, 0. 60 inch.
March 14	7 a. m.	28. 95	56	------	Nim.	10	S.	0	------		------	
	1 p. m.	28. 72	51	------	Cir st.	10	SW.	3	------		------	
	9 p. m.	28. 74	40	------	Nim.	10	SW.	3	------		------	
March 15	7 a. m.	28. 97	33	------		10	W.	5	------		------	
	1 p. m.	29. 15	39	------	u.	8	NW.	5	------		------	
	9 p. m.	29. 34	34	------		0	------		------		------	
March 16	7 a. m.	29. 45	31	------		0	------		------		------	
	1 p. m.	29. 36	57	------	Cir.	5	W.	0	------		------	
	9 p. m.	29. 29	47	------	Cir. st.	10	W.	0	------		------	
March 17	7 a. m.	29. 22	50	------	Cir.	8	SW.	0	------		------	
	1 p. m.	29. 08	63	------	Cir. st.	10	S.	0	------		------	
	9 p. m.	28. 90	40	------	Cir. st.	10	W.	0	------		------	
March 18	7 a. m.	28. 73	34	----	Nim.	10	W.	3	------		------	
	1 p. m.	28. 71	33	-----	Nim.	10	NW.	5	------		------	
	9 p. m.	28. 86	32	------	Nim.	10	NW.	3	------		------	
March 19	7 a. m.	29. 06	30	------	Nim.	10	NW.	3	------		------	
	1 p. m.	29. 20	35	-----	Cu.	10	NW.	3	------		------	

STORM No. 1, MARCH, 1859.

OTTAWA POINT, MICHIGAN.

Month and day.	Hour.	Barom'r corrected to 32° F.	Thermometer.	Force of vapor.	Cloudiness.		Motion of clouds.		Winds.		Relative humidity.	REMARKS.
March 13	6 p. m.	29. 65	37	. 178		3		0	NE.	5	81	14th. Rain? from 3 to 5 p. m.; amount, 0. 08 inch.
March 14	6 a. m.	29. 29	34	. 155		10	N.	5	NE.	6	79	18th. Rain? from 3. 30 to 10. 25 a. m.; amount, 0. 16 inch.
	9 a. m.	29. 18	35	. 162		10	NW.	7	NE.	6	80	
	3 p. m.	28. 76	39	. 195		10		0	E.	3	82	
	6 p. m.	28. 81	42	. 222		7	N.	5	SW.	7	83	
March 15	6 a. m.	28. 80	34	. 155		10		0	SSW.	7	79	
	9 a. m.	28. 85	34	. 175		10	NE.	7	SSW.	7	89	
	3 p. m.	29. 05	31	. 136		10	E.	8	WNW.	7	78	
	6 p. m.	29. 18	30	. 130		10	E.	7	WNW.	5	78	
March 16	6 a. m.	29. 57	27	. 147		0		0	WNW.	0	100	
	9 a. m.	29. 58	28	. 142		0		0	W.	0	88	
	3 p. m.	29. 52	41	. 203		0		0	S.	3	82	
	6 p. m.	29. 49	38	. 178		1		0	ESE.	2	81	
March 17	6 a. m.	29. 38	34	. 155		10		0	S.	0	79	
	9 a. m.	29. 35	36	. 170		9	NE.	6	SSW.	3	80	
	3 p. m.	29. 20	51	. 296		2		0	ESE.	2	79	
	6 p. m.	29. 18	47	. 249		3		0	S.	2	77	
March 18	6 a. m.	28. 86	37	. 178		10		0	N.	3	81	
	9 a. m.	28. 73	36	. 191		10		0	NNW.	5	90	
	3 p. m.	28. 67	38	. 186		10	S.	7	NW.	7	81	
	6 p. m.	28. 68	37	. 178		10	S.	7	NW.	7	81	
March 19	6 a. m.	28. 72	29	. 142		10	SE.	8	NW.	8	88	
	9 a. m.	28. 77	29	. 142		10	E.	8	NW.	8	88	
	3 p. m.	29. 05	34	. 155		5	NE.	8	WNW.	8	79	

PORT HURON, MICHIGAN.

Month and day.	Hour.	Barom'r corrected to 32° F.	Thermometer.	Force of vapor.	Cloudiness.		Motion of clouds.		Winds.		Relative humidity.	REMARKS.
March 13	9 p. m.	......	33	......	Cir.	1	....		NE.	3	......	Storm began at 10 a. m. the 14th, and ended in the a. m. of the 15th.
March 14	7 a. m.	......	40	......	Nim.	10	S.	3	SE.	3	......	16th. Lunar halo all the evening.
	2 p. m.	......	52	......	......		....		....		......	Storm commenced at 10½ p. m. the 17th, and ended in the evening of the 18th.
	9 p. m.	......	47	......	Nim.	10	....		SW.	4	......	
March 15	7 a. m.	......	38	......	Nim.	10	SW.	5	SW.	5	......	
	2 p. m.	......	38	......	Nim.	10	W.	5	W.	5	......	
	9 p. m.	......	35	......	Nim.	10	W.	4	W.	3	......	
March 16	7 a. m.	......	29	......		0		0	W.	3	......	
	2 p. m.	......	47	......		0		0	SE.	3	......	
	9 p. m.	......	39	......	Cu.	5	....		SE.	3	......	
March 17	7 a. m.	......	40	......	Nim.	10	....		S.	3	......	
	2 p. m.	......	63	......	Nim.	10	....		S.	3	......	
	9 p. m.	......	52	......	Nim.	10	....		S.	3	......	
March 18	7 a. m.	......	......	......	Nim.	10	....		S.	3	......	
	2 p. m.	......	......	......	Nim.	10	....		N.	3	......	
	9 p. m.	......	......	......	Nim.	10	....		....		......	
March 19	7 a. m.	......	......	......	Nim.	10	....		NW.	6	....	
	2 p. m.	......	......	......	Nim.	8	NW		NW.	5	......	

YPSILANTI, MICHIGAN.

Month and day.	Hour.	Barom'r corrected to 32° F.	Thermometer.	Force of vapor.	Cloudiness.		Motion of clouds.		Winds.		Relative humidity.	REMARKS.
March 13	9 p. m.	29. 157	40	. 136		0		0	E.	1	52	13th. Rain, 3½ to 4 p. m; amount, 0. 30 inch.
March 14	7 a. m.	28. 857	40	. 182	Cu.	10	SE.	2	E.	1	73	17th. Slight solar halo most of the day; snow storm from 8¾ p. m. to 9½ p. m. on the 18th; amount in water, 0. 72 inch.
	2 p. m.	28. 857	54	. 308	Cu.	10	S.	3	SE.	3	79	
	9 p. m.	28. 537	41	. 177	Cir. cu.	9	SW.	5	SW.	1	66	
March 15	7 a. m.	28. 598	35. 5	. 149	Cir. cu.	10	SW.	4	SW.	3	71	
	2 p. m.	28. 598	36	. 142	Cir. cu.	10	W.	4	W.	4	70	
	9 p. m.	29. 016	31	. 102	Cu.	1	W.	1	W.	1	49	
March 16	7 a. m.	29. 201	29	. 133		0		0	W.	1	78	
	2 p. m.	29. 201	51	. 126		0		0	SE.	3	34	
	9 p. m.	29. 140	37	. 171	Cir.	1	W.	1	SE.	1	68	

STORM No. 1, MARCH, 1859.

YPSILANTI, MICHIGAN—Continued.

Month and day.	Hour.	Barom'r corrected to 32° F.	Thermometer.	Force of vapor.	Cloudiness.		Motion of clouds.		Winds.		Relative humidity.	REMARKS.
March 17	7 a. m.	29. 053	38	. 184	Cir. cu.	9	W.	3	S.	1	77	
	2 p. m.	29. 053	65	. 176	St.	10		0	SW.	2	32	
	9 p. m.	28. 772	49	. 296	Nim.	10	SE.	1	SE.	2	82	
March 18	7 a. m.	28. 403	46	. 286	Cir.	10	E ------		ENE.	1	92	
	2 p. m.	28. 403	30. 5	. 215	Cir. cu.	10	NW.	1	NNW.	3	80½	
	9 p. m.	28. 316	32	. 179	Overcast	10	NW ------		NW.	4	94	
March 19	7 a. m.	28. 496	32	. 168	Cir. cu.	10	NW.	5	WNW.	5	89	
	2 p. m.	28. 496	35	. 142	{ Cir. { Cir. cu.	2 5	NW. W.	1 } 5 }	WNW.	5	70	

THUNDER BAY ISLAND, MICHIGAN.

Month and day.	Hour.	Barom'r corrected to 32° F.	Thermometer.	Force of vapor.	Cloudiness.	Motion of clouds.	Winds.		Relative humidity.	REMARKS.
March 13	6 p. m.	29. 64	31	. 136	6	------------	NNE.	3	78	18th. Storm from 9 a. m. to 2 p. m; amount, 0. 14 inch.
March 14	6 a. m.	29. 36	32	. 143	5	SE ------	SE.	5	79	
	9 a. m.	29. 24	34	. 155	10	------------	SE.	7	79	
	3 p. m.	28. 83	36	. 180	10	SE ------	SE.	7	85	
	6 p. m.	28. 76	36	. 170	10	------------	SE.	7	80	
March 15	6 a. m.	28. 80	33	. 150	5	N ------	S.	5	80	
	9 a. m.	28. 95	35	. 159	10	------------	S.	4	79	
	3 p. m.	29. 09	29	. 123	10	WNW ------	NW.	6	77	
	6 p. m.	29. 55	28	. 117	10	------------	NW.	5	76	
March 16	6 a. m.	29. 52	30	. 130	0	------------	NW.	3	78	
	9 a. m.	29. 50	32	. 143	0	------------	NW.	2	79	
	3 p. m.	29. 49	34. 5	. 155	0	------------	SSW.	6	79	
	6 p. m.	29. 44	34	. 155	6	S ------	S.	6	79	
March 17	6 a. m.	29. 34	34. 5	. 155	10	------------	SW.	4	79	
	9 a. m.	29. 31	39	. 184	6	------------	S.	6	77	
	3 p. m.	29. 19	42	. 211	0	------------	S.	7	78	
	6 p. m.	29. 12	38	. 186	10	N ------	S.	5	81	
March 18	6 a. m.	28. 86	34	. 155	10	------------	NE.	5	79	
	9 a. m.	28. 70	35	. 162	10	NE ------	NNE.	4	80	
	3 p. m.	28. 66	34	. 155	10	------------	NE.	7	79	
	6 p. m.	28. 64	34	. 155	10	N ------	NNE.	8	79	
March 19	6 a. m.	28. 62	26	. 105	10	N ------	N.	9	75	
	9 a. m.	28. 74	26	. 105	10	N ------	NNW.	8	75	
	3 p. m.	28. 95	31	. 136	6	N ------	N.	7	78	

AURORA, INDIANA.

Month and day.	Hour.	Barom'r corrected to 32° F.	Thermometer.	Force of vapor.	Cloudiness.	Motion of clouds.	Winds.	Relative humidity.	REMARKS.
March 13	9 p. m.	29. 50	54	------	------------	------------	------------	------	14th. Stormy; amount of rain, 0. 875 inch.
March 14	6 a. m.	29. 15	52	------	------------	------------	W ------------	------	15th. Windy and variable.
	2 p. m.	29. 01	62	------	------------	------------	------------	------	16th. Clear.
	9 p. m.	29. 02	52	------	------------	------------	------------	------	
March 15	6 a. m.	29. 30	42	------	------------	------------	W ------------	------	
	2 p. m.	29. 41	46	------	------------	------------	------------	------	
	9 p. m.	29. 56	40	------	------------	------------	------------	------	
March 16	6 a. m.	29. 60	32	------	------------	------------	SE ------------	------	
	2 p. m.	29. 63	58	------	------------	------------	------------	------	
	9 p. m.	29. 58	49	------	------------	------------	------------	------	
March 17	6 a. m.	29. 53	46	------	------------	------------	------------	------	
	2 p. m.	------	57	------	------------	------------	------------	------	
	9 p. m.	------	53	------	------------	------------	------------	------	
March 18	6 a. m.	------	------	------	------------	------------	------------	------	
	2 p. m.	------	------	------	------------	------------	------------	------	
	9 p. m.	------	------	------	------------	------------	------------	------	
March 19	6 a. m.	------	------	------	------------	------------	------------	------	
	2 p. m.	------	------	------	------------	------------	------------	------	
	9 p. m.	------	------	------	------------	------------	------------	------	

STORM No. 1, MARCH, 1859.

CANNELTON, INDIANA.

Month and day.	Hour.	Barom'r corrected to 32° F.	Thermometer.	Force of vapor.	Cloudiness.		Motion of clouds.		Winds.		Relative humidity.	REMARKS.
March 13	9 p. m.	29. 48	58. 2	------	Nim.	10	----------		SE.	½	------	
March 14	7 a. m.	29. 25	61	------	Nim.	10	S.	3	SE.	2	------	13th. Rain during the night; am't, 0. 26 inch.
	2 p. m.	29. 20	63. 7	------	Cu. st.	7	SW.	4	S.	4	------	
	9 p. m.	29. 38	49. 8	------		0	----------		S.	4	------	18th. Snowing from 2 to 6 p. m., melting as it fell; amount in water, 0. 82 inch.
March 15	7 a. m.	29. 57	40. 3	------	Cir. st.	3	W.	3	W.	3	------	
	2 p. m.	29. 69	47. 9	------		0	----------		W.	3	------	
	9 p. m.	29. 79	40. 4	------		0	----------		SE.	1	------	
March 16	7 a. m.	29. 86	37. 2	------		0	----------		SE.	1	------	
	2 p. m.	29. 72	63. 8	------	St.	1	----------		E.	1	------	
	9 p. m.	29. 68	52. 6	------	Nim.	10	S.	3	SE.	1	------	
March 17	7 a. m.	29. 61	57	------	Nim.	10	S.	2	S.	1	------	
	2 p. m.	29. 38	53. 2	------	Nim.	10	----------		E.	2	------	
	9 p. m.	29. 11	51. 5	------	Nim.	10	----------		SE.	1	------	
March 18	7 a. m.	29. 02	43	------	Nim.	10	W.	3	W.	2	------	
	2 p. m.	29. 18	33. 9	------	Nim.	10	----------		W.	3	------	
	9 p. m.	29. 46	34. 5	------	Nim.	10	W.	4	W.	3	------	
March 19	7 a. m.	29. 61	33. 9	------	Nim.	10	W.	3	W.	3	------	
	2 p. m.	29. 67	42	------	Cu. st.	1	W.	3	W.	3	------	

LOGANSPORT, INDIANA.

Month and day.	Hour.	Barom'r corrected to 32° F.	Thermometer.	Force of vapor.	Cloudiness.		Motion of clouds.		Winds.		Relative humidity.	REMARKS.
March 13	9 p. m.	------	57	------	St.	10	SW.	1	E.	1	------	14th. Rain from 7 a. m. to 4 p. m.; amount, 0. 15 inch.
March 14	7 a. m.	------	59	------	Nim.	10	N.	3	SW.	4	------	
	2 p. m.	------	55	------	Nim.	10	E.	4	W.	5	------	17th. Began to rain at 8.30 p. m., and ended at 6.30 a. m. on the 18th; snow from 11.30 a. m. to 8 p. m. the 18th; amount in water, 0. 90 inch.
	9 p. m.	------	39	------	Cu.	10	E.	5	W.	6	------	
March 15	7 a. m.	------	35	------	Cu.	10	E.	4	NW.	5	------	
	2 p. m.	------	44	------	Cir.	7	E.	4	NW.	5	------	
	9 p. m.	------	36	------		0	SE.	1	NW.	1	------	
March 16	7 a. m.	------	34	------		0	SW.	1	NE.	1	------	
	2 p. m.	------	61	------		0	NE.	3	SW.	4	------	
	9 p. m.	------	53	------	Cir.	10	SW.	1	NE.	1	------	
March 17	7 a. m.	------	47	------	Cir.	10	NE.	1	SE.	1	------	
	2 p. m.	------	64	------	Cir. st.	10	E.	1	SW.	2	------	
	9 p. m.	------	51	------	Nim.	10	E	1	SW.	1	------	
March 18	7 a. m.	------	42	------	Nim.	10	SE.	1	NE.	2	------	
	2 p. m.	------	37	------	Cu. st.	1	SE.	2	NW.	3	------	
	9 p. m.	------	32	------	Cu. st.	10	S.	2	NW.	4	------	
March 19	7 a. m.	------	30	------	Cir. st.	10	SE.	3	NW.	4	------	
	2 p. m.	------	36	------	Cir.	5	E.	1	NW.	2	------	

NEW HARMONY, INDIANA.

Month and day.	Hour.	Barom'r corrected to 32° F.	Thermometer.	Force of vapor.	Cloudiness.		Motion of clouds.		Winds.		Relative humidity.	REMARKS.
March 13	9 p. m.	29. 477	59	. 323		10	----------		----------		65	13th. Rain in the night; amount, 0. 15 inch.
March 14	7 a. m.	29. 234	59	. 469		8	----------		SW.	3	94	
	2 p. m.	29. 174	56	. 204		0	----------		W----------		45	Rain from 3 p. m. the 17th to 7 a. m. on the 18th; amount, 0. 50 inch.
	9 p. m.	29. 380	52	. 183		10	----------		W.	4	47	
March 15	7 a. m.	29. 619	38	. 165		0	----------		SW.	2	72	
	2 p. m.	29. 765	50	. 234		0	----------		SW.	1	65	18th. Snow from 7 a. m. to 5 p. m.; amount in water, 0. 42 inch.
	9 p. m.	29. 831	39	. 216		0	----------		SW----------		91	
March 16	7 a. m.	29. 839	35	. 183		0	----------		SW----------		90	
	2 p. m.	29. 690	62	. 370		5	----------		SE ----------		66	
	9 p. m.	29. 670	56	. 23		10	----------		SE ----------		51	
March 17	7 a. m.	29. 597	52	. 208		10	----------		S.----------		53	
	2 p. m.	29. 425	56	. 336		10	----------		SE ----------		75	
	9 p. m.	29. 172	52	. 388		10	----------		NW ----------		100	
March 18	7 a. m.	29. 061	40	. 248		10	----------		NW ----------		100	
	2 p. m.	29. 241	38	. 186		10	----------		W.	2	81	
	9 p. m.	29. 487	36	. 149		10	----------		W.	2	71	
March 19	7 a. m.	29. 672	33	. 168		0	----------		NW ----------		89	
	2 p. m.	29. 736	44	. 196		2	----------		SW----------		68	

STORM No. 1, MARCH, 1859.

RICHMOND, INDIANA.*

Month and day.	Hour.	Barom'r corrected to 32° F.	Thermometer.	Force of vapor.	Cloudiness.	Motion of clouds.	Winds.	Relative humidity.	REMARKS.
March 13	9 p. m.	------	56	------	------	------	------	------	13th. Rain; amount, 0. 40 inch.
March 14	Sunrise.	------	50	------	------	------	------	------	16th. Rain in the night; wind SE.; amount, 0. 20 inch.
	2 p. m.	------	56	------	------	------	------	------	
	9 p. m.	------	47	------	------	------	------	------	18th. Rain; wind SE.; amount, 1. 00 inch.
March 15	Sunrise.	------	36	------	------	------	------	------	
	2 p. m.	------	38	------	------	------	------	------	
	9 p. m.	------	36	------	------	------	------	------	
March 16	Sunrise.	------	26	------	------	------	------	------	
	2 p. m.	------	56	------	------	------	------	------	
	9 p. m.	------	46	------	------	------	------	------	
March 17	Sunrise.	------	46	------	------	------	------	------	
	2 p. m.	------	54	------	------	------	------	------	
	9 p. m.	------	48	------	------	------	------	------	
March 18	Sunrise.	------	48	------	------	------	------	------	
	2 p. m.	------	42	------	------	------	------	------	
	9 p. m.	------	36	------	------	------	------	------	
March 19	Sunrise.	------	27	------	------	------	------	------	
	2 p. m.	------	36	------	------	------	------	------	

RICHMOND, INDIANA.†

Month and day.	Hour.	Barom'r corrected to 32° F.	Thermometer.	Force of vapor.	Cloudiness.	Motion of clouds.	Winds.	Relative humidity.	REMARKS.
March 14	6 a. m.	------	52	------	Rain 10	S. 4	S. 3	------	15th. Wind and clouds W. 3 and 5 all day; showers of snow and rain.
	1 p. m.	------	60	------	10	S. 4	S. 3	------	
March 15	6 a. m.	------	38	------	10	W. 4	W. 4	------	
	1 p. m.	------	37	------	10	W. 4	W. 4	------	17th. Rain p. m. and night.
March 16	6 a. m.	------	28	------	1	------	NE. 1	------	18th. Rain all day; 5 p. m. snow from W.
	1 p. m.	------	56	------	0	------	S. 1	------	
March 17	6 a. m.	------	47	------	10	WSW. 1	NE. 1	------	19th. 6 a. m. snow 3 inches deep; storm all day and night.
	1 p. m.	------	55	------	Rain 10	S. 1	S. 1	------	
March 18	6 a. m.	------	52	------	10	SSW. 2	SSW. 1	------	
	1 p. m.	------	48	------	10	NW. 3	NW. 2	------	
March 19	6 a. m.	------	28	------	10	NW. 2	NW ------	------	
	1 p. m.	------	36	------	9	------	------	------	

WISHAWAKA, INDIANA.

Month and day.	Hour.	Barom'r corrected to 32° F.	Thermometer.	Force of vapor.	Cloudiness.	Motion of clouds.	Winds.	Relative humidity.	REMARKS.
March 13	6 p. m.	------	------	------	Cir. st. 8	------	SE. 2	------	14th. Rain from 11½ a. m. to 3 p. m.
March 14	6 a. m.	------	------	------	Cir. st. 6	------	S. 3	------	15th. Snow from 5 to 9 a. m.; depth. 0. 50 inch.
	1 p. m.	------	------	------	Nim. 10	------	SW. 6	------	
	6 p. m.	------	------	------	Nim. 10	------	W. 5	------	17th. Rain at 10 p. m.
March 15	6 a. m.	------	------	------	Nim. 10	------	W. 4	------	18th. Snow at 1 p. m., continued till 7 a. m. on the 19th; depth, 3 inches.
	1 p. m.	------	39	------	Cir. 8	------	W. 4	------	
	6 p. m.	------	30½	------	0	------	W. 1	------	
March 16	6 a. m.	------	24	------	0	------	W. 1	------	
	1 p. m.	------	59	------	St. 2	------	S. 2	------	
	6 p. m.	------	49	------	St. 2	------	SE. 2	------	
March 17	6 a. m.	------	42	------	St. 2	------	S. 2	------	
	1 p. m.	------	60	------	St. 2	------	S. 2	------	
	6 p. m.	------	51	------	Cir. st. 6	------	S. 2	------	
March 18	6 a. m.	------	43	------	Nim. 10	------	S. 3	------	
	1 p. m.	------	41	------	Nim. 10	------	W. 3	------	
	6 p. m.	------	31	------	Nim. 10	------	NW. 3	------	
March 19	6 a. m.	------	29	------	Nim. 10	------	W. 2	------	
	1 p. m.	------	34	------	Cir. 6	------	W. 2	------	

* Moore, observer.

† Austin, observer.

STORM No. 1, MARCH, 1859.

AUGUSTA, ILLINOIS.

Month and day.	Hour.	Barom'r corrected to 32° F.	Thermometer.	Force of vapor.	Cloudiness.		Motion of clouds.		Winds.		Relative humidity.	REMARKS.
March 13	2 p. m.	......	61	.249	Cir. cu.	10	SE.	2	SE.	4	47	13th. Light thunder shower, accompanied by lightning at 7 p. m.; amount, 0.165 inch.
	9 p. m.	......	54	.362	Cir. cu.	9	W.	1	SE.	4	87	14th. Snow squalls from 3 to 8 p. m; amount in water, 0.13 inch.
March 14	7 a. m.	......	39	.155	Nim.	10	SW.	3	SW.	5	68	17th. Cold rain, began to freeze at 6 p. m., turned to snow at 7 p. m, continued in the night, ceased at 2 a. m. next morning; amount in water, 0.72 inch.
	2 p. m.	......	35	.162	Nim.	10	SW.	3	SW.	6	80	19th. Showery p. m.
	9 p. m.	......	33	.144	Nim.	10	W.	3	W.	5	75	
March 15	7 a. m.	......	30	.111		0	....		W.	4	67	
	2 p. m.	......	47	.115		0	....		W.	4	36.5	
	9 p. m.	......	39	.144		0	....		E.	2	63	
March 16	7 a. m.	......	39	.100		0	....		SE.	3	42	
	2 p. m.	......	65	.176	Cir.	2		0	SE.	4	29	
	9 p. m.	......	54	.206	Nim.	10	....		SE.	3	49	
March 17	7 a. m.	......	49	.284	Cir. cu.	8	S.	2	S.	2	82	
	2 p. m.	......	41	.235	Nim.	10	NE.	2	NE.	3	91	
	9 p. m.	......	33	.188	Nim.	10	Snow		NW.	4	100	
March 18	7 a. m.	......	28	.091	Nim.	10	NW.	3	NW.	4	39	
	2 p. m.	......	33	.152	Cir. cu.	9	NW.	3	NW.	4	79.5	
	9 p. m.	......	32	.150	Nim.	10	....		SW.	4	80	
March 19	7 a. m.	......	22	.101		0	....		W.	2	86	

AURORA, ILLINOIS.

Month and day.	Hour.	Barom'r corrected to 32° F.	Thermometer.	Force of vapor.	Cloudiness.		Motion of clouds.		Winds.		Relative humidity.	REMARKS.
March 13	2 p. m.	......	50	......	Cir. cu.	8	S.	3	NE.	4	......	Storm commenced at 9 p. m. the 13th and ended at 11 a. m. on the 14th; recommenced at 6 p. m and ended at 11 p. m.; amount in water, 0.61 inch.
	9 p. m.	......	41	......	Cir. st.	9	S.	3	NE.	4	......	Snow storm from 9½ p. m. the 17th to 2 p. m. on the 18th; amount in water, 0.32 inch.
March 14	7 a. m.	......	51	......	St.	10	SE.	4	SE.	4	......	16th. Halo at night.
	2 p. m.	......	37	......	St.	10	SW.	4	SW.	4	......	17th. Very hazy all day.
	9 p. m.	......	34	......	Snow	10	SW.	5	SW.	5	......	
March 15	7 a. m.	......	32	......	St.	10	W.	4	W.	4	......	
	2 p. m.	......	40	......	St.	1	NW.	5	NW.	5	......	
	9 p. m.	......	33	......		0	....		W.	1	......	
March 16	7 a. m.	......	32	......		0	....		SE.	2	......	
	2 p. m.	......	59	......	Cir.	2	W.	1	S.	5	......	
	9 p. m.	......	46	......		0	....		SE.	4	......	
March 17	7 a. m.	......	41	......	Cir. cu.	4	SW.	4	SE.	2	......	
	2 p. m.	......	59	......	Cir. st.	10	SW.	1	SW.	3	......	
	9 p. m.	......	39	......	Cir. st.	10	SW.	4	N.	5	......	
March 18	7 a. m.	......	32	......	Snow	10	....		N.	5	......	
	2 p. m.	......	34	......	Cir. st.	10	NW.	4	NW.	4	......	
	9 p. m.	......	31	......	Cir. st.	6	NW.	4	NW.	4	......	
March 19	7 a. m.	......	25	......		0	....		W.	4	......	

BATAVIA, ILLINOIS.

Month and day.	Hour.	Barom'r corrected to 32° F.	Thermometer.	Force of vapor.	Cloudiness.		Motion of clouds.		Winds.		Relative humidity.	REMARKS.
March 13	2 p. m.	29.327	52	.308		3	NE.	2	N.	2	74	Storm commenced in the night of the 14th and ended on the 15th at night; amount, 0.58 inch.
	9 p. m.	29.100	38	.190		10	SW.	2	NE.	2	74	16th. Mock moon at 9 p. m.
March 14	7 a. m.	28.619	50	.348	Cu. st.	10	SSE.	1	SSE.	1	86	Storm commenced at 9 p. m. the 17th and ended at 1 p. m. on the 18th; amount in water, 0.46 inch.
	2 p. m.	28.611	38	.097	Cu. st.	10	SW.	2	N.	2	39	
	9 p. m.	28.633	32	.155		10	SW.	2	SW.	2	79	
March 15	7 a. m.	28.868	39	.136		10	NW.	2	NW.	2	78	
	2 p. m.	29.080	40	.134	Cir. cu.	1	W.	2	W.	2	50	
	9 p. m.	29.212	33	.149		0	....		W.	1	71	
March 16	7 a. m.	29.210	33	.142	Cir. cu.	1	SSW.	1	SW.	1	70	
	2 p. m.	29.151	60	.284	Cir., cir. st.	5	SSW.	2	SSW.	2	51	
	9 p. m.	29.099	48	.210	Cir. st.	1	SW.	1	SW.	1	58	
March 17	7 a. m.	29.048	42	.241	Cu. st.	5	SW.	1	SW.	1	84	
	2 p. m.	28.950	52	.282		10	SW.	1	SW.	1	67	
	9 p. m.	28.884	37	.203		10	NE.	1	NE.	1	82	
March 18	7 a. m.	28.750	30	.181	St.	10	NE.	1	NE.	1	100	
	2 p. m.	28.770	31	.150	St., cu. st.	10	NW.	1	NW.	1	80	
	9 p. m.	28.970	28	.130	Cir. cu.	2	NW.	1	NW.	1	78	
March 19	7 a. m.	29.035	23	.117		0	....		NW.	1	87	

STORM No. 1, MARCH, 1859.

EDGINGTON, ILLINOIS.

Month and day.	Hour.	Barom'r corrected to 32° F.	Thermometer.	Force of vapor.	Cloudiness.	Motion of clouds.	Winds.	Relative humidity.	REMARKS.
March 13	2 p. m.	------	54	------	Cir. 10	SE. 2	E. 2	------	13th. Rain from 6½ to 8 p m.
	9 p. m.	------	52	------	Cir. 10	SW. 1	SE. 2	------	14th. Rain and snow at 7½ a. m.
March 14	7 a. m.	------	44	------	Nim. 10	SW. 3	SW. 3	------	15th Rain at 1 p. m.; snow at 1½ p. m
	2 p. m.	------	35	------	Nim. 10	SW. 4	W. 4	------	17th. Began to rain at 8 a. m; wind NW., continued till 1 p. m., then changed to a heavy snow storm, reaching far into the night, leaving 3 inches of snow in addition to what melted as it fell.
	9 p. m.	------	34	------	Nim. 10	NW. 5	NW. 5	------	
March 15	7 a. m.	------	29	------	0	0	NW. 5	------	
	2 p. m.	------	46	------	0	0	NW. 4	------	
	9 p. m.	------	36	------	0	0	NW. 3	------	
March 16	7 a. m.	------	40	------	Cir. 1	SW. 4	SW. 4	------	
	2 p. m.	------	58	------	Cir. 5	SW. 3	SW. 3	------	
	9 p. m.	------	42	------	Cir. st. 10	S. 3	S. 3	------	
March 17	7 a. m.	------	45	------	Nim. 10	NW. 3	NW. 3	------	
	2 p. m.	------	35	------	Nim. 10	NW. 4	NW. 4	------	
	9 p. m.	------	34	------	Nim. 10	NW. 5	NW. 4	------	
March 18	7 a. m.	------	32	------	Cir. 10	NW. 3	NW. 3	------	
	2 p. m.	------	34	------	Cir. 8	NW. 3	NW. 3	------	
	9 p. m.	------	32	------	Cir. st. 6	NW. 3	NW. 3	------	
March 19	7 a. m.	------	22	------	Cir. 6	NW. 3	NW. 3	------	

CARTHAGE, ILLINOIS.

Month and day.	Hour.	Barom'r corrected to 32° F.	Thermometer.	Force of vapor.	Cloudiness.	Motion of clouds.	Winds.	Relative humidity.	REMARKS.
March 13	1 p. m.	------	64	------	10	------	------	------	15th. Very windy.
	7 p. m.	------	57	------	10	------	------	------	
March 14	7 a. m.	------	42	------	------	------	------	------	
	1 p. m.	------	36	------	------	------	------	------	
	7 p. m.	------	34	------	------	------	------	------	
March 15	7 a. m.	------	36	------	------	------	------	------	
	1 p. m.	------	50	------	------	------	------	------	
	7 p. m.	------	38	------	------	------	------	------	
March 16	7 a. m.	------	34	------	------	------	------	------	
	1 p. m.	------	64	------	------	------	------	------	
	7 p. m.	------	56	------	5	------	------	------	
March 17	7 a. m.	------	50	------	10	------	------	------	
	1 p. m.	------	38	------	10	------	------	------	
	7 p. m.	------	32	------	10	------	------	------	
March 18	7 a. m.	------	28	------	10	------	------	------	
	1 p. m.	------	35	------	10	------	------	------	
	7 p. m.	------	32	------	10	------	------	------	
March 19	7 a. m.	------	23	------	------	------	------	------	

ELGIN, ILLINOIS.

Month and day.	Hour.	Barom'r corrected to 32° F.	Thermometer.	Force of vapor.	Cloudiness.	Motion of clouds.	Winds.	Relative humidity.	REMARKS.
March 13	2 p. m.	------	47	------	Cir. cu. 9	NE. 2	NE. 4	------	13th. A few small hail stones fell at 6 p m.; shower in the night.
	9 p. m.	------	41	------	Cu. st. 10	------	NE. 4	------	14th. Rained till 10 a. m., then a light fall of snow; began to snow at 3 p. m and continued till 1 a. m. the following day; amount, 0.417 inch.
March 14	7 a. m.	------	48	------	10	------	S. 3	------	Snow, with an occasional shower of rain, from 9.30 p. m the 17th to 11 a. m on the 18th; amount in water, 0.55 inch.
	2 p. m.	------	38	------	Cu. st. 10	------	SW. 4	------	
	9 p. m.	------	33	------	Snow 10	------	SW. 3	------	
March 15	7 a. m.	------	31	------	Cu. st. 10	------	NW. 4	------	
	2 p. m.	------	41	------	Cu. 1	------	NW. 6	------	
	9 p. m.	------	34	------	0	------	NW. 2	------	
March 16	7 a. m.	------	30	------	0	------	SW. 1	------	
	2 p. m.	------	59	------	Cir. st. 2	------	SW. 6	------	
	9 p. m.	------	47	------	Thin, st. 10	------	S. 3	------	
March 17	7 a. m.	------	44	------	Cu st. 10	------	S. 1	------	
	2 p. m.	------	55	------	10	------	NW. 1	------	
	9 p. m.	------	37	------	St. 10	------	NW. 5	------	
March 18	7 a. m.	------	32	------	Snow 10	------	NW. 3	------	
	2 p. m.	------	34	------	St. 10	------	4	------	
	9 p. m.	------	31	------	Cu. st. 9	------	4	------	
March 19	7 a. m.	------	25	------	0	------	3	------	

STORM No. 1, MARCH, 1859.

MANCHESTER, ILLINOIS.

Month and day.	Hour.	Barom'r corrected to 32° F.	Thermometer.	Force of vapor.	Cloudiness.		Motion of clouds.		Winds.		Relative humidity.	REMARKS.
March 13	1 p. m.	28. 70	57	. 295	Cir. st.	10	S.........		S.	3	63	13th. Rain, accompanied by thunder, from 7 to 7½ p. m.; amount, 0. 13 inch.
	9 p. m.	28. 59	54	. 418	Nim.	10	S.........		S.	2	100	
March 14	7 a. m.	28. 39	39	. 238	Cu.	4	SW.......		SW.	2	100	
	1 p. m.	28. 33	38	. 186	Cu.	10	SW.......		SW.	3	81	16th. Snow and rain; halo about the moon.
	9 p. m.	28. 55	34	. 196	Cu.	10	W........		W.	4	100	
March 15	7 a. m.	28. 78	31	. 174		0		0	W.	3	100	17th. Began to rain at 6½ p. m., and ended in the night; amount, 0. 47 inch.
	1 p. m.	28. 91	48	. 212	Cir.	1	W........		W.	2	63	
	9 p. m.	28. 91	34	. 196		0		0	S.	1	100	
March 16	7 a. m.	28. 86	38	. 229	Cu.	2	S.........		S.	2	100	19th. Halo about the moon.
	1 p. m.	28. 78	62	. 312	Cir. cu.	2	S.........		S.	3	56	
	9 p. m.	28. 76	51	. 374	Haze		....		S.	2	100	
March 17	7 a. m.	28. 67	49	. 272	Cir. cu.	10	S.........		S.	1	78	
	1 p. m.	28. 59	56	. 391	Nim.	10	S.........		S.	1	87	
	9 p. m.	28. 51	32	. 181	Nim.	10	N		N.	3	100	
March 18	7 a. m.	28. 52	28	. 153	Nim.	10	NW		NW.	3	100	
	1 p. m.	28. 57	32	. 181	Nim.	10	NW		NW.	3	100	
	9 p. m.	28. 70	30	. 167	Cu.	10	N		N.	3	100	
March 19	7 a. m.	28. 88	26	. 141	Cu.	4	NW		NW.	2	100	

MARENGO, ILLINOIS.

Month and day.	Hour.	Barom'r corrected to 32° F.	Thermometer.	Force of vapor.	Cloudiness.		Motion of clouds.		Winds.		Relative humidity.	REMARKS.
March 13	2 p. m.	28. 95	47	......	St.	1	....		SE.	3	......	Rain from 10 p. m. the 13th to 1 p. m. on the 14th; amount, 0. 29 inch.
	9 p. m.	28. 84	38	......		10	....		E.	3	......	
March 14	7 a. m.	28. 41	48	......		10	....		SE.	3	......	
	2 p. m.	28. 34	37	......		10	....		S.	3	......	14th. Snow from 5 to 7 p. m.
	9 p. m.	28. 31	32	......		10	....		SW.	2	......	17th. Snow at night; depth, 3½ inches.
March 15	7 a. m.	28. 59	31	......		10	....		SW.	3	......	
	2 p. m.	28. 79	42	......	Cu.	1	....		SW.	3	......	
	9 p. m.	28. 91	33	......		0	....		SW.	1	......	
March 16	7 a. m.	28. 95	35	......		0	....		SE.	2	......	
	2 p. m.	28. 89	58	......		0	....		S.	3	......	
	9 p. m.	28. 86	49	......	St.	3	....		SW.	2	......	
March 17	7 a. m.	28. 79	44	......		10	....		S.	3	......	
	2 p. m.	28. 72	50	......		10	....		SW.	2	......	
	9 p. m.	28. 67	38	......		10	....		SW.	3	......	
March 18	7 a. m.	28. 54	30	......		10	....		W.	3	......	
	2 p. m.	28. 51	36	......		10	....		W.	3	......	
	9 p. m.	28. 61	28	......	Cu. st.	4	....		W.	3	......	
March 19	7 a. m.	28. 76	26	......		0	....		SW.	2	......	

OTTAWA, ILLINOIS.

Month and day.	Hour.	Barom'r corrected to 32° F.	Thermometer.	Force of vapor.	Cloudiness.		Motion of clouds.		Winds.		Relative humidity.	REMARKS.
March 13	2 p. m.	......	59	......	Cir.	2	SW.	1	SE.	3	......	13th. Rain, accompanied by thunder in SW., at 6 p. m.
	9 p. m.	......	43	......		10	....		SE.	3	......	
March 14	7 a. m.	......	......	......		10	....		SE.	3	......	14th. Little rain in p. m.
	2 p. m.	......	38	......	Cu.	10	SW.	6	SW.	4	......	15th. Rain; amount, 0. 32 inch.
	9 p. m.	......	34	......		10	....		SW.	4	......	16th. Large lunar halo in the evening.
March 15	7 a. m.	......	32	......	Cu.	10	SW.	5	SW.	4	......	
	2 p. m.	......	44	......	Cu.	1	NW.	7	NW.	4	......	Rain and snow at intervals from 0. 10 p. m. the 17th to 11. 30 a. m. on the 18th; amount, 0. 538 inch.
	9 p. m.	......	38	......		0	....		SW.	......	......	
March 16	7 a. m.	......	34	......		0	....		SE.	4	......	
	2 p. m.	......	59	......	Cir.	2	SW........		S.	4	......	
	9 p. m.	......	49	......	Haze		....		SE.	2	......	
March 17	7 a. m.	......	40	......	Cu.	10	NW.	5	W.	1	......	
	2 p. m.	......	55	......	Cu.	10	NW.	6	SW.	2	......	
	9 p. m.	......	38	......	Cu.	10	....		N.	3	......	
March 18	7 a. m.	......	31	......	Cu.	10	NW.	5	NW.	3	......	
	2 p. m.	......	34	......	Cir.	2	NW.	6	NW.	4	......	
	9 p. m.	......	32	......		1	....		NW.	3	......	
March 19	7 a. m.	......	30	......	Cir.	6	....		NW.	3	......	

STORM No. 1, MARCH, 1859.

PEKIN, ILLINOIS.

Month and day.	Hour.	Barom'r corrected to 32° F.	Thermometer.	Force of vapor.	Cloudiness.	Motion of clouds.	Winds.	Relative humidity.	REMARKS.
March 13	2 p. m.		64		Cu. 2	SW. 1	SE. 4		13th. Shower at 5.20 a. m.; wind, E. 4; 9 to 9.30 p. m. several flashes of diffused lightning, followed by low rolling thunder in west.
	9 p. m.		37		Cu., nim. 10		SE. 4		
March 14	7 a. m.		43		Nim. 10	S. 4	S. 4		
	2 p. m.		39		Nim. 10	SW. 6	SW. 6		
	9 p. m.		34		Nim. 10	SW. 5	SW. 6 to 7		
March 15	7 a. m.		31		Cir. 9	NW. 5	NW. 5		14th. Rain from 5 to 10 a. m.; wind, SW. 5, increased to 6 and to 7, with sleet at 4 p. m.; storm ceased at 8.30 p. m; amount, 0.186 inch.
	2 p. m.		45		0	0	NW. 2 to 5		
	9 p. m.		34		0	0	S. 1		
March 16	7 a. m.		40		Haze	0	S. 2		
	2 p. m.		65		Cu. 5	W. 1	S. 5		
	9 p. m.		48		Haze 5		S. 3		17th. Gentle rain at 4.40 p. m., from SW. 1; wind, NE. 3; 5.20 p. m., from N. 3; wind, 3; 5.40 p. m., from N. 5; wind, 3; changed to snow in the night, and continued till 5 a. m. next morning; amount, in water, 0.75 inch.
March 17	7 a. m.		46		Cu. 9	SW. 2	S. 2		
	2 p. m.		58		Cu. 10	SW. 2	S. 4		
	9 p. m.		34		Nim. 10	W. 5	N. 5		
March 18	7 a. m.		32		Cu. 10	N. 5	N. 5		
	2 p. m.		32		Nim. 10	NW	NW. 5		
	9 p. m.		31		Cu. 10	N. 2	N. 4		
March 19	7 a. m.		25		0	0	NW. 3		18th. Slight snow from 10.30 to 12 m.

PEORIA, ILLINOIS.

Month and day.	Hour.	Barom'r corrected to 32° F.	Thermometer.	Force of vapor.	Cloudiness.	Motion of clouds.	Winds.	Relative humidity.	REMARKS.
March 13	2 p. m.		59	.140	Cir., cu. st. 3		S. 2	28	13th. Thunder SW. and NE. at 9 p. m.
	9 p. m.		54.5	.355	Nim. 8		SW. 2	84	
March 14	7 a. m.		43.5	.224	Nim. 10		SW. 3	79	14th. Rain from before sunrise to 9 a. m.; amount, 0.40 inch.
	2 p. m.		43	.132	Nim. 10		SW. 6	48	
	9 p. m.		36.5	.143	Cu. 10		SW. 5	66	15th. Snow before sunrise; amount, in water, 0.28 inch.
March 15	7 a. m.		33.5	.116	Cu. 3	W., E. 4	W. 3	60	
	2 p. m.		49	.130	Cu. 1	W., E. 2	W. 3	37	
	9 p. m.		37	.167	0		W. 1	76	
March 16	7 a. m.		40	.118	0		E. 2	48	
	2 p. m.		64	.176	Cir. 3		E. 3	29	
	9 p. m.		53	.206	St. 5		E. 1	52	
March 17	7 a. m.		52	.183	Cu. 5		E. 1	47	
	2 p. m.		57	.216	Cu. st. 10		W. 1	46	
	9 p. m.		35.5	.182	Nim. 10		N. 2	87	
March 18	7 a. m.		34	.155	Nim. 10		N. 2	79	
	2 p. m.		37.5	.110	Cu. st. 10		W. 4	49	
	9 p. m.		33	.168	St. 10		W. 4	89	
March 19	7 a. m.		27	.111	Cu. 1		W. 3	75	

RILEY, ILLINOIS.

Month and day.	Hour.	Barom'r corrected to 32° F.	Thermometer.	Force of vapor.	Cloudiness.	Motion of clouds.	Winds.	Relative humidity.	REMARKS.
March 13	2 p. m.		38		Cir. 2		E. 3		13th. High wind, E; clouds, N, slow.
	9 p. m.		38		Cir. 2		E. 4		
March 14	7 a. m.		43		Nim. 10		SE. 2		14th. Rain at daybreak; rain for half an hour at 9 a. m.; rain at 10 a. m.; wind, W., strong; rain changed to snow; thermometer fell to 12°.
	2 p. m.		36		Cu. st. 10		S. 4		
	9 p. m.		32		Nim. 10		SW. 5		
March 15	7 a. m.		30		Cir. 6		W. 2		
	2 p. m.		42		0		W. 4		
	9 p. m.		31		0		SW. 1		15th. Snow squalls and rain; high wind, W.
March 16	7 a. m.		29		0		SW. 1		
	2 p. m.		60		0		SW. 6		16th. White frost; strong wind, S.; 9 p. m. large circle round the moon till 10½ p. m.
	9 p. m.		45		Hazy		S. 3		
March 17	7 a. m.		40		Cu. st. 6		SW. 2		
	2 p. m.		50		Hazy 3		N. 2		17th. Sky red at 7 a. m.; rain at 6 p. m.
	9 p. m.		34		Cu. 10		N. 3		
March 18	7 a. m.		30		Cu. 10		N. 3		18th. Two inches of snow, and very wet.
	2 p. m.		34		Cu. 10		N. 3		
	9 p. m.		29		Cir. st. 2		N. 2		
March 19	7 a. m.		30		0		NW. 2		

STORM No. 1, MARCH, 1859.

SANDWICH, ILLINOIS.

Month and day.	Hour.	Barom'r corrected to 32° F.	Thermometer.	Force of vapor.	Cloudiness.	Motion of clouds.	Winds.	Relative humidity.	REMARKS.
March 13	2 p. m.	------	54	------	Cir. st. 2	----------	NE. 3	------	14th. Hail storm from 9 to 10 a. m.; not violent; hail stones half inch in diameter; thermometer fell from 40° to 30°, 10 to 11 a. m., concluding in a thunder storm, accompanied by lightning; began to snow at 1 a. m.; storm ended at noon on the 15th; amount in water, 1. 02 inch. 16th. Lunar halo. Snow storm from 8 p. m. the 17th till noon on the 18th; amount in water, 0. 03 inch.
	9 p. m.	------	42	------	Cu. st. 10	W--------	NE. 3	------	
March 14	7 a. m.	------	50	------	Cu. st. 10	W-------	SE. 2	------	
	2 p. m.	------	38	------	Cir. st. 10	----------	SW. 3	------	
	9 p. m.	------	32	------	Cu. st. 10	W--------	SE. 4	------	
March 15	7 a. m.	------	31	------	Cir. st. 10	----------	NW. 3	------	
	2 p. m.	------	40	------	0	----------	NW. 4	------	
	9 p. m.	------	33	------	0	----------	NW-------	------	
March 16	7 a. m.	------	30	------	0	----------	E-------	------	
	2 p. m.	------	60	------	0	----------	SW--------	------	
	9 p. m.	------	49	------	Cir. st. 10	----------	S. 2	------	
March 17	7 a. m.	------	38	------	Cir. st. 8	----------	SE-------	------	
	2 p. m.	------	56	------	Cu. st. 10	W--------	NW. 2	------	
	9 p. m.	------	38	------	Cu. 10	NW------	NE. 3	------	
March 18	7 a. m.	------	31	------	Cu. cir. 10	----------	NE. 2	------	
	2 p. m.	------	34	------	Cir. st. 10	W--------	NE. 3	------	
	9 p. m.	------	30	------	Cir. cu. 10	----------	NW. 2	------	
March 19	7 a. m.	------	25	------	0	----------	NW. 2	------	

UPPER ALTON, ILLINOIS.

Month and day.	Hour.	Barom'r corrected to 32° F.	Thermometer.	Force of vapor.	Cloudiness.	Motion of clouds.	Winds.	Relative humidity.	REMARKS.
March 13	2 p. m.	29. 37	55	. 433	------------	----------	------------	100	Storm on the 18th; amount, 0. 40 inch.
	9 p. m.	29. 20	58	. 365	------------	----------	------------	76	
March 14	7 a. m.	29. 09	42	. 222	------------	----------	------------	83	
	2 p. m.	28. 93	42	. 244	------------	----------	------------	91	
	9 p. m.	29. 23	39	. 195	------------	----------	------------	82	
March 15	7 a. m.	29. 45	32	. 162	------------	----------	------------	89	
	2 p. m.	29. 55	50	. 258	------------	----------	------------	71	
	9 p. m.	29. 55	35	. 183	------------	----------	------------	90	
March 16	7 a. m.	29. 53	39	. 216	------------	----------	------------	91	
	2 p. m.	29. 42	64	. 464	------------	----------	------------	77	
	9 p. m.	29. 39	53	. 375	------------	----------	------------	93	
March 17	7 a. m.	29. 25	58	. 229	------------	----------	------------	47	
	2 p. m.	29. 20	50	. 361	------------	----------	------------	100	
	9 p. m.	29. 09	36	. 191	------------	----------	------------	90	
March 18	7 a. m.	29. 25	33	. 168	------------	----------	------------	89	
	2 p. m.	29. 25	35	. 142	------------	----------	------------	70	
	9 p. m.	29. 37	36	. 149	------------	----------	------------	71	
March 19	7 a. m.	29. 53	28	. 135	------------	----------	------------	88	

WAYNESVILLE, ILLINOIS.

Month and day.	Hour.	Barom'r corrected to 32° F.	Thermometer.	Force of vapor.	Cloudiness.	Motion of clouds.	Winds.	Relative humidity.	REMARKS.
March 13	2 p. m.	------	64	------	0	----------	S. 3	------	14th. Snow; at 5 p. m. light shower. 17th. Snow and rain at 10 p. m.; continued till 5 p. m. on the 18th; depth of snow, 2 inches.
	9 p. m.	------	59	------	St. 10	S. 1	S. 1	------	
March 14	7 a. m.	------	46	------	Rain 10	0	W. 5	------	
	2 p. m.	------	39	------	Cu. 10	W. 1	W. 5	------	
	9 p. m.	------	33	------	Nim. 10	S. 1	W. 3	------	
March 15	7 a. m.	------	30	------	Nim. 10	W. 1	W. 3	------	
	2 p. m.	------	46	------	0	----------	W. 5	------	
	9 p. m.	------	42	------	Rain 10	0	W. 1	------	
March 16	7 a. m.	------	31	------	0	----------	S. 1	------	
	2 p. m.	------	62	------	0	----------	S. 3	------	
	9 p. m.	------	58	------	St. 3	0	S. 1	------	
March 17	7 a. m.	------	45	------	Nim. 10	S. 1	S. 1	------	
	2 p. m.	------	55	------	Nim. 10	S. 1	E. 2	------	
	9 p. m.	------	50	------	Rain 10	0	NW. 1	------	
March 18	7 a. m.	------	31	------	Nim. 10	N. 1	N. 3	------	
	2 p. m.	------	31	------	Snow 10	N-------	N. 3	------	
	9 p. m.	------	30	------	St. 10	0	N. 3	------	
March 19	7 a. m.	------	22	------	Cu. 3	NW. 2	W. 3	------	

STORM No. 1, MARCH, 1859.

WEST SALEM, ILLINOIS.

Month and day.	Hour.	Barom'r corrected to 32° F.	Thermometer.	Force of vapor.	Cloudiness.	Motion of clouds.	Winds.	Relative humidity.	REMARKS.
March 13	2 p. m.	......	66	......	Cir. st. 8	SW. 4	SE. 2	......	13th. Distant thunder and light-
	9 p. m.	......	59	......	Cir. st. 9	SW. 5	SE. 2	......	ning in the SW., from 9 to 11
March 14	7 a. m.	......	60	......	Cir., nim. 9	SW. 8	S. 3	......	p. m.
	2 p. m.	......	56	......	Cu. st. 3		SW. 5	......	14th. Shower at 8 a. m. and at 2
	9 p. m.	......	46	......	Cu. st. 9	....	SW. 6	......	a. m.; ? amount, 0. 27 inch.
March 15	7 a. m.	......	38	......	Cu. st. 4	....	W. 4	......	Rain from 4. 45 p. m. the 17th to
	2 p. m.	......	50	......	0	....	NW. 4	......	4½ a. m. on the 18th; amount,
	9 p. m.	......	43	......	0	....	0	......	0. 26 inch.
March 16	7 a. m.	......	39	......	0	....	SE. 1	......	18th. A furious snow storm from 7
	2 p. m.	......	68	......	Cir. 4	SW. 6	SE. 3	......	a. m. to 4. 30 p. m.; amount in
	9 p. m.	......	57	......	Cir. st. 9	SW. 6	SE. 1	......	water, 0. 30 inch.
March 17	7 a. m.	......	54	......	Cir. st. 8	SW. 5	SE. 1	......	
	2 p. m.	......	60	......	Cir. st. 10	....	SE. 2	......	
	9 p. m.	......	52	......	Nim. 10	....	S. 2	......	
March 18	7 a. m.	......	36	......	Nim. 10	....	NW. 3	......	
	2 p m.	......	33	......	Cir.st.,nim. 10	....	NW. 5	......	
	9 p. m.	......	33	......	Cir. st. 9	....	NW. 4	......	
March 19	7 a. m.	......	31	......	Cir. st. 1	....	NW. 3	......	

WHEATON, ILLINOIS.

Month and day.	Hour.	Barom'r corrected to 32° F.	Thermometer.	Force of vapor.	Cloudiness.	Motion of clouds.	Winds.	Relative humidity.	REMARKS.
March 13	2 p. m.	29. 27	49	. 130	Cir. cu. 3	....	E. 3	37	Storm commenced at 7 p. m. the
	9 p. m.	29. 09	40	. 193	Nim. 10	....	NE. 4	77	13th, and ended on the 14th in
March 14	7 a. m.	28. 63	51	. 296	Nim. 10	....	SE. 4	79	the night; amount, 0. 64 inch.
	2 p. m.	28. 59	39	. 158	Nim. 10	....	SW. 5	68	16th. Lunar halo at 9 p. m.
	9 p. m.	28. 56	33	. 182	Nim. 10	....	SW. 5	95	Storm commenced at 9. 30 p. m.
March 15	7 a m.	28. 89	30	. 127	Nim. 10	....	NW. 5	73	the 17th, and ended on the 18th;
	2 p. m.	29. 08	40	. 122	Cir. 1	NW. 5	NW. 4	50	amount in water, 0. 46 inch.
	9 p. m.	29 26	35	. 140	0	....	W. 2	70	
March 16	7 a. m.	29. 31	33	. 156	0	....	SE. 1	85	
	2 p. m.	29. 18	57	. 203	Cir. 3	....	S. 5	42	
	9 p m.	29. 14	48	. 190	Cir. 9	....	SE. 2	59	
March 17	7 a m.	29. 06	42	. 189	Cir. cu. 9	SW. 2	S. 2	64	
	2 p. m.	28. 93	59	. 249	Cir.cu.,nim. 10	....	SW. 2	51	
	9 p. m.	28. 86	37	. 193	Nim. 10	....	WNW. 5	85	
March 18	7 a. m.	28. 69	32	. 181	Nim. 10	....	N. 7	100	
	2 p m.	28. 71	32	. 152	Nim. 10	....	NW. 6	85	
	9 p. m.	28. 86	29	. 127	Cir. cu. 10	....	NW. 5	77	
March 19	7 a. m.	29. 04	24	. 114	St. 1	....	W. 3	87	

WINNEBAGO, ILLINOIS.

Month and day.	Hour.	Barom'r corrected to 32° F.	Thermometer.	Force of vapor.	Cloudiness.	Motion of clouds.	Winds.	Relative humidity.	REMARKS.
March 13	2 p. m.	......	50. 5	......	Cir. cu. 10	SW. 2	SE. 3	......	13th. Began to rain at 8. 20 p. m;
	9 p. m.	......	39	......	Nim. 10	SW. 2	NE. 3	......	continued during the night; wind
March 14	7 a. m.	......	48	......	Nim. 10	....	SE. 3	......	changed at 8 a. m. on the 14th
	2 p. m.	......	35	......	Nim. 10	....	SW. 2	......	from SE., 3, to S. & SW., 4 to 5,
	9 p. m.	......	33	......	Nim. 10	....	SW. 3	......	with heavy rain; snow from SW.;
March 15	7 a. m.	......	30	......	Cir. st. 10	NW. 3	NW. 3	......	storm ended in the night; am't
	2 p. m.	......	41. 5	......	0	....	NW. 5	......	in water, 0. 95 inch.
	9 p. m.	......	32	......	0	....	SW. 1	......	16th. Solar halo at 2 p. m.; lunar
March 16	7 a. m.	......	33	......	Cu. 1	....	SE. 2	......	halo at 9 p. m., followed by rain.
	2 p. m.	......	62	......	Cir. 5	SW. 0	S. 5	......	17th. Storm commenced at 5 a. m.;
	9 p. m.	......	50	......	Cir. 5	SW. 1	SE. 3	......	wind changed at 7.30 a. m. from
March 17	7 a. m.	......	44	......	Cir. 10	SW. 2	SE. 2	......	SE. 2, to S. and SW. 1, to W.
	2 p. m.	......	38	......	Nim. 10	....	N. 3	......	at 10 a. m., and to NW. and N.
	9 p. m.	......	33. 5	......	Nim. 10	....	N. 4	......	2 at 11. 30 a. m.; light rain from
March 18	7 a m.	......	31	......	Nim. 10	....	N. 3	......	2 to 7 p. m., then heavy snow
	2 p. m.	......	35	......	Cu. st. 10	....	N. 3	......	storm; ended at 10 a. m. on the
	9 p. m.	......	31. 5	......	Cir. st. 10	....	N. 3	......	18th; amount in water, 0. 37
March 19	7 a. m.	......	24	......	0	....	NW. 2	......	inch.

STORM No. 1, MARCH, 1859.

WEST URBANA, ILLINOIS

Month and day.	Hour.	Barom'r corrected to 32° F.	Thermometer.	Force of vapor.	Cloudiness.		Motion of clouds.		Winds.		Relative humidity.	REMARKS.
March 13	2 p. m.	29. 201	62	......	Cir. cu.	4	....		SE.	4	......	14th. Snow at 5 p. m.
	9 p. m.	29. 098	54	......	Cu. st.	10	....		SE.	2	......	17th. Frost.
March 14	7 a. m.	28. 763	60	......	Cu. st.	10	N.	4	SE.	2	......	18th. Snow at 7½ a. m.; rain at 9 p. m.; amount, 0. 25 inch.
	2 p. m.	28. 733	46	......	Cir. cu.	10	....		SW.	7	......	
	9 p. m.	28. 773	36	......	Cu. st.	10	....		SW.	6	......	
March 15	7 a. m.	28. 988	32	......	Cu. st.	10	....		SW.	4	......	
	2 p. m.	29. 180	45	......	Cu.	1	....		W.	4	......	
	9 p. m.	29. 283	36	......	Clear	0	....		SW.	2	......	
March 16	7 a. m.	29. 325	31	......	Clear	0	....		SE.	2	......	
	2 p. m.	29. 271	42	......	Cir.	5	....		S.	3	......	
	9 p. m.	29. 191	49	......	Cir.	9	....		S.	3	......	
March 17	7 a. m.	29. 133	41	......	Cir.	9	....		SE.	1	......	
	2 p. m.	29. 001	59	......	St.	10	....		S.	2	......	
	9 p. m.	29. 191	59	......	St.	10	....		S.	0	......	
March 18	7 a. m.	28. 720	32	......	St.	10	....		NW.	6	......	
	2 p. m.	28. 690	29	......	St.	10	....		NW.	6	......	
	9 p. m.	28. 930	29	......	St.	10	....		NW.	5	......	
March 19	7 a. m.	29. 080	26	......	Cu.	1	....		NW.	4	......	

ST. LOUIS, MISSOURI.

Month and day.	Hour.	Barom'r corrected to 32° F.	Thermometer.	Force of vapor.	Cloudiness.		Motion of clouds.		Winds.		Relative humidity.	REMARKS.
March 13	2 p. m.	29. 37	52. 5	. 354		10	....		E.	2	90	13th. Rain from 11 a. m. to 3 p. m.; amount, 0. 03 inch. Storm commenced at 6 p. m. the 17th and ended at 9 a. m. on the 18th; amount in water, 0. 60 inch.
	9 p. m.	29. 20	56	. 391		10	....		SE.	2	87	
March 14	7 a. m.	29. 11	42	. 131		0	....		SW.	5	50	
	2 p. m.	29. 09	43. 5	. 114		10	....		SW.	7	40	
	9 p. m.	29. 29	41	. 136		9	....		SW.	5	52	
March 15	7 a. m.	29. 53	36	. 106		0	....		W.	4	50	
	2 p. m.	29. 62	52. 5	. 106		0	....		W.	3	27	
	9 p. m.	29. 63	44	. 173		0	....		SW.	2	60	
March 16	7 a. m.	29. 62	42. 5	. 171		0	....		SW.	3	62	
	2 p. m.	29. 47	63	. 163		5	....		SW.	5	28	
	9 p. m.	29. 45	56	. 204		10	....		SW.	1	45	
March 17	7 a. m.	29. 39	48	. 200		8	....		SW.	2	59	
	2 p. m.	29. 20	54. 5	. 262		10	....		SW.	2	61	
	9 p. m.	29. 13	40	. 225		10	....		SW.	3	91	
March 18	7 a. m.	29. 19	32	. 162		10	....		W.	4	89	
	2 p. m.	29. 30	35	. 127		10	....		W.	5	62	
	9 p. m.	29. 43	35	. 134		9	....		W.	4	66	
March 19	7 a. m.	29. 56	29	. 123		0	....		W.	2	77	

APPLETON, WISCONSIN.

Month and day.	Hour.	Barom'r corrected to 32° F.	Thermometer.	Force of vapor.	Cloudiness.		Motion of clouds.		Winds.		Relative humidity.	REMARKS.
March 13	2 p. m.	28. 90	36	. 186	Cir. st.	4	NE.	2	NE.	2	81	Storm commenced at 8 p. m. the 13th and ended at 2 p. m. on the 14th; amount in water, 0. 906 inch.
	9 p. m.	29. 00	31	. 150	Nim. st.	10	NE.	3	NE.	3	80	15th and 16th. Showers of rain and snow.
March 14	7 a. m.	28. 53	35	. 178	Cu. nim.	8	E.	2	E.	3	81	Storm commenced at 11. 30 a. m. the 17th and ended at 10 a. m. on the 18th; amount in water, 0. 281 inch.
	2 p. m.	28. 18	38	. 203	Cu. nim.	9	SW.	2	SW.	2	82	
	9 p. m.	28. 19	34	. 191	St.	10	SW.	2	SW.	2	90	
March 15	7 a. m.	28. 50	33	. 162	St.	8	NW.	2	NW.	2	80	
	2 p. m.	28. 78	40	. 244	Cu.	2	N.	1	N.	1	91	
	9 p. m.	29. 00	31	. 150		0		0	N.	1	80	
March 16	7 a. m.	29. 01	29	. 155		0		0	SW.	1	89	
	2 p. m.	28. 84	58	. 181		0		0	S.	2	43	
	9 p. m.	28. 89	36	. 186	Cu.	6	SW.	2	SW.	2	81	
March 17	7 a. m.	28. 78	40	. 244	Nim.	10	SW.	1	SW.	1	91	
	2 p. m.	28. 79	35	. 199	Nim.	10	N.	2	N.	2	90	
	9 p. m.	28. 89	35	. 178	Nim.	10	N.	1	N.	1	81	
March 18	7 a. m.	28. 75	33	. 162	Nim.	10	N.	1	N.	1	80	
	2 p. m.	28. 75	36	. 067	Cir. nim.	8	N.	1	N.	1	28	
	9 p. m.	28. 76	31	. 143	St.	2	N.	4	N.	1	79	
March 19	7 a. m.	28. 76	28	. 130	Cu. st.	5	NW.	2	NW.	2	78	

STORM No. 1, MARCH, 1859.

BAYFIELD, WISCONSIN.

Month and day.	Hour.	Barom'r corrected to 32° F.	Thermometer.	Force of vapor.	Cloudiness.	Motion of clouds.	Winds.	Relative humidity.	REMARKS.
March 13	2 p. m.	......	27	......	St. 5	NE. 3	NE. 3	......	Snow from 8 p. m. the 13th to 11 p. m. on the 14th; depth, 12 inches.
	9 p. m.	......	28	......	......	......	......	......	
March 14	7 a. m.	......	28	......	Nim. 10	......	NE. 5	......	
	2 p. m.	......	29	......	Nim. 10	......	NE. 6	......	
	9 p. m.	......	28	......	......	......	......	......	
March 15	7 a. m.	......	24	......	St. 4	......	NW. 2	......	
	2 p. m.	......	32	......	0	......	NW. 2	......	
	9 p. m.	......	25	......	......	......	......	......	
March 16	7 a. m.	......	23	......	Cir. cu. 3	NW. 2	NW. 1	......	
	2 p. m.	......	44	......	Cir. 3	SW. 2	SW. 3	......	
	9 p. m.	......	34	......	......	......	......	......	
March 17	7 a. m.	......	27	......	Cu. 6	SW. 3	SW. 2	......	
	2 p. m.	......	42	......	Cir. cu. 4	SW. 3	SW. 2	......	
	9 p. m.	......	30	......	......	......	......	......	
March 18	7 a. m.	......	26	......	Cu. 8	NW. 3	NW. 3	......	
	2 p. m.	......	29	......	Cu. 2	NW. 4	NW. 5	......	
	9 p. m.	......	27	......	......	......	......	......	
March 19	7 a. m.	......	22	......	0	0	NW. 1	......	

BAY CITY, WISCONSIN.

Month and day.	Hour.	Barom'r corrected to 32° F.	Thermometer.	Force of vapor.	Cloudiness.	Motion of clouds.	Winds.	Relative humidity.	REMARKS.
March 13	2 p. m.	......	28	......	Cir. st. 10	W. 1	E. 2	......	Snow from 7 p. m. the 13th to 10 p. m. on the 14th.; depth, 10 inches.
	9 p. m.	......	28	......	Fog 10	0	E. 2	......	
March 14	7 a. m.	......	28	......	Fog 10	0	NE. 4	......	
	2 p. m.	......	30	......	Fog 10	0	NE. 4	......	
	9 p. m.	......	28	......	10	0	NE. 3	......	
March 15	7 a. m.	......	22	......	None 0	0	NW. 2	......	
	2 p. m.	......	30	......	0	......	NW. 2	......	
	9 p. m.	......	20	......	0	......	S. 1	......	
March 16	7 a. m.	......	8	......	None 0	......	SE. 1	......	
	2 p. m.	......	48	......	Cir. 5	NE. 1	SW. 2	...	
	9 p. m.	......	28	......	None 0	0	S. 1	......	
March 17	7 a. m.	......	30	......	Cu. 5	NE. 1	SW. 2	......	
	2 p. m.	......	42	......	Cu. 5	NE. 1	SW. 2	......	
	9 p. m.	......	30	......	Cu. 3	E. 1	W. 2	......	
March 18	7 a. m.	......	26	......	Cu. 5	SW. 1	NE. 1	......	
	2 p. m.	......	30	......	Cu. 5	SW. 1	NE. 2	......	
	9 p. m.	......	22	......	Cu. 5	S. 1	N. 2	......	
March 19	7 a. m.	......	26	......	None 0	0	SW. 1	......	

BELOIT, WISCONSIN.

Month and day.	Hour.	Barom'r corrected to 32° F.	Thermometer.	Force of vapor.	Cloudiness.	Motion of clouds.	Winds.	Relative humidity.	REMARKS.
March 13	2 p. m.	29. 109	50	......	6	......	E. 3	......	13th. Rain in the night and on the following morning; amount, 0.75 inch.
	9 p. m.	29. 004	37	......	9	......	SE. 3	......	17th. Rain in the night; amount, 0. 325 inch.
March 14	7 a. m.	28. 508	48	......	9	......	W. 2	......	
	2 p. m.	29. 490	38	......	9	......	W. 3	......	
	9 p. m.	28. 460	34	......	9	......	W. 2	......	
March 15	7 a. m.	28. 666	30	......	5	......	W. 1	......	
	2 p. m.	28. 960	44	......	0	......	W. 3	......	
	9 p. m.	29. 149	30	......	0	......	W. 1	......	
March 16	7 a. m.	29. 047	34	......	0	......	SW. 2	......	
	2 p. m.	28. 986	60	......	4	......	S. 2	......	
	9 p. m.	28. 976	48	......	6	......	S. 2	......	
March 17	7 a. m.	28. 936	43	......	9	......	S. 1	......	
	2 p. m.	28. 934	40	......	9	......	N. 2	......	
	9 p. m.	28. 853	34	......	10	......	N. 2	......	
March 18	7 a. m.	28. 698	34	......	10	......	NW. 2	......	
	2 p. m.	28. 703	38	......	9	......	NW. 2	......	
	9 p. m.	28. 825	30	......	7	......	NW. 2	......	
March 19	7 a. m.	28. 956	24	......	0	......	W. 1	......	

STORM No. 1, MARCH, 1859.

KENOSHA, WISCONSIN.

Month and day.	Hour.	Barom'r corrected to 32° F.	Thermometer.	Force of vapor.	Cloudiness.		Motion of clouds.		Winds.		Relative humidity.	REMARKS.
March 13	2 p. m.	......	40½	......		0	....		E.	2	......	13th. Rain in the night.
	9 p. m.	......	38½	......		10	....		NE.	5	......	14th. Rain.
March 14	7 a. m.	29. 03	42	......		10	....		SE.	2	......	18th. Rain in the night.
	2 p. m.	28. 95	40	......		10	....		W.	5	......	19th. Rain in the morning.
	9 p. m.	......	35	......		10	....		W.	6	......	
March 15	7 a. m.	29. 16	33	......		10	....		W.	7	......	
	2 p. m.	29. 35	42	......		0	....		W.	7	......	
	9 p. m.	29. 56	35	......		0	....		W.	1	......	
March 16	7 a. m.	29. 60	35	......		0	....		SW.	1	......	
	2 p. m.	29. 50	50	......		0	....		S.	4	......	
	9 p. m.	......	44	......		0	....			0	......	
March 17	7 a. m.	29. 40	46	......		0	....		SW.	1	......	
	2 p. m.	......	57	......		10	....			0	......	
	9 p. m.	......	38	......		10	....		NE.	6	......	
March 18	7 a. m.	......	32	......		10	....		N.	6	......	
	2 p. m.	......	36	......		10	....		N.	2	......	
	9 p. m.	29. 16	31½	......		5	....		N.	4	......	
March 19	7 a. m.	29. 28	27	......		0	....		W.	4	......	

MADISON, WISCONSIN.

Month and day.	Hour.	Barom'r corrected to 32° F.	Thermometer.	Force of vapor.	Cloudiness.		Motion of clouds.		Winds.		Relative humidity.	REMARKS.
March 13	2 p. m.	29. 104	47	. 179		5	....		SE.	1	55	13th. Rain during night.
	9 p. m.	28. 884	38	. 173	Cu.	4	....		W.	1	73	14th. Rain and snow from 8 a. m.
March 14	7 a. m.	28. 405	40	. 257	Nim.	10	....		SW.	2	100	to 10 p. m.
	2 p. m.	28. 322	34	. 162	Nim.	10	....		SW.	3	80	17th. Snow during the day after
	9 p. m	28. 305	33	. 168	Nim.	10	....		SW.	3	89	11 a. m.
March 15	7 a. m.	28. 649	30	. 111		9	....		NW.	4	67	18th. Snow at 7 a. m.; amount in
	2 p. m.	28. 858	40	. 097	Cir.	1	....		NW.	4	39	water, 0.32 inch.
	9 p. m.	29. 057	34	. 108		0	....		W.	2	53	
March 16	7 a. m.	29. 035	33	. 155	St.	1	....		SE.	3	79	
	2 p. m.	28. 873	58	. 178	Cu. st.	9	....		SE.	3	37	
	9 p. m.	28. 382	45	. 228	Cu. st.	9	....		SW.	3	76	
March 17	7 a. m.	28. 882	39	. 160	Nim.	10	....		NW.	3	64	
	2 p. m.	28. 841	33	. 196	Nim.	10	....		NW.	2	100	
	9 p. m.	28. 326	31	. 174	Nim.	10	....		NW.	3	100	
March 18	7 a. m.	28. 637	32	. 155		10	....			4	89	
	2 p. m.	28. 609	35	. 108		9	....			5	53	
	9 p. m.	28. 711	27	. 099	St.	1	....			4	64	
March 19	7 a. m.	28. 944	28	. 099	St.	1	....			4	64	

MANITOWOC, WISCONSIN.

Month and day.	Hour.	Barom'r corrected to 32° F.	Thermometer.	Force of vapor.	Cloudiness.		Motion of clouds.		Winds.		Relative humidity.	REMARKS.
March 13	2 p. m.	28. 060	36	......	Cir.	5	W.	3	NE.	5	......	13th. Hail from 9 to 10 p. m.;
	9 p. m.	27. 113	35	......	Cu.	10	....		NE.	4	......	changed to rain and continued
March 14	7 a. m.	27. 590	36	......	Cu. st.	10	....		E.	5	......	till 1 p. m. on the 14th; thunder
	2 p. m.	27. 300	43	......	Cu.	10	....		S.	7	......	storm on the 14th, from 11 to
	9 p. m.	27. 320	36	......	Cu.	5	....		W.	2	......	11.15 a. m., SE.; snow in the
March 15	7 a. m.	27. 570	29	......	Cu.	5	....		NW.	4	......	night; depth, 0.10 inch.
	2 p. m.	27. 820	42	......	Cu.	5	....		NW.	3	......	16th. Lunar halo in the evening.
	9 p. m.	27. 109	35	......		0	....		W.	1	......	17th. Rain from 2 30 to 4 p. m.;
March 16	7 a. m.	27. 116	32	......		0	....		SE.	3	......	then snow and rain in the night,
	2 p. m.	27. 100	44	......	Cir.	5	SW.	2	S.	6	......	and snow till 10 a. m. on the
	9 p. m.	27. 980	44	......	St.	5	....		S.	1	......	18th.
March 17	7 a. m.	27. 850	42	......	Cir. st.	10	SW.	4	N.	1	......	
	2 p. m.	27. 860	41	......	Cu. st.	10	....		NW.	3	......	
	9 p. m.	27. 840	37	......	Nim.	10	....		NW.	2	......	
March 18	7 a. m.	27. 580	33	......	Nim.	10	....		N.	5	......	
	2 p. m.	27. 540	38	......	Cu.	10	....		NW.	6	......	
	9 p. m.	27. 630	33	......	Cir. st.	5	N.	3	NW.	7	......	
March 19	7 a. m.	27. 770	29	......	Cu.	5	....		NW.	5	......	

STORM No. 1, MARCH, 1859.

MILWAUKEE, WISCONSIN.*

Month and day.	Hour.	Barom'r corrected to 32° F.	Thermometer.	Force of vapor.	Cloudiness.	Motion of clouds.	Winds.	Relative humidity.	REMARKS.
March 13	2 p. m.	29.44	38	------	3	----------	NE. 2	------	Storm on the 14th; amount in water, 0.61 inch.
	9 p. m.	29.27	36	------	6	----------	NNE. 4	------	
March 14	7 a. m.	28.83	39	------	10	----------	NE. 1	------	
	2 p. m.	28.68	39	------	9	----------	W. 1	------	
	9 p. m.	28.61	34	------	9	----------	SW. 2	------	
March 15	7 a. m.	28.91	31	------	7	----------	NW. 1	------	
	2 p. m.	29.10	41	------	1	----------	NW. 2	------	
	9 p. m.	29.31	33	------	0	----------	NW. 0	------	
March 16	7 a. m.	29.36	36	------	0	----------	S. 1	------	
	2 p. m.	29.26	47	------	1	----------	SE. 2	------	
	9 p. m.	29.20	50	------	2	----------	SW. 1	------	
March 17	7 a. m.	29.14	47	------	5	----------	SW. 1	------	
	2 p. m.	29.09	49	------	8	----------	NE. 1	------	
	9 p. m.	29.00	36	------	8	----------	N. 2	------	
March 18	7 a. m.	28.87	32	------	10	----------	N. 2	------	
	2 p. m.	29.81	36	------	10	----------	N. 1	------	
	9 p. m.	28.90	31	------	3	----------	NW. 1	------	
March 19	7 a. m.	28.97	30	------	0	----------	NW. 1	------	

MILWAUKEE, WISCONSIN. †

Month and day.	Hour.	Barom'r corrected to 32° F.	Thermometer.	Force of vapor.	Cloudiness.	Motion of clouds.	Winds.	Relative humidity.	REMARKS.
March 13	2 p. m.	------	39	------	7	----------	NE --------	------	14th. Rain and snow at intervals all day.
	9 p. m.	------	36	------	10	----------	NE --------	------	18th. Snow.
March 14	7 a. m.	------	34	------	10	Rain & snow	SE --------	------	
	2 p. m.	------	39	------	10	Rain & snow	S --------	------	
	9 p. m.	------	33	------	10	Rain & snow	SW --------	------	
March 15	7 a. m.	------	32	------	10	----------	SW --------	------	
	2 p. m.	------	39	------	10	----------	SW --------	------	
	9 p. m.	------	33	------	3	----------	SW --------	------	
March 16	7 a. m.	------	32	------	4	----------	SE --------	------	
	2 p. m.	------	36	------	2	----------	SE --------	------	
	9 p. m.	------	34	------	1	----------	SE --------	------	
March 17	7 a. m.	------	38	------	10	----------	SW --------	------	
	2 p. m.	------	39	------	9	----------	SW --------	------	
	9 p. m.	------	33	------	10	----------	NE --------	------	
March 18	7 a. m.	------	34	------	Snow 10	----------	NW --------	------	
	2 p. m.	------	36	------	Snow 10	----------	NW --------	------	
	9 p. m.	------	30	------	10	----------	NW --------	------	
March 19	7 a. m.	------	28	------	7	----------	NE --------	------	

NEW DANEMORA, WISCONSIN.

Month and day.	Hour.	Barom'r corrected to 32° F.	Thermometer.	Force of vapor.	Cloudiness.	Motion of clouds.	Winds.	Relative humidity.	REMARKS.
March 13	Noon ...	------	38.5	------	9	----------	------------	------	13th. Rain and snow from 10.30 to 12 p. m.
	6 p. m.	------	41	------	9	----------	------------	------	14th. Snow in the night; depth, 2.00 inches.
March 14	6 a. m.	------	34.5	------	10	----------	------------	------	
	Noon ...	------	35.5	------	10	----------	------------	------	
	6 p. m.	------	33	------	10	----------	W. 5	------	
March 15	6 a. m.	------	24.5	------	2	----------	------------	------	
	Noon ...	------	39	------	2	----------	------------	------	
	6 p. m.	------	32.5	------	2	----------	------------	------	
March 16	6 a. m.	------	26.5	------	5	----------	------------	------	
	Noon ...	------	60	------	2	----------	------------	------	
	6 p. m.	------	50.5	------	2	----------	------------	------	
March 17	6 a. m.	------	34.5	------	------------	----------	------------	------	
	Noon ...	------	40	------	10	----------	NW --------	------	
	6 p. m.	------	38.5	------	------------	----------	------------	------	
March 18	6 a. m.	------	29.5	------	9	----------	------------	------	
	Noon ...	------	36.5	------	2	----------	NW --------	------	
	6 p. m.	------	31	------	2	----------	NW --------	------	
March 19	6 a. m.	------	20	------	------------	----------	------------	------	

* Winkler, observer.

† Pomeroy, observer.

STORM No. 1, MARCH, 1859.

PLATTEVILLE, WISCONSIN.

Month and day.	Hour.	Barom'r corrected to 32° F.	Thermometer.	Force of vapor.	Cloudiness.		Motion of clouds.		Winds.		Relative humidity.	REMARKS.
March 13	2 p. m.	......	50	......	Cir. st.	10	E.	4	E.	4	......	Snow storm from 5.45 p. m. the 13th, to the 14th at night; am't, in water, 0. 87 inch. 17th. Snow storm commenced at 7 a. m. and ended in the night; amount in water, 0. 331 inch. 18th and 19th. Faint aurora in the evening.
	9 p. m.	......	39	......	Nim.	10	E.	4	E.	4	......	
March 14	7 a. m.	......	45	......	Nim.	10	SE.	2	SE.	2	......	
	2 p. m.	......	39	......	Nim.	10	S.	3	S.	2	......	
	9 p. m.	......	30	......	St.	10	SW.	2	SW.	2	......	
March 15	7 a. m.	......	26	......		0	....		NW.	3	......	
	2 p. m.	......	42	......		0	....		NW.	2	......	
	9 p. m.	......	35	......		0	....		NW.	1	......	
March 16	7 a. m.	......	36	......		0	....		SE.	1	......	
	2 p. m.	......	59	......	Cir.	2	W.	1	SE.	4	......	
	9 p. m.	......	48	......	Cir. st.	9	S.	3	SE.	3	......	
March 17	7 a. m.	......	42	......	Nim.	10	NW.	2	NW.	2	......	
	2 p. m.	......	46	......	Nim.	10	N.	3	NW.	2	......	
	9 p. m.	......	33	......	Nim.	10	N.	2	N.	2	......	
March 18	7 a. m.	......	28	......	Cir. st.	8	NW.	2	NW.	3	......	
	2 p. m.	......	35	......	Cir. st.	5	NW.	2	NW.	3	......	
	9 p. m.	......	28	......		0	....		NW.	2	......	
March 19	7 a. m.	......	22	......		0	....		NW.	2	......	

WAUSAU, WISCONSIN.

Month and day.	Hour.	Barom'r corrected to 32° F.	Thermometer.	Force of vapor.	Cloudiness.		Motion of clouds.		Winds.		Relative humidity.	REMARKS.
March 13	2 p. m.	......	33	......	Cir. cu.	2	SE.	2	NE.	3	......	Storm commenced at 8.30—? the 13th, and ended at 2 a. m. on the 15th; amount, in water, 3. 50 inches. 17th and 18th. Overcast.
	9 p. m.	......	30	......		0	....		....		......	
March 14	7 a. m.	......	36	......	Nim.	10		0	NE.	2	......	
	2 p. m.	......	37	......	Nim.	10		4	E.	5	......	
	9 p. m.	......	31	......		0	....		S.	6	......	
March 15	7 a. m.	......	27	......		8	E.	3	W.	5	......	
	2 p. m.	......	38	......	Cir. cu.	2	S.	2	W.	5	......	
	9 p. m.	......	25	......		0	....		SW.	2	......	
March 16	7 a. m.	......	31	......		0		0	E.	2	......	
	2 p. m.	......	57	......	Cir.	2	W.	6	E.	6	......	
	9 p. m.	......	36	......		0	....		....		......	
March 17	7 a. m.	......	37	......	Nim.	9		0	NW.	1	......	
	2 p. m.	......	43	......	Nim.	10		2	NW.	2	......	
	9 p. m.	......	37	......	Cu. st.	5	S.	3	W.	1	......	
March 18	7 a. m.	......	30	......		8	....		N.	4	......	
	2 p. m.	......	29	......		8	S.	3	N.	3	......	
	9 p. m.	......	26	......		0	....		N.	3	......	
March 19	7 a. m.	......	28	......	Cir. st.	8	S.	2	NW.	3	......	

WAUKESHA, WISCONSIN.

Month and day.	Hour.	Barom'r corrected to 32° F.	Thermometer.	Force of vapor.	Cloudiness.		Motion of clouds.		Winds.		Relative humidity.	REMARKS.
March 13	2 p. m.	29. 26	48	. 236	Cir. st.	3	....		....		70	14th. Rain.
	9 p. m.	29. 18	35	. 162	Cir.	8	....		....		80	
March 14	7 a. m.	28. 60	42	. 177	Nim.	10	....		....		65	
	2 p. m.	28. 46	35	. 162	Nim.	10	....		....		80	
	9 p. m.	28. 54	37	. 116	Nim.	10	....		....		53	
March 15	7 a. m.	28. 77	30	. 148	Cir.	10	....		....		89	
	2 p. m.	28. 93	41	. 147	....		....		....		57	
	9 p. m.	29. 15	35	. 162	Cu.	4	....		....		80	
March 16	7 a. m.	28. 87	32	. 143	Cir. cu.	8	NE.	3	....		79	
	2 p. m.	28. 98	44	. 196		0	....		....		68	
	9 p. m.	29. 03	37	. 178	Cu.	10	....		....		81	
March 17	7 a. m.	28. 99	34	. 155	Cu. cir.	8	NE.	2	....		79	
	2 p. m.	29. 03	48	. 260	Cu. st.	10	....		....		78	
	9 p. m.	28. 90	37	. 136	Cu. st.	3	....		....		62	
March 18	7 a. m.	28. 72	32	. 162	Nim.	10	....		....		89	
	2 p. m.	28. 77	46	. 238	Cir.	10	....		....		77	
	9 p. m.	28. 77	39	. 110	Nim.	10	....		....		46	
March 19	7 a. m.	28. 93	32	. 162	St.	3	....		....		89	

STORM No. 1, MARCH, 1859.

BURLINGTON, IOWA.

Month and day.	Hour.	Barom'r corrected to 32° F.	Thermometer.	Force of vapor.	Cloudiness.		Motion of clouds.		Winds.		Relative humidity.	REMARKS.
March 13	2 p. m.	......	62	......	Cir.	8	NE.	2	SE.	3	......	13th. Rain, snow, and hail occasionally.
	9 p. m.	......	54	......	Nim.	10	....		SE		......	
March 14	7 a. m.	......	41	......	Cir. st.	10	NE.	5	SW.	6	......	14th. Storm from 1 to 9 p. m.; high gale; storm scud near the earth, driving NE.; upper strata E.
	2 p. m.	......	36	......	Cir. cu.	10	NE.	3	SW.	6	......	
	9 p. m.	......	36	......		10	....		NW.	4	......	
March 15	7 a. m	......	32	......		0	....		NW.	5	......	16th. Commenced raining at 7 a. m., and rained and snowed until 8 p. m. of the 17th; am't, 2 inches.
	2 p. m.	......	48	......		0	....		NW.	4	......	
	9 p. m.	......	42	......		0	....		NW.	1	......	
March 16	7 a. m.	......	44	......		6	....		SE.	3	......	
	2 p. m.	......	66	......	Cir. cu.	5	NE.	3	S.	4	......	
	9 p. m.	......	56	......	St.	8	....		S.	1	......	
March 17	7 a. m.	......	50	......	St. Nim.	10	....		NW.	2	......	
	2 p. m.	......	38	......	Cir. cu.	10	....		NW.	3	......	
	9 p. m.	......	34	......		0	....		NW.	5	......	
March 18	7 a. m.	......	30	......	Cir. st., cu.	0	....		NW.	3	......	
	2 p. m.	......	38	......	Cir. cu.	9	....		NW.	4	......	
	9 p. m.	......	34	......	Cir. cu.	10	....		NW.	3	......	
March 19	7 a m.	......	26	......		0	....		NW.	2	......	

DUBUQUE, IOWA.

Month and day.	Hour.	Barom'r corrected to 32° F.	Thermometer.	Force of vapor.	Cloudiness.		Motion of clouds.		Winds.		Relative humidity.	REMARKS.
March 13	2 p m.	29.24	51	......	Nim.	10	SE.	4	SF.	4	......	13th. Slight rain at 7 p. m.; snow and sleet during the night.
	9 p. m.	29.14	42	......	Nim.	10	W.	3	SE.	2	......	
March 14	7 a. m.	29.63	42	......	Cir. st.	8	S.	5	SE.	2	......	17th. Storm from 8 a. m. to 6 p. m.
	2 p. m.	29.61	37	......	Cir. st.	9	S.	4	SE.	3	......	
	9 p m.	29.69	34	......	Nim.	10	....		S.	2	......	
March 16	7 a. m.	29.13	32	......	Cir. cu.	1	N.	1	SE.	3	......	
	2 p. m.	29.32	45	......	Cir.	2	W.	3	W.	4	......	
	9 p. m.	29.37	36	......	Cir.	6	W.	2	NW.	2	......	
March 16	7 a. m.	29.26	42	......	Cir.	3	NW.	1	SE.	3	......	
	2 p. m.	29.13	60	......	Cir. st.	9	SW.	4	S.	4	......	
	9 p m	29.15	54	......	Nim.	10	....		SW.	2	......	
March 17	7 a. m.	29.20	40	......	Nim.	10	SE.	4	NW.	4	......	
	2 p. m.	29.16	33	......	Nim.	10	SW.	4	NW.	2	......	
	9 p. m.	29.16	36	......	Hazy		....		NE.	2	......	
March 18	7 a. m.	29.02	30	......		0	....		N.	4	......	
	2 p. m.	29.02	35	......		0	....		N.	4	......	
	9 p. m.	29.13	32	......		0	....		N.	2	......	
March 19	7 a. m.	29.25	24	......		0	....		N.	4	......	

BELLEVUE, IOWA.

Month and day.	Hour.	Barom'r corrected to 32° F.	Thermometer.	Force of vapor.	Cloudiness.		Motion of clouds.		Winds.		Relative humidity.	REMARKS.
March 13	2 p. m.	......	52	......	Cu. st.	9	....		E.	4	......	13th. Rain at 7 p. m.; shower at 9 p. m., with thunder and diffused lightning from the S.; rain and snow during the night.
	9 p. m.	......	40	......	Nim.	10	....		E.	4	......	
March 14	7 a. m.	......	42	......	Nim.	10	....		SW.	5	......	
	2 p. m.	......	35	......	Nim.	10	....		SW.	4	......	
	9 p. m.	......	34	......	Nim.	10	....		SW.	3	......	14th. Snow and rain during the day; amount in water, 1.20 inch.
March 15	7 a. m.	......	32	......		0	....		NW.	3	......	
	2 p m.	......	45	......		0	....		NW.	4	......	17th. Snow and rain at 7.30 a. m., during the day and in the night; amount in water, 0.55 inch.
	9 p. m.	......	28	......		0	....		NW.	3	......	
March 16	7 a. m.	......	40	......		0	....		SE.	3	......	
	2 p. m.	......	61	......	Cir st.	8	....		S.	5	......	
	9 p. m.	......	54	......		8	....		S.	2	......	
March 17	7 a m.	......	44	......	Nim.	10	....		NW.	3	......	
	2 p. m.	......	34	......	Nim.	10	....		NW.	4	......	
	9 p. m.	......	34	......		10	....		NW.	3	......	
March 18	7 a. m.	......	34	......	Cu. st.	9	....		NW.	4	......	
	2 p. m.	......	37	......	Cu. st.	10	....		NW.	3	......	
	9 p. m.	......	30	......		10	....		NW.	3	......	
March 19	7 a. m.	......	33	......	St.	2	....		NW.	2	......	

STORM No. 1, MARCH, 1859.

BORDER PLAINS, IOWA.

Month and day.	Hour.	Barom'r corrected to 32° N.	Thermometer.	Force of vapor.	Cloudiness.		Motion of clouds.		Winds.		Relative humidity.	REMARKS.
March 13	2 p. m.	28.54	53	......	Cu. st.	10	SW.	4	E.	3	......	14th. Rain from midnight till 8 p. m ; amount in water, 0.75 inch.
	9 p. m.	28.41	44	......		0	....		E.	4	......	
March 14	7 a. m.	28.08	35	......	Nim.	10	....		SW.	3	......	
	2 p. m.	28.08	33	......	Nim.	10	....		NW.	6	......	
	9 p. m.	28.45	28	......	Cir. st.	9	....		NW.	6	......	
March 15	7 a. m.	28.73	24	......		0	....		NW.	1	......	
	2 p. m.	28.77	43	......		0	....		S.	1	......	
	9 p. m.	28.64	39	......		0	....		SE.	4	......	
March 16	7 a. m.	28.47	41	......		0	....		SE.	4	......	
	2 p. m.	28.53	58	......		0	....		S.	3	......	
	9 p. m.	28.62	36	......		9	....		NW.	3	......	
March 17	7 a. m.	28.73	37	......	Nim.	10	....		NW.	3	......	
	2 p. m.	28.72	43	......	Nim.	10	....		NW.	4	......	
	9 p. m.	28.72	31	......	Nim.	10	....		NW.	3	......	
March 18	7 a. m.	28.70	29	......	Cir. cu.	9	....		NW.	4	......	
	2 p. m.	28.78	38	......	Cir. cu.	8	....		NW.	4	......	
	9 p. m.	28.75	27	......	Cir. cu.	9	....		NW.	4	......	
March 19	7 a. m.	28.81	21	......	Nim.	9	....		NW.	1	......	

FAIRFIELD, IOWA.

Month and day.	Hour.	Barom'r corrected to 32° N.	Thermometer.	Force of vapor.	Cloudiness.		Motion of clouds.		Winds.		Relative humidity.	REMARKS.
March 13	2 p m.	27.03	59	.165		10	....		SE.	4	33	13th. Storm in the night, commencing at 9.30 p m.
	9 p. m.	26 95	53	.295		10	....		SE.	2	73	
March 14	7 a m.	26.78	36	.129		10	....		SW.	4	61	14th. Storm from 10 a. m. till noon.
	2 p. m.	26.74	35	.142		10	....		SW.	3	70	
	9 p. m.	27.04	32	.106		10	....		W.	5	58	15th. Storm from 5 to 7 p. m ; total depth of snow, 2 inches.
March 15	7 a m.	27.25	33	.159		0		0	NW.	3	80	
	2 p. m.	27.25	47	.112		0		0	NW.	2	34	Snow storm on the 16th and 17th; depth of snow, 4 inches.
	9 p. m.	27.28	38	.125		0		0		0	54	
March 16	7 a m.	27.21	44	.151		0		0	SE.	4	52	
	2 p. m.	27.02	64	.124	Cir.	5	....		SW.	4	21	
	9 p. m.	27.04	54	.157		10	....		SW.	2	38	
March 17	7 a. m.	27.07	39	.131	Rain	10	....		NW.	2	55	
	2 p. m.	27.09	33	.150	Snow	10	....		NE.	3	80	
	9 p. m.	27.18	33	.131		10	....		NW.	2	70	
March 18	7 a. m.	27.18	29	.123		5	....		NW.	4	77	
	2 p. m.	27.14	35	.142	Cu.	8	....		NW.	4	70	
	9 p. m.	27.17	32	.125	Cu.	5		0	NW.	4	69	
March 19	7 a. m.	27.29	32	.106		0		0	NW.	1	58	

FORT MADISON, IOWA.

Month and day.	Hour.	Barom'r corrected to 32° N.	Thermometer.	Force of vapor.	Cloudiness.		Motion of clouds.		Winds.		Relative humidity.	REMARKS.
March 13	12 m.	......	59	......	Cir.	3	S.	2	E.	2	......	13th. Shower at 7 p. m.; amount, 0.20 inch.
	7 p. m.	......	54	......	Nim.	10	S.	1	SW.	2	......	
March 14	6 a. m.	......	40	......	Cir. st.	10	SW.	3	SW.	2	......	14th. Rain and melted snow, 0.04 inch.
	12 m.	......	36	......	Nim.	10	SE.	2	SW.	3	......	
	7 p. m.	......	34	......	Nim.	10	NW.	2	NW.	3	......	17th. Rain and snow from 6.30 a. m. to 5 p. m.; amount in water, 1.19 inch.
March 15	6 a. m.	......	29	......		0		0	NW.	2	......	
	12 m.	......	40	......		0		0	W.	1	......	
	7 p. m.	......	39	......		0		0	SW.	1	......	
March 16	6 a. m.	......	38	......		0		0	SE.	1	......	
	12 p. m.	......	62	......	Cir.	5	SW.	1	SW.	2	......	
	7 p. m.	......	54	......	Cir.	8	S.	1	SE.	2	......	
March 17	6 a. m.	......	49	......	Nim.	9	SW.	1	SW.	1	......	
	12 p. m.	......	38	......	Nim.	10	N.	3	NW.	2	......	
	7 p m.	......	32	......	Nim.	10	N.	3	NW.	4	......	
March 18	6 a. m.	......	28	......	Nim.	10	N.	1	NW.	3	......	
	12 p m.	......	32	......	Cir. cu.	10	NW.	2	NW.	3	......	
	7 p. m.	......	32	......	Cir. st.	9	N.	1	NW.	3	......	
March 19	6 a. m.	......	22	......		0		0	NW.	1	......	

STORM No. 1, MARCH, 1859.

MUSCATINE, IOWA.

Month and day.	Hour.	Barom'r corrected to 32° F.	Thermometer.	Force of vapor.	Cloudiness.	Motion of clouds.	Winds.	Relative humidity.	REMARKS.
March 13	2 p. m.	29.26	60	.256	St. 5	SW. 2	SE. 2	61	13th. Storm commenced with rain at 5 p. m. and ended with snow at 4 p. m. on the 14th; amount of rain, 0.05 inch; depth of snow, 0.45 inch.
	9 p. m.	29.23	54	.321	10	....	SE. 1	86	
March 14	7 a. m.	28.85	38	.309	10	....	SE. 2	85	
	2 p. m.	28.81	35	.262	10	....	SW. 3	84	
	9 p. m.	28.97	34	.218	10	....	SW. 3	76	
March 15	7 a. m.	29.31	30	.262	0	....	SW. 2	84	Rain and snow from 8 a. m. the 17th to 4 a. m on the 18th; amount of rain, 0.40 inch; depth of snow 3 inches.
	2 p. m.	29.49	44	.178	0	....	W. 2	81	
	9 p. m.	29.48	28	.212	0	....	W. 0	82	
March 16	7 a. m.	29.43	40	.203	0	....	S. 1	82	
	2 p. m.	29.31	61	.270	Cu. st. 5	S. 2	S. 2	72	
	9 p. m.	29.32	52	.283	10	....	S. 1	78	
March 17	7 a. m.	29.32	42	.285	10	....	S. 1	85	
	2 p. m.	29.27	35	.228	10	....	N. 2	76	
	9 p. m.	29.28	32	.235	10	....	N. 3	91	
March 18	7 a. m.	29.19	24	.162	0	....	N. 3	80	
	2 p. m.	29.19	33	.162	Nim. 8	SW. 2	NW. 3	80	
	9 p. m.	29.30	32	.162	Nim. 8	SW. 3	NW. 2	80	
March 19	7 a. m.	29.40	23	.143	0	....	NW. 1	79	

PLEASANT PLAIN, IOWA.

Month and day.	Hour.	Barom'r corrected to 32° F.	Thermometer.	Force of vapor.	Cloudiness.	Motion of clouds.	Winds.	Relative humidity.	REMARKS.
March 13	2 p. m.	......	58	......	Cir. 1	S. 4	SE. 3	......	13th. Sleet.
	9 p. m.	......	52	......	9	....	S. 2	......	16th. Snow; amount in water, 0.70 inches.
March 14	7 a. m.	......	35	......	Nim. 10	SW. 2	SW. 4	......	
	2 p. m.	......	36	......	Nim. 10	SW. 3	SW. 3	......	
	9 p. m.	......	34	......	8	....	SW. 2	......	
March 15	7 a. m.	......	28	......	0	....	SW. 2	......	
	2 p. m.	......	55	......	0	....	W. 2	......	
	9 p. m.	......	36	......	0	....	W. 1	......	
March 16	7 a. m.	......	40	......	0	....	S. 3	......	
	2 p. m.	......	65	......	Cu. 10	SW. 3	S. 2	......	
	9 p. m.	......	55	......	Cir. 10	SW. 3	SW. 2	......	
March 17	7 a. m.	......	38	......	Nim. 10	SW. 2	SW. 2	......	
	2 p. m.	......	32	......	Nim. 10	NW. 2	NW. 3	......	
	9 p. m.	......	32	......	Nim. 10	NE. 2	NE. 2	......	
March 18	7 a. m.	......	28	......	Cir. 4	NW. 3	NW. 3	......	
	2 p. m.	......	38	......	Cir. 10	NW. 2	NW. 3	......	
	9 p. m.	......	30	......	Cir. 8	NW. 2	W. 3	......	
March 19	7 a. m.	......	23	......	Cir. 2	S. 2	S. 2	......	

ROSSVILLE, IOWA.

Month and day.	Hour.	Barom'r corrected to 32° F.	Thermometer.	Force of vapor.	Cloudiness.	Motion of clouds.	Winds.	Relative humidity.	REMARKS.
March 13	2 p. m.	......	46.2	......	8	....	E. 4	......	Storm commenced at 5.36 p. m. the 13th; at 9 a. m. the 14th snowing fast and large flakes; storm ended at 10.20 a. m.; snow at 5 p. m.; amount in water, 1.20 inch.
	9 p. m.	......	39	......	10	....	E. 3	......	
March 14	7 a. m.	......	35.2	......	10	....	N. 3	......	
	2 p. m.	......	00.0	......	10	....	SW. 2	......	
	9 p. m.	......	29.1	......	10	....	W. 5	......	
March 15	7 a. m.	......	22.9	......	1	....	W. 4	......	
	2 p. m.	......	37.1	......	0	....	W. 4	......	16th. Very dull; halo at 11 a. m.
	9 p. m.	......	30	......	0	....	0	......	
March 16	7 a. m.	......	35.3	......	1	....	S. 3	......	
	2 p. m.	......	59	......	2	....	SW. 4	......	
	9 p. m.	......	47.9	......	10	....	W. 1	......	
March 17	7 a. m.	......	35.1	......	10	....	NW. 3	......	
	2 p. m.	......	36.7	......	10	....	NW. 3	......	
	9 p. m.	......	34.1	......	10	....	NW. 2	......	
March 18	7 a. m.	......	28.8	......	6	....	NW. 3	......	
	2 p. m.	......	32.3	......	8	....	NW. 4	......	
	9 p. m.	......	27.5	......	1	....	NW. 3	......	
March 19	7 a. m.	......	20.6	......	0	....	NW. 3	......	

STORM No. 1, MARCH, 1859.

BEAVER BAY, MINNESOTA.*

Month and day.	Hour.	Barom'r corrected to 32° F.	Thermometer.	Force of vapor.	Cloudiness.	Motion of clouds.	Winds.	Relative humidity.
March 13	8 a. m.	29. 485	34	. 139	------------	----------	N. 1 to 3	83
	12 m.	------	------	------	------------	----------	NE. 2 to 3	------
	2 p. m.	29. 49	28	. 117	Nim., Z. M. 9 Cir. st. H. 1	NE. 2 --------	NE. 2	76. 8
	9 p. m.	29. 42	28	. 127	Nim. 9	----------	NE. 3	82. 7
March 14	7 a. m.	29. 07	28. 5	. 156	Nim. 10	----------	NE. 3	100
	2 p. m.	28. 75	31	. 174	Nim, D. 9	NE. 1	NE. 2	100
	9 p. m.	28. 80	27. 5	. 141	Nim. 9	----------	N. 2	94. 1
March 15	7 a. m.	28. 87	22. 5	. 112	Cir. st., D. 8	N. 1	N. 1	93. 1
	2 p. m.	29. 04	40	. 128	0	----------	W. 1	51. 7
	9 p. m.	29. 18	26. 5	. 135	Cir. M. 1	NW. 1	N. 1	94
March 16	7 a. m.	29. 14	25	. 131	Cir. Z. 2	SW. 2	N. 1	96. 8
	2 p. m.	28. 97	36. 5	. 163	0	----------	NNE. 2	75. 6
	9 p. m.	29. 02	33	. 168	Cir. Z. 5 St. H. 2	SW. 2 --------	Calm. ------	89. 3
March 17	7 a. m.	29. 11	28	. 148	Cir. Z. 1 St. H. 1	W. 2 --------	W. 0	97. 1
	2 p. m.	29. 03	37	. 136	Cir. Z. 1 Cir. st. H. 2	SW. 2 --------	SW. 2	61. 9
	9 p. m.	29. 09	34. 5	. 134	Cir. cu. Z. 3 St. H. 3	NW. 2 --------	W. 1	66. 9
March 18	7 a. m.	29. 11	26	. 109	Nim. Z. 5 St. H. 2	N. 1 --------	N. 0	75. 7
	2 p. m.	29. 06	33. 5	. 135	Cu. H. 1	N. 2	N. 2	70. 7
	9 p. m.	29. 15	25. 5	. 112	Cu. M. 5	N. 6	N. 3	81. 2
March 19	7 a. m.	29. 19	22	. 069	St. H. 1	----------	N. 1	58. 4

REMARKS.

Snow from 8½ p. m. the 13th to 2 p. m. on the 14th; amount in water, 0. 55 inch; recommenced at 6 p. m. the 14th, and ended in the night; amount in water, 0. 184 inch.

17th. At 10 a. m. bar. 29. 11, ther. 35°, wind SW. 2, cloudiness 2, SW. 1; diffuse cirrus; solar halo of the ordinary size, 45°, and colors, accompanied with an arc; the diameter of the halo, resting tangentially on the upper limb at their junction; the light is equal to a bright parhelion; at 12 m. the whole was distinct, with a bright parhelion in addition on the lower limb of the halo; gradually faded away at about 3 p. m.; at sunset ther. 40°, bar. 29.05, cloudiness 5, NW. cir., wind W. 0.

18th. 8. 30 p. m. clouds over the lake, apparently 10 miles off, move from N. to S. 10° in forty seconds of time, 2⅔ miles per minute; but assuming the clouds to be but 5 miles off, their velocity is 75 miles per hour; the surface wind rates at 3 or 30 miles per hour; the 9 p. m. observations apply to this state of winds and clouds since the 15th; flakes of snow at 6 a. m.; amount in water, 0. 001 inch.

BURLINGTON, MINNESOTA.

Month and day.	Hour.	Barom'r corrected to 32° F.	Thermometer.	Force of vapor.	Cloudiness.	Motion of clouds.	Winds.	Relative humidity.
March 13	2 p. m.	------	33	------	Cr. st., cr. cu. 7	W. 2	E ------------	------
	9 p. m.	------	27	------	Nim. 10	3	NE ------------	------
March 14	7 a. m.	------	29	------	Nim. 10	3	E ------------	------
	2 p. m.	------	33	------	Nim. 10	3	E ------------	------
	9 p. m.	------	28	------	Cu. 10	W. 1	E ------------	------
March 15	7 a. m.	------	22	------	Cir. 3	E. 1	W ------------	------
	2 p. m.	------	38	------	0	1	W ------------	------
	9 p. m.	------	24	------	Cir. 2	E. 1	W ------------	------
March 16	7 a. m.	------	24	------	Cr. cu., cr. st. 3	E. 2	E ------------	------
	2 p. m.	------	39	------	0	2	E ------------	------
	9 p. m.	------	32	------	Cir. cu. 5	E. 1	W ------------	------
March 17	7 a. m.	------	26	------	Cir. & cu. 3	E. 1	W ------------	------
	2 p. m.	------	45	------	Cir. 1	E. 1	W ------------	------
	9 p. m.	------	30	------	Cr. st., cr. cu. 4	E. 1	W ------------	------
March 18	7 a. m.	------	27	------	Cu. 9	E. 1	W ------------	------
	2 p. m.	------	35	------	Cir. st. 1	E. 1	W ------------	------
	9 p. m.	------	24	------	Cir. 1	S. 1	N ------------	------
March 19	7 a. m.	------	16	------	St. 1	----------	------------	------

Snow from 9 p. m. the 13th to 6 p. m. on the 14th; depth of snow, 5. 25 inches.

16. Dark singular clouds at 7 a. m. in the N. and NE., and several kinds cir., cir. st., and cu. in different parts of the horizon, all moving to the E.; a very rapid wind a little N. of E.; good breeze at 8 a. m.; sky nearly clear; 9 a. m. sky nearly covered with clouds, cir. cu. secondary forms, moving E. rapidly; 10 a. m. only one small cloud, and that a very curious one; at noon sky perfectly clear; 2 p. m. clear; 4 p. m. sky all cloudy, cu., looks like rain; 6 p. m. nearly clear, cir. st. various forms; 9 p. m. about one-half cloudy, cir. and cu. clouds moving E.; ther. from 25° to 39°, and down to 32°.

18th. 7 a. m. clouds very dark, moving E.; 9 a. m. nearly clear, clouds cir.; at noon dry cir.; 4 p. m. clear; 6 p. m. little dry cu.

19th. 7 a. m. one small cloud in the SE. stratus; 9 a. m. perfectly clear; at noon clear, wind S.

*Clark, observer.

NOTE.—Abbreviations: Z, zenith; M, midway between zenith and horizon; H, horizon; D, diffused.

STORM No. 1, MARCH, 1859.

BEAVER BAY, MINNESOTA.*

Month and day.	Hour.	Barom'r corrected to 32° F.	Thermometer.	Force of vapor.	Cloudiness.	Motion of clouds.	Winds.	Relative humidity.	REMARKS.
March 13	2 p. m.		34	.196				100	
	9 p. m.		26	.141				100	
March 14	7 a. m.		28	.153				100	
	2 p. m.		30	.167				100	
	9 p. m.		26	.141				100	
March 15	7 a. m.		20	.108				100	
	2 p. m.		44	.241				83.6	
	9 p. m.		22	.118				100	
March 16	7 a. m.		33	.168				89.3	
	2 p. m.		46	.262				84.3	
	9 p. m.		33	.188				100	
March 17	7 a. m.		34	.155				79.2	
	2 p. m.		46	.262				84.3	
	9 p. m.		34	.155				79.2	
March 18	7 a. m.		26	.141				100	
	2 p. m.		32	.181				100	
	9 p. m.		24	.129				100	

FOREST CITY, MINNESOTA.

Month and day.	Hour.	Barom'r corrected to 32° F.	Thermometer.	Force of vapor.	Cloudiness.	Motion of clouds.	Winds.	Relative humidity.	REMARKS.
March 13	2 p. m.		26		8		E. 4		Snow from 2 p. m. the 13th to 7 p. m. on the 14th; depth, 4 inches.
	9 p. m.		29		8		E. 4		
March 14	7 a. m.		28		8		NE. 5		
	2 p. m.		31		8		NE. 5		
	9 p. m.		24		0		NW. 2		
March 15	7 a. m.		24		0		0		
	2 p. m.		36		0		0		
	9 p. m.		25		0		E. 2		
March 16	7 a. m.		41		2		SE. 3		
	2 p. m.		47		0		SE. 3		
	9 p. m.		34		3		0		
March 17	7 a. m.		27		0		0		
	2 p. m.		38		0		NW. 3		
	9 p. m.		28		2		0		
March 18	7 a. m.		33		0		W. 3		
	2 p. m.		33		0		W. 3		
	9 p. m.		16		0		W. 2		
March 19	7 a. m.		27		0		0		

HAZLEWOOD, MINNESOTA.

Month and day.	Hour.	Barom'r corrected to 32° F.	Thermometer.	Force of vapor.	Cloudiness.	Motion of clouds.	Winds.	Relative humidity.	REMARKS.
March 13	2 p. m.		28		Nim. 10	NE	NE. 3		13th. Snow storm at 11 a. m.; ended on the 14th; depth, 3.50 inches; amount in water, 0.47 inch.
	9 p. m.		26		Nim. 10	NE	NE. 3		
March 14	7 a. m.		26		Nim. 10	NE	NE. 4		
	2 p. m.		26		Nim. 10	NE	NE. 5		
	9 p. m.		24		Cu. 4		NE. 5		
March 15	7 a. m.		12		0		W. 2		
	2 p. m.		32		Cu. 1		SW. 3		
	9 p. m.		28		St. 1		S. 4		
March 16	7 a. m.		29		Cu. 3		S. 2		
	2 p. m.		36		Cu. cir. 5		NW. 3		
	9 p. m.		28		Cir. cu. 7		NW. 2		
March 17	7 a. m.		24		Cir. cu. 8		W. 2		
	2 p. m.		36		Cir. 4		NW. 2		
	9 p. m.		26		0		NW. 2		
March 18	7 a. m.		21		St. 1		NW. 4		
	2 p. m.		22		Cu. 4		NW. 5		
	9 p. m.		20				NW. 2		
March 19	7 a. m.		16		Cu. cir. 9		S. 1		

* Wieland, observer.

STORM No. 1, MARCH, 1859.

PRINCETON, MINNESOTA.

Month and day.	Hour.	Barom'r corrected to 32° F.	Thermometer.	Force of vapor.	Cloudiness.		Motion of clouds.		Winds.		Relative humidity.	REMARKS.
March 13	2 p. m.	------	30	------	Nim.	10	----------		NE.	2	------	13th. Snow at 12.45 p m.; amount, 0.40 inch.
	9 p. m.	------	30	------	Nim.	10	----------		NE.	2	------	
March 14	7 a. m.	------	29	------	Nim.	10	----------		NE.	2	------	
	2 p. m.	------	33	------	Nim.	10	----------		N.	3	------	
	9 p. m.	------	28	------	Cir. cu.	10	W.	2	NW.	4	------	
March 15	7 a. m.	------	26	------		0	----------		NW.	2	------	
	2 p. m.	------	38	------		0	----------		W.	2	------	
	9 p. m.	------	30	------		0	----------		W.	1	------	
March 16	7 a. m.	------	32	------	Cu. st.	2	NW ------		E.	2	------	
	2 p. m.	------	47	------		0	----------			0	------	
	9 p. m.	------	40	------	Cir.	8	----------		S.	1	------	
March 17	7 a. m.	------	29	------	Cu. st.	5		0	W.	2	------	
	2 p. m.	------	38	------	Cir.	3		0	W.	2	------	
	9 p. m.	------	32	------	Cir. cu.	8	NW.	2	NW.	2	------	
March 18	7 a. m.	------	28	------	Cu. cir.	8	NW.	2	NW.	2	------	
	2 p. m.	------	34	------	Cu.	2	NE.	3	N.	3	------	
	9 p. m.	------	27	------		0	----------		N.	3	------	
March 19	7 a. m.	------	12	------		0	----------		W.	1	------	

BELLEVUE, NEBRASKA.

Month and day.	Hour.	Barom'r corrected to 32° F.	Thermometer.	Force of vapor.	Cloudiness.		Motion of clouds.		Winds.		Relative humidity.	REMARKS.
March 13	7 a. m.	------	40	------	Cu. st.	10	Hazy ------		NE.	2	------	14th. Snow at 6 p. m.; amount, in water, 0.05 inch.
	2 p. m.	------	43	------	Cu. st.	10	S.	2	NE.	2	------	15th. Temperature 20° at sunrise.
	9 p. m.	------	39	------	Cu. st.	8	SE.	4	NE.	1	------	
March 14	7 a. m.	------	36	------	Snow	10	N -------		N.	4	------	
	2 p. m.	------	29	------	Snow	10	N -------		N.	5	------	
	9 p. m.	------	29	------	------------		----------		N.	2	------	
March 15	7 a. m.	------	29	------	------------		----------		W.	1	------	
	2 p. m.	------	52	------	------------		----------		S.	2	------	
	9 p. m.	------	45	------	------------		----------		S.	3	------	
March 16	7 a. m.	------	42	------	------------		----------		S.	4	------	
	2 p. m.	------	50	------	St.	3	W.	2	W.	3	------	
	9 p. m.	------	40	------	Cir. cu.	6	SW.	3	N.	4	------	
March 17	7 a. m.	------	41	------	Nim.	10	N.	2	N.	3	------	
	2 p. m.	------	32	------	Cir. cu.	5	N.	3	N.	3	------	
	9 p. m.	------	27	------	Cir. cu.	6	N.	3	N.	4	------	
March 18	7 a. m.	------	26	------	Cir. cu.	5	N.	4	N.	3	------	
	2 p. m.	------	32	------	Cu.	4	----------		N.	3	------	
	9 p. m.	------	27	------	------------		----------		N.	1	------	

BROWNVILLE, NEBRASKA.

Month and day.	Hour.	Barom'r corrected to 32° F.	Thermometer.	Force of vapor.	Cloudiness.		Motion of clouds.		Winds.		Relative humidity.	REMARKS.
March 13	7 a. m.	------	40	------		5	NE.	1	SE.	2	------	13th. Rain from 7.30 to 8 p. m.
	2 p. m.	------	54	------		5	NE.	1	SW.	2	------	14th. Snow from 6.30 a. m. to 2.30 p. m., accompanied by a perfect gale of wind; depth, 1.50 inch.
	9 p. m.	------	39	------	Nim.	10	S.	1	NW.	1	------	17th. Snow from 5 to 10 a. m.; depth, 2 inches.
March 14	7 a. m.	------	32	------	Snow	10	S.	1	NW.	2	------	
	2 p. m.	------	33	------	Snow	10	SE.	1	NW.	6	------	
	9 p. m.	------	29	------		0	----------		SE.	3	------	
March 15	7 a. m.	------	26	------		0	----------		NW.	2	------	
	2 p. m.	------	55	------		0	----------		SE.	4	------	
	9 p. m.	------	49	------		0	----------		NW.	5	------	
March 16	7 a. m.	------	47	------	Cir.	5	NE.	1	SW.	4	------	
	2 p. m.	------	63	------	Cir. st.	5	NE.	1	NW.	4	------	
	9 p. m.	------	41	------	Cir. st.	5	E.	2	NW.	3	------	
March 17	7 a. m.	------	33	------	Snow	10	S.	1	NE.	3	------	
	2 p. m.	------	55	------	Nim.	10	SE.	1	NW.	3	------	
	9 p. m.	------	34	------	Nim.	10	SE.	1	SW.	2	------	
March 18	7 a. m.	------	29	------	Cir. st.	5	SE.	2	NW.	2	------	
	2 p. m.	------	48	------		0	----------		NW.	2	------	
	9 p. m.	------	37	------		0	----------		SE.	3	------	

STORM No. 1, MARCH, 1859.

ELKHAM, NEBRASKA.

Month and day.	Hour.	Barom'r corrected to 32° F.	Thermometer.	Force of vapor.	Cloudiness.		Motion of clouds.	Winds.		Relative humidity.	REMARKS.
March 13	7 a. m.	------	33	------	Nim.	10	3	NE.	3	------	13th. Several spits of sleet and rain; rain, with distant thunder and lightning, in the evening. 14th. Wind changed in the night, with snow and sleet; snow from 6 a. m. to 2. 30 p. m.; wind moderated; began to clear in the west at 3 p. m.; 10 a. m. temperature 25°; sunset red; blue and yellow rays thirty minutes after sunset. 15th. 6 a. m. temperature 20°; 2 p. m. clouds WSW. 16th. 7 a. m. hazy; 9 a. m. wind suddenly changed to NW., and thermometer fell from 44° to 42°. 17th. Morning cold and raw; 9 p. m. clouds to SE.
	2 p. m.	------	34	------	Nim.	10	3	NE.	3	------	
	9 p. m.	------	32	------	Cir. st.	7	3	NE.	3	------	
March 14	7 a. m.	------	28	------	Nim.	10	6	N.	6	------	
	2 p. m.	------	28	------	Nim.	10	6	NW.	6	------	
	9 p. m.	------	28	------		0	0	W.	2	------	
March 15	7 a. m.	------	21	------		0	0	W.	1	------	
	2 p. m.	------	42	------	Cir.	1	2	SE.	2	------	
	9 p. m.	------	40	------		0	0	SE.	3	------	
March 16	7 a. m.	------	40	------	Cir.	4	3	S.	3	------	
	2 p. m.	------	43	------	Cu.	9	3	NW.	3	------	
	9 p. m.	------	33	------	Cu. st.	4	SW. 2	NE.	2	------	
March 17	7 a. m.	------	33	------	St.	10	2	N.	2	------	
	2 p. m.	------	42	------	Cu. st.	7	3	N.	3	------	
	9 p. m.	------	28	------	Cir.	1	1	NW.	1	------	
March 18	7 a. m.	------	27	------	St.	1	2	NW.	2	------	
	2 p. m.	------	35	------	Cu. st.	6	3	NW.	3	------	
	9 p. m.	------	26	------	Cir. st.	1	1	NW.	1	------	

18th. 7 a. m. clouds to N. and E.; 10 a. m. spit of snow; 9 p. m. clouds to E. 19th. Frost.

PIONEER GROVE, NEBRASKA.

Month and day.	Hour.	Barom'r corrected to 32° F.	Thermometer.	Force of vapor.	Cloudiness.		Motion of clouds.		Winds.		Relative humidity.	REMARKS.
March 13	7 a. m.	------	34	------	Cir. st.	10	----------		NE.	3	------	13th. Light frost; one flash of lightning and one clap of thunder N. at 7 p. m.; clouds nim., S. 3.; wind, N. 3; a few drops of rain before the thunder. 14th. Snow from 6 a. m. to 1. 30 p. m; amount, in water, 0. 26 inch. 15th and 16th. Frost. 19th. Light white frost.
	2 p. m.	------	38	------	Nim.	10	----------		NE.	2	------	
	9 p. m.	------	34	------	Nim.	8	S.	3	N.	3	------	
March 14	7 a. m.	------	32	------	Nim.	10	----------		N.	5	------	
	2 p. m.	------	28	------	Cir. st.	8	----------		NW.	6	------	
	9 p. m.	------	28	------		0	----------		NW.	2	------	
March 15	7 a. m.	------	25	------		0	----------		W.	1	------	
	2 p. m.	------	42	------		0	----------		W.	2	------	
	9 p. m.	------	45	------		0	----------		SW.	3	------	
March 16	7 a. m.	------	47	------		0	----------		S.	3	------	
	2 p. m.	------	56	------	Cir. st.	8	----------		S.	4	------	
	9 p. m.	------	46	------	Cu. st.	10	----------		SW.	2	------	
March 17	7 a. m.	------	44	------	St.	8	----------		SW.	1	------	
	2 p. m.	------	54	------	Cir. st.	8	----------		W.	2	------	
	9 p. m.	------	45	------	Cir. st.	10	----------		NW.	1	------	
March 18	7 a. m.	------	36	------	St.	4	----------		W.	2	------	
	2 p. m.	------	40	------	Cir.	6	----------		SW.	3	------	
	9 p. m.	------	34	------	Cir. st.	8	----------		S.	4	------	

LAWRENCE, KANSAS.

Month and day.	Hour.	Barom'r corrected to 32° F.	Thermometer.	Force of vapor.	Cloudiness.		Motion of clouds.	Winds.		Relative humidity.	REMARKS.
March 13	7 a. m.	28. 88	48	. 231	St.	6	----------	S.	3	55	14th. Flurries of snow. 16th. Rain in the night. 17th. Sleet in the morning; snow at 2 p. m.
	2 p. m.	28. 71	60	. 268	Cu.	8	----------	S.	4	58	
	9 p. m.	28. 69	42	. 282	Clear	0	----------	S.	4	67	
March 14	7 a. m.	28. 56	32	. 136	Nim.	8	----------	W.	6	35	
	2 p. m.	28. 81	38	. 177	Cu. st.	10	----------	NW.	6	66	
	9 p. m.	29. 08	36	. 151	Clear	0	----------	W.	3	52	
March 15	7 a. m.	29. 18	30	. 164	Clear	0	----------	W.	2	59	
	2 p. m.	29. 10	62	. 257	Clear	0	----------	S.	3	43	
	9 p. m.	29. 03	47	. 369	Clear	0	----------	S.	3	41	
March 16	7 a. m.	28. 94	48	. 382	Cir. st.	4	----------	S.	4	44	
	2 p. m.	28. 84	65	. 261	Cu.	4	----------	S.	4	38	
	9 p. m.	28. 98	62	. 318	Cu. st.	6	----------	S.	4	37	
March 17	7 a. m.	28. 93	34	. 306	Nim.	10	----------	NE.	4	43	
	2 p. m.	28. 95	36	. 283	Nim.	10	----------	N.	4	35	
	9 p. m.	29. 03	36	. 242	Cir.	5	----------	N.	4	45	
March 18	7 a. m.	29. 08	32	. 113	Clear	0	----------	NW.	4	29	
	2 p. m.	29. 09	44	. 190	Cir.	2	----------	NW.	5	29	
	9 p. m.	29. 14	36	. 305	Clear	0	----------	N.	2	34	

STORM No. 1, MARCH, 1859.

MANHATTAN, KANSAS.

Month and day.	Hour.	Barom'r corrected to 32° F.	Thermometer.	Force of vapor.	Cloudiness.	Motion of clouds.	Winds.	Relative humidity.	REMARKS.
March 13	7 a. m.	......	44	......	Nim. 10	SW. 3	SE. 1	......	14th. Snow from 6.30 to 9.30 a. m; amount in water, 0. 05 inch. 17th. Snow from 2.30 a. m. till noon ; amount in water, 0. 28 inch.
	2 p. m.	......	63	......	Cir. cu. 6	SW. 3	S. 2	......	
	9 p. m.	......	40	......	Nim. 10	S. 3	S. 3	......	
March 14	7 a. m.	......	31	......	Nim. 10	NW. 5	NW. 6	......	
	2 p. m.	......	44	......	Cu. 9	NW. 4	NW. 3	......	
	9 p. m.	......	36	......	Cir. cu. 7	SW. 2	SW. 2	......	
March 15	7 a. m.	......	31	......	0	0	0	......	
	2 p. m.	......	62	......	0	0	SW. 4	......	
	9 p. m.	......	45	......	Cir. st. 3	SW. 3	S. 3	......	
March 16	7 a. m.	......	54	......	Cir. cu. 7	SW. 3	S. 4	......	
	2 p. m.	......	46	......	Cir. cu. 7	SW. 2	S. 5	......	
	9 p. m.	......	44	......	Nim. 10	S. 4	N. 3	......	
March 17	7 a. m.	......	33	......	Nim. 10	N. 2	NW. 3	......	
	2 p. m.	......	43	......	Cu. 9	W. 2	N. 4	......	
	9 p. m.	......	32	......	0	0	0	......	
March 18	7 a. m.	......	32	......	0	0	NW. 2	......	
	2 p. m.	......	48	......	Cu. 9	N. 2	NW. 2	......	
	9 p. m.	......	32	......	0	0	0	......	

BURLINGAME, KANSAS.

Month and day.	Hour.	Barom'r corrected to 32° F.	Thermometer.	Force of vapor.	Cloudiness.	Motion of clouds.	Winds.	Relative humidity.	REMARKS.
March 13	7 a. m.	......	40	......	4	....	SE. 1	......	17th. Storm commenced at 2 a. m. and ended at 2 p. m.; amount, 0. 06 inch.
	2 p. m.	......	60	......	8	....	S. 4	......	
	9 p. m.	......	39	......	6	....	SW. 5	......	
March 14	7 a. m.	......	32	......	10	....	NW. 7	......	
	2 p. m.	......	40	......	1	....	NW. 6	......	
	9 p. m.	......	36	......	0	....	NW. 1	......	
March 15	7 a. m.	......	26	......	0	....	0	......	
	2 p. m.	......	54	......	0	....	S. 2	......	
	9 p. m.	......	48	......	0	....	S. 4	......	
March 16	7 a. m.	......	44	......	2	....	S. 3	......	
	2 p. m.	......	61	......	2	....	S. 5	......	
	9 p. m.	......	47	......	10	....	S. 3	......	
March 17	7 a. m.	......	34	......	10	....	N. 4	......	
	2 p. m.	......	36	......	8	....	N. 4	......	
	9 p. m.	......	36	......	5	....	NW. 3	......	
March 18	7 a. m.	......	31	......	0	....	N. 1	......	
	2 p. m.	......	45	......	0	....	N. 4	......	
	9 p. m.	......	42	......	0	....	N. 1	......	

NEOSHO FALLS, KANSAS.

Month and day.	Hour.	Barom'r corrected to 32° F.	Thermometer.	Force of vapor.	Cloudiness.	Motion of clouds.	Winds.	Relative humidity.	REMARKS.
March 13	7 a. m.	......	48	......	Cir. cu. 8	....	SE. 2	......	17th. Rain and snow at intervals from 4 a. m. to 3 p. m.; amount in water, 0. 58 inch.
	2 p. m.	......	61	......	Cir. 5	....	S. 2	......	
	9 p. m.	......	37	......	0	....	SW. 2	......	
March 14	7 a. m.	......	33	......	Cir. st. 9	....	W. 6	......	
	2 p. m.	......	44	......	Cu. st. 4	....	NW. 4	......	
	9 p. m.	......	39	......	0	....	NW	......	
March 15	7 a. m.	......	31	......	0	....	Calm	......	
	2 p. m.	......	59	......	0	....	SW. 2	......	
	9 p. m.	......	48	......	0	....	S. 4	......	
March 16	7 a. m.	......	44	......	Cir. 5	....	SE. 4	......	
	2 p. m.	......	61	......	Cir. cu. 8	....	S. 4	......	
	9 p. m.	......	53	......	Cir. 9	....	SE. 2	......	
March 17	7 a. m.	......	35	......	Nim. 10	....	NE. 4	......	
	2 p. m.	......	34	......	Nim. 10	....	N. 2	......	
	9 p. m.	......	37	......	Cir. 6	....	NW. 2	......	
March 18	7 a. m.	......	33	......	0	....	NW. 2	......	
	2 p. m.	......	46	......	Cir. 1	....	NW. 2	......	
	9 p. m.	......	33	......	0	....	Calm	......	

STORM No. 1, MARCH, 1859.

GREAT SALT LAKE CITY, UTAH.

13th. A. m. clear and cold; a few clouds continued all day. 14th. A. m. clear, which continued fine all day. 15th. A. m. hazy; cloudy p. m. 16th. A. m. clear; alternately clear and cloudy all day. 17th. A. m. clear; clear rest of the day. 18th. A. m. hazy; noon warm; p. m. springlike. 19th. Snowing at 7, and continued ten hours, with a fall 12¼ inches.

MAYSVILLE, CALIFORNIA.

Month and day.	Hour.	Barom'r corrected to 32° F.	Thermometer.	Force of vapor.	Cloudiness.	Motion of clouds.	Winds.	Relative humidity.	REMARKS.
March 13	7 a. m.	......	43	......	2	....	N	......	
	2 p. m.	......	64	......	1	....	SE	......	
	9 p. m.	......	53	......	1	....	SE	......	
March 14	7 a. m.	......	46	......	2	....	S.	......	
	2 p. m.	......	65	......	1	....	S.	......	
	9 p. m.	......	52	......	2	....	S.	......	
March 15	7 a. m.	......	44	......	3	....	S.	......	
	2 p. m.	......	64	......	2	....	S.	......	
	9 p. m.	......	50	......	3	....	S.	......	
March 16	7 a. m.	......	45	......	2	....	S.	......	
	2 p. m.	......	64	......	3	....	S.	......	
	9 p. m.	......	51	......	3	....	S.	......	
March 17	7 a. m.	......	46	......	2	....	N	......	
	2 p. m.	......	63	......	3	....	N	......	
	9 p. m.	......	49	......	4	....	N	......	
March 18	7 a. m.	......	43	......	5	....	N	......	
	2 p. m.	......	62	......	5	....	N	......	
	9 p. m.	......	47	......	6	....	N	......	

SACRAMENTO, CALIFORNIA.

Month and day.	Hour.	Barom'r corrected to 32° F.	Thermometer.	Force of vapor.	Cloudiness.		Motion of clouds.		Winds.		Relative humidity.	REMARKS.
March 13	7 a. m.	30.300	41	.182	Cir. st.	1		0	NE.	3	73	18th. Sprinkle of rain at 3.45 p. m.
	2 p. m.	30.289	51	.234		0		0	SW.	2	65	
	9 p. m.	30.263	53	.282		0		0	SE.	1	73	
March 14	7 a. m.	30.268	47	.215		0		0	SE.	2	69	
	2 p. m.	30.174	54	.321		0		0	SW.	2	80	
	9 p. m.	30.096	52	.296	St.	0		0	SW.	3	79	
March 15	7 a. m.	30.119	48	.273	Nim.	10		0	W.	3	85	
	2 p. m.	30.085	56	.193		0		0	NW.	4	44	
	9 p. m.	30.064	52	.245		0		0	N.	2	65	
March 16	7 a. m.	30.137	46	.182		0		0	NW.	4	61	
	2 p. m.	30.128	62	.216		0		0	N.	3	40	
	9 p. m.	30.163	56	.295		0		0	N.	1	68	
March 17	7 a. m.	30.221	51	.231	Cir.	1		0	N.	2	65	
	2 p. m.	30.153	61	.367	Cir. st.	5	SW.	2	SE.	2	71	
	9 p. m.	30.111	59	.365	Cir., cu.	2	SW.	2	S.	1	76	
March 18	7 a. m.	30.059	54	.308	Cir. cu.	8	SW.	1	S.	3	74	
	2 p. m.	29.999	62	.340	Nim.	9	W.	2	SW.	5	61	
	9 p. m.	30.050	52	.245	Cu.	3	W.	2	W.	3	65	

STORM No. 1, MARCH, 1859.

SAN FRANCISCO, CALIFORNIA.

Month and day.	Hour.	Barom'r corrected to 32° F.	Thermometer.	Force of vapor.	Cloudiness.		Motion of clouds.		Winds.		Relative humidity.	REMARKS.
March 13	7 a. m.	30.192	48	.099		0		0	S.	1	29	
	2 p. m.	30.187	60	.127		0		0	N.	1	25	
	9 p. m.	30.190	49	.272		0		0	W.	1	78	
March 14	7 a. m.	30.182	46	.262	Cir. cu.	2	W.	2	W.	1	84	
	2 p. m.	30.102	57	.268		0		0	W.	2	58	
	9 p. m.	30.050	49	.272		0		0		0	78	
March 15	7 a. m.	30.060	47	.156	Cir. cu.	8	NW.	2	N.	2	48	
	2 p. m.	30.016	57	.216		0		0	N.	2	46	
	9 p. m.	29.961	49	.199		0		0		0	57	
March 16	7 a. m.	30.073	49	.199		0		0		0	57	
	2 p. m.	30.054	59	.190		0		0	N.	2	38	
	9 p. m.	30.073	52	.334		0		0		0	86	
March 17	7 a. m.	30.107	48	.310		0		0		0	92	
	2 p. m.	30.085	67	.303	Cir.	4	W.	1	N.	1	46	
	9 p. m.	30.046	56	.391		0		0		0	87	
March 18	7 a. m.	29.998	49	.297	Cu. st.	10	W.	1	W.	1	85	
	2 p. m.	29.994	54	.362	Cir. cu.	9	W.	3	W.	3	87	
	9 p. m.	29.996	54	.362		0		0	W.	1	87	

MINATITLAN, MEXICO.

Month and day.	Hour.	Barom'r corrected to 32° F.	Thermometer.	Force of vapor.	Cloudiness.		Motion of clouds.		Winds.		Relative humidity.
March 13	7 a. m.	29.83	75	.772	Nim., cu.	10	SW.	2		0	86
	2 p. m.	29.78	93	.894	Cu.	1	S.	2	SSW.	2	64
	9 p. m.	29.80	79	.904	Cu.	8	S.	1		0	83
March 14	7 a. m.	29.76	72	.636	Cir.	0		0		0	79
	2 p. m.	29.86	83	.739	Cir. cu.	5	----------		NNE.	5	62
	9 p. m.	30.02	73	.591	Nim., cu.	9	NNE.	8	NNE.	5	68
March 15	7 a. m.	29.99	70	.595	N., cu., cir st.	9	N.	8		0	76
	2 p. m.	29.97	75.5	.635	Nim., cu.	9	----------			0	75
	9 p. m.	29.98	68	.551	Cir. st.	7	ESE. / NNE.	4 / 12		0	75
March 16	7 a. m.	29.82	66.5	.550	Cir. st.	9	NNE.	6	SSE.	1	82
	2 p. m.	29.87	85	.684	Cu.	5	SE.	2	ESE.	2	67
	9 p. m.	29.83	67	.608		0		0		0	80
March 17	7 a. m.	29.84	69	.624	Thick fog....		----------		SW.	1	90
	2 p. m.	29.85	82.5	.788	Cu.	1	NNE. -----		NNE.	3	71
	9 p. m.	29.94	71	.705	Cir.	7	----------			0	81
March 18	7 a. m.	30.02	70.5	.663	Cir. st.	9	N.	1		0	88
	2 p. m.	30.07	78	.704	Nim., cu.	10	N.	20	N.	5	73
	9 p. m.	30.16	71	.839	Nim., cu.	10	NE.	8	NE.	2	100

REMARKS.

14th. In the a. m a breeze came from every point of compass; but at noon, all at once, a high wind rose from NNE., and the thermometer fell from 90° to 83°; from 3 to 9 p. m. it blew 6; at midnight the wind ceased.

15th. About 8 a. m. it sprinkled for 30 minutes.

16th. Till noon a light breeze from SSE.; thermometer 88°; at and after 9 p. m. there was a distinct white circle round the moon, about 45° in diameter; the moon, though nearly full and on the zenith, shown very clear.

18th About noon it rained, but not sufficiently to lay the dust; then a wind arose, which grew stronger and stronger, and lasted till 3 p. m; at 9 p. m. it rained a little; amount, 0.01 inch.

CATHARINA SOPHIA, SURINAM, SOUTH AMERICA.

Month and day.	Hour.	Barom'r corrected to 32° F.	Thermometer.	Force of vapor.	Cloudiness.		Motion of clouds.		Winds.		Relative humidity.
March 13	6 a. m.	29.950	75	.745		5	E.	1	SE.	1	86
	2 p. m.	......	87	.836		5	NE.	3	NE.	3	65
	6 p. m.	29.871	80	.886		4	SE.	1	NNE.	3	87
March 14	6 a. m.	29.905	75	.785		8	E.	3	E.	2	90
	2 p. m.	29.899	86	.805		6	NE.	2	NE.	3	65
	6 p. m.	29.894	80	.843		4	NE.	2	NE.	2	83
March 15	6 a. m.	29.942	74	.798		8	SE.	2	SE.	1	95
	2 p. m.	29.929	87	.836		5	NE.	3	NE.	3	65
	6 p. m.	29.901	80	.886		4	E.	1	E.	1	87
March 16	6 a. m.	29.912	76	.812		7	SE.	2	SE.	1	91
	2 p. m.	29.905	85	.863		7	NE.	3	NNE.	3	72
	6 p. m.	29.890	79	.856		6	NE.	3	NNE.	2	87
March 17	6 a. m.	29.952	76	.772		6	E.	2	E.	1	86
	2 p. m.	29.929	84	.877		7	NE.	3	NNE.	3	75
	6 p. m.	29.901	80	.843		5	NE.	2	NNE.	2	83
March 18	6 a. m.	29.948	76	.812		8	SE.	2	E	1	91
	2 p. m.	29.907	83	.936		9	NE.	3	N.	3	83
	6 p. m.	29.862	75	.868		10	NE.	3	NE.	3	100

REMARKS.

14th. Rain from 5.25 to 6.10 a. m; amount, 0 10 inch.

15th. Rain from 2 to 3.50 a. m; amount, 0.426 inch.

16th. Rain from 3 a. m. to 4 p. m.; amount, 0.048 inch.

18th. Rain from 1 a. m. to 11 p. m; amount, 2 40 inches.

19th Rain from 12 a. m. to 5 p. m; amount, 1.39 inch.

STORMS Nos. 2 AND 3, SEPTEMBER, 1859.

FORT SIMPSON, HUDSON BAY TERRITORY, BRITISH AMERICA.

Month and day.	Hour.	Barom'r corrected to 32° F.	Thermometer.	Force of vapor.	Cloudiness.		Motion of clouds.	Winds.		Relative humidity.	REMARKS.
Sept. 11	7 a. m.	......	56	......	Cir. cu.	3	NW. to SE.	NW.	1	......	11th. Faint aurora.
	2 p. m.	......	68	......	Cir. cu.	5	....	SE.	1	......	13th. Heavy rain from 6½ a. m. to 10 p. m.
	9 p. m.	......	40	......	Cir. st.	1	....	S.	2	......	
Sept. 12	7 a. m.	......	47	......	Cir. st.	3	....	SE.	7	......	14th. Light rain from 1 to 11½ a. m.
	2 p. m.	......	58	......	Cir. st.	1	....	NW.	1	......	15th. Light rain from 2½ to 3 p. m.
	9 p. m.	......	45	......	Nim.	10	....	W.	4	......	Heavy rain from the 16th to 11 a. m. on the 18th.
Sept. 13	7 a. m.	......	44	......	Nim.	9	W. to E.	NW.	1	......	
	2 p. m.	......	46	......	Nim.	10	....	E.	6	......	19th. Heavy rain from daybreak to 9 p. m.
	9 p. m.	......	42	......	Nim.	8	....	SE.	4	......	
Sept. 14	7 a. m.	......	41	......	Nim.	10	....	N	2	......	20th. Rain at intervals all day.
	2 p. m.	......	45	......	Nim.	10	....	NW.	2	......	21st Showery all day.
	9 p. m.	......	42	......	Nim.	10	....	NW.	5	......	19th. Well-defined arch in zenith, and broken arch in NE. at 9 p. m.; colors yellow and various shades; active.
Sept. 15	7 a. m.	......	43	......	Nim.	10	....	NW.	3	......	
	2 p. m.	......	48	......	Nim.	8	....	N.	2	......	
	9 p. m.	......	41	......	Nim.	10	....	N.	1	......	
Sept. 16	7 a. m.	......	40	......	Cir. cu.	8	E. to W. 1	NE.	2	......	
	2 p. m.	......	44	......	Nim.	10	....	NW.	2	......	
	9 p. m.	......	40	......	Nim.	10	....	NW.	3	......	
Sept. 17	7 a. m.	......	41	......	Nim.	10	....	NE.	3	......	
	2 p. m.	......	43	......	Nim.	10	....	NE.	3	......	
	9 p. m.	......	40	......	Nim.	10	....	NE.	6	......	
Sept. 18	7 a. m.	......	40	......	Nim.	10	....	NE.	3	......	
	2 p. m.	......	48	......	Nim.	10	....	NE.	1	......	
	9 p. m.	......	39	......	Cu. st.	5	....	NE.	4	......	
Sept. 19	7 a. m.	......	38	......	Nim.	10	....	NE.	2	......	
	2 p. m.	......	42	......	Cu. st.	10	....	NE.	2	......	
	9 p. m.	......	48	......	Cu. st.	3	....	NE.	2	......	
Sept. 20	7 a. m.	......	37	......	Cu. st.	6	....	NW.	2	......	
	2 p. m.	......	45	......	Nim.	5	....	N.	3	......	
	9 p. m.	......	36	......	Nim.	10	....	N.	1	......	
Sept. 21	7 a. m.	......	42	......	Nim.	10	....	NE.	3	......	
	2 p. m.	......	45	......	Cu. st.	8	....	NW.	3	......	
	9 p. m.	......	40	......	Cu. st.	8	....	NW.	2	......	

HAMILTON, CANADA.

Month and day.	Hour.	Barom'r corrected to 32° F.	Thermometer.	Force of vapor.	Cloudiness.	Motion of clouds.	Winds.	Relative humidity.	REMARKS.
Sept. 14	9 p. m.	29.90	46	......	....	....	....	......	14th. Fair and clear.
Sept. 15	9 a. m.	30.04	46	......	....	....	....	......	15th. Partly cloudy.
	9 p. m.	29.94	48	......	....	....	....	......	16th Cloudy.
Sept. 16	9 a. m.	29.84	50	......	....	....	....	......	17th. Mostly cloudy; morning and evening foggy.
	9 p. m.	29.70	54	......	....	....	....	......	
Sept. 17	9 a. m.	29.64	55	......	....	....	....	......	18th. Partly cloudy.
	9 p. m.	29.66	56	......	....	....	....	......	19th. Mostly cloudy; slight shower at noon; thunder shower at night.
Sept. 18	9 a. m.	29.72	58	......	....	....	....	......	
	9 p. m.	29.60	57	......	....	....	....	......	20th. Cloudy, windy, slight showers morning and evening.
Sept. 19	9 a. m.	29.44	56	......	....	....	....	......	
	9 p. m.	29.38	60	......	....	....	....	......	21st. Rainy.
Sept. 20	9 a. m.	29.56	54	......	....	....	....	......	22d. Slight shower at noon.
	9 p. m.	29.68	54	......	....	....	....	......	23d. Mostly cloudy.
Sept. 21	9 a. m.	29.65	51	......	....	....	....	......	24th. Partly cloudy.
	9 p. m.	29.53	54	......	....	....	....	......	
Sept. 22	9 a. m.	29.50	54	......	....	....	....	......	
	9 p. m.	29.64	60	......	....	....	....	......	
Sept. 23	9 a. m.	29.70	60	......	....	....	....	......	
	9 p. m.	29.70	62	......	....	....	....	......	
Sept. 24	9 a. m.	29.70	62	......	....	....	....	......	
	9 p. m.	29.67	60	......	....	....	....	......	
Sept. 25	9 a. m.	29.69	60	......	....	....	....	......	

STORMS Nos. 2 AND 3, SEPTEMBER, 1859.

MONTREAL, CANADA.

Month and day.	Hour.	Barom'r corrected to 32° F.	Thermometer.	Force of vapor.	Cloudiness.	Motion of clouds.	Winds.	Relative humidity.	REMARKS.
Sept. 14	9 p. m.	29.999	40.5	.169	0	0	NW. 4	65	
Sept. 15	7 a. m.	30.281	40	.139	0	0	NW. 3	56	
	2 p. m.	.287	49.5	.247	Cu. 1	W. 2	W. 2	71	
	9 p. m.	.297	45	.160	Cir. st. 2	WSW. 2	WSW. 2	53	
Sept. 16	7 a. m.	.294	41	.212	Cir. st., cu. st. 8	NNW. 1	NNW. 1	82	
	2 p. m.	.247	55	.208	0	0	SSW. 1	53	
	9 p. m.	.111	50.5	.234	Cu. st. 7	SSW. 1	SSW. 1	65	
Sept. 17	7 a. m.	.031	51.8	.348	Cu. st. 10	SSW. 1	SSW. 1	93	
	2 p. m.	29.931	55.6	.376	Cu. st. 10	N. 1	N. 1	87	
	9 p. m.	.931	53	.361	Cu. st. 10	N. 2	N. 2	93	
Sept. 18	7 a. m.	30.108	51	.335	Cu. st. 10	N. 1	N. 1	93	
	2 p. m.	29.920	62.8	.383	0	0	NNE. 1	71	
	9 p. m.	.909	57.2	.322	0	0	NNE. 1	69	
Sept. 19	7 a. m.	.832	51.6	.321	Cu. st. 5	N. 1	N. 1	86	
	2 p. m.	.723	69	.393	0	0	SSE. 1	59	
	9 p. m.	.661	62.5	.460	Cu. 10	SSE. 1	SSE. 1	83	
Sept. 20	7 a. m.	.856	51.5	.348	Nim. 10	N. 1	N. 1	93	
	2 p. m.	30.023	57	.242	Cir. st. 6	NNE. 1	NNE. 2	52	
	9 p. m.	.145	50.4	.234	St. 1	ENE. 1	ENE. 3	65	
Sept. 21	7 a. m.	.195	44.7	.196	Cu. st. 10	ENE. 5	ENE. 5	68	
	2 p. m.	.186	48.6	.310	Nim. 10	ENE. 4	ENE. 4	92	
	9 p. m.	.167	50	.322	Nim. 10	ENE. 4	ENE. 4	92	
Sept. 22	7 a. m.	.103	49	.348	Nim. 10	ENE. 3	ENE. 3	100	
	2 p. m.	.060	56	.433	Nim. 10	ENE. 3	ENE. 3	100	
	9 p. m.	.056	54.6	.418	Nim. 10	NE. 3	NE. 3	100	
Sept. 23	7 a. m.	29.986	51	.374	Nim. 10	NNE. 3	NNE. 3	100	
	2 p. m.	30.010	55	.405	Nim. 10	N. 3	N. 3	94	
	9 p. m.	.017	53	.375	Nim. 10	N. 3	N. 3	93	
Sept. 24	7 a. m.	29.974	57	.378	Cu. st. 10	N. 1	N. 1	81	
	2 p. m.	.920	61	.426	Cu. st. 10	N. 1	N. 1	82	
	9 p. m.	.941	57.8	.423	Cu. st. 10	N. 1	N. 1	88	
Sept. 25	7 a. m.	.967	56.8	.420	Cu. st. 10	NNE. 1	Calm	94	
	2 p. m.	.922	63	.460	Cu. st. 10	NNE. 1	NNE. 1	83	

RED RIVER SETTLEMENT, BRITISH AMERICA.

Month and day.	Hour.	Barom'r corrected to 32° F.	Thermometer.	Force of vapor.	Cloudiness.	Motion of clouds.	Winds.	Relative humidity.	REMARKS.
Sept. 14	9 p. m.	......	......	......	0	......	S. 1	......	Rain from 6 p. m. the 17th to 8 a. m. on the 18th; amount, 3.00 inches. Thunder and lightning in the evening of the 24th.
Sept. 15	7 a. m.	......	56	......	Cu. 10	S. 3	S. 2	......	
	2 p. m.	......	65.5	......	Cu. 10	N. 3	N. 1	......	
	9 p. m.	......	......	......	10	0	0	......	
Sept. 16	7 a. m.	......	57	......	Cu. 9	S. 1	S.	......	
	2 p. m.	......	62	......	Cu. 10	NW. 2	S. 1	......	
	9 p. m.	......	......	......	0	0	0	......	
Sept. 17	7 a. m.	......	57	......	Cu. 10	S. 1	S. 1	......	
	2 p. m.	......	75	......	Cu. 10	NE. 2	E. 1	......	
	9 p. m.	......	......	......	Nim. 10	N. 2	N. 1	......	
Sept. 18	7 a. m.	......	48	......	Nim. 10	N. 3	N. 3	......	
	2 p. m.	......	48	......	Cu. 10	N. 2	N. 3	......	
	9 p. m.	......	42	......	0	0	N. 1	......	
Sept. 19	7 a. m.	......	33	......	0	0	S.	......	
	2 p. m.	......	56	......	0	0	S.	......	
	9 p. m.	......	......	......	0	0	0	......	
Sept. 20	7 a. m.	......	42	......	0	0	S. 3	......	
	2 p. m.	......	61	......	0	0	S. 3	......	
	9 p. m.	......	53	......	Cir. 4	......	S. 2	......	
Sept. 21	7 a. m.	......	52	......	0	0	S. 2	......	
	2 p. m.	......	66	......	0	0	S. 2	......	
	9 p. m.	......	53	......	0	0	S. 1	......	
Sept. 22	7 a. m.	......	52	......	Cir. 3	S. 1	S. 1	......	
	2 p. m.	......	72.5	......	Cir. 2	S. 3	S. 1	......	
	9 p. m.	......	......	......	0	0	0	......	

STORMS Nos. 2 AND 3, SEPTEMBER, 1859.

RED RIVER SETTLEMENT, BRITISH AMERICA—Continued.

Month and day.	Hour.	Barom'r corrected to 32° F.	Thermometer.	Force of vapor.	Cloudiness.	Motion of clouds.	Winds.	Relative humidity.	REMARKS.
Sept. 23	7 a. m.	......	53.5	......	0	0	S.	......	
	2 p. m.	......	75.5	......	Cir. 2	......	S.	......	
	9 p. m.	......	63	......	St. 10	......	S.	......	
Sept. 24	7 a. m.	......	60	......	Nim. 10	SW. 2	E.		
	2 p. m.	......	65	......	Cir. 4	S. 1	S. 1	......	
	9 p. m.	......	49	......	0	0	0	......	

ST. JOHN'S, NEWFOUNDLAND.

Month and day.	Hour.	Barom'r corrected to 32° F.	Thermometer.	Force of vapor.	Cloudiness.	Motion of clouds.	Winds.	Relative humidity.	REMARKS.
Sept. 15	9 p. m.	29.51	48	......	Cu. 2	0	W. 4	......	14th. Showery all day; raining hard at 4 p. m.; cleared off at 8 p. m; northern lights; amount, 1.32 inch. 15th. Cold and blustering. 16th. Cold sharp breeze. 17th. Morning very cold; light breeze; night cold and dark. 18th. Morning rainy; day fine; evening foggy; amount, 0.32 inch. 19th. Morn fine; dull; fog over the town; eve raining hard; amount, 0.46 inch. 20th. Morn fine but foggy; night cleared off; dark. 21st. Clear and cold. 22d. Clear and cold; high wind. 23d. Morn dull; eve cold. 24th. Fine clear and cold; northern lights. 25th. Fine fresh breeze; night quite warm; northern lights. 26th. Morn dull; evening raining hard; amount, 0.40 inch. 27th. Heavy rain all day and night; amount, 2.18 inches.
Sept. 16	7 a. m.	.67	50	......	Cir. 8	1	W. 3	......	
	2 p. m.	.70	54	......	Cir. 8	0	NW. 4	......	
	9 p. m.	.72	54	......	0	0	W. 3	......	
Sept. 17	7 a. m.	.83	45	......	Cir. 3	NE. 2	W. 3	......	
	2 p. m.	.80	54	......	Cu. st. 1	0	NW. 3	......	
	9 p. m.	.81	48	......	Cu. 8	0	NW. 3	......	
Sept. 18	7 a. m.	.71	55	......	Cu. 10	0	SW. 1	......	
	2 p. m.	.67	62	......	Cu. 9	0	SW. 2	......	
	9 p. m.	.62	54	......	St. 10	0	SW. 2	......	
Sept. 19	7 a. m.	.65	56	......	St. 8	0	SSW. 1	......	
	2 p. m.	.57	58	......	St. 9	0	SSW. 1	......	
	9 p. m.	.49	54	......	St. 9	0	SW. 1	......	
Sept. 20	7 a. m.	.39	60	......	Cir. 9	0	NE. 2	......	
	2 p. m.	.39	70	......	0	0	NE. 3	......	
	9 p. m.	.40	54	......	0	0	N. 3	......	
Sept. 21	7 a. m.	.61	47	......	0	0	NW. 4	......	
	2 p. m.	.62	56	......	0	0	NW. 5	......	
	9 p. m.	.81	46	......	St. 10	0	NW. 4	......	
Sept. 22	7 a. m.	.92	45	......	Cu. 3	NW. 9	NNW. 4	......	
	2 p. m.	.91	50	......	Cir. 2	NW. 7	NNW. 3	......	
	9 p. m.	30.00	39	......	0	0	NW. 2	......	
Sept. 23	7 a. m.	29.52	51	......	Cir. 8	0	W. 2	......	
	2 p. m.	.78	60	......	Cu. 3	0	NW. 2	......	
	9 p. m.	.80	32	......	0	0	NW. 2	......	
Sept. 24	7 a. m.	.82	45	......	Cu. 3	0	N. 3	......	
	2 p. m.	.80	48	......	0	0	N. 3	......	
	9 p. m.	.79	39	......	0	0	SE. 1	......	
Sept. 25	7 a. m.	.71	52	......	Cir. 4	0	W. 4	......	
	2 p. m.	.70	62	......	Cu. 4	NW. 3	NW. 4	......	
	9 p. m.	.70	38	......	Cu. st. 10	W. 3	NNW. 4	......	
Sept. 26	7 a. m.	.76	58	......	St. 7	0	NW. 1	......	
	2 p. m.	.72	72	......	Cu. 6	0	NW. 2	......	
	9 p. m.	.73	60	......	Cu. 5	0	W. 2	......	
Sept. 27	7 a. m.	.50	62	......	Cu. 9	0	S. 4	......	
	2 p. m.	.49	69	......	St. 9	0	SE. 3	......	

ST. MARTIN, CANADA.

Month and day.	Hour.	Barom'r corrected to 32° F.	Thermometer.	Force of vapor.	Cloudiness.	Motion of clouds.	Winds.	Relative humidity.	REMARKS.
Sept. 14	10 p. m.	29.850	38.1	.186	Clear	Aurora	W.	81	14th. Snow, with hail.
Sept. 15	6 a. m.	30.083	37.2	.178	Clear, frost	....	WNW	81	
	2 p. m.	.107	20	.139	Clear	....	W. by N.	39	
	10 p. m.	.154	38.4	.165	Cir. 4	....	SW.	72	
Sept. 16	6 a. m.	.120	34.2	.144	Cir. cu st. 8	....	SE	75	
	2 p. m.	.044	61.3	.249	Clear	....	ESE	47	
	10 p. m.	29.998	44.6	.241	Clear	....	ESE	84	
Sept. 17	6 a. m.	.856	42	.228	Cu. st. 10	....	E	87	
	2 p. m.	.789	58.2	.387	Cu. st. 10	....	E. by N.	80	
	10 p. m.	.834	52.2	.361	Cu. st. 10	....	NE. by E.	93	

STORMS Nos. 2 AND 3, SEPTEMBER, 1859.

ST. MARTIN, CANADA--Continued.

Month and day.	Hour.	Barom'r corrected to 32° F.	Thermometer.	Force of vapor.	Cloudiness.	Motion of clouds.	Winds.	Relative humidity.	REMARKS.
Sept. 18	6 a. m.	29.840	48	.303	Cu. st. 10	....	W..........	89	
	2 p. m.	.862	75.7	.574	Clear	....	S..........	70	
	10 p. m.	.848	50.4	.290	Clear	F't aurora.	S. by W.....	82	
Sept. 19	6 a. m.	.640	45.2	.211	Clear	....	E	72	
	2 p. m.	.629	77	.534	Clear	....	S by E	59	
	10 p. m.	.610	61.7	.442	Cu. st. 9	....	SE. by E	83	
Sept. 20	6 a. m.	.632	55.5	.405	Rain	....	N	94	
	2 p. m.	.814	62.4	.429	Cu. st. 10	....	NE	77	
	10 p. m.	.973	46.3	.238	Clear	Aurora ...	ENE	77	
Sept. 21	6 a. m.	30.008	43	.215	Cu. st. 8	....	ENE	79	
	2 p. m.	29.943	47	.291	Rain	....	NE. by E....	89	
	10 p. m.	.986	48	.316	Slight rain...	....	NE. by E....	96	
Sept. 22	6 a. m.	.940	45.2	.294	Rain	....	NE. by E....	99	
	2 p. m.	.880	54.3	.396	Rain	....	NE. by E....	96	
	10 p. m.	.887	53.6	.397	C. st. 10	....	NE. by E....	95	
Sept. 23	6 a. m.	.840	50.0	.341	Rain	....	NE. by E....	96	
	2 p. m.	.844	55.2	.383	Rain	....	NE. by E....	90	
	10 p. m.	.887	52.6	.361	Cu. st. 10	....	NE. by E....	93	
Sept. 24	6 a. m.	.834	50.9	.348	Cu. st. 9	....	N	92	
	2 p. m.	.800	63.2	.429	Cu. st. 6	....	NE. by E....	77	
	10 p. m.	.791	55.2	.383	Cu. st. 10	....	NE. by E....	90	
Sept. 25	6 a. m.	.870	53	.354	Cu st. 10	....	ESE	90	
	2 p. m.	.864	62.3	.436	Cu. st. 9	....	ESE	80	

STANBRIDGE, CANADA.

Month and day.	Hour.	Barom'r corrected to 32° F.	Thermometer.	Force of vapor.	Cloudiness.	Motion of clouds.	Winds.	Relative humidity.	REMARKS.
Sept. 14	9 p. m.	......	39	......	5	....	W. 2	......	Rain, more or less, on the 14th, 17th, 20th, 21st, 22d, 23d, and 25th.
Sept. 15	7 a. m.	......	32	......	3	....	W. 2	......	
	2 p. m.	......	45	......	4	....	W. 3	......	
	9 p. m.	......	36	......	3	....	W. 2	......	
Sept. 16	7 a. m.	......	37	......	8	....	SE. 1	......	
	2 p. m.	......	53	......	2	....	E. 1	......	
	9 p. m.	......	42	......	4	....	SE. 1	......	
Sept. 17	7 a. m.	......	48	......	10	....	SE. 1	......	
	2 p. m.	......	57	......	10	....	SE. 1	......	
	9 p. m.	......	40	......	10	....	NE. 1	......	
Sept. 18	7 a. m.	......	46	......	10	Fog	N 1	......	
	2 p. m.	......	62	......	1	....	NW. 2	......	
	9 p. m	......	47	......	0	....	E. 1	......	
Sept. 19	7 a. m.	......	45	......	2	....	SE. 1	......	
	2 p. m.	......	70	......	0	....	S. 3	......	
	9 p. m.	......	63	......	3	....	S. 2	......	
Sept. 20	7 a. m.	......	58	......	10	....	N. 2	......	
	2 p. m.	......	53	......	9	....	NE. 2	......	
	9 p. m.	......	48	......	8	....	NE. 2	......	
Sept. 21	7 a. m.	......	46	......	10	....	NE. 1	......	
	2 p. m.	......	54	......	10	....	E. 1	......	
	9 p. m.	......	51	......	10	....	NE. 1	......	
Sept. 22	7 a. m.	......	51	......	10	....	SE. 1	......	
	2 p. m.	......	61	......	9	....	SE. 2	......	
	9 p. m.	......	56	......	10	....	SE. 1	......	
Sept. 23	7 a. m.	......	55	......	10	....	SE. 1	......	
	2 p. m.	......	61	......	10	....	SE. 1	......	
	9 p. m.	......	57	......	10	....	W. 1	......	
Sept. 24	7 a. m.	......	52	......	10	Fog	W. 1	......	
	2 p. m.	......	57	......	10	....	SE. 1	......	
	9 p. m.	......	55	......	10	....	NE. 1	......	
Sept. 25	7 a. m.	......	55	......	10	....	N. 1	......	
	2 p. m.	......	63	......	8	....	SW. 1	......	

STORMS Nos. 2 AND 3, SEPTEMBER, 1859.

WINDSOR, NOVA SCOTIA.

Month and day.	Hour.	Barom'r corrected to 32° F.	Thermometer.	Force of vapor.	Cloudiness.		Motion of clouds.	Winds.		Relative humidity.
Sept. 14	9 p. m.	29.593	43	.254	Nim.	1		W.	4	92
Sept. 15	7 a. m.	.886	43.5	.191	Cu.	7		W.	4	67
	2 p. m.	.881	47.5	.184	Cu.	6		W.	3	56
	9 p. m.	30.148	38.5	.191		0			0	81
Sept. 16	7 a. m.	.244	35	.173		0		W.	1	85
	2 p. m.	.225	56	.363	Cu.	5		W.	2	81
	9 p. m.	.222	39.5	.210		0			0	86
Sept. 17	7 a. m.	.229	34.5	.179	St. or cir.	5			0	89
	2 p. m.	.080	60	.283	Cir., st.	4		S.	1	54
	9 p. m.	.019	48	.297	Nim.	10				89
Sept. 18	7 a. m.	29.836	47.5	.316	Nim.	10		S.	2	96
	2 p. m.	.812	58	.467	Nim.	10		SE.	2	97
	9 p. m.	.787	55	.419	Nim.	10		SE.	2	97
Sept. 19	7 a. m.	.756	55.5	.427	Nim.	10		S.	1	97
	2 p. m.	.767	57.5	.400	Nim., cu.	10		E.	1	84
	9 p. m.	.713	49.5	.355		0			0	100
Sept. 20	7 a. m.	.816	45.5	.305	Cir. cu.	5				100
	2 p. m.	.8[illegible]8	63	.510	Nim., cu.	10		S.	1	88
	9 p. m.	.990	60.5	.480	Nim.	10		SW.	4	99
Sept. 21	7 a. m.	30.244	47.5	.267	Cu.	8		NE.	1	81
	2 p. m.	.279	55.5	.288	Nim., cu.	9		NE.	1	65
	9 p. m.	.321	49	.309	Nim.	10		NE.	1	89
Sept. 22	7 a. m.	.311	45.5	.280	Nim.	10		E.	1	92
	2 p. m.	.317	53	.375	Nim.	10		E.	1	93
	9 p. m.	.241	47	.323	Nim.	10		E.	1	100
Sept. 23	7 a. m.	.165	51.5	.368	Nim.	10		E.	1	96
	2 p. m.	.126	59	.469	Nim.	10		E.	1	94
	9 p. m.	30.049	54.5	.411	Nim.	10		E.	1	97
Sept. 24	7 a. m.	.015	54.5	.426	Nim.	10		E.	1	100
	2 p. m.	29.990	62.5	.485	Nim.	10		E.	2	86
	9 p. m.	.945	57	.466	Nim.	10		E.	2	100
Sept. 25	7 a. m.	.887	60.5	.511	Nim.	10		E.	1	97
	2 p. m.	.873	73	.600	Nim., cu.	7				74
	9 p. m.	.937	59.5	.493	Nim., cu.	8				97
Sept. 26	7 a. m.	.922	56.5	.443	Nim., cu.	8			0	97

REMARKS.

14th. Rain from early morning till 6 p. m.

Began to rain at 6 p. m. the 17th and ended in the night of the 18th.

Storm commenced at 6 p. m. the 21st and ended before day on the 25th.

WOLFVILLE, NOVA SCOTIA.

Month and day.	Hour.	Barom'r corrected to 32° F.	Thermometer.	Force of vapor.	Cloudiness.		Motion of clouds.		Winds.		Relative humidity.
Sept. 14	9 p. m.	29.623	42	.155	St.	7	SW.	3	NW.	4	58
Sept. 15	7 a. m.	.163	40	.181					W.	2	73
	2 p. m.	.781	55	.295	Cir. cu.	3	SW.	2	NW.	3	68
	9 p. m.	.806	40	.181							73
Sept. 16	7 a. m.	.839	37	.157	Cir.	2			W.	1	71
	2 p. m.	.094	62	.429	Haze, cir	10			SW.	2	77
	9 p. m.	.543	45	.251	Nim.	10					84
Sept. 17	7 a. m.	.597	48	.322	Nim.	10			E.	1	96
	2 p. m.	.564	56	.449	Nim.	10			E.	1	100
	9 p. m.	.538	54	.418	Nim.	10			E.	1	100
Sept. 18	7 a. m.	.511	56	.363	St.	10	NE.	3	NE.	3	81
	2 p. m.	.488	68	.577	St.	10					84
	9 p. m.	.491	57	.350							75
Sept. 19	7 a. m.	.485	53	.295	Cir. cu.	5	W.	3	W.	3	73
	2 p. m.	.526	64.5	.522	Nim.	10	W.	3	W.	3	86
	9 p. m.	.435	55	.349	St.	10			W.	1	80
Sept. 20	7 a. m.	.952	49.5	.240	Cir. cu.	10	W.	3	E.	1	68
	2 p. m.	.990	56.5	.356	St.	10			E.	2	78
	9 p. m.	30.045	50	.309	Nim.	10					86
Sept. 21	7 a. m.	.115	48.5	.316	Nim.	10					93
	2 p. m.	.025	51	.374	Nim.	10			E.	1	100
	9 p. m.	29.811	47	.323	Nim.	10			E.	2	100

REMARKS.

Heavy rain, with high wind, from $2\frac{1}{2}$ a. m. to $3\frac{1}{4}$ a. m. on the 14th; amount, 0.30 inch.

15th. Violent gale, with torrents of rain and hail at $3\frac{1}{4}$ p. m.; lasted but a few moments.

17th. Heavy frost in the morning; began to rain at 6 p. m., and continued till the a. m. of the 19th; amount, 2.51 inches.

20th. Rain from $1\frac{1}{4}$ to 3 p. m.; amount, 0.30 inch.

Storm commenced at 6 p. m. the 21st, and ended in the a. m. of the 25th; amount, 2.30 inches.

Rain from 2 p. m. the 26th to a. m. on the 27th; amount, 1.02 inch.

STORMS Nos. 2 AND 3, SEPTEMBER, 1859.

WOLFVILLE, NOVA SCOTIA—Continued.

Month and day.	Hour.	Barom'r corrected to 32° F.	Thermometer.	Force of vapor.	Cloudiness.	Motion of clouds.	Winds.	Relative humidity.	REMARKS.
Sept. 22	7 a. m.	29. 875	52	. 388	Nim. 10	----------	E. 1	100	
	2 p. m.	. 825	55	. 433	Nim. 10	----------	E. 2	100	
	9 p. m.	. 714	55	. 433	Nim. 10	----------	E. 1	100	
Sept. 23	7 a. m.	. 685	54. 5	. 411	Nim. 10	----------	E. 2	97	
	2 p. m.	. 524	56	. 391	Nim. 10	----------	SE. 2	87	
	9 p. m.	. 561	56	. 420	Nim. 5	SE. 2	SE. 2	93	
Sept. 24	7 a. m.	. 465	65	. 516	St. 10	----------	----------	84	
	2 p. m.	. 446	66. 5	. 529	St. 5	S. 1	NE. 1	81	
	9 p. m.	. 480	62	. 523	St. 9	S. 1	NE. 1	94	
Sept. 25	7 a. m.	. 614	62	. 491	St. 10	----------	----------	88	
	2 p. m.	. 388	64	. 562	Nim. 10	----------	E. 1	94	
	9 p. m.	. 415	61	. 505	Nim. 10	----------	E. 1	94	
Sept. 26	7 a. m.	. 445	65	. 583	St. 10	W. 2	W. 1	94	

BELFAST, MAINE.

Month and day.	Hour.	Barom'r corrected to 32° F.	Thermometer.	Force of vapor.	Cloudiness.	Motion of clouds.	Winds.	Relative humidity.	REMARKS.
Sept. 14	6 p. m.	------	44	------	Cu. 2	0	NW. 5	------	14th. 9 a. m. ther. 51° ; heavy rain clouds rolling to NE. and W.; force, 6; 10½ a. m. hurricane, wind NW., ther. 53°; 10. 35 a. m. hurricane, accompanied by rain, ther. 50°, wind NW.; 10. 40 a. m. heavy fall of hail, size of peas, ther. 44°, wind NW., 7 ; 10. 45 a. m. ther. 42°, wind NW., 5 ; 10. 50 a. m. ther. 42°, raining, wind 5 ; 10. 55 a. m. sprinkling, ther. 42° ; 11 a. m. rain ceased, ther. 43°; violent gale from noon to 2 p. m., and from 2½ p. m. till sunset, wind NW.; amount of rain, 0.12 inch. 15th. Ther. 33° at sunrise ; first frost of the season ; gale all day. 16th. Ther. 33° at sunrise ; water congealed for the first time this season ; very heavy frost. 17th. Rain at intervals from 2 p. m. till some time in the night ; amount, 0. 25 inch. 19th and 20th. Misty all day. 21st. Began to rain at noon, wind NE. by E. ; rain continued without interruption till in the night of the 24th ; during that period the sun was not visible; constant heavy fog ; amount of rain, 3. 20 inches. 25th. Slight shower of rain at 3 p.m.
Sept. 15	7 a. m.	------	49	------	Cu. st. 1	----------	NW. 4	------	
	Noon.	------	47. 5	------	St. 1	----------	NW. 6	------	
	6 p. m.	------	44	------	Cir., cu. st. 8	NE. 1	NW. 3	------	
Sept. 16	7 a. m.	------	46	------	Cir. 2	NE. 1	SW. 1	------	
	Noon.	------	54	------	Cir. st. 4	E. 2	W. 3	------	
	6 p. m.	------	45	------	Nim. 5	NE. 2	W. 4	------	
Sept. 17	7 a. m.	------	48. 4	------	Nim. 10	N. 1	S. 1	------	
	Noon.	------	57	------	Nim. 10	N. 2	S. 3	------	
	6 p. m.	------	48. 5	------	Nim. 10	NW. 1	SE. 2	------	
Sept. 18	7 a. m.	------	47	------	Nim. 9	SE. 1	N. 2	------	
	Noon.	------	57. 6	------	Cu. 2	S. 3	N. 5	------	
	6 p. m.	------	61	------	0	----------	N. 2	------	
Sept. 19	7 a. m.	------	57	------	St. 2	S. 1	S. 1	------	
	Noon.	------	67. 2	------	Cir. 1	----------	E. 0	------	
	6 p. m.	------	58	------	0	----------	S. 0	------	
Sept. 20	7 a. m.	------	58	------	Nim. 10	N. 2	NE. 2	------	
	Noon.	------	73	------	Nim. 10	SW. 2	S. 2	------	
	6 p. m.	------	63	------	Nim. 10	SW. 3	E. 3	------	
Sept. 21	7 a. m.	------	43	------	Nim. 10	S. 2	NE. 2	------	
	Noon.	------	45	------	Nim. 10	SW. 2	NE. 2	------	
	6 p. m.	------	44	------	Nim. 10	SW. 2	NE. 2	------	
Sept. 22	7 a. m.	------	45	------	Nim. 10	S. 2	E. 2	------	
	Noon.	------	48	------	Nim. 10	SW. 2	E. 2	------	
	6 p. m.	------	48	------	Nim. 10	W. 3	E. 2	------	
Sept. 23	7 a. m.	------	49	------	Nim. 10	W. 2	NE. 2	------	
	Noon.	------	52	------	Nim. 10	W. 2	NE. 2	------	
	6 p. m.	------	53	------	Nim. 10	SW. 2	NE. 2	------	
Sept. 24	7 a. m.	------	53	------	Nim. 10	SW. 2	NE. 2	------	
	Noon.	------	57	------	Nim. 10	SW. 2	NE. 2	------	
	6 p. m.	------	57	------	Nim. 10	W. 2	E. 2	------	
Sept. 25	7 a. m.	------	57	------	Nim. 10	SW. 1	NE. 2	------	
	Noon.	------	64	------	Cir. st. 10	S. 1	N. 1	------	
	6 p. m.	------	58	------	Cu. st. 3	S. 2	N. 2	------	

STORMS Nos. 2 AND 3, SEPTEMBER, 1859.

CORNISH, MAINE.

Month and day.	Hour.	Barom't corrected to 32° F.	Thermometer.	Force of vapor.	Cloudiness.	Motion of clouds.	Winds.	Relative humidity.	REMARKS.
Sept. 14	9 p. m.		42		Cu. st. 4		NW. 2		14th. Rainbow at 7½ a. m.; began
Sept. 15	7 a. m.		35		Cir. st. 1		NW		to rain at 8 a. m.; squalls of sleet
	2 p. m.		47		Cir. 4		NW. 1		from 9 to 11 a. m.; snow at 3 p.
	9 p. m.		40		Cir. 4		W		m.; several snow squalls in the
Sept. 16	7 a. m.		37		Cir. 5		W		afternoon.
	2 p. m.		54		Cir. 3		W. 1		15th. Heavy frost; cold and win-
	9 p. m.		44		Cir. 5		SW		try during the day.
Sept. 17	7 a. m.		47		Nim. 9		SW		16th. Heavy frost in the morning;
	2 p. m.		50		Nim. 10		E		hazy; solar halo most of the p m.
	9 p. m.		46		Nim. 10		NE		17th. Began to rain at 10 a. m.;
Sept. 18	7 a. m.		48		Cir. st. 8		N. 1		constant rain in the p. m.; heavy
	2 p. m.		66		Cir. st. 1		N. 1		in the evening; amount, 0.56
	9 p. m.		58		0		N		inch.
Sept. 19	7 a. m.		51		Cir. 1	W. 1	SW		20th. Hazy a. m.; solar halo at 11
	2 p. m.		68		Cir. 1		S. 1		a. m.; clouds thickened in the
	9 p. m.		56		Cir. st. 1		S		p. m.; began to rain at 5 p. m.,
Sept. 20	7 a. m.		60		St. 3	W. 3	SW. 2		clouds SW.
	2 p. m.		71		Cir. st. 8		SW. 1		21st. Drizzling rain.
	9 p. m.		61		Nim. 10		NE. 1		22d. Drizzling rain.
Sept. 21	7 a. m.		42		Nim. 10		NE. 2		23d. Drizzling rain till 4½ p. m.;
	2 p. m.		40		Nim. 10		NE. 1		commenced again at 5¼ p. m.;
	9 p. m.		40		Nim. 10		NE. 2		wind E. by N.
Sept. 22	7 a. m.		44		Nim. 10		NE. 2		24th. Showers at intervals during
	2 p. m.		47		Nim. 10		NE. 2		the day; wind varying from N.
	9 p. m.		46		Nim. 10		NE. 2		to NW.
Sept. 23	7 a. m.		47		Nim. 10		N. 2		25th. Partially clear in the morn-
	2 p. m.		52		Nim. 10		N. 1		ing; clouded up; began to break
	9 p. m.		50		Nim. 10		N. 1		away at 10 a. m.; fair and plea-
Sept. 24	7 a. m.		51		Nim. 10		N. 1		sant in the p. m.; amount of rain
	2 p. m.		57		Nim. 10		N. 1		recorded since the 17th, 2.625
	9 p. m.		55		Nim. 10		N. 1		inches.
Sept. 25	7 a. m.		56		Cir. st. 9		NW		
	2 p. m.		66		Cir. st. 5		W. 1		
	9 p. m.		58		Cir. st. 3		SE		

CORNISHVILLE, MAINE.

Month and day.	Hour.	Barom't corrected to 32° F.	Thermometer.	Force of vapor.	Cloudiness.	Motion of clouds.	Winds.	Relative humidity.	REMARKS.
Sept. 14	9 p. m.		44		Cu. 5		NW. 3		14th. Snow squall at 10 a. m.
Sept. 15	7 a. m.		36		Cir. st. 5		NW. 3		16th. Solar halo from 1 to 4 p. m.
	2 p. m.		49		Cir. 5		NW. 2		Rain from 11 a. m. the 17th to 1
	9 p. m.		43		Cu. 5		NW. 1		a. m. on the 18th; amount, 0.53
Sept. 16	7 a. m.		43		Cir. cu. 5		W. 1		inch.
	2 p. m.		57		Cir. st. 5		SW. 2		Storm commenced at 6 p. m. the
	9 p. m.		45		Cir. cu. 5		S. 1		20th, and ended at 2 p. m. on
Sept. 17	7 a. m.		48		Nim. 10		S. 1		the 25th; amount, 2.04 inches.
	2 p. m.		57		Nim. 10		SE. 2		
	9 p. m.		46		Nim. 10		SE. 1		
Sept. 18	7 a. m.		48		Nim. 10		NE. 3		
	2 p. m.		67		0		NE. 3		
	9 p. m.		57		0		NE. 1		
Sept. 19	7 a. m.		54		0		W. 2		
	2 p. m.		71		0		S. 3		
	9 p. m.		60		0		S. 3		
Sept. 20	7 a. m.		61		Cir. cu. & st. 5		W. 2		
	2 p. m.		73		Nim. 10		S. 3		
	9 p. m.		65		Nim. 10		S. 2		
Sept. 21	7 a. m.		45		Nim. 10		E. 2		
	2 p. m.		44		Nim. 10		E. 2		
	9 p. m.		43		Nim. 10		NE. 2		
Sept. 22	7 a. m.		44		Nim. 10		NE. 2		
	2 p. m.		49		Nim. 10		NE. 3		
	9 p. m.		48		Nim. 10		NE. 2		

STORMS Nos. 2 AND 3, SEPTEMBER, 1859.

CORNISHVILLE, MAINE—Continued.

Month and day.	Hour.	Barom'r corrected to 32° F.	Thermometer.	Force of vapor.	Cloudiness	Motion of clouds.	Winds.	Relative humidity.	REMARKS.
Sept. 23	7 a. m.	------	48	------	Nim. 10	----------	NE. 2	------	
	2 p. m.	------	53	------	Nim. 10	----------	NE. 2	------	
	9 p. m.	------	51	------	Nim. 10	----------	NE. 2	------	
Sept. 24	7 a. m.	------	53	------	St. 10	----------	N. 3	------	
	2 p. m.	------	60	------	Nim. 10	----------	N. 2	------	
	9 p. m.	------	56	------	Nim. 10	----------	N. 2	------	
Sept. 25	7 a. m.	------	57	------	Nim. 10	----------	N. 1	------	
	2 p. m.	------	66	------	Nim. 10	----------	N. 1	------	
	9 p. m.	------	60	------	Nim. 5	----------	N. 1	------	

DEXTER, MAINE.

Month and day.	Hour.	Barom'r corrected to 32° F.	Thermometer.	Force of vapor.	Cloudiness	Motion of clouds.	Winds.	Relative humidity.	REMARKS.
Sept. 14	9 p. m.	------	------	------	0	----------	NW. 4		14th. Rain from 10 a. m. till noon;
Sept. 15	7 a. m.	------	------	------	Cir. st. 5	----------	W. 3	------	amount, 0. 125 inch.
	2 p. m.	------	------	------	Cir. st. 5	----------	W. 3	------	17th. Sprinkle of rain at 1 p. m.
	9 p. m.	------	------	------	St. 2	----------	NW. 2	------	Rain from 2 p. m. the 21st to 10
Sept. 16	7 a. m.	------	------	------	Cir. st. 3	----------	W. 1	------	p. m. on the 25th; amount,
	2 p. m.	------	------	------	Cir. cu. 5	----------	W. 3	------	2. 50 inches.
	9 p. m.	------	------	------	Cir. st. 2	----------	NW. 1	------	
Sept. 17	7 a. m.	------	------	------	Cir. st. 9	----------	SW. 2	------	
	2 p. m.	------	------	------	Nim. 10	----------	SW. 2	------	
	9 p. m.	------	------	------	Nim. 10	----------	0	------	
Sept. 18	7 a. m.	------	------	------	Nim. 10	----------	E. 3	------	
	2 p. m.	------	------	------	St. 1	----------	NE. 4	------	
	9 p. m.	------	------	------	0	----------	NW. 2	------	
Sept. 19	7 a. m.	------	------	------	Cir. st. 5	----------	NW. 1	------	
	2 p. m.	------	------	------	Cir. st. 3	----------	W. 2	------	
	9 p. m.	------	------	------	Cir. st. 2	----------	SW. 2	------	
Sept. 20	7 a. m.	------	------	------	Fog 10	----------	S. 3	------	
	2 p. m.	------	------	------	Cir. cu. 10	----------	NE. 2	------	
	9 p. m.	------	------	------	Nim. 9	----------	NE. 2	------	
Sept. 21	7 a. m.	------	------	------	Cir. st. 10	----------	N. 4	------	
	2 p. m.	------	------	------	Nim. 10	----------	NE. 3	------	
	9 p. m.	------	------	------	Nim. 10	----------	NE. 3	------	
Sept. 22	7 a. m.	------	------	------	Nim. 10	----------	NE. 3	------	
	2 p. m.	------	------	------	Nim. 10	----------	NE. 3	------	
	9 p. m.	------	------	------	Nim. 10	----------	NE. 2	------	
Sept. 23	7 a. m.	------	------	------	Nim. 10	----------	NE. 3	------	
	2 p. m.	------	------	------	Nim. 10	----------	NE. 3	------	
	9 p. m.	------	------	------	Nim. 10	----------	NE. 3	------	
Sept. 24	7 a. m.	------	------	------	Nim. 10	----------	NE. 3	------	
	2 p. m.	------	------	------	Nim. 10	----------	NE. 2	------	
	9 p. m.	------	------	------	Nim. 10	----------	NE. 2	------	
Sept. 25	7 a. m.	------	------	------	Nim. 10	----------	NE. 3	------	
	2 p. m.	------	------	------	Cir. cu. 9	----------	E. 3	------	
	9 p. m.	------	------	------	Cir. st. 8	----------	NW. 1	------	

LISBON, MAINE.

Month and day.	Hour.	Barom'r corrected to 32° F.	Thermometer.	Force of vapor.	Cloudiness	Motion of clouds.	Winds.	Relative humidity.	REMARKS.
Sept. 14	9 p. m.	------	43	------	0	----------	NW. 3	------	14th. Very strong breezes west-
Sept. 15	7 a. m.	------	42	------	0	----------	W. 3	------	ward, with heavy squalls of
	2 p. m.	------	52	------	Cir. 2	NW. 3	NW. 4	------	snow and hail.
	9 p. m.	------	43	------	Cir. 4	NW. 2	NW. 3	------	15th. Fresh breezes during the
Sept. 16	7 a. m.	------	38	------	Cir. st. 10	W. 1	NW. 2	------	past night; light frost.
	2 p. m.	------	54	------	Cir. 3	W. 2	SW. 3	------	16th. Severe frost last night, kill-
	9 p. m.	------	42	------	Cir. st. 2	W. 2	S. 2	------	ing vegetation, &c.; at noon
Sept. 17	7 a. m.	------	48	------	Nim. 10	S. 1	S. 2	------	wind south, and quite mild.
	2 p. m.	------	55	------	Nim. 10	S. 1	S. 2	------	17th. Rain from 1 to 12 p. m.;
	9 p. m.	------	48	------	Nim. 10	SE. 2	SE. 2	------	amount, 0. 50 inch.

STORMS Nos. 2 AND 3, SEPTEMBER, 1859.

LISBON, MAINE—Continued.

Month and day.	Hour.	Barom'r corrected to 32° F.	Thermometer.	Force of vapor.	Cloudiness.	Motion of clouds.	Winds.	Relative humidity.	REMARKS.
Sept. 18	7 a. m.	......	52	......	Nim. 4	N. 4	N. 5	......	19th. 10 a. m. wind south.
	2 p. m.	......	68	......	0	....	N. 5	......	20th. 10 a. m. wind W.; 3 p. m. north.
	9 p. m.	......	53	......	0	....	N. 2	......	Storm commenced at 10 a. m. the 21st, and ended at 9 p. m. on the 24th; amount, 4. 10 inches.
Sept. 19	7 a. m.	......	46	......	0	....	N. 2	......	
	2 p. m.	......	70	......	0	....	S. 3	......	
	9 p. m.	......	54	......	0	....	S. 1	......	
Sept. 20	7 a. m.	......	59	......	Fog 10	S. 1	S. 2	......	
	2 p. m.	......	78	......	Cu. 6	N. 2	W. 2	......	
	9 p. m.	......	61	......	Nim. 10	N. 3	N. 5	......	
Sept. 21	7 a. m.	......	48	......	Nim. 10	NE. 2	NE. 3	......	
	2 p. m.	......	46	......	Nim. 10	NE. 2	NE. 3	......	
	9 p. m.	......	47	......	Nim. 10	NE. 2	NE. 3	......	
Sept. 22	7 a. m.	......	49	......	Nim. 10	NE. 2	NE. 2	......	
	2 p. m.	......	53	......	Nim. 10	NE. 2	NE. 2	......	
	9 p. m.	......	52	......	Nim. 10	NE. 2	NE. 2	......	
Sept. 23	7 a. m.	......	50	......	Nim. 10	N. 3	N. 3	......	
	2 p. m.	......	55	......	Nim. 10	NE. 2	NE. 2	......	
	9 p. m.	......	55	......	Nim. 10	NE. 2	NE. 2	......	
Sept. 24	7 a. m.	......	56	......	Nim. 10	N. 2	N. 2	......	
	2 p. m.	......	62	......	Nim. 10	N. 1	N. 2	......	
	9 p. m.	......	59	......	Nim. 10	N. 2	N. 2	......	
Sept. 25	7 a. m.	......	60	......	Nim. cum. 10	N. 2	N. 2	......	
	2 p. m.	......	68	......	Nim. cum. 10	N. 2	N. 2	......	
	9 p. m.	......	55	......	0	....	N. 1	......	

GARDINER, MAINE.

Month and day.	Hour.	Barom'r corrected to 32° F.	Thermometer.	Force of vapor.	Cloudiness.	Motion of clouds.	Winds.	Relative humidity.	REMARKS.
Sept. 14	9 p. m.	29. 84	52	. 244	Clear 0	....	NW. 5	91	14th. Very violent squalls; amount of rain, 0. 060 inch.
Sept. 15	7 a. m.	30. 10	43	. 164	Cir. 1	NW. 4	NW. 3	59	17th. Began to rain at 12½ p. m., and ended in the night; amount, 0. 296 inch.
	2 p. m.	29. 13	49	. 107	Cir. 4	NW. 4	NW. 5	31	18th. Aurora, with faint streamers.
	9 p. m.	30. 25	43	. 186	Cu. st. 10	NW. 1	WNW. 2	67	Storm commenced at 11½ a. m. the 21st, and ended at 8 a. m. on the 25th; amount, 1. 347 inch.
Sept. 16	7 a. m.	30. 30	40½	. 175	Cir. 9	NW. 3	SE. 1	69	
	2 p. m.	30. 21	56	. 282	Cir. 4	W. 3	W. 2	63	
	9 p. m.	30. 17	42	. 244	Overcast 10	....	SW. 2	91	
Sept. 17	7 a. m.	30. 11	46	. 311	Nim. 10	SE. 3	SW. 1	100	
	2 p. m.	30. 01	53	. 375	Rain 10	....	SSE. 2	93	
	9 p. m.	29. 88	47	. 323	Rain 10	....	ESE. 2	100	
Sept. 18	7 a. m.	29. 78	47	. 298	{ Cir. ...... { Cu. st. 9	SW. 1 NE. 6	} NE. 5	92	
	2 p. m.	29. 73	64	. 403	St. 1	....	NE. 4	67	
	9 p. m.	29. 81	53	. 375	Clear 0	....	NW. 3	93	
Sept. 19	7 a. m.	29. 85	47	. 298	Fog 10	....	Calm	92	
	2 p. m.	29. 78	66	. 471	Clear 0	....	SW. 3	73	
	9 p. m.	29. 79	53	. 403	Clear 0	....	ESE. 3	100	
Sept. 20	7 a. m.	29. 76	56	. 449	Fog 10	....	SE. 3	100	
	2 p. m.	29. 82	69	. 635	Nim. 10	SSW. 1	SSW. 1	90	
	9 p. m.	30. 04	58	. 365	Nim. 10	....	NNE. 4	76	
Sept. 21	7 a. m.	30. 26	46	. 215	Nim. 10	....	NNE. 2	69	
	2 p. m.	30. 30	45	. 275	Rain 10	....	NE. 2	92	
	9 p. m.	30. 25	45	. 300	Rain 10	....	NE. 2	100	
Sept. 22	7 a. m.	30. 17	47	. 297	Rain 10	....	NE. 3	85	
	2 p. m.	30. 14	52	. 388	Rain 10	....	NE. 3	100	
	9 p. m.	30. 15	50	. 361	Rain 10	....	NE. 2	100	
Sept. 23	7 a. m.	30. 03	49	. 348	Rain 10	....	NE. 2	100	
	2 p. m.	29. 96	53	. 403	Rain 10	NE. 5	NE. 3	100	
	9 p. m.	29. 94	53½	. 396	Rain 10	....	NE. 2	96	
Sept. 24	7 a. m.	29. 87	54	. 418	Rain 10	....	NE. 2	100	
	2 p. m.	29. 85	60	. 487	Nim. 10	NNE. 4	NE. 3	94	
	9 p. m.	29. 82	57	. 466	Drizzle......	....	NE. 2	100	
Sept. 25	7 a. m.	29. 85	58	. 452	Nim. 10	....	NE. 1	94	
	2 p. m.	29. 85	64	. 563	Cu. 6	NNE. 4	NNE. 2	94	
	9 p. m.	29. 89	56	. 449	Clear 0	....	WNW. 2	100	

STORMS Nos. 2 AND 3, SEPTEMBER, 1859.

HARTLAND, MAINE.

Month and day.	Hour.	Barom'r corrected to 32° F.	Thermometer.	Force of vapor.	Cloudiness.	Motion of clouds.	Winds.		Relative humidity.	REMARKS.
Sept. 14	9 p. m.				0		W.	2		15th. Heavy frost.
Sept. 15	7 a. m.				1		NW.	2		Storm from 2 p. m. the 21st to 12
	2 p. m.				0		NW.	5		p. m. on the 24th.
	9 p. m.				0		NW.	1		
Sept. 16	7 a. m.				0		NW.	1		
	2 p. m.				5		SW.	3		
	9 p. m.				4		W.	1		
Sept. 17	7 a. m.				2		NW.	2		
	2 p. m.				4		SW.	4		
	9 p. m.				0		W.	2		
Sept. 18	7 a. m.				4		W.	3		
	2 p. m.				5		W.	3		
	9 p. m.				4		NW.	3		
Sept. 19	7 a. m.				2		NW.	1		
	2 p. m.				5		NW.	2		
	9 p. m.				0		W.	2		
Sept. 20	7 a. m.				10		SW.	1		
	2 p. m.				10		NW.	2		
	9 p. m.				5		W.	1		
Sept. 21	7 a. m.				10		NW.	1		
	2 p. m.				10		NE.	2		
	9 p. m.				10		NE.	2		
Sept. 22	7 a. m.				10		NE.	1		
	2 p. m.				10		NE.	2		
	9 p. m.				10		NE.	1		
Sept. 23	7 a. m.				10		NE.	2		
	2 p. m.				10		NE.	2		
	9 p. m.				10		NE.	1		
Sept. 24	7 a. m.				10		NE.	1		
	2 p. m.				10		NE.	2		
	9 p. m.				10		NE.	1		
Sept. 25	7 a. m.				5		NW.	3		
	2 p. m.				8		NE.	2		
	9 p. m.				7		W.	2		

LIMINGTON, MAINE.

Month and day.	Hour.	Barom'r corrected to 32° F.	Thermometer.	Force of vapor.	Cloudiness.	Motion of clouds.	Winds.		Relative humidity.	REMARKS.
Sept. 14					4		NW.	4		14th. Very cold; snow squalls dur-
Sept. 15					2		NW.	2		ing the day.
					3		W.	3		15th and 16th. Very cold.
					6		NW.	2		17th. Rain from 2 to 12 p. m.;
Sept. 16					5		NW.	2		amount, 0. 20 inch.
					8		W.	2		18th and 19th. Mild and pleasant.
					5		SW.	4		20th. Commenced raining at 6 p.
Sept. 17					9		W.	2		m.; amount, 0. 50 inch.
					10		NW.	2		21st. Moderate rain all day; am't,
					10		NE.	4		0. 20 inch.
Sept. 18					9		N.	2		22d. Heavy rain most of the day;
					2		NE.	2		amount, 0. 40 inch.
					1		N.	2		23d. Amount of rain, 0. 30 inch;
Sept. 19					0		NW.	1		no appearances of fair weather.
					1		W.	2		24th. Amount of rain, 0. 10 inch;
					0		S.	1		has an appearance at times of
Sept. 20					5		W.	2		clearing off.
					9		NW.	2		25th. Cleared up last night.
					10		NE.	3		
Sept. 21					10		NE.	2		
					10		NE.	3		
					10		NE.	3		
Sept. 22					10		NE.	3		
					10		NE.	3		
					10		NE.	3		

STORMS Nos. 2 AND 3, SEPTEMBER, 1859.

LIMINGTON, MAINE—Continued.

Month and day.	Hour.	Barom'r corrected to 32° F.	Thermometer.	Force of vapor.	Cloudiness.	Motion of clouds.	Winds.	Relative humidity.	REMARKS.
Sept. 23					10		NE. 3		
					10		NE. 3		
					10		NE. 3		
Sept. 24					10		NE. 2		
					10		NE. 2		
					10		NE. 3		
Sept. 25					5		NW. 1		
					2		SW. 1		
					2		SE. 1		

NEW CASTLE, MAINE.

Month and day.	Hour.	Barom'r corrected to 32° F.	Thermometer.	Force of vapor.	Cloudiness.	Motion of clouds.	Winds.	Relative humidity.	REMARKS.
Sept. 14	9 p. m.		40		0		W. 1		14th. A severe squall passed over
Sept. 15	7 a. m.		47		1		W. 2		at 10 a. m.; moved to N. of E.;
	2 p. m.		62		3		W. 3		when it came up the wind was
	9 p. m.				0		SW. 1		nearly SW., but changed to S.,
Sept. 16	7 a. m.		49		8		W. 1		and blew with tremendous force.
	2 p. m.		69		5		W. 1		The course of the squall cloud
	9 p. m.		60		0		W. 1		during the gale was the same for
Sept. 17	7 a. m.				10		SW. 1		some distance, at least 6 miles N.
	2 p. m.				10		SW. 1		and 8 S., and also for ten miles
	9 p. m.				10		SW. 2		E. to W.
Sept. 18	7 a. m.				8		NE. 1		15th. Slight frost.
	2 p. m.				2		NW. 1		16th. Heavy frost.
	9 p. m.				0		NW. 1		17th. Rain from noon to 11 p. m.;
Sept. 19	7 a. m.		68		0		NW. 1		amount, 1. 00 inch.
	2 p. m.		80		0		NW. 1		Storm from 6 a. m. the 21st to —
	9 p. m.		60		0		NW. 1		a. m. on the 25th; amount, 3.00
Sept. 20	7 a. m.				10		SE. 2		inches.
	2 p. m.				5		SW. 1		
	9 p. m.				5		SW. 2		
Sept. 21	7 a. m.				10		NW. 2		
	2 p. m.				10		SW. 1		
	9 p. m.				10		SE. 1		
Sept. 22	7 a. m.				10		NE. 1		
	2 p. m.				10		NE. 1		
	9 p. m.				10		NE. 1		
Sept. 23	7 a. m.				10		NE. 1		
	2 p. m.				10		NE. 1		
	9 p. m.				10		NE. 1		
Sept. 24	7 a. m.				10		NE. 1		
	2 p. m.				10		NE. 1		
	9 p. m.				10		NE. 1		
Sept. 25	7 a. m.				10		NW. 1		
	2 p. m.				10		NW. 1		
	9 p. m.				10		NW. 1		

NORTH BELGRADE, MAINE.

Month and day.	Hour.	Barom'r corrected to 32° F.	Thermometer.	Force of vapor.	Cloudiness.	Motion of clouds.	Winds.	Relative humidity.	REMARKS.
Sept. 14	9 p. m.				1		NW. 3		13th. Rain in the eve.
Sept. 15	7 a. m.				1		NW. 3		14th. Hail and rain at 10 a. m.;
	2 p. m.				2		NW. 3		slight shower and heavy wind p.
	9 p. m.				3		NW. 2		m.
Sept. 16	7 a. m.				5		NW. 2		16th. Slight frost.
	2 p. m.				2		S. 2		17th. Light rain most of the day.
	9 p. m.				1		S. 2		20th. Fog at 7 a. m.; rain p. m.
Sept. 17	7 a. m.				10		SE. 1		Commenced raining at noon the
	2 p. m.				10		SE. 2		21st, and ended at night on the
	9 p. m.				10		S. 1		25th.

STORMS Nos. 2 AND 3, SEPTEMBER, 1859.

NORTH BELGRADE, MAINE—Continued.

Month and day.	Hour.	Barom'r corrected to 32° F.	Thermometer.	Force of vapor.	Cloudiness.	Motion of clouds.	Winds.	Relative humidity.	REMARKS.
Sept. 18	7 a. m.	------	------	------	9	----------	NE. 3	------	
	2 p. m.	------	------	------	1	----------	NE. 3	------	
	9 p. m.	------	------	------	1	----------	NW. 2	------	
Sept. 19	7 a. m.	------	------	------	1	----------	NE. 1	------	
	2 p. m.	------	------	------	1	----------	S. 2	------	
	9 p. m.	------	------	------	1	----------	S. 2	------	
Sept. 20	7 a. m.	------	------	------	10	----------	S. 2	------	
	2 p. m.	------	------	------	8	----------	N. 2	------	
	9 p. m.	------	------	------	8	----------	NE. 3	------	
Sept. 21	7 a. m.	------	------	------	10	----------	NE. 3	------	
	2 p. m.	------	------	------	10	----------	NE. 2	------	
	9 p. m.	------	------	------	10	----------	NE. 1	------	
Sept. 22	7 a. m.	------	------	------	10	----------	NE. 3	------	
	2 p. m.	------	------	------	10	----------	NE. 3	------	
	9 p. m.	------	------	------	10	----------	NE. 2	------	
Sept. 23	7 a. m.	------	------	------	10	----------	NE. 2	------	
	2 p. m.	------	------	------	10	----------	NE. 2	------	
	9 p. m.	------	------	------	10	----------	NE. 2	------	
Sept. 24	7 a. m.	------	------	------	10	----------	NE. 2	------	
	2 p. m.	------	------	------	10	----------	NE. 2	------	
	9 p. m.	------	------	------	10	----------	NW. 2	------	
Sept. 25	7 a. m.	------	------	------	10	----------	N. 2	------	
	2 p. m.	------	------	------	10	----------	NE. 1	------	
	9 p. m.	------	------	------	2	----------	NW. 1	------	

NORWAY, MAINE.

Month and day.	Hour.	Barom'r corrected to 32° F.	Thermometer.	Force of vapor.	Cloudiness.	Motion of clouds.	Winds.	Relative humidity.	REMARKS.
Sept. 14	9 p. m.	------	------	------	2	----------	NW. 4	------	14th. Cold and squally, a little rain,
Sept. 15	7 a. m.	------	------	------	2	----------	NW. 5	------	and considerable wind.
	2 p. m.	------	------	------	2	----------	NW. 5	------	15th. Cold and windy; frost in
	9 p. m.	------	------	------	1	----------	N. 2	------	night.
Sept. 16	7 a. m.	------	------	------	9	----------	NW. 2	------	16th. Fair; rather cool.
	2 p. m.	------	------	------	1	----------	NW. 3	------	17th. Drizzling rain most of the
	9 p. m.	------	------	------	3	----------	SW. 2	------	day.
Sept. 17	7 a. m.	------	------	------	10	----------	SW. 2	------	18th. Frost; pleasant.
	2 p. m.	------	------	------	10	----------	SW. 2	------	19th. Cloudy, with slight rain both
	9 p. m.	------	------	------	10	----------	SW. 3	------	in day and night.
Sept. 18	7 a. m.	------	------	------	1	----------	NW. 3	------	20th. Cold, cloudy, drizzling all day;
	2 p. m.	------	------	------	0	----------	NW. 3	------	some rain in night.
	9 p. m.	------	------	------	2	----------	NW. 2	------	21st. Same as preceding day.
Sept. 19	7 a. m.	------	------	------	8	----------	SW. 1	------	22d. Rain all day.
	2 p. m.	------	------	------	10	----------	SW. 2	------	23d. Rain all day.
	9 p. m.	------	------	------	10	----------	NE. 2	------	24th. Rather drizzly.
Sept. 20	7 a. m.	------	------	------	10	----------	NE. 3	------	
	2 p. m.	------	------	------	10	----------	SE. 3	------	
	9 p. m.	------	------	------	10	----------	SE. 3	------	
Sept. 21	7 a. m.	------	------	------	10	----------	NE. 3	------	
	2 p. m.	------	------	------	10	----------	SE. 3	------	
	9 p. m.	------	------	------	10	----------	SE. 3	------	
Sept. 22	7 a. m.	------	------	------	10	----------	SE. 2	------	
	2 p. m.	------	------	------	10	----------	SE. 2	------	
	9 p. m.	------	------	------	10	----------	NE. 2	------	
Sept. 23	7 a. m.	------	------	------	10	----------	NE. 3	------	
	2 p. m.	------	------	------	10	----------	NE. 3	------	
	9 p. m.	------	------	------	10	----------	NE. 2	------	
Sept. 24	7 a. m.	------	------	------	10	----------	NE. 2	------	
	2 p. m.	------	------	------	10	----------	NE. 2	------	
	9 p. m.	------	------	------	10	----------	NE. 1	------	
Sept. 25	7 a. m.	------	------	------	8	----------	SE. 2	------	
	2 p. m.	------	------	------	8	----------	SE. 2	------	
	9 p. m.	------	------	------	1	----------	SE. 2	------	

STORMS Nos. 2 AND 3, SEPTEMBER, 1859.

PERRY, MAINE.

Month and day.	Hour.	Barom'r corrected to 32° F.	Thermometer.	Force of vapor.	Cloudiness.	Motion of clouds.	Winds.	Relative humidity.	REMARKS.
Sept. 14	9 p. m.	29.67	42	.199	0	----------	NW. 6	74	18th. Storm in the night; amount, 0.17 inch.
Sept. 15	7 a. m.	------	36	------	0	----------	NW. 6	------	
	2 p. m.	------	54	------	0	----------	NW. 6	------	Storm of rain, mist, fog, &c., commenced at 5 p. m. the 21st and ended at 2 p. m. on the 25th; amount, 2.05 inches.
	9 p. m.	30.17	38	.165	0	----------	NW. 1	72	
Sept. 16	7 a. m.	30.31	37	.178	0	----------	SW. 1	81	
	2 p. m.	30.21	56	.155	Cir. st. 8	SW. 1	W. 2	34	
	9 p. m.	30.21	42	.199	0	----------	W. 1	74	
Sept. 17	7 a. m.	30.17	37	.178	Cir. st. 8	W. 1	W. 1	81	
	2 p. m.	30.07	56	.308	St. 10	SW. 1	SW. 2	69	
	9 p. m.	29.97	47	.310	10	----------	SW. 1	92	
Sept. 18	7 a. m.	29.90	47	.298	St. 10	NE. 1	NE. 2	92	
	2 p. m.	29.78	61	.383	St. 10	NE. 1	NE. 2	71	
	9 p. m.	29.79	53	.348	St. 3	NE. 1	NE. 3	86	
Sept. 19	7 a. m.	29.83	46	.311	St. 10	N. 1	NE. 2	100	
	2 p. m.	------	------	------	0	----------	----------	------	
	9 p. m.	29.83	47	.298	0	----------	NW. 1	92	
Sept. 20	7 a. m.	29.77	54	.418	Fog 10	----------	SW. 3	100	
	2 p. m.	------	------	------	----------	----------	----------	------	
	9 p. m.	------	------	------	----------	----------	----------	------	
Sept. 21	7 a. m.	------	------	------	Thick ------	----------	----------	------	
	2 p. m.	------	------	------	----------	----------	----------	------	
	9 p. m.	------	------	------	----------	----------	----------	------	
Sept. 22	7 a. m.	------	------	------	Thick ------	----------	NE. 5	------	
	2 p. m.	30.26	49	.348	----------	----------	NE. 5	100	
	9 p. m.	30.21	49	------	----------	----------	NE. 2	100	
Sept. 23	7 a. m.	30.12	50	.361	Thick ------	----------	NE. 2	100	
	2 p. m.	30.07	50	.361	----------	----------	NE. 2	100	
	9 p. m.	29.99	53	.403	----------	----------	NE. 1	100	
Sept. 24	7 a. m.	30.04	54	.418	Thick ------	----------	NE. 1	100	
	2 p. m.	29.89	56	.449	----------	----------	NE. 1	100	
	9 p. m.	29.88	55	.433	----------	----------	NE. 1	100	
Sept. 25	7 a. m.	29.88	55	.403	Thick ------	----------	NE. 1	100	
	2 p. m.	29.89	60	.518	----------	----------	NE. 0	100	
	9 p. m.	29.93	53	.403	----------	----------	NE. 1	100	

PORTLAND, MAINE.*

Month and day.	Hour.	Barom'r corrected to 32° F.	Thermometer.	Force of vapor.	Cloudiness.	Motion of clouds.	Winds.	Relative humidity.	REMARKS.
Sept. 14	9 p. m.	------	------	------	0	----------	W. 35	------	13th. Showers during the night.
Sept. 15	7 a. m.	------	------	------	0	----------	S. 12	------	14th. First frost.
	2 p. m.	------	------	------	0	----------	S. 12	------	15th. Very cold.
	9 p. m.	------	------	------	0	----------	S. 12	------	17th. Began to rain at 9 p. m. and ended in the night.
Sept. 16	7 a. m.	------	------	------	0	----------	S. 4	------	
	2 p. m.	------	------	------	0	----------	S. 2	------	Storm commenced at 9 p. m. the 20th and ended at 6 p. m. on the 24th.
	9 p. m.	------	------	------	5	----------	S. 2	------	
Sept. 17	7 a. m.	------	------	------	10	----------	S. 4	------	
	2 p. m.	------	------	------	10	----------	SE. 4	------	
	9 p. m.	------	------	------	10	----------	S. 2	------	
Sept. 18	7 a. m.	------	------	------	0	----------	N. 35	------	
	2 p. m.	------	------	------	0	----------	N. 35	------	
	9 p. m.	------	------	------	0	----------	N. 12	------	
Sept. 19	7 a. m.	------	------	------	0	----------	NE. 2	------	
	2 p. m.	------	------	------	0	----------	S. 4	------	
	9 p. m.	------	------	------	2	----------	S. 2	------	
Sept. 20	7 a. m.	------	------	------	7	----------	S. 12	------	
	2 p. m.	------	------	------	8	----------	S. 12	------	
	9 p. m.	------	------	------	10	----------	S. 12	------	
Sept. 21	7 a. m.	------	------	------	10	----------	NE. 12	------	
	2 p. m.	------	------	------	10	----------	NE. 12	------	
	9 p. m.	------	------	------	10	----------	NE. 12	------	
Sept. 22	7 a. m.	------	------	------	10	----------	NE. 12	------	
	2 p. m.	------	------	------	10	----------	N. 12	------	
	9 p. m.	------	------	------	10	----------	N. 12	------	

* Adams, observer.

STORMS Nos. 2 AND 3, SEPTEMBER, 1859.

PORTLAND, MAINE—Continued.

Month and day.	Hour.	Barom'r corrected to 32° F.	Thermometer.	Force of vapor.	Cloudiness.	Motion of clouds.	Winds.	Relative humidity.	REMARKS.
Sept. 23	7 a. m.	------	------	------	10	----------	N. 12	------	
	2 p. m.	------	------	------	10	----------	NE. 12	------	
	9 p. m.	------	------	------	10	----------	N. 4	------	
Sept. 24	7 a. m.	------	------	------	10	----------	NE. 4	------	
	2 p. m.	------	------	------	10	----------	N. 4	------	
	9 p. m.	------	------	------	9	----------	N. 4	------	
Sept. 25	7 a. m.	------	------	------	8	----------	N. 2	------	
	2 p. m.	------	------	------	3	----------	SE. 2	------	
	9 p. m.	------	------	------	2	----------	N. 2	------	

PORTLAND, MAINE.*

Month and day.	Hour.	Barom'r corrected to 32° F.	Thermometer.	Force of vapor.	Cloudiness.	Motion of clouds.	Winds.	Relative humidity.	REMARKS.
Sept. 14	9 p. m.	29.90	44	.162	3	W. 3	W. 3	55	A storm of rain and hail commenced in the night of the 14th and continued till 11.45 a. m. on the 15th; amount, 0.290 inch.
Sept. 15	7 a. m.	30.15	38	.154	0	----------	NW. 1	67½	
	2 p. m.	30.18	50.5	.132	Cir. 7	W. 1	NW. 1	36	
	9 p. m.	30.28	42	.177	Cu. 4	NW. 1	NW. 1	66	
Sept. 16	7 a. m.	30.33	40	.182	Cir. cu., cu. 8	W. 1	W. 1	73	
	2 p. m.	30.26	51	.161	9	----------	SE. 2	42	17th. Began to rain at 11 a. m. and ended in the night; amount, 0.770 inch.
	9 p. m.	30.19	45	.240	Cir. 5	----------	S. 1	80	
Sept. 17	7 a. m.	30.13	48.5	.278	Light fog. 10	----------	SW. 1	81	
	2 p. m.	29.97	51	.348	Rain 10	----------	SE. 2	93	Storm commenced at 8.30 p. m. the 20th and ended in the night of the 24th; amount, 2.60 inches.
	9 p. m.	29.81	45	.287	Rain 10	----------	E. 4	96	
Sept. 18	7 a. m.	29.76	50	.309	Cu. 10	----------	NE. 4	85	
	2 p. m.	29.73	64.5	.366	Cu. 1	----------	N. 2	60	
	9 p. m.	29.81	58	.337	0	----------	W. 1	70	
Sept. 19	7 a. m.	29.86	52	.334	Cir. 1	----------	N. 1	86	
	2 p. m.	29.81	64	.343	0	----------	S. 1	57	
	9 p. m.	29.80	54	.390	0	----------	S. 1	93	
Sept. 20	7 a. m.	29.76	59	------	Cu. 8	W. 1	W. 1	------	
	2 p. m.	29.80	75	.591	Cu. 9	SW. 1	NW.	68	
	9 p. m.	29.99	61	.398	Rain 10	----------	NE. 3	74	
Sept. 21	7 a. m.	30.22	46	.250	Rain 10	----------	NE. 2	80	
	2 p. m.	30.22	45.5	.280	Rain 10	----------	NE. 3	92	
	9 p. m.	30.21	46	.299	Rain 10	----------	NE. 3	96	
Sept. 22	7 a. m.	30.16	47	.323	Rain 10	----------	NE. 1	100	
	2 p. m.	30.13	51.5	.368	Rain 10	----------	NE. 2	96	
	9 p. m.	------	------	------	Rain 10	----------	NE -------	------	
Sept. 23	7 a. m.	30.02	49	.348	Rain 10	----------	NE. 1	100	
	2 p. m.	29.84	59	------	Rain 10	----------	NNE. 1	------	
	9 p. m.	29.94	53	.403	Rain 10	----------	NE. 1	100	
Sept. 24	7 a. m.	29.90	53	.403	Rain 10	----------	N ----------	100	
	2 p. m.	29.87	58	.423	Rain 10	----------	NE. 1	88	
	9 p. m.	------	------	------	10	----------	----------	------	
Sept. 25	7 a. m.	29.88	58	.452	Cu. 9	W. 1	NW. 1	94	
	2 p. m.	29.86	65	.500	Cu. 9	W. 1	S. 1	81	
	9 p. m.	29.91	56.5	.428	Cu. 9	----------	S. 1	94	

STEUBEN, MAINE.

Month and day.	Hour.	Barom'r corrected to 32° F.	Thermometer.	Force of vapor.	Cloudiness.	Motion of clouds.	Winds.	Relative humidity.	REMARKS.
Sept. 14	9 p. m.	29.74	40	.182	St. 1	NW. 1	NW. 3	73	14th. Violent tornado, with rain and hail, from 11½ a. m. till noon; gale continued all the afternoon; amount, 0.20 inch.
Sept. 15	7 a. m.	29.94	40	.139	St. 1	NW. 1	NW. 4	56	
	2 p. m.	30.06	44	.196	St. 1	NW. 1	NW. 3	68	
	9 p. m.	30.21	38	.144	0	0	NW. 2	63	
Sept. 16	7 a. m.	30.32	38	.165	Nim. 3	a	SW. 1	72	17th. Began to rain at 3 p. m. and ended in the night; amount, 0.50 inch.
	2 p. m.	30.29	51	.245	Nim. 5	a	SW. 2	65	
	9 p. m.	30.22	37	.178	Nim. 8	SW. 1	SW. 1	81	
Sept. 17	7 a. m.	30.13	41	.037	Nim. 9	SW. 1	SW. 1	14	18th. Rainbow at 4½ p. m; rain at intervals from 1 p. m. the 20th till the night of the 23d; am't, 2.70 inches.
	2 p. m.	30.10	52	.282	Nim. 10	SW. 1	SW. 1	73	
	9 p. m.	29.93	47	.273	Rain 10	Thick	SW. 1	85	
Sept. 18	7 a. m.	29.75	48	.285	Cir. cu. 2	NE	NE. 3	85	

* Willis, observer.

STORMS Nos. 2 AND 3, SEPTEMBER, 1859.

STEUBEN, MAINE—Continued.

Month and day.	Hour.	Barom'r corrected to 32° F.	Thermometer.	Force of vapor.	Cloudiness.	Motion of clouds.	Winds.	Relative humidity.	REMARKS.
Sept. 18	2 p. m.	29.72	64	.373	Nim. 9	NE. 3	NE. 3	62	
	9 p. m.	29.77	58	.365	St. 2	NE ------	NE. 2	76	
Sept. 19	7 a. m.	29.89	51	.321	St. 2	SW. 1	NE. 1	86	
	2 p. m.	29.80	61	.383	St. 1	a	SW. 2	71	
	9 p. m.	29.81	47	.298	0	0	0	92	
Sept. 20	7 a. m.	29.75	56	.420	Fog 10	----------	SW. 2	94	
	2 p. m.	29.80	63	.478	Fog 10	----------	NE. 2	83	
	9 p. m.	29.86	46	.262	Fog 10	----------	NE. 1	84	
Sept. 21	7 a. m.	------	------	------	Fog 10	----------	NE. 2	------	
	2 p. m.	------	------	------	Fog & rain 10	----------	NE. 3	------	
	9 p. m.	------	------	------	Fog & rain 10	----------	NE. 1	------	
Sept. 22	7 a. m.	------	------	------	Fog 10	----------	NE. 1	------	
	2 p. m.	------	------	------	Fog 10	----------	NE. 1	------	
	9 p. m.	------	------	------	Fog 10	----------	NE. 1	------	
Sept. 23	7 a. m.	29.93	50	.335	Fog & mist 10	----------	NE. 1	93	
	2 p. m.	30.00	53	.403	Thick 10	Rain ------	NE. 1	100	
	9 p. m.	29.95	54	.390	Fog & rain 10	----------	NE. 2	93	
Sept. 24	7 a. m.	29.89	54	.390	Rain 10	----------	NE. 1	93	
	2 p. m.	29.81	58	.452	Fog 10	----------	NE. 1	94	
	9 p. m.	29.88	56	.391	Fog 10	----------	NE. 1	87	
Sept. 25	7 a. m.	29.89	54	.390	Fog 10	----------	NE. 1	93	
	2 p. m.	29.87	60	.426	Fog 10	----------	SW. 1	82	
	9 p. m.	29.97	55	.405	Fog 10	----------	SW. 1	94	

TOPSHAM, MAINE.

Month and day.	Hour.	Barom'r corrected to 32° F.	Thermometer.	Force of vapor.	Cloudiness.	Motion of clouds.	Winds.	Relative humidity.	REMARKS.
Sept. 14	9 p. m.	------	------	------	0	----------	NW. 1	------	14th. Heavy squall at $10\frac{1}{2}$ a. m. from W. to E.; wind, 7 to 8; slight snow; p. m. clear and cool.
Sept. 15	7 a. m.	------	------	------	0	----------	NW. 1	------	
	2 p. m.	------	------	------	0	----------	NW. 2	------	
	9 p. m.	------	------	------	1	----------	NW. 1	------	15th. Heavy frost; clear and cool; aurora.
Sept. 16	7 a. m.	------	------	------	0	----------	SW. 1	------	
	2 p. m.	------	------	------	2	----------	SW. 1	------	17th. Gentle rain commenced at noon; heavy wind 4 to 5 p. m.; storm ended in the night.
	9 p. m.	------	------	------	2	----------	SW. 1	------	
Sept. 17	7 a. m.	------	------	------	10	----------	SW. 1	------	
	2 p. m.	------	------	------	10	----------	SW. 1	------	18th and 19th. Pleasant, light winds.
	9 p. m.	------	------	------	10	----------	SW. 1	------	
Sept. 18	7 a. m.	------	------	------	0	----------	NW. 4	------	20th. Cloudy, stratus; mild.
	2 p. m.	------	------	------	0	----------	NW. 3	------	21st. Gentle rain all day.
	9 p. m.	------	------	------	0	----------	NW. 1	------	22d. Rain all day; heavy shower at 9 p. m.
Sept. 19	7 a. m.	------	------	------	0	----------	N. 1	------	
	2 p. m.	------	------	------	0	----------	W. 2	------	23d. Rain at intervals; some very heavy showers.
	9 p. m.	------	------	------	0	----------	SW. 2	------	
Sept. 20	7 a. m.	------	------	------	10	----------	NE. 1	------	24th. Storm ended in the night—a very warm storm for a north-easter.
	2 p. m.	------	------	------	10	----------	NE. 1	------	
	9 p. m.	------	------	------	10	----------	NE. 1	------	
Sept. 21	7 a. m.	------	------	------	10	----------	NE. 2	------	
	2 p. m.	------	------	------	10	----------	NE. 1	------	
	9 p. m.	------	------	------	10	----------	NE. 2	------	
Sept. 22	7 a. m.	------	------	------	10	----------	NE. 1	------	
	2 p. m.	------	------	------	10	----------	NE. 1	------	
	9 p. m.	------	------	------	10	----------	NE. 1	------	
Sept. 23	7 a. m.	------	------	------	10	----------	NE. 2	------	
	2 p. m.	------	------	------	10	----------	NE. 2	------	
	9 p. m.	------	------	------	10	----------	NE. 2	------	
Sept. 24	7 a. m.	------	------	------	10	----------	NE. 2	------	
	2 p. m.	------	------	------	10	----------	NE. 2	------	
	9 p. m.	------	------	------	10	----------	NE. 2	------	
Sept. 25	7 a. m.	------	------	------	10	----------	NE. 2	------	
	2 p. m.	------	------	------	9	----------	N. 1	------	
	9 p. m.	------	------	------	1	----------	SW. 1	------	

STORMS Nos. 2 AND 3, SEPTEMBER, 1859.

VASSALBORO', MAINE.

Month and day.	Hour.	Barom'r corrected to 32° F.	Thermometer.	Force of vapor.	Cloudiness.	Motion of clouds.	Winds.		Relative humidity.	REMARKS.
Sept. 14	9 p. m.	......	......	......	0	....	W.	6	......	14th. Squally. 16th. Frost; blustering. 17th. Drizzling rain from 10 a. m. to 12 p. m. 21st. Commenced raining at 11 a. m. and ceased at 11 p. m. on the 24th.
Sept. 15	7 a. m.	......	......	......	1	....	W.	4	......	
	2 p. m.	......	......	......	3	....	W.	3	......	
	9 p. m.	......	......	......	5	....	W.	2	......	
Sept. 16	7 a. m.	......	......	......	7	....	W.	2	......	
	2 p. m.	......	......	......	3	....	W.	3	......	
	9 p. m.	......	......	......	5	....	W.	2	......	
Sept. 17	7 a. m.	......	......	......	10	....	S.	2	......	
	2 p. m.	......	......	......	10	....	S.	1	......	
	9 p. m.	......	......	......	10	....	S.	2	......	
Sept. 18	7 a. m.	......	......	......	9	....	E.	2	......	
	2 p. m.	......	......	......	4	....	E.	3	......	
	9 p. m.	......	......	......	6	....	N.	2	......	
Sept. 19	7 a. m.	......	......	......	7	....	N.	9	......	
	2 p. m.	......	......	......	0	....	N.	3	......	
	9 p. m.	......	......	......	1	....	W.	1	......	
Sept. 20	7 a. m.	......	......	......	10	....	S.	2	......	
	2 p. m.	......	......	......	5	....	S.	2	......	
	9 p. m.	......	......	......	9	....	W.	2	......	
Sept. 21	7 a. m.	......	......	......	10	....	NE.	2	......	
	2 p. m.	......	......	......	10	....	E.	3	......	
	9 p. m.	......	......	......	10	....	E.	3	......	
Sept. 22	7 a. m.	......	......	......	10	....	E.	2	......	
	2 p. m.	......	......	......	10	....	E.	3	......	
	9 p. m.	......	......	......	10	....	E.	2	......	
Sept. 23	7 a. m.	......	......	......	10	....	E.	3	......	
	2 p. m.	......	......	......	10	....	E.	2	......	
	9 p. m.	......	......	......	10	....	E.	2	......	
Sept. 24	7 a. m.	......	......	......	10	....	N.	2	......	
	2 p. m.	......	......	......	10	....	N.	2	......	
	9 p. m.	......	......	......	10	....	N.	2	......	
Sept. 25	7 a. m.	......	......	......	10	....	N.	2	......	
	2 p. m.	......	......	......	8	....	N.	2	......	
	9 p. m.	......	......	......	5	....	N.	1	......	

WARREN, MAINE.

Month and day.	Hour.	Barom'r corrected to 32° F.	Thermometer.	Force of vapor.	Cloudiness.	Motion of clouds.	Winds.		Relative humidity.	REMARKS.
Sept. 14	9 p. m.	......	......	......	0	....	W.	2	......	14th. Rain during past night; a violent wind prevailed from 10 p. m. till midnight; began to subside before 2 a. m. 17th. Began to rain at noon, and ended in the night. 20th. Fog morning and evening. 21st. Began to rain before day, and ended at 7 p. m. on the 24th.
Sept. 15	7 a. m.	......	......	......	1	....	NW.	3	......	
	2 p. m.	......	......	......	3	....	NW.	5	......	
	9 p. m.	......	......	......	6	....	NW.	2	......	
Sept. 16	7 a. m.	......	......	......	2	....	NW.	1	......	
	2 p. m.	......	......	......	2	....	SW.	2	......	
	9 p. m.	......	......	......	6	....	SW.	1	......	
Sept. 17	7 a. m.	......	......	......	8	....	SW.	1	......	
	2 p. m.	......	......	......	10	....	SW.	1	......	
	9 p. m.	......	......	......	10	....	SW.	1	......	
Sept. 18	7 a. m.	......	......	......	8	....	W.	4	......	
	2 p. m.	......	......	......	0	....	N.	4	......	
	9 p. m.	......	......	......	0	....	N.	3	......	
Sept. 19	7 a. m.	......	......	......	3	....	NW.	3	......	
	2 p. m.	......	......	......	3	....	W.	3	......	
	9 p. m.	......	......	......	1	....	SW.	3	......	
Sept. 20	7 a. m.	......	......	......	10	....	SW.	3	......	
	2 p. m.	......	......	......	10	....	SW.	2	......	
	9 p. m.	......	......	......	10	....	SW.	3	......	
Sept. 21	7 a. m.	......	......	......	10	....	E.	2	......	
	2 p. m.	......	......	......	10	....	NE.	3	......	
	9 p. m.	......	......	......	10	....	NE.	2	......	
Sept. 22	7 a. m.	......	......	......	10	....	NE.	4	......	
	2 p. m.	......	......	......	10	....	NE.	4	......	
	9 p. m.	......	......	......	10	....	NE.	3	......	

STORMS Nos. 2 AND 3, SEPTEMBER, 1859.

WARREN, MAINE—Continued.

Month and day.	Hour.	Barom'r corrected to 32° F.	Thermometer.	Force of vapor.	Cloudiness.	Motion of clouds.	Winds.	Relative humidity.	REMARKS.
Sept. 23	7 a. m.	------	------	------	10	----------	NE. 3	------	
	2 p. m.	------	------	------	10	----------	NE. 3	------	
	0 p. m.	------	------	------	10	----------	NE. 1	------	
Sept. 24	7 a. m.	------	------	------	10	----------	NE. 3	------	
	2 p. m.	------	------	------	10	----------	NE. 3	------	
	9 p. m.	------	------	------	10	----------	E. 2	------	
Sept. 25	7 a. m.	------	------	------	10	----------	NE. 1	------	
	2 p. m.	------	------	------	16	----------	SE. 2	------	
	9 p. m.	------	------	------	10	----------	SW. 1	------	

CLAREMONT, NEW HAMPSHIRE.

Month and day.	Hour.	Barom'r corrected to 32° F.	Thermometer.	Force of vapor.	Cloudiness.	Motion of clouds.	Winds.	Relative humidity.	REMARKS.
Sept. 14	9 p. m.	29.30	44	------	Cu. 6	E. 2	NW. 2	------	14th. High wind from NW.
Sept. 15	7 a. m.	.49	39	------	Cir. 2	SE. 4	NW. 4	------	16th. At 11 a. m. a thin cir. cloud surrounded the sun at about 25° distant.
	2 p. m.	.57	53	------	Cir. st. 8	SE. 2	NW. 3	------	
	9 p. m.	.60	41	------	Cir. 1	3	NW. 1	------	
Sept. 16	7 a. m.	.65	40	------	Nim. 10	E. 4	W. 1	------	17th. Rain from 6 a. m. to 11 p. m.; amount, 0.37 inch.
	2 p. m.	.59	60	------	Cir. cu. 8	E. 4	W. 3	------	
	9 p. m.	.51	52	------	Nim. 10	----------	SE. 3	------	Rain from 9½ p. m. the 20th to 1 p. m. on the 23d; amount, 2.75 inches.
Sept. 17	7 a. m.	.42	52	------	Nim. 10	N. 3	S. 2	------	
	2 p. m.	.34	55	------	Nim. 10	N. 2	E. 4	------	
	9 p. m.	.17	52	------	Nim. 10	----------	E. 4	------	
Sept. 18	7 a. m.	.17	53	------	Nim. 10	S. 4	N. 5	------	
	2 p. m.	.21	65	------	Cir. 1	S. 3	NW. 4	------	
	9 p. m.	.23	58	------	0	----------	N. 2	------	
Sept. 19	7 a. m.	.21	48	------	Cir. 2	W. 3	E. 3	------	
	2 p. m.	.19	67	------	0	----------	S. 2	------	
	9 p. m.	.16	63	------	Cu. st. 1	----------	S. 2	------	
Sept. 20	7 a. m.	.15	65	------	Nim. 10	NE. 3	S. 1	------	
	2 p. m.	.19	73	------	Cu. st. 10	E. 1	S. 1	------	
	9 p. m.	.32	56	------	Nim. 10	----------	W. 3	------	
Sept. 21	7 a. m.	.46	50	------	Nim. 10	W. 4	E. 5	------	
	2 p. m.	.49	50	------	Nim. 10	W. 4	E. 4	------	
	9 p. m.	.48	46	------	Nim. 10	----------	E. 4	------	
Sept. 22	7 a. m.	.46	52	------	Nim. 10	NW. 6	E. 5	------	
	2 p. m.	.45	55	------	Nim. 10	NW. 4	SE. 5	------	
	9 p. m.	.43	52	------	Nim. 10	----------	E. 5	------	
Sept. 23	7 a. m.	.36	55	------	Nim. 10	----------	E. 1	------	
	2 p. m.	.34	62	------	Nim. 10	W. 1	E. 2	------	
	9 p. m.	.32	55	------	Nim. 10	----------	SE. 2	------	
Sept. 24	7 a. m.	.29	60	------	Nim. 9	----------	SE. 2	------	
	2 p. m.	.24	71	------	Cu. 9	SE. 2	NE. 1	------	
	9 p. m.	.23	59	------	Cir. cu. 2	----------	NE. 1	------	
Sept. 25	7 a. m.	.26	60	------	Nim. 10	----------	N. 1	------	
	2 p. m.	.26	72	------	Cir. cu. 8	SW. 1	NE. 2	------	

MOUNT WASHINGTON, NEW HAMPSHIRE.

Month and day.	Hour.	Barom'r corrected to 32° F.	Thermometer.	Force of vapor.	Cloudiness.	Motion of clouds.	Winds.	Relative humidity.	REMARKS.
Sept. 14	9 p. m.	23.481	17.25	.096	Mist --------	----------	W. 7	100	14th. Max. ther., 24°; min., 15°.
Sept. 15	7 a. m.	23.613	10.00	.071	Mist --------	----------	NW. 5	100	
	2 p. m.	------	------	------	------------	----------	------------	------	
	9 p. m.	------	------	------	------------	----------	------------	------	

STORMS Nos. 2 AND 3, SEPTEMBER, 1859.

SHELBURNE, NEW HAMPSHIRE.

Month and day.	Hour.	Barom'r corrected to 32° F.	Thermometer.	Force of vapor.	Cloudiness.	Motion of clouds.	Winds.	Relative humidity.	REMARKS.
Sept. 14	9 p. m.	------	------	------	------------	----------	------------	------	14th. Snow squalls from 9 to 11 a. m.; wind W. 5.
Sept. 15	Sunrise.	29. 91	------	------	Cu. 10	NW. 2	W. 3	------	
	Noon.	. 99	------	------	Cu. 6	NW. 1	W. 3	------	17th. Smart showers from 10 a. m. to 4 p. m.
	9 p. m.	30. 08	------	------	Cir. st. 3	0	W. 3	------	
Sept. 16	Sunrise	. 11	------	------	Cir. cu. 8	0	0	------	20th. Began to rain at 10.30 p. m.; continued till sunrise next morning.
	Noon.	. 08	------	------	Cir. st. 3	0	E 1	------	
	9 p. m.	. 04	------	------	Nim. 9	0	W. 1	------	
Sept. 17	Sunrise.	29. 97	------	------	Nim. 10	0	0	------	21st. Fine rain from 11. 25 a. m. till noon; moderate rain all p. m. till 9 in the evening.
	Noon.	. 89	------	------	Nim. 10	0	E. 1	----	
	9 p. m.	. 78	------	------	10	Overcast --	E. 1	----	
Sept. 18	Sunrise.	. 71	------	------	Nim. 10	E. 2	W. 2	------	Rain continued in the night of the 21st, and during the a. m. of the 22d.
	Noon.	. 69	------	------	------------	Clear -----	W. 2	------	
	9 p. m.	. 70	------	------	0	W. clear ---	W. 1	------	
Sept. 19	Sunrise.	. 75	------	------	Foggy ------	----------	0	------	22d. Fine rain in the p. m., and some during the night.
	Noon.	. 69	------	------	W. clear ----	----------	E. 2	------	
	9 p. m.	. 64	------	------	Cu. 2	NW. 1	E. 1	------	23d. Fine rain in the morning till 8. 30 a. m; rain in torrents at from 8. 37 to 8. 42 a. m., then steady rain till 10. 20 a. m.
Sept. 20	Sunrise.	. 64	------	------	Nim. 10	0	0	------	
	Noon.	. 66	------	------	Nim. 10	0	W. 3	------	
	9 p. m.	. 85	------	------	Nim. 10	WSW. 3	W. 3	------	
Sept. 21	Sunrise.	30. 02	------	------	Nim. 10	E. 1	E. 1	------	
	Noon.	. 07	------	------	10	Overcast ---	E. 2	------	
	9 p. m.	. 08	------	------	10	Overcast ---	E. 1	------	
Sept. 22	Sunrise.	. 05	------	------	10	Overcast ---	E. 3	------	
	Noon.	. 04	------	------	Nim. 10	E. 2	E. 2	------	
	9 p. m.	. 03	------	------	10	Overcast ---	E. 1	------	
Sept. 23	Sunrise.	. 03	------	------	10	Overcast ---	E. 1	------	
	Noon.	29. 90	------	------	Nim. 10	E. 1	E. 1	------	
	9 p. m.	. 86	------	------	10	Overcast ---	E. 1	------	
Sept. 24	Sunrise.	. 82	------	------	10	Overcast ---	0	------	
	Noon.	------	------	------	------------	----------	------------	------	
	9 p. m.	. 74	------	------	10	Overcast ---	0	------	
Sept. 25	Sunrise	. 74	------	------	Cu. 9	SE. 1	W. 2	------	

STRATFORD, NEW HAMPSHIRE.

Month and day.	Hour.	Barom'r corrected to 32° F.	Thermometer.	Force of vapor.	Cloudiness.	Motion of clouds.	Winds.	Relative humidity.	REMARKS.
Sept. 14	9 p. m.	------	37	------	Nim. 10	----------	W. 2	------	14th. Rain; amount, 0.16 inch.
Sept. 15	7 a. m.	------	32	------	Nim. 9	SW. 4	NW. 4	------	16th. Hard frost.
	2 p. m.	------	44	------	Cu. cir. 5	W. 2	W. 2	------	17th. Rain; amount, 0.15 inch.
	9 p. m.	------	30	------	0	----------	0	------	21st. Rain; amount, 0.32 inch.
Sept. 16	7 a. m.	------	30	------	Nim. 10	----------	0	------	22d. Rain; amount, 0.50 inch.
	2 p. m.	------	55	------	Cir. st. 1	----------	E. 1	------	23d. Amount of rain recorded, 1.30 inch.
	9 p m.	------	39	------	0	----------	E. 1	------	
Sept. 17	7 a. m.	------	43	------	Nim. 10	----------	0	------	24th. Rain; amount, 0.07 inch.
	2 p. m.	------	50	------	Nim. 10	----------	E. 2	------	
	9 p. m.	------	47	------	Nim. 9	----------	NE. 1	------	
Sept. 18	7 a. m.	------	48	------	Nim. 10	----------	0	------	
	2 p. m.	------	68	------	Cu. 1	W. 2	NW. 3	------	
	9 p. m.	------	53	------	0	----------	NE. 1	------	
Sept. 19	7 a. m.	------	40	------	Cir. 1	----------	0	------	
	2 p. m.	------	70	------	0	----------	SW. 3	------	
	9 p. m.	------	58	------	Cir. st. 2	----------	SE. 1	------	
Sept. 20	7 a. m.	------	59	------	Nim. 9	SW. 1	SE. 1	------	
	2 p. m.	------	63	------	Nim. 10	----------	SE. 1	------	
	9 p. m.	------	52	------	Nim. 10	----------	E. 1	------	
Sept. 21	7 a. m.	------	46	------	Nim. 10	----------	NE. 3½	------	
	2 p. m.	------	45	------	Nim. 10	----------	NE. 2	------	
	9 p. m.	------	42	------	Nim. 10	----------	NE. 3	------	
Sept. 22	7 a. m.	------	47	------	Nim. 10	----------	NE. 1	------	
	2 p. m.	------	50	------	Nim. 10	----------	E. 3	------	
	9 p. m.	------	48	------	Nim. 10	----------	NE. 2	------	

STORMS Nos. 2 AND 3, SEPTEMBER, 1859.

STRATFORD, NEW HAMPSHIRE—Continued.

Month and day.	Hour.	Barom'r corrected to 32° F.	Thermometer.	Force of vapor.	Cloudiness.		Motion of clouds.		Winds.		Relative humidity.	REMARKS.
Sept. 23	7 a. m.	......	51	......	Nim.	10	....		NE.	2	......	
	2 p. m.	......	58	......	Nim.	10	....		NE.	1	......	
	9 p. m.	......	54	......	Nim.	10	....		NE.	1	......	
Sept. 24	7 a. m.	......	52	......	Nim.	10	....			0	......	
	2 p. m.	......	65	......	Nim.	10	....		W.	1	......	
	9 p. m.	......	58	......	Nim.	10	....			0	......	
Sept. 25	7 a. m.	......	55	......	Nim.	9	....			0	......	
	2 p. m.	......	65	......	Nim.	8	....		NW.	1	......	

STRATHAM, NEW HAMPSHIRE.

Month and day.	Hour.	Barom'r corrected to 32° F.	Thermometer.	Force of vapor.	Cloudiness.		Motion of clouds.		Winds.		Relative humidity.	REMARKS.
Sept. 14	9 p. m.	......	......	......		2	....		SW.	2	......	14th. Very cold.
Sept. 15	7 a. m.	......	......	......		3	....		W.	2	......	15th. Cold.
	2 p. m.	......	......	......		2	....		NW.	3	......	17th. Rain from 10 a. m. to 9 p. m.
	9 p. m.	......	......	......		9	....		NW.	1	......	Storm commenced at 9 p. m. the
Sept. 16	7 a. m.	......	......	......		3	....		W.	1	......	20th and ended at 9 p. m. on
	2 p. m.	......	......	......		2	....		W.	1	......	the 23d.
	9 p. m.	......	......	......		9	....		SW.	1	......	
Sept. 17	7 a. m.	......	......	......		10	....		SE.	2	......	
	2 p. m.	......	......	......		10	....		SE.	2	......	
	9 p. m.	......	......	......		10	....		SE.	2	......	
Sept. 18	7 a. m.	......	......	......		8	....		N.	3	......	
	2 p. m.	......	......	......		3	....		N.	3	......	
	9 p. m.	......	......	......		1	....		NW.	1	......	
Sept. 19	7 a. m.	......	......	......		3	....		W.	2	......	
	2 p. m.	......	......	......		2	....		W.	1	......	
	9 p. m.	......	......	......		1	....		W.	1	......	
Sept. 20	7 a. m.	......	......	......		6	....		SW.	2	......	
	2 p. m.	......	......	......		9	....		SW.	1	......	
	9 p. m.	......	......	......		10	....		SE.	1	......	
Sept. 21	7 a. m.	......	......	......		10	....		NE.	2	......	
	2 p. m.	......	......	......		10	....		NE.	2	......	
	9 p. m.	......	......	......		10	....		NE.	2	......	
Sept. 22	7 a. m.	......	......	......		10	....		NE.	2	......	
	2 p. m.	......	......	......		10	....		NE.	2	......	
	9 p. m.	......	......	......		10	....		NE.	2	......	
Sept. 23	7 a. m.	......	......	......		10	....		NE.	2	......	
	2 p. m.	......	......	......		10	....		NE.	2	......	
	9 p. m.	......	......	......		10	....		NE.	2	......	
Sept. 24	7 a. m.	......	......	......		10	....		N.	2	......	
	2 p. m.	......	......	......		9	....		N.	2	......	
	9 p. m.	......	......	......		9	....		N.	1	......	
Sept. 25	7 a. m.	......	......	......		10	....		NW.	1	......	
	2 p. m.	......	......	......		3	....		NW.	2	......	
	9 p. m.	......	......	......			....		....		......	

BRANDON, VERMONT.

Month and day.	Hour.	Barom'r corrected to 32° F.	Thermometer.	Force of vapor.	Cloudiness.		Motion of clouds.		Winds.		Relative humidity.	REMARKS.
Sept. 14	9 p. m.	......	40	......	Cu.	1	....		NW.	1	......	14th. Rain till 6 a. m.; strong
Sept. 15	7 a. m.	......	32. 5	......		0	....		NW.	1	......	wind all day from W. and NW.
	2 p. m.	......	50	......	Cu.	3	NW.	1	NW.	1	......	15th. Thermometer 30° at sunrise;
	9 p. m.	......	36. 5	......	Cir.	1	NW.	1	SW.	1	......	heavy frost and ice.
Sept. 16	7 a. m.	......	41	......	Cir. cu.	8	NW.	1	SE.	1	......	17th. Rain from early morn till
	2 p. m.	......	59. 5	......	Cir. cu.	9	NW.	1	S.	1	......	2 p. m.; amount, 0.36 inch.
	9 p. m.	......	51	......		10	....		SW.	1	......	Storm commenced at 6 p. m. the
Sept. 17	7 a. m.	......	48	......	Nim.	10	....		S.	1	......	20th and ended before day on
	2 p. m.	......	53. 5	......	Cu.	10	SW.	1	S.	1	......	the 24th; amount, 2.625 inches.
	9 p. m.	......	51	......		1	....		N.	1	......	

STORMS Nos. 2 AND 3, SEPTEMBER, 1859.

BRANDON, VERMONT—Continued.

Month and day.	Hour.	Barom'r corrected to 32° F.	Thermometer.	Force of vapor.	Cloudiness.	Motion of clouds.	Winds.	Relative humidity.	REMARKS.
Sept. 18	7 a. m.	------	51	------	Cu. 10	N. 3	N. 2	------	
	2 p. m.	------	60	------	0	----------	N. 2	------	
	9 p. m.	------	49. 5	------	Cir. 1	----------	SE ----------	------	
Sept. 19	7 a. m.	------	47	------	Cir. 1	----------	SE. 1	------	
	2 p. m.	------	74. 5	------	0	----------	S. 1	------	
	9 p. m.	------	62	------	9	----------	S. 1	------	
Sept. 20	7 a. m.	------	65. 5	------	Cu. 10	WNW. 1	0	------	
	2 p. m.	------	53	------	Cu. 10	NW. 2	NW. 2	------	
	9 p. m.	------	49	------	Nim. 10	----------	N. 1	------	
Sept. 21	7 a. m.	------	47	------	Nim. 10	----------	N. 1	------	
	2 p. m.	------	54	------	Cu. 10	S. 1	S. 1	------	
	9 p. m.	------	49	------	Nim. 10	----------	0	------	
Sept. 22	7 a. m.	------	48. 5	------	Nim. 10	----------	S. 2	------	
	2 p. m.	------	64	------	Cu. 10	SW. 1	S. 2	------	
	9 p. m.	------	52	------	Nim. 10	----------	S. 3	------	
Sept. 23	7 a. m.	------	52	------	Nim. 10	----------	S. 1	------	
	2 p. m.	------	62	------	Nim. 10	----------	S. 1	------	
	9 p. m.	------	58	------	10	----------	0	------	
Sept. 24	7 a. m.	------	55	------	Fog 10	----------	NW. 1	------	
	2 p. m.	------	63	------	Cu. 8	NW. 1	NW. 1	------	
	9 p. m.	------	54	------	Cu. 1	----------	NW. 1	------	
Sept. 25	7 a. m.	------	57	------	Cu. 10	----------	0	------	
	2 p. m.	------	69. 5	------	2	{ N. 1 / S. 1 }	NW. 1	------	

BURLINGTON, VERMONT.

Month and day.	Hour.	Barom'r corrected to 32° F.	Thermometer.	Force of vapor.	Cloudiness.	Motion of clouds.	Winds.	Relative humidity.	REMARKS.
Sept. 14	9 p. m.	29. 686	40	. 177	1	----------	NW. 3	66	
Sept. 15	7 a. m.	. 943	33	. 115	1	----------	NW. 2	54	
	2 p. m.	. 952	45	. 202	4	----------	NW. 2	62	
	9 p. m.	30. 000	34	. 116	3	----------	W. 1	53	
Sept. 16	7 a. m.	29. 955	36	. 173	8	----------	W. 1	73	
	2 p. m.	. 840	57	. 255	3	----------	S. 1	49	
	9 p. m.	. 815	49	. 296	8	----------	S. 1	79	
Sept. 17	7 a. m.	. 726	48	. 309	10	----------	S. 1	85	
	2 p. m.	. 624	53	. 349	10	----------	S. 1	81	
	9 p. m.	. 547	50	. 334	10	----------	S. 1	86	
Sept. 18	7 a. m.	. 654	47	. 335	10	----------	N. 1	93	
	2 p. m.	. 598	58	. 367	1	----------	N. 1	71	
	9 p. m.	. 583	48	. 335	0	----------	N. 1	93	
Sept. 19	7 a. m.	. 547	43	. 262	0	----------	N. 1	84	
	2 p. m.	. 493	69	. 436	0	----------	S. 3	57	
	9 p. m.	. 384	64	. 407	2	----------	SW. 3	63	
Sept. 20	7 a. m.	. 467	62	. 549	10	----------	S. 1	89	
	2 p. m.	. 650	50	. 308	10	----------	N. 2	79	
	9 p. m.	. 744	51	. 269	10	----------	N. 1	67	
Sept. 21	7 a. m.	. 823	44. 5	. 298	10	----------	N. 1	92	
	2 p. m.	. 810	52	. 390	10	----------	NE. 1	93	
	9 p. m.	. 778	50	. 361	10	----------	NE. 1	93	
Sept. 22	7 a. m.	. 755	49	. 361	10	----------	S. 1	93	
	2 p. m.	. 700	62	. 451	10	----------	S. 1	73	
	9 p. m.	. 688	55	. 423	10	----------	S. 1	88	
Sept. 23	7 a. m.	. 659	54	. 420	10	----------	S. 1	94	
	2 p. m.	. 633	60	. 478	10	----------	S. 1	83	
	9 p. m.	. 646	55	. 423	10	----------	S. 1	88	
Sept. 24	7 a. m.	. 736	52	. 376	10	----------	N. 1	87	
	2 p. m.	. 600	60	. 429	10	----------	N. 1	74	
	9 p. m.	. 597	56	. 452	10	----------	N. 1	94	
Sept. 25	7 a. m.	. 614	57	. 500	10	----------	S. 1	100	
	2 p. m.	. 586	61	. 478	10	----------	S. 1	83	

STORMS Nos. 2 AND 3, SEPTEMBER, 1859.

CRAFTSBURY, VERMONT.

Month and day.	Hour.	Barom'r corrected to 32° F.	Thermometer.	Force of vapor.	Cloudiness.	Motion of clouds.	Winds.	Relative humidity.	REMARKS.
Sept. 14	9 p. m.	------	36	------	Nim. 8	NW. 3	NW. 3	------	14th. Amount of rain, 0. 17 inch.
Sept. 15	7 a. m.	------	30	------	Nim. 8	NW. 3	NW. 3	------	17th. Rain; amount, 0. 08 ? inch.
	2 p. m.	------	42	------	Cu. st. 2	NW. 3	NW. 3	------	Rain from 11 p. m. the 21st to the 24th; amount, 2. 28 inches.
	0 p. m.	------	30	------	0	----------	S. 1	------	
Sept. 16	7 a. m.	------	33	------	Cir. cu. 8	W. 2	SE. 1	------	
	2 p. m.	------	58	------	Cir. st. 1	SW. 1	SE. 1	------	
	9 p. m.	------	44	------	Cir. cu. 7	W. 1	S. 2	------	
Sept. 17	7 a. m.	------	44	------	Nim. 10	S. 3	S. 1	------	
	2 p. m.	------	49	------	Nim. 10	S. 2	S. 2	------	
	9 p. m.	------	48	------	Nim. 10	----------	NE. 3	------	
Sept. 18	7 a. m.	------	50	------	Nim. 8	NE. 4	NE. 3	------	
	2 p. m.	------	63	------	0	----------	NE. 3	------	
	9 p. m.	------	52	------	0	----------	S. 1	------	
Sept. 19	7 a. m.	------	47	------	Cir. 4	W. 1	SW. 1	------	
	2 p. m.	------	73	------	0	----------	S. 2	------	
	9 p. m.	------	60	------	St. 1	----------	S. 2	------	
Sept. 20	7 a. m.	------	61	------	Nim. 8	W. 3	S. 1	------	
	2 p. m.	------	54	------	Nim. 10	----------	NE. 3	------	
	9 p. m.	------	50	------	Nim. 10	----------	NE. 3	------	
Sept. 21	7 a. m.	------	46	------	Nim. 10	----------	NE. 1	------	
	2 p. m.	------	52	------	Nim. 10	S. 2	S. 1	------	
	9 p. m.	------	49	------	Nim. 10	----------	NW. 1	------	
Sept. 22	7 a. m.	------	47	------	Nim. 10	----------	0	------	
	2 p. m.	------	53	------	Nim. 10	S. 3	S. 2	------	
	9 p. m.	------	53	------	Nim. 10	----------	S. 1	------	
Sept. 23	7 a. m.	------	50	------	Nim. 10	----------	SW. 1	------	
	2 p. m.	------	56	------	Nim. 10	----------	S. 1	------	
	9 p. m.	------	56	------	Nim. 10	----------	S. 1	------	
Sept. 24	7 a. m.	------	54	------	Nim. 10	W. 2	SW. 1	------	
	2 p. m.	------	61	------	Nim. 9	NW. 2	NW. 1	------	
	9 p. m.	------	56	------	Nim. 9	----------	NE. 1	------	
Sept. 25	7 a. m.	------	54	------	Nim. 9	NW. 1	NW. 1	------	
	2 p. m.	------	64	------	Nim. 9	S. 1	N. 1	------	

LUNENBURG, VERMONT.

Month and day.	Hour.	Barom'r corrected to 32° F.	Thermometer.	Force of vapor.	Cloudiness.	Motion of clouds.	Winds.	Relative humidity.	REMARKS.
Sept. 14	9 p. m.	28. 78	------	------	6	----------	W----------	------	17th. Rain from 11 a. m. to 10 p. m.; amount, 0. 40 inch.
Sept. 15	7 a. m.	28. 88	23	------	1	----------	W----------	------	21st. Rain in the night; amount, 0. 40 inch.
	1 p. m.	28. 94	72	------	1	----------	W----------	------	22d. Rain from morn to 1 p. m.; amount, 0. 60 inch.
	9 p. m.	28. 94	------	------	0	----------	SW----------	------	23d. Rain all day; amount, 1. 25 inch.
Sept. 16	7 a. m.	29. 16	23	------	3	----------	S----------	------	24th. Rain from 6 a. m. till 2 p. m.; amount, 0. 25 inch.
	1 p. m.	28. 94	60	------	1	----------	S----------	------	
	9 p. m.	28. 94	------	------	1	----------	S----------	------	
Sept. 17	7 a. m.	28. 78	40	------	9	----------	E----------	------	
	1 p. m.	28. 68	74	------	10	----------	E----------	------	
	9 p. m.	28. 68	------	------	10	----------	E----------	------	
Sept. 18	7 a. m.	28. 69	38	------	3	----------	NW----------	------	
	1 p. m.	28. 73	80	------	2	----------	NW----------	------	
	9 p. m.	28. 69	------	------	0	----------	NW----------	------	
Sept. 19	7 a. m.	28. 70	40	------	2	----------	SW----------	------	
	1 p. m.	28. 64	71	------	4	----------	SW----------	------	
	9 p. m.	28. 59	------	------	4	----------	W----------	------	
Sept. 20	7 a. m.	28. 63	40	------	10	W. 2	N----------	------	
	1 p. m.	28. 68	52	------	10	W. 2	NE----------	------	
	9 p. m.	28. 83	------	------	10	----------	NE----------	------	
Sept. 21	7 a. m.	28. 93	50	------	10	E. 2	E. 2	------	
	1 p. m.	29. 43	65	------	10	E. 2	E. 2	------	
	9 p. m.	28. 93	------	------	10	E. 2	E. 2	------	
Sept. 22	7 a. m.	28. 93	45	------	10	E. 2	E. 2	------	
	1 p. m.	28. 85	70	------	10	E. 2	E. 2	------	
	9 p. m.	28. 85	------	------	10	SE. 2	SE. 2	------	

STORMS Nos. 2 AND 3, SEPTEMBER, 1859.

LUNENBURG, VERMONT—Continued.

Month and day.	Hour.	Barom'r corrected to 32° F.	Thermometer.	Force of vapor.	Cloudiness.	Motion of clouds.	Winds.	Relative humidity.	REMARKS.
Sept. 23	7 a. m.	28.76	45	------	10	E. 2	E. 2	------	
	1 p. m.	28.75	69	------	10	E. 2	E. 2	------	
	9 p. m.	28.75	------	------	10	E. 2	E. 2	------	
Sept. 24	7 a. m.	28.75	49	------	10	E. 2	E. 2	------	
	1 p. m.	28.72	72	------	10	SW. 3	E. 2	------	
	9 p. m.	28.72	------	------	10	SW. 3	S. 2	------	
Sept. 25	7 a. m.	28.69	45	------	10	E. 3	SW. 1	------	
	1 p. m.	28.73	80	------	10	2	SW. 1	------	

RUPERT, VERMONT.

Month and day.	Hour.	Barom'r corrected to 32° F.	Thermometer.	Force of vapor.	Cloudiness.	Motion of clouds.	Winds.	Relative humidity.	REMARKS.
Sept. 14	9 p. m.	------	42	------	Cir. 4	W. 1	------------	------	
Sept. 15	7 a. m.	------	36	------	0	0	------------	------	
	2 p. m.	------	60	------	Cir. 3	W. 1	------------	------	
	9 p. m.	------	56	------	Cir. 6	SW. 1	------------	------	
Sept. 16	7 a. m.	------	50	------	Cir. 4	SW. 1	------------	------	
	2 p. m.	------	62	------	Cir. 5	SW. 1	------------	------	
	9 p. m.	------	60	------	Cir. st. 6	SW. 1	------------	------	
Sept. 17	7 a. m.	------	54	------	Nim. 10	SW. 1	------------	------	
	2 p. m.	------	60	------	Nim. 10	N. 1	------------	------	
	9 p. m.	------	58	------	Cu. st. 10	NE. 1	------------	------	
Sept. 18	7 a. m.	------	56	------	Cu. st. 10	SW. 1	------------	------	
	2 p. m.	------	62	------	Cu. 2	N. 1	------------	------	
	9 p. m.	------	62	------	0	0	------------	------	
Sept. 19	7 a. m.	------	62	------	Cu. 6	SW. 1	------------	------	
	2 p. m.	------	72	------	Cir. 4	SW. 1	------------	------	
	9 p. m.	------	68	------	Cu. st. 3	SW. 1	------------	------	
Sept. 20	7 a. m.	------	62	------	Cu. st. 10	SW. 1	------------	------	
	2 p. m.	------	60	------	St. 10	N. 1	------------	------	
	9 p. m.	------	58	------	Cu. st. 10	N. 1	------------	------	
Sept. 21	7 a. m.	------	58	------	Nim. 10	SE. 1	------------	------	
	2 p. m.	------	58	------	Nim. 10	SE. 2	------------	------	
	9 p. m.	------	58	------	Nim. 10	SE. 1	------------	------	
Sept. 22	7 a. m.	------	60	------	Nim. 10	SE. 1	------------	------	
	2 p. m.	------	70	------	Cu. st. 10	SW. 1	------------	------	
	9 p. m.	------	64	------	Nim. 10	SW. 1	------------	------	
Sept. 23	7 a. m.	------	56	------	Nim. 10	SW. 1	------------	------	
	2 p. m.	------	68	------	Nim. 10	SW. 1	------------	------	
	9 p. m.	------	62	------	Nim. 10	SW. 1	------------	------	
Sept. 24	7 a. m.	------	58	------	Cu. st. 10	SW. 1	------------	------	
	2 p. m.	------	68	------	Cir. 7	SW. 1	------------	------	
	9 p. m.	------	64	------	Cu. st. 10	SW. 1	------------	------	
Sept. 25	7 a. m.	------	58	------	St. 10	SW. 1	------------	------	
	2 p. m.	------	68	------	Cir. st. 8	SW. 1	------------	------	

ST. JOHNSBURY, VERMONT.

Month and day.	Hour.	Barom'r corrected to 32° F.	Thermometer.	Force of vapor.	Cloudiness.	Motion of clouds.	Winds.	Relative humidity.	REMARKS.
Sept. 14	9 p. m.	29.38	39	------	Nim. 5	W. 1	W. 0	------	14th. Rain and snow from 4 to — a. m.
Sept. 15	7 a. m.	29.66	35	------	Cu. 5	W. 2	W. 3	------	
	2 p. m.	29.68	46	------	Cir. cu. 3	W. 2	W. 3	------	17th. Rain from 2 a. m. to 3 p. m.; amount, 0.80 inch.
	9 p. m.	29.75	31	------	0	0	NW. 1	------	
Sept. 16	7 a. m.	29.76	32	------	Cir. cu. 10	W. 1	W. 0	------	Rain on the 21st, 22d, 23d, and 24th; amount, 2.00 inches.
	2 p. m.	29.64	57	------	0	0	S. 2	------	
	9 p. m.	29.61	40	------	Nim. 10	0	S. 1	------	
Sept. 17	7 a. m.	29.50	45	------	Nim. 10	0	SE. 2	------	
	2 p. m.	29.40	49	------	Nim. 10	0	SE. 2	------	
	9 p. m.	29.29	48	------	Thick haze.--	----------	W. 0	------	
Sept. 18	7 a. m.	29.32	52	------	Nim. 10	0	NW. 1	------	
	2 p. m.	29.26	69	------	0	0	NW. 3	------	

STORMS Nos. 2 AND 3, SEPTEMBER, 1859.

ST. JOHNSBURY, VERMONT—Continued.

Month and day.	Hour.	Barom'r corrected to 32° F.	Thermometer.	Force of vapor.	Cloudiness.	Motion of clouds.	Winds.	Relative humidity.	REMARKS.
Sept. 18	9 p. m.	29.33	47	......	0	0	NW. 0	......	
Sept. 19	7 a. m.	29.34	44	......	Foggy......	......	NW. 0	......	
	2 p. m.	......	......	......	......	......	......	......	
	9 p. m.	29.17	64	......	......	......	......	......	
Sept. 20	7 a. m.	......	......	......	......	......	......	......	
	2 p. m.	......	......	......	......	......	......	......	
	9 p. m.	29.34	53	......	......	......	......	......	
Sept. 21	7 a. m.	......	......	......	......	......	......	......	
	2 p. m.	......	......	......	......	......	......	......	
	9 p. m.	29.56	47	......	......	......	......	......	
Sept. 22	7 a. m.	......	......	......	Nim. 10	0	......	......	
	2 p. m.	......	......	......	......	......	......	......	
	9 p. m.	29.53	52	......	......	......	......	......	
Sept. 23	7 a. m.	29.32	56	......	Nim. 10	0	......	......	
	2 p. m.	......	......	......	......	......	......	......	
	9 p. m.	......	......	......	......	......	......	......	
Sept. 24	7 a. m.	......	......	......	Nim. 10	0	......	......	
	2 p. m.	......	......	......	Nim. 8	0	......	......	
	9 p. m.	29.31	59	......	Nim. 10	0	0	......	
Sept. 25	7 a. m.	29.34	56	......	Nim. 10	0	0	......	
	2 p. m.	29.33	68	......	Nim. 5	0	E. 0	......	

AMHERST, MASSACHUSETTS.

Month and day.	Hour.	Barom'r corrected to 32° F.	Thermometer.	Force of vapor.	Cloudiness.	Motion of clouds.	Winds.	Relative humidity.	REMARKS.
Sept. 14	9 p. m.	29.835	43	.211	St. 5	......	NW. 1	77	Rain from 8 p. m. the 16th till sometime during the night of the 17th; amount, 1.158 inch.
Sept. 15	7 a. m.	30.042	41	.156	Cir. 1	......	W. 3	60	Storm commenced at 8 p. m. the 20th, and ended at 10 a. m. on the 23d; amount, 2.734 inches.
	2 p. m.	30.060	52	.390	St. 5	......	NW. 3	50	24th. Sprinkles in p. m.
	9 p. m.	30.114	40	.218	St. 5	......	NW. 2	92	
Sept. 16	7 a. m.	30.135	38	.204	St. 7	W. 2	W. 1	88	
	2 p. m.	30.079	56	......	St. 9	......	SE. 1	......	
	9 p. m.	30.005	50	.351	St. 10	......	......	97	
Sept. 17	7 a. m.	29.864	49	.330	Nim. 10	......	......	100	
	2 p. m.	29.663	50	.368	Nim. 10	NE. 5	NE. 2	97	
	9 p. m.	29.496	51	.361	10	......	NE. 3	94	
Sept. 18	7 a. m.	29.578	53.5	.380	St. 7	NW	NW. 4	90	
	2 p. m.	29.589	65.9	.421	0	......	NW. 4	64	
	9 p. m.	29.675	56.7	.411	0	......	NW. 1	88	
Sept. 19	7 a. m.	29.715	45.2	.308	Fog. 3	......	SE. 2	100	
	2 p. m.	29.632	70	.550	St. 1	......	SE. 3	73	
	9 p. m.	29.638	61	.526	St. 1	......	SE. 3	97	
Sept. 20	7 a. m.	29.640	63.7	.574	St. 10	......	SE. 3	95	
	2 p. m.	29.658	71.4	.716	St. 10	......	SE. 3	97	
	9 p. m.	29.772	66	.638	Nim. 10	......	......	98	
Sept. 21	7 a. m.	29.955	51.8	.357	10	......	E. 3	88	
	2 p. m.	29.950	48.2	.330	Nim. 10	......	E. 2	96	
	9 p. m.	29.934	47.4	.325	Nim. 10	......	NE. 3	96	
Sept. 22	7 a. m.	29.902	48.4	.349	Nim. 10	NE 5	N. 2	100	
	2 p. m.	29.898	53.5	.393	Nim. 10	......	NE. 2	90	
	9 p. m.	29.895	51.4	.371	Nim. 10	......	NE. 1	95	
Sept. 23	7 a. m.	29.800	51	.385	Nim. 10	E. 3	N. 2	100	
	2 p. m.	29.754	58.5	.445	St. 9	NE. 5	NW. 3	89	
	9 p. m.	29.762	57.8	.424	St. 10	......	N. 2	86	
Sept. 24	7 a. m.	29.743	55.4	.445	St. 9	......	NW. 2	99	
	2 p. m.	29.749	70.4	.566	Cu. 3	......	NW. 2	74	
	9 p. m.	29.677	60.1	.516	St. 3	......	......	95	
Sept. 25	7 a. m.	29.707	53.6	.423	St. 2	......	NW. 1	100	
	2 p. m.	29.675	68.3	.523	St. 5	NW	NW. 1	72	

STORMS Nos. 2 AND 3, SEPTEMBER, 1859.

CAMBRIDGE, MASSACHUSETTS.

Month and day.	Hour.	Barom'r corrected to 32° F.	Thermometer.	Force of vapor.	Cloudiness.	Motion of clouds.	Winds.	Relative humidity.	REMARKS.
Sept. 14	9 p. m.	30. 03	45	......	Cir. st. 4	....	W. 1	......	17th. Began to rain at 6 a. m.;
Sept. 15	7 a. m.	30. 23	42	......	Cir. st. 6	....	NW. 1	81	violent NE. storm, lasted during
	2 p. m.	30. 26	52	......	Cir.st.,cir.cu. 4	....	WNW. 1	67. 6	the night; amount, 2. 26 inches.
	9 p. m.	30. 26	45	......	Cir. cu. 6	....	Calm 0	74. 3	22d. Heavy rain 11 to 12 a. m.;
Sept. 16	7 a. m.	30. 35	41	......	Cir. cu. 8	....	NW. 1	86. 8	amount, 0. 92 inch.
	2 p. m.	30. 24	57	......	Cir. cu. 10	....	SE. 1	75	23d. Very heavy rain from 4 to 7
	9 p. m.	30. 17	51	......	Cir. cu. 10	....	S. 1	82. 5	a. m.; amount, 0. 74 inch.
Sept. 17	7 a. m.	30. 06	52	......	Rain 10	....	E. 1	91. 2	24th. Aurora at 9 p. m.
	2 p. m.	29. 92	54	......	Rain 10	....	E. 1	99. 8	
	9 p. m.	29. 66	48	......	Rain 10	....	NE. 3	102	
Sept. 18	7 a. m.	29. 66	51	......	Rain 10	....	NNE. 3	102. 5	
	2 p. m.	......	......	......	....	....	....	......	
	9 p. m.	29. 85	57	......	Clear 0	....	Calm 0	94	
Sept. 19	7 a. m.	29. 87	52	......	Clear 0	....	Calm 0	97. 7	
	2 p. m.	29. 85	68	......	Clear 0	....	E. 1	85. 7	
	9 p. m.	29. 90	59	......	Cir. st. 1	....	SW. 1	94. 5	
Sept. 20	7 a. m.	29. 84	65	......	Cu. st. 10	....	SW. 1	102	
	2 p. m.	29. 81	73	......	Cu. st. 10	....	S. 1	96. 1	
	9 p. m.	29. 91	67	......	Cu. 10	....	Calm 0	98. 8	
Sept. 21	7 a. m.	30. 12	52	......	Cir. st. 10	....	NE. 2	96. 9	
	2 p. m.	30. 13	49	......	Rain 10	....	NE. 1	100. 1	
	9 p. m.	30. 14	52	......	Rain 10	....	NE. 3	103	
Sept. 22	7 a. m.	......	50	......	Rain 10	....	NE. 1	102	
	2 p. m.	30. 17	53	......	Rain 10	....	NNE. 1	102	
	9 p. m.	30. 10	51	......	Cu. st. 10	....	NNE. 1	102	
Sept. 23	7 a. m.	29. 95	52	......	Cu. 10	....	NE. 1	102. 5	
	2 p. m.	29. 86	56	......	Nim. 10	....	NE. 1	101. 5	
	9 p. m.	29. 95	55	......	Fog 10	....	NE. 1	101. 8	
Sept. 24	7 a. m.	29. 93	56	......	Cu. st. 10	....	NE. 1	102. 8	
	2 p. m.	29. 83	64	......	Cu. 10	....	E. 1	97. 1	
	9 p. m.	29. 84	55	......	Cu. st. 1	....	E. 1	100	
Sept. 25	7 a. m.	......	......	......	Cu. 10	....	Calm 0	......	
	2 p. m.	29. 90	65	......	Cu. st.......	....	Calm 0	95. 6	

FLORIDA, MASSACHUSETTS.

Month and day.	Hour.	Barom'r corrected to 32° F.	Thermometer.	Force of vapor.	Cloudiness.	Motion of clouds.	Winds.	Relative humidity.	REMARKS.
Sept. 14	9 p. m.	......	......	......	10	....	NW. 8	......	14th. High winds.
Sept. 15	7 a. m.	......	......	......	7	....	NW. 5	......	15th. Windy and cold; a very
	2 p. m.	......	......	......	8	....	NW. 4	......	large halo at 9 p. m.
	9 p. m.	......	......	......	8	....	NW. 4	......	16th. Cloudy all day; cool and un-
Sept. 16	7 a. m.	......	......	......	10	....	E. 1	......	comfortable; commenced raining
	2 p. m.	......	......	......	10	....	E. 2	......	at 9 p. m.
	9 p. m.	......	......	......	10	....	E. 2	......	17th. Rain till 9 p. m.
Sept. 17	7 a. m.	......	......	......	10	....	NE. 4	......	18th. Windy a. m.; p. m. clear and
	2 p. m.	......	......	......	10	....	NE. 5	......	pleasant.
	9 p. m.	......	......	......	10	....	NE. 5	......	19th. Very pleasant.
Sept. 18	7 a. m.	......	......	......	10	....	N. 2	......	20th. Some clouds, but warm and
	2 p. m.	......	......	......	0	....	NW. 4	......	pleasant.
	9 p. m.	......	......	......	6	....	NW. 4	......	21st. Rain in p. m., from SW. and
Sept. 19	7 a. m.	......	......	......	1	....	N. 1	......	SE.; rain from NE. at night.
	2 p. m.	......	......	......	2	....	N. 2	......	22d. Rain all day.
	9 p. m.	......	......	......	3	....	N. 2	......	23d. Cloudy; rain in a. m.
Sept. 20	7 a. m.	......	......	......	5	....	W. 3	......	24th. Cool at night, and very warm
	2 p. m.	......	......	......	4	....	W. 3	......	at noon.
	9 p. m.	......	......	......	6	....	W. 2	......	
Sept. 21	7 a. m.	......	......	......	10	....	SW. 4	......	
	2 p. m.	......	......	......	10	....	SE. 2	......	
	9 p. m.	......	......	......	10	....	NE. 3	......	
Sept. 22	7 a. m.	......	......	......	10	....	NE. 4	......	
	2 p. m.	......	......	......	10	....	NE. 4	......	
	9 p. m.	......	......	......	10	....	NE. 5	......	

STORMS Nos. 2 AND 3, SEPTEMBER, 1859.

FLORIDA, MASSACHUSETTS—Continued.

Month and day.	Hour.	Barom'r corrected to 32° F.	Thermometer.	Force of vapor.	Cloudiness.		Motion of clouds.		Winds.		Relative humidity.	REMARKS.
Sept. 23	7 a. m.	......	......	......		10	....		SE.	3	......	
	2 p. m.	......	......	......		10	....		SW.	2	......	
	9 p. m.	......	......	......		10	....		W.	0	......	
Sept. 24	7 a. m.	......	......	......		10	....		W.	2	......	
	2 p. m.	......	......	......		7	....		W.	2	......	
	9 p. m.	......	......	......		4	....		W.	3	......	
Sept. 25	7 a. m.	......	......	......		3	....		W.	3	......	
	2 p. m.	......	......	......		4	....		W.	2	......	

LAWRENCE, MASSACHUSETTS.

Month and day.	Hour.	Barom'r corrected to 32° F.	Thermometer.	Force of vapor.	Cloudiness.		Motion of clouds.		Winds.		Relative humidity.	REMARKS.
Sept. 14	9 p. m.	29.83	44	.175	Cir. st.	3	....		NW.	2	60	17th. Began to rain at 6 a. m.; amount, 1.60 inch.
Sept. 15	7 a. m.	30.05	43	.142	St.	1	....		NW.	2	51	21st. Rain in the evening.
	2 p. m.	30.08	53	.123	Cir.	4	....		NW.	3	30	22d. Rain all day; amount, 1.15 inch.
	9 p. m.	30.13	44	.151	Cu.	0	....		NW.	2	52	23d. Rain; amount, 0.61 inch.
Sept. 16	7 a. m	30.15	39	.131	St.	3	....		NW.	2	55	
	2 p. m.	30.11	57	.191	Overcast	10	....		SW.	2	41	
	9 p. m.	30.13	50	.231	St.	5	....		SW.	2	65	
Sept. 17	7 a. m.	29.93	48	.310	Overcast	10	....		NE.	2	92	
	2 p. m.	29.80	52	.388	Rain	10	....		NE.	2	100	
	9 p. m.	29.65	45	.300	Rain	10	....		NE.	3	100	
Sept. 18	7 a. m.	29.62	51	.321	Overcast	10	....		NE.	3	86	
	2 p. m.	29.60	67	.393	St. cu.	6	....		NE.	3	59	
	9 p. m.	29.67	57	.295	St.	2	....		NE.	2	63	
Sept. 19	7 a. m.	29.74	52	.282	Fog	0	....		SW.	2	73	
	2 p. m.	29.72	72	.422		0	....		SW.	3	54	
	9 p. m.	29.65	60	.367	St.	1	....		SW.	2	71	
Sept. 20	7 a. m.	29.71	63	.478	St., nim.	10	....		SW.	2	83	
	2 p. m.	29.73	72	.559	Overcast	9	....		SW.	2	72	
	9 p. m.	29.79	68	.543	Overcast	9	....		SW.	2	79	
Sept. 21	7 a. m.	30.08	49	.297	Nim.	10	....		NE	....	85	
	2 p. m.	30.03	45	.275	Rain	10	....		NE.	2	92	
	9 p. m.	30.01	47	.323	Rain	10	....		NE.	2	100	
Sept. 22	7 a. m.	30.02	47	.298	Rain	10	....		NE.	2	92	
	2 p. m.	29.97	51	.348	Rain	10	....		NE.	3	93	
	9 p. m.	29.96	50	.361	Rain	10	....		NE.	2	100	
Sept. 23	7 a. m.	29.87	50	.361	Rain	10	....		NE.	2	100	
	2 p. m.	29.85	55	.405	Nim.	10	....		NE.	2	94	
	9 p. m.	29.82	54	.390		10	....		NE.	2	93	
Sept. 24	7 a. m.	29.82	55	.405	Overcast	10	....		NE.	2	94	
	2 p. m.	29.75	64	.464	Nim., st.	10	....		NE.	2	77	
	9 p. m.	29.76	57	.378	Overcast	10	....		NE.	2	81	
Sept. 25	7 a. m.	29.67	56	.363	Overcast	10	....		NW.	2	81	
	2 p. m.	29.75	67	.457	Cu. st.	6	....		SW.	2	69	

MENDON, MASSACHUSETTS.

Month and day.	Hour.	Barom'r corrected to 32° F.	Thermometer.	Force of vapor.	Cloudiness.		Motion of clouds.		Winds.		Relative humidity.	REMARKS.
Sept. 14	9 p. m.	......	42	......	Nim.	6	SW.	1	SW.	1	......	
Sept. 15	7 a. m.	......	42	......	Cir. st.	1	SW.	1	SW.	1	......	
	2 p. m.	......	58	......	Nim	6	SW.	1	SW.	1	......	
	9 p. m.	......	42	......	Nim.	10	SW.	1	SW.	1	......	
Sept. 16	7 a. m.	......	42	......	Nim.	10	NE.	3	NE.	2	......	
	2 p. m.	......	59	......	Nim.	10	NW.	3	NE.	3	......	
	9 p. m.	......	52	......	Nim.	10	NE.	3	NE.	2	......	
Sept. 17	7 a. m.	......	50	......	Cir.	10	NE.	1	NE.	1	......	
	2 p. m.	......	53	......	Nim.	10	NE.	2	NE.	2	......	
	9 p. m.	......	48	......	Nim.	10	NE.	1	NE.	1	......	

STORMS Nos. 2 AND 3, SEPTEMBER, 1859.

MENDON, MASSACHUSETTS—Continued.

Month and day.	Hour.	Barom'r corrected to 32° F.	Thermometer.	Force of vapor.	Cloudiness.	Motion of clouds.	Winds.	Relative humidity.	REMARKS.
Sept. 18	7 a. m.	......	54	......	Cir. 10	NE. 1	NW. 1	......	
	2 p. m.	......	61	......	Nim. 2	NW. 1	NW. 1	......	
	9 p. m.	......	58	......	Nim. 1	NW. 1	NW. 1	......	
Sept. 19	7 a. m.	......	60	......	Nim. 1	W. 1	W. 1	......	
	2 p. m.	......	72	......	Nim. 1	W. 1	W. 2	......	
	9 p. m.	......	60	......	Nim. 1	W. 1	W. 1	......	
Sept. 20	7 a. m.	......	64	......	Cir. 10	SW. 1	SW. 1	......	
	2 p. m.	......	72	......	Cir. 10	SW. 1	SW. 1	......	
	9 p. m.	......	67	......	Nim. 10	NE. 1	NE. 1	......	
Sept. 21	7 a. m.	......	54	......	Nim. 10	NE. 1	NE. 1	......	
	2 p. m.	......	58	......	Nim. 10	NE. 1	NE. 2	......	
	9 p. m.	......	50	......	Nim. 10	NE. 1	NE. 1	......	
Sept. 22	7 a. m.	......	48	......	Nim. 10	NE. 1	NE. 1	......	
	2 p. m.	......	50	......	Nim. 10	NE. 1	NE. 1	......	
	9 p. m.	......	50	......	Nim. 10	NE. 1	NE. 1	......	
Sept. 23	7 a. m.	......	51	......	Nim. 10	E. 1	E. 1	......	
	2 p. m.	......	56	......	Nim. 10	E. 1	E. 2	......	
	9 p. m.	......	54	......	Nim. 10	NE. 1	E 1	......	
Sept. 24	7 a. m.	......	54	......	Nim. 10	NE. 3	NE. 1	......	
	2 p. m.	......	63	......	Nim. 10	NE. 3	NE. 2	......	
	9 p. m.	......	60	......	Nim. 10	NE. 2	NE. 1	......	
Sept. 25	7 a. m.	......	57	......	Nim. 10	NE. 3	NE. 1	......	
	2 p. m.	......	65	......	Nim. 10	NE. 2	NE. 1	......	

NANTUCKET, MASSACHUSETTS.

Month and day.	Hour.	Barom'r corrected to 32° F.	Thermometer.	Force of vapor.	Cloudiness.	Motion of clouds.	Winds.	Relative humidity.	REMARKS.
Sept. 14	9 p. m.	30.03	54	.231	Cir. 2	....	NW. 5	55	14th. Amount of rain, 0.009 inch.
Sept. 15	7 a. m.	.23	52.5	.165	Cir. 2	....	NW. 4	41	17th. Rain in the p. m.; amount,
	2 p. m.	.25	56.5	.173	St. 2	....	NW. 3	38	1.130 inch.
	9 p. m.	.28	48.5	.241	Clear 0	....	Calm 0	70	18th. Amount of rain; 1.110 inch.
Sept. 16	7 a m.	.32	54	.181	8	....	ENE. 1	43	23d. Rain in the p. m.; amount,
	2 p m.	.29	59.5	.209	Cir. 10	....	NE. 1	41	0 95 inch.
	9 p. m.	.23	54	.282	Cir. 10	....	0	67	
Sept. 17	7 a. m.	.07	56	.336	Slight rain 10	....	E. 2	75	
	2 p. m.	29.83	58	.423	Rain 10	....	E. by N. 4	88	
	9 p. m.	.54	64	.529	St. 9	....	0	89	
Sept. 18	7 a. m.	.50	57	.392	10	....	N. 7	84	
	2 p. m.	.68	56	.363	Drizzle 10	....	N. 6	81	
	9 p. m.	.84	59	.410	Slight driz. 10	....	N. 2	82	
Sept. 19	7 a. m.	30.00	61	.457	Clear 0	....	NNW. 1	85	
	2 p. m.	29.94	70.5	.410	Clear 0	....	Calm 0	55	
	9 p. m.	.90	62	.491	Clear 0	....	Calm 0	88	
Sept. 20	7 a. m.	.93	66	.502	Cu. 10	....	SW. 3	78	
	2 p. m.	.97	72	.455	Cir. 5	....	SSW. 2	58	
	9 p. m.	30.01	64	.529	Cir. 7	....	0	89	
Sept. 21	7 a. m.	.07	62	.491	Slight rain 10	....	E. 3	88	
	2 p. m.	.06	61.5	.466	Slight rain 10	....	NE. 3	85	
	9 p. m.	.04	60.5	.464	Fog 10	....	NE. 1	88	
Sept. 22	7 a. m.	.04	64	.529	Rain 10	....	SE. 1	89	
	2 p. m.	.04	65	.500	Fog 10	....	N. 2	81	
	9 p m.	.06	61.5	.466	Intense fog 10	....	Calm 0	85	
Sept. 23	7 a. m.	.06	66	.552	Intense fog 10	....	Calm 0	87	
	2 p. m.	29.92	68.5	.389	Intense fog 10	....	NNW. 2	56	
	9 p. m.	.91	58.5	.431	10	....	NNW. 2	88	
Sept. 24	7 a. m.	.92	57.5	.372	High fog 10	....	NW. 2	78	
	2 p m.	.90	64	.403	High fog 10	....	NW. 3	67	
	9 p. m.	.92	61.5	.421	High fog 10	....	Calm 0	77	
Sept. 25	7 a. m.	.95	64	.403	High fog 7	....	WNW. 1	67	
	2 p. m.	.91	67.7	.448	9	....	N. 1	66	

STORMS Nos. 2 AND 3, SEPTEMBER, 1859.

NEW BEDFORD, MASSACHUSETTS.

Month and day.	Hour.	Barom'r corrected to 32° F.	Thermometer.	Force of vapor.	Cloudiness.	Motion of clouds.	Winds.	Relative humidity.	REMARKS.
Sept. 14	9 p. m.	29.97	47	.179	Cir. st. 9	W.	NW. 1	55	Began to rain in the night of the 17th, and ended at 1 p. m. on the 18th; amount, 2.75 inches.
Sept. 15	7 a. m.	30.19	42.5	.215	Cir. st. 4	NW. ½	NW. ½	79	20th. Began to rain at 9½ p. m., and ended in the night; amount, 0.21 inch.
	2 p. m.	30.20	55.5	.137	Cir. st. 8	W. 1	W. by N. 1	31	Commenced raining at 9 p. m. the 22d, and ended at 6 a. m. on the 23d; amount, 0.14 inch.
	9 p. m.	30.26	41	.235	Cir. st. 3	NW. 2	NNW. 1	91	24th. Began to rain at 7 p. m., and ended in the night; amount, 0.25 inch.
Sept. 16	7 a. m.	30.31	43	.209	Cir. st. 8		NNW. 1	75	
	2 p. m.	30.25	58	.255	Cir. st. 10		SE. ½	53	
	9 p. m.	30.16	53.5	.275	5		SE. 1	67	
Sept. 17	7 a. m.	30.04	55	.405	Rain 10		ESE. 1	94	
	2 p. m.	29.78	54	.418	Rain 10		ENE. 3	100	
	9 p. m.	29.51	54.5	.425	Drizzle 10		NE. 4	100	
Sept. 18	7 a. m.	29.56	50	.361	Thick 10		NNE. 5	100	
	2 p. m.	29.67	60	.411	Cir. st. 10	N. 3	N. by E. 4	79½	
	9 p. m.	29.80	58	.423	Horizon ¼		NNW. ½	88	
Sept. 19	7 a. m.	29.85	55	.376	St., & cu. 1	Horizon	NNW. 1	87	
	2 p. m.	29.83	68.5	.469	St. & haze 1	Horizon	SSW. 2	67	
	9 p. m.	29.83	61	.537	Haze 1	Horizon	WSW. 2	100	
Sept. 20	7 a. m.	29.85	64	.596	Cir. 10	SW. 3	SW. 2	100	
	2 p. m.	29.85	73.5	.611	Cir. st. 7	WNW. 1	SW. 3	75	
	9 p. m.	29.92	65	.618	10		WSW. ½	100	
Sept. 21	7 a. m.	30.03	56	.449	Fog 10	Thick	NE. 2	100	
	2 p. m.	30.03	55	.419	Drizzle 10		NNE. 3	97	
	9 p. m.	30.01	55.5	.441	Rain 10		NNE. 2	100	
Sept. 22	7 a. m.	30.02	55.5	.449	Thick 10		NE. 2	100	
	2 p. m.	30.02	59	.469	10		NNE. 2½	94	
	9 p. m.	30.06	54	.418	Drizzle 10		NNE. 3	100	
Sept. 23	7 a. m.	29.91	54	.418	Drizzle 10		NNE. 2	100	
	2 p. m.	29.87	59	.469	Thick 10		N. 2	94	
	9 p. m.	29.88	53	.403	Thick 10		NNW. 2	100	
Sept. 24	7 a. m.	29.88	54.5	.425	Cir. cu. 10	N. 3	NW. 1	100	
	2 p. m.	29.84	60.5	.515	Cir. cu. 10	N. 1	NNW. 1	97	
	9 p. m.	29.86	58	.483	St. 3	Horizon	WSW. ½	100	
Sept. 25	7 a. m.	29.86	60.5	.511	Cir. st. 10	W.	W. by S. ½	97	
	2 p. m.	29.85	65.5	.542	Cir. st. 10	W. 1	SSE. ½	87	

SPRINGFIELD, MASSACHUSETTS.

Month and day.	Hour.	Barom'r corrected to 32° F.	Thermometer.	Force of vapor.	Cloudiness.	Motion of clouds.	Winds.	Relative humidity.	REMARKS.
Sept. 14	9 p. m.				4		N. 1		14th. Variable; slight showers; cold winds.
Sept. 15	7 a. m.				3		NW. 1		15th. Temperature 35° at 7 a. m., 60° at 1 p. m.
	2 p. m.				2		N. 4		17th. Rain from 12 past night to 11 p. m.; temperature 8° to 10° colder than last year.
	9 p. m.				4		W. 1		18th and 19th. Fine and clear.
Sept. 16	7 a. m.				8		W. 0		20th. Warm; heavy rain one hour p. m.
	2 p. m.				7		N. 1		21st. Cooler; rain most of the time, day and night.
	9 p. m.				10		N. 1		22d and 23d. Rain day and night.
Sept. 17	7 a. m.				10		NE. 1		24th. Warm; hazy; slight aurora at 9 p. m.
	2 p. m.				10		NE. 2		
	9 p. m.				8		W. 3		
Sept. 18	7 a. m.				3		W. 4		
	2 p. m.				2		N. 2		
	9 p. m.				2		W. 1		
Sept. 19	7 a. m.				3		S. 2		
	2 p. m.				3		S. 1		
	9 p. m.				4		S. 1		
Sept. 20	7 a. m.				10		S. 2		
	2 p. m.				6		S. [illegible]		
	9 p. m.				8		SW. 3		
Sept. 21	7 a. m.				10		NW. 3		
	2 p. m.				10		NW. 2		
	9 p. m.				10		NW. 2		
Sept. 22	7 a. m.				10		N. 2		
	2 p. m.				10		NE. 1		
	9 p. m.				10		NE. 3		

STORMS Nos. 2 AND 3, SEPTEMBER, 1859.

SPRINGFIELD, MASSACHUSETTS—Continued.

Month and day.	Hour.	Barom'r corrected to 32° F.	Thermometer.	Force of vapor.	Cloudiness.	Motion of clouds.	Winds.	Relative humidity.	REMARKS.
Sept. 23	7 a. m.	......	......	......	10	....	NE. 3	......	
	2 p. m.	......	......	......	8	....	NE. 2	......	
	9 p. m.	......	......	......	9	....	NE. 2	......	
Sept. 24	7 a. m.	......	......	......	8	....	NE. 0	......	
	2 p. m.	......	......	......	4	....	SW. 0	......	
	9 p. m.	......	......	......	2	....	SW. 0	......	
Sept. 25	7 a. m.	......	......	......	3	....	S. 0	......	
	2 p. m.	......	......	......	2	....	S. 1	......	

WESTFIELD, MASSACHUSETTS.

Month and day.	Hour.	Barom'r corrected to 32° F.	Thermometer.	Force of vapor.	Cloudiness.	Motion of clouds.	Winds.	Relative humidity.	REMARKS.
Sept. 14	9 p. m.	29. 97	42	. 234	Cir. cu. 5	....	W..........	85	14th. Hard frost.
Sept. 15	7 a. m.	30. 16	37	. 136	Cu. 5	....	SW..........	59	Rain from 8 p m the 16th to 9 p. on the 17th; amount, 1. 92 inch.
	2 p. m.	. 15	53	. 113	Cir. 5	....	W..........	28	20th. Rain from 8 to 11 p. m.; amount, 0. 07 inch.
	9 p. m.	. 25	40	. 177	Cir. 5	....	W..........	69	Rain from 1 p. m. the 21st to 10 a. m. on the 23d; amount, 2. 75 inches.
Sept. 16	7 a. m.	. 24	37	. 136	Cir. 10	....	NW	59	
	2 p. m.	. 13	53	. 221	Cir. 10	....	W..........	54	
	9 p. m.	. 10	48	. 326	Nim. 10	....	W..........	93	
Sept. 17	7 a. m.	29. 94	57	. 316	Nim. 10	....	NE..........	100	
	2 p. m.	. 64	58	. 349	Nim. 10	....	NE..........	100	
	9 p. m.	. 61	50	. 361	Nim. 10	....	NE..........	100	
Sept. 18	7 a. m.	. 69	56	. 364	Cir. 5	....	N	78	
	2 p. m.	. 68	66	. 661	Cir. 5	....	NE..........	63	
	9 p. m.	. 78	55	. 376	0	....	NW	83	
Sept. 19	7 a. m.	. 82	44	. 252	0	....	NW	85	
	2 p. m	. 77	72	. 435	0	....	SE	54	
	9 p. m.	. 78	61	. 521	Cir. 5	....	SE	95	
Sept. 20	7 a. m.	. 75	64	. 544	Cir. 10	....	SE	90	
	2 p. m.	. 78	72	. 624	Cir. 10	....	SE	78	
	9 p. m.	. 88	66	. 581	Nim. 10	....	SE	95	
Sept. 21	7 a. m.	30. 03	50	. 337	Cir. 10	....	NE..........	94	
	2 p. m.	. 03	47	. 327	Nim. 10	....	NE..........	100	
	9 p. m.	. 12	46	. 327	Nim. 10	....	NE..........	100	
Sept. 22	7 a. m.	. 03	47	. 337	Nim. 10	....	N	100	
	2 p. m.	. 02	51	. 373	Nim. 10	....	N	100	
	9 p. m.	. 01	50	. 361	Nim. 10	....	N	100	
Sept. 23	7 a. m.	29. 95	50	. 373	Nim. 10	....	N	100	
	2 p. m.	. 86	59	. 433	Cir. 5	....	N	84	
	9 p. m.	. 87	56	. 442	Cu. 10	....	N	94	
Sept. 24	7 a. m.	. 86	56	. 469	Cir. 5	NW	E	100	
	2 p. m.	. 78	71	. 477	Cir. 5	....	E	62	
	9 p. m.	. 84	55	. 351	Cir. 5	....	NW	77	
Sept. 25	7 a. m.	. 83	51	. 361	0	....	NW	94	
	2 p. m.	. 81	69	. 471	Cir. 5	....	NW	65	

WILLIAMSTOWN, MASSACHUSETTS.

Month and day.	Hour.	Barom'r corrected to 32° F.	Thermometer.	Force of vapor.	Cloudiness.	Motion of clouds.	Winds.	Relative humidity.	REMARKS.
Sept. 14	9 p. m.	29. 308	47. 7	......	Cir. 6	....	NW. 2	......	Rain from 7 p. m. the 16th till 9 p. m. on the 17th; amount. 1.171 inch.
Sept. 15	7 a. m.	29. 571	37. 3	......	Cir. st. 1	....	NW. 2	......	
	2 p. m.	29. 593	47. 2	......	Cir. cu. 7	....	NW. 2	......	
	9 p. m.	29. 813	41. 2	......	Cir. cu. 6	....	0	......	Storm commenced at 2 p. m. the 20th, and ended at 8 p. m. on the 23d; amount, 2,276 inches.
Sept. 16	7 a. m.	29. 841	38. 3	......	Cir. cu. 9	....	S. 1	......	
	2 p. m.	29. 465	54. 6	......	Cir. st. 10	....	SW. 3	......	
	9 p. m.	29. 014	45. 9	......	Nim. 10	....	0	......	
Sept. 17	7 a. m.	29. 346	46. 2	......	Nim. 10	....	SE. 3	......	
	2 p. m.	29. 201	48. 5	......	Nim. 10	....	0	......	
	9 p. m.	29. 084	48. 6	......	Nim. 10	....	0	......	
Sept. 18	7 a. m.	29. 182	51. 65	......	Nim. 10	....	NW. 1	......	
	2 p. m.	29. 190	59	......	Cu. 2	....	N. 2	......	
	9 p. m	29. 218	49. 3	......	0	....	0	......	

STORMS Nos. 2 AND 3, SEPTEMBER, 1859.

WILLIAMSTOWN, MASSACHUSETTS—Continued.

Month and day.	Hour.	Barom'r corrected to 32° F.	Thermometer.	Force of vapor.	Cloudiness.	Motion of clouds.	Winds.	Relative humidity.	REMARKS.
Sept. 19	7 a. m.	29. 238	42	......	Cir. 1	....	S. 1	......	
	2 p. m.	29. 137	68. 9	......	0	....	S. 3	......	
	9 p. m.	29. 140	62	......	Cir. cu. 2	....	S. 2	......	
Sept. 20	7 a. m.	29. 158	62	......	Nim. 10	....	S. 1	......	
	2 p. m.	29. 186	69. 95	......	Nim. 10	....	S. 1	......	
	9 p. m.	29. 254	57	......	Nim. 10	....	0	......	
Sept. 21	7 a. m.	29. 422	53. 4	......	Nim. 10	....	SE. 3	......	
	2 p. m.	28. 909	51	......	Nim. 10	....	SE. 2	......	
	9 p. m.	28. 896	46. 5	......	Nim. 10	....	SE. 2	......	
Sept. 22	7 a. m.	28. 902	47. 65	......	Nim. 10	....	SE. 3	......	
	2 p. m.	29. 367	55. 6	......	Nim. 9	....	E. 3	......	
	9 p. m.	29. 345	51. 45	......	Nim. 10	....	E. 3	......	
Sept. 23	7 a m.	29. 806	51. 5	......	Nim. 10	....	SE. 2	......	
	2 p. m.	28. 773	61. 65	......	Nim. 10	....	SE. 1	......	
	9 p. m.	28. 756	58. 85	......	Nim. 10	....	0	......	
Sept. 24	7 a. m.	28. 766	56. 2	......	Nim. 9	....	NW. 1	......	
	2 p. m.	29. 229	64. 6	......	Nim. 8	....	NW. 2	......	
	9 p. m.	29. 220	54. 8	......	Nim. 1	....	0	......	
Sept. 25	7 a. m.	29. 245	53	......	Nim. 9	....	0	......	
	2 p. m.	29. 219	65. 8	......	Cir. 4	....	N. 2	......	

WORCESTER, MASSACHUSETTS.

Month and day.	Hour.	Barom'r corrected to 32° F.	Thermometer.	Force of vapor.	Cloudiness.	Motion of clouds.	Winds.	Relative humidity.	REMARKS.
Sept. 14	9 p. m	29. 500	54½	. 379	Cir. st. 8	....	NW. 1	89	15th. Frost a. m.
Sept. 15	7 a. m.	. 704	41	. 214	Cir. st. 1	....	NW. 2	84	16th. Severe frost; foggy 6½ to 7½
	2 p. m.	. 714	50½	. 268	Cir. st. 3	NW	NW. 3	74	a. m.
	9 p. m.	. 767	44	. 250	Cir. cu. 8	NW	NW. 1	88	17th. Drizzling rain commencing
Sept. 16	7 a. m.	. 791	40	. 245	Cir. st. 7	....	NW. 1	100	before day, varying in intensity;
	2 p. m.	. 749	55½	. 352	Cir. st. 8	....	SE. 1	82	ceased at 7 a. m. on the 18th;
	9 p. m.	. 698	51	. 347	St. 10	....	SE. 1	93	amount, 2. 07 inches.
Sept. 17	7 a. m.	. 568	48	. 335	St. 10	....	NE. 1	100	18th. Fog 5½ to 8 a. m.
	2 p. m.	. 385	52	......	Nim. 10	....	NE. 2	......	Began to rain at 9 p. m. the 20th,
	9 p. m.	. 158	47	......	Nim. 10	....	NE. 4	......	and ended at 5½ p. m. on the 23d;
Sept. 18	7 a. m.	. 208	52½	. 389	St. 10	NE	NE. 3	100	amount, 1. 70 inch.
	2 p. m.	. 246	66	. 512	Cir. cu. 3	NE	NE. 2	80	24th. Light shower at 8½ p. m.
	9 p. m.	. 335	60	. 450	0	....	NE. 1	89	25th. Dense fog falling at 5 a. m.;
Sept. 19	7 a m.	. 377	49	. 347	Cir. st. 1	....	N. 1	100	rising at 10 a. m.
	2 p. m.	. 310	72	. 635	0	....	SW. 1	81	
	9 p. m.	. 325	60	. 513	Cir. st. 10	....	SW. 1	100	
Sept. 20	7 a. m.	. 322	64	. 596	St. 10	....	SW. 1	100	
	2 p. m.	. 336	73½	. 759	St. 9	SW	SW. 1	94	
	9 p. m.	. 444	67	. 355	St. 10	....	SW. 1	100	
Sept. 21	7 a. m.	. 648	49	. 348	St. 10	....	NE. 2	100	
	2 p. m.	. 608	46½	. 316	Nim. 10	....	NE. 1	100	
	9 p m.	. 615	47	......	Nim. 10	....	NE. 1	......	
Sept. 22	7 a m.	. 601	47	......	Nim. 10	....	NE. 1	......	
	2 p. m.	. 588	51	......	Nim. 10	....	NE. 1	......	
	9 p. m.	. 588	50½	. 364	Nim. 10	....	NE. 1	100	
Sept. 23	7 a. m.	. 498	50½	......	Nim. 10	....	NE. 1	......	
	2 p. m	. 446	56	. 446	Nim. 10	....	NE. 1	100	
	9 p. m.	. 434	55	. 430	St. 10	NE	NE. 1	100	
Sept. 24	7 a. m.	. 433	55	......	St. 9	....	NE. 1	......	
	2 p. m.	. 342	68½	. 584	Cir. cu. 7	NW	NE. 1	86	
	9 p m.	. 350	61½	. 538	Cir. st. 9	....	NE. 1	99	
Sept. 25	7 a. m.	. 391	56½	......	....	....	NE. 1	......	
	2 p. m.	. 374	65	. 597	Cir. cu. 9	SE	SE. 1	97	

STORMS Nos. 2 AND 3, SEPTEMBER, 1859.

PROVIDENCE, RHODE ISLAND.

Month and day.	Hour.	Barom'r corrected to 32° F.	Thermometer.	Force of vapor.	Cloudiness.	Motion of clouds.	Winds.	Relative humidity.*
Sept. 14	10 p. m.	30. 00	46	------	4	----------	NW. 2	------
Sept. 15	6 a. m.	30. 14	39	------	1	----------	NW. 2	------
	2 p. m.	30. 15	57	------	5	----------	NW. 2	48
	10 p. m.	30. 24	43	------	0	----------	NW. 1	------
Sept. 16	6 a. m.	30. 23	39	------	8	----------	NW. 1	------
	2 p. m.	30. 20	63	------	10	----------	Southwest'y 1	41. 7
	10 p. m	30. 17	52	------	10	----------	SW. 1	------
Sept. 17	6 a. m.	30. 03	51	------	Rain--------	----------	NE. 2	------
	2 p. m.	29. 72	54	------	Rain--------	----------	Northeast'ly 4	41. 7
	10 p. m.	29. 50	52	------	Rain--------	----------	NE. 5	------
Sept. 18	6 a. m.	29. 58	52	------	Rain--------	----------	NE. 4	------
	2 p m.	29. 69	67	------	8	----------	NNE. 3	91
	10 p. m	29. 82	59	------	0	----------	NW. 1	------
Sept. 19	6 a. m.	29. 82	50	------	0	----------	NW. 1	------
	2 p. m.	29. 80	72	------	0	----------	SW. 3	76. 3
	10 p. m.	29. 83	62	------	1	----------	NW. 1	------
Sept. 20	6 a. m.	29. 80	65	------	7	----------	SW. 2	------
	2 p. m.	29. 83	78	------	10	----------	SW. 3	88. 2
	10 p. m.	29. 97	66	------	10	----------	SW. 1	------
Sept. 21	6 a. m.	30. 00	54	------	10	----------	NE. 3	------
	2 p. m.	30. 05	51	------	Rain --------	----------	NE. 4	76. 9
	10 p. m.	30. 03	53	------	Rain--------	----------	NE. 2	------
Sept. 22	6 a. m.	30. 00	50	------	Mist --------	----------	Northeast'ly 2	------
	2 p. m.	30. 00	54	------	Mist --------	----------	NE. 2	88. 3
	10 p. m.	30. 00	52	------	Rain--------	----------	NE. 2	------
Sept. 23	6 a. m.	29. 90	52	------	Rain--------	----------	NE. 1	------
	2 p. m.	29. 86	58	------	Mist --------	----------	NE. 2	93
	10 p. m.	29. 87	56	------	10	----------	Northerly 1	------
Sept. 24	6 a. m.	29. 84	56	------	10	----------	Northerly 2	------
	2 p. m.	29. 80	70	------	5	----------	NW. 1	89. 4
	10 p. m.	29. 87	62	------	10	----------	NW. 1	------
Sept. 25	6 a. m.	29. 87	61	------	10	----------	NW. 1	------
	2 p. m.	29. 88	65	------	10	----------	NW. 1	72. 8

REMARKS.

17th. Began to rain at sunrise and continued all day—very heavy p. m , with high wind; amount, 2. 40 inches

18th. Light rain and mist in the morning; cloudy p. m ; evening clear and mild.

19th. Very fine.

20th. Warm and sultry.

21st. Began to rain moderately at sunrise; rain fine and misty, with strong wind; in the evening wind abated and rain increased.

22d. Mist, and occasional light showers.

23d. Clouds, with occasional rain; amount of rain, 1. 45 inch.

COLUMBIA, CONNECTICUT.

Month and day.	Hour.	Barom'r corrected to 32° F.	Thermometer.	Force of vapor.	Cloudiness.	Motion of clouds.	Winds.	Relative humidity.
Sept. 14	9 p. m.	------	42	------	Nim. 10	0	0	------
Sept. 15	7 a. m.	------	40	------	------------	----------	NW. 2	------
	2 p. m.	------	58	------	St. 5	NW. 2	NW. 2	------
	9 p. m.	------	36	------	------------	----------	0	------
Sept. 16	7 a. m.	------	38	------	Nim. 10	NE. 1	N. 3	------
	2 p. m.	------	56	------	Nim. 10	NE. 1	NE. 2	------
	9 p. m.	------	38	------	Nim. 10	----------	0	------
Sept. 17	7 a m.	------	48	------	Nim. 10	NE. 2	NE. 2	------
	2 p. m.	------	52	------	Nim. 10	NE. 3	NE. 3	------
	9 p. m.	------	49	------	Nim. 10	NE. 3	NE. 3	------
Sept. 18	7 a. m.	------	56	------	Nim. 10	NE. 0	NE. 4	------
	2 p. m.	------	76	------	Nim. 5	NW. 3	NW. 3	------
	9 p. m.	------	55	------	0	0	0	------
Sept. 19	7 a. m.	------	55	------	0	0	0	------
	2 p. m.	------	72	------	0	0	S. 2	------
	9 p m.	------	64	------	Nim. 10	S. 2	S. 3	------
Sept. 20	7 a. m.	------	62	------	Nim. 10	S. 2	S. 3	------
	2 p. m.	------	74	------	Nim. 10	S. 2	S. 2	------
	9 p. m.	------	64	------	Nim. 10	0	0	------
Sept. 21	7 a. m.	------	50	------	Nim. 10	NE. 2	NE. 4	------
	2 p. m.	------	48	------	Nim. 10	NE. 1	NE. 2	------
	9 p. m.	------	46	------	Nim. 10	NE. 1	NE. 2	------
Sept. 22	7 a. m.	------	48	------	Nim. 10	NE. 2	NE. 1	------
	2 p. m.	------	52	------	Nim. 10	NE. 1	NE. 2	------
	9 p. m.	------	50	------	Nim. 10	NE. 1	NE. 2	------

REMARKS.

17th. Rain from 1 to 10 p. m.

Rain from 2 p. m. the 21st till 10 a. m. on the 23d.

* Mean for the day.

STORMS Nos. 2 AND 3, SEPTEMBER, 1859.

COLUMBIA, CONNECTICUT—Continued.

Month and day.	Hour.	Barom'r corrected to 32° F.	Thermometer.	Force of vapor.	Cloudiness.	Motion of clouds.	Winds.	Relative humidity.	REMARKS.
Sept. 23	7 a. m.	......	51	......	Nim. 10	NE. 1	NE. 1	......	
	2 p. m.	......	57	......	Nim. 10	0	NE. 1	......	
	9 p. m.	......	54	......	Nim. 10	SW. 1	NE. 1	......	
Sept. 24	7 a. m.	......	54	......	Nim. 10	NW. 2	0	......	
	2 p. m.	......	74	......	Cu. 8	NW. 2	NE. 2	......	
	9 p. m.	......	60	......	Cu. 5	NE. 1	NE. 2	......	
Sept. 25	7 a. m.	......	64	......	Cu. 7	NW. 2	NE. 2	......	
	2 p. m.	......	71	......	Cu. 6	SW. 2	NW. 1	......	

MIDDLETOWN, CONNECTICUT.

Month and day.	Hour.	Barom'r corrected to 32° F.	Thermometer.	Force of vapor.	Cloudiness.	Motion of clouds.	Winds.	Relative humidity.	REMARKS.
Sept. 14	9 p. m.	29.903	43.4	.208	Cu. 4	....	NW. 1	74	14th. Amount of rain recorded, 0.03 inch.
Sept. 15	7 a. m.	30.127	41	.179	Cu. 1	W. 2	0	69	Storm commenced in the a. m. of the 17th, and ended in the a. m. of the 18th; amount, 1.96 inch.
	2 p. m.	30.115	57.4	.115	Cu. 1	W. 1	NW. 1	24	Rain on the 21st and 22d; amount, 2.07 inches.
	9 p. m.	30.162	41	.210	0	....	0	81	
Sept. 16	7 a. m.	30.135	37.4	.220	Cu. 9	W........	0	98	
	2 p. m.	30.174	58	.229	Cu. 9	....	0	47	
	9 p. m.	30.128	52.2	.305	10	....	SE. 1	78	
Sept. 17	7 a. m.	30.047	52.5	.333	Nim. 10	....	E. 1	84	
	2 p. m.	29.674	54	.367	Nim. 10	....	NE. 2	88	
	9 p. m.	29.580	49.7	.320	Nim. 10	....	NE. 3	90	
Sept. 18	7 a. m.	29.431	55	.327	10	....	N. 3	75	
	2 p. m.	29.579	71	.403	Cu. 2	NW. 3	N. 2	54	
	9 p. m.	29.695	54.4	.381	0	....	0	89	
Sept. 19	7 a. m.	29.727	46.1	.312	Cu. 1	....	0	100	
	2 p. m.	29.756	76.4	.464	0	....	S. 1	51	
	9 p. m.	29.715	62.6	.516	Cu. 9	....	SW. 2	90	
Sept. 20	7 a. m.	29.712	65	.552	Nim. 10	....	SW. 2	90	
	2 p. m.	29.703	79	.628	Cir. cu. 4	W. 3	SW. 2	64	
	9 p. m.	29.727	65.6	.582	Nim. 10	....	0	93	
Sept. 21	7 a. m.	29.809	57	.356	Nim. 10	....	NE. 2	76	
	2 p. m.	29.914	51.8	.311	Nim. 10	....	NE. 2	80	
	9 p. m.	29.922	48.3	.321	Nim. 10	....	NE. 1	95	
Sept. 22	7 a. m.	29.929	49	.320	Nim. 10	....	NE. 2	91	
	2 p. m.	29.904	54.5	.383	Nim. 10	....	NE. 1	90	
	9 p. m.	29.906	52.4	.372	Nim. 10	....	NE. 1	94	
Sept. 23	7 a. m.	29.910	51.9	.341	Nim. 10	....	N. 1	88	
	2 p. m.	29.822	57.6	.411	10	....	N. 1	86	
	9 p. m.	29.796	56.1	.431	10	....	0	96	
Sept. 24	7 a. m.	29.811	56.4	.414	9	....	0	91	
	2 p. m.	29.805	75.2	.467	Cu. 3	W. 1	0	54	
	9 p. m.	29.720	62.5	.533	10	....	0	94	
Sept. 25	7 a. m.	29.726	55.5	.407	Foggy	....	0	93	
	2 p. m.	29.761	75.2	.464	Cu. 3	NW. 2	0	53	

POMFRET, CONNECTICUT.

Month and day.	Hour.	Barom'r corrected to 32° F.	Thermometer.	Force of vapor.	Cloudiness.	Motion of clouds.	Winds.	Relative humidity.	REMARKS.
Sept. 14	9 p. m.	29.443	43	.231	Cu. st. 6	....	NW. 1	83	13th. Rain from 5 to 6 p. m; am't, 0.04 inch.
Sept. 15	7 a. m.	29.641	39	.195	Cir. st. 3	NW. 1	NW. 1	82	Rain from 4 a. m. the 17th to 8 a. m. on the 18th; amount, 1.62 inch.
	2 p. m.	29.678	49.5	.234	Cu. 4	NW. 2	NW. 2	65	Storm commenced at 6½ p. m. the 20th and ended in the night of the 23d; amount, 1 20 inch.
	9 p. m.	29.715	41	.212	Cir. cu. 5	NW. 2	NW. 2	82	24th. Rain from 5 to 6½ p. m.; amount, 0.070 inch.
Sept. 16	7 a. m.	29.731	38.5	.216	Cir. st. 8	SW. 1	NE. 2	91	25th. Rain at 7½ p. m.
	2 p. m.	29.706	54	.362	Cir. st. 10	NW. 1	SE. 2	87	
	9 p. m.	29.630	49	.348	Cir. cu. 10	NW. 1	SE. 1	100	
Sept. 17	7 a. m.	29.264	47	.323	Nim. 10	NE. 2	NE. 2	100	
	2 p. m.	29.239	51	.374	Nim. 10	NE. 3	NE. 3	100	
	9 p. m.	29.030	47	.323	Nim. 10	NE. 5	NE. 5	100	
Sept. 18	7 a. m.	29.127	51.5	.374	Nim. 10	W. 4	N. 4	78	
	2 p. m.	29.183	64.5	.483	Cu. 6	NE. 2	NW. 3	88	
	9 p. m.	29.287	58	.423	0	....	NW. 1	100	

STORMS Nos. 2 AND 3, SEPTEMBER, 1859.

POMFRET, CONNECTICUT—Continued.

Month and day.	Hour.	Barom'r corrected to 32° F.	Thermometer.	Force of vapor.	Cloudiness.	Motion of clouds.	Winds.	Relative humidity.	REMARKS.
Sept. 19	7 a. m.	29.332	51.5	.388	0	....	NW. 1	85	
	2 p. m.	29.283	68	.577	Cu. 2	SW. 2	SW. 2	100	
	9 p. m.	29.290	58	.483	Cir. st. 10	SW. 2	SW. 2	100	
Sept. 20	7 a. m.	29.293	62	.556	Cir. st. 10	SW. 1	SW. 1	25	
	2 p. m.	29.310	71	.720	Cir st., cir. 5	SW. 1	SW. 1	100	
	9 p. m.	29.384	64	.596	Nim. 10	S. 1	S. 1	100	
Sept. 21	7 a. m.	29.527	49	.348	Nim. 10	NE. 4	NE. 4	100	
	2 p. m.	29.525	46	.311	Nim. 10	NE. 4	NE. 4	100	
	9 p. m.	29.508	46	.311	Nim. 10	NE. 4	NE. 4	100	
Sept. 22	7 a. m.	29.497	47	.323	Nim. 10	NE. 4	NE. 4	100	
	2 p. m.	29.488	50	.361	Nim. 10	NE. 3	NE. 3	100	
	9 p. m.	29.497	48	.335	Nim. 10	NE. 3	NE. 3	100	
Sept. 23	7 a. m.	29.401	49	.348	Nim. 10	NE. 3	NE. 3	100	
	2 p. m.	29.367	54	.418	Nim. 10	NE. 2	NE. 2	100	
	9 p. m.	29.373	53	.403	Nim. 10	NE. 2	NE. 2	100	
Sept. 24	7 a. m.	29.366	50.5	.374	St. 10	NW. 1	NW. 1	100	
	2 p. m.	29.304	65	.563	Cu. 5	NW. 2	E. 1	94	
	9 p. m.	29.300	57	.466	Cu. st. 9	SE. 1	SE. 1	100	
Sept. 25	7 a. m.	29.334	54	.418	St. 10	NW. 1	NW. 1	100	
	2 p. m.	29.309	63.2	.543	Cu. st., cu. 7	NW. 1	E. 1	94	

SAYBROOK, CONNECTICUT.

Month and day.	Hour.	Barom'r corrected to 32° F.	Thermometer.	Force of vapor.	Cloudiness.	Motion of clouds.	Winds.	Relative humidity.	REMARKS.
Sept. 14	9 p. m.	------	50	------	7	----------	NW. 4	------	14th. Large lunar halo at 9 p. m.
Sept. 15	7 a. m.	------	42	------	Cir. 2	NW. 3	NW. 2	------	Rain from 4 a. m. the 17th to 6 a. m. on the 18th; amount, 2.41 inches.
	2 p. m.	------	58	------	Cir. 2	W. 3	NW. 4	------	
	9 p. m.	------	48	------	0	0	NW. 3	------	
Sept. 16	7 a. m.	------	47	------	Nim., cu. 9	----------	NE. 2	------	Rain storm from 2 p. m. the 21st till 10 p. m. on the 23d; amount, 1.50 inch.
	2 p. m.	------	62	------	Nim. 10	----------	E. 4	------	
	9 p. m.	------	57	------	Nim. 10	----------	E. 4	------	
Sept. 17	7 a. m.	------	58	------	Nim. 10	----------	E. 6	------	
	2 p. m.	------	56	------	Nim. 10	----------	E. 7	------	
	9 p. m.	------	54	------	Nim. 10	----------	NE. 8	------	
Sept. 18	7 a. m.	------	54	------	Nim. 10	N. 5	N. 6	------	
	2 p. m.	------	68	------	Cir. 4	----------	NNW. 5	------	
	9 p. m.	------	60	------	0	0	NW. 1	------	
Sept. 19	7 a. m.	------	52	------	Cir. 1	S. 1	N. 2	------	
	2 p. m.	------	68	------	0	0	SE. 2	------	
	9 p. m.	------	64	------	7	----------	SW. 1	------	
Sept. 20	7 a. m.	------	65	------	Nim. 10	----------	S. 1	------	
	2 p. m.	------	75	------	Cir., nim. 8	----------	SE. 1	------	
	9 p. m.	------	66	------	Nim. 10	----------	E. 1	------	
Sept. 21	7 a. m.	------	56	------	Nim. 10	W. 1	NE. 6	------	
	2 p. m.	------	55	------	Nim. 10	E. 6	ENE. 7	------	
	9 p. m.	------	54	------	Nim. 10	----------	NNW. 1	------	
Sept. 2	7 a. m.	------	54	------	Nim. 10	----------	NNE. 5	------	
	2 p. m.	------	58	------	Nim. 10	----------	E. 3	------	
	9 p. m.	------	55	------	Nim. 10	----------	E. 3	------	
Sept. 23	7 a. m.	------	54	------	Nim. 10	----------	E. 3	------	
	2 p. m.	------	62	------	Nim. 10	----------	NE. 2	------	
	9 p. m.	------	48	------	Nim. 8	----------	E. 2	------	
Sept. 24	7 a. m.	------	56	------	Nim. 10	NNE. 2	0	------	
	2 p. m.	------	70	------	3	----------	SW. 2	------	
	9 p. m.	------	62	------	Nim. 5	----------	S. 2	------	
Sept. 25	7 a. m.	------	60	------	Cir. st. 4	NW. 1	N. 1	------	
	2 p. m.	------	------	------	------------	----------	------------	------	

STORMS Nos. 2 AND 3, SEPTEMBER, 1859.

WALLINGFORD, CONNECTICUT.

Month and day.	Hour.	Barom'r corrected to 32° F.	Thermometer.	Force of vapor.	Cloudiness.		Motion of clouds.		Winds.		Relative humidity.
Sept. 14	9 p. m.	30. 00	44	. 218	Cir.	4	W.	1	NW.	0	76
Sept. 15	7 a. m.	30. 21	39. 5	. 225	Cir. cu	1	W.	2	NW.	1	91
	2 p. m.	30. 20	56	. 118	Cir. st.	1	W.	2	NW.	2	26
	9 p. m.	30. 24	42	. 177	Cir. st.	1	W.	2	N.	0	66
Sept. 16	7 a. m.	30. 26	39	. 188	Cir. st.	8	W.	2	N.	1	77
	2 p. m.	30. 10	56	. 266		10	----------		SE.	2	57
	9 p. m.	30. 11	53	. 295		10	----------		SE.	0	73
Sept. 17	7 a. m.	29. 92	51	. 368	Nim.	10	----------		NNE.	1	96
	2 p. m.	29. 63	53	. 403	Nim.	10	----------		N.	3	100
	9 p. m.	29. 48	49	. 348		10	----------		NNE.	3	100
Sept. 18	7 a. m.	29. 66	57	. 350	Scuds.	9	NE.	6	N.	4	75
	2 p. m.	29. 72	68	. 443	Scuds.	1	NE.	5	NNW.	4	65
	9 p. m.	29. 80	53	. 361		0		0	NW.	0	90
Sept. 19	7 a. m.	29. 83	47	. 310		0		0	N.	1	96
	2 p. m.	29. 78	75	. 449		0		0	SW.	2	52
	9 p. m	29. 79	63	. 543		10	----------		SSW.	2	94
Sept. 20	7 a. m.	29. 79	64. 5	. 596		10	Foggy. ----		SSW.	1	100
	2 p. m.	29. 78	74. 5	. 641	Cir. st.	8	----------		SSW.	2	77
	9 p. m.	29. 89	65	. 590		10	----------		S.	2	97
Sept. 21	7 a. m.	29. 96	57	. 413	Nim.	10	----------		NE.	2	90
	2 p. m.	29. 99	50. 5	. 335	Nim.	10	----------		NE.	3	93
	9 p. m.	30. 00	48	. 322	Nim.	10	----------		N.	2	96
Sept. 22	7 a. m.	29. 99	48. 5	. 329	Nim.	10	----------		NNE.	2	96
	2 p. m.	29. 96	53	. 403	Nim.	10	NE.	5	NE.	2	100
	9 p. m.	29. 98	51. 5	. 374	Nim.	10	----------		NNE.	2	100
Sept. 23	7 a. m.	29. 88	51. 5	. 388	Nim.	10	----------		N.	2	100
	2 p. m.	29. 84	58. 5	. 446	Nim.	10	----------		N.	3	91
	9 p. m.	29. 88	56	. 435	St.	1	----------		N.	0	97
Sept. 24	7 a. m.	29. 87	57	. 452		10	W.	1	N.	0	94
	2 p. m	29. 89	75	. 422	Cu.	1	NW.	2	N.	2	49
	9 p. m.	29. 80	61	. 530	Nim.	10	----------		S.	1	97
Sept. 25	7 a. m.	29. 83	54. 5	. 418	Fog	0		0	NW.	0	100
	2 p. m.	29. 89	68	. 476	Nim.	9	W.	1	SE.	2	69

REMARKS.

17th. Began to rain last night; light wind NE ; steady fall of barometer during the a. m.; rapid fall of rain from 11 a. m. to 12 m.; more moderate previously; 3 p. m. wind NE. 3; 4 p. m. N. E. 3; still raining; rain during the evening; amount, 2.57 inches.

18th. 7 a. m. clouds broken.

20th. Rain from 5 to 8 p. m.; am't, 0 09 inch.

21st. Began to rain at 11.30 a. m.; wind and clouds from NE. ; storm continued till 9 p. m. on the 22d; remarkable high barometer during the storm; am't of rain, 1.91 inch.

23d. Rain from 12 midnight till 7 a. m; misty during the a. m.; amount, 0.61 inch.

25th. Rain from 2 to 3 p. m ; amount, 0.19 inch.

ADAMS CENTRE, NEW YORK.

Month and day.	Hour.	Barom'r corrected to 32° F.	Thermometer.	Force of vapor.	Cloudiness.		Motion of clouds.		Winds.		Relative humidity.
Sept. 14	9 p m.	------	------	------		2	----------		NW.	1	------
Sept. 15	7 a. m.	------	------	------		0	----------		Still ----------		------
	2 p. m.	------	------	------		4	----------		NW.	1	------
	9 p. m.	------	------	------	------------		----------		NW.	1	------
Sept. 16	7 a. m.	------	------	------		3	----------		SE.	2	------
	2 p. m.	------	------	------		10	----------		SE.	4	------
	9 p. m.	------	------	------		10	----------		SE.	1	------
Sept. 17	7 a. m.	------	------	------		10	----------		SE.	2	------
	2 p m.			------		10	----------		SE.	2	------
	9 p. m.	------	------	------		10	----------		N.	1	------
Sept. 18	7 a. m.	------	------	------		10	----------		N.	1	------
	2 p. m.	------	------	------		0	----------		NW.	1	------
	9 p. m.	------	------	------		0	----------		Still ----------		------
Sept. 19	7 a. m.	------	------	------		0	----------		S.	1	------
	2 p. m.	------	------	------		0	----------		SW.	1	------
	9 p. m.	------	------	------		10	----------		S.	1	------
Sept. 20	7 a. m.	------	------	------		10	----------		N.	3	------
	2 p m.	------	------	------		10	----------		NE.	2	------
	9 p. m.	------	------	------		10	----------		NE.	1	------
Sept. 21	7 a. m.	------	------	------		10	----------		NE.	2	------
	2 p. m.	------	------	------		10	----------		NE.	2	------
	9 p. m.	------	------	------		10	----------		NE.	1	------
Sept. 22	7 a. m.	------	------	------		9	----------		S.	1	------
	2 p m.	------	------	------		8	----------		S.	2	------
	9 p. m.	------	------	------		10	----------		S.	1	------

REMARKS.

14th. Very high wind all night, with some rain.

15th. Heavy frost.

17th. Rain from 3. 30 to 11 a. m.; amount, 0. 30 inch.

19th Some thunder and lightning in the evening; began to rain at 8 p. m.

20th. Storm ended at 0 a. m.; amount, 0. 90 inch.

Rain from 8 a. m. the 22d to 5 a. m. on the 23d; amount, 0.70 inch.

24th. Sprinkle of rain two or three times during the day.

STORMS Nos. 2 AND 3, SEPTEMBER, 1859.

ADAMS CENTRE, NEW YORK—Continued

Month and day.	Hour.	Barom'r corrected to 32° F.	Thermometer.	Force of vapor.	Cloudiness.		Motion of clouds.		Winds.		Relative humidity.	REMARKS.
Sept. 23	7 a. m.	------	------	------		7	----------		SW.	1	------	
	2 p. m.	------	------	------		0	----------		SW.	2	------	
	9 p. m.	------	------	------		9	----------		Still -------		------	
Sept. 24	7 a. m.	------	------	------		10	----------		N.	1	------	
	2 p. m.	------	------	------		10	----------		N.	3	------	
	9 p. m.	------	------	------		10	----------		N.	1	------	
Sept. 25	7 a. m.	------	------	------		10	----------		N.	1	------	

BALDWINSVILLE, NEW YORK.

Month and day.	Hour.	Barom'r corrected to 32° F.	Thermometer.	Force of vapor.	Cloudiness.		Motion of clouds.		Winds.		Relative humidity.	REMARKS.
Sept. 14	9 p. m.	------	44	------	Cir. cu.	2	W.	1	NW.	2	------	Moderate rain from 8 p. m. the 16th till 5 p. m. on the 17th.
Sept. 15	7 a. m.	------	37	------	Cir.	1	NW.	0	N.	1	------	20th. Light rain during the night.
	2 p. m.	------	50	------	Cu.	5	NW.	1	NW.	2	------	21st. Light rain during the day.
	9 p. m.	------	42	------	Cu.	8	W.	0	W.	0	------	22d. Very light rain from 2 to 3 p. m.
Sept. 16	7 a. m.	------	42	------	St.	5	W.	0	SE.	0	------	
	2 p. m.	------	51	------	St.	10	SE.	2	SE.	1	------	
	9 p. m.	------	50	------		10	----------		SE.	1	------	
Sept. 17	7 a. m.	------	50	------	Nim.	10	SE.	0	SE.	0	------	
	2 p. m.	------	54	------	Nim.	10	SE.	0	SE.	0	------	
	9 p. m.	------	55	------		10	----------		SE.	0	------	
Sept. 18	7 a. m.	------	54	------	Cu.	8	N.	3	N.	1	------	
	2 p. m.	------	61	------	Cu.	4	N.	2	N.	1	------	
	9 p. m.	------	54	------		0	----------		N.	0	------	
Sept. 19	7 a. m.	------	49	------		0	----------		S.	0	------	
	2 p. m.	------	66	------	Cir.	2	W.	0	S.	1	------	
	9 p. m.	------	67	------	St.	10	W.	0	SW.	2	------	
Sept. 20	7 a. m.	------	64	------	Nim.	10	W.	0	E.	0	------	
	2 p. m.	------	61	------	Nim.	10	W.	0	E	0	------	
	9 p. m.	------	57	------	Nim.	10	W.	0	E.	0	------	
Sept. 21	7 a. m.	------	56	------	Nim.	10	W.	0	SE.	1	------	
	2 p. m.	------	60	------	Nim.	10	SE.	3	SE.	1	------	
	9 p. m.	------	56	------	Nim.	10	E --------		NE	2	------	
Sept. 22	7 a. m.	------	53	------	Cir ------ Nim.	 2	SW SE.	0 3	SE.	0	------	
	2 p. m.	------	65	------	Nim.	8	SE.	3	SE.	1	------	
	9 p. m.	------	60	------	Nim.	10	E.	2	E.	0	------	
Sept. 23	7 a. m.	------	58	------	Nim.	8	W.	1	W.	0	------	
	2 p. m	------	67	------	Cu.	8	W.	1	W.	0	------	
	9 p. m.	------	59	------		0	----------		W.	0	------	
Sept. 24	7 a. m.	------	58	------	Nim.	10	W.	1	W.	1	------	
	2 p. m.	------	67	------	Cu.	5	W.	1	W.	1	------	
	9 p. m.	------	60	------	Cu.	3	W.	1	W.	0	------	
Sept. 25	7 a. m.	------	59	------	Nim.	8	W.	0	W.	0	------	

BELLPORT, LONG ISLAND, NEW YORK.

Month and day.	Hour.	Barom'r corrected to 32° F.	Thermometer.	Force of vapor.	Cloudiness.		Motion of clouds.		Winds.		Relative humidity.	REMARKS.
Sept. 14	9 p. m.	29.41	45	.210		5	----------		NW.	2	68½	13th. Rain from 5 to 6½ p. m.; amount, 0.16 inch.
Sept. 15	7 a. m.	29.46	53	.194		0	----------		SW.	2	48	Began to rain at 11 a. m the 16th, and ended at 3 p. m. on the 18th; amount, 2.87 inches.
	2 p. m.	29.38	49	.162		0	----------		SW.	1	45	Commenced raining at 11 a. m. the 21st, and ended at 3 p. m. on the 23d; amount, 2.40 inches.
	9 p. m.	29.49	44	.192		0	----------		SW.	1	62	
Sept. 16	7 a. m.	29.56	52.5	.276		10	----------		NE.	1	70	
	2 p. m.	29.52	58	.365		10	----------		SE.	2	76	
	9 p. m.	29.47	57	.407		10	----------		NE.	4	87	
Sept. 17	7 a. m.	29.26	59	.469		10	E -------		E.	5	94	
	2 p. m.	28.96	58	.423		10	E -------		E.	7	88	
	9 p. m.	28.89	55	.377		10	----------		N.	1	87	
Sept. 18	7 a. m.	29.09	60	.396		3	N -------		N.	8	76	
	2 p. m.	29.15	67	.457		3	N -------		N.	7	69	
	9 p. m.	29.22	56	.420		0	----------		N.	1	94	

STORMS Nos. 2 AND 3, SEPTEMBER, 1859.

BELLPORT, LONG ISLAND, NEW YORK—Continued.

Month and day.	Hour.	Barom'r corrected to 32° F.	Thermometer.	Force of vapor.	Cloudiness.	Motion of clouds.	Winds.	Relative humidity.	REMARKS.
Sept. 19	7 a. m.	29.22	54	.390	0	....	0	93	
	2 p. m.	29.24	68	.522	0	....	SW. 2	79	
	9 p. m.	29.23	64	.529	3	W........	SW. 2	89	
Sept. 20	7 a. m.	29.26	65	.549	0	SW.......	SW. 0	89	
	2 p. m.	29.21	72	.631	6	SW.......	SW. 4	81	
	9 p. m.	29.26	68	.577	10	S.........	S. 2	85	
Sept. 21	7 a. m.	29.29	65	.549	10	SE	E. by N. 5	89	
	2 p. m.	29.31	55	.405	10	NE.......	NE. 7	94	
	9 p. m.	29.33	56	.391	10	....	NE. 5	87	
Sept. 22	7 a. m.	29.34	55	.405	10	....	E. by N. 5	94	
	2 p. m.	29.34	60	.487	10	E	E. by N. 4	94	
	9 p. m.	29.31	68	.612	10	E	E. 4	90	
Sept. 23	7 a. m.	29.26	57	.436	10	....	E. 4	94	
	2 p. m.	29.26	60	.439	10	NE.......	NE. 3	88	
	9 p. m.	29.29	56	.420	2	NW	NW. 2	94	
Sept. 24	7 a. m.	29.29	58	.423	6	....	0	88	
	2 p. m.	29.25	64	.433	3	S.........	SW. 3	73	
	9 p. m.	29.24	59	.469	2	W........	W. 1	94	
Sept. 25	7 a. m.	29.24	62	.523	5	....	S. 1	94	

BEVERLY, NEW YORK.

Month and day.	Hour.	Barom'r corrected to 32° F.	Thermometer.	Force of vapor.	Cloudiness.	Motion of clouds.	Winds.	Relative humidity.	REMARKS.
Sept. 14	9 p. m.	......	49	......	Cu. 9	SW. 1	NW. 1	......	Storm commenced at 8 p. m. the 16th, and ended in the night of the 17th; amount, 2.78 inches.
Sept. 15	7 a. m.	......	42	......	Cu. 5	SW. 1	NW. 1	......	
	2 p. m.	......	55	......	Cir. 2	SW. 2	NW. 2	......	
	9 p. m.	......	44	......	Cir. 2	NW. 1	NW. 1	......	Storm commenced at 5 p. m. the 20th, and ended at 10 a. m. on the 23d; amount, 3.03 inches.
Sept. 16	7 a. m.	......	45	......	Cu 10	SW. 2	SW. 1	......	
	2 p. m.	......	......	......	....	....	....	......	
	9 p. m.	......	52	......	Cu. 10	SE. 3	SW. 2	......	
Sept. 17	7 a. m.	......	51	......	Cu. 10	NE. 3	NE. 3	......	
	2 p. m.	......	52	......	Cu. 10	NE. 3	NE. 3	......	
	9 p. m.	......	50	......	Cu. 10	N. 5	NE. 5	......	
Sept. 18	7 a. m.	......	55	......	Cu. st. 1	NW. 2	NW. 4	......	
	2 p. m.	......	66	......	0		NW. 2	......	
	9 p. m.	......	54	......	0	....	NW. 1	......	
Sept. 19	7 a. m.	......	50	......	Cir. 1	NE. 1	N. 1	......	
	2 p. m.	......	......	......	....	....	....	......	
	9 p. m.	......	......	......	....	....	....	......	
Sept. 20	7 a. m.	......	63	......	Cu. 10	SE. 1	SE. 2	......	
	2 p. m.	......	......	......	....	....	....	......	
	9 p. m.	......	63	......	Cu. 10	SE. 2	SE. 3	......	
Sept. 21	7 a. m.	......	58	......	Cu. 10	E. 3	NE. 3	......	
	2 p. m.	......	54	......	Cu. 10	NE. 2	NE. 3	......	
	9 p. m.	......	50	......	Cu. 10	NE. 3	NE. 2	......	
Sept. 22	7 a. m.	......	51	......	10	....	NE. 1	......	
	2 p. m.	......	57	......	Cu. 10	....	NE. 1	......	
	9 p. m.	......	55	......	10	....	NE. 1	......	
Sept. 23	7 a. m.	......	55	......	Cu. 10	NE. 2	NE. 2	......	
	2 p. m.	......	65	......	Cu. 9	NW. 4	NW. 2	......	
	9 p. m.	......	58	......	St. 1	W. 1	NW. 1	......	
Sept. 24	7 a. m.	......	59	......	Cu. 10	S. 1	SW. 1	......	
	2 p. m.	......	68	......	Cu. st. 8	SW. 2	N. 1	......	
	9 p. m.	......	60	......	St. 2	SW. 1	N. 1	......	
Sept. 25	7 a. m.	......	59	......	Cir. cu. 7	NW. 1	NW. 1	......	

STORMS Nos. 2 AND 3, SEPTEMBER, 1859.

BUFFALO, NEW YORK.

Month and day.	Hour.	Barom'r corrected to 32° F.	Thermometer.	Force of vapor.	Cloudiness.	Motion of clouds.	Winds.	Relative humidity.	REMARKS.
Sept. 14	9 p. m.	29. 559	46	. 146	0	....	W. 2	47	14th. Frost. 17th. A fine mist nearly all day; foggy at 9 p. m. 18th. Foggy till 8 a. m. 19th. Rain, accompanied by thunder and lightning from the S. at 5. 40 p. m.; continued fifteen minutes; slight rain at 9 p. m. 20th. Rain from 3 a. m. till 10 a. m., and from 5 p. m. till 4. 30 p. m. on the 21st; wind NE., fresh; amount of rain, 1. 20 inch. 23d. Slight rain at daylight. 24th. Slight rain at 5 a. m.
Sept. 15	8 a. m.	. 737	44	. 108	Cir. st. 5	2	NE. 2	37	
	2 p. m.	. 668	53	. 123	Cir. st. 5	2	NE. 2	30	
	9 p. m.	. 622	46	. 169	Cir. st. 8	....	SE. 2	54	
Sept. 16	8 a. m.	. 507	51	. 245	Cir. st. 3	2	E. 1	65	
	2 p. m.	. 421	62	. 340	Cir. st. 10	....	E. 1	61	
	9 p. m.	. 346	56	. 420	Cir. st. 10	....	SE. 1	94	
Sept. 17	8 a. m.	. 303	61	. 354	Cir. st. 10	....	N. 1	66	
	2 p. m.	. 271	57	. 407	Cir. st. 10	....	N. 1	87	
	9 p. m.	. 341	54	. 362	0	....	....	87	
Sept. 18	8 a. m.	. 422	56	......	St 10	....	W. 1	......	
	2 p. m.	. 360	58	......	Cir. cu. 5	....	....	......	
	9 p. m.	......	......	......	0	....	SW. 1	......	
Sept. 19	8 a. m.	. 118	61	. 442	0	....	S. 2	83	
	2 p. m.	. 040	73	. 545	Cir. cu. 10	....	S. 1	67	
	9 p. m.	. 067	67	. 556	Nim. 10	....	S. 2	84	
Sept. 20	8 a. m.	. 230	54	. 418	Nim. 10	....	NE. 2	100	
	2 p. m.	. 253	52	. 361	St. 10	....	NE. 3	93	
	9 p. m.	. 303	53	. 375	St. 10	....	NE. 4	93	
Sept. 21	8 a. m.	. 278	54	. 418	Nim. 10	....	NE. 3	100	
	2 p. m.	. 218	59	. 500	Nim. 10	....	NE. 3	100	
	9 p. m.	. 168	60	. 487	Cu. st. 4	....	NE. 2	94	
Sept. 22	8 a. m.	. 220	64	. 497	0	....	SE. 1	83	
	2 p. m.	. 250	65	. 516	Cir. cu. 5	4	SW. 2	84	
	9 p. m.	. 348	62	. 491	Cir. st. 5	....	SW. 2	88	
Sept. 23	8 a. m.	. 411	61	. 473	Cir. st. 5	....	SW. 1	88	
	2 p. m.	. 382	63	. 478	Cir. st. 8	....	SW. 2	83	
	9 p. m.	. 400	62	. 460	Cir. st. 7	....	SW. 3	83	
Sept. 24	8 a. m.	. 360	60	. 487	Cir. cu. 5	....	SE. 2	94	
	2 p. m.	. 302	66	. 438	Cu. st. 6	SW. 3	E. 2	68	
	9 p. m.	. 348	61	. 473	0	....	E. 2	88	
Sept. 25	8 a. m.	......	......	......	St. 10	....	....	......	

BUFFALO, NEW YORK, (PINE HILL.)

Month and day.	Hour.	Barom'r corrected to 32° F.	Thermometer.	Force of vapor.	Cloudiness.	Motion of clouds.	Winds.	Relative humidity.	REMARKS.
Sept. 14	9 p. m.	......	......	......	4	....	N. 1	......	14th. Very cold; clear p. m. 15th. Frost. 16th. Fine day; appearance of rain in the evening. 17th. Dark, and sometimes foggy; light rain. 18th. Fine day. 19th. Fine and warm a. m., dark p. m.; shower, accompanied by lightning, NW., from 5 to 6 p. m. 20th. Light rain from 3 a. m. to 9 p. m. 21st. Rain from 3 to 9 a. m.; some rain in p. m. 22d. Shower at 1 p. m; very warm. 23d and 24th. Very fine; moderately warm.
Sept. 15	7 a. m.	......	......	......	4	....	N. 1	......	
	2 p. m.	......	......	......	3	....	NE. 3	......	
	9 p. m.	......	......	......	5	....	NE. 2	......	
Sept. 16	7 a. m.	......	......	......	5	....	NW. 1	......	
	2 p. m.	......	......	......	2	....	NW. 3	......	
	9 p. m.	......	......	......	10	....	NW. 2	......	
Sept. 17	7 a. m.	......	......	......	10	....	N. 2	......	
	2 p. m.	......	......	......	10	....	N. 3	......	
	9 p. m.	......	......	......	2	....	N. 1	......	
Sept. 18	7 a. m.	......	......	......	10	....	SW. 2	......	
	2 p. m.	......	......	......	2	....	SW. 3	......	
	9 p. m.	......	......	......	2	....	W. 0	......	
Sept. 19	7 a. m.	......	......	......	1	....	SW 1	......	
	2 p. m.	......	......	......	10	....	SW. 3	......	
	9 p. m.	......	......	......	3	....	SW. 1	......	
Sept. 20	7 a. m.	......	......	......	10	....	NE. 3	......	
	2 p. m.	......	......	......	10	....	NE. 4	......	
	9 p. m.	......	......	......	10	....	NE. 3	......	
Sept. 21	7 a. m.	......	......	......	10	....	SE. 3	......	
	2 p. m.	......	......	......	10	....	SE. 4	......	
	9 p. m.	......	......	......	5	....	SE 3	......	
Sept. 22	7 a. m.	......	......	......	3	....	SW. 2	......	
	2 p. m.	......	......	......	6	....	SW. 4	......	
	9 p. m.	......	......	......	5	....	SW. 1	......	
Sept. 23	7 a. m.	......	......	......	10	....	SW. 2	......	
	2 p. m.	......	......	......	9	....	SW. 2	......	
	9 p. m.	......	......	......	5	....	SW. 1	......	
Sept. 24	7 a. m.	......	......	......	9	....	SW. 1	......	
	2 p. m.	......	......	......	5	....	SW. 3	......	
	9 p. m.	......	......	......	4	....	SW. 0	......	
Sept. 25	7 a. m.	......	......	......	10	....	SW. 0	......	

STORMS Nos. 2 AND 3, SEPTEMBER, 1859.

CAZENOVIA, NEW YORK.

Month and day.	Hour.	Barom'r corrected to 32° F.	Thermometer.	Force of vapor.	Cloudiness.	Motion of clouds.	Winds.	Relative humidity.	REMARKS.
Sept. 14	9 p. m.	28.71	38	.144	Cir. 3	NW. 1	NW. 1	63	14th. Cold winds; strong all
Sept. 15	7 a. m.	28.91	32.5	.110	0	----------	N. 1	59	night.
	2 p. m.	28.92	46 5	.078	Cir. cu. 8	NW. 2	NW. 2	25½	15th. Frost.
	9 p. m.	28.90	34.5	.169	Cir. cu. 6	NW. 2	NW. 1	84	Rain from 11 a. m. the 16th, till 2
Sept. 16	7 a. m.	28.84	42	.166	St. 5	W. 2	SE. 1	61	p. m. on the 17th; amount,
	2 p. m.	28.79	46.5	.250	Nim, st. 10	S. 3	S. 3	80	1.00 inch.
	9 p. m.	28.71	46.5	.299	Nim. 10	S. 2	S. 2	96	19th. Heavy dew.
Sept. 17	7 a. m.	28.57	52.3	.375	Nim. 10	SE. 3	SE. 1	96	Storm commenced at 6½ a. m. the
	2 p. m.	28.49	51	.361	Nim. 10	SE. 2	SE. 1	96	20th, and ended at 8 a. m. on
	9 p. m.	28.48	53	.396	Fog 10	W. 2	W. 2	100	the 23d; amount, 1.34 inch.
Sept. 18	7 a. m.	28.57	49.5	.341	Mist, nim. 10	NW. 2	NW. 2	96	
	2 p. m.	28.58	64	.317	St. 3	NW. 3	NW. 3	54	
	9 p. m.	28.54	47.5	.316	Cir. 1	NW. 1	NW. 1	96	
Sept. 19	7 a. m.	28.50	52	.348	Hazy, wet ---	----------	SW. 1	96	
	2 p. m.	28.39	74.8	.446	Cir. 3	W. 1	S. 3	54	
	9 p. m.	28.39	65.5	.509	Nim. 10	S. 2	S. 3	81	
Sept. 20	7 a. m.	28.45	62.5	.540	Nim. 10	S. 2	S. 1	97	
	2 p. m.	28.49	61	.511	Nim. 10	SW. 2	SW. 1	97	
	9 p. m.	28.55	55.2	.433	10	? 0	0	100	
Sept. 21	7 a. m.	28.45	56	.368	Nim. 10	SE. 2	SE. 2	93	
	2 p. m.	28.48	61.5	.473	Nim. 10	SE. 3	SE. 2	88	
	9 p. m.	28.52	55	.390	Nim. 10	SE. 3	SE. 1	93	
Sept. 22	7 a. m.	28.73	55.5	.405	Mist, nim. 10	SE. 3	SE 1	94	
	2 p. m.	28.47	64.5	.529	Nim. 10	SE. 3	SE. 2	89	
	9 p. m.	28.59	59.5	.496	Nim. 10	SE.-------	SE. 1	99	
Sept. 23	7 a. m.	28.65	56.5	.446	St., nim-----	NW. 2	NW. 2	99	
	2 p. m.	28.64	64.5	.433	St. 9	NW. 2	NW. 2	73	
	9 p. m.	28.65	52.5	.375	St. 1	NW. 1	NW. 1	96	
Sept. 24	7 a. m.	28.61	55	.397	St. 10	NW. 2	NW. 1	93	
	2 p. m.	------	------	------	St. 5	NW. 2	NW. 1	------	
	9 p. m.	28.57	52.5	.384	St. 8	NW. 1	NW. 1	99	
Sept. 25	7 a. m.	28.58	56	.437	Mist, st. 10	NW. 2	NW. 1	99	

CHARLOTTE, NEW YORK.

Month and day.	Hour.	Barom'r.*	Thermometer.	Force of vapor.	Cloudiness.	Motion of clouds.	Winds.	Relative humidity.	REMARKS.
Sept. 14	6 p. m.	29.90	61	.165	3	W. 5	NW. 3	49	15th. Heavy frost last night, which
Sept. 15	6 a. m.	30.15	57	.126	4	NW. 3	NNE. 4	49	did considerable damage.
	9 a. m.	30.21	59	.160	4	W. 2	NE. 3	53	17th. Amount in rain, 0.15 inch.
	3 p. m.	30.16	61	.185	8	W. 1	NE. 3	47	Rain on the 20th, 21st, and 22d;
	6 p. m.	30.13	60	.234	3	W. 1	E. 3	65	amount, 1.13 inch.
Sept. 16	6 a. m.	30.01	59	.196	8	W. 3	E. 3	68	20th. Very cloudy all day; could
	9 p. m.	29.98	59	.175	9	W. 2	ESE. 2	50	not discern the movement of the
	3 p. m.	29.90	61	.356	9	W. 1	SE. 3	62	clouds; a light, though steady
	6 p. m.	29.87	61	.337	10	----------	SE. 3	70	gale from NE.
Sept. 17	6 a. m.	29.77	60	.349	10	----------	SE. 2	81	
	9 p. m.	29.75	60	.407	10	----------	SE. 1	87	
	3 p. m.	29.71	61	.456	10	----------	NNE. 3	88	
	6 p. m.	29.71	60	.423	10	----------	NNE. 2	88	
Sept. 18	6 a. m.	29.81	58	.375	10	----------	WNW. 1	93	
	9 p. m.	29.86	58	.405	8	NE. 2	WNW. 1	94	
	3 p. m.	29.81	61	.429	0	----------	E. 1	77	
	6 p. m.	29.77	61	.464	3	W. 1	N. 1	77	
Sept. 19	6 a. m.	29.63	59	.309	2	----------	SSE. 2	85	
	9 p. m.	29.58	59	.456	2	----------	S. 1	88	
	3 p. m.	29.49	60	.527	9	SW. 2	S. 2	57	
	6 p. m.	29.49	60	.662	10	W. 2	ENE. 1	100	
Sept. 20	6 a. m.	29.64	60	.439	10	----------	NE. 5	88	
	9 p. m.	29.73	60	.391	10	----------	NE. 6	87	
	3 p. m.	29.77	60	.376	10	----------	NE. 5	87	
	6 p. m.	29.78	60	.376	10	----------	NE. 6	87	

* Barometer not corrected for temperature.

STORMS Nos. 2 AND 3, SEPTEMBER, 1859.

CHARLOTTE, NEW YORK—Continued.

Month and day.	Hour.	Barom'r corrected to 32° F.	Thermometer.	Force of vapor.	Cloudiness.	Motion of clouds.	Winds.	Relative humidity.	REMARKS.
Sept. 21	6 a. m.	29 76	60	.376	10	....	NE. 5	87	
	9 p. m.	29.76	59	.376	10	....	ENE. 4	87	
	3 p. m.	29.74	59	.407	10	E. 3	E. 4	87	
	6 p. m.	29.71	59	.405	10	....	E. 4	94	
Sept. 22	6 a. m.	29.68	60	.420	8	SW. 3	ESE. 2	94	
	9 p. m.	29.68	60	.510	3	S. 3	SE. 3	88	
	3 p. m.	29.68	62	.551	4	SW. 2	S. 3	75	
	6 p. m.	29.72	62	.529	7	SW. 2	NW. 1	75	
Sept. 23	6 a. m.	29.83	62	.407	3	S. 2	SW. 1	87	
	9 p. m.	29.86	63	.426	2	S. 1	SW. 1	82	
	3 p. m.	29.85	64	.563	8	SW. 1	NNE. 1	94	
	6 p. m.	29.84	64	.556	8	SW. 1	N. 1	100	
Sept. 24	6 a. m.	29.82	63	.456	8	SW. 1	SW. 1	88	
	9 p. m.	29.83	63	.473	8	NW. 1	W. 2	88	
	3 p. m.	29.77	64	.478	7	NW. 1	N. 1	83	
	6 p. m.	29.77	64	.478	8	NW. 1	Calm 0	83	
Sept. 25	6 a. m.	29.79	63	.407	10	....	NW. 1	25	

CLYDE, NEW YORK.

Month and day.	Hour.	Barom'r corrected to 32° F.	Thermometer.	Force of vapor.	Cloudiness.	Motion of clouds.	Winds.	Relative humidity.	REMARKS.
Sept. 14	9 p. m.	29.61	42	......	5	....	....	......	14th. Cold and windy.
Sept. 15	7 a. m.	29.78	38	......	3	....	S. 2	......	15th. White frost.
	2 p. m.	29.82	54	......	3	....	NW. 2	......	17th. Rainy most of the day.
	9 p. m.	29.78	41	......	5	....	....	......	19th. Cloudy; wind SW.; rain and
Sept. 16	7 a. m.	29.65	43	......	8	....	S. 2	......	lightning in the evening till near
	2 p. m.	29.63	55	......	10	....	S. 25	......	9 p. m.
	9 p. m.	29.56	51	......	10	....	S. 12	......	20th. Rainy most of the day.
Sept. 17	7 a. m.	29.44	51	......	10	....	S. 2	......	22d. Rainbow SE. at 6 p. m.
	2 p. m.	29.36	58	......	10	....	S. 4	......	
	9 p. m.	29.39	56	......	10	....	N. 12	......	
Sept. 18	7 a. m.	29.47	54	......	8	....	NW. 2	......	
	2 p. m.	29.45	70	......	1	....	S. 2	......	
	9 p. m.	29.41	52	......	0	....	....	......	
Sept. 19	7 a. m.	29.32	51	......	1	....	SE. 2	......	
	2 p. m.	29.19	76	......	5	....	S. 12	......	
	9 p. m.	29.23	68	......	1	....	....	......	
Sept. 20	7 a. m.	29.29	64	......	10	....	S. 2	......	
	2 p. m.	29.38	55	......	10	....	N. 4	......	
	9 p. m.	29.41	54	......	10	....	N. 4	......	
Sept. 21	7 a. m.	29.42	56	......	10	....	NW. 2	......	
	2 p. m.	29.41	61	......	10	....	SE. 4	......	
	9 p. m.	29.38	58	......	10	....	SE. 4	......	
Sept. 22	7 a. m.	29.38	59	......	8	....	SE. 4	......	
	2 p. m.	29.37	73	......	5	....	SE. 12	......	
	9 p. m.	29.42	65	......	10	....	NW. 2	......	
Sept. 23	7 a. m.	29.48	60	......	3	....	Calm	......	
	2 p. m.	29.49	64	......	5	....	N. 2	......	
	9 p. m.	29.49	56	......	2	....	Calm	......	
Sept. 24	7 a. m.	29.47	55	......	8	....	S. 2	......	
	2 p. m.	29.41	71	......	5	....	NW. 4	......	
	9 p. m.	29.43	58	......	3	....	....	......	
Sept. 25	7 a. m.	29.43	58	......	10	....	SE. 2	......	

STORMS Nos. 2 AND 3, SEPTEMBER, 1859.

DANSVILLE, NEW YORK.

Month and day.	Hour.	Barom'r corrected to 32° F.	Thermometer.	Force of vapor.	Cloudiness.		Motion of clouds.		Winds.		Relative humidity.	REMARKS.
Sept. 14	9 p. m.	29.515	47	.090	Cir.	5		0	N.	3	27.6	17th. Began to rain last night, and ended at 10 a. m; amount, 0.87 inch.
Sept. 15	7 a. m.	.646	37	.178	Cir.	1	W.	1	S.	1	80.7	
	2 p. m.	.631	53	.244	Cir.	2		0	S.	1	69	
	9 p. m.	.588	45	.182	Cir.	8	W.	0	S.	1	60.7	20th. Rain from 10 a. m. till 5.40 p. m.; amount, 1.08 inch.
Sept. 16	7 a. m.	.506	48	.236	Cu.	10	W.	1	S.	1	70	
	2 p. m.	.455	57	.407	Cu.	10	S.	1	S.	2	87.4	21st. Rain from 9 to 10 p. m; amount, 0.04 inch.
	9 p. m.	.352	54	.335	Cu. st.	10		0	S.	1	80.2	
Sept. 17	7 a. m.	.265	54	.418	Nim.	10		0		0	100	23d. Rain from 5 to 5.40 p. m.; amount, 0.07 inch.
	2 p. m.	.167	59	.500	Nim.	10	N.	1	N.	1	100	
	9 p. m.	.248	55	.433	Nim.	10	N.	1	N.	1	100	24th. Rain from 5.30 to 6.30 p. m.; amount, 1.05 inch.
Sept. 18	7 a. m.	.366	52	.388	Nim.	10		0		0	100	
	2 p. m.	.296	63	.416		0		0	N.	1	72.3	
	9 p. m.	.225	54	.384		0		0	N.	1	93.3	
Sept. 19	7 a. m.	.131	52	.361	Cir.	3		0	S.	1	93	
	2 p. m.	.982	82	.497	Cir.	4	W.	1	S.	1	45.5	
	9 p. m.	.077	68	.543	Nim.	10		0	S.	1	79.3	
Sept. 20	7 a. m.	.120	64	.596	Nim.	10		0	S.	1	100	
	2 p. m.	.231	55	.433	Nim.	10		0	N.	1	100	
	9 p. m.	.255	53	.403	Nim.	10		0	N.	1	100	
Sept. 21	7 a. m.	.221	54	.418	Nim.	10		0	N.	1	100	
	2 p. m.	.198	62	.522	Nim.	10		0	N.	1	94.2	
	9 p. m.	.160	62	.556	Nim.	10		0	N.	1	100	
Sept. 22	7 a. m.	.230	61	.537	Nim.	10		0	NE.	3	100	
	2 p. m.	.195	74	.568	Nim.	10		0	NW.	1	67	
	9 p. m.	.296	63	.542	Nim.	10		0	S.	3	94.2	
Sept. 23	7 a. m.	.362	60	.487	Cu.	10		0	SE.	1	94	
	2 p. m.	.346	67	.522	Cu. st.	10		0	N.	1	79	
	9 p. m.	.366	57	.466	Nim.	10		0	N.	1	100	
Sept. 24	7 a. m.	.337	58	.457	Cu. st.	10	NW.	1	S.	1	96.8	
	2 p. m.	.267	69.5	.526	Cu.	5	N.	1	S.	1	76.6	
	9 p. m.	.364	58	.482	Nim.	10		0	S.	1	100	
Sept. 25	7 a. m.	.317	57.5	.473	Nim.	10		0	W.	1	100	

EAST HENRIETTA, NEW YORK.

Month and day.	Hour.	Barom'r corrected to 32° F.	Thermometer.	Force of vapor.	Cloudiness.		Motion of clouds.		Winds.		Relative humidity.
Sept. 14	9 p. m.	28.97	40	.203	----------		----------		NW.	1	82
Sept. 15	7 a. m.	29.00	48	.310	Cir.	1	W.	2	SW.	2	92
	2 p. m.	28.99	52	.136	Cu.	2	SW.	2	W.	1	35
	9 p. m.	29.00	49	.086	----------		----------		W.	1	24
Sept. 16	7 a. m.	28.99	46	.215	Cir.	2	S.	1	S.	1	69
	2 p. m.	28.96	63	.356	Cir.	3	SE.	1	SE.	1	62
	9 p. m.	29.33	52	.388	----------		----------		S.	1	100
Sept. 17	7 a. m.	29.25	54	.390	Cu.	9	S.	2	SW.	1	93
	2 p. m.	29.19	59	.439	Cu.	9		0	N.	1	88
	9 p. m.	29.30	55	.405	----------		----------		S.	1	94
Sept. 18	7 a. m.	29.36	60	.456	Cu.	8		0	NW.	1	88
	2 p. m.	29.28	66	.438	Cu.	2	NW.	1	NW.	1	68
	9 p. m.	29.25	56	.391	----------		----------		N.	1	87
Sept. 19	7 a. m.	29.12	64	.556	Cir. st.	1		0	SW.	1	100
	2 p. m.	29.01	82	.534	Cir. cu.	3	SW.	2	SW.	1	49
	9 p. m.	29.05	68	.577	----------		----------		S.	2	85
Sept. 20	7 a. m.	29.14	59	.500	Nim.	10		0	NW.	2	100
	2 p. m.	29.26	53	.375	St.	8		0	NW.	2	93
	9 p. m.	29.26	54	.362	----------		----------		NE.	2	87
Sept. 21	7 a. m.	29 26	55	.435	Nim.	10		0	NW.	2	100
	2 p. m.	29.21	62	.523	Nim.	10		0	N.	2	94
	9 p. m.	29.28	61	.505	----------		----------		NE.	1	94
Sept. 22	7 a. m.	29.25	60	.518	Cir.	2	SW.	1	SW.	1	100
	2 p. m.	29.29	75	.591	Cu.	8	SW.	2	SW.	1	68
	9 p. m.	29.29	62	.491	----------		----------		SW.	1	88

STORMS Nos. 2 AND 3, SEPTEMBER, 1859.

EAST HENRIETTA, NEW YORK—Continued.

Month and day.	Hour.	Barom'r corrected to 32° F.	Thermometer.	Force of vapor.	Cloudiness.	Motion of clouds.	Winds.	Relative humidity.	REMARKS.
Sept. 23	7 a. m.	29. 34	68	. 612	Cu. 1	W. 1	W. 1	90	
	2 p. m.	29. 34	65	. 485	Nim. 6	SW. 1	N. 1	78	
	9 p. m.	29. 35	60	. 456	-----------	----------	NW. 1	88	
Sept. 24	7 a. m.	29. 30	60	. 487	Nim. 8	NW. 1	W. 1	94	
	2 p. m.	29. 29	66	. 502	Cu. 5	NW. 2	NW. 2	78	
	9 p. m.	29. 30	50	. 361	-----------	----------	N. 1	100	
Sept. 25	7 a. m.	29. 30	58	. 423	Cir. 3	N. 2	SW. 1	88	

FISHKILL LANDING, NEW YORK.

Month and day.	Hour.	Barom'r corrected to 32° F.	Thermometer.	Force of vapor.	Cloudiness.	Motion of clouds.	Winds.	Relative humidity.	REMARKS.
Sept. 14	9 p. m.	30. 25	50	------	Cir. 4	E. 1	NW. 5	------	17th. Rain from 1 a. m. to 10 p. m.; amount, 3. 16 inches.
Sept. 15	7 a. m.	30. 60	42	------	Cu. 3	NE. 2	SW. 1	------	
	2 p. m.	30. 55	56	------	Cu. st. 2	NE. 2	E. 1	------	Rain from 4 p. m. the 20th to 9 p. m. on the 22d; amount, 2. 98 inches.
	9 p. m.	30. 55	48	------	St. 2	----------	NE. 2	------	
Sept. 16	7 a. m.	30. 55	45	------	Nim. 4	E. 2	NE. 2	------	
	2 p. m.	30. 55	56	------	Nim. 9	----------	E. 1	------	24th. Shower at 6 p. m.; amount, 0. 12 inch.
	9 p. m.	30. 50	51	------	Nim. 10	----------	NE. 2	------	
Sept. 17	7 a. m.	30. 30	51	------	Nim. 10	SW. 3	NE. 3	------	
	2 p. m.	29. 97	53	------	Nim. 10	SW. 4	NE. 7	------	
	9 p. m.	29. 91	57	------	Nim. 10	----------	NE. 8	------	
Sept. 18	7 a. m.	30. 07	56	------	Cu. 4	SW. 5	NE. 7	------	
	2 p. m.	30. 15	67	------	0	----------	NE. 3	------	
	9 p. m.	30. 19	57	------	0	----------	NE. 2	------	
Sept. 19	7 a. m.	30. 18	50	------	Fog -------	----------	NE. 1	------	
	2 p. m.	30. 13	71	------	Cu. 2	E. 3	S. 3	------	
	9 p. m.	30. 15	65	------	Cu. 6	S. 4	SE. 5	------	
Sept. 20	7 a. m.	30. 13	64	------	Nim. 10	NE. 2	S. 3	------	
	2 p. m.	30. 13	72	------	Nim. 10	N. 2	SE. 1	------	
	9 p. m.	30. 13	64	------	Nim. 10	----------	S. 2	------	
Sept. 21	7 a. m.	30. 22	55	------	10	----------	NE. 2	------	
	2 p. m.	30. 30	55	------	10	----------	NE. 4	------	
	9 p. m.	30. 27	50	------	10	----------	NE. 4	------	
Sept. 22	7 a. m.	30. 25	51	------	10	----------	NE. 4	------	
	2 p. m.	30. 23	57	------	10	----------	NE. 3	------	
	9 p. m.	30. 21	55	------	10	----------	NE. 1	------	
Sept. 23	7 a. m.	30. 27	50	------	Nim. 10	E. 1	NE. 2	------	
	2 p. m.	30. 25	65	------	Nim. 6	NE. 2	NE. 2	------	
	9 p. m.	30. 25	51	------	Cu. 3	----------	NE. 1	------	
Sept. 24	7 a. m.	30. 30	59	------	Fog -------	----------	N. 1	------	
	2 p. m.	30. 18	71	------	Cu. 4	SW. 2	W. 1	------	
	9 p. m.	30. 11	61	------	Cu. st. 4	----------	W. 1	------	
Sept. 25	7 a. m.	30. 20	57	------	Fog -------	----------	SW. 1	------	

FLATBUSH, NEW YORK.

Month and day.	Hour.	Barom'r corrected to 32° F.	Thermometer.	Force of vapor.	Cloudiness.	Motion of clouds.	Winds.	Relative humidity.	REMARKS.
Sept. 14	9 p. m.	30. 005	51	------	Cir. st. 2	----------	NW. 2	------	14th and 15th. Pleasant.
Sept. 15	7 a. m.	. 240	46. 9	------	St., cir. cu. 3	W. 2	W. 1	------	16th. Slight rain at intervals during the p. m.; more constant in the evening.
	2 p. m.	. 226	52. 2	------	Cir cu., cr. st. 3	W. 5	W. 1	------	
	9 p. m.	. 207	45. 8	------	Cir. 5	SW. 1	S. 0	------	
Sept. 16	7 a. m.	. 242	49. 1	------	Nim. 10	----------	E. 1	------	17th. Very heavy rain; ended in the night; amount, 2. 76 inches.
	2 p. m.	. 203	54. 6	------	Nim. 10	E 2	E. 2	------	
	9 p. m.	. 046	57	------	Nim. 10	SE. 2	SW. 2	------	18th and 19th. Pleasant.
Sept. 17	7 a. m.	29. 872	59. 1	------	Nim. 10	SE. 8	E. 3	------	20th. Began to rain at 2½ p. m; moderate rain at intervals during the p. m. and evening.
	2 p. m.	. 406	57. 4	------	Nim. 10	E. 8	NE. 4	------	
	9 p. m.	. 494	53	------	Nim. 10	----------	N. 4	------	
Sept. 18	7 a. m.	. 796	57. 2	------	0	----------	N. 2	------	21st. Moderate rain a. m., more p. m. and evening.
	2 p. m.	. 820	70	------	Cir. 2	N. 4	NW. 2	------	
	9 p. m.	. 875	56	------	0	----------	NW. 0	------	22d. Rainy all day.
Sept. 19	7 a. m.	. 915	53. 6	------	St., cir. st. 1	----------	NW. 0	------	23d. Storm ended at 10 a. m.; damp, slight sprinkle at dark; amount, 3. 60 inches.
	2 p. m.	. 843	69. 7	------	Cu. 1	----------	S. 2	------	
	9 p. m.	. 883	62	------	Nim. 2	----------	S. 2	------	

STORMS Nos. 2 AND 3, SEPTEMBER, 1859.

FLATBUSH, NEW YORK—Continued.

Month and day.	Hour.	Barom'r corrected to 32° F.	Thermometer.	Force of vapor.	Cloudiness.	Motion of clouds.	Winds.	Relative humidity.	REMARKS.
Sept. 20	7 a. m.	29.859	62.3	......	Nim. 9	W. 3	SE. 0	......	24th. Slight sprinkles during the
	2 p. m.	.861	71.4	......	Nim. 10	SW. 1	S. 2	......	day ; lightning in the evening.
	9 p. m.	.872	65.5	......	Nim. 10	S. 1	SE. 0	......	25th. Pleasant.
Sept. 21	7 a. m.	.902	67.1	......	Nim. 10	SE. 5	E. 2	......	
	2 p. m.	.937	57.3	......	Nim. 10	E. 5	E. 3	......	
	9 p. m.	.968	54	......	Nim. 10	....	NE. 1	......	
Sept. 22	7 a. m.	.974	55.5	......	Nim. 10	SE. 3	E. 1	......	
	2 p. m.	.956	60	......	Nim. 10	E. 3	E. 1	......	
	9 p. m.	.940	57.5	......	Nim. 10	....	E. 2	......	
Sept. 23	7 a. m.	.931	55.1	......	Nim. 10	NE. 5	NE. 2	......	
	2 p. m.	.919	66.9	......	Nim., cir.cu. 8	N. 3	NE. 1	......	
	9 p. m.	.922	61	......	St. 1	....	E. 0	......	
Sept. 24	7 a. m.	.924	59.9	......	Nim. 10	....	E. 1	......	
	2 p. m.	.889	68.9	......	Nim., cir.cu. 9	W. 2	S. 1	......	
	9 p. m.	.920	58.8	......	St 2	....	S. 0	......	
Sept. 25	7 a. m.	.915	59.9	......	Nim. 10	....	NE. 0	......	

FORT NIAGARA, NEW YORK.

Month and day.	Hour.	Barom'r corrected to 32° F.	Thermometer.	Force of vapor.	Cloudiness.	Motion of clouds.	Winds.	Relative humidity.	REMARKS.
Sept. 14	6 p. m.	29.23	50	.335	7	N. 3	N. 5	93	17th. Heavy fog off the lake from
Sept. 15	6 a. m.	29.24	41	.235	8	....	NE. 4	91	5 a. m. till 3 p. m.
	9 a. m.	29.23	47	.179	8	....	W. 2	55	18th. Heavy fog off the lake from
	3 p. m.	29.24	47	.249	6	....	NE. 4	77	5 to 11 a. m.
	6 p. m.	29.23	46	.192	10	....	N. 3	62	19th. Rain from 1 to 2 p. m. ;
Sept. 16	6 a. m.	29.25	42	.244	10	....	N. 2	91	amount, 0.12 inch; heavy thun-
	9 a. m.	29.24	50	.234	10	....	NE. 2	65	der, with lightning from S. E.,
	3 p. m.	29.24	55	.321	6	....	NE. 3	74	from 7 to 9 p. m.
	6 p. m.	29.24	54	.362	10	....	NE. 1	87	20th. Rain from 6 to 7 p. m. ;
Sept. 17	6 a. m.	29.34	54	.362	10	....	N. 1	87	amount, 0.20 inch.
	9 a. m.	29.34	54	.390	10	....	NE. 2	93	21st. Rain from 7 to 8 p. m. ;
	3 p. m.	29.34	56	.420	10	....	NE. 2	94	amount, 0.82 inch.
	6 p. m.	29.34	56	.420	5	....	N. 1	94	23d. Slight shower of rain.
Sept. 18	6 a. m.	29.36	58	.483	10	....	S. 1	100	24th. Heavy fog off the lake from
	9 a. m.	29.32	51	.374	10	....	S. 1	100	NW. from 6 to 9 a. m.
	3 p. m.	29.44	58	.485	5	....	SE. 2	100	25th. Red sky on the horizon from
	6 p. m.	29.49	61	.413	5	....	W. 1	77	S. to E. for 20 minutes.
Sept. 19	6 a. m.	29.43	65	.244	5	....	S. 2	39	
	9 a. m.	29.42	62	.460	5	....	S. 2	83	
	3 p. m.	29.43	65	.549	10	....	W. 1	89	
	6 p. m.	29.42	64	.529	10	....	W.	89	
Sept. 20	6 a. m.	29.42	53	.321	10	....	NE. 4	80	
	9 a. m.	29.43	51	.374	10	....	NE. 4	100	
	3 p. m.	29.43	51	.321	8	N. 4	N. 5	86	
	6 p. m.	29.43	52	.361	10	....	E. 5	93	
Sept. 21	6 a. m.	29.44	50	.361	10	....	N. 3	100	
	9 a. m.	29.43	49	.348	10	....	NE. 4	100	
	3 p. m.	29.43	50	.361	10	....	NE. 4	100	
	6 p. m.	29.43	50	.361	10	....	NE. 5	100	
Sept. 22	6 a. m.	29.44	60	.487	10	....	NE. 2	94	
	9 a. m.	29.43	60	.338	10	....	N. 2	65	
	3 p. m.	29.63	68	.543	5	....	W. 2	79	
	6 p. m.	29.64	65	.516	7	....	W. 1	84	
Sept. 23	6 a. m.	29.64	59	.469	8	....	S. 1	94	
	9 a. m.	29.64	66	.470	8	....	S. 1	73	
	3 p. m.	29.65	65	.483	10	....	N. 1	78	
	6 p. m.	29.64	63	.510	10	....	S. 1	88	
Sept. 24	6 a. m.	29.64	58	.452	5	....	W. 1	94	
	9 a. m.	29.60	64	.497	8	....	SW.	83	
	3 p. m.	29.64	64	.529	8	....	E. 1	89	
	6 p. m.	29.63	62	.491	6	....	N. 1	88	
Sept. 25	6 a. m.	29.64	57	.295	10	....	S. 1	63	

STORMS Nos. 2 AND 3, SEPTEMBER, 1859.

GREAT VALLEY, NEW YORK.

Month and day.	Hour.	Barom'r corrected to 32° F.	Thermometer.	Force of vapor.	Cloudiness.	Motion of clouds.	Winds.	Relative humidity.	REMARKS.
Sept. 14	9 p. m.				6		SW. 1		14th. Cold wind all day.
Sept. 15	7 a. m.				7		W. 1		15th. Hard frost.
	2 p. m.				1		SE. 2		16th. Mild; appearance of rain
	9 p. m.				5		NW. 1		17th. Misty, foggy, and dark.
Sept. 16	7 a. m.				10		SW. 1		18th. Fine day.
	2 p. m.				10		S. 2		19th. Fine day; began to rain at
	9 p. m.				10		S. 2		7 p. m; storm in the evening,
Sept. 17	7 a. m.				10		NW. 1		accompanied by thunder and zig-
	2 p. m.				10		N. 2		zag lightning from NW.
	9 p. m.				10		N. 2		20th. Rain continues.
Sept. 18	7 a. m.				10		S. 1		21st Rain till 6 a. m.; slight mist
	2 p. m.				0		S. 2		most of the day.
	9 p. m.				0		0		22d. Several sprinkles of rain.
Sept. 19	7 a. m.				0		N. 1		23d. Slight mist a. m.
	2 p. m.				10		S. 3		24th. Slight mist p. m.
	9 p. m.				10		SW. 1		
Sept. 20	7 a. m.				10		N. 1		
	2 p. m.				10		N. 1		
	9 p. m.				10		S. 1		
Sept. 21	7 a. m.				10		0		
	2 p. m.				10		S. 1		
	9 p. m.				10		SE. 1		
Sept. 22	7 a. m.				10		S. 1		
	2 p. m.				10		S. 3		
	9 p. m.				5		N. 1		
Sept. 23	7 a. m.				10		W. 1		
	2 p. m.				10		SW. 1		
	9 p. m.				10		SW. 1		
Sept. 24	7 a. m.				10		W. 1		
	2 p. m.				10		S. 1		
	9 p. m.				10		S. 1		
Sept. 25	7 a. m.				10		0		

HAVANA, NEW YORK.

Month and day.	Hour.	Barom'r corrected to 32° F.	Thermometer.	Force of vapor.	Cloudiness.	Motion of clouds.	Winds.	Relative humidity.	REMARKS.
Sept. 14	9 p. m.		44		0		N. 1		17th. Rain from 5 a. m. till 6½
Sept. 15	7 a. m.		35		Cir. st. 3		NE. 1		p. m.
	2 p. m.		50		Cir. st. 2		NE. 3		20th. Rain from 8 a. m. till 5½
	9 p. m.		40		Cir. st. 5		E. 1		p. m.
Sept. 16	7 a. m.		43		Cu. 10		SW. 3		21st. Rain from 5 to 11½ a. m.
	2 p. m.		44		Nim. 10		SW. 3		24th. Rain from 5 to 6 a. m.
	9 p. m.		34		Nim. 10		E. 1		
Sept. 17	7 a. m.		46		Nim. 10		N. 3		
	2 p. m.		56		Nim. 10		N. 1		
	9 p. m.		48		1		W. 1		
Sept. 18	7 a. m.		49		Nim. 10		N. 3		
	2 p. m.		61		0		N. 1		
	9 p. m.		62		0		W. 1		
Sept. 19	7 a. m.		52		0		S. 2		
	2 p. m.		80		Cir. st. 4		SW. 4		
	9 p. m.		51		0		S. 1		
Sept. 20	7 a. m.		64		Nim. 10		S. 3		
	2 p. m.		56		Nim. 10		NW. 3		
	9 p. m.		45		Nim. 10		S. 2		
Sept. 21	7 a. m.		56		Nim. 10		SE. 3		
	2 p. m.		68		Cir. st. 10		S. 5		
	9 p. m.		58		Nim. 10		N. 2		
Sept. 22	7 a. m.		58		Nim. 10		SE. 2		
	2 p. m.		70		Nim. 10		S. 3		
	9 p. m.		62		Nim. 8		W. 1		
Sept. 23	7 a. m.		57		Cu. 8		NE. 1		
	2 p. m.		70		Nim. 10		N. 2		
	9 p. m.		47		Cu. 10		N. 1		
Sept. 24	7 a. m.		62		Cu. 10		N. 1		
	2 p. m.		70		Nim. 9		N. 1		
	9 p. m.		58		Cu. 10		N. 2		
Sept. 25	7 a. m.		61		Nim. 10		NW. 2		

STORMS Nos. 2 AND 3, SEPTEMBER, 1859.

IBION, NEW YORK

Month and day.	Hour.	Barom'r corrected to 32° F.	Thermometer.	Force of vapor.	Cloudiness.	Motion of clouds.	Winds.		Relative humidity.	REMARKS.
Sept. 14	9 p. m.	------	------	------	3	----------	W.	4	------	Severe storm on the 13th.
Sept. 15	7 a. m.	------	------	------	3	----------	W.	3	------	14th. Very cold for the season;
	2 p. m.	------	------	------	8	----------	W.	3	------	snow on high lands.
	9 p. m.	------	------	------	5	----------	W.	2	------	15th. Black frost; cool.
Sept. 16	7 a. m.	------	------	------	10	----------	NE.	2	------	16th. Signs of rain; drizzling rain
	2 p. m.	------	------	------	10	----------	NE.	2	------	at 0 45 p. m.
	9 p. m.	------	------	------	10	----------	E.	2	------	17th. Clear and warm.
Sept. 17	7 a. m.	------	------	------	10	----------	W.	2	------	18th. Warm and pleasant; wind
	2 p. m.	------	------	------	3	----------	W.	3	------	increased at 9 30 p. m.
	9 p. m.	------	------	------	0	----------	SW.	2	------	19th. Warm and pleasant.
Sept. 18	7 a. m.	------	------	------	10	----------	E.	2	------	20th. Commenced raining at 9.15
	2 p. m.	------	------	------	2	----------	SE.	3	------	a. m.; heavy still rain p. m.;
	9 p. m.	------	------	------	1	----------	S.	3	------	storm ended at 6 p. m.
Sept. 19	7 a. m.	------	------	------	10	----------	E.	2	------	21st. Rain all day and night;
	2 p. m.	------	------	------	2	----------	S.	3	------	colder in p. m.; wind rises.
	9 p. m.	------	------	------	2	----------	S.	2	------	22d. Showers and drizzles all day;
Sept. 20	7 a. m.	------	------	------	10	----------	E.	2	------	warm for the season.
	2 p. m.	------	------	------	10	----------	SE.	2	------	23d. Rain till 9.30 a. m., then
	9 p. m.	------	------	------	10	----------	S.	1	------	clears warm and fine.
Sept. 21	7 a. m.	------	------	------	10	----------	E.	2	------	24th. Pleasant and warm.
	2 p. m.	------	------	------	10	----------	E.	3	------	
	9 p. m.	------	------	------	10	----------	E.	3	------	
Sept. 22	7 a. m.	------	------	------	10	----------	E.	2	------	
	2 p. m.	------	------	------	10	----------	E.	3	------	
	9 p. m.	------	------	------	10	----------	E.	2	------	
Sept. 23	7 a. m.	------	------	------	10	----------	E.	2	------	
	2 p. m.	------	------	------	5	----------	W.	2	------	
	9 p. m.	------	------	------	1	----------	W.	1	------	
Sept. 24	7 a. m.	------	------	------	10	----------	W.	1	------	
	2 p. m.	------	------	------	2	----------	W.	1	------	
	9 p. m.	------	------	------	5	----------	W.	0	------	
Sept. 25	7 a. m.	------	------	------	10	----------	W.	1	------	

LYONS, NEW YORK.

Month and day.	Hour.	Barom'r corrected to 32° F.	Thermometer.	Force of vapor.	Cloudiness.		Motion of clouds.		Winds.		Relative humidity.	REMARKS.
Sept. 14	9 p. m.	29.62	38	------	Cir. cu.	5	E.	1	W.	5	------	13th Slight showers all day.
Sept. 15	7 a. m.	29.74	36	------	Cir.	3	E.	2	W.	1	------	14th. Shower at 3 a. m.
	2 p. m.	29.75	53	------	Cu. st.	6	E.	1	W.	1	------	17th. Rain from 1½ a. m. till 10
	9 p. m.	29.75	39	------	Cu. st.	9	NE.	1	W.	2	------	p. m.
Sept. 16	7 a. m.	29.62	42	------	Cu. st.	8	NE.	1	E.	2	------	Storm commenced at 10 p. m. the
	2 p. m.	29.54	62	------	Cu. st.	9	N.	3	SE.	2	------	19th and ended at 12 p. m. on
	9 p. m.	29.51	51	------	St.	10		0	S.	3	------	the 21st.
Sept. 17	7 a. m.	29.39	52	------	Nim.	10		0	S.	1	------	25th. Rain from 2 to 2¾ p. m.
	2 p. m.	29.32	66	------	St.	10		0	E.	1	------	
	9 p. m.	29.38	56	------	Nim.	10		0	E	1	------	
Sept. 18	7 a. m.	29.45	53	------	Cu.	5	S.	2	N.	3	------	
	2 p. m.	29.42	65	------	Cu.	2	S.	1	N.	1	------	
	9 p. m.	29.39	50	------		0		0	N.	1	------	
Sept. 19	7 a. m.	29.46	62	------	Cir.	3		0	SE.	2	------	
	2 p. m.	29.16	77	------	Cir.	2		0	SE.	2	------	
	9 p. m.	29.20	66	------	St.	3		0	SE.	1	------	
Sept. 20	7 a. m.	29.27	60	------	St.	10		0	E.	3	------	
	2 p. m.	29.34	54	------	St.	10		0	N.	3	------	
	9 p. m.	29.39	52	------	St.	10		0	N.	1	------	
Sept. 21	7 a. m.	29.41	54	------	Nim.	10		0	N.	2	------	
	2 p. m.	29.34	62	------	St.	10		0	E.	2	------	
	9 p. m.	29.44	58	------	St.	10		?	E.	1	------	
Sept. 22	7 a. m.	29.35	62	------	Cu. st.	8	W.	2	E.	1	------	
	2 p. m.	29.34	76	------	Cu. st.	2	W.	1	E.	2	------	
	9 p. m.	29.38	64	------	Cu. st.	8	E.	2	E.	1	------	

STORMS Nos. 2 AND 3, SEPTEMBER, 1859.

LYONS, NEW YORK—Continued.

Month and day.	Hour.	Barom'r corrected to 32° F.	Thermometer.	Force of vapor.	Cloudiness.	Motion of clouds.	Winds.	Relative humidity.	REMARKS.
Sept. 23	7 a. m.	29.46	61	------	Cu. st. 2	E. 2	W. 1	------	
	2 p. m.	29.48	70	------	Cu. st. 3	E. 2	E. 1	------	
	9 p. m.	29.47	56	------	Cu. st. 8	E. 3	E. 1	------	
Sept. 24	7 a. m.	29.46	58	------	Cu. 6	SE. 3	S. 1	------	
	2 p. m.	29.37	64	------	Cu. 3	S. 2	W. 1	------	
	9 p. m.	29.40	54	------	St. 10	0	S. 1	------	
Sept. 25	7 a. m.	29.43	54	------	Cu. st. 8	SE. 2	SW. 1	------	

MADRID, NEW YORK.

Month and day.	Hour.	Barom'r corrected to 32° F.	Thermometer.	Force of vapor.	Cloudiness.	Motion of clouds.	Winds.	Relative humidity.	REMARKS.
Sept. 14	9 p. m.	------	------	------	------------	----------	W. 1	------	14th. Rain; amount, 0.18 inch.
Sept. 15	7 a. m.	30.06	------	------	0	----------	W. 3	------	17th Misty.
	2 p. m.	30.03	------	------	10	----------	W. 3	------	18th. Fog in the morning.
	9 p. m.	30.06	------	------	------------	----------	W. 1	------	21st Began to rain at 9 a. m. and continued all day.
Sept. 16	7 a. m.	30.03	------	------	Cir. 5	SW. 3	NE. 1	------	
	2 p. m.	29.90	------	------	Cir. 3	SW. 3	NE. 2	------	22d. Rain all day.
	9 p. m.	29.81	------	------	St. 10	SW. 2	W. 1	------	23d. Misty.
Sept. 17	7 a. m.	29.73	------	------	Nim. 10	NE. 2	NE. 2	------	24th. Foggy all day; amount rain, 1.64 inch.
	2 p. m.	29.65	------	------	Nim. 10	NE. 2	NE. 2	------	
	9 p. m.	29.64	------	------	10	NE. 3	NE. 3	------	25th. Rain in the a. m.; amount, 0.14 inch.
Sept. 18	7 a. m.	29.73	------	------	10	----------	0	------	
	2 p. m.	------	------	------	0	----------	NE. 1	------	
	9 p. m.	29.63	------	------	0	----------	0	------	
Sept. 19	7 a. m.	29.56	------	------	------------	----------	------------	------	
	2 p. m.	29.41	------	------	Cir. 6	SW. 4	SW. 4	------	
	9 p. m.	29.39	------	------	Cu. 10	SW. 2	0	------	
Sept. 20	7 a. m.	29.73	------	------	10	----------	NE. 2	------	
	2 p. m.	------	------	------	10	----------	NE. 3	------	
	9 p. m.	29.81	------	------	10	----------	NE. 3	------	
Sept. 21	7 a. m.	29.83	------	------	Nim. 10	NE. 4	NE. 4	------	
	2 p. m.	29.72	------	------	Nim. 10	NE. 5	NE. 5	------	
	9 p. m.	29.77	------	------	10	----------	NE. 5	------	
Sept. 22	7 a. m.	29.72	------	------	10	----------	NE. 1	------	
	2 p. m.	29.72	------	------	10	----------	NE. 2	------	
	9 p. m.	29.70	------	------	Nim. 10	NE. 3	NE. 2	------	
Sept. 23	7 a. m.	29.71	------	------	10	----------	NE. 1	------	
	2 p. m.	29.73	------	------	10	----------	NE. 1	------	
	9 p. m.	29.73	------	------	10	----------	0	------	
Sept. 24	7 a. m.	------	------	------	Fog 10	----------	0	------	
	2 p. m.	------	------	------	St. 10	NE. 2	NE. 1	------	
	9 p. m.	29.67	------	------	St. 10	----------	0	------	
Sept. 25	7 a. m.	29.67	------	------	St. 10	----------	NE. 1	------	

MORRISANIA, NEW YORK.

Month and day.	Hour.	Barom'r corrected to 32° F.	Thermometer.	Force of vapor.	Cloudiness.	Motion of clouds.	Winds.	Relative humidity.	REMARKS.
Sept. 14	9 p. m.	------	52	------	Cu. 5	0	W. 3	------	16th. Rain at intervals during the whole day.
Sept. 15	7 a. m.	------	46	------	0	0	SW. 2	------	
	2 p. m.	------	63	------	0	0	W. 2	------	17th. Rain at intervals during the day.
	9 p. m.	------	60	------	0	0	W. 1	------	
Sept. 16	7 a. m.	------	49	------	Nim. 10	NE. 4	N. 1	------	Storm commenced at 7 p. m. the 20th, and ended at 5 a. m. on the 23d.
	2 p. m.	------	57	------	Nim. 10	NE. 4	NE. 2	------	
	9 p. m.	------	54	------	Nim. 10	NE. 4	NE. 3	------	
Sept. 17	7 a. m.	------	58	------	Nim. 10	NE. 4	NE. 4	------	
	2 p. m.	------	56	------	Nim. 10	NE. 4	NE. 8	------	
	9 p. m.	------	54	------	Nim. 10	NE. 4	NE. 8	------	
Sept. 18	7 a. m.	------	58	------	0	0	NW. 4	------	
	2 p. m.	------	73	------	0	0	W. 2	------	
	9 p. m.	------	64	------	0	0	NW. 1	------	

STORMS Nos. 2 AND 3, SEPTEMBER, 1859.

MORRISANIA, NEW YORK—Continued.

Month and day.	Hour.	Barom'r corrected to 32° F.	Thermometer.	Force of vapor.	Cloudiness.		Motion of clouds.		Winds.		Relative humidity.	REMARKS.
Sept. 19	7 a. m.	------	53	------		0		0	NW.	0	------	
	2 p. m.	------	80	------		0		0	SE.	2	------	
	9 p. m.	------	68	------	Cir.	4	W.	2	SE.	1	------	
Sept. 20	7 a. m.	------	66	------	Nim.	5	E.	1	S.	0	------	
	2 p. m.	------	82	------	Nim.	10	E.	1	SE.	1	------	
	9 p. m.	------	66	------	Nim.	10	E.	1	E.	1	------	
Sept. 21	7 a. m.	------	66	------	Nim.	10	E.	1	NE.	3	------	
	2 p. m.	------	56	------	Nim.	10	E.	1	NE.	4	------	
	9 p. m.	------	54	------	Nim.	10	E.	1	NE.	4	------	
Sept. 22	7 a. m.	------	55	------	Nim.	10	E.	1	NE.	3	------	
	2 p. m.	------	58	------	Nim.	10	E.	1	NE.	4	------	
	9 p. m.	------	58	------	Nim.	10	E.	1	NE.	5	------	
Sept. 23	7 a. m.	------	54	------		10	E.	0	NE.	1	------	
	2 p. m.	------	78	------	Nim.	10	E.	1	NE.	2	------	
	9 p. m.	------	64	------	Nim.	10	E.	1	NE.	2	------	
Sept. 24	7 a. m.	------	62	------		0		0	NE.	0	------	
	2 p. m.	------	77	------		0		0	S.	1	------	
	9 p. m.	------	62	------		0		0	S.	0	------	
Sept. 25	7 a. m.	------	60	------	Cu.	10		0	SW.	1	------	

NEW YORK CITY, NEW YORK.

Month and day.	Hour.	Barom'r corrected to 32° F.	Thermometer.	Force of vapor.	Cloudiness.		Motion of clouds.		Winds.		Relative humidity.	REMARKS.
Sept. 14	9 p. m.	30. 093	53	. 136	Cir.	4	W.	1	NW.	2	35	14th. Parhelion at sunset, about
Sept. 15	7 a. m.	. 317	48. 2	. 179	Cir. st.	5	W.	1	NW.	1	52	45° N. of the sun; cirrus clouds
	2 p. m.	. 356	63	. 256		0	----------		W.	2	44	just above the horizon; lunar
	9 p. m.	. 316	56. 2	. 205		0	----------		W.	1	45½	halo from 8. 20 to 11 p. m., and
Sept. 16	7 a. m.	. 331	51. 8	. 152	Cir. & nim.	10	SW.	1	NE.	1	40	very large; a thin haze, just suf-
	2 p. m.	. 324	58	. 282	Nim.	10	W.	1	NE.	2	58	ficient to dim or almost obscure
	9 p. m.	. 284	56	. 443	Nim.	10	W.	1	NE.	2	100	the stars, covering the sky; light
Sept. 17	7 a. m.	. 198	58. 4	. 474	Nim.	10	W.	1	NE.	4	97	frost a. m.
	2 p. m.	29. 687	55. 8	. 408	Nim.	10	W.	1	NE.	8	91	Violent storm; commenced raining
	9 p. m.	. 612	53	. 406	Nim.	10	W.	1	NE.	6	100	very moderately at 11 a. m. the
Sept. 18	7 a. m.	. 832	59. 2	. 398		0	----------		W.	3	79	16th, but on the morning of the
	2 p. m.	. 845	70. 2	. 451		0	----------		W.	2	61	17th the wind and rain increased
	9 p. m.	. 894	61. 7	. 470		0	----------		W.	1	85½	NE., and about 4 p. m. blew in
Sept. 19	7 a. m.	. 889	56. 2	. 378	Cir. st.	3	W.	1	NW.	1	84	terrific gusts, doing much damage
	2 p. m.	. 884	71. 5	. 479	Cir.	1	W.	1	SE.	2	62	to shipping, buildings, &c.; it
	9 p. m.	. 906	65	. 566	Cir.	2	W.	1	SE.	1	92	ceased about 10 p. m., when the
Sept. 20	7 a. m.	. 859	65. 3	. 569	Fog	10	W.	1	NE.	1	92	wind changed to NW., and blew
	2 p. m.	. 893	74	. 622	Cir. & nim.	9	SW.	1	NE.	1	74	strong in the night; amount rain,
	9 p. m.	. 968	67. 1	. 618	Nim.	10	W.	1	NE.	1	94½	3. 36 inches.
Sept. 21	7 a. m.	. 941	67	. 633	Nim.	10	W.	1	NE.	2	97	Storm commenced at 3. 40 p. m. the
	2 p. m.	. 996	58	. 433	Nim.	10	W.	1	NE.	4	91	20th, and ended at 10 a. m. on
	9 p. m.	. 996	55. 3	. 415	Nim.	10	W.	1	NE.	3	95	the 23d; amount, 2. 76 inches.
Sept. 22	7 a. m.	30. 024	56. 4	. 427	Nim.	10		1	NE.	3	93½	24th. Slight showers; lightning in
	2 p. m.	. 071	58	. 482	Nim.	10	W.	1	NE.	2	100	the W from 10. 45 to 11 p. m.
	9 p. m.	29. 991	59. 5	. 477	Nim.	10	W.	1	NE.	2	94	25th. Slight shower.
Sept. 23	7 a. m.	. 866	57. 2	. 436	Nim.	10		1	NE.	1	94	
	2 p. m.	. 986	68	. 577	Cir. cu.	3	W.	1	NW.	1	84	
	9 p. m.	30. 009	64	. 549	Cir. st.	1	W.	1	W.	1	92	
Sept. 24	7 a. m.	29. 961	62	. 488	Fog	10	W.	1	W.	1	88	
	2 p. m.	. 941	70. 2	. 559	Cir. cu.	5	W.	1	SE.	1	76	
	9 p. m.	. 946	64. 4	. 504		0	----------		SE.	1	83	
Sept. 25	7 a. m.	. 909	60. 2	. 496	Fog	10	----------		N.	0	97	

STORMS Nos. 2 AND 3, SEPTEMBER, 1859.

NICHOLS, NEW YORK.

Month and day.	Hour.	Barom'r corrected to 32° F.	Thermometer.	Force of vapor.	Cloudiness.	Motion of clouds.	Winds.	Relative humidity.
Sept. 14	9 p. m.	------	37	------	Cir. 6	S. 0	S. 1	------
Sept. 15	7 a. m.	------	37	------	Cir. & cu. 4	N. 1	E. 3	------
	2 p. m.	------	54	------	Cir. cu. 3	NW. 3	NW. 2	------
	9 p. m.	------	39	------	Cir. cu. 4	S. 1	S. 2	------
Sept. 16	7 a. m.	------	44	------	Nim. 10	0	NW. 2	------
	2 p. m.	------	50	------	Nim. 10	SE. 6	SE. 3	------
	9 p. m.	------	51	------	Nim. 10	SE. 0	SE. 3	------
Sept. 17	7 a. m.	------	55	------	Nim. 10	SE. 5	SE. 2	------
	2 p. m.	------	58	------	Nim. 10	NE. 5	N. 2	------
	9 p. m.	------	55	------	Nim. 10	0	NE. 4	------
Sept. 18	7 a. m.	------	54	------	Cu. st. 10	NW. 5	NW. 4	------
	2 p. m.	------	69	------	Cir. 1	S. 1	NW. 3	------
	9 p. m.	------	50	------	Cir. 2	NE. 0	SE. 3	------
Sept. 19	7 a. m.	------	46	------	Cir. 1	NW. 1	SE. 3	------
	2 p. m.	------	78	------	Cir. 3 Cu. 1	N. 1 S. 5	SE. 4	------
	9 p. m.	------	66	------	Nim. 10	NW. 0	SE. 3	------
Sept. 20	7 a. m.	------	67	------	Cu. st. 10	SE. 5	SE. 2	------
	2 p. m.	------	74	------	Cu. st. 10	S. 5	S. 2	------
	9 p. m.	------	62	------	Cu. st. 10	NW. 4	NW. 2	------
Sept. 21	7 a. m.	------	66	------	Nim. 10	S. 6	S. 1	------
	2 p. m.	------	66	------	Cu. st. 10	SE. 6	SE. 4	------
	9 p. m.	------	58	------	Nim. 10	SE. 5	SE. 3	------
Sept. 22	7 a. m.	------	60	------	Nim. 10	SE. 5	SE. 2	------
	2 p. m.	------	66	------	Nim. 10	SE. 6	SE. 3	------
	9 p. m.	------	62	------	Nim. 10	SE. 6	SE. 3	------
Sept. 23	7 a. m.	------	60	------	Cu. 8	N. 3	N. 3	------
	2 p. m.	------	70	------	Cu. 7	N. 3	N. 2	------
	9 p. m.	------	59	------	Cu. 5	N. 2	N. 2	------
Sept. 24	7 a. m.	------	60	------	Cu. st. 10	N. 4	N. 2	------
	2 p. m.	------	74	------	Cu. st. 8	N. 2	N. 3	------
	9 p. m.	------	59	------	Cu. 9	S. 1	N. 3	------
Sept. 25	7 a. m.	------	59	------	Fog 0	0	N. 1	------

REMARKS.

14th. Cu. and cir. cu at sunrise; light rain at 6 a. m.; thick cir. cu. for a short time; afterwards scattering cu S. and SW.; cu. in all directions at 6 p. m.; cold day; evening partly clear.

15th. Heavy frost; cir cu. in various directions, some of a purple shade, in the morning; before noon the sky was entirely covered with cir. st.; scattering cir. and cir. cu p. m.; a few cir. cu. in the evening.

16th. Clouds half way between cir. cu and nim. 9 to 10 a. m.; they soon, however, assumed more the appearance of nim., and began to move rapidly from SE.; mist from 11 a m. to 5 p. m.; heavy rain all night.

17th. Rain from SE.; clouds moved rapidly from 9 to 10 a. m.; nim. from NE.; wind NW.; clouds more the form of cu.; rain ceased at 2 p. m.; evening misty.

18th. Thick nim. and fine mist till 9 or 10 a. m.; then began to clear from N.; from 1 to 3 p. m. clear, with the exception of a small bank of cir. in the S; cir. clouds in the NW. late p. m; small cir. in N. and S in the evening.

19th. Fog till near 7 a. m.; small cir. shower in SW.; middle of a. m. cir. NW.; p. m. cir. from NW., and very small cu. from S., the cir. moving rapidly and the cu. very slow; nim. cloud in N. near night; evening quite thick.

20th. Thick nim. and cu. st. all a. m, moving rapidly from the SE.; a few drops of rain at break of day; near noon dark nim. in N.; began to rain at 12 o'clock and continued 60 or 70 minutes; broken cu. p. m. at times very fast from S. and SE.; evening cloudy.

21st. Began to rain heavily from SE. at 2 or 3 a. m.; nim. clouds very swift; rain ceased at 9 a. m.; light shower at noon; p. m. clouds more broken; heavy rain in the evening; clouds swift from S.

22d. Thick nim. at daybreak; began to rain about 2 a. m.; clouds swift from SE; rain heavy from 8 to 9 a. m.; rain at short intervals during the p. m. and evening.

23d. Rain at intervals during the past night; wind and clouds changed to N. in the night; at 8 a. m. clouds more in W. and NW., and moving rapidly, while those in the E. scarcely move at all; kind of clouds nim. and cu., but afterwards dark cu.

24th. Thick fog till 9 a. m., then a few drops of rain; a. m. dark cu., with but little motion N.; p. m. clouds more broken; two or three currents of wind from N. and from S.; cu. clouds from the S in the evening.

25th. Thick fog on high places till 9 or 10 a. m.; dark cu. from NW.; light shower of rain between 3 and 4 p. m. from NW.; light shower from SE. just before night.

OGDENSBURG, NEW YORK.

Month and day.	Hour.	Barom'r corrected to 32° F.	Thermometer.	Force of vapor.	Cloudiness.	Motion of clouds.	Winds.	Relative humidity.	Remarks.
Sept. 14	9 p. m.	------	------	------	------------	----------	W. 3	------	14th. Cloudy.
Sept. 15	7 a. m.	------	------	------	0	W ----------	N. 3	------	15th. Clear and cold.
	2 p. m.	------	------	------	------------	----------	N. 3	------	16th. Cloudy; clear at 10 a. m.
	9 p. m.	------	------	------	------------	----------	N. 3	------	17th. Light, misty rain; clouds moving W.
Sept. 16	7 a. m.	------	------	------	5	----------	NE. 2	------	
	2 p. m.	------	------	------	4	NE ------	NE. 2	------	18th. Clear.
	9 p. m.	------	------	------	10	----------	NE. 2	------	

STORMS Nos. 2 AND 3, SEPTEMBER, 1859.

OGDENSBURG, NEW YORK—Continued.

Month and day.	H. m.	Barom'r corrected to 32° F.	Thermometer.	Force of vapor.	Cloudiness.	Motion of clouds.	Winds.	Relative humidity.	REMARKS.
Sept. 17	7 a. m.				10		NE. 2		19th. Morning mild and clear; a little before noon a few cirrus clouds made their appearance; 1 p. m., a few radiated clouds in the NW; an hour or two after this the cirrus clouds in the NW. formed into strata and became dense; at 4 p. m., the southern portion of the hemisphere was covered with small fleecy clouds, cirro-cumulus; sometime before midnight it began to rain and continued at intervals till 11 a. m. on the 20th. 21st. Cloudy; drizzling rain at 9 a. m.; rained most of the night. 23d. Cloudy. 24th. Cloudy; more mild; amount rain, 1. 795 inch.
	2 p. m.				10		NE. 2		
	9 p. m.								
Sept. 18	7 a. m.				Cir. 2		N. 2		
	2 p. m.				Cir. 3		N. 2		
	9 p. m.								
Sept. 19	7 a. m.				Cir. 2		E 2		
	2 p. m.				Cir. 3		W. 3		
	9 p. m.								
Sept. 20	7 a. m.				Nim. 10		NE. 3		
	2 p. m.				10		NE. 3		
	9 p. m.						NE. 2		
Sept. 21	7 a. m.				Overcast 10		NE. 3		
	2 p. m.				10		NE. 3		
	9 p. m.						NE. 3		
Sept. 22	7 a. m.				10		NE. 3		
	2 p. m.				Overcast 10		NE. 2		
	9 p. m.						NE. 3		
Sept. 23	7 a. m.				10		NE. 1		
	2 p. m.						NE. 2		
	9 p. m.								
Sept. 24	7 a. m.				10		NE. 2		
	2 p. m.				10		NE. 2		
	9 p. m.								
Sept. 25	7 a. m.				10		N. 2		

OSWEGO, NEW YORK.

Month and day.	H. m.	Barom'r corrected to 32° F.	Thermometer.	Force of vapor.	Cloudiness.	Motion of clouds.	Winds.	Relative humidity.	REMARKS.
Sept. 14	9 p. m.	29. 354	46		5		W. 6		16th. Rain in the night. 17th. Showery; amount, 0.24 inch. Showers on the 19th, 20th, and 21st; amount, 0. 89 inch.
Sept. 15	7 a. m.	. 597	41		0		NE. 4		
	2 p. m.	. 668	48		5		NE. 2		
	9 p. m.	. 624	42		10		E. 1		
Sept. 16	7 a. m.	. 463	53		10		E. 5		
	2 p. m.	. 442	57		10		SE 5		
	9 p. m.	. 401	50		10		SE. 5		
Sept. 17	7 a. m.	. 271	50		10		E. 1		
	2 p. m.	. 184	61		10		E. 2		
	9 p. m.	. 202	56		10		NE. 5		
Sept. 18	7 a. m.	. 264	55		10		NE. 2		
	2 p. m.	. 284	60		5		NW. 2		
	9 p. m.	. 221	51		0		SE. 1		
Sept. 19	7 a. m.	. 120	58		0		SE. 4		
	2 p. m.	28. 980	74		8		SSE. 4		
	9 p. m.	. 995	69		10		W. 2		
Sept. 20	7 a. m.	29. 066	57		10		NE. 5		
	2 p. m.	. 109	52		10		NE. 5		
	9 p. m.	. 275	54		10		NE. 4		
Sept. 21	7 a. m.	. 226	57		10		NE. 3		
	2 p. m.	. 193	62		10		E. 5		
	9 p. m.	. 206	57		10		SE. 4		
Sept. 22	7 a. m.	. 174	54		10		S. 2		
	2 p. m.	. 106	75		8		SE 4		
	9 p. m.	. 198	60		6		S. 3		
Sept. 23	7 a. m.	. 245	60		10		SW. 1		
	2 p. m.	. 255	64		8		NW. 2		
	9 p. m.	. 250	55		8		SW. 1		
Sept. 24	7 a. m.	. 245	57		10		SW. 1		
	2 p. m.	. 301	65		8		N. 2		
	9 p. m.	. 214	60		10		NE. 2		
Sept. 25	7 a. m.	. 214	61		10		SW. 1		

STORMS Nos. 2 AND 3, SEPTEMBER, 1859.

PENN YAN, NEW YORK.

Month and day.	Hour.	Barom'r corrected to 32° F.	Thermometer.	Force of vapor.	Cloudiness.	Motion of clouds.	Winds.	Relative humidity.	REMARKS.
Sept. 14	Sunset ..	29. 55	44	------	9	----------	NW --------	------	17th. Amount rain, 1. 14 inch.
Sept. 15	Sunrise ..	. 80	34	------	8	----------	NE --------	------	20th. Amount rain, 0. 95 inch.
	2 p. m.	. 84	56	------	10	----------	NE --------	------	21st. Amount rain, 0. 21 inch.
	Sunset ..	. 79	42	------	0	----------	NE --------	------	23d and 24th. Amount rain, 0. 04 inch.
Sept. 16	Sunrise ..	. 70	41	------	0	----------	SW --------	------	
	2 p. m.	. 65	52	------	0	----------	SW --------	------	
	Sunset ..	. 67	49	------	0	----------	SW --------	------	
Sept. 17	Sunrise ..	. 46	52	------	0	----------	NE --------	------	
	2 p. m.	. 40	54	------	0	----------	NE --------	------	
	Sunset ..	. 40	54	------	0	----------	NE --------	------	
Sept. 18	Sunrise ..	. 52	51	------	9	----------	SW --------	------	
	2 p. m.	. 50	64	------	10	----------	SW --------	------	
	Sunset ..	. 48	60	------	6	----------	SW --------	------	
Sept. 19	Sunrise ..	. 40	50	------	9	----------	S --------	------	
	2 p. m.	. 29	79	------	10	----------	S --------	------	
	Sunset ..	. 30	71	------	0	----------	S --------	------	
Sept. 20	Sunrise ..	. 35	61	------	0	----------	NE --------	------	
	2 p. m.	. 45	53	------	0	----------	NE --------	------	
	Sunset ..	. 45	51	------	0	----------	NE --------	------	
Sept. 21	Sunrise ..	. 45	55	------	0	----------	NE --------	------	
	2 p. m.	. 40	64	------	0	----------	N --------	------	
	Sunset ..	. 42	61	------	0	----------	S --------	------	
Sept. 22	Sunrise ..	. 42	55	------	1	----------	SW --------	------	
	2 p. m.	. 45	69	------	1	----------	SW --------	------	
	Sunset ..	. 45	64	------	4	----------	SW --------	------	
Sept. 23	Sunrise ..	. 55	57	------	0	----------	SW --------	------	
	2 p. m.	. 53	67	------	1	----------	SW --------	------	
	Sunset ..	. 53	59	------	1	----------	SW --------	------	
Sept. 24	Sunrise ..	. 52	55	------	0	----------	SW --------	------	
	2 p. m.	. 48	64	------	1	----------	SW --------	------	
	Sunset ..	. 47	61	------	0	----------	SW --------	------	
Sept. 25	Sunrise ..	. 49	54	------	0	----------	SW --------	------	

ROCHESTER, NEW YORK.*

Sept. 14	9 p. m.	29. 38	------	45	Cir.	4	N.	1	N.	2	------	14th. High wind; NW. gale till 9 a. m.
Sept. 15	7 a. m.	29. 61	------	43	Cir.	6	NE.	1	NE.	2	------	
	2 p. m.	29. 59	------	53	Cir.	7	E.	0	E.	2	------	15th. Hard frost; began to rain at 8 p. m.; continued till 9 a. m. on the 16th; amount, 0.31 inch.
	9 p. m.	29. 56	------	45	Cir. st.	9	E.	1	E.	1	------	
Sept. 16	7 a. m.	29. 47	------	45	Cir.	9	SE.	0	SE.	1	------	
	2 p. m.	29. 36	------	65	Cir. st.	9	SE.	1	SE.	1	------	17th. Rain from before day till 9 a. m.; misty day.
	9 p. m.	29. 32	------	55	St.	10		0	SE.	1	------	
Sept. 17	7 a. m.	29. 23	------	54	St.	10		0	SE.	1	------	18th. Dense fog.
	2 p. m.	29. 16	------	58	St.	10	NE.	2	NE.	1	------	19th. Heavy dew; rain at 7 p. m.; thunder from 8 to 9 p. m.
	9 p. m.	29. 22	------	56	t.	10		0	NE.	1	------	
Sept. 18	7 a. m.	29. 33	------	53	St.	10		0	NW.	1	------	20th. Heavy thunder shower at 2⅔ a. m. from W.; at sunrise, NE. wind and rain during the day, and all night from NE.; amount 0. 43 inch.
	2 p. m.	29. 25	------	66	Cir.	1		0	NW.	1	------	
	9 p. m.	29. 18	------	57		0		0	W.	1	------	
Sept. 19	7 a. m.	29. 12	------	52	Cir.	1	S.	1	S.	1	------	
	2 p. m.	28. 98	------	79	Cir.	1		0	S.	1	------	
	9 p. m.	28. 99	------	66	St.	10	SW.	1	SW.	1	------	22d. Rain at 7 a. m; distant showers in the p. m.; amount 0. 54 inch.
Sept. 20	7 a. m.	29. 13	------	58	St.	10		0	NE.	1	------	
	2 p. m.	29. 22	------	54	St.	10		0	NE.	1	------	
	9 p. m.	29. 24	------	55	St.	10		0	NE.	1	------	23d. Appearance of rain; distant showers in p. m.
Sept. 21	7 a. m.	29. 23	------	55	St.	10	NE.	0	NE.	1	------	
	2 p. m.	29. 16	------	61	St.	10	NE.	2	NE	1	------	24th. Rain from 11½ a. m. till 12½ noon; amount, 0. 74 inch.
	9 p. m.	29. 14	------	60	St.	10		0	NE	1	------	
Sept. 22	7 a. m.	29. 17	------	58	Cir.	3	SW.	3	E.	1	------	
	2 p. m.	29. 14	------	77	Cu.	2	S.	0	SE.	1	------	
	9 p. m.	29. 23	------	65	Cir.	6		0	SE.	1	------	

* Dewey, observer.

STORMS Nos. 2 AND 3, SEPTEMBER, 1859.

ROCHESTER, NEW YORK—Continued.

Month and day.	Hour.	Barom'r corrected to 32° F.	Thermometer.	Force of vapor.	Cloudiness.	Motion of clouds.	Winds.	Relative humidity.	REMARKS.
Sept. 23	7 a. m.	29.30	......	59	Cir. 1	0	W. 1	......	
	2 p. m.	29.28	......	65	Cir. st. 8	NW. 1	NW. 1	......	
	9 p. m.	29.29	......	61	St. 9	0	NW. 1	......	
Sept. 24	7 a. m.	29.26	......	58	St. 9	NW. 2	NW. 1	......	
	2 p. m.	29.22	......	65	Cir. cu. 8	0	NE. 1	......	
	9 p. m.	29.24	......	59	St. 10	0	0	......	
Sept. 25	7 a. m.	29.26	......	59	St. 10	W. 1	NW. 1	......	

ROCHESTER, NEW YORK.*

Month and day.	Hour.	Barom'r corrected to 32° F.	Thermometer.	Force of vapor.	Cloudiness.	Motion of clouds.	Winds.	Relative humidity.	REMARKS.
Sept. 14	9 p. m.	29.61	42	.134	Cir. cu. 5	NW. 3	NW. 3	50	15th. Frost
Sept. 15	7 a. m.	29.80	43	.121	6	----------	NE. 3	43	Rain from 7.45 p. m. the 16th to 9 a. m. on the 17th ; amount, 0.27 inch.
	2 p. m.	29.78	49	.107	Cir. st. 6	W. 2	NE. 3	31	
	9 p. m.	29.74	44	.130	Cu. st. 9	W. 3	E. 3	45	
Sept. 16	7 a. m.	29.64	46	.192	Cir. 7	W. 2	SE. 4	62	Moderate rain from 8.15 p. m. the 19th till the night of the 21st; amount, 0.88 inch.
	2 p. m.	29.54	66	.316	Cu. 10	W. 3	SE. 4	49	
	9 p. m.	29.50	52	.361	Nim. 10	----------	SE. 3	93	
Sept. 17	7 a. m.	29.40	54	.418	Nim. 10	----------	SE. 3	100	24th. Heavy showers; amount, 0.27 inch.
	2 p. m.	29.33	58	.394	Nim. 10	----------	NE. 4	82	
	9 p. m.	29.39	56	.420	Nim. 10	----------	NE. 3	94	
Sept. 18	7 a. m.	29.48	52	.388	----------	----------	----------	100	
	2 p. m.	29.43	65	.359	Cu. 1	----------	NE. 1	58	
	9 p. m.	29.36	55	.376	Cu. 1	----------	0	87	
Sept. 19	7 a. m.	29.24	53	.375	Cir. st. 1	----------	S. 3	93	
	2 p. m.	29.13	81	.438	Cir. cu. 4	S. 2	SW. 4	41	
	9 p. m.	29.19	65	.549	Nim. 10	----------	SW. 2	89	
Sept. 20	7 a. m.	29.30	57	.466	Nim. 10	----------	NE. 5	100	
	2 p. m.	29.38	53	.375	Nim. 10	NE. 7	NE. 5	93	
	9 p. m.	29.41	55	.349	Nim. 10	----------	NE. 4	81	
Sept. 21	7 a. m.	29.38	56	.449	Nim. 10	----------	NE. 4	100	
	2 p. m.	29.33	61	.473	Nim. 10	NE. 7	NE. 3	88	
	9 p. m.	29.32	60	.487	Nim. 10	----------	NE. 3	94	
Sept. 22	7 a. m.	29.32	58	.483	Cir. st. 1	----------	SE. 5	100	
	2 p. m.	29.32	76	.505	Cir. cu. 2	SW. 5	S. 4	56	
	9 p. m.	29.42	64	.464	Nim. 10	----------	NW. 3	77	
Sept. 23	7 a. m.	29.47	59	.500	Cir. st. 1	----------	SW. 1	100	
	2 p. m.	29.46	65	.420	Nim. 9	W. 5	NE. 2	68	
	9 p. m.	29.48	59	.469	Cir. st. 8	----------	0	94	
Sept. 24	7 a. m.	29.45	58	.483	Cu. st. 9	NW. 4	SW. 2	100	
	2 p. m.	29.40	66	.438	Cu. st. 6	W. 1	NE. 2	68	
	9 p. m.	29.42	58	.452	Cu. 3	----------	0	94	
Sept. 25	7 a. m.	29.43	58	.423	Cu. st. 10	N. 1	NW. 2	88	

SACKETT'S HARBOR, NEW YORK.

Month and day.	Hour.	Barom'r corrected to 32° F.	Thermometer.	Force of vapor.	Cloudiness.	Motion of clouds.	Winds.	Relative humidity.	REMARKS.
Sept. 14	6 p. m.	29.77	49	.175	5	6	NW. 6	50	14th. High wind; amount rain, 0 16 inch.
Sept. 15	6 a. m.	30.10	38.5	.169	2	3	N. 3	72	
	9 a. m.	30.05	41	.147	4	3	NNE. 3	57	17th. Rain; amount, 0.06 inch.
	3 p. m.	29.99	50	.258	5	1	SW. 1	71	Rain on the 20th, 21st, and 22d; amount, 1.46 inch.
	6 p. m.	30.06	49.5	.192	4	1	SW. 1	54	
Sept. 16	6 a. m.	30.03	43	.186	1	2	E. by N. 2	67	
	9 a. m.	30.01	51.5	.239	3	1	ENE. 1	63	
	3 p. m.	29.93	56	.282	10	2	S. by E. 2	63	
	6 p. m.	29.88	53	.244	10	2	S. by E. 2	60	
Sept. 17	6 a. m.	29.74	53	.348	10	1	E. by S. 1	86	
	9 a. m.	29.71	56.5	.357	9	1	ENE. 1	78	
	3 p. m.	29.64	60	.396	8	3	NE. 3	76	
	6 p. m.	29.64	58	.394	10	4	NE. 4	82	
Sept. 18	6 a. m.	29.75	53	.348	10	3	NNE. 3	86	
	9 a. m.	29.78	54	.335	8	2	NE. 2	80	

* Mathews, observer.

STORMS Nos. 2 AND 3, SEPTEMBER, 1859.

SACKETT'S HARBOR, NEW YORK—Continued.

Month and day.	Hour.	Barom'r corrected to 32° F.	Thermometer.	Force of vapor.	Cloudiness.	Motion of clouds.	Winds.	Relative humidity.	REMARKS.
Sept. 18	3 p. m.	29. 69	64	. 403	1	2	W. by S. 2	67	
	6 p. m.	29. 68	64	. 418	1	1	W. by S. 1	70½	
Sept. 19	6 a. m.	29. 60	50	. 309	2	1	SSE. 1	85	
	9 a. m.	29. 53	64	. 403	1	2	S. by W. 2	67	
	3 p. m.	29. 43	75	. 519	3	2	S. by W. 2	60	
	6 p. m.	29. 44	73. 5	. 504	8	W. 1	S. by E. 1	61	
Sept. 20	6 a. m.	29. 60	55	. 376	10	4	NE. 4	87	
	9 a. m.	29. 59	52	. 308	9	5	NE. 5	79	
	3 p. m.	29. 61	53. 5	. 288	9	6	NE. 6	70	
	6 p. m.	29. 62	52	. 282	10	6	NE. 6	73	
Sept. 21	6 a. m.	29. 77	50	. 283	10	6	NE. 6	78	
	9 a. m.	29. 78	50	. 309	10	6	NE. 6	85	
	3 p. m.	29. 73	52	. 334	10	6	NE. 6	86	
	6 p. m.	29. 72	52	. 308	10	6	NE. 6	79	
Sept. 22	6 a. m.	29. 69	56	. 363	10	4	NE. 4	81	
	9 a. m.	29. 68	59	. 410	5	4	NE. 4	82	
	3 p. m.	29. 67	69. 5	. 557	8	2	SE. 2	77	
	6 p. m.	29. 68	68	. 543	3	0	0	79	
Sept. 23	6 a. m.	29. 75	61	. 442	8	2	SW. 2	83	
	9 a. m.	29. 76	64	. 433	3	1	SW. 1	73	
	3 p. m.	29. 75	66. 5	. 463	4	3	SW. 3	71	
	6 p. m.	29. 76	65	. 420	2	1	SW. 1	68	
Sept. 24	6 a. m.	29. 76	59	. 439	10	1	S. 1	88	
	9 a. m.	29. 75	62	. 491	8	1	SW. 1	88	
	3 p. m.	29. 72	63	. 478	4	1	W. 1	83	
	6 p. m.	29. 62	63. 5	. 455	5	1	NW. 1	77	
Sept. 25	6 a. m.	29. 70	59. 5	. 403	7	1	NW. 1	79	

SARATOGA, NEW YORK.

Month and day.	Hour.	Barom'r corrected to 32° F.	Thermometer.	Force of vapor.	Cloudiness.	Motion of clouds.	Winds.	Relative humidity.	REMARKS.
Sept. 14	9 p. m.	29. 54	52	------	St. 0	W. 0	W. 2	------	Rain from 5 a. m. the 17th to 9 p. m. on the 18th; amount, 0.30 inch.
Sept. 15	7 a. m.	29. 82	36	------	St. 0	W. 0	W. 1	------	
	2 p. m.	29. 81	43	------	Cir. 5	SW. 0	SW. 1	------	
	9 p. m.	29. 84	46	------	St. 0	SW. 0	SW. 1	------	Rain on the 20th and 23d.
Sept. 16	7 a. m.	29. 86	38	------	Cir. 0	N. 0	N. 1	------	
	2 p. m.	29. 82	54	------	Cu. 5	SW. 0	SW. 1	------	
	9 p. m.	------	------	------	------	------	------	------	
Sept. 17	7 a. m.	29. 67	52	------	Cir. 10	SW. 0	SW. 1	------	
	2 p. m.	29. 40	54	------	Cu. 10	N. 0	N. 2	------	
	9 p. m.	29. 42	60	------	St. 0	SW. 0	------	------	
Sept. 18	7 a. m.	29. 48	55	------	0	SW. 1	NE. 1	------	
	2 p. m.	------	60	------	------	------	------	------	
	9 p. m.	------	------	------	------	NE. 1	------	------	
Sept. 19	7 a. m.	29. 43	54	------	St. 0	NE. 0	N. 1	------	
	2 p. m.	29. 35	67	------	St. 0	NE. 0	NE. 1	------	
	9 p. m.	------	------	------	------	------	NE. 1	------	
Sept. 20	7 a. m.	29. 40	62	------	St. 10	SE. 5	SE. 1	------	
	2 p. m.	29. 45	65	------	Cu. 0	NE. 0	NE. 2	------	
	9 p. m.	------	------	------	Cu. 10	NE. 0	NE. 1	------	
Sept. 21	7 a. m.	29. 61	54	------	St. 10	NE. 0	NE. 1	------	
	2 p. m.	29. 62	60	------	Cu. 10	NE. 0	NE. 1	------	
	9 p. m.	------	60	------	St. 10	NE. 0	NE. 1	------	
Sept. 22	7 a. m.	29. 62	56	------	St. 10	NE. 0	NE. 1	------	
	2 p. m.	29. 57	60	------	Cu. 10	NE. 0	NE. 1	------	
	9 p. m.	------	61	------	St. 10	NE. 0	NE. 1	------	
Sept. 23	7 a. m.	29. 52	58	------	St. 10	NE. 0	NE. 1	------	
	2 p. m.	29. 46	62	------	Cu. 10	NE. 0	NE. 1	------	
	9 p. m.	------	60	------	St. 10	NE. 0	NE. 1	------	
Sept. 24	7 a. m.	29. 52	59	------	St. 5	NE. 0	NE. 1	------	
	2 p. m.	29. 46	64	------	Cu. 0	NE. 0	SE. 1	------	
	9 p. m.	------	------	------	------	------	------	------	
25	7 a. m.	------	------	------	------	------	------	------	

STORMS Nos. 2 AND 3, SEPTEMBER, 1859.

SCHENECTADY, NEW YORK.

Month and day.	Hour.	Barom'r corrected to 32° F.	Thermometer.	Force of vapor.	Cloudiness.	Motion of clouds.	Winds.	Relative humidity.	REMARKS.
Sept. 14	9 p. m.				Cu. st. 10	W. 1	W. 1		14th. Shower from 6 to 6½ a. m. Rain from 5.50 p. m. the 16th to 6.10 p. m. on the 17th. 19th. Rain from 1.40 p. m. to 6.10 p. m. 20th. Misty all day. Began to rain at 7 a. m. the 21st; continued very heavy during the night and at short intervals on the 22d. 24th. Northern lights visible at 8.20 p. m., shooting up from behind a black cloud; disappeared about 9.05 p. m.
Sept. 15	7 a. m.				Cir. 3	W. 1	NW. 1		
	2 p. m.				Cu. st. 10	W. 1	W. 1		
	9 p. m.				Cir. 2	W. 2	W. 1		
Sept. 16	7 a. m.				Cir. st. 8	W. 1	W. 1		
	2 p. m.				Cu. st. 10	W. 1	S. 1		
	9 p. m.				Cu. st. 10	W. 1	SE. 1		
Sept. 17	7 a. m.				Nim., cu. st. 10	SE. 2	E. 1		
	2 p. m.				Cu. st. 10	E. 2	NE. 1		
	9 p. m.				Cu. st. 9	E. 1	NE. 2		
Sept. 18	7 a. m.				Cu. st. 9½	NE. 1	N. 1		
	2 p. m.				0	0	NE. 1		
	9 p. m.				Cu. st. 1	W. 1			
Sept. 19	7 a. m.				0	0			
	2 p. m.				0	0	S. 2		
	9 p. m.		65		Cir. st. 2	W. 1	S. 1		
Sept. 20	7 a. m.		61			Fog	S. 1		
	2 p. m.		72		Nim. 4	SW. 1	SE. 1		
	9 p. m.		54						
Sept. 21	7 a. m.		52		Cu. st. 10	N. 3	NE. 2		
	2 p. m.		56		Cu. st., nim. 10	NE. 1	E. 1		
	9 p. m.		52		10		E. 1		
Sept. 22	7 a. m.		52		Cu. st. 10	NE. 1	SE. 1		
	2 p. m.		62		Cu. st., nim. 10	E. 1	E. 1		
	9 p. m.		58		Thick fog				
Sept. 23	7 a. m.				Thick fog				
	2 p. m.		69		Cu. st. 10	W. 1			
	9 p. m.		62		Cu. st. 1	W. 1	NW. 1		
Sept. 24	7 a. m.		59			W. 1	NW. 1		
	2 p. m.		72		Cu. 9	W. 1	W. 1		
	9 p. m.		64		Cu. st. 4	W. 1			
Sept. 25	7 a. m.		60		Cu. st. 10	E. 1			

SPENCERTOWN, NEW YORK.

Month and day.	Hour.	Barom'r corrected to 32° F.	Thermometer.	Force of vapor.	Cloudiness.	Motion of clouds.	Winds.	Relative humidity.	REMARKS.
Sept. 14	9 p. m.	29.421	43.2	.158	Nim 10	N. 2	N. 2	52	16th. Rain from 6 a. m. to 9 p. m. 17th. Rain from 3 a. m. to 10 p. m.; amount, 0.887 inch. Rain from 5 p. m. the 20th to 4 a. m. on the 23d; amount, 1.398 inch.
Sept. 15	7 a. m.	29.620	34	.140	Cir. st. 2	0	N. 2	67	
	2 p. m.	29.655	45.5	.109	Nim. 8	N. 2	N. 2	33	
	9 p. m.	29.659	34.8	.170	0		N. 1	80	
Sept. 16	7 a. m.	29.658	44	.176	Nim. 10	0	SW. 1	57	
	2 p. m.	29.625	53.2	.220	Nim. 10	0	S. 1	51	
	9 p. m.	29.532	46.5	.297	Nim. 10	0	S. 1	88	
Sept. 17	7 a. m.	29.369	47.5	.297	Nim. 10	0	SE. 2	85	
	2 p. m.	29.180	49	.315	Nim. 10	0	E. 1	85	
	9 p. m.	29.095	49	.328	Nim. 10	0	E. 1	80	
Sept. 18	7 a. m.	29.228	52.2	.341	Nim. 10	0	N. 2	83	
	2 p. m.	29.226	62.8	.328	0		N. 2	55	
	9 p. m.	29.258	48.6	.288	0		N. 1	80	
Sept. 19	7 a. m.	29.269	54.6	.349	0		N. 1	80	
	2 p. m.	29.207	67.6	.398	0		S. 2	56	
	9 p. m.	29.185	63.2	.497	0		S. 2	83	
Sept. 20	7 a. m.	29.189	63.8	.549	Nim. 8	S. 3	S. 1	89	
	2 p. m.	29.225	70.5	.612	Nim. 10	0	S. 1	78	
	9 p. m.	29.340	55.2	.398	Nim. 10	0	S. 1	90	
Sept. 21	7 a. m.	29.483	55	.394	Nim. 10	SE. 3	SE. 3	87	
	2 p. m.	29.419	54.2	.324	Nim. 10	SE. 3	SE. 2	76	
	9 p. m.	29.416	49	.304	Nim. 10	0	SE. 2	84	
Sept. 22	7 a. m.	29.383	52	.344	Nim. 10	0	SE. 1	88	
	2 p. m.	29.482	57.2	.363	Nim. 10	0	SE. 1	81	
	9 p. m.	29.412	56.5	.385	Nim. 10	0	SE. 1	84	

STORMS Nos. 2 AND 3, SEPTEMBER, 1859.

SPENCERTOWN, NEW YORK—Continued.

Month and day.	Hour.	Barom'r corrected to 32° F.	Thermometer.	Force of vapor.	Cloudiness.	Motion of clouds.	Winds.	Relative humidity.	REMARKS.
Sept. 23	7 a. m.	29.345	55	.394	Nim. 10	0	SE. 1	89	
	2 p. m.	29.329	61.5	.457	Nim. 10	0	SE. 1	82	
	9 p. m.	29.323	61.5	.491	Nim. 10	0	SE. 1	88	
Sept. 24	7 a. m.	29.323	56	.413	Nim. 8	0	SE. 1	90	
	2 p. m.	29.264	67.2	.443	Cu. 8	N. 3	N. 1	65	
	9 p. m.	29.258	56.2	.392	Nim. 3	0	N. 1	84	
Sept. 25	7 a. m.	29.304	56.2	.421	Dense fog ---	----------	N. 1	90	

WAMPSVILLE, NEW YORK.

Month and day.	Hour.	Barom'r corrected to 32° F.	Thermometer.	Force of vapor.	Cloudiness.	Motion of clouds.	Winds.	Relative humidity.	REMARKS.
Sept. 14	9 p. m.	------	39	------	St. 3	W. 1	W. 1	------	16th. Rain from noon till 9 p. m.; amount, 0.08 inch.
Sept. 15	7 a. m.	------	34	------	St. 4	NW. 1	NW. 1	------	17th. Rain from 9 p. m. till midnight; amount, 1.88 inch.
	2 p. m.	------	50	------	8	NE. 1	NW. 1	------	20th. Rain from 2 to 5 p. m.; am't, 0.10 inch. Began to rain again in the night and ended at noon on the 21st; amount, 1.80 inch. Commenced again in the night of the 21st and ended at 9 p. m. on the 22d; amount, 0.80 inch.
	9 p. m.	------	38	------	6	W. 1	W. 1	------	23d. Rain till 8 a. m.; amount, 0.30 inch.
Sept. 16	7 a. m.	------	42	------	3	E. 1	W. 1	------	25th. Frost.
	2 p. m.	------	49	------	10	E. 1	E. 1	------	
	9 p. m.	------	45	------	10	E. 1	E. 1	------	
Sept. 17	7 a. m.	------	48	------	10	E. 1	E. 1	------	
	2 p. m.	------	52	------	10	E. 1	E. 1	------	
	9 p. m.	------	55	------	10	E. 1	E. 1	------	
Sept. 18	7 a. m.	------	54	------	9	W. 1	W. 1	------	
	2 p. m.	------	64	------	1	W. 1	W. 1	------	
	9 p. m.	------	51	------	0	0	W. 1	------	
Sept. 19	7 a. m.	-----	48	------	0	0	S. 1	------	
	2 p. m.	------	74	------	Cir. cu. 4	S. 1	S. 2	------	
	9 p. m.	------	68	------	Cu. st. 8	S. 2	S. 1	------	
Sept. 20	7 a. m.	------	64	------	Cir. 10	NW. 1	NW. 1	------	
	2 p. m.	------	68	------	Cu. 6	NW. 1	SW. 1	------	
	9 p. m.	------	57	------	Cu. 10	SW. 1	SW. 1	------	
Sept. 21	7 a. m.	------	55	------	Cir. 10	E. 1	E. 1	------	
	2 p. m.	------	60	------	Cir. 10	E. 1	E. 2	------	
	9 p. m.	------	52	------	Cu. 10	E. 1	E. 1	------	
Sept. 22	7 a. m.	------	53	------	Cir. 10	E. 1	E. 1	------	
	2 p. m.	------	60	------	Cu. 10	E. 1	E. 2	------	
	9 p. m.	------	57	------	Cu. 10	E. 1	E. 1	------	
Sept. 23	7 a. m.	------	60	------	Cir. 10	E. 1	E. 1	------	
	2 p. m.	------	68	------	Cir. cu. 9	W. 1	W. 2	------	
	9 p. m.	------	52	------	0	0	W. 1	------	
Sept. 24	7 a. m.	------	56	------	Cir. cu. 8	W. 1	W. 1	------	
	2 p. m.	------	66	------	Cu. st. 6	W. 1	W. 1	------	
	9 p. m.	------	56	------	Cu. 5	W. 1	W. 1	------	
Sept. 25	7 a. m.	------	58	------	Cir. cu. 10	W. 1	W. 1	------	

WATERFORD, NEW YORK.

Month and day.	Hour.	Barom'r corrected to 32° F.	Thermometer.	Force of vapor.	Cloudiness.	Motion of clouds.	Winds.	Relative humidity.	REMARKS.
Sept. 14	9 p. m.	30.004	48	.260	Cir. cu. 3	----------	W----------	78	Rain from 6 p. m. the 16th to 7 p. m. on the 17th; amount, 0.84 inch.
Sept. 15	7 a. m.	.261	43	.199	0	----------	NW---- ----	74	Rain from 1¾ p. m. the 20th to 7 a. m. on the 22d; amount, 1.47 inch; began to rain again at 1 p. m. the 22d, and ended at 7 a. m. on the 23d; amount, 1.49 inch.
	2 p. m.	.261	54	.237	Cir. st. 7	----------	NW. 2	58	23d. Rain till 7 a. m.; amount, 0.02 inch.
	9 p. m.	.249	47	.249	St. 1	----------	N. 1	77	
Sept. 16	7 a. m.	.270	40	.225	9	----------	N---- ------	91	
	2 p. m.	.210	55	.218	Cir. st. 10	----------	S. 3	50	
	9 p. m.	.181	49	.322	Nim. 10	----------	S. 1	92	
Sept. 17	7 a. m.	.032	50	.361	Nim. 10	----------	NW---- ----	100	
	2 p. m.	29.857	52	.361	Nim. 10	----------	NE. 3	93	
	9 p. m.	.790	53	.348	Nim. 10	----------	NE---- ----	86	
Sept. 18	7 a. m.	.836	55	.349	Cir. st. 10	----------	NE. 3	81	
	2 p. m.	.838	64	.433	0	----------	NE. 2	73	
	9 p. m.	.861	57	.378	0	----------	N---- ------	81	

STORMS Nos. 2 AND 3, SEPTEMBER, 1859.

WATERFORD, NEW YORK—Continued.

Month and day.	Hour.	Barom'r corrected to 32° F.	Thermometer.	Force of vapor.	Cloudiness.	Motion of clouds.	Winds.	Relative humidity.	REMARKS.
Sept. 19	7 a. m.	29.885	46	.286	0	----------	N.	92	
	2 p. m.	.757	74	.429	Cir. st. 0	----------	SE. 4	51	
	9 p. m.	.754	66	.522	5	----------	S.	79	
Sept. 20	7 a. m.	.780	65	.549	Cir. st. 10	----------	S. 2	89	
	2 p. m.	.787	72	.662	10	----------	SW. 6	83	
	9 p. m.	.944	53	.348	Nim. 10	----------	N. 4	86	
Sept. 21	7 a. m.	30.255	50	.354	Nim. 10	----------	NE. 3	96	
	2 p. m.	.003	56	.420	Nim. 10	----------	N. 2	94	
	9 p. m.	.021	53	.403	Nim. 10	----------	0	100	
Sept. 22	7 a. m.	.029	52	.388	Nim. 10	----------	N.	100	
	2 p. m.	.001	59	.500	Nim. 10	----------	NW.	100	
	9 p. m.	29.988	58	.452	Nim. 10	----------	S.	94	
Sept. 23	7 a. m.	.964	58	.452	Nim. 10	----------	W.	94	
	2 p. m.	.913	66	.509	Cir. st. 9	----------	SW. 2	81	
	9 p. m.	.923	62	.549	Cir. st. 10	----------	S.	97	
Sept. 24	7 a. m.	.934	58	.452	Cu. st. 7	----------	SW.	94	
	2 p. m.	.871	70	.551	Cu. st. 2	----------	NE. 1	75	
	9 p. m.	.871	62	.523	Cir. st. 9	----------	NW.	94	
Sept. 25	7 a. m.	.907	59	.469	Cu. st. 8	----------	N.	94	

WILSON, NEW YORK.

Month and day.	Hour.	Barom'r corrected to 32° F.	Thermometer.	Force of vapor.	Cloudiness.	Motion of clouds.	Winds.	Relative humidity.	REMARKS.
Sept. 14	9 p. m.	------	45	------	St. 3	----------	NNW. 3	------	19th. Thunder shower at 7.30 p. m.; lightning near and vivid; showery since 2 p. m.; at 11 a. m. mercury rose suddenly to 79°; at 1 p. m. it stood at 69°; 9 p. m. both diffused and chain lightning in the NW., N., and NE. 20th. Rain from 7.35 to 9 a. m.; commenced again in the night, and ended at 3 p. m. on the 21st. 24th. Aurora at 7.20 p. m., from NW. to NE., appeared like a st. cloud streaked with vermillion; some fog was observed at the same time.
Sept. 15	7 a. m.	------	43	------	Cir. st. 4	----------	ENE. 2	------	
	2 p. m.	------	50.5	------	St. 8	----------	ENE. 2	------	
	9 p. m.	------	45	------	St. 9	----------	E. 1	------	
Sept. 16	7 a. m.	------	44.5	------	Cu. st. 9	----------	SE. 1	------	
	2 p. m.	------	60	------	Cu. st. 9	SW. 2	NE. 3	------	
	9 p. m.	------	56	------	St. 10	----------	SW. 1	------	
Sept. 17	7 a. m.	------	56	------	St. 10	----------	E.	------	
	2 p. m.	------	56	------	Fog 10	----------	NE. 2	------	
	9 p. m.	------	50	------	Fog 3	----------	SW.	------	
Sept. 18	7 a. m.	------	52.5	------	Fog 10	----------	SW. 1	------	
	2 p. m.	------	59	------	Fog 5	----------	NE. 2	------	
	9 p. m.	------	54.5	------	St. 1	----------	S. 1	------	
Sept. 19	7 a. m.	------	55	------	Cir. st. 2	----------	S. 2	------	
	2 p. m.	------	74	------	Nim. 8	----------	SW. 3	------	
	9 p. m.	------	64	------	Cu. 10	----------	SW. 1	------	
Sept. 20	7 a. m.	------	52	------	Nim. 10	----------	NE. 3	------	
	2 p. m.	------	52	------	Nim. 10	----------	NE. 2	------	
	9 p. m.	------	53	------	St. 9	----------	NE. 3	------	
Sept. 21	7 a. m.	------	49	------	Nim. 10	----------	NE. 3	------	
	2 p. m.	------	53	------	Nim. 10	----------	NE. 3	------	
	9 p. m.	------	56	------	Nim. 10	----------	E. 2	------	
Sept. 22	7 a. m.	------	58	------	Cu. st. 8	SW. 2	E. 1	------	
	2 p. m.	------	72	------	Cu. 5	SW. 2	SW. 2	------	
	9 p. m.	------	60.5	------	Cu. 1	----------	SW. 2	------	
Sept. 23	7 a. m.	------	60	------	St. 3	----------	SW. 1	------	
	2 p. m.	------	68	------	Cu. 8	----------	SW. 1	------	
	9 p. m.	------	61	------	Nim. 10	----------	SW.	------	
Sept. 24	7 a. m.	------	60	------	Nim. 5	NE. 1	SSE. 1	------	
	2 p. m.	------	66	------	Cu. st. 6	----------	SW. 1	------	
	9 p. m.	------	56	------	St. 3	----------	S. 1	------	
Sept. 25	7 a. m.	------	59	------	Cu. st. 8	----------	S. 1	------	

CINNAMINSON, NEW JERSEY.

Month and day.	Hour.	Barom'r corrected to 32° F.	Thermometer.	Force of vapor.	Cloudiness.	Motion of clouds.	Winds.	Relative humidity.	REMARKS.
Sept. 14	9 p. m.	------	------	------	3	----------	W. 2	------	16th. Moderate rain after 9 a. m.; heavy in the night. 17th. Heavy rain, with strong gale from E., till 9 p. m.
Sept. 15	7 a. m.	------	------	------	4	----------	NW. 2	------	
	2 p. m.	------	------	------	2	----------	NW. 2	------	
	9 p. m.	------	------	------	8	----------	SE. 2	------	

STORMS Nos. 2 AND 3, SEPTEMBER, 1859.

CINNAMINSON, NEW JERSEY—Continued.

Month and day.	Hour.	Barom'r corrected to 32° F.	Thermometer.	Force of vapor.	Cloudiness.	Motion of clouds.	Winds.	Relative humidity.	REMARKS.
Sept. 16	7 a. m.	......	......	......	10	....	NE. 2	......	20th. Rain from 1 to 2 p. m.
	2 p. m.	......	......	......	10	....	NE. 1	......	21st. Heavy rain; commenced at 9 a. m.; continued all day and night.
	9 p. m.	......	......	......	10	....	NE. 1	......	22d. Still raining; considerable thunder in SW.; at $1\frac{3}{4}$ p. m. wind shifted to a gale, SW.; lasted about five minutes, and returned to NE.; a heavy shower followed, and continued near 3 p. m; rain again from 8 to 9 p. m., and a heavy shower from 10 to 11 p. m.
Sept. 17	7 a. m.	......	......	......	10	....	E. 3	......	
	2 p. m.	......	......	......	10	....	NE. 7	......	
	9 p. m.	......	......	......	10	....	N. 7	......	
Sept. 18	7 a. m.	......	......	......	0	....	NW. 4	......	
	2 p. m.	......	......	......	5	....	NW. 3	......	
	9 p. m.	......	......	......	0	....	0	......	
Sept. 19	7 a. m.	......	......	......	3	....	NW. 1	......	
	2 p. m.	......	......	......	7	....	SW. 2	......	
	9 p. m.	......	......	......	2	....	S. 3	......	
Sept. 20	7 a. m.	......	......	......	10	....	S. 2	......	
	2 p. m.	......	......	......	10	....	SE. 2	......	
	9 p. m.	......	......	......	10	....	E. 1	......	
Sept. 21	7 a. m.	......	......	......	10	....	SE. 2	......	
	2 p. m.	......	......	......	10	....	E. 5	......	
	9 p. m.	......	......	......	10	....	NE. 5	......	
Sept. 22	7 a. m.	......	......	......	10	....	NE. 2	......	
	2 p. m.	......	......	......	10	....	NE. 3	......	
	9 p. m.	......	......	......	10	....	NE. 3	......	
Sept. 23	7 a. m.	......	......	......	10	....	NE. 1	......	
	2 p. m.	......	......	......	10	....	NE. 1	......	
	9 p. m.	......	......	......	5	....	NW. 1	......	
Sept. 24	7 a. m.	......	......	......	9	....	N. 1	......	
	2 p. m.	......	......	......	5	....	W. 1	......	
	9 p. m.	......	......	......	8	....	SW. 1	......	
Sept. 25	7 a. m.	......	......	......	8	....	N. 2	......	

LAMBERTVILLE, NEW JERSEY.

Month and day.	Hour.	Barom'r corrected to 32° F.	Thermometer.	Force of vapor.	Cloudiness.	Motion of clouds.	Winds.	Relative humidity.	REMARKS.
Sept. 14	9 p. m.	30.07	49.5	......	10	....	NW. 1	......	Rain from 10 a m. the 16th, to 9 p. m. the 17th; amount in inches, 3.46.
Sept. 15	7 a. m.	30.24	44.7	......	10	....	NW. 1	......	Storm commenced at 10 a. m. the 20th, and ended on the morning of the 23d; amount, 3.97 inches.
	2 p. m.	30.29	59.4	......	7	....	NW. 1	......	Rain, accompanied by thunder at intervals, from $8\frac{3}{4}$ p. m. the 24th, to $6\frac{3}{4}$ p. m. on the 25th; amount, 0.35 inch.
	9 p. m.	30.28	50.8	......	....	....	NW. 1	......	
Sept. 16	7 a. m.	30.25	49	......	4	....	NNE. 1	......	
	2 p. m.	30.25	57.1	......	9	....	NE. 1	......	
	9 p. m.	30.15	54.2	......	....	....	NE. 1	......	
Sept. 17	7 a. m.	29.86	59.5	......	0	....	NE. 3	......	
	2 p. m.	29.54	55.8	......	0	....	NE. 3	......	
	9 p. m.	29.63	54.4	......	0	....	....	......	
Sept. 18	7 a. m.	29.86	57.5	......	0	....	NW. 1	......	
	2 p. m.	29.89	67.7	......	0	....	NW. 2	......	
	9 p. m.	29.92	54.2	......	0	....	NW. 1	......	
Sept. 19	7 a. m.	29.91	49.9	......	9	....	SW. 1	......	
	2 p. m.	29.90	77	......	10	....	S. 2	......	
	9 p. m.	29.91	65.2	......	8	....	S. 2	......	
Sept. 20	7 a. m.	29.89	64	......	Fog 10	....	SSW. 1	......	
	2 p. m.	29.89	73.3	......	3	....	E. 1	......	
	9 p. m.	29.91	67.3	......	....	....	....	......	
Sept. 21	7 a. m.	29.91	67.8	......	0	....	ESE. 3	......	
	2 p. m.	29.94	62.2	......	0	....	ESE. 2	......	
	9 p. m.	29.98	55.2	......	0	....	E. 2	......	
Sept. 22	7 a. m.	29.96	55.2	......	0	....	E. 1	......	
	2 p. m	29.97	61	......	0	....	NE. 2	......	
	9 p. m.	29.98	60.3	......	0	....	ENE. 1	......	
Sept. 23	7 a. m.	29.97	58.6	......	0	....	N. 1	......	
	2 p. m.	29.95	72.4	......	0	....	NNW. 1	......	
	9 p. m.	29.99	63.5	......	0	....	....	......	
Sept. 24	7 a. m.	29.98	62.2	......	0	....	N. 1	......	
	2 p. m.	29.95	74.4	......	0	....	N. 1	......	
	9 p. m.	29.95	62.8	......	....	....	N	......	
Sept. 25	7 a. m.	29.93	60.7	......	....	....	NNE. 1	......	

STORMS Nos. 2 AND 3, SEPTEMBER, 1859.

NEWARK, NEW JERSEY.

Month and day.	Hour.	Barom'r corrected to 32° F.	Thermometer.	Force of vapor.	Cloudiness.	Motion of clouds.	Winds.	Relative humidity.	REMARKS.
Sept. 14	6 p. m.	29. 88	------	------	Fair	----------	NW. 3	------	Rain from 0.30 p. m. on the 16th to 11.30 p. m. on the 17th; amount, 2. 985 inches.
Sept. 15	7 a. m.	30. 26	------	------	Fair	----------	N. 4	------	Rain from 3 p. m. the 20th to 9 a. m. on the 23d; amount, 3.405 inches.
	6 p. m.	30. 26	------	------	Fair	----------	N. 2	------	24th. Began to rain at 3 p. m., and ended in the night; amount, 0. 225 inch.
Sept. 16	7 a. m.	30. 26	------	------	Cloudy	----------	NE. 2	------	
	6 p. m.	------	------	------	Rain	----------	NE. 3	------	
Sept. 17	7 a. m.	29. 84	------	------	Cloudy	----------	NE. 3	------	
	6 p. m.	29. 46	------	------	Rain	----------	NE. 6	------	
Sept. 18	7 a. m.	29. 82	------	------	Fair	----------	NE. to NW. 3	------	
	6 p. m.	29. 84	------	------	Fair	----------	NW. 2	------	
Sept. 19	7 a. m.	29. 91	------	------	Fair	----------	NE. 2	------	
	6 p. m.	29. 82	------	------	Fair	----------	SE. 2	------	
Sept. 20	7 a. m.	29. 89	------	------	Overcast	----------	SW. 1	------	
	6 p. m.	29. 87	------	------	Cloudy, rain after 3 p. m.	----------	S. to NE. 1	------	
Sept. 21	7 a. m.	29. 92	------	------	Rain	----------	ENE. 3	------	
	6 p. m.	29. 94	------	------	Cloudy	----------	NE. 3	------	
Sept. 22	7 a. m.	29. 95	------	------	Cloudy, mist	----------	NE. 3	------	
	6 p. m.	29. 96	------	------	Cloudy	----------	NE. 3	------	
Sept. 23	7 a. m.	29. 93	------	------	Cloudy	----------	NE. 2	------	
	6 p. m.	29. 93	------	------	Cloudy	----------	NE. 1	------	
Sept. 24	7 a. m.	29. 93	------	------	Cloudy, foggy	----------	SE. 1	------	
	6 p. m.	29. 97	------	------	Cloudy	----------	SW. 2	------	
Sept. 25	7 a. m.	29. 91	------	------	Cloudy	----------	NE. 1	------	

NEW BRUNSWICK, NEW JERSEY.

Month and day.	Hour.	Barom'r corrected to 32° F.	Thermometer.	Force of vapor.	Cloudiness.	Motion of clouds.	Winds.	Relative humidity.	REMARKS.
Sept. 14	9 p. m.	------	------	------	4	----------	NW. 2	------	16th. Rain lightly at intervals from 8 a. m. to 4 p. m., then with increased violence till 10 p. m.
Sept. 15	7 a. m.	------	------	------	5	----------	NW. 2	------	Rain at intervals from 2 p. m. the 20th to 6 a. m. on the 23d.
	2 p. m.	------	------	------	4	----------	W. 2	------	23d. Shower at 5 p. m.
	9 p. m.	------	------	------	1	----------	S. 1	------	24th. Showery during the day; lightning SW. in the evening.
Sept. 16	7 a. m.	------	------	------	10	----------	NE. 3	------	25th. Thunder in N. at 3 p. m.
	2 p. m.	------	------	------	10	----------	NE. 1	------	
	9 p. m.	------	------	------	10	----------	NE. 2	------	
Sept. 17	7 a. m.	------	------	------	10	----------	NE. 5	------	
	2 p. m.	------	------	------	10	----------	NE. 8	------	
	9 p. m.	------	------	------	10	----------	N. 6	------	
Sept. 18	7 a. m.	------	------	------	1	----------	NW. 3	------	
	2 p. m.	------	------	------	2	----------	NW. 1	------	
	9 p. m.	------	------	------	1	----------	NW. 2	------	
Sept. 19	7 a. m.	------	------	------	1	----------	S. 1	------	
	2 p. m.	------	------	------	5	----------	SW. 2	------	
	9 p. m.	------	------	------	4	----------	S. 2	------	
Sept. 20	7 a. m.	------	------	------	9	----------	E. 1	------	
	2 p. m.	------	------	------	10	----------	S. 3	------	
	9 p. m.	------	------	------	10	----------	NE. 4	------	
Sept. 21	7 a. m.	------	------	------	10	----------	NE. 3	------	
	2 p. m.	------	------	------	10	----------	NE. 5	------	
	9 p. m.	------	------	------	10	----------	NE. 4	------	
Sept. 22	7 a. m.	------	------	------	10	----------	NE. 3	------	
	2 p. m.	------	------	------	10	----------	S. 3	------	
	9 p. m.	------	------	------	10	----------	NE. 6	------	
Sept. 23	7 a. m.	------	------	------	10	----------	NE. 3	------	
	2 p. m.	------	------	------	9	----------	N. 2	------	
	9 p. m.	------	------	------	9	----------	NE. 1	------	
Sept. 24	7 a. m.	------	------	------	10	----------	N. 1	------	
	2 p. m.	------	------	------	9	----------	N. 1	------	
	9 p. m.	------	------	------	3	----------	NE. 1	------	
Sept. 25	7 a. m.	------	------	------	10	----------	NE. 1	------	

STORMS Nos. 2 AND 3, SEPTEMBER, 1859.

BEDFORD, PENNSYLVANIA.

Month and day.	Hour.	Barom'r corrected to 32° F.	Thermometer.	Force of vapor.	Cloudiness.		Motion of clouds.		Winds.		Relative humidity.	REMARKS.
Sept. 14	9 p. m.	------	52	------	------------		----------			0	------	Rain from 1 a. m. the 15th to 2 p. m. on the 17th; amount, 4. 30 inches.
Sept. 15	7 a. m.	------	42	------		0		0		0	------	20th. Rain commencing at 10 p. m.; amount, 1. 95 inch.
	2 p. m.	------	70	------	Nim.	2	S.	1	SE.	2	------	24th. Began to rain at 8 p. m.; amount, 0. 10 inch.
	9 p. m.	------	57	------	Nim.	6	S.	1	SE.	2	------	
Sept. 16	7 a. m.	------	58	------	Nim.	10	S.	0	S.	1	------	
	2 p. m.	------	60	------	Nim.	10	S.	0	S.	1	------	
	9 p. m.	------	54	------	Nim.	10	S.	0	S.	1	------	
Sept. 17	7 a. m.	------	50	------	Nim.	10	N.	0	N.	1	------	
	2 p. m.	------	62	------	Nim.	10	N.	0	N.	1	------	
	9 p. m.	------	61	------	Nim.	10	N.	2	N.	2	------	
Sept. 18	7 a. m.	------	53	------	Cu.	2	W.	1		0	------	
	2 p. m.	------	65	------		0		0		0	------	
	9 p. m.	------	59	------	Nim.	8	W.	2		0	------	
Sept. 19	7 a. m.	------	56	------		0		0		0	------	
	2 p. m.	------	72	------	Nim.	5	W.	0		0	------	
	9 p. m.	------	67	------	Nim.	10	W.	1		0	------	
Sept. 20	7 a. m.	------	64	------	Nim.	10	S.	1		0	------	
	2 p. m.	------	71	------	Nim.	9	SE.	2	SE.	2	------	
	9 p. m.	------	66	------	Nim.	10	SE.	2	SE.	2	------	
Sept. 21	7 a. m.	------	66	------	Nim.	10	SE.	0		0	------	
	2 p. m.	------	77	------	Nim.	10	SE.	3	SE.	1	------	
	9 p. m.	------	64	------	Nim.	10	SE.	0		0	------	
Sept. 22	7 a. m.	------	62	------	Nim.	10	E.	0		0	------	
	2 p. m.	------	78	------	Nim.	8	E.	0		0	------	
	9 p. m.	------	64	------	Nim.	10	E.	0		0	------	
Sept. 23	7 a. m.	------	62	------	Cu.	5	NW.	0		0	------	
	2 p. m.	------	67	------	Cu.	2	N.	0		0	------	
	9 p. m.	------	62	------	Nim.	10	N.	0		0	------	
Sept. 24	7 a. m.	------	59	------	Nim.	10	N.	0		0	------	
	2 p. m.	------	66	------	Nim.	9	SE.	2		0	------	
	9 p. m.	------	60	------	Nim.	10	SE.	0		0	------	
Sept. 25	7 a. m.	------	59	------	Nim.	10		0		0	------	

BERWICK, PENNSYLVANIA.

Month and day.	Hour.	Barom'r corrected to 32° F.	Thermometer.	Force of vapor.	Cloudiness.		Motion of clouds.		Winds.		Relative humidity.	REMARKS.
Sept. 14	9 p. m.	29. 42	51	. 234	Cir. st.	1	----------		W.	1	65	Rain from 6 a. m. the 16th to 7 p. m. on the 17th; amount, 2. 30 inches.
Sept. 15	7 a. m.	29. 77	44	. 231	Cu. st.	4	----------		E.	0	83	Rain from 8 a. m. the 20th to 3 p. m. on the 25th; amount, 3. 62 inches.
	2 p. m.	29. 77	60	. 242	Cir. cu.	1	----------		N.	1	48	
	9 p. m.	29. 58	49	. 236		0	----------		E.	1	70	
Sept. 16	7 a. m.	29. 58	52	. 270	Nim.	9	----------		E.	2	72	
	2 p. m.	29. 58	51	. 321	Nim.	10	----------		E.	2	86	
	9 p. m.	29. 42	54	. 375	Nim.	10	----------		E.	1	93	
Sept. 17	7 a. m.	29. 17	56	. 376	Nim.	10	----------		E.	2	87	
	2 p. m.	29. 00	66	. 382	Nim.	10	N.	6	N.	2	63	
	9 p. m.	29. 17	59	. 410	Cu. st.	7	----------		NW.	1	82	
Sept. 18	7 a. m.	29. 25	59	. 423	Cu. st.	8	----------		NW.	2	88	
	2 p. m.	29. 33	66	. 451	Cu. st.	2	----------		W.	0	73	
	9 p. m.	29. 33	57	. 407	St.	1	----------			0	87	
Sept. 19	7 a. m.	29. 25	50	. 335	Fog --------		----------		E.	0	93	
	2 p. m.	29. 17	76	. 641	Cu. st.	3	----------		S.	3	77	
	9 p. m.	29. 17	69	. 599	------------		----------		E.	0	85	
Sept. 20	7 a. m.	29. 17	70	. 635	Nim.	10	----------		E.	0	90	
	2 p. m.	29. 17	70	. 658	Nim.	10	E.	4	E.	2	90	
	9 p. m.	29. 25	67	. 591	Nim.	10	----------		E.	0	89	
Sept. 21	7 a. m.	29. 25	66	. 604	Nim.	10	E.	6	E.	1	94	
	2 p. m.	29. 25	65	. 529	Nim.	10	E.	5	E.	4	89	
	9 p. m.	29. 25	58	. 436	Nim.	10	----------		E.	5	94	
Sept. 22	7 a. m.	29. 25	62	. 473	Nim.	9	----------		E.	2	88	
	2 p. m.	29. 25	66	. 549	Nim.	10	----------		E.	1	89	
	9 p. m.	29. 33	63	. 543	Nim.	10	----------		E.	2	94	

STORMS Nos. 2 AND 3, SEPTEMBER, 1859.

BERWICK, PENNSYLVANIA—Continued.

Month and day.	Hour.	Barom'r corrected to 32° F.	Thermometer.	Force of vapor.	Cloudiness.	Motion of clouds.	Winds.	Relative humidity.	REMARKS.
Sept. 23	7 a. m.	29. 33	61	. 505	Nim. 10	----------	E. 1	94	
	2 p. m.	29. 33	71	. 608	Nim. 9	----------	E. 1	80	
	9 p. m.	29. 33	64	. 520	Nim. 0	----------	W. 1	89	
Sept. 24	7 a. m.	29. 33	60	. 487	Fog --------	----------	W. 0	94	
	2 p. m.	29. 25	74	. 581	Cu. st. 5	----------	W. 2	72	
	9 p. m.	29. 25	63	. 510	Cu. st. 5	----------	W. 0	88	
Sept. 25	7 a. m.	29. 33	64	. 529	Nim. 9	----------	W. 1	89	

CANNONSBURG, PENNSYLVANIA.

Month and day.	Hour.	Barom'r corrected to 32° F.	Thermometer.	Force of vapor.	Cloudiness.	Motion of clouds.	Winds.	Relative humidity.	REMARKS.
Sept. 14	9 p. m.	28. 96	56	------	Cir. cu. 9	----------	W. 1	------	Rain from 5 a. m. the 16th to 11 a. m. on the 17th ; 1. 070 inch.
Sept. 15	7 a. m.	28. 92	52	------	St., cir cu. 9	----------	E. 2	------	Rain from 5 p. m. the 19th till noon on the 20th ; amount, 0.840 inch.
	2 p. m.	28. 97	68	------	9	----------	E. 2	------	21st. Rain from 8½ to 11 a. m.; amount, 0. 260 inch.
	9 p. m.	28. 94	61	------	Overcast 10	----------	E. 1	------	
Sept. 16	7 a. m.	28. 89	59	------	Nim. 10	----------	E. 1	------	
	2 p. m.	28. 82	60	------	Nim. 10	----------	E. 1	------	
	9 p. m.	28. 76	61	------	Nim. 10	----------	E. 1	------	
Sept. 17	7 a. m.	28. 76	56	------	Nim. 10	----------	E. 1	------	
	2 p. m.	28. 67	61	------	Overcast 10	----------	E. 2	------	
	9 p. m.	28. 75	59	------	Overcast 10	----------	NE. 1	------	
Sept. 18	7 a. m.	28. 85	55	------	Foggy ------	----------	NE. 1	------	
	2 p. m.	28. 89	65	------	0	----------	NE. 1	------	
	9 p. m.	28. 74	62	------	St. 1	----------	NE. 1	------	
Sept. 19	7 a. m.	28. 63	54	------	Cir. 5	----------	W. 1	------	
	2 p. m.	28. 58	72	------	Overcast 10	----------	W. 1	------	
	9 p. m.	28. 57	65	------	Nim. 10	----------	W. 1	------	
Sept. 20	7 a. m.	28. 55	63	------	Nim. 10	----------	E. 1	------	
	2 p. m.	28. 54	68	------	Overcast 10	----------	E. 2	------	
	9 p. m.	28. 55	63	------	Overcast 10	----------	E. 1	------	
Sept. 21	7 a. m.	28. 56	64	------	Cu. st., cr. cu. 8	----------	E. 1	------	
	2 p. m.	28. 54	74	------	St., cu. st. 8	----------	E. 1	------	
	9 p. m.	28. 54	69	------	Overcast 9	----------	E. 1	------	
Sept. 22	7 a. m.	28. 63	63	------	Cir. cu. 9	----------	W. 2	------	
	2 p. m.	28. 72	67	------	Overcast 9	----------	W. 2	------	
	9 p. m.	28. 80	60	------	St., cir. cu. 9	----------	W. 1	------	
Sept. 23	7 a. m.	28. 87	56	------	Overcast 10	----------	W. 1	------	
	2 p. m.	28. 86	63	------	Overcast 10	----------	W. 2	------	
	9 p. m.	28. 87	58	------	St. 4	----------	W. 1	------	
Sept. 24	7 a. m.	28. 85	59	------	Nim. 10	----------	W. 1	------	
	2 p. m.	28. 87	60	------	Nim. 10	----------	W. 1	------	
	9 p. m.	28. 76	60	------	Overcast 10	----------	W. 1	------	
Sept. 25	7 a. m.	28. 78	58	------	Overcast 10	----------	E. 1	------	

CARLISLE, PENNSYLVANIA.

Month and day.	Hour.	Barom'r corrected to 32° F.	Thermometer.	Force of vapor.	Cloudiness.	Motion of clouds.	Winds.	Relative humidity.	REMARKS.
Sept. 14	9 p. m.	------	------	------	------------	----------	------------	------	16th. Began to rain in the night and ended at 6½ p. m. on the 17th; amount, 6.60 inches.
Sept. 15	7 a. m.	29. 447	49	. 175	Cir. st. 6	W. 1	NE. 1	50. 5	
	2 p. m.	29. 442	61	. 297	0	----------	SW. 1	55. 3	
	9 p. m.	29. 401	52	. 282	Hazy 9	----------	0	72. 7	20th. Began to rain at 8 a. m. and ended in the night; amount, 1.465 inch.
Sept. 16	7 a. m.	29. 406	52	. 361	Nim. 10	SE. 2	SE. 2	93	
	2 p. m.	29. 287	54	. 535	Rain 10	----------	NE. 2	80. 2	
	9 p. m.	29. 098	54	. 362	Raining -----	----------	NW. 1	86. 7	Storm commenced at 9 a. m. the 21st, continued during the 22d, and ended in the night. Several showers on the 23d; amount, 1.26 inch.
Sept. 17	7 a. m.	29. 911	58	. 422	Rain 10	----------	NE. 3	87. 6	
	2 p. m.	29. 705	56	. 367	Rain 10	----------	NW. 3	70. 8	
	9 p. m.	29. 953	60	. 456	Nim 10	NW. 3	NW. 3	88	
Sept. 18	7 a. m.	29. 098	60	. 456	Cir. st. 4	W. 2	W. 0	88	
	2 p. m.	29. 099	70	. 416	Cir. 3	W. 1	W. 1	57	
	9 p. m.	29. 075	60	. 456	Cir. 3	0	0	88	

STORMS Nos. 2 AND 3, SEPTEMBER, 1859.

CARLISLE, PENNSYLVANIA—Continued.

Month and day.	Hour.	Barom'r corrected to 32° F.	Thermometer.	Force of vapor.	Cloudiness.		Motion of clouds.		Winds.		Relative humidity.	REMARKS.
Sept. 19	7 a. m.	29.061	57½	.371	Fog	0	....		SE.	1	78.4	
	2 p. m.	28.960	76	.614	Cir. cu.	7	SW.	3	SE.	3	68.5	
	9 p. m.	28.977	70	.586	Nim.	9		0		0	79.9	
Sept. 20	7 a. m.	28.965	69	.599	Nim.	10	SE.	2	SE.	1	84.6	
	2 p. m.	28.927	70½	.544	Cir. st.	9	SE.	1	SE.	2	72.9	
	9 p. m.	28.985	69	.564	Rain	10	....		W.	1	79.6	
Sept. 21	7 a. m.	28.989	69	.635	Nim.	9	SE.	2	SE.	2	89.6	
	2 p. m.	28.992	74	.718	Nim.	10	SE.	3	SE.	2	85.6	
	9 p. m.	......	.....	......	....		....		....		......	
Sept. 22	7 a. m.	29.075	56	.449	Nim.	10	SE.	2	SE.	2	100	
	2 p. m.	29.101	61	.443	Nim.	10	SE.	1	SE.	1	82.5	
	9 p. m.	29.120	61	.473	Nim.	10		0		0	88.2	
Sept. 23	7 a. m.	29.151	63	.510	Nim.	10		0		0	88.6	
	2 p. m.	29.166	70	.449	Cu. st.	9	SW.	1	SW.	2	61.3	
	9 p. m.	29.153	65	.451	Nim.	10		0		0	73.1	
Sept. 24	7 a. m.	29.174	62	.429	Cir. st.	6	SW.	1	SW.	1	77.2	
	2 p. m.	29.110	66	.438	Cir. st.	7	W.	2	W.	2	68.5	
	9 p. m.	29.115	65	.456	Nim.	10		0		0	88	
Sept. 25	7 a. m.	29.105	60	.385	Cir. st.	8	W.	2	W.	1	52.5	

CHAMBERSBURG, PENNSYLVANIA.

Month and day.	Hour.	Barom'r corrected to 32° F.	Thermometer.	Force of vapor.	Cloudiness.		Motion of clouds.		Winds.		Relative humidity.	REMARKS.
Sept. 14	9 p. m.	29.46	60	.433	Hazy		....		W.	1	73	14th. Rain from 2.20 to 2.40 p. m.;
Sept. 15	7 a. m.	29.68	52	.269	Cir. cu.	6	W.	2	NW.	1	67	amount, 0.188 inch.
	2 p. m.	29.57	62	.242	Cir.	2	W.	1	SE.	1	45.2	Severe storm from 8 a. m. the 16th
	9 p. m.	29.58	62	.369	Cir.	2	W.	1	W.	2	66.5	till 8 p. m. on the 17th; amount,
Sept. 16	7 a. m.	29.54	53	.396	Nim.	10	NE.	4	E.	1	71.5	7.116 inches.
	2 p. m.	29.49	54	.497	Nim.	10	NE.	2	E.	2	83	Rain from 4.30 p. m. the 20th to
	9 p. m.	29.40	54	.509	Nim.	10	NE.	2	E.	1	74.3	2 p. m. the 21st; amount, 2.55
Sept. 17	7 a. m.	29.03	57	.536	Nim.	10	NE.	4	E.	3	83.8	inches.
	2 p. m.	29.58	58	.583	Nim.	10	N.	4	W.	1	94	22d. Rain from 9 a. m. till noon;
	9 p. m.	29.19	62	.595	Nim.	10	N.	3	W.	1	75.8	amount, 0.166 inch.
Sept. 18	7 a. m.	29.33	60	.522	Clear		....		W.	1	79	24th. Rain from 9.45 to 10.30
	2 p. m.	29.29	73	.476	Cir.	7	W.	1	W.	1	69	a. m.; amount, 0.050 inch.
	9 p. m.	29.29	60	.489	St.	1	W.	1	W.	1	74	
Sept. 19	7 a. m.	29.22	56	.422	Foggy		....		SW.	1	87.6	
	2 p. m.	29.25	76	.489	Cu.	10	S.	2	SW.	1	75	
	9 p. m.	29.17	72	.679	Nim.	10	S.	1	SW.	1	81	
Sept. 20	7 a. m.	29.15	67	.612	Nim.	10	S.	1	Calm		89.5	
	2 p. m.	29.14	70	.617	Nim.	10	SE.	1	SW.	1	77	
	9 p. m.	29.19	68	.668	Nim.	10	S.	2	SW.	1	85	
Sept. 21	7 a. m.	29.16	68	.635	Nim.	10	S.	1	W.	1	90	
	2 p. m.	29.15	73	.759	Nim.	10	S.	2	S.	1	100	
	9 p. m.	29.19	65	.599	Nim.	10		0	S.	1	84.6	
Sept. 22	7 a. m.	29.11	60	.491	Nim.	10	S.	2	SE.	1	89.9	
	2 p. m.	29.28	65	.463	Nim.	10	NE.	2	SE.	1	56	
	9 p. m.	29.33	62	.591	Nim.	10	W.	1	Calm		89.3	
Sept. 23	7 a. m.	29.35	64	.569	Nim.	10	W.	1	Calm		88.4	
	2 p. m.	29.34	72	.604	Cu. st.	10	W.	1	E.	1	94	
	9 p. m.	29.39	64	.599	Cu. st.	10	W.	1	Calm		85	
Sept. 24	7 a. m.	29.36	62	.516	Cu. st.	8	W.	1	E.	1	89.1	
	2 p. m.	29.30	69	.516	Cu.	6	W.	1	E.	1	70	
	9 p. m.	29.31	66	.591	Cir. st.	5	NW.	1	E.	1	89.3	
Sept. 25	7 a. m.	29.31	64	.569	Cir. cu.	8	NE.	1	Calm		83.6	

STORMS Nos. 2 AND 3, SEPTEMBER, 1859.

FLEMING, PENNSYLVANIA.

Month and day.	Hour.	Barom'r corrected to 32° F.	Thermometer.	Force of vapor.	Cloudiness.	Motion of clouds.	Winds.	Relative humidity.	REMARKS.
Sept. 14	9 p. m.	------	46	------	C. cu., cir. st. 4	W. 1	W. 2	------	Rain from 6½ a. m. the 17th to 3 p. m. on the 18th; amount, 3.18 inches.
Sept. 15	7 a. m.	------	42	------	Cir. cu. 1	W. 1	SW. 1	------	20th. Rain from 7 a. m. till 2 p. m.; amount, 0.10 inch. Began again at 9 p. m. and ended at 9 p. m. on the 21st; amount, 0.775 inch.
	2 p. m.	------	62	------	0	----------	SW. 3	------	22d. Rain at 7 a. m.; amount, 0.175 inch.
	9 p. m.	------	44	------	Cir. st. 5	W. 1	W. 1	------	23d. Sprinkle of rain in the morning.
Sept. 16	7 a. m.	------	50	------	Nim. 10	SW. 3	E. 1	------	24th. Sprinkle in the evening.
	2 p. m.	------	54	------	Nim. 10	SE. 2	E. 1	------	25th. Rain from 4 to 5 p. m.; am't, 0.113 inch.
	9 p. m.	------	52	------	Nim. 10	0	E. 1	------	
Sept. 17	7 a. m.	------	54	------	Nim. 10	E. 2	E. 1	------	
	2 p. m.	------	62	------	Nim. 10	E. 2	NW. 2	------	
	9 p. m.	------	61	------	Nim. 10	NE. 1	NW. 2	------	
Sept. 18	7 a. m.	------	56	------	0	----------	E. 2	------	
	2 p. m.	------	74	------	Cir., cir. st. 8	NW. 2	SE. 2	------	
	9 p. m.	------	54	------	St. 2	0	NW. 1	------	
Sept. 19	7 a. m.	------	51	------	Fog 10	0	E. 1	------	
	2 p. m.	------	80	------	Cir., cir. cu. 5	W. 2	SW. 2	------	
	9 p. m.	------	66	------	Nim. 10	SW. 2	W. 1	------	
Sept. 20	7 a. m.	------	67	------	Nim. 9	SW. 3	E. 2	------	
	2 p. m.	------	77	------	Nim. 10	SE. 2	SE. 2	------	
	9 p. m.	------	68	------	Nim. 10	W. 1	W. 1	------	
Sept. 21	7 a. m.	------	66	------	Nim. 10	W. 2	E. 2	------	
	2 p. m.	------	76	------	Nim. 10	SE. 3	SE. 2	------	
	9 p. m.	------	64	------	Nim. 10	SE. 2	SE. 2	------	
Sept. 22	7 a. m.	------	60	------	Nim. 10	SE. 1	E. 2	------	
	2 p. m.	------	74	------	Nim., cu. 10	SW. 2	E. 2	------	
	9 p. m.	------	65	------	Nim. 8	W. 1	W. 1	------	
Sept. 23	7 a. m.	------	63	------	Nim. 10	NE. 2	SW. 1	------	
	2 p. m.	------	71	------	Nim., cu. 10	SW. 1	E. 2	------	
	9 p. m.	------	62	------	Cu., nim. 10	W. 1	W. 2	------	
Sept. 24	7 a. m.	------	60	------	Cu. 7	W. 1	W. 1	------	
	2 p. m.	------	75	------	Cu. 6	W. 1	NW. 2	------	
	9 p. m.	------	59	------	St., cir. st. 5	0	SW. 1	------	
Sept. 25	7 a. m.	------	59	------	Nim. 10	E. 2	E. 2	------	

GERMANTOWN, PENNSYLVANIA.

Month and day.	Hour.	Barom'r corrected to 32° F.	Thermometer.	Force of vapor.	Cloudiness.	Motion of clouds.	Winds.	Relative humidity.	REMARKS.
Sept. 14	9 p. m.	------	------	------	------------	----------	----------	----	13th. Showery p. m.
Sept. 15	7 a. m.	------	------	------	8	----------	N. 1	------	16th. Light rain at 6½ p. m.; halos at 8½ p. m.
	2 p. m.	------	------	------	1	----------	W. 1	------	17th. Heavy rain.
	9 p. m.	------	------	------	8	----------	W. 1	------	20th. Light rain at noon.
Sept. 16	7 a. m.	------	------	------	10	----------	SW. 1	------	21st. Heavy rain.
	2 p. m.	------	------	------	10	----------	S. 1	------	22d. Showery.
	9 p. m.	------	------	------	10	----------	SE. 1	------	24th. Clear at sunrise.
Sept. 17	7 a. m.	------	------	------	10	----------	SE. 2	------	25th. Thunder shower from 6 to 9 p. m.
	2 p. m.	------	------	------	10	----------	SE. 3	------	
	9 p. m.				10	----------	NE. 5	------	
Sept. 18	7 a. m.	------	------	------	3	----------	NW. 1	------	
	2 p. m.	------	------	------	3	----------	NW. 2	------	
	9 p. m.	------	------	------	2	----------	W. 2	------	
Sept. 19	7 a. m.	------	------	------	0	----------	NW. 1	------	
	2 p. m.	------	------	------	5	----------	SW 0	------	
	9 p. m.	------	------	------	5	----------	SW. 1	------	
Sept. 20	7 a. m.	------	------	------	10	----------	E. 1	------	
	2 p. m.	------	------	------	10	----------	E. 1	------	
	9 p. m.	------	------	------	10	----------	SE. 1	------	
Sept. 21	7 a. m.	------	------	------	10	----------	S. 1	------	
	2 p. m.	------	------	------	10	----------	SE. 1	------	
	9 p. m.	------	------	------	10	----------	SE. 3	------	
Sept. 22	7 a. m.	------	------	------	10	----------	NE. 1	------	
	2 p. m.	------	------	------	10	----------	E. 1	------	
	9 p. m.	------	------	----	10	----------	SE. 1	------	

STORMS Nos. 2 AND 3, SEPTEMBER, 1859.

GERMANTOWN, PENNSYLVANIA—Continued.

Month and day.	Hour.	Barom'r corrected to 32° F.	Thermometer.	Force of vapor.	Cloudiness.		Motion of clouds.		Winds.		Relative humidity.	REMARKS.
Sept. 23	7 a. m.	......	......	......		10	....		NW.	1	......	
	2 p. m.	......	......	......		10	....		NW.	1	......	
	9 p. m.	......	......	......		8	....		NW.	1	......	
Sept. 24	7 a. m.	......	......	......		8	....		NW.	1	......	
	2 p. m.	......	......	......		5	....		NW.	1	......	
	9 p. m.	......	......	......		5	....		NW.	1	......	
Sept. 25	7 a. m.	......	......	......		5	....		NW.	1	......	

GETTYSBURG, PENNSYLVANIA.

Month and day.	Hour.	Barom'r corrected to 32° F.	Thermometer.	Force of vapor.	Cloudiness.		Motion of clouds.		Winds.		Relative humidity.	REMARKS.
Sept. 14	9 p. m.	29.565	57	......	Cir.	10	W.	2	NW.	1	......	Began to rain at 3½ a. m. the 16th and ended at 7 p. m. on the 17th; amount, 3.386 inches.
Sept. 15	7 a. m.	.785	47	......	Cir. cu.	5	W.	3	N.	1	......	
	2 p. m.	.753	61	......		0	....		N.	1	......	
	9 p. m.	.619	57	......	Cir. st.	10	SW.	2	SW.	1	......	20th. Began to rain at 8 a. m. and ended at 11 a. m.; amount, 0.335 inch.
Sept. 16	7 a. m.	.705	50	......	Cir. st.	10		?	NNE.	1	......	
	2 p. m.	.706	54	......	Cir. st.	10		?	NNE.	1	......	
	9 p. m.	.541	67	......	Cu. st.	10		?	NE.	1	......	Commenced again at 6 p. m. and ended at 3 a. m. on the 21st; amount, 0.75 inch.
Sept. 17	7 a. m.	.170	58	......	Cu. st.	10	NE.	3	NNE.	3	......	
	2 p. m.	.092	56	......	Cu. st.	10	NE.	3	NNE.	4	......	
	9 p. m.	.320	58	......	Cir. cu.	5	N.	2	NW.	3	......	21st. Showery; rain from 5 p. m. till 5 a. m. on the 22d; amount, 0.90 inch.
Sept. 18	7 a. m.	.444	57	......		0	....		NW.	2	......	
	2 p. m.	.431	71	......	Cir. st.	5	W.	2	N.	1	......	
	9 p. m.	.434	60	......	Cir.	2	W.	1		0	......	22d. Rain from 8½ to 11½ a. m. and from 1 to 7 p. m.; amount, 0.716 inch.
Sept. 19	7 a. m.	.392	54	......	Fog	1	....		NNE.	1	......	
	2 p. m.	.276	78	......	Cu	4	SW.	3	SSW.	2	......	
	9 p. m.	.292	68	......	Cu. st.	9	W.	1	SSW.	2	......	23d. Shower at 11 a. m.; amount, 0.005 inch.
Sept. 20	7 a. m.	.270	67	......	Cu. st.	10	SSW.	2	S.	1	......	
	2 p. m.	.268	72	......	Cu. st.	10	S.	2	SSE.	1	......	
	9 p. m.	.316	66	......	Cu. st.	10	S.	2	SSE.	1	......	
Sept. 21	7 a. m.	.309	69	......	{ Cir. st..... { Cu. st.	10	S. S.	3 2	S.	1	......	
	2 p. m.	.304	75	......	Cu. st.	10	S.	2	S.	2	......	
	9 p. m.	.326	61	......	Cu. st.	10	S.	2	SSE.	2	......	
Sept. 22	7 a. m.	.394	59	......	Cu. st.	10		?	NNE.	1	......	
	2 p. m.	.427	64	......	Cir. st.	10	NE.	3	NNE.	1	......	
	9 p. m.	.437	63	......	Cir. st.	10	NE.	2	NNE.	1	......	
Sept. 23	7 a. m.	.489	63	......	Cir st.	10	NW.	1	NNE.	1	......	
	2 p. m.	.516	72	......	{ Cir......... { Cu. st.	6	NW. NW.	1 3	NNE.	1	......	
	9 p. m.	.536	65	......	Cir. st.	10		?	NNE.	1	......	
Sept. 24	7 a. m.	.632	60	......	Cir. st.	6	W.	1	NW.	1	......	
	2 p. m.	.451	69	......	Cu. st.	10	W.	2	NW.	1	......	
	9 p. m.	.527	61	......	Cu. st.	3	W.	1	NW.	1	......	
Sept. 25	7 a. m.	.552	57	......	Cir. cu.	9	W.	1	W.	1	......	

HARRISBURG, PENNSYLVANIA.*

Month and day.	Hour.	Barom'r corrected to 32° F.	Thermometer.	Force of vapor.	Cloudiness.		Motion of clouds.		Winds.		Relative humidity.	REMARKS.
Sept. 14	9 p. m.	29.82	55	.168	Nim.	9	....		W..........		39	Rain from 4 a. m. the 16th till 2 a. m. on the 18th; amount, 3.63 inches.
Sept. 15	7 a. m.	30.03	45.5	.176	Cir.	5	....		N.	1	57	
	2 p. m.	30.00	61	.164		0	....		SE.	1	30	
	9 p. m.	29.98	53	.244	Nim.	10	....		SE		60	20th. Rain from 8½ a. m. to 11½ a. m.; amount, 0.20 inch.
Sept. 16	7 a. m.	29.94	53	.321	Rain	10	....		NE.	1	80	
	2 p. m.	29.88	53	.321	Rain	10	W.	2	E.	1	80	Rain from 2½ p. m. the 21st to 7½ p m. on the 22d; amount, 4.09 inches.
	9 p. m.	29.78	56	.391	Rain	10	....		E.	2	87	
Sept. 17	7 a. m.	29.44	60	.456	Rain	10	....		E.	3	88	
	2 p. m.	29.35	58	.394	Rain	10	W.	3	E.	3	82	
	9 p. m.	29.51	62.5	.408	Nim.	10	....		N.	3	72	

* Hickok, observer.

STORMS Nos. 2 AND 3, SEPTEMBER, 1859.

HARRISBURG, PENNSYLVANIA—Continued.

Month and day.	Hour.	Barom'r corrected to 32° F.	Thermometer.	Force of vapor.	Cloudiness.	Motion of clouds.	Winds.	Relative humidity.	REMARKS.
Sept. 18	7 a. m.	29.68	62	.370	Cir. st. 10	----------	N. 1	66	
	2 p. m.	29.64	68.5	.373	Cir. 7	----------	N. 3	54	
	9 p. m.	29.63	61	.442	Cir. st. 9	----------	N. 2	83	
Sept. 19	7 a. m.	29.63	52	.334	0	----------	SE. 2	86	
	2 p. m.	29.50	79	.612	Cir. cu. 5	----------	E. 1	62	
	9 p. m.	29.54	70	.551	4	----------	----------	75	
Sept. 20	7 a. m.	29.52	69	.599	Nim. 10	----------	E ----------	85	
	2 p. m.	29.51	71.5	.601	Rain 10	----------	E. 2	78	
	9 p. m.	29.57	67.5	.571	----------	----------	E. 1	82	
Sept. 21	7 a. m.	29.55	70	.658	Rain 10	----------	E. 1	90	
	2 p. m.	29.53	74	.680	Rain 10	W. 2	E. 1	81	
	9 p. m.	29.61	60.5	.434	Rain 10	----------	SE. 3	82	
Sept. 22	7 a. m.	29.66	57	.407	Rain 10	----------	E. 1	87	
	2 p. m.	29.65	63	.478	Rain 10	----------	E. 1	83	
	9 p. m.	29.66	63	.510	Nim. 10	----------	E. 2	88	
Sept. 23	7 a. m.	29.71	64	.529	Nim. 10	----------	W. 1	89	
	2 p. m.	29.70	70	.516	Cu. 9	E --------	W. 2	70	
	9 p. m.	29.74	66	.502	Nim. 10	----------	W. 2	78	
Sept. 24	7 a. m.	29.70	61	.413	Cir. cu. 3	----------	W. 1	77	
	2 p. m.	29.64	69.5	.391	Nim. 9	----------	W. 1	54	
	9 p. m.	29.65	65	.500	9	----------	W ----------	81	
Sept. 25	7 a. m.	29.67	61	.442	Cir. cu. 5	----------	W. 1	83	

HARRISBURG, PENNSYLVANIA.*

Month and day.	Hour.	Barom'r corrected to 32° F.	Thermometer.	Force of vapor.	Cloudiness.	Motion of clouds.	Winds.	Relative humidity.	REMARKS.
Sept. 14	9 p. m.	29.85	61	------	Cir. cu. 8	NW. 1	NW. 1	------	Rain on the 16th and 17th; amount, 5.063 inches.
Sept. 15	7 a. m.	30.07	49	------	Cir. 5	S. 1	S. 1	------	Rain from 8½ a. m the 20th to 8 p. m. on the 22d; amount, 3.83 inches.
	2 p. m.	30.06	62	------	0	----------	S. 1	------	
	9 p. m.	30.04	58	------	10	----------	S. 1	------	
Sept. 16	7 a. m.	30.01	56	------	10	----------	E. 1	------	
	2 p. m.	29.97	56	------	10	----------	E. 1	------	
	9 p. m.	29.84	56	------	10	----------	E. 2	------	
Sept. 17	7 a. m.	29.52	61	------	10	----------	E. 3	------	
	2 p. m.	29.40	59	------	10	----------	NE. 3	------	
	9 p. m.	29.57	61	------	10	----------	N. 2	------	
Sept. 18	7 a. m.	29.69	62	------	Cu. 6	W. 1	W. 1	------	
	2 p. m.	29.72	70	------	St. 6	W. 1	W 2	------	
	9 p. m.	29.69	64	------	0	----------	W 1	------	
Sept. 19	7 a. m.	29.68	56	------	0	----------	S. 1	------	
	2 p. m.	29.58	78	------	Cu. 5	SW. 1	SW. 1	------	
	9 p. m	29.57	72	------	8	SW. 1	SW. 1	------	
Sept. 20	7 a. m.	29.57	72	------	10	----------	S. 1	------	
	2 p. m.	29.58	73	------	10	----------	S. 2	------	
	9 p. m.	29.59	70	------	10	----------	E. 1	------	
Sept. 21	7 a. m.	29.60	73	------	10	----------	E. 2	------	
	2 p. m.	29.50	76	------	10	----------	E. 2	------	
	9 p. m.	29.64	62	------	10	----------	NE. 2	------	
Sept. 22	7 a. m.	29.68	58	------	10	----------	NE. 2	------	
	2 p. m.	29.70	64	------	10	----------	SE. 1	------	
	9 p. m.	29.71	64	------	10	----------	W. 1	------	
Sept. 23	7 a. m.	29.74	66	------	10	----------	W. 1	------	
	2 p. m.	29.76	72	------	Cu. 5	NW. 2	NW. 2	------	
	9 p. m.	29.77	68	------	10	----------	0	------	
Sept. 24	7 a. m.	29.77	65	------	St. 4	NW. 1	NW. 1	------	
	2 p. m.	29.71	72	------	Cir. st. 8	W. 1	W. 1	------	
	9 p. m.	29.68	68	------	Cu. 5	0	0	------	
Sept. 25	7 a. m.	29.69	63	------	Cir. 8	W. 1	W. 1	------	

* Heisely, observer.

STORMS Nos. 2 AND 3, SEPTEMBER, 1859.

LEWISBURG, PENNSYLVANIA.

Month and day.	Hour.	Barom'r corrected to 32° F.	Thermometer.	Force of vapor.	Cloudiness.	Motion of clouds.	Winds.	Relative humidity.	REMARKS.
Sept. 14	9 p. m.	29.679	48.1	.185	7	----------	0	55	Rain from 8½ a.m the 16th to 5 p.m. on the 17th; amount, 2.48 inches.
Sept. 15	7 a. m.	.883	43.4	.205	Cu., cu. st. 8	----------	E. 1	73	
	2 p. m.	.840	56.3	.185	Cu. cir. 4	----------	W. 1	41	
	9 p. m.	.812	46.1	.223	6	----------	0	71	
Sept. 16	7¼ a. m.	.793	48.7	.271	Nim. 10	----------	0	79	
	2 p. m.	.737	50.0	.338	Nim. 10	----------	NE. 1	94	
	9 p. m.	.639	52.6	.383	Nim. 10	----------	0	96	
Sept. 17	7 a. m.	.407	55.5	.421	Nim. 10	----------	SE. 3	96	
	2 p. m.	.267	57.2	.442	Nim. 10	----------	NW. 4	95	
	9 p. m.	.394	60.4	.409	Nim. 10	NW. 4	N. 3	78	
Sept. 18	7 a. m.	.522	56.6	.347	Nim. 10	NW. 4	N. 2	76	
	2 p. m.	.502	65.9	.452	Cu. st. 7	----------	SE. 1	71	
	9 p. m.	.485	56.5	.428	Cir. st. 8	----------	NE. 1	94	
Sept. 19	7 a. m.	.466	49.9	.351	Thick fog ---	----------	0	98	
	2 p. m.	.351	74.5	.616	Cu st., nim. 8	S. 7	S. 3	73	
	9 p. m.	.356	68.2	.565	9	----------	SW. 2	82	
Sept. 20	7 a. m.	.352	67.1	.600	Nim. 10	----------	NE. 1	90	
	2 p. m.	.273	72.8	.591	Nim. 10	----------	S. 1	74	
	9 p. m.	.415	66.7	.585	Nim. 10	----------	NE. 3	80	
Sept. 21	7 a. m.	.420	66.4	.596	Nim. 10	----------	NE. 2	92	
	2 p. m.	.412	68.7	.554	Nim. 10	SE 8	SE. 5	79	
	9¾ p. m.	.463	58.0	.435	Nim 10	----------	NE. 2	90	
Sept. 22	7 a. m.	.489	57.8	.455	Nim. 10	----------	N. 1	95	
	2¾ p. m.	.499	63.8	.552	Nim. 10	----------	0	93	
	9 p. m.	.523	62.9	.544	Nim. 10	----------	0	95	
Sept. 23	7 a. m.	.548	62.6	.548	Fog --------	----------	0	96	
	2 p. m.	.545	70.4	.494	Nim , cu. 10	----------	0	66	
	9 p. m.	.574	62.6	.509	5	----------	S. 1	89	
Sept. 24	7 a. m.	.561	58.5	.479	Cu. 8	----------	0	98	
	2 p. m.	.472	69.8	.512	Nim., cu. 9	----------	0	70	
	9 p. m.	.484	60.1	.473	Nim. 4	----------	0	91	
Sept. 25	7½ a. m.	.519	55.4	.422	Thick fog----	----------	NW. 1	96	

MORRISVILLE, PENNSYLVANIA.

Month and day.	Hour.	Barom'r corrected to 32° F.	Thermometer.	Force of vapor.	Cloudiness.	Motion of clouds.	Winds.	Relative humidity.	REMARKS.
Sept. 14	9 p. m.	30.100	51	------	Haze 5	W. 1	NE. 1	------	14th. Cool temperature; 46° in the morning.
Sept. 15	7 a. m.	30.300	44	------	Cu. 1	W. 1	W. 1	------	
	2 p. m.	30.300	62	------	Cir. 1	W. 1	S. 1	------	15th. Temperature, 42° in the morning.
	9 p. m.	30.300	50	------	Nim. 10	W. 1	SE. 1	------	
Sept. 16	7 a. m.	30.300	50	------	Nim. 10	E 1	E. 2	------	Began to rain at 7½ a.m. the 16th and ended at 11 p.m. on the 17th; amount, 3 inches; storm very severe on the 17th.
	2 p. m.	30.250	55	------	Nim. 10	SE. 3	E. 1	------	
	9 p. m.	30.150	55	------	Nim. 10	SE. 2	SE. 1	------	
Sept. 17	7 a. m.	29.900	60	------	Nim. 10	E. 2	E. 2	------	
	2 p. m.	29.500	58	------	Nim. 10	NE. 6	NE. 6	------	Storm commenced at 1 p.m. the 20th and ended at 4 a.m. on the 23d; thunder at 3 p.m. on the 22d; amount of rain, 5 inches.
	9 p. m.	29.650	54	------	Nim. 10	NE. 5	NE. 5	------	
Sept. 18	7 a. m.	29.875	58	------	0	----------	N. 2	------	
	2 p. m.	29.900	69	------	Cu. 2	NW. 2	NW. 2	------	
	9 p. m.	29.950	57	------	0	----------	0	------	24th. Winds variable; misty; sprinkle of rain at 11½ a.m.; shower from 7½ to 8½ p.m.; amount, 0.20 inch.
Sept. 19	7 a. m.	29.925	52	------	Fog 5	0	0	------	
	2 p. m.	29.900	75	------	Cu. 1	SW. 2	S. 2	------	
	9 p. m.	29.900	64	------	Cir. 1	SW. 1	SW. 1	------	
Sept. 20	7 a. m.	29.900	63	------	Nim. 5	SW. 1	SW. 1	------	25th. Dense fog and damp; shower 7 to 8 p.m; amount, 0.10 inch.
	2 p. m.	29.900	68	------	Nim. 10	S. 2	S. 2	------	
	9 p. m.	29.900	66	------	Nim. 10	SE. 1	SE. 1	------	
Sept. 21	7 a. m.	29.900	66	------	Nim. 10	SE. 2	SE. 2	------	
	2 p. m.	30.000	60	------	Nim. 10	SE. 4	SE. 4	------	
	9 p. m.	30.000	55	------	Nim. 10	E. 4	E. 4	------	
Sept. 22	7 a. m.	29.975	56	------	Nim. 10	E. 3	E. 3	------	
	2 p. m.	30.000	62	------	Nim. 10	E. 3	E. 3	------	
	9 p. m.	29.970	60	------	Nim. 10	NE. 3	NE. 3	------	
Sept. 23	7 a. m.	30.000	56	------	Nim. 10	E. 2	E. 2	------	
	2 p. m.	30.000	66	------	Nim. 10	W. 1	W. 1	------	

STORMS Nos. 2 and 3, SEPTEMBER, 1859.

MORRISVILLE, PENNSYLVANIA—Continued.

Month and day.	Hour.	Barom'r corrected to 32° F.	Thermometer.	Force of vapor.	Cloudiness.		Motion of clouds.		Winds.		Relative humidity.	REMARKS.
Sept. 23	9 p. m.	30.000	61	------	Cu.	3	W.	1		0	------	
Sept. 24	7 a. m.	30.000	61	------	Cu.	8	SW.	1	SE.	1	------	
	2 p. m.	29.950	70	------	Cu.	5	SW.	1	S.	1	------	
	9 p. m.	29.925	62	------	Cu.	3	NW.	2	N.	1	------	
Sept. 25	7 a. m.	29.925	59	------	Fog.	10		0		0	------	

MOUNT JOY, PENNSYLVANIA.

Month and day.	Hour.	Barom'r corrected to 32° F.	Thermometer.	Force of vapor.	Cloudiness.		Motion of clouds.		Winds.		Relative humidity.	REMARKS.
Sept. 14	9 p. m.	29.770	56½	------	Cir. cu.	3	SE. ------			1	------	14th. Large halo in the evening.
Sept. 15	7 a. m.	29.960	48	.308	St.	6	W.	1		1	74	16th. Rain from 4 to 10 a. m.; amount, 0.05 inch.
	2 p. m.	29.940	66	.516	------------		----------			1	70	
	9 p. m.	29.960	60	------	Nim.	10	NW.	3	------------		------	17th. Rain from 4 a. m. to 8 p. m.; amount, 6.10 inches
Sept. 16	7 a. m.	29.900	55	.349	Nim.	10	SE.	1	SE.	2	81	
	2 p. m.	29.830	58	.426	Nim.	10	SE.	3	SE.	1	82	? Rain from 1 a. m. the 18th to 8 p. m. on the 22d; ? amount, 4.68 inches.
	9 p. m.	29.740	64	.456	St.	10	SE.	1	------------		88	
Sept. 17	7 a. m.	29.360	62	.473		10		1	W.	6	88	
	2 p. m.	29.230	59	.473		10		3	N.	7	88	25th. Rain from 1½ to 3 p. m.; amount, 0.12 inch.
	9 p. m.	29.440	65	.473	Cir.	10	N.	2	------------		88	
Sept. 18	7 a. m.	29.600	63	.469	------------		----------		------------		94	
	2 p. m.	29.600	70	.577	------------		----------		------------		85	
	9 p. m.	29.600	62	.516	------------		----------		------------		84	
Sept. 19	7 a. m.	29.560	56	.407	------------		----------		------------		87	
	2 p. m.	29.500	81	.718	Cu.	0	NE.	1	------------		86	
	9 p. m.	29.525	71	.644	------------		----------		E.	3	86	
Sept. 20	7 a. m.	29.520	72	.635	St.	5	NE.	1	------------		90	
	2 p. m.	29.500	71	.635		10		2	N.	2	90	
	9 p. m.	29.560	70	.682	Nim.	10	N.	2	SE.	1	90	
Sept. 21	7 a. m.	29.550	71	.658	Nim.	10	SE.	2	SE.	1	90	
	2 p. m.	29.555	71	.758	Nim.	10	SE.	3	SE.	3	90	
	9 p. m.	29.600	61	.549		10	NE.	2	NE.	3	89	
Sept. 22	7 a. m.	29.600	60	.510		10		2		2	88	
	2 p. m.	29.620	62	.549		10		2		1	89	
	9 p. m.	29.630	64	.542	------------		----------		------------		87	
Sept. 23	7 a. m.	29.665	63	.510	Thick fog----		----------		------------		88	
	2 p. m.	29.680	73	------	Cu.	9	NW.	2	NW.	2	------	
	9 p. m.	29.710	67	.599	Nim.	10	NE.	3	------------		85	
Sept. 24	7 a. m.	29.690	65	.510	------------		----------		------------		88	
	2 p. m.	29.620	75	.668	St.	3	W.	1	------------		86	
	9 p. m.	29.615	65	.556	Cu.	1	----------		------------		84	
Sept. 25	7 a. m.	29.600	61½	.478	Cir.	2	N------		------------		83	

NAZARETH, PENNSYLVANIA.

Month and day.	Hour.	Barom'r corrected to 32° F.	Thermometer.	Force of vapor.	Cloudiness.		Motion of clouds.		Winds.		Relative humidity.	REMARKS.
Sept. 14	9 p. m.	29.51	------	------	Cu. st.	8		0	N.	1	------	14th. Lunar halo in the east at 10 p. m.; diameter, about 45°.
Sept. 15	7 a. m.	29.72	------	------	Cu. st.	3	SE.	1	NW.	1	------	
	2 p. m.	29.68	------	------	Cu. st.	5	E.	1	N.	1	------	Storm commenced at 11 a. m. the 16th, and ended at 11 p. m. on the 17th; at noon on the 17th the storm reached its height; it was very severe, causing much damage; amount, 1.17 inch.
	9 p. m.	29.66	------	------	Cir. st.	4		0		0	------	
Sept. 16	7 a. m.	29.68	------	------	Nim.	9	SW.	1	N.	2	------	
	2 p. m.	29.59	------	------	Nim.	10	SW.	1	NE.	1	------	
	9 p. m.	29.52	------	------	Nim.	10	----------		NE.	1	------	
Sept. 17	7 a. m.	29.26	------	------	Nim.	10	SW.	2	NE.	2	------	
	2 p. m.	28.92	------	------	Nim.	10	SW.	1	NE.	6	------	Rain from 10.30 a. m. the 20th till 12 p. m. on the 22d; amount, 5.07 inches.
	9 p. m.	29.10	------	------	Nim.	10	----------		N.	3	------	
Sept. 18	7 a. m.	29.23	------	------	St.	3	SW.	3	NW.	4	------	
	2 p. m.	29.30	------	------	Cu. st.	4	SE.	1	NW.	1	------	24th. Showers from 11 a. m. to 12 m.
	9 p. m.	29.31	------	------		3	----------		NW.	1	------	
Sept. 19	7 a. m.	29.32	------	------	Foggy ------		----------			0	------	25th. Rain, accompanied with zig-zag lightning, from 2.30 to 3.30 p. m.; wind, W. 2; am't, 0.19 inch.
	2 p. m.	29.26	------	------	Cu. st.	8	NE.	2	S.	2	------	
	9 p. m.	29.24	------	------	Nim.	10	----------			0	------	

STORMS Nos. 2 AND 3, SEPTEMBER, 1859.

NAZARETH, PENNSYLVANIA—Continued.

Month and day.	Hour.	Barom'r corrected to 32° F.	Thermometer.	Force of vapor.	Cloudiness.	Motion of clouds.	Winds.	Relative humidity.	REMARKS.
Sept. 20	7 a. m.	29. 25	------	------	Nim. 10	----------	S. 1	------	
	2 p. m.	29. 26	------	------	Nim. 8	NW. 2	SE. 1	------	
	9 p m.	29. 25	------	------	Nim. 10	----------	------------	------	
Sept. 21	7 a. m.	29. 31	------	------	Nim. 10	W. 3	E. 2	------	
	2 p m.	29. 35	------	------	Nim. 10	SW. 4	NE. 2	------	
	9 p. m.	29. 36	------	------	Nim. 10	----------	NE. 2	------	
Sept. 22	7 a. m.	29. 36	------	------	Nim. 10	SW. 2	NE. 3	------	
	2 p. m.	29. 36	------	------	Nim. 10	SW. 2	NE. 2	------	
	9 p. m.	29. 36	------	------	Nim. 10	----------	NE. 2	------	
Sept. 23	7 a. m.	29. 36	------	------	Nim. 10	SW. 1	NE. 1	------	
	2 p. m.	29. 35	------	------	Nim. 10	SW. 1	NE. 1	------	
	9 p. m.	29. 36	------	------	Nim. 9	----------	NW. 1	------	
Sept. 24	7 a. m.	29. 37	------	------	Cu. st. 10	SE. [illegible]	NW. 1	------	
	2 p m.	29. 29	------	------	Cu. st. 7	SE. 2	NW. 1	------	
	9 p m.	29. 31	------	------	Cu. st. 9	----------	NW. 1	------	
Sept. 25	7 a. m.	29. 33	------	------	Cu. st. 8	0	NW. 1	------	

NORRISTOWN, PENNSYLVANIA.

Month and day.	Hour.	Barom'r corrected to 32° F.	Thermometer.	Force of vapor.	Cloudiness.	Motion of clouds.	Winds.	Relative humidity.	REMARKS.
Sept. 14	9 p. m.	29. 896	54	. 206	Cu. 8	W. 1	W. 1	49	16th. Storm from the E.; commenced at 6 a. m; drizzled heavily till near sunset, when the rain and wind increased in violence; the storm grew heavier gradually until noon on the 17th, when the wind shifted to the NW. and gradually abated; ended at midnight; amount, 4. 16 inches.
Sept. 15	7 a. m.	30. 235	48	. 143	St. 1	W. 1	W. 1	43	
	2 p m.	. 209	59	. 140	St. 3	W. 1	W. 1	28	
	9 p. m.	. 218	53	. 231	Nim. 10	E. 1	E. 2	55	
Sept. 16	7 a. m.	. 193	51	. 257	Nim. 10	SE. 2	SE. 2	66	
	2 p. m.	. 113	54	. 362	Nim. 10	SE. 2	SE. 2	87	
	9 p. m.	29. 970	57	. 436	Nim. 10	SE. 2	SE. 2	94	
Sept. 17	7 a. m.	. 675	61	. 505	Nim. 10	E. 3	E. 3	94	
	2 p. m.	. 295	61	. 419	Nim. 10	NE. 3	NE. 5	77	
	9 p. m.	. 581	57	. 407	Nim. 10	NE. 3	NW. 5	87	Rain from 12½ p. m. the 20th till near midnight on the 22d; amount, 3. 58 inches.
Sept. 18	7 a. m.	------	------	------	------------	----------	------------	------	
	2 p. m.	------	------	------	------------	----------	------------	------	
	9 p. m.	------	------	------	------------	----------	------------	------	
Sept. 19	7 a. m.	. 839	62	. 523	Foggy ------	----------	SE. 1	94	
	2 p m.	. 759	74	. 532	Cir. st. 3	SW. 2	SW. 1	63	
	9 p m.	. 776	67	. 591	Nim. 10	SE. 2	S. 2	89	
Sept. 20	7 a. m.	. 769	66	. 604	Foggy ------	----------	SE. 1	94	
	2 p. m.	. 746	66	. 604	Nim. 10	SW. 2	SE. 1	94	
	9 p. m.	. 796	68	. 655	Nim. 10	SW. 2	S. 1	97	
Sept. 21	7 a. m.	. 796	68	. 648	Nim. 10	SE. 2	SE. 1	95	
	2 p m.	. 816	61	. 505	Nim. 10	E. 1	E. 2	94	
	9 p m.	. 851	57	. 450	Nim. 10	E. 1	NE. 2	84	
Sept. 22	7 a. m.	. 869	67	. 626	Nim. 10	E. 2	E. 1	95	
	2 p. m.	. 869	62	. 523	Nim. 10	E. 2	E. 2	94	
	9 p. m.	. 845	61	. 511	Nim. 10	E. 2	E. 1	97	
Sept. 23	7 a. m.	. 877	60	. 456	Nim. 10	W. 2	W. 1	88	
	2 p. m.	. 881	68	. 543	Cu. 10	W. 1	W. 1	79	
	9 p. m.	. 900	64	. 529	Cu. st. 7	W. 1	W. 1	89	
Sept. 24	7 a. m.	. 931	63	. 478	Cu. st. 4	W. 1	W. 1	83	
	2 p. m.	. 879	71	. 436	Cu. 4	W. 3	W. 2	57	
	9 p. m.	. 879	63. 5	. 503	Nim----------	W. 18	W. 1	86	
Sept. 25	7 a. m.	------	------	------	------------	----------	------------	------	

NORTH WHITEHALL, PENNSYLVANIA.

Month and day.	Hour.	Barom'r corrected to 32° F.	Thermometer.	Force of vapor.	Cloudiness.	Motion of clouds.	Winds.	Relative humidity.	REMARKS.
Sept. 14	Sunset.	------	52	------	Cir. st. 4	----------	W. 1	------	14th and 15th. Fair.
Sept. 15	Sunrise	------	40	------	Cu st. 8	----------	0	------	Rain from 11 a. m. the 16th to 5 p. m. on the 17th. ; amount not given.
	Noon.	------	55	------	Cu. 2	----------	NE. 1	------	
	Sunset.	------	52	------	Clear 0	----------	E. 1	------	
Sept. 16	Sunrise.	------	47	------	Nim. 10	E ---- ----	E. 2	------	Storm commenced at 11 a. m. the 20th ; continued heavy during the 21st and 22d.
	Noon.	------	48	------	Nim. 10	E ---- ----	E. 1	------	
	Sunset.	------	52	------	Rain 10	E ---- ----	E. 1	------	

STORMS Nos. 2 AND 3, SEPTEMBER, 1859.

NORTH WHITEHALL, PENNSYLVANIA—Continued.

Month and day.	Hour.	Barom'r corrected to 32° F.	Thermometer.	Force of vapor.	Cloudiness.	Motion of clouds.	Winds.	Relative humidity.	REMARKS.
Sept. 17	Sunrise	......	55	......	Rain 10	NE.	NE. 2	......	23d, 24th, and 25th. Cloudy.
	Noon.	......	53	......	Rain 10	NE.	NE. 3	......	
	Sunset.	......	57	......	Nim. 10	NE.	NE. 2	......	
Sept. 18	Sunrise	......	56	......	Cu. st. 4	N.	N. 2	......	
	Noon.	......	63	......	Cir. 4	N.	N. 2	......	
	Sunset.	......	70	......	Cir. st. 2	....	0	......	
Sept. 19	Sunrise	......	45	......	Clear, foggy 0	....	0	......	
	Noon.	......	78	......	Cu. 6	SW.	SW. 1	......	
	Sunset.	......	72	......	Cu. st. 8	SW.	0	......	
Sept. 20	Sunrise.	......	70	......	Nim., foggy 10	....	0	......	
	Noon.	......	70	......	Rain 10	....	E. 1	......	
	Sunset.	......	67	......	Rain 10	....	0	......	
Sept. 21	Sunrise	......	65	......	Rain 10	....	NE. 1	......	
	Noon.	......	62	......	Rain 10	E.	E. 2	......	
	Sunset.	......	58	......	Rain 10	....	NE. 2	......	
Sept. 22	Sunrise	......	53	......	Rain 10	....	0	......	
	Noon.	......	59	......	Rain 10	E.	E. 1	......	
	Sunset.	......	59	......	Nim. 10	....	0	......	
Sept. 23	Sunrise	......	59	......	Nim. 10	....	0	......	
	Noon.	......	78	......	Cu. st. 8	NE.	0	......	
	Sunset.	......	65	......	Cu. st. 8	....	0	......	
Sept. 24	Sunrise	......	60	......	Nim. 10	....	0	......	
	Noon.	......	76	......	Cu. 6	....	0	......	
	Sunset.	......	66	......	Cu. st. 7	....	0	......	
Sept. 25	Sunrise.	......	57	......	Cu. st. 8	....	0	......	

PHILADELPHIA, PENNSYLVANIA.

Month and day.	Hour.	Barom'r corrected to 32° F.	Thermometer.	Force of vapor.	Cloudiness.	Motion of clouds.	Winds.	Relative humidity.	REMARKS.
Sept. 14	9 p. m.	29.947	56	.229	8	....	NW. 2	51	16th. Drizzling rain all day; during the night became heavier; amount, 0.90 inch.
Sept. 15	7 a. m.	30.124	48½	.181	Cir.cu., cir st. 3	NW. 2	NW. 2	53	
	2 p. m.	.088	65	.215	Haze 4	....	NW. 2	35	
	9 p. m.	.086	56	.281	Cu. st. 10	....	NE. 2	63	17th. Raining hard all day; the amount, 3.202 inches, that fell on this day was nearly as great as the general average of rain for the month of September for the last nine years.
Sept. 16	7 a. m.	.099	54½	.301	10	....	NE. 2	71	
	2 p. m.	.055	60	.426	Nim. 10	....	E. 2	82	
	9 p. m.	29.950	59	.454	Nim. 10	....	SE. 2	91	
Sept. 17	7 a. m.	.638	62	.540	Nim. 10	....	ENE. 2	97	
	2 p. m.	.338	61	.473	Nim. scud. 10	NE. 5	NE. 3	88	
	9 p. m.	.542	58	.422	Nim. 10	....	NNE. 3	88	20th. Rain from 10½ a. m. to 3½ p. m.; thunder at 1 and 2 p. m.; began to rain again at 4½ p. m., and ceased at 3 p. m on the 22d; Commenced again at 8 p m. and ended at 8 a. m. on the 23d; amount, 3.217 inches.
Sept. 18	7 a. m.	.714	59½	.402	0	....	NW. 3	79	
	2 p. m.	.747	71	.468	Cir. cu. 3	NW. 2	NW. 2	62	
	9 p. m.	.816	62	.491	6	....	NW. 1	88	
Sept. 19	7 a. m.	.804	57	.436	Heavy fog 10	....	N. 1	94	
	2 p. m.	.732	78	.549	Cu. 4	....	SW. 1	57	
	9 p. m.	.724	68	.594	5	....	SW. 2	87	
Sept. 20	7 a. m.	.711	67	.591	Cir.cu., cu. 10	S. 1	S. 1	89	25th. Rain from 5¼ to 9½ p. m.; amount, 0.110 inch.
	2 p. m.	.735	70	.658	Nim. 10	....	SW. 2	90	
	9 p. m.	.738	70	.658	Nim. 10	....	SW. 1	90	
Sept. 21	7 a. m.	.747	70	.658	Nim. 10	....	SE. 2	90	
	2 p. m.	.750	68	.612	Nim. 10	....	NE. 2	89	
	9 p. m.	.803	60	.487	Nim. 10	....	NE. 2	94	
Sept. 22	7 a. m.	.814	60	.487	Nim. 10	....	NE. 2	91	
	2 p. m.	.801	65	.549	Nim. 10	....	NNE. 2	89	
	9 p. m.	.796	64½	.589	Fog, nim. 10	....	NE. 2	97	
Sept. 23	7 a. m.	.791	60½	.480	Nim. 10	....	N. 2	91	
	2 p. m.	.891	71	.608	Cu. nim. 10	....	NNW. 1	80	
	9 p. m.	.833	67	.591	10	....	NW. 1	89	
Sept. 24	7 a. m.	.813	64	.529	Cir. cu. 10	NW. 1	NNW. 1	89	
	2 p. m.	.744	76½	.497	Cu. 5	SW. 1	SW. 1	54	
	9 p. m.	.754	66½	.529	10	....	SW. 1	81	
Sept. 25	7 a. m.	.776	63½	.520	Haze 10	....	WNW. 1	89	

STORMS Nos. 2 AND 3, SEPTEMBER, 1859.

PITTSBURG, (MARINE HOSPITAL,) PENNSYLVANIA.

Month and day.	Hour.	Barom'r corrected to 32° F.	Thermometer.	Force of vapor.	Cloudiness.	Motion of clouds.	Winds.	Relative humidity.
Sept. 14	9 p. m.	29. 13	52	......	7	NW. 1	NW. 2	......
Sept. 15	7 a. m.	29. 14	48	......	9	0	NF. 1	......
	2 p. m.	29. 11	62	......	5	0	NE. 2	......
	9 p. m.	29. 11	60	......	10	0	SE. 2	......
Sept. 16	7 a. m.	29. 02	58	......	10	E. 2	E. 1	......
	2 p. m.	29. 01	62	......	10	SE 4	ESE. 2	......
	9 p. m.	28. 91	60	......	10	0	SW. 1	......
Sept. 17	7 a. m.	28. 81	58	......	10	W. 1	W. 1	......
	2 p. m.	28. 81	63	......	10	NW. 4	W. 2	......
	9 p. m.	28. 91	61	......	3	0	NW. 2	......
Sept. 18	7 a. m.	29. 03	55	......	10	0	N. 1	......
	2 p. m.	29. 00	64	......	9	E. 1	E. 1	......
	9 p. m.	28. 92	58	......	1	0	NW. 1	......
Sept. 19	7 a. m.	28. 73	54	......	8	S. 1	SSE 1	......
	2 p. m.	28. 67	74	......	9	S. 2	S. 1	......
	9 p. m.	28. 69	68	......	10	0	NW. 1	......
Sept. 20	7 a. m.	28. 70	65	......	10	SW. 1	W. 1	......
	2 p m.	28. 68	71	......	9	E. 3	E. 2	......
	9 p m.	28. 69	68	......	10	0	SE. 1	......
Sept. 21	7 a. m.	28. 70	67	......	8	E. 3	SE. 1	......
	2 p. m.	28. 67	76	......	8	SE. 4	E. 2	......
	9 p. m.	28. 68	71	......	10	0	E. 1	......
Sept. 22	7 a. m.	28. 80	67	......	5	SW. 4	SSE. 3	......
	2 p. m.	28. 88	74	......	9	W. 1	W. 1	......
	9 p. m.	28. 90	64	......	0	0	NNW. 1	......
Sept. 23	7 a. m.	28. 92	58	......	Foggy	0	W. 1	......
	2 p. m.	29. 01	67	......	8	S. 2	S. 2	......
	9 p. m.	29. 01	61	......	10	0	NW. 2	......
Sept. 24	7 a. m.	29. 01	60	......	10	S. 4	S. 1	......
	2 p. m.	28. 90	65	......	10	S. 2	S. 1	......
	9 p. m.	28. 91	63	......	9	0	NW. 1	......
Sept. 25	7 a. m.	28. 92	60	......	8	E. 1	ESE. 1	......

REMARKS.

16th. Began to rain at 5. 10 a m., and ended in the night; amount, 0. 752 inch.

17th. Rain from 6. 40 to 9. 05 a. m.; amount, 0. 040 inch.

19th Light fog at 7 a. m.; rain from 4. 45 p. m till in the night; amount, 0. 638 inch.

20th. Began to rain at 7 a. m. and ended in the night; amount, 0. 388 inch.

21st. Rain from 10. 40 to 11. 15 a. m.; amount, 0. 013 inch.

24th. Rain from 6. 40 a. m. to 5. 35 p. m.; amount, 0. 275 inch.

25th. Rain from noon till 1 p. m.; amount, 0. 012 inch.

POCOPSON, PENNSYLVANIA.

Month and day.	Hour.	Barom'r corrected to 32° F.	Thermometer.	Force of vapor.	Cloudiness.	Motion of clouds.	Winds.	Relative humidity.
Sept. 14	9 p. m.	......	54	......	Cir. st. 9	....	NW. 2	......
Sept. 15	7 a. m.	......	51	......	Cir. 4	N. 1	NE. 4	......
	2 p. m.	......	66	......	Cir. 2	NW. 1	NW. 1	......
	9 p. m.	......	57	......	9	....	NE. 1	......
Sept. 16	7 a. m.	......	55	......	10	....	NE. 1	......
	2 p. m.	......	60	......	10	....	E. 2	......
	9 p. m.	......	59	......	10	....	SE. 1	......
Sept. 17	7 a. m.	......	63	......	10	....	E	......
	2 p. m.	......	57	......	10	....	NE. 7	......
	9 p. m.	......	58	......	10	....	N. 5	......
Sept. 18	7 a. m.	......	62	......	0	....	N. 3	......
	2 p. m.	......	70	......	0	....	N. 3	......
	9 p. m.	......	58	......	4	....	NW. 2	......
Sept. 19	7 a. m.	......	55	......	10	....	....	......
	2 p. m.	......	78	......	Cu. 4	SW. 3	SW. 4	......
	9 p. m.	......	66	......	4	....	S. 1	......
Sept. 20	7 a. m.	......	68	......	10	....	S. 1	......
	2 p. m.	......	72	......	10	....	SW. 4	......
	9 p. m.	......	69	......	10	....	E. 2	......
Sept. 21	7 a. m.	......	70	......	10	....	SE. 1	......
	2 p. m.	......	65	......	10	....	E. 4	......
	9 p m.	......	60	......	10	....	E 3	......
Sept. 22	7 a m.	......	62	......	10	....	NE. 1	......
	2 p. m.	......	64½	......	10	....	N. 3	......
	9 p. m.	......	64	......	10	....	N. 1	......
Sept. 23	7 a. m.	......	62	......	10	....	N. 2	......
	2 p. m.	......	73	......	Cu., cir. 3	S. 1	N. 2	......

REMARKS.

14th. Lunar halo at 9½ p. m

Began to rain at 6 a. m. the 16th and ended at midnight on the 17th; amount, 5 inches.

20th. Rain from 8 a. m. till near midnight; generally moderate, sometimes heavy; amount, 0.29 inch

21st. Commenced raining about 4 a. m.; very heavy at times, and at other times moderate and fine; storm ended at 6½ a. m on the 23d; amount, 2 90 inches.

24th. Aurora at 8 p m.

25th Rain from 1 to 4 p. m.; amount, 0.12 inch.

STORMS Nos. 2 AND 3, SEPTEMBER, 1859.

POCOPSON, PENNSYLVANIA—Continued.

Month and day.	Hour.	Barom'r corrected to 32° F.	Thermometer.	Force of vapor.	Cloudiness.	Motion of clouds.	Winds.	Relative humidity.	REMARKS.
Sept. 23	9 p. m.	......	65	......	8	....	N. 1	......	
Sept. 24	7 a. m.	......	63	......	Cu. 5	SW. 2	NW. 1	......	
	2 p. m.	......	72	......	Cu. 6	....	W. 2	......	
	9 p. m.	......	64	......	Cu. 4	....	SW. 1	......	
Sept. 25	7 a. m.	......	60	......	Fog. 10	....	W. 1	......	

SHAMOKIN, PENNSYLVANIA.

Month and day.	Hour.	Barom'r corrected to 32° F.	Thermometer.	Force of vapor.	Cloudiness.	Motion of clouds.	Winds.	Relative humidity.	REMARKS.
Sept. 14	9 p. m.	......	50	......	St. 5	E. 1	S. 1	......	15th. Hard frost.
Sept. 15	7 a. m.	......	32	......	Cir. 2	E. 1	S. 1	......	16th. Rain all day; amount, 0.28
	2 p. m.	......	60	......	0	....	W. 1	......	inch.
	9 p. m.	......	49	......	Cu. st. 3	E. 1	W. 1	......	17th. Rain all night and day till
Sept. 16	7 a. m.	......	49	......	Nim. 10	E 1	S. 1	......	evening; amount, 2.50 inches.
	2 p. m.	......	50	......	Nim. 10	E. 1	S. 1	......	Rain most of the time from the
	9 p. m.	......	51	......	Nim. 10	E 2	SE. 3	......	20th to the 23d; thunder on the
Sept. 17	7 a. m.	......	57	......	Nim. 10	E. 1	SE. 1	......	23d; amount, 2.586 inches.
	2 p. m.	......	54	......	Nim. 10	E. 1	S. 1	......	
	9 p. m.	......	56	......	Nim. 10	E. 2	W. 2	......	
Sept. 18	7 a. m.	......	55	......	Cir. st. 8	E. 1	W. 2	......	
	2 p. m.	......	58	......	Cir. 10	W. 1	W. 1	......	
	9 p. m.	......	52	......	Cir. cu. 8	E. 1	S. 1	......	
Sept. 19	7 a. m.	......	39	......	0	....	S. 1	......	
	2 p. m.	......	75	......	Cir. cu. 5	E. 2	S. 1	......	
	9 p. m.	......	68	......	Cu. 2	E. 1	W. 1	......	
Sept. 20	7 a. m.	......	67	......	St. 8	SE. 1	S. 1	......	
	2 p. m.	......	68	......	Nim. 10	E. 1	S. 1	......	
	9 p. m.	......	66	......	Cu. 8	E 2	E 2	......	
Sept. 21	7 a. m.	......	68	......	Cu. st. 10	E 1	SE. 1	......	
	2 p. m.	......	68	......	Nim. 10	E. 2	S. 2	......	
	9 p. m.	......	68	......	Nim. 10	W. 2	E 3	......	
Sept. 22	7 a. m.	......	66	......	Nim. 10	E. 1	S. 1	......	
	2 p. m.	......	60	......	Nim. 10	E. 2	SE. 2	......	
	9 p. m.	......	61	......	Nim. 10	E. 1	S. 1	......	
Sept. 23	7 a. m.	......	58	......	Nim. 10	....	S. 1	......	
	2 p. m.	......	66	......	Nim. 10	E. 1	S. 1	......	
	9 p. m.	......	62	......	Cir. 8	E. 1	S. 1	......	
Sept. 24	7 a. m.	......	56	......	Cu. st. 10	E. 1	S. 1	......	
	2 p. m.	......	68	......	Cu. 5	E. 1	S. 1	......	
	9 p. m.	......	62	......	St. 8	E. 1	S. 1	......	
Sept. 25	7 a. m.	......	56	......	Cir. 10	E. 1	S. 1	......	

SOMERSET, PENNSYLVANIA.

Month and day.	Hour.	Barom'r corrected to 32° F.	Thermometer.	Force of vapor.	Cloudiness.	Motion of clouds.	Winds.	Relative humidity.	REMARKS.
Sept. 14	9 p. m.	27.750	48	......	Cu. st. 10	W. 3	0	......	Rain from early morn the 16th to
Sept. 15	7 a. m.	.845	47	......	Cu. 5	W. 2	E. 1	......	10 a. m. on the 17th; amount,
	2 p. m.	.833	63	......	Cir. cu. 4	W. 2	SE. 2	......	2.218 inches.
	9 p. m.	.813	53	......	Cu. st. 10	W. 1	S. 1	......	18th. Clouds variable.
Sept. 16	7 a. m.	.765	53	......	Nim. 10	SE. 2	0	......	19th. Moderate rain; thunder and
	2 p. m.	.745	54	......	Nim. 10	SE. 2	SE. 1	......	lightning at 5½ p. m. to 7½ p. m;
	9 p. m.	.652	55	......	Nim. 10	....	SE. 1	......	amount, 0.253 inch.
Sept. 17	7 a. m.	.494	54	......	Nim. 10	....	0	......	20th. Rain from early morn till 7
	2 p. m.	.492	58	......	Nim. 10	NW. 2	NNW. 2	......	a. m.; drizzly rain in the night;
	9 p. m.	.572	56	......	Nim. 10	NW. 4	NW. 3	......	amount, 0 203 inch.
Sept. 18	7 a. m.	.659	53	......	Cu. st. 10	NW. 2	0	......	21st. Heavy showers from 10 a. m.
	2 p. m.	.650	75	......	Cir. st. 9	W. 1	NW. 1	......	to 0.30 p. m.; amount, 0.631
	9 p. m.	.615	58	......	Cu. st. 10	W. 1	0	......	inch.
Sept. 19	7 a. m.	.537	53	......	Cir. 7	W. 1	0	......	22d. Cumulus clouds.
	2 p. m.	.485	80	......	Cu st. 10	SW. 2	SW. 1	......	23d. Cloudy; rain in the night;
	9 p. m.	.510	66	......	Nim. 10	....	0	......	amount, 0 025 inch.

STORMS Nos. 2 AND 3, SEPTEMBER, 1859.

SOMERSET, PENNSYLVANIA—Continued.

Month and day.	Hour.	Barom'r corrected to 32° F.	Thermometer.	Force of vapor.	Cloudiness.	Motion of clouds.	Winds.	Relative humidity.	REMARKS.
Sept. 20	7 a. m.	27.460	63	......	{ Nim ...... / Vapory 10 }	{ S. 2 / S. 6 }	S. 1	......	24th. Rain from 11 a. m. to 5 p. m.; amount, 0.304 inch.
	2 p. m.	.455	69	......	Cu. st. 10	SSE. 3	SSE. 2	......	25th. Morn foggy; variable.
	9 p. m.	.457	63	......	Nim. 10	....	SE. 2	......	
Sept. 21	7 a. m.	.457	64	......	Nim. 10	....	0	......	
	2 p. m.	.452	71	......	Cu. st. 10	SE. 6	SE. 2	......	
	9 p. m.	.465	65	......	Cu. st. 10	SE. 3	SE. 1	......	
Sept. 22	7 a. m.	.532	62	......	Cu. 5	S. 6	S. 1	......	
	2 p. m.	.568	77	......	Cu. 8	SSW. 2	W. 2	......	
	9 p. m.	.655	62	......	Cu. 10	W. 2	W. 2	......	
Sept. 23	7 a. m.	.689	58	......	{ Cir. cu .... / Vapory 8 }	{ W. 1 / WNW. 4 }	W. 1	......	
	2 p. m.	.689	69	......	Cu. st. 10	W. 2	W. 2	......	
	9 p. m.	.709	58	......	Cu. st. 10	W. 2	0	......	
Sept. 24	7 a. m.	.686	54	......	Nim. 10	W. 3	W. 1	......	
	2 p. m.	.639	59	......	Nim. 10	W. 4	W. 2	......	
	9 p. m.	.624	56	......	Cu. st. 10	W. 3	WSW. 1	......	
Sept. 25	7 a. m.	.624	56	......	Nim. 10	....	W. 1	......	

TARENTUM, PENNSYLVANIA.

Month and day.	Hour.	Barom'r corrected to 32° F.	Thermometer.	Force of vapor.	Cloudiness.	Motion of clouds.	Winds.	Relative humidity.	REMARKS.
Sept. 14	9 p. m.	......	46	......	Cir. cu. 4	W. 5	N. 1	......	16th. Rain at 6.30 a. m. and ended at noon on the 17th.
Sept. 15	7 a. m.	......	49	......	Cir. cu. 8	W. 2	0	......	Rain from 8.45 p. m. the 19th to 11 a. m on the 20th.
	2 p. m.	......	68	......	Cir. cu. 3	W. 1	NE. 2	......	24th. Rain from daylight till 5.30 p. m. ?; shower at 9 p. m.
	9 p. m.	......	56	......	Cu. st. 9	W. 4	0	......	
Sept. 16	7 a. m.	......	55	......	Nim. 10	SE. 7	0	......	
	2 p. m.	......	59	......	Nim. 10	SE 8	S. 2	......	
	9 p. m.	......	57	......	Nim. 10	....	0	......	
Sept. 17	7 a. m.	......	56	......	Nim. 10	NW. 1	W. 1	......	
	2 p. m.	......	62	......	Cu. st. 10	NW. 6	W. 2	......	
	9 p. m.	......	59	......	Cu. st. 10	....	NW. 2	......	
Sept. 18	7 a. m.	......	54	......	Fog	....	0	......	
	2 p. m.	......	66	......	Cir. cu. 5	NW. 2	W. 1	......	
	9 p. m.	......	52	......	Cir. cu. 3	....	0	......	
Sept. 19	7 a. m.	......	50	......	Fog	....	0	......	
	2 p. m.	......	78	......	Cu. st. 10	SW. 3	SW. 2	......	
	9 p. m.	......	69	......	Nim. 10	SE. 5	0	......	
Sept. 20	7 a. m.	......	65	......	Nim. 10	SE. 8	0	......	
	2 p. m.	......	73	......	Cu. st. 10	S. 5	S. 2	......	
	9 p. m.	......	66	......	Cu. st. 10	SE. 5	NE. 1	......	
Sept. 21	7 a. m.	......	68	......	Cir. cu. 8	SE. 5	0	......	
	2 p. m.	......	78	......	Cir. cu. 9	SE. 8	E. 2	......	
	9 p. m.	......	66	......	Cir. cu. 4	SE. 7	SE. 1	......	
Sept. 22	7 a. m.	......	66	......	Cu. st. 10	S. 6	S. 2	......	
	2 p. m.	......	73	......	Cu. 4	SW. 2	S. 1	......	
	9 p. m.	......	60	......	Cir. cu. 3	W. 6	0	......	
Sept. 23	7 a. m.	......	58	......	Fog	....	0	......	
	2 p. m.	......	66	......	Cu. st. 10	S. 3	S. 1	......	
	9 p. m.	......	58	......	Cu. st. 10	SW. 6	0	......	
Sept. 24	7 a. m.	......	59	......	Cu. st. 10	SW. 8	SW. 2	......	
	2 p. m.	......	62	......	Nim. 10	SW. 9	0	......	
	9 p. m.	......	59	......	Nim. 10	....	0	......	
Sept. 25	7 a. m.	......	59	......	Cu. st. 10	W. 6	0	......	

WEST HAVERFORD, PENNSYLVANIA.

Month and day.	Hour.	Barom'r corrected to 32° F.	Thermometer.	Force of vapor.	Cloudiness.	Motion of clouds.	Winds.	Relative humidity.	REMARKS.
Sept. 14	9 p. m.	......	......	......	....	....	....	......	Storm commenced at 6½ a. m. the 16th and ended in the night of the 18th; amount, 4.63 inches.
Sept. 15	7 a. m.	......	44	......	Cir. cu. 6	NW. 3	NE. 2	......	Storm commenced at 12 m. the 20th and ended in the night of the 23d; amount, 3.90 inches.
	2 p. m.	......	60	......	Cir. 1	W. 2	NE. 2	......	
	9 p. m.	......	......	......	....	....	....	......	
Sept. 16	7 a. m.	......	52	......	Cu. 10	SE. 4	E. 3	......	
	2 p. m.	......	56	......	10	....	E. 3	......	

STORMS Nos. 2 AND 3, SEPTEMBER, 1859.

WEST HAVERFORD, PENNSYLVANIA—Continued.

Month and day.	Hour.	Barom'r corrected to 32° F.	Thermometer.	Force of vapor.	Cloudiness.	Motion of clouds.	Winds.	Relative humidity.	REMARKS.
Sept. 16	9 p. m.	......	......	......	......	......	......	......	
Sept. 17	7 a. m.	......	61	......	10	E	E. 4	......	
	2 p. m.	......	59	......	10	......	NE. 3	......	
	9 p. m.	......	......	......	......	......	NW. 5	......	
Sept. 18	7 a. m.	......	61	......	10	......	NW. 2	......	
	2 p. m.	......	70	......	Cir. cu. 4	NW. 8	NW. 3	......	
	9 p. m.	......	......	......	......	......	......	......	
Sept. 19	7 a. m.	......	60	......	0	......	W. 1	......	
	2 p. m.	......	75	......	Cu. 4	W. 4	SW. 3	......	
	9 p. m.	......	......	......	......	......	......	......	
Sept. 20	7 a. m.	......	70	......	Fog	......	S. 1	......	
	2 p. m.	......	70	......	Cu. 10	SE. 3	SE. 4	......	
	9 p. m.	......	......	......	......	......	......	......	
Sept. 21	7 a. m.	......	68	......	10	......	SE. 4	......	
	2 p. m.	......	63	......	10	......	SE. 4	......	
	9 p. m.	......	......	......	......	......	......	......	
Sept. 22	7 a. m.	......	57	......	10	......	NE. 2	......	
	2 p. m.	......	64	......	10	......	E. 2	......	
	9 p. m.	......	......	......	......	......	......	......	
Sept. 23	7 a. m.	......	58	......	10	......	NE. 3	......	
	2 p. m.	......	72	......	Cu. 8	NW. 6	NE. 2	......	
	9 p. m.	......	......	......	......	......	......	......	
Sept. 24	7 a. m.	......	62	......	Cu. st. 10	NW. 3	0	......	
	2 p. m.	......	75	......	Cu. 8	NW. 3	S. 7	......	
	9 p. m.	......	......	......	......	......	......	......	
Sept. 25	7 a. m.	......	60	......	Fog	......	NE. 1	......	

WORTHINGTON, PENNSYLVANIA.

Month and day.	Hour.	Barom'r corrected to 32° F.	Thermometer.	Force of vapor.	Cloudiness.	Motion of clouds.	Winds.	Relative humidity.	REMARKS.
Sept. 14	9 p. m.	......	48	......	Cir. 5	NW. 1	NW. 1	......	16th. Rain from 1 a. m. to 2 p. m.; amount, 1.50 inch.
Sept. 15	7 a. m.	......	43	......	Cir. 10	NW. 2	E. 3	......	
	2 p. m.	......	67	......	Cir. 2	W. 1	E. 3	......	18th. Lightning in the SW. at 8 p. m.
	9 p. m.	......	57	......	Nim. 10	0	E. 2	......	
Sept. 16	7 a. m.	......	55	......	Nim. 10	W. 0	E. 1	......	19th. Rain from 5 a. m. till 2 p. m.; amount, 1.75 inch.
	2 p. m.	......	57	......	Nim. 10	ESE. 8	ESE. 4	......	
	9 p. m.	......	56	......	Nim. 10	0	E. 1	......	21st. Rain from 4 to 6 a. m.; amount, 0.25 inch.
Sept. 17	7 a. m.	......	56	......	Nim. 10	ESE. 2	E. 1	......	
	2 p. m.	......	61	......	Nim. 10	N. 4	N. 2	......	24th. Rain from 3 a. m. to 5 p. m.; amount, 0.25 inch.
	9 p. m.	......	58	......	Nim. 10	0	N. 1	......	
Sept. 18	7 a. m.	......	55	......	Cir. 6	NW. 2	N. 1	......	
	2 p. m.	......	68	......	Cir. 8	NW. 1	N. 2	......	
	9 p. m.	......	58	......	Cir. 4	W. 1	0	......	
Sept. 19	7 a. m.	......	56	......	Cir. 5	W. 2	0	......	
	2 p. m.	......	76	......	Nim. 10	SW. 1	SE. 3	......	
	9 p. m.	......	69	......	Nim. 10	0	E. 1	......	
Sept. 20	7 a. m.	......	66	......	Nim. 10	E. 4	E. 1	......	
	2 p. m.	......	78	......	Nim. 10	SE. 2	SE. 2	......	
	9 p. m.	......	66	......	Nim. 10	SE. 2	SE. 1	......	
Sept. 21	7 a. m.	......	66	......	Nim. 10	SE. 3	E. 2	......	
	2 p. m.	......	78	......	Cir. 5	S. 3	SE. 3	......	
	9 p. m.	......	69	......	Cir. 6	S. 1	SE. 2	......	
Sept. 22	7 a. m.	......	74	......	Cu. 5	SW. 4	E. 4	......	
	2 p. m.	......	70	......	Cir. 6	SW. 4	S. 3	......	
	9 p. m.	......	60	......	0	0	0	......	
Sept. 23	7 a. m.	......	60	......	Nim. 10	W. 3	SW. 1	......	
	2 p. m.	......	64	......	Nim. 8	SW. 2	SW. 4	......	
	9 p. m.	......	60	......	Nim. 0	W. 0	0	......	
Sept. 24	7 a. m.	......	58	......	Nim. 10	SW. 4	E. 2	......	
	2 p. m.	......	62	......	Nim. 10	SW. 4	0	......	
	9 p. m.	......	59	......	Nim. 10	NW. 2	0	......	
Sept. 25	7 a. m.	......	58	......	Nim. 10	W. 1	NW. 1	......	

STORMS Nos. 2 AND 3, SEPTEMBER, 1859.

ANNAPOLIS, MARYLAND.

Month and day.	Hour.	Barom'r corrected to 32° F.	Thermometer.	Force of vapor.	Cloudiness.	Motion of clouds.	Winds.	Relative humidity.
Sept. 14	9 p. m.	29. 90	68	. 349	10	----------	NNE. 2	51
Sept. 15	7 a. m.	30. 10	54	. 231	Cr., cr.st., cu. 8	SW. 1	NE. 3	55
	2 p. m.	30. 10	61. 5	. 235	Cr., cr.st., cu. 6	WSW. 2	NE. 2	43
	9 p. m.	30. 07	61	. 354	10	----------	E. 3	66
Sept. 16	7 a. m.	30. 02	63	. 510	10	----------	NE. 2	88
	2 p. m.	29. 95	65	. 549	10	----------	ESE. 3	89
	9 p. m.	29. 83	64	. 563	10	----------	ENE. 3	94
Sept. 17	7 a. m.	29. 40	67	. 662	10	----------	NE. 3	100
	2 p. m.	29. 26	60	. 487	10	----------	N. 4	94
	9 p. m.	29. 62	63	. 543	10	----------	NW. 2	94
Sept. 18	7 a. m.	29. 76	57. 5	. 459	0	----------	NW. 1	97
	2 p. m.	29. 74	72. 5	. 517	Cr., cr.st., cu. 3	SW. 1	N. 1	64
	9 p. m.	29. 75	65	. 549	Cir. st., cu. 3	----------	N. 1	89
Sept. 19	7 a. m.	29. 75	57. 5	. 459	0	----------	0	97
	2 p. m.	29. 67	76	. 652	Cir. and cu. 2	SW. 2	S. 2	73
	9 p. m.	29. 66	72	. 668	10	----------	S. 2	86
Sept. 20	7 a. m.	29. 65	70	. 695	10	----------	S. 1	95
	2 p. m.	29. 62	73	. 732	10	----------	S. 1	90
	9 p. m.	29. 65	71. 5	. 752	10	----------	SSE. 2	98
Sept. 21	7 a. m.	29. 66	71. 5	. 752	10	----------	SE. 1	98
	2 p. m.	29. 65	76	. 812	10	----------	S. 1	91
	9 p. m.	29. 67	73	. 771	10	----------	E. 2	95
Sept. 22	7 a. m.	29. 70	72. 5	. 778	Cr., cr.st., cu. 6	SW. 1	S. 1	98
	2 p. m.	29. 72	74	. 718	10	----------	NE. 2	86
	9 p. m.	29. 74	70	. 658	Cr., cr.st., cu 7	----------	NNE. 1	90
Sept. 23	7 a. m.	29. 80	64. 5	. 590	Cr., cr.st., cu. 5	SW. 1	N. 1	97
	2 p. m.	29. 79	71. 5	. 638	Cr., cr.st., cu. 7	SW. 1	NE. 1	83
	9 p m.	29. 82	73	. 732	10	----------	0	90
Sept. 24	7 a. m.	29. 82	63	. 543	10	----------	NW. 1	94
	2 p. m.	29. 75	74. 5	. 561	10	----------	WSW. 1	65
	9 p m.	29. 75	72	. 595	10	----------	SW. 1	76

REMARKS.

16th. Rain at intervals from 5 a. m till 9 p. m.; steady till 9 p. m. on the 17th, then at intervals till 10. 30 p. m ; amount, 5. 27 inches.

20th. Rain at intervals from 6. 20 a m. to 9 p. m , then light rain at intervals till 8 p m. on the 21st ; then again light rain from 10. 30 p. m. during the night, or nearly so.

22d. Rain from 8. 40 a. m. at intervals till 8 p. m.; amount from 20th to 22d inclusive, 1. 69 inch.

24th. Sprinkle of rain at 8. 50 a. m. and 9. 40 p. m.

25th. Heavy dew.

BLADENSBURG, MARYLAND.

Month and day.	Hour.	Barom'r corrected to 32° F.	Thermometer.	Force of vapor.	Cloudiness.	Motion of clouds.	Winds.	Relative humidity.
Sept. 14	9 p. m.	------	60	------	------------	----------	------------	------
Sept. 15	7 a. m.	------	51	------	------------	----------	NE --------	------
	2 p. m.	------	65	------	------------	----------	E----------	------
	9 p. m.	------	55	------	------------	----------	------------	------
Sept. 16	7 a. m.	------	59	------	------------	----------	E----------	------
	2 p. m.	------	66	------	8	----------	E----------	------
	9 p. m.	------	62	------	10	----------	NE --------	------
Sept. 17	7 a. m.	------	66	------	10	----------	E----------	------
	2 p. m.	------	60	------	10	----------	NW --------	------
	9 p. m.	------	60	------	10	----------	NW --------	------
Sept. 18	7 a. m.	------	58	------	10	----------	NW --------	------
	2 p. m.	------	74	------	10	----------	------------	------
	9 p. m.	------	57	------	10	----------	------------	------
Sept. 19	7 a. m.	------	54	------	1	----------	------------	------
	2 p. m.	------	------	------	5	----------	------------	------
	9 p. m.	------	67	------	2	----------	E----------	------
Sept. 20	7 a. m.	------	67	------	------------	----------	------------	------
	2 p. m.	------	------	------	------------	----------	------------	------
	9 p. m.	------	69	------	4	----------	------------	------
Sept. 21	7 a. m.	------	69	------	10	----------	SE----------	------
	2 p m.	------	79	------	10	----------	SE----------	------
	9 p. m.	------	69	------	10	----------	------------	------
Sept. 22	7 a. m.	------	70	------	10	----------	------------	------
	2 p. m.	------	74	------	10	----------	SW----------	------
	9 p. m.	------	66	------	10	----------	------------	------
Sept. 23	7 a. m.	------	------	------	10	----------	------------	------
	2 p. m.	------	------	------	10	----------	------------	------
	9 p. m.	------	65	------	10	----------	------------	------
Sept. 24	7 a. m.	------	63	------	------------	----------	NW --------	------
	2 p. m.	------	77	------	------------	----------	------------	------
	9 p. m.	------	62	------	10	----------	------------	------

16th and 17th. Amount of rain, 3. 95 inches.

21st and 22d. Amount, 1. 37 inch.

STORMS Nos. 2 AND 3, SEPTEMBER, 1859.

FREDERICK, MARYLAND.

Month and day.	Hour.	Barom'r corrected to 32° F.	Thermometer.	Force of vapor.	Cloudiness.		Motion of clouds.		Winds.		Relative humidity.
Sept. 14	9 p. m.	29. 838	62	------	Nim.	9	----------			0	------
Sept. 15	7 a. m.	30. 061	51	------	Cir. st.	9	W.	3	NE.	2	------
	2 p. m.	29. 998	63. 5	------	Cir.	5	W.	1	SE.	2	------
	9 p. m.	. 993	59	------		10	----------		NE.	2	------
Sept. 16	7 a. m.	. 338	53	------	Nim.	10	----------		NE.	3	------
	2 p. m.	. 847	57	------	Nim.	10	----------		N.	2	------
	9 p. m.	. 766	60	------	Nim.	10	----------		NE.	2	------
Sept. 17	7 a. m.	. 317	59. 5	------	Nim.	10	----------		N.	4	------
	2 p. m.	. 362	59	------	Nim.	10	N.	5	N.	3	------
	9 p. m.	. 589	59. 7	------	Cir. st.	9	W.	2	NW.	2	------
Sept. 18	7 a. m.	. 786	58. 5	------		0		0		0	------
	2 p. m.	. 667	68. 5	------	Cir.	7	W.	2	W.	2	------
	9 p. m.	. 667	61	------	Cir. st.	3	W.	1		0	------
Sept. 18	7 a. m.	. 626	56. 5	------		0		0	N.	1	------
	2 p. m.	. 526	71	------	Cir. cu.	8	S.	3	S.	3	------
	9 p. m.	. 548	69	------	Nim.	10	----------		NE.	2	------
Sept. 19	7 a. m.	. 535	67. 5	------	Nim.	10	S.	2	S.	1	------
	2 p. m.	. 515	71. 5	------	Nim.	10	SE.	3	SE.	2	------
	9 p. m.	. 541	86. 7	------	Nim.	10	----------		NE.	2	------
Sept. 20	7 a. m.	. 553	69. 5	------	Nim.	10	S.	2	NE.	2	------
	2 p. m.	. 533	75	------	Cir. st.	9	S.	2	SE.	2	------
	9 p. m.	. 558	68. 5	------	Nim.	10	----------		NE.	1	------
Sept. 21	7 a. m.	. 642	61	------	Nim.	10	----------		NE.	2	------
	2 p. m.	. 645	65. 5	------	Nim.	10	NE.	2	NE.	2	------
	9 p. m.	. 680	64. 8	------	Nim.	10	----------		NE.	1	------
Sept. 22	7 a. m.	. 741	64. 5	------	Cir. st.	9	N.	1		0	------
	2 p. m.	. 730	71. 5	------	Cir. cu.	6	NW.	2	N.	1	------
	9 p. m.	. 756	65. 5	------	Cir. st.	10	----------			0	------
Sept. 23	7 a. m.	. 765	63	------	Cir. st.	8	W.	2	W.	2	------
	2 p. m.	. 668	69	------	Cir. cu.	9	W.	2	NW.	2	------
	9 p. m.	. 669	64. 5	------	Cir. st.	9	W.	1		0	------
Sept. 24	7 a. m.	. 677	59. 5	------	Cir. st.	8	W.	2	W.	1	------
	2 p. m.	. 645	69. 5	------	Cir. st.	8	W.	1	W.	3	------
	9 p. m.	. 677	64	------	St.	2	----------		W.	1	------

REMARKS.

Storm commenced in the night of the 15th, and ended at 9 p. m. on the 17th; amount, 7. 89 inches.

Rain from 6. 45 a. m. the 20th, to 7 a. m. on the 21st; amount, 1. 506 inch.

Rain from 2 p. m. the 21st, to 7 a. m. on the 22d; amount, 1. 00 inch.

23d. Rain during past night; am't, 0. 63 inch.

LEITERSBURG, MARYLAND.

Month and day.	Hour.	Barom'r corrected to 32° F.	Thermometer.	Force of vapor.	Cloudiness.		Motion of clouds.		Winds.		Relative humidity.
Sept. 14	9 p. m.	------	58	------	St.	8	?		NE.	2	------
Sept. 15	7 a. m.	------	46	------	Cir. st.	6	W.	3	NW.	1	------
	2 p. m.	------	64	------	Cir. st.	3	W.	3	SW.	2	------
	9 p. m.	------	56	------	St.	10	SW.	3	S.	2	------
Sept. 16	7 a. m.	------	52	------	Nim.	10	E.	4	NW.	1	------
	2 p. m.	------	58	------	Nim.	10	E.	3	SE.	2	------
	9 p. m.	------	60	------	Nim.	10	E.	3	SE.	2	------
Sept. 17	7 a. m.	------	60	------	Nim.	10	NE.	6	NE.	5	------
	2 p. m.	------	58	------	Nim.	10	N.	5	NW.	3	------
	9 p. m.	------	60	------	Nim.	10	W ?-------		W.	1	------
Sept. 18	7 a. m.	------	58	------	Cir.	1	NW.	1		0	------
	2 p. m.	------	71	------	Cir.	8	NW.	2	NW.	2	------
	9 p. m.	------	59	------	Cir.	3	?		W.	1	------
Sept. 19	7 a. m.	------	54	------		0		0		0	------
	2 p. m.	------	80	------	Cir. cu.	5	{ W. { SW.	2 } 4 }	S.	3	------
	9 p. m.	------	72	------	Cir. st.	10	?		S.	4	------
Sept. 20	7 a. m.	------	70	------	St.	10	SW.	3	S.	3	------
	2 p. m.	------	77	------	Nim.	8	SE.	2	SE.	2	------
	9 p. m.	------	68	------	Nim.	10	SE.	3	E.	2	------
Sept. 21	7 a. m.	------	70	------	St.	10	{ W. { SW.	1 } 3 }	S.	2	------
	2 p. m.	------	78	------	Nim.	9	S.	2	S.	3	------
	9 p. m.	------	66	------	Nim.	10	SE.	4	SE.	4	------

REMARKS.

Began to rain moderately some time during the night of the 15th; continued in showers E. and SE. during the 16th; storm increased after dark; wind shifted to the N. strong; considerable rain fell in the night, (16th.)

17th. High wind and heavy rain till 2 p. m.; after that time the storm abated gradually and ceased at 7 p. m.; three inches and two-tenths of rain fell from 6 a. m. to 6 p. m.; amount rain during the storm, 5. 35 inches.

20th. Moderate showers during the day and evening; amount, 0. 72 inch.

21st. Slight showers in a. m.; 3½ p. m. dashing rain SW. and S., wind shifting to SE.; heavy showers in fore part of night; amount, 1. 63 inch.

STORMS Nos. 2 AND 3, SEPTEMBER, 1859.

LEITERSBURG, MARYLAND—Continued.

Month and day.	Hour.	Barom'r corrected to 32° F.	Thermometer.	Force of vapor.	Cloudiness		Motion of clouds.		Winds.		Relative humidity.	REMARKS.
Sept. 22	7 a. m.	------	64	------	St.	10	SW.	3	SE.	2	------	22d. Showers and sunshine during the day; wind E. in the morning; then S and SW. and N. in the evening; amount, 0. 40 inch.
	2 p. m.	------	72	------	St.	8	SW.	3	W.	2	------	
	9 p. m.	------	64	------	Cir. st.	5	?		N.	1	------	
Sept. 23	7 a. m.	------	64	------	St.	10	W.	2	W.	1	------	
	2 p. m.	------	74	------	Cu.	8	W.	2	NW.	2	------	24th. Low fog till 9 a. m.; rain from 7 to 9 p. m; amount, 0. 03 inch.
	9 p. m.	------	64	------	St.	9	NW.	1	W.	1	------	
Sept. 24	7 a. m.	------	62	------	Cir. st.	3	NW.	3	W.	1	------	
	2 p. m.	------	72	------	Cir. st.	7	NW.	2	W.	2	------	25th. Low fog till 9 a. m.; course NE. to SW.
	9 p. m.	------	62	------	Nim.	9	NW.	2	W.	1	------	

LEONARDTOWN, MARYLAND.

Month and day.	Hour.	Barom'r corrected to 32° F.	Thermometer.	Force of vapor.	Cloudiness		Motion of clouds.		Winds.		Relative humidity.	REMARKS.
Sept. 14	9 p. m.	29. 67	65	------	Cir. cu.	7	NW.	2	NE.	1	------	Began to rain in the night of the 16th, and ended at 10 p. m. on the 17th.
Sept. 15	7 a. m.	29. 85	56	------	Cir.	3	W.	1	NW.	4	------	
	2 p. m.	29. 87	66	------		10		0	E.	1	------	
	9 p. m.	29. 87	62	------		10		0	NE.	4	------	20th. Showers.
Sept. 16	7 a. m.	29. 85	64	------		10		0	E.	2	------	21st. Showers; lightning SW. after night.
	2 p. m.	29. 80	67	------		10		0	E.	2	------	
	9 p. m.	29. 70	65	------		10		0	E.	4	------	22d. Showers.
Sept. 17	7 a. m.	29. 23	72	------		10		0	SE.	4	------	25th. Heavy showers during the day.
	2 p. m.	29. 14	66	------		10		0	WNW.	8	------	
	9 p. m.	29. 45	64	------		10		0	NW.	5	------	
Sept. 18	7 a. m.	29. 60	67	------	Cir.	1		0	NW.	2	------	
	2 p. m.	29. 63	80	------	Cir.	1		0	W.	3	------	
	9 p. m.	29. 63	64	------	Cir. st.	5		0	SE.	0	------	
Sept. 19	7 a. m.	29. 63	70	------	Cir.	5		0	S.	1	------	
	2 p. m.	------	------	------	------		------		------		------	
	9 p. m.	29. 58	70	------	Cir.	4		0	SE.	3	------	
Sept. 20	7 a. m.	29. 56	74	------		10		0	SE.	1	------	
	2 p. m.	29. 56	74	------		10		0	SE.	1	------	
	9 p. m.	29. 58	72	------		10		0	SE.	1	------	
Sept. 21	7 a. m.	29. 54	73	------		10		0	SE.	2	------	
	2 p. m.	29. 54	------	------		10		0	SE.	1	------	
	9 p. m.	29. 54	73	------		10		0	SE.	1	------	
Sept. 22	7 a. m.	29. 55	73	------		10		0	SE.	1	------	
	2 p. m.	29. 56	74	------		10		0	SE.	1	------	
	9 p. m.	29. 57	70	------		10		0	NE.	1	------	
Sept. 23	7 a. m.	29. 63	69	------		10		0	NW.	1	------	
	2 p. m.	29. 65	73	------	Cir. st.	8		0	SW.	2	------	
	9 p. m.	29. 65	71	------	Cu. st.	3		0	E.	0	------	
Sept. 24	7 a. m.	29. 65	67	------		10		0	NW.	1	------	
	2 p. m.	29. 65	70	------		10		0	SE.	1	------	
	9 p. m.	29. 65	70	------		10		0	W.	2	------	

SYKESVILLE, MARYLAND.

Month and day.	Hour.	Barom'r corrected to 32° F.	Thermometer.	Force of vapor.	Cloudiness		Motion of clouds.		Winds.		Relative humidity.	REMARKS.
Sept. 14	9 p. m.	------	60	------	Nim.	10	SW.	1	S.	1	------	Began to rain in the night of the 16th and rained in torrents till 10 p. m. on the 17th; amount, 5. 00 inches.
Sept. 15	7 a. m.	------	49	------	Cu.	6	W.	2	NE.	3	------	
	2 p. m.	------	65	------	Cir. st.	8	SW.	2	NE.	2	------	
	9 p. m.	------	58	------	Nim.	10	NE.	1	NE.	3	------	
Sept. 16	7 a. m.	------	55	------	Nim.	10	NE.	2	NE.	3	------	20th. Began to rain at 7 a. m.; storm ended at 6 p. m. on the 22d; thunder and lightning at 5 p. m. on the 21st, and very heavy rain during the night; amount, 3. 00 inches.
	2 p. m.	------	65	------	Nim.	10	NE.	2	NE.	4	------	
	9 p. m.	------	60	------	Nim.	10	NE.	1	W.	2	------	
Sept. 17	7 a. m.	------	63	------	Nim.	10	NE.	2	NW.	2	------	
	2 p. m.	------	57	------	Nim.	10	N.	3	NW.	2	------	
	9 p. m.	------	58	------	Nim.	10	W.	2	NW.	2	------	
Sept. 18	7 a. m.	------	58	------	St.	1	W.	1	N.	2	------	24th. Lightning at 7 p. m.
	2 p. m.	------	68	------	St.	4	W.	2	S.	3	------	25th. Showery from 1 to 6 p. m; amount, 0. 25 inch.
	9 p. m.	------	61	------	St.	2	W.	2	SE.	3	------	

STORMS Nos. 2 AND 3, SEPTEMBER, 1859.

SYKESVILLE, MARYLAND—Continued.

Month and day.	Hour.	Barom'r corrected to 32° F.	Thermometer.	Force of vapor.	Cloudiness.	Motion of clouds.	Winds.	Relative humidity.	REMARKS.
Sept. 19	7 a. m.	......	55	......	Fog 9	W. 1	SE. 2	......	
	2 p. m.	......	75	......	St. 4	W. 1	SE. 3	......	
	9 p. m.	......	70	......	Cu. st. 5	SW. 2	SE. 2	......	
Sept. 20	7 a. m.	......	65	......	Nim. 10	SE. 2	W. 1	......	
	2 p. m.	......	70	......	Nim. 9	SE. 2	E. 2	......	
	9 p. m.	......	68	......	Nim. 10	SE. 2	NE. 3	......	
Sept. 21	7 a. m.	......	70	......	Cu. 9	S. 3	S. 2	......	
	2 p. m.	......	76	......	Cu. 9	SE. 2	S. 1	......	
	9 p. m.	......	68	......	Nim. 10	SE. 2	N. 1	......	
Sept. 22	7 a. m.	......	70	......	Cu. 9	S. 2	N. 2	......	
	2 p. m.	......	72	......	Cu. 9	S. 1	NW. 3	......	
	9 p. m.	......	66	......	St. 2	W. 1	W. 2	......	
Sept. 23	7 a. m.	......	64	......	Cu. st. 4	W. 2	NE. 2	......	
	2 p. m	......	74	......	Cu. 5	NW. 3	W. 2	......	
	9 p. m.	......	67	......	Cu. st. 4	W. 2	W. 2	......	
Sept. 24	7 a. m.	......	60	......	Cu. st. 8	W. 1	W. 2	......	
	2 p. m.	......	73	......	Cir. 5	W. 2	S. 2	......	
	9 p. m.	......	64	......	Cu. 4	W. 1	W. 1	......	

WASHINGTON, DISTRICT OF COLUMBIA.

Month and day.	Hour.	Barom'r corrected to 32° F.	Thermometer.	Force of vapor.	Cloudiness.	Motion of clouds.	Winds.	Relative humidity.	REMARKS.
Sept. 14	9 p. m.	30.071	65	.330	Haze	....	NE. 1	53	Rain from 1 a. m. the 16th to 3 p. m. on the 17th; amount, 4.00 inches
Sept. 15	7 a. m.	30.273	52	.232	Cir. cu. 8	....	NE. 2	60	
	2 p. m.	30.273	61	.216	Cu. st. 10	....	NE. 3	40	
	9 p. m.	30.241	59	.296	Overcast 10	....	NE. 2	59	17th. Rain from 3 to 9½ p. m.; amount, 0.34 inch.
Sept. 16	7 a. m.	30.175	60	.487	Nim. 10	....	NE. 2	94	
	2 p. m.	30.086	67	.556	Nim. 10	....	SE. 3	84	Rain, with intermissions from 7 a. m. the 20th till 10 a. m. on the 21st; amount, 0.57 inch.
	9 p. m.	29.962	63	.543	Nim. 10	....	NE. 4	94	
Sept. 17	7 a. m.	29.498	69	.671	Nim. 10	....	NE. 4	95	
	2 p. m.	29.498	61	.505	Nim. 10	....	NW. 4	94	21st. Showers in past night and this morning; rain from 1 to 6 p. m.; amount, 0.55 inch.
	9 p. m.	29.779	62	.523	Nim. 10	....	NW. 4	94	
Sept. 18	7 a. m.	29.917	61	.442	0	....	NW	83	
	2 p. m.	29.899	71	.503	Cir. 3	....	NW. 1	66	24th. Sprinkle a. m.
	9 p. m.	29.907	64	.563	0	....	0	94	
Sept. 19	7 a. m.	29.891	58	.452	0	....	0	94	
	2 p. m.	29.805	77	.601	Cir. cu. 8	....	S. 3	65	
	9 p. m.	29.815	70	.658	Haze	....	S. 2	90	
Sept. 20	7 a. m.	29.801	69	.635	Nim. 10	....	SE. 1	90	
	2 p. m.	29.783	73	.782	Nim. 10	....	SE. 1	90	
	9 p. m.	29.789	70	.695	Nim. 10	....	E. 3	95	
Sept. 21	7 a. m.	29.813	71	.720	Nim. 10	....	SE. 3	95	
	2 p. m.	29.805	77	.758	Cu. st. 10	....	SE. 2	82	
	9 p. m.	29.813	73	.771	Nim. 10	....	SE. 2	95	
Sept. 22	7 a. m.	29.873	72	.745	Nim. 10	....	S. 1	95	
	2 p. m.	29.895	73	.655	Nim. 10	....	NW. 2	81	
	9 p. m.	29.921	68	.648	0	....	NW. 1	95	
Sept. 23	7 a. m.	29.983	66	.570	Cir. cu. 6	....	NW. 1	89	
	2 p. m.	29.957	75	.519	Cu. 8	....	NW. 3	60	
	9 p. m.	29.993	69	.564	Overcast 10	....	NW. 3	79	
Sept. 24	7 a. m.	30.001	64	.497	Overcast 10	....	NW. 3	83	
	2 p. m.	30.919	73	.409	Cu. st. 10	....	NW. 2	50	
	9 p. m.	30.911	67	.556	Overcast 10	....	NW. 1	84	

CRICHTON'S STORE, VIRGINIA.

Month and day.	Hour.	Barom'r corrected to 32° F.	Thermometer.	Force of vapor.	Cloudiness.	Motion of clouds.	Winds.	Relative humidity.	REMARKS.
Sept. 14	6 p. m.	......	......	......	1	....	N	......	16th. Rain in the a. m., commencing at 5½ o'clock; amount, 0.50 inch.
Sept. 15	7½ a. m.	......	62	......	Cir. cu. 9	SW. 3	NE. 1	......	
	12 m.	......	73	......	Cir. 8	SW. 2	NE. 2	......	19th Heavy dew.
	6 p. m.	......	......	......	10	....	NE. 1	......	Began to rain in the a. m of the 20th and ended at 10 a. m. on the 22d; thunder in the evening of the 20th and 21st; amount of rain, 1.05 inch.
Sept. 16	7½ a. m.	......	67	......	10	....	NE. 1	......	
	12 m.	......	69	......	10	....	NE. 2	......	
	6 p. m.	......	67	......	10	....	NE. 2	......	
Sept. 17	7½ a. m.	......	66	......	Cir. cu. 1	W. 3	W. 4	......	

STORMS Nos. 2 AND 3, SEPTEMBER, 1859.

CRICHTON'S STORE, VIRGINIA—Continued.

Month and day.	Hour.	Barom'r corrected to 32° F.	Thermometer.	Force of vapor.	Cloudiness.	Motion of clouds.	Winds.	Relative humidity.	REMARKS.
Sept. 17	12 m.	------	------	------	5	----------	W. 4	------	24th. At 7 a. m. wind N., but rain and wind clouds SW. 3; 8.15 a. m. upper stratus SW. 2, cir. st.; next under stratus SW. 3; cir. st. lower, NE. 5; perhaps these were the real rain and wind clouds; occasional showers, which I believe sometimes came from the under stratus from N., and at others from the highest from SW.; showers from 8 a. m. till evening; two rainbows at 5 p. m.; amount of rain, 0.10 inch. 25th. Sprinkle in the a. m.
	6 p. m.	------	------	------	1	----------	W. 1	------	
Sept. 18	7½ a. m.	------	67	------	0	----------	NE. 1	------	
	12 m.	------	78	------	4	----------	NE. 1	------	
	6 p. m.	------	75	------	Cir. cu. 4	SW. 2	NE. ----------	------	
Sept. 19	7½ a. m.	------	66	------	3	----------	SW. 1	------	
	12 m.	------	84	------	3	----------	S. 2	------	
	6 p. m.	------	78	------	Cir. 8	W. 2	S ----------	------	
Sept. 20	7½ a. m.	------	71	------	10	----------	S. 1	------	
	12 m.	------	76	------	10	----------	S. 1	------	
	6 p. m.	------	72	------	10	----------	S. ----------	------	
Sept. 21	7½ a. m.	------	73	------	10	----------	SE. 1	------	
	12 m.	------	76	------	10	----------	S. 2	------	
	6 p. m.	------	72	------	10	----------	S ----------	------	
Sept. 22	7½ a. m.	------	72	------	10	----------	S ----------	------	
	12 m.	------	70	------	10	----------	SW. 1	------	
	6 p. m.	------	76	------	Cir. st. 2	W. 2	SW. 1	------	
Sept. 23	7½ a. m.	------	65	------	10	----------	N. 1	------	
	12 m.	------	74	------	Cir. st. 5	W. 2	N. 1	------	
	6 p. m.	------	76	------	1	----------	SW ----------	------	
Sept. 24	7½ a. m.	------	60	------	10	----------	N. 1	------	
	12 m.	------	64	------	10	----------	N ----------	------	
	6 p. m.	------	68	------	Cir. st. 9	SW. 3	N ----------	------	

CROSS CREEK, VIRGINIA.

Month and day.	Hour.	Barom'r corrected to 32° F.	Thermometer.	Force of vapor.	Cloudiness.	Motion of clouds.	Winds.	Relative humidity.	REMARKS.
Sept. 14	9 p. m.	------	51	------	------------	W --------	2	------	Rain from 2 a. m. the 16th to 6 a. m. on the 17th; amount, 0.96 inch. Storm commenced at 5 p. m. the 19th and ended at 3 a. m. on the 25th; amount, 1.95 inch.
Sept. 15	7 a. m.	------	47	------	------------	W --------	1	------	
	2 p. m.	------	64	------	------------	W --------	2	------	
	9 p. m.	------	55	------	------------	SW --------	0	------	
Sept. 16	7 a. m.	------	52	------	------------	S --------	1	------	
	2 p. m.	------	------	------	------------	E --------	1	------	
	9 p. m.	------	62	------	------------	E --------	1	------	
Sept. 17	7 a. m.	------	60	------	------------	SW --------	0	------	
	2 p. m.	------	60	------	------------	SW --------	1	------	
	9 p. m.	------	------	------	------------	0	1	------	
Sept. 18	7 a. m.	------	52	------	------------	W --------	1	------	
	2 p. m.	------	71	------	------------	W --------	1	------	
	9 p. m.	------	56	------	------------	0	1	------	
Sept. 19	7 a. m.	------	58	------	------------	0	0	------	
	2 p. m.	------	74	------	------------	SW --------	0	------	
	9 p. m.	------	68	------	------------	S --------	1	------	
Sept. 20	7 a. m.	------	66	------	------------	S --------	1	------	
	2 p. m.	------	70	------	------------	S --------	1	------	
	9 p. m.	------	68	------	------------	S --------	0	------	
Sept. 21	7 a. m.	------	62	------	------------	S --------	1	------	
	2 p. m.	------	76	------	------------	S --------	1	------	
	9 p. m.	------	65	------	------------	0	0	------	
Sept. 22	7 a. m.	------	64	------	------------	S --------	1	------	
	2 p. m.	------	70	------	------------	S --------	1	------	
	9 p. m.	------	58	------	------------	0	1	------	
Sept. 23	7 a. m.	------	62	------	------------	SW --------	0	------	
	2 p. m.	------	60	------	------------	SW --------	1	------	
	9 p. m.	------	58	------	------------	SW --------	1	------	
Sept. 24	7 a. m.	------	63	------	------------	SW --------	1	------	
	2 p. m.	------	64	------	------------	W --------	2	------	
	9 p. m.	------	60	------	------------	NW --------	1	------	

STORMS Nos. 2 AND 3, SEPTEMBER, 1859.

FALMOUTH, VIRGINIA.

Month and day.	Hour.	Barom'r corrected to 32° F.	Thermometer.	Force of vapor.	Cloudiness.	Motion of clouds.	Winds.	Relative humidity.	REMARKS.
Sept. 14	9 p. m.		63						Rain from 3 a. m. the 16th to 6 p. m. on the 17th; amount, 4.30 inches.
Sept. 15	7 a. m.		52						
	2 p. m.		70						
	9 p. m.		60						20th. Rain from 1 to 6 p. m.; amount, 0.85 inch.
Sept. 16	7 a. m.		62						
	2 p. m.		65						Rain from 1 p. m. the 21st to 4½ p. m. on the 22d; amount 2.65 inches.
	9 p. m.		64						
Sept. 17	7 a. m.		64						
	2 p. m.		69						24th and 25th. Drops of rain several times during the day.
	9 p. m.		66						
Sept. 18	7 a. m.		65						
	2 p. m.		79						
	9 p. m.		67						
Sept. 19	7 a. m.		70						
	2 p. m.		82						
	9 p. m.		71						
Sept. 20	7 a. m.		70						
	2 p. m.		71						
	9 p. m.		71						
Sept. 21	7 a. m.		70						
	2 p. m.		76						
	9 p. m.		72						
Sept. 22	7 a. m.		68						
	2 p. m.		69						
	9 p. m.		68						
Sept. 23	7 a. m.		70						
	2 p. m.		78						
	9 p. m.		67						
Sept. 24	7 a. m.		66						
	2 p. m.		76						
	9 p. m.		64						

FREDERICKSBURG, VIRGINIA.

Month and day.	Hour.	Barom'r corrected to 32° F.	Thermometer.	Force of vapor.	Cloudiness.	Motion of clouds.	Winds.	Relative humidity.	REMARKS.
Sept. 14	9 p. m.				9		NE. 2		14th. Pleasant; thermometer 78° at 5 p. m.
Sept. 15	7 a. m.				3		NE. 2		
	2 p. m.				7		NE. 3		15th. Pleasant; thermometer 74° at 4 p. m.
	9 p. m.				10		NE. 2		
Sept. 16	7 a. m.				10		NE. 1		16th. Cool; began to rain at 0.30 p. m.; thermometer 67° at 3 p. m.
	2 p. m.				10		NE. 3		
	9 p. m.				10		NW. 4		
Sept. 17	7 a. m.				10		NW. 5		17th. Cool; rain till 3 p. m.; temperature 68° at 3 p. m.
	2 p. m.				10		NW. 5		
	9 p. m.				10		NW. 1		18th. Warm; thermometer 83° at 4 p. m.
Sept. 18	7 a. m.				0		NE. 1		
	2 p. m.				0		NE. 2		19th. Temperature 82° at 4 p. m; storm commenced at 5 a. m.
	9 p. m.				0		SE. 1		
Sept. 19	7 a. m.				0		S. 1		20th. Cool; thermometer at 4 p. m., 74°.
	2 p. m.				5		S. 1		
	9 p. m.				10		E. 2		21st. Thermometer 83° at 4 p. m.
Sept. 20	7 a. m.				10		E. 1		22d. Cool; thermometer 73° at 4 p. m.; storm ended at 5 p. m.
	2 p. m.				10		E. 2		
	9 p. m.				10		E. 1		23d. Pleasant; thermometer 77° at 4 p. m.
Sept. 21	7 a. m.				10		NE. 1		
	2 p. m.				10		S. 3		24th. Pleasant; thermometer 78° at 3 p. m.
	9 p. m.				10		S. 2		
Sept. 22	7 a. m.				10		SW. 1		25th. Pleasant; thermometer 77° at 4 p. m
	2 p. m.				10		E. 2		
	9 p. m.				10		NE. 1		
Sept. 23	7 a. m.				3		N. 1		
	2 p. m.				6		N. 2		
	9 p. m.				10		NE. 0		

STORMS Nos. 2 AND 3, SEPTEMBER, 1859.

FREDERICKSBURG, VIRGINIA—Continued.

Month and day.	Hour.	Barom'r corrected to 32° F.	Thermometer.	Force of vapor.	Cloudiness.	Motion of clouds.	Winds.	Relative humidity.	REMARKS.
Sept. 21	7 a. m.	......	......	......	10	....	NE. 1	......	
	2 p. m.	......	......	......	9	....	SE. 2	......	
	9 p. m.	......	......	......	9	....	SE. 1	......	

LEWINSVILLE, VIRGINIA.

Month and day.	Hour.	Barom'r corrected to 32° F.	Thermometer.	Force of vapor.	Cloudiness.	Motion of clouds.	Winds.	Relative humidity.	REMARKS.
Sept. 14	7 a. m.	......	60	......	Cu. 0	....	NE. 1	......	Rain from the 16th to the 19th inclusive; amount, 5.44 inches.
Sept. 15	7 a. m.	......	49	......	St. 9	....	SE. 0	......	
	2 p. m.	......	64	......	Cir. 2	....	SE. 0	......	
	9 p. m.	......	57	......	Cir. st. 4	....	NE. 1	......	
Sept. 16	7 a. m.	......	54	......	Nim. 10	Rain......	ESE. 2	......	
	2 p. m.	......	65	......	Nim. 10	Rain......	SE. 2	......	
	9 p. m.	......	60	......	Nim. 10	Rain......	NE. 1	......	
Sept. 17	7 a. m.	......	64	......	Nim. 10	Rain......	NE. 1	......	
	2 p. m.	......	60	......	Nim. 10	Rain......	N. 0	......	
	9 p. m.	......	60	......	Nim. 10	Rain......	NE. 1	......	
Sept. 18	7 a. m.	......	62	......	....	....	....	......	
	2 p. m.	......	72	......	....	....	....	......	
	9 p. m.	......	63	......	....	....	....	......	
Sept. 19	7 a. m.	......	60	......	Cir. 8	....	NE. 1	......	
	2 p. m.	......	82	......	Cu. 5	....	E. 2	......	
	9 p. m.	......	69	......	Cir. 8	....	NE. 2	......	
Sept. 20	7 a. m.	......	60	......	Cir. 6	....	ESE. 0	......	
	2 p. m.	......	72½	......	Cu. 5	....	E. 2	......	
	9 p. m.	......	68	......	Nim. 10	Rain......	ENE. 2	......	
Sept. 21	7 a. m.	......	72½	......	Nim. 10	....	E. 0	......	
	2 p. m.	......	77	......	0	....	E. 2	......	
	9 p. m.	......	69	......	Nim. 10	....	S. 2	......	
Sept. 22	7 a. m.	......	72	......	Nim. 10	....	W. 1	......	
	2 p. m.	......	67	......	Nim. 10	....	W. 1	......	
	9 p. m.	......	64	......	0	Clear	W. 1	......	
Sept. 23	7 a. m.	......	65	......	Cu. nim. 8	....	NWN. 1	......	
	2 p. m.	......	70	......	Cu. 6	....	SW. 1	......	
	9 p. m.	......	66½	......	Nim. 10	Sprinkle...	WNW. 0	......	
Sept. 24	7 a. m.	......	63	......	Cir. st. 8	....	WNW. 1	......	
	2 p. m.	......	72	......	Cu. 9	....	W. 2	......	
	9 p. m.	......	63	......	Nim. 5	....	NW. 0	......	

MONTROSS, VIRGINIA.

Month and day.	Hour.	Barom'r corrected to 32° F.	Thermometer.	Force of vapor.	Cloudiness.	Motion of clouds.	Winds.	Relative humidity.	REMARKS.
Sept. 14	9 p. m.	......	60	.456	St. 10	W. 3	W. 2	88	Rain from 9 a. m. the 16th to 7 p. m. on the 17th; amount, 2.20 inches. Storm commenced at 11 p. m. the 19th and ended at 4½ p. m. on the 22d; amount, 0.96 inch.
Sept. 15	7 a. m.	......	56	.308	St. 4	W. 1	NE. 12	69	
	2 p. m.	......	65	.451	Cir. st. 3	SE. 3	E. 6	73	
	9 p. m.	......	62	.460	Cir. st. 10	0	E. 8	83	
Sept. 16	7 a. m.	......	64	.596	Nim. 10	0	E. 4	100	
	2 p. m.	......	64	.596	Nim. 10	0	E. 15	100	
	9 p. m.	......	65	.618	Nim. 10	0	E. 15	100	
Sept. 17	7 a. m.	......	70	.733	Nim. 10	0	SE. 15	100	
	2 p. m.	......	66	.570	Nim. 10	0	NW. 25	89	
	9 p. m.	......	62	.523	Nim. 10	0	NW. 15	94	
Sept. 18	7 a. m.	......	62	.491	0	0	NW. 6	88	
	2 p. m.	......	71	.608	Cir. 4	W. 1	NW. 4	80	
	9 p. m.	......	62	.491	0	0	0	88	
Sept. 19	7 a. m.	......	63	.543	0	0	W. 4	94	
	2 p. m.	......	77	.717	Cu. 5	S. 2	S. 6	77	
	9 p. m.	......	70	.658	Cir. 9	0	E. 4	90	
Sept. 20	7 a. m.	......	68	.685	Nim. 10	0	0	100	
	2 p. m.	......	72	.745	Cu. st. 10	SW. 4	E. 6	95	
	9 p. m.	......	71	.720	Nim. 10	0	E. 4	95	

STORMS Nos. 2 AND 3, SEPTEMBER, 1859.

MONTROSS, VIRGINIA—Continued.

Month and day.	Hour.	Barom'r corrected to 32° F.	Thermometer.	Force of vapor.	Cloudiness.		Motion of clouds.		Winds.		Relative humidity.	REMARKS.
Sept. 21	7 a. m.	......	70	.733	St.	10	S.	2		0	100	
	2 p. m.	......	76	.812	St.	10	SE.	5	SE.	12	91	
	9 p. m.	......	71	.720	St.	9	S.	5	SE.	12	95	
Sept. 22	7 a. m.	......	72	.745	Cir. st.	10	S.	4		0	95	
	2 p. m.	......	68	.648	Cir.	10	SE.	4		0	95	
	9 p. m.	......	66	.604	Cir.	2		0		0	94	
Sept. 23	7 a. m.	......	05	.018	Nim.	10		0	W.	2	100	
	2 p. m.	......	75	.628	Cu.	8	NW.	3	W.	4	73	
	9 p. m.	......	66	.570		0		0		0	89	
Sept. 24	7 a. m.	......	64	.497	St.	10	W.	2		0	83	
	2 p. m.	......	72	.559	St.	6	W.	1		0	72	
	9 p. m.	......	64	.570	Nim.	10		0		0	89	

MONTVIEW, VIRGINIA.

Month and day.	Hour.	Barom'r corrected to 32° F.	Thermometer.	Force of vapor.	Cloudiness.		Motion of clouds.		Winds.		Relative humidity.	REMARKS.
Sept. 14	9 p. m.	......	65	......		0	....			2	......	Rain from 1 a. m. the 16th till 8 a.
Sept. 15	7 a. m.	......	56	......		0	....		N.	2	......	m. on the 17th ; amount, 4.50 (?)
	2 p. m.	......	71	......	Cir. st.	6	....		NE.	2	......	inches ; probably six inches of
	9 p. m.	......	56	......	Nim.	10	NE.	1	NE.	2	......	water fell during that period, for
Sept. 16	7 a. m.	......	56	......	Nim.	10	NE.	1	NE.	2	......	the rain gauge was running over
	2 p. m.	......	61	......	Nim.	10	NE.	1		2	......	at the time of measurement.
	9 p. m.	......	60	......		10	NE.	1		2	......	Heavy rain from 1 a. m. the 20th
Sept. 17	7 a. m.	......	60	......		10	NW.	7	NW.	8	......	to 6 p. m. on the 21st; amount,
	2 p. m.	......	70	......	Cu.	6	NW.	2	NW.	4	......	2 30 inches.
	9 p. m.	......	62	......		0	....		N.	2	......	Showery from the 22d to the 25th,
Sept. 18	7 a. m.	......	60	......		0	....		W.	2	......	inclusive ; amount, 1.50 inch.
	2 p. m.	......	74	......	Cir. st.	4	....		W.	2	......	
	9 p. m.	......	65	......		0	....		W.	2	......	
Sept. 19	7 a. m.	......	58	......		0	....			2	......	
	2 p. m.	......	80	......		0	....		SW.	2	......	
	9 p. m.	......	69	......	Nim.	8	SE.	1	S.	2	......	
Sept. 20	7 a. m.	......	60	......	Nim.	10	SE.	1	S.	2	......	
	2 p. m.	......	71	......	Nim.	10	SE.	1	S.	2	......	
	9 p. m.	......	70	......	Nim.	10		1	SE.	2	......	
Sept. 21	7 a. m.	......	70	......		10		1	SE.	2	......	
	2 p. m.	......	76	......		10		1	SE.	2	......	
	9 p. m.	......	70	......		10		1		2	......	
Sept. 22	7 a. m.	......	64	......		10	S.	1	S.	2	......	
	2 p. m.	......	75	......	Cu.	6	SW.	1	SW.	2	......	
	9 p. m.	......	65	......		0	....		SW.	2	......	
Sept. 23	7 a. m.	......	64	......		10	SW.	1	SW.	2	......	
	2 p. m.	......	77	......	Nim.	8		1		2	......	
	9 p. m.	......	66	......	Nim.	10	S.	1		2	......	
Sept. 24	7 a. m.	......	63	......		10		1		2	......	
	2 p. m.	......	76	......		10		1		2	......	
	9 p. m.	......	65	......		10		1		2	......	

MUSTAPHA, VIRGINIA.

Month and day.	Hour.	Barom'r corrected to 32° F.	Thermometer.	Force of vapor.	Cloudiness.		Motion of clouds.		Winds.		Relative humidity.	REMARKS.
Sept. 15	7 a. m.	......	......	......		7	....		S.	2	......	14th. Cool morning.
	2 p. m.	......	......	......		3	....		SW.	3	......	15th. Cool and dry.
Sept. 16	7 a. m.	......	......	......		0	....		N.	6	......	16th. Appearance of rain.
	2 p. m.	......	......	......		0	....		N.	6	......	17th. Appearance of rain.
Sept. 17	7 a. m.	......	......	......		0	....		S.	6	......	18th. Foggy morning.
	2 p. m.	......	......	......		7	....		S.	1	......	19th. Began to rain at 5 p. m. and
Sept. 18	7 a. m.	......	......	......		0	....		N.	2	......	continued at intervals during the
	2 p. m.	......	......	......		5	....		NW.	5	......	night, accompanied by distant
Sept. 19	7 a. m.	......	......	......		9	....		N.	2	......	thunder.
	2 p. m.	......	......	......		10	....		SW.	2	......	20th. Showery.

STORMS Nos. 2 AND 3, SEPTEMBER, 1859.

MUSTAPHA, VIRGINIA—Continued.

Month and day.	Hour.	Barom'r corrected to 32° F.	Thermometer.	Force of vapor.	Cloudiness.	Motion of clouds.	Winds.	Relative humidity.	REMARKS.
Sept. 20	7 a. m.	......	......	......	10	....	S. 5	......	21st Heavy thunder shower in the
	2 p. m.	......	......	......	10	....	S. 4	......	night.
Sept. 21	7 a. m.	......	......	......	10	....	0	......	22d. Some rain in the night.
	2 p. m.	......	......	......	6	....	S. 2	......	24th. Sultry and rainy.
Sept. 22	7 a. m.	......	......	......	10	....	S. 1	......	25th. A little rainy.
	2 p. m.	......	......	......	8	....	S. 2	......	
Sept. 23	7 a. m.	......	......	......	10	....	S. 5	......	
	2 p. m.	......	......	......	10	....	S. 2	......	
Sept. 24	7 a. m.	......	......	......	10	....	S. 1	......	
	2 p. m.	......	......	......	9	....	SW. 2	......	

POPLAR GROVE, VIRGINIA.

Month and day.	Hour.	Barom'r corrected to 32° F.	Thermometer.	Force of vapor.	Cloudiness.	Motion of clouds.	Winds.	Relative humidity.	REMARKS.
Sept. 14	9 p. m.	......	55	......	0	0	0	......	Rain from 12 a. m. the 16th to 9
Sept. 15	7 a. m.	......	55	......	Cir. st. 8	SW. 3	E. 2	......	a. m. on the 17th; amount, 2
	2 p. m.	......	78	......	Cir. cu. 7	SW. 3	E. 4	......	inches.
	9 p. m.	......	63	......	Cir. st. 10	0	E. 1	......	20th. Rain from 6 a. m. till 2½ p.
Sept. 16	7 a. m.	......	65	......	Cir. st. 10	SSE. 2	E. 2	......	m.; amount, 1.50 inch.
	2 p. m.	......	67	......	Nim. 10	Dense, raining	W. 2	......	21st. Rain from 5 to 6 a. m. and 6 to 8 p. m; amount, 1.00 inch.
	9 p. m.	......	62	......	St. 10	Dense 0	0	......	23d. Rain from 5 to 6 a. m.;
Sept. 17	7 a. m.	......	62	......	St. 10	0	W. 1	......	amount, 0.33 inch.
	2 p. m.	......	71	......	Cu. st. 9	N. 3	W. 2	......	24th. Rain from 4 to 8 p. m.;
	9 p. m.	......	62	......	Fog 10	Dense 0	0	......	amount, 1.00 inch.
Sept. 18	7 a. m.	......	61	......	Fog 10	Dense 0	E. 2	......	
	2 p. m.	......	75	......	Cir. 2	SW. 3	E. 2	......	
	9 p. m.	......	61	......	0	0	E. 1	......	
Sept. 19	7 a. m.	......	63	......	Cir. 2	W. 2	E. 1	......	
	2 p. m.	......	77	......	Cu. st. 9	SW. 4	E. 1	......	
	9 p. m.	......	69	......	St. 10	Dense 0	E. 1	......	
Sept. 20	7 a. m.	......	68	......	St. 10	SE. 3	E. 1	......	
	2 p. m.	......	73	......	Cu. st. 10	S. 4	W. 2	......	
	9 p. m.	......	67	......	Cir. st. 2	W. 2	W. 1	......	
Sept. 21	7 a. m.	......	66	......	St. 10	NE. 3	W. 1	......	
	2 p. m.	......	77	......	Cir. cu. 3	E. 3	W. 3	......	
	9 p. m.	......	67	......	St. 4	W. 2	W. 1	......	
Sept. 22	7 a. m.	......	63	......	Cu. st. 9	SW. 8	E. 1	......	
	2 p. m.	......	68	......	Cu. st. 10	W. 2	W. 2	......	
	9 p. m.	......	63	......	Cir. st. 10	Dense 0	0	......	
Sept. 23	7 a. m.	......	63	......	Cu. st. 10	W. & NE. 1	0	......	
	2 p. m.	......	68	......	Cir. cu. 9	SW. 4	W. 2	......	
	9 p. m.	......	60	......	St. 10	0	0	......	
Sept. 24	7 a. m.	......	61	......	Cir. cu. 8	NW. 3	0	......	
	2 p. m.	......	68	......	Cir. st. 10	NW. 2	W. 1	......	
	9 p. m.	......	59	......	Nim. 10	NW. 0	0	......	

PORTSMOUTH, VIRGINIA.

Month and day.	Hour.	Barom'r corrected to 32° F.	Thermometer.	Force of vapor.	Cloudiness.	Motion of clouds.	Winds.	Relative humidity.	REMARKS.
Sept. 14	9 p. m.	30.08	59	......	3	....	NW. 2	......	Rain from 8 a. m. the 16th to 9 a.
Sept. 15	7 a. m.	30.19	60	......	1	....	NE. 2	......	m. on the 17th; amount, 1.04
	2 p. m.	30.19	79	......	4	....	NE. 3	......	inch.
	9 p. m.	30.20	62	......	3	....	NE. 3	......	20th Showers; thunder and light-
Sept. 16	7 a. m.	30.13	60	......	9	....	NE. 4	......	ning at 10 p. m.; amount, 0.22
	2 p. m.	29.94	73	......	10	....	E. 4	......	inch.
	9 p. m.	29.98	69	......	10	....	SE. 4	......	21st. Showers; thunder and light-
Sept. 17	7 a. m.	29.49	70	......	4	....	SW. 4	......	ning at night; amount, 0.18 inch.
	2 p. m.	29.48	74	......	3	....	WSW. 5	......	24th. Showers at night; amount,
	9 p. m.	29.83	65	......	4	....	W. 3	......	0.27 inch.

STORMS Nos. 2 AND 3, SEPTEMBER, 1859.

PORTSMOUTH, VIRGINIA—Continued.

Month and day.	Hour.	Barom'r corrected to 32° F.	Thermometer.	Force of vapor.	Cloudiness.	Motion of clouds.	Winds.	Relative humidity.	REMARKS.
Sept. 18	7 a. m.	30.07	61	------	0	----------	NW. 3	------	
	2 p. m.	30.07	81	------	1	----------	NW. 1	------	
	9 p. m.	30.08	61	------	2	----------	W. 1	------	
Sept. 19	7 a. m.	29.94	62	------	1	----------	SW. 2	------	
	2 p. m.	29.91	83	------	1	----------	SW. 3	------	
	9 p. m.	29.91	65	------	1	----------	SW. 2	------	
Sept. 20	7 a. m.	29.89	64	------	6	----------	SE. 2	------	
	2 p. m.	29.76	85	------	2	----------	SE. 3	------	
	9 p. m.	29.66	71	------	5	----------	SE. 3	------	
Sept. 21	7 a. m.	29.78	70	------	6	----------	SSE. 2	------	
	2 p. m.	29.79	70	------	7	----------	SE. 3	------	
	9 p. m.	29.97	65	------	6	----------	SE. 2	------	
Sept. 22	7 a. m.	29.98	74	------	9	----------	SE. 2	------	
	2 p. m.	29.90	77	------	8	----------	SE. 2	------	
	9 p. m.	29.93	64	------	2	----------	SE. 2	------	
Sept. 23	7 a. m.	29.95	68	------	Fog --------	----------	------------	------	
	2 p. m.	29.94	78	------	2	----------	SE. 1	------	
	9 p. m.	29.87	64	------	1	----------	SE. 1	------	
Sept. 24	7 a. m.	29.98	68	------	5	----------	------------	------	
	2 p. m.	29.93	76	------	7	----------	SW. 2	------	
	9 p. m.	29.93	63	------	5	----------	E. 1	------	

ROUGEMONT, VIRGINIA.

Month and day.	Hour.	Barom'r corrected to 32° F.	Thermometer.	Force of vapor.	Cloudiness.	Motion of clouds.	Winds.	Relative humidity.	REMARKS.
Sept. 14	9 p. m.	------	66	------	Cir. st. 8	0	NE. 3	------	Began to rain in the night of the 14th, and ended at 10 a. m. on the 17th; amount, 4.90 inches.
Sept. 15	7 a. m.	------	56	------	Cir. cu. 3	W. 3	N. 3	------	
	2 p. m.	------	71	------	Cir. st. 10	W. 2	NE. 3	------	
	9 p. m.	------	60	------	Nim. 10	0	N. 2	------	Rain from 6 a. m. the 20th to 2½ p. m. on the 22d; amount, 5.20 inches.
Sept. 16	7 a. m.	------	59	------	Rain'g hard 10	----------	NE. 1	------	
	2 p. m.	------	69	------	Raining 10	----------	NE. 2	------	
	9 p. m.	------	64	------	Raining 10	----------	E. 2	------	23d. Showers last night; amount, 0.32 inch.
Sept. 17	7 a. m.	------	61	------	Rain 10	----------	NW. 8	------	
	2 p. m.	------	72	------	Cu. 5	NW. 6	NW. 5	------	24th. Showery; amount, 0 28 inch.
	9 p. m	------	68	------	Cu. 6	NW. 4	NW. 3	------	25th. Slight showers; amount, 0 30 inch.
Sept. 18	7 a. m.	------	64	------	Cir. 3	NW. 1	NE. 3	------	
	2 p. m.	------	78	------	Cir. st. 9	0	E. 1	------	
	9 p. m.	------	70	------	Cir. st. 4	W. 1	NW. 1	------	
Sept. 19	7 a. m.	------	64	------	Cir. 3	W. 2	W. 1	------	
	2 p. m.	------	------	------	------------	----------	------------	------	
	9 p. m.	------	74	------	Nim. 10	W. 3	SW. 2	------	
Sept. 20	7 a. m.	------	69	------	Nim. 10	0	NE. 1	------	
	2 p. m.	------	72	------	Rain 10	----------	NE. 1	------	
	9 p. m.	------	69	------	Rain 10	----------	NE. 1	------	
Sept. 21	7 a. m.	------	71	------	Heavy fog----	----------	S. 1	------	
	2 p. m.	------	74	------	Rain 10	----------	NE. 1	------	
	9 p. m.	------	71	------	Nim. 10	E. 6	E. 1	------	
Sept. 22	7 a. m.	------	68	------	Nim. 10	0	N. 1	------	
	2 p. m.	------	78	------	Nim. 10	SE. 3	SE. 3	------	
	9 p. m.	------	69	------	St. 4	0	SE. 2	------	
Sept. 23	7 a. m.	------	------	------	------------	----------	------------	------	
	2 p. m.	------	------	------	------------	----------	------------	------	
	9 p. m.	------	------	------	------------	----------	------------	------	
Sept. 24	7 a. m.	------	64	------	Nim. 10	W. 3	W. 1	------	
	2 p. m.	------	------	------	------------	----------	------------	------	
	9 p. m.	------	64	------	Nim. 9	W. 2	W. 2	------	

STORMS Nos. 2 AND 3, SEPTEMBER, 1859.

SMITHFIELD, VIRGINIA.

Month and day.	Hour.	Barom'r corrected to 32° F.	Thermometer.	Force of vapor.	Cloudiness.	Motion of clouds.	Winds.	Relative humidity.	REMARKS.
Sept. 14	9 p. m.		61		Cir. st. 2	NW. 1	SE. 1		Rain from 7 a. m. the 16th to 9 a. m. on the 17th; amount, 0.935 inch.
Sept. 15	7 a. m.		61		Cu. st. 5	NE. 2	NE. 1		
	2 p. m.		70		Cu. nim. 9	E. 2	NE. 2		
	9 p. m.		67		Cu. nim. 4	NW. 1	E. 1		Rain from 4 p. m. the 20th till 4 p. m. on the 22d; amount, 1.407 inch.
Sept. 16	7 a. m.		69		Cu. nim. 10	E. 2	E. 2		
	2 p. m.		70.5		Cu. nim. 10	E. 2	E. 3		
	9 p. m.		68		Nim. 10		E. 3		23d. Rain in the night; amount, 0.010 inch.
Sept. 17	7 a. m.		72		Cu. nim. 10	S. 2	S. 3		
	2 p. m.		74		Cu. nim. 9	NW. 2	W. 3		24th. Began to rain at 4 p. m. and ended in the night; amount, 0.355 inch.
	9 p. m.		65		Cir. st. 2	N. 1	NW. 1		
Sept. 18	7 a. m.		64		Cu. cir. 1	NW. 1	N. 2		
	2 p. m.		73.8		Cir. st. 5	NW. 1	NE. 1		
	9 p. m.		65		Nim. st. 6		S. 1		
Sept. 19	7 a. m.		61.7		Cir. st. 2		S. 1		
	2 p. m.		77		Cir. cu. 6	SW. 1	SW. 1		
	9 p. m.		70.7		Cir. st. 2		S. 1		
Sept. 20	7 a. m.		70		Cir. nim. 10	S. 1	SE. 1		
	2 p. m.		78.3		Cu. nim. 9	SW. 1	S. 1		
	9 p. m.		73		Cu. nim 10	SW. 1	S. 2		
Sept. 21	7 a. m.		70		Nim. st. 10	SW. 1	S. 1		
	2 p. m.		73.5		Cu. nim. 10	S. 1	SE. 1		
	9 p. m.		70.5		Cir. nim. 10	S. 1	S. 2		
Sept. 22	7 a. m.		71		Nim. st. 10	S. 1	S. 1		
	2 p. m.		74.5		Nim. st. 10	S. 2	S. 1		
	9 p. m.		66.1		0		SW. 1		
Sept. 23	7 a. m.		64.5		Fog		SW. 1		
	2 p. m.		75		Cir cu. 5	NW. 1	NW. 1		
	9 p. m.		66.5		Cir. st. 1		S. 1		
Sept. 24	7 a m.		64.8		Cir. st. 7	NW. 1	NW. 1		

WESTWOOD, VIRGINIA.

Month and day.	Hour.	Barom'r corrected to 32° F.	Thermometer.	Force of vapor.	Cloudiness.	Motion of clouds.	Winds.	Relative humidity.	REMARKS.
Sept. 14	9 p. m.								16th. Cloudy; some rain; stormy night.
Sept. 15	7 a. m.								
	2 p. m.								17th. Rain till 1 p. m; amount, 1.375 inch.
	9 p. m.								
Sept. 16	7 a. m.						NE. 4		18th. Fine day.
	2 p. m.		71				NE. 4		19th. Foggy morning; rather cloudy; began to rain in the night.
	9 p. m.		67						
Sept. 17	7 a. m.		72						
	2 p. m.		76			NW. 7	NW. 35		20th. Rainy day; light showers; heavy at night; amount, 1.50 inch.
	9 p. m.		66						
Sept. 18	7 a. m.		60						
	2 p. m.		76						21st. Cloudy morning; light showers; rain at night.
	9 p. m.		68						
Sept. 19	7 a. m.		62						22d. Cloudy; showers; amount, 0.50 inch.
	2 p. m.		82						
	9 p. m.								23d. Clear.
Sept. 20	7 a. m.		70				S. 2		24th. Light showers about 7 a. m.; another at 4 p. m.; amount, 0.25 inch.
	2 p. m.		75				S. 2		
	9 p. m.		72						
Sept. 21	7 a. m.		71						25th. Clear and calm.
	2 p. m.		80				S. 2		
	9 p. m.		74						
Sept. 22	7 a. m.		72						
	2 p. m.		71				S. 2		
	9 p. m.		68						
Sept. 23	7 a m.		66						
	2 p. m.		79			NW. 2	N		
	9 p. m.		70						
Sept. 24	7 a. m.		64						
	2 p. m.		76			N			
	9 p. m.		64						

STORMS Nos. 2 AND 3, SEPTEMBER, 1859.

CHAPEL HILL, NORTH CAROLINA.

Month and day.	Hour.	Barom'r corrected to 32° F.	Thermometer.	Force of vapor.	Cloudiness.	Motion of clouds.	Winds.	Relative humidity.	REMARKS.
Sept. 14	9 p. m.	29.589	65	......	....	W. 1	W. 1	......	Began to rain at 6 a. m. the 16th and ended before day on the 17th; amount, 1.528 inch.
Sept. 15	7 a. m.	.696	62	......	10	NE. 2	NE. 2	......	19th. Colored halo at 7½ p. m; colors bright as ordinary rain bows, and about an arc of 60°.
	2 p. m.	.704	76	......	8	SE. 2	NE. 2	......	Began to rain at 6 a. m. the 20th; thunder in W. at 0.½ p. m; storm ended at 1 p. m. on the 21st; very dense fog at 6 p. m. on the 21st; amount, 1.486 inch.
	9 p. m.	.705	68	......	10	Invisible ..	N. 2	......	22d. Rain during the past night; amount of water included in the above.
Sept. 16	7 a. m.	.630	66	......	10	Invisible ..	NE. 2	......	
	2 p. m.	.526	70	......	10	Invisible ..	NE. 1	......	
	9 p. m.	.322	68	......	10	Invisible ..	E. 2	......	
Sept. 17	7 a. m.	.228	66	......	....	....	NW. 3	......	
	2 p. m.	.318	80	......	6	NW. 2	NW. 3	......	
	9 p. m.	.455	69	......	....	....	NW. 0	......	
Sept. 18	7 a. m.	.533	65	......	5	NW. 1	N. 2	......	
	2 p. m.	.518	78	......	7	SW. 1	NW. 1	......	
	9 p. m.	.506	65	......	....	....	S. 1	......	
Sept. 19	7 a. m.	.477	61	......	5	W. 1	W. 1	......	
	2 p. m.	.409	83	......	7	SW. 2	SW. 1	......	
	9 p. m.	.385	70	......	10	Invisible ..	E. 2	......	
Sept. 20	7 a. m.	.323	68	......	10	S. 2	S. 1	......	
	2 p. m.	.241	78	......	10	S. 2	S. 1	......	
	9 p. m.	.292	67	......	10	Invisible ..	NE. 1	......	
Sept. 21	7 a. m.	.330	72	......	10	Invisible ..	S. 1	......	
	2 p. m.	.297	74	......	10	S. 1	S. 1	......	
	9 p. m.	.351	71	......	....	....	SE. 2	......	
Sept. 22	7 a. m.	.434	69	......	10	S. 1	S. 1	......	
	2 p. m.	.429	80	......	7	SW. 1	S. 1	......	
	9 p. m.	.498	67	......	....	....	W. 1	......	
Sept. 23	7 a. m.	.570	65	......	3	W. 1	W. 1	......	
	2 p. m.	.565	78	......	8	SW. 1	SW. 1	......	
	9 p. m.	.575	68	......	....	....	SW. 1	......	
Sept. 24	7 a. m.	.575	66	......	10	N. 1	N. 1	......	
	2 p. m.	.511	76	......	6	W. 2	W. 2	......	
	9 p. m.	.507	65	......	3	W. 1	W. 2	......	

GREEN PLAINS, NORTH CAROLINA.

Month and day.	Hour.	Barom'r corrected to 32° F.	Thermometer.	Force of vapor.	Cloudiness.	Motion of clouds.	Winds.	Relative humidity.	REMARKS.
Sept. 14	9 p. m.	......	60	......	....	....	....	......	Rain on the 16th and 17th; amount, 1.30 inch.
Sept. 15	7 a. m.	......	60	......	....	....	....	......	Rain, accompanied by lightning, on the 20th, 21st, and 22d; amount, 1.67 inch.
	2 p. m.	......	72	......	....	....	....	......	
	9 p. m.	......	64	......	....	....	....	......	
Sept. 16	7 a. m.	......	64	......	....	....	....	......	
	2 p. m.	......	68	......	....	....	....	......	
	9 p. m.	......	68	......	....	....	....	......	
Sept. 17	7 a. m.	......	69	......	....	....	....	......	
	2 p. m.	......	80	......	....	....	....	......	
	9 p. m.	......	69	......	....	....	....	......	
Sept. 18	7 a. m.	......	70	......	....	....	....	......	
	2 p. m.	......	82	......	....	....	....	......	
	9 p. m.	......	64	......	....	....	....	......	
Sept. 19	7 a. m.	......	62	......	....	....	....	......	
	2 p. m.	......	80	......	....	....	....	......	
	9 p. m.	......	65	......	....	....	....	......	
Sept. 20	7 a. m.	......	70	......	....	....	....	......	
	2 p. m.	......	82	......	....	....	....	......	
	9 p. m.	......	70	......	....	....	....	......	
Sept. 21	7 a. m.	......	70	......	....	....	....	......	
	2 p. m.	......	76	......	....	....	....	......	
	9 p. m.	......	70	......	....	....	....	......	
Sept. 22	7 a. m.	......	72	......	....	....	....	......	
	2 p. m.	......	80	......	....	....	....	......	
	9 p. m.	......	62	......	....	....	....	......	
Sept. 23	7 a. m.	......	64	......	....	....	....	......	
	2 p. m.	......	80	......	....	....	....	......	

STORMS Nos. 2 AND 3, SEPTEMBER, 1859.

GREEN PLAINS, NORTH CAROLINA—Continued.

Month and day.	Hour.	Barom'r corrected to 32° F.	Thermometer.	Force of vapor.	Cloudiness.	Motion of clouds.	Winds.	Relative humidity.	REMARKS.
Sept. 23	9 p. m.	------	66	------	------	------	------	------	
Sept. 24	7 a. m.	------	64	------	------	------	------	------	
	2 p m.	------	82	------	------	------	------	------	
	9 p. m.	------	64	------	------	------	------	------	

MURFREESBOROUGH, NORTH CAROLINA.

Month and day.	Hour.	Barom'r corrected to 32° F.	Thermometer.	Force of vapor.	Cloudiness.	Motion of clouds.	Winds.	Relative humidity.	REMARKS.
Sept. 14	9 p. m.	------	------	------	------	------	------	------	16th. Rain from 6 a. m. till noon; amount, 0. 60 inch.
Sept. 15	7 a m.	29. 30	63	. 529	Cir. st. 3	W. 1	W. 1	89	
	2 p. m.	29. 23	76	. 691	Cu. 8	NE. 2	SE. 1	77	17th. Rain from 4 to 8 a. m.; amount, 0. 50 inch.
	9 p. m.	29. 24	68	. 682	0	------	NE. 1	90	
Sept. 16	7 a m.	29. 19	69	. 695	Nim. 10	E. 2	E. 2	95	Rain from 7 p. m. the 20th, to 9 a. m. on the 21st; amount, 1.30 inch.
	2 p. m.	29. 14	70	. 682	Cir. st. 10	NE. 3	NE. 3	90	
	9 p. m.	29. 09	69	. 695	Nim. 10	E. 2	E. 2	95	
Sept. 17	7 a. m.	28. 79	72	. 745	Nim. 10	SW. 4	SE. 4	95	22d. Rain from 6 a. m. to 1 p. m.; amount, 0. 70 inch.
	2 p m.	28. 86	82	. 787	Cu. 4	NW. 3	NW. 3	74	
	9 p. m.	28. 99	71	. 631	0	------	NW. 1	81	
Sept. 18	7 a. m.	29. 10	63	. 529	0	------	NW. 1	89	
	2 p. m.	29. 08	76	. 652	Cu. st. 2	0	NW. 1	73	
	9 p. m.	29. 09	68	. 644	0	------	NW. 1	86	
Sept. 19	7 a. m.	------	------	------	------	------	------	------	
	2 p. m.	------	------	------	------	------	------	------	
	9 p. m.	------	------	------	------	------	------	------	
Sept. 20	7 a. m.	28. 98	75	. 758	Cu. 8	SW. 2	SW. 1	90	
	2 p. m.	28. 86	85	. 891	Cu. st. 6	0	S. 1	79	
	9 p. m.	------	------	------	------	------	------	------	
Sept. 21	7 a. m.	29. 08	72	. 771	Nim. 10	S. 2	S. 1	95	
	2 p. m.	29. 07	77	. 841	Nim. 8	SW. 3	SE. 2	91	
	9 p. m.	28. 98	73	. 785	0	------	SE. 1	90	
Sept. 22	7 a. m.	28. 98	72	. 758	Nim. 10	SW. 2	SW. 1	90	
	2 p. m.	29. 03	75	. 758	Cir. st. 5	W. 1	S. 1	90	
	9 p. m.	29. 03	70	. 758	0	------	SW. 1	90	
Sept. 23	7 a. m.	------	------	------	------	------	------	------	
	2 p m.	------	------	------	------	------	------	------	
	9 p. m.	------	------	------	------	------	------	------	
Sept. 24	7 a. m.	29. 11	64	. 563	0	------	N. 1	94	
	2 p. m.	------	------	------	------	------	------	------	
	9 p. m.	------	------	------	------	------	------	------	

RALEIGH, NORTH CAROLINA.

Month and day.	Hour.	Barom'r corrected to 32° F.	Thermometer.	Force of vapor.	Cloudiness.	Motion of clouds.	Winds.	Relative humidity.	REMARKS.
Sept. 14	9 p. m.	------	------	------	1	------	0	------	14th and 15th. Pleasant.
Sept. 15	7 a. m.	------	------	------	0	------	0	------	16th. Rain from 7 a. m? to 6 p. m.?; strong wind in the night from NNE.
	2 p. m.	------	------	------	0	------	0	------	
	9 p. m.	------	------	------	0	------	0	------	
Sept. 16	7 a. m.	------	------	------	10	------	N. 3	------	17th. White clouds flying all day from NE. to SE.
	2 p. m.	------	------	------	10	------	NW. 3	------	
	9 p. m.	------	------	------	10	------	N. 3	------	18th. Cold; very cold from 5 to 9 a. m.
Sept. 17	7 a. m.	------	------	------	10	------	N. 3	------	
	2 p. m.	------	------	------	5	------	0	------	19th. Warm rain all day.
	9 p. m.	------	------	------	0	------	0	------	20th. Showery all day and night; clouds from W.
Sept. 18	7 a. m.	------	------	------	0	------	0	------	
	2 p. m.	------	------	------	0	------	0	------	21st. Cloudy.
	9 p. m.	------	------	------	0	------	0	------	22d. Sunshine all day.
Sept. 19	7 a. m.	------	------	------	10	------	W. 3	------	23d. Very warm for the season; thermometer 80° at 2 p. m.
	2 p. m.	------	------	------	10	------	W. 2	------	
	9 p. m.	------	------	------	9	------	W. 4	------	24th and 25th. Pleasant.
Sept. 20	7 a. m.	------	------	------	10	------	0	------	
	2 p. m.	------	------	------	9	------	0	------	
	9 p. m.	------	------	------	10	------	0	------	

STORMS Nos. 2 AND 3, SEPTEMBER, 1859.

RALEIGH, NORTH CAROLINA—Continued.

Month and day.	Hour.	Barom'r corrected to 32° F.	Thermometer.	Force of vapor.	Cloudiness.	Motion of clouds.	Winds.	Relative humidity.	REMARKS.
Sept. 21	7 a. m.	------	------	------	10	----------	SW. 2	------	
	2 p. m.	------	------	------	9	----------	S. 1	------	
	9 p. m.	------	------	------	5	----------	SW. 1	------	
Sept. 22	7 a. m.	------	------	------	0	----------	SW. 1	------	
	2 p. m.	------	------	------	1	----------	W. 2	------	
	9 p. m.	------	------	------	0	----------	0	------	
Sept. 23	7 a. m.	------	------	------	0	----------	0	------	
	2 p. m.	------	------	------	1	----------	0	------	
	9 p. m.	------	------	------	0	----------	W. 1	------	
Sept. 24	7 a. m.	------	------	------	1	----------	S. 1	------	
	2 p. m.	------	------	------	1	----------	0	------	
	9 p. m.	------	------	------	0	----------	0	------	

AIKEN, SOUTH CAROLINA.

Month and day.	Hour.	Barom'r corrected to 32° F.	Thermometer.	Force of vapor.	Cloudiness.	Motion of clouds.	Winds.	Relative humidity.	REMARKS.
Sept. 14	9 p. m.	------	72	------	0	----------	E. 2	------	15th. Amount of rain, 0. 85 inch.
Sept. 15	7 a. m.	------	------	------	----------	----------	----------	------	16th. Amount, 0. 94 inch.
	2 p. m.	------	72	------	Nim. 10	----------	E. 1	------	
	9 p. m.	------	66	------	Nim. 10	----------	NE. 3	------	
Sept. 16	7 a. m.	------	73	------	Nim. 10	----------	NE. 4	------	
	2 p. m.	------	80	------	Nim. 10	----------	SE. 4	------	
	9 p. m.	------	66	------	0	----------	W. 4	------	
Sept. 17	7 a. m.	------	67	------	0	----------	W. 3	------	
	2 p. m.	------	81	------	0	----------	W. 3	------	
	9 p. m.	------	69	------	Cir. cu. 2	----------	NW. 1	------	
Sept. 18	7 a. m.	------	69	------	Cu. 4	----------	NE. 3	------	
	2 p. m.	------	86	------	Cu. 5	----------	E. 2	------	
	9 p. m.	------	72	------	0	----------	E. 3	------	
Sept. 19	7 a. m.	------	69	------	Cir. 4	----------	E. 2	------	
	2 p. m.	------	------	------	----------	----------	----------	------	
	9 p. m.	------	------	------	----------	----------	----------	------	
Sept. 20	7 a. m.	------	------	------	----------	----------	----------	------	
	2 p. m.	------	------	------	----------	----------	----------	------	
	9 p. m.	------	------	------	----------	----------	----------	------	
Sept. 21	7 a. m.	------	------	------	----------	----------	----------	------	
	2 p. m.	------	------	------	----------	----------	----------	------	
	9 p. m.	------	------	------	----------	----------	----------	------	
Sept. 22	7 a. m.	------	61	------	0	----------	----------	------	
	2 p. m.	------	74	------	5	----------	----------	------	
	9 p. m.	------	61	------	0	----------	----------	------	
Sept. 23	7 a. m.	------	------	------	----------	----------	----------	------	
	2 p. m.	------	80	------	0	----------	----------	------	
	9 p. m.	------	61	------	0	----------	----------	------	
Sept. 24	7 a. m.	------	61	------	0	----------	----------	------	
	2 p. m.	------	79	------	Cir. 1	----------	SW. 3	------	
	9 p. m.	------	64	------	0	----------	SW. 1	------	

ALL SAINTS, SOUTH CAROLINA.

Month and day.	Hour.	Barom'r corrected to 32° F.	Thermometer.	Force of vapor.	Cloudiness.	Motion of clouds.	Winds.	Relative humidity.	REMARKS.
Sept. 14	9 p. m.	29. 96	62	. 491	----------	----------	S. 1	88	16th. Amount of rain, 0. 22 inch.
Sept. 15	7 a. m.	30. 01	67	. 626	3	W. 1	N. 1	95	20th. Amount of rain, 1. 32 inch.
	2 p. m.	30. 03	79	. 945	0	----------	SE. 1	95	21st. Amount of rain, 1. 90 inch.
	9 p. m.	29. 94	77	. 841	0	----------	E. 1	91	
Sept. 16	7 a. m.	29. 95	79	. 900	----------	----------	S. 1	91	
	2 p. m.	29. 88	83	1. 079	----------	----------	S. 3	96	
	9 p. m.	29. 78	80	. 931	----------	----------	SW. 3	91	
Sept. 17	7 a. m.	29. 79	72	. 745	----------	----------	W. 2	95	
	2 p. m.	29. 78	82	1. 014	----------	----------	W. 2	96	
	9 p. m.	29. 83	71	. 720	----------	----------	W. 1	95	

STORMS Nos. 2 AND 3, SEPTEMBER, 1859.

ALL SAINTS, SOUTH CAROLINA—Continued.

Month and day.	Hour.	Barom'r corrected to 32° F.	Thermometer.	Force of vapor.	Cloudiness.	Motion of clouds.	Winds.	Relative humidity.	REMARKS.
Sept. 18	7 a. m.	29.91	68	.648	....	....	N. 1	95	
	2 p. m.	29.91	78	.914	....	....	S. 1	95	
	9 p. m.	29.93	68	.612	....	....	S. 1	90	
Sept. 19	7 a. m.	29.90	67	.626	....	....	S. 1	95	
	2 p. m.	29.81	77	.884	....	....	S. 1	95	
	9 p. m.	29.81	74	.798	....	....	S. 1	95	
Sept. 20	7 a. m.	29.73	76	.854	....	....	S. 2	95	
	2 p. m.	29.68	80	.931	....	....	S. 1	91	
	9 p. m.	29.70	72	.706	....	....	S. 1	90	
Sept. 21	7 a. m.	29.73	74	.758	....	....	SW. 1	90	
	2 p. m.	29.72	78	.785	5	SW. 1	SW. 2	82	
	9 p. m.	29.79	74	.758	....	....	S. 1	90	
Sept. 22	7 a. m.	29.85	69	.635	8	W. 2	NW. 1	90	
	2 p. m.	29.98	78	.914	4	W. 1	S. 2	95	
	9 p. m.	29.93	67	.591	1	....	S. 1	89	
Sept. 23	7 a. m.	30.01	67	.591	1	W. 1	W. 1	89	
	2 p. m.	30.05	77	.841	2	W. 1	W. 1	91	
	9 p. m.	29.99	78	.870	....	....	S. 1	91	
Sept. 24	7 a. m.	29.96	68	.577	....	....	S. 1	85	
	2 p. m.	29.89	78	.588	3	S. 1	S. 1	62	
	9 p. m.	29.89	70	.621	....	....	S. 1	85	

CHARLESTON, SOUTH CAROLINA.

Month and day.	Hour.	Barom'r corrected to 32° F.	Thermometer.	Force of vapor.	Cloudiness.	Motion of clouds.	Winds.	Relative humidity.	REMARKS.
Sept. 14	9 p. m.	30.07	78	......	....	....	....	......	15th. Rain, accompanied by thunder; amount, 0.65 inch.
Sept. 15	7 a. m.	30.10	76	......	....	....	E...........	......	16th. Gusty showers; amount, 0.05 inch.
	2 p. m.	30.12	80	......	....	....	Cloudy......	......	19th. Rain, accompanied by thunder; amount, 0.30 inch.
	9 p. m.	30.11	78	......	....	....	....	......	20th. Rain, with thunder; amount, 0.75 inch.
Sept. 16	7 a. m.	30.16	80	......	....	....	SE..........	......	
	2 p. m.	29.94	84	......	....	....	Cloudy......	......	
	9 p. m.	29.86	80	......	....	....	Fresh	......	
Sept. 17	7 a. m.	29.90	73	......	....	....	NW	......	
	2 p. m.	29.90	83	......	....	....	Clear	......	
	9 p. m.	29.99	78	......	....	....	Calm	......	
Sept. 18	7 a. m.	30.00	72	......	....	....	NE	......	
	2 p. m.	30.01	81	......	....	....	Clear	......	
	9 p. m.	30.03	76	......	....	....	Clear	......	
Sept. 19	7 a. m.	30.01	72	......	....	....	NE	......	
	2 p. m.	29.92	80	......	....	....	Clear	......	
	9 p. m.	29.89	76	......	....	....	Calm	......	
Sept. 20	7 a. m.	29.96	79	......	....	....	S...........	......	
	2 p. m.	29.78	84	......	....	....	Cloudy......	......	
	9 p. m.	29.83	78	......	....	....	Gusty......	......	
Sept. 21	7 a. m.	29.82	76	......	....	....	SW..........	......	
	2 p. m.	29.85	80	......	....	....	Cloudy......	......	
	9 p. m.	29.90	76	......	....	....	Clear	......	
Sept. 22	7 a. m.	29.96	68	......	....	....	SE	......	
	2 p. m.	30.00	75	......	....	....	Clear	......	
	9 p. m.	30.07	75	......	....	....	Calm	......	
Sept. 23	7 a. m.	30.12	66	......	....	....	W...........	......	
	2 p. m.	30.08	78	......	....	....	Clear	......	
	9 p. m.	30.05	74	......	....	....	Calm	......	
Sept. 24	7 a. m.	30.10	66	......	....	....	W...........	......	
	2 p. m.	30.00	79	......	....	....	Clear	......	
	9 p. m.	30.01	74	......	....	....	Calm	......	

STORMS Nos. 2 AND 3, SEPTEMBER, 1859.

COLUMBIA, SOUTH CAROLINA.*

Month and day.	Hour.	Barom'r corrected to 32° F.	Thermometer.	Force of vapor.	Cloudiness.	Motion of clouds.	Winds.	Relative humidity.	REMARKS.
Sept. 14	9 p. m.	------	71	.720	Nim. 10	----------	------------	95	Storm commenced at 4½ p. m. the
Sept. 15	7 a. m.	------	70	.658	0	0	E. 3	90	15th, ended in the night of the
	2 p. m.	------	83	.983	Nim. 8	----------	3	87	17th; amount, 1.80 inch.
	9 p. m.	------	72	.745	------------	----------	2	95	19th. Began to rain in the night,
Sept. 16	7 a. m.	------	73	.732	Cir. 3	0	W. 6	90	continued during greater part of
	2 p. m.	------	78	.870	10	----------	5	91	next day, and ended in the night
	9 p. m.	------	68	.648	0	----------	12	95	of the 21st; amount, 1.00 inch.
Sept. 17	7 a. m.	------	66	.604	Nim. 10	0	NE. 0	94	
	2 p. m.	------	85	.942	Cir. st. 3	----------	NW. 3	76	
	9 p. m.	------	72	.706	------------	----------	------------	90	
Sept. 18	7 a. m.	------	65	.583	0	0	SE ---------	94	
	2 p. m.	------	82	.996	Cir. 4	----------	SW. 0	91	
	9 p. m.	------	73	.771	Nim. 10	----------	------------	95	
Sept. 19	7 a. m.	------	69	.671	Cir. 4	0	------------	95	
	2 p. m.	------	83	1.030	Cu. st. 4	----------	SE. 3	91	
	9 p. m.	------	72	.706	Cir. st. 6	0	------------	90	
Sept. 20	7 a. m.	------	73	.732	Nim. 7	----------	2	90	
	2 p. m.	------	79	.945	0	0	S. 0	95	
	9 p. m.	------	69	.671	Nim. 10	0	------------	95	
Sept. 21	7 a. m.	------	72	.785	Cu. st. 4	NE. 2	NW. 0	100	
	2 p. m.	------	81	.963	------------	----------	SW. 3	91	
	9 p. m.	------	74	.758	10	----------	------------	90	
Sept. 22	7 a. m.	------	69	.635	5	----------	W. 2	90	
	2 p. m.	------	78	.870	------------	----------	2	91	
	9 p. m.	------	68	.612	Cir. 3	0	------------	90	
Sept. 23	7 a. m.	------	67	.556	0	0	NW. 1	84	
	2 p. m.	------	82	.904	------------	----------	W----------	83	
	9 p. m.	------	64	.563	------------	----------	------------	94	
Sept. 24	7 a. m.	------	59	.469	Cir. st. 3	----------	0	94	
	2 p. m.	------	78	.870	------------	----------	NW. 3	91	
	9 p. m.	------	70	.658	0	----------	------------	90	

* White, observer.

ST. JOHN'S, SOUTH CAROLINA.

Month and day.	Hour.	Barom'r corrected to 32° F.	Thermometer.	Force of vapor.	Cloudiness.	Motion of clouds.	Winds.	Relative humidity.	REMARKS.
Sept. 14	9 p. m.	30.14	72	.631	0	----------	SE. 2	81	15th. Drizzling rain at 1.15 p. m.;
Sept. 15	7 a. m.	------	------	------	Nim. 8	----------	NE. 2	------	distant thunder from 6 to 7 a. m.
	2 p. m.	30.23	81	.873	Nim. 10	W. 1	NE. 2	83	16th. Between 8 and 9 a. m. wind
	9 p. m.	30.21	76	.812	Nim. 10	----------	SE. 2	91	came up in scuds with appear-
Sept. 16	7 a. m.	30.14	76	.854	Nim. 9	SW. 2	SE. 1	95	ances of an approaching gale,
	2 p. m.	30.03	84	.891	Nim. 10	SW. 4	SE. 4	79	and continued all day; while
	9 p. m.	29.92	80	.800	Nim. 9	----------	E. 5	78	the higher clouds passed slowly
Sept. 17	7 a. m.	29.96	71	.644	Cir. st. 2	----------	NW. 2	86	from SW., light, watery, lower
	2 p. m	30.02	82	.650	0	----------	NW. 3	59	clouds passed in the same direc-
	9 p. m.	30.03	70	.682	0	----------	W. 2	90	tion very quickly, at a velocity
Sept. 18	7 a. m.	30.04	66	.591	Cir. st. 2	----------	NE. 1	89	of about 7 or 8; barometer fell
	2 p. m.	30.13	83	.624	Cir. st. 6	NW. 2	NW. 2	59	very quickly after 7 a. m. to
	9 p. m.	30.07	70	.658	0	----------	SE. 2	90	about what is noted at 2 p. m.;
Sept. 19	7 a. m.	30.00	65	.549	Cir. st. 2	W. 1	SE. 2	89	appearance quite threatening
	2 p. m.	30.03	83	.624	Cir. 2	W. 1	SE. 3	59	late at night, but passed off be-
	9 p. m.	29.96	72	.668	Nim. 6	----------	SE. 2	86	fore morning; amount, 0.09 inch.
Sept. 20	7 a. m.	29.88	74	.798	Nim. 10	----------	SW. 5	95	19th. Distant diffused lightning
	2 p. m.	29.87	81	.873	Nim. 9	W. 2	SW. 4	83	near the horizon SW. from 9 to
	9 p. m.	29.88	75	.785	Nim. 7	----------	SE. 2	90	11 p. m.
Sept. 21	7 a. m.	29.90	74	.798	Nim. 10	SW. 3	SE. 1	59	20th. Shower at 5.40 a. m.; soon
	2 p. m.	29.93	82	.624	Cir. 3	SW. 3	SW. 3	59	after this the wind rose and was
	9 p. m.	29.98	74	.718	Nim. 10	----------	SW. 2	86	quite squally, blowing about
Sept. 22	7 a. m.	30.00	67	.591	Cir. st. 2	----------	NW. 2	89	the tree tops in scuds; occasional
	2 p. m.	30.08	77	.601	Cir. 4	SW. 2	SW. 2	65	thunder from 9 to 11 a. m., and
	9 p. m.	30.12	69	.621	0	----------	SW. 2	85	diffused lightning late at night;
Sept. 23	7 a. m.	30.12	61	.505	Cir. st. 2	----------	NW. 1	94	showery; amount, 0.54 inch.

STORMS Nos. 2 AND 3, SEPTEMBER, 1859.

ST. JOHN'S SOUTH CAROLINA—Continued.

Month and day.	Hour.	Barom'r corrected to 32° F.	Thermometer.	Force of vapor.	Cloudiness.	Motion of clouds.	Winds.	Relative humidity.	REMARKS.
Sept. 23	2 p. m.	30.19	77	.564	Cir. 1	W. 2	NW. 2	61	21st. Rain about 4 a. m., and thunder from 7 to 8 a. m.; rain again at 9.45 p. m.; thunder and diffused lightning; amount 0.22 inch.
	9 p. m.	30.14	66	.536	0	----------	SW. 2	84	
Sept. 24	7 a. m.	30.08	60	.473	0	----------	NW. 1	88	
	2 p. m.	30.09	79	.564	Cir. 3	W. 2	NW. 2	61	
	9 p. m.	30.05	68	.599	0	----------	SE. 2	85	

23d. Meteor about 9.30 p. m., passing from SW. to NE., not very large or brilliant, and no explosion heard after it.

ATHENS, GEORGIA.

Month and day.	Hour.	Barom'r corrected to 32° F.	Thermometer.	Force of vapor.	Cloudiness.	Motion of clouds.	Winds.	Relative humidity.	REMARKS.
Sept. 14	9 p. m.	29.26	71.8	.552	0	----------	0	71	Rain from 11.40 a. m. the 15th to 6.30 p. m. on the 16th; amount, 3.104 inches. Rain from 2.20 p. m the 19th to 7½ a. m. on the 20th; amount, 0.667 inch.
Sept. 15	7 a. m.	29.33	65	.489	Cir. st. 4	0	NE. 3	79	
	2 p. m.	29.35	69	.670	Nim. 10	----------	0	94	
	9 p. m.	29.32	66	.615	Nim. 10	----------	NE. 3	96	
Sept. 16	7 a. m.	29.11	64.5	.700	Nim. 10	----------	NE. 4	98	
	2 p. m.	28.93	71	.723	Nim. 10	SW. 5	SW. 4	94	
	9 p. m.	29.01	65	.587	0	----------	NW. 2	94	
Sept. 17	7 a. m.	29.18	66.5	.559	0	----------	NW. 3	85	
	2 p. m.	------	------	------	------------	----------	NW. 3	------	
	9 p. m.	29.29	71	.240	0	----------	NW. 1	86	
Sept. 18	7 a. m.	29.25	64.8	.562	Cir. 7	NW. 1	0	90	
	2 p. m.	29.23	77.8	.602	Cir. cu. 3	NW. 1	NW -------	64	
	9 p. m.	29.21	68.5	.661	0	----------	0	97	
Sept. 19	7 a. m.	29.17	66.5	.608	Cir. cu. 8	W. 1	0	93	
	2 p. m.	29.05	78	.704	Cu. st. 10	SW. 1	SW. 2	72	
	9 p. m.	29.05	69	.684	Nim. 10	----------	0	96	
Sept. 20	7 a. m.	29.06	68.5	.686	Nim. 10	SW. 2	SW---------	97	
	2 p. m.	28.94	76.5	.437	Cu. st. 9	----------	SW---------	68½	
	9 p. m.	29.06	68.5	.645	Nim. 8	NW. 1	NW. 1	92	
Sept. 21	7 a. m.	29.03	62.5	.506	0	----------	NW. 1	89	
	2 p. m.	29.04	71	.495	Cu. 6	W. 3	W. 3	65	
	9 p. m.	29.13	61	.476	0	----------	NW. 1	89	
Sept. 22	7 a. m.	29.18	58.9	.468	Cu. st. 6	----------	NW. 2	92	
	2 p. m.	29.22	71	.493	Cu. 6	NW. 2	NW. 1	64	
	9 p. m.	29.29	60	.473	0	----------	0	93	
Sept. 23	7 a. m.	29.37	60	.459	0	----------	0	87	
	2 p. m.	29.32	73	.461	Cu. st. 2	----------	0	57	
	9 p. m.	29.33	62.5	.462	0	----------	S. 1	83	
Sept. 24	7 a. m.	29.34	57.5	.414	0	----------	------------	85	
	2 p. m.	------	------	------	------------	----------	------------	------	
	9 p. m.	29.24	65	.539	0	----------	0	91	

ATLANTA, GEORGIA.

Month and day.	Hour.	Barom'r corrected to 32° F.	Thermometer.	Force of vapor.	Cloudiness.	Motion of clouds.	Winds.	Relative humidity.	REMARKS.
Sept. 14	9 p. m.	30.05	70	------	0	----------	W---------	------	Amount of rain on the 15th, 0.150 inch. 16th. Amount, 3.87 inches. 19th. Amount, 0.37 inch. 20th. Amount, 0.25 inch.
Sept. 15	7 a. m.	30.03	62	------	5	----------	SW---------	------	
	2 p. m.	30.08	70	------	10	----------	E ---------	------	
	9 p. m.	30.05	64	------	10	----------	E---------	------	
Sept. 16	7 a. m.	29.80	62	------	10	----------	E ---------	------	
	2 p. m.	29.70	78	------	10	----------	E ---------	------	
	9 p. m.	29.80	70	------	5	----------	NW --------	------	
Sept. 17	7 a. m.	29.93	64	------	0	----------	W---------	------	
	2 p. m.	30.05	80	------	0	----------	W---------	------	
	9 p. m.	30.00	70	------	0	----------	W---------	------	
Sept. 18	7 a. m.	30.00	66	------	0	----------	W---------	------	
	2 p. m.	30.05	76	------	0	----------	W---------	------	
	9 p. m.	30.00	68	------	0	----------	SW---------	------	
Sept. 19	7 a. m.	29.90	66	------	0	----------	SW---------	------	
	2 p. m.	29.90	74	------	10	----------	SW---------	------	
	9 p. m.	29.90	68	------	10	----------	SW---------	------	

STORMS Nos. 2 AND 3, SEPTEMBER, 1859.

ATLANTA, GEORGIA—Continued.

Month and day.	Hour.	Barom'r corrected to 32° F.	Thermometer.	Force of vapor.	Cloudiness.	Motion of clouds.	Winds.	Relative humidity.	REMARKS.
Sept. 20	7 a. m.	29.77	58	------	5	----------	W----------	------	
	2 p. m.	29.75	68	------	5	----------	W----------	------	
	9 p. m.	29.75	58	------	5	----------	W----------	------	
Sept. 21	7 a. m.	29.77	56	------	5	----------	W----------	------	
	2 p. m.	29.80	68	------	5	----------	W----------	------	
	9 p. m.	29.80	58	------	5	----------	W----------	------	
Sept. 22	7 a. m.	29.90	56	------	5	----------	W----------	------	
	2 p. m.	30.05	68	------	5	----------	SW----------	------	
	9 p. m.	30.05	62	------	0	----------	W----------	------	
Sept. 23	7 a. m.	30.05	54	------	0	----------	S----------	------	
	2 p. m.	30.09	68	------	0	----------	W----------	------	
	9 p. m.	30.10	60	------	0	----------	W----------	------	
Sept. 24	7 a. m.	30.00	52	------	0	----------	SW----------	------	
	2 p. m.	30.09	72	------	0	----------	SW----------	------	
	9 p. m.	30.08	68	------	0	----------	W----------	------	

AUGUSTA, GEORGIA.

Month and day.	Hour.	Barom'r corrected to 32° F.	Thermometer.	Force of vapor.	Cloudiness.		Motion of clouds.		Winds.		Relative humidity.	REMARKS.
Sept. 14	9 p. m.	30.21	74	.717	Cu. st.	10	SW.	2	W.	0	70	16th. Rain; amount, 1.88 inch.
Sept. 15	7 a m.	30.18	72.5	.604	Cu.	10	SE.	2	W.	0	73	17th. Amount, 0 42 inch.
	2 p. m.	30.11	75	.738	Cu.	10	S.	3	W.	0	76	20th. Amount, 1.34 inch.
	9 p m.	30.06	72	.717	Cu.	10	SW.	2	W.	0	77	21st. Amount, 2.25 inches.
Sept. 16	7 a. m.	29.97	74	.717		0		0	SE.	3	77	
	2 p. m.	29.91	79	.793		0		0	SE.	2	76	
	9 p. m.	29.88	73	.772		0		0	SW.	2	86	
Sept. 17	7 a. m.	29.91	69	.595		0		0	W.	0	76	
	2 p. m.	29.97	88	.724	St.	6	SW.	2	W.	1	65	
	9 p m	30.02	72	.731		0		0	W.	0	74	
Sept. 18	7 a. m.	30.01	74.5	.641		0		0	W.	0	77	
	2 p. m.	30.01	89	.711	Cu.	5	SW.	2	W.	0	62	
	9 p. m.	30.27	72	.829	Cu. st.	10	SW.	2	W.	0	79	
Sept. 19	7 a. m.	30.02	70	.623	Cu.	10	SE.	2	W.	0	75	
	2 p. m.	29.99	87	.782	Cu.	10	SW.	3	SE.	2	67	
	9 p. m.	30.02	77	.758	Cu.	6	SW.	2	SE.	1	74	
Sept. 20	7 a m.	29.97	75	.744	Cir. st.	9	SW.	1	SE.	0	78	
	2 p. m.	29.99	88	.816	Cu.	6	SW.	2	S.	1	75	
	9 p. m.	29.89	72	.717		0		0	SW.	0	77	
Sept. 21	7 a. m.	29.88	71	.673		0		0	SW.	0	79	
	2 p. m.	29.97	81	.542	Cu.	4	SW.	2	SW.	2	53	
	9 p. m.	30.08	------	.678		0		0	SW.	0	73	
Sept. 22	7 a. m.	30.05	68	.493		0		0	SW.	0	72	
	2 p. m.	30.02	77	.554	Cu.	4	SW.	2	SW.	1	64	
	9 p. m.	30.06	66	.600		0		0	SW.	0	74½	
Sept. 23	7 a. m.	30.08	62	.466		0		0	SW.	0	73	
	2 p. m.	30.05	85	.588	Cu.	4	NW.	2	SW.	0	62	
	9 p. m.	30.12	68	.581		0		0	SW.	0	7[illegible]	
Sept. 24	7 a. m.	30.10	62.5	.480		0		0	SW.	0	74	
	2 p. m.	30.06	83	.600	Cu.	4	NW.	2	SW.	1	62	
	9 p. m.	30.13	68.5	.617	Cu. st.	2	W.	1	SW.	0	77	

CLARKSVILLE, GEORGIA.

Month and day.	Hour.	Barom'r corrected to 32° F.	Thermometer.	Force of vapor.	Cloudiness.	Motion of clouds.	Winds.		Relative humidity.	REMARKS.
Sept. 14	9 p. m.	------	71	.608	0	----------	SW.	1	80	Heavy rain from 4 p m the 15th to 6 p. m. on the 16th.
Sept. 15	7 a. m.	------	66	.502	5	----------	E.	2	78	Rain from 3 p m. the 19th to 6 a. m. on the 20th.
	2 p m.	------	72	.559	8	----------	E.	3	72	
	9 p. m.	------	68	.612	10	----------	E.	2	90	
Sept. 16	7 a. m.	------	65	.583	10	----------	E.	5	94	
	2 p. m.	------	66	.639	10	----------	E.	5	100	
	9 p. m.	------	68	.577	3	----------	W.	4	85	

STORMS Nos. 2 AND 3, SEPTEMBER, 1859.

CLARKSVILLE, GEORGIA—Continued.

Month and day.	Hour.	Barom'r corrected to 32° F.	Thermometer.	Force of vapor.	Cloudiness.	Motion of clouds.	Winds.	Relative humidity.	REMARKS.
Sept. 17	7 a. m.	......	64	.529	0	....	NW. 3	89	
	2 p. m.	......	76	.691	2	....	W. 2	77	
	9 p. m.	......	70	.621	0	....	W. 1	85	
Sept. 18	7 a. m.	......	66	.570	5	....	W. 2	89	
	2 p. m.	......	78	.704	2	....	W. 1	73	
	9 p. m.	......	72	.631	0	....	S. 1	81	
Sept. 19	7 a. m.	......	62	.491	10	....	SW. 1	88	
	2 p. m.	......	74	.758	10	....	SW. 2	90	
	9 p. m.	......	70	.658	10	....	SW. 1	90	
Sept. 20	7 a. m.	......	68	.612	2	....	SW. 1	90	
	2 p. m.	......	78	.626	5	....	W. 3	65	
	9 p. m.	......	68	.577	0	....	W. 1	85	
Sept. 21	7 a. m.	......	62	.429	0	....	W. 1	77	
	2 p. m.	......	70	.551	5	....	SW. 3	75	
	9 p. m.	......	65	.549	0	....	SW. 1	89	
Sept. 22	7 a. m.	......	56	.391	0	....	SW. 1	87	
	2 p. m.	......	70	.551	0	....	SW. 2	75	
	9 p. m.	......	65	.483	0	....	W. 1	78	
Sept. 23	7 a. m.	......	58	.282	0	....	W. 1	58	
	2 p. m.	......	70	.551	3	....	W. 2	75	
	9 p. m.	......	60	.426	0	....	N. 2	82	
Sept. 24	7 a. m.	......	51	.348	0	....	W. 1	93	
	2 p. m.	......	72	.524	3	....	NW. 3	66	
	9 p. m.	......	60	.456	0	....	W. 1	88	

COVINGTON, GEORGIA.

Month and day.	Hour.	Barom'r corrected to 32° F.	Thermometer.	Force of vapor.	Cloudiness.	Motion of clouds.	Winds.	Relative humidity.	REMARKS.
Sept. 14	9 p. m.	......	......	......	0	....	N. 2	......	15th. Rain from 11 a. m. to 5½ p. m., and during the night.
Sept. 15	7 a. m.	......	......	......	1	....	NE. 4	......	
	2 p. m.	......	......	......	10	....	NE. 4	......	16th. Rain continued, with low flying clouds, till 5½ p. m.
	9 p. m.	......	......	......	10	....	SW. 2	......	
Sept. 16	7 a. m.	......	......	......	10	....	SE. 8	......	19th. Gentle shower from 5 to 10 p. m.; clouds from S. and SW.
	2 p. m.	......	......	......	10	....	SW. 8	......	
	9 p. m.	......	......	......	1	....	NW. 8	......	
Sept. 17	7 a. m.	......	......	......	0	....	NW. 4	......	
	2 p. m.	......	......	......	1	....	NW. 4	......	
	9 p. m.	......	......	......	0	....	NW. 2	......	
Sept. 18	7 a. m.	......	......	......	0	....	NW. 2	......	
	2 p. m.	......	......	......	1	....	E. 2	......	
	9 p. m.	......	......	......	0	....	SE. 2	......	
Sept. 19	7 a. m.	......	......	......	1	....	SW. 4	......	
	2 p. m.	......	......	......	7	....	SW. 4	......	
	9 p. m.	......	......	......	10	....	NE. 2	......	
Sept. 20	7 a. m.	......	......	......	1	....	SW. 4	......	
	2 p. m.	......	......	......	3	....	SW. 4	......	
	9 p. m.	......	......	......	1	....	SW. 2	......	
Sept. 21	7 a. m.	......	......	......	3	....	SW. 4	......	
	2 p. m.	......	......	......	2	....	SW. 8	......	
	9 p. m.	......	......	......	0	....	SW. 4	......	
Sept. 22	7 a. m.	......	......	......	1	....	SW. 2	......	
	2 p. m.	......	......	......	4	....	SW. 4	......	
	9 p. m.	......	......	......	0	....	SW. 2	......	
Sept. 23	7 a. m.	......	......	......	0	....	W. 2	......	
	2 p. m.	......	......	......	0	....	W. 4	......	
	9 p. m.	......	......	......	0	....	NW. 2	......	
Sept. 24	7 a. m.	......	......	......	0	....	NW. 2	......	
	2 p. m.	......	......	......	2	....	NW. 4	......	
	9 p. m.	......	......	......	0	....	NW. 2	......	

STORMS Nos. 2 AND 3, SEPTEMBER, 1859.

SAVANNAH, GEORGIA.

Month and day.	Hour.	Barom'r corrected to 32° F.	Thermometer.	Force of vapor.	Cloudiness.	Motion of clouds.	Winds.	Relative humidity.
Sept. 14	9 p. m.	30. 023	77	. 740	Coj. 6	----------	SE --------	82
Sept. 15	7 a. m.	. 071	74	. 795	M. 10	----------	NNE -------	94
	2 p. m.	. 071	80	. 857	Mk. 10	----------	E. 2	84
	9 p. m.	. 076	76. 6	. 849	Dark 10	----------	SE. 1	92
Sept. 16	7 a. m.	29. 969	79. 3	. 891	Hm. 10	----------	SE. 4	87
	2 p. m.	. 832	81. 6	. 926	Ol. 10	----------	S. 4	85
	9 p. m.	. 843	75. 1	. 760	Dark 10	----------	S. 3	86
Sept. 17	7 a. m.	. 926	70. 5	. 644	H. 1	----------	SW. 2	85
	2 p. m.	. 881	82. 9	. 641	0	----------	WNW. 2	59
	9 p. m.	. 953	75. 0	. 705	Great light 10	NE. -------	WNW ------	80
Sept. 18	7 a. m.	. 985	70. 5	. 651	0	----------	WNW. -----	86
	2 p. m.	. 973	81. 9	. 704	Kc. 8	----------	SE. 1	64
	9 p. m.	. 981	74. 5	. 708	H. 1	----------	SE --------	83
Sept. 19	7 a. m.	. 960	78	. 675	0	----------	SE --------	68
	2 p. m.	. 862	82. 7	. 648	Kc. 3	----------	SSE. 1	58
	9 p. m.	. 854	76. 8	. 738	0	----------	SSE. 1	79
Sept. 20	7 a. m.	. 757	76. 1	. 864	Ih. 10	----------	S. --------	87
	2 p. m.	. 746	78. 7	. 767	M. 10	----------	S. 2	79
	9 p. m.	. 761	75	. 693	H. 5	----------	S. 1	80
Sept. 21	7 a. m.	. 817	72. 5	. 728	Hgd. 8	----------	SW. 2	88
	2 p. m.	. 796	82. 6	. 591	K. 4	----------	SW. 3	51
	9 p. m.	. 860	76. 1	. 686	Dark 10	----------	SW. 1	77
Sept. 22	7 a. m.	. 967	66	. 496	0	----------	W. 1	77
	2 p. m.	. 967	80. 3	. 492	K. 5	----------	SW. 1	47
	9 p. m.	30. 052	72	. 573	0	----------	SW --------	73
Sept. 23	7 a. m.	. 130	68	. 544	0	----------	NW. 1	77
	2 p. m.	. 055	80. 5	. 490	Kh. 7	SW. ------	WNW. 2	46
	9 p. m.	. 075	72. 1	. 607	0	----------	W ---------	77
Sept. 24	7 a. m.	. 064	66. 5	. 514	0	----------	NW. 1	79
	2 p. m.	. 968	79	. 465	K. 1	----------	NNW. 1	46
	9 p. m.	. 973	71. 5	. 607	0	----------	NW -------	80

REMARKS.

14th. Rain in the night; amount, 2. 991 inches
15th. Rain from 7 a. m. to 2 p. m.; amount, 0. 10 inch.
16th. Showery after 10 a. m.; amount, 0. 56 inch.
19th. Rain in the night; amount, 0. 103 inch.
20th. Showery from 10 a. m. till noon; amount, 0. 038 inch.

☞ In kind of clouds a signifies curled cirrus; b, cirrus in straight threads; c, gauze cirrus; d, cirro cumulus; e, thin cir. stratus with fleecy edges; f, dense cir. stratus in long narrow bands; g, cimoid cir. st.; gs, mackerel sky; h, cir. st. in loose fleecy masses; hd, cir. st. like cir. cum.; i, cir. st. with sharp wavy edges; j, thin cir. st., with halos, circles, &c.; k, cumulus; l, cum. st.; m, nimbus, (with or without rain;) n, stratus; o, scud; cr, like roads across the sky; th, thunder; l, lightning; r, rain; spr, sprinkle.

SPARTA, GEORGIA.

Month and day.	Hour.	Barom'r corrected to 32° F.	Thermometer.	Force of vapor.	Cloudiness.	Motion of clouds.	Winds.	Relative humidity.
Sept. 14	9 p. m	------	70	------	Cir. 1	NW. 1	N. 1	------
Sept. 15	7 a. m	------	65	------	Cir. cu. 7	NW. 1	E. 1	------
	2 p. m	------	72	------	Nim. 10	S. 2	NE. 2	------
	9 p. m	------	69	------	Nim. 10	SW. 1	E. 4	------
Sept. 16	7 a. m	------	70	------	Nim. 10	S. 3	SE. 1	------
	2 p. m	------	74	------	Nim. 10	SW. 4	SW. 3	------
	9 p. m	------	69	------	Nim. 10	W. 3	SW. 4	------
Sept. 17	7 a. m	------	63	------	0	----------	W. 1	------
	2 p. m	------	83	------	0	----------	NW. 3	------
	9 p. m	------	71	------	0	----------	NE. 1	------
Sept. 18	7 a. m	------	63	------	0	----------	NE. 1	------
	2 p. m	------	88	------	Cu. 9	NE. 1	SW. 1	------
	9 p. m	------	70	------	0	----------	SW. 1	------
Sept. 19	7 a. m	------	66	------	Cir. cu. 3	SW. 1	S. 1	------
	2 p. m	------	88	------	Cu.&cir.cu. 10	SW. 2	SW. 2	------
	9 p. m	------	73	------	Nim. 10	S. 2	S. 1	------
Sept. 20	7 a. m	------	70	------	Nim. 10	SW. 4	SW. 1	------
	2 p. m	------	76	------	Nim. 10	SW. 1	SW. 1	------
	9 p. m	------	70	------	Cu. 2	SW. 1	SW. 1	------
Sept. 21	7 a. m	------	62	------	Cir. cu. 3	SW. 3	SW. 1	------
	2 p. m	------	75	------	Cu. 3	SW. 2	SW. 2	------
	9 p. m	------	63	------	0	----------	SW. 1	------
Sept. 22	7 a. m	------	55	------	0	----------	W. 1	------
	2 p. m	------	71	------	Cu. 5	SW. 2	SW. 2	------
	9 p. m	------	61	------	0	----------	W. 1	------
Sept. 23	7 a. m	------	54	------	0	----------	SW. 1	------
	2 p. m	------	77	------	0	----------	W. 3	------
	9 p. m	------	64	------	0	----------	NW. 1	------
Sept. 24	7 a. m	------	54	------	0	----------	NW. 1	------
	2 p. m	------	77	------	Cu. 4	N. 1	N. 2	------
	9 p. m	------	65	------	0	----------	NW. 1	------

REMARKS.

15th. Rain p. m. and night; am't, 2. 71 inches.
16th. Rain during the day; am't, 0. 50 inch.
19th. Rain p. m. and night; am't, 0. 52 inch.
20th. Rain p. m.; amount, 0.26 inch.

STORMS Nos. 2 AND 3, SEPTEMBER, 1859.

THOMASTON, GEORGIA.

Month and day.	Hour.	Barom'r corrected to 32° F.	Thermometer.	Force of vapor.	Cloudiness.	Motion of clouds.	Winds.	Relative humidity.	REMARKS.
Sept. 14	9 p. m.	28. 92	80	. 800	0	----------	SE. 0	78	Rain from 2 p. m. the 14th to 9 a. m. on the 15th; amount, 3. 35 inches.
Sept. 15	7 a. m.	28. 94	72	. 631	St. 10	----------	E. 1	81	
	2 p. m.	28. 93	76	. 897	10	----------	NE. 2	100	
	9 p. m.	28. 94	72	. 668	10	----------	NE. 4	86	
Sept. 16	7 a. m.	28. 69	73	. 771	10	----------	S. 5	95	
	2 p. m.	28. 68	74	. 758	10	----------	S. 4	90	
	9 p. m.	28. 89	71	. 644	0	----------	NW --------	86	
Sept. 17	7 a. m.	28. 90	70	. 658	10	----------	NE. --------	90	
	2 p. m.	28. 86	84	. 746	1	----------	NW --------	64	
	9 p. m.	28. 88	77	. 799	0	----------	NW--------	86	
Sept. 18	7 a. m.	28. 90	70	. 621	St. 1	----------	NW--------	85	
	2 p. m.	28. 86	84	. 746	5	----------	NE--------	64	
	9 p. m.	28. 88	77	. 799	0	----------	SE. 0	86	
Sept. 19	7 a. m.	28. 88	76	. 731	1	----------	S--------	81	
	2 p. m.	28. 76	83	. 891	10	----------	S. 3	79	
	9 p. m.	28. 77	79	. 813	10	----------	S. 1	82	
Sept. 20	7 a. m.	28. 74	74	. 758	9	----------	SW. 0	90	
	2 p. m.	28. 67	79	. 772	9	----------	NW. 0	78	
	9 p. m.	28. 69	74	. 680	1	----------	W--------	81	
Sept. 21	7 a. m.	28. 76	65	. 549	Cu. 9	----------	W. 3	89	
	2 p. m.	28. 79	72	. 631	Cir. st. 9	----------	W. 2	81	
	9 p. m.	28. 80	67	. 591	10	----------	NE--------	89	
Sept. 22	7 a. m.	28. 87	60	. 456	0	----------	NW. 1	88	
	2 p. m.	28. 89	72	. 595	1	----------	SW. 2	76	
	9 p. m.	28. 94	71	. 644	0	----------	NW. 0	86	
Sept. 23	7 a. m.	29. 02	62	. 491	0	----------	N. 1	88	
	2 p. m.	29. 03	74	. 641	0	----------	N. 1	77	
	9 p. m.	29. 04	72	. 595	0	----------	N. 0	76	
Sept. 24	7 a. m.	28. 99	68	. 443	1	----------	NE--------	65	
	2 p. m.	28. 98	75	. 666	3	----------	NE--------	77	
	9 p. m.	28. 99	73	. 655	0	----------	N--------	81	

WHITEMARSH ISLAND, GEORGIA.

Month and day.	Hour.	Barom'r corrected to 32° F.	Thermometer.	Force of vapor.	Cloudiness.	Motion of clouds.	Winds.	Relative humidity.	REMARKS.
Sept. 14	9 p. m.	------	75	------	Cir. 4	----------	0	------	14th. Fine, clear day
Sept. 15	7 a. m.	------	73	------	Nim. 10	WSW. 3	W. 1	------	15th. Rain commenced in the night, but was hardest after daylight; a great deal of thunder all the while; amount, 1.35 inch.
	2 p. m.	------	80	------	Nim. 10	----------	NE. 3	------	
	9 p. m.	------	77	------	Nim. 10	----------	SE. 3	------	
Sept. 16	7 a. m.	------	77	------	Nim. 10	S. 1	S. 4	------	
	2 p. m.	------	82	------	Cir. cu. 8	S. 1	S. 5	------	16th. Wind fresh from S. at an early hour; sky very stormy, but grew no worse in the p. m.; sky nearly clear at 8 p. m; wind began to haul to westward; very soon it clouded up from W., and a little rain fell; amount, 0.08 inch.
	9 p. m.	------	79	------	Nim. 10	----------	WSW. 5	------	
Sept. 17	7 a. m.	------	72	------	Cir. 2	SW. 1	WNW. 3	------	
	2 p. m.	------	83	------	Cir. cu. 2	----------	NNW. 3	------	
	9 p. m.	------	75	------	0	----------	0	------	
Sept. 18	7 a. m.	------	73	------	Cu. st. 1	----------	W. 2	------	
	2 p. m.	------	81	------	Cir. 4	NW. 1	SE. 2	------	
	9 p. m.	------	75	------	Cu. st. 2	----------	0	------	
Sept. 19	7 a. m.	------	75	------	Cir. cu. 4	NW. 1	SE. 2	------	17th. The sky was cleared by daylight, except a bank of clouds at SSE, which remained all day.
	2 p. m.	------	82	------	Cir. 4	WNW. 1	SSE. 3	------	
	9 p. m.	------	77	------	Cu. st. 3	----------	S. 3	------	
Sept. 20	7 a. m.	------	77	------	Nim. 10	SW. 2	SW. 2	------	18th. Rain cloud in the N. about 1 p. m.
	2 p. m.	------	80	------	Nim. 10	----------	W. 3	------	
	9 p. m.	------	76	------	Nim. 9	----------	W. 1	------	20th. Cloudy, with frequent dropping of rain; amount, 0.42 inch.
Sept. 21	7 a. m.	------	74	------	Cir. cu. 5	SW. 3	SW. 3	------	
	2 p. m.	------	81	------	Cir. cu. 3	SW. 3	W. 3	------	21st. Few drops of rain; amount, 0.04 inch.
	9 p. m.	------	75	------	Nim. 10	----------	0	------	
Sept. 22	7 a. m.	------	68	------	Cir. cu. 3	W. 3	NW. 2	------	23d Clear; cool.
	2 p. m.	------	78	------	Cu. st. 3	W. 3	NNW. 2	------	24th and 25th. Clear and fine.
	9 p. m.	------	71	------	Cu. st. 1	----------	0	------	
Sept. 23	7 a. m.	------	68	------	Cir. 1	----------	W. 1	------	
	2 p. m.	------	79	------	Cu. st. 3	W. 3	WNW. 3	------	
	9 p. m.	------	71	------	0	----------	0	------	
Sept. 24	7 a. m.	------	67	------	Cir. st. 1	----------	W. 1	------	
	2 p. m.	------	80	------	Cu. st. 3	----------	NW. 2	------	
	9 p. m.	------	68	------	0	----------	0	------	

STORMS Nos. 2 AND 3, SEPTEMBER, 1859.

ATSENA, FLORIDA.

Month and day.	Hour.	Barom'r corrected to 32° F.	Thermometer.	Force of vapor.	Cloudiness.	Motion of clouds.	Winds.	Relative humidity.	REMARKS.
Sept. 14	9 p. m.	29.78	80	......	8	0	0	......	14th. Rain from 7 to 8 p. m.;
Sept. 15	7 a. m.	29.78	80	......	Cir. 10	E. 2	E. 3	......	amount, 0.10 inch.
	2 p. m.	29.77	85	......	Cir. 9	SE. 1	SE. 2	......	Began to rain in the night of the
	9 p. m.	29.77	81	......	Nim. 10	SE. 4	SE. 4	......	16th and ended at 10 a. m. on
Sept. 16	7 a. m.	29.76	76	......	Nim. 10	SE. 2	SE. 3	......	the 17th; amount, 3.20 inches.
	2 p. m.	29.71	81	......	Cu., cir. cu. 7	SW. 3	SW. 3	......	17th Light rain at night.
	9 p. m.	29.73	80	......	Cir. 7	SW. 3	SW. 4	......	
Sept. 17	7 a. m.	29.77	77	......	Cir. 4	NW. 2	NW. 2	......	
	2 p. m.	29.75	82	......	Cir. 5	W. 2	W. 2	......	
	9 p. m.	29.74	79	......	Cir. 2	WNW. 1	WNW. 2	......	
Sept. 18	7 a. m.	29.75	76	......	0	0	E. 2	......	
	2 p. m.	29.76	85	......	Cir. 1	NW. 1	WSW. 2	......	
	9 p. m.	29.73	82	......	0	0	NW. 2	......	
Sept. 19	7 a. m.	29.75	79	......	Cu. 5	SE. 1	SE. 2	......	
	2 p. m.	29.67	84	......	Cu. 1	SE. 1	SW. 3	......	
	9 p. m.	29.65	80	......	Cu. 5	W. 3	W. 3	......	
Sept. 20	7 a. m.	29.57	80	......	Cu. 5	SW. 3	SW. 4	......	
	2 p. m.	29.55	83	......	Nim. 8	SW. 3	SW. 4	......	
	9 p. m.	29 56	77	......	St. 1	WNW. 1	WNW. 2	......	
Sept. 21	7 a. m.	29.60	77	......	Cir. 8	WSW. 2	WSW. 2	......	
	2 p. m.	29.60	77	......	Nim. 10	WNW. 1	WNW. 1	......	
	9 p. m.	29.67	74	......	0	0	0	......	
Sept. 22	7 a. m.	29.67	70	......	Cir. cu. 4	NE. 2	NE. 2	......	
	2 p. m.	29.77	80	......	Cir. cu. 2	SW. 1	SW. 1	......	
	9 p. m.	29.80	74	......	0	0	NE. 1	......	
Sept. 23	7 a. m.	29.82	71	......	Cir. cu. 3	SW. 3	NE. 2	......	
	2 p. m.	29.85	80	......	St. 1	1	W. 3	......	
	9 p. m.	29.85	78	......	0	0	WNW. 2	......	
Sept. 24	7 a. m.	29.80	71	......	Cir. cu. 1	NW. 1	NE. 2	......	
	2 p. m.	29.82	80	......	Cu. 1	NW. 2	NW. 2	......	
	9 p. m.	29.72	75	......	0	0	NE. 2	......	

BELAIR, FLORIDA.

Month and day.	Hour.	Barom'r corrected to 32° F.	Thermometer.	Force of vapor.	Cloudiness.	Motion of clouds.	Winds.	Relative humidity.	REMARKS.
Sept. 14	9 p. m.	......	74	......	......	......	......	......	
Sept. 15	7 a. m.	......	76	......	......	......	......	......	
	2 p. m.	......	88	......	......	......	......	......	
	9 p. m	......	75	......	......	......	......	......	
Sept. 16	7 a. m.	......	74	......	......	......	......	......	
	2 p. m.	......	88	......	......	......	......	......	
	9 p. m.	......	73	......	......	......	......	......	
Sept. 17	7 a. m.	......	74	......	......	......	......	......	
	2 p. m.	......	88	......	......	......	......	......	
	9 p. m.	......	75	......	......	......	......	......	
Sept. 18	7 a. m.	......	74	......	......	......	......	......	
	2 p. m.	......	89	......	......	......	......	......	
	9 p. m.	......	73	......	......	......	......	......	
Sept. 19	7 a. m.	......	69	......	......	......	......	......	
	2 p. m.	......	86	......	......	......	......	......	
	9 p. m.	......	70	......	......	......	......	......	
Sept. 20	7 a. m.	......	69	......	......	......	......	......	
	2 p. m.	......	86	......	......	......	......	......	
	9 p. m.	......	68	......	......	......	......	......	
Sept. 21	7 a. m.	......	67	......	......	......	......	......	
	2 p. m.	......	86	......	......	......	......	......	
	9 p. m.	......	68	......	......	......	......	......	
Sept. 22	7 a. m.	......	68	......	......	......	......	......	
	2 p. m.	......	86	......	......	......	......	......	
	9 p. m.	......	69	......	......	......	......	......	
Sept. 23	7 a. m.	......	68	......	......	......	......	......	
	2 p. m.	......	86	......	......	......	......	......	
	9 p. m.	......	69	......	......	......	......	......	
Sept. 24	7 a. m.	......	68	......	......	......	......	......	
	2 p. m.	......	88	......	......	......	......	......	
	9 p. m.	......	70	......	......	......	......	......	

STORMS Nos. 2 AND 3, SEPTEMBER, 1859.

JACKSONVILLE, FLORIDA.

Month and day.	Hour.	Barom'r corrected to 32° F.	Thermometer.	Force of vapor.	Cloudiness.	Motion of clouds.	Winds.	Relative humidity.	REMARKS.
Sept. 14	9 p. m.	30.044	81	.963	Nim ,cir.cu. 9	SW. 1	SW. 3	91	14th. Thunder shower in SW. at 7 p m.
Sept. 15	7 a. m.	.080	83	.936	Cir. cu. 4	SW. 1	NE. 2	83	16th. Thunder shower at 7 a. m. and p. m ; amount, 0.30 inch.
	2 p. m.	.028	89	1.046	Cir.cu.,nim. 8	SE. 2	SE. 3	77	20th. Sprinkle at 10 a. m. and p. m ; amount, 0.20 inch.
	9 p. m.	.019	81	.963	Cir. cu. 3	SE. 1	SE. 2	91	21st. Sprinkle p. m.; amount, 0.05 inch.
Sept. 16	7 a. m.	.009	81	.963	Cir.cu.,nim. 10	SE. 3	SSW. 3	91	
	2 p. m.	29.959	81	.918	Cir. cu. 10	SW. 2	SW. 3	87	
	9 p. m.	.962	79	.900	Cir. cu. 5	SW. 2	SW. 4	91	
Sept. 17	7 a. m.	30.017	79	.813	Cir.cu.,nim. 5	SW. 1	SW. 1	82	
	2 p. m.	.939	88	.962	St., cir. cu. 5	SW. 1	NW. 1	73	
	9 p. m.	.007	82	.950	0	0	SE. 1	87	
Sept. 18	7 a. m.	.008	81	.918	0	0	NE. 1	87	
	2 p. m.	.968	89	.948	Cir. cu., st. 3	SW. 1	NE. 3	69	
	9 p. m.	30.001	78	.827	0	0	SE. 1	86	
Sept. 19	7 a. m.	29.970	79	.856	Cir. cu. 4	S. 2	NE. 1	87	
	2 p. m.	.896	88	.868	Cir. cu. 4	SW. 2	SE. 3	66	
	9 p. m.	.909	80	.931	Cir. cu. 6	SW. 2	SW. 1	91	
Sept. 20	7 a. m.	.824	81	.918	Cir. cu. 3	SW. 3	SW. 3	87	
	2 p. m.	.784	83	.936	Cir.cu.,nim. 9	SW. 2	SW. 3	83	
	9 p. m.	.835	78	.827	0	0	SW. 3	86	
Sept. 21	7 a. m.	.873	77	.799	Cir. cu. 4	SW. 3	SW. 1	86	
	2 p. m.	.844	83	.891	Cir. cu. 10	SW. 1	SW. 1	79	
	9 p. m.	.913	74	.718	0	0	NW. 1	86	
Sept. 22	7 a. m.	30.006	70	.621	Cir. st. 1	....	NW. 1	85	
	2 p. m.	29.987	81	.787	Cir. cu. 5	SW. 2	SW. 1	74	
	9 p. m.	30.083	74	.718	0	0	NW. 1	86	
Sept. 23	7 a. m.	.111	72	.706	Cir. cu. 5	SW. 2	NW. 1	90	
	2 p. m.	.061	84	.877	Cu. st. 2	SW. 2	NE. 1	75	
	9 p. m.	.107	74	.718	0	0	NE. 1	86	
Sept. 24	7 a. m.	.083	74	.718	0	0	NW. 1	86	
	2 p. m.	29.977	85	.775	Cir. cu. 3	SW. 1	N. 1	65	
	9 p. m.	.993	72	.668	0	0	NW. 1	86	

LAKE CITY, FLORIDA.

Month and day.	Hour.	Barom'r corrected to 32° F.	Thermometer.	Force of vapor.	Cloudiness.	Motion of clouds.	Winds.	Relative humidity.	REMARKS.
Sept. 14	9 p. m.	------	78	------	Nim. 10	0	0	------	14th. Rain from 5½ to 9 p. m.; lightning and thunder in all directions during the p. m ; amount, in rain, 0.50 inch.
Sept. 15	7 a. m.	------	79	------	Cir. 5	0	SE. 1	------	16th. Rain from 4 a. m. to 6 p. m.; amount, 1.60 inch.
	2 p. m.	------	87	------	Nim. 10	S. 2	S. 2	------	20th. Rain from 9 a. m. till noon ; amount, 0.70 inch.
	9 p. m.	------	75	------	Nim. 8	S. 2	S. 2	------	21st. Rain from 3 to 5 p. m.; lightning in NW. from 7 to 9 p. m ; amount, 0.60 inch.
Sept. 16	7 a. m.	------	74	------	Nim. 10	S. 4	S. 3	------	
	2 p. m.	------	82	------	Cir. 6	S. 3	SW. 5	------	
	9 p. m.	------	78	------	Nim. 10	S. 2	SW. 2	------	
Sept. 17	7 a. m.	------	76	------	Cir. 5	0	SW. 1	------	
	2 p. m.	------	88	------	Cir. 2	SW. 1	0	------	
	9 p. m.	------	76	------	0	0	0	------	
Sept. 18	7 a. m.	------	76	------	0	0	SW. 1	------	
	2 p. m.	------	88	------	Cu. 3	0	SW. 1	------	
	9 p. m.	------	81	------	0	0	SW. 1	------	
Sept. 19	7 a. m.	------	76	------	0	0	SE. 1	------	
	2 p. m.	------	89	------	Cu. 4	0	SE. 1	------	
	9 p. m.	------	80	------	0	0	SE. 1	------	
Sept. 20	7 a. m.	------	80	------	Nim. 8	SW. 4	SW. 2	------	
	2 p. m.	------	83	------	Nim. 6	SW. 2	SW. 1	------	
	9 p. m.	------	77	------	Nim. 6	SW. 2	SW. 2	------	
Sept. 21	7 a. m.	------	70	------	Cir. 2	SW. 3	SE. 2	------	
	2 p. m.	------	80	------	St. 8	S. 3	S. 1	------	
	9 p. m.	------	75	------	0	0	SE. 1	------	
Sept. 22	7 a. m.	------	68	------	Cu. 4	SW. 2	SE. 1	------	
	2 p. m.	------	82	------	Cu. 5	SW. 2	W. 2	------	
	9 p. m.	------	76	------	0	0	0	------	
Sept. 23	7 a. m.	------	72	------	0	0	SW. 1	------	
	2 p. m.	------	83	------	Cu. 5	W. 2	SW. 2	------	
	9 p. m.	------	74	------	0	0	0	------	
Sept. 24	7 a. m.	------	68	------	0	0	W. 3	------	
	2 p. m.	------	82	------	Cu. 4	W. 2	W. 1	------	
	9 p. m.	------	72	------	0	0	0	------	

STORMS Nos. 2 AND 3, SEPTEMBER, 1859.

MICANOPY, FLORIDA.

Month and day.	Hour.	Barom'r corrected to 32° F.	Thermometer.	Force of vapor.	Cloudiness.	Motion of clouds.	Winds.	Relative humidity.
Sept. 14	9 p. m.	29.929	76	.791	Cu., cu. st. 10	....	SW.	88
Sept. 15	7 a. m.	.934	75.5	.819	Cir., cir. st., cu. st., st. 2	....	SE. 3	92
	2 p. m.	.800	87	.836	Cir. cu., cir st. 10	....	SE. 2	65
	9 p. m.	.916	74.5	.731	Cu., cir., cir. st. 10	....	SE. 2	85
Sept. 16	7 a. m.	.935	74	.744	Nim. 10	....	W., SW. 5	90
	2 p. m.	.847	76.5	.793	Cu., cu. st. 9	....	SE. 3	86
	9 p. m.	.872	75	.803	Cir., cir. cu., cu., cu. st. 5	....	S. 2	95
Sept. 17	7 a. m.	30.000	76	.833	Cir., cir. st., cir. cu., cu. st. 6	W. 2	NW. 3	92
	2 p. m.	.842	84.5	.656	Cir., cir. cu., cir. st., st. 7	....	NW. 2	55
	9 p. m.	.879	76	.737	Cir. cu., cir st., st. 3	....	W. 1	83
Sept. 18	7 a. m.	.891	77.5	.651	St. 1	....	NW. 2	69
	2 p. m.	.864	87.5	.678	Cu., cu. st., cir cu. 3	....	SW. 1	52
	9 p. m.	.870	78.5	.761	0	....	E. 1	78
Sept. 19	7 a. m.	.851	74.3	.770	Cir. st. 3	NE. 1	SE. 2	90
	2 p. m.	.759	87.6	.692	Cir., cir. st, cu. 4	0	SE. 3	52
	9 p. m.	.772	78.5	.790	Cir. st., cir. 1	....	SW. 1	82
Sept. 20	7 a. m.	.711	75.5	.798	Cu., cir. cu., cu. st., st. 4	....	S. 3	90
	2 p. m.	.666	77.5	.834	Nim., cu. 10	....	SE. 3	88
	9 p. m.	.708	73.2	.752	Cu., cu. st. 8	....	SE. 2	92
Sept. 21	7 a. m.	.755	73	.752	Cu., cu. st. 2	....	SE. 2	93
	2 p. m.	.739	75	.731	Nim., cu., cu. st. 10	....	NW. 3	85
	9 p. m.	.800	69	.625	0	....	N. 1	89
Sept. 22	7 a. m.	.882	65.5	.587	Cu. st. 1	....	NE. 1	93
	2 p. m.	.896	81	.604	Cu. 5	....	SE. 1	57
	9 p. m.	.947	72	.621	Cu., cu. st. 1	....	NW. 1	80
Sept. 23	7 a. m.	.988	68	.595	Cu. st., cu. 2	SW. 4	NW. 2	86
	2 p. m.	.955	83.6	.518	Cu., cu. st. 5	....	NW. 1	44
	9 p. m.	.980	74.8	.691	Cu., cu. st. 1	....	0	81
Sept. 24	7 a. m.	.973	70.4	.636	Cu. st. 1	....	NE. 3	84
	2 p. m.	.871	82.5	.493	Cu., cu. st. 4	....	N. 2	44
	9 p. m.	.875	71	.597	0	....	E. 1	80

REMARKS.

14th. Rain from 5½ to 7¾ p. m.; amount, 0.90 inch.

15th Barom'r falling in the evening; at 7 p. m., wind, S. 4; at 7.05, bar. 30.07; wind, SE. 5; at 7.10, bar. 30.078; open air ther. 77°; wind, S. 4, with rain; at 7.15, bar. 30.068; open air ther. 75°.5; wind, SSE. 4; rain; at 7.20, bar. 30.065; ther. attached 77°; open air ther. 75°.3; wind, SSE. 3; light rain; at 7.30, rain ceased; bar. 30.063; open air ther. 75°.5; wind, SSE. 3; bar. fell during the night; amount of rain, 0.16 inch.

16th. Sudden wind sprung up in the morning from NW. 4; bar. 30.055; at 7.05 a. m., bar. 30.062; wind, SW. 6; at 7.15 wind abated; bar. rose some then; fell again; very red sky at sunset; rain from 7 a. m. to 1½ p. m., and from 4.35 to 6 p. m.; amount, 0.82 inch.

20th. Barom'r lower than usual; at 6 a. m., bar. 29.740; attached ther. 77°; at 7 a. m., bar. 29.843; attached ther. 77°.8; at 8.15, bar. 29.85; attached ther. 81°.5; wind, S. 2; at 9 a. m., bar. 29.86; attached ther. 82°; wind, S. 3; at 11 a. m., bar. 29.853; attached ther. 79°.5; wind, S. 4, with rain; some thunder and lightning; at 1 p. m., bar. 29.832; attached ther. 79°; wind, SW. 3; rain from 9¼ to 10 a. m., and showers from 11.10 a. m. till 7½ p. m.; amount, 1.11 inch.

21st. Rain from 0.½ to 1½ p. m; amount, 0.05 inch.

ST. AUGUSTINE, FLORIDA.

Month and day.	Hour.	Barom'r corrected to 32° F.	Thermometer.	Force of vapor.	Cloudiness.	Motion of clouds.	Winds.	Relative humidity.
Sept. 14	9 p. m.	29.90	81	......	Cu. 8	SW. 1	SW. 1	......
Sept. 15	7 a. m.	29.95	84	......	Cu. 7	SE. 2	SE. 2	......
	2 p. m.	29.94	86	......	Cu. 8	SE. 3	SE. 4	......
	9 p. m.	29.95	84	......	Cu. 10	SE. 3	SE. 4	......
Sept. 16	7 a. m.	29.90	83	......	Cu. 7	S. 2	S. 3	......
	2 p. m.	29.86	78	......	Cu. 9	SW. 3	SW. 3	......
	9 p. m.	29.83	77	......	Cu. 10	SW. 2	SW. 2	......
Sept. 17	7 a. m.	29.85	80	......	Cir. st. 4	NW. 2	NW. 2	......
	2 p. m.	29.84	90	......	Cir. st. 4	SW. 2	SW. 3	......
	9 p. m.	29.85	81	......	Cu. 3	SW. 1	SW. 1	......
Sept. 18	7 a. m.	29.85	82	......	Cu. 1	N. 1	N. 1	......
	2 p. m.	29.84	84	......	Cu. 2	E. 2	E. 3	......
	9 p. m.	29.85	82	......	Cu. 1	NE. 2	NE. 2	......
Sept. 19	7 a. m.	29.85	80	......	Cu. 3	S. 1	S. 1	......
	2 p. m.	29.80	85	......	St. 2	SE. 2	SE. 3	......
	9 p. m.	29.75	82	......	Cu. 4	SE. 2	SE. 2	......

REMARKS.

16th. Rain from 11 a. m. to 1 p. m.; amount, 0.40 inch.

20th. Rain from noon till 7 p. m.; amount, 0.50 inch.

21st. Rain from 1½ to 5 p. m.; amount, 0.55 inch.

STORMS Nos. 2 AND 3, SEPTEMBER, 1859.

ST. AUGUSTINE, FLORIDA—Continued.

Month and day.	Hour.	Barom'r corrected to 32° F.	Thermometer.	Force of vapor.	Cloudiness.	Motion of clouds.	Winds.	Relative humidity.	REMARKS.
Sept. 20	7 a. m	29. 75	80	------	Cu. 4	NW. 2	NW. 1	------	
	2 p. m	29. 71	78	------	Cu. 9	NW. 2	NW. 2	------	
	9 p. m	29. 67	75	------	Cu. 6	NW. 2	NW. 2	------	
Sept. 21	7 a. m	29. 76	80	------	Cir. cu. 4	NW. 2	NW. 2	------	
	2 p. m	29. 75	82	------	Cu. 10	SE. 2	SE. 2	------	
	9 p. m	29. 77	75	------	Cu. 4	SW. 2	SW. 2	------	
Sept. 22	7 a. m	29. 86	74	------	St. 1	NW. 1	NW. 2	------	
	2 p. m	29. 85	82	------	Cu. 3	SE. 2	SE. 2	------	
	9 p. m	29. 87	76	------	Cu. 3	SE. 2	SE. 1	------	
Sept. 23	7 a. m	29. 96	76	------	Cir. cu. 2	NW. 1	NW. 1	------	
	2 p. m	29. 95	84	------	Cu. 4	NE. 2	NE. 3	------	
	9 p. m	29. 96	80	------	Cu. 2	NE. 2	NE. 1	------	
Sept. 24	7 a. m	29. 96	75	------	Cir. cu. 3	N. 1	N. 1	------	
	2 p. m	29. 90	82	------	Cir. cu. 2	NE. 2	NE. 3	------	
	9 p. m	29. 86	79	------	0	0	NE. 2	------	

SALT PONDS, FLORIDA.

Month and day.	Hour.	Barom'r corrected to 32° F.	Thermometer.	Force of vapor.	Cloudiness.	Motion of clouds.	Winds.	Relative humidity.	REMARKS.
Sept. 15	7 a. m	29. 66	81	------	10	----------	SE. 4	------	14th. Shower at 9 a. m.; sprinkle at 5 p. m; amount, 0. 09 inch.
	2 p. m	29. 70	87	------	4	----------	SE. 5	------	16th. Wind high at 10 a. m.
Sept. 16	7 a. m	29. 65	82	------	4	----------	SE. 3	------	18th. Squall passed to the N. at 9 p. m.
	2 p. m	29. 68	88	------	4	----------	S. 3	------	19th. Lightning in the N. at 7 p. m.; bank of clouds in the N. at dark.
Sept. 17	7 a. m	29. 62	82	------	3	----------	E. 1	------	20th. Light showers at 8 a. m.
	2 p. m	29. 68	88	------	2	----------	E. 2	------	21st. Lightning in the N. and SE. after dark; heavy squall and light shower from the S. at 10 p. m.
Sept. 18	7 a. m	29. 60	81	------	3	----------	E. 1	------	22d. Wind came round to N. at sunset
	2 p. m	29. 65	89	------	3	----------	SE. 2	------	23d. Heavy shower from 11½ a. m. till 1 p. m.; light shower from 4 p. m. till 5 p. m.; shower at 7 p. m.; squall and shower from 11 to 11½ p. m.; amount, 1. 50 inch.
Sept. 19	7 a. m	29. 58	82	------	4	----------	E. 1	------	24th. Shower at 8 p. m.
	2 p. m	29. 60	88	------	2	----------	S. 2	------	25th. Squall and shower at 4 a. m.; amount, 0. 15 inch.
Sept. 20	7 a. m	29. 52	83	------	3	----------	SE. 3	------	
	2 p. m	29. 56	88	------	1	----------	SW. 3	------	
Sept. 21	7 a. m	29. 52	82	------	2	----------	S. 3	------	
	2 p. m	29. 58	89	------	3	----------	SW. 4	------	
Sept. 22	7 a. m	29. 58	82	------	2	----------	S. 2	------	
	2 p. m	29. 69	88	------	2	----------	SW. 2	------	
Sept. 23	7 a. m	29. 68	82	------	5	----------	NE. 2	------	
	2 p. m	29. 70	88	------	5	----------	SE. 1	------	
Sept. 24	7 a. m	29. 63	80	------	3	----------	NE. 3	------	
	2 p. m	29. 65	86	------	2	----------	N. 3	------	

WARRINGTON, FLORIDA.

Month and day.	Hour.	Barom'r corrected to 32° F.	Thermometer.	Force of vapor.	Cloudiness.	Motion of clouds.	Winds.	Relative humidity.	REMARKS.
Sept. 14	9 p. m.	29. 859	84	1. 101	Cir. 2; Nim. 5	SW. 0; 1	NE. 3	91	15th. A severe gale came up from NE. at 6 a. m.; increased gradually as the wind shifted to SE., which occurred at 10 a. m.; wind at its height about 11 p. m; showers from 1 a. m till 3 a. m. on the 16th; wind shifted to the S., and after 1 a. m. the 16th gradually decreased; at 3 a. m. the wind had slackened and came from the W.; amount of rain, 3. 65 inches.
Sept. 15	7 a. m	. 827	75	. 958	Nim. 10	SW. 4	NE. 6	100	Rain from 9 a. m. the 19th to 4 a. m. on the 20th; amount, 2. 15 inches.
	2 p. m	. 602	80	. 977	Nim. 10	NW. 6	SE. 7	96	
	9 p. m	. 524	81	1. 010	Nim. 10	NW. 8	SE. 8	96	
Sept. 16	7 a. m	. 762	76	. 841	Cir. cu. 5	0	SW. 5	91	
	2 p. m	. 769	88	1. 111	0	0	SW. 3	84	
	9 p. m	. 879	84	1. 101	Cir. 3	0	SW. 2	91	
Sept. 17	7 a. m	. 942	79	1. 044	0	0	NE. 2	96	
	2 p. m	. 931	86	1. 003	0	0	SW. 3	83	
	9 p. m	. 917	83	1. 030	Cu. 3	NE. 1	SW. 3	91	
Sept. 18	7 a. m	. 907	81	. 996	0	0	NE. 1	91	
	2 p. m	. 921	89	1. 038	0	0	SW. 2	84	
	9 p. m	. 891	83	1. 030	Cir. 4	0	SW. 3	91	
Sept. 19	7 a. m	. 809	83	1. 010	Cu. 3	NW. 1	SE. 2	96	
	2 p. m	. 770	78	. 945	Nim. 10	NW. 1	SE. 3	95	
	9 p. m	. 752	76	. 914	Nim. 10	NW. 1	SE. 3	95	
Sept. 20	7 a. m	. 748	72	. 884	0	0	NW. 3	94	
	2 p. m	. 684	82	1. 010	0	0	SW. 2	96	
	9 p. m	. 715	72	. 914	Cu. 5	SE. 1	NW. 3	95	

STORMS Nos. 2 AND 3, SEPTEMBER, 1859.

WARRINGTON, FLORIDA—Continued.

Month and day.	Hour.	Barom'r corrected to 32° F.	Thermometer.	Force of vapor.	Cloudiness.	Motion of clouds.	Winds.	Relative humidity.	REMARKS.
Sept. 21	7 a. m.	29.828	66	.745	Cu. 8	SE. 1	NW. 2	95	
	2 p. m.	.818	80	.785	Nim. 5	NE. 1	SW. 3	90	
	9 p. m.	.800	72	.785	Cu. 5	SE. 1	NW. 2	90	
Sept. 22	7 a. m.	.929	65	.658	Nim. 8	SW. 1	NE. 3	90	
	2 p. m.	.955	76	.799	0	0	E. 3	86	
	9 p. m.	.943	72	.854	0	0	SE. 2	95	
Sept. 23	7 a. m.	30.061	70	.771	0	0	NE. 2	95	
	2 p. m.	.025	81	1.010	0	0	E. 3	96	
	9 p. m.	.002	78	.945	Cir. 2	0	SW. 2	95	
Sept. 24	7 a. m.	.051	68	.771	0	0	NE. 2	95	
	2 p. m.	29.995	80	.873	0	0	NW. 3	83	
	9 p. m.	.919	78	.931	0	0	NW. 2	91	

CAHAWBA, ALABAMA.

Month and day.	Hour.	Barom'r corrected to 32° F.	Thermometer.	Force of vapor.	Cloudiness.	Motion of clouds.	Winds.	Relative humidity.	REMARKS.
Sept. 14	9 p. m.	......	......	......	1	....	NW. 1	......	14th. Cool morning; day bright and warm; evening hazy.
Sept. 15	7 a. m.	......	......	......	10	....	NE. 3	......	15th. Sky overcast from NE.; rain storm commenced at 9 a. m.
	2 p. m.	......	......	......	10	....	NE. 2	......	16th The rain storm yesterday, after increasing both in wind and rain all day, became a violent NE. gale, and blew with great fury all night, attended by hard driving rain; about 8 a. m. this morning the wind veered to the W., the rain ceased, and by noon the day was fine.
	9 p. m.	......	......	......	10	....	NE. 5	......	17th. Pleasant; sky deep blue; a few snowy clouds about noon.
Sept. 16	7 a. m.	......	......	......	10	....	NE. 6	......	18th. Hazy.
	2 p. m.	......	......	......	3	....	NW. 2	......	19th. Masses of watery clouds boiling up from SW. till 11 a. m, when heavy showers commenced and continued, with very short intervals between them, till 6 p. m.; the last and hardest of the showers came up from the NW.; all the others from SW.
	9 p. m.	......	......	......	0	....	NW. 1	......	20th. Strong cool NW. wind all p. m.; night clear and still.
Sept. 17	7 a. m.	......	......	......	0	....	NW. 1	......	21st. Sky overcast with thin high clouds till sunset; night clear.
	2 p. m.	......	......	......	1	....	NW. 1	......	22d. Pleasant; hot sun and cool shade.
	9 p. m.	......	......	......	0	....	NW. 1	......	23d. Same as preceding day.
Sept. 18	7 a. m.	......	......	......	0	....	NW. 1	......	24th. Clear; not a cloud visible.
	2 p. m.	......	......	......	5	....	W. 2	......	
	9 p. m	......	......	......	0	....	SW. 1	......	
Sept. 19	7 a. m.	......	......	......	10	....	NW. 2	......	
	2 p. m.	......	......	......	10	....	S. 3	......	
	9 p m.	......	......	......	5	....	SW. 1	......	
Sept. 20	7 a. m.	......	......	......	2	....	NW. 2	......	
	2 p. m.	......	......	......	2	....	NW. 4	......	
	9 p. m.	......	......	......	1	....	NW. 1	......	
Sept. 21	7 a. m.	......	......	......	10	....	NW. 2	......	
	2 p. m.	......	......	......	10	....	NW. 2	......	
	9 p. m.	......	......	......	1	....	NW. 1	......	
Sept. 22	7 a. m.	......	......	......	1	....	NW. 1	......	
	2 p. m.	......	......	......	3	....	NW. 2	......	
	9 p. m.	......	......	......	0	....	NW. 1	......	
Sept. 23	7 a. m.	......	......	......	0	....	NW. 1	......	
	2 p. m.	......	......	......	3	....	NW. 2	......	
	9 p. m.	......	......	......	0	....	NW. 1	......	
Sept. 24	7 a. m.	......	......	......	0	....	NW. 1	......	
	2 p. m.	......	......	......	0	....	NW. 3	......	
	9 p. m.	......	......	......	0	....	NW. 1	......	

CARLOWVILLE, ALABAMA.

Month and day.	Hour.	Barom'r corrected to 32° F.	Thermometer.	Force of vapor.	Cloudiness.	Motion of clouds.	Winds.	Relative humidity.	REMARKS.
Sept. 14	9 p. m.	......	78	......	Cir. st. 3	0	N. 2	......	Rain from 7 a. m. the 15th to 6 a. m on the 16th; amount, 7.80 inches.
Sept. 15	7 a. m.	......	68	......	Nim. 10	0	E. 3	......	20th. Rain from 9 a m. till 1 p. m.; amount, 3.00 inches.
	2 p. m.	......	72	......	Nim. 10	0	E. 1	......	
	9 p. m.	......	68	......	Nim. 10	0	E. 1	......	
Sept. 16	7 a m.	......	70	......	Nim. 10	0	E. 2	......	
	2 p. m.	......	80	......	Cu. 4	E. 1	N. 2	......	
	9 p m.	......	74	......	0	0	E. 1	......	
Sept. 17	7 a. m.	......	73	......	St. 2	0	E. 1	......	
	2 p. m.	......	80	......	0	0	NE. 1	......	
	9 p. m.	......	78	......	0	0	E. 2	......	

STORMS Nos. 2 AND 3, SEPTEMBER, 1859.

CARLOWVILLE, ALABAMA—Continued.

Month and day.	Hour.	Barom'r corrected to 32° F.	Thermometer.	Force of vapor.	Cloudiness.	Motion of clouds.	Winds.	Relative humidity.	REMARKS.
Sept. 18	7 a m.	......	74	......	Cu. 4	N. 1	S. 1	......	
	2 p. m.	......	86	......	Cu. 4	E. 1	S. 0	......	
	9 p. m.	......	78	......	Cu. 4	0	S. 0	......	
Sept. 19	7 a. m.	......	76	......	Cu. 8	N. 2	S. 2	......	
	2 p. m.	......	88	......	Cir. 3	0	S. 0	......	
	9 p. m.	......	78	......	0	0	S. 0	......	
Sept. 20	7 a. m.	......	74	......	Nim. 10	0	S. 1	......	
	2 p. m.	......	84	......	Cu. 8	N. 1	NW. 1	......	
	9 p m.	......	74	......	Cu. 4	0	E. 0	......	
Sept. 21	7 a. m.	......	72	......	Cir. 1	0	E. 1	......	
	2 p. m.	......	86	......	0	0	W. 1	......	
	9 p. m.	......	76	......	0	0	E. 1	......	
Sept. 22	7 a. m.	......	60	......	1	0	E. 1	......	
	2 p. m.	......	80	......	Cir. cu. 3	E. 1	S. 0	......	
	9 p. m.	......	74	......	0	0	W. 1	......	
Sept. 23	7 a. m.	......	62	......	0	0	E. 0	......	
	2 p. m.	......	80	......	Cir. 2	0	S. 1	......	
	9 p. m.	......	74	......	Cir. 3	0	N. 1	......	
Sept. 24	7 a. m.	......	60	......	St. 2	0	SE. 1	......	
	2 p. m.	......	81	......	Cu. 3	0	SE. 2	......	
	9 p. m.	......	76	......	Cu. 4	0	N. 2	......	

GREENE SPRINGS, ALABAMA.

Month and day.	Hour.	Barom'r corrected to 32° F.	Thermometer.	Force of vapor.	Cloudiness.	Motion of clouds.	Winds.	Relative humidity.	REMARKS.
Sept. 14	9 p. m.	......	73	......	....	....	W. 4	......	Rain from noon the 15th to 8 a. m. on the 16th; amount, 3. 17 inches.
Sept. 15	7 a. m.	......	......	......	Nim. 10	....	....	......	
	2 p. m.	......	75	......	Nim. 10	....	....	......	
	9 p. m.	......	71	......	Nim. 10	....	....	......	19th. Rain from 8 to 11 a. m , and 2 to 3 p. m.; amount, 0.96 inch.
Sept. 16	7 a. m.	......	66	......	....	....	....	......	
	2 p. m.	......	......	......	....	....	....	......	
	9 p. m.	......	......	......	....	....	....	......	
Sept. 17	7 a. m.	......	......	......	....	....	....	......	
	2 p. m.	......	86	......	Cu. 2	....	W. 1	......	
	9 p. m.	......	......	......	....	....	....	......	
Sept. 18	7 a. m.	......	69	......	6	SW. 1	SE. 1	......	
	2 p. m.	......	87	......	1	....	SE. 2	......	
	9 p. m.	......	76	......	8	....	NE. 1	......	
Sept. 19	7 a. m.	......	70	......	....	....	....	......	
	2 p. m.	......	74	......	....	....	....	......	
	9 p. m.	......	70	......	....	....	....	......	
Sept. 20	7 a. m.	......	......	......	Nim. 10	SW. 1	E. 2	......	
	2 p. m.	......	......	......	Nim. 10	SW. 2	SW. 3	......	
	9 p. m.	......	62	......	3	....	W. 2	......	
Sept. 21	7 a. m.	......	61	......	10	N. 1	N. 2	......	
	2 p. m.	......	......	......	10	N. 1	N. 2	......	
	9 p. m.	......	58	......	9	....	W. 2	......	
Sept. 22	7 a. m.	......	53	......	10	NW. 1	W. 2	......	
	2 p. m.	......	70	......	....	....	....	......	
	9 p. m.	......	60	......	0	....	SE. 1	......	
Sept. 23	7 a. m.	......	54	......	10	....	....	......	
	2 p. m.	......	75	......	10	....	NE. 1	......	
	9 p. m.	......	63	......	0	....	E. 1	......	
Sept. 24	7 a. m.	......	58	......	....	....	....	......	
	2 p. m.	......	......	......	....	....	....	......	
	9 p. m.	......	64	......	0	....	....	......	

STORMS Nos. 2 AND 3, SEPTEMBER, 1859.

GREENSBOROUGH, ALABAMA.

Month and day.	Hour.	Barom'r corrected to 32° F.	Thermometer.	Force of vapor.	Cloudiness.	Motion of clouds.	Winds.	Relative humidity.	REMARKS.
Sept. 14	9 p. m.	......	78	......	0	0	....	......	15th. Heavy storm, commencing at 10 a. m., continued during the day; rain fell in torrents during the night; high wind.
Sept. 15	7 a. m.	......	69	......	St. 9	E. 3	E. 2	......	16th. Wind changed to the W. at 6½ a. m.; rain ceased at 7½ a. m.
	2 p. m.	......	73	......	Nim. 10	SE. 3	E. 2	......	19th. Rain from 9. 30 a. m. to 5 p. m.
	9 p. m.	......	69	......	Nim. 10	SE. 4	SE. 4	......	
Sept. 16	7 a. m.	......	68	......	St. 10	W. 4	W. 3	......	
	2 p. m.	......	79	......	Patches 5	NW. 4	NW. 2	......	
	9 p. m.	......	74	......	0	0	NW. 1	......	
Sept. 17	7 a. m.	......	68	......	0	0	SW. 1	......	
	2 p. m.	......	86	......	2	SE. 1	S. 1	......	
	9 p. m.	......	75. 5	......	0	0	NW. 1	......	
Sept. 18	7 a. m.	......	71	......	Cir., cir. st. 2	W. 3	SW. 2	......	
	2 p. m.	......	86	......	{ Cu ...... / Cir. 2 }	{ SW. 1 / W. 3 }	SW. 1	......	
	9 p. m.	......	78	......	St. 2	....	SE. 1	......	
Sept. 19	7 a. m.	......	73	......	St. 10	SW. 3	WSW. 2	......	
	2 p. m.	......	78	......	Nim. 10	SSW. 3	SW. 2	......	
	9 p. m.	......	72. 5	......	0	0	NW. 1	......	
Sept. 20	7 a. m.	......	61. 5	......	Patches 1	NW. 5	NW. 2	......	
	2 p. m.	......	67	......	St. 10	W. 2	NNW. 2½	......	
	9 p. m.	......	62	......	St. 1	....	NW. 2	......	
Sept. 21	7 a. m.	......	59. 5	......	St. 4	NW. 4	NW. 2	......	
	2 p. m.	......	64	......	St. 10	NW. 3	NW. 2	......	
	9 p. m.	......	60. 5	......	0	0	NW. 2	......	
Sept. 22	7 a. m.	......	55. 5	......	10	....	NW. 1	......	
	2 p. m.	......	69	......	Dense st. 3	E. 3	N. 2	......	
	9 p. m.	......	63. 5	......	0	0	NW. 1	......	
Sept. 23	7 a. m.	......	58	......	0	0	NW. 1	......	
	2 p. m.	......	76	......	St. 4	NE. 2	SE. 1	......	
	9 p. m.	......	67	......	0	0	SE. 1	......	
Sept. 24	7 a. m.	......	57. 5	......	0	0	SW. 1	......	
	2 p. m.	29. 64	77	. 492	0	0	NW. 2	53	
	9 p. m.	29. 65	62. 5	. 533	0	0	NW. 1	94	

LIVINGSTON, ALABAMA.

Month and day.	Hour.	Barom'r corrected to 32° F.	Thermometer.	Force of vapor.	Cloudiness.	Motion of clouds.	Winds.	Relative humidity.	REMARKS.
Sept. 14	9 p. m.	......	......	......	1	....	NE. 2	......	15th. Began to rain at noon; very heavy in the night, with strong wind.
Sept. 15	7 a. m.	......	......	......	7	....	NE. 1	......	16th. Pleasant.
	2 p. m.	......	......	......	10	....	NE. 1	......	17th. Quite clear about 8½; white caps afterwards.
	9 p. m.	......	......	......	10	....	E. 8	......	19th. Heavy rain in the morning and most of the day.
Sept. 16	7 a. m.	......	......	......	10	....	N. 3	......	20th. Morning bright; day dark; damp, and sometimes misty.
	2 p. m.	......	......	......	3	....	NW. 1	......	21st. Dark, cool day.
	9 p. m.	......	......	......	0	....	0	......	22d. Pleasant.
Sept. 17	7 a. m.	......	......	......	2	....	N. 1	......	24th. Pleasant.
	2 p. m.	......	......	......	1	....	N. 1	......	
	9 p. m.	......	......	......	0	....	S. 1	......	
Sept. 18	7 a. m.	......	......	......	0	....	E. 1	......	
	2 p. m.	......	......	......	0	....	NE. 1	......	
	9 p. m.	......	......	......	2	....	E. 1	......	
Sept. 19	7 a. m.	......	......	......	9	....	SW. 1	......	
	2 p. m.	......	......	......	10	....	SW. 1	......	
	9 p. m.	......	......	......	3	....	NE. 2	......	
Sept. 20	7 a. m.	......	......	......	0	....	NW. 1	......	
	2 p. m.	......	......	......	10	....	N. 1	......	
	9 p. m.	......	......	......	9	....	W. 2	......	
Sept. 21	7 a. m.	......	......	......	10	....	NE. 1	......	
	2 p. m.	......	......	......	10	....	N. 1	......	
	9 p. m.	......	......	......	1	....	NW. 1	......	
Sept. 22	7 a. m.	......	......	......	2	....	NE. 1	......	
	2 p. m.	......	......	......	5	....	S. 1	......	
	9 p. m.	......	......	......	0	....	S. 1	......	
Sept. 23	7 a. m.	......	......	......	1	....	E. 1	......	
	2 p. m.	......	......	......	4	....	E. 1	......	

STORMS Nos. 2 AND 3, SEPTEMBER, 1859.

LIVINGSTON, ALABAMA—Continued.

Month and day.	Hour.	Barom'r corrected to 32° F.	Thermometer.	Force of vapor.	Cloudiness.	Motion of clouds.	Winds.	Relative humidity.	REMARKS.
Sept. 23	9 p. m.	------	------	------	0	----------	0	------	
Sept. 24	7 a. m.	------	------	------	0	----------	W. 1	------	
	2 p. m.	------	------	------	0	----------	NW. 1	------	
	9 p. m.	------	------	------	0	----------	0	------	

MONTGOMERY, ALABAMA.

Month and day.	Hour.	Barom'r corrected to 32° F.	Thermometer.	Force of vapor.	Cloudiness.	Motion of clouds.	Winds.	Relative humidity.	REMARKS.
Sept. 14	9 p. m.	------	------	------	1	----------	NW. 1	------	15th. Clouds generally from NE.; rain at 9 a. m., during night.
Sept. 15	7 a. m.	------	------	------	10	----------	E. 1	------	16th. Rain till 9 a. m.; wind 5 till 10 a. m.
	2 p. m.	------	------	------	10	----------	NE. 2	------	17th and 18th. Warm and pleasant.
	9 p. m.	------	------	------	10	----------	NE -------	------	19th. Rain SW. from 11½ a. m. to 9 p. m.
Sept. 16	7 a. m.	------	------	------	10	----------	NE. 3	------	20th. Cool and pleasant.
	2 p. m.	------	------	------	9	----------	NW. 2	------	21st. Cool.
	9 p. m.	------	------	------	0	----------	NW. 1	------	22d. Cool and foggy.
Sept. 17	7 a. m.	------	------	------	0	----------	NW. 1	------	23d and 24th. Cool.
	2 p. m	------	------	------	2	----------	NW. 2	------	
	9 p. m.	------	------	------	1	----------	NW. 1	------	
Sept. 18	7 a. m.	------	------	------	0	----------	NW. 1	------	
	2 p. m.	------	------	------	2	----------	NW. 2	------	
	9 p. m.	------	------	------	1	----------	NE. 1	------	
Sept. 19	7 a. m.	------	------	------	3	----------	NW. 1	------	
	2 p. m.	------	------	------	10	----------	SW. 2	------	
	9 p. m.	------	------	------	10	----------	SE. 2	------	
Sept. 20	7 a. m	------	------	------	10	----------	N. 2	------	
	2 p. m.	------	------	------	8	----------	N. 2	------	
	9 p. m.	------	------	------	0	----------	NW. 1	------	
Sept. 21	7 a. m.	------	------	------	10	----------	N. 2	------	
	2 p. m.	------	------	------	10	----------	NW. 2	------	
	9 p. m.	------	------	------	0	----------	NW. 2	------	
Sept. 22	7 a. m.	------	------	------	0	----------	NW. 2	------	
	2 p. m.	------	------	------	0	----------	NW. 2	------	
	9 p. m.	------	------	------	0	----------	NW. 1	------	
Sept. 23	7 a. m.	------	------	------	0	----------	NW. 1	------	
	2 p. m.	------	------	------	0	----------	NW. 2	------	
	9 p. m.	------	------	------	0	----------	NW. 1	------	
Sept. 24	7 a. m.	------	------	------	0	----------	NW. 1	------	
	2 p. m.	------	------	------	0	----------	NW. 2	------	
	9 p. m.	------	------	------	0	----------	NW. 1	------	

SELMA, ALABAMA.

Month and day.	Hour.	Barom'r corrected to 32° F.	Thermometer.	Force of vapor.	Cloudiness.	Motion of clouds.	Winds.	Relative humidity.	REMARKS.
Sept. 14	9 p. m.	------	78	.478	Cir. 1	SW. 1	NE. 3	50	Rain from 9.40 a. m. the 15th till 6¼ a. m. on the 16th; amount, 4.061 inches.
Sept. 15	7 a. m.	------	70	.551	Nim. 10	E. 2	NE. 3	75	16th. Rain from 8 to 9 a. m.; amount, 0.192 inch.
	2 p. m.	------	73	.545	Nim. 10	E. 2	NE. 3	67	19th. Rain from 10½ a. m. to 7 p. m.; amount, 3 inches.
	9 p. m.	------	70	.551	Nim. 10	E. 2	N. 4	75	
Sept. 16	7 a. m.	------	69	.564	Nim. 10	E. 2	NW. 4	79	
	2 p. m.	------	79	.465	Cu. 5	E. 2	NW. 3	47	
	9 p. m.	------	75	.519	0	----------	NW. 3	60	
Sept. 17	7 a. m.	------	68	.577	0	----------	NW. 2	85	
	2 p. m.	------	84	.397	Cu. 4	W. 1	NW. 2	34	
	9 p. m.	------	77	.492	0	----------	NW. 2	53	
Sept. 18	7 a. m.	------	68	.577	0	----------	W. 2	85	
	2 p. m.	------	87	.393	Dim cir. 1	W. 1	W. 1	31	
	9 p. m.	------	71	.537	0	----------	W. 1	71	
Sept. 19	7 a. m.	------	73	.476	Nim. 10	SE. 2	S. 2	59	
	2 p. m.	------	76	.541	Nim. 9	SE. 2	S. [illegible]	60	
	9 p. m.	------	75	.519	Nim. 10	SE. 2	S. 3	60	
Sept. 20	7 a. m.	------	65	.549	Nim. 10	N. 3	NW. 3	89	
	2 p. m.	------	71	.537	Nim. 10	N. 2	NW. 3	71	
	9 p. m.	------	64	.497	Nim. 10	N. 2	NW. 2	83	

STORMS Nos. 2 AND 3, SEPTEMBER, 1859.

SELMA, ALABAMA—Continued.

Month and day.	Hour.	Barom'r corrected to 32° F.	Thermometer.	Force of vapor.	Cloudiness.	Motion of clouds.	Winds.	Relative humidity.	REMARKS.
Sept. 21	7 a. m.	------	61	.473	Nim. 10	NW. 3	NW. 3	88	
	2 p. m.	------	64	.464	Nim. 10	NW. 3	NW. 3	77	
	9 p. m.	------	62	.491	0	----------	NW. 3	88	
Sept. 22	7 a. m.	------	56	.420	0	----------	NW. 3	94	
	2 p. m.	------	70	.449	Cir ------ Cu. 6	E. 2 W. 2	NW. 3	61	
	9 p. m.	------	64	.497	0	----------	NW. 3	83	
Sept. 23	7 a. m.	------	59	.439	0	----------	N. 2	88	
	2 p. m.	------	76	.505	Cir. 2	N. 2	N. 3	56	
	9 p. m.	------	67	.556	0	----------	N. 2	84	
Sept. 24	7 a. m.	------	59	.439	0	----------	N. 1	88	
	2 p. m.	------	76	.505	0	----------	N. 2	56	
	9 p. m.	------	69	.564	0	----------	N. 2	79	

COLUMBUS, MISSISSIPPI.

Month and day.	Hour.	Barom'r corrected to 32° F.	Thermometer.	Force of vapor.	Cloudiness.	Motion of clouds.	Winds.	Relative humidity.	REMARKS.
Sept. 14	9 p. m.	29.762	72.8	.545	Cir. st. 3	W. 2	N. 1	67	15th. Commenced raining at 5 p. m. and ended ?; amount, 0.108 inch.
Sept. 15	7 a. m.	.773	67.5	.543	Cir. cu. 6	S. 2	SE. 2	79	
	2 p. m.	.735	77.9	.725	Cu. st. 10	SE. 3	SE. 3	75	
	9 p. m.	.651	70.6	.704	Nim. 10	----------	E. 3	94	19th. Rain from 4 a. m. till noon; amount, 1.99 inch.
Sept. 16	7 a. m.	.613	70.3	.615	Cu. st. 10	N. 3	N. 3	83	
	2 p. m.	.638	85.1	.595	Cu. 3	N. 3	N. 3	49	
	9 p. m.	.699	72.6	.709	0	----------	N. 1	88	
Sept. 17	7 a. m.	.801	66.6	.619	0	----------	N. 1	94	
	2 p. m.	.740	88.1	.707	Cir. cu. 4	E. 2	S. 2	53	
	9 p. m.	.742	74.3	.715	St. 1	----------	E. 2	85	
Sept. 18	7 a. m.	.793	68.9	.607	Cir. 3	W. 2	S. 2	86	
	2 p. m.	.701	88.7	.752	Cu. 4	W. 2	S. 3	56	
	9 p. m.	.652	77.2	.738	Cir. st. 2	----------	E. 2	79	
Sept. 19	7 a. m.	.598	70.6	.717	Nim. 10	SE. 1	SE. 2	95	
	2 p. m.	.492	78.5	.863	Cu. st. 7	S. 2	NW. 2	89	
	9 p. m.	.556	68.8	.599	St. 1	----------	NW. 2	85	
Sept. 20	7 a. m.	.611	62.3	.500	Cu. st. 9	NW. 3	NW. 2	88	
	2 p. m.	.589	65.8	.470	Cu. st. 10	NW. 3	NW. 3	73	
	9 p. m.	.631	60.3	.480	Cir. cu. 6	----------	N. 2	91	
Sept. 21	7 a. m.	.686	57.7	.394	Cu. st. 5	W. 3	W. 2	82	
	2 p. m.	.628	65.8	.470	Cu. st. 9	W. 3	W. 2	73	
	9 p. m.	.707	61.6	.495	Cu. st. 7	----------	W. 1	90	
Sept. 22	7 a. m.	.815	59.8	.456	Cir. st. 1	W. 2	W. 2	88	
	2 p. m.	.802	71.4	.514	Cu. 6	W. 2	W. 2	66	
	9 p. m.	.835	61.8	.523	St. 1	----------	N. 1	94	
Sept. 23	7 a. m.	.965	56.1	.434	St. 1	----------	N. 2	95	
	2 p. m.	.910	76.4	.516	Cu. 3	N. 2	N. 2	56	
	9 p. m.	.912	62.9	.533	St. 1	----------	N. 1	93	
Sept. 24	7 a. m.	.972	56	.428	0	----------	W. 1	94	
	2 p. m.	.874	77.3	.506	Cu. 1	N. 2	N. 1	54	
	9 p. m.	.834	65.5	.593	0	----------	N. 1	01	

NATCHEZ, MISSISSIPPI.

Month and day.	Hour.	Barom'r corrected to 32° F.	Thermometer.	Force of vapor.	Cloudiness.	Motion of clouds.	Winds.	Relative humidity.	REMARKS.
Sept. 14	9 p. m.	29.50	76	------	0	0	N. 2	------	14th. Morning clouds, cirri and cumuli; at noon, cumuli innumerable; in the evening, cumuli of every form.
Sept. 15	7 a. m.	.48	70	------	Cir. cu. 8	NW. 1	NE. 4	------	
	2 p. m.	.40	87	------	Cir. 5	SW. 1	N. 12	------	
	9 p. m.	.40	78	------	10	----------	N. 4	------	
Sept. 16	7 a. m.	.40	72	------	0	0	NE. 2	------	15th. Morning, cirri and cumuli; at noon, cirri of every form; evening, overcast; a light sprinkle of rain at 6 p. m.
	2 p. m.	.50	85	------	0	0	NE. 4	------	
	9 p. m.	.50	78	------	0	0	NE. 2	------	
Sept. 17	7 a. m.	.55	70	------	------------	----------	NE. 2	------	
	2 p. m.	.55	86	------	Cir. 3	NW. 1	W. 12	------	16th. Morning very clear, a cloudless sky.
	9 p. m.	.55	78	------	0	0	SW. 2	------	

STORMS Nos. 2 AND 3, SEPTEMBER, 1859.

NATCHEZ, MISSISSIPPI—Continued.

Month and day.	Hour.	Barom'r corrected to 32° F.	Thermometer.	Force of vapor.	Cloudiness.		Motion of clouds.		Winds.		Relative humidity.	REMARKS.
Sept. 18	7 a. m.	29. 55	72	------	Cir. cu.	5	NW.	1	S.	2	------	17th. Morning hazy; at noon large cumuli; in the evening cir.; hazy.
	2 p. m.	. 50	87	------	Cir. cu.	5	SW.	1	SW.	12	------	
	9 p. m.	. 55	78	------		10	----------		SW.	1	------	18th. Morning cirri and cumuli; at noon cirri cumuli; overcast all the evening; at 9 p. m. began to drizzle.
Sept. 19	7 a. m.	. 40	74	------		10	----------		SW.	4	------	
	2 p. m.	. 35	82	------	Cir.	8	SW.	2	NW.	12	------	
	9 p. m.	. 40	70	------		0		0	N.	4	------	
Sept. 20	7 a. m.	. 40	62	------	Cir.	8	NW.	1	N.	4	------	19th. Morning overcast and rainy till 9 a. m.; amount rain, 0.51 inch; at noon large cumuli; evening a few cumuli and strati; at 9 p. m. clear, with lightning in SE.
	2 p. m.	. 38	68	------		10	----------		N.	4	------	
	9 p. m.	. 40	64	------		10	----------		NW.	4	------	
Sept. 21	7 a. m.	. 45	60	------		10	----------		N.	4	------	
	2 p. m.	. 45	70	------	Cu.	8	NW.	1	NW.	4	------	
	9 p. m.	. 45	60	------		0		0	N.	2	------	20th. Morning large cumuli; at noon overcast; at 5 p. m. a light sprinkle of rain.
Sept. 22	7 a. m.	. 50	55	------		0		0	SE.	4	------	
	2 p. m.	. 53	74	------	Cir. cu	5	NW.	1	SW.	2	------	
	9 p. m.	. 55	68	------		0		0	SW.	2	------	21st. Morning overcast; at noon large cumuli; evening clear; brilliant sunset.
Sept. 23	7 a. m.	. 65	66	------		10	----------		SE.	2	------	
	2 p. m.	. 65	78	------	Cu.	5	NW.	1	SW.	4	------	
	9 p. m.	. 65	70	------		0		0	NE.	2	------	22d. Morning clear and cool; at noon cirri cumuli; in the evening fleecy cirri; at 9 p m. very clear.
Sept. 24	8 a. m.	. 70	64	------		0		0	E.	4	------	
	2 p. m.	. 70	80	------	Cu.	3	NE.	1	N.	4	------	
	9 p. m.	. 60	70	------		0		0	N.	2	------	23d. Equinox, overcast; at noon cumuli cirri; clear sunset.
												24th. Clear; at noon cumuli; clear sunset.

PAULDING, MISSISSIPPI.

Month and day.	Hour.	Barom'r corrected to 32° F.	Thermometer.	Force of vapor.	Cloudiness.		Motion of clouds.		Winds.		Relative humidity.	REMARKS.
Sept. 14	9 p. m.	29. 64	81. 6	. 677		3	SW.	1	NE.	2	66	15th. Cumulus clouds SE. from NE. at 7 p. m.; top just visible SE. 4; wind at 6 p. m. NE. 5, clouds same; began to rain at noon and ended at 1 a. m. on the 16th; amount, 1.65 inch.
Sept. 15	7 a. m.	29. 62	71	. 621	St.	10	SW.	2	NE.	3	85	
	2 p. m.	29. 58	76	. 771	Nim.	10	NE	4	NE.	4	90	
	9 p. m.	29. 42	71	. 759	Nim.	10	NE.	1	NE.	4	100	
Sept. 16	7 a. m.	29. 52	71. 5	. 702	Nim.	7	NW.	3	NW.	2	97	
	2 p. m.	29. 57	87	. 829	Cu.	3	NW.	3	NW.	3	79	
	9 p. m.	29. 62	80	. 870	Cu.	1	NE.	1	NE.	1	91	19th. Rain from 7 a. m. to 3 p. m.; lightning at 9 p. m.; amount rain, 3.50 inches.
Sept. 17	7 a. m.	29. 68	73. 5	. 758	St.	1	SW.	1	NE.	1	90	
	2 p. m.	------	------	------		0		0	------------		------	
	9 p. m.	29. 64	82. 5	. 820		0	----------		E.	2	81	20th. Mist from 9 to 10. 30 a. m.; after 2 p. m. light showers from NW.
Sept. 18	7 a. m.	29. 66	76	. 818	St.	1	W.	1	W.	1	93	
	2 p. m.	29. 62	92. 5	. 683	Cu.	5	SW.	2	SW.	2	100	
	9 p. m.	29. 59	82	. 813	Nim.	6	SW.	2	SW.	2	82	
Sept. 19	7 a. m.	29. 52	76	. 839	Nim.	10	SW.	4	SW.	2	100	
	2 p. m.	29. 46	76. 6	. 839	Nim.	10	SW.	4	SW.	2	100	
	9 p. m.	29. 49	72	. 713		1	NW.	2	NW.	3	92	
Sept. 20	7 a. m.	29. 51	62. 5	. 592	Cu.	1	NW.	3	NW.	1	98	
	2 p. m.	29. 50	69. 5	. 635		10	NW.	3	NW.	2	90	
	9 p. m.	29. 54	62. 3	. 596		2	NW.	1	NW.	1	100	
Sept. 21	7 a. m.	29. 58	59	. 487	Nim.	6	NW.	3	NW.	1	94	
	2 p. m.	29. 59	67. 5	. 556		10	NW.	1	NW.	1	84	
	9 p. m.	29. 61	62	. 546	St.	1	NE.	1	NE.	1	92	
Sept. 22	7 a. m.	29. 68	56. 5	. 500		0	----------		E.	1	100	
	2 p. m.	29. 69	77	. 595	Cu.	5	NE.	2	NE.	2	76	
	9 p. m.	29. 71	68	. 591		1	E.	1	E.	2	89	

WESTVILLE, MISSISSIPPI.

Month and day.	Hour.	Barom'r corrected to 32° F.	Thermometer.	Force of vapor.	Cloudiness.		Motion of clouds.		Winds.		Relative humidity.	REMARKS.
Sept. 14	9 p. m.	------	85	------	Nim.	2		0	SE.	2	------	14th and 15th. Pleasant.
Sept. 15	7 a. m.	------	74	------	Nim.	8	E.	1	E.	1	------	16th. Cool; soft rain; clear sunset.
	2 p. m.	------	82	------	Nim.	10	NW.	3	W.	1	------	
	9 p. m.	------	70	------	------------		----------		------------		------	
Sept. 16	7 a. m.	------	70	------	Cu. st.	9	SE.	3	S.	3	------	
	2 p. m.	------	90	------	Fleecy	1	S.	4	W.	4	------	
	9 p. m.	------	84	------	Hazy	0		0		0	------	

STORMS Nos. 2 AND 3, SEPTEMBER, 1859.

WESTVILLE, MISSISSIPPI—Continued.

Month and day.	Hour.	Barom'r corrected to 32° F.	Thermometer.	Force of vapor.	Cloudiness.		Motion of clouds.		Winds.		Relative humidity.	REMARKS.
Sept. 17	7 a. m.	------	73	------		0		0		0	------	19th. Rain all day; cool and
	2 p. m.	------	94	------		4	WSW.	2	SW.	2	------	showery.
	9 p. m.	------	90	------	------------		----------		W.	0	------	20th. Cool rain.
Sept. 18	7 a. m.	------	82	------		0		0	E.	1	------	22d. Variablo.
	2 p. m.	------	90	------	Cir. st.	3	W.	3	W.	3	------	23d. Thin fleecy stratus clouds,
	9 p. m.	------	------	------	------------		----------			0	------	floating
Sept. 19	7 a. m.	------	68	------	Nim.	10	WSW.	3	ESE.	1	------	24th and 25th. Clear and pleasant;
	2 p. m.	------	80	------	Cu. st.	9	SW.	2	NE.	2	------	cool mornings and nights.
	9 p. m.	------	78	------	St.	7		0		0	------	
Sept. 20	7 a. m.	------	64	------	Nim	10	SW.	4	WSW.	2	------	
	2 p. m.	------	70	------	Cir. cu.	10	SE.	3	SE.	3	------	
	9 p. m.	------	67	------	------------		----------		S.	2	------	
Sept. 21	7 a. m.	------	60	------	Nim.	9	SSW.	2	SW.	2	------	
	2 p. m.	------	66	------	Cir. cu.	10		0	------------		------	
	9 p. m.	------	68	------	------------		----------			0	------	
Sept. 22	7 a m.	------	51	------		0		0	SE.	1	------	
	2 p. m.	------	78	------		2		0		0	------	
	9 p. m.	------	66	------	Cu.	2		0		0	------	
Sept. 23	7 a. m.	------	57	------	Cir. st.	3		0	SW.	2	------	
	2 p. m.	------	82	------	Cu.	4	SE.	1	------------		------	
	9 p. m.	------	70	------	------------		----------			0	------	
Sept. 24	7 a. m.	------	70	------	St.	2		0	SE.	1	------	
	2 p. m	------	85	------		0		0		0	------	
	9 p. m.	------	73	------		0		0	SW.	1	------	

NEW ORLEANS, LOUISIANA.

Month and day.	Hour.	Barom'r corrected to 32° F.	Thermometer.	Force of vapor.	Cloudiness.	Motion of clouds.	Winds.	Relative humidity.	REMARKS.
Sept. 14	3 p. m.	------	87	------	------------	----------	SE.	------	14th. Clear.
Sept. 15	9 a. m.	------	80	------	------------	----------	NE.	------	15th. Rain
	12 m	------	79	------	------------	----------	NE.	------	16th. Clear.
	3 p. m.	------	77	------	------------	----------	NE.	------	17th and 18th. Rain.
Sept. 16	9 a. m.	------	79	------	------------	----------	NW.	------	19th to 24th. Clear.
	12 m	------	83	------	------------	----------	NW	------	
	3 p. m.	------	86	------	------------	----------	SW.	------	
Sept. 17	9 a. m.	------	83	------	------------	----------	SW.	------	
	12 m	------	85	------	------------	----------	SE.	------	
	3 p. m.	------	88	------	------------	----------	SE	------	
Sept. 18	9 a. m.	------	80	------	------------	----------	SW.	------	
	12 m.	------	87	------	------------	----------	SE	------	
	3 p. m.	------	84	------	------------	----------	NE.	------	
Sept. 19	9 a. m.	------	78	------	------------	----------	SW.	------	
	12 m.	------	78	------	------------	----------	SW.	------	
	3 p. m.	------	81	------	------------	----------	SW.	------	
Sept. 20	9 a. m.	------	71	------	------------	----------	NW	------	
	12 m.	------	73	------	------------	----------	NE.	------	
	3 p. m.	------	75	------	------------	----------	NW	------	
Sept. 21	9 a. m.	------	68	------	------------	----------	NE.	------	
	12 m	------	70	------	------------	----------	NE.	------	
	3 p. m.	------	73	------	------------	----------	NE.	------	
Sept. 22	9 a. m.	------	70	------	------------	----------	NE.	------	
	12 m	------	75	------	------------	----------	NE.	------	
	3 p. m.	------	77	------	------------	----------	NE.	------	
Sept. 23	9 a. m.	------	75	------	------------	----------	NE.	------	
	12 m.	------	79	------	------------	----------	NE.	------	
	3 p. m.	------	81	------	------------	----------	SE.	------	
Sept. 24	9 a. m.	------	76	------	------------	----------	SE.	------	
	12 m	------	81	------	------------	----------	SE.	------	
	3 p. m.	------	82	------	------------	----------	SE.	------	

STORMS Nos. 2 AND 3, SEPTEMBER, 1859.

POYDRAS COLLEGE, LOUISIANA.

Month and day.	Hour.	Barom'r corrected to 32° F.	Thermometer.	Force of vapor.	Cloudiness.	Motion of clouds.	Winds.		Relative humidity.	REMARKS.
Sept. 14	9 p. m.	------	------	------	1	----------	N.	2	------	
Sept. 15	7 a. m.	------	------	------	4	----------	N.	3	------	
	2 p. m.	------	------	------	10	----------	N.	2	------	
	9 p. m.	------	------	------	4	----------	N.	3	------	
Sept. 16	7 a. m.	------	------	------	5	----------		0	------	
	2 p. m.	------	------	------	0	----------		0	------	
	9 p. m.	------	------	------	5	----------		0	------	
Sept. 17	7 a. m.	------	------	------	4	----------	S.	1	------	
	2 p. m.	------	------	------	5	----------		0	------	
	9 p. m.	------	------	------	2	----------	S.	1	------	
Sept. 18	7 a. m.	------	------	------	4	----------	N.	1	------	
	2 p. m.	------	------	------	10	----------	N.	2	------	
	9 p. m.	------	------	------	10	----------	N.	2	------	
Sept. 19	7 a. m.	------	------	------	6	----------	N.	2	------	
	2 p. m.	------	------	------	10	----------	N.	4	------	
	9 p. m.	------	------	------	10	----------	N.	3	------	
Sept. 20	7 a. m.	------	------	------	2	----------	S.	2	------	
	2 p. m.	------	------	------	3	----------	S.	3	------	
	9 p. m.	------	------	------	4	----------		0	------	
Sept. 21	7 a. m	------	------	------	2	----------	S.	1	------	
	2 p. m.	------	------	------	1	----------		0	------	
	9 p. m.	------	------	------	0	----------		0	------	
Sept. 22	7 a. m.	------	------	------	3	----------	NW.	1	------	
	2 p. m.	------	------	------	6	----------	NW.	2	------	
	9 p. m.	------	------	------	0	----------	NW.	3	------	
Sept. 23	7 a. m.	------	------	------	2	----------	NW.	1	------	
	2 p. m.	------	------	------	0	----------	NW.	2	------	
	9 p. m.	------	------	------	0	----------	NW.	2	------	
Sept. 24	7 a. m.	------	------	------	3	----------	S.	1	------	
	2 p. m.	------	------	------	0	----------	S.	2	------	
	9 p. m.	------	------	------	0	----------	S.	1	------	

TICKFAW STATION, LOUISIANA.

Month and day.	Hour.	Barom'r corrected to 32° F.	Thermometer.	Force of vapor.	Cloudiness.	Motion of clouds.	Winds.		Relative humidity.	REMARKS.
Sept. 14	9 p. m.	------	------	------	4	----------	SW.	2	------	19th. Heavy rain from 3 to 10 a. m.
Sept. 15	7 a. m.	------	------	------	1	----------	SW.	1	------	
	2 p. m.	------	------	------	0	----------	SW.	1	------	
	9 p. m.	------	------	------	2	----------	SW.	0	------	
Sept. 16	7 a. m.	------	------	------	0	----------	SW.	2	------	
	2 p. m.	------	------	------	3	----------	W.	3	------	
	9 p. m.	------	------	------	1	----------	W.	3	------	
Sept. 17	7 a. m.	------	------	------	1	----------	W.	1	------	
	2 p. m.	------	------	------	0	----------	W.	1	------	
	9 p. m.	------	------	------	2	----------	W.	1	------	
Sept. 18	7 a. m.	------	------	------	0	----------	W.	1	------	
	2 p. m.	------	------	------	8	----------	W.	2	------	
	9 p. m.	------	------	------	10	----------	SW.	0	------	
Sept. 19	7 a. m.	------	------	------	10	----------	SW.	1	------	
	2 p. m.	------	------	------	10	----------	SW.	3	------	
	9 p. m.	------	------	------	10	----------	W.	1	------	
Sept. 20	7 a. m.	------	------	------	8	----------	W.	2	------	
	2 p. m.	------	------	------	8	----------	NW.	2	------	
	9 p. m.	------	------	------	7	----------	NW.	2	------	
Sept. 21	7 a. m.	------	------	------	6	----------	N.	2	------	
	2 p. m.	------	------	------	5	----------	N.	3	------	
	9 p. m.	------	------	------	4	----------	N.	1	------	
Sept. 22	7 a. m.	------	------	------	3	----------	N.	2	------	
	2 p. m.	------	------	------	2	----------	NW.	2	------	
	9 p. m.	------	------	------	4	----------	NW.	0	------	
Sept. 23	7 a. m.	------	------	------	0	----------	NW.	1	------	
	2 p. m.	------	------	------	0	----------	NW.	2	------	
	9 p. m.	------	------	------	1	----------	NW.	1	------	
Sept. 24	7 a. m.	------	------	------	0	----------	NW.	1	------	
	2 p. m.	------	------	------	1	----------	N.	2	------	
	9 p. m.	------	------	------	1	----------	N.	1	------	

STORMS Nos. 2 AND 3, SEPTEMBER, 1859.

AUSTIN CITY, TEXAS.*

Month and day.	Hour.	Barom'r corrected to 32° F.	Thermometer.	Force of vapor.	Cloudiness.	Motion of clouds.	Winds.	Relative humidity.	REMARKS.
Sept. 14	9 p. m.	29.39	73	.507	Cir. cu. 3	NW. 1	NW. 0	43	14th. Shower at 5 p. m.; distant thunder, S. W., from 4 to 5 p. m. 17th. Shower about noon. 23d. Lightning from 4 to 5 p. m., NE 24th. Shower, with lightning, NW., from 4 to 5 p. m.
Sept. 15	7 a. m.	29.42	75	.666	0	0	S. 0	77	
	2 p. m.	29.34	89	.529	Cu. 2	W. 1	SE. 1	36	
	9 p. m.	29.36	78	.077	0	0	W. 0	66	
Sept. 16	7 a. m.	29.41	79	.717	0	0	SE. 0	70	
	2 p. m.	29.35	91	.542	Cu. 1	0	SE. 0	35	
	9 p. m.	29.38	80	.664	Cu. 2	S. 2	E. 0	62	

* Swante Palm, observer.

AUSTIN, TEXAS.*

Month and day.	Hour.	Barom'r corrected to 32° F.	Thermometer.	Force of vapor.	Cloudiness.	Motion of clouds.	Winds.	Relative humidity.	REMARKS.
Sept. 14	9 p. m.	------	74.5	.792	Cir., nim. 4	NW. 1	W. 2	93	14th. Distant thunder at noon; 2 p. m. loud and near; 4.30 p. m. light shower SW.; S. and SE. heavy rain; amount, 0.21 inch. 18th. Shower at 7 a. m; amount, 0.07 inch; shower from 2.20 to 2.50 p. m.; amount, 0.52 inch; thunder and forked lightning in the evening. 23d. Few drops rain from 8.30 to 9 p. m. 24th. Showers at 7 and 9 a. m.; wind, thunder, and rain at 3.30 p. m.; diffused lightning in the evening; amount, 0.35 inch.
Sept. 15	7 a. m.	------	73	.732	0	----------	N. 1	90	
	2 p. m.	------	90	.707	Cu. 3	N. 1	S. 1	51	
	9 p. m.	------	79.5	.807	0	----------	N. 1	80	
Sept. 16	7 a. m.	------	76	.731	Cir. 1	0	W. 1	81	
	2 p. m.	------	92	.596	Cu. 2	0	S. 2	40	
	9 p. m.	------	80.5	.751	Cir. and cu. 1	0	SW. 1	72	
Sept. 17	7 a. m.	------	76.5	.805	Cir. cu. 1	0	S. 1	88	
	2 p. m.	------	91	.610	Cu. 2	S. 1	S. 3	42	
	9 p. m.	------	75	.666	Nim. 1	----------	S. 2	77	
Sept. 18	7 a. m.	------	74	.798	Nim. 10	S. 2	S. 0	95	
	2 p. m.	------	85	.774	Nim. 10	0	S. 1	65	
	9 p. m.	------	74.5	.792	Nim. 10	----------	W. 1	93	
Sept. 19	7 a. m.	------	71	.503	Cir. 1	----------	N. 3	66	
	2 p. m.	------	81	.369	Cir. 1	----------	N. 3	35	
	9 p. m.	------	70	.323	0	----------	N. 3	44	
Sept. 20	7 a. m.	------	64	.433	0	----------	NW. 3	73	
	2 p. m.	------	80.5	.376	St. 1	0	NW. 3	36	
	9 p. m.	------	64.5	.396	0	----------	W. 2	65	
Sept. 21	7 a. m.	------	60	.456	0	----------	N. 1	88	
	2 p. m.	------	81	.335	0	----------	S. 2	32	
	9 p. m.	------	64	.433	0	----------	W. 1	73	
Sept. 22	7 a. m.	------	60	.456	Cir. 8	SW. 1	0	88	
	2 p. m.	------	82	.497	Cir. 9	0	S. 3	45	
	9 p. m.	------	72	.489	Nim. 1	----------	S. 3	62	
Sept. 23	7 a. m.	------	66	.570	Cir. cu. 7	W. 1	N. 1	89	
	2 p. m.	------	89	.596	Cu. 3	S. 1	S. 3	43	
	9 p. m.	------	77.5	.792	Cu. 10	----------	E. 3	84	
Sept. 24	7 a. m.	------	75	.826	Nim. 10	----------	E. 1	95	
	2 p. m.	------	84	.789	Cu. 3	S. 2	N. 2	68	
	9 p. m.	------	73	.771	Nim. 10	----------	S. 3	95	

* Van Nostrand, observer.

BOSTON, TEXAS.

Month and day.	Hour.	Barom'r corrected to 32° F.	Thermometer.	Force of vapor.	Cloudiness.	Motion of clouds.	Winds.	Relative humidity.	REMARKS.
Sept. 14	9 p. m.	------	------	------	9	----------	S. 1	------	14th. Light rain and lightning S., (distant.)
Sept. 15	7 a. m.	------	------	------	0	----------	SE. 1	------	
	2 p. m.	------	------	------	3	----------	S. 1	------	
	9 p. m.	------	------	------	1	----------	S. 1	------	
Sept. 16	7 a. m.	------	------	------	0	----------	S. 1	------	
	2 p. m.	------	------	------	3	----------	E. 1	------	
	9 p. m.	------	------	------	0	----------	S. 1	------	
Sept. 17	7 a. m.	------	------	------	1	----------	S. 1	------	
	2 p. m.	------	------	------	4	----------	S. 1	------	
	9 p. m.	------	------	------	3	----------	SE. 1	------	

STORMS Nos. 2 AND 3, SEPTEMBER, 1859.

BOSTON, TEXAS—Continued.

Month and day.	Hour.	Barom'r corrected to 32° F.	Thermometer.	Force of vapor.	Cloudiness.	Motion of clouds.	Winds.		Relative humidity.	REMARKS.
Sept. 18	7 a. m.	......	......	......	2	....	S.	1	......	19th. Cloudy and cold.
	2 p. m.	......	......	......	5	....	SE.	2	......	22d. Autumn weather.
	9 p. m.	......	......	......	9	....	S.	1	......	24th. Pleasant.
Sept. 19	7 a. m.	......	......	......	7	....	W.	3	......	
	2 p. m.	......	......	......	5	....	NW.	3	......	
	9 p. m.	......	......	......	2	....	NE.	1	......	
Sept. 20	7 a. m	......	......	......	9	....	N.	1	......	
	2 p. m.	......	......	......	3	....	NW.	2	......	
	9 p. m.	......	......	......	1	....	NW.	1	......	
Sept. 21	7 a. m.	......	......	......	8	....	N.	1	......	
	2 p. m.	......	......	......	3	....	NW.	1	......	
	9 p m.	......	......	......	0	....	E.	1	......	
Sept. 22	7 a. m.	......	......	......	4	....	NW.	1	......	
	2 p. m.	......	......	......	2	....	W.	1	......	
	9 p. m.	......	......	......	2	....	W.	1	......	
Sept. 23	7 a. m.	......	......	......	4	....	S.	1	......	
	2 p. m.	......	......	......	3	....	SE.	1	......	
	9 p. m.	......	......	......	0	....	NE.	1	......	
Sept. 24	7 a. m.	......	......	......	3	....	SE.	1	......	
	2 p. m.	......	......	......	4	....	S.	1	......	
	9 p. m.	......	......	......	3	....	S.	1	......	

BURKEVILLE, TEXAS.

Month and day.	Hour.	Barom'r corrected to 32° F.	Thermometer.	Force of vapor.	Cloudiness.	Motion of clouds.	Winds.		Relative humidity.	REMARKS.
Sept. 14	9 p. m.	......	......	......	5	....		0	......	14th. Cool and pleasant.
Sept. 15	7 a m.	......	......	......	5	....		0	......	15th. Warm.
	2 p m.	......	......	......	4	....	SW.	1	......	16th. Very warm and sultry.
	9 p m.	......	......	......	0	....		0	......	17th. Thick fog till 9 a. m.; very warm.
Sept. 16	7 a. m.	......	......	......	0	....		0	......	
	2 p. m.	......	......	......	0	....		0	......	18th. Shower at 11 a. m.; foggy morning; gentle rain all night.
	9 p. m.	......	......	......	5	....		0	......	
Sept. 17	7 a m.	......	......	......	10	....		0	......	19th. Rain ceased with hard shower at 6 a. m.; cool, pleasant day.
	2 p. m.	......	......	......	4	....	SE.	1	......	
	9 p. m.	......	......	......	5	....		0	......	20th. Cool; heavy dew.
Sept. 18	7 a. m.	......	......	......	5	....		0	......	21st, 22d, and 23d. Cool and pleasant.
	2 p. m.	......	......	......	10	....	SE.	1	......	
	9 p. m.	......	......	......	10	....	NE.	1	......	24th. Warm and pleasant.
Sept. 19	7 a. m.	......	......	......	0	....	NE.	2	......	
	2 p. m.	......	......	......	1	....	NE.	3	......	
	9 p. m.	......	......	......	0	....	N.	2	......	
Sept. 20	7 a. m.	......	......	......	0	....	N.	2	......	
	2 p. m.	......	......	......	4	....	NE.	2	......	
	9 p. m.	......	......	......	0	....	NW.	1	......	
Sept. 21	7 a. m.	......	......	......	0	....	N.	1	......	
	2 p. m.	......	......	......	4	....		0	......	
	9 p. m.	......	......	......	3	....	NW.	1	......	
Sept. 22	7 a. m.	......	......	......	4	....	NW.	1	......	
	2 p. m.	......	......	......	8	....	W.	1	......	
	9 p. m.	......	......	......	5	....	N.	1	......	
Sept. 23	7 a. m.	......	......	......	5	....	N.	1	......	
	2 p. m.	......	......	......	0	....	NW.	1	......	
	9 p. m.	......	......	......	2	....	N.	1	......	
Sept. 24	7 a. m.	......	......	......	6	....	NE.	1	......	
	2 p. m.	......	......	......	4	....	SW.	2	......	
	9 p. m.	......	......	......	4	....		0	......	

STORMS Nos. 2 AND 3, SEPTEMBER, 1859.

GILMER, TEXAS.

Month and day.	Hour.	Barom'r corrected to 32° F.	Thermometer.	Force of vapor.	Cloudiness.	Motion of clouds.	Winds.	Relative humidity.
Sept. 14	9 p. m.	......	......	......	8	....	....	......
Sept. 15	7 a. m.	......	74	......	....	....	SW. 1	......
	2 p. m.	......	87	......	1	....	S. 1	......
	9 p. m.	......	......	......	....	....	....	......
Sept. 16	7 a. m.	......	75	......	....	....	....	......
	2 p. m.	......	89	......	1	....	S. 1	......
	9 p. m.	......	......	......	....	....	....	......
Sept. 17	7 a. m.	......	74	......	....	....	S. 1	......
	2 p. m.	......	87	......	1	....	S. 2	......
	9 p. m.	......	......	......	....	....	SW. 2	......
Sept. 18	7 a. m.	......	72	......	4	....	SW. 2	......
	2 p. m.	......	75	......	10	....	NW. 2	......
	9 p. m.	......	......	......	5	....	....	......
Sept. 19	7 a. m.	......	60	......	....	....	N. 2	......
	2 p. m.	......	78	......	2	....	NW. 3	......
	9 p. m.	......	......	......	....	....	N. 3	......
Sept. 20	7 a. m.	......	56	......	....	....	N. 3	......
	2 p. m.	......	79	......	5	....	N. 3	......
	9 p. m.	......	......	......	....	....	....	......
Sept. 21	7 a. m.	......	48	......	....	....	SE. 2	......
	2 p. m.	......	84	......	....	....	S. 1	......
	9 p. m.	......	......	......	....	....	....	......
Sept. 22	7 a. m.	......	54	......	3	....	S. 1	......
	2 p. m.	......	82	......	5	....	S. 2	......
	9 p. m.	......	......	......	3	....	....	......
Sept. 23	7 a. m.	......	62	......	5	....	S. 1	......
	2 p. m.	......	86	......	3	....	S. 2	......
	9 p. m.	......	......	......	....	....	....	......
Sept. 24	7 a. m.	......	64	......	1	....	S. 2	......
	2 p. m.	......	83	......	9	....	S. 1	......
	9 p. m.	......	......	......	1	....	....	......

REMARKS.

14th. Heavy fog at daylight; rain, accompanied by thunder, in the evening.
18th. Rain at 2 p. m; heavy thunder; wind NW; cool.
19th Cool, fresh breeze from NW.; thin clouds from same direction.
20th. Cool, fresh breeze from N.; thick clouds at 8 p. m. from N.
22d. Hazy, clouds NW.
23d. Clouds from SW. in the morning, clear in the evening.
24th. Light showers from 2 to 3.30 p. m.; clouds from NW.

GONZALES, TEXAS.

Month and day.	Hour.	Barom'r corrected to 32° F.	Thermometer.	Force of vapor.	Cloudiness.	Motion of clouds.	Winds.	Relative humidity.
Sept. 14	9 p. m.	......	......	......	0	....	N. 1	......
Sept. 15	7 a. m.	......	......	......	0	....	N. 1	......
	2 p. m.	......	......	......	0	....	S. 1	......
	9 p. m.	......	......	......	0	....	W. 1	......
Sept. 16	7 a. m.	......	......	......	0	....	N. 1	......
	2 p. m.	......	......	......	0	....	SW. 1	......
	9 p. m.	......	......	......	0	....	W. 1	......
Sept. 17	7 a. m.	......	......	......	1	....	E. 1	......
	2 p. m.	......	......	......	6	....	S. 3	......
	9 p. m.	......	......	......	10	....	S. 1	......
Sept. 18	7 a. m.	......	......	......	10	....	S. 2	......
	2 p. m.	......	......	......	10	....	S. 1	......
	9 p. m.	......	......	......	10	....	E. 1	......
Sept. 19	7 a. m.	......	......	......	0	....	N. 3	......
	2 p. m.	......	......	......	1	....	N. 2	......
	9 p. m.	......	......	......	2	....	N. 1	......
Sept. 20	7 a. m.	......	......	......	0	....	N. 1	......
	2 p. m.	......	......	......	0	....	N. 1	......
	9 p. m.	......	......	......	1	....	N. 1	......
Sept. 21	7 a. m.	......	......	......	0	....	N. 1	......
	2 p. m.	......	......	......	0	....	SE. 1	......
	9 p. m.	......	......	......	0	....	E. 1	......
Sept. 22	7 a. m.	......	......	......	0	....	E. 1	......
	2 p. m.	......	......	......	5	....	S. 2	......
	9 p. m.	......	......	......	8	....	E. 2	......

REMARKS.

18th. Showery; lightning N. in the night.

STORMS Nos. 2 AND 3, SEPTEMBER, 1859.

GONZALES, TEXAS—Continued.

Month and day.	Hour.	Barom'r corrected to 32° F.	Thermometer.	Force of vapor.	Cloudiness.	Motion of clouds.	Winds.	Relative humidity.	REMARKS.
Sept. 23	7 a. m.	------	------	------	5	----------	E. 1	------	24th. Showery; lightning E. in the night.
	2 p. m.	------	------	------	6	----------	S. 3	------	
	9 p. m.	------	------	------	10	----------	E. 2	------	
Sept. 24	7 a. m.	------	------	------	10	----------	S. 1	------	
	2 p. m.	------	------	------	10	----------	S. 1	------	
	9 p. m.	------	------	------	8	----------	S. 1	------	

GREENVILLE, TEXAS.

Month and day.	Hour.	Barom'r corrected to 32° F.	Thermometer.	Force of vapor.	Cloudiness.	Motion of clouds.	Winds.	Relative humidity.	REMARKS.
Sept. 14	9 p. m.	------	------	------	0	----------	W. 1	------	14th. Rain from 2 to 3 p. m.
Sept. 15	7 a. m.	------	------	------	0	----------	SE. 1	------	15th. Heavy fog till 8 a. m.
	2 p. m.	------	------	------	8	----------	SE. 2	------	17th. Several days warm.
	9 p. m.	------	------	------	0	----------	SE. 1	------	18th. Norther.
Sept. 16	7 a. m.	------	------	------	8	----------	SE. 1	------	
	2 p. m.	------	------	------	4	----------	SE. 2	------	
	9 p. m.	------	------	------	0	----------	SE. 1	------	
Sept. 17	7 a. m.	------	------	------	0	----------	SE. 1	------	
	2 p. m.	------	------	------	4	----------	SE. 2	------	
	9 p. m.	------	------	------	0	----------	SE. 1	------	
Sept. 18	7 a. m.	------	------	------	0	----------	SE. 1	------	
	2 p. m.	------	------	------	4	----------	SE. 1	------	
	9 p. m.	------	------	------	0	----------	N. 4	------	
Sept. 19	7 a. m.	------	------	------	0	----------	N. 3	------	
	2 p. m.	------	------	------	0	----------	N. 2	------	
	9 p. m.	------	------	------	0	----------	N. 2	------	
Sept. 20	7 a. m.	------	------	------	0	----------	N. 2	------	
	2 p. m.	------	------	------	0	----------	N. 2	------	
	9 p. m.	------	------	----	0	----------	SE. 1	------	
Sept. 21	7 a. m.	------	------	------	0	----------	SE. 3	------	
	2 p. m.	------	------	------	0	----------	SE. 3	------	
	9 p. m.	------	------	------	0	----------	SE. 3	------	
Sept. 22	7 a. m.	------	------	------	0	----------	SE. 2	------	
	2 p. m.	------	------	------	4	----------	SE. 2	------	
	9 p. m.	------	------	------	0	----------	SE. 2	------	
Sept. 23	7 a. m.	------	------	------	0	----------	S. 3	------	
	2 p. m.	------	------	------	4	----------	S. 4	------	
	9 p. m.	------	------	------	0	----------	S. 1	------	
Sept. 24	7 a. m.	------	------	------	0	----------	S. 1	------	
	2 p. m.	------	------	------	5	----------	S. 3	------	
	9 p. m.	------	------	------	8	----------	S. 1	------	

LARISSA, TEXAS.

Month and day.	Hour.	Barom'r corrected to 32° F.	Thermometer.	Force of vapor.	Cloudiness.	Motion of clouds.	Winds.	Relative humidity.	REMARKS.
Sept. 14	9 p. m.	------	77	.841	Cir. --------	----------	SE. 1	91	Rain on the 13th and 25th, but none recorded from the 14th to the 24th.
Sept. 15	7 a. m.	------	72½	.778	0	0	E. ½	98	
	2 p. m.	------	89¾	.755	Cu. st. 3	----------	NW. 1	54	
	9 p. m.	------	78	.744	0	0	S. 1	78	
Sept. 16	7 a. m.	------	75	.776	0	0	S. ½	89	
	2 p. m.	------	91¼	.734	Cu. st. 2	1	NE. 1	50	
	9 p. m.	------	80	.677	0	0	S. 1	66	
Sept. 17	7 a. m.	------	76½	.765	0	0	S. ½	84	
	2 p. m.	------	92	.712	Cu. st. 2	S. 4	S. 3	47½	
	9 p. m.	------	80	.652	0	0	S. ½	64	
Sept. 18	7 a. m.	------	78	.785	Nim. 8	S. 2	S. 2½	82	
	2 p. m.	------	76	.772	Nim. 10	SW. 2	SW. 1	86	
	9 p. m.	------	74	.773	Nim. 10	----------	N. 2	93	
Sept. 19	7 a. m.	------	62¾	.498	Cir. st. 1	0	NW. 3	87	
	2 p. m.	------	76	.419	Cu. st. 2	NW. 5	NW. 3	46½	
	9 p. m.	------	67¾	.415	0	0	N. 3	61	

STORMS Nos. 2 AND 3, SEPTEMBER, 1859.

LARISSA, TEXAS—Continued.

Month and day.	Hour.	Barom'r corrected to 32° F.	Thermometer.	Force of vapor.	Cloudiness.	Motion of clouds.	Winds.	Relative humidity.	REMARKS.
Sept. 20	7 a. m.	------	57½	.425	0	0	NW. 3	91	
	2 p. m.	------	69	.447	Cu. st. 2	NW. 6	NW. 3	63	
	9 p. m.	------	64½	.466	0	0	S. 1	76	
Sept. 21	7 a. m.	------	55¾	.395	0	0	SW. ⅛	88	
	2 p. m.	------	75	.342	0	0	NW. 3	39	
	9 p. m.	------	65½	.429	0	0	S. 1	68	
Sept. 22	7 a. m.	------	60¼	.452	Cir. cu. 7	NW. 1	SE. 2	86	
	2 p. m.	------	82¼	.527	Cir. cu. 4	W. 2	S. 4	48	
	9 p. m.	------	71	.503	St. ----------	0	SE. 2	66	
Sept. 23	7 a. m.	------	67¾	.566	{ Cir. cu. 4; Cu. st. 2 }	SW. 1	SE. 3	83	
	2 p. m.	------	86¼	.717	Cu. st. 5	SW. 5	SW. 3	77	
	9 p. m.	------	75½	.710	St. ----------	0	S. 1	95	
Sept. 24	7 a. m.	------	71½	.601	Nim. 3	SW. 2	SE. 1	78	
	2 p. m.	------	84	.832	Nim. 2	0	S. 1	72	
	9 p. m.	------	75	.591	0	0	SE. 2	68	

PRESTON, TEXAS.

Month and day.	Hour.	Barom'r corrected to 32° F.	Thermometer.	Force of vapor.	Cloudiness.	Motion of clouds.	Winds.	Relative humidity.	REMARKS.
Sept. 14	9 p. m.	------	------	------	5	----------	0	------	17th. Rain from 4.15 to 5 p. m.; wind E. at 6.
Sept. 15	7 a. m.	------	------	------	5	----------	0	------	
	2 p. m.	------	------	------	3	----------	S. 1	------	20th. Indian summer.
	9 p. m.	------	------	------	0	----------	0	------	24th. Rain from 3.15 to 4 p. m.
Sept. 16	7 a. m.	------	------	------	0	----------	0	------	
	2 p. m.	------	------	------	0	----------	S. 1	------	
	9 p. m.	------	------	------	0	----------	0	------	
Sept. 17	7 a. m.	------	------	------	0	----------	0	------	
	2 p. m.	------	------	------	6	----------	S. 1	------	
	9 p. m.	------	------	------	5	----------	S. 2	------	
Sept. 18	7 a. m.	------	------	------	0	----------	S. 2	------	
	2 p. m.	------	------	------	1	----------	SE. 2	------	
	9 p. m.	------	------	------	0	----------	0	------	
Sept. 19	7 a. m.	------	------	------	3	----------	N. 1	------	
	2 p. m.	------	------	------	2	----------	N. 2	------	
	9 p. m.	------	------	------	0	----------	N. 1	------	
Sept. 20	7 a. m.	------	------	------	0	----------	N. 1	------	
	2 p. m.	------	------	------	0	----------	N. 1	------	
	9 p. m.	------	------	------	0	----------	0	------	
Sept. 21	7 a. m.	------	------	------	0	----------	SE. 1	------	
	2 p. m.	------	------	------	0	----------	SE. 2	------	
	9 p. m.	------	------	------	3	----------	0	------	
Sept. 22	7 a. m.	------	------	------	0	----------	SW. 1	------	
	2 p. m.	------	------	------	0	----------	W. 1	------	
	9 p. m.	------	------	------	0	----------	W. 2	------	
Sept. 23	7 a. m.	------	------	------	0	----------	SW. 1	------	
	2 p. m.	------	------	------	0	----------	S. 1	------	
	9 p. m.	------	------	------	0	----------	S. 4	------	
Sept. 24	7 a. m.	------	------	------	1	----------	E. 1	------	
	2 p. m.	------	------	------	2	----------	SE. 2	------	
	9 p. m.	------	------	------	3	----------	SE. 3	------	

SAN PATRICIO, TEXAS.

Month and day.	Hour.	Barom'r corrected to 32° F.	Thermometer.	Force of vapor.	Cloudiness.	Motion of clouds.	Winds.	Relative humidity.	REMARKS.
Sept. 14	9 p. m.	------	------	------	0	----------	SE. 1	------	14th. Diffused lightning NE. and W. p. m.; extremely warm.
Sept. 15	7 a. m.	------	------	------	0	----------	SE. 1	------	
	2 p. m.	------	------	------	0	----------	SE. 1	------	15th and 16th. Extremely warm.
	9 p. m.	------	------	------	0	----------	SE. 1	------	
Sept. 16	7 a. m.	------	------	------	0	----------	SE. 1	------	
	2 p. m.	------	------	------	0	----------	SE. 2	------	
	9 p. m.	------	------	------	0	----------	SE. 2	------	

STORMS Nos. 2 AND 3, SEPTEMBER, 1859.

SAN PATRICIO, TEXAS—Continued.

Month and day.	Hour.	Barom'r corrected to 32° F.	Thermometer.	Force of vapor.	Cloudiness.	Motion of clouds.	Winds.	Relative humidity.	REMARKS.
Sept. 17	7 a. m.	------	------	------	0	----------	SE. 1	------	17th. Rain from noon to 1 p. m.; very warm.
	2 p. m.	------	------	------	0	----------	SE. 3	------	18th. Lightning diffused N. and NE., W. and SW. p. m.; very warm.
	9 p. m.	------	------	------	0	----------	SE. 2	------	19th and 20th. Cold.
Sept. 18	7 a. m.	------	------	------	0	----------	N. 1	------	21st. Morning cold, day pleasant.
	2 p. m.	------	------	------	0	----------	SE. 1	------	22d and 23d. Pleasant.
	9 p. m.	------	------	------	0	----------	SE. 1	------	24th. Lightning zigzag, NW. and W , p. m.
Sept. 19	7 a. m.	------	------	------	0	----------	N. 2	------	
	2 p. m.	------	------	-----	0	----------	N. 3	------	
	9 p. m.	------	------	------	0	----------	N. 3	------	
Sept. 20	7 a. m.	------	------	------	0	----------	N. 2	------	
	2 p. m.	------	------	------	0	----------	N. 2	------	
	9 p. m.	------	------	------	0	----------	N. 1	------	
Sept. 21	7 a. m.	------	------	------	0	----------	N. 1	------	
	2 p. m.	------	------	------	0	----------	S. 1	------	
	9 p. m.	------	------	------	0	----------	SE. 2	------	
Sept. 22	7 a. m.	------	------	------	0	----------	SE. 3	------	
	2 p. m.	------	------	------	0	----------	SE. 3	------	
	9 p. m.	------	------	------	0	----------	SE. 3	------	
Sept 23	7 a. m.	------	------	------	0	----------	SE. 3	------	
	2 p. m.	------	------	------	0	----------	SE. 3	------	
	9 p. m.	------	------	------	0	----------	SE. 3	------	
Sept. 24	7 a. m.	------	------	------	0	----------	SE. 3	------	
	2 p. m.	------	------	------	0	----------	SE. 3	------	
	9 p. m.	------	------	------	0	----------	SE. 3	------	

SISTERDALE, TEXAS.

Month and day.	Hour.	Barom'r corrected to 32° F.	Thermometer.	Force of vapor.	Cloudiness.	Motion of clouds.	Winds.	Relative humidity.	REMARKS.
Sept. 14	9 p. m.	28. 626	73. 2	. 690	Cu. st. 2	0	NW. 1	84	14th. Thunder storm SE. and SW., from 0½ to 7 p. m.
Sept. 15	7 a. m.	. 614	70	. 621	0	0	W. 1	85	18th. Heat lightning from 6 to 8 p. m ; S. and SE.
	2 p. m.	. 542	92	. 552	Cir. cu. 4	0	SE. 1	37	24th. Thunder storm from 2 to 5 p. m., N.; heat lightning from 5 to 7 p. m., W. and NE.
	9 p. m.	. 599	72	. 624	0	0	NW. 1	80	
Sept. 16	7 a. m.	. 613	72	. 602	Cir. st. 1	0	N. 1	77	
	2 p. m.	. 551	95	. 535	Cir. cu. 5	0	SE. 1	33	
	9 p. m.	. 601	72. 3	. 598	0	0	NE. 1	76	
Sept. 17	7 a. m.	. 636	71	. 609	0	0	NE. 1	80	
	2 p. m.	. 551	91. 3	. 577	Cir. cu. 1	0	S. 3	39	
	9 p. m.	. 575	74	. 699	Cu. 1	0	S. 2	83	
Sept. 18	7 a. m.	. 612	77. 4	. 754	Cir. cu. 2	0	S. 1	81	
	2 p. m.	. 519	84. 3	. 666	Nim. 7	0	NW. 1	57	
	9 p. m.	. 615	75	. 584	Cu. 1	0	N. 1	67	
Sept. 19	7 a. m.	. 701	67. 8	. 398	Cir. st. 1	0	NE. 3	58	
	2 p. m.	. 686	82	. 223	Cir. 1	0	NE. 4	21	
	9 p. m.	. 682	60. 2	. 344	0	0	NW. 1	66	
Sept. 20	7 a. m.	. 744	62	. 340	0	0	SW. 1	61	
	2 p. m.	. 644	80. 9	. 290	0	0	NE. 3	27	
	9 p. m.	. 636	57. 5	. 350	0	0	NW. 1	74	
Sept. 21	7 a. m.	. 650	52	. 290	0	0	NW. 1	75	
	2 p. m.	. 533	86. 5	. 318	Cir. 1	0	SW. 1	25	
	9 p. m.	. 525	59. 2	. 392	0	0	NW. 1	78	
Sept. 22	7 a. m.	. 554	56. 3	. 364	Cir. st. 2	0	NW. 1	78	
	2 p. m.	. 485	84. 8	. 437	Cir. st. 7	0	S. 3	37	
	9 p. m.	. 563	70	. 456	Cir. st. 1	0	SE. 1	62	
Sept. 23	7 a. m.	. 644	65. 4	. 553	Cir. st. 5	SE. 3	NW. 1	88	
	2 p. m.	. 619	82. 9	. 616	Nim. 9	0	SE. 2	54	
	9 p. m.	. 678	76	. 739	Cir. cu. 3	0	S. 2	82	
Sept. 24	7 a. m.	. 695	74	. 717	Cir. cu. 9	0	SE. 1	86	
	2 p. m.	. 614	87. 5	. 657	Cu. 5	0	SE. 2	50	
	9 p. m.	. 652	74. 6	. 718	10	0	SE. 2	84	

STORMS Nos. 2 AND 3, SEPTEMBER, 1859.

TARRANT, TEXAS.

Month and day.	Hour.	Barom'r corrected to 32° F.	Thermometer.	Force of vapor.	Cloudiness.	Motion of clouds.	Winds.	Relative humidity.	REMARKS.
Sept. 14	9 p. m.	......	......	......	2	....	E. 2	......	18th. Light showers W. from 8 to 9 a. m.
Sept. 15	7 a. m.	......	......	......	2	....	E. 1	......	
	2 p. m.	......	......	......	2	....	S. 2	......	
	9 p. m.	......	......	......	3	....	S. 2	......	
Sept. 16	7 a. m.	......	......	......	3	....	S. 2	......	
	2 p. m.	......	......	......	4	....	S. 2	......	
	9 p. m.	......	......	......	2	....	S. 2	......	
Sept. 17	7 a. m.	......	......	......	0	....	S. 2	......	
	2 p. m.	......	......	......	0	....	S. 2	......	
	9 p. m.	......	......	......	0	....	S. 2	......	
Sept. 18	7 a. m.	......	......	......	10	....	SW. 2	......	
	2 p. m.	......	......	......	10	....	SW. 2	......	
	9 p. m.	......	......	......	4	....	S. 2	......	
Sept. 19	7 a. m.	......	......	......	5	....	N. 4	......	
	2 p. m.	......	......	......	5	....	N. 4	......	
	9 p. m.	......	......	......	5	....	N. 4	......	
Sept. 20	7 a. m.	......	......	......	2	....	N. 4	......	
	2 p. m.	......	......	......	1	....	N. 4	......	
	9 p. m.	......	......	......	0	....	N. 2	......	
Sept. 21	7 a. m.	......	......	......	0	....	E. 2	......	
	2 p. m.	......	......	......	0	....	S. 2	......	
	9 p. m.	......	......	......	0	....	S. 2	......	
Sept. 22	7 a. m.	......	......	......	0	....	S. 2	......	
	2 p. m.	......	......	......	0	....	S. 2	......	
	9 p. m.	......	......	......	0	....	S. 2	......	
Sept. 23	7 a. m.	......	......	......	5	....	S. 2	......	
	2 p. m.	......	......	......	5	....	S. 3	......	
	9 p. m.	......	......	......	2	....	S. 2	......	
Sept. 24	7 a. m.	......	......	......	5	....	S. 1	......	
	2 p. m.	......	......	......	5	....	S. 1	......	
	9 p. m.	......	......	......	5	....	S. 2	......	

UNION HILL, TEXAS.

Month and day.	Hour.	Barom'r corrected to 32° F.	Thermometer.	Force of vapor.	Cloudiness.	Motion of clouds.	Winds.	Relative humidity.	REMARKS.
Sept. 14	9 p. m.	......	74	......	Nim. 9	W. 1	W. 2	......	15th. Rain from 6 to 8 p. m.; amount, 1. 125 inch.
Sept. 15	7 a. m.	......	74	......	Fog	....	N. 1	......	19th. Rain from 5 to 6 p. m.; amount, 0. 875 inch.
	2 p. m.	......	92	......	Cu. st. 6	SW. 1	S. 3	......	24th. Heavy rain all around us during the afternoon.
	9 p. m.	......	82	......	0	0	W. 1	......	
Sept. 16	7 a. m.	......	76	......	0	0	W. 3	......	
	2 p. m.	......	92	......	Cu. st. 5	S. 1	S. 2	......	
	9 p. m.	......	82	......	0	0	S. 3	......	
Sept. 17	7 a. m.	......	74	......	0	0	S. 1	......	
	2 p. m.	......	92	......	Cu. st. 5	S. 2	S. 2	......	
	9 p. m.	......	82	......	St. 4	S. 1	S. 1	......	
Sept. 18	7 a. m.	......	76	......	Cu. st. 5	S. 1	S. 1	......	
	2 p. m.	......	84	......	Cu. st. 4	N. 1	N. 2	......	
	9 p. m.	......	74	......	Cu. st. 9	N. 1	N. 2	......	
Sept. 19	7 a. m.	......	62	......	Cir. 2	W. 1	N. 3	......	
	2 p. m.	......	78	......	0	0	N. 5	......	
	9 p. m.	......	68	......	0	0	N. 2	......	
Sept. 20	7 a. m.	......	58	......	0	0	N. 2	......	
	2 p. m.	......	76	......	0	0	N. 4	......	
	9 p. m.	......	66	......	0	0	N. 1	......	
Sept. 21	7 a. m.	......	57	......	0	0	W. 1	......	
	2 p. m.	......	80	......	0	0	S. 2	......	
	9 p. m.	......	69	......	0	0	S. 1	......	
Sept. 22	7 a. m.	......	58	......	Cir. 4	W. 1	S. 1	......	
	2 p. m.	......	84	......	St. 9	S. 1	S. 3	......	
	9 p. m.	......	72	......	Cu. 1	0	S. 1	......	
Sept. 23	7 a. m.	......	70	......	Cir. 4	W. 1	E. 2	......	
	2 p. m.	......	85	......	Cu. st. 9	S. 2	S. 5	......	
	9 p. m.	......	78	......	St. 4	S. 2	S. 2	......	
Sept. 24	7 a. m.	......	72	......	Nim. 9	S. 2	SE. 3	......	
	2 p. m.	......	80	......	Nim. 8	S. 1	S. 2	......	
	9 p. m.	......	74	......	Cu. st. 1	S. 2	S. 2	......	

STORMS Nos. 2 AND 3, SEPTEMBER, 1859.

WASHINGTON, TEXAS.

Month and day.	Hour.	Barom'r corrected to 32° F.	Thermometer.	Force of vapor.	Cloudiness.		Motion of clouds.		Winds.		Relative humidity.	REMARKS.
Sept. 14	9 p. m.	29. 56	73	------	Nim.	10		0	N.	1	------	19th. Amount of rain, 0.23 inch.
Sept. 15	7 a. m.	29. 55	72	------		0		0	NW.	1	------	
	2 p. m.	29. 48	96	------	Cu.	2		0	NW.	1	------	
	9 p. m.	29. 51	77	------		0		0	E.	1	------	
Sept. 16	7 a. m.	29. 54	74	------		0		0		0	------	
	2 p. m.	29. 48	96	------	Cu.	2		0	S.	1	------	
	9 p. m.	29. 55	78	------		0		0	S.	1	------	
Sept. 17	7 a. m.	29. 59	75	------	Dense fog	---		0		0	------	
	2 p. m.	29. 51	94	------	Cir.	2		0	S.	2	------	
	9 p. m.	29. 55	76	------	Cir.	2		0	S.	1	------	
Sept. 18	7 a. m.	29. 56	78	------	Nim.	10	S.	1	S.	1	------	
	2 p. m.	29. 50	89	------	Cir., nim.	8		0	S.	2	------	
	9 p. m.	29. 52	79	------	Nim.	0		0		0	------	
Sept. 19	7 a. m.	29. 56	70	------	St.	1		0	W.	2	------	
	2 p. m.	29. 58	80	------	St.	1		0	W.	2	------	
	9 p. m.	29. 61	63	------		0		0	W.	1	------	
Sept. 20	7 a. m.	29. 66	65	------		0		0	W.	2	------	
	2 p. m.	29. 54	79	------		0		0	W.	2	------	
	9 p. m.	29. 59	59	------		0		0		0	------	
Sept. 21	7 a. m.	29. 58	58	------		0		0		0	------	
	2 p. m.	29. 50	80	------		0		0	W.	1	------	
	9 p. m.	29. 52	58	------		0		0		0	------	
Sept. 22	7 a. m.	29. 55	68	------	Cir.	1		0		0	------	
	2 p. m.	29. 51	86	------	Cir.	3		0	S.	2	------	
	9 p. m.	29. 56	72	------	Nim.	4		0	S.	2	------	
Sept. 23	8 a. m.	29. 64	76	------	Cir.	1		0	S.	2	------	
	2 p. m.	29. 64	83	------	Nim.	9	S.	1	S.	4	------	
	9 p. m.	29. 68	72	------	St.	2		0	S.	1	------	
Sept. 24	8 a. m.	29. 68	79	------	Nim.cir.&cir.	8		0	S.	1	------	
	2 p. m.	29. 65	82	------	Nim.	9		0	S.	2	------	
	9 p. m.	29. 66	70	------	St.	1		0		0	------	

WEBBERVILLE, TEXAS.

Month and day.	Hour.	Barom'r corrected to 32° F.	Thermometer.	Force of vapor.	Cloudiness.		Motion of clouds.	Winds.		Relative humidity.	REMARKS.
Sept. 14	9 p. m.	29. 37	80	------		0	----------	Calm	-------	------	18th. Showery at 2 p. m.
Sept. 15	7 a. m.	29. 38	72	------		0	----------	NE.	1	------	
	2 p. m.	29. 33	90	------		5	W--------	Calm	-------	------	
	9 p. m.	29. 32	80	------		0	----------	Calm	-------	------	
Sept. 16	7 a. m.	29. 36	73	------		0	----------	Calm	-------	------	
	2 p. m.	29. 31	94	------		0	----------	S.	1	------	
	9 p. m.	29. 33	82	------		5	----------	S.	2	------	
Sept. 17	7 a. m.	29. 34	89	------		5	SE. ------	S.	1	------	
	2 p. m.	29. 33	93	------		5	----------	S.	2	------	
	9 p. m.	29. 36	77	------		5	----------	S.	2	------	
Sept. 18	7 a. m.	29. 37	66	------	------------		----------	------------		------	
	2 p. m.	29. 34	86	------		10	----------	W.	1	------	
	9 p. m.	29. 37	74	------		0	----------	Calm	-------	------	
Sept. 19	7 a. m.	29. 44	66	------		0	----------	NW.	4	------	
	2 p. m.	29. 46	81	------		0	----------	NW.	4	------	
	9 p. m.	29. 46	65	------		0	----------	Calm	-------	------	
Sept. 20	7 a. m.	29. 50	63	------		0	----------	NW.	3	------	
	2 p. m.	29. 43	80	------		0	----------	NW.	3	------	
	9 p. m.	29. 43	66	------		0	----------	Calm	-------	------	
Sept. 21	7 a. m.	29. 35	55	------		0	----------	NW.	1	------	
	2 p. m.	29. 36	80	------		0	----------	NW.	1	------	
	9 p. m.	29. 36	67	------		0	----------	NW.	1	------	
Sept. 22	7 a. m.	29. 38	58	------		0	----------	Calm	-------	------	
	2 p. m.	29. 33	84	------		5	W--------	S.	2	------	
	9 p. m.	29. 35	73	------		0	----------	Calm	-------	------	
Sept. 23	7 a. m.	29. 40	67	------		5	W--------	SE.	1	------	
	2 p. m.	29. 41	88	------		5	----------	S.	2	------	
	9 p. m.	29. 47	78	------		5	----------	S.	2	------	
Sept. 24	7 a. m.	29. 47	77	------		10	----------	E.	1	------	
	2 p. m.	29. 42	86	------		5	S---------	E.	2	------	
	9 p. m.	29. 44	76	------		0	----------	S.	2	------	

STORMS Nos. 2 AND 3, SEPTEMBER, 1859.

WHEELOCK, TEXAS.

Month and day.	Hour.	Barom'r corrected to 32° F.	Thermometer.	Force of vapor.	Cloudiness.	Motion of clouds.	Winds.	Relative humidity.	REMARKS.
Sept. 14	9 p. m.				10		W. 1		14th. Foggy, nimbus a. m.; showery, nimbus p. m.; diffused lightning N. and W., from 8 to 10 p. m.
Sept. 15	7 a. m.				0		S. 1		
	2 p. m.				5		W. 1		
	9 p. m.				0		W. 1		
Sept. 16	7 a. m.				1				15th. Hazy cu. st., ther. 104°; nimbus thunder clouds from 12 m. to 10 p. m.; incessant thunder N. and S. from 7 to 10 p. m.; red diffuse lightning SW.
	2 p. m.				4		E. 1		
	9 p. m.				2		S. 2		
Sept. 17	7 a. m.				2		S. 1		
	2 p. m.				3		S. 1		
	9 p. m.				2		S. 2		16th. Cu. st., cir. a. m.; clear p. m.
Sept. 18	7 a. m.				7		S. 1		17th. Gray haze, cu. st. and cumulus.
	2 p. m.				9		E. 1		
	9 p. m.				10		E. 1		18th. Nimbus thunder clouds all day; diffused lightning from 4.30 to 9 p. m., W., NW., N., and NE.; forked lightning SSE., from 8 to 10 p. m.
Sept. 19	7 a. m.				1		N. 1		
	2 p. m.				0		N. 2		
	9 p. m.				0		N. 1		
Sept. 20	7 a. m.				0		N. 2		
	2 p. m.				1		N. 3		19th. Clear.
	9 p. m.				0		N. 1		20th. Cir. SE. to SW., 3 p. m.
Sept. 21	7 a. m.				0		N. 1		21st. Cir. W., 8 to 9 a. m.
	2 p. m.				0		S. 1		22d. Cu. st. and cir.
	9 p. m.				0		S. 1		23d. Cu. st. and nimbus.
Sept. 22	7 a. m.				7		S. 1		24th. Nim. cu. st. and cir.
	2 p. m.				6		S. 2		
	9 p. m.				5		S. 4		
Sept. 23	7 a. m.				5		S. 2		
	2 p. m.				6		S. 2		
	9 p. m.				4		S. 2		
Sept. 24	7 a. m.				9		S. 2		
	2 p. m.				10		E. 3		
	9 p. m.				10		E. 1		

ARKADELPHIA, ARKANSAS.

Month and day.	Hour.	Barom'r corrected to 32° F.	Thermometer.	Force of vapor.	Cloudiness.	Motion of clouds.	Winds.	Relative humidity.	REMARKS.
Sept. 14	9 p. m.				5		N. & E. 1		18th. Thunder storm from 8 to 8. 30 p. m., W. to E.
Sept. 15	7 a. m.				1		N. & E. 1		
	2 p. m.				1		N. & E. 1		
	9 p. m.				0		N. & E. 1		
Sept. 16	7 a. m.				1		E. 1		
	2 p. m.				2		E. 2		
	9 p. m.				1		S. & E. 1		
Sept. 17	7 a. m.				1		S. & E. 1		
	2 p. m.				1		S. & E. 2		
	9 p. m.				1		S. & E. 1		
Sept. 18	7 a. m.				0		S. & W. 1		
	2 p. m.				8		S. & W. 2		
	9 p. m.				10		S. & W. 1		
Sept. 19	7 a. m.				0		N. 1		
	2 p. m.				4		N. 3		
	9 p. m.				2		N. 1		
Sept. 20	7 a. m.				10		N. 1		
	2 p. m.				10		N. 3		
	9 p. m.				10		N. 1		
Sept. 21	7 a. m.				5		N. & E. 1		
	2 p. m.				3		N. & E. 2		
	9 p. m.				0		S. & E. 1		
Sept. 22	7 a. m.				1		N. 1		
	2 p. m.				1		N. & E. 2		
	9 p. m.				0		S. & E. 1		
Sept. 23	7 a. m.				1		E. 1		
	2 p. m.				1		S. & E. 3		
	9 p. m.				0		N. & E. 1		
Sept. 24	7 a. m.				1		S. & E. 1		
	2 p. m.				1		S. & E. 2		
	9 p. m.				0		S. & E. 1		

STORMS Nos. 2 AND 3, SEPTEMBER, 1859.

BENTONVILLE, ARKANSAS.

Month and day.	Hour.	Barom'r corrected to 32° F.	Thermometer.	Force of vapor.	Cloudiness.	Motion of clouds.	Winds.	Relative humidity.
Sept. 14	9 p. m.				9			
Sept. 15	7 a. m.				8			
	2 p. m.				7			
	9 p. m.				3			
Sept. 16	7 a. m.				1			
	2 p. m.				4		S. 3	
	9 p. m.				4			
Sept. 17	7 a. m.				1		S. 5	
	2 p. m.				4		SW. 3	
	9 p. m.				10			
Sept. 18	7 a. m.				1		S. 4	
	2 p. m.				10		W. 6	
	9 p. m.				0			
Sept. 19	7 a. m.				10		N. 3	
	2 p. m.				10		N. 4	
	9 p. m.				10			
Sept. 20	7 a. m.				10		N. 4	
	2 p. m.				10			
	9 p. m.				10			
Sept. 21	7 a. m.				10			
	2 p. m.				9			
	9 p. m.				5			
Sept. 22	7 a. m.				0			
	2 p. m.				0			
	9 p. m.				0			
Sept. 23	7 a. m.				0			
	2 p. m.				3			
	9 p. m.				0			
Sept. 24	7 a. m.				2		W. 3	
	2 p. m.				5		SW. 1	
	9 p. m.				0			

REMARKS.

14th. Rain from 2 to 3 p. m.
16th. Fair and warm.
17th. Cloudy and sultry in the evening.
18th. Distant thunder S. and W. at 7 a. m.; clear sky, but strong winds, fitful and sudden gusts, alternately clear and cloudy during the day; south wind, and southern horizon rather hazy; indications of a severe storm.
19th and 20th. Cold and cloudy.
22d. Slight frost.
23d. Pleasant and warm.
24th. Temperature at 2 p. m., 81°.

BROWNSVILLE, ARKANSAS.

Month and day.	Hour.	Barom'r corrected to 32° F.	Thermometer.	Force of vapor.	Cloudiness.	Motion of clouds.	Winds.	Relative humidity.
Sept. 14	9 p. m.				2		S. 1	
Sept. 15	7 a. m.				8		W. 2	
	2 p. m.				3		SW. 2	
	9 p. m.				3		S. 1	
Sept. 16	7 a. m.				3		SW. 1	
	2 p. m.				2		SW. 2	
	9 p. m.				0		S. 1	
Sept. 17	7 a. m.				2		SW. 2	
	2 p. m.				2		SW. 2	
	9 p. m.				1		S. 1	
Sept. 18	7 a. m.				6		SW. 2	
	2 p. m.				8		W. 3	
	9 p. m.				10		W. 2	
Sept. 19	7 a. m.				10		SW. 1	
	2 p. m.				9		SW. 2	
	9 p. m.				10		SW. 2	
Sept. 20	7 a. m.				10		NE. 1	
	2 p. m.				10		NE. 2	
	9 p. m.				10		S. 2	
Sept. 21	7 a. m.				10		SW. 2	
	2 p. m.				10		S. 1	
	9 p. m.				4		S. 2	
Sept. 22	7 a. m.				1		SW. 2	
	2 p. m.				0		SW. 3	
	9 p. m.				0		S. 2	
Sept. 23	7 a. m.				0		SW. 3	
	2 p. m.				2		SW. 2	
	9 p. m.				0		SW. 1	
Sept. 24	7 a. m.				1		SW. 1	
	2 p. m.				0		NW. 2	
	9 p. m.				1		W. 1	

REMARKS.

14th. Morning cool.
15th. Warm.
16th. Very warm.
17th. Warm.
18th. Cool; rain from noon to 3.15 p. m.
19th, 20th, and 21st. Cool.
22d. Morning cold; warm towards noon.
23d. Warm during the day; night cool.
24th. Warm; cool night.

STORMS Nos. 2 AND 3, SEPTEMBER, 1859.

JACKSONPORT, ARKANSAS.

Month and day.	Hour.	Barom'r corrected to 32° F.	Thermometer.	Force of vapor.	Cloudiness.	Motion of clouds.	Winds.	Relative humidity.	REMARKS.
Sept. 14	9 p. m.	------	------	------	0	----------	N. 1	------	18th. Began to r in at 4 p. m.; strong gale and lightning in the north at 5 p. m.; continued till 9 p. m.; wind from SW.; very cold at night. 20th. Cold all day.
Sept. 15	7 a. m.	------	------	------	9	----------	N. 2	------	
	2 p. m.	------	------	------	2	----------	N. 2	------	
	9 p. m.	------	------	------	1	----------	NE. 2	------	
Sept. 16	7 a. m.	------	------	------	8	----------	N. 1	------	
	2 p. m.	------	------	------	3	----------	NE. 2	------	
	9 p. m.	------	------	------	0	----------	E. 1	------	
Sept. 17	7 a. m.	------	------	------	2	----------	SE. 1	------	
	2 p. m.	------	------	------	2	----------	S. 1	------	
	9 p. m.	------	------	------	3	----------	E. 1	------	
Sept. 18	7 a. m.	------	------	------	0	----------	S. 3	------	
	2 p. m.	------	------	------	3	----------	SW. 4	------	
	9 p. m.	------	------	------	6	----------	S. 1	------	
Sept. 19	7 a. m.	------	------	------	3	----------	NW. 3	------	
	2 p. m.	------	------	------	9	----------	NW. 4	------	
	9 p. m.	------	------	------	9	----------	N. 3	------	
Sept. 20	7 a. m.	------	------	------	10	----------	N. 4	------	
	2 p. m.	------	------	------	10	----------	N. 4	------	
	9 p. m.	------	------	------	10	----------	N. 2	------	
Sept. 21	7 a. m.	------	------	------	10	----------	NW. 3	------	
	2 p. m.	------	------	------	10	----------	NW. 2	------	
	9 p. m.	------	------	------	10	----------	S. 2	------	
Sept. 22	7 a. m.	------	------	------	10	----------	S. 3	------	
	2 p. m.	------	------	------	7	----------	S. 3	------	
	9 p. m.	------	------	------	4	----------	S. 2	------	
Sept. 23	7 a. m.	------	------	------	0	----------	E. 2	------	
	2 p. m.	------	------	------	3	----------	SW. 2	------	
	9 p. m.	------	------	------	0	----------	E. 2	------	
Sept. 24	7 a. m.	------	------	------	0	----------	E. 1	------	
	2 p. m.	------	------	------	3	----------	SW. 2	------	
	9 p. m.	------	------	------	0	----------	S. 2	------	

PERRYVILLE, ARKANSAS.

Month and day.	Hour.	Barom'r corrected to 32° F.	Thermometer.	Force of vapor.	Cloudiness.	Motion of clouds.	Winds.	Relative humidity.	REMARKS.
Sept. 14	9 p. m.	------	------	------	2	----------	E. 1	------	20th. Several slight showers during the day; wind W. 4.
Sept. 15	7 a. m.	------	------	------	2	----------	E. 1	------	
	2 p. m.	------	------	------	1	----------	E. 1	------	
	9 p. m.	------	------	------	1	----------	E. 1	------	
Sept. 16	7 a. m.	------	------	------	1	----------	E. 1	------	
	2 p. m.	------	------	------	1	----------	E. 1	------	
	9 p. m.	------	------	------	1	----------	SE. 1	------	
Sept. 17	7 a. m.	------	------	------	1	----------	S. 1	------	
	2 p. m.	------	------	------	1	----------	S. 1	------	
	9 p. m.	------	------	------	1	----------	S. 2	------	
Sept. 18	7 a. m.	------	------	------	3	----------	S. 2	------	
	2 p. m.	------	------	------	2	----------	S. 2	------	
	9 p. m.	------	------	------	5	----------	S. 2	------	
Sept. 19	7 a. m.	------	------	------	9	----------	NW. 2	------	
	2 p. m.	------	------	------	10	----------	NW. 3	------	
	9 p. m.	------	------	------	10	----------	NW. 4	------	
Sept. 20	7 a. m.	------	------	------	10	----------	N. 3	------	
	2 p. m.	------	------	------	10	----------	N. 3	------	
	9 p. m.	------	------	------	10	----------	NE. 1	------	
Sept. 21	7 a. m.	------	------	------	9	----------	N. 1	------	
	2 p. m.	------	------	------	3	----------	N. 1	------	
	9 p. m.	------	------	------	1	----------	N. 1	------	
Sept. 22	7 a. m.	------	------	------	1	----------	N. 1	------	
	2 p. m.	------	------	------	2	----------	N. 1	------	
	9 p. m.	------	------	------	1	----------	N. 1	------	
Sept. 23	7 a. m.	------	------	------	1	----------	N. 1	------	
	2 p. m.	------	------	------	1	----------	S. 1	------	
	9 p. m.	------	------	------	1	----------	S. 1	------	
Sept. 24	7 a. m.	------	------	------	1	----------	S. 1	------	
	2 p. m.	------	------	------	1	----------	S. 1	------	
	9 p. m.	------	------	------	1	----------	S. 1	------	

STORMS Nos. 2 AND 3, SEPTEMBER, 1859.

SPRINGFIELD, ARKANSAS.

Month and day.	Hour.	Barom'r corrected to 32° F.	Thermometer.	Force of vapor.	Cloudiness.	Motion of clouds.	Winds.		Relative humidity.
Sept. 14	9 p. m.	......	......	......	10	....	NW.	1	......
Sept. 15	7 a. m.	......	......	......	5	....	SE.	1	......
	2 p. m.	......	......	......	6	....	NW.	1	......
	9 p. m.	......	......	......	0	....		0	......
Sept. 16	7 a. m.	......	......	......	1	....		0	......
	2 p. m.	......	92	......	3	....	SW. to W.	1	......
	9 p. m.	......	......	......	0	....		0	......
Sept. 17	7 a. m.	......	72	......	2	....		0	......
	2 p. m.	......	96	......	3	....	S. to SW.	2	......
	9 p. m.	......	......	......	2	....		0	......
Sept. 18	7 a. m.	......	78	......	1	....	S.	1	......
	2 p. m.	......	80	......	10	....		0	......
	9 p. m.	......	......	......	10	....	NW.	1	......
Sept. 19	7 a. m.	......	70	......	0	....	NW.	1	......
	2 p. m.	......	......	......	....	....	....		......
	9 p. m.	......	......	......	10	....	NW.	1	......
Sept. 20	7 a. m.	......	64	......	10	....	NW.	1	......
	2 p. m.	......	69	......	10	....	NW.	1	......
	9 p. m.	......	......	......	6	....		0	......
Sept. 21	7 a. m.	......	61	......	2	....		0	......
	2 p. m.	......	71	......	3	....	SE.	1	......
	9 p. m.	......	......	......	0	....		0	......
Sept. 22	7 a. m.	......	62	......	[illegible]	....		0	......
	2 p. m.	......	79	......	2	....	SE. to SW.	2	......
	9 p. m.	......	......	......	0	....		0	......
Sept. 23	7 a. m.	......	64	......	4	....		0	......
	2 p. m.	......	84	......	3	....	SE.	3	......
	9 p. m.	......	......	......	0	....		0	......
Sept. 24	7 a. m.	......	65	......	9	....		0	......
	2 p. m.	......	85	......	5	....	NE	2	......
	9 p. m.	......	......	......	0	....		0	......

REMARKS.

14th. Thunder cloud and diffused lightning W. to N.

17th. Very dry.

18th. Light shower NW. from 1.30 to 1.40 p. m.; dark thunder cloud passed from S. to E. from 2 to 3 p. m.; heavy thunder NW. from 5 to 8 p. m.

24th. A few small shooting stars.

Note.—Thermometer observations taken at 7 a. m. and 3 p. m.

WALDRON, ARKANSAS.

Month and day.	Hour.	Barom'r corrected to 32° F.	Thermometer.	Force of vapor.	Cloudiness.	Motion of clouds.	Winds.		Relative humidity.
Sept. 14	9 p. m.	......	......	......	10	....	SW.	1	......
Sept. 15	7 a. m.	......	......	......	0	....	N.	1	......
	2 p. m.	......	......	......	0	....	N.	1	......
	9 p. m	......	......	......	0	....	N.	1	......
Sept. 16	7 a. m.	......	......	......	8	....	N.	1	......
	2 p. m.	......	......	......	0	....	N.	1	......
	9 p. m.	......	......	......	0	....	N.	1	......
Sept. 17	7 a. m.	......	......	......	0	....	E.	1	......
	2 p. m.	......	......	......	0	....	E.	1	......
	9 p. m.	......	......	......	0	....	E.	1	......
Sept. 18	7 a. m.	......	......	......	0	....	SW.	3	......
	2 p. m.	......	......	......	4	....	SW.	3	......
	9 p. m.	......	......	......	0	....	W.	1	......
Sept. 19	7 a. m.	......	......	......	10	....	NW.	3	......
	2 p. m.	......	......	......	8	....	NW.	3	......
	9 p. m.	......	......	......	10	....	NW.	4	......
Sept. 20	7 a. m.	......	......	......	9	....	NW.	3	......
	2 p. m.	......	......	......	4	....	NW.	3	......
	9 p. m.	......	......	......	0	....	W.	1	......
Sept. 21	7 a. m.	......	......	......	0	....	S.	2	......
	2 p. m.	......	......	......	0	....	S.	2	......
	9 p. m.	......	......	......	0	....	S.	1	......
Sept. 22	7 a. m.	......	......	......	0	....	E.	1	......
	2 p. m.	......	......	......	0	....	E.	1	......
	9 p. m.	......	......	......	0	....	E.	1	......
Sept. 23	7 a. m.	......	......	......	0	....	S.	1	......
	2 p. m.	......	......	......	0	....	S.	1	......
	9 p. m.	......	......	......	0	....	N.	1	......
Sept. 24	7 a. m.	......	......	......	0	....	N.	1	......
	2 p. m.	......	......	......	4	....	N.	1	......
	9 p. m.	......	......	......	0	....	W.	1	......

14th. Rain from 5 to 6 p. m.

17th. Diffused lightning NE. at 9 p. m.

18th. Rain from 3 to 3. 30 p. m.

STORMS Nos. 2 AND 3, SEPTEMBER, 1859.

GLENWOOD, TENNESSEE.

Month and day.	Hour.	Barom'r corrected to 32° F.	Thermometer.	Force of vapor.	Cloudiness.		Motion of clouds.		Winds.		Relative humidity.
Sept. 14	9 p. m.	29.598	58.2	.365	Cir. st.	9	— WSW.	1		0	76
Sept. 15	7 a. m.	.568	55.3	.342	Cir. 0	5	W. 0	1 0	E.	1	78
	2 p. m.	.485	79.2	.476	Cir. 0	8	W. 0	1 0	SE.	1	47
	9 p. m.	.485	71	.627	St.	10	— W.	1	SE.	1	83
Sept. 16	7 a. m.	.448	66	.587	St. Scud	9	W. E.	1 2	E.	1	92
	2 p. m.	.380	79.4	.561	St. Cu.	5	W. NE.	1 2	NE.	1	55
	9 p. m.	.417	69	.617		0		0		0	88
Sept. 17	7 a. m.	.533	64	.546	Cir. st. 0	1	NNW. 0	1 0	S.	1	92
	2 p. m.	.455	84	.570	Cir. Cu.	3	W. NNW.	1 1	W.	1	47
	9 p. m.	.529	72	.650	St.	10	— —	?	W.	1	83
Sept. 18	7 a. m.	.480	69	.644	Cir. st. 0	1	W. 0	1 0	SSE.	1	88
	2 p. m.	.379	86.2	.583	Cu.	4	0 SW.	2	SSE.	3	42
	9 p. m.	.334	77.2	.362	St.	10	— SW.	1	SSE.	3	67
Sept. 19	7 a. m.	.275	69.3	.690	St.	10	— W.	2		0	97
	2 p. m.	.215	76.5	.534	Cu.	5	0 W.	2	WNW.	3	59
	9 p. m.	.264	65	.507	St.	1	0 W.	1	WNW.	1	83
Sept. 20	7 a. m.	.295	60.3	.556	St.	10	— NW.	2	NW.	2	88
	2 p. m.	.325	58.6	.446	St.	10	NNW.	2	NW.	1	91
	9 p. m.	.345	57.2	.428	St.	10	— —	?	NW.	1	94
Sept. 21	7 a. m.	.341	55.8	.427	Nim.	10	— —	?	W.	1	97
	2 p. m.	.376	59	.469	Nim.	10	NW.	2	NW.	1	94
	9 p. m.	.428	56.6	.428	St.	10	— —	?	W.	1	94
Sept. 22	7 a. m.	.541	55.8	.413	St.	10	— W.	1	W.	1	94
	2 p. m.	.585	61.8	.449	St. Scud	10	— NW.	? 2	SW.	1	80
	9 p. m.	.582	59.5	.469	St.	10	— —	?	E.	1	94
Sept. 23	7 a. m.	.700	58.7	.461	St.	10	— W.	1	SSE.	1	94
	2 p. m.	.637	71	.446	Cu.	8	0 WNW.	2	S.	1	57
	9 p. m.	.669	60	.478		0	0 0	0		0	94
Sept. 24	7 a. m.	.686	56.3	.436	Fog	0	0 0	0	S.	1	97
	2 p. m.	.574	77	.521	Cu.	6	0 WNW.	2	SW.	2	55
	9 p. m.	.557	64.5	.546		0	0 0	0		0	92

REMARKS.

18th. At 7.30 p. m. a storm cloud arose in the W. with active lightning, and passed round by NW. to N.; the lightning continued to westward round the horizon to the southward; at 9 p. m. there was active lightning, with distant thunder, all along the western horizon, passing from SW.; at 10 p. m. the clouds spread over us, and rain commenced falling.

19th. Rain continued during last night in light showers, and up to 6.45 a. m.; amount, 0.554 inch.

20th. Gentle rain from 2 to 5 a.m.; recommenced at 11 p. m. in light showers.

21st. Rain continued in sprinkling misty showers during last night and to-day.

22d. Showers of mist and drizzling rain continued during the past night; this morning it appears to be a little denser; rain ceased about 10 a. m.; amount, 0.809 inch.

24th. Fog at sunrise, and for some time after.

MEMPHIS, TENNESSEE.

Month and day.	Hour.	Barom'r corrected to 32° F.	Thermometer.	Force of vapor.	Cloudiness.		Motion of clouds.	Winds.		Relative humidity.
Sept. 14	9 p. m.	29.766	65	.516		0	----------		0	84
Sept. 15	7 a. m.	.727	63	.478	Cu. st.	5	----------	N.	2	83
	2 p. m.	.676	83	.637	Cir. cu.	4	----------	N.	2	56
	9 p. m.	.640	73	.693	Cu. & nim.	6	----------		0	85
Sept. 16	7 a. m.	.639	71	.682		0	----------		0	90
	2 p. m.	.621	84	.704	Cir.	3	----------	NW.	2	60
	9 p. m.	.651	74	.798		0	----------		0	95

STORMS Nos. 2 AND 3, SEPTEMBER, 1859.

MEMPHIS, TENNESSEE—Continued.

Month and day.	Hour.	Barom'r corrected to 32° F.	Thermometer.	Force of vapor.	Cloudiness.		Motion of clouds.		Winds.		Relative humidity.	REMARKS.
Sept. 17	7 a. m.	29.703	71	.720		0	----------			0	95	Rain on the 17th; amount, 0.15 inch.
	2 p. m.	.657	89	.637	Cir.	4	----------		W.	1	47	
	9 p. m.	.674	79	.813	Cu. & nim.	4	----------			0	82	
Sept. 18	7 a. m.	.664	76	.691		0	----------		S.	2	77	
	2 p. m.	.580	90	.751	Cir.	3	----------		S.	3	53	
	9 p. m.	.553	76	.812	Nim.	6	----------		SW.	1	91	
Sept. 19	7 a. m.	.525	69	.599	Cir. cu.	2	----------		W.	2	85	
	2 p. m.	.515	72	.595	Cu. & nim.	7	----------		SW.	3	76	
	9 p. m.	.568	65	.483	Nim.	10	----------		NW.	3	78	
Sept. 20	7 a. m.	.563	59	.439	Cu. & nim.	6	----------		N.	3	88	
	2 p. m.	.571	63	.416	Cu. & nim.	9	----------		N.	3	72	
	9 p. m.	.516	56	.449	Nim.	5	----------		N.	2	100	
Sept. 21	7 a. m.	.620	56	.420	Nim.	10	----------		N.	2	94	
	2 p. m.	.621	61	.442	Nim.	10	----------		NW.	2	83	
	9 p. m.	.661	58	.452	Nim.	10	----------			0	94	
Sept. 22	7 a. m.	.717	57	.466	Cir. cu.	8	----------		E.	1	100	
	2 p. m.	.706	73	.442	Cir.	4	----------		W.	1	55	
	9 p. m.	.744	62	.523		0	----------			0	94	
Sept. 23	7 a. m.	.899	58	.423		0	----------			0	88	
	2 p. m.	.855	77	.527	Cir.	3	----------		W.	1	57	
	9 p. m.	.860	65	.549		0	----------			0	89	
Sept. 24	7 a. m.	.907	60	.456		0	----------			0	88	
	2 p. m.	.830	79	.501	Cir.	2	----------		NW.	1	51	
	9 p. m.	.797	67	.556		0	----------			0	84	

WINCHESTER, TENNESSEE.

Month and day.	Hour.	Barom'r corrected to 32° F.	Thermometer.	Force of vapor.	Cloudiness.		Motion of clouds.		Winds.		Relative humidity.	REMARKS.
Sept. 14	9 p. m.	------	------	------		5	----------		N.	1	------	14th. Cold
Sept. 15	7 a. m.	------	------	------		5	----------		SE.	1	------	16th. Rain during most of the a. m., commencing in the past night.
	2 p. m.	------	------	------		5	----------		S.	2	------	
	9 p. m.	------	------	------		10	----------		S.	2	------	
Sept. 16	7 a. m.	------	------	------		10	----------		S.	2	------	19th. Rain during the day.
	2 p. m.	------	------	------		10	----------		N.	4	------	20th. Cold and rainy nearly all day.
	9 p. m.	------	------	------		5	----------		N.	1	------	
Sept. 17	7 a. m.	------	------	------		5	----------		S.	1	------	
	2 p. m.	------	------	------		3	----------		S.	1	------	
	9 p. m.	------	------	------		2	----------		S.	1	------	
Sept. 18	7 a. m.	------	------	------		5	----------		W.	1	------	
	2 p. m.	------	------	------		5	----------		W.	3	------	
	9 p. m.	------	------	------		5	----------		W.	1	------	
Sept. 19	7 a. m.	------	------	------		10	----------		S.	1	------	
	2 p. m.	------	------	------		8	----------		S.	3	------	
	9 p. m.	------	------	------		10	----------		S.	1	------	
Sept. 20	7 a. m.	------	------	------		10	----------		W.	2	------	
	2 p. m.	------	------	------		8	----------		NW.	2	------	
	9 p. m.	------	------	------		10	----------		NW.	3	------	
Sept. 21	7 a. m.	------	------	------		10	----------		W.	1	------	
	2 p. m.	------	------	------		10	----------		W.	1	------	
	9 p. m.	------	------	------		10	----------		W.	1	------	
Sept. 22	7 a. m.	------	------	------		10	----------		NW.	1	------	
	2 p. m.	------	------	------		5	----------		N.	1	------	
	9 p. m.	------	------	------		5	----------		NW.	1	------	
Sept. 23	7 a. m.	------	------	------		8	----------		W.	1	------	
	2 p. m.	------	------	------		5	----------		W.	1	------	
	9 p. m.	------	------	------		5	----------		NW.	2	------	
Sept. 24	7 a. m.	------	------	------		5	----------		N.------	---	------	
	2 p. m.	------	------	------		3	----------		N.	1	------	
	9 p. m.	------	------	------		1	----------		NW.	1	------	

BARDSTOWN, KENTUCKY.

Month and day.	Hour.	Barom'r corrected to 32° F.	Thermometer.	Force of vapor.	Cloudiness.		Motion of clouds.		Winds.		Relative humidity.	REMARKS.
Sept. 14	9 p. m.	29.376	59	.323	Cir. cu.	5	SSW.	1	E.----	------	65	16th. Dense fog, passing off at 8.15 a. m.
Sept. 15	7 a. m.	.404	57	.350	Cir. cu.	8	W.	1	NW.	2	75	
	2 p. m.	.435	75	.449	St.	5	SW.	1	WSW.	2	52	
	9 p. m.	.411	68	.509	Cir. st.	10	S.	0	ENE.	1	75	
Sept. 16	7 a. m.	.356	67	.591	St.	10		0	NW.	1	89	
	2 p. m.	------	------	------	----------	----	----------		----------	---	------	
	9 p. m.	.283	65	.583	Cir. st.	3		0	S.	1	94	

STORMS Nos. 2 AND 3, SEPTEMBER, 1859.

BARDSTOWN, KENTUCKY—Continued.

Month and day.	Hour.	Barom'r corrected to 32° F.	Thermometer.	Force of vapor.	Cloudiness.		Motion of clouds.		Winds.		Relative humidity.	REMARKS.
Sept. 17	7 a. m.	29.331	62	.491		0		0	W.	1	88	19th. Rain at intervals, general, sometimes heavy, then drizzling showers; at 2 p. m. two strata of clouds, lower (cum.) moving from SW., the upper (st.) apparently stationary; rain ceased at 4 p. m.; amount, 0.883 inch. 20th. Two strata of clouds, the upper (st.) moving slowly from SW., the lower (cirri) rapidly from NW.; at 1 p. m. heavy storm of wind and rain from NW. for about ten minutes; rain continued till 8.15 p. m. on the 21st; amount, 1.413 inch. 21st. Two strata of clouds, the upper (st.) from S., the lower (cirri) from W. 24th. Light fog; two strata of clouds at 2 p. m.; upper moving from NW., lower from SSE.; both cu. st.
	2 p. m.	.338	79	.537	Cir. st.	5	NNW.	1	WNW.	1	54	
	9 p. m.	.383	64	.529	St.	3		0		0	89	
Sept. 18	7 a. m.	.381	64	.529	Cir. st.	3		0	SSE-------		89	
	2 p. m.	.290	86	.677	Cir. st.	4	SSW.	1	S.	1	54	
	9 p. m.	.242	73	.617	St.	2		0	SE.	1	77	
Sept. 19	7 a. m.	.180	65	.583	Nim.	10	SSW.	2	S.	1	94	
	2 p. m.	.112	75	.666	St.	9		0	SE.	2	77	
	9 p. m.	.132	65.5	.611	Cir. st.	4		0		0	97	
Sept. 20	7 a. m.	.150	62	.491	Cir. cu.	5	SW.	1	WNW.	1	88	
	2 p. m.	.157	64.5	.590	Nim.	8		0	NW.	1	97	
	9 p. m.	.193	62	.523	Cu. st.	7		0	WSW.	3	94	
Sept. 21	7 a. m.	.211	57	.407	Nim.	10	NW.	4	NW.	3	87	
	2 p. m.	.201	66	.470	St.	9	S.	1	NW.	1	73	
	9 p. m.	.251	60	.487	St.	10		0		0	94	
Sept. 22	7 a. m.	.344	57	.436	St.	10	W.	2	NW.	1	94	
	2 p. m.	------	------	------	------------		----------		------------		------	
	9 p. m.	.444	59	.469	St.	10		0	W.----------		94	
Sept. 23	7 a. m.	.534	59	.469	St.	10		0	SSW.	1	94	
	2 p. m.	.514	69	.529	Cu. st.	7	NE.	1	S.----------		75	
	9 p. m.	.517	57	.436	St.	3	SW.	1	NE.---------		94	
Sept. 24	7 a. m.	.497	58	.452	Cu. st.	7	NW.	2	SSW--------		94	
	2 p. m.	.418	77	.492	Cu. st.	4	NW.	1	NW.	1	53	
	9 p. m.	.401	62.5	.549	St.	2		0	NE.---------		97	

DANVILLE, KENTUCKY.

Month and day.	Hour.	Barom'r corrected to 32° F.	Thermometer.	Force of vapor.	Cloudiness.		Motion of clouds.		Winds.		Relative humidity.	REMARKS.
Sept. 14	9 p. m.	29.10	64	------	St.	5	NW.	2	NE.	2	------	Commenced raining in the night of the 18th and ended in the night of the 19th; amount, 1.561 inch.
Sept. 15	7 a. m.	29.10	60	------	Cir. st.	3	W.	3	NE.	2	------	
	2 p. m.	29.08	79	------	St.	2	SW.	3	E.	1	------	
	9 p. m.	29.05	70	------	Cu. st.	7	S.	2	SE.	1	------	
Sept. 16	7 a. m.	29.01	70	------	St.	10	S.	1	SE.	1	------	
	2 p. m.	28.95	76	------	St.	10	E.	3	E.	2	------	
	9 p. m.	28.89	66	------	St.	2	SE.	1	SE	1	------	
Sept. 17	7 a. m.	28.93	64	------	Cu. st.	5	NW.	6	NW.	3	------	
	2 p. m.	28.96	82	------	Cu. st.	3	NW.	3	NW.	4	------	
	9 p. m.	28.98	66	------		0	----------		NW.	1	------	
Sept. 18	7 a. m.	29.01	62	------	Cir. st.	3	W.	2	E.	1	------	
	2 p. m.	28.97	87	------	Cu.	3	NW.	3	S.	2	------	
	9 p. m.	28.89	73	------		0	----------		S.	1	------	
Sept. 19	7 a. m.	28.82	68	------	St.	10	SW.	3	SW.	1	------	
	2 p. m.	28.78	72	------	St.	10	SW.	6	S.	4	------	
	9 p. m.	28.73	68	------	Cu. st.	10	SW.	3	S.	2	------	
Sept. 20	7 a. m.	28.75	65	------	St.	5	NW.	6	W.	2	------	
	2 p. m.	28.77	74	------	Cu. st.	6	SE.	2	W.	2	------	
	9 p. m.	28.78	65	------		10	----------		W.	1	------	
Sept. 21	7 a. m.	28.80	61	------	St.	10	----------		N.	1	------	
	2 p. m.	28.82	65	------	St.	10	NW.	6	N.	2	------	
	9 p. m.	28.84	62	------	St.	10	----------		N.	1	------	
Sept. 22	7 a. m.	28.93	62	------	St.	10	SW.	2	NW.	1	------	
	2 p. m.	28.99	66	------	St.	10	SW.	3	SW.	1	------	
	9 p. m.	29.06	60	------	St.	4	SW.	1	SW.	1	------	
Sept. 23	7 a. m.	29.15	60	------	St.	10	NW.	2	SW.	1	------	
	2 p. m.	29.16	62	------	Cu. st.	10	W.	1	SW.	2	------	
	9 p. m.	29.14	64	------	St.	10	W.	1	W.	1	------	
Sept. 24	7 a. m.	29.14	64	------	Cu. st.	5	NW.	4	SW.	1	------	
	2 p. m.	29.06	79	------	Cu. st.	4	NW.	3	SW.	2	------	
	9 p. m.	29.01	66	------		0	----------		NW.	1	------	

STORMS Nos. 2 AND 3, SEPTEMBER, 1859.

HARDINSBURG, KENTUCKY.

Month and day.	Hour.	Barom'r corrected to 32° F.	Thermometer.	Force of vapor.	Cloudiness.	Motion of clouds.	Winds.	Relative humidity.	REMARKS.
Sept. 14	9 p. m.	......	......	......	5	....	NE. 6	......	15th. Sprinkle of rain at noon;
Sept. 15	7 a. m.	......	......	......	5	....	SE. 12	......	sprinkle of rain and diffused
	2 p. m.	......	......	......	7	....	NE. 10	......	lightning in the N. at 6 p. m.
	9 p. m.	......	......	......	5	....	SE. 10	......	17th. Thunder and diffused light-
Sept. 16	7 a. m.	......	......	......	9	....	NE. 10	......	ning in the N.
	2 p. m.	......	......	......	4	....	N. 8	......	18th. Thunder shower from noon
	9 p. m.	......	......	......	0	....	N. 5	......	to 5 p. m.
Sept. 17	7 a. m.	......	......	......	0	....	SW. 10	......	20th. Light showers all day.
	2 p. m.	......	......	......	4	....	NW. 8	......	22d. Rain from 5 to 8 a. m.
	9 p. m.	......	......	......	2	....	NW. 5	......	23d. Very warm for the season.
Sept. 18	7 a. m.	......	......	......	2	....	SW. 10	......	
	2 p. m.	......	......	......	4	....	SW. 10	......	
	9 p. m.	......	......	......	2	....	SW. 5	......	
Sept. 19	7 a. m.	......	......	......	10	....	SW. 6	......	
	2 p. m.	......	......	......	4	....	W. 10	......	
	9 p. m.	......	......	......	4	....	SW. 8	......	
Sept. 20	7 a. m.	......	......	......	10	....	NW. 8	......	
	2 p. m.	......	......	......	8	....	NW. 10	......	
	9 p. m.	......	......	......	8	....	NW. 8	......	
Sept. 21	7 a. m.	......	......	......	10	....	NE. 10	......	
	2 p. m.	......	......	......	8	....	NW. 10	......	
	9 p. m.	......	......	......	10	....	N. 10	......	
Sept. 22	7 a. m.	......	......	......	9	....	W. 8	......	
	2 p. m.	......	......	......	10	....	SW. 11	......	
	9 p. m.	......	......	......	10	....	S. 10	......	
Sept. 23	7 a. m.	......	......	......	10	....	N. 4	......	
	2 p. m.	......	......	......	5	....	NW. 12	......	
	9 p. m.	......	......	......	0	....	S. 5	......	
Sept. 24	7 a. m.	......	......	......	5	....	NW. 6	......	
	2 p. m.	......	......	......	5	....	SW. 10	......	
	9 p. m.	......	......	......	0	....	SW. 8	......	

LEXINGTON, KENTUCKY.

Month and day.	Hour.	Barom'r corrected to 32° F.	Thermometer.	Force of vapor.	Cloudiness.	Motion of clouds.	Winds.	Relative humidity.	REMARKS.
Sept. 14	9 p. m.	29.07	59	......	7	SW. 1	....	......	19th. Began to rain at 5 a. m. and
Sept. 15	7 a. m.	29.08	56	......	5	SW. 1	NE. 3	......	ended late at night; amount, 2.04
	2 p. m.	29.02	76	......	5	SW. 1	NE. 2	......	inches.
	9 p. m.	28.99	66	......	10	SW. 1	NE. 1	......	21st. Began to rain at 2.45 p. m.
Sept. 16	7 a. m.	28.95	66	......	10	SW. 1	NE. 1	......	and ended late in the night;
	2 p. m.	28.86	75	......	10	SW. 2	NE. 1	......	amount, 0.262 inch.
	9 p. m.	28.85	66	......	4	SW. 2	NE. 2	......	
Sept. 17	7 a. m.	28.90	64	......	3	SW. 2	SW. 2	......	
	2 p. m.	28.92	70	......	3	SW. 2	SW. 2	......	
	9 p. m.	28.96	63	......	3	Imp	NE. 2	......	
Sept. 18	7 a. m.	28.98	63	......	4	SW. 1	NE. 1	......	
	2 p. m.	28.87	83	......	3	SW. 2	SW. 2	......	
	9 p. m.	28.82	73	......	0	....	S. [illegible]	......	
Sept. 19	7 a. m.	28.76	66	......	10	Imp	S. 2	......	
	2 p. m.	28.68	69	......	10	S. 2	S. 2	......	
	9 p. m.	28.67	65	......	10	Imp	....	......	
Sept. 20	7 a. m.	28.70	60	......	Dense fog 10	....	SW. 2	......	
	2 p. m.	28.69	68	......	10	Imp	NW. 2	......	
	9 p. m.	28.77	61	......	10	....	....	......	
Sept. 21	7 a. m.	28.77	56	......	10	Imp	....	......	
	2 p. m.	28.76	62	......	10	....	NW. 1	......	
	9 p. m.	28.79	59	......	10	....	....	......	
Sept. 22	7 a. m.	28.92	58	......	10	SW. 2	SW. 1	......	
	2 p. m.	28.96	62	......	10	....	SW. 2	......	
	9 p. m.	29.02	57	......	0	....	....	......	
Sept. 23	7 a. m.	29.11	57	......	10	SW. 1	SW. 1	......	
	2 p. m.	29.09	65	......	10	W. 1	W. 1	......	
	9 p. m.	29.11	60	......	10	Imp	....	......	
Sept. 24	7 a. m.	29.07	59	......	10	W. 2	SE. 1	......	
	2 p. m.	28.98	73	......	8	W. 2	W. 2	......	
	9 p. m.	28.98	62	......	0	....	SW. 2	......	

STORMS Nos. 2 AND 3, SEPTEMBER, 1859.

PADUCAH, KENTUCKY.

Month and day.	Hour.	Barom'r corrected to 32° F.	Thermometer.	Force of vapor.	Cloudiness.		Motion of clouds.		Winds.		Relative humidity.	REMARKS.
Sept. 14	9 p. m.	......	......	......		1	......		......		......	14th. Very fine day.
Sept. 15	7 a. m.	......	......	......		0	......		......		......	15th and 16th. Very warm.
	2 p. m.	......	......	......		1	......		......		......	17th. Rain from 7 to 10 p. m.; very
	9 p. m.	......	......	......		0	......		......		......	warm; thunder NW. at 5 p. m.;
Sept. 16	7 a. m.	......	......	......		0	......		......		......	wind 4 at 7 p. m.; heavy rain
	2 p. m.	......	......	......		1	......		......		......	with very loud thunder passing
	9 p. m.	......	......	......		0	......		......		......	from NW. to SE.
Sept. 17	7 a. m.	......	......	......		0	......		......		......	18th. Cool; thunder in the W. from
	2 p. m.	......	......	......		1	......		......		......	2 to 4 p. m; passed off to N.;
	9 p. m.	......	......	......		10	......		......		......	distant lightning in all points at
Sept. 18	7 a. m.	......	......	......		0	......		......		......	9 p. m.
	2 p. m.	......	......	......		1	......		S.	3	......	19th. Cool and pleasant.
	9 p. m.	......	......	......		10	......		......		......	20th. Very cold.
Sept. 19	7 a. m.	......	......	......		0	......		......		......	21st. Very unpleasant.
	2 p. m.	......	......	......		10	......		S.	3	......	22d. Fine day, but cloudy.
	9 p. m.	......	......	......		10	......		NW.	2	......	23d Very fine.
Sept. 20	7 a. m.	......	......	......		10	......		NW.	3	......	24th. Delightful day.
	2 p. m.	......	......	......		10	......		NW.	3	......	
	9 p. m.	......	......	......		10	......		N.	2	......	
Sept. 21	7 a. m.	......	......	......		10	......		N.	2	......	
	2 p. m.	......	......	......		10	......		N.	2	......	
	9 p. m.	......	......	......		10	......		......		......	
Sept. 22	7 a. m.	......	......	......		10	......		S.	1	......	
	2 p. m.	......	......	......		10	......		......		......	
	9 p. m.	......	......	......		5	......		......		......	
Sept. 23	7 a. m.	......	......	......		10	......		......		......	
	2 p. m.	......	......	......		0	......		......		......	
	9 p. m.	......	......	......		0	......		......		......	
Sept. 24	7 a. m.	......	......	......		0	......		......		......	
	2 p. m.	......	......	......		0	......		NE.	1	......	
	9 p. m.	......	......	......		0	......		......		......	

PARIS, KENTUCKY.

Month and day.	Hour.	Barom'r corrected to 32° F.	Thermometer.	Force of vapor.	Cloudiness.		Motion of clouds.		Winds.		Relative humidity.	REMARKS.
Sept. 14	9 p. m.	29.28	57	......	Cu.	8	NW.	1	NW.	1	......	15th. Slight shower at night.
Sept. 15	7 a. m.	.28	54	......	Cir. cu.	7	SW.	1	NE.	1	......	16th. Hazy and smoky.
	2 p. m.	.24	71	......	Cir.	5	SW.	1	NE.	1	......	17th. Dense fog.
	9 p. m.	.20	66	......	Cu.	9	S.	1	NE.	1	......	18th. Began to rain at 5 a. m., and
Sept. 16	7 a. m.	.16	64	......	Nim.	10	W.	1	NE.	1	......	ended in the night; diffuse light-
	2 p. m.	.05	72	......	Nim.	10	E.	1	NE.	1	......	ning W. & N. at 8 p. m.; amount,
	9 p. m.	.05	65	......		0	......		NE.	1	......	1.81 inch.
Sept. 17	7 a. m.	.06	61	......	Cu.	8	W.	2	NE.	1	......	20th. Shower at 8 p. m.
	2 p. m.	.04	74	......	Cu.	2	NW.	1	NW.	1	......	21st. Commenced raining at 4.30
	9 p. m.	.15	62	......		0	......		NW.	1	......	p. m, and ended in the night;
Sept. 18	7 a. m.	.16	59	......	Cu.	5	W.	1	NW.	1	......	amount, 0.210 inch.
	2 p. m.	.10	79	......	Cu.	1		0	SE.	1	......	23d. Rain in the night; amount,
	9 p. m.	......	......	......	......		......		......		......	0.10 inch.
Sept. 19	7 a. m.	28.93	68	......	Nim.	10	W.	1	SW.	1	......	
	2 p. m.	.89	69	......	Nim.	10	W.	2	S.	1	......	
	9 p. m.	.89	67	......	Nim.	10		0	SE.	1	......	
Sept. 20	7 a. m.	.86	62	......	Cu.	1	SE.	1	SW.	1	......	
	2 p. m.	.88	71	......	Cu.	5	W.	1	W.	1	......	
	9 p. m.	.93	60	......	Nim.	10		0	NW.	2	......	
Sept. 21	7 a. m.	.99	57	......	Nim.	10		0	NW.	1	......	
	2 p. m.	.98	61	......	Nim.	9	NW.	1	NW.	1	......	
	9 p. m.	.98	60	......	Nim.	9		0	NW.	1	......	
Sept. 22	7 a. m.	29.10	59	......	Nim.	10	W.	1	W.	1	......	
	2 p. m.	.14	62	......	Nim.	10	W.	1	SW.	2	......	
	9 p. m.	.22	58	......	St.	1		0	SW.	1	......	
Sept. 23	7 a. m.	.28	58	......	Nim.	10	W.	1	SW.	1	......	
	2 p. m.	......	......	......	......		......		......		......	
	9 p. m.	.29	61	......	Nim.	10		0	SW.	1	......	
Sept. 24	7 a. m.	.26	60	......	Nim.	10	W.	2	SW.	1	......	
	2 p. m.	.19	69	......	Cu.	9	W.	2	SW.	1	......	
	9 p. m.	.21	61	......		0	......		SW.	1	......	

STORMS Nos. 2 AND 3, SEPTEMBER, 1859.

SPRINGDALE, KENTUCKY.

Month and day.	Hour.	Barom'r corrected to 32° F.	Thermometer.	Force of vapor.	Cloudiness.	Motion of clouds.	Winds.	Relative humidity.	REMARKS.
Sept. 14	9 p. m.	29.49	64	.399	4	----------	0	72	18th. Began to rain in the night, and ended at 2 p. m. on the 19th; amount, 0.38 inch. 20th. Rain from 2.30 to 5 p. m.; amount, 0.53 inch.
Sept. 15	7 a. m.	29.52	54	.321	3	----------	NE. 2	80	
	2 p. m.	29.43	76	.409	3	----------	E. 3	50	
	9 p. m.	29.41	69	.509	7	----------	E. 1	75	
Sept. 16	7 a. m.	29.37	63	.491	10	----------	E. 1	88	
	2 p. m.	29.27	80	.812	9	----------	0	91	
	9 p. m.	29.25	75	.668	6	----------	0	81	
Sept. 17	7 a. m.	29.32	60	.456	Fog-------	----------	0	88	
	2 p. m.	29.34	79	.505	5	----------	W. 3	56	
	9 p. m.	29.33	71	.577	3	----------	0	85	
Sept. 18	7 a. m.	29.36	59	.423	3	----------	0	88	
	2 p. m.	29.28	87½	.691	3	----------	SW. 3	57	
	9 p. m.	29.20	79	.601	7	----------	SW. 2	65	
Sept. 19	7 a. m.	29.11	66½	.604	10	----------	SSW. 2	94	
	2 p. m.	29.06	74	.693	7	----------	WSW. 3	85	
	9 p. m.	29.05	71	.564	0	----------	WSW. 1	79	
Sept. 20	7 a. m.	29.11	59	.423	0	----------	0	88	
	2 p. m.	29.11	71	.430	9	----------	WSW. 2	43	
	9 p. m.	29.15	63	.510	9	----------	W. 3	88	
Sept. 21	7 a. m.	29.19	56	.376	10	----------	NNE. 3	87	
	2 p. m.	29.20	63	.429	10	----------	NNE. 2	77	
	9 p. m.	29.21	61	.426	8	----------	ENE. 1	82	
Sept. 22	7 a. m.	29.32	57	.391	10	----------	NW. 2	87	
	2 p. m.	29.39	62	.396	10	----------	ENE. 1	76	
	9 p. m.	29.43	60	.380	10	----------	0	76	
Sept. 23	7 a. m.	29.52	57	.391	10	----------	0	87	
	2 p. m.	29.52	68½	.438	10	----------	NE. 1	68	
	9 p. m.	29.49	66	.433	8	----------	WSW. 1	73	
Sept. 24	7 a. m.	29.51	58	.407	8	----------	0	87	
	2 p. m.	29.39	77	.497	4	----------	W. 2	59	
	9 p. m.	29.39	72	.496	0	----------	WSW. 1	64	

AVON, OHIO.

Month and day.	Hour.	Barom'r corrected to 32° F.	Thermometer.	Force of vapor.	Cloudiness.	Motion of clouds.	Winds.	Relative humidity.	REMARKS.
Sept. 14	9 p. m.	29.278	45	.251	------------	----------	E---- ------	84	20th. Showers after 8 a. m.; occasional showers during the 21st, 22d, & 23d; amount, 2.05 inches.
Sept. 15	7 a. m.	.320	56	.230	Cu. st-------	----------	NE. 2	51	
	2 p. m.	.282	57.5	.482	Cu. nim. 9	----------	SW---------	66	
	9 p. m.	.176	55	.376	Cu. nim. 10	W. 1	NE. 1	87	
Sept. 16	7 a. m.	.173	62	.370	Cu. st. 3	1	SE. 1	66	
	2 p. m.	.100	70	.403	Cir. st , nim. 9	SW. 1	NE---------	67	
	9 p. m.	28.908	64	.433	Cu. nim. 10	NW. 0	SE. 1	73	
Sept. 17	7 a. m.	29.018	64	.403	Nim. 10	NE--------	NE. 2	67	
	2 p. m.	.058	64	.403	Nim. 10	N. 1	N. 1	67	
	9 p. m.	.111	57	.276	3	----------	NE. 0	79	
Sept. 18	7 a. m.	------	------	------	Cu. st. 5	SW. 1	SW. 2	------	
	2 p. m.	------	------	------	Cir.cu., nim. 5	SW. 1	------------	------	
	9 p. m.	28.936	62	.496	Cu. st. 2	SE -------	SE. 1	77	
Sept. 19	7 a. m.	.715	71	.436	------------	----------	SW. 2	57	
	2 p. m.	.752	79	.527	------------	----------	SW. 2	54	
	9 p. m.	.823	68	.476	Nim. 9	SW. 1	SW. 1	69	
Sept. 20	7 a. m.	.745	65	.483	Nim. 10	NE. 1	NE. 1	78	
	2 p. m.	.870	62	.635	Nim. 10	NE. 1	NE---------	90	
	9 p. m.	.918	62	.429	Nim. 10	NE. 2	NE. 2	77	
Sept. 21	7 a. m.	.913	62	.460	Nim. 10	NE. 2	NE. 2	83	
	2 p. m.	.888	64	.529	Nim. 10	NE. 1	NE. 2	89	
	9 p. m.	.895	62	.525	Nim. 10	NE. 1	NE. 1	94	
Sept. 22	7 a. m.	.918	61	.442	Nim. 10	NW. 2	NW. 1	53	
	2 p. m.	.922	64.5	.523	Cir.cu., nim. 10	W. 1	W. 1	86	
	9 p. m.	29.038	60	.487	Nim. 10	W. 1	W. 1	94	
Sept. 23	7 a. m.	.133	59	.439	Cir. cu. 10	W. 1	SW. 1	88	
	2 p. m.	.233	63.7	.536	Cu. nim. 10	W. 1	SW. 1	92	
	9 p. m.	.105	60	.487	Nim. 10	W. 1	S. 0	94	
Sept. 24	7 a. m.	.078	50	.487	Cir.cu., nim. 10	W. 1	NW. 1	94	
	2 p. m.	.038	60	.571	Nim. 10	NW. 1	NW. 1	97	
	9 p. m.	.078	61	.473	Cir , nim. 9	NW. 1	------------	88	

STORMS Nos. 2 AND 3, SEPTEMBER, 1859.

BELLEFONTAINE, OHIO.

Month and day.	Hour.	Barom'r corrected to 32° F.	Thermometer.	Force of vapor.	Cloudiness.	Motion of clouds.	Winds.	Relative humidity.	REMARKS.
Sept. 14	9 p. m.	------	51	------	Nim. 9	SW. 2	NE. 4	------	Rain from 3 a. m. the 20th to 7 a. m. on the 22d; amount, 0.75 inch.
Sept. 15	7 a. m.	------	48	------	Cir. 6	NE. 2	SW. 2	------	
	2 p. m.	------	56	------	Cu. 10	SE. 2	W. 2	------	
	9 p. m.	------	53	------	Cir. 5	0	SW. 1	------	
Sept. 16	7 a. m.	------	56	------	Cir. 5	NW. 1	SW. 2	------	
	2 p. m.	------	74	------	Cu. 8	SE. 2	SW. 3	------	
	9 p. m.	------	54	------	Nim. 10	NE. 1	SW. 1	------	
Sept. 17	7 a. m.	------	64	------	Nim. 10	SW. 1	NE. 1	------	
	2 p. m.	------	69	------	Nim. 5	NE. 2	SE. 3	------	
	9 p. m.	------	59	------	0	0	SE. 1	------	
Sept. 18	7 a. m.	------	62	------	Cu. st 8	NW. 2	SE. 2	------	
	2 p. m.	------	78	------	Cir. 6	NW. 2	SE. 2	------	
	9 p. m.	------	68	------	Nim. 10	NE. 2	SE. 1	------	
Sept. 19	7 a. m.	------	66	------	Nim. 9	SW. 3	SE. 2	------	
	2 p. m.	------	73	------	Cir. 5	NW. 2	NE. 3	------	
	9 p. m.	------	64	------	Nim. 6	0	NE. 2	------	
Sept. 20	7 a. m.	------	61	------	Nim. 10	SE. 2	NW. 4	------	
	2 p. m.	------	64	------	Nim. 10	SW. 2	NE. 4	------	
	9 p. m.	------	52	------	Nim. 10	0	NE. 3	------	
Sept. 21	7 a. m.	------	54	------	Nim. 10	0	NW. 1	------	
	2 p. m.	------	65	------	Nim. 10	SE. 2	NW. 2	------	
	9 p. m.	------	57	------	Nim. 10	SE. 1	W. 2	------	
Sept. 22	7 a. m.	------	56	------	Nim. 10	NE 3	SW. 3	------	
	2 p. m.	------	67	------	Nim. 9	NE. 3	SW. 2	------	
	9 p. m.	------	58	------	Nim. 10	NE. 1	SW. 1	------	
Sept. 23	7 a. m.	------	57	------	Nim. 10	NW. 2	SW. 2	------	
	2 p. m.	------	68	------	Nim. 9	NE. 1	W. 3	------	
	9 p. m.	------	58	------	Nim. 10	NE. 1	SW. 1	------	
Sept. 24	7 a. m.	------	59	------	Nim. 10	NE. 3	SW. 2	------	
	2 p. m.	------	67	------	Nim. 10	NE. 2	SW. 3	------	
	9 p. m.	------	59	------	Nim. 10	NE. 1	W. 2	------	

BETHEL, OHIO.

Month and day.	Hour.	Barom'r corrected to 32° F.	Thermometer.	Force of vapor.	Cloudiness.	Motion of clouds.	Winds.	Relative humidity.	REMARKS.
Sept. 14	9 p. m.	------	------	------	2	----------	------------	------	14th. Dim halo at 9 a. m.; slight frost. 15th. Slight rain at 11 p. m.; warm. 18th. Appearances of rain; lightning NW. at 8 p. m. 19th. Warm rain from 4 a. m to 8 p. m.; amount, 1.00 inch. 20th. Very cold at night.
Sept. 15	7 a. m.	------	------	------	7	----------	E. 2	------	
	2 p. m.	------	------	------	4	----------	E. 3	------	
	9 p. m.	------	------	------	------------	----------	------------	------	
Sept. 16	7 a. m.	------	------	------	5	----------	1	------	
	2 p. m.	------	------	------	3	----------	NE. 2	------	
	9 p. m.	------	------	------	2	----------	------------	------	
Sept. 17	7 a. m.	------	------	------	7	----------	NE. 1	------	
	2 p. m.	------	------	------	2	----------	2	------	
	9 p. m.	------	------	------	------------	----------	------------	------	
Sept. 18	7 a. m.	------	------	------	6	----------	E. 1	------	
	2 p. m.	------	------	------	3	----------	E. 2	------	
	9 p. m.	------	------	------	5	----------	------------	------	
Sept. 19	7 a. m.	------	------	------	10	----------	SE. 2	------	
	2 p. m.	------	------	------	7	----------	S. 3	------	
	9 p. m.	------	------	------	4	----------	SW. 1	------	
Sept. 20	7 a. m.	------	------	------	10	----------	N. 1	------	
	2 p. m.	------	------	------	5	----------	N. 2	------	
	9 p. m.	------	------	------	------------	----------	N. 3	------	
Sept. 21	7 a. m.	------	------	------	10	----------	SW. 1	------	
	2 p. m.	------	------	------	6	----------	SW. 2	------	
	9 p. m.	------	------	------	10	----------	------------	------	
Sept. 22	7 a. m.	------	------	------	10	----------	1	------	
	2 p. m.	------	------	------	7	----------	2	------	
	9 p. m.	------	------	------	10	----------	------------	------	
Sept. 23	7 a. m.	------	------	------	10	----------	W. 2	------	
	2 p. m.	------	------	------	10	----------	W. 3	------	
	9 p. m.	------	------	------	10	----------	------------	------	
Sept. 24	7 a. m.	------	------	------	10	----------	1	------	
	2 p. m.	------	------	------	6	----------	NW. 3	------	
	9 p. m.	------	------	------	3	----------	------------	------	

STORMS Nos. 2 AND 3, SEPTEMBER, 1859.

BOWLING GREEN, OHIO.

Month and day.	Hour.	Barom'r corrected to 32° F.	Thermometer.	Force of vapor.	Cloudiness.	Motion of clouds.	Winds.	Relative humidity.
Sept. 14	9 p. m.	29.409	48.6	------	Cu. 10	0	0	------
Sept. 15	7 a. m.	.477	48	------	Cu. 9	W. 1	SE. 2	------
	2 p. m.	.434	57	------	Cir. cu. 7	W. 1	E. 2	------
	9 p. m.	.373	56.4	------	Cu. 9	0	0	------
Sept. 16	7 a. m.	.299	58	------	Fog 10	----------	E. 1	------
	2 p. m.	.203	69.3	------	Cir. 7	0	E. 1	------
	9 p. m.	.157	62.6	------	10	----------	0	------
Sept. 17	7 a. m.	.202	62	------	Fog 10	----------	N. 1	------
	2 p. m.	.193	70	------	Cu. 1	NW. 1	NW. 1	------
	9 p. m.	.221	55	------	0	0	0	------
Sept. 18	7 a. m.	.223	54.7	------	Cu. 9	W. 1	SW. 1	------
	2 p. m.	.239	77	------	Cir. cu. 1	0	S. 1	------
	9 p. m.	.044	59	------	Cu. 10	W. 2	S. 2	------
Sept. 19	7 a. m.	28.898	64	------	Cir. cu., st. 10	W. 1	S. 1	------
	2 p. m.	.848	75	------	Cu. 5	SW. 1	S. 2	------
	9 p. m.	.815	64.2	------	Cu. 1	----------	0	------
Sept. 20	7 a. m.	29.045	54.3	------	? 10	NW. 3	NW. 3	------
	2 p. m.	.036	54.5	------	? 10	NE. 2	NE. 2	------
	9 p. m.	.062	52	------	Nim. 10	----------	0	------
Sept. 21	7 a. m.	.031	64	------	Nim. 10	NE. 2	NE. 2	------
	2 p. m.	.034	62	------	Mist.clouds 10	NE. 2	NE. 1	------
	9 p. m.	.032	56	------	Nim. 10	----------	0	------
Sept. 22	7 a. m.	.120	60.5	------	? 10	SW. 2	SW. 1	------
	2 p. m.	.146	67.5	------	10	SW. 1	W. 1	------
	9 p. m.	.227	58	------	Cu. 10	----------	0	------
Sept. 23	7 a. m.	.288	60.5	------	Cu. st. 10	W. 2	SW. 1	------
	2 p. m.	.265	66	------	Cu. 10	W. 2	SW. 1	------
	9 p. m.	.380	60.5	------	10	----------	0	------
Sept. 24	7 a. m.	.254	60.5	------	? 10	NW. 2	0	------
	2 p. m.	.224	67	------	Cu. 10	NW. 1	0	------
	9 p. m.	.233	56	------	0	0	0	------

REMARKS.

18th. Diffused lightning in the W. from 8 to 9 p. m.; dense black cloud at 9 p. m.; light dashes of rain in the night.
19th. Alternate showers and sunshine till noon, then mostly clear till night; amount, 0.08 inch.
20th. Rain from NE., commencing at 7 a. m.; amount, 0.40 inch.
21st. Amount of rain, 0.935 inch.
22d. Amount of rain, 0.142 inch.
24th. Aurora in the evening; am't of rain, 0.093 inch.

CINCINNATI, OHIO.*

Month and day.	Hour.	Barom'r corrected to 32° F.	Thermometer.	Force of vapor.	Cloudiness.	Motion of clouds.	Winds.	Relative humidity.
Sept. 14	9 p. m.	29.33	61	.383	Cu. 10	----------	NW --------	71
Sept. 15	7 a. m.	29.38	54	.308	Cu. st. 8	----------	NE----------	74
	2 p. m.	29.38	76	.541	Cu. 5	----------	NE----------	60
	9 p. m.	29.36	65	.451	Nim. 10	----------	E.----------	73
Sept. 16	7 a. m.	29.21	56	.420	Nim. 10	----------	NE----------	94
	2 p. m.	29.11	76	.614	------------	----------	NE----------	68
	9 p. m.	29.07	67	.522	------------	----------	E.----------	79
Sept. 17	7 a. m.	29.16	65	.483	Nim. 10	----------	NE--------	78
	2 p. m.	29.15	74	.641	Cu. 5	----------	N.----------	77
	9 p. m.	29.19	65	.583	0	----------	E.----------	94
Sept. 18	7 a. m.	29.21	66	.570	Cir. cu., st. 8	----------	SE --------	89
	2 p. m.	29.13	86	.850	Nim. 3	----------	SW--------	68
	9 p. m.	29.00	75	.666	Nim. 5	----------	S.----------	77
Sept. 19	7 a. m.	28.91	68	.648	Nim. 10	SW. 3	SW. 3	95
	2 p. m.	28.89	77	.799	Cu. 5	----------	SW--------	86
	9 p. m.	28.90	67	.655	Nim. 5	----------	SW--------	97
Sept. 20	7 a. m.	28.91	63	.543	Nim. 8	----------	N ----------	94
	2 p. m.	28.93	65	.549	Nim. 10	----------	N ----------	89
	9 p. m.	29.02	57	.436	Nim. 10	----------	N. 4	94
Sept. 21	7 a. m.	29.01	55	.405	Nim. 10	----------	N ----------	94
	2 p. m.	29.00	66	.502	Nim. 10	----------	N ----------	78
	9 p. m.	29.01	61	.505	Nim. 10	----------	N ----------	94
Sept. 22	7 a. m.	29.13	60	.426	Nim. 10	----------	W. 2	82
	2 p. m.	29.20	65	.483	Nim. 10	----------	SW--------	78
	9 p. m.	29.25	60	.456	Nim. 10	----------	SW--------	88
Sept. 23	7 a. m.	29.35	60	.456	Nim. 10	----------	SW. 2	88
	2 p. m.	29.29	73	.510	Nim. 10	----------	W----------	63
	9 p. m.	29.31	63	.510	Nim. 10	----------	W----------	88
Sept. 24	7 a. m.	29.29	62	.491	Cu. 8	----------	W. 1	88
	2 p. m.	29.19	75	.745	Nim. 8	----------	W. 3	86
	9 p. m.	29.24	60	.456	0	----------	W----------	88

REMARKS.

16th. Sprinkle before day.
19th. Showery from before day till after 9 a. m.; rain from 3.30 to 5 p. m.; amount, 0.66 inch.
20th. Rain from 11 a. m. to 0.30 p. m.; amount, 0.75 inch.

* Harper, observer.

STORMS Nos. 2 AND 3, SEPTEMBER, 1859.

CINCINNATI, OHIO.*

Month and day.	Hour.	Barom'r corrected to 32° F.	Thermometer.	Force of vapor.	Cloudiness.	Motion of clouds.	Winds.	Relative humidity.	REMARKS.
Sept. 14	9 p. m.	29.47	62	------	Cir. 5	NE-------	0	------	19th. Rain from 3 a. m. to 4.30 p. m.; amount, 0.75 inch.
Sept. 15	7 a. m.	29.49	65	------	Cir. 10	E---- ----	E. 2	------	
	2 p. m.	29.47	74	------	Cir. 4	NE-------	NE. 4	------	
	9 p. m.	29.30	68	------	Cir. 9	NE-------	S. 4	------	
Sept. 16	7 a. m.	29.39	60	------	Nim. 10	E -------	SE. 2	------	
	2 p. m.	29.37	76	------	0	0	S. 2	------	
	9 p. m.	29.37	70	------	0	0	NW. 8	------	
Sept. 17	7 a. m.	29.28	66	------	Nim. 10	E---- ----	SW. 4	------	
	2 p. m.	29.26	76	------	Cu. 6	E---- ----	W. 4	------	
	9 p. m.	29.27	68	------	0	0	0	------	
Sept. 18	7 a. m.	29.38	60	------	Cu. 4	NE-------	SW. 2	------	
	2 p. m.	29.25	82	------	0	0	SW. 4	------	
	9 p. m.	29.16	76	------	0	0	0	------	
Sept. 19	7 a. m.	29.07	70	------	Nim. 10	NE-------	SW. 6	------	
	2 p. m.	29.07	78	------	Cu. 6	NE-------	S. 2	------	
	9 p. m.	29.07	68	------	0	0	0	------	
Sept. 20	7 a. m.	29.08	66	------	Nim. 10	NE. ------	0	------	
	2 p. m.	29.07	70	------	Cu. 8	S.--------	0	------	
	9 p. m.	29.18	60	------	Nim. 10	SE. ------	0	------	
Sept. 21	7 a. m.	29.18	58	------	Nim. 10	NE. ------	NW. 6	------	
	2 p. m.	29.17	64	------	Nim. 10	E---- ----	NW. 6	------	
	9 p. m.	29.17	64	------	Nim. 10	SE -------	0	------	
Sept. 22	7 a. m.	29.29	62	------	Nim. 10	E -------	NW. 2	------	
	2 p. m.	29.27	64	------	Nim. 10	NE------	SW. 6	------	
	9 p. m.	29.37	62	------	Nim. 10	NE-------	0	------	
Sept. 23	7 a. m.	29.49	64	------	Nim. 10	E -------	0	------	
	2 p. m.	29.48	68	------	Cu. 10	E -------	SW. 4	------	
	9 p. m.	29.47	64	------	Nim. 10	NE-------	0	------	
Sept. 24	7 a. m.	29.38	64	------	Cir. 8	E -------	0	------	
	2 p. m.	29.36	74	------	Cu. 6	E -------	SW. 2	------	
	9 p. m.	29.37	64	------	0	0	0	------	

* Phillips, observer.

CLEVELAND, OHIO.

Month and day.	Hour.	Barom'r corrected to 32° F.	Thermometer.	Force of vapor.	Cloudiness.	Motion of clouds.	Winds.	Relative humidity.	REMARKS.
Sept. 14	9 p. m.	29.19	49	------	Cir. cu. 9	W. 2	NE. 1	------	14th, 15th, and 16th. Cloudy.
Sept. 15	7 a. m.	29.26	46½	------	Cir. st. 10	W. 2	SE.--- ----	------	17th. Mist; cloudy; rain from 8.30 to 11 a. m.; amount, 0.01 inch.
	2 p. m.	29.19	60	------	Cir. st. 10	----------	NE. 2	------	
	9 p. m.	29.15	55	------	Cir. cu. 10	W. 2	SE. 1	------	18th and 19th. Cloudy.
Sept. 16	7 a. m.	29.06	55	------	Cir. st. 10	NE. 3	NE. 3	------	20th. Rain from early a. m. to 3 p. m.; amount, 0.23 inch.
	2 p. m.	29.00	67	------	Cu. st. 10	NE. 3	NE. 2	------	
	9 p. m.	28.96	63½	------	10	----------	S. 1	------	21st. Cloudy.
Sept. 17	7 a. m.	28.94	63	------	10	----------	SE. 2	------	22d. Cloudy to 8 a. m. and shower about 3 p. m.
	2 p. m.	28.97	64	------	Cir. 8	W. 2	S. 2	------	
	9 p. m.	28.99	58½	------	0	----------	SE. 2	------	23d. Rainy.
Sept. 18	7 a. m.	29.03	57	------	Cir. 9	W. 2	S. 2	------	24th. Rain till 4 p. m.; amount, 0.72 inch.
	2 p. m.	28.96	73	------	10	----------	S. 4	------	
	9 p. m.	28.87	65	------	5	----------	NE---------	------	
Sept. 19	7 a. m.	28.74	62	------	10	----------	NE. 3	------	
	2 p. m.	28.71	79	------	10	----------	NE. 4	------	
	9 p. m.	28.75	70	------	10	----------	NE. 3	------	
Sept. 20	7 a. m.	28.78	65	------	10	----------	NE. 2	------	
	2 p. m.	28.80	60	------	10	----------	NE. 3	------	
	9 p. m.	28.85	60½	------	10	----------	N. 1	------	
Sept. 21	7 a. m.	28.83	60	------	10	W. 3	NW. 2	------	
	2 p. m.	28.80	67	------	10	----------	W. 2	------	
	9 p. m.	28.80	62½	------	10	----------	S.----------	------	
Sept. 22	7 a. m.	28.86	60	------	10	----------	SW. 2	------	
	2 p. m.	28.94	63	------	10	----------	W. 2	------	
	9 p. m.	29.02	61½	------	10	----------	S. 1	------	
Sept. 23	7 a. m.	29.08	59½	------	10	----------	SW. 2	------	
	2 p. m.	29.07	64½	------	10	W. 3	W. 2	------	
	9 p. m.	29.05	60½	------	2	----------	N. 3	------	
Sept. 24	7 a. m.	29.02	59½	------	Cir. st. 10	NE. 3	N. 2	------	
	2 p. m.	28.98	63	------	Cu. 6	NW. 3	NW. 2	------	
	9 p. m.	29.02	62½	------	0	----------	S.------- ----	------	

STORMS Nos. 2 AND 3, SEPTEMBER, 1859.

COLLINGWOOD, OHIO.

Month and day.	Hour.	Barom'r corrected to 32° F.	Thermometer.	Force of vapor.	Cloudiness.	Motion of clouds.	Winds.	Relative humidity.	REMARKS.
Sept. 14	9 p. m.	------	60	------	------	------	------	------	
Sept. 15	7 a. m.	------	52	------	------	------	------	------	
	2 p. m.	------	60	------	------	------	------	------	
	9 p. m.	------	54	------	------	------	------	------	
Sept. 16	7 a. m.	------	62	------	------	------	------	------	
	2 p. m.	------	65	------	------	------	------	------	
	9 p. m.	------	66	------	------	------	------	------	
Sept. 17	7 a. m.	------	62	------	------	------	------	------	
	2 p. m.	------	80	------	------	------	------	------	
	9 p. m.	------	56	------	------	------	------	------	
Sept. 18	7 a. m.	------	54	------	------	------	------	------	
	2 p. m.	------	75	------	------	------	------	------	
	9 p. m.	------	64	------	------	------	------	------	
Sept. 19	7 a. m.	------	52	------	------	------	------	------	
	2 p. m.	------	66	------	------	------	------	------	
	9 p. m.	------	64	------	------	------	------	------	
Sept. 20	7 a. m.	------	50	------	------	------	------	------	
	2 p. m.	------	60	------	------	------	------	------	
	9 p. m.	------	50	------	------	------	------	------	
Sept. 21	7 a. m.	------	54	------	------	------	------	------	
	2 p. m.	------	68	------	------	------	------	------	
	9 p. m.	------	58	------	------	------	------	------	
Sept. 22	7 a. m.	------	60	------	------	------	------	------	
	2 p. m.	------	64	------	------	------	------	------	
	9 p. m.	------	64	------	------	------	------	------	
Sept. 23	7 a. m.	------	62	------	------	------	------	------	
	2 p. m.	------	65	------	------	------	------	------	
	9 p. m.	------	45	------	------	------	------	------	
Sept. 24	7 a. m.	------	62	------	------	------	------	------	
	2 p. m.	------	68	------	------	------	------	------	
	9 p. m.	------	56	------	------	------	------	------	

COLLEGE HILL, OHIO.*

Month and day.	Hour.	Barom'r corrected to 32° F.	Thermometer.	Force of vapor.	Cloudiness.	Motion of clouds.	Winds.	Relative humidity.	REMARKS.
Sept. 14	9 p. m.	28.75	60	------	9	W. 2	W. 2	------	17th. Amount of rain, 0.90 inch.
Sept. 15	7 a. m.	28.80	54	------	5	W. 2	E. 3	------	21st. Rain from 3 to 4 p. m.; amount, 0.50 inch.
	2 p. m.	28.80	68	------	4	W. 3	E. 3	------	
	9 p. m.	28.80	60	------	9	E. 2	E. 2	------	23d. Sprinkle.
Sept. 16	7 a. m.	28.71	56	------	10	E. 2	E. 1	------	
	2 p. m.	28.64	74	------	9	SE. 2	SE. 2	------	
	9 p. m.	28.64	60	------	9	SE. 2	NE. 2	------	
Sept. 17	7 a. m.	28.60	62	------	9	NW. 2	NE. 1	------	
	2 p. m.	28.60	76	------	5	NE. 2	NE. 2	------	
	9 p. m.	28.60	62	------	9	NE. 2	NE. 1	------	
Sept. 18	7 a. m.	28.64	64	------	8	NW. 2	NW. 3	------	
	2 p. m.	28.56	82	------	8	SE. 3	SE. 3	------	
	9 p. m.	28.56	74	------	8	SE. 2	SE. 2	------	
Sept. 19	7 a. m.	28.48	68	------	10	S. 2	S. 2	------	
	2 p. m.	28.40	72	------	8	S. 4	S. 3	------	
	9 p. m.	28.40	60	------	8	S. 3	S. 2	------	
Sept. 20	7 a. m.	28.40	64	------	10	N. 3	N. 4	------	
	2 p. m.	28.40	66	------	10	N. 4	N. 4	------	
	9 p. m.	28.46	56	------	10	N. 2	N. 2	------	
Sept. 21	7 a. m.	28.47	56	------	10	N. 2	N. 2	------	
	2 p. m.	28.48	66	------	10	N. 3	N. 3	------	
	9 p. m.	28.49	56	------	10	N. 2	N. 2	------	
Sept. 22	7 a. m.	28.55	58	------	10	W. 2	W. 2	------	
	2 p. m.	28.56	66	------	10	W. 2	W. 2	------	
	9 p. m.	28.58	56	------	10	NW. 2	W. 2	------	
Sept. 23	7 a. m.	28.71	58	------	9	NW. 2	S. 1	------	
	2 p. m.	28.80	68	------	10	S. 2	S. 2	------	
	9 p. m.	28.80	64	------	10	SW. 2	SW. 2	------	
Sept. 24	7 a. m.	28.76	64	------	3	NW. 3	SW. 3	------	
	2 p. m.	28.70	69	------	4	W. 4	N. 4	------	
	9 p. m.	28.70	60	------	4	W. 2	N. 2	------	

* Wilson, observer.

STORMS Nos. 2 AND 3, SEPTEMBER, 1859.

COLLEGE HILL, OHIO.*

Month and day.	Hour.	Barom'r corrected to 32° F.	Thermometer.	Force of vapor.	Cloudiness.	Motion of clouds.	Winds.		Relative humidity.	REMARKS.
Sept. 14	9 p. m.				6		NW.	1		14th. Frost; cool evening.
Sept. 15	7 a. m.				5		NE.	1		15th. Frost; cool evening.
	2 p. m.				5		NE.	2		16th. Shower from 4 to 9 a. m.
	9 p. m.				4		NE.	2		17th and 18th. Pleasant.
Sept. 16	7 a. m.				10		W.	2		19th. Fine rain at 2 a. m.
	2 p. m.				5		W.	2		20th. Cloudy; signs of rain.
	9 p. m.				4		W.	2		21st. Light rain, commencing at 4
Sept. 17	7 a. m.				10		NW.	3		a. m.
	2 p. m.				5		NW.	2		22d, 23d, and 24th. Cloudy.
	9 p. m.				0		NW.	2		
Sept. 18	7 a. m.				6		SE.	1		
	2 p. m.				0		SE.	1		
	9 p. m.				10		SW.	1		
Sept. 19	7 a. m.				10		SW.	2		
	2 p. m.				3		SW.	3		
	9 p. m.				10		SW.	2		
Sept. 20	7 a. m.				10		W.	2		
	2 p. m.				10		NW.	3		
	9 p. m.				10		N.	3		
Sept. 21	7 a. m.				10		N.	2		
	2 p. m.				10		NE.	2		
	9 p. m.				10		N.	2		
Sept. 22	7 a. m.				10		NW.	1		
	2 p. m.				10		NW.	1		
	9 p. m.				10		NW.	2		
Sept. 23	7 a. m.				10		SW.	1		
	2 p. m.				10		SW.	1		
	9 p. m.				6		SW.	1		
Sept. 24	7 a. m.				3		NW.	2		
	2 p. m.				7		NW.	5		
	9 p. m.				5		N.	2		

* Hammitt, observer.

DALLASBURG, OHIO.

Month and day.	Hour.	Barom'r corrected to 32° F.	Thermometer.	Force of vapor.	Cloudiness.	Motion of clouds.	Winds.		Relative humidity.	REMARKS.
Sept. 14	9 p. m.				6		W.	1		16th. Rain from 4 to 9 p. m.
Sept. 15	7 a. m.				2		W.	1		19th. Rain from 3 a. m. to 9 p. m.
	2 p. m.				3		SW.	2		20th, 21st, and 22d. Drizzling rain.
	9 p. m.				2		S.	2		24th. Aurora 7.30 to 8.30 p. m;
Sept. 16	7 a. m.				10		SW.	2		small diffused light.
	2 p. m.				8		S.	1		
	9 p. m.				6		S.	2		
Sept. 17	2 a. m.				10		S.	1		
	7 p. m.				6		SW.	2		
	9 p. m.				2		SW.	1		
Sept. 18	7 a. m.				4		NW.	1		
	2 p. m.				2		NW.	1		
	9 p. m.				3		W.	1		
Sept. 19	7 a. m.				10		NE.	1		
	2 p. m.				10		NE.	1		
	9 p. m.				10		E.	1		
Sept. 20	7 a. m.				8		SW.	1		
	2 p. m.				9		SW.	1		
	9 p. m.				10		SW.	1		
Sept. 21	7 a. m.				8		NW.	1		
	2 p. m.				8		W.			
	9 p. m.				8		W.	1		
Sept. 22	7 a. m.				9		NW			
	2 p. m.				9		W.	1		
	9 p. m.				9		W.	1		
Sept. 23	7 a. m.				10		W.	1		
	2 p. m.				10		SW.	1		
	9 p. m.				10		SW.	1		
Sept. 24	7 a. m.				9		W.	2		
	2 p. m.				6		N.	1		
	9 p. m.				4		N.	2		

STORMS Nos. 2 AND 3, SEPTEMBER, 1859.

ELKRUN, OHIO.

Month and day.	Hour.	Barom'r corrected to 32° F.	Thermometer.	Force of vapor.	Cloudiness.	Motion of clouds.	Winds.	Relative humidity.
Sept. 14	9 p. m.	28.61	47	.273	Cir. cu. 6	W. 3	NW. 1	85
Sept. 15	7 a. m.	28.74	43	.209	Cir. cu. 9	W. 1	E. 1	75
	2 p. m.	28.60	69	.398	Cir. 2	W. 3	E. 1	56
	9 p. m.	28.59	57	.407	Cir. st. 10	W. 2	NE. 1	87
Sept. 16	7 a. m.	28.54	55	.376	Cir. st. 10	W. 1	E. 1	87
	2 p. m.	28.48	61	.505	Nim. 10	----------	E. 1	94
	9 p. m.	28.43	60	.487	Nim. 10	----------	E. 2	94
Sept. 17	7 a. m.	28.35	58.5	.491	Nim. 10	----------	NE. 1	100
	2 p. m.	28.37	63	.478	Cu. st. 10	----------	N. 1	83
	9 p. m.	28.45	55	.405	Cir. st. 1	NW. 2	NE. 1	94
Sept. 18	7 a. m.	28.57	43	.375	Fog 10	----------	0	93
	2 p. m.	28.45	66	.502	Cir. st. 7	----------	SE. 1	78
	9 p. m.	28.38	57	.378	0	0	NW. 1	81
Sept. 19	7 a. m.	28.27	54	.390	Cir. st. 8	NW. 2	N. 1	97
	2 p. m.	28.21	74	.641	Cir. st 10	SW. 1	SE. 2	77
	9 p. m.	28.24	67	.522	Cu. st. 8	SW. 3	S. 3	79
Sept. 20	7 a. m.	28.22	65	.583	Nim. 10	----------	NE. 2	94
	2 p. m.	28.22	69	.599	St. 10	----------	NE. 1	85
	9 p. m.	28.24	67	.556	Nim. 10	----------	NE. 3	84
Sept. 21	7 a. m.	28.26	69	.599	Nim. 10	----------	E. 1	85
	2 p. m.	28.23	75	.666	Cir. st 7	SE. 6	NE. 2	77
	9 p. m.	28.22	68	.612	10	----------	N. 2	90
Sept. 22	7 a. m.	28.28	64	.529	Nim. 10	----------	S. 2	89
	2 p. m.	28.36	79	.362	Cir. cu. 9	----------	S. 1	36
	9 p. m.	28.45	59	.469	St. 3	SW. 1	NW. 1	94
Sept. 23	7 a. m.	28.51	58	.423	Cu. st. 10	----------	SW. 1	88
	2 p. m.	28.51	62	.491	Cu. st. 9	----------	SW. 2	83
	9 p. m.	28.51	59	.469	10	----------	NW. 1	88
Sept. 24	7 a. m.	28.47	59	.439	Nim. 10	----------	E. 1	88
	2 p. m.	28.40	63	.478	Nim. 10	----------	SW. 1	79
	9 p. m.	28.42	60	.456	10	----------	0	94

REMARKS.

16th. Rain from early morn till 2 p. m.; amount, 0.12 inch.
17th. Amount, 0.45 inch.
18th. Rain from early night till 9 to 10 a. m.; amount 0.01 inch.
20th. Rain from 2 p. m. to 11 a. m.; ?? amount, 0 81 inch.
21st. Rain from early night to 12 noon; amount, 0.46 inch
22d. Rain from early night to 11 a.m.; amount, 0.28 inch.
23d. Rain from 7.30 a. m. to 2 p. m; amount, 0.05 inch.
24th. Rain at 2 p. m.; amount, 0.71 inch.

FREEDOM, OHIO.

Month and day.	Hour.	Barom'r corrected to 32° F.	Thermometer.	Force of vapor.	Cloudiness.	Motion of clouds.	Winds.	Relative humidity.
Sept. 14	9 p. m.	28.74	40	------	Cir. cu. 9	E. 2	E. 4	------
Sept. 15	7 a. m.	28.84	43	------	Cir. cu. 10	E. 2	SE. 12	------
	2 p. m.	28.51	60	------	Cir. cu. 5	SE. 12	N. 4	------
	9 p. m.	28.62	50	------	Cir. cu. 8	SE. 4	N. 12	------
Sept. 16	7 a. m.	28.82	55	------	Cu. 5	S. 4	NE. 12	------
	2 p. m.	28.81	60	------	Cu. nim. 8	E. 4	NE. 12	------
	9 p. m.	28.31	60	------	Nim. 10	E. 4	N. 12	------
Sept. 17	7 a. m.	28.12	50	------	Nim. 10	E. 4	S. 12	------
	2 p. m.	28.11	60	------	Cir. cu. 5	S. 4	S. 12	------
	9 p. m.	28.42	50	------	Cir. 1	E. 2	E. 4	------
Sept. 18	7 a. m.	28.52	50	------	Cir. cu. 10	E. 4	W. 4	------
	2 p. m.	28.09	70	------	Cir. 3	E. 2	S. 4	------
	9 p. m.	28.21	59	------	Cu. 1	S. 2	S. 4	------
Sept. 19	7 a. m.	28.10	63	------	Cir. 8	NE. 4	N. 2	------
	2 p. m.	27.82	79	------	Cir. 8	NE. 12	NW. 12	------
	9 p. m.	27.89	69	------	Cir. cu. 9	E. 2	E. 2	------
Sept. 20	7 a. m.	28.10	67	------	Nim. 10	N. 2	W. 12	------
	2 p. m.	27.89	70	------	Nim. 10	NE. 12	N. 12	------
	9 p. m.	28.21	57	------	Nim. 10	E. 2	N. 14	------
Sept. 21	7 a. m.	28.41	59	------	Nim. 10	NE. 2	N. 14	------
	2 p. m.	28.11	60	------	Nim. 10	NE. 4	N. 12	------
	9 p. m.	28.11	62	------	Nim. 10	E. 2	E. 4	------
Sept. 22	7 a. m.	28.16	61	------	Nim. 10	E. 2	NE. 2	------
	2 p. m.	27.89	70	------	Cir. cu. 8	E. 2	NE. 12	------
	9 p. m.	28.31	60	------	Cir. 4	E. 2	N. 2	------
Sept. 23	7 a. m.	28.11	60	------	Nim. 10	N. 2	N. 2	------
	2 p. m.	28.39	70	------	Cir. cu. 8	E. 2	W. 12	------
	9 p. m.	28.12	55	------	Nim. 10	E. 2	N. 4	------
Sept. 24	7 a. m.	28.41	60	------	Nim. 10	E. 2	N. 2	------
	2 p. m.	28.29	70	------	Nim. 10	E. 4	SE. 12	------
	9 p. m.	28.69	58	------	Cir. 5	SE. 4	E. 12	------

REMARKS.

Storm from 7 p. m. the 15th to 1 p. m. on the 16th; amount, 0.25 inch.
17th. Partially overcast; dry and dusty.
18th. Pleasant most of the day.
19th. Rain; portion of the day some diffuse lightning.
20th. Began to rain at 5 a. m.; storm ended at 6 p m. on the 23d; amount, 1.50 inch.
24th. Stormy most of the day.

STORMS Nos. 2 AND 3, SEPTEMBER, 1859.

HILLSBOROUGH, OHIO.*

Month and day.	Hour.	Barom'r corrected to 32° F.	Thermometer.	Force of vapor.	Cloudiness.	Motion of clouds.	Winds.	Relative humidity.	REMARKS.
Sept. 14	9 p. m.	------	------	------	8	----------	NE. 1	------	14th. Slight frost at 4 30 a. m.
Sept. 15	7 a. m.	------	------	------	10	----------	NE. 3	------	16th. Halo at 10 p. m.
	2 p. m.	------	------	------	1	----------	N. 3	------	17th. Halo at 11 p. m.
	0 p. m.	------	------	------	10	----------	NE. 3	------	18th. Warm.
Sept. 16	7 a. m.	------	------	------	10	----------	SE. 1	------	19th. Rain from 8 to 11 a. m., and at night.
	2 p. m.	------	------	------	10	----------	E. 3	------	
	9 p. m.	------	------	------	8	----------	------------	------	20th. Rain from 7 to 10 a. m.; showery.
Sept. 17	7 a. m.	------	------	------	10	----------	N. 2	------	
	2 p. m.	------	------	------	2	----------	------------	------	21st. Cool; heavy rain in the night
	9 p. m.	------	------	------	2	----------	W. 1	------	22d. Cold.
Sept. 18	7 a. m.	------	------	------	5	----------	W. 1	------	23d. Cold and cloudy; damp and chilly.
	2 p. m.	------	------	------	5	----------	SW. 2	------	
	9 p. m.	------	------	------	2	----------	SW. 1	------	
Sept. 19	7 a. m.	------	------	------	10	----------	W. 3	------	
	2 p. m.	------	------	------	10	----------	NW. 2	------	
	9 p. m.	------	------	------	10	----------	NW. 1	------	
Sept. 20	7 a. m.	------	------	------	10	----------	NW. 2	------	
	2 p. m.	------	------	------	10	----------	W. 2	------	
	9 p. m.	------	------	------	10	----------	NW. 2	------	
Sept. 21	7 a. m.	------	------	------	10	----------	NW. 2	------	
	2 p. m.	------	------	------	10	----------	NW. 2	------	
	9 p. m.	------	------	------	8	----------	NW. 1	------	
Sept. 22	7 a. m.	------	------	------	10	----------	NW. 3	------	
	2 p. m.	------	------	------	10	----------	W. 2	------	
	9 p. m.	------	------	------	10	----------	SW. 3	------	
Sept. 23	7 a. m.	------	------	------	10	----------	SW. 2	------	
	2 p. m.	------	------	------	10	----------	SW. 2	------	
	9 p. m.	------	------	------	10	----------	W. 1	------	
Sept. 24	7 a. m.	------	------	------	10	----------	W. 2	------	
	2 p. m.	------	------	------	10	----------	W. 2	------	
	9 p. m.	------	------	------	0	----------	W. 1	------	

* Gamble, observer.

HILLSBOROUGH, OHIO.*

Month and day.	Hour.	Barom'r corrected to 32° F.	Thermometer.	Force of vapor.	Cloudiness.	Motion of clouds.	Winds.	Relative humidity.	REMARKS.
Sept. 14	9 p. m.	28. 40	57½	.337	Cir. st. 2	----------	NE. 2	70	16th. Rain in a. m.; amount, 0.610 inch.
Sept. 15	7 a. m.	28. 46	47½	.212	Cir. st. 8	----------	NE. 2	63	
	2 p. m.	28. 37	63	.285	Cir. st. 2	----------	NE. 3	48	19th. Rain in a. m. and p. m.; amount, 0.228 inch.
	9 p. m.	28. 34	59½	.297	Cu. 8	----------	NE. 3	57	
Sept. 16	7 a. m.	28. 33	54	.411	St. 10	----------	NE. 2	97	20th. Rain in a. m.; amount, 1.365 inch.
	2 p. m.	28. 21	69½	.586	St. 8	----------	SE. 2	80	
	9 p. m.	28. 17	63	.563	St. 2	----------	SE. 1	94	21st. Rain from 11 to 12 p. m; amount, 0.465 inch.
Sept. 17	7 a. m.	28. 22	62	.563	St. 10	----------	NW. 1	94	
	2 p. m.	28. 24	70	.537	St. 8	NW. 1	SW. 3	71	
	9 p. m.	28. 27	63	.543	St. 1	----------	SW. 2	94	
Sept. 18	7 a. m.	28. 27	57	.452	St. 3	----------	SE. 1	94	
	2 p. m.	28. 19	75	.591	Cir. 1	----------	SE. 1	08	
	9 p. m.	28. 15	67	.522	St. 1	----------	SW. 1	79	
Sept. 19	7 a. m.	28. 09	66	.591	Nim. 10	----------	SW. 1	89	
	2 p. m.	28. 04	67½	.612	St. 10	----------	SW. 3	90	
	9 p. m.	28. 04	65½	.587	St. 10	----------	SW. 1	92	
Sept. 20	7 a. m.	27. 99	63	.580	St. 8	----------	NW. 1	97	
	2 p. m.	28. 01	66	.489	St. 8	----------	NW. 3	75	
	9 p. m.	28. 09	56	.405	St. 10	----------	NW. 3	90	
Sept. 21	7 a. m.	28. 10	53	.396	Fog 10	----------	NW. 2	96	
	2 p. m.	28. 10	61	.460	St. 10	----------	NW. 1	83	
	9 p. m.	28. 10	58½	.439	St. 10	----------	NW. 1	88	
Sept. 22	7 a. m.	28. 20	57	.436	St. 10	----------	SW. 1	94	
	2 p. m.	28. 26	61½	.453	St. 10	----------	SW. 1	80	
	9 p. m.	28. 30	57	.429	St. 3	----------	SW. 1	91	

* Matthews, observer.

STORMS Nos. 2 AND 3, SEPTEMBER, 1859.

HILLSBOROUGH, OHIO—Continued.

Month and day.	Hour.	Barom'r corrected to 32° F.	Thermometer.	Force of vapor.	Cloudiness.	Motion of clouds.	Winds.	Relative humidity.	REMARKS.
Sept. 23	7 a. m.	28.40	55½	.420	St. 10	....	SW. 1	94	
	2 p. m.	28.39	62	.399	St. 10	....	SW. 2	72	
	9 p. m.	28.40	59	.439	St. 8	....	NE. 1	88	
Sept. 24	7 a. m.	28.37	58½	.454	St. 9	....	SW. 2	91	
	2 p. m.	28.29	66½	.489	St. 10	....	SW. 1	75	
	9 p. m.	28.29	57	.407	Cu. 1	....	NW. 2	87	

HOCKING PORT, OHIO.

Month and day.	Hour.	Barom'r corrected to 32° F.	Thermometer.	Force of vapor.	Cloudiness.	Motion of clouds.	Winds.	Relative humidity.	REMARKS.
Sept. 14	9 p. m.	......	......	......	8	....	1	......	14th. Cirrus clouds.
Sept. 15	7 a. m.	......	......	......	7	....	NE. 3	......	15th. Cirro stratus clouds.
	2 p. m.	......	......	......	4	....	NW. 1	......	16th. Rain from 7 a. m. to 9 p. m.;
	9 p. m.	......	......	......	8	....	NW. 1	......	cirru clouds.
Sept. 16	7 a. m.	......	......	......	10	....	SE. 1	......	17th. Cir. stratus.
	2 p. m.	......	......	......	10	....	NE. 1	......	18th. Foggy.
	9 p. m.	......	......	......	10	....	SW. 1	......	19th. Frequent showers from 4 to
Sept. 17	7 a. m.	......	......	......	10	....	NE. 1	......	9 p. m.; distant thunder S. and
	2 p. m.	......	......	......	4	....	NE. 1	......	SW. at 5 p. m.; cirro stratus
	9 p. m.	......	......	......	0	....	....	......	clouds.
Sept. 18	7 a. m.	......	......	......	10	....	SE. 1	......	20th. Showery.
	2 p. m.	......	......	......	3	....	1	......	21st. Showery; distant thunder and
	9 p. m.	......	......	......	0	....	Calm 0	......	lightning in SW. at 9 p. m.
Sept. 19	7 a. m.	......	......	......	4	....	NE. 1	......	22d. Rain till 11 a. m.; nimbus
	2 p. m.	......	......	......	10	....	SE. 1	......	clouds.
	9 p. m.	......	......	......	10	....	W. 1	......	23d. Cool; cirro stratus.
Sept. 20	7 a. m.	......	......	......	10	....	NE. 1	......	24th. Rain from 3 to 5 p. m.
	2 p. m.	......	......	......	7	....	S. 1	......	
	9 p. m.	......	......	......	5	....	SW. 2	......	
Sept. 21	7 a. m.	......	......	......	10	....	W. 1	......	
	2 p. m.	......	......	......	5	....	SE. 1	......	
	9 p. m.	......	......	......	4	....	2	......	
Sept. 22	7 a. m.	......	......	......	10	....	SW. 2	......	
	2 p. m.	......	......	......	6	....	SW. 1	......	
	9 p. m.	......	......	......	....	....	....	......	
Sept. 23	7 a. m.	......	......	......	7	....	SW. 1	......	
	2 p. m.	......	......	......	9	....	2	......	
	9 p. m.	......	......	......	8	....	W. 1	......	
Sept. 24	7 a. m.	......	......	......	9	....	SE. 1	......	
	2 p. m.	......	......	......	7	....	2	......	
	9 p. m.	......	......	......	9	....	SE. 1	......	

HUDSON, OHIO.

Month and day.	Hour.	Barom'r corrected to 32° F.	Thermometer.	Force of vapor.	Cloudiness.	Motion of clouds.	Winds.	Relative humidity.	REMARKS.
Sept. 14	9 p. m.	28.91	47.6	......	Cu. 5	....	E. 1	......	16th. Slight rain in the evening;
Sept. 15	7 a. m.	29.10	43.2	......	St. and cu. 9	....	E. 2	......	amount, 0.03 inch.
	2 p. m.	29.02	56	......	Cir. and cu. 4	....	E. 1	......	Storm commenced in the night of
	9 p. m.	28.96	52.8	......	Aurora 10	....	NE. 1	......	the 19th, and ended at 7.30 p. m.
Sept. 16	7 a. m.	28.89	53.3	......	Cu. 10	....	E. 2	......	on the 24th; amount, 0.50 inch.
	2 p. m.	28.82	65.8	......	Cu. 10	....	E. 1	......	
	9 p. m.	28.76	61.5	......	Nim. 10	....	E. 0	......	
Sept. 17	7 a. m.	20.70	00.4	......	Aurora 10	....	N. 0	......	
	2 p. m.	28.76	65	......	Cu. 10	....	NW. 2	......	
	9 p. m.	......	......	......	....	....	....	......	
Sept. 18	7 a. m.	......	......	......	....	....	....	......	
	2 p. m.	......	......	......	....	....	....	......	
	9 p. m.	......	......	......	....	....	....	......	
Sept. 19	7 a. m.	28.57	62	......	Cu. 10	....	S. 1	......	
	2 p. m.	28.52	73.2	......	Cu. 7	....	SW. 2	......	
	9 p. m.	28.52	64.1	......	Cir. st. 9	....	SE. 1	......	

STORMS Nos. 2 AND 3, SEPTEMBER, 1859.

HUDSON, OHIO—Continued.

Month and day.	Hour.	Barom'r corrected to 32° F.	Thermometer.	Force of vapor.	Cloudiness.	Motion of clouds.	Winds.	Relative humidity.	REMARKS.
Sept. 20	7 a. m.	28. 57	66. 7	------	Nim. 10	----------	E. 0	------	
	2 p. m.	28. 55	65. 2	------	Aurora 9	----------	NE. 2	------	
	9 p. m.	28. 58	63. 4	------	Nim. 10	----------	NE. 0	------	
Sept. 21	7 a. m.	28. 61	62. 3	------	Nim. 10	----------	NE. 0	------	
	2 p. m.	28. 55	73. 0	------	Aurora 9	----------	E. 0	------	
	9 p. m.	28. 60	64	------	Nim. 10	----------	NW. 0	------	
Sept. 22	7 a. m.	28. 55	62. 1	------	Nim. 10	----------	W. 1	------	
	2 p. m.	28. 74	66. 8	------	Nim. 10	----------	SW. 1	------	
	9 p. m.	28. 84	61. 2	------	Cu. 10	----------	SW. 1	------	
Sept. 23	7 a. m.	28. 89	59. 5	------	Aurora 10	----------	SW. 1	------	
	2 p. m.	28. 87	62. 8	------	Cu. 10	----------	W. 1	------	
	9 p. m.	28. 87	60. 7	------	Nim. 10	----------	SW. 1	------	
Sept. 24	7 a. m.	28. 84	60	------	Nim. 10	----------	SW. 1	------	
	2 p. m.	28. 79	61. 2	------	Nim. 10	----------	NW. 1	------	
	9 p. m.	28. 81	58. 8	------	0	----------	N. 1	------	

IBERIA, OHIO.

Month and day.	Hour.	Barom'r corrected to 32° F.	Thermometer.	Force of vapor.	Cloudiness.	Motion of clouds.	Winds.	Relative humidity.	REMARKS.
Sept. 14	9 p. m.	------	------	------	------------	----------	------------	------	15th. Rain from 6.25 to 7.15 p.m.; amount, 0. 10 inch. 16th. Rainy. 18th. Light fog at 6 a. m.; diffused lightning at 7 p. m. 19th. Diffused lightning NW. at 6 p. m.; remote thunder NW. at 7 p. m ; rain from 8 to 8.15 a. m. 20th. Continued rain from 4 a. m. to 9.15 p. m.; occasionally very heavy, with wind; amount, 4.50 inches. 21st. Fog very dense till 10 a. m., then ascended, and remained in dense clouds all day. 22d. Diffused rapid lightning at 1 a. m.; heavy thunder, moving NE. to SW.; rain from 1 to 6 a. m.; amount, 2.00 inches. 23d. Rainy all day; direction NNW.; drops fine; shower heavy from 5.15 to 6 p. m.; lightning very sharp; amount, 0.25 inch. 24th. Drizzling rain all day from NW.; amount, 0.50 inch.
Sept. 15	7 a. m.	------	47	------	Cir. cu. 7	SW. 2	ENE. 4	------	
	2 p. m.	------	64	------	Cu. st. 7	----------	NE. 4	------	
	9 p. m.	------	54	------	Nim. 10	----------	NE. 3	------	
Sept. 16	7 a. m.	------	56	------	Nim. 8	NE. 1	NE. 1	------	
	2 p. m.	------	------	------	Cu. st. 4	----------	------------	------	
	9 p. m.	------	62	------	0	----------	NE. 2	------	
Sept. 17	7 a. m.	------	66	------	Nim. 10	NE. 2	NNE. 1	------	
	2 p. m.	------	72	------	Cir. 4	----------	NNW. 2	------	
	9 p. m.	------	52	------	0	----------	ENE. 1	------	
Sept. 18	7 a. m.	------	52	------	Dense fog 6	----------	NE. 3	------	
	2 p. m.	------	80	------	Cir. cu. 2	----------	S. 1	------	
	9 p. m.	------	66	------	0	----------	SSE. 3	------	
Sept. 19	7 a. m.	------	70	------	Nim. 9	NE. 1	S. 4	------	
	2 p. m.	------	74	------	Nim. 6	----------	NW. 4	------	
	9 p. m.	------	68	------	Nim. 9	----------	S. 1	------	
Sept. 20	7 a. m.	------	60	------	Nim. 10	NW ------	NE. 3	------	
	2 p. m.	------	64	------	Nim. 10	NW. 2	NNW. 3	------	
	9 p. m.	------	59	------	Nim. 10	----------	NE. 2	------	
Sept. 21	7 a. m.	------	63	------	Fog 10	----------	NNE. 2	------	
	2 p. m.	------	70	------	Nim. 10	----------	NNW. 1	------	
	9 p. m.	------	62	------	Nim. 10	----------	NNW. 1	------	
Sept. 22	7 a. m.	------	59	------	Nim. 10	----------	W. 2	------	
	2 p. m.	------	63	------	Nim. 10	NW. 2	SW. 1	------	
	9 p. m.	------	59	------	Nim. 9	----------	SW. 1	------	
Sept. 23	7 a. m.	------	58	------	Nim. 10	----------	SW. 2	------	
	2 p. m.	------	62	------	Nim. 10	----------	W. 2	------	
	9 p. m.	------	59	------	Nim. 10	----------	W. 2	------	
Sept. 24	7 a. m.	------	60	------	Nim. 10	----------	W. 4	------	
	2 p. m.	------	68	------	Nim. 10	----------	NW. 4	------	
	9 p. m.	------	60	------	Nim. 10	----------	NW. 3	------	

JACKSON, MONROE COUNTY, OHIO.

Month and day.	Hour.	Barom'r corrected to 32° F.	Thermometer.	Force of vapor.	Cloudiness.	Motion of clouds.	Winds.	Relative humidity.	REMARKS.
Sept. 14	9 p. m.	------	55	------	3	----------	S. 1	------	16th. Began to rain at 1 a. m.; amount, 0.25 inch.
Sept. 15	7 a. m.	------	------	------	------------	----------	------------	------	
	2 p. m.	------	------	------	------------	----------	S. 2	------	
	9 p. m.	------	65	------	------------	----------	------------	------	
Sept. 16	7 a. m.	------	------	------	10	----------	------------	------	
	2 p. m.	------	------	------	10	----------	S. 0	------	
	9 p. m.	------	63	------	10	----------	S. 1	------	

STORMS Nos. 2 AND 3, SEPTEMBER, 1859.

JACKSON, MONROE COUNTY, OHIO—Continued.

Month and day.	Hour.	Barom'r corrected to 32° F.	Thermometer.	Force of vapor.	Cloudiness.	Motion of clouds.	Winds.	Relative humidity.	REMARKS.
Sept. 17	7 a. m.	......	60	......	10				17th. Rain in a. m.; amount, 0.05 inch.
	2 p. m.	......	......	......	......	......	......	......	
	9 p. m.	......	......	......	......	......	......	......	Storm commenced at 4 p. m. the 19th, and ended in the a. m. of the 22d; amount, 4.00 inches.
Sept. 18	7 a. m.	......	......	......	......	......	......	......	
	2 p. m.	......	......	......	......	......	......	......	
	9 p. m.	......	......	......	......	......	......	......	24th. Rain from 4 a. m. till — p. m.; amount, 0.20 inch.
Sept. 19	7 a. m.	......	......	......	......	......	......	......	
	2 p. m.	......	......	......	......	......	......	......	
	9 p. m.	......	64	......	10	......	......	......	
Sept. 20	7 a. m.	......	......	......	......	......	......	......	
	2 p. m.	......	72	......	10	......	......	......	
	9 p. m.	......	67	......	10	......	......	......	
Sept. 21	7 a. m.	......	65	......	10	......	......	......	
	2 p. m.	......	......	......	......	......	......	......	
	9 p. m.	......	64	......	1	......	......	......	
Sept. 22	7 a. m.	......	......	......	......	......	......	......	
	2 p. m.	......	......	......	......	......	......	......	
	9 p. m.	......	......	......	......	......	......	......	
Sept 23	7 a. m.	......	......	......	10	......	......	......	
	2 p. m.	......	......	......	10	......	......	......	
	9 p. m.	......	59	......	10	......	......	......	
Sept. 24	7 a. m.	......	62	......	10	......	......	......	
	2 p. m.	......	......	......	10	......	......	......	
	9 p. m.	......	59	......	10	......	......	......	

KELLEY'S ISLAND, OHIO.

Month and day.	Hour.	Barom'r corrected to 32° F.	Thermometer.	Force of vapor.	Cloudiness.	Motion of clouds.	Winds.	Relative humidity.	REMARKS.
Sept. 14	9 p. m.	29.42	51	......	Cir. cu., cir st. 8	......	N. 1	......	18th. Lightning in the W. at 9 p. m.
Sept. 15	7 a. m.	29.50	52	......	St., cir. cu., cu. st. 7	......	ESE. 5	......	19th. Slight shower at 10 a. m.
	2 p. m.	29.49	58	......	Cir.cu.,cu.st.6	......	E. 6	......	20th. 8.30 a. m. wind changed to NE., and commenced raining very hard; continued without intermission till 6 p. m., wind blowing a gale; very dark through the day.
	9 p. m.	29.39	58	......	Nim. 8	......	E. 5	......	
Sept. 16	7 a. m.	29.34	58	......	Cir. st. 3	......	E. 2	......	
	2 p. m.	29.23	57	......	Cu. st. 8	......	ENE. 3	......	
	9 p. m.	29.20	65	......	Cu. st. 4	......	E. 1	......	
Sept. 17	7 a. m.	29.20	62	......	Cu. st. 5	......	NE. 3	......	
	2 p. m.	29.23	66	......	Cu. 2	......	W. 2	......	21st. 7 a. m. still very dark, and wind blowing strong from NE., with drizzling rain; continued all day, but decreasing gradually; 9 p. m. light wind from the N.
	9 p. m.	29.24	57	......	0	......	0	......	
Sept. 18	7 a. m.	29.28	60	......	St., cu. st. 7	......	ESE. 2	......	
	2 p. m.	29.20	76	......	Cir.cu.,cir.st.5	......	ESE. 2	......	
	9 p. m.	29.12	66	......	Cu. st. 4	......	SE. 2	......	
Sept. 19	7 a. m.	28.98	65	......	St., cir. st., nim. 9	......	ESE. 2	......	22d. 7 a. m. still raining; wind light from the W.; storm ceased at 9.30 a. m.; am't, 2.03 inches.
	2 p. m.	28.94	70	......	Haze, cir., cir. cu., nim. 9	......	W. 4	......	Rain from 8.30 p. m. the 23d to 7 a. m. on the 24th; amount, 0.10 inch.
	9 p. m.	28.97	67	......	Cu. st., nim. 9	......	0	......	
Sept. 20	7 a. m.	29.06	58	......	Nim. 10	......	N. 4	......	
	2 p. m.	29.08	55	......	Nim. 10	......	NE. 8	......	
	9 p. m.	29.09	57	......	Nim. 10	......	NE. 8	......	
Sept. 21	7 a. m.	29 09	61	......	Nim. 10	......	NE. 6	......	
	2 p. m.	29.07	63	......	Nim. 10	......	NE. 5	......	
	9 p. m.	29.08	58	......	Nim. 10	......	N. 1	......	
Sept. 22	7 a. m.	29.12	58	......	Nim. 10	......	W. 2	......	
	2 p. m.	29.19	63	......	Nim. 10	......	SW. 2	......	
	9 p. m.	29.26	61	......	Nim., st. 10	......	W. 1	......	
Sept. 23	7 a. m.	29.29	60	......	St., cir. cu. 9	......	W. 2	......	
	2 p. m.	29.29	64	......	Nim. 10	......	SW. 3	......	
	9 p. m.	29.32	60	......	Nim. 10	......	SW. 2	......	
Sept. 24	7 a. m.	29.29	59	......	Nim., st. 10	......	NW. 4	......	
	2 p. m.	29.29	62	......	Nim., st. 10	......	NW. 2	......	
	9 p. m.	29.29	60	......	St. 1	......	N. 1	......	

STORMS Nos. 2 AND 3, SEPTEMBER, 1859.

MADISON, OHIO.*

Month and day.	Hour.	Barom'r corrected to 32° F.	Thermometer.	Force of vapor.	Cloudiness.	Motion of clouds.	Winds.	Relative humidity.	REMARKS.
Sept. 14	9 p. m.	------	------	------	St. 3	0	0	------	19th. Thunder at intervals during the p. m , SE. 20th. Wind shifted from SE. to NE. at 8 a. m.; began to rain at 6 a. m., and continued at intervals till the 24th ; amount, 1.50 inch. 22d. Wind shifted from NW. to W. at 8 a. m., then to SW., and back to W. again during the day. 24th. Aurora, single arch, well defined and steady, at 8 30 p. m.
Sept. 15	7 a. m.	------	54	------	St. 10	0	SE. 2	------	
	2 p. m.	------	58	------	Cir. cu. 8	0	NE. 3	------	
	9 p. m.	------	53	------	Cu. st. 8	----------	NE. 3	------	
Sept. 16	7 a. m.	------	56	------	St. 10	0	SE. 1	------	
	2 p. m.	------	78	------	St. 10	0	SE. 2	------	
	9 p. m.	------	62	------	St. 10	----------	SE. 1	------	
Sept. 17	7 a. m.	------	60	------	St. 10	0	0	------	
	2 p. m.	------	64	------	St. 10	NE. 2	NE. 3	------	
	9 p. m.	------	51	------	0	----------	NE. 1	------	
Sept. 18	7 a. m.	------	54	------	Cir. 8	0	0	------	
	2 p. m.	------	72	------	Cir. 3	0	SE. 2	------	
	9 p. m.	------	59	------	Cir. 7	----------	SE. 2	------	
Sept. 19	7 a. m.	------	63	------	Cir. st. 9	0	SE. 3	------	
	2 p. m.	------	80	------	Cir. st. 10	SW. 3	SE. 3	------	
	9 p. m.	------	68	------	St. 10	----------	0	------	
Sept. 20	7 a. m.	------	65	------	Nim. 10	0	SE. 1	------	
	2 p. m.	------	56	------	Nim. 10	0	NE. 4	------	
	9 p. m.	------	58	------	St. 10	----------	NE. 5	------	
Sept. 21	7 a. m.	------	58	------	St. 10	0	NE. 3	------	
	2 p. m.	------	64	------	St. 10	0	NE. 2	------	
	9 p. m.	------	63	------	St. 10	----------	NE. 1	------	
Sept. 22	7 a. m.	------	62	------	Nim. 10	NE. 2	NE. 1	------	
	2 p. m.	------	63	------	St. 10	0	SW. 3	------	
	9 p. m.	------	61	------	St. 10	----------	W. 2	------	
Sept. 23	7 a. m.	------	58	------	St. 10	0	0	------	
	2 p. m.	------	60	------	Cir. st. 8	0	W. 2	------	
	9 p. m.	------	60	------	St. 10	----------	0	------	
Sept. 24	7 a. m.	------	60	------	Nim. 10	0	SW. 1	------	
	2 p. m.	------	63	------	St. 10	----------	SW. 2	------	
	9 p. m.	------	59	------	Cir. st. 8	----------	0	------	

* Atkins, observer.

MADISON, OHIO.*

Month and day.	Hour.	Barom'r corrected to 32° F.	Thermometer.	Force of vapor.	Cloudiness.	Motion of clouds.	Winds.	Relative humidity.	REMARKS.
Sept. 14	9 p. m.	------	48	------	------------	----------	SE. 1	------	Storm from 5 a. m. the 20th to 8 a. m. on the 23d ; amount, 1.75 inch.
Sept. 15	7 a. m.	------	53	------	Cir. 4	SE. 1	SE. 1	------	
	2 p. m.	------	58	------	Cir. 3	SE. 3	SE. 2	------	
	9 p. m.	------	52	------	Cir. --------	SE. ------	N. 1	------	
Sept. 16	7 a. m.	------	52	------	Cir. 7	NW. 1	NW. 1	------	
	2 p. m.	------	67	------	Nim. 10	NW. 1	NW. 1	------	
	9 p. m.	------	60	------	Nim. 10	N. -------	N. 1	------	
Sept. 17	7 a. m.	------	57	------	Nim. 10	N. 1	N. 1	------	
	2 p. m.	------	62	------	------------	----------	------------	------	
	9 p. m.	------	50	------	------------	----------	------------	------	
Sept. 18	7 a. m.	------	78	------	Nim. 2	----------	NW. 1	------	
	2 p. m.	------	70	------	Nim. 2	SW. 1	SW. 1	------	
	9 p. m.	------	52	------	1	0	0	------	
Sept. 19	7 a. m.	------	62	------	Cir. 5	NE. 1	N. 1	------	
	2 p. m.	------	80	------	Cir. cu. 3	SW. 1	N. 1	------	
	9 p. m.	------	64	------	Nim. 10	0	0	------	
Sept. 20	7 a. m.	------	56	------	Nim. 10	NW. 1	NW. 1	------	
	2 p. m.	------	56	------	Nim. 10	SW. 3	SW. 1	------	
	9 p. m.	------	66	------	Nim. 1	NW. 1	------------	------	
Sept. 21	7 a. m.	------	58	------	10	NW. 1	------------	------	
	2 p. m.	------	60	------	------------	----------	------------	------	
	9 p. m.	------	59	------	------------	----------	------------	------	

*Mrs. A. C. King, observer.

STORMS Nos. 2 AND 3, SEPTEMBER, 1859.

MADISON, OHIO—Continued.

Month and day.	Hour.	Barom'r corrected to 32° F.	Thermometer.	Force of vapor.	Cloudiness.	Motion of clouds.	Winds.	Relative humidity.	REMARKS.
Sept. 22	7 a. m.	......	60	......	Nim. 10	NE. 1	NE. 1	......	
	2 p. m.	......	63	......	Nim. 10	NE. 1	NE. 1	......	
	9 p. m.	......	60	......	Nim........	....	....	......	
Sept. 23	7 a. m.	......	56	......	Nim. 9	0	0	......	
	2 p. m.	......	66	......	Nim........	NE. 1	NE. 1	......	
	9 p. m.	......	58	......	Nim. 10	....	....	......	
Sept. 24	7 a. m.	......	56	......	Nim. 10	0	0	......	
	2 p. m.	......	64	......	Nim. 8	NE. 1	NE. 1	......	
	9 p. m.	......	56	......	Nim. 6	....	0	......	

MONTVILLE, OHIO.

Month and day.	Hour.	Barom'r corrected to 32° F.	Thermometer.	Force of vapor.	Cloudiness.	Motion of clouds.	Winds.	Relative humidity.	REMARKS.
Sept. 14	9 p. m.	28.873	44	......	Cir. cu. 6	SW. 1	SE. 1	......	15th. Shower in the night. 16th. Misty; sprinkle in the night. 17th. Misty. 19th. Light shower in the a. m.; commenced raining at 10 p. m.; wind light, SE. 20th. Rain till 10 a. m., and at intervals till 1 p. m.; wind changed to NE. and NW. 21st. Sprinkle in the a. m., and rain at night. 22d. Sprinkle in the morning. 23d. Began to rain at 6 p. m.; continued during the night. 24th. Occasional showers in the a. m.; amount of rain from 15th to 24th, 1.854 inch.
Sept. 15	7 a. m.	.963	45	......	Cir. cu. 8	W. 1	SW. 1	......	
	2 p. m.	.874	48.5	......	Cir. st. 5	W. 1	NE. 1	......	
	9 p. m.	.816	53	......	Cu. st. 10	....	NE. 1	......	
Sept. 16	7 a. m.	.787	52	......	Cir. cu. 10	W. 1	SE. 1	......	
	2 p. m.	.641	66	......	Cu. st. 10	....	SE. 2	......	
	9 p. m.	.624	63	......	10	....	SE. 2	......	
Sept. 17	7 a. m.	.599	60.5	......	Fog 10	....	NE. 2	......	
	2 p. m.	.538	62.5	......	Cu. 9	NW. 2	NW. 2	......	
	9 p. m.	.679	54	......	0	....	SE. 1	......	
Sept. 18	7 a. m.	.746	54	......	10	....	SE. 1	......	
	2 p. m.	.632	70	......	Cir. cu. 5	....	S. 2	......	
	9 p. m.	.577	63	......	Cu. 1	....	SW. 3	......	
Sept. 19	7 a. m.	.421	63	......	Cir. cu. 8	SW. 2	SE. 3	......	
	2 p. m.	.430	73	......	Cir. cu. 8	SW. 2	SW. 3	......	
	9 p. m.	.409	68	......	10	....	SE. 2	......	
Sept. 20	7 a. m.	.407	65	......	Cu. st. 9	NE. 2	NE. 2	......	
	2 p. m.	.432	64	......	10	....	NE. 2	......	
	9 p. m.	.504	58	......	10	....	NW. 1	......	
Sept. 21	7 a. m.	.477	61	......	Fog 10	....	NW. 1	......	
	2 p. m.	.435	69	......	Cu. 8	....	NE. 1	......	
	9 p. m.	.489	62	......	10	....	N 2	......	
Sept. 22	7 a. m.	.540	59	......	10	....	NW. 2	......	
	2 p. m.	.626	63	......	10	....	SE. 1	......	
	9 p. m.	.702	58.5	......	St. 9	....	SE. 1	......	
Sept. 23	7 a. m.	.766	57.5	......	St. 10	....	SW........	......	
	2 p. m.	.694	64	......	Cu. st. 10	....	SW. 2	......	
	9 p. m.	.740	58.5	......	St. 10	....	SW. 2	......	
Sept. 24	7 a. m.	.702	59	......	10	....	NW. 1	......	
	2 p. m.	.668	61	......	Cu. 8	NW. 1	NW. 1	......	
	9 p. m.	.670	59	......	St. 10	....	NE. 3	......	

NEWARK, OHIO.

Month and day.	Hour.	Barom'r corrected to 32° F.	Thermometer.	Force of vapor.	Cloudiness.	Motion of clouds.	Winds.	Relative humidity.	REMARKS.
Sept. 14	9 p. m.	......	......	......	5	....	N. 1	......	14th. Wind variable, SE. to N. 15th. Cool. 16th. Rain till 8 a. m. 18th. Lightning from light clouds in W.
Sept. 15	7 a. m.	......	......	......	7	....	NE. 2	......	
	2 p. m.	......	......	......	5	....	NE. 2	......	
	9 p. m.	......	......	......	9	....	NE. 1	......	
Sept. 16	7 a. m.	......	......	......	10	....	NE. 2	......	
	2 p. m.	......	......	......	10	....	NE. 1	......	
	9 p. m.	......	......	......	10	....	NW. 1	......	
Sept. 17	7 a. m.	......	......	......	10	....	N. 1	......	
	2 p. m.	......	......	......	6	....	NE. 1	......	
	9 p. m.	......	......	......	0	....	SE. 1	......	
Sept. 18	7 a. m.	......	......	......	7	....	NE. 1	......	
	2 p. m.	......	......	......	2	....	S. 1	......	
	9 p. m.	......	......	......	6	....	S. 1	......	

STORMS Nos. 2 AND 3, SEPTEMBER, 1859.

NEWARK, OHIO—Continued.

Month and day.	Hour.	Barom'r corrected to 32° F.	Thermometer.	Force of vapor.	Cloudiness.	Motion of clouds.	Winds.	Relative humidity.
Sept. 19	7 a. m.	......	......	......	9	....	S. 2	......
	2 p. m.	......	......	......	9	....	S. 3	......
	9 p. m.	......	......	......	10	....	S. 2	......
Sept. 20	7 a. m.	......	......	......	10	....	NE. 1	......
	2 p. m.	......	......	......	10	....	N. 2	......
	9 p. m.	......	......	......	10	....	SW. 1	......
Sept. 21	7 a. m.	......	......	......	10	....	S. 1	......
	2 p. m.	......	......	......	9	....	SW. 1	......
	9 p. m.	......	......	......	2	....	SW. 1	......
Sept. 22	7 a. m.	......	......	......	10	....	SW. 1	......
	2 p. m.	......	......	......	10	....	SW. 3	......
	9 p. m.	......	......	......	10	....	SW. 1	......
Sept. 23	7 a. m.	......	......	......	10	....	SW. 1	......
	2 p. m.	......	......	......	9	....	SW. 1	......
	9 p. m.	......	......	......	10	....	SW. 1	......
Sept. 24	7 a. m.	......	......	......	10	....	SW. 1	......
	2 p. m.	......	......	......	9	....	W. 2	......
	9 p. m.	......	......	......	4	....	W. 1	......

REMARKS.

19th. Sprinkling rain from 8.20 a. m. to 9.15 p. m.
20th. Steady rain.
21st. Very warm; lightning in the NW.; morning dark and misty; moderate rain during night.
22d and 23d. Rainy.
24th. Rainy night and morning till 1 p. m.; at 7.40 p. m. there was an opening of the clouds N., through which an aurora shone like a rising moon; this continued for an hour and a half, until the northern sky became clear; that horizon was then lighter than elsewhere.

NEW LISBON, OHIO.

Month and day.	Hour.	Barom'r corrected to 32° F.	Thermometer.	Force of vapor.	Cloudiness.	Motion of clouds.	Winds.	Relative humidity.
Sept. 14	9 p. m.	29.08	47	......	Cu. 6	W. 0	W. 0	......
Sept. 15	7 a. m.	29.14	45	......	Nim. 8	N. 2	N. 0	......
	2 p. m.	29.08	69	......	Cir. st. 3	NE. 0	NE. 0	......
	9 p. m.	29.00	57	......	Cu. 2	NE. 0	NE. 0	......
Sept. 16	7 a. m.	28.97	68	......	Nim. 10	SE. 1	SE. 0	......
	2 p. m.	28.90	72	......	Nim. 10	SE. 0	SE. 0	......
	9 p. m.	28.87	60	......	Nim. 10	SE. 0	SE. 0	......
Sept. 17	7 a. m.	28.80	57	......	Nim. 10	NE. 0	NE. 0	......
	2 p. m.	28.82	65	......	Nim. 10	N. 0	N. 0	......
	9 p. m.	28.85	52	......	St. 1	NW. 0	NW. 0	......
Sept. 18	7 a. m.	28.95	52	......	Nim. 10	N. 0	N. 0	......
	2 p. m.	28.90	65	......	Cu. 4	N. 0	N. 0	......
	9 p. m.	28.81	58	......	0	0	N. 0	......
Sept. 19	7 a. m.	28.70	56	......	Cu. 2	SE. 0	SE. 0	......
	2 p. m.	28.66	76	......	Cu. 6	S. 0	S. 0	......
	9 p. m.	28.67	67	......	Nim. 8	SE. 0	SE. 0	......
Sept. 20	7 a. m.	28.66	65	......	Nim. 10	SSE. 1	SSE. 0	......
	2 p. m.	28.68	72	......	Nim. 8	SE. 3	SE. 0	......
	9 p. m.	28.69	68	......	Nim. 5	E. 0	E. 0	......
Sept. 21	7 a. m.	28.70	68	......	Nim. 9	E. 3	E. 0	......
	2 p. m.	28.68	76	......	Cu. 4	E. 1	E. 0	......
	9 p. m.	28.68	72	......	0	0	E. 0	......
Sept. 22	7 a. m.	28.75	74	......	Nim. 10	S. 1	S. 0	......
	2 p. m.	28.82	72	......	Cu. 8	SW. 0	SW. 1	......
	9 p. m.	28.92	59	......	Nim. 1	SW. 0	SW. 0	......
Sept. 23	7 a. m.	28.95	54	......	Nim. 8	SW. 0	SW. 0	......
	2 p. m.	28.98	80	......	Nim. 5	SW. 0	SW. 0	......
	9 p. m.	28.98	60	......	Nim. 10	SW. 0	SW. 0	......
Sept. 24	7 a. m.	28.90	59	......	Nim. 10	SW. 1	SW. 0	......
	2 p. m.	28.85	60	......	Nim. 10	NW. 3	NW. 0	......
	9 p. m.	28.85	60	......	Nim. 8	W. 0	NW. 0	......

REMARKS.

14th. Little frost.
15th. Cool.
16th. Amount of rain, 2.25 inches.
17th. Damp.
19th. Fair; began to rain in the night, and ended in the a. m. of the 20th; amount, 0.75 inch.
21st. Rain from 10.30 to 11.30 a. m.; amount 0.33 inch.
22d. Began to rain last night, and ended at 9 a. m. this morning; amount, 0.15 inch.
23d. Damp.
24th. Rain from 4 a. m. to 9 p. m.; amount, 0.80 inch.

STORMS Nos. 2 AND 3, SEPTEMBER, 1859.

NORTH BEND, OHIO

Month and day.	Hour.	Barom'r corrected to 32° F.	Thermometer.	Force of vapor.	Cloudiness.	Motion of clouds.	Winds.	Relative humidity.	REMARKS.
Sept. 14	9 p. m.				4		NE. 1		16th. Rain from 3 to 9 a. m.; amount, 0.56 inch. 17th. Amount of rain, 0.161 inch. 19th. Rain from 2 to 8 a. m.; amount, 0.214 inch. 22d. Cloudy all day. 24th. Rain in the night; amount, 0.022 inch.
Sept. 15	7 a. m.				6		0		
	2 p. m.				3		NW. 1		
	9 p. m.				9		0		
Sept. 16	7 a. m.				0		E. 2		
	2 p. m.				8		S. 1		
	9 p. m.				6		0		
Sept. 17	7 a. m.				7		0		
	2 p. m.				1		0		
	9 p. m.				4		E. 1		
Sept. 18	7 a. m.				2		SE. 1		
	2 p. m.				1		S. 2		
	9 p. m.				6		SE. 2		
Sept. 19	7 a. m.				10		SE. 3		
	2 p. m.				8		SE. 2		
	9 p. m.				0		0		
Sept. 20	7 a. m.				4		0		
	2 p. m.				7		NE. 2		
	9 p. m.				3		N. 3		
Sept. 21	7 a. m.				9		NE. 1		
	2 p. m.				9		0		
	9 p. m.				10		0		
Sept. 22	7 a. m.				10		0		
	2 p. m.				10		SW. 1		
	9 p. m.				10		0		
Sept. 23	7 a. m.				10		0		
	2 p. m.				10		SW. 1		
	9 p. m.				10		0		
Sept. 24	7 a. m.				9		0		
	2 p. m.				5		W. 3		
	9 p. m.				3		N. 0		

NORTHWOOD, OHIO.

Month and day.	Hour.	Barom'r corrected to 32° F.	Thermometer.	Force of vapor.	Cloudiness.	Motion of clouds.	Winds.	Relative humidity.	REMARKS.
Sept. 14	9 p. m.	28.94			Cir. 5	SW. 1	NE. 2		20th. Amount of rain, 0.50 inch.
Sept. 15	7 a. m.	29.01			Cir. 9	W. 1	E. 3		
	2 p. m.				Cir. 10	W. 1			
	9 p. m.	28.94			Cir. 9	1	W. 1		
Sept. 16	7 a. m.	28.82			Nim. 10				
	2 p. m.				Cir. 9				
	9 p. m.	28.73			Nim. 10		SE. 1		
Sept. 17	7 a. m.	28.71			Nim. 10		NW. 1		
	2 p. m.	28.75			Nim. 9		NW. 1		
	9 p. m.	28.77			0		NW. 1		
Sept. 18	7 a. m.	28.80			Cir. 3	NW. 1	SE. 2		
	2 p. m.	28.68			Cir. 1	W. 1	W. 1		
	9 p. m.	28.65			St. 3	SW. 1	SW. 3		
Sept. 19	7 a. m.	28.53			Nim. 10		SE. 2		
	2 p. m.				Cir. 9	SW. 1	SW. 1		
	9 p. m.	28.50			Cir. 2	W. 1	W. 1		
Sept. 20	7 a. m.	28.53			Nim. 10		NW. 1		
	2 p. m.	28.54			Nim. 10		NW. 1		
	9 p. m.	28.57			Nim. 10		NE. 1		
Sept. 21	7 a. m.	28.49			Nim. 10		W. 1		
	2 p. m.				Nim. 10		NW. 1		
	9 p. m.	28.58			Nim. 10		SE. 1		
Sept. 22	7 a. m.	28.67			Nim. 10	SW. 1	SW. 1		
	2 p. m.				Nim. 10	SW. 1	SW. 1		
	9 p. m.	28.80			Nim. 10	SW. 1	SW. 1		
Sept. 23	7 a. m.	28.88			Nim. 10	SW. 1	SW. 1		
	2 p. m.				Nim. 10	SW. 1	SW. 1		
	9 p. m.	28.87			Nim. 10	SW. 1	SW. 1		
Sept. 24	7 a. m.								
	2 p. m.								
	9 p. m.								

STORMS Nos. 2 AND 3, SEPTEMBER, 1859.

PORTSMOUTH, OHIO.

Month and day.	Hour.	Barom'r corrected to 32° F.	Thermometer.	Force of vapor.	Cloudiness.		Motion of clouds.		Winds.		Relative humidity.	REMARKS.
Sept. 14	9 p. m.	29.38	58	......	Cir.	10	SW.	1	NW.	1	......	16th. Rain from 5 to 6 a. m., and
Sept. 15	7 a. m.	29.41	54	......	Cir.	10	SW.	1	NE.	2	......	from 8 to 8.30 a. m.; amount,
	2 p. m.	29.35	76	......	Cir.	4	SW.	1	E.	1	......	0.09 inch.
	9 p. m.	29.29	62	......	Cir.	7	SW.	1	N.	1	......	19th. Rain from 12 m. to 11 p. m.;
Sept. 16	7 a. m.	29.30	60	......	Nim.	10	SW.	1	N.	1	......	amount, 0.44 inch.
	2 p. m.	29.21	72	......	Nim.	10	SW.	1	E.	1	......	21st. Rain from 0.30 to 11 p. m.
	9 p. m.	29.17	64	......	Cir.	5	SW.	1	N.	1	......	22d. Rain from 9.15 to 9.45 a. m.;
Sept. 17	7 a. m.	29.22	68	......	Cir.	9	SW.	1	N.	1	......	amount, 0.11 inch.
	2 p. m.	29.21	79	......	Cir. cu.	9	NW.	1	N.	1	......	
	9 p. m.	29.25	62	......		0		0	NE.	1	......	
Sept. 18	7 a. m.	29.30	64	......	Cir.	4	SW.	1	E.	1	......	
	2 p. m.	29.23	82	......		0		0	SE.	1	......	
	9 p. m.	29.14	66	......	Cir.	1	SW.	1	SW.	1	......	
Sept. 19	7 a. m.	29.12	68	......	Nim.	10	SW.	2	NW.	1	......	
	2 p. m.	29.08	73	......	Nim.	10	SW.	1	SE.	1	......	
	9 p. m.	29.06	68	......	Nim.	10	SW.	1	SW.	1	......	
Sept. 20	7 a. m.	29.04	70	......	Nim.	10	NW.	1	E.	1	......	
	2 p. m.	29.04	76	......	Cir.	2	NW.	2	N.	1	......	
	9 p. m.	29.11	62	......	Nim.	10	NW.	1	N.	1	......	
Sept. 21	7 a. m.	29.12	60	......	Nim.	10	NW.	1	NW.	1	......	
	2 p. m.	29.09	70	......	Nim.	10	NW.	1	SW.	1	......	
	9 p. m.	29.13	64	......	Nim.	10	NW.	1	SW.	1	......	
Sept. 22	7 a. m.	29.22	64	......	Nim.	10	SW.	1	SW.	1	......	
	2 p. m.	29.22	72	......	Nim.	10	SW.	1	W..........		......	
	9 p. m.	29.31	60	......	Nim.	10	SW.	1	W.	1	......	
Sept. 23	7 a. m.	29.38	61	......	Cir.	8	SW.	1	SW.	1	......	
	2 p. m.	29.36	72	......	Nim.	9	SW.	1	SW.	2	......	
	9 p. m.	29.36	62	......	Nim.	10	SW.	1	SW.	1	......	
Sept. 24	7 a. m.	29.34	74	......	Cir.	10	SW.	3	SW.	3	......	
	2 p. m.	29.27	76	......	Nim.	9	NW.	2	SW.	2	......	
	9 p. m.	29.29	58	......		0		0	SW.	1	......	

SAVANNAH, OHIO.

Month and day.	Hour.	Barom'r corrected to 32° F.	Thermometer.	Force of vapor.	Cloudiness.		Motion of clouds.		Winds.		Relative humidity.	REMARKS.
Sept. 14	9 p. m.	29.04	45	.218	Cir. st.	10	NW.	3	NW.	2	76	14th. Solar halo.
Sept. 15	7 a. m.	29.12	50	.273	Cir. st.	8	NW.	3	NW.	3	85	Rain from 10 p. m. the 15th to 1
	2 p. m.	29.07	68	.257	St.	10	W.	2	W.	3	43	a. m. on the 16th; amount, 0.106
	9 p. m.	29.03	54	.270	St.	10	W.	3	W.	2	72	inch.
Sept. 16	7 a. m.	28.93	54	.321	Cir. st.	10	W.	2	SW.	2	86	16th. Mild and cloudy.
	2 p. m.	28.83	73	.529	St.	10	W.	2	SW.	2	75	17th. Pleasant.
	9 p. m.	28.80	65	.497	St.	10	SW.	3	SW.	2	83	18th. Thunder NW. in the evening.
Sept. 17	7 a. m.	28.77	64	.510	St.	10	SW.	2	SW.	2	88	19th. Rain from 3 to 4.15 p. m ;
	2 p. m.	28.81	75	.390	Cir. st.	8	SW.	2	SW.	3	50	thunder and lightning in the
	9 p. m.	28.84	54	.348		0	....		W.	1	86	evening ; amount, 0.225 inch.
Sept. 18	7 a. m.	28.88	52	.335	Cir. st.	8	NW.	3	SE.	1	93	20th. Rain from 4 a. m. to 8 p. m.;
	2 p. m.	28.78	78	.463	Cir. st.	6	SW.	3	SW.	3	56	amount, 1.20 inch.
	9 p. m.	28.73	66	.373	St.	2	SW.	2	SW.	3	62	21st. Rain from 2 to 6 a. m.; fine
Sept. 19	7 a. m.	28.60	66	.510	Cir. st.	10	W.	3	SW.	2	88	rain during the day and heavy
	2 p. m.	28.55	80	.554	St.	10	SW.	4	SW.	4	64	at night.
	9 p. m.	28.57	70	.502	St.	10	SW.	3	SW.	3	78	22d. Rain very heavy early; thun-
Sept. 20	7 a. m.	28.57	65	.618	Nim.	10	W.	3	N.	3	100	der ; mild day ; amount, 1.25
	2 p. m.	28.57	63	.518	St.	10	N.	4	N.	4	100	inch.
	9 p. m.	28.64	59	.466	St.	10	N.	3	N.	3	100	Rain from 6 p. m. the 23d to 11
Sept. 21	7 a. m.	28.64	61	.518	St.	10	N.	2	N.	2	100	a. m. on the 24th ; amount, 0.675
	2 p. m.	28.63	69	.549	St.	10	SW.	2	SW.	2	89	inch.
	9 p. m.	28.63	67	.662	Nim.	10	NW.	3	NW.	3	100	
Sept. 22	7 a. m.	28.70	60	.451	Nim.	10	W.	3	NW.	3	97	
	2 p. m.	28.77	69	.570	St.	10	NW.	2	NW.	3	89	
	9 p. m.	28.75	61	.452	St.	10	NW.	2	SW.	2	94	
Sept. 23	7 a. m.	28.93	61	.456	St.	10	W.	2	NW.	3	88	
	2 p. m.	28.92	65	.413	St.	10	NW.	3	NW.	3	77	
	9 p. m.	28.92	60	.483	Nim.	10	NW.	3	NW.	3	100	
Sept. 24	7 a. m.	28.88	60	.500	St.	10	NW.	3	NW.	3	100	
	2 p. m.	28.86	63	.491	St.	10	NW.	3	NW.	3	88	
	9 p. m.	28.87	60	.469	St.	10	NW.	3	NW.	2	94	

STORMS Nos. 2 AND 3, SEPTEMBER, 1859.

SHARONVILLE, OHIO.

Month and day.	Hour.	Barom'r corrected to 32° F.	Thermometer.	Force of vapor.	Cloudiness.	Motion of clouds.	Winds.	Relative humidity.	REMARKS.
Sept. 14	9 p. m.				7		S. 1		16th. Rain from 4 to 8 a. m.
Sept. 15	7 a. m.				5		W. 1		18th. Very warm.
	2 p. m.				5		W. 1		19th. Rain from 6 a. m. to 4 p. m.
	9 p. m.				10		W. 1		20th. Light rain all night.
Sept. 16	7 a. m.				10		W. 1		22d. Heavy showers in the night.
	2 p. m.				10		1		24th. Cool.
	9 p. m.								
Sept. 17	7 a. m.				3		N. 1		
	2 p. m.				4		N. 1		
	9 p. m.				5		N. 1		
Sept. 18	7 a. m.				3		W. 1		
	2 p. m.				5		W. 1		
	9 p. m.				6				
Sept. 19	7 a. m.				10		S. 2		
	2 p. m.				10		S. 1		
	9 p. m.				10		S. 1		
Sept. 20	7 a. m.						1		
	2 p. m.						1		
	9 p. m.								
Sept. 21	7 a. m.				5		W. 1		
	2 p. m.				5		W. 1		
	9 p. m.				5		W. 1		
Sept. 22	7 a. m.						1		
	2 p. m.								
	9 p. m.								
Sept. 23	7 a. m.				4		SW. 1		
	2 p. m.				4		SW. 1		
	9 p. m.				10		SW. 1		
Sept. 24	7 a. m.				5		N. 1		
	2 p. m.				5		N. 1		
	9 p. m.				5		N. 1		

TOLEDO, OHIO.

Month and day.	Hour.	Barom'r corrected to 32° F.	Thermometer.	Force of vapor.	Cloudiness.	Motion of clouds.	Winds.	Relative humidity.	REMARKS.
Sept. 14	9 p. m.				9				20th to 23d. Rainy.
Sept. 15	7 a. m.				8				
	2 p. m.				7				
	9 p. m.				10				
Sept. 16	7 a. m.				9				
	2 p. m.				7				
	9 p. m.				8				
Sept. 17	7 a. m.				7				
	2 p. m.				3				
	9 p. m.				3				
Sept. 18	7 a. m.				5				
	2 p. m.				6				
	9 p. m.				7				
Sept. 19	7 a. m.				10				
	2 p. m.				8				
	9 p. m.				10				
Sept. 20	7 a. m.				10				
	2 p. m.				10				
	9 p. m.				10				
Sept. 21	7 a. m.				10				
	2 p. m.				10				
	9 p. m.				10				
Sept. 22	7 a. m.				10				
	2 p. m.				10				
	9 p. m.				10				
Sept. 23	7 a. m.				10				
	2 p. m.				10				
	9 p. m.				10				
Sept. 24	7 a. m.				10				
	2 p. m.				6				
	9 p. m.				2				

STORMS Nos. 2 AND 3, SEPTEMBER, 1859.

TROY, OHIO.

Month and day.	Hour.	Barom'r corrected to 32° F.	Thermometer.	Force of vapor.	Cloudiness.	Motion of clouds.	Winds.	Relative humidity.	REMARKS.
Sept. 14	9 p. m.	29.92	55	------	Cir. 10	W. 4	Calm. 0	------	16th. Rain from 2 to 2.30 a. m.;
Sept. 15	7 a. m.	30.04	49	------	Cir. 10	W. 6	W. 2	------	amount, 0.15 inch.
	2 p. m.	30.01	67	------	Cir. 10	W. 5	W. 4	------	19th. Rain from 3.30 to 4 p. m.;
	9 p. m.	29.93	56	------	Cir. 10	W. 4	Calm. 0	------	amount, 0.19 inch.
Sept. 16	7 a. m.	29.88	54	------	0	0	W. 2	------	20th. Rain from 1 to 3 a. m.;
	2 p. m.	29.79	76	------	Cir. 5	W. 2	W. 1	------	amount, 0.43 inch.
	9 p. m.	29.79	60	------	Cir. 10	W. 6	W. 2	------	
Sept. 17	7 a. m.	29.81	63	------	Foggy ------	----------	W. 4	------	
	2 p. m.	29.79	70	------	Foggy ------	----------	W. 2	------	
	9 p. m.	29.82	57	------	Foggy ------	----------	W. 4	------	
Sept. 18	7 a. m.	29.71	64	------	0	0	W. 12	------	
	2 p. m.	29.77	80	------	0	0	W. 12	------	
	9 p. m.	29.69	70	------	Cir. 10	W. 5	W. 12	------	
Sept. 19	7 a. m.	29.44	70	------	Cir. 10	W. 10	W. 2	------	
	2 p. m.	29.54	76	------	Cir. 5	W. 10	N. 12	------	
	9 p. m.	29.56	63	------	Cir. 10	W. 6	N. 12	------	
Sept. 20	7 a. m.	29.56	62	------	Cir. 10	W. 6	W. 4	------	
	2 p. m.	29.59	69	------	Cir. 10	W. 10	W. 2	------	
	9 p. m.	29.53	53	------	Cir. 10	W. 10	W. 0	------	
Sept. 21	7 a. m.	29.63	56	------	Cir. 10	W. 8	W. 4	------	
	2 p. m.	29.60	69	------	Cir. 10	W. 5	W. 12	------	
	9 p. m.	29.62	62	------	Cir. 10	W. 4	W. 4	------	
Sept. 22	7 a. m.	29.72	60	------	Cir. 10	W. 4	W. 12	------	
	2 p. m.	29.74	66	------	Cir. 10	W. 5	W. 12	------	
	9 p. m.	29.90	69	------	Cir. 10	W. 5	W. 2	------	
Sept. 23	7 a. m.	29.90	69	------	Cir. 10	W. 3	W. 12	------	
	2 p. m.	29.88	70	------	Cir. 10	W. 4	W. 12	------	
	9 p. m.	29.93	60	------	Cir. 10	W. 3	W. 2	------	
Sept. 24	7 a. m.	29.93	60	------	Cir. 6	W. 4	N. 12	------	
	2 p. m.	29.92	63	------	Cir. 10	W. 8	W. 2	------	
	9 p. m.	29.71	58	------	Cir. 2	W. 3	W. 2	------	

URBANA, OHIO.

Month and day.	Hour.	Barom'r corrected to 32° F.	Thermometer.	Force of vapor.	Cloudiness.	Motion of clouds.	Winds.	Relative humidity.	REMARKS.
Sept. 14	9 p. m.	29.01	55	------	St. 10	W. 1	0	------	15th. Rain at night.
Sept. 15	7 a. m.	29.08	48	------	St. 10	W. 1	E. 3	------	18th. Lightning in the evening.
	2 p. m.	29.02	68	------	St. 10	W. 2	NE. 4	------	19th. Rain, accompanied by thun-
	9 p. m.	28.98	58	------	St. 10	SW. 2	NE. 2	------	der, from 5 to 6.30 p. m.; am't,
Sept. 16	7 a. m.	28.91	56	------	St. 10	W. 1	0	------	0.95 inch.
	2 p. m.	28.81	77	------	St. 10	S. 2	SE. 1	------	20th. Rainy and misty all day;
	9 p. m.	28.80	67	------	St. 9	S. 3	0	------	rain and thunder in the night;
Sept. 17	7 a. m.	28.78	64	------	St. 10	NW. 3	0	------	storm ended at 8 a. m. on the
	2 p. m.	28.83	72	------	St. 10	NW. 3	NE. 2	------	21st; amount, 0.27 inch.
	9 p. m.	28.87	58	------	0	0	0	------	23d. Misty from 6 to 7 p. m.; rain
Sept. 18	7 a. m.	28.88	54	------	St. 10	W. 1	0	------	in the night.
	2 p. m.	28.79	80	------	St. 1	W. 1	SE. 5	------	24th. Showery till noon; amount,
	9 p. m.	28.71	70	------	St. 8	S. 3	SE. 5	------	0.05 inch.
Sept. 19	7 a. m.	28.59	69	------	Rain 10	S. 7	S. 5	------	
	2 p. m.	28.57	73	------	St. 10	SSW. 6	SSW. 5	------	
	9 p. m.	28.57	64	------	St. 5	S. 4	0	------	
Sept. 20	7 a. m.	28.57	63	------	Rain 10	NNE. 8	NNE. 4	------	
	2 p. m.	28.63	59	------	St. 10	NNW. 5	NNW. 5	------	
	9 p. m.	28.67	52	------	Rain 10	NNW. 5	NNW. 2	------	
Sept. 21	7 a. m.	28.68	54	------	Misty 10	NNW. 4	0	------	
	2 p. m.	28.66	68	------	St. 10	NNW. 4	NNW. 2	------	
	9 p. m.	28.66	52	------	St. 10	?	0	------	
Sept. 22	7 a. m.	28.74	58	------	Misty 10	W. 6	WSW. 3	------	
	2 p. m.	28.82	67	------	St. 9	WSW. 4	WSW. 2	------	
	9 p. m.	28.89	60	------	St. 10	WSW. 3	0	------	
Sept. 23	7 a. m.	28.97	57	------	St. 10	W. 5	0	------	
	2 p. m.	28.98	68	------	St. 10	W. 2	W. 1	------	
	9 p. m.	28.97	60	------	St. 10	W. 2	0	------	
Sept. 24	7 a. m.	28.93	59	------	St. 10	NW. 5	0	------	
	2 p. m.	28.90	66	------	St. 10	NW. 4	W. 2	------	
	9 p. m.	28.90	60	------	St. 10	NW. 5	0	------	

STORMS Nos. 2 AND 3, SEPTEMBER, 1859.

WELCHFIELD, OHIO.

Month and day.	Hour.	Barom'r corrected to 32° F.	Thermometer.	Force of vapor.	Cloudiness.		Motion of clouds.	Winds.		Relative humidity.
Sept. 14	9 p. m.	------	40	------	Cir.	1	0	NW.	1	------
Sept. 15	7 a. m.	------	42	------	Cir. st.	10	0	SE.	1	------
	2 p. m.	------	60	------	Cir. cu.	3	0	SE.	2	------
	9 p. m.	------	48	------	Nim.	10	0	N.	2	------
Sept. 16	7 a. m.	------	53	------	Nim.	10	0	SE.	2	------
	2 p. m.	------	55	------	Nim.	3	0	SE.	1	------
	9 p. m.	------	58	------	Nim.	10	0	SE.	1	------
Sept. 17	7 a. m.	------	58	------	Nim.	10	0	SE.	1	------
	2 p. m.	------	63	------	Nim.	10	0	NW.	1	------
	9 p. m.	------	51	------		0	0	N.	1	------
Sept. 18	7 a. m.	------	55	------	Fog	10	0	SE.	1	------
	2 p. m.	------	72	------	Cir.	3	0	SE.	2	------
	9 p. m.	------	56	------		0	0	S.	2	------
Sept. 19	7 a. m.	------	62	------	Cir.	3	0	SE.	1	------
	2 p. m.	------	80	------	Nim.	10	0	SE.	1	------
	9 p. m.	------	66	------	Nim.	10	0	S.	2	------
Sept. 20	7 a. m.	------	66	------	Nim.	10	0	SE.	2	------
	2 p. m.	------	61	------	Nim.	10	0	N.	2	------
	9 p. m.	------	56	------	Nim.	10	0	N.	2	------
Sept. 21	7 a. m.	------	59	------	Nim.	10	0	SE.	2	------
	2 p. m.	------	73	------	Nim.	10	0	SE.	1	------
	9 p. m.	------	60	------	Fog	10	0	NW.	2	------
Sept. 22	7 a. m.	------	60	------	Nim.	10	0	NW.	2	------
	2 p. m.	------	72	------	Nim.	10	0	SW.	2	------
	9 p. m.	------	57	------		0	0	W.	1	------
Sept. 23	7 a. m.	------	57	------	Fog	10	0	SW.	1	------
	2 p. m.	------	64	------	Nim.	10	0	W.	1	------
	9 p. m.	------	56	------	Nim.	10	0	SW.	1	------
Sept. 24	7 a. m.	------	56	------	Nim.	10	0	SW.	1	------
	2 p. m.	------	64	------	Nim.	10	0	N.	2	------
	9 p. m.	------	58	------		0	0	N.	2	------

REMARKS.

15th. Rain from 7.30 to 10 p. m.; amount, 0.062 inch.
Dense fog from 6 p. m. the 17th to 11.30 a. m. on the 18th.
20th. Began to rain at 1 a. m.; thunder and diffused lightning from 8 to 10 p. m.; storm ended at 11 a. m on the 22d; amount, 1.255 inch.
Rain from 8 p. m. the 23d to 1 p. m. on the 24th; amount, 0.438 inch.

WINDHAM, OHIO.

Month and day.	Hour.	Barom'r corrected to 32° F.	Thermometer.	Force of vapor.	Cloudiness.	Motion of clouds.	Winds.	Relative humidity.
Sept. 14	9 p. m.	------	43	------	------	------	------	------
Sept. 15	7 a. m.	------	42	------	------	------	------	------
	2 p. m.	------	63	------	------	------	------	------
	9 p. m.	------	54	------	------	------	------	------
Sept. 16	7 a. m.	------	54	------	------	------	------	------
	2 p. m.	------	62	------	------	------	------	------
	9 p. m.	------	61	------	------	------	------	------
Sept. 17	7 a. m.	------	60	------	------	------	------	------
	2 p. m.	------	64	------	------	------	------	------
	9 p. m.	------	56	------	------	------	------	------
Sept. 18	7 a. m.	------	54	------	------	------	------	------
	2 p. m.	------	71	------	------	------	------	------
	9 p. m.	------	55	------	------	------	------	------
Sept. 19	7 a. m.	------	54	------	------	------	------	------
	2 p. m.	------	75	------	------	------	------	------
	9 p. m.	------	69	------	------	------	------	------
Sept. 20	7 a. m.	------	65	------	------	------	------	------
	2 p. m.	------	60	------	------	------	------	------
	9 p. m.	------	58	------	------	------	------	------
Sept. 21	7 a. m.	------	59	------	------	------	------	------
	2 p. m.	------	63	------	------	------	------	------
	9 p. m.	------	62	------	------	------	------	------
Sept. 22	7 a. m.	------	57	------	------	------	------	------
	2 p. m.	------	65	------	------	------	------	------
	9 p. m.	------	60	------	------	------	------	------
Sept. 23	7 a. m.	------	58	------	------	------	------	------
	2 p. m.	------	65	------	------	------	------	------
	9 p. m.	------	58	------	------	------	------	------
Sept. 24	7 a. m.	------	58	------	------	------	------	------
	2 p. m.	------	68	------	------	------	------	------
	9 p. m.	------	62	------	------	------	------	------

REMARKS.

15th. Evening showery.
16th. Sprinkling most of the day.
17th. Drizzling a. m.; heavy fog at night.
18th. Fog till 9 a. m.
19th. Rain most of the night.
20th. Drizzled all day; heavy rain in the night.
21st. Showery a. m.; rainbow at 4 p. m.; heavy shower at 5 p. m.
22d. Drizzling rain most of the day.
23d. Drizzled and showered during the day; rain in the night.
24th. Drizzling rain most of the day.

STORMS Nos. 2 AND 3, SEPTEMBER, 1859.

WESTERVILLE, OHIO.

Month and day.	Hour.	Barom'r corrected to 32° F.	Thermometer.	Force of vapor.	Cloudiness.		Motion of clouds.		Winds.		Relative humidity.
Sept. 14	9 p. m.	29.03	50½	.215	Cir.	5	W.	3	N.	2	58
Sept. 15	7 a. m.	29.08	48	.200	Cir. st.	9	W.	1	E.	2	59
	2 p. m.	29.02	63	.216	Cir.	8	----------		NE.	2	37
	9 p. m.	28.08	58½	.289	St.	10	NW.	2	E.	2	58
Sept. 16	7 a. m.	28.90	55½	.383	St.	10	SW.	1	E.	1	87
	2 p. m.	28.82	75	.519	Cu. st.	10	W.	1	E.	1	60
	9 p. m.	28.78	71	.590	St.	10	----------		SE.	1	78
Sept. 17	7 a. m.	28.78	66	.570	Cir. st.	10	N.	3	NW.	2	89
	2 p. m.	28.81	71	.519	Cir. st.	9	N.	1	NW.	2	68
	9 p. m.	28.86	58	.423		0	----------		N.	1	88
Sept. 18	7 a. m.	28.87	68	.476	Cir.	8	NW.	1	NW.	1	69
	2 p. m.	28.80	75½	.584	Cir. cu.	4	SW.	1	W.	1	66
	9 p. m.	28.73	71	.608	St.	4	----------		SW.	1	80
Sept. 19	7 a. m.	28.61	67½	.584	St.	9	SW.	2	SW.	1	87
	2 p. m.	28.56	73	.581	Cu. st.	10	W.	2	S.	4	72
	9 p. m.	28.59	69	.671	St.	10	----------		SW.	1	95
Sept. 20	7 a. m.	28.56	64½	.590	St.	10	N.	3	N.	2	97
	2 p. m.	------	------	------	----------		----------		----------		------
	9 p. m.	28.65	58½	.476	St.	10	N.	3	N.	1	97
Sept. 21	7 a. m.	28.64	60½	.511	Fog	10	----------		NE.	1	97
	2 p. m.	28.64	70	.551	Cu. st.	9	W.	1	SE.	1	75
	9 p. m.	28.65	63	.543	St.	10	W.	1	NW.	1	94
Sept. 22	7 a. m.	28.73	62	.507	St.	10	NW.	2	NW.	1	91
	2 p. m.	28.82	66	.438	St.	10	W.	2	W.	1	68
	9 p. m.	28.89	64	.563	St.	10	NW ------		NW.	1	94
Sept. 23	7 a. m.	28.96	61	.489	St.	10	SW.	1	S.	1	91
	2 p. m.	28.94	66	.570	St.	10	SW.	2	SW.	1	89
	9 p. m.	28.97	62½	.549	St.	10	SW-------		SW.	1	97
Sept. 24	7 a. m.	28.91	59½	.477	St.	10	SW.	1	SW.	1	94
	2 p. m.	28.84	64	------	St.	10	W.	2	SW.	1	------
	9 p. m.	28.89	58½	.460	St.	3	----------		W.	1	94

REMARKS.

14th. Frost.

Began to rain in the night of the 15th, and ended at 8 a. m. on the 16th; amount, 0.10 inch. Lightning in the N. at 9 p. m.

20th. A very wet day; lightning at night.

21st. Dense fog in the morning; rain till 8 a. m.; rain in the night.

22d. Rain at night.

24th. Rainy; amount of rain since the 20th, 3.00 inches.

BATTLE CREEK, MICHIGAN.

Month and day.	Hour.	Barom'r corrected to 32° F.	Thermometer.	Force of vapor.	Cloudiness.		Motion of clouds.		Winds.		Relative humidity.
Sept. 14	9 p. m.	29.28	46	------	Cir. st.	7	W.	1	E.	2	------
Sept. 15	7 a. m.	29.33	52	------	Cir.	2	W.	1	SE.	2	------
	2 p. m.	29.35	56	------	Cir. st.	7	W.	1	SE.	2	------
	9 p. m.	29.25	52	------	Cir. cu.	4	W.	1	SE.	2	------
Sept. 16	7 a. m.	29.14	50	------	Cir. cu.	2	W.	1	SE.	2	------
	2 p. m.	29.07	71	------	Cir. st.	2	W.	1	SE.	2	------
	9 p. m.	29.03	62	------	Cir. st.	4	W.	1	SE.	1	------
Sept. 17	7 a. m.	29.09	50	------		0	----------		W.	1	------
	2 p. m.	29.06	72	------		0	----------		E.	1	------
	9 p. m.	29.08	58	------		0	----------			0	------
Sept. 18	7 a. m.	29.04	60	------	Cir.	1	W.	1	S.	2	------
	2 p. m.	28.93	76	------	Cir. st.	3	W.	2	S.	4	------
	9 p. m.	28.85	64	------	Nim.	10	W.	2	S.	3	------
Sept. 19	7 a. m.	28.72	66	------	Cir. cu.	4	SW.	2	S.	2	------
	2 p. m.	28.77	75	------	Cir. st.	3	W.	2	SW.	2	------
	9 p. m.	28.84	63	------	Cu. st.	4	SW.	2	E.	1	------
Sept. 20	7 a. m.	28.98	51	------	St.	10	NE.	3	NE.	3	------
	2 p. m.	29.00	50	------	St.	10	NE.	3	NE.	3	------
	9 p. m.	29.01	49	------	Nim.	10	NE.	1	NE.	3	------
Sept. 21	7 a. m.	28.99	50	------	Nim.	10	NE.	2	NE.	2	------
	2 p. m.	28.98	54	------	Nim.	10	NE.	2	NE.	3	------
	9 p. m.	28.97	54	------	Nim.	10	NE.	2	NE.	2	------
Sept. 22	7 a. m.	29.00	56	------	Nim.	10	W.	1	W.	1	------
	2 p. m.	29.02	62	------	Cir. st.	10	W.	2	W.	2	------
	9 p. m.	29.07	59	------	St.	10	W.	2	W.	1	------
Sept. 23	7 a. m.	29.16	58	------	Mist	10	W.	2	W.	1	------
	2 p. m.	29.15	62	------	Nim.	10	NW.	2	NW.	2	------
	9 p. m.	29.15	59	------	Cu. st.	8	NW.	2	NW.	2	------
Sept. 24	7 a. m.	29.17	59	------	St.	9	NW.	1	NW.	1	------
	2 p. m.	29.15	63	------	St.	8	NW.	1	NW.	2	------
	9 p. m.	29.16	60	------	St.	7	NW.	1	W.	1	------

REMARKS.

18th. Rain from 10½ a. m. till noon; began to rain at 4 p. m. and ended in the night; amount, 1.02 inch.

20th. Rain from 7½ to 9 p. m.; amount, 0.26 inch.

21st. Rain from 8 a. m. to 5 p. m.; Amount, 0.60 inch.

23d. Shower at 4 p. m.; amount, 0.03 inch.

STORMS Nos. 2 AND 3, SEPTEMBER, 1859.

CORUNNA, MICHIGAN.

Month and day.	Hour.	Barom'r corrected to 32° F.	Thermometer.	Force of vapor.	Cloudiness.		Motion of clouds.		Winds.		Relative humidity.	REMARKS.
Sept. 14	9 p. m.	......	......	......	......		......		......		......	15th. Sprinkled all day; slight amount of rain fell.
Sept. 15	7 a. m.	......	......	......	Cir.	9	E.	3	E.	3	......	18th. Began sprinkling at 2 p. m.; began to rain at dark.
	2 p. m.	......	......	......	Cir. st.	10	......		E.	2	......	19th. Ceased raining about 4 a. m.; commenced again at 5 p. m. and rained at intervals till 4 a. m. on the 20th.
	9 p. m.	......	......	......	......		......		......		......	21st. Began to rain lightly about 11 a. m., and ended at 4 a. m. on the 22d.
Sept. 16	7 a. m.	......	......	......		0	......		E.	2	......	22d. Sprinkle at 6 p. m.
	2 p. m.	......	......	......	Cir. cu.	9	......		E.	2	......	
	9 p. m.	......	......	......	......		......		......		......	
Sept. 17	7 a. m.	......	......	......	Fog		......		W.	1	......	
	2 p. m.	......	......	......		0	......		E.	2	......	
	9 p. m.	......	......	......	......		......		......		......	
Sept. 18	7 a. m.	......	......	......	......		......		......		......	
	2 p. m.	......	......	......	......		......		......		......	
	9 p. m.	......	......	......	......		......		......		......	
Sept. 19	7 a. m.	......	......	......	Nim.	9	S.	7	S.	2	......	
	2 p. m.	......	......	......	Cu.	5	SW.	4	SW.	4	......	
	9 p. m.	......	......	......	......		......		......		......	
Sept. 20	7 a. m.	......	......	......	Cir. st.	10	......		N.	4	......	
	2 p. m.	......	......	......	Cir. st.	9	NE.	3	NE.	4	......	
	9 p. m.	......	......	......	......		......		......		......	
Sept. 21	7 a. m.	......	......	......	Nim.	10	......		NE.	2	......	
	2 p. m.	......	......	......	Nim.	10	......		NE.	2	......	
	9 p. m.	......	......	......	......		......		......		......	
Sept. 22	7 a. m.	......	......	......	......		......		......		......	
	2 p. m.	......	......	......	Nim.	9	SW.	1	SW.	2	......	
	9 p. m.	......	......	......	......		......		......		......	
Sept. 23	7 a. m.	......	......	......	Nim.	10		0	S.	2	......	
	2 p. m.	......	......	......	Cu.	9	W.	3	W.	3	......	
	9 p. m.	......	......	......	......		......		......		......	
Sept. 24	7 a. m.	......	......	......	Nim.	10		0	W.	1	......	
	2 p. m.	......	......	......	Cu.	9	S.	2	SW.	2	......	
	9 p. m.	......	......	......	......		......		......		......	

DETROIT, MICHIGAN.

Month and day.	Hour.	Barom'r corrected to 32° F.	Thermometer.	Force of vapor.	Cloudiness.		Motion of clouds.		Winds.		Relative humidity.	REMARKS.
Sept. 14	9 p. m.	29.37	53	.157	St.	4	SE.	1	N.	2	37	Rain at intervals from 8.16 p. m. on the 18th, to 2.16 p. m. on the 21st; amount, 1.52 inch.
Sept. 15	7 a. m.	29.76	50	.258	Nim.	9	S.	1	E.	3	71	Rain from 9 a. m. on the 21st, to 9.30 a. m. on the 22d; amount, 0.15 inch.
	2 p. m.	29.67	62	.312	Nim.	6	SE.	2	E.	2	56	
	9 p. m.	29.70	52	.219	Cu. st.	2	N.	1	E.	2	54	
Sept. 16	7 a. m.	29.59	52	.321	Cir.	1	E.	1	E.	2	85	
	2 p. m.	29.53	65	.346	Cu. st.	9	SE.	1	E.	1	54	
	9 p. m.	29.63	63	.399	St.	8	E.	1	E.	1	72	
Sept. 17	7 a. m.	29.48	59	.393	St.	10	E.	1	NE.	2	81	
	2 p. m.	29.56	71	.436	St.	1	S.	1	NE.	1	57	
	9 p. m.	29.49	56	.308		0	......		E.	1	68	
Sept. 18	7 a. m.	29.41	54	.335	Cu.	9	E.	2	SE.	1	80	
	2 p. m.	29.50	75	.462	Cir. cu.	5	E.	1	SE.	1	55	
	9 p. m.	29.50	66	.470	Nim.	8	E.	1	SW.	1	73	
Sept. 19	7 a. m.	29.38	65	.497	Nim.	10	NE.	1	S.	1	83	
	2 p. m.	29.17	72	.668	Nim.	3	E.	1	S.	2	85	
	9 p. m.	29.36	64	.465	Nim.	2	E.	1	SE.	1	78	
Sept. 20	7 a. m.	29.36	54	.375	Nim.	10	W.	3	NE.	3	93	
	2 p. m.	29.40	52	.257	Nim.	10	SW.	5	NE.	2	66	
	9 p. m.	29.27	53	.334	Nim.	10	SW.	5	NE.	3	86	
Sept. 21	7 a. m.	29.37	52	.334	Nim.	10	SW.	4	E.	2	86	
	2 p. m.	29.34	55	.349	Nim.	10	SW.	3	E.	2	80	
	9 p. m.	29.43	56	.362	Nim.	10	SW.	2	E.	1	86	
Sept. 22	7 a. m.	29.38	57	.335	Nim.	10	SE.	3	W.	2	74	
	2 p. m.	29.42	62	.386	Nim.	8	E.	1	W.	1	67	
	9 p. m.	29.33	57	.350	Nim.	9	E.	1	W.	1	75	
Sept. 23	7 a. m.	29.55	61	.426	Cu. st.	8	SE.	1	S.	2	82	
	2 p. m.	29.51	70	.449	Cu. st.	4	SW.	2	SW.	2	61	
	9 p. m.	29.51	64	.497	Cu. st.	7	W.	1	SW.	1	83	
Sept. 24	7 a. m.	29.55	62	.426	Cu. st.	7	NW.	1	SW.	1	82	
	2 p. m.	29.53	71	.595	Nim.	10	W.	2	SW.	2	76	
	9 p. m.	29.55	63	.416	Nim.	10	W.	2	W.	1	82	

STORMS Nos. 2 AND 3, SEPTEMBER, 1859.

GRAND RAPIDS, MICHIGAN.

Month and day.	Hour.	Barom'r corrected to 32° F.	Thermometer.	Force of vapor.	Cloudiness.	Motion of clouds.	Winds.	Relative humidity.	REMARKS.
Sept. 14	9 p. m.	------	47	------	Cir. st. 4	W. 2	W. 1	------	14th. Frost; windy; solar halo.
Sept. 15	7 a. m.	------	42	------	Cir. cu. 6	W. 2	SE. 1	------	18th. Rain at intervals all day; thunder and lightning in the p. m.; amount, 1.05 inch.
	2 p. m.	------	62	------	Cu. st. 8	W. 2	SE. 2	------	
	9 p. m.	------	52	------	Cu. st. 9	W. 2	E. 1	------	
Sept. 16	7 a. m.	------	50	------	Cu. st. 9	W. 2	E. 1	------	19th. Rain at intervals all day; strong wind at night, changed to E; amount, 0.17 inch.
	2 p. m.	------	70	------	Cu. st. 9	W. 2	E. 1	------	
	9 p. m.	------	61	------	Cu. st. 9	W. 2	E. 1	------	
Sept. 17	7 a. m.	------	53	------	0	----------	E. 1	------	20th. Cloudy; cool rain at night.
	2 p. m.	------	76	------	0	----------	E. 1	------	21st. Rain at intervals all day; slight rain at night.
	9 p. m.	------	57	------	0	----------	SW. 1	------	
Sept. 18	7 a. m.	------	62	------	{ Cu. st. / Cir. st. } 7	W. 2 / S. 3	S. 1	------	22d. Drizzling rain at intervals all day.
	2 p. m.	------	75	------	{ Nim. / Cir. st. } 10	W. 2 / S. 3	S. 1	------	23d. Drizzling rain. 24th. Drizzling rain in the morning; amount of rain, 0.69 inch.
	9 p. m.	------	63	------	{ Cu. st. / Cir. st. } 6	W. 2 / S. 3	S. 1	------	
Sept. 19	7 a. m.	------	64	------	Nim. 9	S. 2	S. 1	------	
	2 p. m.	------	70	------	Nim. 10	SW. 2	SW. 1	------	
	9 p. m.	------	66	------	Nim. 10	S. 3	E. 3	------	
Sept. 20	7 a. m.	------	46	------	Cu. st. 10	NE. 2	NE. 2	------	
	2 p. m.	------	52	------	{ Cir. cu. / Cu. st. } 8	W. 1 / N. 2	NE. 2	------	
	9 p. m.	------	49	------	Nim. 10	NE. 2	NE. 2	------	
Sept. 21	7 a. m.	------	49	------	Cu. st. 10	E. 2	NE. 1	------	
	2 p. m.	------	54	------	Nim. 10	E. 2	NE. 2	------	
	9 p. m.	------	51	------	Cu. st. 10	E. 2	NE. 1	------	
Sept. 22	7 a. m.	------	52	------	Cu. st. 10	W. 2	S. 1	------	
	2 p. m.	------	64	------	Nim. 10	W. 2	SW. 1	------	
	9 p. m.	------	57	------	Nim. 10	W. 2	W. 1	------	
Sept. 23	7 a. m.	------	56	------	Cu. st. 10	W. 2	W. 1	------	
	2 p. m.	------	64	------	Nim. 10	W. 2	W. 1	------	
	9 p. m.	------	57	------	Nim. 10	W. 2	W. 1	------	
Sept. 24	7 a. m.	------	56	------	Cu. st. 10	N. 2	N. 1	------	
	2 p. m.	------	69	------	Cu. st. 9	N. 2	N. 1	------	
	9 p. m.	------	57	------	0	----------	N. 1	------	

GRAND HAVEN, MICHIGAN.

Month and day.	Hour.	Barom'r corrected to 32° F.	Thermometer.	Force of vapor.	Cloudiness.	Motion of clouds.	Winds.	Relative humidity.	REMARKS.
Sept. 14	9 p. m.	29.62	48	.335	9	----------	NE. 1	100	19th. Amount of rain, 0.90 inch.
Sept. 15	7 a. m.	29.67	44	.196	9	E. 1	E. 2	68	20th. Amount, 0.06 inch.
	2 p. m.	29.48	59	.269	10	E. 1	E. 1	54	21st. Amount, 0.12 inch.
	9 p. m.	29.56	55	.243	10	NW. 2	E. 1	56	22d. Amount, 0.12 inch.
Sept. 16	7 a. m.	29.48	50	.258	10	----------	E. 1	71	
	2 p. m.	29.41	65	.330	10	----------	E. 1	53	
	9 p. m.	29.36	61	.354	10	----------	E. 1	66	
Sept. 17	7 a. m.	29.36	55	.321	0	----------	E. 1	74	
	2 p. m.	29.31	59	.323	0	----------	E. 1	65	
	9 p. m.	29.31	60	.396	3	----------	E. 1	76	
Sept. 18	7 a. m.	29.31	64	.464	9	W. 3	W. 1	77	
	2 p. m.	29.09	68	.577	10	W. 2	S. 2	85	
	9 p. m.	29.11	66	.570	10	W. 2	SW. 2	89	
Sept. 19	7 a. m.	28.97	64	.563	10	SW. 2	SW. 1	94	
	2 p. m.	------	63	.510	10	W. 4	W. 2	88	
	9 p. m.	29.17	53	.375	10	----------	NE. 8	93	
Sept. 20	7 a. m.	29.39	49	.297	10	NE. 7	NE. 7	85	
	2 p. m.	29.37	56	.308	10	NE. 2	NE. 3	69	
	9 p. m.	29.41	52	.232	10	----------	NE. 7	60	
Sept. 21	7 a. m.	29.35	50	.309	10	----------	NE. 5	85	
	2 p. m.	29.30	56	.391	10	----------	E. 3	87	
	9 p. m.	29.30	54	.362	10	----------	E. 1	87	
Sept. 22	7 a. m.	29.30	52	.361	10	----------	SE. 1	93	
	2 p. m.	29.34	56	.391	10	----------	SE. 1	87	
	9 p. m.	29.42	55	.405	10	----------	NW. 1	94	

STORMS Nos. 2 AND 3, SEPTEMBER, 1859.

GRAND HAVEN, MICHIGAN—Continued.

Month and day.	Hour.	Barom'r corrected to 32° F.	Thermometer.	Force of vapor.	Cloudiness.	Motion of clouds.	Winds.	Relative humidity.	REMARKS.
Sept. 23	7 a. m.	29.48	56	.391	10	NW. 2	NE. 1	87	23d. Amount of rain, 0.06 inch.
	2 p. m.	29.46	58	.452	10	----------	W. 1	94	24th. Amount, 0.02 inch.
	9 p. m.	29.50	54	.362	0	----------	S. 1	87	
Sept. 24	7 a. m.	29.51	55	.405	10	NE. 2	NE. 2	94	
	2 p. m.	29.47	63	.446	9	NW. 1	NW. 1	77	
	9 p. m.	29.47	56	.449	2	----------	SE. 1	100	

LAKE GEORGE, MICHIGAN.

Month and day.	Hour.	Barom'r corrected to 32° F.	Thermometer.	Force of vapor.	Cloudiness.	Motion of clouds.	Winds.	Relative humidity.	REMARKS.
Sept. 14	9 p. m.	29.62	34	------	Nim. 8	----------	NW. 1	------	14th. Heavy frost.
Sept. 15	7 a. m.	29.71	32	------	Cir. cu. 0	----------	NW. 1	------	15th. Frost; two circles in the fir-
	2 p. m.	29.69	54	------	Cir. cu. 2	----------	SE. 1	------	mament at 7 p. m. resembling
	9 p. m.	29.56	49	------	Clear 1	----------	SE. 2	------	rainbows—one of them started
Sept. 16	7 a. m.	29.60	43	------	Clear 1	----------	E. 1	------	from E. to SW., and the other
	2 p. m.	29.41	65	------	Cu. 0	----------	SE. 1	------	from E. to NW.
	9 p. m.	29.42	51	------	Cir. 1	----------	SE. 1	------	18th. Aurora at 8½ p. m., a black
Sept. 17	7 a. m.	29.43	40	------	Nim. 10	----------	Calm 0	------	cloud underneath, continued till
	2 p. m.	29.40	73	------	Nim. 5	----------	Calm 0	------	11 p. m.
	9 p. m.	29.39	56	------	Nim. 10	----------	Calm 0	------	19th. Severe gale and very heavy
Sept. 18	7 a. m.	29.38	51	------	Nim. 9	----------	NE. 1	------	rain; amount, 1.62 inch.?
	2 p. m.	29.12	62	------	Nim. 10	----------	SE. 2	------	20th. Frost.
	9 p. m.	29.18	59	------	Nim. 10	----------	NE. 1	------	21st. Heavy rain and wind; am't,
Sept. 19	7 a. m.	29.08	58	------	Clear 0	----------	NE. 2	------	0.90 inch.
	2 p. m.	29.21	47	------	Cir. 0	----------	NE. 6	------	
	9 p. m.	29.40	42	------	Clear 2	----------	NE. 4	------	
Sept. 20	7 a. m.	29.55	31	------	Cir. st. 10	----------	N. 2	------	
	2 p. m.	29.43	58	------	Cir. st. 3	----------	N. 2	------	
	9 p. m.	29.51	47	------	Nim. 4	----------	NE. 1	------	
Sept. 21	7 a. m.	29.52	41	------	Nim. 10	----------	N. 2	------	
	2 p. m.	29.33	68	------	Nim. 10	----------	Calm 0	------	
	9 p. m.	29.38	58	------	Nim. 10	----------	Calm 0	------	
Sept. 22	7 a. m.	29.31	53	------	Nim. 5	----------	N. 2	------	
	2 p. m.	29.30	57	------	Nim. 10	----------	E. 1	------	
	9 p. m.	29.37	56	------	Nim. 10	----------	Calm 0	------	
Sept. 23	7 a. m.	29.31	53	------	Fog. 10	----------	Calm 0	------	
	2 p. m.	29.32	62	------	Nim. 3	----------	Calm 0	------	
	9 p. m.	29.34	56½	------	Nim. 10	----------	Calm 0	------	
Sept. 24	7 a. m.	29.48	51	------	Nim. 10	----------	NW. 1	------	
	2 p. m.	29.46	73	------	Cu. 10	----------	Calm 0	------	
	9 p. m.	29.45	61	------	Nim. 8	----------	Calm 0	------	

MARQUETTE, MICHIGAN.

Month and day.	Hour.	Barom'r corrected to 32° F.	Thermometer.	Force of vapor.	Cloudiness.	Motion of clouds.	Winds.	Relative humidity.	REMARKS.
Sept. 14	9 p. m.	29.58	35.2	.142	St. 1	W. 1	WSW. 1	70	14th. Snow in the morning, cloudy
Sept. 15	7 a. m.	29.59	43.1	.208	Nim. 10	----------	S. 2	74	and cold; fine hail and very little
	2 p. m.	29.51	58.1	.254	St. cu. 7	N. 1	SSW. 3	53	ice.
	9 p. m.	29.49	49	.244	Cir. 10	----------	S. 1	69	15th. Thick, hazy clouds, in long
Sept. 16	7 a. m.	29.41	50.2	.296	Cir. 9	W. 1	S. 2	81	bands across the sky.
	2 p. m.	29.33	65	.304	St. 1	0	S. 3	50	16th. Faint aurora at 10 p. m.
	9 p. m.	29.29	52.1	.126	0	----------	WSW. 3	32	18th. Rain at night; amount, 0.94
Sept. 17	7 a. m.	29.30	53	.284	St. 1	----------	NW. 1	71	inch.
	2 p. m.	29.25	71.3	.394	St. 4	----------	ESE. 2	51	19th. Strong north wind and rough
	9 p. m.	29.22	57.8	.330	Cu. 7	----------	SW. 1	70	sea.
Sept. 18	7 a. m.	20.10	57	.466	Nim. 10	----------	SE. 1	100	20th. A few scattering cirrus clouds
	2 p. m.	29.08	66	.516	Nim. 10	----------	SSW. 2	84	in the morning, very high, and
	9 p. m.	29.07	52.2	.376	Nim. 10	----------	WSW. 4	96	coming from the west with great
Sept. 19	7 a. m.	29.23	42.7	.255	Nim. 10	----------	N. 7	93	velocity.
	2 p. m.	29.34	43.8	.239	Cir. cu. 10	----------	N. 8	83	21st. White frost.
	9 p. m.	29.46	44.6	.207	10	----------	NW. 4	70	23d. Misty rain; amount, 0.05 inch.
Sept. 20	7 a. m.	29.52	44.3	.219	Cir. 10	E. 1	E. 4	76	24th. Pale aurora.
	2 p. m.	29.54	51	.226	0	----------	NE. 3	60	
	9 p. m.	29.51	35	.188	0	----------	N. 2	90	

STORMS Nos. 2 AND 3, SEPTEMBER, 1859.

MARQUETTE, MICHIGAN—Continued.

Month and day.	Hour.	Barom'r corrected to 32° F.	Thermometer.	Force of vapor.	Cloudiness.		Motion of clouds.		Winds.		Relative humidity.	REMARKS.
Sept. 21	7 a. m.	29.52	38	.170		0	....		WNW.	1	72	
	2 p. m.	29.36	73	.346		0	....		WNW.	1	50	
	9 p. m.	29.33	41.3	.212	Cir.	1	Shower....		WNW.	1	81	
Sept. 22	7 a. m.	29.27	30	.239	St.	8	Still	0	NE.	1	66	
	2 p. m.	29.28	54	.335	Nim.	10		0	NE.	2	80	
	9 p. m.	29.47	52.3	.327	Nim.	10		0	NE.	1	86	
Sept. 23	7 a. m.	29.41	51	.357	St.	10	....		NE.	0	94	
	2 p. m.	29.40	62.4	.369	Nim.	10	....		NE.	1	66	
	9 p. m.	29.43	47.2	.295		0	....		NW.	1	91	
Sept. 24	7 a. m.	29.42	46.4	.283		0	....		NW.	0	91	
	2 p. m.	29.40	62.1	.419	Cu.	1	Shower	1	NE.	1	73	
	9 p. m.	29.33	49.1	.321		0	....		NW.	0	89	

MONROE, MICHIGAN.*

Month and day.	Hour.	Barom'r corrected to 32° F.	Thermometer.	Force of vapor.	Cloudiness.		Motion of clouds.		Winds.		Relative humidity.	REMARKS.
Sept. 14	9 p. m.	......	......	......	Cir. cu.	5	N.	1	N.	2	......	15th. Slight sprinkle at 8 p. m.
Sept. 15	7 a. m.	......	......	......	Cir. st.	9	N.	2	N.	3	......	18th. Began to rain at 8½ p. m. and ended some time in the night.
	2 p. m.	......	......	......	Cir. cu.	6	N.	3	N.	3	......	19th. Light showers in rapid succession all day.
	9 p. m.	......	......	......	Nim.	10	NE.	1	NE.	1	......	20th. Drizzling rain all day; showers at night, with lightning.
Sept. 16	7 a. m.	......	......	......	Cir. st.	1	E.	1	E.	2	......	
	2 p. m.	......	......	......	Cir.	1	E.	2	E.	2	......	
	9 p. m.	......	......	......	Cir. st.	7	E.	1	E.	1	......	
Sept. 17	7 a. m.	......	......	......	Light fog,	10	E.	1	E.	2	......	
	2 p. m.	......	......	......	Cir.	5	E.	1	E.	2	......	
	9 p. m.	......	......	......		0		0	E.	2	......	
Sept. 18	7 a. m.	......	......	......	Cir. cu.	6	SW.	2	SW.	2	......	
	2 p. m.	......	......	......	Cir. cu.	4	SW.	2	SW.	1	......	
	9 p. m.	......	......	......	Nim.	9	SW.	2	SW.	2	......	
Sept. 19	7 a. m.	......	......	......	Nim.	10	SW.	1	SW.	2	......	
	2 p. m.	......	......	......	Cir. cu.	3	SE.	1	SE.	3	......	
	9 p. m.	......	......	......		0		0	SE.	1	......	
Sept. 20	7 a. m.	......	......	......	Nim.	10	NE.	2	NE.	4	......	
	2 p. m.	......	......	......	Nim.	10	NE.	2	NE.	3	......	
	9 p. m.	......	......	......	Nim.	10	NE.	2	NE.	2	......	
Sept. 21	7 a. m.	......	......	......	Nim.	10	NE.	2	NE.	2	......	
	2 p. m.	......	......	......	Nim.	10	NW.	2	NW.	2	......	
	9 p. m.	......	......	......	Nim.	10	NW.	2	NW.	2	......	
Sept. 22	7 a. m.	......	......	......	Nim.	10	W.	1	NW.	2	......	
	2 p. m.	......	......	......	Nim.	10	W.	2	W.	2	......	
	9 p. m.	......	......	......	Cir. st.	9	W.	2	W.	2	......	
Sept. 23	7 a. m.	......	......	......	Nim.	10	W.	1	W.	2	......	
	2 p. m.	......	......	......	Nim.	10	W.	1	W.	2	......	
	9 p. m.	......	......	......	Nim.	10	W.	1	W.	2	......	
Sept. 24	7 a. m.	......	......	......	Nim.	10	W.	2	NW.	2	......	
	2 p. m.	......	......	......	Nim.	10	NW.	1	NW.	2	......	
	9 p. m.	......	......	......	Nim.	10	NW.	1	NW.	2	......	

* Whelpley, observer.

MONROE, MICHIGAN.*

Month and day.	Hour.	Barom'r corrected to 32° F.	Thermometer.	Force of vapor.	Cloudiness.		Motion of clouds.		Winds.		Relative humidity.	REMARKS.
Sept. 14	9 p. m.	......	50	......	Cir. cu.	8		0		0	......	18th. Rain in the evening, accompanied by thunder and zigzag lightning.
Sept. 15	7 a. m.	......	49	......	Nim.	8		0	E.	1	......	
	2 p. m.	......	56	......	Cu.	6		0	E.	4	......	
	9 p. m.	......	53	......	Cu.	7		0		0	......	
Sept. 16	7 a. m.	......	47	......	Cir.	1		0	E.	1	......	
	2 p. m.	......	67	......	Cu.	4		0	NE.	1	......	
	9 p. m.	......	63	......	Diffuse	8		0		0	......	
Sept. 17	7 a. m.	......	60	......	Diffuse	10		0	W.	1	......	
	2 p. m.	......	72	......	Cu. and cir.	1		0	SE.	1	......	
	9 p. m.	......	61	......		0		0		0	......	
Sept. 18	7 a. m.	......	58	......	Cir.	3		0	E.	1	......	
	2 p. m.	......	68	......	Cir. and cu.	4		0	E.	1	......	
	9 p. m.	......	66	......	Nim.	8		0		0	......	

* Bowlsby, observer.

STORMS Nos. 2 AND 3, SEPTEMBER, 1859.

MONROE, MICHIGAN—Continued.

Month and day.	Hour.	Barom'r corrected to 32° F.	Thermometer.	Force of vapor.	Cloudiness.	Motion of clouds.	Winds.	Relative humidity.	REMARKS.
Sept. 19	7 a. m.	------	66	------	Nim. 10	0	SE. 1	------	20th to 27th. Rain more or less, at longer or shorter intervals each day.
	2 p. m.	------	71	------	Cu. and nim. 7	0	SE. 1	------	
	9 p. m.	------	69	------	Cu. 7	0	0	------	
Sept. 20	7 a. m.	------	64	------	Nim. 10	0	SW. 1	------	
	2 p. m.	------	70	------	Nim. 9	0	SW. 1	------	
	9 p. m.	------	68	------	Nim. 9	0	0	------	
Sept. 21	7 a. m.	------	67	------	Nim. 10	0	SW. 1	------	
	2 p. m.	------	70	------	Nim. 10	0	SW. 1	------	
	9 p. m.	------	67	------	Nim. 10	0	0	------	
Sept. 22	7 a. m.	------	62	------	Nim. 10	0	SW. 1	------	
	2 p. m.	------	71	------	Nim. 10	0	SW. 1	------	
	9 p. m.	------	66	------	Nim. 10	0	0	------	
Sept. 23	7 a. m.	------	59	------	Nim. 10	0	SW. 1	------	
	2 p. m.	------	68	------	Nim. 10	0	SW. 1	------	
	9 p. m.	------	66	------	Nim. 10	0	0	------	
Sept. 24	7 a. m.	------	58	------	Nim. 10	0	SW. 1	------	
	2 p. m.	------	66	------	Nim. 10	0	SW. 1	------	
	9 p. m.	------	63	------	Nim. 10	0	0	------	

MONROE PIERS, MICHIGAN.

Month and day.	Hour.	Barom'r corrected to 32° F.	Thermometer.	Force of vapor.	Cloudiness.	Motion of clouds.	Winds.	Relative humidity.	REMARKS.
Sept. 14	6 p. m.	29. 60	53. 5	. 175	9	W. 1	WNW. 2	42	17th. Light fog falling at 5. 30 a. m.; rising at 9. 30 a. m. 18th. Heavy mist at sunrise; disappeared at 7 a. m.; rain at intervals during the night, commencing, with a thunder shower from the south, at 9 p. m.; amount, 0. 42 inch. 19th. Frequent showers from the south, commencing at 9 a. m. and ending at 3. 30 p. m.; rainbow in the NE. at 3 p. m.; amount, 0. 29 inch. 20th. A general rain from 9 a. m. till noon; thunder shower from the SE. between 9 and 10 p. m.; amount, 1. 01 inch. 21st. Drizzling rain from 10 a. m. till noon; amount, 0. 01 inch. 22d. Drizzling rain from 7 to 8. 30 a. m.; amount, 0. 03 inch. 23d. Rain in the night; amount, 0. 01 inch.
Sept. 15	6 a. m.	29. 70	53. 5	. 315	10	----------	NE. 5	77	
	9 a. m.	29. 73	53. 5	. 301	9	----------	E. 5	73	
	3 p. m.	39. 66	55	. 269	8	SW. 2	NE. 6	62	
	6 p. m.	29. 62	54. 5	. 263	8	SW. 2	NE. 6	61½	
Sept. 16	6 a. m.	29. 50	52	. 321	3	SW. 2	N. 5	83	
	9 a. m.	29. 49	55. 5	. 356	1	----------	N. 4	81	
	3 p. m.	29. 39	63. 5	. 440	5	SW. 4	NE. 5	75	
	6 p. m.	29. 38	62	. 444	9	SW. 3	NE. 5	80	
Sept. 17	6 a. m.	29. 36	59. 5	. 462	10	----------	NW. 3	91	
	9 a. m.	29. 40	60. 5	. 434	9	SW. 3	NW. 2	82	
	3 p. m.	29. 41	65	. 467	3	SW. 2	SE. 3	75	
	6 p. m.	29. 39	65. 5	. 493	2	----------	SSE. 2	78	
Sept. 18	6 a. m.	29. 44	57	. 407	9	----------	S. 1	87	
	9 a. m.	29. 42	60. 5	. 390	8	----------	SE. 3	74	
	3 p. m.	29. 32	67	. 489	7	S. 1	ENE. 3	75	
	6 p. m.	29. 24	65. 5	. 526	8	W. 2	E. 4	84	
Sept. 19	6 a. m.	29. 06	64. 5	. 539	10	W. 2	ESE. 3	89	
	9 a. m.	29. 08	65	. 549	10	S. 3	SSE. 2	89	
	3 p. m.	29. 03	68	. 612	4	----------	S. by E. 2	90	
	6 p. m.	29. 08	69	. 599	5	----------	SW. 1	85	
Sept. 20	6 a. m.	29. 25	53. 5	. 355	10	----------	NW. 4	86	
	9 a. m.	29. 27	54. 5	. 369	10	----------	NW. 5	87	
	3 p. m.	29. 26	54	. 376	10	----------	NNW. 7	90	
	6 p. m.	29. 29	53. 5	. 382	10	----------	NW. 6	93	
Sept. 21	6 a. m.	29. 28	54	. 390	10	NE. 7	NNW. 6	93	
	9 a. m.	29. 28	54	. 390	10	----------	NNW. 4	93	
	3 p. m.	29. 24	55. 5	. 370	10	----------	NNW. 3	84	
	6 p. m.	29. 26	55. 5	. 412	10	----------	WNW. 3	94	
Sept. 22	6 a. m.	29. 27	56	. 405	10	----------	WSW. 2	90	
	9 a. m.	29. 30	57. 5	. 429	9	----------	WSW. 1	91	
	3 p. m.	29. 35	60	. 441	10	----------	SW. 2	85	
	6 p. m.	29. 39	59. 5	. 447	10	----------	SW. 3	88	
Sept. 23	6 a. m.	29. 49	57. 5	. 429	9	----------	SW. 2	91	
	9 a. m.	29. 50	59. 5	. 418	10	----------	SW. 2	82	
	3 p. m.	29. 46	61. 5	. 482	10	----------	S. 3	88	
	6 p. m.	29. 47	61	. 489	10	----------	SW. 1	91	
Sept. 24	6 a. m.	29. 45	57	. 421	10	----------	WNW. 2	90	
	9 a. m.	29. 46	58. 5	. 416	10	----------	SSW. 1	85	
	3 p. m.	29. 44	63	. 462	4	SW. 3	SW. 1	80	
	6 p. m.	29. 45	61. 5	. 436	1	NW. 2	W. 2	80	

STORMS Nos. 2 AND 3, SEPTEMBER, 1859.

NEW BUFFALO, MICHIGAN.

Month and day.	Hour.	Barom'r corrected to 32° F.	Thermometer.	Force of vapor.	Cloudiness.	Motion of clouds.	Winds.	Relative humidity.	REMARKS.
Sept. 14	9 p. m.	29.47	48	------	Cu. 6	NW. 0	------------	------	Rain from 2 p. m. the 18th to 9 a. m. on the 19th; amount, 0.69 inch.
Sept. 15	7 a. m.	.51	53	------	Cu. st. 10	NW. 1	------------	------	Rain from 1 a. m. the 21st to 11 a. m. on the 23d; amount, 0.45 inch.
	2 p. m.	.47	58	------	Nim. 10	NW. 0	------------	------	24th. Faint aurora at 7 p. m.
	9 p. m.	.41	56	------	Cir. cu. 9	SW. 1	------------	------	
Sept. 16	7 a. m.	.34	53	------	Nim. 10	SW. 0	------------	------	
	2 p. m.	.27	56	------	10	W. 0	------------	------	
	9 p. m.	.23	54	------	Cir. st. 1	W. 0	------------	------	
Sept. 17	7 a. m.	.27	58	------	0	----------	------------	------	
	2 p. m.	.21	70	------	Cir. 8	W. 0	------------	------	
	9 p. m.	.27	59	------	Cir. 7	W. 0	------------	------	
Sept. 18	7 a. m.	.18	66	------	Nim. 10	W. 1	------------	------	
	2 p. m.	.12	72	------	Nim. 10	SW. 0	------------	------	
	9 p. m.	.01	66	------	Nim. 10	SW. 1	------------	------	
Sept. 19	7 a. m.	28.89	68	------	Nim. 10	S. 6	------------	------	
	2 p. m.	.91	70	------	10	SW. 4	------------	------	
	9 p. m.	29.02	58	------	Cir. st. 9	SW. 2	------------	------	
Sept. 20	7 a. m.	.27	52	------	10	E. 4	------------	------	
	2 p. m.	------	------	------	10	NE. 1	------------	------	
	9 p. m.	.26	48	------	Nim. 10	N. 1	------------	------	
Sept. 21	7 a. m.	.20	50	------	Nim. 10	NE. 0	------------	------	
	2 p. m.	.16	58	------	Nim. 10	NE. 3	------------	------	
	9 p. m.	.16	54	------	10	NE. 2	------------	------	
Sept. 22	7 a. m.	.19	56	------	10	SW. 3	------------	------	
	2 p. m.	.23	64	------	10	W. 4	------------	------	
	9 p. m.	.32	56	------	10	W. 4	------------	------	
Sept. 23	7 a. m.	.38	57	------	10	W. 4	------------	------	
	2 p. m.	.40	68	------	10	W. 0	------------	------	
	9 p. m.	.39	65	------	10	W. 0	------------	------	
Sept. 24	7 a. m.	.42	59	------	Cu. st. 10	W. 0	------------	------	
	2 p. m.	.41	62	------	Cu. 10	NW. 0	------------	------	
	9 p. m.	.35	48	------	0	----------	------------	------	

ONTONAGON, MICHIGAN.

Month and day.	Hour.	Barom'r corrected to 32° F.	Thermometer.	Force of vapor.	Cloudiness.	Motion of clouds.	Winds.	Relative humidity.	REMARKS.
Sept. 14	3 p. m.	29.65	48	.189	5	----------	NW. 1	56	18th. Amount of rain, 0.64 inch.
Sept. 15	9 a. m.	29.65	48	.236	9	----------	S. 2	70	
	3 p. m.	29.61	55	.295	9	----------	S. 2	68	
Sept. 16	9 a. m.	29.36	51	.296	9	----------	S. 1	79	
	3 p. m.	------	------	------	------------	----------	------------	------	
Sept. 17	9 a. m.	29.29	56	.363	9	----------	S. 1	81	
	3 p. m.	29.24	65	.420	8	----------	N. 2	68	
Sept. 18	9 a. m.	29.05	61	.442	6	----------	S 1	83	
	3 p. m.	29.03	61	.413	9	----------	N. 1	77	
Sept. 19	9 a. m.	29.47	44	.218	10	----------	NE. 5	76	
	3 p. m.	29.47	49	.247	3	----------	NE. 5	71	
Sept. 20	9 a. m.	29.52	45	.251	2	----------	NE. 1	84	
	3 p. m.	29.53	53	.269	1	----------	NE. 1	67	
Sept. 21	9 a. m.	29.53	41	.257	1	----------	NE. 1	100	
	3 p. m.	29.34	67	.218	1	----------	W. 1	33	
Sept. 22	9 a. m.	29.34	45	.300	3	----------	W. 1	100	
	3 p. m.	29.34	59	.380	1	----------	S. 1	76	
Sept. 23	9 a. m.	29.30	53	.348	7	----------	S. 1	86	
	3 p. m.	29.31	62	.429	1	----------	S. 2	77	
Sept. 24	9 a. m.	29.52	60	.426	1	----------	S. 2	82	
	3 p. m.	29.53	67	.425	2	----------	S. 1	64	

STORMS Nos. 2 AND 3, SEPTEMBER, 1859.

OTSEGO, MICHIGAN.

Month and day.	Hour.	Barom'r corrected to 32° F.	Thermometer.	Force of vapor.	Cloudiness.		Motion of clouds.		Winds.		Relative humidity.
Sept. 14	9 p. m.	------	------	------		6	----------			0	------
Sept. 15	7 a. m.	------	------	------		7	----------		NE.	2	------
	2 p. m.	------	------	------		10	----------		E.	3	------
	9 p. m.	------	------	------		9	----------		SE.	3	------
Sept. 16	7 a. m.	------	------	------		5	----------		E.	2	------
	2 p. m.	------	------	------		9	----------		NE.	2	------
	9 p. m.	------	------	------		5	----------			0	------
Sept. 17	7 a. m.	------	------	------		0	----------		E.	1	------
	2 p. m.	------	------	------		2	----------		S.	2	------
	9 p. m.	------	------	------	----------		----------		E.	1	------
Sept. 18	7 a. m.	------	------	------		3	----------		SE.	2	------
	2 p. m.	------	------	------		4	----------		S.	3	------
	9 p. m.	------	------	------		10	----------		S.	3	------
Sept. 19	7 a. m.	------	------	------		6	----------		S.	3	------
	2 p. m.	------	------	------		8	----------		SW.	2	------
	9 p. m.	------	------	------		7	----------			0	------
Sept. 20	7 a. m.	------	------	------		10	----------		NE.	3	------
	2 p. m.	------	------	------		10	----------		NE.	3	------
	9 p. m.	------	------	------		10	----------		NE.	2	------
Sept. 21	7 a. m.	------	------	------		10	----------		NE.	1	------
	2 p. m.	------	------	------		10	----------		NE.	2	------
	9 p. m.	------	------	------		10	----------			0	------
Sept. 22	7 a. m.	------	------	------		10	----------		SW.	1	------
	2 p. m.	------	------	------		10	----------			0	------
	9 p. m.	------	------	------		10				0	------
Sept. 23	7 a. m.	------	------	------		10				0	------
	2 p. m.	------	------	------		10	----------		SW.	2	------
	9 p. m.	------	------	------		10	----------		SW.	1	------
Sept. 24	7 a. m.	------	------	------		10	----------		NW.	1	------
	2 p. m.	------	------	------		10	----------		N.	1	------
	9 p. m.	------	------	------		5	----------			0	------

REMARKS.

15th. Slight rain at 1 p. m.
18th. Rain from 9. 30 a. m. to 11. 40 a. m.; heavy thunder shower from W. and SW. about 4 p. m.
Rain most of the time from 7½ p. m. the 20th to 4. 30 p. m. on the 21st.
22d and 23d. Sprinkles of rain.

OTTAWA POINT, MICHIGAN.

Month and day.	Hour.	Barom'r corrected to 32° F.	Thermometer.	Force of vapor.	Cloudiness.		Motion of clouds.		Winds.		Relative humidity.
Sept. 14	6 p. m.	29. 57	50	. 162	Cu.	8	NW.	2	NW.	3	45
Sept. 15	6 a. m.	29. 72	39	. 195	Nim.	10	----------		N.	2	82
	9 a. m.	29. 73	46	. 215	Nim.	10	----------		SE.	2	69
	3 p. m.	29. 67	54	. 231	Cir. st.	10	----------		ENE.	1	55
	6 p. m.	29. 64	52	. 232	Cir. st.	10	SW.	5	ESE.	4	60
Sept. 16	6 a. m.	29. 57	51	. 245	Cir. st.	10	SW.	1	E.	2	65
	9 a. m.	29. 55	53	. 244	Cir. cu.	8	----------		NE.	2	60
	3 p. m.	29. 43	62	. 284	Cir. st.	8	W.	2	NE.	3	51
	6 p. m.	29. 39	57	. 322	Cir. st.	5	W.	2	NE.	2	69
Sept. 17	6 a. m.	29. 40	51	. 296	Cir. st.	10	W.	2	N.	2	79
	9 a. m.	29. 40	58	. 394	Cu.	1	----------		NE.	2	82
	3 p. m.	29. 37	66	. 376	Cir.	1	----------		E.	2	59
	6 p. m.	29. 38	62	. 340	Cir. st.	3	----------		E.	2	61
Sept. 18	6 a. m.	29. 38	56	. 363	Cir. st.	6	----------		SSE.	1	81
	9 a. m.	29. 36	63	. 416	Cir.	8	----------		S.	2	72
	3 p. m.	29. 17	68	. 509	Cir. st.	8	S.	1	SSE.	2	75
	6 p. m.	29. 17	68	. 476	Nim.	10	S.	2	SSE.	2	69
Sept. 19	6 a. m.	29. 06	62	. 491	Nim.	10	----------		SE.	1	88
	9 a. m.	29. 01	64	. 497	Cir. st.	9	S.	2	SE.	1	83
	3 p. m.	29. 01	71	. 572	Cir. st.	9	SW.	1	NNE.	2	76
	6 p. m.	29. 12	57	. 407	Nim.	10	----------		NNE.	4	87
Sept. 20	6 a. m.	29. 38	45	. 275	Nim.	10	----------		NNE.	7	92
	9 a. m.	29. 43	45	. 251	Cir. st.	9	NNE.	8	NNE.	8	84
	3 p. m.	29. 42	49	. 247	Cir. st.	9	----------		NNE.	9	71
	6 p. m.	29. 43	49	. 247	Cir. st.	6	SW.	7	NNE.	8	71
Sept. 21	6 a. m.	29. 37	52	. 308	Cu. st.	10	----------		NE.	8	79
	9 a. m.	29. 37	52	. 361	Nim.	10	NE.	8	NE.	7	93
	3 p. m.	29. 30	52	. 361	Nim.	10	----------		NNE.	6	93
	6 p. m.	29. 28	53	. 375	Nim.	10	----------		NNE.	5	93

REMARKS.

15th. Sun rose faint into dark, nimbus clouds; air quite raw; barometer 29. 77 and rising steady. 7. 25 a. m. a perfect calm. 7. 40, light breeze sprung up from SE. 10. 15, wind S. 11. 30 a. m. shower, 7 or 8 miles passing N.; wind S., force 3; barometer stationary at 29. 79; cloudiness 10; velocity 2, ENE.; a few drops of rain falling on the Point. 6. 03 p. m. sun's rays struggling through a narrow line of red; set behind a line of dark stratus; barometer falling; sky covered with a thick, impenetrable cu. st.; sun set in a narrow line of st.; small, red lines above, increasing in width to the N., thus ending a very pleasant day.

16th. No dew; sun rose pale in a narrow line scarcely his own width, into dark stratus.

17th. Light dew; sun rose in a clear line into a belt of stratus; sky covered with thick cir.; wind N. 2, which, at 7. 10 a. m., hauled to NE.; sky gradually cleared up, except a little light

STORMS Nos. 2 AND 3, SEPTEMBER, 1859.

OTTAWA POINT, MICHIGAN—Continued.

Month and day.	Hour.	Barom'r corrected to 32° F.	Thermometer.	Force of vapor.	Cloudiness.	Motion of clouds.	Winds.	Relative humidity.
Sept. 22	6 a. m.	29. 22	54	. 390	Nim. 10	....	NNW. 2	93
	9 a. m.	29. 23	55	. 405	Nim. 10	....	NW. 0	94
	3 p. m.	29. 26	59	. 430	Cu. st. 10	SSW. 2	S. 1	88
	6 p. m.	29. 32	59	. 439	Cu. st. 10	SW. 1	SSW. 1	88
Sept. 23	6 a. m.	29. 42	56	. 420	Cir. st. 10	SW. 1	WSW. 2	94
	9 a. m.	29. 44	57	. 436	Cir. st. 10	SW. 1	SW. 1	94
	3 p. m.	29. 41	60	. 456	Cir. st. 10	SW. 1	SSW. 1	88
	6 p. m.	29. 42	60	. 487	Nim. 10	....	W. 0	94
Sept. 24	6 a. m.	29. 43	56	. 391	Nim. 10	W. 1	NNW. 1	87
	9 a. m.	29. 45	57	. 407	Cir. st. 10	NW. 2	NNW. 1	87
	3 p. m.	29. 43	62	. 491	Nim. 10	....	ENE. 1	88
	6 p. m.	29. 43	59	. 469	10	....	ENE. 1	94

REMARKS.

cir. SE.; sun set behind a wide belt of dark st. 8. 20 p. m. observed one star shoot from 15° SW. of zenith in a straight line S. to the horizon, and in two or three directions.

18th. Light dew; sun came up in a bank of red st., the sky half covered with a white light cir. 3. 15 p. m. a dense fog came down on land and lake; sun disappeared behind a dark mass of cir. st. clouds, but, for the absence of lines on the horizon, the zenith covered over with thick cir.; at sunset fog lifting from the shore and becoming more dense on land. 8. 40 p. m. a moderate rain of 25 minutes duration; barometer 29. 16 and falling; night dark; wind SSE. 2; a heavy sea setting on the shore. 8. 45 p. m. began a general fine rain; wind SE. 1.

19th. Thick, cloudy weather, drizzling rain. 6. 25 a. m. ceased raining; light fog falling round the shore and on the land. 8 a. m spots of blue sky appearing in the W. 9. 05 a. m. fog falling with more density on land and lake. 3. 45 p. m. a heavy shower to 12 miles passing S.; barometer rising slowly, a faint electric detonation from a dark cloud NE.

19th. 4. 27 p. m. a general rain, small drops; wind NNE. and increasing. 7 p. m. blowing a heavy gale. 10. 30 p. m. gale unabated. 12 m. moderating a little, rain fine, but drifting.

20th. A heavy gale NNE.; vane oscillating 2 points; sky thickly covered with nimbus clouds. 9. 30 a. m. a few blue spots NW.; gale increasing; barometer 29. 50 and rising fast; thermometer attached 55°; sun set in a clear, narrow belt on the horizon, below a mass of dark cumuli.

21st. No dew; gale continuing with slight abatement; a fine, misty rain. 8 a. m. mist coming down on land and lake. 9 a. m. rain and mist increasing; clouds driving fast from NE.; barometer and thermometer stationary since 6 a. m. 9. 35, clearing up a little. 2. 50 p. m. wind NNE. 6; misty rain; weather thick; barometer falling. 6 p. m. fair weather; thick and damp mist hanging on the land; a narrow, pale red line on the eastern horizon. 7. 20 p. m. general rain; moderate.

22d. Thick, misty rain; a small, light spot NW. 8. 40 p. m. perfect calm; wind vane NW.; sky covered thick with dark gray nimbus, without motion; barometer 29. 30 and rising; day closed with a light air SSW.

23d. Light air; cloudy morning; wind WSW. 3. 10 p. m. shower, 3 or 4 miles west, going N. 4 p. m. a perfect calm on this point; a shower going N., 5 or 6 miles W.; sky thickly covered with dark cumulus stratus. 6 p. m. drizzling rain; quite calm and cloudy; amount of rain from the 18th to the 25th, 0. 87 inch.

THUNDER BAY ISLAND, MICHIGAN.

Month and day.	Hour.	Barom'r corrected to 32° F.	Thermometer.	Force of vapor.	Cloudiness.	Motion of clouds.	Winds.	Relative humidity.
Sept. 14	6 p. m.	29. 57	42	. 155	St. 3	....	N. 5	58
Sept. 15	6 a. m.	29. 69	44	. 218	Cu. st. 7	NW. 2	S. 2	76
	9 a. m.	29. 74	50	. 234	Cir. cu. 8	S. 2	SE. 4	65
	3 p. m.	29. 67	50. 5	. 246	Cu. 10	S. 2	SE. 5	68
	6 p. m.	29. 64	48	. 260	Cu. st. 10	S. 3	S. 6	78
Sept. 16	6 a. m.	29. 55	49	. 284	Cu. st. 8	SW. 2	SE. 5	81½
	9 a. m.	29. 54	57	. 281	Cir. cu. 5	NW. 2	SE. 5	60
	3 p. m.	29. 43	55	. 269	Cu. 10	SE. 1	SE. 3	62
	6 p. m.	29. 42	52	. 295	Cu. 7	W. 2	E. 2	76
Sept. 17	6 a. m.	29. 38	51	. 321	St. 1	....	NE. 2	86
	9 a. m.	29. 38	56	. 363	0	....	E. 1	81
	3 p. m.	29. 33	63	. 386	Cir. 3	NE. 1	SE. 2	67
	6 p. m.	29. 36	56	. 363	St. 2	....	S. 3	81
Sept. 18	6 a. m.	29. 33	56	. 443	Cir. cu. 8	NW. 1	S. 4	97
	9 a. m.	29. 34	61	. 413	Cir. 7	N. 2	S. 5	77
	3 p. m.	29. 21	62	. 444	Cu. 10	NW. 3	SE. 6	80
	6 p. m.	29. 08	60	. 441	Cu. st. 10	NW. 2	SE. 7	85
Sept. 19	6 a. m.	29. 02	59	. 439	Nim. 10	....	SE. 6	88
	9 a. m.	29. 01	60	. 441	Nim. 10	....	SE. 2	85
	3 p. m.	29. 05	52	. 308	Nim. 10	....	NE. 8	79
	6 p. m.	29. 16	48	. 272	Nim. 10	....	NE. 9	81
Sept. 20	6 a. m.	29. 46	42	. 210	Cu. 7	NE. 4	NE. 7	78
	9 a. m.	29. 49	44	. 218	Cu. 8	E. 5	E. 8	76
	3 p. m.	29. 45	50	. 216	Cir. 6	SE. 2	E. 7	61
	6 p. m.	29. 46	50	. 283	Cir. st. 6	N. 1	E. 6	78

18th. Rain from 4. 30 to 7 p. m.; amount, 0. 17 inch.

19th. Rain from 4. 30 to 11 p. m.; amount, 0. 42 inch.

STORMS Nos. 2 AND 3, SEPTEMBER, 1859.

THUNDER BAY ISLAND, MICHIGAN—Continued.

Month and day.	Hour.	Barom'r corrected to 32° F.	Thermometer.	Force of vapor.	Cloudiness.	Motion of clouds.	Winds.	Relative humidity.	REMARKS.
Sept. 21	6 a. m.	29. 39	49	. 259	Cu. st. 8	SE. 3	E. 7	74	22d. Rain from 1 to 6 a. m.; am't,
	9 a. m.	29. 40	47	. 280	Cu. 8	E. 4	E. 7	88	0. 33 inch.
	3 p. m.	29. 33	52	. 308	Nim. 10	....	E. 6	79	23d. Rain from 9 to 11 a. m.; am't,
	6 p. m.	29. 28	54	. 294	Nim. 10	....	E. 6	70	0. 42 inch.
Sept. 22	6 a. m.	29. 20	52	. 334	Nim. 10	....	E. 7	86	24th. Rain from 2 to 8 a. m ; am't,
	9 a. m.	29. 22	53	. 348	Nim. 10	....	SE. 4	86	0. 07 inch.
	3 p. m.	29. 29	55	. 362	Nim. 10	....	SE. 1	84	
	6 p. m.	29. 31	54	. 362	Nim. 10	....	N. 1	87	
Sept. 23	6 a. m.	29. 39	52	. 334	Nim. 10	....	Calm 0	86	
	9 a. m.	29. 40	54	. 348	Nim. 10	....	Calm 0	83	
	3 p. m.	29. 40	56	. 391	Nim. 10	Fog	E. 2	87	
	6 p. m.	29. 41	53	. 348	Nim. 10	Fog	SE. 1	86	
Sept. 24	6 a. m.	29. 41	54	. 348	Nim. 10	Fog	NE. 3	83	
	9 a. m.	29. 43	55	. 390	Nim. 10	Fog	NE. 4	90	
	3 p. m.	29. 43	56. 5	. 377	Cir. 4	N. 2	N. 3	84	
	6 p. m.	29. 45	56	. 391	Cu. 8	N. 2	N. 3	87	

NEW HARMONY, INDIANA.

Month and day.	Hour.	Barom'r corrected to 32° F.	Thermometer.	Force of vapor.	Cloudiness.	Motion of clouds.	Winds.	Relative humidity.	REMARKS.
Sept. 14	9 p. m.	29. 744	58	. 483	5	....	NW	100	17th. Slight shower at 7 p. m.
Sept. 15	7 a. m.	29. 722	58	. 423	6	....	NE. 2	88	18th. Shower from 2. 30 to 3 p. m.;
	2 p. m.	29. 655	74	. 568	5	....	SE	67	amount, 0. 04 inch. Began to
	9 p. m.	29. 618	70	. 658	10	....	S..........	90	rain again at 6. 30 p. m. and
Sept. 16	7 a. m.	29. 583	62	. 556	2	....	S.	100	ended in the night; amount,
	2 p. m.	29. 500	79	. 691	3	....	NW	69	0. 80 inch.
	9 p. m.	29. 495	70	. 695	5	....	....	95	Rain from 7. 30 p. m. the 20th to
Sept. 17	7 a. m.	29. 591	65	. 583	2	....	....	94	7 a. m. on the 21st; amount,
	2 p. m	29. 559	82	. 773	8	....	....	71	0. 07 inch.
	9 p. m.	29. 562	74	. 758	10	....	....	90	22d. Showery; amount, 0. 01 inch.
Sept. 18	7 a. m.	29. 553	70	. 658	9	....	SE	90	
	2 p. m.	29. 427	86	. 850	6	....	SW. 3	68	
	9 p. m.	29. 372	74	. 680	10	....	....	81	
Sept. 19	7 a. m.	29. 335	67	. 591	10	....	SW.........	89	
	2 p. m.	29. 310	71	. 572	10	....	W	76	
	9 p. m.	29. 331	63	. 510	10	....	....	88	
Sept. 20	7 a. m	29. 389	58	. 452	10	....	W	94	
	2 p. m.	29. 426	62	. 491	10	....	W	88	
	9 p. m.	29. 431	60	. 518	10	....	....	100	
Sept. 21	7 a. m.	29. 452	57	. 466	10	....	NW	100	
	2 p. m.	29. 454	58	. 452	10	....	NW	94	
	9 p. m.	29. 476	56	. 436	10	....	....	94	
Sept. 22	7 a. m.	29. 562	57	. 436	10	....	SE	94	
	2 p. m.	29. 616	63	. 523	10	....	SE	94	
	9 p. m.	29. 646	61	. 537	10	....	....	100	
Sept. 23	7 a. m.	29. 786	60	. 518	10	....	SW.........	100	
	2 p. m.	29. 735	75	. 628	3	....	S...........	73	
	9 p. m.	29. 761	63	. 576	0	....	....	100	
Sept. 24	7 a. m.	29. 774	62	. 523	0	....	S...........	94	
	2 p. m.	29. 780	80	. 677	5	....	NW	66	
	9 p. m.	29. 668	67	. 662	6	....	....	100	

YPSILANTI, MICHIGAN.

Month and day.	Hour.	Barom'r corrected to 32° F.	Thermometer.	Force of vapor.	Cloudiness.	Motion of clouds.	Winds.	Relative humidity.	REMARKS.
Sept. 14	9 p. m.	29. 16	42. 5	. 204	St. 2	0	N. 1	68	
Sept. 15	7 a. m.	29. 25	44	. 218	Cir. cu. 7	W. 1	E. 2	76	
	2 p. m.	29. 22	60	. 255	Cir. cu. 8	SE. 1	SE. 1	53	
	9 p. m.	29. 19	49	. 244	Cir. cu. 9	W. 1	E. 1	60	
Sept. 16	7 a. m.	29. 08	48	. 202	Cir. cu. 4	W. 1	ENE. 2	62	
	2 p. m.	29. 00	70	. 333	Cir. cu. 5	SW. 1	E. 1	50	
	9 p. m.	28. 97	58	. 398	Overcast 10	....	E. 1	74	
Sept. 17	7 a. m.	28. 95	58	. 429	Overcast 10	Foggy	N. 1	91	
	2 p. m.	28. 94	74	. 436	Cu. 5	W. 1	W. 2	57	
	9 p m.	......	......	......	....	....	....	......	

STORMS Nos. 2 AND 3, SEPTEMBER, 1859.

YPSILANTI, MICHIGAN—Continued.

Month and day.	Hour.	Barom'r corrected to 32° F.	Thermometer.	Force of vapor.	Cloudiness.	Motion of clouds.	Winds.	Relative humidity.	REMARKS.
Sept. 18	7 a. m.	29. 01	53	. 362	Overcast 10	Foggy	E. 1	84	18th. Began to rain at 8½ p. m. and ended in the night; amount, 0.35 inch.
	2 p. m.	28. 87	79	. 479	Cir. cu. 5	W. 1	SE. 2	57	Commenced raining at 1 p. m. the 20th and ended at night on the 21st; amount, 0.81 inch.
	9 p. m.	28. 86	61	. 497	Overcast 10		N. 1	83	
Sept. 19	7 a. m.	28. 67	63	. 538	Overcast 10	SE. 1	E. 1	86	
	2 p. m.								
	9 p. m.								
Sept. 20	7 a. m.	28. 89	51	. 334	Overcast 10	NE. 1	NE. 4	89	
	2 p. m.	28. 90	50	. 335	Overcast 10	NE. 3	NE. 3	93	
	8½ p. m.	28. 22	49	. 341	Overcast 10		NE. 3	96	
Sept. 21	7 a. m.								
	2 p. m.	28. 83	54	. 418	Overcast 10	NE. 2	NE. 3	100	
	9 p. m.	28. 87	54	. 405	Overcast 10		NE. 1	94	
Sept. 22	7 a. m.	28. 86	56	. 386	Overcast 10	SW. 4	WSW. 2	81	
	2 p. m.	28. 89	60	. 413	Cu. 10	SW. 1	SSW. 2	77	
	9 p. m.	29. 00	58	. 413	Overcast 10	SW. 1	SW. 1	77	
Sept. 23	7 a. m.	29. 03	60	. 441	Cu. 10	SW. 4	SW. 1	85	
	2 p. m.	29. 03	67	. 500	Cu. 10	SW. 3	SW. 1	81	
	9 p. m.	29. 05	58	. 429	Overcast 10		W. 1	77	
Sept. 24	7 a. m.	29. 02	57	. 407	Cu. 10	NW. 3	NW. 2	87	
	2 p. m.	29. 01	63	. 416	Cu. 9	NW. 3	W. 3	72	
	9 p. m.	29. 02	54. 5	. 407	St. 1		NW. 1	87	

AURORA, INDIANA.

Month and day.	Hour.	Barom'r corrected to 32° F.	Thermometer.	Force of vapor.	Cloudiness.	Motion of clouds.	Winds.	Relative humidity.	REMARKS.
Sept. 14	9 p. m.	29. 62	60				W.		14th and 15th. Variable.
Sept. 15	6 a. m.	29. 66	50				W.		16th. Amount rain, 0.125 inch.
	2 p. m.	29. 61	74						17th and 18th. Clear.
	9 p. m.	29. 60	63						19th. Variable; rain; amount, 0.25 inch.
Sept. 16	6 a. m.	29. 53	54				W.		20th to 24th. Cloudy.
	2 p. m.	29. 52	84						
	9 p. m.	29. 49	67						
Sept. 17	6 a. m.	29. 49	65				W.		
	2 p. m.	29. 50	81						
	9 p. m.	29. 53	72						
Sept. 18	6 a. m.	29. 52	70				SW.		
	2 p. m.	29. 46	90						
	9 p. m.	29. 44	80						
Sept. 19	6 a. m.	29. 30	68				S.		
	2 p. m.	29. 23	82						
	9 p. m.	29. 22	70						
Sept. 20	6 a. m.	29. 26	68				W.		
	2 p. m.	29. 27	64						
	9 p. m.	29. 31	60				N		
Sept. 21	6 a. m.	29. 32	60				N		
	2 p. m.	29. 33	66						
	9 p. m.	29. 36	62				W.		
Sept. 22	6 a. m.	29. 44	60				W.		
	2 p. m.	29. 50	62						
	9 p. m.	29. 52	60						
Sept. 23	6 a. m.	29. 66	60				W.		
	2 p. m.	29. 64	67						
	9 p. m.	29. 65	60						
Sept. 24	6 a. m.	29. 61	62				SW.		
	2 p. m.	29. 54	78						
	9 p. m.	29. 56	60						

CANNELTON, INDIANA.

Month and day.	Hour.	Barom'r corrected to 32° F.	Thermometer.	Force of vapor.	Cloudiness.	Motion of clouds.	Winds.	Relative humidity.	REMARKS.
Sept. 14	9 p. m.	29. 713	59. 2		Cir. cu. 8	SW. 2	SW. 1		
Sept. 15	7 a. m.	29. 707	60. 8		St. 1		SE. 2		
	2 p. m.	29. 624	73. 4		St. 1	SE. 2	SE. 2		
	9 p. m.	29. 588	68. 8		Nim. 9	S. 2	SE. 1		

STORMS Nos. 2 AND 3, SEPTEMBER, 1859.

CANNELTON, INDIANA—Continued.

Month and day.	Hour.	Barom'r corrected to 32° F.	Thermometer.	Force of vapor.	Cloudiness.		Motion of clouds.		Winds.		Relative humidity.	REMARKS.
Sept. 16	7 a. m.	29.556	68	------	Nim.	10	E.	1	E.	1	------	18th. Rain, with violent gale from SW. during the night, began at 9¼ p. m.; amount, 0.48 inch.
	2 p. m.	29.466	79	------	Cu. st.	4	E.	2	SE.	2	------	
	9 p. m.	29.498	67.4	------		0	----------		NW.	1	------	
Sept. 17	7 a. m.	29.598	65	------	Cir.	1	NE.	1	NE.	1	------	
	2 p. m.	29.552	80	------	Cir. st.	8	W.	1	W.	1	------	
	9 p. m.	29.584	68.2	------	Nim.	8	SE.	1	SE.	1	------	
Sept. 18	7 a. m.	29.562	71.5	------	St.	1	----------		SE.	1	------	
	2 p. m.	29.411	86	------	Cu. st.	4	SE.	2	SE.	2	------	
	9 p. m.	29.378	77.7	------	Nim.	1	SW. ------		S.	2	------	
Sept. 19	7 a. m.	29.329	70.5	------	Nim.	9	SW.	4	SW.	2	------	
	2 p. m.	29.302	74.1	------	Cu. st.	8	SW.	4	W.	3	------	
	9 p. m.	29.341	66.1	------	Nim.	10	Lightning -		W.	2	------	
Sept. 20	7 a. m.	29.389	61	------	Nim.	10	NW.	4	NW.	2	------	
	2 p. m.	29.395	63.2	------	Nim.	10	W.	3	W.	2	------	
	9 p. m.	29.408	62	------	Nim.	10	----------		N.	1	------	
Sept. 21	7 a. m.	29.430	58.5	------	Nim.	10	NW.	3	N.	2	------	
	2 p. m.	29.429	62.5	------	Nim.	10	NW.	3	NW.	2	------	
	9 p. m.	29.480	67.2	------	Drizzling	10	----------		NW.	1	------	
Sept. 22	7 a. m.	29.584	60	------	Nim.	10	----------		W.	1	------	
	2 p. m.	29.584	63	------	Nim.	10	SW.	2	SW.	1	------	
	9 p. m.	29.675	59	------	Nim.	10	----------		W.	1	------	
Sept. 23	7 a. m.	29.767	60.5	------	Nim.	10	NW.	2	E.	2	------	
	2 p. m.	29.730	71.2	------	Cu. st.	4	W.	2	W.	2	------	
	9 p. m.	29.748	60.4	------		0	----------		SE.	1	------	
Sept. 24	7 a. m.	29.740	63	------	Cu. st.	4	NW.	2	NW.	1	------	
	2 p. m.	29.623	77.4	------	Cu.	3	W.	3	W.	3	------	
	9 p. m.	29.621	65.3	------	Cu.	2	----------		E.	1	------	

GREENCASTLE, INDIANA.

Month and day.	Hour.	Barom'r corrected to 32° F.	Thermometer.	Force of vapor.	Cloudiness.		Motion of clouds.	Winds.		Relative humidity.	REMARKS.
Sept. 14	9 p. m.	------	------	------		4	----------	E ----------		------	18th. Began to rain at 3 p. m. and ended in the night.
Sept. 15	7 a. m.	------	------	------		3	----------	E.	3	------	19th. Showery p. m.
	2 p. m.	------	------	------		4	----------	E.	3	------	20th. Rainy.
	9 p. m.	------	------	------		3	----------	E.	3	------	
Sept. 16	7 a. m.	------	------	------		2	----------	SE.	1	------	
	2 p. m.	------	------	------		3	----------	S.	2	------	
	9 p. m.	------	------	------		2	----------	S.	1	------	
Sept. 17	7 a. m.	------	------	------		2	----------	N.	2	------	
	2 p. m.	------	------	------		4	----------	N.	3	------	
	9 p. m.	------	------	------		1	----------	----------		------	
Sept. 18	7 a. m.	------	------	------		2	----------	SW.	1	------	
	2 p. m.	------	------	------		5	----------	SW.	2	------	
	9 p. m.	------	------	------		10	----------	SW.	2	------	
Sept. 19	7 a. m.	------	------	------		8	----------	SW.	2	------	
	2 p. m.	------	------	------		11	----------	SW.	2	------	
	9 p. m.	------	------	------		8	----------	SW. ----------		------	
Sept. 20	7 a. m.	------	------	------		9	----------	N.	2	------	
	2 p. m.	------	------	------		10	----------	N.	2	------	
	9 p. m.	------	------	------		10	----------	N.	2	------	
Sept. 21	7 a. m.	------	------	------		10	----------	N.	1	------	
	2 p. m.	------	------	------		10	----------	N.	1	------	
	9 p. m.	------	------	------		10	----------	N.	1	------	
Sept. 22	7 a. m.	------	------	------		10	----------	SW.	2	------	
	2 p. m.	------	------	------		10	----------	SW.	1	------	
	9 p. m.	------	------	------		10	----------	SW.	1	------	
Sept. 23	7 a. m.	------	------	------		10	----------	S.	1	------	
	2 p. m.	------	------	------		6	----------	S.	1	------	
	9 p. m.	------	------	------		2	----------	S.	1	------	
Sept. 24	7 a. m.	------	------	------		3	----------	NW.	1	------	
	2 p. m.	------	------	------		2	----------	NW.	1	------	
	9 p. m.	------	------	------		0	----------	NW.	1	------	

STORMS Nos. 2 AND 3, SEPTEMBER, 1859.

LOGANSPORT, INDIANA.*

Month and day.	Hour.	Barom'r corrected to 32° F.	Thermometer.	Force of vapor.	Cloudiness.	Motion of clouds.	Winds.	Relative humidity.	REMARKS.
Sept. 14	9 p. m.	------	51	------	0	W --------	W. 1	------	18th. Rain from 7.45 to 8.15 a. m.; amount, 0.25 inch.
Sept. 15	7 a. m.	------	57	------	Cir. cu. 10	SW. 2	NE. 2	------	
	2 p. m.	------	53	------	Cir. st. 10	W. 2	NE. 3	------	19th. Rain from 2 a. m.? to 3 p. m.;? amount, 1.10 inch.
	9 p. m.	------	61	------	Cu. 10	SW. 1	E. 1	------	
Sept. 16	7 a. m.	------	55	------	0	W --------	E. 1	------	Rain from 2.50 p. m. the 20th, to 3 a. m. on the 21st, amount, 0.60 inch.
	2 p. m.	------	74	------	0	W --------	SE. 2	------	
	9 p. m.	------	63	------	0	W --------	SE. 1	------	
Sept. 17	7 a. m.	------	55	------	Cu. 9	NW. 2	NW. 2	------	
	2 p. m.	------	77	------	0	W --------	SW. 3	------	
	9 p. m.	------	66	------	St. 10	SE. 1	E. 1	------	
Sept. 18	7 a. m.	------	67	------	Nim. 10	NE. 2	SW. 3	------	
	2 p. m.	------	81	------	Nim. 10	SW. 3	SE. 4	------	
	9 p. m.	------	66	------	St. 10	NE. 2	SW. 2	------	
Sept. 19	7 a. m.	------	70	------	Cu. 10	E. 1	SW. 2	------	
	2 p. m.	------	70	------	Cu. 10	SE. 4	SW. 3	------	
	9 p. m.	------	65	------	St. 10	NW. 2	SW. 1	------	
Sept. 20	7 a. m.	------	61	------	Nim. 10	NE. 1	NE. 1	------	
	2 p. m.	------	67	------	St. 10	SW. 2	NE. 3	------	
	9 p. m.	------	57	------	Nim. 10	SW. 2	NE. 3	------	
Sept. 21	7 a. m.	------	52	------	Nim. 10	SW. 1	NE. 2	------	
	2 p. m.	------	60	------	Nim. 10	SW. 2	NE. 2	------	
	9 p. m.	------	58	------	Nim. 10	SW. 1	NE. 1	------	
Sept. 22	7 a. m.	------	57	------	Nim. 10	NE. 1	SW. 2	------	
	2 p. m.	------	63	------	Nim. 10	E. 1	W. 1	------	
	9 p. m.	------	59	------	Cu. 10	SE. 1	W. 1	------	
Sept. 23	7 a. m.	------	59	------	Cu. 10	SE. 1	SW. 1	------	
	2 p. m.	------	67	------	St. 10	SE. 1	NW. 1	------	
	9 p. m.	------	58	------	0	E. 1	SW. 1	------	
Sept. 24	7 a. m.	------	61	------	Cir. cu. 7	S. 2	NW. 2	------	
	2 p. m.	------	66	------	Cu. 10	SE. 2	NW. 2	------	
	9 p. m.	------	68	------	0	S. 1	W. 1	------	

* Bartlett, observer.

LOGANSPORT, INDIANA.

Month and day.	Hour.	Barom'r corrected to 32° F.	Thermometer.	Force of vapor.	Cloudiness.	Motion of clouds.	Winds.	Relative humidity.	REMARKS.
Sept. 14	9 p. m.	------	------	------	0	----------	WSW. 1	------	14th. Clear at sunrise; light fog clouds at 7 a. m.; thermometer at 2 p. m. 54°, at 9 p. m. 65°.
Sept. 15	7 a. m.	------	------	------	10	----------	NE. 2	------	
	2 p. m.	------	------	------	10	----------	NE. 3	------	
	9 p. m.	------	------	------	0	----------	ESE. 1	------	15th. Cool day.
Sept. 16	7 a. m.	------	------	------	0	----------	E. 1	------	16th. Cool and very pleasant.
	2 p. m.	------	------	------	0	----------	SE. 2	------	17th. Light clouds and fog early; pleasant till 4 p. m., then cloudy.
	9 p. m.	------	------	------	0	----------	ESE. 1	------	
Sept. 17	7 a. m.	------	------	------	9	----------	NW. 2	------	18th. Heavy rain, accompanied by thunder and sharp forked lightning, W. and N. at 6 a. m.
	2 p. m.	------	------	------	0	----------	SW. 3	------	
	9 p. m.	------	------	------	10	----------	E. 1	------	
Sept. 18	7 a. m.	------	------	------	10	----------	SSW. 3	------	3 p. m. Heavy rain, thunder, and sharp lightning from SW.; am't, 0.25 inch.
	2 p. m.	------	------	------	10	----------	SSE. 4	------	
	9 p. m.	------	------	------	10	----------	SSW. 2	------	
Sept. 19	7 a. m.	------	------	------	10	----------	WSW. 2	------	19th. Light showers during the day; amount, 0.60 inch.
	2 p. m.	------	------	------	10	----------	SW 3	------	
	9 p. m.	------	------	------	10	----------	WSW. 2	------	Rain from 2.30 p. m. the 20th, to 3 a. m. on the 21st; amount, 0.60 inch.
Sept. 20	7 a. m.	------	------	------	10	----------	NE. 3	------	
	2 p. m.	------	------	------	10	----------	NNE. 3	------	
	9 p. m.	------	------	------	10	----------	NE. 1	------	21st. Showery.
Sept. 21	7 a. m.	------	------	------	10	----------	NE. 2	------	22d. Light showers from W.; close, misty.
	2 p. m.	------	------	------	10	----------	NNE. 2	------	
	9 p. m.	------	------	------	10	----------	ESE. 1	------	23d. Cloudy and warm; misty; showers from W.; night clear.
Sept. 22	7 a. m.	------	------	------	10	----------	SW. 2	------	
	2 p. m.	------	------	------	10	----------	WSW. 1	------	24th. Warm, and flying clouds.
	9 p. m.	------	------	------	10	----------	WSW. 1	------	
Sept. 23	7 a. m.	------	------	------	10	----------	SW. 1	------	
	2 p. m.	------	------	------	10	----------	WNW. 1	------	
	9 p. m.	------	------	------	0	----------	WNW. 1	------	
Sept. 24	7 a. m.	------	------	------	7	----------	NW. 2	------	
	2 p. m.	------	------	------	10	----------	WSW. 2	------	
	9 p. m.	------	------	------	0	----------	W. 1	------	

STORMS Nos. 2 AND 3, SEPTEMBER, 1859.

MICHIGAN CITY, INDIANA.

Month and day.	Hour.	Barom'r corrected to 32° F.	Thermometer.	Force of vapor.	Cloudiness.	Motion of clouds.	Winds.	Relative humidity.	REMARKS.
Sept. 14	6 p. m.	29.35	60	.338	3	SW. 1	NE. 1	65	Amount of rain on the 19th and 20th, 0.50 inch.
Sept. 15	6 a. m.	29.37	60	.367	2	NE. 1	N. 1	71	23d. Amount, 0.12 inch.
	9 a. m.	29.35	58	.309	2	NE. 1	N. 1	64	
	3 p. m.	29.35	58	.309	0	0	NE. 1	64	
	6 p. m.	29.37	56	.308	0	0	N. 1	69	
Sept. 16	6 a. m.	29.35	58	.309	2	NE. 1	N. 2	64	
	9 a. m.	29.35	56	.308	1	SE. 1	N. 1	69	
	3 p. m.	29.37	58	.309	1	SE. 1	N. 1	64	
	6 p. m.	29.37	56	.336	1	SE. 1	NE. 1	75	
Sept. 17	6 a. m.	29.37	64	.433	2	NE. 1	N. 2	73	
	9 a. m.	29.35	64	.403	0	0	NE. 2	67	
	3 p. m.	29.39	52	.388	0	0	N. 1	100	
	6 p. m.	29.39	62	.429	0	0	N. 1	77	
Sept. 18	6 a. m.	29.43	64	.433	2	E. 1	N. 1	73	
	9 a. m.	29.37	64	.433	2	E. 1	NE. 1	73	
	3 p. m.	29.35	66	.438	2	SE. 1	N. 1	68	
	6 p. m.	29.37	64	.403	2	SW. 1	NE. 1	67	
Sept. 19	6 a. m.	29.35	68	.543	4	E. 2	NW. 1	79	
	9 a. m.	29.37	64	.497	6	SE. 3	NW. 2	83	
	3 p. m.	29.33	65	.483	6	SE. 2	N. 3	78	
	6 p. m.	29.36	62	.429	4	SE. 2	N. 3	77	
Sept. 20	6 a. m.	29.23	56	.336	4	E. 2	N. 4	75	
	9 a. m.	29.27	54	.335	3	SE. 1	NW. 3	80	
	3 p. m.	29.33	56	.336	2	E. 1	N. 2	75	
	6 p. m.	29.27	54	.335	1	SE. 1	N. 2	80	
Sept. 21	6 a. m.	29.25	54	.335	8	SE. 2	N. 3	80	
	9 a. m.	29.24	56	.336	5	SE. 2	E. 2	75	
	3 p. m.	29.27	58	.337	4	SE. 2	NW. 2	70	
	6 p. m.	29.28	58	.309	3	SE. 1	N. 2	64	
Sept. 22	6 a. m.	29.26	54	.335	2	SE. 1	NW. 1	80	
	9 a. m.	29.26	58	.365	3	E. 1	W. 2	76	
	3 p. m.	49.33	60	.396	8	E. 1	SW. 2	76	
	6 p. m.	29.33	58	.394	6	SE. 1	SW. 2	82	
Sept. 23	6 a. m.	29.43	58	.394	8	SE. 2	SE. 1	82	
	9 a. m.	29.45	58	.423	8	SE. 2	SE. 3	88	
	3 p. m.	29.43	64	.464	8	E. 1	W. 1	77	
	6 p. m.	29.45	63	.446	1	SE. 1	NW. 1	77	
Sept. 24	6 a. m.	29.45	58	.394	6	SE. 2	N. 2	82	
	9 a. m.	29.45	58	.394	6	SE. 1	NW. 1	82	
	3 p. m.	29.42	62	.460	6	SE. 1	N. 1	83	
	6 p. m.	29.45	62	.429	2	SE. 1	NE. 1	77	

MISHAWAKA, INDIANA.

Month and day.	Hour.	Barom'r corrected to 32° F.	Thermometer.	Force of vapor.	Cloudiness.	Motion of clouds.	Winds.	Relative humidity.	REMARKS.
Sept. 14	9 p. m.	------	52	------	Cir. st. 6	SW. 2	SW. 2	------	18th. Amount of rain, 3.40 inches.
Sept. 15	7 a. m.	------	51	------	Cir. st. 6	SE. 2	SE. 2	------	20th. Amount of rain, 0.50 inch.
	2 p. m.	------	63	------	Cir. st. 5	SE. 2	SE. 2	------	
	9 p. m.	------	52	------	Cir. st. 8	SE. 2	SE. 2	------	
Sept. 16	7 a. m.	------	57	------	Cir. st. 4	SE. 2	SE. 2	------	
	2 p. m.	------	71	------	Cir. st. 6	SE. 2	SE. 2	------	
	9 p. m.	------	64	------	Cir. st. 7	SE. 2	SE. 2	------	
Sept. 17	7 a. m.	------	54	------	Cir. st. 4	SE. 2	SE. 2	------	
	2 p. m.	------	73	------	Cir. st. 5	SE. 2	SE. 2	------	
	9 p. m.	------	64	------	Cir. st. 4	SE. 2	SE. 2	------	
Sept. 18	7 a. m.	------	53	------	Cir. st. 8	SW. 3	SW. 3	------	
	2 p. m.	------	79	------	Cir. st. 8	SW. 3	SW. 3	------	
	9 p. m.	------	60	------	Cir. st. 10	SE. 2	SE. 2	------	
Sept. 19	7 a. m.	------	60	------	Cir. st. 8	SW. 2	SW. 2	------	
	2 p. m.	------	74	------	Cir. st. 7	SW. 2	SW. 2	------	
	9 p. m.	------	62	------	Cir. st. 3	W. 2	W. 2	------	
Sept. 20	7 a. m.	------	56	------	Cir. st. 10	NE. 3	NE. 3	------	
	2 p. m.	------	54	------	Cir. st. 10	NE. 2	NE. 2	------	
	9 p. m.	------	49	------	Cir. st. 10	NE. 3	NE. 3	------	

STORMS Nos. 2 AND 3, SEPTEMBER, 1859.

MISHAWAKA, INDIANA—Continued.

Month and day.	Hour.	Barom'r corrected to 32° F.	Thermometer.	Force of vapor.	Cloudiness.	Motion of clouds.	Winds.	Relative humidity.	REMARKS.
Sept. 21	7 a. m.	------	52	------	Cir. st. 10	E. 2	E. 2	------	23d. Began to rain at 4 a. m.; am't, 0.75 inch.
	2 p. m.	------	54	------	Cir. st. 10	E. 2	E. 2	------	
	9 p. m.	------	52	------	Cir. st. 10	E. 2	E. 2	------	
Sept. 22	7 a. m.	------	53	------	Cir. st. 10	W. 2	W. 2	------	
	2 p. m.	------	60	------	Cir. st. 10	W. 2	W. 2	------	
	9 p. m.	------	58	------	Cir. st. 10	W. 2	W. 2	------	
Sept. 23	7 a. m.	------	60	------	Nim. 10	W. 2	W. 2	------	
	2 p. m.	------	65	------	Cir. st. 10	W. 2	W. 2	------	
	9 p. m.	------	61	------	Cir. st. 10	W. 2	W. 2	------	
Sept. 24	7 a. m.	------	58	------	Cir. st. 10	W. 2	W. 2	------	
	2 p. m.	------	64	------	Cir. 8	W. 2	W. 2	------	
	9 p. m.	------	60	------	Cir. 6	W. 2	W. 2	------	

NEW ALBANY, INDIANA.

Month and day.	Hour.	Barom'r corrected to 32° F.	Thermometer.	Force of vapor.	Cloudiness.	Motion of clouds.	Winds.	Relative humidity.	REMARKS.
Sept. 14	9 p. m.	------	58	------	Cir. cu. 7	0	Calm ------	------	18th. Distant diffused lightning in the W. and NW. from 7 to 9 p. m.; continued to lighten till 12 p. m., then began to rain; rained heavily till 4 a. m. on the 19th.
Sept. 15	7 a. m.	------	57	------	Cir. cu. 7	W. 1	E. 1	------	20th. Heavy shower from noon to 1½ p. m.; rain from 3½ to 5 p. m.
	2 p. m.	------	75	------	Cir. 4	W. 1	E. 1	------	22d. Shower at 1. 45 p. m.
	9 p. m.	------	66	------	Cir., cir. cu. 9	0	Calm ------	------	
Sept. 16	7 a. m.	------	65	------	Nim. 10	0	E. 1	------	
	2 p. m.	------	80	------	------------	----------	------------	------	
	9 p. m.	------	69	------	St. 1	0	Calm ------	------	
Sept. 17	7 a. m.	------	65	------	Cir. 1	0	SW. 1	------	
	2 p. m.	------	------	------	------------	----------	------------	------	
	9 p. m.	------	67	------	St. 3	0	Calm ------	------	
Sept. 18	7 a. m.	------	65	------	Cir. and st. 4	0	SW. 1	------	
	2 p. m.	------	------	------	------------	----------	------------	------	
	9 p. m.	------	75	------	Cu. and st. 3	0	Calm ------	------	
Sept. 19	7 a. m.	------	68	------	Nim. 10	0	W. 1	------	
	2 p. m.	------	79	------	Cu. 3	0	NW. 2	------	
	9 p. m.	------	66	------	Nim., cu. 9	0	NW. 3	------	
Sept. 20	7 a. m.	------	64	------	Nim. 10	0	W. 1	------	
	2 p. m.	------	70	------	Cir. cu., nim. 7	0	NW. 2	------	
	9 p. m.	------	62	------	Nim. 10	0	NW. 4	------	
Sept. 21	7 a. m.	------	57	------	Nim. 10	0	NE. 2	------	
	2 p. m.	------	------	------	------------	0	------------	------	
	9 p. m.	------	60	------	Nim. 10	0	NW. 1	------	
Sept. 22	7 a. m.	------	58	------	Nim. 10	0	W. 1	------	
	2 p. m.	------	63	------	Nim. 10	0	W. 2	------	
	9 p. m.	------	60	------	8	0	Calm ------	------	
Sept. 23	7 a. m.	------	60	------	St., nim. 10	0	SW. 1	------	
	2 p. m.	------	71	------	Cir. cu. 10	0	SW. 2	------	
	9 p. m.	------	62	------	Nim. 9	0	SW. 2	------	
Sept. 24	7 a. m.	------	65	------	Cir., cir. cu. 3	NW. 1	W. 2	------	
	2 p. m.	------	80	------	Cu. 5	NW. 1	NW. 3	------	
	9 p. m.	------	------	------	------------	----------	------------	------	

RICHMOND, INDIANA.*

Month and day.	Hour.	Barom'r corrected to 32° F.	Thermometer.	Force of vapor.	Cloudiness.	Motion of clouds.	Winds.	Relative humidity.	REMARKS.
Sept. 15	6 a. m.	------	52	------	9	W. 1	NE. 1	------	15th. Showery at night.
	1 p. m.	------	64	------	10	----------	------------	------	16th. Showery a. m.
Sept. 16	6 a. m.	------	58	------	10	SW. 1	NE. 1	------	18th. Cloudy; began to rain at 8 p. m.
	1 p. m.	------	73	------	9	----------	SE. 1	------	
Sept. 17	6 a. m.	------	64	------	Fog 10	----------	N. 1	------	
	1 p. m.	------	72	------	10	N. 2	N. 1	------	
Sept. 18	6 a. m.	------	------	------	------------	----------	------------	------	
	1 p. m.	------	------	------	------------	----------	------------	------	

* Austin, observer.

STORMS Nos. 2 AND 3, SEPTEMBER, 1859.

RICHMOND, INDIANA—Continued.

Month and day.	Hour.	Barom'r corrected to 32° F.	Thermometer.	Force of vapor.	Cloudiness.	Motion of clouds.	Winds.	Relative humidity.	REMARKS.
Sept. 19	6 a. m.	......	70	......	10	SW. 4	SW. 1	......	19th. Showery a. m. and night.
	1 p. m.	......	72	......	10	SW. 1	S. 1	......	20th. Showery a. m.
Sept. 20	6 a. m.	......	63	......	10	NE. 3	SW. 1	......	
	1 p. m.	......	61	......	10	....	N. 1	......	
Sept. 21	6 a. m.	......	55	......	Mist 10	NNE. 1	N. 1	......	
	1 p. m.	......	63	......	10	N	N. 1	......	
Sept. 22	6 a. m.	......	61	......	10	SW. 2	SW. 1	......	
	1 p. m.	......	64	......	10	SW. 2	SW. 1	......	
Sept. 23	6 a. m.	......	62	......	10	S..........	S. 1	......	
	1 p. m.	......	68	......	10	NW. 2	NW. 1	......	
Sept. 24	6 a. m.	......	61	......	4	NW. 2	0	......	
	1 p. m.	......	66	......	10	N. 2	N. 2	......	

RICHMOND, INDIANA.*

Month and day.	Hour.	Barom'r corrected to 32° F.	Thermometer.	Force of vapor.	Cloudiness.	Motion of clouds.	Winds.	Relative humidity.	REMARKS.
Sept. 14	9 p. m.	28.80	64	......	5	....	NE. 1	......	14th. Smoky; cool at 7 a. m.
Sept. 15	7 a. m.	28.90	60	......	7	....	NE. 3	......	16th. Appearances of rain.
	2 p. m.	28.90	67	......	5	....	E. 2	......	17th. Pleasant.
	9 p. m.	28.90	64	......	7	....	NE. 1	......	18th. Bank of thick clouds in W.
Sept. 16	7 a. m.	28.80	60	......	10	....	E. 1	......	at 9 p. m.; rain, accompanied by
	2 p. m.	28.90	75	......	4	....	E. 1	......	thunder and sheet and zigzag
	9 p. m.	28.70	75	......	6	....	E. 1	......	lightning.
Sept. 17	7 a. m.	28.70	66	......	Fog	....	NE. 1	......	19th. Appearances of rain at 2
	2 p. m.	28.70	73	......	3	....	Calm	......	p. m.
	9 p. m.	28.80	70	......	0	....	NW. 1	......	20th. Misty at 2 p. m.
Sept. 18	7 a. m.	28.80	65	......	9	....	NE. 2	......	21st. Mist at 9 a. m.
	2 p. m.	28.70	80	......	5	....	SW. 3	......	22d. Dull, cloudy weather.
	9 p. m.	28.70	75	......	10	....	SW. 4	......	23d and 24th. Same as 22d.
Sept. 19	7 a. m.	28.60	70	......	10	....	SW. 1	......	
	2 p. m.	28.50	73	......	10	....	SW. 2	......	
	9 p. m.	28.50	70	......	7	....	W. 1	......	
Sept. 20	7 a. m.	28.50	65	......	10	....	NE. 2	......	
	2 p. m.	28.60	64	......	10	....	NW. 3	......	
	9 p. m.	28.60	63	......	10	....	SW. 2	......	
Sept. 21	7 a. m.	28.60	63	......	10	....	N. 1	......	
	2 p. m.	28.60	62	......	10	....	NE. 1	......	
	9 p. m.	28.60	61	......	10	....	SE. 1	......	
Sept. 22	7 a. m.	28.70	64	......	9	....	E. 1	......	
	2 p. m.	28.70	64	......	10	....	SE. 1	......	
	9 p. m.	28.80	65	......	10	....	E. 1	......	
Sept. 23	7 a. m.	28.80	63	......	10	....	Calm	......	
	2 p. m.	28.80	66	......	10	....	N. 2	......	
	9 p. m.	28.90	70	......	4	....	Calm	......	
Sept. 24	7 a. m.	28.80	67	......	7	....	E. 1	......	
	2 p. m.	28.80	65	......	10	....	NW. 2	......	
	9 p. m.	28.90	62	......	8	....	NW. 1	......	

* Haines, observer.

SHELBYVILLE, INDIANA.

Month and day.	Hour.	Barom'r corrected to 32° F.	Thermometer.	Force of vapor.	Cloudiness.	Motion of clouds.	Winds.	Relative humidity.	REMARKS.
Sept. 14	9 p. m.	......	......	......	8	....	SE. 1	......	14th. Light frost; cool.
Sept. 15	7 a. m.	......	......	......	9	....	E. 2	......	15th. A. m. quite cool.
	2 p. m.	......	......	......	5	....	E. 3	......	16th. Morning cool; day quite
	9 p. m.	......	......	......	9	....	E. 1	......	warm.
Sept. 16	7 a. m.	......	......	......	9	....	E. 1	......	
	2 p. m.	......	......	......	8	....	E. 1	......	
	9 p. m.	......	......	......	0	....	NE. 1	......	

STORMS Nos. 2 AND 3, SEPTEMBER, 1859.

SHELBYVILLE, INDIANA—Continued.

Month and day.	Hour.	Barom'r corrected to 32° F.	Thermometer.	Force of vapor.	Cloudiness.	Motion of clouds.	Winds.		Relative humidity.	REMARKS.
Sept. 17	7 a. m.	------	------	------	10	----------	NE.	1	------	17th. Very warm.
	2 p. m.	------	------	------	4	----------	S.	2	------	18th. Very warm from 6 to 9 p. m.;
	9 p. m.	------	------	------	5	----------	SW.	1	------	diffused lightning WNW. and N.;
Sept. 18	7 a. m.	------	------	------	8	----------	SE.	1	------	began to rain at 11 p. m.; showery
	2 p. m.	------	------	------	8	----------	SW.	3	------	during the night.
	9 p. m.	------	------	------	9	----------	SW.	1	------	19th. Rain till 5 a. m.
Sept. 19	7 a. m.	------	------	------	9	----------	W.	1	------	20th. Heavy rain from 5 a. m. to
	2 p. m.	------	------	------	4	----------	W.	3	------	0. 30 p. m.
	9 p. m.	------	------	------	9	----------	W.	1	------	21st. Cool.
Sept. 20	7 a. m.	------	------	------	10	----------	SW.	1	------	22d. Cloudy, cool, and unpleasant.
	2 p. m.	------	------	------	10	----------	N.	2	------	23d. Warm.
	9 p. m.	------	------	------	10	----------	N.	1	------	24th. Pleasant.
Sept. 21	7 a. m.	------	------	------	10	----------	N.	2	------	
	2 p. m.	------	------	------	10	----------	N.	1	------	
	9 p. m.	------	------	------	10	----------	N.	1	------	
Sept. 22	7 a. m.	------	------	------	10	----------	W.	1	------	
	2 p. m.	------	------	------	10	----------	W.	1	------	
	9 p. m.	------	------	------	10	----------	W.	1	------	
Sept. 23	7 a. m.	------	------	------	10	----------	SE.	1	------	
	2 p. m.	------	------	------	10	----------	S.	2	------	
	9 p. m.	------	------	------	6	----------	S.	1	------	
Sept. 24	7 a. m.	------	------	------	4	----------	S.	1	------	
	2 p. m.	------	------	------	4	----------	NE.	3	------	
	9 p. m.	------	------	------	6	----------	N.	1	------	

SOUTH BEND, INDIANA.

Month and day.	Hour.	Barom'r corrected to 32° F.	Thermometer.	Force of vapor.	Cloudiness.	Motion of clouds.	Winds.		Relative humidity.	REMARKS.
Sept. 14	9 p. m.	------	------	------	10	----------		0	------	15th. Rain from noon to 1 p. m.
Sept. 15	7 a. m.	------	------	------	10	----------	W.	2	------	18th. Rain from 8 a. m. to 6 p. m.
	2 p. m.	------	------	------	10	----------	SE.	3	------	19th. Dashes of rain from 1 to 6
	9 p. m.	------	------	------	10	----------	E.	2	------	p. m.
Sept. 16	7 a. m.	------	------	------	8	----------	W.	1	------	20th. Showers from 1 to 3 a. m.
	2 p. m.	------	------	------	9	----------	W.	1	------	21st. Misty, rainy, and damp.
	9 p. m.	------	------	------	2	----------		0	------	22d. Constant rain and mist.
Sept. 17	7 a. m.	------	------	------	5	----------	W.	1	------	23d. Rain and mist at short inter-
	2 p. m.	------	------	------	8	----------	W.	1	------	vals.
	9 p. m.	------	------	------	2	----------		0	------	24th. Rain from 2 to 4 p. m.; aurora
Sept. 18	7 a. m.	------	------	------	9	----------	W.	1	------	early in the evening; three per-
	2 p. m.	------	------	------	10	----------	W.	1	------	pendicular columns rising from
	9 p. m.	------	------	------	10	----------	W.	1	------	a low arch of light at the horizon,
Sept. 19	7 a. m.	------	------	------	10	----------	W.	1	------	which disappeared before 11 p. m.
	2 p. m.	------	------	------	8	----------	W.	2	------	
	9 p. m.	------	------	------	8	----------	----------		------	
Sept. 20	7 a. m.	------	------	------	8	----------	E.	1	------	
	2 p. m.	------	------	------	9	----------	E.	2	------	
	9 p. m.	------	------	------	10	----------	E.	1	------	
Sept. 21	7 a. m.	------	------	------	10	----------		0	------	
	2 p. m.	------	------	------	9	----------	SE.	1	------	
	9 p. m.	------	------	------	9	----------		0	------	
Sept. 22	7 a. m.	------	------	------	10	----------		0	------	
	2 p. m.	------	------	------	9	----------	SE.	1	------	
	9 p. m.	------	------	------	10	----------		0	------	
Sept. 23	7 a. m.	------	------	------	9	----------	----------		------	
	2 p. m.	------	------	------	10	----------		0	------	
	9 p. m.	------	------	------	10	----------		0	------	
Sept. 24	7 a. m.	------	------	------	6	----------		0	------	
	2 p. m.	------	------	------	10	----------	SW.	1	------	
	9 p. m.	------	------	------	10	----------		0	------	

STORMS Nos. 2 AND 3, SEPTEMBER, 1859.

AUGUSTA, ILLINOIS.

Month and day.	Hour.	Barom'r corrected to 32° F.	Thermometer.	Force of vapor.	Cloudiness.		Motion of clouds.		Winds.		Relative humidity.
Sept. 14	9 p. m.	......	59	.395	Nim.	10	....		SW.	2	79
Sept. 15	7 a. m.	......	54	.369	Nim.	10	E.	2	E.	2	90
	2 p. m.	......	66	.547	Nim.	10	E.	2	E.	2	79
	9 p. m.	......	62	.466	Nim.	10	....		E.	2	85
Sept. 16	7 a. m.	......	57	.413	Cir. cu.	6	W.	3	NE.	2	90
	2 p. m.	......	75	.566	Cir. cu.	4	W.	2	W.	2	64
	9 p. m.	......	64	.510		0	....		SE.	2	88
Sept. 17	7 a. m.	......	61	.505	Nim.	7	W.	1	SE.	2	94
	2 p. m.	......	69	.714	Cir. cu.	7	NW.	2	SE.	3	97
	9 p. m.	......	67	.573	Nim.	5	....		SE.	3	87
Sept. 18	7 a. m.	......	67	.637	Cir. cu.	9	SW.	3	SW.	3	95
	2 p. m.	......	65	.628	Nim.	10	SW.	2	SE.	1	100
	9 p. m.	......	61	.537	Nim.	10	....			(	100
Sept. 19	7 a. m.	......	57	.443	Nim.	10	W.	3	W.	3	97
	2 p. m.	......	56	.449	Nim.	10	NW.	3	NW.	3	100
	9 p. m.	......	49	.354	Nim.	10	....		NW.	2	100
Sept. 20	7 a. m.	......	45	.270	Nim.	10	NE.	3	NE.	3	92
	2 p. m.	......	51	.348	Nim.	10	NE.	2	NE.	3	93
	9 p. m.	......	50	.341		0	....			0	96
Sept. 21	7 a. m.	......	49	.310	Nim.	9	NE.	2	NE.	2	92
	2 p. m.	......	57	.350	Nim.	9	NE.	2	NE.	3	75
	9 p. m.	......	54	.396	Nim.	10	....		NE.	2	96
Sept. 22	7 a. m.	......	54	.390	Cu. st.	9	....			0	93
	2 p. m.	......	67	.431	Cir. cu.	2	SW.	2	SE.	2	66
	9 p. m.	......	59	.423		0	....			0	88
Sept. 23	7 a. m.	......	53	.369		0	....		SE.	1	90
	2 p. m.	......	65	.407		0	....		E.	1	63
	9 p. m.	......	65	.527		0	....			0	91
Sept. 24	7 a. m.	......	57	.428		0	....			0	94
	2 p. m.	......	77	.704	Cir. cu.	1	S.	2	S.	2	73
	9 p. m.	......	66	.513		0	....			0	86

REMARKS.

15th. Rain from 1 to 3 a. m.; amt., 0.145 inch.

17th. Rain from 8 to 11.50 a. m.; amount, 0 995 inch.

18th. Rain from 4½ to 6 a. m., 8.20 to 11 a. m., 1.15 to 9 p. m.; amount, 0 893 inch.

19th. Rain from 8.40 a. m. to 10½ p. m.; amount, 0.275 inch.

AURORA, ILLINOIS.

Month and day.	Hour.	Barom'r corrected to 32° F.	Thermometer.	Force of vapor.	Cloudiness.		Motion of clouds.		Winds.		Relative humidity.
Sept. 14	9 p. m.	......	51	......	Cir. st.	9	NW.	2	NE.	4	......
Sept. 15	7 a. m.	......	54	......	Cir. st.	10	W.	2	E.	2	......
	2 p. m.	......	63	......	Cir. st.	10	W.	2	E.	4	......
	9 p. m.	......	55	......	Cir. st.	10	SW.	3	SE.	4	......
Sept. 16	7 a. m.	......	55	......	Cir.	10	SE.	2	E.	2	......
	2 p. m.	......	69	......	Cir. st.	9	W.	2	NE.	3	......
	9 p. m.	......	52	......		0	....		NE.	2	......
Sept. 17	7 a. m.	......	51	......		0	....		E.	1	......
	2 p. m.	......	76	......	Cir.	8	W.	2	S.	3	......
	9 p. m.	......	63	......	Cir. st.	7	SW.	4	S.	3	......
Sept. 18	7 a. m.	......	65	......	Cu. st.	8	SW.	3	SW.	3	......
	2 p. m.	......	74	......	Cir.	6	SW.	4	S.	4	......
	9 p. m.	......	67	......	Cir. st.	7	SW.	4	S.	6	......
Sept. 19	7 a. m.	......	61	......	Nim.	10	SW.	3	SW.	3	......
	2 p. m.	......	61	......	Nim.	10	SW.	3	N.	4	......
	9 p. m.	......	48	......	Nim.	10	....		N.	5	......
Sept. 20	7 a. m.	......	51	......	Nim.	10	....		NE.	6	......
	2 p. m.	......	49	......	Nim.	10	....		NE.	5	......
	9 p. m.	......	49	......	Cir. st.	4	NE.	3	N.	5	......
Sept. 21	7 a. m.	......	50	......	Misty	10	....		NE.	4	......
	2 p. m.	......	54	......	Misty	10	....		NE.	4	......
	9 p. m.	......	51	......	St.	10	....		N.	3	......
Sept. 22	7 a. m.	......	53	......	Misty	10	....		NW.	3	......
	2 p. m.	......	58	......	Nim.	10	W.	3	W.	3	......
	9 p. m.	......	57	......	St.	10	....		W.	1	......
Sept. 23	7 a. m.	......	58	......	Cir. st.	9	NW.	1	SE.	1	......
	2 p. m.	......	66	......	Cir. st.	6	NW.	4	SW.	2	......
	9 p. m.	......	60	......	Cir. cu.	9	NW.	4	W.	1	......
Sept. 24	7 a. m.	......	55	......		0	....		NE.	2	......
	2 p. m.	......	72	......	Cu.	1	N.	3	NE.	1	......
	9 p. m.	......	57	......		0	....		SE.	2	......

REMARKS.

16th. Bright meteor at 8½ p. m.; that portion of its path observed was about 20° in length, descending from towards the zenith, to within about 30° of the southern horizon; it had a bright blue color, and appeared to have a sort of tumbling or unsteady motion at the termination of its course.

18th. Rain from 10.30 a. m. to 1 p. m.; amount, 0.34 inch.

19th. Rain from 7 a. m. to 9 p. m.; amount, 1.48 inch.

20th. Misty a portion of the day.

21st. Misty all day; amount, 0.03 inch.

22d. Light showers till 3 p. m.; amount, 0.06 inch.

24th. Aurora, as a bright twilight.

STORMS Nos. 2 AND 3, SEPTEMBER, 1859.

BATAVIA, ILLINOIS.

Month and day.	Hour.	Barom'r corrected to 32° F.	Thermometer.	Force of vapor.	Cloudiness.	Motion of clouds.	Winds.	Relative humidity.	REMARKS.
Sept. 14	9 p. m.	29.300	50	.283	Cu. st. 9	SW. 1	NE. 7	78	18th. Storm commenced in the night and ended at 6 a. m. on the 23d ; amount, 1 93 inch.
Sept. 15	7 a. m.	29.324	50	.309	9	W. 1	ESE. 1	85	22d. Heat lightning in the east.
	2 p. m.	29.289	64	.359	Cir. st. 10	W. 3	ESE. 3	58	
	9 p. m.	29.246	56	.308	10	WNW. 1	SW. 1	69	
Sept. 16	7 a. m.	29.206	52	.308	Cu. st. 10	SW. 1	NE. 1	79	
	2 p. m.	29.146	76	.577	Cir. cu. 5	SW. 1	NE. 1	64	
	9 p. m.	29.118	51	.348	0	----------	NE. 1	93	
Sept. 17	7 a. m.	29.109	49	.322	St. 1	NE. 1	NE. 1	92	
	2 p. m.	29.112	84	.623	Cir. st. 2	SE. 1	SE. 1	53	
	9 p. m.	29.088	66	.570	Cir. st. 2	SE. 1	SE. 1	89	
Sept. 18	7 a. m.	28.991	71	.631	Cu. st. 9	SW. 1	SW. 1	81	
	2 p. m.	28.932	78	.758	Cu. st. 10	SW. 1	SW. 1	74	
	9 p. m.	28.892	69	.635	St. 9	SW. 1	SW. 2	90	
Sept. 19	7 a. m.	28.722	62	.556	St. 10	SW. 1	SW. 2	100	
	2 p. m.	28.845	52	.388	St. 10	NE. 3	NE. 3	100	
	9 p. m.	28.930	49	.322	St. 10	NE. 2	NE. 2	92	
Sept. 20	7 a. m.	29.032	52	.361	St. 10	NE. 2	NE. 2	93	
	2 p. m.	29.095	50	.335	St. 10	NE. 2	NE. 2	93	
	9 p. m.	29.103	51	.321	St. 10	NE. 2	NE. 2	86	
Sept. 21	7 a. m.	29.073	50	.361	St. 10	NE. 1	NE. 1	100	
	2 p. m.	29.047	54	.405	St. 10	NE. 1	NE. 1	94	
	9 p. m.	29.050	52	.388	St. 10	NE. 1	NE. 1	100	
Sept. 22	7 a. m.	29.055	53	.403	St. 10	NW. 1	NE. 1	100	
	2 p. m.	29.070	58	.469	St. 10	NW. 1	NW. 1	94	
	9 p. m.	29.158	58	.423	St. 10	NW. 1	NW. 1	88	
Sept. 23	7 a. m.	29.198	60	.518	Cu. st. 10	NW. 1	NW. 1	100	
	2 p. m.	29.185	68	.543	Cu. st. 10	WNW. 1	NW. 1	79	
	9 p. m.	29.188	60	.491	St. 10	SE. 1	NE. 1	88	
Sept. 24	7 a. m.	29.223	52	.375	0	----------	NE. 1	93	
	2 p. m.	29.170	79	.612	0	----------	ESE. 1	62	
	9 p. m.	29.173	56	.420	0	----------	NE. 1	94	

BLOOMINGTON, ILLINOIS.

Month and day.	Hour.	Barom'r corrected to 32° F.	Thermometer.	Force of vapor.	Cloudiness.	Motion of clouds.	Winds.	Relative humidity.	REMARKS.
Sept. 14	9 p. m.	------	------	------	10	----------	E. 2	------	14th. Cool, foggy morning; and warm day.
Sept. 15	7 a. m.	------	------	------	10	----------	----------	------	
	2 p. m.	------	------	------	8	----------	E. 2	------	18th. Rain at 7 p. m.
	9 p. m.	------	------	------	10	----------	S. 2	------	19th. Gentle rain.
Sept. 16	7 a. m.	------	------	------	5	----------	----------	------	20th. Rain from 5 to 9 a. m., p. m. windy.
	2 p. m.	------	------	------	4	----------	----------	------	
	9 p. m.	------	------	------	----------	----------	SE. 2	------	21st. Some rain, misty all day.
Sept. 17	7 a. m.	------	------	------	0	----------	----------	------	22d. Cloudy.
	2 p. m.	------	------	------	10	----------	----------	------	23d. Fair weather.
	9 p. m.	------	------	------	10	----------	----------	------	
Sept. 18	7 a. m.	------	------	------	4	----------	SW. 2	------	
	2 p. m.	------	------	------	8	----------	SW. 2	------	
	9 p. m.	------	------	------	10	----------	----------	------	
Sept. 19	7 a. m.	------	------	------	10	----------	SW. 2	------	
	2 p. m.	------	------	------	10	----------	SW. 3	------	
	9 p. m.	------	------	------	10	----------	W. 4	------	
Sept. 20	7 a. m.	------	------	------	10	----------	NE. 4	------	
	2 p. m.	------	------	------	10	----------	N. 3	------	
	9 p. m.	------	------	------	10	----------	E. 3	------	
Sept. 21	7 a. m.	------	------	------	10	----------	N. 1	------	
	2 p. m.	------	------	------	9	----------	N. 1	------	
	9 p. m.	------	------	------	10	----------	E. 2	------	
Sept. 22	7 a. m.	------	------	------	10	----------	----------	------	
	2 p. m.	------	------	------	10	----------	E. 1	------	
	9 p. m.	------	------	------	10	----------	----------	------	
Sept. 23	7 a. m.	------	------	------	8	----------	----------	------	
	2 p. m.	------	------	------	3	----------	----------	------	
	9 p. m.	------	------	------	2	----------	----------	------	
Sept. 24	7 a. m.	------	------	------	2	----------	NW. 1	------	
	2 p. m.	------	------	------	2	----------	----------	------	
	9 p. m.	------	------	------	----------	----------	S. 2	------	

STORMS Nos. 2 AND 3, SEPTEMBER, 1859.

CARBON CLIFF, ILLINOIS.

Month and day.	Hour.	Barom'r corrected to 32° F.	Thermometer.	Force of vapor.	Cloudiness.	Motion of clouds.	Winds.		Relative humidity.	REMARKS.
Sept. 14	9 p. m.				5		W.	2		14th. Cool, clouds thick, a. m.; appearance of rain, clouds thin, at noon. 15th. Pleasant but cool; clouds thin. 16th. Cool a. m.; air moist and warm at noon; clouds like rain p. m. 17th. Warm. rain; the heaviest showers at 6 and 7.15 a. m. and 4 and 7 p. m. 18th. Rainy, dark, and cold; some thunder and a few flashes of lightning accompanied the rain; heaviest showers at 6, 7, and 11 a. m., 12 m., and 6 and 10 p. m. 19th. Rain from 3 a. m. to 10 p. m., with the exception of a few brief intervals. 20th. Appeared like rain all day; clouds dark and heavy; cool. 21st. Slight fall of snowy hail at 10 a. m. 22d. Cloudy all day, though not heavy, some warmer. 23d. Clouds in broken masses; fog in the valley; warm and pleasant. 24th. Fog in the valley; quite warm; clouds in rolling masses.
Sept. 15	7 a. m.				4		W.	2		
	2 p. m.				3		W.	3		
	9 p. m.				3		W.	2		
Sept. 16	7 a. m.				4		E.	2		
	2 p. m.				4		E.	3		
	9 p. m.				8		E.	2		
Sept. 17	7 a. m.				10		E.	3		
	2 p. m.				10		E.	4		
	9 p. m.				10		SE.	2		
Sept. 18	7 a. m.				10		W.	2		
	2 p. m.				10		W.	3		
	9 p. m.				10		W.	2		
Sept. 19	7 a. m.				10		W.	4		
	2 p. m.				10		W.	3		
	9 p. m.				10		NW.	2		
Sept. 20	7 a. m.				10		NE.	2		
	2 p. m.				10		NE.	3		
	9 p. m.				10		E.	2		
Sept. 21	7 a. m.				10		N.	1		
	2 p. m.				10		E.	2		
	9 p. m.				10		E.	2		
Sept. 22	7 a. m.				8		E.	2		
	2 p. m.				10		E.	2		
	9 p. m.				10		SE.	2		
Sept. 23	7 a. m.				2		N.	1		
	2 p. m.				4		W.	2		
	9 p. m.				1		E.	2		
Sept. 24	7 a. m.				3		E.	2		
	2 p. m.				4		SW.	2		
	9 p. m.				4		SE.	2		

CARTHAGE, ILLINOIS.

Month and day.	Hour.	Barom'r corrected to 32° F.	Thermometer.	Force of vapor.	Cloudiness.	Motion of clouds.	Winds.	Relative humidity.
Sept. 14	9 p. m.		60					
Sept. 15	7 a. m.		54		10			
	2 p. m.		70		4			
	9 p. m.		63		5			
Sept. 16	7 a. m.		60					
	2 p. m.		79					
	9 p. m.		66					
Sept. 17	7 a. m.		58		10			
	2 p. m.		65		10			
	9 p. m.		68		5			
Sept. 18	7 a. m.		70		9			
	2 p. m.		68		10			
	9 p. m.		62		10			
Sept. 19	7 a. m.		68		10			
	2 p. m.		57		10			
	9 p. m.		50		10			
Sept. 20	7 a. m.		46					
	2 p. m.		52		5			
	9 p. m.		50					
Sept. 21	7 a. m.		47		4			
	2 p. m.		59		8			
	9 p. m.		56		5			
Sept. 22	7 a. m.		56					
	2 p. m.		72					
	9 p. m.		60		5			
Sept. 23	7 a. m.		58		4			
	2 p. m.		82					
	9 p. m.		70		6			
Sept. 24	7 a. m.		66					
	2 p. m.		85					
	9 p. m.		71					

STORMS Nos. 2 AND 3, SEPTEMBER, 1859.

CLEAVERVILLE, ILLINOIS.

Month and day.	Hour.	Barom'r corrected to 32° F.	Thermometer.	Force of vapor.	Cloudiness.	Motion of clouds.	Winds.		Relative humidity.	REMARKS.
Sept. 14	9 p. m.	------	------	------	4	----------	SE.	4	------	18th. Rain from 11.45 a. m. to 2 p. m.
Sept. 15	7 a. m.	------	------	------	5	----------	SE.	1	------	19th. Rain at 9 a. m.
	2 p. m.	------	------	------	5	----------	SE.	2	------	
	9 p. m.	------	------	------	5	----------	SE.	1	------	
Sept. 16	7 a. m.	------	------	------	10	----------	SE.	1	------	
	2 p. m.	------	------	------	5	----------	SE.	2	------	
	9 p. m.	------	------	------	0	----------	SE.	1	------	
Sept. 17	7 a. m.	------	------	------	0	----------	W.	1	------	
	2 p. m.	------	------	------	3	----------	SW.	1	------	
	9 p. m.	------	------	------	4	----------	SW.	1	------	
Sept. 18	7 a. m.	------	------	------	6	----------	SW.	3	------	
	2 p. m.	------	------	------	10	----------	SE.	5	------	
	9 p. m.	------	------	------	10	----------	SE.	2	------	
Sept. 19	7 a. m.	------	------	------	5	----------	SW.	2	------	
	2 p. m.	------	------	------	10	----------	NE.	4	------	
	9 p. m.	------	------	------	10	----------	NE.	5	------	
Sept. 20	7 a. m.	------	------	------	10	----------	NE.	5	------	
	2 p. m.	------	------	------	10	----------	NE.	4	------	
	9 p. m.	------	------	------	10	----------	NE.	4	------	
Sept. 21	7 a. m.	------	------	------	10	----------	NE.	3	------	
	2 p. m.	------	------	------	10	----------	NE.	3	------	
	9 p. m.	------	------	------	10	----------	NE.	1	------	
Sept. 22	7 a. m.	------	------	------	10	----------	NW.	1	------	
	2 p. m.	------	------	------	10	----------	NW.	1	------	
	9 p. m.	------	------	------	10	----------	NW.	1	------	
Sept. 23	7 a. m.	------	------	------	10	----------	SW.	1	------	
	2 p. m.	------	------	------	10	----------	SW.	1	------	
	9 p. m.	------	------	------	10	----------	SW.	1	------	
Sept. 24	7 a. m.	------	------	------	0	----------	W.	1	------	
	2 p. m.	------	------	------	0	----------	NE.	1	------	
	9 p. m.	------	------	------	3	----------	NE.	1	------	

DIXON, ILLINOIS.

Month and day.	Hour.	Barom'r corrected to 32° F.	Thermometer.	Force of vapor.	Cloudiness.	Motion of clouds.	Winds.		Relative humidity.	REMARKS.
Sept. 14	9 p. m.	------	------	------	4	----------	NE.	1	------	15th. Sprinkle of rain at 8 a. m.
Sept. 15	7 a. m.	------	------	------	8	----------	SE.	1	------	18th. Thunder in NW. at 7 a. m.; rain at intervals all day.
	2 p. m.	------	------	------	6	----------	SE.	1	------	19th. Rain at intervals till 5.30 p. m.; very cold p. m.
	9 p. m.	------	------	------	4	----------	SE.	1	------	22d. Rain from 6 to 7 a. m.
Sept. 16	7 a. m.	------	------	------	8	----------	SE.	1	------	
	2 p. m.	------	------	------	8	----------	SE.	1	------	
	9 p. m.	------	------	------	4	----------	SE.	1	------	
Sept. 17	7 a. m.	------	------	------	4	----------	SE.	1	------	
	2 p. m.	------	------	------	8	----------	SE.	1	------	
	9 p. m.	------	------	------	8	----------	SE.	4	------	
Sept. 18	7 a. m.	------	------	------	10	----------	SW.	1	------	
	2 p. m.	------	------	------	10	----------	SW.	1	------	
	9 p. m.	------	------	------	10	----------	SW.	1	------	
Sept. 19	7 a. m.	------	------	------	10	----------	SE.	1	------	
	2 p. m.	------	------	------	10	----------	NE.	5	------	
	9 p. m.	------	------	------	10	----------	N.	5	------	
Sept. 20	7 a. m.	------	------	------	10	----------	N.	1	------	
	2 p. m.	------	------	------	5	----------	N.	1	------	
	9 p. m.	------	------	------	8	----------	N.	1	------	
Sept. 21	7 a. m.	------	------	------	8	----------	N.	1	------	
	2 p. m.	------	------	------	8	----------	NE.	1	------	
	9 p. m.	------	------	------	10	----------	NE.	1	------	
Sept. 22	7 a. m.	------	------	------	10	----------	NE.	1	------	
	2 p. m.	------	------	------	8	----------	NE.	1	------	
	9 p. m.	------	------	------	8	----------	NE.	1	------	
Sept. 23	7 a. m.	------	------	------	8	----------	E.	1	------	
	2 p. m.	------	------	------	6	----------	SE.	1	------	
	9 p. m.	------	------	------	6	----------	SE.	1	------	
Sept. 24	7 a. m.	------	------	------	8	----------	SE.	1	------	
	2 p. m.	------	------	------	2	----------	S.	1	------	
	9 p. m.	------	------	------	0	----------	S.	1	------	

STORMS Nos. 2 AND 3, SEPTEMBER, 1859.

EDGINGTON, ILLINOIS.

Month and day.	Hour.	Barom'r corrected to 32° F.	Thermometer.	Force of vapor.	Cloudiness.	Motion of clouds.	Winds.	Relative humidity.	REMARKS.
Sept. 14	9 p. m.	......	58	......	Cir. 10	E. 2	E. 2	......	15th and 16th. Rain.
Sept. 15	7 a. m.	......	54	......	Cir. 10	E. 1	E. 1	......	Drizzling rain on the 17th, 18th, and 19th; amount, 1. 20 inch.
	2 p. m.	......	62	......	Cir. 10	E. 1	E. 1	......	
	9 p. m.	......	58	......	Cir. 10	E. 1	E. 1	......	
Sept. 16	7 a. m.	......	54	......	Cir. 10	E. 1	E. 1	......	
	2 p. m.	......	77	......	Cir. 10	SE. 3	SE. 3	......	
	9 p. m.	......	61	......	Cir. 5	SW. 2	SE. 2	......	
Sept. 17	7 a. m.	......	60	......	Cir. st. 10	SW. 2	SW. 2	......	
	2 p. m.	......	72	......	Cir. st. 10	SW. 2	SW. 2	......	
	9 p. m.	......	66	......	Cir. 10	SW. 1	SW. 1	......	
Sept. 18	7 a. m.	......	66	......	St. 10	SW. 3	SW. 3	......	
	2 p. m.	......	73	......	Cir. st. 10	SW. 3	SW. 3	......	
	9 p. m.	......	67	......	Nim. 10	SW. 3	SW. 3	......	
Sept. 19	7 a. m.	......	60	......	Nim. 10	SW. 2	SW. 3	......	
	2 p. m.	......	56	......	Cir. st. 10	W. 3	W. 3	......	
	9 p. m.	......	50	......	Cir. st. 10	NW. 3	NW. 3	......	
Sept. 20	7 a. m.	......	44	......	Cir. 10	N. 3	N. 3	......	
	2 p. m.	......	52	......	Cir. st. 10	N. 3	N. 3	......	
	9 p. m.	......	52	......	Cir. st. 3	N. 3	N. 3	......	
Sept. 21	7 a. m.	......	42	......	Cir. st. 2	NE. 3	NE. 3	......	
	2 p. m.	......	55	......	Cir. st. 10	NE. 3	NE. 3	......	
	9 p. m.	......	56	......	Cir. st. 8	NE. 2	NE. 2	......	
Sept. 22	7 a. m.	......	55	......	Cir. st. 6	SW. 1	SW. 1	......	
	2 p. m.	......	69	......	Cir. cu. 9	SW. 1	SW. 1	......	
	9 p. m.	......	62	......	Cir. st. 9	SW. 1	SW. 1	......	
Sept. 23	7 a. m.	......	54	......	Cir. cu. 1	SW. 1	SW. 1	......	
	2 p. m.	......	82	......	Cir. cu. 1	SW. 1	SW. 1	......	
	9 p. m.	......	67	......	Cir. 7	SW. 1	SW. 1	......	
Sept. 24	7 a. m.	......	69	......	Cir. 1	SW. 1	SW. 1	......	
	2 p. m.	......	87	......	Cir. cu. 2	SW. 2	SW. 2	......	
	9 p. m.	......	69	......	Cir. 1	SW. 1	SE. 2	......	

ELGIN, ILLINOIS.

Month and day.	Hour.	Barom'r corrected to 32° F.	Thermometer.	Force of vapor.	Cloudiness.	Motion of clouds.	Winds.	Relative humidity.	REMARKS.
Sept. 14	9 p. m.	......	44	......	5	....	NE. 1	......	15th. Rain from 10. 30 a. m. till noon; amount, 0. 01 inch.
Sept. 15	7 a. m.	......	48	......	10	....	SE. 2	......	
	2 p. m.	......	68	......	10	....	SW. 1	......	18th. Rain from 4 a. m. to 2 p. m.; amount, 0. 48 inch.
	9 p. m.	......	46	......	5	....	0	......	
Sept. 16	7 a. m.	......	47	......	Fog 10	....	SE. 1	......	19th. Began to rain at 3 a. m.; ended ?; amount, 1. 125 inch.
	2 p. m.	......	75	......	3	....	SW. 2	......	
	9 p. m.	......	48	......	0	....	SW. 2	......	22d. Amount, 0. 03 inch.
Sept. 17	7 a. m.	......	50	......	5	....	SE. 1	......	
	2 p. m.	......	74	......	4	....	SW. 2	......	
	9 p. m.	......	61	......	5	....	E. 1	......	
Sept. 18	7 a. m.	......	66	......	Nim. 10	....	SE. 1	......	
	2 p. m.	......	74	......	Cir. st. 8	....	S. 2	......	
	9 p. m.	......	68	......	Cir. 10	....	S. 2	......	
Sept. 19	7 a. m.	......	61	......	Nim. 10	....	S. 2	......	
	2 p. m.	......	52	......	Nim. 10	....	NE. 3	......	
	9 p. m.	......	47	......	Nim. 10	....	NE. 4	......	
Sept. 20	7 a. m.	......	50	......	Nim. 10	....	NE. 3	......	
	2 p. m.	......	48	......	Mist 10	....	NE. 3	......	
	9 p. m.	......	49	......	Cu. 9	....	NE. 3	......	
Sept. 21	7 a. m.	......	49	......	Mist 10	....	NE. 3	......	
	2 p. m.	......	53	......	St. 10	....	NE. 2	......	
	9 p. m.	......	51	......	St. 10	....	N. 2	......	
Sept. 22	7 a. m.	......	52	......	Mist 10	....	N. 1	......	
	2 p. m.	......	58	......	Mist 10	....	SW. 1	......	
	9 p. m.	......	56	......	Mist 10	....	S. 1	......	
Sept. 23	7 a. m.	......	56	......	Mist 10	....	SE. 1	......	
	2 p. m.	......	67	......	Mist 10	....	SW. 2	......	
	9 p. m.	......	60	......	Cu. st. 10	....	E. 1	......	
Sept. 24	7 a. m.	......	49	......	Fog 10	....	N. 1	......	
	2 p. m.	......	74	......	Cu. 1	....	NE. 2	......	
	9 p. m.	....	55	......	Cu. 1	....	0	......	

STORMS Nos. 2 AND 3, SEPTEMBER, 1859.

GALENA, ILLINOIS.

Month and day.	Hour.	Barom'r corrected to 32° F.	Thermometer.	Force of vapor.	Cloudiness.	Motion of clouds.	Winds.	Relative humidity.	REMARKS.
Sept. 14	9 p. m.	------	------	------	------------	----------	------------	------	
Sept. 15	7 a. m.	------	------	------	Nim. 10	----------	------------	------	
	2 p. m.	------	------	------	Nim. 10	----------	------------	------	
	9 p. m.	------	------	------	Nim. 10	----------	------------	------	
Sept. 16	7 a. m.	------	------	------	------------	----------	------------	------	
	2 p. m.	------	------	------	Cu. 5	----------	------------	------	
	9 p. m.	------	------	------	0	----------	------------	------	
Sept. 17	7 a. m.	------	------	------	0	----------	------------	------	
	2 p. m.	------	------	------	Nim. 10	----------	NE. 3	------	
	9 p. m.	------	------	------	Nim. 10	----------	NE. 3	------	
Sept. 18	7 a. m.	------	------	------	Nim. 10	----------	NE. 3	------	
	2 p. m.	------	------	------	Nim. 10	----------	NE. 3	------	
	9 p. m.	------	------	------	Nim. 10	----------	NE ---- ----	------	
Sept. 19	7 a. m.	------	------	------	Nim. 10	----------	------------	------	
	2 p. m.	------	------	------	0	----------	------------	------	
	9 p. m.	------	------	------	0	----------	------------	------	
Sept. 20	7 a. m.	------	------	------	Nim. 10	----------	------------	------	
	2 p. m.	------	------	------	Nim. 10	----------	------------	------	
	9 p. m.	------	------	------	Nim. 10	----------	------------	------	
Sept. 21	7 a. m.	------	------	------	Nim. 10	----------	------------	------	
	2 p. m.	------	------	------	------------	----------	------------	------	
	9 p. m.	------	------	------	------------	----------	------------	------	
Sept. 22	7 a. m.	------	------	------	------------	----------	------------	------	
	2 p. m.	------	------	------	------------	----------	------------	------	
	9 p. m.	------	------	------	------------	----------	------------	------	
Sept. 23	7 a. m.	------	------	------	------------	----------	------------	------	
	2 p. m.	------	------	------	------------	----------	------------	------	
	9 p. m.	------	------	------	------------	----------	------------	------	
Sept. 24	7 a. m.	------	------	------	------------	----------	------------	------	
	2 p. m.	------	------	------	------------	----------	------------	------	
	9 p. m.	------	------	------	------------	----------	------------	------	

MANCHESTER, ILLINOIS.

Month and day.	Hour.	Barom'r corrected to 32° F.	Thermometer.	Force of vapor.	Cloudiness.	Motion of clouds.	Winds.	Relative humidity.	REMARKS.
Sept. 14	9 p. m.	28.92	58	.423	St. 4	SW -- ----	SE. 1	88	17th. Distant thunder all the morning in the W.; rain from 11 a. m. to 3 p. m; amount, 0.59 inch.
Sept. 15	7 a. m.	28.93	58	.483	Cir. cu. 4	W--------	SE. 1	100	
	1 p. m.	28.86	70	.551	Cir. cu. 1	W--------	S. 2	75	
	9 p. m.	28.81	63	.576	0	0	SE. 1	100	18th. Rain during the day; amount, 0.48 inch.
Sept. 16	7 a. m.	28.80	61	.473	Cu. st. 8	W--------	S. 1	88	
	1 p. m.	28.76	77	.758	Nim. 10	S---------	N. 1	82	19th. Rain during the day; amount, 0.08 inch.
	9 p. m.	28.72	66	.570	Cu. 5	S---------	E. 1	89	
Sept. 17	7 a. m.	28.76	58	.483	Cu. 8	SW-------	S. 1	100	20th. Rain during the day; amount, 0.67 inch.
	1 p. m.	28.77	68	.685	Nim. 10	S---------	S. 3	100	
	9 p. m.	28.62	65	.618	Nim. 8	S---------	S. 3	100	17th. Diffused lightning in the W. at night.
Sept. 18	7 a. m.	28.69	66	.639	Nim. 10	W--------	S. 2	100	
	1 p. m.	28.61	67	.626	Nim. 10	SW-------	S. 1	95	18th. Thunder, distant, all the morning, W.; diffused lightning in the SE. at night.
	9 p. m.	28.51	64	.596	Nim. 10	N --------	S. 3	100	
Sept. 19	7 a. m.	28.55	58	.483	Nim. 8	W--------	W. 2	100	
	1 p. m.	28.54	60	.518	Nim. 8	SW-------	SW. 3	100	
	9 p. m.	28.65	49	.348	Nim. 6	N --------	N. 4	100	
Sept. 20	7 a. m.	28.75	46	.311	Nim. 10	N --------	N. 3	100	
	1 p. m.	28.73	52	.388	Nim. 10	N --------	N. 3	100	
	9 p. m.	28.78	50	.361	Nim. 10	N --------	N. 1	100	
Sept. 21	7 a. m.	28.75	52	.388	Nim. 10	N --------	N. 1	100	
	1 p. m.	28.73	54	.335	Nim. 10	N --------	N. 1	80	
	9 p. m.	28.72	53	.403	Nim. 10	N --------	N. 1	100	
Sept. 22	7 a. m.	28.78	54	.418	Nim. 10	N --------	SE. 1	100	
	1 p. m.	28.78	66	.570	Cir. cu. 10	NE -------	S. 1	89	
	9 p. m.	28.84	56	.449	0	0	E. 1	100	
Sept. 23	7 a. m.	28.92	58	.483	Dense fog ---	--- ------	S. 1	100	
	1 p. m.	28.89	77	.758	Cu. 2	SW-------	SW. 1	82	
	9 p. m.	28.92	65	.618	0	0	S. 1	100	
Sept. 24	7 a. m.	28.93	60	.518	0	0	S. 1	100	
	1 p. m.	28.89	80	.800	Cir. 2	SW-------	W. 1	78	
	9 p. m.	28.85	65	.583	0	0	SW. 1	94	

STORMS Nos. 2 AND 3, SEPTEMBER, 1859.

MARENGO, ILLINOIS.

Month and day.	Hour.	Barom'r corrected to 32° F.	Thermometer.	Force of vapor.	Cloudiness.		Motion of clouds.		Winds.		Relative humidity.	REMARKS.
Sept. 14	9 p. m.	------	58	------	------		------		------		------	Rain from 8.30 a. m. the 17th to 10 p. m. on the 18th; amount, 1.02 inch.
Sept. 15	7 a. m.	29.14	56	------	------		------		------		------	21st. Rain from 9 to 10 a. m.
	2 p. m.	29.08	61	------	------		------		------		------	
	9 p. m.	29.06	51	------	------		------		------		------	
Sept. 16	7 a. m.	29.05	60	------	------		------		------		------	
	2 p. m.	29.05	66	------	------		------		------		------	
	9 p. m.	28.94	52	------	------		------		------		------	
Sept. 17	7 a. m.	28.96	66	------	------		------		------		------	
	2 p. m.			------	------		------		------		------	
	9 p. m.	------	------	------	------		------		------		------	
Sept. 18	7 a. m.	28.82	65	------	Nim.	9	------		SE.	2	------	
	2 p. m.	28.72	74	------		10	------		S.	3	------	
	9 p. m.	28.67	67	------		10	------		------		------	
Sept. 19	7 a. m.	28.57	62	------		10	------		S.	1	------	
	2 p. m.	28.74	67	------		10	------		NE.	2	------	
	9 p. m.	28.88	50	------		10	------		NE.	3	------	
Sept. 20	7 a. m.	28.96	48	------	Cir.	8	------		E.	5	------	
	2 p. m.	29.01	54	------	Cir.	6	------		E.	3	------	
	9 p. m.	29.02	51	------		0	------		NE.	3	------	
Sept. 21	7 a. m.	------	64	------		10	------		NE.	4	------	
	2 p. m.	------	72	------		10	------		NE.	3	------	
	9 p. m.	------	60	------		6	------		NE.	2	------	
Sept. 22	7 a. m.	------	64	------		10	------		NE.	2	------	
	2 p. m.	------	71	------		10	------		W.	2	------	
	9 p. m.	------	58	------	Cir.	2	------		W.	1	------	
Sept. 23	7 a. m.	29.03	63	------	Cu.	10	------		W.	2	------	
	2 p. m.	29.03	68	------		10	------		W.	2	------	
	9 p. m.	29.03	58	------	Cu.	4	------		SW.	1	------	
Sept. 24	7 a. m.	29.07	49	------	Foggy	------	------		------		------	
	2 p. m.	29.02	74	------	------		------		W.	1	------	
	9 p. m.	29.03	52	------	------		------		SW.	1	------	

NAPERVILLE, ILLINOIS.

Month and day.	Hour.	Barom'r corrected to 32° F.	Thermometer.	Force of vapor.	Cloudiness.		Motion of clouds.		Winds.		Relative humidity.	REMARKS.
Sept. 14	9 p. m.	------	------	------	St.	8		0	NE.	2	------	15th. Sprinkle at 9.45 a. m.
Sept. 15	7 a. m.	------	56	------	Nim.	9		0	SE.	3	------	18th. Rain from 10.30 a. m. till noon.
	2 p. m.	------	60	------	St.	10	S.	1	NE.	2	------	19th. Rain from 7 a. m. to 6 p. m.
	9 p. m.	------	56	------	Cu. st.	9		0	SE.	3	------	20th. Sprinkle at 1 p. m.
Sept. 16	7 a. m.	------	59	------	Nim.	10		0	NE.	1	------	
	2 p. m.	------	65	------	Cir. cu.	3		0	E.	1	------	
	9 p. m.	------	54	------		0		0	SE.	1	------	
Sept. 17	7 a. m.	------	60	------	St.	2		0	E.	1	------	
	2 p. m.	------	78	------	Cir. st.	6	E.	1	SW.	2	------	
	9 p. m.	------	55	------	------		------		------		------	
Sept. 18	7 a. m.	------	58	------	------		------		------		------	
	2 p. m.	------	74	------	Cu. st.	7	NE.	1	SW.	1	------	
	9 p. m.	------	70	------	Nim.	9	NE.	1	S.	1	------	
Sept. 19	7 a. m.	------	62	------	Nim.	9	NE.	2	SW.	3	------	
	2 p. m.	------	65	------	Nim.	10	S.	2	NNE.	3	------	
	9 p. m.	------	50	------	Nim.	10	S.	1	NNE.	3	------	
Sept. 20	7 a. m.	------	52	------	Nim.	10	S.	2	N.	3	------	
	2 p. m.	------	52	------	Nim.	10	SW.	2	NE.	2	------	
	9 p. m.	------	52	------	Nim.	10	SW.	2	NE.	2	------	
Sept. 21	7 a. m.	------	53	------	Nim.	10	SW.	2	NW.	1	------	
	2 p. m.	------	56	------	Nim.	10	SW.	2	NNE.	3	------	
	9 p. m.	------	52	------	Nim.	10	S.	1	NE.	1	------	
Sept. 22	7 a. m.	------	57	------	Nim.	10	SSE.	1	NNW.	1	------	
	2 p. m.	------	62	------	Nim.	10	SW.	2	NNE.	3	------	
	9 p. m.	------	57	------	Nim.	10		0	NNE.	1	------	
Sept. 23	7 a. m.	------	59	------	Cu.	3	SSE.	1	NNW.	1	------	
	2 p. m.	------	70	------	Cu.	5	E.	1	NW.	2	------	
	9 p. m.	------	60	------		0		0		0	------	
Sept. 24	7 a. m.	------	55	------	Cir. cu.	4		0	SE.	1	------	
	2 p. m.	------	75	------	Cir. st.	4	N.	1	SW.	2	------	
	9 p. m.	------	64	------	Nim.	10	N.	1	SSW.	2	------	

STORMS Nos. 2 AND 3, SEPTEMBER, 1859.

OTTAWA, ILLINOIS.

Month and day.	Hour.	Barom'r corrected to 32° F.	Thermometer.	Force of vapor.	Cloudiness.	Motion of clouds.	Winds.	Relative humidity.
Sept. 14	9 p. m.		56		10		NE. 2	
Sept. 15	7 a. m.		48		Cu. 10		NE. 1	
	2 p. m.		62		Cir. cu. 10	SE. 4	SE. 2	
	9 p. m.		56		10		SE. 2	
Sept. 16	7 a. m.		54		Cu. 10		NE. 1	
	2 p. m.		66		Cir. cu. 4	W. 1	NE. 1	
	9 p. m.		58				NE. 1	
Sept. 17	7 a. m.		46		Fog		NE.	
	2 p. m.		74		Cu. 10	SW. 1	S. 1	
	9 p. m.		66		10		SE. 2	
Sept. 18	7 a. m.		66		Cu. 10		SW. 2	
	2 p. m.		75		Cu. 10		SW. 2	
	9 p. m.		66		10		SW. 3	
Sept. 19	7 a. m.		61		Cu. 10	SW. 8	SW. 3	
	2 p. m.		63.4		10		SW. 1	
	9 p. m.		49		10		NE. 3	
Sept. 20	7 a. m.		51		10		NE. 3	
	2 p. m.		53		Cu. 10	NE. 5	NE. 3	
	9 p. m.		51.5		10		NE. 3	
Sept. 21	7 a. m.		49		Hazy		NE. 3	
	2 p. m.		56		Cu. 10	NE. 5	NE. 2	
	9 p. m.		53		10			
Sept. 22	7 a. m.		52		Cu. 10	NW. 3	NW. 1	
	2 p. m.		59		Hazy		NW. 1	
	9 p. m.		57		10		0	
Sept. 23	7 a. m.		57		10		0	
	2 p. m.		67		Cu. 9	NW. 2	SW. 1	
	9 p. m.		61		Cu. 1		0	
Sept. 24	7 a. m.		53		Fog		SE. 1	
	2 p. m.		73		Cu. 1		NE. 1	
	9 p. m.		62		0		NE. 1	

REMARKS.

15th. Began to rain at 7.05 a. m. and ended on the 16th ?; am't, 0.178 inch.

18th. Storm commenced at 9.40 a. m. and ended on the 23d, ??; amount, 0.497 inch.

PEKIN, ILLINOIS.

Month and day.	Hour.	Barom'r corrected to 32° F.	Thermometer.	Force of vapor.	Cloudiness.	Motion of clouds.	Winds.	Relative humidity.
Sept. 14	9 p. m.		58		Cir. 9	SW. 1	E. 2	
Sept. 15	7 a. m.		53		Cu. & nim. 10	SW. 1	NE. 1	
	2 p. m.		74		Cu. 9	SW. 2	NE. 2	
	9 p. m.		51		Nim. 10	SW. 2	NE. 1	
Sept. 16	7 a. m.		57		Cir. 8	W. 2	N. 1	
	2 p. m.		73		Cu. 9	NW. 3	NE. 1	
	9 p. m.		62		0	0	E. 2	
Sept. 17	7 a. m.		63		Cir. cu. 5	W. 2	E. 1	
	2 p. m.		66		Cu. 1 Nim. 9	 SW. 2	SE. 2	
	9 p. m.		64		Cir. cu. & cu. 4	S. 1	E. 1	
Sept. 18	7 a. m.		67		Cir. 4 Nim. 5	N. W. 2	0	
	2 p. m.		74		Cir. cu. & cu. 4	SW. 3	SW. 3	
	9 p. m.		62		Cu. 1	SW. 1	SW. 1	
Sept. 19	7 a. m.		61		Nim. 10	W. 5	W. 5	
	2 p. m.		60		Nim. 10	NW. 4	NW. 4	
	9 p. m.		50		Nim. 10	N. 5	N. 5	
Sept. 20	7 a. m.		48		Nim. 10		N. 3	
	2 p. m.		56		Nim. 10	N. 3	NE. 3	
	9 p. m.		52		Nim. 10		N. 3	
Sept. 21	7 a. m.		51		Nim. 10	NE. 3	N. 1	
	2 p. m.		53		Nim. 10	NE. 3	NW. 2	
	9 p. m.		55		Nim. 10		N. 1	
Sept. 22	7 a. m.		54		Nim. 10	NE. 2	0	
	2 p. m.		70		Cu. 10	SW. 1	NW. 1	
	9 p. m.		61		Nim. 10		S. 1	

REMARKS.

15th. 4 to 8 a. m. slight rain from SW. 1, wind from NE. 1; two flashes of lightning (diffused) at 8 p. m., followed by low rolling thunder in W.; nimbus clouds 10, from E. 1; slight rain at 8.15 p. m.; ceased raining at 8.30 p. m.; low rolling thunder and diffused lightning at 9 p. m. in NE., at short intervals; am't, 0.10 inch.

17th. 9 a. m. frequent rolling thunder low in W., increasing gradually to almost a continuous roll at 9.30 a. m.; bank of hazy nimbus clouds about 20° high in W.; thunder at longer intervals, higher and louder, at 10 a. m.; at 11.40 a. m. sprinkling, clouds one mass; wind from NE. 1; rain at intervals from 11.40 a. m to 2.30 p. m.; amount, 0.01 inch.

18th. Low rolling thunder and faint diffused lightning at short intervals about 5.20 a. m.; low in W. clouds about 20° high going N. and gradually rising; at 7.20 a. m. sprinkling from W. 2, contin-

STORMS Nos. 2 AND 3, SEPTEMBER, 1859.

PEKIN, ILLINOIS—Continued.

Month and day.	Hour.	Barom'r corrected to 32° F.	Thermometer.	Force of vapor.	Cloudiness.		Motion of clouds.		Winds.		Relative humidity.	REMARKS.
Sept. 23	7 a. m.	......	61	......	Cu.	9	NW.	1	S.	2	......	uous rolling thunder, and some
	2 p. m.	......	73	......	Cu.	1	NW.	1	W.	1	......	diffused lightning; at 8.50 a. m.
	9 p. m.	......	66	......	Cu.	1	SW.	1	S.	1	......	rolling thunder about half of the
Sept. 24	7 a. m.	......	64	......	Cu.	1	NW.	1		0	......	time from SW.; at 7 p. m. thun-
	2 p. m.	......	77	......	Cu.	3	NW.	2	N.	1	......	der storm going east; 7.20 p. m.
	9 p. m.	......	64	......		0		0	N.	2	......	slight rain from SW. 3, wind the

same; rain from 7.20 to 9 a. m.; amount, 0.06 inch.
19th. 9.20 a. m. slight fine rain, increasing gradually to a brisk fine rain at noon; wind W. 5.
20th. Rain till 11 a. m.; amount, 0.625 inch.
21st. 8.25 a. m. slight fine rain from NE. 3, wind same; ceased raining at 10 a. m; amount 0.01 inch. 1 p. m. wind N. 2; 2 p. m. slight rain from NE. 3.
24th. Aurora from 7 to 7.30 p. m.

PEORIA, ILLINOIS.

Month and day.	Hour.	Barom'r corrected to 32° F.	Thermometer.	Force of vapor.	Cloudiness.		Motion of clouds.		Winds.		Relative humidity.	REMARKS.
Sept. 14	9 p. m.	......	61	.340	Cu.	6	....		NE.	1	64	15th. Rain at 5 a. m. and at 9
Sept. 15	7 a. m.	......	53. 5	.341	Cu. st.	10	....		NE.	2	83	p. m.; amount, 0. 17 inch; thun-
	2 p. m.	......	71. 5	.397	Cu.	8	....		NE.	2	52	der at 9 p. m.
	9 p. m.	......	62. 5	.392	Cu. nim.	7	....		NE.	2	69	17th. Thunder storm NW. at 2
Sept. 16	7 a. m.	......	60. 5	.390	Cu.	6	....		NE.	2	74	p. m.; amount, 0. 01 inch.
	2 p. m.	......	73. 5	.469	Cu.	5	....		NE.	3	57	18th. Thunder storm SW. and NE.
	9 p. m.	......	66. 5	.463		0	....		NE.	1	71	at 9 a. m; rain from 8 to 9 p. m.;
Sept. 17	7 a. m.	......	62. 5	.453	Cir.	3	....		SE.	1	80	amount, 0. 16 inch.
	2 p. m.	......	71. 5	.566	Cu. nim.	10	....		NE.	1	74	Rain from noon the 19th to 7 a. m.
	9 p. m.	......	68	.560	Cir. st.	3	....		SE.	1	82	on the 20th; amount, 0.34 inch.
Sept. 18	7 a. m.	......	69	.599	Cir. st.	2	....		E.	1	85	
	2 p. m.	......	72. 5	.624	Cu. nim.	10	....		SW.	3	79	
	9 p. m.	......	64. 5	.556	Cu.	5	....		SW.	1	92	
Sept. 19	7 a. m.	......	64. 5	.458	Cu.	10	....		SW.	3	75	
	2 p. m.	......	62. 5	.485	Nim. st.	10	....		W.	2	86	
	9 p. m.	......	50	.335	Nim.	10	....		NE.	2	93	
Sept. 20	7 a. m.	......	50	.309	Nim.	10	....		N.	2	85	
	2 p. m.	......	55. 5	.342	Cu. nim.	10	....		N.	3	78	
	9 p. m.	......	54. 5	.275	Cu.	5	....		N.	1	65	
Sept. 21	7 a. m.	......	53	.321	Cu.	10	....		NE.	2	80	
	2 p. m.	......	55. 5	.342	Cu.	10	....		N.	2	78	
	9 p. m.	......	55. 5	.342	Cu.	8	....		NE.	2	78	
Sept. 22	7 a. m.	......	55. 5	.288	Cu.	10	....		W.	1	65	
	2 p. m.	......	65	.420	Cu.	8	....		W.	2	68	
	9 p. m.	......	62. 5	.453	Cu.	10	....		E.	1	80	
Sept. 23	7 a. m.	......	62. 5	.453	Cu.	10	....		W.	1	80	
	2 p. m.	......	74. 5	.422	Cu.	2	W.	1	W.	1	49	
	9 p. m.	......	68	.509	Cu.	5	....		SE.	1	75	
Sept. 24	7 a. m.	......	61. 5	.466	St.	1	....		S.	1	85	
	2 p. m.	......	79	.537	Cu.	4	....		E.	2	54	
	9 p. m.	......	69	.462		0	....		SE.	1	65	

RILEY, ILLINOIS.

Month and day.	Hour.	Barom'r corrected to 32° F.	Thermometer.	Force of vapor.	Cloudiness.		Motion of clouds.		Winds.		Relative humidity.	REMARKS.
Sept. 14	9 p. m.	......	57	......	....		....		....		......	14th, 15th, and 16th. Cool and
Sept. 15	7 a. m.	......	50	......	....		....		....		......	cloudy most of the day.
	2 p. m.	......	57	......	....		....		....		......	17th. Foggy; pleasant.
	9 p. m.	......	55	......	....		....		....		......	18th. Sprinkle of rain and thunder
Sept. 16	7 a. m.	......	55	......	....		....		....		......	and lightning N. at 7. 30 a. m.;
	2 p. m.	......	71	......	....		....		....		......	rain from 8. 30 a. m. to 1 p. m.;
	9 p. m.	......	54	......		0		0		0	......	amount, 0. 53 inch.
Sept. 17	7 a. m.	......	53	......		0	....			0	......	19th. Rain from 11 a. m. till sun-
	2 p. m.	......	76	......	Hazy	2	....		SE.	3	......	set; amount, 0. 51 inch.
	9 p. m.	......	62	......	Cu. st.	2	....		SE.	2	......	24th. Dense fog till 8 a. m.
Sept. 18	7 a. m.	......	64	......	Nim.	10	....		S.	2	......	
	2 p. m.	......	78	......	Nim.	10	....		SE.	1	......	
	9 p. m.	......	67	......	Cu.	7	....		SE.	3	......	

STORMS Nos. 2 AND 3, SEPTEMBER, 1859.

RILEY, ILLINOIS—Continued.

Month and day.	Hour.	Barom'r corrected to 32° F.	Thermometer.	Force of vapor.	Cloudiness.		Motion of clouds.	Winds.		Relative humidity.	REMARKS.
Sept. 19	7 a. m.		61		Nim.	10		SE.	2		
	2 p. m.		54		Nim.	10		NE.	3		
	9 p. m.		46		Nim.	10		ENE.	3		
Sept. 20	7 a. m.		47		Nim.	10		NE.	4		
	2 p. m.		60		Cu. st.	8		NE.	3		
	9 p. m.		51		Cu. st.	2		NW.	1		
Sept. 21	7 a. m.		60		Nim.	10		ENE.	3		
	2 p. m.		64		Cu.	10		NE.	3		
	9 p. m.		51		Cu.	8			0		
Sept. 22	7 a. m.		52		Mist & haze	10		NW.	2		
	2 p. m.		62		Cu. st.	10					
	9 p. m.		57		Cu.	10					
Sept. 23	7 a. m.		59		Mottled	6			0		
	2 p. m.		68		Cu.	8		W.			
	9 p. m.		58		Cu. st.	6			0		
Sept. 24	7 a. m.		50		Dense fog				0		
	2 p. m.		76			0		SW.	2		
	9 p. m.		53			0		S.	1		

SANDWICH, ILLINOIS.

Month and day.	Hour.	Barom'r corrected to 32° F.	Thermometer.	Force of vapor.	Cloudiness.		Motion of clouds.	Winds.		Relative humidity.	REMARKS.
Sept. 14	9 p. m.		52		Cir. cu.	10	W	E.	3		14th. Lunar halo.
Sept. 15	7 a. m.		52		St.	10	W	NE			16th. Mock sun at 6. 30 p. m; shooting stars at 9 p. m., brilliant and beautiful.
	2 p. m.		64		Cu. st.	10	W	E			
	9 p. m.		57		Cir. cu.	10	W	E			
Sept. 16	7 a. m.		57		St.	5	SW	SE			17th. Fog falling.
	2 p. m.		74		Cu. st.	10	W	SE			18th. Rain from 10. 30 to 11 a. m. and from 1 to 2 p. m.; amount, 0. 25 inch.
	9 p. m.		57			0		S.			
Sept. 17	7 a. m.		50		Cu. st.	10	W	SE			
	2 p. m.		80		Cir. cu.	5	W	SE			19th. Rain from 6 a. m. to 4 p. m.; amount, 2. 00 inches.?
	9 p. m.		66		Cu. st.	10	W	SE			
Sept. 18	7 a. m.		68		Cu. st.	10		SE			20th, 21st, and 22d. Drizzling rain.
	2 p. m.		78		Cir. st.	5	SW	SW			
	9 p. m.		70		Cu. st.	10	W	SE			
Sept. 19	7 a. m.		66		St.	10		SW			
	2 p. m.		66		St.	10	W	NE			
	9 p. m.		54			0		N.	3		
Sept. 20	7 a. m.		54		St.	10	W	NE			
	2 p. m.		52		St.	10		NE			
	9 p. m.		50		Cu. st.	10	W	NE			
Sept. 21	7 a. m.		52		St.	10		NE			
	2 p. m.		57		St.	10		SW			
	9 p. m.		54		Cu. st.	10	W	NE			
Sept. 22	7 a. m.		54		Cu. st.	10		N			
	2 p. m.		62		St.	10	W	SE			
	9 p. m.		58		Cu. st.	10	W	SW			
Sept. 23	7 a. m.		60			0		SE			
	2 p. m.		70		St.	10	NE	NE			
	9 p. m.		64		Cu. st.	7	W	SE			
Sept. 24	7 a. m.		60		Cir. cu.	2	W	SE			
	2 p. m.		78		St.	7	W	SE			
	9 p. m.		60		St.	10	W	NE			

TISKILWA, ILLINOIS.

Month and day.	Hour.	Barom'r corrected to 32° F.	Thermometer.	Force of vapor.	Cloudiness.		Motion of clouds.	Winds.		Relative humidity.	REMARKS.
Sept. 14	9 p. m.					10		NE.	2		14th. Cloudy all day.
Sept. 15	7 a. m.					10		SE.	2		15th. Cloudy all day; rain from 8 to 9 p. m.
	2 p. m.					10		SE.	2		
	9 p. m.					10		SE.	3		17th. Several showers during the day.
Sept. 16	7 a. m.					10		SE.	1		
	2 p. m.					9		SE.	2		19th. Cloudy; rain from 11 a. m. to 9 p. m.
	9 p. m.					1		SE.	1		

STORMS Nos. 2 AND 3, SEPTEMBER, 1859.

TISKILWA, ILLINOIS—Continued.

Month and day.	Hour.	Barom'r corrected to 32° F.	Thermometer.	Force of vapor.	Cloudiness.	Motion of clouds.	Winds.		Relative humidity.	REMARKS.
Sept. 17	7 a. m.	......	......	......	1	....	SE.	1	......	20th. Cloudy and cool; wind NE. all day.
	2 p. m.	......	......	......	10	....	SE.	2	......	21st. Cloudy, misty early a. m.; NE. wind all day.
	9 p. m.	......	......	......	7	....	SE.	1	......	21st. Cloudy.
Sept. 18	7 a. m.	......	......	......	9	....	SE.	2	......	24th. Nearly clear and warm all day.
	2 p. m.	......	......	......	9	....	SW.	3	......	
	9 p. m.	......	......	......	10	....	SW.	2	......	
Sept. 19	7 a. m.	......	......	......	10	....	SW.	2	......	
	2 p. m.	......	......	......	10	....	W.	4	......	
	9 p. m.	......	......	......	10	....	NE.	3	......	
Sept. 20	7 a. m.	......	......	......	10	....	NE.	2	......	
	2 p. m.	......	......	......	10	....	NE.	3	......	
	9 p. m.	......	......	......	10	....	NE.	1	......	
Sept. 21	7 a. m.	......	......	......	10	....	NE.	3	......	
	2 p. m.	......	......	......	10	....	NE.	3	......	
	9 p. m.	......	......	......	10	....	NE.	1	......	
Sept. 22	7 a. m.	......	......	......	10	....	NW.	1	......	
	2 p. m.	......	......	......	10	....	NW.	2	......	
	9 p. m.	......	......	......	10	....	NW.	1	......	
Sept. 23	7 a. m.	......	......	......	10	....	SW.	1	......	
	2 p. m.	......	......	......	7	....	SW.	2	......	
	9 p. m.	......	......	......	1	....	SW.	1	......	
Sept. 24	7 a. m.	......	......	......	2	....	SW.	1	......	
	2 p. m.	......	......	......	3	....	SW.	2	......	
	9 p. m.	......	......	......	1	....	SE.	2	......	

UPPER ALTON, ILLINOIS.

Month and day.	Hour.	Barom'r corrected to 32° F.	Thermometer.	Force of vapor.	Cloudiness.		Motion of clouds.		Winds.		Relative humidity.	REMARKS.
Sept. 14	9 p. m.	29.56	54	.388		0	NW.	2	NW.	2	100	14th. Rain from 2 to 7 a. m.; amount, 0.15 inch.
Sept. 15	7 a. m.	29.56	56	.391	Nim.	10	SW.	1	SW.	1	87	17th. Rain from 2 to 3 p. m.; amount, 0.05 inch.
	2 p. m.	29.49	73	.655	Cir. st.	5	W.	1	W.	1	81	Rain from 5 p. m. the 18th to 7 a. m. on the 19th; amount, 0.40 inch.
	9 p. m.	29.46	64	.529	Cir. st.	10	W.	1	W.	1	89	20th. Rain at 7 a. m.; amount, 0.018 inch.
Sept. 16	7 a. m.	29.44	60	.456		0	W.	1	W.	1	88	
	2 p. m.	29.39	78	.827		0	W.	1	W.	1	86	
	9 p. m.	29.39	66	.536		0	W.	1	W.	1	84	
Sept. 17	7 a. m.	29.40	62	.523		0	SW.	1	SW.	1	94	
	2 p. m.	29.49	66	.570	Nim.	10	NW.	2	NW.	2	89	
	9 p. m.	29.39	63	.543	Nim.	10	W.	1	W.	1	94	
Sept. 18	7 a. m.	29.30	64	.563	Cir. cu.	5	SW.	1	SW.	1	94	
	2 p. m.	29.23	76	.691	Nim.	10	SW.	2	SW.	2	77	
	9 p. m.	29.17	64	.529	Cir. cu.	5	SW.	2	SW.	2	89	
Sept. 19	7 a. m.	29.19	64	.497	Cir. st.	10	W.	3	W.	3	83	
	2 p. m.	29.20	62	.491	Nim.	10	SW.	2	SW.	2	88	
	9 p. m.	29.39	52	.334	Nim.	10	NW.	2	NW.	2	86	
Sept. 20	7 a. m.	29.33	47	.298	Nim.	10	NW.	3	NW.	3	92	
	2 p. m.	29.38	54	.362	Nim.	10	NW.	3	NW.	3	87	
	9 p. m.	29.43	53	.375	Nim.	10	NW.	2	NW.	2	93	
Sept. 21	7 a. m.	29.37	52	.334	Nim.	10	NE.	2	NE.	2	86	
	2 p. m.	29.44	58	.423	Nim.	10	NW.	2	NW.	2	88	
	9 p. m.	29.37	52	.334	Nim.	10	NW.	2	NW.	2	86	
Sept. 22	7 a. m.	29.43	54	.362	Nim.	10		1		0	87	
	2 p. m.	29.40	72	.668	Nim.	10	SW.	1	SW.	1	86	
	9 p. m.	29.51	55	.376		0	SW.	2	SW.	2	87	
Sept. 23	7 a. m.	29.58	52	.361		0	SW.	1	SW.	1	93	
	2 p. m.	29.55	75	.591		0	NE.	1	NE.	1	68	
	9 p. m.	29.47	60	.487		0	SW.	1	SW.	1	94	
Sept. 24	7 a. m.	29.60	54	.362		0	SW.	1	SW.	1	87	
	2 p. m.	29.55	78	.785		0	SW.	1	SW.	1	82	
	9 p. m.	29.50	64	.529		0	SW.	1	SW.	1	89	

STORMS Nos. 2 AND 3, SEPTEMBER, 1859.

WEST SALEM, ILLINOIS.

Month and day.	Hour.	Barom'r corrected to 32° F.	Thermometer.	Force of vapor.	Cloudiness.	Motion of clouds.	Winds.	Relative humidity.	REMARKS.
Sept. 14	9 p. m.	------	58	------	Cu. st. 7	W. 5	0	------	17th. Distant thunder in W. from 3 to 6 p. m.
Sept. 15	7 a. m.	------	60	------	Cir. st. 7	----------	NE. 2	------	18th. Thunder and lightning, with rain, in W. and S. from 2 to 3 p. m; thunder storm from SW. about 3 p. m.; thunder and lightning, with rain, in W. and NW. from 7 to 9 p. m.; rain in the night; amount, 1. 33 inch.
	2 p. m.	------	75	------	Cir. st. 6	W. 3	E. 2	------	Rain from 4 p. m. the 20th to 9 a. m. on the 21st; amount, 0. 25 inch.
	9 p. m.	------	68	------	Cir. st. 9	W. 4	0	------	22d. Rain at 4 p. m.; amount, 0. 01 inch.
Sept. 16	7 a. m.	------	60	------	Cir. 1	SW. 8	0	------	
	2 p. m.	------	83	------	Cir. st. 3	----------	NW. 1	------	
	9 p. m.	------	69	------	0	----------	0	------	
Sept. 17	7 a. m.	------	67	------	Cir. 2	W. 5	S. ?	------	
	2 p. m.	------	83	------	Cir. 6	W. 5	NW. 1	------	
	9 p. m.	------	74	------	Cir. 9	W. 5	0	------	
Sept. 18	7 a. m.	------	70	------	Cir. 8	W. 4	SE. 1	------	
	2 p. m.	------	90	------	Cir., cu. st. 6	SW. 5	S. 4	------	
	9 p. m.	------	70	------	Cir. st. 10	SW. 6	SE. 1	------	
Sept. 19	7 a. m.	------	67	------	Nim., cir. st. 9	----------	W. 1	------	
	2 p. m.	------	74	------	Cir.st.,cu.st. 8	----------	W. 1	------	
	9 p. m.	------	63	------	Cir. st. 3	----------	SW. 1	------	
Sept. 20	7 a. m.	------	58	------	Cir.st.,nim. 10	----------	0	------	
	2 p. m.	------	68	------	Nim., cir. st. 9	----------	W. 1	------	
	9 p. m.	------	58	------	Nim. 10	----------	N. 2	------	
Sept. 21	7 a. m.	------	55	------	Nim. 10	----------	0	------	
	2 p. m.	------	59	------	Nim. 10	----------	NW. 1	------	
	9 p. m.	------	57	------	Nim. 10	----------	0	------	
Sept. 22	7 a. m.	------	56	------	Nim. 10	----------	0	------	
	2 p. m.	------	66	------	Nim.,cu.st. 10	----------	SW. 1	------	
	9 p. m.	------	60	------	Nim.,cu.st. 10	----------	0	------	
Sept. 23	7 a. m.	------	61	------	Cir. st. 9	----------	0	------	
	2 p. m.	------	78	------	Cu. st. 3	----------	W. 1	------	
	9 p. m.	------	64	------	0	----------	0	------	
Sept. 24	7 a. m.	------	63	------	0	----------	0	------	
	2 p. m.	------	82	------	Cu. st. 4	----------	SW. 1	------	
	9 p. m.	------	69	------	0	----------	0	------	

WEST URBANA, ILLINOIS.

Month and day.	Hour.	Barom'r corrected to 32° F.	Thermometer.	Force of vapor.	Cloudiness.	Motion of clouds.	Winds.	Relative humidity.	REMARKS.
Sept. 14	9 p. m.	29. 201	58	------	Cir. 3	----------	NW. 1	20*	19th. Rain from 7 to 9 p. m.; amount, 0.27 inch.
Sept. 15	7 a. m.	29. 221	54	------	St. 10	----------	NE. 1	21	20th. Rain at 9 p. m.; amount, 0.17 inch.
	2 p. m.	29. 191	66	------	Cu. 10	----------	E. 3	18	21st. Showery; amount, 0.07 inch.
	9 p. m.	29. 138	61	------	St. 10	----------	E. 3	20	
Sept. 16	7 a. m.	29. 101	59	------	Cir. cu. 3	----------	E. 1	22	
	2 p. m.	29. 038	74	------	Cu. 0	----------	N. 1	19	
	9 p. m.	29. 021	69	------	Cu. 0	----------	N. 1	20	
Sept. 17	7 a. m.	29. 091	59	------	Cir. st. 2	----------	N. 1	21	
	2 p. m.	29. 054	75	------	Cir. st. 10	----------	W. 1	20	
	9 p. m.	28. 994	67	------	Cir. 3	----------	SE. 1	20	
Sept. 18	7 a. m.	28. 976	73	------	Cir. cu. 3	----------	SE. 4	27	
	2 p. m.	28. 904	77	------	Cir. cu. 8	----------	S. 2	18	
	9 p. m.	28. 824	66	------	St. 10	----------	S. 3	23	
Sept. 19	7 a. m.	28. 791	64	------	Cir. cu. 9	----------	SW. 3	28	
	2 p. m.	28. 768	67	------	Cir. st. 10	----------	SW. 3	23	
	9 p. m.	28. 818	55	------	Cu. st. 10	----------	N. 2	27	
Sept. 20	7 a. m.	28. 923	55	------	St. 10	----------	N. 3	33	
	2 p. m.	28. 931	58	------	Cu. st. 10	----------	NE. 5	30	
	9 p. m.	28. 971	54	------	St. 10	----------	NE. 3	35	
Sept. 21	7 a. m.	28. 990	50	------	St. 10	----------	NE. 1	42	
	2 p. m.	28. 951	58	------	St. 10	----------	N. 2	35	
	9 p. m.	28. 951	56	------	St. 10	----------	NW. 1	38	
Sept. 22	7 a. m.	29. 001	54	------	St. 10	----------	NW. 1	30	
	2 p. m.	29. 041	64	------	Cu. st. 10	----------	NW. 2	36	
	9 p. m.	29. 098	59	------	Cu. st. 10	----------	SW. 1	36	
Sept. 23	7 a. m.	29. 188	60	------	Cu. st. 10	----------	SW. 1	41	
	2 p. m.	29. 196	71	------	Cir. cu. 3	----------	NW. 2	31	
	9 p. m.	29. 184	62	------	Cir. cu. 5	E. 2	E. 2	33	
Sept. 24	7 a. m.	29. 188	63	------	Cir. cu. 5	SE. 2	NE. 2	30	
	2 p. m.	29. 144	75	------	Cir. cu. 2	----------	S. 1	25	
	9 p. m.	29. 126	64	------	Cu. 0	----------	SW. 1	25	

* Dalton's hygrometer.

STORMS Nos. 2 AND 3, SEPTEMBER, 1859.

WHEATON, ILLINOIS.

Month and day.	Hour.	Barom'r corrected to 32° F.	Thermometer.	Force of vapor.	Cloudiness.	Motion of clouds.	Winds.	Relative humidity.	REMARKS.
Sept. 14	9 p. m.	29. 392	49	. 247	Nim. 10	----------	NE. 2	71	15th. Shower at 6 a. m. 18th. Thunder in the morning, commencing at 6 a. m.; rain from 11 a. m. to 1 p. m.; amount, 0.38 inch. Rain from 3 a. m. the 19th to 4 p. m. on the 20th; amount, 0.70 inch. 21st. Rain at 1 a. m. and after; amount, 0.07 inch.
Sept. 15	7 a. m.	29. 405	49. 5	. 240	Nim. 10	----------	E. 1	68	
	2 p. m.	29. 321	59. 2	. 187	Nim. 10	----------	E. 4	37	
	9 p. m.	29. 303	50	. 228	Nim. 10	----------	E. 4	64	
Sept. 16	7 a. m.	29. 236	58. 5	. 222	Nim. 10	----------	E. 1	45	
	2 p. m.	29. 170	63	. 386	Nim. 10	----------	NE. 2	67	
	9 p. m.	29. 176	53	. 348	0	----------	NE. 1	86	
Sept. 17	7 a. m.	29. 203	53	. 375	Fog. 10	----------	0	93	
	2 p. m.	------	------	------	------------	----------	------------	------	
	9 p. m.	29. 111	61	. 442	Cir. st. 1	----------	E. 1	83	
Sept. 18	7 a. m.	29. 033	68	. 526	Cir. & nim. 10	----------	S. 3	77	
	2 p. m.	28. 922	75	. 685	Cir. st. nim. 10	----------	S. 2	79	
	9 p. m.	28. 820	68. 5	. 571	------------	----------	------------	82	
Sept. 19	7 a. m.	28. 716	62. 5	. 485	Nim. 9	----------	SW. 3	86	
	2 p. m.	28. 859	55	. 405	Nim. 10	----------	N. 4	94	
	9 p. m.	28. 989	48	. 322	Nim. 10	----------	N. 3	96	
Sept. 20	7 a. m.	29. 116	51	. 348	Nim. 10	----------	N. 4	93	
	2 p. m.	29. 161	50	. 309	Nim. 10	----------	NE. 4	85	
	9 p. m.	29. 168	52. 5	. 328	Nim. 10	----------	NE. 3	83	
Sept. 21	7 a. m.	29. 109	51	. 348	Nim. 10	----------	N. 2	93	
	2 p. m.	29. 061	54	. 362	Nim. 10	----------	NE. 2	87	
	9 p. m.	29. 065	51. 5	. 368	Nim. 10	----------	NW. 2	96	
Sept. 22	7 a. m.	29. 101	52. 5	. 354	Nim. 10	----------	NW. 1	90	
	2 p. m.	29. 133	58	. 379	Nim. 10	----------	W. 1	78	
	9 p. m.	29. 213	57	. 421	Nim. 10	----------	W. 1	90	
Sept. 23	7 a. m.	29. 288	58	. 423	Nim. 10	----------	W. 1	88	
	2 p. m.	29. 270	67	. 425	Nim. 10	----------	W. 1	64	
	9 p. m.	29. 295	61	. 458	Nim. 6	----------	NE. 2	85	
Sept. 24	7 a. m.	29. 329	51. 5	. 368	St. 1	----------	NE. 1	96	
	2 p. m.	29. 252	72. 5	. 416	Cir. & cir. st. 3	----------	NE. 1	52	
	9 p. m.	29. 257	55	. 376	Cir. st. 1	----------	E. 1	87	

WILLOW CREEK, ILLINOIS.

Month and day.	Hour.	Barom'r corrected to 32° F.	Thermometer.	Force of vapor.	Cloudiness.	Motion of clouds.	Winds.	Relative humidity.	REMARKS.
Sept. 14	9 p. m.	------	------	------	10	----------	E. 3	------	15th. Gentle rain 9 to 10 a. m. 16th. Bright meteor at 8.45 p. m., course SE., two distinct flashes, very bright; aurora at 9.15 p. m., columns of light very distinct for a few minutes, although the moon shone brightly. 17th. Fog early in the morning; distant lightning W. from 7 to 9 p. m., (diffuse.) 18th. Showers, accompanied by thunder and lightning, at intervals from 8.10 a. m. to 1 p. m. Rain from 4 a. m. the 19th to 8 a. m. on the 20th. 21st. Rain and mist, morning and evening. 23d. Clouds broke up in the p. m. 24th. Aurora in the early part of the evening, arch formed about 7.30 p. m., quite brilliant.
Sept. 15	7 a. m.	------	------	------	10	----------	E. 3	------	
	2 p. m.	------	63	------	10	----------	E. 3	------	
	9 p. m.	------	------	------	10	----------	E. 2	------	
Sept. 16	7 a. m.	------	------	------	10	----------	E. 2	------	
	2 p. m.	------	75	------	10	----------	SE. 2	------	
	9 p. m.	------	------	------	3	----------	E. 1	------	
Sept. 17	7 a. m.	------	------	------	0	----------	SE. 2	------	
	2 p. m.	------	78	------	0	----------	S. 3	------	
	9 p. m.	------	------	------	8	----------	S. 4	------	
Sept. 18	7 a. m.	------	------	------	6	----------	S. 3	------	
	2 p. m.	------	77	------	10	----------	S. 3	------	
	9 p. m.	------	------	------	10	----------	SE. 4	------	
Sept. 19	7 a. m.	------	------	------	10	----------	SW. 3	------	
	2 p. m.	------	54	------	10	----------	SE. 5	------	
	9 p. m.	------	------	------	10	----------	N. 5	------	
Sept. 20	7 a. m.	------	------	------	10	----------	NE. 3	------	
	2 p. m.	------	51	------	10	----------	NE. 3	------	
	9 p. m.	------	------	------	10	----------	NE. 1	------	
Sept. 21	7 a. m.	------	------	------	10	----------	NE. 2	------	
	2 p. m.	------	55	------	10	----------	NE. 2	------	
	9 p. m.	------	------	------	10	----------	NE. 1	------	
Sept. 22	7 a. m.	------	------	------	10	----------	NW. 1	------	
	2 p. m.	------	------	------	10	----------	NW. 1	------	
	9 p. m.	------	------	------	10	----------	------------	------	
Sept. 23	7 a. m.	------	------	------	10	----------	W. 1	------	
	2 p. m.	------	70	------	10	----------	SW. 1	------	
	9 p. m.	------	------	------	8	----------	------------	------	
Sept. 24	7 a. m.	------	------	------	0	----------	E. 1	------	
	2 p. m.	------	------	------	0	----------	E. 1	------	
	9 p. m.	------	------	------	0	----------	SE. 1	------	

STORMS Nos. 2 AND 3, SEPTEMBER, 1859.

WINNEBAGO, ILLINOIS.

Month and day.	Hour.	Barom'r corrected to 32° F.	Thermometer.	Force of vapor.	Cloudiness.	Motion of clouds.	Winds.	Relative humidity.
Sept. 14	9 p. m.	......	50	......	Cir. cu. 9	WSW. 1	E. 2	......
Sept. 15	7 a. m.	......	53	......	Cir. cu. 10	......	SE. 3	......
	2 p. m.	......	62	......	Cir. cu. 10	......	SE. 3	......
	9 p. m.	......	57	......	Cir. cu. 10	......	SE. 2	......
Sept. 16	7 a. m.		54.5	......	Cir. cu. 9	SW. 1	SE. 2	......
	2 p. m.	......	70.5	......	Cir. cu. 6	W. 1	E 1	......
	9 p. m.	......	55	......	0	......	E. 1	......
Sept. 17	7 a. m.	......	53	......	St. 1	......	E. 2	......
	2 p. m.	......	77	......	Cir. & cir. cu. 9	W. 1	S. 2	......
	9 p. m.	......	65	......	Cir. cu. 3	W. 0	SE. 3	......
Sept. 18	7 a. m.	......	54.5	......	Nim. 10	......	SE. 1	......
	2 p. m.	......	70	......	Nim. 9	......	E. 3	......
	9 p. m.	......	65.5	......	Nim. 10	......	SW. 1	......
Sept. 19	7 a. m.	......	62	......	Nim. 10	......	SE. 0	......
	2 p. m.	......	51	......	Nim. 10	......	NE. 4	......
	9 p. m.	......	45.5	......	Nim. 10	......	N. 4	......
Sept. 20	7 a. m.	......	47	......	Cir. st. 10	......	N. 3	......
	2 p. m.	......	59	......	Cu. st. 5	......	N. 3	......
	9 p. m.	......	52	......	Cir. st. 5	......	NE. 3	......
Sept. 21	7 a. m.	......	47	......	Cir. st. 9	......	N. 2	......
	2 p. m.	......	55	......	Cu. st. 10	......	NE. 2	......
	9 p. m.	......	50	......	Nim. 10	......	NE. 1	......
Sept. 22	7 a. m.	......	52	......	Nim. 10	......	W. 1	......
	2 p. m.	......	59	......	Cir. st. 10	......	NW. 2	......
	9 p. m.	......	57	......	Cir. st. 10	......	SW. 0	......
Sept. 23	7 a. m.	......	56	......	Cir. cu. 8	NW. 1	SW. 1	......
	2 p. m.	......	68	......	Cir. cu. 8	NW. 1	W. 1	......
	9 p. m.	......	60	......	Cir. st. 1	......	NW. 0	......
Sept. 24	7 a. m.	......	50	......	St. 1	......	NE. 0	......
	2 p. m.	......	76	......	Cir. 1	......	SW. 1	......
	9 p. m.	......	61	......	0	......	SE. 2	......

REMARKS.

14th. Solar halo at 11 a. m.

17th. Solar halo at 11 a. m.; lightning in the NW. near the horizon at 9 p. m.; lunar halo at 10 p. m.

18th. Light showers, accompanied by thunder, at intervals from 7 a. m. to 2 p. m.; a general rain commenced at 7.30 p. m.; am't, 0.88 inch.

19th. Rain from 11 a. m. to 10 p. m.; amount, 0.16 inch.

Rain from 9 p. m. the 21st to 5 a. m. on the 22d; amount, 0.32 inch.

24th. Aurora from 7.30 to 8.30 p. m.

WOODSTOCK, ILLINOIS.

Month and day.	Hour.	Barom'r corrected to 32° F.	Thermometer.	Force of vapor.	Cloudiness.	Motion of clouds.	Winds.	Relative humidity.
Sept. 14	9 p. m.	......	......	......	......	......	......	......
Sept. 15	7 a. m.	......	54	......	10	......	SE. 2	......
	2 p. m.	......	52	......	10	......	SE. 3	......
	9 p. m.	......	56	......	10	......	SE. 1	......
Sept. 16	7 a. m.	......	56	......	10	......	ESE. 1	......
	2 p. m.	......	......	......	......	......	......	......
	9 p. m.	......	54	......	Cir. 2	0	ESE. 0	......
Sept. 17	7 a. m.	......	50	......	0	......	E. 0	......
	2 p. m.	......	62	......	Cu. 8	0	SSE. 2	......
	9 p. m.	......	58	......	10	......	S. 1	......
Sept. 18	7 a. m.	......	66	......	Nim. 8	W. 5	SSW. 2	......
	2 p. m.	......	76	......	Nim. 8	SW. 7	SW. 1	......
	9 p. m.	......	70	......	......	......	......	......
Sept. 19	7 a. m.	......	66	......	Cu. st. 9	SW. 3	S. 1	......
	2 p. m.	......	52		10	......	NE. 5	......
	9 p. m.	......	46	......	10	......	NE. 5	......
Sept. 20	7 a. m.	......	48	......	10	......	NE. 5	......
	2 p. m.	......	50	......	Cu. 9	NE. 4	NE. 3	......
	9 p. m.	......	48	......	Cir. st. 9	NE. 1	NE. 3	......
Sept. 21	7 a. m.	......	48	......	10	......	NE. 2	......
	2 p. m.	......	56	......	10	......	NE. 1	......
	9 p. m.	......	42	......	10	......	NE. 2	......
Sept. 22	7 a. m.	......	54	......	10	......	NE. 0	......
	2 p. m.	......	62	......	Cu. 9	NW. 2	NE. 1	......
	9 p. m.	......	58	......	10	......	NE. 1	......
Sept. 23	7 a. m.	......	60	......	Cu. 9	W. 2	NE. 1	......
	2 p. m.	......	68	......	Cir. cu. 9	NW. 3	NE. 2	......
	9 p. m.	......	58	......	Cir. st. 5	W. 1	......	......
Sept. 24	7 a. m.	......	54	......	Cu. 3	N. 5	NW. 0	......
	2 p. m.	......	78	......	St. 2	N. 3	NW. 1	......
	9 p. m.	......	56	......	St. 2	N. 0	NW. 1	......

REMARKS.

15th. Sprinkle of rain three times during the day.

16th. Appearance of rain.

17th. Very heavy fog in the morning.

18th. Storm of rain and hail, accompanied by thunder and lightning, from 1 to 7 a. m.; amount, 1.00 inch.

20th. Amount of rain, from 6 last evening to 7 this morning, 0.06 inch; very windy; rain continues.

21st. Rain from 7 a. m. to 9 p. m; amount, 0.25 inch.

24th. Aurora from 7 to 7.30 p. m.

STORMS Nos. 2 AND 3, SEPTEMBER, 1859.

AUGUSTA, MISSOURI.

Month and day.	Hour.	Barom'r corrected to 32° F.	Thermometer.	Force of vapor.	Cloudiness.	Motion of clouds.	Winds.		Relative humidity.	REMARKS.
Sept. 14	9 p. m.	------	------	------	4	----------	E. to S.	4	------	17th. At 1 p. m. dark clouds rose from NE., going SW.; a gale; thunder and faint lightning; separated clouds and rain followed till 3 p. m.; in the evening distant lightning S. in a cloud on the horizon. 18th. Heavy thunder storm from 2 to 5 p. m.; wind, E; clouds came up from NW. Storm commenced at 6 a. m. the 19th, and ended at 8 a. m. on the 21st.
Sept. 15	7 a. m.	------	------	------	6	----------	E. to S.	2	------	
	2 p. m.	------	------	------	4	----------	E. to S.	2	------	
	9 p. m.	------	------	------	6	----------	E. to S.	2	------	
Sept. 16	7 a. m.	------	------	------	4	----------	E.	2	------	
	2 p. m.	------	------	------	4	----------	E.	2	------	
	9 p. m.	------	------	------	4	----------	E.	2	------	
Sept. 17	7 a. m.	------	------	------	2	----------	N. to E.	2	------	
	2 p. m.	------	------	------	10	----------	N. to E.	6	------	
	9 p. m.	------	------	------	4	----------	E.	2	------	
Sept. 18	7 a. m.	------	------	------	4	----------	S.	3	------	
	2 p. m.	------	------	------	10	----------	E.	2	------	
	9 p. m.	------	------	------	0	----------	W. to N.	2	------	
Sept. 19	7 a. m.	------	------	------	8	----------	W.	2	------	
	2 p. m.	------	------	------	10	----------	N. to E.	2	------	
	9 p. m.	------	------	------	10	----------	N. to E.	2	------	
Sept. 20	7 a. m.	------	------	------	10	----------	E.	2	------	
	2 p. m.	------	------	------	8	----------	W.	2	------	
	9 p. m.	------	------	------	10	----------	W. to N.	2	------	
Sept. 21	7 a. m.	------	------	------	8	----------	W. to N.	2	------	
	2 p. m.	------	------	------	6	----------	N.	2	------	
	9 p. m.	------	------	------	4	----------	N.	2	------	
Sept. 22	7 a. m.	------	------	------	4	----------	N. to E.	2	------	
	2 p. m.	------	------	------	2	----------	N. to E.	2	------	
	9 p. m.	------	------	------	0	----------	N. to E.	2	------	
Sept. 23	7 a. m.	------	------	------	0	----------	E.	1	------	
	2 p. m.	------	------	------	0	----------	S.	2	------	
	9 p. m.	------	------	------	0	----------	W. to N.	2	------	
Sept. 24	7 a. m.	------	------	------	0	----------	W. to N.	2	------	
	2 p. m.	------	------	------	2	----------	W.	1	------	
	9 p. m.	------	------	------	0	----------	N. to W.	3	------	

BETHANY, MISSOURI.

Month and day.	Hour.	Barom'r corrected to 32° F.	Thermometer.	Force of vapor.	Cloudiness.	Motion of clouds.	Winds.		Relative humidity.	REMARKS.
Sept. 14	9 p. m.	------	------	------	------------	----------	------------		------	17th. Rain and hail from 10½ to 12 p. m. 18th. Rain from 11 a. m. to 12 noon. 24th. Diffuse lightning NW. at 7 p. m.
Sept. 15	7 a. m.	------	------	------	------------	----------	------------		------	
	2 p. m.	------	------	------	------------	----------	------------		------	
	9 p. m.	------	------	------	------------	----------	------------		------	
Sept. 16	7 a. m.	------	------	------	------------	----------	------------		------	
	2 p. m.	------	------	------	------------	----------	------------		------	
	9 p. m.	------	------	------	------------	----------	------------		------	
Sept. 17	7 a. m.	------	------	------	1	----------	S.	2	------	
	2 p. m.	------	------	------	2	----------	S.	4	------	
	9 p. m.	------	------	------	6	----------	S.	1	------	
Sept. 18	7 a. m.	------	------	------	4	----------	S.	1	------	
	2 p. m.	------	------	------	8	----------	SW.	2	------	
	9 p. m.	------	------	------	8	----------	W.	3	------	
Sept. 19	7 a. m.	------	------	------	10	----------	W.	2	------	
	2 p. m.	------	------	------	8	----------	W.	2	------	
	9 p. m.	------	------	------	8	----------	W.	2	------	
Sept. 20	7 a. m.	------	------	------	0	----------	SW.	2	------	
	2 p. m.	------	------	------	1	----------	SW.	2	------	
	9 p. m.	------	------	------	0	----------	NW.	1	------	
Sept. 21	7 a. m.	------	------	------	1	----------		0	------	
	2 p. m.	------	------	------	1	----------	W.	1	------	
	9 p. m.	------	------	------	0	----------		0	------	
Sept. 22	7 a. m.	------	------	------	0	----------		0	------	
	2 p. m.	------	------	------	0	----------	NW.	1	------	
	9 p. m.	------	------	------	0	----------		0	------	
Sept. 23	7 a. m.	------	------	------	1	----------	SE.	1	------	
	2 p. m.	------	------	------	0	----------	SE.	2	------	
	9 p. m.	------	------	------	0	----------	SE.	2	------	
Sept. 24	7 a. m.	------	------	------	2	----------	S.	2	------	
	2 p. m.	------	------	------	1	----------	S.	2	------	
	9 p. m.	------	------	------	2	----------	S.	2	------	

STORMS Nos. 2 AND 3, SEPTEMBER, 1859.

BOLIVAR, MISSOURI.

Month and day.	Hour.	Barom'r corrected to 32° F.	Thermometer.	Force of vapor.	Cloudiness.	Motion of clouds.	Winds.	Relative humidity.	REMARKS.
Sept. 14	9 p. m.				10		SE. 3		14th. Rain from 4 to 9 p. m.
Sept. 15	7 a. m.				10		SE. 2		15th. Rain from 7 to 7½ a. m.
	2 p. m.						SE. 2		Drizzling rain from 7½ a. m. the 18th to the evening of the 19th.
	9 p. m.				4		SE. 2		
Sept. 16	7 a. m.				1		SE. 2		
	2 p. m.				5		SE. 2		
	9 p. m.				4		SW. 1		
Sept. 17	7 a. m.				2		S. 1		
	2 p. m.				4		SE. 2		
	9 p. m.				3		SE. 1		
Sept. 18	7 a. m.				10		SW. 3		
	2 p. m.				9		SW. 5		
	9 p. m.				10		SW. 3		
Sept. 19	7 a. m.				10		SW. 3		
	2 p. m.				10		NW. 3		
	9 p. m.				10		NW. 3		
Sept. 20	7 a. m.				10		NW. 3		
	2 p. m.				10		NW. 2		
	9 p. m.				10		NW. 3		
Sept. 21	7 a. m.				10		E		
	2 p. m.				10		E		
	9 p. m.				0				
Sept. 22	7 a. m.				10		SE. 2		
	2 p. m.				9		S. 2		
	9 p. m.				0		SW. 2		
Sept. 23	7 a. m.				2		SW. 1		
	2 p. m.				3		SE. 2		
	9 p. m.				4		SE. 2		
Sept. 24	7 a. m.				3		SE. 2		
	2 p. m.				2		SE. 3		
	9 p. m.				2		SE. 1		

BOONVILLE, MISSOURI.

Month and day.	Hour.	Barom'r corrected to 32° F.	Thermometer.	Force of vapor.	Cloudiness.	Motion of clouds.	Winds.	Relative humidity.	REMARKS.
Sept. 14	9 p. m.				9		SE. 2		18th. Thunder showers from 6.30 a. m. to 4 p. m.
Sept. 15	7 a. m.				10		SE. 3		19th. Drizzling rain from 11 a. m. to 11 p. m.
	2 p. m.				5		SE. 2		23d. Warm.
	9 p. m.				8		SE. 1		24th. Warm; thermometer 86° at 2 p. m.
Sept. 16	7 a. m.				2		SE. 2		
	2 p. m.				2		SE. 1		
	9 p. m.				1		SE. 1		
Sept. 17	7 a. m.				1		SE. 1		
	2 p. m.				4		SE. 2		
	9 p. m.				4		SE. 2		
Sept. 18	7 a. m.				10		SE. 2		
	2 p. m.				6		SE. 2		
	9 p. m.				10		SE. 1		
Sept. 19	7 a. m.				10		NW. 2		
	2 p. m.				10		NW. 2		
	9 p. m.				10		NW. 1		
Sept. 20	7 a. m.				10		NE. 3		
	2 p. m.				10		NE. 3		
	9 p. m.				0		NE. 1		
Sept. 21	7 a. m.				3		NW. 2		
	2 p. m.				6		NW. 1		
	9 p. m.				0		S. 1		
Sept. 22	7 a. m.				0		NW. 2		
	2 p. m.				0		SE. 1		
	9 p. m.				0		SE. 1		
Sept. 23	7 a. m.				0		SE. 1		
	2 p. m.				0		SE. 2		
	9 p. m.				0		SE. 1		
Sept. 24	7 a. m.				0		NW. 1		
	2 p. m.				0		SE. 1		
	9 p. m.				0		SE. 1		

STORMS Nos. 2 AND 3, SEPTEMBER, 1859.

BURLINGTON, MISSOURI.

Month and day.	Hour.	Barom'r corrected to 32° F.	Thermometer.	Force of vapor.	Cloudiness.	Motion of clouds.	Winds.	Relative humidity.
Sept. 14	9 p. m.	......	......	......	2	....	NE. 1	......
Sept. 15	7 a. m.	......	......	......	5	....	NE. 1	......
	2 p. m.	......	......	......	5	....	NE. 1	......
	9 p. m.	......	......	......	7	....	NE. 1	......
Sept. 16	7 a. m.	......	......	......	7	....	E. 1	......
	2 p. m.	......	......	......	6	....	SE. 1	......
	9 p. m.	......	......	......	0	....	NE. 1	......
Sept. 17	7 a. m.	......	......	......	0	....	NE. 1	......
	2 p. m.	......	......	......	1	....	S. 1	......
	9 p. m.	......	......	......	1	....	SE. 1	......
Sept. 18	7 a. m.	......	......	......	8	....	SE. 1	......
	2 p. m.	......	......	......	9	....	SW. 1	......
	9 p. m.	......	......	......	10	....	SE. 1	......
Sept. 19	7 a. m.	......	......	......	10	....	SW. 1	......
	2 p. m.	......	......	......	10	....	N. 2	......
	9 p. m.	......	......	......	10	....	N. 3	......
Sept. 20	7 a. m.	......	......	......	10	....	N. 4	......
	2 p. m.	......	......	......	3	....	N. 3	......
	9 p. m.	......	......	......	3	....	N. 3	......
Sept. 21	7 a. m.	......	......	......	10	....	N. 2	......
	2 p. m.	......	......	......	10	....	N. 1	......
	9 p. m.	......	......	......	10	....	N. 1	......
Sept. 22	7 a. m.	......	......	......	10	....	N. 1	......
	2 p. m.	......	......	......	10	....	SW. 1	......
	9 p. m.	......	......	......	10	....	SW. 1	......
Sept. 23	7 a. m.	......	......	......	8	....	W. 1	......
	2 p. m.	......	......	......	9	....	W. 1	......
	9 p. m.	......	......	......	9	....	NE. 1	......
Sept. 24	7 a. m.	......	......	......	0	....	N. 1	......
	2 p. m.	......	......	......	1	....	W. 1	......
	9 p. m.	......	......	......	10	....	SE. 1	......

REMARKS.

14th. Cold.
15th. Appearance of storm.
16th. Clouds from SW.
18th. Light shower, accompanied with lightning and heavy thunder, before sunrise; clouds from SW.; light showers during the day.
19th. Rain NE. from 10 a. m. to 2.30 p. m.
20th. Clouds from NW.
21st. Clouds from NE.; cool dull weather, with occasional mist.
22d. Clouds from SE. in the afternoon.
23d. Clouds from NE.
24th. Clouds from NW. till sunset; fog in the evening from SE.

CARROLLTON, MISSOURI.

Month and day.	Hour.	Barom'r corrected to 32° F.	Thermometer.	Force of vapor.	Cloudiness.	Motion of clouds.	Winds.	Relative humidity.
Sept. 14	9 p. m.	......	......	......	10	....	S. 2	......
Sept. 15	7 a. m.	......	......	......	10	....	S. 2	......
	2 p. m.	......	......	......	5	....	S. 2	......
	9 p. m.	......	......	......	5	....	S. 2	......
Sept. 16	7 a. m.	......	......	......	5	....	S. 2	......
	2 p. m.	......	......	......	2	....	S. 2	......
	9 p. m.	......	......	......	2	....	S. 2	......
Sept. 17	7 a. m.	......	......	......	5	....	S. 2	......
	2 p. m.	......	......	......	2	....	SW. 4	......
	9 p. m.	......	......	......	5	....	SW. 4	......
Sept. 18	7 a. m.	......	......	......	10	....	SE. 2	......
	2 p. m.	......	......	......	10	....	SW. 2	......
	9 p. m.	......	......	......	10	....	W. 2	......
Sept. 19	7 a. m.	......	......	......	10	....	W. 4	......
	2 p. m.	......	......	......	10	....	W. 2	......
	9 p. m.	......	......	......	10	....	W. 2	......
Sept. 20	7 a. m.	......	......	......	5	....	N. 4	......
	2 p. m.	......	......	......	5	....	N. 4	......
	9 p. m.	......	......	......	5	....	N. 2	......
Sept. 21	7 a. m.	......	......	......	5	....	N. 2	......
	2 p. m.	......	......	......	8	....	N. 2	......
	9 p. m.	......	......	......	8	....	N. 2	......
Sept. 22	7 a. m.	......	......	......	0	....	W. 2	......
	2 p. m.	......	......	......	0	....	S. 2	......
	9 p. m.	......	......	......	8	....	S. 2	......
Sept. 23	7 a. m.	......	......	......	8	....	S. 2	......
	2 p. m.	......	......	......	0	....	SW. 2	......
	9 p. m.	......	......	......	0	....	SW. 2	......
Sept. 24	7 a. m.	......	......	......	0	....	SW. 2	......
	2 p. m.	......	......	......	8	....	SW. 2	......
	9 p. m.	......	......	......	8	....	SW. 2	......

REMARKS.

18th. Began to rain at 3 a. m.
19th Began to rain at 10 a. m.
20th. Very cool.

STORMS Nos. 2 AND 3, SEPTEMBER, 1859.

CASSVILLE, MISSOURI.

Month and day.	Hour.	Barom'r corrected to 32° F.	Thermometer.	Force of vapor.	Cloudiness.	Motion of clouds.	Winds.		Relative humidity.	REMARKS.
Sept. 14	9 p. m.	------	64	------	10	----------		0	------	14th. Rain; amount, 0.125 inch. 17th. Clouds in layers, with lightning passing up and down towards zenith at 7 p. m.
Sept. 15	7 a. m.	------	62	------	8	----------		0	------	
	2 p. m.	------	74	------	5	----------	SE.	1	------	
	9 p. m.	------	66	------	2	----------		0	------	
Sept. 16	7 a. m.	------	65	------	4	----------		0	------	
	2 p. m.	------	80	------	2	----------	SE.	1	------	
	9 p. m.	------	64	------	2	----------		0	------	
Sept. 17	7 a. m.	------	75	------	5	----------		0	------	
	2 p. m.	------	82	------	5	----------	S.	1	------	
	9 p. m.	------	79	------	3	----------		0	------	
Sept. 18	7 a. m.	------	75	------	5	----------	SW.	3	------	
	2 p. m.	------	79	------	3	----------	S.	1	------	
	9 p. m.	------	69	------	2	----------		0	------	
Sept. 19	7 a. m.	------	62	------	10	----------	W.	3	------	
	2 p. m.	------	69	------	10	----------	SW.	2	------	
	9 p. m.	------	64	------	10	----------		0	------	
Sept. 20	7 a. m.	------	54	------	10	----------	NW.	2	------	
	2 p. m.	------	60	------	10	----------	NW.	1	------	
	9 p. m.	------	60	------	10	----------	NW.	1	------	
Sept. 21	7 a. m.	------	54	------	10	----------		0	------	
	2 p. m.	------	58	------	10	----------	NW.	1	------	
	9 p. m.	------	54	------	0	----------		0	------	
Sept. 22	7 a. m.	------	53	------	Foggy------ -	----------		0	------	
	2 p. m.	------	70	------	1	----------	S.	1	------	
	9 p. m.	------	53	------	0	----------		0	------	
Sept. 23	7 a. m.	------	67	------	0	----------	S.	1	------	
	2 p. m.	------	76	------	3	----------	S.	1	------	
	9 p. m.	------	70	------	0	----------		0	------	
Sept. 24	7 a. m.	------	60	------	5	----------		0	------	
	2 p. m.	------	76	------	2	----------	S.	1	------	
	9 p. m.	------	65	------	0	----------		0	------	

EMERSON, MISSOURI.

Month and day.	Hour.	Barom'r corrected to 32° F.	Thermometer.	Force of vapor.	Cloudiness.	Motion of clouds.	Winds.		Relative humidity.	REMARKS.
Sept. 14	9 p. m.	------	------	------	5	----------	SW.	1	------	17th. Heavy shower, accompanied by thunder and lightning, from 7 to 9 a. m. 18th. Rain at intervals during the day after 8 a. m. 19th. Rain after 9 a. m. during the day.
Sept. 15	7 a. m.	------	------	------	0	----------	NW.	1	------	
	2 p. m.	------	------	------	10	----------	W.	1	------	
	9 p. m.	------	------	------	4	----------	SW.	1	------	
Sept. 16	7 a. m.	------	------	------	8	----------	W.	1	------	
	2 p. m.	------	------	------	1	----------	SW.	1	------	
	9 p. m.	------	------	------	0	----------	SW.	1	------	
Sept. 17	7 a. m.	------	------	------	10	----------	NW.	3	------	
	2 p. m.	------	------	------	3	----------	SW.	2	------	
	9 p. m.	------	------	------	1	----------	SW.	3	------	
Sept. 18	7 a. m.	------	------	------	10	----------	SW.	3	------	
	2 p. m.	------	------	------	10	----------	SW.	2	------	
	9 p. m	------	------	------	10	----------	SW.	1	------	
Sept. 19	7 a. m.	------	------	------	10	----------	NW.	2	------	
	2 p. m.	------	------	------	10	----------	NW.	2	------	
	9 p. m.	------	------	------	10	----------	NW.	1	------	
Sept. 20	7 a. m.	------	------	------	10	----------	N.	3	------	
	2 p m.	------	------	------	10	----------	N.	1	------	
	9 p. m.	------	------	------	10	----------	N.	1	------	
Sept. 21	7 a. m.	------	------	------	10	----------	N.	1	------	
	2 p. m.	------	------	------	2	----------	N.	1	------	
	9 p. m.	------	------	------	4	----------	NW.	1	------	
Sept. 22	7 a. m.	------	------	------	6	----------	W.	1	------	
	2 p. m.	------	------	------	1	----------	SW.	1	------	
	9 p. m.	------	------	------	0	----------	SW.	1	------	
Sept. 23	7 a. m.	------	------	------	2	----------	S.	1	------	
	2 p. m.	------	------	------	2	----------	SW.	1	------	
	9 p. m.	------	------	------	1	----------	SW.	1	------	
Sept. 24	7 a. m.	------	------	------	6	----------	W.	1	------	
	2 p. m.	------	------	------	4	----------	W.	1	------	
	9 p. m.	------	------	------	3	----------	W.	1	------	

STORMS Nos. 2 AND 3, SEPTEMBER, 1859.

FARMINGTON, MISSOURI.

Month and day.	Hour.	Barom'r corrected to 32° F.	Thermometer.	Force of vapor.	Cloudiness.	Motion of clouds.	Winds.		Relative humidity.	REMARKS.
Sept. 14	9 p. m.	......	......	......	5	....	NE.	1	......	15th. Rain 6 to 7 a. m.
Sept. 15	7 a. m.	......	......	......	10	....	NE.	2	......	17th. Rain NW. 3 to 5 p. m.; heavy thunder and forked lightning SW. at 3 p. m.
	2 p. m.	......	......	......	5	....	E.	2	......	
	9 p. m.	......	......	......	10	....	E.	1	......	
Sept. 16	7 a. m.	......	......	......	10	....	SE.	1	......	18th. Rain from 4 to 6 p. m. W.; heavy thunder and forked lightning at 4 p. m.
	2 p. m.	......	......	......	10	....	SE.	3	......	
	9 p. m.	......	......	......	10	....	SE.	1	......	
Sept. 17	7 a. m.	......	......	......	10	....	S.	1	......	19th. Rain from 5 p. m. to 12 midnight.
	2 p. m.	......	......	......	10	....	W.	4	......	
	9 p. m.	......	......	......	10	....	W.	3	......	20th. Rain from 6 a. m. to 9 p. m.
Sept. 18	7 a. m.	......	......	......	10	....	SW.	1	......	21st. Rain from 4 a. m. to 2 p. m.
	2 p. m.	......	......	......	5	....	S.	2	......	
	9 p. m.	......	......	......	10	....	SW.	2	......	
Sept. 19	7 a. m.	......	......	......	10	....	S.	1	......	
	2 p. m.	......	......	......	8	....	SW.	1	......	
	9 p. m.	......	......	......	10	....	NW.	4	......	
Sept. 20	7 a. m.	......	......	......	10	....	N.	1	......	
	2 p. m.	......	......	......	10	....	NE.	1	......	
	9 p. m.	......	......	......	10	....	NE.	1	......	
Sept. 21	7 a. m.	......	......	......	10	....	NE.	1	......	
	2 p. m.	......	......	......	10	....	E.	1	......	
	9 p. m.	......	......	......	10	....	SE.	1	......	
Sept. 22	7 a. m.	......	......	......	6	....	W.	1	......	
	2 p. m.	......	......	......	2	....	SW.	3	......	
	9 p. m.	......	......	......	0	....	S.	1	......	
Sept. 23	7 a. m.	......	......	......	0	....	S.	1	......	
	2 p. m.	......	......	......	5	....	S.	2	......	
	9 p. m.	......	......	......	0	....	S.	1	......	
Sept. 24	7 a. m.	......	......	......	0	....	S.	2	......	
	2 p. m.	......	......	......	2	....	SW.	3	......	
	9 p. m.	......	......	......	0	....	SW.	1	......	

GREENFIELD, MISSOURI.

Month and day.	Hour.	Barom'r corrected to 32° F.	Thermometer.	Force of vapor.	Cloudiness.	Motion of clouds.	Winds.		Relative humidity.	REMARKS.
Sept. 14	9 p. m.	......	......	......	10	....	SE.	4	......	14th. Heavy rain from 5 to 7½ p. m.
Sept. 15	7 a. m.	......	......	......	8	....	SE.	4	......	
	2 p. m.	......	......	......	8	....	SE.	4	......	16th. Thermometer 88° at 3 p. m.
	9 p. m.	......	......	......	10	....	S.	2	......	17th. Thermometer 88° at 3 p. m.; sheet lightning N. and E. at night.
Sept. 16	7 a. m.	......	......	......	9	....	S.	4	......	
	2 p. m.	......	......	......	4	....	SE.	4	......	
	9 p. m.	......	......	......	5	....	S.	2	......	18th. Brisk shower, accompanied by thunder and lightning, 11 to 11½ a. m.
Sept. 17	7 a. m.	......	......	......	2	....	SW.	4	......	
	2 p. m.	......	......	......	5	....	SW.	4	......	
	9 p. m.	......	......	......	5	....	S.	2	......	20th. Cloudy; thermometer 71° at 7 a. m.
Sept. 18	7 a. m.	......	......	......	10	....	S.	12	......	
	2 p. m.	......	......	......	5	....	SE.	4	......	22d. Dense fog at 6 a. m, thermometer 45°; thermometer at 2 p. m. 74°.
	9 p. m.	......	......	......	5	....	SE.	2	......	
Sept. 19	7 a. m.	......	......	......	10	....	S.	12	......	
	2 p. m.	......	......	......	10	....	SE.	12	......	24th. Sheet lightning W.
	9 p. m.	......	......	......	10	....	W.	4	......	
Sept. 20	7 a. m.	......	......	......	10	....	NW.	12	......	
	2 p. m.	......	......	......	7	....	NW.	12	......	
	9 p. m.	......	......	......	10	....	NW.	2	......	
Sept. 21	7 a. m.	......	......	......	10	....	W.	2	......	
	2 p. m.	......	......	......	10	....	E.	2	......	
	9 p. m.	......	......	......	0	....	SE.	2	......	
Sept. 22	7 a. m.	......	......	......	10	....	S.	4	......	
	2 p. m.	......	......	......	0	....	S.	4	......	
	9 p. m.	......	......	......	0	....	S.	2	......	
Sept. 23	7 a. m.	......	......	......	1	....	S.	2	......	
	2 p. m.	......	......	......	5	....	S.	12	......	
	9 p. m.	......	......	......	0	....	S.	2	......	
Sept. 24	7 a. m.	......	......	......	5	....	S.	2	......	
	2 p. m.	......	......	......	3	....	SW.	12	......	
	9 p. m.	......	......	......	3	....	SW.	2	......	

STORMS NOS. 2 AND 3, SEPTEMBER, 1859.

GREENVILLE, MISSOURI.

Month and day.	Hour.	Barom'r corrected to 32° F.	Thermometer.	Force of vapor.	Cloudiness.	Motion of clouds.	Winds.	Relative humidity.	REMARKS.
Sept. 14	9 p. m.				10		SE. 4		14th. Cloudy and cold.
Sept. 15	7 a. m.				10		SW. 4		15th. Slight rain in the morning;
	2 p. m.				6		SW. 4		cool.
	9 p. m.				2		SW. 4		16th. Clear and warm.
Sept. 16	7 a. m.				0		SW. 4		17th. Rain, with brisk wind in the
	2 p. m.				0		SW. 4		evening.
	9 p. m.				0		SW. 4		18th. Rain, accompanied by heavy
Sept. 17	7 a. m.				0		SW. 4		thunder and lightning.
	2 p. m.				0		SW. 4		19th. Cloudy and cold.
	9 p. m.				10		SW. 25		20th and 21st. Cloudy and cold.
Sept. 18	7 a. m.				0		SW. 4		22d and 23d. Cloudy and warm.
	2 p. m.				2		SW. 4		24th. Warm.
	9 p. m.				10		NE. 12		
Sept. 19	7 a. m.				10		SW. 4		
	2 p. m.				10		SW. 4		
	9 p. m.				10		SW. 4		
Sept. 20	7 a. m.				10		SW. 4		
	2 p. m.				10		SW. 4		
	9 p. m.				10		SW. 4		
Sept. 21	7 a. m.				10		SW. 4		
	2 p. m.				10		SW. 4		
	9 p. m.				10		SW. 4		
Sept. 22	7 a. m.				10		SW. 4		
	2 p. m.				10		SW. 4		
	9 p. m.				6		SW. 4		
Sept. 23	7 a. m.				2		SW. 4		
	2 p. m.				2		SW. 4		
	9 p. m.				2		SW. 4		
Sept. 24	7 a. m.				2		SW. 4		
	2 p. m.				2		SW. 4		
	9 p. m.				2		SW. 4		

HERMAN, MISSOURI.

Month and day.	Hour.	Barom'r corrected to 32° F.	Thermometer.	Force of vapor.	Cloudiness.	Motion of clouds.	Winds.	Relative humidity.	REMARKS.
Sept. 14	9 p. m.				9		E. 2		14th. Shower at 7 a. m.
Sept. 15	7 a. m.				10		E. 1		16th. Shower at 7 a. m.
	2 p. m.				6		E. 1		17th. Thunder storm in the dis-
	9 p. m.				4		E. 1		tance at 6. 30 a. m.; E., no rain;
Sept. 16	7 a. m.				10		E. 1		gale from N. to W. and E. 11. 30
	2 p. m.				4		E. 1		a. m. to 12 noon; heavy rain
	9 p. m.				1		E. 1		and hail from 12 noon to 0. 45
Sept. 17	7 a. m.				7		E. 1		p. m.; hail stone ½ inch in di-
	2 p. m.				10		E. 1		ameter.
	9 p. m.				6		E. 2		18th. Rain from 11 a. m. to 4 p. m.;
Sept. 18	7 a. m.				5		NW. 2		thunder storm in the distance,
	2 p. m.				10		SE. 1		N. and S.; diffuse lightning N.
	9 p. m.				5		SE. 3		and NE. at 9 p. m.
Sept. 19	7 a. m.				10		W. 2		19th. Cool; rain from 1 to 7 p. m.
	2 p. m.				10		W. 1		20th. Cool; rain from 8 to 9 a. m.
	9 p. m.				10		W. 3		21st. Cool.
Sept. 20	7 a. m.				10		N. 2		22d. Pleasant.
	2 p. m.				10		N. 2		23d. Fog till 7 a. m.; warm.
	9 p. m.				10		N. 2		24th. Fog till 7 a. m.; warm.
Sept. 21	7 a. m.				10		NW. 1		
	2 p. m.				9		N. 1		
	9 p. m.				10		N. 1		
Sept. 22	7 a. m.				8		N. 1		
	2 p. m.				4		NE. 2		
	9 p. m.				0		E. 1		
Sept. 23	7 a. m.				0		E. 1		
	2 p. m.				3		E. 1		
	9 p. m.				0		E. 1		
Sept. 24	7 a. m.				0		S. 1		
	2 p. m.				2		SW. 2		
	9 p. m.				0		SW. 1		

STORMS Nos. 2 AND 3, SEPTEMBER, 1859.

HORNERSVILLE, MISSOURI.

Month and day.	Hour.	Barom'r corrected to 32° F.	Thermometer.	Force of vapor.	Cloudiness.	Motion of clouds.	Winds.	Relative humidity.
Sept. 14	9 p. m.				0		NW. 1	
Sept. 15	7 a. m.				8		NW. 1	
	2 p. m.				3		E. 1	
	9 p. m.				4		NE. 1	
Sept. 16	7 a. m.				1		NW. 1	
	2 p. m				4		NW. 1	
	9 p. m.				0		NW. 1	
Sept. 17	7 a. m.				1		SE. 1	
	2 p. m.				3		SE. 1	
	9 p. m.				4		NW. 3	
Sept. 18	7 a. m.				7		S. 2	
	2 p. m.				3		S. 3	
	9 p. m.				10		S. 2	
Sept. 19	7 a. m.				1		NW. 2	
	2 p. m.				6		NW. 2	
	9 p. m.				10		NW. 1	
Sept. 20	7 a. m.		60		10		NW. 1	
	2 p. m.		66		9		N. 3	
	9 p. m.		54		10		N. 1	
Sept. 21	7 a. m.		58		10		SW. 2	
	2 p. m.		60		10		W. 2	
	9 p. m.		60		10		NW. 2	
Sept. 22	7 a. m.				8		SW. 2	
	2 p. m.				6		SW. 2	
	9 p. m.				5		NW. 1	
Sept. 23	7 a. m.				1		W. 1	
	2 p. m.				2		SW. 1	
	9 p. m.				0		NW. 1	
Sept. 24	7 a. m.				1		NW. 1	
	2 p. m.				4		S. 2	
	9 p. m.				0		S. 1	

REMARKS.

14th. Morning cloudy and cool; evening clear and cool.
15th. Morning clouds from NW.; evening variable.
16th. Morning clouds SE.; evening clear and warm.
17th. Variable; lightning NW. at 9 p. m.
18th. Rain from 5.30 a. m. to 9 p. m.; thunder cloud and lightning in W. at 7 a. m.; heavy rain at 6.30 p. m.; cloud rose in SW., direction NE.; wind S. 4, continued about fifteen minutes, then all was calm. The thunder was heavy and the lightning zig-zag.
19th. Sprinkle rain in the evening; cloudy.
20th. Cloudy; misty.
21st. Cloudy and cool.
22d. Variable.
23d. Changeable.
24th. Cloudy a. m.; evening clear.

HARRISONVILLE, MISSOURI.

Month and day.	Hour.	Barom'r corrected to 32° F.	Thermometer.	Force of vapor.	Cloudiness.	Motion of clouds.	Winds.	Relative humidity.
Sept. 14	9 p. m.				9		E. 3	
Sept. 15	7 a. m.				10		SE. 2	
	2 p. m.				4		SE. 3	
	9 p. m.				9		SE. 2	
Sept. 16	7 a. m.				8		E. 2	
	2 p. m.				7		SE. 3	
	9 p. m.				9		E. 3	
Sept. 17	7 a. m.				8		S. 3	
	2 p. m.				7		S. 3	
	9 p. m.				2		SE. 3	
Sept. 18	7 a. m.				7		E. 3	
	2 p. m.				8		NW. 3	
	9 p. m.				2		NW. 3	
Sept. 19	7 a. m.				9		NW. 4	
	2 p. m.				10		NW. 3	
	9 p. m.				10		NW. 4	
Sept. 20	7 a. m.				0		N. 3	
	2 p. m.				4		N. 2	
	9 p. m.				9		E. 2	
Sept. 21	7 a. m.				4		N. 1	
	2 p. m.				8		SW. 1	
	9 p. m.				1		SW. 1	
Sept. 22	7 a. m.				1		NE. 2	
	2 p. m.				0		SE. 2	
	9 p. m.				0		E. 2	
Sept. 23	7 a. m.				3		S. 2	
	2 p. m.				3		S. 3	
	9 p. m.				0		SE. 2	
Sept. 24	7 a. m.				4		SE. 3	
	2 p. m.				3		SE. 3	
	9 p. m.				4		S. 3	

REMARKS.

14th. Light shower at 3.04 a. m.; light rain from 9 to 9.30 p. m.
16th. Warm.
17th. Distant thunder W. at 6 a. m., extending towards the S., and continued till about 7 a. m., a heavy cloud in the W. at the same time; the wind changing from SE. to SW., the cloud dispersed towards the E.; also, at the same time, three arch beams, two of them distinctly visible W., extending from S. to N., the southern limbs most distinct; only a few drops of rain.
18th. NW. storm at 4.45 a. m.; the wind continued about ten minutes, with a dashing rain; a few minutes after another of the same kind, accompanied by diffuse lightning NE. and heavy peals of thunder; distant thunder SE. at 1 p. m.; about that time the wind changed from E. to NW.; distant thunder W. at 2.30 p. m., wind N.; about fifteen minutes later a heavy shower came up from the NW., with strong wind; some thunder and lightning over head; this lasted about fifteen minutes; clouds driven SE.; rain from 4.45 a. m. to 7 a. m. and from 2.43 to 3 p. m. 19th to 22d. Cold. 23d and 24th. Pleasant.

STORMS Nos. 2 AND 3, SEPTEMBER, 1859.

KIRKSVILLE, MISSOURI.

Month and day.	Hour.	Barom'r corrected to 32° F.	Thermometer.	Force of vapor.	Cloudiness.	Motion of clouds.	Winds.		Relative humidity.
Sept. 14	9 p. m.				8		E.	1	
Sept. 15	7 a. m.				10		SE.	2	
	2 p. m.				4		SE.	3	
	9 p. m.				5		SE.	1	
Sept. 16	7 a. m.				9		SE.	1	
	2 p. m.				2		SE.	2	
	9 p. m.				0		SE.	1	
Sept. 17	7 a. m.				9		SE.	2	
	2 p. m.				10		SE.	4	
	9 p. m.				5		SE.	3	
Sept. 18	7 a. m.				10		SE.	1	
	2 p. m.				10		SE.	3	
	9 p. m.				9		NW.	1	
Sept. 19	7 a. m.				10		NW.	3	
	2 p. m.				10		N.	3	
	9 p. m.				10		NE.	4	
Sept. 20	7 a. m.				10		N.	3	
	2 p. m.				10		N.	3	
	9 p. m.				9		N.	1	
Sept. 21	7 a. m.				1		NW.	1	
	2 p. m.				3		NE.	2	
	9 p. m.				9		NE.	1	
Sept. 22	7 a. m.				1		SE.	1	
	2 p. m.				2		S.	2	
	9 p. m.				0		S.	1	
Sept. 23	7 a. m.				3		S.	1	
	2 p. m.				1		S.	1	
	9 p. m.				0		S.	1	
Sept. 24	7 a. m.				1		SE.	1	
	2 p. m.				2		SE.	1	
	9 p. m.				3		SE.	1	

REMARKS.

14th. Slight shower of rain at 10 p. m.

17th. Rain, with diffuse and zig-zag lightning NE. from 5 to 11 a. m.

18th. Rain from 4 a. m. to 7 p. m.; diffuse zig-zag and forked lightning from all points of compass; heavy thunder all day.

19th. Rain from 7. 30 a. m. to 6 p. m.

22d. Dense fog early.

LANCASTER, MISSOURI.

Month and day.	Hour.	Barom'r corrected to 32° F.	Thermometer.	Force of vapor.	Cloudiness.	Motion of clouds.	Winds.		Relative humidity.
Sept. 14	9 p. m.				10		E.	4	
Sept. 15	7 a. m.				10		E.	2	
	2 p. m.				10		E.	2	
	9 p. m.				10		E.	2	
Sept. 16	7 a. m.				10		E.	2	
	2 p. m.				5		S.	2	
	9 p. m.				0		NE.	2	
Sept. 17	7 a. m.				10		E.	4	
	2 p. m.				5		SW.	2	
	9 p. m.				5		W		
Sept. 18	7 a. m.				10		E.	4	
	2 p. m.				10		W.	2	
	9 p. m.				10		W		
Sept. 19	7 a. m.				10		W.	12	
	2 p. m.				10		NW.	4	
	9 p. m.				10		NW		
Sept. 20	7 a. m.				10		N.	4	
	2 p. m.				10		N.	4	
	9 p. m.				10		N.	2	
Sept. 21	7 a. m.				0		N.	2	
	2 p. m.				0		N.	2	
	9 p. m.				5		N.	2	
Sept. 22	7 a. m.				10		E.	2	
	2 p. m.				0		S.	2	
	9 p. m.				0		S.	2	
Sept. 23	7 a. m.				0		S.	2	
	2 p. m.				0		S.	2	
	9 p. m.				0		S.	2	
Sept. 24	7 a. m.				0		S.	2	
	2 p. m.				0		S.	2	
	9 p. m.				0		S.	2	

REMARKS.

14th. 7 a. m., cool; 2 p. m., more moderate; 9 p. m., pleasant.

16th. Pleasant.

17th. Rain 6 to 10 a. m.; pleasant and warm; 6 to 10 a. m. forked lightning, heavy thunder, and a copious shower of rain.

18th. Rain 6 to 9 a. m.

19th. Rain 6 to 9 a. m.; cool.

20th. Cool and cloudy.

21st. Light frost; warm and pleasant.

22d, 23d, and 24th. Pleasant.

STORMS Nos. 2 AND 3, SEPTEMBER, 1859.

LEXINGTON, MISSOURI.

Month and day.	Hour.	Barom'r corrected to 32° F.	Thermometer.	Force of vapor.	Cloudiness.	Motion of clouds.	Winds.		Relative humidity.
Sept. 14	9 p. m.	------	------	------	10	----------	E.	4	------
Sept. 15	7 a. m.	------	------	------	10	----------	NE.	4	------
	2 p. m.	------	------	------	5	----------	N.	2	------
	9 p. m.	------	------	------	9	----------	NE.	4	------
Sept. 16	7 a. m.	------	------	------	6	----------	N.	2	------
	2 p. m.	------	------	------	7	----------	E.	2	------
	9 p. m.	------	------	------	8	----------	SE.	8	------
Sept. 17	7 a. m.	------	------	------	5	----------	SE.	12	------
	2 p. m.	------	------	------	3	----------	SW.	10	------
	9 p. m.	------	------	------	4	----------	S.	12	------
Sept. 18	7 a. m.	------	------	------	9	----------	SE.	8	------
	2 p. m.	------	------	------	9	----------	NW.	6	------
	9 p. m.	------	------	------	10	----------	W.	8	------
Sept. 19	7 a. m.	------	------	------	10	----------	NW.	20	------
	2 p. m.	------	------	------	10	----------	NW.	15	------
	9 p. m.	------	------	------	10	----------	NW.	15	------
Sept. 20	7 a. m.	------	------	------	2	----------	N.	10	------
	2 p. m.	------	------	------	5	----------	N.	8	------
	9 p. m.	------	------	------	8	----------	E.	4	------
Sept. 21	7 a. m.	------	------	------	7	----------	N.	2	------
	2 p. m.	------	------	------	3	----------	N.	4	------
	9 p. m.	------	------	------	1	----------	NW.	2	------
Sept. 22	7 a. m.	------	------	------	1	----------	E.	2	------
	2 p. m.	------	------	------	1	----------	S.	2	------
	9 p. m.	------	------	------	0	----------	SE.	4	------
Sept. 23	7 a. m.	------	------	------	1	----------	S.	2	------
	2 p. m.	------	------	------	2	----------	S.	8	------
	9 p. m.	------	------	------	1	----------	SE.	2	------
Sept. 24	7 a. m.	------	------	------	2	----------	S.	4	------
	2 p. m.	------	------	------	3	----------	S.	6	------
	9 p. m.	------	------	------	2	----------	S.	4	------

REMARKS.

14th. Very cool; rain from 3 to 4½ a. m.

15th. Cool and pleasant.

16th Rather sultry.

17th. Sultry; heavy bank of clouds N. and W. at sunset; diffuse lightning, very vivid; fresh breeze from SE.; same at 9 p. m.

18th. Rain from 3 to 7 a. m.; warm, with occasional showers.

19th. Cold and damp; driving mist and showers.

20th. Cold and dry; blustering.

21st. Cool and pleasant.

22d. Warm and pleasant.

24th. Warm all day.

LURAY, MISSOURI.

Month and day.	Hour.	Barom'r corrected to 32° F.	Thermometer.	Force of vapor.	Cloudiness.	Motion of clouds.	Winds.		Relative humidity.
Sept. 14	9 p. m.	------	------	------	10	----------	SE.	1	------
Sept. 15	7 a. m.	------	------	------	10	----------	SE.	2	------
	2 p. m.	------	------	------	9	----------	SE.	1	------
	9 p. m.	------	------	------	10	----------	SE.	1	------
Sept. 16	7 a. m.	------	------	------	5	----------	SE.	1	------
	2 p. m.	------	------	------	4	----------	SE.	1	------
	9 p. m.	------	------	------	1	----------	SE.	1	------
Sept. 17	7 a. m.	------	------	------	10	----------	SW.	2	------
	2 p. m.	------	------	------	4	----------	SE.	1	------
	9 p. m.	------	------	------	3	----------	SE.	1	------
Sept. 18	7 a. m.	------	------	------	10	----------	SW.	2	------
	2 p. m.	------	------	------	10	----------	SW.	2	------
	9 p. m.	------	------	------	10	----------	SW.	1	------
Sept. 19	7 a. m.	------	------	------	10	----------	W.	4	------
	2 p. m.	------	------	------	10	----------	NW.	4	------
	9 p. m.	------	------	------	10	----------	N.	2	------
Sept. 20	7 a. m.	------	------	------	10	----------	N.	3	------
	2 p. m.	------	------	------	10	----------	N.	1	------
	9 p. m.	------	------	------	10	----------	N.	1	------
Sept. 21	7 a. m.	------	------	------	2	----------	N.	1	------
	2 p. m.	------	------	------	10	----------	NW.	1	------
	9 p. m.	------	------	------	9	----------	NW.	1	------
Sept. 22	7 a. m.	------	------	------	10	----------	NE.	1	------
	2 p. m.	------	------	------	4	----------	NE.	1	------
	9 p. m.	------	------	------	1	----------	E.	1	------
Sept. 23	7 a. m.	------	------	------	1	----------	SE.	1	------
	2 p. m.	------	------	------	1	----------	SE.	1	------
	9 p. m.	------	------	------	1	----------	SE.	1	------
Sept. 24	7 a. m.	------	------	------	1	----------	S.	1	------
	2 p. m.	------	------	------	1	----------	S.	1	------
	9 p. m.	------	------	------	1	----------	S.	1	------

REMARKS.

14th. Cool; rain from 9 to 11 p. m.; amount, 0.625 inch.

15th. Cool; misty; some light sprinkles about 6 p. m.

16th. Variable.

17th. Heavy rain, with high wind NW., from 6 to 11½ a. m.; am't, 2.25 inches.

18th. Rain from 6 to 9 a. m., and 2 to 6 p. m.; amount, 2.00 inches.

19th. Drizzling rain all day; cold and disagreeable.

20th. Very cool.

21st. Little warmer.

22d. Warmer still.

23d. Very pleasant.

24th. Warm for the season.

STORMS Nos. 2 AND 3, SEPTEMBER, 1859.

PARIS, MISSOURI.

Month and day.	Hour.	Barom'r corrected to 32° F.	Thermometer.	Force of vapor.	Cloudiness.	Motion of clouds.	Winds.	Relative humidity.	REMARKS.
Sept. 14	9 p. m.	------	------	------	9	----------	E. 2	------	14th. Rather cool; light rain at 9 p. m.
Sept. 15	7 a. m.	------	------	------	10	----------	SE. 2	------	
	2 p. m.	------	------	------	10	----------	SE. 2	------	16th. Warmer than usual.
	9 p. m.	------	------	------	2	----------	0	------	17th. Lightning NW. at 4 a. m., diffuse; occasional thunder up to 10 a. m., and for a few moments considerable wind; at 9 a. m. wind N. for a short time; lightning again at 9 p. m. NW., diffuse; slight rain at 9 a. m.
Sept. 16	7 a. m.	------	------	------	10	----------	SE. 1	------	
	2 p. m.	------	------	------	3	----------	SE. 2	------	
	9 p. m.	------	------	------	1	----------	0	------	
Sept. 17	7 a. m.	------	------	------	5	----------	SE. 2	------	
	2 p. m.	------	------	------	2	----------	SE. 3	------	
	9 p. m.	------	------	------	2	----------	SE. 2	------	
Sept. 18	7 a. m.	------	------	------	10	----------	SW. 2	------	18th. Showers all day; amount, 0. 20 inch.
	2 p. m.	------	------	------	9	----------	SW. 3	------	
	9 p. m.	------	------	------	5	----------	W. 2	------	19th. Cool, cloudy, and disagreeable; light showers, am't, 0. 20 inch.
Sept. 19	7 a. m.	------	------	------	10	----------	NW. 2	------	
	2 p. m.	------	------	------	10	----------	NE. 2	------	
	9 p. m.	------	------	------	10	----------	NW. 4	------	20th. Nearly cold enough for frost.
Sept. 20	7 a. m.	------	------	------	10	----------	N. 2	------	21st. Stars very numerous; galaxy quite distinct; direction, NE. and SW.
	2 p. m.	------	------	------	10	----------	NE. 2	------	
	9 p. m.	------	------	------	10	----------	NW. 1	------	
Sept. 21	7 a. m.	------	------	------	9	----------	NE. 2	------	23d. Pleasant; light red streaks diverging from the W. after sunset.
	2 p. m.	------	------	------	3	----------	NW. 1	------	
	9 p. m.	------	------	------	8	----------	0	------	
Sept. 22	7 a. m.	------	------	------	3	----------	SW. 1	------	
	2 p. m.	------	------	------	4	----------	S. 1	------	
	9 p. m.	------	------	------	0	----------	SE. 2	------	
Sept. 23	7 a. m.	------	------	------	1	----------	S. 1	------	
	2 p. m.	------	------	------	2	----------	SW. 2	------	
	9 p. m.	------	------	------	1	----------	0	------	
Sept. 24	7 a. m.	------	------	------	0	----------	0	------	
	2 p. m.	------	------	------	2	----------	SW. 1	------	
	9 p. m.	------	------	------	0	----------	0	------	

ST. LOUIS, MISSOURI.

Month and day.	Hour.	Barom'r corrected to 32° F.	Thermometer.	Force of vapor.	Cloudiness.	Motion of clouds.	Winds.	Relative humidity.	REMARKS.
Sept. 14	9 p. m.	29. 60	60	. 367	9	----------	NE. 2	71	15th. Rain from 5 to 9 a. m.; am't, 0.08 inch.
Sept. 15	7 a. m.	29. 60	57. 5	. 415	10	----------	NE. 1	87	
	2 p. m.	29. 51	74	. 463	8	----------	E. 1	56	17th. Thunder shower from 1 to 1.15 p. m.; amount, 0.35 inch.
	9 p. m.	29. 48	57	. 522	10	----------	E. 1	79	
Sept. 16	7 a. m.	29. 46	66. 5	. 431	3	----------	E. 2	66	18th. Rain, accompanied by violent thunder, from 2.30 to 7 p. m.; amount, 1.54 inch.
	2 p. m.	29. 41	78. 5	. 581	3	----------	E. 2	60	
	9 p. m.	29. 41	69	. 635	0	----------	E. 1	90	
Sept. 17	7 a. m.	29. 47	68. 5	. 405	1	----------	E. 2	58	19th. Rain from 4 to 9 p. m.; am't, 0.15 inch.
	2 p. m.	29. 46	69	. 653	10	----------	W. 3	92	
	9 p. m.	29. 42	68	. 612	6	----------	SE. 1	90	
Sept. 18	7 a. m.	29. 34	70	. 640	4	----------	SE. 1	88	
	2 p. m.	29. 21	80. 5	. 670	8	----------	N. 2	64	
	9 p. m.	29. 21	68. 5	. 606	2	----------	N. 2	88	
Sept. 19	7 a. m.	29. 22	63. 5	. 471	10	----------	W. 3	81	
	2 p. m.	29. 25	62. 5	. 437	10	----------	W. 3	77	
	9 p. m.	29. 33	55	. 376	10	----------	W. 3	87	
Sept. 20	7 a. m.	29. 39	48	. 310	10	----------	NW. 3	92	
	2 p. m.	29. 49	53. 5	. 352	10	----------	NW. 3	86	
	9 p. m.	29. 45	53	. 375	10	----------	NW. 2	93	
Sept. 21	7 a. m.	29. 42	51	. 348	10	----------	NW. 2	93	
	2 p. m.	29. 38	57. 5	. 343	10	----------	NW. 2	72	
	9 p. m.	29. 40	55	. 376	10	----------	NW. 2	87	
Sept. 22	7 a. m.	29. 46	56	. 420	10	----------	SE. 1	94	
	2 p. m.	29. 46	69	. 447	9	----------	SE. 1	63	
	9 p. m.	29. 52	58. 5	. 446	0	----------	SE. 1	91	
Sept. 23	7 a. m.	29. 63	58	. 423	2	----------	SE. 1	88	
	2 p. m.	29. 59	76	. 505	0	----------	S. 1	56	
	9 p. m.	29. 60	66	. 536	0	----------	S. 1	84	
Sept. 24	7 a. m.	29. 65	62	. 491	0	----------	S. 1	88	
	2 p. m.	29. 55	81	. 547	2	----------	SW. 2	52	
	9 p. m.	29. 53	68	. 630	0	----------	SW. 1	92	

STORMS Nos. 2 AND 3, SEPTEMBER, 1859.

STOCKTON, MISSOURI.

Month and day.	Hour.	Barom'r corrected to 32° F.	Thermometer.	Force of vapor.	Cloudiness.	Motion of clouds.	Winds.	Relative humidity.	REMARKS.
Sept. 14	9 p. m.	------	65	------	Nim. 10	NW. 1	NE. 2	------	15th. Thunder in NE.
Sept. 15	7 a. m.	------	63	------	Nim. 10	0	E. 1	------	17th. Thunder and lightning in E.
	2 p. m.	------	77	------	Cu. 5	0	E. 1	------	at 6 a. m.
	9 p. m.	------	70	------	Cu. st. 8	0	SE. 1	------	18th. Light shower at 6 a. m.
Sept. 16	7 a. m.	------	68	------	0	0	SE. 1	------	
	2 p. m.	------	86	------	Cu. 5	W. 1	E. 1	------	
	9 p. m.	------	72	------	Cir. 1	0	S. 1	------	
Sept. 17	7 a. m.	------	76	------	Cir. 3	W. 3	S. 2	------	
	2 p. m.	------	86	------	Cu. 9	0	S. 1	------	
	9 p. m.	------	78	------	Cu. 4	----------	S. 1	------	
Sept. 18	7 a. m.	------	68	------	Nim. 10	S. 5	W. 3	------	
	2 p. m.	------	78	------	Cu. 5	W. 3	W. 3	------	
	9 p. m.	------	64	------	Nim. 8	0	0	------	
Sept. 19	7 a. m.	------	58	------	Nim. 8	W. 2	NW. 2	------	
	2 p. m.	------	------	------	------------	----------	------------	------	
	9 p. m.	------	------	------	------------	----------	------------	------	
Sept. 20	7 a. m.	------	------	------	------------	----------	------------	------	
	2 p. m.	------	------	------	------------	----------	------------	------	
	9 p. m.	------	------	------	------------	----------	------------	------	
Sept. 21	7 a. m.	------	60	------	Cu. 8	0	NW. 1	------	
	2 p. m.	------	64	------	Cu. 10	W. 1	NW. 1	------	
	9 p. m.	------	56	------	0	0	0	------	
Sept. 22	7 a. m.	------	68	------	Fog -------	----------	0	------	
	2 p. m.	------	79	------	0	0	SW. 1	------	
	9 p. m.	------	64	------	0	0	0	------	
Sept. 23	7 a. m.	------	64	------	Cir. 2	0	SW. 1	------	
	2 p. m.	------	------	------	------------	----------	------------	------	
	9 p. m.	------	------	------	------------	----------	------------	------	
Sept. 24	7 a. m.	------	------	------	Cu. 5	0. 1	SW. 1	------	
	2 p. m.	------	------	------	0	0	SW. 1	------	
	9 p. m.	------	70	------	Cu. 0	0	0	------	

TUSCUMBIA, MISSOURI.

Month and day.	Hour.	Barom'r corrected to 32° F.	Thermometer.	Force of vapor.	Cloudiness.	Motion of clouds.	Winds.	Relative humidity.	REMARKS.
Sept. 14	9 p. m.	------	------	------	8	----------	E. 2	------	14th. Damp and cool.
Sept. 15	7 a. m.	------	------	------	8	----------	SE. 1	------	15th, 16th, and 17th. Pleasant.
	2 p. m.	------	------	------	3	----------	S. 1	------	18th. Showers; wind SW.; cool and
	9 p. m.	------	------	------	6	----------	Calm	------	damp.
Sept. 16	7 a. m.	------	------	------	4	----------	S. 1	------	19th. Cool; heavy mist.
	2 p. m.	------	------	------	6	----------	SW. 1	------	20th and 21st. Cool and cloudy.
	9 p. m.	------	------	------	3	----------	S. 2	------	22d. Pleasant.
Sept. 17	7 a. m.	------	------	------	3	----------	E. 1	------	23d and 24th. Clear and pleasant.
	2 p. m.	------	------	------	1	----------	SE. 1	------	
	9 p. m.	------	------	------	4	----------	S. 1	------	
Sept. 18	7 a. m.	------	------	------	8	----------	S. 2	------	
	2 p. m.	------	------	------	9	----------	SW. 3	------	
	9 p. m.	------	------	------	4	----------	S. 1	------	
Sept. 19	7 a. m.	------	------	------	10	----------	SE. 1	------	
	2 p. m.	------	------	------	10	----------	SE. 1	------	
	9 p. m.	------	------	------	10	----------	S. 1	------	
Sept. 20	7 a. m.	------	------	------	10	----------	NW. 1	------	
	2 p. m.	------	------	------	10	----------	W. 1	------	
	9 p. m.	------	------	------	10	----------	SW. 1	------	
Sept. 21	7 a. m.	------	------	------	10	----------	Calm	------	
	2 p. m.	------	------	------	9	----------	SW. 1	------	
	9 p. m.	------	------	------	10	----------	SW. 1	------	
Sept. 22	7 a. m.	------	------	------	2	----------	SE. 1	------	
	2 p. m.	------	------	------	0	----------	SW. 1	------	
	9 p. m.	------	------	------	3	----------	S. 1	------	
Sept. 23	7 a. m.	------	------	------	0	----------	Calm	------	
	2 p. m.	------	------	------	1	----------	SW. 1	------	
	9 p. m.	------	------	------	0	----------	Calm	------	
Sept. 24	7 a. m.	------	------	------	0	----------	Calm	------	
	2 p. m.	------	------	------	0	----------	SW. 1	------	
	9 p. m.	------	------	------	0	----------	S. 1	------	

STORMS Nos. 2 AND 3, SEPTEMBER, 1859.

WARRENTON, MISSOURI.

Month and day.	Hour.	Barom'r corrected to 32° F.	Thermometer.	Force of vapor.	Cloudiness.	Motion of clouds.	Winds.	Relative humidity.	REMARKS.
Sept. 14	9 p. m.	......	......	......	5	....	NE. 1	......	14th. Rain from 7.45 to 8.30 a. m.
Sept. 15	7 a. m.	......	......	......	8	....	NE. 1	......	15th. Rain from 5 to 7.30 a. m.
	2 p. m.	......	......	......	8	....	E. 1	......	16th. Rain from 6 to 8.30 a. m. and 9.15 to 10 a. m.
	9 p. m.	......	......	......	7	....	NE. 1	......	
Sept. 16	7 a. m.	......	......	......	8	....	NE. 1	......	17th. Heavy rain, with violent wind and lightning and thunder W., at 11.30 a. m.; clouds driving from NW. to SE.; diffuse lightning at 9 p. m. SE. to S.; rain from 7 to 7.30 a. m. and 0.30 to 3 p. m.
	2 p. m.	......	......	......	5	....	E. 0	......	
	9 p. m.	......	......	......	1	....	E. 2	......	
Sept. 17	7 a. m.	......	......	......	5	....	E. 1	......	
	2 p. m.	......	......	......	9	....	NE. 5	......	
	9 p. m.	......	......	......	7	....	SSE.	......	
Sept. 18	7 a. m.	......	......	......	7	....	S. 3	......	
	2 p. m.	......	......	......	10	....	NE. 4	......	18th. Heavy rain, accompanied by forked lightning and thunder, commencing at 9 30 a. m. and continued with but little intermission till 6 p. m , from N. to W.; diffuse lightning after sunset from E. to S. The direction of the wind had been at 6 a. m. ESE., passed through S. at 7 a. m., became SW. at 10 a. m., moved through N. to NE. at 2 p. m., at 6 p. m. it passed to E , and at 9 p. m. was S.
	9 p. m.	......	......	......	5	....	S. 4	......	
Sept. 19	7 a. m.	......	......	......	10	....	NW. 5	......	
	2 p. m.	......	......	......	7	....	W. 3	......	
	9 p. m.	......	......	......	8	....	SW. 3	......	
Sept. 20	7 a. m.	......	......	......	10	....	NW. 2	......	
	2 p. m.	......	......	......	10	....	NW. 3	......	
	9 p. m.	......	......	......	9	....	NW. 2	......	
Sept. 21	7 a. m.	......	......	......	10	....	NW. 1	......	
	2 p. m.	......	......	......	5	....	NW. 2	......	
	9 p. m.	......	......	......	8	....	NW. 1	......	
Sept. 22	7 a. m.	......	......	......	4	....	NNE. 1	......	
	2 p. m.	......	......	......	5	....	W. 1	......	
	9 p. m.	......	......	......	0	....	NE. 1	......	Storm commenced at 8 a. m on the 19th, and continued almost without intermission till noon on the 22d.
Sept. 23	7 a. m.	......	......	......	0	....	NE. 1	......	
	2 p. m.	......	......	......	2	....	SSE. 1	......	
	9 p. m.	......	......	......	0	....	S. 1	......	
Sept. 24	7 a. m.	......	......	......	0	....	S. 0	......	
	2 p. m.	......	......	......	3	....	SW. 1	......	
	9 p. m.	......	......	......	0	....	SSW. 1	......	

WAYNESVILLE, MISSOURI.

Month and day.	Hour.	Barom'r corrected to 32° F.	Thermometer.	Force of vapor.	Cloudiness.	Motion of clouds.	Winds.	Relative humidity.	REMARKS.
Sept. 14	9 p. m.	......	......	......	5	....	NW. 1	......	18th. Quite a heavy shower in the afternoon.
Sept. 15	7 a. m.	......	......	......	6	....	W. 1	......	
	2 p. m.	......	......	......	3	....	S. 1	......	19th. Rain late in the evening.
	9 p. m.	......	......	......	2	....	S. 1	......	
Sept. 16	7 a. m.	......	......	......	1	....	S. 2	......	
	2 p. m.	......	......	......	3	....	S. 2	......	
	9 p. m.	......	......	......	2	....	SW. 2	......	
Sept. 17	7 a. m.	......	......	......	3	....	SW. 2	......	
	2 p. m.	......	......	......	4	....	SW. 3	......	
	9 p. m.	......	......	......	2	....	SW. 2	......	
Sept. 18	7 a. m.	......	......	......	5	....	SW. 3	......	
	2 p. m.	......	......	......	8	....	SW. 4	......	
	9 p. m.	......	......	......	5	....	SW. 3	......	
Sept. 19	7 a. m.	......	......	......	8	....	NW. 2	......	
	2 p. m.	......	......	......	7	....	NW. 3	......	
	9 p. m.	......	......	......	8	....	NW. 2	......	
Sept. 20	7 a. m.	......	......	......	9	....	NW. 2	......	
	2 p. m.	......	......	......	8	....	NW. 2	......	
	9 p. m.	......	......	......	8	....	N. 2	......	
Sept. 21	7 a. m.	......	......	......	8	....	NW. 2	......	
	2 p. m.	......	......	......	8	....	NW. 2	......	
	9 p. m.	......	......	......	5	....	NW. 1	......	
Sept. 22	7 a. m.	......	......	......	1	....	NW. 1	......	
	2 p. m.	......	......	......	1	....	NW. 2	......	
	9 p. m.	......	......	......	2	....	NW. 1	......	
Sept. 23	7 a. m.	......	......	......	1	....	NW. 1	......	
	2 p. m.	......	......	......	0	....	NW. 1	......	
	9 p. m.	......	......	......	0	....	NW. 1	......	
Sept. 24	7 a. m.	......	......	......	0	....	W. 1	......	
	2 p. m.	......	......	......	2	....	W. 2	......	
	9 p. m.	......	......	......	2	....	W. 1	......	

STORMS Nos. 2 AND 3, SEPTEMBER, 1859.

WET AU GLAIZE, MISSOURI.

Month and day.	Hour.	Barom'r corrected to 32° F.	Thermometer.	Force of vapor.	Cloudiness.	Motion of clouds.	Winds.	Relative humidity.	REMARKS.
Sept. 14	9 p. m.	------	------	------	10	----------	SW. --------	------	14th. Several showers during the day.
Sept. 15	7 a. m.	------	------	------	10	----------	SE. 1	------	
	2 p. m.	------	------	------	2	----------	SE. 2	------	15th. Two or three light showers in the a. m.
	9 p. m.	------	------	------	2	----------	SE --------	------	
Sept. 16	7 a. m.	------	------	------	1	----------	S. 1	------	16th. Warm.
	2 p. m.	------	------	------	1	----------	S. 1	------	17th. Warm; lightning E. & SE. at 9 p. m.; shower in the night.
	9 p. m.	------	------	------	1	----------	S. --------	------	
Sept. 17	7 a. m.	------	------	------	0	----------	SE. 1	------	18th. Rain from 11 a. m. to 1.30 p. m.
	2 p. m.	------	------	------	0	----------	SE. 2	------	
	9 p. m.	------	------	------	1	----------	SE. 1	------	19th. Drizzling rain all day.
Sept. 18	7 a. m.	------	------	------	5	----------	SE. 2	------	20th. Cool.
	2 p. m.	------	------	------	7	----------	S. 3	------	21st to 24th. Pleasant.
	9 p. m.	------	------	------	0	----------	SW. 2	------	
Sept. 19	7 a. m.	------	------	------	10	----------	NW. 2	------	
	2 p. m.	------	------	------	10	----------	NW. 3	------	
	9 p. m.	------	------	------	10	----------	NW. 3	------	
Sept. 20	7 a. m.	------	------	------	10	----------	NW. 1	------	
	2 p. m.	------	------	------	10	----------	NW. 2	------	
	9 p. m.	------	------	------	10	----------	NW --------	------	
Sept. 21	7 a. m.	------	------	------	10	----------	NW. 1	------	
	2 p. m.	------	------	------	10	----------	NW. 2	------	
	9 p. m.	------	------	------	10	----------	NW --------	------	
Sept. 22	7 a. m.	------	------	------	0	----------	SE. 1	------	
	2 p. m.	------	------	------	1	----------	S. 2	------	
	9 p. m.	------	------	------	0	----------	SW. --------	------	
Sept. 23	7 a. m.	------	------	------	0	----------	S. 1	------	
	2 p. m.	------	------	------	0	----------	S. 2	------	
	9 p. m.	------	------	------	0	----------	S. --------	------	
Sept. 24	7 a. m.	------	------	------	0	----------	SW. 1	------	
	2 p. m.	------	------	------	1	----------	SW. 2	------	
	9 p. m.	------	------	------	0	----------	SW. --------	------	

APPLETON, WISCONSIN.

Month and day.	Hour.	Barom'r corrected to 32° F.	Thermometer.	Force of vapor.	Cloudiness.	Motion of clouds.	Winds.	Relative humidity.	REMARKS.
Sept. 14	9 p. m.	29. 24	44	. 251	Cu. st. 8	----------	E. 1	84	17th and 18th. Showers; amount, 0.25 inch.
Sept. 15	7 a. m.	29. 15	47	. 247	Cu. st. 8	E. 1	E. 2	71	
	2 p. m.	29. 11	64	. 438	St. 8	E. 2	E. 2	68	Began to rain in the night of the 19th and ended in the night of the 20th; amount, 1.00 inch.
	9 p. m.	29. 14	54	. 391	Nim. 10	----------	E. 1	87	
Sept. 16	7 a. m.	29. 03	56	. 337	Cu. st. 8	SE. 2	SE. 1	70	
	2 p. m.	28. 89	69	. 340	St. 5	S. 1	S. 1	45	22d. Rain from 6 a. m. to 3 p. m.; amount, 0.125 inch.
	9 p. m.	28. 95	49	. 321	0	0	S. 1	86	
Sept. 17	7 a. m.	28. 94	50	. 334	0	0	S. 1	86	24th. Aurora.
	2 p. m.	28. 92	70	. 396	0	S. 1	S. 1	48	
	9 p. m.	28. 90	64	. 391	St. 5	SW. 1	SE. 1	87	
Sept. 18	7 a. m.	28. 67	68	. 658	Cu. st. 4	S. 2	S. 2	90	
	2 p. m.	28. 58	72	. 758	Nim. 10	SW. 1	SW. 1	90	
	9 p. m.	28. 60	65	. 591	Nim. 10	E. 1	SW. 1	89	
Sept. 19	7 a. m.	28. 54	50	. 334	Nim. 10	NE. 2	NE. 2	86	
	2 p. m.	28. 65	48	. 232	Nim. 10	NE. 3	NE. 3	60	
	9 p. m.	29. 01	42	. 196	Nim. 10	----------	NW. 4	68	
Sept. 20	7 a. m.	29. 02	40	. 222	St. 3	NE. 2	NE. 2	83	
	2 p. m.	29. 08	56	. 203	0	----------	NE. 4	42	
	9 p. m.	29. 05	42	. 196	0	----------	NE. 4	68	
Sept. 21	7 a. m.	29. 02	42	. 241	St. 4	NE. 2	NE. 2	84	
	2 p. m.	28. 96	63	. 389	0	----------	NE. 1	63	
	9 p. m.	28. 94	52	. 362	Nim. 10	----------	NE. 2	87	
Sept. 22	7 a. m.	28. 84	53	. 376	Nim. 10	NE. 1	NE. 1	87	
	2 p. m.	28. 84	55	. 350	Nim. 10	NE. 1	NE. 1	75	
	9 p. m.	28. 95	53	. 405	Nim. 10	----------	NW. 1	94	
Sept. 23	7 a. m.	28. 99	54	. 336	Cu. 8	NNW. 1	NNW. 1	75	
	2 p. m.	29. 02	58	. 367	St. 8	NE. 1	NE. 1	71	
	9 p. m.	29. 04	52	. 375	0	0	NW. 1	93	
Sept. 24	7 a. m.	29. 04	53	. 349	0	SW. 1	SW. 1	81	
	2 p. m.	28. 98	74	. 591	0	0	SW. 1	68	
	9 p. m.	29. 04	52	. 362	0	0	SW. 1	87	

STORMS Nos. 2 AND 3, SEPTEMBER, 1859.

BAY CITY, WISCONSIN.

Month and day.	Hour.	Barom'r corrected to 32° F.	Thermometer.	Force of vapor.	Cloudiness.		Motion of clouds.		Winds.		Relative humidity.	REMARKS.
Sept. 14	9 p. m.	------	34	------		0		0	S.	1	------	17th. Rain from 4 to 6 p. m.; amount, 0.80 inch.
Sept. 15	7 a. m.	------	44	------	St.	10		0	SW.	1	------	18th. Rain from 4 to 10 a. m.; amount, 0 15 inch.
	2 p. m.	------	60	------	Cir. st.	10		0	SW.	2	------	
	9 p. m.	------	46	------	Cir. cu.	5		0	S.	1	------	
Sept. 16	7 a. m.	------	50	------	St.	10		0	SW.	1	------	
	2 p. m.	------	64	------	Cir.	5	SW.	1	SW.	2	------	
	9 p. m.	------	56	------	St.	10		0	S.	1	------	
Sept. 17	7 a. m.	------	56	------	St.	10		0	SW.	1	------	
	2 p. m.	------	60	------	Cu. st.	10	SW.	1	NE.	2	------	
	9 p. m.	------	52	------		0		0	NE.	2	------	
Sept. 18	7 a. m.	------	52	------	Cu. st.	10		0	S.	1	------	
	2 p. m.	------	55	------	Cu. st.	10		0	NE.	1	------	
	9 p. m.	------	48	------	St.	10		0	NE.	3	------	
Sept. 19	7 a. m.	------	42	------	Cu. st.	10	NE.	3	NE.	5	------	
	2 p. m.	------	43	------		0		0	NE.	4	------	
	9 p. m.	------	34	------		0		0	S.	1	------	
Sept. 20	7 a. m.	------	32	------		0		0	SW.	1	------	
	2 p. m.	------	42	------		0		0	NE.	3	------	
	9 p. m.	------	35	------		0		0	S.	1	------	
Sept. 21	7 a. m.	------	30	------		0		0	SW.	1	------	
	2 p. m.	------	48	------		0		0	NE.	3	------	
	9 p. m.	------	34	------		0		0	S.	1	------	
Sept. 22	7 a. m.	------	48	------	Fog	10		0	S.	1	------	
	2 p. m.	------	50	------		0		0	NE.	2	------	
	9 p. m.	------	39	------		0		0	S.	1	------	
Sept. 23	7 a. m.	------	42	------		0		0	SW.	1	------	
	2 p. m.	------	56	------		0		0	NE.	2	------	
	9 p. m.	------	42	------		0		0	S.	1	------	
Sept. 24	7 a. m.	------	42	------		0		0	SW.	1	------	
	2 p. m.	------	54	------		0		0	NE.	2	------	
	9 p. m.	------	50	------	Cu.	5		0	S.	1	------	

BELOIT, WISCONSIN.

Month and day.	Hour.	Barom'r corrected to 32° F.	Thermometer.	Force of vapor.	Cloudiness.	Motion of clouds.	Winds.		Relative humidity.	REMARKS.
Sept. 14	9 p. m.	29.361	48	------	9	----------	SE.	1	------	18th. Showers at 11 a. m. and 1½ p. m.
Sept. 15	7 a. m.	.358	52	------	9	----------	E.	1	------	19th. Rain in the evening; amount, 0. 47 inch.
	2 p. m.	.286	66	------	8	----------	SE.	2	------	20th. Rain at intervals; amount, 0. 28 inch.
	9 p. m.	.253	56	------	9	----------	SE.	1	------	21st. Amount of rain, 0. 05 inch.
Sept. 16	7 a. m.	.213	56	------	8	----------	E.	1	------	
	2 p. m.	.150	72	------	3	----------	E.	2	------	
	9 p. m.	.145	54	------	0	----------	E.	2	------	
Sept. 17	7 a. m.	.153	46	------	0	----------	SE.	1	------	
	2 p. m.	.135	81	------	6	----------	S.	2	------	
	9 p. m.	.067	65	------	1	----------	S.	2	------	
Sept. 18	7 a. m.	28.992	62	------	8	----------	S.	1	------	
	2 p. m.	.887	76	------	7	----------	S.	2	------	
	9 p. m.	.817	66	------	10	----------	S.	2	------	
Sept. 19	7 a. m.	.697	62	------	9	----------	SW.	1	------	
	2 p. m.	.900	49	------	9	----------	N.	2	------	
	9 p. m.	.050	45	------	10	----------	NW.	1	------	
Sept. 20	7 a. m.	29.139	49	------	10	----------	N.	2	------	
	2 p. m.	.115	62	------	3	----------	N.	2	------	
	9 p. m.	.188	46	------	0	----------	N.	2	------	
Sept. 21	7 a. m.	.130	49	------	9	----------	N.	1	------	
	2 p. m.	.083	54	------	8	----------	N.	1	------	
	9 p. m.	.078	52	------	10	----------	N.	2	------	
Sept. 22	7 a. m.	.081	52	------	9	----------	N.	1	------	
	2 p. m.	.116	58	------	9	----------	N.	1	------	
	9 p. m.	.168	52	------	9	----------	N.	2	------	
Sept. 23	7 a. m.	.251	52	------	5	----------	N.	1	------	
	2 p. m.	.220	72	------	7	----------	N.	1	------	
	9 p. m.	.265	58	------	0	----------	N.	1	------	
Sept. 24	7 a. m.	.291	48	------	0	----------	NE.	1	------	
	2 p. m.	.230	72	------	0	----------	SE.	1	------	
	9 p. m.	.225	58	------	0	----------	N.	1	------	

STORMS Nos. 2 AND 3, SEPTEMBER, 1859.

GREEN BAY, WISCONSIN.

Month and day.	Hour.	Barom'r corrected to 32° F.	Thermometer.	Force of vapor.	Cloudiness.		Motion of clouds.		Winds.		Relative humidity.
Sept. 14	9 p. m.	......	49	......	Cir. cu.	10	SW.	1	SW.	1	......
Sept. 15	7 a. m.	......	43	......		10	....		S.	1	......
	2 p. m.	......	64	......		10	....		S.	1	......
	9 p. m.	......	51	......		10	....			0	......
Sept. 16	7 a. m.	......	56	......		0		0		0	......
	2 p. m.	......	62	......		0		0	NE.	1	......
	9 p. m.	......	50	......		0		0		0	......
Sept. 17	7 a. m.	......	58	......	Dense fog		....			0	......
	2 p. m.	......	67	......		0		0	N.	1	......
	9 p. m.	......	54	......		0		0		0	......
Sept. 18	7 a. m.	......	61	......		10	....		S.	1	......
	2 p. m.	......	68	......		10	....		S.	1	......
	9 p. m.	......	66	......		10	S			0	......
Sept. 19	7 a. m.	......	47	......	Nim.	10	N		N.	6	......
	2 p. m.	......	50	......	Nim.	10	N		N.	6	......
	9 p. m.	......	42	......	St.	10	N.	2	N.	7	......
Sept. 20	7 a. m.	......	42	......	St.	4	NE.	2	NE.	4	......
	2 p. m.	......	54	......		0	....		NE.	5	......
	9 p. m.	......	46	......	St.	10	N.	1	N.	3	......
Sept. 21	7 a. m.	......	50	......	St.	10	N.	1	N.	3	......
	2 p. m.	......	55	......	St.	10	N.	1	NE.	3	......
	9 p. m.	......	54	......		10	....		N.	2	......
Sept. 22	7 a. m.	......	51	......	Nim.	10	....		N.	1	......
	2 p. m.	......	54	......	Nim.	10	N.	1	NE.	1	......
	9 p. m.	......	54	......		10	....			0	......
Sept. 23	7 a. m.	......	56	......	Nim.	10	....		N.	1	......
	2 p. m.	......	60	......	St.	10	N.	1	N.	1	......
	9 p. m.	......	52	......		0		0		0	......
Sept. 24	7 a. m.	......	58	......	Thick fog		....			0	......
	2 p. m.	......	69	......	....			0		0	......
	9 p. m.	......	53	......		0		0		0	......

REMARKS.

19th. Rain in the night, with heavy gale, and ended at 6 p. m. on the 20th; amount, 1. 00 inch. Amount of rain from storm ending at 9 a. m. on the 23d, 0. 75 inch.

JANESVILLE, WISCONSIN.

Month and day.	Hour.	Barom'r corrected to 32° F.	Thermometer.	Force of vapor.	Cloudiness.		Motion of clouds.		Winds.		Relative humidity.
Sept. 14	9 p. m.	......	52	......	St.	2	....		N.	2	......
Sept. 15	7 a. m.	......	44	......	St.	5	E.	3	NE.	3	......
	2 p. m.	......	68	......	St., nim.	7	NE.	3	E.	4	......
	9 p. m.	......	58	......	....		....		E.	2	......
Sept. 16	7 a. m.	......	53	......	St.	7	NW.	2	SE.	2	......
	2 p. m.	......	72	......	Cir.	2	....		E.	3	......
	9 p. m.	......	53	......	Cir. cu.	2	SE.	3	E.	2	......
Sept. 17	7 a. m.	......	43	......		0	....		E.	2	......
	2 p. m.	......	70	......	Cir.	2	....		S.	3	......
	9 p. m.	......	64	......	St.	4	E.	2	SE.	2	......
Sept. 18	7 a. m.	......	73	......	Nim.	7	E.	3	SE.	3	......
	2 p. m.	......	73	......	Nim.	6	NE.	4	SE.	3	......
	9 p. m.	......	66	......	Nim.	8	NE.	5	SE.	1	......
Sept. 19	7 a. m.	......	62	......	Nim.	9	....		SE		......
	2 p. m.	......	52	......	Nim.	8	SW.	6	NE.	4	......
	9 p. m.	......	48	......	Nim.	9	SW.	4	NE.	4	......
Sept. 20	7 a. m.	......	43	......	Nim.	8	....		NE.	3	......
	2 p. m.	......	65	......	Cir.	3	SW.	4	NE.	3	......
	9 p. m.	......	47	......	Nim.	3	....		NE.	2	......
Sept. 21	7 a. m.	......	41	......	St.	8	....		NE.	3	......
	2 p. m.	......	63	......	St.	8	....		NE.	3	......
	9 p. m.	......	55	......	St.	7	....		NE.	1	......
Sept. 22	7 a. m.	......	50	......	Nim.	8	....		N.	1	......
	2 p. m.	......	70	......	Nim.	8	....		N.	1	......
	9 p. m.	......	65	......	Nim.	8	....		N.	1	......
Sept. 23	7 a. m.	......	51	......	Cu.	6	E.	2	NW.	1	......
	2 p. m.	......	70	......	Cu., nim.	7	E.	3	W.	2	......
	9 p. m.	......	57	......		0	....		N		......
Sept. 24	7 a. m.	......	45	......	Cu.	3	....			0	......
	2 p. m.	......	73	......	....		....			0	......
	9 p. m.	......	50	......		0	....		SW.	2	......

REMARKS.

17th. Diffused lightning and little thunder in west at 6 p. m.

18th. Commenced raining during past night; continued and general.

19th. Drizzling rain.

20th. Clouds cleared away at noon.

21st. Cloudy.

22d. Rain during the night.

STORMS Nos. 2 AND 3, SEPTEMBER, 1859.

KENOSHA, WISCONSIN.

Month and day.	Hour.	Barom'r corrected to 32° F.	Thermometer.	Force of vapor.	Cloudiness.	Motion of clouds.	Winds.	Relative humidity.
Sept. 14	9 p. m.	------	51	------	5	----------	E. 2	------
Sept. 15	7 a. m.	------	57	------	10	----------	SE. 2	------
	2 p. m.	------	61	------	10	----------	SE. 3	------
	9 p. m.	29. 64	58	------	10	----------	E. 3	------
Sept. 16	7 a. m.	29. 56	58	------	10	----------	SE. 2	------
	2 p. m.	------	------	------	0	----------	----------	------
	9 p. m.	29. 52	52	------	0	----------	SE. 2	------
Sept. 17	7 a. m.	29. 54	49	------	0	----------	E. 1	------
	2 p. m.	29. 51	70	------	0	----------	SE. 1	------
	9 p. m.	29. 45	62½	------	0	----------	SE. 1	------
Sept. 18	7 a. m.	29. 38	62	------	10	----------	S. 3	------
	2 p. m.	------	66	------	10	----------	S. 3	------
	9 p. m.	------	66	------	10	----------	S. 3	------
Sept. 19	7 a. m.	29. 07	63	------	10	----------	SW. 1	------
	2 p. m.	29. 20	53½	------	10	----------	N. 5	------
	9 p. m.	29. 32	51	------	10	----------	N. 5	------
Sept. 20	7 a. m.	29. 44	51	------	10	----------	SE. 5	------
	2 p. m.	29. 49	51½	------	10	----------	NE. 3	------
	9 p. m.	29. 50	54	------	10	----------	NE. 4	------
Sept. 21	7 a. m.	29. 44	52	------	10	----------	E. 3	------
	2 p. m.	29. 39	54	------	10	----------	E. 2	------
	9 p. m.	------	53½	------	10	----------	NE. 2	------
Sept. 22	7 a. m.	29. 42	54	------	10	----------	E. 2	------
	2 p. m.	------	63	------	10	----------	E. 1	------
	9 p. m.	29. 51	57½	------	10	----------	E. 1	------
Sept. 23	7 a. m.	29. 56	57½	------	10	----------	S. 1	------
	2 p. m.	29. 56	70	------	5	----------	S. 2	------
	9 p. m.	29. 62	57½	------	10	----------	E. 1	------
Sept. 24	7 a. m.	29. 60	51	------	0	----------	NE. 1	------
	2 p. m.	------	62½	------	0	----------	NE. 1	------
	9 p. m.	29. 57	57	------	10	----------	E. 1	------

REMARKS.

18th. Rain, commencing before daylight, accompanied by thunder and lightning.
19th. Rain last night and to-day; amount, 1. 25 inch.
20th. Rain last night.
21st. Slight rain; amount, 0. 28 inch.

LAKE MILLS, WISCONSIN.

Month and day.	Hour.	Barom'r corrected to 32° F.	Thermometer.	Force of vapor.	Cloudiness.	Motion of clouds.	Winds.	Relative humidity.
Sept. 14	9 p. m.	------	------	------	6	----------	SE. 1	------
Sept. 15	7 a. m.	------	------	------	7	----------	SE. 3	------
	2 p. m.	------	------	------	7	----------	E. 2	------
	9 p. m.	------	------	------	9	----------	SE. 1	------
Sept. 16	7 a. m.	------	------	------	10	----------	W. 0	------
	2 p. m.	------	------	------	8	----------	W. 1	------
	9 p. m.	------	------	------	5	----------	W. 2	------
Sept. 17	7 a. m.	------	------	------	1	----------	SW. 0	------
	2 p. m.	------	------	------	2	----------	SW. 2	------
	9 p. m.	------	------	------	10	----------	S. 1	------
Sept. 18	7 a. m.	------	------	------	10	----------	S. 1	------
	2 p. m.	------	------	------	10	----------	S. 1	------
	9 p. m.	------	------	------	10	----------	S. 0	------
Sept. 19	7 a. m.	------	------	------	10	----------	S. 0	------
	2 p. m.	------	------	------	10	----------	S. 2	------
	9 p. m.	------	------	------	10	----------	SE. 5	------
Sept. 20	7 a. m.	------	------	------	10	----------	NE. 6	------
	2 p. m.	------	------	------	2	----------	NE. 3	------
	9 p. m.	------	------	------	1	----------	E. 2	------
Sept. 21	7 a. m.	------	------	------	10	----------	NE. 3	------
	2 p. m.	------	------	------	10	----------	NE. 0	------
	9 p. m.	------	------	------	10	----------	NE. 0	------
Sept. 22	7 a. m.	------	------	------	10	----------	SE. 0	------
	2 p. m.	------	------	------	10	----------	SE. 0	------
	9 p. m.	------	------	------	10	----------	SE. 0	------
Sept. 23	7 a. m.	------	------	------	10	----------	S. 0	------
	2 p. m.	------	------	------	3	----------	S. 0	------
	9 p. m.	------	------	------	0	----------	S. 0	------
Sept. 24	7 a. m.	------	------	------	0	----------	S. 0	------
	2 p. m.	------	------	------	0	----------	S. 0	------
	9 p. m.	------	------	------	0	----------	S. 0	------

REMARKS.

16th. Dash of rain at 7 a. m.
17th. Lightning SW. at 8 p. m.: continued to increase till 3 a. m. on the 18th, then rained for about one hour; considerable chain lightning and heavy thunder during the storm.
18th. Rain from 3 to 4 p. m.
19th. Rain from 7 to 10 a. m.; slight showers during the day.
20th. Pleasant and warm.
21st. Appearances of rain.
22d. A very little rain at 4 p. m.
23d and 24th. Pleasant and quite warm all day.

STORMS NOS. 2 AND 3, SEPTEMBER, 1859.

MANITOWOC, WISCONSIN.

Month and day.	Hour.	Barom'r corrected to 32° F.	Thermometer.	Force of vapor.	Cloudiness.	Motion of clouds.	Winds.	Relative humidity.	REMARKS.
Sept. 14	9 p. m.	28 1.0	48	......	Cir. st. 5	....	E. 3	......	18th. Thunder shower from 4½ to 7½ a. m.
Sept. 15	7 a. m.	28 1.4	51	......	Cir. 5	W. 2	SE. 3	......	Began to rain at 9½ p. m. and ended at 6 p. m. on the 19th.
	2 p. m.	28 0.8	61	......	Cir. cu. 5	W. 3	S. 3	......	Showers from 11 a. m. the 21st to 10 a. m. on the 23d.
	9 p. m.	28 0.4	56	......	Cir. cu. 10	....	E. 5	......	
Sept. 16	7 a. m.	27 11.4	56	......	Cir. 5	W. 4	SE. 2	......	
	2 p. m.	27 10.5	62	......	Cir. cu. 10	....	SE. 2	......	
	9 p. m.	27 10.4	55	......	Cir. 10	....	SE. 1	......	
Sept. 17	7 a. m.	27 10.6	45	......	Foggy 0	....	W. 1	......	
	2 p. m.	27 10.2	64	......	Cir. st. 5	W. 3	SE. 2	......	
	9 p. m.	27 10.0	57	......	Cir. 5	....	E. 1	......	
Sept. 18	7 a. m.	27 8.4	61	......	Nim. 10	....	S. 5	......	
	2 p. m.	27 7.5	66	......	Nim. 10	....	SW. 4	......	
	9 p. m.	27 6.7	63	......	Nim. 10	....	S. 3	......	
Sept. 19	7 a. m.	27 6.1	57	......	Cu. st. 10	....	NE. 6	......	
	2 p. m.	27 7.7	48	......	Nim. 10	....	N. 7	......	
	9 p. m.	27 10.0	46	......	Fog, cu. st. 10	....	N. 7	......	
Sept. 20	7 a. m.	27 11.0	48	......	Cu. 5	....	NE. 5	......	
	2 p. m.	27 11.3	55	......	Cir. st. 5	....	NE. 5	......	
	9 p. m.	27 11.4	52	......	Cu. st. 5	....	NE. 4	......	
Sept. 21	7 a. m.	27 10.5	46	......	Cir. st. 5	....	N. 2	......	
	2 p. m.	27 10.0	57	......	Cu. 10	....	N. 3	......	
	9 p. m.	27 9.6	53	......	Nim. 10	....	N. 2	......	
Sept. 22	7 a. m.	27 9.3	54	......	Nim. 10	....	NE. 2	......	
	2 p. m.	27 9.8	58	......	Nim. 10	....	NE. 2	......	
	9 p. m.	27 10.7	55	......	Cu. st. 10	....	N. 1	......	
Sept. 23	7 a. m.	27 11.1	56	......	Nim. 10	....	SE. 1	......	
	2 p. m.	27 11.5	58	......	Fog, cu. st. 10	....	E. 1	......	
	9 p. m.	27 11.8	56	......	0	....	NW. 1	......	
Sept. 24	7 a. m.	28 0.0	53	......	Fog, nim. 10	....	W. 2	......	
	2 p. m.	27 11.3	63	......	Nim. 10	....	SE. 2	......	
	9 p. m.	27 11.5	50	......	Fog 0	....	W. 1	......	

MILWAUKEE, WISCONSIN.*

Month and day.	Hour.	Barom'r corrected to 32° F.	Thermometer.	Force of vapor.	Cloudiness.	Motion of clouds.	Winds.	Relative humidity.	REMARKS.
Sept. 14	9 p. m.	......	51	.220	....	....	....	59	
Sept. 15	7 a. m.	......	57	.322	....	....	....	69	
	2 p. m.	......	63	.356	....	....	....	62	
	9 p. m.	......	57	.407	....	....	....	87	
Sept. 16	7 a. m.	......	58	.365	....	....	....	76	
	2 p. m.	......	62	.369	....	....	....	66	
	9 p. m.	......	54	.362	....	....	....	87	
Sept. 17	7 a. m.	......	49	.271	....	....	....	78	
	2 p. m.	......	66	.407	....	....	....	64	
	9 p. m.	......	64	.497	....	....	....	83	
Sept. 18	7 a. m.	29.217	64	.529	....	....	....	89	
	10 a. m.	29.196	......	......	....	....	....	......	
	12 m.	29.167	......	......	....	....	....	......	
	1 p. m.	29.136	......	......	....	....	....	......	
	2 p. m.	29.107	69	.635	....	....	....	90	
	4 p. m.	29.062	......	......	....	....	....	......	
	5 p. m.	29.056	......	......	....	....	....	......	
	6 p. m.	29.051	......	......	....	....	....	......	
	8 p. m.	29.026	......	......	....	....	....	......	
	9 p. m.	29.007	67	.591	....	....	....	89	
Sept. 19	1 a. m.	28.908	......	......	....	....	....	......	
	5½ a. m.	28.885	......	......	....	....	....	......	
	7 a. m.	......	64	.529	....	....	....	89	
	8 a. m.	28.908	......	......	....	....	....	......	
	10 a. m.	28.971	......	......	....	....	....	......	
	12 m.	29.031	......	......	....	....	....	......	
	2 p. m.	......	51	.321	....	....	....	86	
	4 p. m.	29.148	......	......	....	....	....	......	

* Lapham, observer.

STORMS Nos. 2 AND 3, SEPTEMBER, 1859.

MILWAUKEE, WISCONSIN—Continued.

Month and day.	Hour.	Barom'r corrected to 32° F.	Thermometer.	Force of vapor.	Cloudiness.	Motion of clouds.	Winds.	Relative humidity.	REMARKS.
Sept. 19	8 p. m.	29. 218	......	......	......	......	......	......	
	9 p. m.	......	49	. 322	......	......	......	93	
Sept. 20	7 a. m.	......	49	. 297	......	......	......	85	
	9 a. m.	29. 417	......	......	......	......	......	......	
	11 a. m.	29. 434	......	......	......	......	......	......	
	2 p. m.	......	52	. 308	......	......	......	79	
	7 p. m.	29. 398	......	......	......	......	......	......	
	9 p. m.	......	53	. 295	......	......	......	73	
Sept. 21	7 a. m.	......	50	. 309	......	......	......	86	
	2 p. m.	......	53	. 321	......	......	......	80	
	9 p. m.	......	54	. 389	......	......	......	93	
Sept. 22	7 a. m.	......	54	. 389	......	......	......	93	
	2 p. m.	29. 309	58	. 452	......	......	......	94	
	9 p. m.	......	57	. 436	......	......	......	94	
Sept. 23	7 a. m.	......	57	. 436	......	......	......	94	
	2 p. m.	......	62	. 429	......	......	......	77	
	9 p. m.	......	57	. 436	......	......	......	94	
Sept. 24	7 a. m.	29. 511	54	. 389	......	......	......	93	
	2 p. m.	29. 472	59	. 439	......	......	......	88	
	9 p. m.	29. 450	56	. 420	......	......	......	93	

MILWAUKEE, WISCONSIN.*

Month and day.	Hour.	Barom'r corrected to 32° F.	Thermometer.	Force of vapor.	Cloudiness.	Motion of clouds.	Winds.	Relative humidity.	REMARKS.
Sept. 14	9 p. m.	29. 32	......	......	Cir. cu., cir and nim. 8	......	E. 2	......	15th. Rain from 4.30 to 5.30 a. m. 17th. Rain from 4 a. m. to 2.30 p. m , and from 7 to 9 p. m. 18th. Storm commenced at 6 a. m. and ended at 6 a. m. on the 20th. Rain from 3 a m. the 21st to 8.45 a. m. on the 23d.
Sept. 15	7 a. m.	29. 35	......	......	Nim., st., cir. cu. 9	......	SE. 2	......	
	2 p. m.	29. 32	......	......	Nim.,cir.st. 10	E. 2	SE. 2	......	
	9 p. m.	29. 30	......	......	Cu., nim. 9	NW. 3	SE. 3	......	
Sept. 16	7 a m.	29. 23	......	......	Nim., cu., cu. st , cir. cu. 8	SE. 2	SE. 1	......	
	2 p. m.	29. 18	......	......	Cir. st., cir. cu. 9	NE. 1	E. 2	......	
	9 p. m.	29. 15	......	......	Cir. cu. 5	E. 1	......	......	
Sept. 17	7 a. m.	29. 16	......	......	......	......	......	......	
	2 p. m.	29. 14	......	......	Nim., cir. st., cu. 6	NE. 3	SE. 2	......	
	9 p. m.	29. 09	......	......	Cir. cu., cir. st. 1	......	......	......	
Sept. 18	7 a m.	29. 01	......	......	Nim., st., cu st. 8	......	SE. 2	......	
	2 p. m.	28. 91	......	......	Nim. 9	NE. 6	SE. 4	......	
	9 p. m.	28. 84	......	......	Nim. 10	......	W. 2	......	
Sept. 19	7 a. m.	28. 67	......	......	Nim ,st., cir. 7	......	......	......	
	2 p. m.	28. 77	......	......	Nim., cir. 10	S. 4	NE. 5	......	
	9 p. m.	28. 94	......	......	Nim. 10	......	NE. 6	......	
Sept. 20	7 a. m.	29. 14	......	......	Nim. 10	SW. 5	NE. 3	......	
	2 p. m.	29. 18	......	......	Cir. st., st. cir. 6	N. 3	NE. 5	......	
	9 p. m.	29. 17	......	......	Nim. 8	......	NE. 4	......	
Sept. 21	7 a. m.	29. 25	......	......	Nim , cir st., cir. 10	SW. 4	NE. 3	......	
	2 p. m.	29. 11	......	......	Nim. st. 10	S. 3	N. 1	......	
	9 p. m.	29. 05	......	......	Nim. 10	......	......	......	
Sept. 22	7 a. m.	29. 07	......	......	Nim. 10	SW. 2	SW. 1	......	
	2 p. m.	29. 15	......	......	Nim. 10	......	NE. 1	......	
	9 p. m.	29. 14	......	......	Nim. 10	......	......	......	
Sept. 23	7 a. m.	29. 21	......	......	Cu., nim.,st. & cir. cu. 10	SE. 2	......	......	
	2 p. m.	29. 22	......	......	Nim., st., cir., st. 9	SW. 2	NE. 2	......	
	9 p. m.	29. 25	......	......	......	......	......	......	

* Larkin, observer.

STORMS Nos. 2 AND 3, SEPTEMBER, 1859.

MILWAUKEE, WISCONSIN—Continued.

Month and day.	Hour.	Barom'r corrected to 32° F.	Thermometer.	Force of vapor.	Cloudiness.	Motion of clouds.	Winds.	Relative humidity.	REMARKS.
Sept. 24	7 a. m.	29. 26	------	------	St., cir., nim., cir. cu.	----------	W. 1	------	24th. Fog from 2 p. m. till midnight.
	2 p. m.	29. 26	------	------	Nim., dense fog 10	SW. 3	NE. 2	------	
	9 p. m.	29. 24	------	------	Nim. 10	----------	------------	------	

MILWAUKEE, WISCONSIN.*

Month and day.	Hour.	Barom'r corrected to 32° F.	Thermometer.	Force of vapor.	Cloudiness.	Motion of clouds.	Winds.	Relative humidity.	REMARKS.
Sept. 14	9 p. m.	29. 46	48	------	4	----------	NE. 2	------	18th. Amount rain, 0.32 inch.
Sept. 15	7 a. m.	29. 50	56	------	7	----------	SE. 2	------	20th. Amount rain, 0.78 inch.
	2 p. m.	29. 44	64	------	7	----------	SE. 2	------	20th and 23d. Amount, 0.41 inch.
	9 p. m.	29. 40	56	------	9	----------	SE. 3	------	
Sept. 16	7 a. m.	29. 41	59	------	4	----------	SE. 1	------	
	2 p. m.	29. 29	65	------	5	----------	SE. 1	------	
	9 p. m.	29. 23	50	------	1	----------	N. 1	------	
Sept. 17	7 a. m.	29. 29	50	------	0	----------	N. 0	------	
	2 p. m.	29. 27	70	------	2	----------	ESE. 1	------	
	9 p. m.	29. 16	61	------	2	----------	SE. 1	------	
Sept. 18	7 a. m.	29. 13	63	------	9	----------	NE. 1	------	
	2 p. m.	29. 02	70	------	8	----------	SE. 1	------	
	9 p. m.	28. 92	66	------	9	----------	SE. 1	------	
Sept. 19	7 a. m.	28. 80	63	------	7	----------	S. 1	------	
	2 p. m.	29. 01	49	------	9	----------	NNE. 4	------	
	9 p. m.	29. 11	47	------	10	----------	NNE. 6	------	
Sept. 20	7 a. m	29. 29	49	------	10	----------	NE. 5	------	
	2 p. m.	29. 30	52	------	8	----------	NE. 4	------	
	9 p. m.	29. 29	52	------	8	----------	NE. 3	------	
Sept. 21	7 a. m.	29. 24	47	------	10	----------	NE. 2	------	
	2 p. m.	29. 21	53	------	10	----------	NE. 2	------	
	9 p. m.	29. 16	52	------	10	----------	NE. 1	------	
Sept. 22	7 a. m.	29. 18	53	------	10	----------	NW. 1	------	
	2 p. m.	29. 21	60	------	10	----------	E. 1	------	
	9 p. m.	29. 26	54	------	10	----------	E. 1	------	
Sept 23	7 a. m.	29. 34	57	------	7	----------	NW. 1	------	
	2 p. m.	29. 35	62	------	6	----------	NW. 2	------	
	9 p. m.	29. 40	55	------	9	----------	NE. 0	------	
Sept. 24	7 a. m.	29. 40	56	------	1	----------	NW. 1	------	
	2 p. m.	29. 38	65	------	10	----------	E. 1	------	
	9 p. m.	29. 33	54	------	10	----------	SW. 1	------	

* Winkler, observer.

OTSEGO, WISCONSIN.

Month and day.	Hour.	Barom'r corrected to 32° F.	Thermometer.	Force of vapor.	Cloudiness.	Motion of clouds.	Winds.	Relative humidity.	REMARKS.
Sept. 14	9 p. m.	------	------	------	5	----------	SE. 4	------	17th. Diffuse lightning NW. and distant thunder at 9 p. m.
Sept. 15	7 a. m.	------	------	------	10	----------	SE. 3	------	18th. Terrific thunder storm at 2 a. m. from SW.; several trees struck by lightning; rain from 2 to 5 a. m., and several slight showers during the day; constant rain from 9 p. m. to 9 p. m. on 19th.
	2 p. m.	------	------	------	10	----------	SE. 4	------	
	9 p. m.	------	------	------	10	----------	SE. 4	------	
Sept. 16	7 a. m.	------	------	------	4	----------	S. 3	------	
	2 p. m.	------	------	------	6	----------	S. 3	------	
	9 p. m.	------	------	------	10	----------	S. 2	------	
Sept. 17	7 a. m.	------	------	------	3	----------	S. 3	------	
	2 p. m.	------	------	------	5	----------	S. 3	------	
	9 p. m.	------	------	------	2	----------	SW. 3	------	
Sept. 18	7 a. m.	------	------	------	8	----------	SW. 3	------	
	2 p. m.	------	------	------	6	----------	S. 3	------	
	9 p. m.	------	------	------	10	----------	SW. 2	------	
Sept. 19	7 a. m.	------	------	------	10	----------	NE. 5	------	
	2 p. m.	------	------	------	10	----------	NE. 5	------	
	9 p. m.	------	------	------	10	----------	NE. 4	------	

STORMS Nos. 2 AND 3, SEPTEMBER, 1859.

OTSEGO, WISCONSIN—Continued.

Month and day.	Hour.	Barom'r corrected to 32° F.	Thermometer.	Force of vapor.	Cloudiness.	Motion of clouds.	Winds.	Relative humidity.	REMARKS.
Sept. 20	7 a. m.	------	------	------	6	----------	NE. 3	------	21st. Misty all day. 22d. Fog in the morning and mist in the afternoon.
	2 p. m.	------	------	------	2	----------	NE. 3	------	
	9 p. m.	------	------	------	0	----------	NE. 2	------	
Sept. 21	7 a. m.	------	------	------	10	----------	NE. 3	------	
	2 p. m.	------	------	------	10	----------	NE. 3	------	
	9 p. m.	------	------	------	10	----------	NE. 2	------	
Sept. 22	7 a. m.	------	------	------	10	----------	NE. 3	------	
	2 p. m.	------	------	------	10	----------	NE. 2	------	
	9 p. m.	------	------	------	8	----------	NE. 1	------	
Sept. 23	7 a. m.	------	------	------	10	----------	NE. 2	------	
	2 p. m.	------	------	------	8	----------	NW. 2	------	
	9 p. m.	------	------	------	0	----------	NW. 1	------	
Sept. 24	7 a. m.	------	------	------	0	----------	NW. 1	------	
	2 p. m.	------	------	------	0	----------	SW. 2	------	
	9 p. m.	------	------	------	1	----------	SW. 1	------	

PLATTEVILLE, WISCONSIN.

Month and day.	Hour.	Barom'r corrected to 32° F.	Thermometer.	Force of vapor.	Cloudiness.	Motion of clouds.	Winds.	Relative humidity.	REMARKS.
Sept. 14	9 p. m.	------	54	------	Cir. st. 9	SE. 1	E. 2	------	Showery from 11 a. m. the 17th to 12 noon on the 19th; amount, 0. 632 inch.
Sept. 15	7 a. m.	------	51	------	Cir. st. 10	SE. 1	SE. 1	------	
	2 p. m.	------	61	------	Cir. cu. 10	SE. 1	SE. 1	------	
	9 p. m.	------	56	------	Cir. cu. 10	SE. 1	SE. 1	------	
Sept. 16	7 a. m.	------	55	------	Cir. st. 10	SE. 1	SE. 1	------	
	2 p. m.	------	70	------	Cir. 7	N. 1	SE. 2	------	
	9 p. m.	------	59	------	0	----------	SE. 1	------	
Sept. 17	7 a. m.	------	54	------	0	----------	SE. 1	------	
	2 p. m.	------	74	------	Nim. 10	NW. 2	SE. 3	------	
	9 p. m.	------	69	------	Nim. 10	NW. 2	SE. 2	------	
Sept. 18	7 a. m.	------	66	------	Nim. 10	NW. 1	SE. 2	------	
	2 p. m.	------	77	------	Nim. 10	NW. 1	SE. 2	------	
	9 p. m.	------	67	------	St. 10	NW. 1	SE. 2	------	
Sept. 19	7 a. m.	------	58	------	Nim. 10	N. 4	N. 4	------	
	2 p. m.	------	52	------	St. 10	N. 3	N. 3	------	
	9 p. m.	------	50	------	St. 10	N. 2	N. 2	------	
Sept. 20	7 a. m.	------	43	------	St. 10	N. 2	N. 2	------	
	2 p. m.	------	59	------	0	----------	N. 3	------	
	9 p. m.	------	48	------	0	----------	N. 1	------	
Sept. 21	7 a. m.	------	40	------	0	----------	N. 1	------	
	2 p. m.	------	54	------	St 10	NE. 2	NE. 2	------	
	9 p. m.	------	54	------	St. 10	NE. 2	NE. 2	------	
Sept. 22	7 a. m.	------	55	------	Cir. st. 10	E. 1	E. 1	------	
	2 p. m.	------	64	------	St. 10	NE. 1	NE. 2	------	
	9 p. m.	------	58	------	St. 10	NE. 1	NE. 1	------	
Sept. 23	7 a. m.	------	59	------	Cir. st 7	NW. 1	NW. 1	------	
	2 p. m.	------	72	------	St. 8	NW. 1	NW. 1	------	
	9 p. m.	------	60	------	0	----------	NW. 1	------	
Sept. 24	7 a. m.	------	58	------	0	----------	E. 1	------	
	2 p. m.	------	76	------	0	----------	SE. 2	------	
	9 p. m.	------	68	------	0	----------	SE. 1	------	

ROCKY RUN, WISCONSIN.

Month and day.	Hour.	Barom'r corrected to 32° F.	Thermometer.	Force of vapor.	Cloudiness.	Motion of clouds.	Winds.	Relative humidity.	REMARKS.
Sept. 14	9 p. m.	------	50	------	4	----------	NE. 2	------	17th. Diffused lightning in the W. at 7 a. m., proceeding from dark muddy clouds just above the horizon, extending from NW. to SE.; 9 p. m., thunder and lightning NW.; wind, SE.
Sept. 15	7 a. m.	------	48	------	10	----------	SE. 2	------	
	2 p. m.	------	65	------	10	----------	SE. 1	------	
	9 p. m.	------	58	------	10	----------	SE. 1	------	
Sept. 16	7 a. m.	------	54	------	3	----------	SE. 1	------	
	2 p. m.	------	72	------	8	----------	SE. 1	------	
	9 p. m.	------	59	------	2	----------	SE. 1	------	
Sept. 17	7 a. m.	------	52	------	0	----------	0	------	
	2 p. m.	------	78	------	7	----------	SE. 1	------	
	9 p. m.	------	68	------	5	----------	SW. 1	------	

STORMS Nos. 2 AND 3, SEPTEMBER, 1859.

ROCKY RUN, WISCONSIN—Continued.

Month and day.	Hour.	Barom'r corrected to 32° F.	Thermometer.	Force of vapor.	Cloudiness.	Motion of clouds.	Winds.	Relative humidity.
Sept. 18	7 a. m.	......	68	......	7	....	SE. 1	......
	2 p. m.	......	69	......	10	....	SW. 1	......
	9 p. m.	......	66	......	10	....	SE. 1	......
Sept. 19	7 a. m	......	61	......	10	....	NE. 3	......
	2 p. m.	......	50	......	10	....	NW. 2	......
	9 p. m.	......	49	......	8	....	NE. 2	......
Sept. 20	7 a. m.	......	49	......	10	....	NE. 2	......
	2 p. m.	......	68	......	2	....	N. 2	......
	9 p. m.	......	51	......	0	....	NE. 1	......
Sept. 21	7 a. m.	......	46	......	10	....	NE. 1	......
	2 p. m.	......	58	......	10	....	NE. 1	......
	9 p. m.	......	53	......	10	....	NE. 1	......
Sept. 22	7 a. m.	......	53	......	10	....	W. 1	......
	2 p. m.	......	72	......	10	....	E. 1	......
	9 p. m.	......	59	......	6	....	....	......
Sept. 23	7 a. m.	......	53	......	10	....	NW. 1	......
	2 p. m.	......	84	......	3	....	NW. 1	......
	9 p. m.	......	63	......	0	....	....	......
Sept. 24	7 a. m.	......	52	......	....	....	....	......
	2 p. m.	......	84	......	....	....	NW. 1	......
	9 p. m.	......	62	......	1	....	....	......

REMARKS.

18th. Thunder storm from SE. from 2 to 3 a. m.; course, NW.; wind, SE.; constant stream of diffuse lightning, accompanied by light thunder; rain 2 to 3 and 9 to 10 a. m., and 1 to 2 p. m.; amount, 0. 81 inch; thunder and lightning W. during the evening.

19th. Rain from 9 p. m. last evening till 7 p. m. to-day; amount, 3. 375 inches.

21st. Drizzling rain most of the day.

24th. Slight display of aurora N. to NE. from 7½ to 8½ p. m.; lightning NW. most of the evening.

SUPERIOR, WISCONSIN.

Month and day.	Hour.	Barom'r corrected to 32° F.	Thermometer.	Force of vapor.	Cloudiness.	Motion of clouds.	Winds.	Relative humidity.
Sept. 14	6 p. m.	29. 49	46	. 238	5	....	NE. 2	77
Sept. 15	6 a. m.	29. 46	45	. 251	5	....	SE. 0	84
	9 a. m.	29. 46	49	. 247	5	....	NE. 1	71
	3 p. m.	29. 40	52	. 308	10	....	NE. 1	79
	6 p. m.	29. 38	50	. 283	10	....	N. 1	78
Sept. 16	6 a. m.	29. 31	50	. 335	10	....	NW. 0	93
	9 a. m.	29. 30	57	. 378	5	....	N. 1	81
	3 p. m.	29. 22	58	. 394	5	....	E. 1	82
	6 p. m.	29. 23	55	. 376	5	....	NW. 0	87
Sept. 17	6 a. m.	29. 24	51	. 348	5	....	N. 0	93
	9 a. m.	29. 22	54	. 362	5	....	NE. 1	87
	3 p. m.	29. 19	54	. 362	10	....	E. 1	87
	6 p. m.	29. 07	54	. 390	8	....	NE. 1	93
Sept. 18	6 a. m.	29. 06	51	. 348	10	....	NE. 0	93
	9 a. m.	29. 04	50	. 335	10	....	NE. 1	93
	3 p. m.	29. 03	51	. 348	10	....	NE. 0	93
	6 p. m.	29. 07	51	. 348	10	....	NW. 1	93
Sept. 19	6 a. m.	29. 33	48	. 260	10	....	N. 2	78
	9 a. m.	29. 41	48	. 236	....	....	NE. 1	70
	3 p. m.	29. 49	51	. 270	....	....	NE. 1	72
	6 p. m.	29. 48	49	. 247	....	....	NW. 1	71
Sept. 20	6 a. m.	29. 18	30	. 167	....	....	SE. 1	100
	9 a. m.	29. 60	43	. 254	....	....	NE. 0	92
	3 p. m.	29. 51	51	. 270	....	....	E. 1	72
	6 p. m.	29. 48	50	. 283	....	....	NE. 1	78
Sept. 21	6 a. m.	29. 34	35	. 204	....	....	SE. 0	100
	9 a. m.	29. 42	45	. 275	10	....	NE. 1	92
	3 p. m.	29. 33	53	. 321	....	....	NE. 1	80
	6 p. m.	29. 30	50	. 283	....	....	NE. 1	78
Sept. 22	6 a. m.	29. 31	47	. 273	10	....	E. 1	85
	9 a. m.	29. 31	48	. 285	10	....	NE. 1	85
	3 p. m.	29. 32	52	. 388	....	....	NE. 1	100
	6 p. m.	29. 31	53	. 321	....	....	NE. 1	80
Sept. 23	6 a. m.	29. 41	36	. 212	....	....	SE. 0	100
	9 a. m.	29. 44	48	. 285	....	....	SE. 0	85
	3 p. m.	29. 39	62	. 370	....	....	SE. 1	66
	6 p. m.	29. 34	60	. 456	10	....	SE. 1	88
Sept. 24	6 a. m.	29. 39	37	. 221	....	....	SE. 0	100
	9 a. m.	29. 37	52	. 334	....	....	NE. 1	86
	3 p. m.	29. 39	59	. 410	....	....	NE. 1	82
	6 p. m.	29. 27	55	. 349	....	....	NE. 1	81

REMARKS.

17th. Rain from noon to 6 p. m.; amount, 0. 34 inch.

Rain from 6 p. m. the 18th to 3 p. m. on the 19th; amount, 0. 54 inch.

24th. Rain from 6 to 10 p. m.; amount, 0. 08 inch.

STORMS Nos. 2 AND 3, SEPTEMBER, 1859.

WARSAW, WISCONSIN.

Month and day.	Hour.	Barom'r corrected to 32° F.	Thermometer.	Force of vapor.	Cloudiness.		Motion of clouds.		Winds.		Relative humidity.	REMARKS.
Sept. 14	9 p. m.	------	48	------	Nim.	10	S.	2	SE.	3	------	15th. Slight sprinkle.
Sept. 15	7 a. m.	------	48	------	Nim.	10	S.	1	SE.	1	------	16th. Slight sprinkle from 8 to 10 a. m.
	2 p. m.	------	58	------	Nim.	10	S.	2	SE.	1	------	Rain from 11 p. m. on the 17th to 9 p. m. on the 18th; amount, ½ in.
	9 p. m.	------	52	------		0		0	NW.	4	------	19th. Rainy.
Sept. 16	7 a. m.	------	53	------		10	SE.	1	SE.	1	------	20th. Slight mist.
	2 p. m.	------	76	------	Cir.	1		1	S.	1	------	24th. Rain from 5 a. m. to 1 p. m.
	9 p. m.	------	52	------	Nim.	10	W.	2		0	------	
Sept. 17	7 a. m.	------	58	------	Cir. st.	3	W.	1		0	------	
	2 p. m.	------	79	------		6		2	SE.	2	------	
	9 p. m.	------	62	------		6		0	SE.	1	------	
Sept. 18	7 a. m.	------	60	------	Nim.	10	SE.	2		0	------	
	2 p. m.	------	66	------	Nim.	10	SE.			2	------	
	9 p. m.	------	65	------	Nim.	10	SE.	2	SE.	3	------	
Sept. 19	7 a. m.	------	46	------		10	NE.	3	NE.	4	------	
	2 p. m.	------	50	------	Cir.	8	NW.	6	N.	4	------	
	9 p. m.	------	42	------		0		0	N.	4	------	
Sept. 20	7 a. m.	------	42	------		8	NW.	2	NW.	1	------	
	2 p. m.	------	51	------	Cu.	5		1	NW.	2	------	
	9 p. m.	------	43	------	Nim.	2	NW.	1	NW.	1	------	
Sept. 21	7 a. m.	------	38	------		10		1		2	------	
	2 p. m.	------	54	------	Cir. cu.	5	W.	1	W.	2	------	
	9 p. m.	------	42	------		1		1		3	------	
Sept. 22	7 a. m.	------	46	------		10		1		2	------	
	2 p. m.	------	72	------		0		0	SW.	1	------	
	9 p. m.	------	56	------	Cir.	9	N.	2		0	------	
Sept. 23	7 a. m.	------	55	------	Cir.	9	N.	2		0	------	
	2 p. m.	------	63	------	Cir.	6	NW.	1		0	------	
	9 p. m.	------	51	------		0		0		0	------	
Sept. 24	7 a. m.	------	44	------		0		0		0	------	
	2 p. m.	------	85	------		1	SW.	1	S.	1	------	
	9 p. m.	------	58	------	Nim.	1	SW.	2	S.	1	------	

BELLEVUE, IOWA.

Month and day.	Hour.	Barom'r corrected to 32° F.	Thermometer.	Force of vapor.	Cloudiness.		Motion of clouds.	Winds.		Relative humidity.	REMARKS.
Sept. 14	9 p. m.	------	57	------		8	----------	S.	4	------	17th. Slight showers during the day; amount, 0. 12 inch.
Sept. 15	7 a. m.	------	51	------	Cu. st.	10	----------	E.	2	------	19th. Showers during the day; amount, 0. 32 inch.
	2 p. m.	------	62	------	Nim.	10	----------	SE.	3	------	22d. Frost.
	9 p. m.	------	57	------		10	----------	E.	2	------	
Sept. 16	7 a. m.	------	54	------	Nim.	10	----------	E.	2	------	
	2 p. m.	------	72	------	Cu. st.	2	----------	SE.	2	------	
	9 p. m.	------	54	------		0	----------	SW.	2	------	
Sept. 17	7 a. m.	------	59	------		0	----------	E.	2	------	
	2 p. m.	------	70	------	Cir. cu.	9	----------	E.	2	------	
	9 p. m.	------	66	------		0	----------	E.	3	------	
Sept. 18	7 a. m.	------	64	------	Nim.	10	----------	E.	2	------	
	2 p. m.	------	72	------	Nim.	10	----------	E.	2	------	
	9 p. m.	------	66	------		10	----------	----------		------	
Sept. 19	7 a. m.	------	63	------	Nim.	10	----------	NW.	2	------	
	2 p. m.	------	54	------	Nim.	10	----------	N.	5	------	
	9 p. m.	------	50	------		10	----------	W.	4	------	
Sept. 20	7 a. m.	------	45	------	Nim.	10	----------	N.	4	------	
	2 p. m.	------	66	------	Cir. st.	1	----------	N.	3	------	
	9 p. m.	------	50	------		0	----------	N.	3	------	
Sept. 21	7 a. m.	------	40	------	Cu. st.	10	----------	NW.	2	------	
	2 p. m.	------	56	------	Cu. st.	10	----------	NW.	3	------	
	9 p. m.	------	54	------		10	----------	----------		------	
Sept. 22	7 a. m.	------	54	------	Nim.	10	----------	W.	2	------	
	2 p. m.	------	62	------	Cu.	10	----------	SW.	2	------	
	9 p. m.	------	60	------		10	----------	----------		------	
Sept. 23	7 a. m.	------	56	------	Cir. st.	4	----------	W.	2	------	
	2 p. m.	------	79	------	Cir.	2	----------	NE.	2	------	
	9 p. m.	------	57	------		0	----------	W.	1	------	
Sept. 24	7 a. m.	------	48	------	Fog -------		----------	W.	1	------	
	2 p. m.	------	78	------	Cir.	3	----------	SE.	2	------	
	9 p. m.	------	60	------		0	----------	SW.	1	------	

STORMS Nos. 2 AND 3, SEPTEMBER, 1859.

BORDER PLAINS, IOWA.

Month and day.	Hour.	Barom'r corrected to 32° F.	Thermometer.	Force of vapor.	Cloudiness.	Motion of clouds.	Winds.	Relative humidity.	REMARKS.
Sept. 14	9 p. m.	29.02	58	------	0	----------	S. 1	------	19th. Rain from 6½ to 8 a. m.; amount, 0.125 inch.
Sept. 15	7 a. m.	28.82	53	------	Cir. 10	SW. 2	SE. 1	------	20th and 21st. Frost.
	2 p. m.	28.78	66	------	Cir. st. 10	----------	SE. 3	------	24th. Diffused lightning 8 to 9 p. m.
	9 p. m.	28.77	57	------	Cir. st. 10	----------	SE. 1	------	
Sept. 16	7 a. m.	28.74	57	------	Cir. cu. 10	----------	SE. 3	------	
	2 p. m.	28.62	78	------	0	----------	SE. 2	------	
	9 p. m.	28.60	66	------	Cir. cu. 2	----------	SE. 1	------	
Sept. 17	7 a. m.	28.58	58	------	Cir. 8	S. 2	SE. 2	------	
	2 p. m.	28.40	80	------	Cir. 3	----------	S. 5	------	
	9 p. m.	28.40	77	------	0	----------	S. 5	------	
Sept. 18	7 a. m.	28.44	64	------	Cir. st. 10	S. 1	S. 1	------	
	2 p. m.	28.44	70	------	Nim. 10	----------	W. 2	------	
	9 p. m.	28.46	60	------	Nim. 10	----------	NW. 4	------	
Sept. 19	7 a. m.	28.54	56	------	Cir. st. 10	----------	NW. 5	------	
	2 p. m.	28.72	61	------	Cir. st. 8	----------	NW. 6	------	
	9 p. m.	28.83	46	------	0	----------	N. 1	------	
Sept. 20	7 a. m.	28.81	42	------	0	----------	NW. 3	------	
	2 p. m.	28.81	69	------	0	----------	N. 3	------	
	9 p. m.	28.71	46	------	0	----------	NW. 1	------	
Sept. 21	7 a. m.	28.80	44	------	0	----------	NW. 1	------	
	2 p. m.	28.65	71	------	0	----------	SE. 2	------	
	9 p. m.	28.66	44	------	0	----------	S. 1	------	
Sept. 22	7 a. m.	28.77	40	------	0	----------	SE. 2	------	
	2 p. m.	28.65	75	------	Cir. cu. 2	----------	SE. 3	------	
	9 p. m.	28.74	55	------	0	----------	SE. 2	------	
Sept. 23	7 a. m.	28.80	78	------	Cir. 6	NW. 2	SE. 2	------	
	2 p. m.	28.76	85	------	Cir. 8	NW. 2	SE. 2	------	
	9 p. m.	28.69	62	------	0	----------	SE. 1	------	
Sept. 24	7 a. m.	28.71	68	------	Cir. 7	SW. 1	SE. 1	------	
	2 p. m.	28.67	83	------	Cir. 8	SW. 1	SE. 3	------	
	9 p. m.	28.60	69	------	Cir. 3	SW. 1	SE. 2	------	

BURLINGTON, IOWA.

Month and day.	Hour.	Barom'r corrected to 32° F.	Thermometer.	Force of vapor.	Cloudiness.	Motion of clouds.	Winds.	Relative humidity.	REMARKS.
Sept. 14	9 p. m.	------	58	------	Nim., cu. 10	W ----------	E. 2	------	14th. Rain from 9 15 to 11 40 p. m.; amount, 0.05 inch.
Sept. 15	7 a. m.	------	52	------	10	SW. 2	SE. 1	------	15th. Rain at intervals.
	2 p. m.	------	78	------	------------	----------	SE. 1	------	17th. Rain from 9 a. m. to 2 p. m.; amount, 0.10 inch.
	9 p. m.	------	59	------	------------	----------	SE. 2	------	18th. Cold drizzling rain from 2 to 10 a. m. and 2½ to 7 p. m.; am't, 2.62 inches.
Sept. 16	7 a. m.	------	56	------	St., cir. cu. 5	W. 3	SE. 2	------	
	2 p. m.	------	76	------	Cir. st. 2	W. 2	SE. 1	------	
	9 p. m.	------	65	------	0	----------	SE. 1	------	
Sept. 17	7 a. m.	------	62	------	St. cu., scud 8	SW. 1	E. 1	------	
	2 p. m.	------	70	------	Cu. 7	W. 2	E. 2	------	
	9 p. m.	------	66	------	Cu. 6	W. 2	SE. 3	------	
Sept. 18	7 a. m.	------	63	------	Nim., cu. 10	SW. 3	SE. 4	------	
	2 p. m.	------	68	------	Cu., nim. 10	SW. 2	NW. 3	------	
	9 p. m.	------	60	------	Cu. 4	SW. 3	NW. 1	------	
Sept. 19	7 a. m.	------	59	------	10	W ----------	NW. 4	------	
	2 p. m.	------	56	------	10	----------	NW. 4	------	
	9 p. m.	------	51	------	------------	----------	NW. 2	------	
Sept. 20	7 a. m.	------	50	------	Cu. st. 10	----------	NW. 3	------	
	2 p. m.	------	54	------	Cu. st. 10	----------	NW. 2	------	
	9 p. m.	------	52	------	Cu., st. 10	----------	NW. 1	------	
Sept. 21	7 a. m.	------	46	------	Cir. cu., st. 3	W. 1	NW. 3	------	
	2 p. m.	------	62	------	Cu. 8	W. 2	NE. 3	------	
	9 p. m.	------	54	------	Cu. st. 7	W. 3	NE. 2	------	
Sept. 22	7 a. m.	------	56	------	Cu., haze 10	W ----------	NW. 2	------	
	2 p. m.	------	65	------	Cir. cu., cu. 7	W. 2	SW. 2	------	
	9 p. m.	------	60	------	Cu. 8	SW. 4	SW. 1	------	
Sept. 23	7 a. m.	------	64	------	Haze 10	----------	E. 1	------	
	2 p. m.	------	69	------	Cir., cir. cu. 6	W. 1	SE. 1	------	
	9 p. m.	------	60	------	Cir. 7	SW. 2	SE ----------	------	
Sept. 24	7 a. m.	------	58	------	St. 4	----------	NE. 1	------	
	2 p. m.	------	80	------	Cu. 4	W. 1	SW. 2	------	
	9 p. m.	------	65	------	St. 2	W. 1	SW ----------	------	

STORMS Nos. 2 AND 3, SEPTEMRER, 1859.

DAVENPORT, IOWA.

Month and day.	Hour.	Barom'r corrected to 32° F.	Thermometer.	Force of vapor.	Cloudiness.	Motion of clouds.	Winds.	Relative humidity.	REMARKS.
Sept. 14	9 p. m.	......	......	......	10	....	N. 1	......	15th. Light shower from 7½ to 8 p. m.
Sept. 15	7 a. m.	......	......	......	10	....	E. 1	......	
	2 p. m.	......	......	......	10	....	0	......	18th. Gentle shower, accompanied by thunder and lightning, with strong wind SW., from 9 to 10½ a. m.; rain all night.
	9 p. m.	......	......	......	10	....	E. 1	......	
Sept. 16	7 a. m.	......	......	......	10	....	E. 1	......	
	2 p. m.	......	......	......	10	....	0	......	
	9 p. m.	......	......	......	10	....	0	......	19th. Strong wind from NW.; cold drizzling rain all day.
Sept. 17	7 a. m.	......	......	......	4	....	E. 1	......	
	2 p. m.	......	......	......	10	....	0	......	20th. Clear and cold at eve.
	9 p. m.	......	......	......	5	....	0	......	
Sept. 18	7 a. m.	......	......	......	8	....	S. 1	......	
	2 p. m.	......	......	......	10	....	S. 2	......	
	9 p. m.	......	......	......	10	....	S. 1	......	
Sept. 19	7 a. m.	......	......	......	10	....	W. 2	......	
	2 p. m.	......	......	......	10	....	NW. 4	......	
	9 p. m.	......	......	......	10	....	NW. 3	......	
Sept. 20	7 a. m.	......	......	......	10	....	NW 3	......	
	2 p. m.	......	......	......	10	....	NW. 3	......	
	9 p. m.	......	......	......	0	....	N. 1	......	
Sept. 21	7 a. m.	......	......	......	1	....	N. 2	......	
	2 p. m.	......	......	......	6	....	N. 2	......	
	9 p. m.	......	......	......	10	....	N. 1	......	
Sept. 22	7 a. m.	......	......	......	10	....	W. 1	......	
	2 p. m.	......	......	......	8	....	S. 1	......	
	9 p. m.	......	......	......	10	....	SE. 1	......	
Sept. 23	7 a. m.	......	......	......	0	....	0	......	
	2 p. m.	......	......	......	3	....	S. 1	......	
	9 p. m.	......	......	......	2	....	0	......	
Sept. 24	7 a. m.	......	......	......	10	....	0	......	
	2 p. m.	......	......	......	2	....	0	......	
	9 p. m.	......	......	......	0	....	0	......	

DUBUQUE, IOWA.

Month and day.	Hour.	Barom'r corrected to 32° F.	Thermometer.	Force of vapor.	Cloudiness.	Motion of clouds.	Winds.	Relative humidity.	REMARKS.
Sept. 14	9 p. m.	29.46	57	......	Cir. cu. 9	SW. 1	S. 1	......	15th. Slight sprinkle at 9 and 11 p. m.
Sept. 15	7 a. m.	29.50	50	.248	Cir. st. 10	SW. 1	SW. 1	66	
	2 p. m.	29.40	62	.287	Cir. st. 10	....	E. 2	51	17th. Slight rain from 5½ p. m. during the night.
	9 p. m.	29.37	56	.258	Nim. 8	SE. 1	SE. 1	54	
Sept. 16	7 a. m.	29.36	54	.302	Cir. st. 10	W. 1	W. 1	72	18th. Showery till 8 p. m.
	2 p. m.	29.24	69	.388	Cir. 4	W. 1	SW. 1	54	19th. Began to rain at 3½ a. m.; 4 a. m. barometer 28.80; drizzling rain continued till 2 p. m.; am't, 0.35 inch.
	9 p. m.	29.26	58	.429	0	....	0	89	
Sept. 17	7 a. m.	29.28	55	.346	0	....	SW. 1	80	
	2 p. m.	29.12	70	.457	Cir. st. 7	SW. 2	S. 3	61	
	9 p. m.	29.11	66	.533	Cir. st. 6	SW. 1	S. 1	83	
Sept. 18	7 a. m.	29.07	66	.587	Cir. st. 10	SW. 2	S. 1	89	
	2 p. m.	28.95	75	.522	Dense cir. st. 7	SW. 4	SW. 4	61	
	9 p. m.	28.90	65	.545	Cir. st. 10	....	S. 1	87	
Sept. 19	7 a. m.	28.84	63	.484	D'se low st. 10	N. 7	N. 4	84	
	2 p. m.	29.11	52	.334	*Nim. 10	N. 0	W. 5	86	
	9 p. m.	29.29	47	.199	Cir. st. 4	N. 4	N. 3	61	
Sept. 20	7 a. m.	29.38	44	.220	St. 9	N. 2	N. 5	76	
	2 p. m.	29.35	61	.247	0	....	N. 2	46	
	9 p. m.	29.38	49	.206	0	....	N. 1	59	
Sept. 21	7 a. m.	29.34	42	.226	Cir. st. 5	SE. 2	0	85	
	2 p. m.	29.25	55	.300	Cir. st. 7	W. 1	0	69	
	9 p. m.	29.24	55	.368	Dense 10	....	....	85	
Sept. 22	7 a. m.	29.26	58	.346	Cir. st. 8	NW. 3	NW. 1	71	
	2 p. m.	29.25	65	.399	Cir. st. 9	NW. 2	E. 2	64	
	9 p. m.	29.34	60	.447	10	....	0	86	
Sept. 23	7 a. m.	29.43	58	.391	0	....	0	81	
	2 p. m.	29.37	73	.439	Cir. st. 3	NW. 2	SE. 1	54	
	9 p. m.	29.43	59	.401	0	....	0	81	
Sept. 24	7 a. m.	29.46	57	.408	Cir. cu. 0	NW. 2	NW. 1	86	
	2 p. m.	29.34	77	.520	Cir. cu. 4	NW. 2	0	55	
	9 p. m.	29.33	65	.514	0	....	0	82	

* Misty rain.

STORMS Nos. 2 AND 3, SEPTEMBER, 1859.

FAIRFIELD, IOWA.

Month and day.	Hour.	Barom'r corrected to 32° F.	Thermometer.	Force of vapor.	Cloudiness.		Motion of clouds.	Winds.		Relative humidity.	REMARKS.
Sept. 14	9 p. m.	27.204	55	.321		10	......		0	74	17th. Thunder storms at 6 a. m., noon, and 1½ p. m., from W. to E; showers and diffused lightning all day and night. 18th. Thunder showers from 7½ to 9½ a. m., and 4 to 7 p. m.; am't rain 17th and 18th, 1.50 inch. 24th. Lightning N.NW and W. from a very small cloud at 11½ p. m.
Sept. 15	7 a. m.	.311	53	.321		10	......	SE.	1	80	
	2 p. m.	......	......	......		10	......	SE.	1	......	
	9 p. m.	.279	58	.365		10	......	SE.	1	76	
Sept. 16	7 a. m.	.266	55	.376	Cu. st.	6	......	SE.	1	87	
	2 p. m.	......	......	......	Cu. st.	5	......	SE.	1	......	
	9 p. m.	.049	62	.429		0	0		0	77	
Sept. 17	7 a. m.	......	......	......	Nim.	10	......	SW.	1	......	
	2 p. m.	26.958	75	.554	Cu.	5	......	SW.	3	64	
	9 p. m.	.902	69	.496	Nim.	10	......	SW.	4	70	
Sept. 18	7 a. m.	.947	63	.478		10	......	SW.	1	83	
	2 p. m.	.993	69	.496		10	......	SW.	2	70	
	9 p. m.	27.008	63	.356		10	......		0	62	
Sept. 19	7 a. m.	.019	58	.337		10	......	NE.	2	70	
	2 p. m.	.038	54	.335	Raining	10	......	NE.	2	80	
	9 p. m.	.076	57	.296		10	......	NW.	3	79	
Sept. 20	7 a. m.	.195	43	.134		10	......	NW.	3	59	
	2 p. m.	.161	53	.269		10	......	NW.	2	67	
	9 p. m.	.198	50	.283		10	......		0	78	
Sept. 21	7 a. m.	.173	48	.212		0	0		0	63	
	2 p. m.	.067	63	.270		10	......		0	47	
	9 p. m.	.086	55	.295		10	......	NE.	1	68	
Sept. 22	7 a. m.	.086	55	.321		0	0		0	74	
	2 p. m.	.050	70	.353	Cu.	5	......	SW.	2	48	
	9 p. m.	.072	61	.383		0	0		0	71	
Sept. 23	7 a. m.	.146	55	.295		0	0		0	68	
	2 p. m.	.111	78	.514	St.	3	......		0	54	
	9 p. m.	.167	63	.478		0	0		0	83	
Sept. 24	7 a. m.	.154	62	.429		0	0		0	77	
	2 p. m.	.099	83	.483	Cir. st.	5	......	SE.	1	43	
	9 p. m.	.112	65	.451	St.	1	......		0	73	

FAYETTE, IOWA.

Month and day.	Hour.	Barom'r corrected to 32° F.	Thermometer.	Force of vapor.	Cloudiness.		Motion of clouds.	Winds.		Relative humidity.	REMARKS.
Sept. 14	9 p. m.	......	......	......		10	......	E.	1	......	17th. Thunder shower from the E. 10½ to 11 a. m.; a very heavy shower from the SW. between 11 and 12 p. m. 18th. Commenced raining about noon and continued all day and evening.
Sept. 15	7 a. m.	......	......	......		10	......	SE.	3	......	
	2 p. m.	......	......	......		10	......	E.	2	......	
	9 p. m.	......	......	......		10	......	E.	1	......	
Sept. 16	7 a. m.	......	......	......		5	......	S.	2	......	
	2 p. m.	......	......	......		3	......	S.	2	......	
	9 p. m.	......	......	......		2	......	S.	1	......	
Sept. 17	7 a. m.	......	......	......		6	......	E.	3	......	
	2 p. m.	......	......	......		9	......	E.	2	......	
	9 p. m.	......	......	......		3	......	E.	2	......	
Sept. 18	7 a. m.	......	......	......		10	......	E.	2	......	
	2 p. m.	......	......	......		10	......	SW.	2	......	
	9 p. m.	......	......	......		10	......	SW.	2	......	
Sept. 19	7 a. m.	......	......	......		10	......	NW.	3	......	
	2 p. m.	......	......	......		10	......	NW.	4	......	
	9 p. m.	......	......	......		2	......	NW.	2	......	
Sept. 20	7 a. m.	......	......	......		1	......	NW.	2	......	
	2 p. m.	......	......	......		3	......	NW.	2	......	
	9 p. m.	......	......	......		1	......	NW.	1	......	
Sept. 21	7 a. m.	......	......	......		0	......	NW.	1	......	
	2 p. m.	......	......	......		3	......	NE.	2	......	
	9 p. m.	......	......	......		10	......	NE.	1	......	
Sept. 22	7 a. m.	......	......	......		10	......	E.	2	......	
	2 p. m.	......	......	......		10	......	E.	2	......	
	9 p. m.	......	......	......		10	......	E.	1	......	
Sept. 23	7 a. m.	......	......	......		2	......	E.	2	......	
	2 p. m.	......	......	......		2	......	E.	1	......	
	9 p. m.	......	......	......		2	......	E.	1	......	
Sept. 24	7 a. m.	......	......	......		2	......	E.	2	......	
	2 p. m.	......	......	......		3	......	S.	2	......	
	9 p. m.	......	......	......		4	......	S.	1	......	

STORMS Nos. 2 AND 3, SEPTEMBER, 1859.

FORESTVILLE, IOWA.

Month and day.	Hour.	Barom'r corrected to 32° F.	Thermometer.	Force of vapor.	Cloudiness.		Motion of clouds.		Winds.		Relative humidity.	REMARKS.
Sept. 14	9 p. m.	------	56	------	Cir.	5	S.	2	S.	2	------	17th. Light thunder shower from
Sept. 15	7 a. m.	------	52	------	Nim.	9	S.	3	S.	3	------	10 to 11 a. m.
	2 p. m.	------	60	------	Nim.	8	SE.	2	SE.	2	------	18th. Light rain during the a. m.;
	9 p. m.	------	56	------	Nim.	8	SE.	2	SE.	2	------	very heavy thunder storm from
Sept. 16	7 a. m.	------	58	------	Cir. cu.	6	S.	2	S.	2	------	the NW. 9½ to 11½ p. m.
	2 p. m.	------	74	------	Cir.	1	SE.	2	SE.	2	------	
	9 p. m.	------	59	------	Cir. st.	1	E.	1	E.	1	------	
Sept. 17	7 a. m.	------	75	------	Nim.	4	SE.	4	SE.	4	------	
	2 p. m.	------	68	------	Nim.	8	SE.	3	SE.	3	------	
	9 p. m.	------	64	------	Nim.	5	SE.	3	SE.	3	------	
Sept. 18	7 a. m.	------	63	------	Nim.	10	SE.	2	SE.	2	------	
	2 p. m.	------	76	------	Cu.	5	S.	3	S.	3	------	
	9 p. m.	------	62	------	Nim.	10	S.	1	S.	1	------	
Sept. 19	7 a. m.	------	53	------	Nim.	8	NW.	6	NW.	6	------	
	2 p. m.	------	53	------	Nim.	8	NW.	5	NW.	5	------	
	9 p. m.	------	46	------		0	----------		NW.	3	------	
Sept. 20	7 a. m.	------	46	------		0	----------		NW.	4	------	
	2 p. m.	------	58	------		0	----------		NW.	3	------	
	9 p. m.	------	44	------		0	----------		NE.	1	------	
Sept. 21	7 a. m.	------	44	------		0	----------		NE.	2	------	
	2 p. m.	------	59	------	Cu.	5	NW.	2	NW.	2	------	
	9 p. m.	------	53	------	Nim.	8	NE.	1	NE.	1	------	
Sept. 22	7 a. m.	------	55	------	Cir. st.	6	NW.	1	NW.	1	------	
	2 p. m.	------	55	------	Cu.	5	S.	1	S.	1	------	
	9 p. m.	------	58	------	Nim.	8	S.	1	S.	1	------	
Sept. 23	7 a. m.	------	54	------		1	S.	1	S.	1	------	
	2 p. m.	------	76	------	Cir.	1	S.	1	S.	1	------	
	9 p. m.	------	------	------	----------		----------		----------		------	
Sept. 24	7 a. m.	------	62	------		0	----------		S.	1	------	
	2 p. m.	------	83	------	Cu.	2	S.	2	SW.	2	------	
	9 p. m.	------	66	------	Cir.	1	S.	2	S.	2	------	

FORT MADISON, IOWA.

Month and day.	Hour.	Barom'r corrected to 32° F.	Thermometer.	Force of vapor.	Cloudiness.		Motion of clouds.		Winds.		Relative humidity.	REMARKS.
Sept. 14	7 p. m.	------	60	------	Cir. st.	9	W.	1	NE.	1	------	14th. Drizzling from 12 p. m. to 4
Sept. 15	6 a. m.	------	52	------	Nim.	10	SE.	2	SE.	1	------	a. m. on the 15th; amount, 0.18
	12 m.	------	68	------	Cir. cu.	10	SE.	1	SE.	2	------	inch.
	7 p. m.	------	61	------	Nim.	10	S.	1	NE.	2	------	17th. Rain, accompanied by thun-
Sept. 16	6 a. m.	------	52	------	Cir.	1	W.	2	NE.	1	------	der and lightning, from 8½ a. m.
	12 m.	------	74	------	Cir.	1	N.	1	SE.	1	------	till noon; amount, 0.21 inch.
	7 p. m.	------	68	------		0		0	SE.	1	------	18th. Rain from 10½ a. m. to 9½ p.
Sept. 17	6 a. m.	------	62	------	Nim.	3	W.	1	SE.	1	------	m.; amount, 1.66 inch.
	12 m.	------	68	------	Nim.	8	SW.	2	SE.	2	------	19th. Showery all day from 6 a.
	7 p. m.	------	70	------	Nim.	9	S.	1	S.	2	------	m.; amount, 0 31 inch.
Sept. 18	6 a. m.	------	68	------	Nim.	5	SW.	1	SE.	1	------	21st. Third frost.
	12 m.	------	74	------	Cir. st.	10	SW.	1	SW.	2	------	
	7 p. m.	------	63	------	Nim.	10	SW.	1	SW.	1	------	
Sept. 19	6 a. m.	------	67	------	Cir. st.	10	W.	3	NW.	2	------	
	12 m.	------	56	------	Nim.	10	NW.	3	NW.	2	------	
	7 p. m.	------	51	------	Nim.	10	N.	3	N.	3	------	
Sept. 20	6 a. m.	------	45	------	Cir. st.	10	N.	1	N.	2	------	
	12 m.	------	51	------	Cir. st.	10	N.	2	N.	2	------	
	7 p. m.	------	52	------	Cir. st.	10	N.	1	N.	1	------	
Sept. 21	6 a. m.	------	43	------		0		0	NE.	1	------	
	12 m.	------	59	------	Cir. st.	10	N.	1	NE.	1	------	
	7 p. m.	------	56	------	Cir.	10	W.	1	NE.	1	------	
Sept. 22	6 a. m.	------	55	------	Cir. st.	10	N.	1	NE.	1	------	
	12 m.	------	69	------	Cir.	4	W.	1	E.	1	------	
	7 p. m.	------	60	------	Cir.	1	W.	1	SE.	1	------	
Sept. 23	6 a. m.	------	53	------		0		0	SE.	1	------	
	12 m.	------	77	------		0		0	SW.	2	------	
	7 p. m.	------	68	------		0		0	SW.	1	------	
Sept. 24	6 a. m.	------	58	------		0		0	SW.	1	------	
	12 m.	------	82	------		0		0	SE.	2	------	
	7 p. m.	------	70	------		0		0	SE.	1	------	

STORMS Nos. 2 AND 3, SEPTEMBER, 1859.

LYONS, IOWA.

Month and day.	Hour.	Barom'r corrected to 32° F.	Thermometer.	Force of vapor.	Cloudiness.	Motion of clouds.	Winds.	Relative humidity.	REMARKS.
Sept. 14	9 p. m.	------	------	------	6	----------	NW. 1	------	14th. Rain during the night; am't, 0.02 inch.
Sept. 15	7 a. m.	------	------	------	7	----------	E. 3	------	
	2 p. m.	------	------	------	8	----------	E. 3	------	15th. Rain in night; amount, 0.30 inch.
	9 p. m.	------	------	------	6	----------	E. 2	------	
Sept. 16	7 a. m.	------	------	------	3	----------	E. 2	------	18th. Rain from 6½ a. m. to 8 p. m.; amount, 0.75 inch.
	2 p. m.	------	------	------	8	----------	SW. 2	------	
	9 p. m.	------	------	------	7	----------	E. 1	------	19th. Rain during the night; am't, 0.54 inch.
Sept. 17	7 a. m.	------	------	------	2	----------	E. 2	------	
	2 p. m.	------	------	------	3	----------	S. 4	------	22d. Slight mist and fog.
	9 p. m.	------	------	------	6	----------	SW. 2	------	24th. Rain during the night.
Sept. 18	7 a. m.	------	------	------	8	----------	SW. 1	------	
	2 p. m.	------	------	------	7	----------	SW. 3	------	
	9 p. m.	------	------	------	10	----------	W. 2	------	
Sept. 19	7 a. m.	------	------	------	10	----------	NW. 3	------	
	2 p. m.	------	------	------	10	----------	N. 6	------	
	9 p. m.	------	------	------	10	----------	N. 2	------	
Sept. 20	7 a. m.	------	------	------	10	----------	N. 3	------	
	2 p. m.	------	------	------	5	----------	N. 3	------	
	9 p. m.	------	------	------	2	----------	N. 1	------	
Sept. 21	7 a. m.	------	------	------	8	----------	N. 2	------	
	2 p. m.	------	------	------	9	----------	N. 3	------	
	9 p. m.	------	------	------	7	----------	0	------	
Sept. 22	7 a. m.	------	------	------	10	----------	S. 1	------	
	2 p. m.	------	------	------	8	----------	S. 2	------	
	9 p. m.	------	------	------	7	----------	S. 1	------	
Sept. 23	7 a. m.	----	------	------	7	----------	SE. 1	------	
	2 p. m.	------	------	------	4	----------	SE. 2	------	
	9 p. m.	------	------	------	3	----------	0	------	
Sept. 24	7 a. m.	------	------	------	5	----------	0	------	
	2 p. m.	------	------	------	1	----------	SE. 1	------	
	9 p. m.	------	------	------	0	----------	0	------	

MUSCATINE, IOWA.

Month and day.	Hour.	Barom'r corrected to 32° F.	Thermometer.	Force of vapor.	Cloudiness.	Motion of clouds.	Winds.	Relative humidity.	REMARKS.
Sept. 14	9 p. m.	29.53	59	.429	10	----------	N. 2	77	Rain from 2 p. m. the 17th to 5 p. m. on the 19th; amount, 1.10 inch.
Sept. 15	7 a. m.	29.72	50	.456	10	----------	W. 1	88	
	2 p. m.	29.68	65	.456	St. 5	W. 1	E. 2	88	
	9 p. m.	29.51	59	.478	St. 3	W. 1	E. 1	83	
Sept. 16	7 a. m.	29.50	55	.429	0	----------	E. 1	77	
	2 p. m.	29.52	70	.529	0	----------	E. 2	89	
	9 p. m.	29.42	56	.604	0	----------	E. 1	94	
Sept. 17	7 a. m.	29.51	62	.570	10	----------	E. 1	89	
	2 p. m.	29.39	66	.604	10	----------	SE. 1	94	
	9 p. m.	29.40	68	.586	10	----------	SE. 2	80	
Sept. 18	7 a. m.	29.30	67	.591	10	----------	SE. 2	89	
	2 p. m.	29.19	66	.706	10	----------	S. 1	90	
	9 p. m.	29.19	65	.658	10	----------	S. 1	90	
Sept. 19	7 a. m.	29.18	59	.577	10	----------	SW. 2	85	
	2 p. m.	29.31	52	.529	St. 5	W. 1	SW. 3	89	
	9 p. m.	29.52	50	.396	Nim. 3	W. 1	N. 2	76	
Sept. 20	7 a. m.	29.44	49	.391	Nim. 5	SW. 2	N. 2	87	
	2 p. m.	29.53	55	.420	Cu. 5	SW. 2	NE. 1	94	
	9 p. m.	29.44	55	.394	0	----------	NE. 0	82	
Sept. 21	7 a. m.	29.53	34	.362	0	----------	NE. 0	87	
	2 p. m.	29.41	40	.391	0	----------	NE. 1	87	
	9 p. m.	29.34	53	.391	0	----------	N. 1	87	
Sept. 22	7 a. m.	29.53	54	.394	0	----------	NE. 0	82	
	2 p. m.	29.52	68	.456	0	----------	NE. 1	88	
	9 p. m.	29.43	60	.491	0	----------	N. 1	88	
Sept. 23	7 a. m.	29.54	46	.426	0	----------	N. 1	82	
	2 p. m.	29.53	70	.658	0	----------	N. 1	90	
	9 p. m.	29.52	60	.591	0	----------	N. 1	89	
Sept. 24	7 a. m.	29.58	51	.529	0	----------	N. 1	89	
	2 p. m.	29.52	81	.612	0	----------	NE. 1	90	
	9 p. m.	29.60	62	.668	0	----------	NE. 1	86	

STORMS Nos. 2 AND 3, SEPTEMBER, 1859.

PLEASANT PLAIN, IOWA.

Month and day.	Hour.	Barom'r corrected to 32° F.	Thermometer.	Force of vapor.	Cloudiness.		Motion of clouds.		Winds.		Relative humidity.	REMARKS.
Sept. 14	9 p. m.	------	58	------	Nim.	10	----------		E.	2	------	Rain from 9 p. m. the 14th to 9 p. m. on the 15th; am't, 0.10 inch.
Sept. 15	7 a. m.	------	53	------	Nim.	10	----------		E.	2	------	
	2 p. m.	------	66	------	Nim.	10	----------		E.	2	------	17th. Rain from 6 a. m. to 12 noon; amount, 0.10 inch; diffused lightning in the evening.
	9 p. m.	------	58	------	Nim.	10	----------		E.	1	------	
Sept. 16	7 a. m.	------	55	------	Cir. cu.	4	----------		E.	2	------	
	2 p. m.	------	76	------	Cir. cu	------	SW.	8	SE.	2	------	Rain from 7½ a. m. the 18th to 5 p. m. on the 19th; am't, 1.10 inch.
	9 p. m.	------	64	------		0	----------		S.	----------	------	
Sept. 17	7 a. m.	------	64	------	Cu., nim.	10	SW.	2	SE.	2	------	24th. At 7 p. m. a pale white light with a few streamers, on a well-defined arch.
	2 p. m.	------	75	------	Cir.	4	SW.	4	SE.	2	------	
	9 p. m.	------	70	------	Cir. cu.	9	SW.	------	S.	2	------	
Sept. 18	7 a. m.	------	66	------	Nim.	10	SW.	3	SW.	2	------	
	2 p. m.	------	80	------	Cu. st.	10	SW.	3	SW.	2	------	
	9 p. m.	------	63	------	Nim.	10	----------		W.	1	------	
Sept. 19	7 a. m.	------	58	------	Nim.	10	----------		NW.	3	------	
	2 p. m.	------	52	------	Nim.	10	----------		N.	3	------	
	9 p. m.	------	50	------	Nim.	10	----------		N.	2	------	
Sept. 20	7 a. m.	------	44	------	Cir. st.	10	----------		NW.	3	------	
	2 p. m.	------	55	------	Cir. st.	10	----------		NW.	3	------	
	9 p. m.	------	52	------	Cir. st.	10	----------		NW.	2	------	
Sept. 21	7 a. m.	------	44	------		0	----------		NW.	2	------	
	2 p. m.	------	68	------	Cir. st.	10	----------		NE.	3	------	
	9 p. m.	------	55	------	Cir. st.	10	----------		NE.	1	------	
Sept. 22	7 a. m.	------	52	------	St.	2	----------		NE	------	------	
	2 p. m.	------	72	------		0	----------		SE.	2	------	
	9 p. m.	------	56	------		0	----------		SE.	1	------	
Sept. 23	7 a. m.	------	57	------		0	----------		SW.	2	------	
	2 p. m.	------	82	------		0	----------		SW.	2	------	
	9 p. m.	------	62	------		0	----------			0	------	
Sept. 24	7 a. m.	------	57	------		0	----------			0	------	
	2 p. m.	------	83	------	Cir. cu.	2	SW.	3	SW.	1	------	
	9 p. m.	------	64	------	St	----------	----------			0	------	

ROSSVILLE, IOWA.

Month and day.	Hour.	Barom'r corrected to 32° F.	Thermometer.	Force of vapor.	Cloudiness.	Motion of clouds.	Winds.		Relative humidity.	REMARKS.
Sept. 14	9 p. m.	------	47.8	------	9	----------	E.	2	------	17th. Rain, accompanied by thunder. at 11.20 a. m.; thunder in N. W. at 8 p. m.; rain and thunder in the night; am't, 0 01 inch.
Sept. 15	7 a. m.	------	48.1	------	10	----------	SE.	2	------	
	2 p. m.	------	61.9	------	10	----------	SE.	3	------	
	9 p. m.	------	52.4	------	10	----------	SE.	2	------	
Sept. 16	7 a. m.	------	52.8	------	10	----------	SE.	2	------	18th. Frequent showers in the W. from 2.11 to 4 p. m ; 7.38 p. m., moderate rain; ended in the night; amount, 1.04 inch.
	2 p. m.	------	74	------	4	----------	SE.	2	------	
	9 p. m.	------	54.8	------	0	----------	E.	2	------	
Sept. 17	7 a. m.	------	57.8	------	2	----------	SE.	2	------	
	2 p. m.	------	73	------	4	----------	S.	4	------	21st. Light frost.
	9 p. m.	------	62.4	------	5	----------	SE.	2	------	23d. Light fog in the morning; rose at 9 a. m.
Sept. 18	7 a. m.	------	62.1	------	10	----------	SE.	2	------	
	2 p. m.	------	66.1	------	10	----------	W.	2	------	24th. Morning, light fog; 7.40 p. m., diffused lightning in the W.; aurora, (dull.)
	9 p. m.	------	62.2	------	10	----------	NW.	1	------	
Sept. 19	7 a. m.	------	50.6	------	10	----------	N.	4	------	
	2 p. m.	------	50.3	------	10	----------	N.	4	------	
	9 p. m.	------	42.0	------	0	----------	N.	3	------	
Sept. 20	7 a. m.	------	36.3	------	0	----------	NE.	3	------	
	2 p. m.	------	58.1	------	0	----------	N.	3	------	
	9 p. m.	------	43.6	------	0	----------	N.	2	------	
Sept. 21	7 a. m.	------	39.8	------	0	----------	N.	2	------	
	2 p. m.	------	62.1	------	1	----------	N.	2	------	
	9 p. m.	------	54.1	------	10	----------	SE.	1	------	
Sept. 22	7 a. m.	------	54.8	------	5	----------	NW.	2	------	
	2 p. m.	------	------	------	----------	----------	----------		------	
	9 p. m.	------	52.2	------	2	----------	E.	2	------	
Sept. 23	7 a. m.	------	57.9	------	1	----------	NE.	1	------	
	2 p. m.	------	77.9	------	1	----------	W.	1	------	
	9 p. m.	------	57.3	------	0	----------	NE.	2	------	
Sept. 24	7 a. m.	------	60.5	------	0	----------	SE.	2	------	
	2 p. m.	------	84.3	------	2	----------	SE.	3	------	
	9 p. m.	------	64.1	------	1	----------	SE.	1	------	

STORMS Nos. 2 AND 3, SEPTEMBER, 1859.

BEAVER BAY, MINNESOTA.*

Month and day.	Hour.	Barom'r corrected to 32° F.	Thermometer.	Force of vapor.	Cloudiness.	Motion of clouds.	Winds.	Relative humidity.	REMARKS.
					Cir. Z.† 1	W. 1			
Sept. 14	9 p. m.	29.411	39.5	.204	Cir. st. H. 3	----------	Calm 0	84	14th. Frost and ice.
Sept. 15	7 a. m.	.364	42	.256	Cir. cu. D. 9	SW. 2	NE. 2	95.7	17th. Thunder in SW. at 10½ a. m.; commenced raining at 1.25 p. m.; thunder during the p. m.; lightning in the SE. at 9 p. m; rain ceased in the night; amount, 0.256 inch.
	2 p. m.	.291	51	.321	Cir. cu. Z. H. 5	S. 2	E. 1	85.9	
					Nim. Z. 3	S. 1			
	9 p. m.	.312	39.5	.199	St. H. 3	----------	Calm 0	81.8	
Sept. 16	7 a. m.	.198	48	.335	Nim. D. 9	S. 1	Calm 0	100	
					Cir. cu. Z. 1	W. 1			
	2 p. m.	.139	53	.348	Cir. st. M. H. 4	----------	E. 1	86.4	18th. Began to rain at 9 a. m. and ended in the evening; amount, 0.06 inch.
	9 p. m.	.122	52	.388	Nim. D. 9	----------	Calm 0	100	
					Nim. D. 9	S. 1			
Sept. 17	7 a. m.	.092	51.5	.341	Haze H. 0	----------	NE. 0	89.5	20th and 21st. Frost.
	2 p. m.	.077	55	.376	Nim. D. 9	SW. 1	E. 1	86.9	24th. Thunder in the W. and SW. at 4 p. m.; lightning in the E. and SE. from 6 to 8 p. m.
	9 p. m.	.056	54.5	.426	Nim. D. 6	W. 1	NE. 1	100	
Sept. 18	7 a. m.	28.967	52	.388	Nim. D. 9	NE. 4	NW. 1	100	
	2 p. m.	.936	53	.389	Nim., fog 10	----------	W. 1	96.6	
	9 p. m.	29.018	51	.374	Nim., fog 10	0	NE. 1	100	
					Cir. cu. Z. 3				
Sept. 19	7 a. m.	.246	45	.275	Cir. H. 3	----------	SW. 1	92	
	2 p. m.	.299	48.5	.218	Cu. H. 1	----------	SW. 1	63.5	
	9 p. m.	.409	38	.229	---------- 0	----------	W. 0	100	
Sept. 20	7 a. m.	.465	35.5	.297	Cu. H. 1	----------	N. 1	92.3	
	2 p. m.	.427	48.5	.253	Haze H. 0	----------	E. 1	74.3	
	9 p. m.	.453	36.5	.216	0	----------	Calm 0	100	
Sept. 21	7 a. m.	.343	35	.204	Cu. H. 1	----------	NE. 1	100	
	2 p. m.	.246	49	.283	Cu. Z. 1	----------	E. 3	81.7	
	9 p. m.	.224	42	.244	0	----------	Calm 0	91.4	
Sept. 22	7 a. m.	.228	40	.258	Cu. st. H. 1	----------	W. 1	71.6	
	2 p. m.	.241	51	.283	Cu. H. 1	----------	E. 2	75.5	
	9 p. m.	.247	43	.265	0	----------	W. 1	95.8	
Sept. 23	7 a. m.	.287	42	.295	Cu. H. 1	----------	NW. 0	76.1	
	2 p. m.	.297	60	.282	0	----------	Calm 0	54.6	
	9 p. m.	.328	48	.335	0	----------	Calm 0	100	
Sept. 24	7 a. m.	.297	48.5	.335	Cir. Z. M. 1	----------	Calm 0	74.7	
					Cir. Z. 2	SW. 1			
	2 p. m.	.238	58	.336	Cir. st. H. 3	----------	NE. 1	69.8	
	9 p. m.	.154	56.5	.413	Nim. 10	----------	NE. 0	90.4	

* Clarke, observer. † D, diffuse; H, horizon; M, midway between the horizon; and Z, zenith.

BEAVER BAY, MINNESOTA.*

Month and day.	Hour.	Barom'r corrected to 32° F.	Thermometer.	Force of vapor.	Cloudiness.	Motion of clouds.	Winds.	Relative humidity.
Sept. 14	9 p. m.	------	34	.155	3	----------	Calm 0	79
Sept. 15	7 a. m.	------	44	.241	9	----------	NE. 1	84
	2 p. m.	------	58	.394	5	----------	SE. 1	82
	9 p. m.	------	50	.335	8	----------	Calm 0	93
Sept. 16	7 a. m.	------	50	.335	9	----------	Calm 0	93
	2 p. m.	------	64	.497	6	----------	SW. 1	83
	9 p. m.	------	56	.420	9	----------	Calm 0	94
Sept. 17	7 a. m.	------	56	.391	8	----------	NE. 1	87
	2 p. m.	------	60	.456	10	----------	NE. 1	88
	9 p. m.	------	55	.405	10	----------	NE. 3	94
Sept. 18	7 a. m.	------	54	.418	10	----------	NE. 1	100
	2 p. m.	------	62	.491	9	----------	NE. 1	88
	9 p. m.	------	55	.405	9	----------	N. 3	94
Sept. 19	7 a. m.	------	45	.228	4	----------	N. 3	76
	2 p. m.	------	58	.282	0	----------	NE. 1	58
	9 p. m.	------	33	.188	0	----------	Calm 0	100
Sept. 20	7 a. m.	------	37	.157	0	----------	Calm 0	71
	2 p. m.	------	56	.308	0	----------	E. 1	69
	9 p. m.	------	33	.188	0	----------	Calm 0	100

* Wieland, observer.

STORMS Nos. 2 AND 3, SEPTEMBER, 1859.

BEAVER BAY, MINNESOTA—Continued.

Month and day.	Hour.	Barom'r corrected to 32° F.	Thermometer.	Force of vapor.	Cloudiness.	Motion of clouds.	Winds.	Relative humidity.	REMARKS.
Sept. 21	7 a. m.	------	39	.195	0	----------	NE. 1	82	
	2 p. m.	------	57	.322	1	----------	NE. 1	69	
	9 p. m	------	34	.175	1	----------	Calm 0	89	
Sept. 22	7 a. m.	------	37	.178	0	----------	Calm 0	81	
	2 p. m.	------	64	.464	0	----------	E. 1	77	
	9 p. m.	------	38	.229	0	----------	Calm 0	100	
Sept. 23	7 a. m.	------	43	.254	0	----------	Calm 0	92	
	2 p. m.	------	74	.568	0	----------	E. 1	67	
	9 p. m.	------	43	.231	0	----------	Calm 0	83	
Sept. 24	7 a. m.	------	42	------	1	----------	Calm 0	------	
	2 p. m.	------	73	.655	3	----------	NE. 1	81	
	9 p. m.	------	56	.449	7	----------	Calm 0	100	

BURLINGTON, MINNESOTA.

Month and day.	Hour.	Barom'r corrected to 32° F.	Thermometer.	Force of vapor.	Cloudiness.	Motion of clouds.	Winds.	Relative humidity.	REMARKS.
Sept. 14	9 p. m.	------	39	------	Cu. 6	E. 3	----------	------	21st. Hard frost.
Sept. 15	7 a. m.	------	43	------	Cir. 3	----------	E. 1	------	24th. Rain in the night; amount, 0.02 inch.
	2 p. m.	------	54	------	Cir. cu. 8	E. 2	E. 3	------	
	9 p. m.	------	48	------	Nim. 8	E. 2	----------	------	
Sept. 16	7 a. m.	------	49	------	Nim. 9	E. 2	E. 2	------	
	2 p. m.	------	60	------	Nim. 5	E. 4	E. 4	------	
	9 p. m.	------	53	------	Nim. 6	----------	----------	------	
Sept. 17	7 a. m.	------	54	------	Nim. 8	E. 1	E. 1	------	
	2 p. m.	------	59	------	Nim. 9	E. 3	E. 4	------	
	9 p. m.	------	50	------	Nim. 9	----------	----------	------	
Sept. 18	7 a. m.	------	50	------	Nim. 8	E. 3	E. 3	------	
	2 p. m.	------	53	------	Fog 9	E. 2	E. 4	------	
	9 p. m.	------	51	------	Nim. 10	E. 1	----------	------	
Sept. 19	7 a. m.	------	46	------	Cir. cu. 7	E. 2	E. 2	------	
	2 p. m.	------	49	------	Cir. 1	N. 1	NW. 1	------	
	9 p. m.	------	40	------	----------	----------	----------	------	
Sept. 20	7 a. m.	------	40	------	St. 1	SW. 1	NW. 1	------	
	2 p. m.	------	49	------	St. 1	N. 1	NW. 2	------	
	9 p. m.	------	38	------	----------	----------	W. 1	------	
Sept. 21	7 a. m.	------	33	------	St. 1	E. 1	NW. 1	------	
	2 p. m.	------	49	------	Cir. 1	NE. 3	NE. 1	------	
	9 p. m.	------	39	------	----------	----------	----------	------	
Sept. 22	7 a. m.	------	39	------	St. 1	E. 2	E. 1	------	
	2 p. m.	------	58	------	----------	----------	NE. 1	------	
	9 p. m.	------	40	------	----------	----------	N. 1	------	
Sept. 23	7 a. m.	------	48	------	----------	----------	----------	------	
	2 p. m.	------	68	------	----------	----------	----------	------	
	9 p. m.	------	48	------	----------	----------	W. 1	------	
Sept. 24	7 a. m.	------	48	------	Cir. 1	W. 1	W. 1	------	
	2 p. m.	------	68	------	Cu. 4	W. 1	NE. 2	------	
	9 p. m.	------	59	------	----------	----------	W. 1	------	

CHATFIELD, MINNESOTA.

Month and day.	Hour.	Barom'r corrected to 32° F.	Thermometer.	Force of vapor.	Cloudiness.	Motion of clouds.	Winds.	Relative humidity.	REMARKS.
Sept. 14	9 p. m.	------	50	------	Cir. 10	W. 1	0	------	14th. Rain from 6 to 10 a. m.
Sept. 15	7 a. m.	------	48	------	Nim. 10	0	S. ----------	------	
	2 p. m.	------	56	------	Nim. 10	S. 2	S. ----------	------	
	9 p. m.	------	53	------	Nim. 10	S. 3	0	------	
Sept. 16	7 a. m.	------	53	------	Nim. 10	S. 1	S. ----------	------	
	2 p. m.	------	'70	------	Nim. 9	S. 1	S. ----------	------	
	9 p. m.	------	52	------	0	----------	0	------	

STORMS Nos. 2 AND 3, SEPTEMBER, 1859.

CHATFIELD, MINNESOTA—Continued.

Month and day.	Hour.	Barom'r corrected to 32° F.	Thermometer.	Force of vapor.	Cloudiness.		Motion of clouds.		Winds.		Relative humidity.	REMARKS.
Sept. 17	7 a. m.	------	59	------	Nim.	2	W.	1	SE.		------	Rain from 7 p. m. the 17th to 3 a. m. on the 19th
	2 p. m.	------	80	------	Nim.	5	W.	2	SE.		------	24th. Rain from 9 a. m. to 3 p. m.
	9 p. m.	------	65	------	Nim.	10	W.	3	SE.		------	
Sept. 18	7 a. m.	------	64	------	Nim.	10	W.	1	S.		------	
	2 p. m.	------	75	------	Nim.	10	NE.	1	SW.		------	
	9 p. m.	------	64	------	Nim.	10	----------		W.		------	
Sept. 19	7 a. m.	------	52	------	Nim.	10	N.	8	N.		------	
	2 p. m.	------	56	------	Nim.	10	N.	5	N.		------	
	9 p. m.	------	44	------		0	----------		W.		------	
Sept. 20	7 a. m.	------	36	------		0	----------		N.		------	
	2 p. m.	------	60	------		0	----------		W.		------	
	9 p. m.	------	38	------		0	----------			0	------	
Sept. 21	7 a. m.	------	35	------		0	----------			0	------	
	2 p. m.	------	60	------		0	----------		S.		------	
	9 p. m.	------	50	------		2	----------			0	------	
Sept. 22	7 a. m.	------	56	------		0	----------			0	------	
	2 p. m.	------	75	------		2	----------		S.		------	
	9 p. m.	------	55	------		0	----------			0	------	
Sept. 23	7 a. m.	------	50	------		0	----------			0	------	
	2 p. m.	------	75	------		0	----------		S.		------	
	9 p. m.	------	54	------		0	----------			0	------	
Sept. 24	7 a. m.	------	53	------		0	----------			0	------	
	2 p. m.	------	83	------		0	----------		S.		------	
	9 p. m.	------	69	------	Nim.	10	S.	1	S.		------	

FOREST CITY, MINNESOTA.

Month and day.	Hour.	Barom'r corrected to 32° F.	Thermometer.	Force of vapor.	Cloudiness.	Motion of clouds.	Winds.		Relative humidity.	REMARKS.
Sept. 14	9 p. m.	------	55	------	2	----------		0	------	15th. Misty all day.
Sept. 15	7 a. m.	------	53	------	6	----------	SE.	2	------	16th. Rain from 3 to 8 p. m.; amount, 1.25 inch.
	2 p. m.	------	55	------	8	----------	SE.	2	------	17th. Hail storm about 4 p. m.; rain from 8 to 9 p. m; amount, 0.15 inch.
	9 p. m.	------	54	------	8	----------		0	------	
Sept. 16	7 a. m.	------	55	------	4	----------	SE.	2	------	
	2 p. m.	------	63	------	4	----------	SE.	2	------	
	9 p. m.	------	58	------	0	----------	NE.	2	------	
Sept. 17	7 a. m.	------	62	------	8	----------	SE.	2	------	
	2 p. m.	------	62	------	8	----------	SE.	2	------	
	9 p. m.	------	63	------	8	----------		0	------	
Sept. 18	7 a. m.	------	60	------	4	----------	SE.	2	------	
	2 p. m.	------	64	------	4	----------	SE.	2	------	
	9 p. m.	------	57	------	8	----------	NW.	3	------	
Sept. 19	7 a. m.	------	49	------	8	----------	NE.	5	------	
	2 p. m.	------	57	------	0	----------	NE.	3	------	
	9 p. m.	------	43	------	0	----------		0	------	
Sept. 20	7 a. m.	------	40	------	0	----------		0	------	
	2 p. m.	------	62	------	0	----------		0	------	
	9 p. m.	------	40	------	0	----------		0	------	
Sept. 21	7 a. m.	------	41	------	0	----------	SE.	2	------	
	2 p. m.	------	67	----	0	----------	SE.	2	------	
	9 p. m.	------	43	------	0	----------		0	------	
Sept. 22	7 a. m.	------	40	------	0	----------		0	------	
	2 p. m.	------	67	------	0	----------	E.	1	------	
	9 p. m.	------	48	------	0	----------		0	------	
Sept. 23	7 a. m.	------	55	------	0	----------		0	------	
	2 p. m.	------	75	------	0	----------	NE.	2	------	
	9 p. m.	------	60	------	4	----------		0	------	
Sept. 24	7 a. m.	------	59	------	4	----------	SE.	2	------	
	2 p. m.	------	68	------	8	----------	S.	2	------	
	9 p. m.	------	65	------	6	----------		0	------	

STORMS Nos. 2 AND 3, SEPTEMRER, 1859.

HAZLEWOOD, MINNESOTA.

Month and day.	Hour.	Barom'r corrected to 32° F.	Thermometer.	Force of vapor.	Cloudiness.	Motion of clouds.	Winds.	Relative humidity.	REMARKS.
Sept. 14	9 p. m.	------	58	------	Cu. 4	----------	S. 2	------	16th. Amount of rain, 0 05 inch.
Sept. 15	7 a. m.	------	54	------	Cir. cu. 9	E -------	SE. 2	------	17th. Began to rain at 4 p. m.; amount, 0.10 inch.
	2 p. m.	------	66	------	Cir. cu. 10	E -------	SE. 2	------	
	9 p. m.	------	58	------	Cu. cir. 5	E -------	E 2	------	24th. Storm commenced at noon and ended (?); am't, 0.69 inch.
Sept. 16	7 a. m.	------	58	------	Nim. 9	E -------	E 2	------	
	2 p. m.	------	70	------	Cir. cu. 9	E -------	SE. 3	------	
	9 p. m.	------	68	------	Cu. 3	----------	SE. 2	------	
Sept. 17	7 a. m.	------	65	------	Nim. 8	E -------	E. 2	------	
	2 p. m.	------	69	------	Cu. cir. 9	----------	E. 2	------	
	9 p. m.	------	60	------	Cu. 3	----------	E. 2	------	
Sept. 18	7 a. m.	------	56	------	Cu. 4	----------	SW. 2	------	
	2 p. m.	------	62	------	Nim. 8	W -------	NW. 3	------	
	9 p. m.	------	58	------	Nim. 10	----------	NW. 2	------	
Sept. 19	7 a. m.	------	52	------	Nim. 10	W -------	NW. 3	------	
	2 p. m.	------	60	------	Cu. 4	----------	NW. 2	------	
	9 p. m.	------	49	------	0	----------	NW. 2	------	
Sept. 20	7 a. m.	------	42	------	0	----------	NW. 2	------	
	2 p. m.	------	66	------	2	----------	S. 2	------	
	9 p. m.	------	48	------	St. 2	----------	S. 2	------	
Sept. 21	7 a. m.	------	40	------	Cu. 3	----------	S. 2	------	
	2 p. m.	------	76	------	Cu. 3	----------	S. 2	------	
	9 p. m.	------	48	------	0	----------	S. 2	------	
Sept. 22	7 a. m.	------	44	------	Cu. 2	----------	SE. 2	------	
	2 p. m.	------	68	------	Cu. 2	----------	S. 2	------	
	9 p. m.	------	58	------	0	----------	S. 2	------	
Sept. 23	7 a. m.	------	54	------	St. 2	----------	S. 2	------	
	2 p. m.	------	78	------	Cu. 3	----------	S. 3	------	
	9 p. m.	------	69	------	0	----------	S. 2	------	
Sept. 24	7 a. m.	------	64	------	0	----------	S. 2	------	
	2 p. m.	------	67	------	Nim. 10	E -------	SE. 2	------	
	9 p. m.	------	58	------	Nim. 9	----------	S. 2	------	

PRINCETON, MINNESOTA.

Month and day.	Hour.	Barom'r corrected to 32° F.	Thermometer.	Force of vapor.	Cloudiness.	Motion of clouds.	Winds.	Relative humidity.	REMARKS.
Sept. 14	9 p. m.	------	53	------	Nim. 6	E. 1	E. 2	------	17th. Slight shower just before day, accompanied by considerable thunder and lightning, passed mostly south; continued to rain moderately till 7 a. m., when a heavy shower came up, and passed off about 8 a. m.; amount, 3.31 inches.
Sept. 15	7 a. m.	------	54	------	Nim. 6	E. 2	E. 2	------	
	2 p. m.	------	59	------	Cir. cu. 10	SE. 2	SE. 3	------	
	9 p. m.	------	51	------	Cir. cu. 10	0	0	------	
Sept. 16	7 a. m.	------	56	------	Cu. cir. 10	0	SE. 2	------	
	2 p. m.	------	66	------	Cir. cu. 9	S. 1	S. 2	------	
	9 p. m.	------	58	------	Cir. cu. 1	H. NW. & N.	S. 1	------	
Sept. 17	7 a. m.	------	58	------	Nim. 10	W. 2	SE. 2	------	
	2 p. m.	------	64	------	Nim. 10	W. NW. 2	NE. 2	------	24th. The past four or five days have been clear and pleasant; to-day quite warm, temperature 83° in p. m.; a shower from W.SW. cooled the air somewhat; this shower was accompanied by considerable thunder and lightning; the wind continued W. for an hour or so after the shower had passed, then went to the S.SE. again; heavy shower at 8½ p. m. and ended in the night; amount, 0.41 inch.
	9 p. m.	------	64	------	Nim. 10	----------	SE. 4	------	
Sept. 18	7 a. m.	------	61	------	Nim. 10	NW. 2	NW. 2	------	
	2 p. m.	------	65	------	Nim. 10	N. 2	NW. 2	------	
	9 p. m.	------	62	------	Nim. 10	----------	N. 2	------	
Sept. 19	7 a. m.	------	50	------	Nim. 10	N. 2	N. 2	------	
	2 p. m.	------	60	------	0	----------	N. 3	------	
	9 p. m.	------	42	------	0	----------	N. 1	------	
Sept. 20	7 a. m.	------	40	------	0	----------	N. 1	------	
	2 p. m.	------	62	------	0	----------	0	------	
	9 p. m.	------	50	------	0	----------	0	------	
Sept. 21	7 a. m.	------	42	------	Cir. 1	0	0	------	
	2 p. m.	------	66	------	Cir. 1	0	NE. 2	------	
	9 p. m.	------	46	------	0	----------	0	------	
Sept. 22	7 a. m.	------	42	------	Cir. cu. 3	S. 2	S. 2	------	
	2 p. m.	------	70	------	Cu. 1	NW. Hor. --	E. 1	------	
	9 p. m.	------	54	------	0	----------	0	------	
Sept. 23	7 a. m.	------	50	------	Thin mist ----	----------	E. 1	------	
	2 p. m.	------	74	------	Cir. 1	0	E. 2	------	
	9 p. m.	------	52	------	Cir. 1	0	E. 1	------	
Sept. 24	7 a. m.	------	60	------	Cir. 2	0	E. 1	------	
	2 p. m.	------	81	------	Nim. 8	W. 2	S. 2	------	
	9 p. m.	------	66	------	Nim. 9	----------	S. 2	------	

STORMS Nos. 2 AND 3, SEPTEMBER, 1859.

BELLEVUE, NEBRASKA.

Month and day.	Hour.	Barom'r corrected to 32° F.	Thermometer.	Force of vapor.	Cloudiness.	Motion of clouds.	Winds.	Relative humidity.	REMARKS.
Sept. 14	9 p. m.	......	60	......	0	0	NE. 2	......	17th. Thunder shower at night; amount, 0.17 inch.
Sept. 15	7 a. m.	......	57	......	Nim. 10	......	NE. 2	......	
	2 p. m.	......	66	......	Nim. 10	NE	NE. 2	......	
	9 p. m.	......	57	......	Nim. 4	NE	NE. 2	......	
Sept. 16	7 a. m.	......	62	......	Nim. 10	NE. 2	NE. 2	......	
	2 p. m.	......	82	......	......	......	S. 1	......	
	9 p. m.	......	69	......	......	......	SW	......	
Sept. 17	7 a. m.	......	70	......	Cir. 1	SW	S. 2	......	
	2 p. m.	......	92	......	......	......	S. 2	......	
	9 p. m.	......	74	......	Nim., st. 6	......	SW. 2	......	
Sept. 18	7 a. m.	......	62	......	Nim. 6	N. 2	N. 2	......	
	2 p. m.	......	67	......	Nim , st. 10	N. 6	N. 2	......	
	9 p. m.	......	58	......	Nim. 10	N. 6	N. 5	......	
Sept. 19	7 a. m.	......	48	......	Nim., st. 10	N. 5	N. 5	......	
	2 p. m.	......	60	......	......	......	N. 4	......	
	9 p. m.	......	49	......	......	......	N. 1	......	
Sept. 20	7 a. m.	......	39	......	......	......	N. 2	......	
	2 p. m.	......	66	......	......	......	N. 2	......	
	9 p. m.	......	49	......	......	......	N	......	
Sept. 21	7 a. m.	......	39	......	......	......	S. 1	......	
	2 p. m.	......	70	......	......	......	S 2	......	
	9 p. m.	......	53	......	......	......	......	......	
Sept. 22	7 a. m.	......	50	......	......	......	S. 1	......	
	2 p. m.	......	75	......	......	......	S. 2	......	
	9 p. m.	......	60	......	......	......	S. 3	......	
Sept. 23	7 a. m.	......	57	......	Cir. st. 2	......	S. 1	......	
	2 p. m.	......	80	......	......	......	S. 2	......	
	9 p. m.	......	67	......	Nim. 3	......	S. 2	......	
Sept. 24	7 a. m.	......	66	......	Nim., st. 9	S. 1	S. 1	......	
	2 p. m.	......	78	......	Cu. 2	S. 1	S. 2	......	
	9 p. m.	......	70	......	Nim., st. 3	......	......	......	

ELKHORN CITY, NEBRASKA.

Month and day.	Hour.	Barom'r corrected to 32° F.	Thermometer.	Force of vapor.	Cloudiness.	Motion of clouds.	Winds.	Relative humidity.	REMARKS.
Sept. 14	9 p. m.	......	58	......	St. 10	2	SE. 2	......	14th. Slight sprinkle in the afternoon.
Sept. 15	7 a. m.	......	59	......	Nim. 10	2	SE. 2	......	
	2 p. m.	......	73	......	Cu. st. 9	1	SE. 1	......	16th. Heavy fog; sprinkle of rain at 10 p. m.
	9 p. m.	......	60	......	St. 3	2	SE. 2	......	
Sept. 16	7 a. m.	......	59	......	Nim. 10	2	SE. 2	......	17th. Gusts to S. and E at 9 p. m.
	2 p. m.	......	86	......	Cu. 4	3	SE. 3	......	18th. Sprinkle at 3 p. m.
	9 p. m.	......	73	......	Cu. st. 5	3	SE. 3	......	20th. Thermometer 32° at 6 a. m.
Sept. 17	7 a. m.	......	71	......	Cir. st. 6	3	SE. 3	......	21st. Thermometer 38° at 5½ a. m.; frost; some fog in ravines.
	2 p. m.	......	95	......	Cir. st. 7	3	SW. 3	......	
	9 p. m.	......	71	......	St. 2	2	NW. 2	......	22d. Heavy fog until 7 a. m.
Sept. 18	7 a. m.	......	63	......	St. 9	3	NW. 3	......	23d. Heavy dew; blue rays at sunset; shower at 10 p. m.
	2 p. m.	......	69	......	St. 9	4	NW. 4	......	
	9 p. m.	......	57	......	St. 10	5	N. 5	......	24th. Several showers in a. m; Gusts in various directions at 9 p. m.
Sept. 19	7 a. m.	......	57	......	Nim. 10	4	NW. 4	......	
	2 p. m.	......	59	......	Cu. st. 8	4	NW. 4	......	
	9 p. m.	......	48	......	0	0	NE. 2	......	
Sept. 20	7 a. m.	......	36	......	0	0	N. 1	......	
	2 p m.	......	66	......	0	0	NE. 2	......	
	9 p. m.	......	48	......	0	0	NE. 1	......	
Sept. 21	7 a. m.	......	42	......	Cir. 1	......	E. 0	......	
	2 p. m.	......	73	......	Cir. 2	2	SE. 0	......	
	9 p. m.	......	53	......	0	0	SE. 2	......	
Sept. 22	7 a. m.	......	51	......	......	......	SE. 2	......	
	2 p. m.	......	76	......	Cir. 1	3	S. 3	......	
	9 p. m.	......	63	......	0	0	SE. 3	......	
Sept. 23	7 a. m.	......	58	......	Cir. st. 3	3	SE. 3	......	
	2 p. m.	......	85	......	Cir. 2	4	SE. 4	......	
	9 p. m.	......	68	......	St. 7	2	S. 1	......	
Sept. 24	7 a. m.	......	75	......	Nim., st. 9	1	S. 1	......	
	2 p. m.	......	85	......	Cu. 3	4	S. 4	......	
	9 p. m.	......	70	......	Cu st., nim. 9	1	S. 1	......	

STORMS Nos. 2 AND 3, SEPTEMBER, 1859.

KANOSHA, NEBRASKA.

Month and day.	Hour.	Barom'r corrected to 32° F.	Thermometer.	Force of vapor.	Cloudiness.	Motion of clouds.	Winds.	Relative humidity.	REMARKS.
Sept. 14	9 p. m.	------	------	------	10	----------	SE. 1	------	17th. A shower, accompanied by
Sept. 15	7 a. m.	------	------	------	10	----------	SE. 1	------	thunder and lightning, at night.
	2 p. m.	------	------	------	10	----------	SE. 1	------	18th. Slight sprinkling of rain sev-
	9 p. m.	------	------	------	1	----------	E. 2	------	eral times during the day.
Sept. 16	7 a. m.	------	------	------	0	----------	SE. 1	------	23d. Light shower at night.
	2 p. m.	------	------	------	3	----------	SE. 2	------	24th. Two or three light showers
	9 p. m.	------	------	------	3	----------	SE. 1	------	in the night.
Sept. 17	7 a. m.	------	------	------	0	----------	SE. 1	------	
	2 p. m.	------	------	------	5	----------	S. 3	------	
	9 p. m.	------	------	------	3	----------	NE. 1	------	
Sept. 18	7 a. m.	------	------	------	3	----------	NE. 1	------	
	2 p. m.	------	------	------	10	----------	NW. 1	------	
	9 p. m.	------	------	------	10	----------	NW. 4	------	
Sept. 19	7 a. m.	------	------	------	10	----------	NW. 3	------	
	2 p. m.	------	------	------	10	----------	NW. 3	------	
	9 p. m.	------	------	------	0	----------	NW. 1	------	
Sept. 20	7 a. m.	------	------	------	0	----------	NW. 1	------	
	2 p. m.	------	------	------	0	----------	NW. 1	------	
	9 p. m.	------	------	------	0	----------	NW. 1	------	
Sept. 21	7 a. m.	------	------	------	0	----------	NW. 1	------	
	2 p. m.	------	------	------	3	----------	SE. 1	------	
	9 p. m.	------	------	------	0	----------	NW. 1	------	
Sept. 22	7 a. m.	------	------	------	0	----------	NW. 1	------	
	2 p. m.	------	------	------	1	----------	SE. 2	------	
	9 p. m.	------	------	------	0	----------	SE. 2	------	
Sept. 23	7 a. m.	------	------	------	0	----------	SE. 1	------	
	2 p. m.	------	------	------	1	----------	SE. 1	------	
	9 p. m.	------	------	------	2	----------	SE. 1	------	
Sept. 24	7 a. m.	------	------	------	4	----------	SE. 1	------	
	2 p. m.	------	------	------	8	----------	SE. 2	------	
	9 p. m.	------	------	------	3	----------	SE. 1	------	

NEBRASKA CITY, NEBRASKA.

Month and day.	Hour.	Barom'r corrected to 32° F.	Thermometer.	Force of vapor.	Cloudiness.	Motion of clouds.	Winds.	Relative humidity.	REMARKS.
Sept. 14	9 p. m.	------	57.6	------	10	----------	SE. 2	------	18th. Amount of rain, 1.34 inch.
Sept. 15	7 a. m.	------	57.2	------	10	----------	SE. 3	------	
	2 p. m.	------	63.3	------	10	----------	SE. 3	------	
	9 p. m.	------	57.5	------	10	----------	S. 3	------	
Sept. 16	7 a. m.	------	57.6	------	5	----------	SE. 2	------	
	2 p. m.	------	80.5	------	3	----------	SE. 3	------	
	9 p. m.	------	73.8	------	5	----------	SE. 3	------	
Sept. 17	7 a. m.	------	73.5	------	3	----------	S. 3	------	
	2 p. m.	------	93	------	8	----------	SW. 4	------	
	9 p. m.	------	75.1	------	10	----------	S. 3	------	
Sept. 18	7 a. m.	------	64.4	------	10	----------	SW. 2	------	
	2 p. m.	------	64.5	------	10	----------	W. 2	------	
	9 p. m.	------	60	------	10	----------	N. 5	------	
Sept. 19	7 a. m.	------	51.3	------	10	----------	N. 3	------	
	2 p. m.	------	57.5	------	10	----------	N. 4	------	
	9 p. m.	------	50.1	------	0	----------	N. 1	------	
Sept. 20	7 a. m.	------	40.4	------	0	----------	NE. 1	------	
	2 p. m.	------	66	------	0	----------	N. 1	------	
	9 p. m.	------	43.2	------	0	----------	0	------	
Sept. 21	7 a. m.	------	41.2	------	0	----------	0	------	
	2 p. m.	------	65.1	------	7	----------	SE. 3	------	
	9 p. m.	------	50.5	------	0	----------	S. 1	------	
Sept. 22	7 a. m.	------	50.1	------	0	----------	SE. 1	------	
	2 p. m.	------	70.1	------	0	----------	S. 3	------	
	9 p. m.	------	60.4	------	0	----------	S. 3	------	
Sept. 23	7 a. m.	------	64.1	------	0	----------	S. 2	------	
	2 p. m.	------	75	------	0	----------	W. 3	------	
	9 p. m.	------	68.5	------	2	----------	0	------	
Sept. 24	7 a. m.	------	67	------	8	----------	S. 1	------	
	2 p. m.	------	77.3	------	10	----------	S. 2	------	
	9 p. m.	------	68.9	------	2	----------	0	------	

STORMS Nos. 2 AND 3, SEPTEMBER, 1859.

OMAHA, NEBRASKA.

Month and day.	Hour.	Barom'r corrected to 32° F.	Thermometer.	Force of vapor.	Cloudiness.	Motion of clouds.	Winds.	Relative humidity.	REMARKS.
Sept. 14	9 p. m.	------	58	------	Nim. 10	----------	SE. 0	------	14th, 15th, and 16th. Light dew.
Sept. 15	7 a. m.	------	56	------	Cir. st. 10	----------	SE. 1	------	17th. Heavy dew; lightning dif-
	2 p. m.	------	64	------	Cir. st. 10	----------	SE. 1	------	fuse and zigzag, W., S., and E.,
	9 p. m.	------	60	------	Cir. st. 8	W. 2	SE. 2	------	with occasional thunder from 6
Sept. 16	7 a. m.	------	58	------	Nim. 10	----------	SE. 1	------	p. m. to 4 a. m. (?)
	2 p. m.	------	84	------	Cir. st. 8	----------	SE. 2	------	18th. Blue hazy atmosphere, with
	9 p. m.	------	76	------	Cir. st. 5	----------	S. 1	------	strong smell of smoke at 6 a. m.;
Sept. 17	7 a. m.	------	68	------	Cir. st. 3	----------	S. 0	------	a few drops of rain at 7 a. m.
	2 p. m.	------	88	------	Cir. cu. 6	----------	S. 3	------	19th. Drizzling rain.
	9 p. m.	------	76	------	Cir. cu. 4	----------	SW. 2	------	20th. Heavy frost; falling star at
Sept. 18	7 a. m.	------	66	------	Nim. 10	----------	W. 1	------	9 p. m.
	2 p. m.	------	68	------	Nim. 10	----------	NW. 3	------	21st. Hoar frost and ice.
	9 p. m.	------	58	------	Nim. 10	----------	NW. 4	------	22d. Heavy dew.
Sept. 19	7 a. m.	------	51	------	Nim. 10	----------	NW. 4	------	23d. Light dew.
	2 p. m.	------	60	------	Nim. 9	----------	NW. 3	------	24th. Thunder S. and W. at 10 a. m.
	9 p. m.	------	50	------	0	----------	N. 2	------	
Sept. 20	7 a. m.	------	32	------	0	----------	N. 0	------	
	2 p. m.	------	55	------	0	----------	N. 2	------	
	9 p. m.	------	41	------	Cir. 1	----------	N. 0	------	
Sept. 21	7 a. m.	------	39	------	Cir. 1	----------	SE. 0	------	
	2 p. m.	------	68	------	Cir. 5	----------	SE. 2	------	
	9 p. m.	------	53	------	St. 1	----------	SE. 0	------	
Sept. 22	7 a. m.	------	42	------	Cir. 1	----------	SE. 0	------	
	2 p. m.	------	74	------	Cir. 3	----------	SE. 3	------	
	9 p. m.	------	63	------	0	----------	SE. 1	------	
Sept. 23	7 a. m.	------	56	------	Cir. 1	----------	SE. 1	------	
	2 p. m.	------	82	------	Cir. 7	----------	SE. 2	------	
	9 p. m.	------	67	------	Cu. st. 4	----------	SE. 1	------	
Sept. 24	7 a. m.	------	69	------	Nim. 8	----------	SE. 1	------	
	2 p. m.	------	82	------	Cir. cu. 8	----------	SE. 3	------	
	9 p. m.	------	71	------	Cu. st. 7	----------	SE. 1	------	

BURLINGAME, KANSAS.

Month and day.	Hour.	Barom'r corrected to 32° F.	Thermometer.	Force of vapor.	Cloudiness.	Motion of clouds.	Winds.	Relative humidity.	REMARKS.
Sept. 14	9 p. m.	------	66	------	10	----------	0	------	17th. Amount of rain 0.25 inch.
Sept. 15	7 a. m.	------	62	------	10	----------	0	------	
	2 p. m.	------	86	------	8	----------	N. 2	------	
	9 p. m.	------	74	------	5	----------	E. 2	------	
Sept. 16	7 a. m.	------	70	------	2	----------	E. 2	------	
	2 p. m.	------	90	------	6	----------	SE. 3	------	
	9 p. m.	------	78	------	3	----------	SE. 3	------	
Sept. 17	7 a. m.	------	54	------	5	----------	S. 3	------	
	2 p. m.	------	76	------	3	----------	S. 4	------	
	9 p. m.	------	68	------	8	----------	S. 3	------	
Sept. 18	7 a. m.	------	58	------	10	----------	0	------	
	2 p. m.	------	62	------	5	----------	N. 4	------	
	9 p. m.	------	56	------	5	----------	N. 4	------	
Sept. 19	7 a. m.	------	42	------	10	----------	N. 4	------	
	2 p. m.	------	64	------	10	----------	N. 4	------	
	9 p. m.	------	48	------	10	----------	N. 2	------	
Sept. 20	7 a. m.	------	42	------	0	----------	N. 3	------	
	2 p. m.	------	70	------	0	----------	N. 3	------	
	9 p. m.	------	50	------	0	----------	0	------	
Sept. 21	7 a. m.	------	58	------	0	----------	0	------	
	2 p. m.	------	70	------	0	----------	SE. 2	------	
	9 p. m.	------	66	------	0	----------	SE. 2	------	
Sept. 22	7 a. m.	------	60	------	0	----------	0	------	
	2 p. m.	------	76	------	0	----------	SE. 3	------	
	9 p. m.	------	66	------	1	----------	SE. 3	------	
Sept. 23	7 a. m.	------	68	------	1	----------	SE. 3	------	
	2 p. m.	------	86	------	0	----------	SE. 3	------	
	9 p. m.	------	70	------	0	----------	SE. 2	------	
Sept. 24	7 a. m.	------	66	------	4	----------	0	------	
	2 p. m.	------	78	------	0	----------	SE. 3	------	
	9 p. m.	------	68	------	10	----------	SE. 2	------	

STORMS Nos. 2 AND 3, SEPTEMBER, 1859.

CELESTVILLE, KANSAS

Month and day.	Hour.	Barom'r corrected to 32° F.	Thermometer.	Force of vapor.	Cloudiness.	Motion of clouds.	Winds.	Relative humidity.	REMARKS.
Sept. 14	9 p. m.	------	------	------	6	----------	E. 2	------	Rain from 11 p. m. the 13th to 3 a. m. on the 14th. 17th. Lightning NW., W., S., N., and E., diffuse, from 7 p. m. to 2 a. m. on the 18th; rain from 11 p. m. to 3 a. m. on the 18th. 18th. 9 a. m., lightning W., N., and E., diffuse; 10½ a. m., thunder W. and NW.; 2 p. m., tornado N. and E., hail-stones large as marbles.
Sept. 15	7 a. m.	------	------	------	4	----------	SE. 1	------	
	2 p. m.	------	------	------	6	----------	E. 2	------	
	9 p. m.	------	------	------	8	----------	NE. 3	------	
Sept. 16	7 a. m.	------	------	------	8	----------	SE. 3	------	
	2 p. m.	------	------	------	7	----------	SE. 2	------	
	9 p. m.	------	------	------	2	----------	SE. 1	------	
Sept. 17	7 a. m.	------	------	------	2	----------	SE. 3	------	
	2 p. m.	------	------	------	8	----------	SW. 3	------	
	9 p. m.	------	------	------	10	----------	SW. 3	------	
Sept. 18	7 a. m.	------	------	------	10	----------	E. 3	------	
	2 p. m.	------	------	------	10	----------	W. 3	------	
	9 p. m.	------	------	------	10	----------	W. 4	------	
Sept. 19	7 a. m.	------	------	------	10	----------	NW. 5	------	
	2 p. m.	------	------	------	10	----------	NW. 3	------	
	9 p. m.	------	------	------	8	----------	NW. 2	------	
Sept. 20	7 a. m.	------	------	------	0	----------	NW. 2	------	
	2 p. m.	------	------	------	4	----------	NW. 1	------	
	9 p. m.	------	------	------	3	----------	NW. 3	------	
Sept. 21	7 a. m.	------	------	------	8	----------	0	------	
	2 p. m.	------	------	------	9	----------	SE. 1	------	
	9 p. m.	------	------	------	0	----------	N. 1	------	
Sept. 22	7 a. m.	------	------	------	0	----------	SE. 3	------	
	2 p. m.	------	------	------	0	----------	SE. 1	------	
	9 p. m.	------	------	------	0	----------	E. 1	------	
Sept. 23	7 a. m.	------	------	------	0	----------	SE. 1	------	
	2 p. m.	------	------	------	0	----------	SE. 3	------	
	9 p. m.	------	------	------	0	----------	S. 1	------	
Sept. 24	7 a. m.	------	------	------	0	----------	0	------	
	2 p. m.	------	------	------	0	----------	S. 1	------	
	9 p. m.	------	------	------	10	----------	SE. 1	------	

FORT RILEY, KANSAS.

Month and day.	Hour.	Barom'r corrected to 32° F.	Thermometer.	Force of vapor.	Cloudiness.	Motion of clouds.	Winds.	Relative humidity.	REMARKS.
Sept. 14	9 p. m.	------	------	------	5	----------	E. 1	------	Rain from 9½ p. m. the 17th to 2 p. m. on the 18th; forked lightning SE. and NW. 24th. Rain from 4 to 5 p. m., accompanied by thunder and forked lightning SE.
Sept. 15	7 a. m.	------	------	------	10	----------	E. 1	------	
	2 p. m.	------	------	------	0	----------	SE. 2	------	
	9 p. m.	------	------	------	2	----------	SE. 1	------	
Sept. 16	7 a. m.	------	------	------	0	----------	SE. 2	------	
	2 p. m.	------	------	------	5	----------	S. 4	------	
	9 p. m.	------	------	------	5	----------	S. 4	------	
Sept. 17	7 a. m.	------	------	------	5	----------	SW. 4	------	
	2 p. m.	------	------	------	2	----------	SW. 5	------	
	9 p. m.	------	------	------	4	----------	SW. 5	------	
Sept. 18	7 a. m.	------	------	------	0	----------	NW. 1	------	
	2 p. m.	------	------	------	4	----------	NW. 4	------	
	9 p. m.	------	------	------	10	----------	NW. 4	------	
Sept. 19	7 a. m.	------	------	------	10	----------	N. 5	------	
	2 p. m.	------	------	------	4	----------	N. 5	------	
	9 p. m.	------	------	------	0	----------	N. 1	------	
Sept. 20	7 a. m.	------	------	------	0	----------	N. 1	------	
	2 p. m.	------	------	------	0	----------	N. 2	------	
	9 p. m.	------	------	------	0	----------	N. 1	------	
Sept. 21	7 a. m.	------	------	------	0	----------	N. 1	------	
	2 p. m.	------	------	------	4	----------	N. 2	------	
	9 p. m.	------	------	------	6	----------	NW. 1	------	
Sept. 22	7 a. m.	------	------	------	0	----------	SW. 4	------	
	2 p. m.	------	------	------	0	----------	SW. 2	------	
	9 p. m.	------	------	------	0	----------	S. 4	------	
Sept. 23	7 a. m.	------	------	------	2	----------	S. 3	------	
	2 p. m.	------	------	------	0	----------	S. 4	------	
	9 p. m.	------	------	------	6	----------	S. 2	------	
Sept. 24	7 a. m.	------	------	------	5	----------	S. 3	------	
	2 p. m.	------	------	------	5	----------	S. 3	------	
	9 p. m.	------	------	------	10	----------	S. 3	------	

STORMS Nos. 2 AND 3, SEPTEMBER, 1859.

LEAVENWORTH, KANSAS.

Month and day.	Hour.	Barom'r corrected to 32° F.	Thermometer.	Force of vapor.	Cloudiness.	Motion of clouds.	Winds.	Relative humidity.	REMARKS.
Sept. 14	9 p. m.	......	......	......	St. 3	SE. 2	SW. 1	......	Rain from 8¼ p. m. the 18th to 5½ a. m. on the 19th; amount, 0.75 inch.
Sept. 15	7 a. m.	......	......	......	St. 8	SE. 2	SE. 2	......	
	2 p. m.	......	......	......	Cu. cir. 5	SW. 2	SE. 2	......	
	9 p. m.	......	......	......	Cu. 2	SW. 2	SW. 2	......	
Sept. 16	7 a. m.	......	......	......	St. 10	SE. 2	SE 2	......	
	2 p m.	......	......	......	Cir. cu. 5	SE. ,E. 2	SW. 2	......	
	9 p. m.	......	......	......	St. 8	SE. 2	SW. 2	......	
Sept. 17	7 a. m.	......	......	......	St. 8	SE. 2	NE. 2	......	
	2 p m.	......	......	......	Cu. st. 4	SE. 2	ENE. 3	......	
	9 p. m.	......	......	......	Cu. st. 9	NE. 2	SE.-NE. 2	......	
Sept. 18	7 a. m.	......	......	......	Cu. 10	SE. 3	SE. 2	......	
	2 p. m.	......	......	......	Cu. 10	SE. 3	SE. 3	......	
	9 p. m.	......	......	......	Cu. 10	NE.-NW. 4	NW. 8	......	
Sept. 19	7 a. m.	......	......	......	Cu. st. 9	SE. 2	SE. 2	......	
	2 p. m.	......	......	......	Cu. st. 9	SE. 1	SE. 3	......	
	9 p. m.	......	......	......	Cu. st. 8	SE. 2	SE. 2	......	
Sept. 20	7 a. m.	......	......	......	St. 5	SE. 2	SE. 1	......	
	2 p. m.	......	......	......	Cir. 3	SW. 1	SW. 1	......	
	9 p. m.	......	......	......	Cir. 1	SW. 1	SW. 1	......	
Sept. 21	7 a. m.	......	......	......	St. 5	SE. 2	SE. 1	......	
	2 p. m.	......	......	......	St. cir. 5	SW. 2	SW. 1	......	
	9 p m.	......	......	......	Cir. 2	SW. 1	SW. 1	......	
Sept. 22	7 a. m.	......	......	......	St. 7	SE. 2	SE. 1	......	
	2 p m.	......	......	......	St. cir. 3	SW. 2	SW. 1	......	
	9 p. m.	......	......	......	Cir. 2	SW. 1	SW. 1	......	
Sept. 23	7 a. m.	......	......	......	St. 8	SE. 1	SE. 1	......	
	2 p. m.	......	......	......	St. cir. 4	SW. 2	SW. 2	......	
	9 p. m.	......	......	......	Cir. 1	SW. 1	SW. 1	......	
Sept. 24	7 a. m.	......	......	......	St. 5	SW. 2	SW. 2	......	
	2 p. m.	......	......	......	0	0	SW. 2	......	
	9 p. m.	......	......	......	0	0	SW. 1	......	

LECOMPTON, KANSAS.

Month and day.	Hour.	Barom'r corrected to 32° F.	Thermometer.	Force of vapor.	Cloudiness.	Motion of clouds.	Winds.	Relative humidity.	REMARKS.
Sept. 14	9 p. m.	......	64	......	8	....	SW. 1	......	19th. Rain all night, accompanied by thunder.
Sept. 15	7 a. m.	......	64	......	3	....	SW. 4	......	
	2 p. m.	......	78	......	2	....	SW. 4	......	
	9 p. m.	......	62	......	4	....	SW. 4	......	
Sept. 16	7 a. m.	......	76	......	3	....	NE. 2	......	
	2 p m.	......	92	......	4	....	NW. 5	......	
	9 p. m.	......	80	......	3	....	NW. 4	......	
Sept. 17	7 a. m.	......	78	......	10	....	NW. 4	......	
	2 p. m.	......	97	......	5	....	NW. 4	......	
	9 p. m.	......	76	......	10	....	NW. 1	......	
Sept. 18	7 a. m.	......	64	......	5	....	NW. 1	......	
	2 p. m.	......	74	......	4	....	NW. 1	......	
	9 p. m.	......	62	......	2	....	NW. 1	......	
Sept. 19	7 a. m.	......	62	......	0	....	NW 1	......	
	2 p. m.	....	61	......	0	....	NW. 1	......	
	9 p. m.	......	56	......	0	....	NW. 1	......	
Sept. 20	7 a. m.	......	54	......	0	....	E. S. 2	......	
	2 p. m.	......	76	......	0	....	SE. 2	......	
	9 p m.	......	54	......	0	....	E. S. 1	......	
Sept. 21	7 a. m.	......	52	......	0	....	SE. 2	......	
	2 p. m.	......	76	......	....	....	SE. 3	......	
	9 p. m.	....	52	......	....	....	SE. 1	......	
Sept. 22	7 a. m.	......	58	......	0	....	SE. 1	......	
	2 p. m.	......	66	......	0	....	SE. 2	......	
	9 p. m.	......	58	......	0	....	SE. 1	......	
Sept. 23	7 a. m.	......	68	......	0	....	SE. 1	......	
	2 p. m.	......	82	......	0	....	SE. 1	......	
	9 p. m.	......	68	......	0	....	SE. 1	......	
Sept. 24	7 a. m.	......	72	......	5	....	NW. 1	......	
	2 p. m.	......	88	......	5	....	NW. 1	......	
	9 p. m.	......	76	......	10	....	NW. 1	......	

STORMS Nos. 2 AND 3, SEPTEMBER, 1859.

MANHATTAN, KANSAS.

Month and day.	Hour.	Barom'r corrected to 32° F.	Thermometer.	Force of vapor.	Cloudiness.	Motion of clouds.	Winds.	Relative humidity.	REMARKS.
Sept. 14	9 p. m.	......	62	......	Nim. 10	S. 1	0	......	14th. Rain from 9 to 11 a. m; amount, 0.08 inch.
Sept. 15	7 a. m.	......	60	......	Nim. 10	S. 2	S. 1	......	Rain from 10 p. m. the 17th to 2 a. m. on the 18th; amount, 0.93 inch.
	2 p. m.	......	80	......	Nim. 10	S. 2	S. 2	......	Rain at intervals from 9 a. m. the 24th to 2 a. m. on the 25th; am't, 0.30 inch.
	9 p. m.	......	68	......	Cu. 5	S. 2	0	......	
Sept. 16	7 a. m.	......	64	......	Nim. 10	S. 2	E. 1	......	
	2 p. m.	......	91	......	Cir. cu. 5	S. 3	SE. 2	......	
	9 p. m.	......	82	......	Nim. 8	S. 1	SE. 4	......	
Sept. 17	7 a. m.	......	77	......	Cir. cu. 3	S. 1	S. 3	......	
	2 p. m.	......	96	......	Cir. cu. 2	S. 1	S. 3	......	
	9 p. m.	......	86	......	Nim. 8	SW. 2	S. 4	......	
Sept. 18	7 a. m.	......	60	......	Nim. 10	N. 2	N. 1	......	
	2 p. m.	......	70	......	Nim. 10	N. 2	N. 2	......	
	9 p. m.	......	68	......	Nim. 8	NW. 1	N. 2	......	
Sept. 19	7 a. m.	......	58	......	Nim. 10	N. 2	N. 3	......	
	2 p. m.	......	72	......	Cir. st. 8	SW. 1	N. 2	......	
	9 p. m.	......	54	......	0	0	0	......	
Sept. 20	7 a. m.	......	46	......	0	0	0	......	
	2 p. m.	......	70	......	Cir. st. 3	NW. 1	N. 1	......	
	9 p. m.	......	42	......	0	0	0	......	
Sept. 21	7 a. m.	......	36	......	Cir. st. 1	NW 2	0	......	
	2 p. m.	......	75	......	St. 3	NW. 1	NE. 1	......	
	9 p. m.	......	50	......	0	0	SE. 1	......	
Sept. 22	7 a. m.	......	42	......	0	0	E. 2	......	
	2 p. m.	......	88	......	Cir. 1	SW. 1	SE. 1	......	
	9 p. m.	......	52	......	Cir. st. 2	SW. 1	S. 2	......	
Sept. 23	7 a. m.	......	46	......	Cir. st. 2	SW. 2	S. 2	......	
	2 p. m.	......	86	......	Cir. cu. 2	S. 2	S. 3	......	
	9 p. m.	......	54	......	0	0	S. 1	......	
Sept. 24	7 a. m.	......	48	......	Nim. 10	N. 2	NW. 1	......	
	2 p. m.	......	80	......	Nim. 10	NW. 2	N. 2	......	
	9 p. m.	......	70	......	Nim. 10	NW. 2	N. 1	......	

MONEKA, KANSAS.

Month and day.	Hour.	Barom'r corrected to 32° F.	Thermometer.	Force of vapor.	Cloudiness.	Motion of clouds.	Winds.	Relative humidity.	REMARKS.
Sept. 15	7 a. m.	......	60	......	Rain cld. 10	NE. 1	S.SE. 2	......	14th. Rain from 1 to 2 p. m; am't, 0.20 inch.
	2 p. m.	......	78	......	Cu. 9	0	0	......	18th. Rain from 3½ to 5 a. m.; amount, 0.33 inch.
Sept. 16	7 a. m.	......	72	......	Cu. 7	E SE. 1	S.SE. 1	......	
	2 p. m.	......	80	......	Cir. st. 5	NE. 1	S. 1	......	
Sept. 17	7 a. m.	......	80	......	Cu. 5	NW. 1	S. SW. 2	......	
	2 p. m.	......	90	......	Cir. st. 9	NE. 1	S. SE. 2	......	
Sept. 18	7 a. m.	......	64	......	Rain cld. 9	N. NE. 2	N. NW. 1	......	
	2 p. m.	......	73	......	Cu. 8	SE. 3	SW., NW. 3	......	
Sept. 19	7 a. m.	......	59	......	Rain cld. 10	SE. 2	N. NW. 3	......	
	2 p. m.	......	59	......	Rain cld. 10	SE. 2	N. NW. 3	......	
Sept. 20	7 a. m.		54		Cu. 1	0	NW. 2	......	
	2 p. m.	......	63	......	Cir. st. 6	SW. 1	NE. 2	......	
Sept. 22	7 a. m.	......	58	......	Nim. 9	0	0	......	
	2 p. m.	......	66	......	Cu. 9	NE. 1	E. NE. 1	......	
Sept. 23	7 a. m.	......	53	......	Cir. st. 1	0	0	......	
	2 p. m.	......	79	......	0	0	SW. 3	......	
Sept. 24	7 a. m.	......	69	......	Cir. st. 2	0	S. SW. 1	......	
	2 p. m.	......	82	......	Cir. st. 2	0	S. SW. 3	......	

STORMS Nos. 2 AND 3, SEPTEMBER, 1859.

NEOSHA FALLS, KANSAS.

Month and day.	Hour.	Barom'r corrected to 32° F.	Thermometer.	Force of vapor.	Cloudiness.	Motion of clouds.	Winds.	Relative humidity.	REMARKS.
Sept. 14	9 p. m.	------	63	------	10	----------	NE. 1	------	
Sept. 15	7 a. m	------	64	------	10	----------	SE. 1	------	
	2 p. m.	------	81	------	6	----------	SE. 1	------	
	9 p. m.	------	70	------	4	----------	SE. 1	------	
Sept. 16	7 a. m.	------	70	------	1	----------	SE. 1	------	
	2 p. m.	------	91	------	3	----------	SE. 2	------	
	9 p. m.	------	79	------	2	----------	SE. 2	------	
Sept. 17	7 a. m.	------	74	------	3	----------	SE. 1	------	
	2 p. m.	------	91	------	3	----------	S. 3	------	
	9 p. m.	------	79	------	4	----------	SE. 3	------	
Sept. 18	7 a. m.	------	66	------	5	----------	SE. 2	------	
	2 p. m.	------	71	------	2	----------	NE. 3	------	
	9 p. m.	------	66	------	4	----------	NE. 2	------	
Sept. 19	7 a. m.	------	60	------	3	----------	NE. 1	------	
	2 p. m.	------	63	------	5	----------	NE. 2	------	
	9 p m	------	58	------	7	----------	NE. 3	------	
Sept. 20	7 a. m.	------	46	------	0	----------	N. 3	------	
	2 p. m.	------	68	------	0	----------	N. 2	------	
	9 p. m.	------	59	------	1	----------	N. 1	------	
Sept. 21	7 a. m.	------	52	------	6	----------	NW. 1	------	
	2 p. m.	------	69	------	2	----------	NE. 1	------	
	9 p. m.	------	61	------	1	----------	NE. 1	------	
Sept. 22	7 a. m.	------	50	------	0	----------	SE. 2	------	
	2 p. m.	------	82	------	0	----------	SE. 2	------	
	9 p. m.	------	65	------	0	----------	S. 1	------	
Sept. 23	7 a. m.	------	59	------	0	----------	E. 1	------	
	2 p. m.	------	87	------	0	----------	SE. 1	------	
	9 p. m.	------	71	------	0	----------	S. 2	------	
Sept. 24	7 a. m.	------	64	------	1	----------	S. 1	------	
	2 p. m.	------	91	------	6	----------	S. 3	------	
	9 p m.	------	73	------	10	----------	S. 1	------	

www.ingramcontent.com/pod-product-compliance
Lightning Source LLC
LaVergne TN
LVHW021239110826
845150LV00002B/357

* 9 7 8 1 4 2 5 5 6 1 9 1 8 *